Social Psychology

Robbie Sutton and Karen Douglas

 macmillan education   palgrave

First published 2013 by
PALGRAVE MACMILLAN

Palgrave Macmillan in the UK is an imprint of Macmillan Publishers Limited,
registered in England, company number 785998, of 4 Crinan Street,
London N1 9XW

Palgrave Macmillan in the US is a division of St Martin's Press LLC,
175 Fifth Avenue, New York, NY 10010.

Palgrave Macmillan is the global academic imprint of the above companies
and has companies and representatives throughout the world.

Palgrave® and Macmillan® are registered trademarks in the United States,
the United Kingdom, Europe and other countries.

ISBN: 978–0–230–21803–1

This book is printed on paper suitable for recycling and made from fully
managed and sustained forest sources. Logging, pulping and manufacturing
processes are expected to conform to the environmental regulations of the
country of origin.

A catalogue record for this book is available from the British Library.

A catalog record for this book is available from the Library of Congress.

To Jamie and Rose

About the authors

Robbie Sutton was born in Wellington, New Zealand and completed undergraduate degrees in English, philosophy and psychology at Victoria University of Wellington, and went on to study for his PhD there. He has had teaching positions at Massey University (NZ), Keele University (UK), and now the University of Kent, where he is Reader in Psychology. He has published over 50 articles and book chapters on topics such as justice, inequality, gender, the fear of crime, feedback and causal explanation. He has also acted as a consultant on projects in environmental and community psychology. He serves on the editorial boards of the *European Journal of Social Psychology*, the *British Journal of Social Psychology* and the *Journal of Language and Social Psychology*. With Matthew Hornsey and Karen Douglas, Robbie edited *Feedback: The Communication of Praise, Criticism and Advice*.

Karen Douglas was born in Blackburn, England and grew up in the Hunter Valley, Australia. She completed her undergraduate degree at the University of Newcastle and her PhD at the Australian National University. Karen moved back to the UK to take up a lectureship at Keele University and later moved to the University of Kent where she is now a Reader in Psychology. Karen has many research interests, most notably on the social psychology of conspiracy theories, language and communication, and the psychology of the internet, having published and taught broadly in these areas. She has been an associate editor for the *European Journal of Social Psychology, Social Psychology* and the *British Journal of Social Psychology*.

Brief contents

v

Contents

List of figures

List of tables

Preface

We have been writing this book for some three or four years. Along the way, we have had help from many people, just some of who are named in our acknowledgements section. We think that we, and this small army of talented and dedicated people, have come up with the best social psychology textbook. Ever. But, then, we would think that, wouldn't we? As you will read, people are wont to make unduly positive assessments of themselves and their creations (Chapter 2). They are also prone to cognitive dissonance: a mental state that can lead people to overvalue decisions and achievements for which they have made insane sacrifices (Chapter 4).

So, it's not for us to assess whether ours really is the best social psychology textbook available. Besides, as teachers, we have found that the textbooks of our 'competitors' often provide excellent introductions to the knowledge that social psychologists have garnered. Several make an effort to discuss how this knowledge can be applied to real-life concerns and, in various ways, try to encourage a critical evaluation of this knowledge.

Nonetheless, we do assert, with perfect seriousness, that our book is unique. We wrote it because we felt that the available textbooks, however excellent, shared one extremely important shortcoming. Namely, they assumed that students are consumers of knowledge. In this model, the students' job is to read, absorb and sometimes critically evaluate the material delivered in the textbook. The problem is that you need to be so much more than this, whether you intend to go on to further academic or professional training in psychology, or embark on a career in another field. Success in so many endeavours depends on being open-minded, creative and persuasive; on being able to find and synthesize information, identify and solve problems, and put solutions to the test. In short, all students should aspire to be producers, as well as consumers, of knowledge. This means they should not be content simply to be taught, but should strive to develop the skills and confidence to teach themselves, and then to communicate their insights to others. This is the philosophy that lies behind our book, and which makes it unique.

Like other textbooks, it sets out to communicate science in a clear and interesting way; something we, as teachers, researchers and consultants, have always loved doing. But it also provides you with many opportunities to find and synthesize information for yourself, to solve real-world problems, to experience and design research, and to communicate your ideas. Textbooks in other disciplines (e.g., maths, statistics) are routinely interactive, in the sense that they provide exercises for students. However, this remains highly unusual in psychology, and no other social psychology textbook is as interactive as ours. This philosophy underpins several exercises and other features that are unusual in social psychology textbooks. The three types of features in this book are feature boxes, within-chapter exercises, and end-of-chapter exercises.

Tour of the book

We hope that by the time you have finished reading this book, you are familiar with the main methods by which findings and ideas are produced in social psychology, conscious of their applicability to real-world problems, able to critically evaluate them, and prepared not just to read but to do research. Our feature boxes address each of these learning objectives. Each one considers a topic in depth and concludes with questions to guide further learning.

Ethics and research methods

The ethics and research features focus on an important ethical or methodological issue relevant to social psychological research. For example, in Chapter 9, we examine the ethical issues surrounding one of social psychology's most famous experiments, where Stanley Milgram had participants believe they were delivering strong electrical shocks to another person.

Social psychology in the real world

Social psychology is a far-reaching discipline and addresses social issues that are relevant to people's everyday lives in the past, present and future. The social psychology in the real world features ask you to consider the social psychological dimension of real-world issues, such as anti-smoking campaigns (Chapter 6), road rage (Chapter 10), homophobia (Chapter 11), racism in politics (Chapter 12), alcohol-fuelled aggression (Chapter 13) and the global financial crisis (Chapter 14).

Critical focus

The critical focus features encourage you to critically examine well-known and influential findings and concepts in social psychology. Some of the features re-examine a 'classic' social psychology study from the 1960s and 70s, the findings and conclusions of which have, until recently, been treated most of the time as accepted wisdom. Other critical focus theories examine some of the most high-profile recent developments in social psychology, such as 'ego depletion' (Chapter 2) and 'embodied social cognition' (Chapter 4), both of which cast doubt on the traditional idea that the mind can be considered separate from the body.

Student projects

As students of psychology, you will probably be required to complete a research project in which you collect and analyse your own data. Chapters 1–14 feature an example from a student who has recently conducted their project on a social psychology topic. Each student explains their research question, why they were interested in answering that question, what methods they used, what their findings were and what they mean. They also tell us what they are doing now and offer some advice based on their experiences. These features are designed to help you prepare for your project with confidence and inspiration. They also highlight how your degree prepares you for a range of career paths.

Within-chapter exercises

Each chapter contains several smaller exercises designed to enable you to gain 'hands-on' experience with social psychological research, and to think critically about the investigations we have highlighted.

Note that your lecturer may give you guidance on how much you should engage with the within-chapter and end-of-chapter questions and exercises. You can read this textbook and learn much from it without completing them. If you do attempt these exercises, it is definitely best to try to work through them independently before seeking guidance. But some of them are more challenging or difficult than others. So don't worry if you get stuck on some.

Try it yourself

In the try it yourself exercises, you have an opportunity to gain practical experience of the studies you are learning about. For example, in Chapter 2, you will have direct experience of experimental procedures designed to make you intensely conscious of the inevitability of your own death. In the same chapter, you will be able to take the creativity test that is used in an experiment described in the text. Questions in the exercises will help you reflect critically and creatively on the research methods you have experienced.

Time to reflect

Time to reflect exercises are designed to encourage active, critical or creative thinking about the material. This kind of thinking can be daunting, so the exercises are set up to guide you through the process. For example, in Chapter 2, you are asked to critically evaluate Gallup's 'mirror test', widely used as an indicator of self-awareness among young children and animals. You are asked to think of reasons why a child or animal might 'fail' the test even though they are self-aware (i.e., the test produces false negatives), and may 'pass' the test even though they are not self-aware in the full sense of the term.

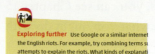

Exploring further Use Google or a similar internet the English riots. For example, try combining terms s attempts to explain the riots. What kinds of explanati

Exploring further

Each chapter features approximately five brief exploring further exercises, designed to encourage you to find out further information about the material, typically using the internet. You may be asked to search the literature for further information about a topic, find online demonstrations, or find relevant material from news, history or popular culture. You are encouraged to develop the skills and mindset of a researcher, and also to enhance your knowledge and understanding of the material. For example, in Chapter 2, there is an exercise on the measurement of self-esteem. You are asked to search the literature to find articles that advocate different ways of measuring self-esteem, and also to find two of these measures and complete them yourselves.

End-of-chapter exercises

At the end of each chapter, we include two exercises designed for you to think about ways of extending existing research.

Applying social psychology

Applying social psychology

Pets and psychological wellbeing: a critical thinking exercise

This exercise is based on the following article:

Herzog, H. (2011) The impact of pets on human health and psychological wellbeing: Fact, fiction or hypothesis? *Current Directions in Psychological Science*, 20, 236–9.

In the applying social psychology exercises, you will explore how the findings and ideas you have read about can be applied to real-life problems. The exercises vary in length and format so that you can practise a range of skills, including critical thinking, synthesis, problem-solving, and communicating your ideas clearly, concisely and persuasively. Often, they put you in the shoes of a professional who needs to solve a problem. For example, you may be asked to imagine you are working for a school that needs to encourage healthy eating by its pupils (Chapter 2), a charity facing a public relations crisis (Chapter 3), or an educational professional who needs to defend social and club activities from budget cuts (Chapter 8).

Blind spot in social psychology

Blind spot in social psychology

Narcissistic leaders and their effects on decision making

In this chapter, we saw how narcissists are overrepresented in the top echelons of business (Chatterjee and Hambrick, 2007). This may not be a bad thing. Narcissists are often enthusiastic and charismatic individuals, and groups containing narcissists may, as

In the blind spot in social psychology exercises, you will encounter untested ideas and neglected topics in the field. Social psychology is a young science in which much remains to be discovered. The joy of this is that it is possible for you to explore new ideas and consider theoretically and practically important studies that have never been done before. These exercises encourage you to consider how the research covered in this book can be extended and how to open up new avenues for research.

The structure of the book

The philosophy behind this book also led us to add a distinctive chapter at its conclusion. Chapter 15 takes an overview of social psychology, summarizing its key points of wisdom. The wisdom of social psychology will help not only in your studies but also in your life beyond university. It discusses some of the main problems and controversies in the discipline. It then covers the skills that you can (and employers do) expect your studies to give you. Thus, you can see Chapter 15 as your guide in reflecting on what you have learned and what you might do with your knowledge.

Before you get to Chapter 15, you'll have read the introductory chapter, which outlines the history, principles and methods of social psychology. The rest of the chapters are organized in four parts; as you move through them, the focus shifts from the individual to larger social groups. Part 1 (Thinking and feeling) explores how individuals understand, evaluate and navigate through their social world. Part 2 (Relating) considers how people influence and bond with each other. Part 3 (Belonging) examines the formation of social groups and their central importance in our lives. Part 4 (Applying) explores how the concepts, findings and methods of social psychology can be applied to improve relations between groups, to reduce aggression and foster cooperation and kindness.

That concludes our guided tour of this book. Now, you are ready to start reading the chapters and engaging with the ideas, findings and techniques of social psychology.

Authors' acknowledgements

There are many individuals without whom this book would not have been possible. First and foremost, we thank the outstanding team at Palgrave Macmillan for their belief, guidance and perseverance over the course of the project. In particular, our thanks go to Anna van Boxel, Catherine Travers, Jamie Joseph, Joanna McGarry, Paul Stevens, Jaime Marshall, Amy Grant and Niki Jayatunga. We would not be so proud of this book, and indeed would not have finished it, were it not for their talent and drive.

Our thanks also go to the team at Aardvark, and in particular the copyeditor Maggie Lythgoe. We also thank Bonny Hartley, Dan Jolley and Kat Wilson for their help with referencing.

We also thank the reviewers who kindly gave their time and expertise to comment on chapters of the book. The end product is all the better for your helpful advice and direction. Particular thanks go to our review panel:

Alison Attrill at De Montfort, University, UK
Jennifer Boldero at the University of Melbourne, Australia
John Drury at the University of Sussex, Brighton, UK
Alex Easton at Durham University, UK
Gareth Hall at Aberystwyth University, UK
Nick Haslam at the University of Melbourne, Australia
Courtney von Hippel at the University of Queensland, Australia
Nicholas Hopkins at the University of Dundee, UK
Konstantinos Kafetsios at the University of Crete, Greece
Anthony Manstead at Cardiff University, UK
Julian Oldmeadow at York University, UK
Jan-Willem van Prooijen, VU University Amsterdam, the Netherlands
Victoria Scaife at the University of East Anglia, Norwich, UK
Fay Short at Bangor University, UK
Val Tuck at Newcastle University, UK
Brady Wagoner at Aalborg University, Denmark
Alison Ziegler at the University of Michigan, USA.

We thank the former students of social psychology for telling us about their student projects and their life paths, and their supervisors for recommending them to us. Each one of these features is an asset to this book.

Thank you to our friends and colleagues for their support and encouragement. In particular, we thank our PhD supervisors John McClure and Craig McGarty for inspiring us and then training us to become social psychologists.

Thanks to our research students who have been fantastically patient and sympathetic, and whose enthusiasm and energy have been an inspiration.

We also both thank our families for their love, inspiration and encouragement.

Publisher's acknowledgements

The authors and publisher are grateful to the following for permission to reproduce copyright material:

Academic Press for permission to reprint Figure 8.3 'Model of group socialization', Moreland, R.L. and Levine, J.M. (1982) 'Socialization in small groups: Temporal changes in individual group relations', *Advances in Experimental Social Psychology*, 15, 137–92.

The American Psychological Association and the named authors for permission to use the following:

Table 1.1 'Characteristics of individualist and collectivist cultures', Markus, H. and Kitayama, S. (1991) 'Culture and the self: Implications for cognition, emotion, and motivation'. *Psychological Review*, 98, 224–53.

Material in the Try it yourself feature in Chapter 2 on p. 58, Campbell, J.D., Trapnell, P.D., Heine, S.J. et al. (1996) 'Self-concept clarity: Measurement, personality correlates, and cultural boundaries'. *Journal of Personality and Social Psychology*, 70(1), 141–56.

Material in the Try it yourself feature in Chapter 2 on p. 67, Friedman, R.S. and Förster, J. (2001) 'The effects of promotion and prevention cues on creativity'. *Journal of Personality and Social Psychology*, 81(6), 1001–13.

Material in the Try it yourself feature in Chapter 7 on p. 333, Collins, N.L. and Read, S.J. (1990) 'Adult attachment, working models and relationship quality in dating couples'. *Journal of Personality and Social Psychology*, 58, 644–63.

Figure 6.1 'Attitude change (persuasion) achieved by likeable and unlikeable communicators' and Figure 6.8 'Attitude change for easy or difficult messages', Chaiken, S. and Eagly, A. (1983) 'Communication modality as a determinant of persuasion: The role of communicator salience'. *Journal of Personality and Social Psychology*, 45(2), 241–56.

Figure 7.11 'Rusbult's (1983) investment model of commitment', Rusbult, C.E. (1983) 'A longitudinal test of the investment model: The development (and deterioration) of satisfaction and commitment in heterosexual involvements'. *Journal of Personality and Social Psychology*, 45, 101–17.

Figure 8.10 'The influence of changing gender roles on personality', adapted from Twenge, J.M. (2001) 'Changes in women's assertiveness in response to status and roles: A cross-temporal meta-analysis, 1931-1993'. *Journal of Personality and Social Psychology*, 81, 133–45.

Figure 8.15 'Mortality salience and the need to belong', Wisman, A. and Koole, S.L. (2003) 'Hiding in the crowd: Can mortality salience promote affiliation with others who oppose one's worldviews?' *Journal of Personality and Social Psychology*, 84(3), 511–26.

Figure 10.11 'The group polarization hypothesis', Moscovici, S. and Zavalloni, M. (1969) 'The group as a polarizer of attitudes'. *Journal of Personality and Social Psychology*, 12(2), 125–35.

Figure 10.12 'Fiedler's contingency theory of leadership', Chemers, M., Hays, R., Rhodewalt, F., Wysocki, J. (1985) 'A person–environment analysis of job stress: A contingency model explanation', *Journal of Personality and Social Psychology*, 49(3), 628–35.

Figure 12.11 'Correlation between level and appropriateness of prejudice', Crandall, C.S., Eshleman, A. and O'Brien, L.O. (2002) 'Social norms and the expression of prejudice: The struggle for internalization'. *Journal of Personality and Social Psychology*, 82, 359–78.

Figure 12.15 'The SIMCA model of group identification', van Zomeren, M., Postmes, T. and Spears, R. (2008) 'Toward an integrative social identity model of collective action: A quantitative research synthesis of three socio-psychological perspectives'. *Psychological Bulletin*, 134(4), 504–35.

Material in the Try it yourself feature in Chapter 13 on pp. 576–7, adapted from Fromme, K., Stroot, E. and Kaplan, D. (1993) 'Comprehensive effects of alcohol: Development and psychometric assessment of a new expectancy questionnaire'. *Psychological Assessment*, 5, 19–26.

Material in the Try it yourself feature in Chapter 13 on p. 601, 'Social dominance orientation scale', Pratto, F., Sidanius, J., Stallworth, L. and Malle, B.F. (1994) 'Social dominance orientation: A personality variable predicting social and political attitudes'. *Journal of Personality and Social Psychology*, 67(4), 741–63.

Figure 14.3 'Decision model of bystander intervention', Darley, J.M. and Latané, B. (1968) 'Bystander intervention in emergencies: Diffusion of responsibility'. *Journal of Personality and Social Psychology*, 8, 377–83.

Figure 14.10, De Cremer, D. and van Vugt, M. (1999) Social identification effects in social dilemmas: A transformation of motives. *European Journal of Social Psychology*, 29, 871–93.

Table 15.1 'Aspects of psychological literacy', McGovern, T.V., Corey, L.A., Cranney, J. et al. (2010) 'Psychologically literate citizens', in D. Halpern (ed.) *Undergraduate Education in Psychology: Blueprint for the Discipline's Future* (pp. 9–27). Washington, DC.

The use of APA information does not imply endorsement by APA. No further reproduction or distribution is permitted without written permission from the American Psychological Association.

Annual Reviews for permission to republish Figure 13.7 'The many paths linking use of violent media to heightened aggression in real life', Bushman, B.J and Anderson, C.A. (2002) 'Human aggression', *Annual Review of Psychology*, 53, 27–51.

Elsevier for permission to reprint Table 2.1 'The self-evaluation maintenance model', Tesser, A. (1988) 'Toward a self-evaluation maintenance model of social behavior', *Advances in Experimental Social Psychology*, 21, 181–227; Figure 4.11 'Effects of affirming versus negating stereotypes', Mbirkou, R., Seibt, S. and Strack, B.F. (2008) 'When "just say no" is not enough: Affirmation versus negation training and the reduction of automatic stereotype activation', *Journal of Experimental Social Psychology*, 44(2), 370–7; Material in the Try it yourself feature in Chapter 5 on p. 248, 'Generalised problematic internet use scale (GPIUS)', Caplan, S.E. (2002) 'Problematic Internet use and psychosocial well-being: Development of a theory-based cognitive-behavioral measurement instrument', *Computers in Human Behaviour*, 18(5), 553–75; Material in the Try it yourself feature in Chapter 6 ('NFCC scale' on p. 275), Roets, A. and van Hiel, A. (2011) 'Item selection and validation of a brief, 15-item version of the need for closure scale', *Personality and Individual Differences*, 50(1), 90–4; Figure 13.6 'A comparison of media violence/aggressive behaviour with other correlations', Huesmann, L.R. (2007) 'The impact of electronic media violence: Scientific theory and research', *Journal of Adolescent Health*, 41(6) (Suppl.), S6–S13; Material in the Try it yourself feature in Chapter 14 on p. 619, Einolf, C.J. (2010) 'Does extensivity form part of the altruistic personality? An empirical test of Oliner and Oliner's theory', *Social Science Research*, 39(1), 142–51.

Peter Glick and Susan Fiske for permission to reproduce the 'Ambivalent sexism inventory' in the Try it yourself feature in Chapter 11 on p. 496.

Michael Hogg for permission to reprint Figure 8.7 'Festinger et al.'s (1950) model of group cohesion', adapted from Festinger, L., Schachter, S. and Back, K. (1950) *Social Pressures in Informal Groups: A Study of a Housing Project*, New York: Harper & Row, in Hogg, M.A. (1992) *The Social Psychology of Group Cohesiveness*, New York: New York University Press.

Hogrefe Publishing for permission to reprint Figure 4.1, 'The Schwarz value circumplex (or "wheel")', Borg, I., Groenen, P.J.F., Jehn, K.A. et al. (2011) 'Embedding the organizational culture profile into Schwartz's theory of universals in values', *Journal of Personnel Psychology*, 10, 1–12.

MIT Press Journals for permission to reproduce Figure 3.10 Engell, A.D., Haxby, J.V. and Todorov, A. (2007) 'Summaries of fMRI scans', *Journal of Cognitive Neuroscience*, 19(9), 1508–19.

Sage Publications for permission to reprint material in the Try it yourself feature in Chapter 12 on pp. 536–7 and Figure 12.8 'Social identity complexity', both from Roccas, S. and Brewer, M.B. (2002) 'Social identity complexity', *Personality and Social Psychology Review,* 6(2), 88–106.

The Society for Personality Research for permission to reprint material in the Try it yourself feature in Chapter 9 'Scale to measure individual differences in conformity' on p. 416, Mehrabian, A. and Stefl, C. (1995) 'Basic temperament components of loneliness, shyness, and conformity', *Social Behavior and Personality: An International Journal,* 23, 253–64.

Taylor and Francis for permission to reprint material in the Try it yourself feature in Chapter 6, 'NFC scale' on p. 281, Cacioppo, J.T., Petty, R.E. and Kao, C.F. (1984) 'The efficient assessment of need for cognition', *Journal of Personality Assessment,* 48, 306–7.

Grant Thornton for permission to reproduce Figure 7.12 'Reasons for divorce in the UK in 2010' from *Matrimonial Survey 2011.*

John Wiley & Sons for permission to reprint material in the Try it yourself feature in Chapter 7 on p. 316, 'Need for affiliation', Buunk, B.P., Zurriaga, R., Peiró, J.M. et al. (2005) 'Social comparisons at work as related to a cooperative social climate and to individual differences in social comparison orientation', *Applied Psychology: An International Review,* 54, 61–80; material in the Try it yourself feature in Chapter 8 on p. 379, 'Scale of group identification', Brown, R., Condor, S., Mathews, A. et al. (1986) 'Explaining intergroup differentiation in an industrial organization', *Journal of Occupational Psychology,* 59, 279–304; Table 12.1 'Ten elements of government apologies that should make them satisfactory to victim groups', Blatz, C.W., Schumann, K. and Ross, M. (2009) 'Government apologies for historical injustices', *Political Psychology,* 30, 219–41.

Yale University Press for permission to reprint Figure 7.8 'Triangular theory of love', Sternberg, R. and Barnes, M. (eds) (1988) *The Psychology of Love* (pp. 264–92), New Haven: Yale University Press.

The publishers are also grateful to the following suppliers of images in the book:

Alamy, Alexandra Milgram, Alice Ferns, Bananastock, Brand X Pictures, ComStock, Corbis, Creatas, Design Pics, Digital Vision, Erin Michelson, Fotolia, Getty, Image 100, Image Source, iStockphoto, James Brunker, John Foxx Images, Macmillan Australia, Macmillan Media Assets Resource Service, Martin Jonathan, Photoalto, PhotoDisc, PhotoSpin, Shutterstock, Stockbyte, Superstock, Tommer Leyvand.

Every effort has been made to trace all the copyright holders but if any have been inadvertently overlooked the publishers will be pleased to make the necessary arrangements at the first opportunity.

1

The discipline of social psychology

This chapter will introduce the discipline of social psychology. It will outline what social psychology is about, provide some information about the history of social psychology and focus on the key topics that social psychologists study. It will also provide an introduction to how social psychologists do research, focusing on the research methods and techniques that social psychologists use. By the end of the chapter, the reader will have a basic knowledge of what social psychology is, and how it is done.

© DIGITAL VISION

Topics covered in this chapter

- What is social psychology?
- Where does social psychology come from?
- Doing social psychological research
- The tools of social psychology
- Issues in conducting social psychological research
- Basic and applied research
- Cultural issues
- Research ethics
- Social psychology and links to other disciplines
- Dissemination of social psychology

Key features

Critical focus The 'crisis' in social psychology

Ethics and research methods Correlation versus causation

Social psychology in the real world Social psychology at work in the classroom

Applying social psychology Pets and psychological wellbeing: a critical thinking exercise

Student project Socially desirable responding

Questions to consider

1. In the midst of the riots in England during August 2011, British Prime Minister David Cameron argued that: 'This is criminality pure and simple, and it must be confronted and defeated.' Many other media reports labelled the incidents as 'mindless violence'. Was this a fair assessment of the situation?

2. A social psychologist is interested in how media representations of gender roles have changed over the past 30 years. What research method(s) would enable the researcher to examine this question and what are the advantages and disadvantages of each?

3. At a party, a social psychologist tells a friend about their research, explaining that most of their findings come from studies where the participants were undergraduates. Their friend says that these findings cannot tell us anything about humans in general. Is the friend correct?

© GETTY

In August 2011, London and other English cities were embroiled in riots and looting. Buildings were burning, cars were being overturned, police were being charged by groups of tens, sometimes hundreds of masked youths, and retail stores were being ransacked – ranging from major department stores and electronic retailers to family-run florists and party suppliers. The theft and disorder were shocking and unprecedented. As social psychologists, we have a professional interest, and arguably a duty, to explain why this happened. Naturally, social psychologists are not alone in wanting to know why these events took place. Residents of affected neighbourhoods saw their streets become a no-go zone and people in the rest of the country were wondering whether the rioting would spread like a contagion and bring chaos to their neighbourhoods. They also worried what the disorder said about the state of the society in which they live. As we shall see throughout this book, when powerful events affect people's lives, they want to know what has caused them.

The media were awash with debate and commentary about what caused the violence and disorder. According to some, the rioting was an inevitable response to disadvantage, despair, frustration and anger among young people, in principally poor and black areas of London. According to others, the rioting should be seen as sheer criminality; government cuts had barely taken effect and helping oneself to a TV from a department store can scarcely be seen as political action. For people advocating this perspective, the rioting reflected the actions of a small minority of people from deprived communities who have been raised with insufficient parental guidance and respect for authority or the rule of law (Reicher and Stott, 2011).

Who is right? In the words of one commentator on a bulletin board: 'Is this really the work of mindless yobs with no cause or the backlash from a frustrated and marginalized youth?' We do not have an easy answer to give you here. However, it is worth pausing to reflect on what it means to think about, and investigate, the causes of events like the riots as a social psychologist. Certainly, one of our main aims in writing this book is that, by its end, you will feel comfortable in adopting a social psychological perspective when thinking about events in your life and in the wider world around you.

A second major lesson we hope you take away from your study of social psychology is that, typically, no one cause, or no one explanation, has a monopoly on the truth. People think, act and feel as they do for many reasons. It is thus perfectly plausible that the riots might be a product of widespread frustration among disadvantaged groups in English cities *and* the actions of a criminal minority, brought up with scant parental discipline. Sometimes multiple causes of our behaviour affect us at the same time, but independently of each other, combining to be a powerful enough force to shape the way we act. Thus, neither disadvantage nor an ill-disciplined upbringing may be enough on their own to get people out on the streets, wreaking havoc. But together, they are enough.

Causes can combine in different ways. Sometimes they interact. The effect of one cause, like poverty, on an outcome such as rioting may depend on the presence, absence or extent of another cause, such as a dysfunctional upbringing. Such

Interaction effect Different causes may interact with each other to produce changes in a dependent variable (A and B interact to bring about changes in C).

Moderation This occurs when the relationship between two variables depends on a third variable (A causes C, but is also dependent on levels of B).

Mediation This occurs when the relationship between two variables is explained by a third variable (A causes B and B causes C).

an **interaction effect** is shown in Figure 1.1a. Here, the relationship between an individual's poverty and the likelihood that they would participate in rioting depends on – in other words, is **moderated** by – their family upbringing. People who have childhoods that have equipped them with self-discipline and concern for others may not respond in the same way to their poverty as children who have not been so fortunate to be born into more functional families. For example, they may engage in lawful political activism, social work, or intensified investment in their education and career.

Sometimes, causes combine to form chains – A causes B and B causes C, like dominoes falling into each other. For example, long-term poverty and disadvantage may mean that a disproportionate number of poorer parents are forced to work long hours, or are beset with social and psychological problems such as addiction and lack of wider family support. Thus, disadvantage and despair, far from being an alternative explanation for the rioting, may actually help explain why so many young people are ill-disciplined. This kind of effect is known as **mediation**. The effect of poverty is mediated by the increase in dysfunctional families (Figure 1.1b). This recognition that normally not one but multiple causes shape our behaviour is one of the key characteristics that makes social psychological explanations different from the ones that people typically come up with in everyday life.

(a) A hypothetical interaction effect

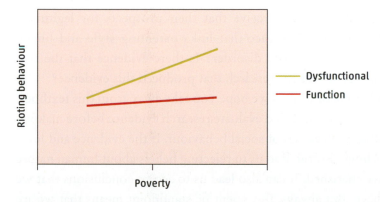

(a) Here, the effect of individuals' poverty on their rioting behaviour is moderated by the type of family they grew up in. Poverty increases the chances of rioting, and being from a dysfunctional family also increases the chances of rioting. However, poverty increases the odds of rioting more strongly when a person is also from a dysfunctional family. Another way to look at the same interaction effect is that the effect of being from a dysfunctional family depends on whether one is poor or not. Family background has little or no effect at low levels of poverty, but has a substantial effect at higher levels. Both ways of looking at the interaction effect may be legitimate, but normally researchers prefer to be informed by theories that tell them which of two or more causes is playing an active role, and which cause operates principally by strengthening, weakening, or even reversing the effect of the other. Researchers normally conduct statistical analyses on their results to see whether the 'main effects' of each variable and the 'interaction effect' of the two combined are greater than would be expected by chance alone. Factorial analysis of variance (ANOVA) is a statistical technique commonly used to do this.

(b) A hypothetical mediation effect

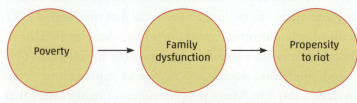

(b) Here, as poverty increases, so does the extent of family dysfunction, which in turn causes rioting. Thus, we can say that poverty causes rioting because it increases family dysfunction. There may also be a 'direct effect' of poverty on rioting, but for the sake of simplicity, this is not shown in the diagram. Once again, researchers will run analyses to test whether 'indirect effects' as shown here are statistically significant, that is, greater than would normally occur by chance alone. It is important to note that mediation and moderation can happen at the same time, that is, both panels may capture an element of the truth about the causes of riots such as those occurring in England in August 2011.

FIGURE 1.1 Two ways variables can combine to produce effects

Another crucial point is that social psychological explanations are informed, and constrained, by research evidence. As social psychologists, we are not entirely free of bias. Nonetheless, we try to select explanations on the basis of whether they are supported by evidence. In other words, we try to select explanations that are most likely to be true, rather than the ones we like the most for other reasons. Although most commentators are united in condemning the looting and rioting of August 2011, their preference for the 'despair' versus 'ill-discipline' explanations seemed, quite clearly, to depend on their political leanings. Conservative or right-wing commentators emphasized the lack of civil order, effective policing, dependency on welfare benefits, and soft punishments in the criminal justice system. Liberal or left-wing commentators, in contrast, tended to point to youth unemployment, government cutbacks, and an alleged increase in the frequency of riots under conservative governments (Reicher and Stott, 2011).

Exploring further Use Google or a similar internet search engine to find different explanations of the causes of the English riots. For example, try combining terms such as '2011', 'riots', 'England' and 'causes'. Find several attempts to explain the riots. What kinds of explanations do you uncover? Do different types of commentators express their explanations more forcefully, and with greater certainty?

As social psychologists, we must, however reluctantly, put our personal preferences aside. Instead, we look for theories and research evidence to guide us in evaluating whether either or both of these causes in tandem can bring about forms of aggressive and antisocial behaviour. We would naturally be sceptical about either explanation until we saw a good deal of corroborating evidence. Is there evidence that similar forms of behaviour are more common under harsh economic conditions, or among people who perceive that their prospects for legitimate advancement are poor? Is there evidence that links parenting style and liberal criminal justice policies to increases in disorder? Is there evidence that the two combine? How well designed was the research that produced this evidence?

Thus, one of the other major lessons we hope you take away from this textbook is that, in social psychology, we seek and evaluate research evidence before making, or accepting, claims about the causes of social behaviour. If the evidence and logic are sufficiently compelling, this can lead us to rejecting beliefs about human nature that we may once have cherished. It can also lead us to accept conclusions that we would rather not believe. But always, this scientific standpoint means that we are aware of uncertainty. Findings are facts, so we can say with confidence that a certain study has produced certain results. As facts and theories accumulate, we can become gradually more certain. However, there is always significant uncertainty when applying this knowledge to explain an event such as the August 2011 English riots. It is difficult to rule out other causes, or to say definitively that ill discipline during childhood has played a significant causal role in this case. This distinguishes scientific and, therefore, social psychological explanations from many that are offered in day-to-day life. Many people will confidently assert that 'these riots have nothing to do with poverty', or 'these riots are the government's chickens coming home to roost'. To put it politely, these assertions are seldom informed by an exhaustive knowledge of fact and theory. In contrast, social psychologists will seldom rule out alternative explanations with such confidence.

Therefore, a third lesson we hope you take away from this book is that the scientific approach taken by most social psychologists means that we recognize uncertainty. We build theories and do research to reduce this uncertainty, but scientific progress always means that we discover not only new facts, but new questions. Social psychology is a relatively young discipline, being barely a century old, and there is much to learn. This presents exciting opportunities for people to learn about the topic. Again and again in this book, we will highlight gaps and blind spots in social psychology, and invite you to think of research that might be done to cast light on unanswered questions. However, much has already been learned. Social psychologists have discovered much about the factors affecting mental health, the quality of relationships, aggression, generosity, love, conflict and peace, to name but a few topics. These insights have been translated into programmes that are bringing about clear improvements to people's lives. Nonetheless, there is always the potential to doubt, to wonder why and what if, not only to satisfy our natural curiosity but also to make possible further improvements and advances in the field.

Now, let us get started. We will begin this chapter by defining social psychology and explaining how it is done, before guiding you through the many topics that have been studied by social psychologists in the following chapters. As we move through this chapter, we will discuss the origins and history of social psychology from the emergence of the discipline at the beginning of the 20th century, through the major influences on the discipline and to the current state of the art. The chapter then focuses on the ways in which social psychological research is done.

What is social psychology?

Social psychology A branch of psychology dedicated to the study of how people think about, influence and relate to each other.

Scholars in many disciplines such as sociology, linguistics, social anthropology, philosophy and biology have long been interested in how people relate to one other and how they negotiate their way through a complex social world. The discipline of **social psychology** has drawn upon insights and knowledge from these academic subjects – and indeed other branches of psychology, such as cognitive, biological, developmental, organizational, clinical, health and personality psychology – to develop an understanding of how people navigate the complexities of their relationships with others and the social environment in which they live. Social psychology is broadly defined as the branch of psychology dedicated to the study of how people think about, influence and relate to each other.

It is an extremely complex and intriguing discipline. No two individuals, social encounters or relationships are exactly the same. Any number of forces operate at once to shape social events, including moods, attitudes, values, stress, the weather, religion, culture and so on. To deal with this variety and complexity, a range of sub-topics are studied under the umbrella of social psychology. In this book, we approach the different sub-topics of social psychology as they have been grouped and studied by social psychologists over the history of the discipline. Of course, there is a significant amount of overlap in the way social psychologists study these particular topics. For example, a researcher interested in communication may also focus on relations between and within groups. A researcher interested in attitudes may also focus on social influence and persuasion. The topics are not therefore mutually exclusive but can nevertheless be organized into general areas that social psychologists have studied in an attempt to understand human social behaviour (see Figure 1.2).

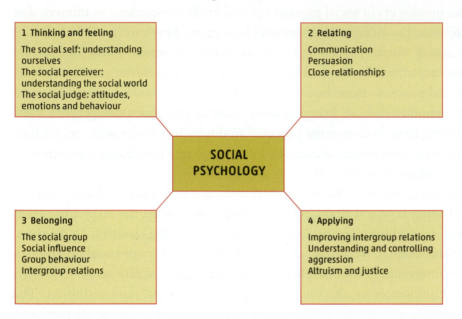

1 Thinking and feeling
The social self: understanding ourselves
The social perceiver: understanding the social world
The social judge: attitudes, emotions and behaviour

2 Relating
Communication
Persuasion
Close relationships

SOCIAL PSYCHOLOGY

3 Belonging
The social group
Social influence
Group behaviour
Intergroup relations

4 Applying
Improving intergroup relations
Understanding and controlling aggression
Altruism and justice

FIGURE 1.2 The different sub-topics of social psychology

Specifically, some social psychologists study processes occurring within the individual, that is, aspects of the self, beliefs and attitudes. The study of these topics is approached in this text as the study of *thinking and feeling* (Part 1), focusing on how people understand themselves and others, and how they judge the social world. Other social psychologists study relation-ships between others, as presented in the part on *relating* (Part 2), focusing on the study of communication, persuasion and close relationships. Further, social psychologists also study people's *belonging* to small and larger social groups, studying how groups influence who we are and how they influence our behaviour (Part 3). Others *apply* basic social psychological knowledge to social issues such as aggression, social harmony and justice, and address societal problems in areas such as business, education and health (Part 4). What ties these sub-disciplines together is the general aim to further knowledge about the relationships between people and the social world. The focus on how people are affected by the actual or implied presence of others (Allport, 1954) is what makes this branch of psychology *social*.

Here, we first focus on social psychology as a **scientific discipline** that uses the scientific method of collecting data, or results, to devise and empirically test **theories** about human nature. Just like the so-called 'hard sciences' such as biology and physics, many social psychologists empirically put theories to the test to make discoveries, draw conclusions and refine theories for future investigations. They test what are thought to be more or less universal laws of human nature. Researchers are typically aware that people from different cultures or with different personali-ties and experiences may behave differently. However, they normally assume that even these differences can be explained by more general principles. To go back to

Scientific discipline A branch of study that involves the gathering of data to test hypotheses that are derived from theories.

Theory A set of principles that aim to explain a phenomenon.

our riots example, you can imagine that a researcher finds that growing up in a dysfunctional family is a major predictor of rioting behaviour, and publishes that finding. The same researcher, or perhaps a different researcher, might then reason that the effect of family dysfunction on rioting may depend on poverty. So they do a study that examines the effects of both variables – family characteristics and economic circumstances. They find the predicted 'interaction effect' and publish those findings. The discipline therefore develops through the same processes as other sciences. Of course, we can use the word 'discipline' here with two different meanings. First, social psychology is a discipline, or subject area of study. Second, as a scientific discipline it also requires rigour that is necessary for scientific enquiry. We therefore spend some time towards the end of the chapter focusing on the methods with which the science of social psychology is done.

However, not all social psychologists consider the discipline to be a science. Specifically, **critical social psychologists** argue that there are no universal laws when it comes to human nature (e.g., Harré, 1997). Critical social psychologists argue that when contexts change (e.g., time and place), so do social rules and conventions. According to this perspective, it is impossible to explain human behaviour using theories of universal principles because these principles constantly change depending on the context. The term 'critical' is not explicitly meant to imply that mainstream social psychologists are *un*critical. Instead, the term is one that is used in sociology (critical theory) which concerns the examination and critique of society and culture. Towards the end of the chapter, we focus on some of the methods used by critical social psychologists to study key issues in social psychology.

The two 'camps' of social psychology, although both address similar issues and are concerned with the same types of social problems, are often in a 'battle' with each other (e.g., Stainton Rogers, 2011). A minority of social psychologists adopt both approaches, but, typically, social psychologists identify themselves as either mainstream or critical social psychologists and, indeed, both feel strongly attached to the epistemological assumptions they make and the methods they use. However, although the two approaches may seem antagonistic and impossible to integrate, it is essential for students of social psychology to understand and appreciate the strengths (and limitations) of both approaches. We explore these throughout the chapter and the book.

Critical social psychology
An alternative to mainstream (often termed experimental) social psychology arguing that mainstream social psychology is limited by its focus on 'universals' of human nature, which do not exist.

Where does social psychology come from?

Although social psychology has drawn on insights from other areas of psychology and other academic disciplines, it is itself a relatively recent discipline. To understand social psychology, some knowledge of its historical context is necessary. This section provides an overview of where social psychology has come from and how it has evolved over the decades. We also present some of the challenges that have faced the discipline over the years.

Early social psychology

The basic questions in social psychology have been the interest of scholars for many centuries. However, it is possible to trace some of the early influences for the discipline of social psychology as we know it today. In the 18th century, British scholars such as David Hume ([1741]1985) and Adam Smith ([1759]2007) wrote about matters related to social psychology. For example, Hume wrote about how people learn to explain events in their lives, by observing what causes tend to correspond with what effects. Hume's writings were, in many respects, the beginning of 'attribution theory', the study of how people explain events, which we will encounter in Chapter 3. Smith wrote about emotions and morality, and their influence on how people trade and exchange goods with each other. His writings have been influential in the social psychological study of emotions (Chapter 4), and justice (Chapter 14). Eighteenth-century German scholars such as Immanuel Kant, Wilhelm von Humboldt and Johann Friedrich Herbart, and the French scholar Auguste Comte also wrote about issues that are of interest to modern-day social psychologists. Kant wrote about the self and the self image, Herbart argued that society was a vital aspect of human existence (Chapter 8), Humboldt stressed the relationship between language and thought (Chapter 5), and Comte argued that social processes could be examined using the same methods as those used in the natural sciences (Chapter 1, and throughout this book). Thus, social psychology has its origins in the British, German and French scholars of the 18th century. Indeed, Herbart and Comte are viewed by many as being the 'fathers' of social psychology.

In the late 19th century, a group of German scholars, largely inspired by the writing of Herbart, began to study the concept of the 'collective mind'. In contrast to the 'individual mind', which was the focus of early forms of general psychology, the collective mind referred to the way in which people think about society, but also the way groups form a 'mind' of their own. Specifically, people who belong to the same social group or groups tend to think in the same way, have the same values and observe the same norms. This discipline was referred to as **Völkerpsychologie** (folk psychology or 'psychology of the people') and is also associated with the work of Wilhelm Wundt, who argued that individual and social psychology were distinct phenomena, and that individual consciousness was influenced by social customs and morals.

Völkerpsychologie also had a significant influence on how early theorists viewed the behaviour of groups. As you will see in Chapter 10 when group behaviour is discussed in detail, theorists such as Gustave Le Bon ([1896]1908) and William McDougall (1920) viewed the group as possessing a 'group mind', in which ideas and notions become 'contagious', much like a disease, and spread throughout the group. According to this view, people in large groups can lose a sense of their individuality and often behave in primitive antisocial ways that they would not even consider when acting alone. As we will see, this perspective led to a rather pessimistic outlook on groups and group behaviour. However, these early ideas helped us to appreciate that in order to understand human behaviour, we need to appreciate individuals as part of collectives and groups (Asch, 1951).

Völkerpsychologie Late 19th-century precursor to social psychology. The study of 'the collective mind'.

Social psychology began to assert its individuality as a discipline with a series of texts written by various authors (e.g., Baldwin, 1897; Bunge, 1903; McDougall, 1919; Orano, 1901), each exploring a variety of social psychological topics such as emotions, morals and individual character. McDougall (1919) argued strongly for the separation of social psychology from sociology and anthropology, while also arguing that social processes should be studied experimentally. Arguably, however, social psychology was first established as a distinct discipline at the beginning of the 20th century with the publication of Floyd Allport's (1924) book *Social Psychology* – an influential book that was subsequently adopted by teachers of psychology for many years. Inspired by the growth of experimental psychology in the USA, Allport argued that social psychology would develop as a discipline if it approached its questions as an experimental science. Others followed this perspective (e.g., Murphy and Murphy, 1931) and this North American approach to social psychology rapidly replaced the German tradition.

Early work in social psychology was also strongly influenced by **behaviourism**. In the early 20th century, there was a surge of research, especially animal research, focusing on the impact of positive and negative events on behaviour. Put quite simply, behaviourists argued that behaviour that was followed with a reward would continue, whereas behaviour that was followed by punishment would not. Animals (and people) could therefore be 'trained' to perform desired behaviours as long as they were rewarded for performing them (Figure 1.3). Much research supported this premise, showing that, for example, pigeons could be trained to move around in a circle, or nod if the behaviour was reinforced with a food reward (Skinner, 1938).

The behaviourist approach has been very influential in social psychology. Many social psychologists argue that people form attitudes and perform behaviours because they either have their own attitudes and behaviours reinforced, or they observe the attitudes and behaviours of others being rewarded. For example, children develop negative attitudes about social groups from observing their parents (Aboud and Doyle, 1996; Castelli, Zogmaister and Tomelleri, 2009; Hughes, Rodriguez, Smith et al., 2006). Children who watch TV programmes or play video games in which characters' violence is rewarded become more violent than children who do not (Anderson, 2002; Eron, 1963; Huesmann, Moise-Titus, Podolski and Eron, 2003). Although the behaviourist approach explains a great deal of social behaviour, it has also been criticized for being simplistic. It is difficult to reconcile some more complex social phenomena (e.g., thoughts, attitudes, emotions) with the simplicity of the social learning approach. For example, a reward may not necessarily lead to behavioural reinforcement for all the right reasons. A child who is rewarded with treats to practise piano may play the piano but rather unwillingly. They may be more motivated by the *extrinsic reward* (the treat) rather than the intended *intrinsic reward* of learning to play the piano well. If you are motivated only by extrinsic rewards, there's a good chance you will not enjoy the task as much, or do it as well, as someone who is motivated by intrinsic rewards (Deci and Ryan, 2000).

Behaviourism Approach based on explaining behaviours in relation to reinforcement.

© GETTY

FIGURE 1.3 Practising the piano for pleasure or reward? Behaviour can be misleading and can be the result of other motivations. For example, promising a child treats in exchange for practising the piano might make them play more but not because of their love of music.

Gestalt psychology Approach proposing that objects are viewed in a holistic sense.

Partly as a consequence of this limitation, **Gestalt psychology** emerged, emphasizing the importance of looking at a whole object and how it appears to people, rather than focusing on specific aspects of the object. The word 'Gestalt' comes from German and means 'shape'. It is a word used in English to refer to the concept of 'wholeness'. Using the example in Figure 1.4, a Gestalt psychologist would argue that it is impossible to see the Dalmatian by focusing on any of the black or white spaces in the picture, nor can it be identified in parts (e.g., the tail, feet, head). When asked to focus on the picture as a whole, the image of the dog emerges to the perceiver and it appears all at once. It can only be perceived and appreciated as a whole object.

PHOTOGRAPHER: RC JAMES

FIGURE 1.4 A Dalmatian emerges as a whole, at once This image demonstrates a principle of Gestalt psychology that the brain is holistic, with self-organizing tendencies.
Source: Gregory, 1970

How is this relevant to social psychology? Gestalt psychologists argued that perception was important in determining attitudes and behaviours. In particular, Kurt Lewin created a framework called **force field analysis** (Lewin, 1943) that expressed human dynamics in the form of a map (see Figure 1.5). The map consists of a person's needs, desires and goals, and arrows indicate the directions and strengths of these forces. All these social forces operated as a Gestalt. Lewin's theory inspired the work of many other social psychologists, such as Muzafer Sherif, Solomon Asch and Leon Festinger, whose work you will read about throughout this book.

Force field analysis Gestalt framework developed by Kurt Lewin to explain human dynamics.

Historical context

It is also important to consider the historical context surrounding the development of social psychology. Earlier, we mentioned William McDougall (1919), whose arguments were largely influenced by Darwinian evolutionary theory – a perspective that was a dominant theme in anthropological and sociological research at the time. However, his arguments about human nature based on evolutionary theory were often ideologically driven and supremacist. Specifically, his social scientific

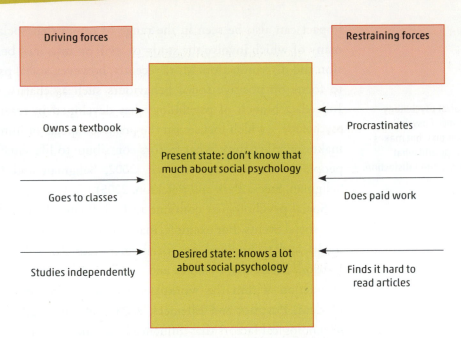

FIGURE 1.5 An example of a Lewinian 'force field' Lewin argued that behaviour is kept in a kind of equilibrium, being held in place by forces that drive change and forces that restrain change. If the number and length of the lines is roughly equal, change is unlikely. If you want to achieve change, you can increase the driving forces (e.g., by attending more classes, or doing more independent reading and exercises), or you can decrease the restraining forces (e.g., by procrastinating less, or taking on less paid work, if possible).

Driving forces

Restraining forces

Owns a textbook

Procrastinates

Present state: don't know that much about social psychology

Goes to classes

Does paid work

Desired state: knows a lot about social psychology

Studies independently

Finds it hard to read articles

explanations, and others at the time, were motivated by the desire to explain the differences between 'civilized' or evolved (that is, Western) people and 'uncivilized' or not yet evolved (that is, non-Western) people (Baumgardner, 1977).

The social backgrounds of the scholars themselves have also strongly influenced the development of social psychology. For example, we spoke earlier about Kurt Lewin's contributions to the influence of Gestalt principles on social psychology. Lewin was born into a Jewish family in Poland and served in the German army during the First World War. Forced to leave Germany in response to Hitler's Nazism, his subsequent research focused on the social problems and other factors that contribute to stereotyping and prejudice. Similarly, the research of Muzafer Sherif into group processes and group conflict (see Chapter 9) was surely influenced by his own experience of Nazi persecution.

The atrocities of Nazi Germany have had a significant influence on social psychology. Much of the theory and research in social psychology has been inspired by the Holocaust (see Figure 1.6). For example, the early work on social influence and conformity (see Chapter 9) was largely a result of researchers wanting to explain why people so readily complied with the requests of their superiors and what processes could possibly explain the atrocities that occurred. Also, the study and theories of social loafing and bystander intervention (see Chapters 10 and 14) have been informed by the events of the Holocaust. For example, how do we explain why people sometimes idly stand by and let bad things happen? This

FIGURE 1.6 Stamp commemorating the Holocaust The atrocities of Nazi Germany have had a significant influence on social psychology, from the work of Kurt Lewin and Muzafer Sherif, to the later work on social influence, conformity, aggression and bystander intervention.

impact can also be seen in the range of topics that social psychologists study – many of which involve the study of 'evil' or antisocial behaviours such as aggression and discrimination. More recently, however, social psychologists have started to focus on positive social behaviours such as charity work and volunteering. Indeed, a branch of psychology has developed in recent years – **positive social psychology** – which focuses on the positive aspects of human nature, such as what makes people happy, what factors contribute to life satisfaction, and the study of people qualities (e.g., Seligman, 2002; Seligman and Csikszentmihalyi, 2000; Seligman, Steen, Park and Peterson, 2005).

Positive social psychology
Branch of social psychology that focuses on what makes people happy and what contributes to life satisfaction.

Social psychologists continue to be influenced by real-world social problems and social events. For example, many social psychologists study the impact of new media and technology on social interaction (e.g., Bargh and McKenna, 2004; Joinson, McKenna, Postmes and Reips, 2007; McKenna and Bargh, 2000). Social interaction within the workplace is also an important area of research (e.g., Haslam, Postmes and Ellemers, 2003; Katz and Kahn, 1978), as are the social psychological factors that influence health behaviours such as the decision to quit smoking (e.g., Fishbein, 1982; Stroebe, 2000). Some social psychologists study the topical issues of rioting and hooliganism (e.g., Cronin and Reicher, 2009; Stott, Adang, Livingstone and Schreiber, 2007). In short, social psychologists 'move with the times' and study important social problems as they emerge. In Chapter 15, we go into depth on some of the ways in which social psychologists address social problems.

Time to reflect We have talked about how social psychology has been inspired by events such as the Holocaust. From what you know about social psychology so far, can you think of two other examples of societal issues, events or problems that might be investigated by a social psychologist?

Doing social psychological research

The need for empirical investigation

Much of social psychology focuses on real-world questions and issues. For example, we want to understand the origins of prejudice and discrimination. We want to know why some people are shy at parties and others are more outgoing. We want to understand how to form better friendships and relationships. We want to know how to persuade someone to go out on a date. The list goes on. Because many social psychological questions lie at the heart of human nature, people have often already formulated some of the answers for themselves. However, with this 'lay understanding' of social psychology comes a problem – many social psychological findings are seen as 'common sense'.

Hindsight bias/the 'I knew it all along' effect The tendency for people to see an outcome as inevitable once the actual outcome is known.

Much of this perception stems from what is known as **hindsight bias**, or the **'I knew it all along' effect**. This refers to the tendency for people to see a given outcome as inevitable once the actual outcome is known (Bernstein, Erdfelder, Meltzoff et al., 2011; Blank, Musch and Pohl, 2008; Bradfield and Wells, 2005; Fischhoff, Gonzalez, Lerner and Small, 2005). It is particularly relevant to social psychology because much of the research in social psychology deals with everyday, ordinary aspects of human thinking and behaviour. Therefore, when a person reads about a social psychological finding in the newspaper, they are likely to see it as something that was obvious, or easy to predict. However, this is, quite simply, a bias. People who are naive to the outcome are significantly less likely to predict it. Some important findings in social psychology may seem obvious in hindsight. We highlight a few examples in the practical activity below.

Try it yourself Here are some common findings in social psychology. Are they obvious, or only in hindsight? You may like to cover the right-hand column and examine the accuracy of your predictions.

Question	Outcome
Is it true, as noted by a common English idiom, that familiarity breeds contempt? Or, do birds of a feather flock together?	In general, we tend to like people with whom we are more familiar. Familiarity is associated with increased liking (Chapter 7)
Does thinking about death make a person feel more helpless, patriotic or selfish?	They are likely to feel more patriotic. Thinking about the inevitability of death makes people think more about the values that are important to them (Chapter 8)
If someone asked you to do a favour for them, would you like them more or less?	If we do a favour for someone, findings suggest that we like them more (Chapter 4)
If someone asked you to write an essay that went against your beliefs, would you feel better about it if you were paid nothing, a little, or a lot?	People tend to feel better about being untrue to their attitudes if they are paid nothing at all, or just a small amount (Chapter 4)

Hypotheses Predictions that are tested empirically.

Research question A question that guides the research that is conducted.

Scientific method A method that involves the formulation of hypotheses, based on theory and research, and the testing of those hypotheses.

As we mentioned earlier, most people see themselves as lay social psychologists. Indeed, people do have a reasonable intuitive understanding of social behaviour even though they fall foul to the hindsight bias. However, a key difference between laypeople and social psychologists is that social psychologists – that is, mainstream social psychologists – devise theories to answer questions scientifically. They use a wide variety of research methods to test **hypotheses**, or testable predictions, about human social processes.

Researchers begin by asking a **research question**. For example, social psychologists might ask if powerlessness makes people more likely to believe in conspiracy theories, or if money makes people happy. The research question guides the research that is done. However, a social psychologist typically has an idea what to expect. The use of the **scientific method** involves the formulation of testable hypotheses (that is, what the social psychologists expect) that are based on theories and previous research, and the testing of those hypotheses with the aim of answering the research question. A simple depiction of the scientific method is presented in Figure 1.7.

A great deal of social psychological work is theory driven, that is, the research question itself derives from a set of assumptions and propositions that organize the findings of previous research. For example, we will talk at length in later chapters about research that has been derived from theories such as social identity theory, system justification theory and social dominance theory. Theories are often modified as a result of the findings of empirical research. For example, if hypotheses are not supported, this means that the theory is also not supported. Either the theory is incorrect (and needs to be revised) or a new investigation

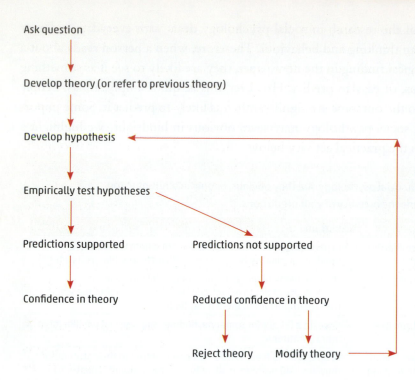

Ask question

Develop theory (or refer to previous theory)

Develop hypothesis

Empirically test hypotheses

Predictions supported   Predictions not supported

Confidence in theory   Reduced confidence in theory

                               Reject theory   Modify theory

FIGURE 1.7 The scientific method This comprises asking questions, devising theories, testing hypotheses and drawing conclusions

needs to be conducted that takes care of some potential flaws in the original investigation. Sometimes, when a study suffers some methodological flaws, these can influence the results and the study may not be a fair test of the hypotheses. Either way, research methods and theories are often modified as a result of empirical findings.

It must be noted, however, that a theory can never be 'proven' to be true. If a theory is supported by empirical findings, its predictive value is strengthened, but it can never completely be proven to be true, or be the one and only explanation for the phenomenon of interest. Instead, it can be said *not to be false*. As Popper (1959) argued, scientific theories cannot be proven beyond doubt but they should nevertheless be *falsifiable*. It must therefore be possible to set up empirical investigations that disprove the theory. A theory can be seen as a plausible explanation of a phenomenon if researchers have failed to disprove it. As you read through this book, you will be able to identify many social psychological theories. As you encounter these theories, perhaps you can take some time to think about ways in which they might be falsified.

On the other hand, some research is only loosely based on theory and is instead driven by a particular social phenomenon or social event. For example, we mentioned earlier a research question involving the connection between powerlessness and beliefs in conspiracy theories. This type of research question is more driven by the motivation to explain a phenomenon (conspiracy beliefs) than applying a particular theoretical perspective. Or, a social psychologist may want to explain why the people of the USA almost universally rejoiced the death of Osama bin Laden in May 2011, but responses across the rest of the world were quite different. Why are people's perceptions of terrorism often so dissimilar? Finally, following the example we used at the beginning of the chapter, a social psychologist may wish to explain why people rioted in England in August 2011. Research in social psychology is sometimes driven by a specific event rather than a theory. Of course, theories are crucial to the formulation of specific hypotheses, but the basic research question itself is sometimes driven by curiosity concerning a particular phenomenon.

To illustrate, immediately after the death of Osama bin Laden, we, together with Karen Douglas's PhD student Mike Wood, became curious about how several of the alternative 'conspiracy theories' about this event contradicted each other. On the one hand, doubters of the official story suggested he was still alive, while on the other, they suggested he had already been killed some years ago.

© SKDIZ/FOTOLIA.COM

Similarly, contradictory conspiracy theories sprang up around the death of Princess Diana in the 1990s (she faked her own death, or was murdered by MI6). We ran a couple of studies showing that, strikingly, people who believed in one conspiracy theory were also more likely to believe in another conspiracy theory, even if the two theories were mutually contradictory (Osama is still alive, and is already dead). This was explained by the fact that people who did not believe the official account of events (that Osama was killed by US forces in Abbotobad) tended to believe in *any* alternative to it (Wood, Douglas and Sutton, 2012). According to some theories in social psychology, commitment to an overall or 'global' belief (e.g., that authorities are deceitful and conspire against the population) will drive people to adopt a range of specific or 'local' beliefs that support it, even though the specific beliefs may contradict each other (Adorno, Frenkel-Brunswik, Levinson and Sanford, 1950). This research was not initially driven by theory, but in the end we were able to derive hypotheses from theory and put them to the test.

Once the research question has been proposed and the hypothesis formulated, the social psychologist then needs to decide how to make the research happen. This leads into a discussion of some of the research 'tools' or methods at the disposal of social psychologists. However, before we move onto a discussion of specific research methods, we must mention one other aspect of the research process – that of critical thinking – and also discuss the critical social psychological approach to research.

Critical thinking

Critical thinking is crucial to learning social psychology. In other words, a scholar of social psychology should appraise each piece of evidence they read and – based on what they know – see if they can develop alternative explanations. This is vital because sometimes a research finding is not everything it appears to be. For example, you might read a research paper arguing that religious people are happier and less stressed than non-religious people. What does this really mean? Are there other explanations? To understand this conclusion, it is necessary to critically examine the argument. To begin, a statement like this seems to imply that religion causes happiness and reduces stress (or the reverse for people with no religious beliefs). However, it is only the case that religious beliefs are *associated* with increased happiness and lower stress levels. It does not mean that one *causes* the other. Further, the statement may imply that the path leading from religion to happiness and low stress is a direct path, that is, no other factors are involved. However, what might really be occurring is an indirect relationship between the two factors through other variables. For instance, religious people may have more opportunity to get together in groups (e.g., at church). Their religious beliefs may also mean that they are more open-minded and creative. It may be these factors – social support and the psychological consequences of having religious beliefs – that lead to happiness and lower stress, rather than the religious beliefs themselves (e.g., Argyle, 1987, 2003). This is another example of the causal mediation we discussed earlier. It demonstrates the importance of thinking critically about findings in social psychology, in other words, to not simply believe what you read.

Question to consider In light of what you have read so far, reread question 1 at the start of the chapter. Critically evaluate the claims that the rioting was 'criminality pure and simple' and 'mindless violence'. Critical thinking involves closely examining other potential explanations. What might some of these have been?

Critical social psychology

As mentioned earlier, not all social psychologists use the scientific method of hypothesis testing. In the 1960s and 70s, many social psychologists became concerned about the prominence of experimental social psychology focusing on social processes that occur at the level of the individual. European researchers such as Henri Tajfel (1972) and Serge Moscovici (1972) argued that because hypothesis testing tends to focus on rules that can predict individuals' thinking and behaviour, social psychology was becoming less 'social' or, more specifically, less about social issues (see also Pepitone, 1981; Taylor and Brown, 1979). This was viewed as a 'crisis' for social psychology and researchers such as Tajfel and Moscovici conducted research endeavouring to put the 'social' back into 'social psychology'. You will learn more about this crisis later in the Critical focus box.

This perspective also led to the development of what we now know as critical social psychology, which focuses on the contexts of social behaviour and emphasizes the study of human behaviour with respect to people's interactions with others. Critical social psychologists often see empirical work in social psychology as driven by a particular agenda, specifically an individualist agenda, and so argue that it is not ideologically neutral. Of course, these are debatable points. Most social psychologists would refuse to accept the criticism that social psychology as an empirical science is asocial. Throughout this textbook you will undoubtedly appreciate the breadth and depth of the investigations conducted by experimental social psychologists in particular. Also, it is a bold statement to criticize a scientist for having an explicit research agenda. Most would argue that empiricism is about discovery rather than simple confirmation of something we think we already know. However, the scientific method is not the only way of gaining knowledge about social psychology and how the social world is determined, in part, by the interactions of people within it (Stainton Rogers, 2011).

A significant minority of social psychologists are critical social psychologists. Many can be further classified as working in the area of **discursive psychology**, which argues that discourse (e.g., talk, written language) is the primary means by which people construct, communicate and interpret social meaning (e.g., Edwards and Potter, 1992). Another type of social psychology relates to **social constructionism**, which is informed by **postmodernism** (Nightingale and Crombie, 1999). Social constructionism emphasizes the way that social phenomena develop in social contexts. A social construct is a concept or activity that is a product (construct) of a particular group (Gergen, 1973, 1999; Jameson, 1991; Nicholson, 1990). Critical social psychologists are informed by Marxist theory and feminist

Discursive psychology
Language is viewed as social action, through which people construct their social world.

Social constructionism
Approach emphasizing the way social phenomena develop in social contexts.

Postmodernism An intentional departure from previously dominant approaches of enquiry, emphasizing that apparent realities are only social constructs and are therefore subject to change.

Social representations
Socially shared beliefs or
widely shared ideas and
values associated with our
cultures.

theory (e.g., Bardwick., 1971; Burman, 2011), and by some of the influential work by Moscovici (1961) on **social representations**, or the study of shared beliefs and values that are held by a culture or group. This research challenges the assumption that people all share a common view, because they often come from radically different cultures with different shared assumptions. Thus, what we may call mainstream social psychologists and critical social psychologists have quite different origins. One thing they do agree on, however, is that the social world is both an antecedent and consequence of the individuals and groups within it.

Time to reflect In the conflict between discursive or critical social psychology and its 'mainstream' counterpart, do you see echoes of the early division between German 'folk psychology' and American experimental social psychology?

CRITICAL FOCUS

The 'crisis' in social psychology

With the development of cognitive psychology in the 1950s and the shift away from behaviourism, the so-called 'cognitive revolution' took place. This brought a new set of research tools and empirical methods to the discipline of social psychology. Methods used by cognitive psychologists to study perception and memory became useful to social psychologists interested in many topics such as emotions, attitudes and stereotyping, allowing easy measurement of social psychological processes with individuals in the laboratory.

This led to the development of the new sub-field of social cognition in the 1970s and 80s, which rapidly became prominent within the field (Taylor, 1998). This development switched the focus of social psychology away from 'macro'-level investigations of social issues to 'micro'-level investigations of social phenomena as they occur at the level of the individual. For some social psychologists, this was seen as an important development that signalled the emergence of social psychology as a scientific discipline. Some argued that the discipline flourished, moving towards an integrated theoretical understanding of cognitive and social processes, and advanced applications of social psychological theory to important societal problems. Reliable and replicable findings in social psychology were an indicator that the discipline had come of age (e.g., Devine, Hamilton and Ostrom, 1994; Fiske and Taylor, 2008).

However, for some social psychologists, this emphasis on cognitive processes came at an unfortunate cost. Specifically, it was argued that as a consequence of using cognitive methods and analysing individuals, social psychology had become less 'social' (Ross, Lepper and Ward, 2010). In focusing on social processes as they occur within the individual, it was argued that the discipline had lost sight of the socially important issues that it was originally developed to address. It reduced complex social phenomena to something much less meaningful (e.g., what does a click of a button really tell us about prejudice?).

Many prominent European and American social psychologists have criticized social psychology for addressing issues of social importance with investigations at the level of the individual. For example, Tajfel (1972) emphasized the importance of the social group in social psychology, arguing for a more collectivist approach to social psychology than the individualistic approach of contemporary North American social psychology. Other theorists, such as Bruner (1990) and Moscovici (1972), emphasized the importance of culture, arguing that culture is both the 'tool and constraint of action and thought, the meeting point of the social and the individual' (Liverta-Sempio and Marchetti, 1997, p. 6). Also, Gergen (1989, p. 463) argued that reducing real-world phenomena to cognitive representations of the world means that social events 'cease to exist for the discipline as legitimate foci of concern'. Finally, in his history of social psychology, Allport (1968) criticized experimental social psychology for its triviality and lack of generalizability. He argued that most studies in experimental social psychology are 'snippets of empiricism, but nothing more' (p. 68). Further, Allport wondered if the objective scientific methods chosen by experimental social psychologists can tell us very much at all about practical problems and social concerns. The new emphasis on the study of social phenomena at the level of the individual seemed to go against Kurt Lewin's attempt to make the discipline socially useful.

Argument about the 'crisis' in social psychology continues to this day. In particular, many critical social psychologists argue that the crisis continues and that mainstream experimental social psychology still does not take the word 'social' seriously enough (Pancer, 1997). Alternative approaches, such as discursive psychology (e.g., Potter and Wetherell, 1987), ethogenics (Harré, 1979) and humanistic psychology (e.g., Shotter, 1984), attempt to understand people as constructions or products of their history, culture and environment. According to this standpoint, all behaviour should be understood within a social context, paying attention to historical, cultural, socioeconomic and political factors. It is argued that investigations at the level of the individual often fail to take such factors into account.

Questions

1 Think critically about the 'crisis' in social psychology, perhaps drawing up a table of the pros and cons of experimentation. What can we learn from experimentation and what can we not learn? Are there some issues in social psychology that are simply not suited to experimentation?

2 Think about the role of culture in social psychology. To what degree does culture hinder the arguably reductionist approach to social phenomena taken by experimental social psychologists?

3 Some alternatives to experimentation argue for more 'deconstructionist' approaches to the study of social psychology, analysing individuals' complex psychological responses in the form of text. Arguably, such analyses are subjective. What are the advantages and disadvantages of subjectivity in social psychological investigations?

The tools of social psychology

Methodology Research methods and their underlying assumptions.

Qualitative methodology Research approach based on interpretations of data generally obtained by observation, use of archives, or interviews. Data are typically verbal (e.g., spoken or written words), but interpretations of pictures, movement and other behaviours may feature in qualitative research.

Quantitative methodology Research approach based on the systematic measurement of events or phenomena and the statistical analysis of data.

Data Information, observations, measurements or responses that are collected, scientifically analysed and interpreted.

We will now focus on the methods of social psychology, beginning with quantitative research methods and then discussing some of the qualitative research methods also used by social psychologists. Once a research question has been proposed and a hypothesis has been formulated, a social psychologist needs to work out the best way to make the research happen. For most social psychologists, this means designing a study to put the hypothesis to the test. This is no small feat. There are many decisions that need to be made, first of which is the type of **methodology** that will best enable the social psychologist to test their hypothesis. A research methodology refers to the general approach taken to provide evidence for a research question. These can generally be seen as either **qualitative** or **quantitative methodologies**.

Qualitative research methods generally involve the collection of information in naturalistic settings. For example, a researcher may observe natural behaviour or language. They assign meaning to what they observe and interpret the behaviours and language in relation to their inherent meaning. On the other hand, quantitative methods involve the collection of **data** – information, quantifiable observations, measurements or responses – for scientific analysis and interpretation. Typically, quantitative social psychologists attempt to control features of the empirical setting in order to directly test the factor of interest.

The choice of whether to use quantitative or qualitative methodology depends largely on the research question being asked. For example, if a researcher wishes to conduct an in-depth examination of a particular social phenomenon, they may be more likely to opt for qualitative methods. If, on the other hand, they are interested in the effect of a discrete event on a particular phenomenon, they may want to measure the factor and therefore conduct a quantitative investigation. The choice of research methodology can also be driven by epistemological assumptions. As we discussed earlier, critical social psychologists do not necessarily believe that there are 'universals' of human nature, so quantitative investigations that attempt to generalize principles across humans are not seen as appropriate. Critical social psychologists, therefore, almost exclusively utilize qualitative methods. Other researchers, however, believe that qualitative methods do not allow researchers to draw conclusions about human nature. If this is viewed as a key goal of social psychology to a researcher, then they will not opt for qualitative methods. On the other hand, there are many social psychologists who use a mixture of both quantitative and qualitative methods.

Quantitative methods

Surveys and questionnaires

Surveys and questionnaires are among the most common research methods used in social psychology. These tools involve simply asking people a series of questions that the researcher has carefully designed and put together to address a specific research question or questions. In surveys, participants are often asked a series of questions in the form of an *interview* in which the investigator records the participants' answers. Alternatively, the survey can be conducted in the form of a *questionnaire*, where the participants record their own responses. A survey or questionnaire can ask for open-ended responses, that is, participants are asked to give their responses freely, in their own words. For example, one might ask participants to freely generate a list of traits that are common to people who seem to be easily persuaded (e.g., Douglas, Sutton and Stathi, 2010). In such a case, the responses may be analysed using qualitative analytical techniques (see later in this chapter), or the researcher may code for specific predetermined responses and analyse the data quantitatively.

On the other hand, some questionnaires ask participants for numerical responses. To use an example from our own research, a questionnaire may be designed to examine the relationship between sexism and restrictive attitudes towards the behaviours of pregnant women, such as the view that they should not drink any alcohol or eat any cheese (e.g., Murphy, Sutton, Douglas and McClellan, 2011; Sutton, Douglas and McClellan, 2011). The researcher carefully chooses the questions asked of the participants in order to test hypotheses. Participants are asked to record their responses to items on what is often referred to as a Likert-type scale, where participants respond with a number indicating their level of agreement or disagreement with a statement. These survey responses are averaged to obtain numerical scores for each participant on the variables of interest, that is, restrictive attitudes and sexism. In survey and questionnaire terminology, the relationship between one 'variable' (the predictor variable) on another (the criterion variable) is examined.

Surveys and questionnaires are a reasonably straightforward way to tap into people's attitudes, values and beliefs and this is one reason for their popularity. Also, they allow researchers to collect a large amount of data, so for the social psychologist interested in making broad conclusions about human nature, they are able to generalize their findings to the broader population. However, surveys and questionnaires are not without their disadvantages. In particular, the investigator chooses the questions to ask in the first place. Question choice may be subject to bias, in that the experimenter chooses a set of questions favouring a particular approach when others may have been fairer. When responses are not anonymous, participants may be reluctant to answer questions honestly and their responses may be subject to **demand characteristics** – they may respond in the way they think the investigator wants them to respond. Further, as we shall see in several chapters, people are not always conscious of all their attitudes (Nisbett and Wilson, 1977), and so are unable to report them in surveys and questionnaires. Also, questionnaires often fall prey to 'response set' – the tendency for people to always respond in the middle of a scale, or to agree to statements without thinking. Sometimes, this can lead to inflated responses (so-called 'ceiling effects') or responses that are too low (so-called 'floor effects'). All these can influence how the results are analysed and interpreted.

The use of surveys and questionnaires also raises the issue of correlation versus causality (see Ethics and research methods box), which is addressed by the use of experiments.

Demand characteristics
Aspects of a study that participants may interpret as 'demanding' a particular response.

ETHICS AND RESEARCH METHODS

Correlation versus causation

The use of questionnaires raises an important issue in social psychological research – that of *correlation versus causation*. In many areas of research, social psychologists are interested in examining the relationships between variables. Specifically, are increased values on one dimension (e.g., sexism) associated with increased values on another (e.g., prescriptive attitudes towards the behaviour of pregnant women, that is, the things that pregnant women should and should not do)? Are religious beliefs associated with happiness?

Correlational research examines the natural association between two or more variables, as in these examples. Such associations differ in their strength, that is, some variables are strongly correlated with each other but others are only weakly associated. Also, some variables are *positively correlated*, that is, as values on one variable increase, values on another variable also increase (see (a) below). However, some variables are *negatively correlated*, meaning that as values on one variable increase, values on the other decrease (see (b) below). Correlations range in size from –1 (perfect negative correlation) through 0 (no correlation) to 1 (perfect correlation). As a general rule of thumb, a correlation of 0.2 (or –0.2) is a small relationship, a correlation of 0.4 (or –0.4) is a moderate relationship and a correlation of 0.6 (or –0.6) is considered a strong relationship. The figures below show what correlational relationships might look like in a *scatterplot* – a graph of values of one variable on the x-axis, set against values of the other variable on the y-axis. Each dot on the graph represents one participant's responses on both variables of interest. In short, correlational studies enable researchers to examine how strong the relationships between variables are.

Correlational research does not, however, inform the researcher about *causality*. In other words, a researcher may hypothesize that sexism causes people to be more prescriptive about the behaviours of pregnant women, or that religion causes happiness, but cause cannot be established. It might be that attitudes towards the behaviour of pregnant women predict sexism, or there may be some third factor involved. It may be that religious beliefs increase people's use of social support networks and it is this factor that makes people happier. To determine whether changes in one variable bring about changes in another, the researcher must conduct **experimental research** in which levels of one variable are manipulated. We will talk more about this under 'Experiments'.

(a) Positive correlation

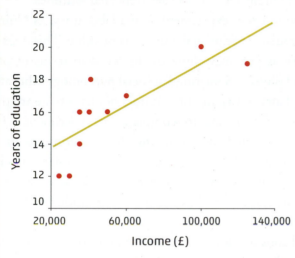

This figure demonstrates a hypothetical strong *positive correlation* between the number of years a person has been educated and their income level. The more years a person studies, the more money they are likely to earn.

(b) Negative correlation

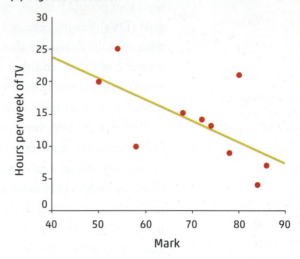

This figure demonstrates a hypothetical strong *negative correlation* between the number of hours a student watches TV and their average mark on leaving university (out of 100). The more hours a person watches TV per week, the lower their grades are likely to be.

Correlational research Examines the relationships or associations between variables.
Experimental research Examines the effect of one variable on another variable(s).

Experiments

Survey and questionnaire studies enable social psychologists to answer a wide range of research questions, but, crucially, they do not allow researchers to infer causality (see Ethics and research methods box). This is often an important question in social psychology. To be sure about which variable 'causes' which, social psychologists conduct experiments in which they control factors in order to measure the direct effect of one variable on another.

For example, consider a study where the researcher examines the effect of power on the pursuit of goals. In a correlational study, the researcher could measure people's feelings of power and the number of goals they pursue over a certain period of time. This would enable the researcher to determine the level of association between the two variables, but it would not answer the question of how power *affects* goal pursuit. To do this, the researcher needs to *manipulate* the variable of power in some way. In an experiment, the variable that is manipulated is called the **independent variable (IV)**. The IV is hypothesized to be the cause of changes in the **dependent variable (DV)**, which the experimenter measures. The

Independent variable (IV)
In an experiment, the IV is the variable that is manipulated and is hypothesized to cause a specific outcome in the dependent variable.

Dependent variable (DV)
In an experiment, the DV is the variable that is measured and is hypothesized to be influenced by the IV.

experimenter chooses how to manipulate the IV and the number of IV levels there should be. For example, Guinote (2007) manipulated power by asking half of the participants to think of a time when they felt in a position of power over someone else (high power) and asking the other half of the participants to think of a time when someone else was in a position of power over them (low power). There were, therefore, two levels of the IV. Guinote (2007, Studies 1 and 2) measured the time that people felt they needed to think about pursuing a goal and to initiate that goal (DVs); results revealed that participants in the high power condition took less time to make decisions about their preferred course of action than those in the low power condition, and that they took less time to initiate the goal. DVs in experiments can be measured in a variety of ways such as behaviours, physiological measures such as heart rate and brain activity, and self-reported attitudes.

Perhaps the best way to conduct an experiment is in a laboratory, as Guinote (2007) did, which ensures as much experimental control as possible. This does not necessarily mean a laboratory as you may think of the word in terms of other sciences such as chemistry and physics. Sometimes, a social psychology laboratory is simply a room with desks, chairs and a computer. It does not have to be anything more than a quiet space for participants to complete an experimental task. However, although we have separated questionnaires and experiments in our discussion, many questionnaires are, in fact, experiments. It is possible to manipulate IVs through verbal instructions in a questionnaire, or by presenting participants with a verbal scenario or story. Not all experiments are conducted by stern scientists wearing white lab coats.

There are various pros and cons of taking an experiment into the laboratory. As we have already mentioned, laboratory experiments allow a researcher as much control over the experiment as possible, therefore allowing for a stringent test of a hypothesis. However, one of the drawbacks is that the experiment can become artificial, thereby compromising the similarity between the experiment and the corresponding natural circumstances of interest in everyday life. This is known as the **external validity** (or **mundane realism**) of an experiment. In other words, when an experiment is so tightly controlled in a laboratory, some would argue that it cannot tell us a great deal about human nature in general which is subject to many complexities that are eliminated in the laboratory.

At the same time, this level of control can be looked at another way – in controlling as many factors as possible, an experimenter is able to focus on one or more specific variables of interest. While it may not be natural per se, the researcher is able to speak with some confidence about the influence of the variable(s) that has been manipulated. In particular, an experiment is said to be high in **internal validity** (or **experimental realism**) if the researcher can be confident that it is the manipulated variable that is having the effect (if any) on the dependent variable(s) in the experiment. Poor external validity is not, therefore, always problematic. Sometimes, creating a bare and artificial experimental setting allows researchers to make specific theoretical and practical points, which would be difficult to make with the presence of other 'noise' in the study. If the 'noise' is controlled and the

External validity/mundane realism The similarity between the situation of the experiment and the situation in which the phenomenon/ phenomena of interest occur in everyday life.

Internal validity/experimental realism The extent to which a researcher can be confident that the variable of interest produced the results.

Manipulation check In an experiment, the researcher takes an additional measure to ensure that the manipulation of an IV has had the desired effect.

Field experiment An experiment that is set up in the 'real world'. Participants are typically unaware that they are participating in an experiment.

Random assignment In an experiment, participants are allocated randomly to groups to avoid any potential effects of participant characteristics (e.g., age, gender) being overrepresented in one group and influencing the results.

Confounding When one (or more) IVs are related to another causal variable, so it is impossible to tell which variable is having an effect.

conditions for participants are different in no way apart from the way determined by the manipulation, then the researcher can be confident that they have fairly put their hypothesis to the test. However, the manipulation must be meaningful and realistic to the participants. For example, understanding the instructions in a manipulation is crucial, otherwise participants' misunderstanding will probably influence the results. For this reason, experimenters often include **manipulation checks** in their studies. For example, in the studies outlined above, after manipulating power, Guinote (2007) asked participants to rate the extent to which they felt in control of the situation they described. If participants in the 'high power' condition reported significantly higher levels of control than those in the 'low power' condition, then the researcher can be confident that participants have understood the manipulation and have responded appropriately. The internal validity of the study is therefore acceptable.

For some research questions, however, external validity is crucial. In many cases, **field experiments** are conducted which take place in the 'real world', but participants may not be aware that they are participating in a study. For example, an experimenter might go out to a shopping centre to examine people's reactions to invasions of their personal space. They may manipulate the magnitude of the invasion but the experiment has a more ecologically valid feel to it because the participants do not know they are participating in a study. If the study was conducted in a laboratory, the participants may get wise to the experimenter's motives and the study may not be a valid test of the hypothesis. Thus, field experiments are important and useful.

Both within and outside the laboratory, experiments have advantages over other methods when social psychologists want to make conclusions about human nature. The main reason for this is that through the **random assignment** of participants to conditions (levels of the IV), the experimenter can be confident that participants in the different conditions are similar. So long as you have enough people, and you randomly assign them to one of two groups, you can be confident that the two groups of people will have much the same age, attitudes, gender and any other traits that might affect the results of your study. Thus, you can be confident that if the two groups of people act differently, it is because of the condition they are assigned to – not because of some other difference between the two groups of people. Except for the influence of the IV, there should be no other differences across experimental conditions.

It is also important that experiments are designed in such a way that they avoid **confounding**, where variables are too closely related within the experiment and it is difficult to know which one is having an effect. For example, imagine an experiment with two different conditions, but everyone in the first condition was female and all participants in the second condition were male. The experimenter cannot be sure which variable is having an effect on the DV: the manipulation of the IV, or differences due to gender. Experimental conditions must therefore be identical in every way apart from the crucial differences that occur with the manipulation of the IV.

Also, experimenters often include a control group or condition, which is equal to the experimental condition in every respect apart from the lack of one 'ingredient' – the crucial feature of the IV that is predicted to directly affect the DV. For example, to determine the influence of positive feedback on a child's motivation at school, a **control condition** where no feedback is given must be included. Any difference between the children's motivation in the control condition and the feedback condition can be directly attributable to the feedback (e.g., Skipper and Douglas, 2011). Sometimes, however, complete experimental control is not possible or necessary. For example, social psychologists often want to investigate the effect of naturally occurring variables (e.g., age, gender, marital status) on various outcomes (e.g., life satisfaction). In such natural experiments, where the IVs of interest occur naturally, the researcher can take advantage of this and measure the DVs of interest.

There are a number of downsides to conducting experiments. For example, experiments are often subject to demand characteristics, as can be the case for surveys and questionnaires. Participants' behaviours and responses may be an artefact of the experimental situation itself rather than a response to the experimental manipulation. For example, participants may infer that the experimenter sees a particular mode of responding as *socially desirable*, and respond accordingly, which may bias the results (Rosenberg, 1969). Similarly, participants may become apprehensive about their responses, which may influence the findings. In both cases, the participants have some knowledge of the hypotheses. It may not be the most accurate knowledge, but it is sufficient enough to have a potential effect on the outcome of the experiment. Thus, it is important for the participants to be as blind to the hypotheses (and research conditions) as possible. Experiments are also subject to *experimenter effects* – effects that occur because the experimenter may inadvertently give the participants 'clues' to the hypotheses. Of course, this is not generally intentional. The researcher simply has knowledge of the experimental conditions and may unintentionally communicate their expectations to participants, potentially biasing the experiment. Therefore, as far as possible, the experimenter should also be blind to experimental conditions. When both experimenter and participant are blind to conditions, this is known as the **double-blind procedure**.

Control condition In an experiment, the control group is similar to a condition in which the IV is manipulated, except that the 'ingredient' that is hypothesized to influence the DV is missing.

Double-blind procedure Procedure in which neither experimenter nor participant have knowledge of the experimental conditions.

Try it yourself Identify the dependent and independent variable(s) in the following examples:

1 An experiment designed to examine the influence of imagined contact with a group on attitudes towards the group.
2 An experiment investigating how advertisement effectiveness is influenced by advertisement length and mode of presentation.
3 An experiment where people judge the attractiveness of faces of different ages and genders.

Techniques that can be quantitative or qualitative

Observations

Some research questions can be answered by merely observing what people do. Many social psychologists' research is informed by observations from which they learn about a particular phenomenon, make hypotheses and then conduct further research. However, observations are often used as a research tool without the use of other methods. For example, social psychologists sometimes use the technique of **participant observation** where they 'get close' to people and observe what they do. This type of research is similar to that conducted by anthropologists, who often study groups (e.g., religious, cultural and occupational groups) and societies by living and interacting with them for an extended period of time and directly observing their behaviour. For example, you may be familiar with the influential work of anthropologist Margaret Mead, who spent a great deal of time in South Pacific and Southeast Asian cultures studying attitudes towards sex and coming of age. Using this technique, the researcher typically observes natural behaviour and does not intervene, staying neutral and non-intrusive so as not to influence what is being observed. The technique of observation is sometimes called the **field study** method.

This method can also include the researcher conducting interviews (see Figure 1.8), discussions, reviewing life histories and reviewing personal documents. Sometimes, observations are purely qualitative, from which researchers draw out themes of observations and interactions, but sometimes observational studies can involve the collection of quantitative data. As mentioned earlier, in social psychology observations are typically used as a tool to generate and develop hypotheses. Unlike anthropologists for whom observations are a primary research method, social psychologists typically use observations more informally with the view to using the information gathered to develop other investigations to test hypotheses. There are good reasons for this. Although observations provide a rich set of information, what an investigator observes is, again, their choice and potentially subject to bias due to a lack of objectivity. If a researcher's goal is to describe human social psychological processes in general, it is difficult to do so based on observations of a small group of people. The observer may also accidentally interact with the people who they are observing, which can also bias the findings.

Case studies

Case studies allow a researcher to analyse a specific event, individual or group, in-depth. They involve a range of the tools we have discussed already, such as observations, surveys, interviews and questionnaires. As such, they have quantitative and qualitative aspects. The advantage to conducting case studies is that they allow for a detailed examination of the subject of interest. They are often used to

Participant observation Research technique in which researchers observe natural behaviour without intervening. It is often referred to as the field study method.

Field study A type of observational study where the researcher goes into the field to observe naturalistic behaviour.

FIGURE 1.8 Interviews These are used in several different types of social psychological research, including surveys, discourse analysis and case studies.

© PHOTODISC

examine phenomena that would be difficult to control in the laboratory, such as cults, criminal behaviour and people's responses to tragedies.

Archival studies

Archival studies involve going back to the 'archives' (as the name suggests) and examining evidence for a hypothesis among existing data. Archives can be many things, such as newspaper reports, political speeches, statistical records and court proceedings, which already exist and can be gathered over a long period of time. Of course, the original information was collected without the hypothesis in mind, so it cannot be biased in terms of how the information was collected. Information can be gathered relatively easily too, but the investigator needs to know what they are looking for, and how to look for it, in order to conduct archival research. Archival research is a rather underutilized tool in social psychology but it can tell us many things. To give one example, Mullen (1986) conducted an archival investigation of 60 newspaper reports of lynching events during the 1800s. Mullen coded the reports for information regarding group composition (number of victims and number of lynchers) and the atrocities performed (occurrence of hangings, shootings, burnings and other atrocities). Results suggested that as the size of the lynch mob, relative to the victims, increased, the mob became more aggressive and performed more atrocities.

Archival research such as this has the advantage of being able to inform social psychologists of social psychological phenomena as they have occurred in the past, and as they occur or change over a period of time. However, archival methods often involve laborious data collection. The researcher is also limited by the amount, and nature, of the information collected originally and may require vital information that is missing. Archival investigations are, therefore, sometimes unreliable. They are also able to answer a smaller range of research questions and so are relatively unpopular among the tools of social psychology.

Qualitative methods

Thematic analysis

As the name suggests, thematic analysis identifies themes in a set of data, usually derived from an interview. The analysis consists of two phases. First, the researcher identifies, analyses and describes patterns or themes within the data and, second, the researcher uses the themes to make further interpretations. This is a complex process of identifying initial themes and then revising and extending the list of themes several times before concluding the analysis and producing a report (Braun and Clarke, 2006). This is one of the most common qualitative methods used in social psychology.

Conversational analysis

Conversational analysis focuses closely on conversational interactions, producing a detailed analysis, classification and notification of the talk. The aim is to examine what people are doing with the language they use, as well as what they are hoping to achieve. Conversational analysis not only analyses the content of what people

are saying, it also analyses how people conduct the conversation, such as how they take turns and use pauses, interruptions and so on. It is designed to give a detailed analysis of how people use language and tailor their talk for specific situations. Typically, conversational analysis uses naturally occurring conversation such as interactions between doctors and patients (West, 1984) and in police interrogations (e.g., Stokoe, 2010).

Narrative analysis

Narrative analysis focuses on how people understand the world through the stories they tell to others. It is based on the idea that telling stories helps people to make meaning out of complex and often chaotic situations (Gergen and Gergen, 1984). Typically, a researcher conducting a narrative analysis will identify some research question or problem and identify the events or situations that will enable them to answer that question. The narratives then need to be collected. The researcher identifies who they want to hear stories from, designs an interview and then conducts the interview. Afterwards, the researcher transcribes the interview and interprets it (Parker, 2005).

Studying text: discourse analysis

Advocates of discourse analysis in social psychology argue that 'text' and 'talk' ought to be the principal focus of social psychology. For example, Potter (1996) has argued that language constructs social and psychological life, rather than being simply a way for researchers to study how people see the world. Language is the means by which people create their social world. Discourse analysis therefore studies language – language obtained from conversations, interviews and text (e.g., newspapers). The text is analysed and interpreted within the context in which it was produced. The researcher can then draw conclusions about what the person is communicating about their thoughts, feelings and experiences (e.g., Edwards and Potter, 1992; Potter, 1996; Potter and Wetherell, 1987). There are two main types of discourse analysis. The first, *micro-discourse analysis*, examines text and talk in fine detail with the aim of understanding what is occurring in particular interactions (e.g., how women deal with sexism). This analysis focuses on the features of the language use, discourse, verbal interaction and communication, and considers the text's syntax, structure and rhetorical devices. From this, researchers can generalize about the discursive practices that people use in specific situations. *Macro-discourse analysis*, on the other hand, aims to identify different discourses that occur surrounding a particular event or topic (e.g., a riot). It is concerned with understanding the broad, societal currents that influence the text being studied. At the middle level, *meso-discourse analysis* attempts to bridge the gap between the smaller details and the societal influences on the text.

Interpretative phenomenological analysis (IPA)

Interpretative phenomenological analysis (IPA) is based on the principle of phenomenology. This philosophy emphasizes the relationship between the world inside the mind and the greater world outside. It considers how people's conscious experience of existing within the world is made up of their feelings, relationships and experiences (e.g., Smith, 2011; Smith, Flowers and Larkin, 2009). This technique consists of extracting people's descriptions of concrete experiences, or narratives about these experiences. IPA uses data obtained from methods such as interviews and sometimes from other forms of text such as letters. In analysing the data, the researcher attempts to identify themes within the text and specifically looks for recurring themes. These themes are then organized into a hierarchy to establish if participants' responses suggest that some themes are more important than others. IPA enables researchers to compare the data from one participant with that of others to establish if there are themes and experiences that are common across people. For example, Rhodes and Smith (2010) gave an interpretative phenomenological analysis of the experience of depression using a case study of one man who had been diagnosed with depression. Interviews with the man were analysed using IPA, enabling the researchers to describe the origins of the illness and the complex effects that followed.

Question to consider Based on what you now know about the various 'tools' of social psychological research, reread question 2 at the start of the chapter. Which research method is the most appropriate and why? What are the strengths and weaknesses of the approach you have chosen?

Issues in conducting social psychological research

We have already discussed some of the issues that occur when conducting social psychological research. For example, experimental social psychologists are often confronted with the dilemma between making their research externally valid, that is, meaningful to something in the 'outside world', and controlling aspects of the context which are not of interest, thereby making the experiment more rigorous but less ecologically valid. We have also discussed the importance of both the participant and experimenter being blind to conditions, in case knowledge of the study objective can bias responses or the way in which the study is run. There are other issues of importance, which we will discuss briefly here. The first relates to how the participants for the studies are selected or sampled.

Sampling

Sampling The process of selecting participants for a study.

How participants are selected or **sampled** for social psychological research is important. To illustrate why this is the case, consider a hypothetical study where a researcher wants to examine the relationship between self-esteem and dieting behaviour among women. The researcher sends the survey to subscribers of a high circulation women's fashion magazine. Why might this not be such a good choice? Well, potentially, this could be a biased sample. One could argue that women who subscribe to fashion magazines are already more focused on issues related to appearance and weight – more so than most women – so they may not be a representative sample from which to test a general hypothesis about female respond-

Random sampling Taking a random group of participants from a population (e.g., giving every British adult the chance to participate in a study of British attitudes towards the government).

ents. To take a representative sample, the researcher would be wise to cast the net more widely in order to test their hypothesis on a range of women with different interests and not such a narrow sample.

Samples should also, where possible, be **random**. Put differently, from a population of interest, everyone should have an equal chance of being able to participate in the research (see Figure 1.9). For example, in a study of British attitudes towards the government, a researcher could not sample from only one region of Britain. A quick glance at the distribution of seats in the House of Commons across the UK (Conservative, Labour, Liberal Democrat, Plaid Cymru, Scottish National Party, Democratic Unionists and so on) suggests that the different regions vote quite differently. A sample of people from the southeast of England may have more positive attitudes towards a Conservative government (because they largely vote for this party), whereas the results may be entirely different in the northern regions of England, Scotland, Northern Ireland or Wales. So, in order to give a fair test of a hypothesis, it is important to sample randomly from the population of interest. Another way this can become a problem is through the issue of **self-selection**. This problem arises when participants select themselves for participation in a study because they are particularly interested or have a vested interest in the topic. For example, if a researcher advertises to the general public a study on conspiracy theories, they may attract a larger number of people who have a personal interest in conspiracy theories, thus potentially not being a representative sample of the population as a whole. Self-selection can influence the result in unpredictable ways. Again, researchers must be careful in their recruitment strategies to avoid potential biases creeping into the study.

Self-selection A problem arising when results in a study become difficult to interpret because participants with certain attitudes or characteristics disproportionately select themselves to participate in the research.

Of course, random sampling is not always possible. As you will notice throughout this book, social psychologists often make claims about human nature in general based on testing **convenience samples** of undergraduate participants. Indeed, critical social psychologists see this as a key weakness of quantitative social psychology and it is a valid point. Not all research questions can be answered by testing the responses of undergraduate psychology students. On the

Convenience sampling Taking a group of participants from an available subgroup (e.g., undergraduate participants).

© PHOTOALTO

FIGURE 1.9 Sampling
In social psychology, sampling should be representative of the population of interest and, where possible, be random.

other hand, it is important to consider the research question. Much of social psychology is concerned with how people think, feel and behave with respect to social situations. Many of the processes of interest should be (and are) universal. In such cases, samples of undergraduate psychology students should respond no differently to samples of non-students. This is a point worth considering as you read this book. In general, convenience samples are used frequently in social psychological research because they are just that – convenient – and mean that the researcher does not have to go to great lengths to randomly sample from larger populations. In many cases, there are no disadvantages in testing these smaller subsets of the population. In Chapter 15, we consider the importance of sampling in more detail.

Another issue related to sampling is exactly how many participants are needed in a social psychological study. In general, this depends largely on the nature of the study. If it is a questionnaire or survey study, there are guidelines for the number of participants that are required based on the number of questions being asked and the level of *statistical significance* the researcher uses as their guideline. We will say more about this later. However, it is useful to note that it is not always necessary to sample a large number of people in order to draw conclusions about a population as a whole. More often than not, a smaller random sample or small convenience sample is enough to draw valid conclusions. For example, the UK population at the time of the 2010 general election was approximately 62 million, and yet exit polls consisted of a random sample of only a few thousand voters across the country. Apart from some notable examples, exit polls tend to provide accurate predictions of electoral outcomes.

Thus far, we have discussed the issue of sampling in quantitative research. Sampling in qualitative studies is a different matter. In qualitative work, sampling is not random – it is *purposive.* As we have discussed earlier, qualitative social psychologists do not deal in universals of human nature and therefore do not have the goal of generalizing their findings. Instead, these researchers are more concerned with people's experiences, so samples will be chosen specifically for people who have had the experiences of interest. The sample does not need to be representative of some larger population. Also, a study may only use one person as a participant (case study) who has been chosen for a particular reason.

Question to consider Reread question 3 at the start of this chapter. Is it a problem that much of social psychological evidence comes from studies of undergraduate students? When might it be a problem and when might it not be an issue?

Reliability and validity

Reliability The extent to which the way a variable is measured is likely to yield consistent results.

Reliability is the extent to which the way a variable is measured, usually in a scale (e.g., extraversion), is likely to bring about consistent results. There are two types of reliability. The first, *test-retest reliability* is the similarity in measurements taken by a single person at different times. In other words, if a person responded to an extraversion scale twice, the scale would be deemed to be reliable if the responses were consistent between time one and time two, assuming that the conditions for taking the test were the same. The second, *internal consistency*, refers to the consistency across items within the scale. In other words, do all the items in the scale measure the same thing? Typically, scales designed to measure social psychological and personality constructs have at least two items, so the internal consistency of a scale can be determined by the correlation between the items within the scale. If the coefficient (Cronbach's alpha statistic is most common here) is high, then the scale is said to be internally consistent. As a general rule of thumb, a Cronbach's alpha score of 0.7 or above signifies a reliable scale (Nunnally, 1978).

Reliability is different to validity. Specifically, while a scale may be reliable, this means that it is consistently measuring something, but we do not necessarily know what. A researcher cannot be sure that the scale is measuring what it is supposed to be measuring. **Construct validity** refers to the relationship between a measure and a particular outcome that the measure is designed to predict. For instance, scores on a scale of extraversion should be related to scores on outcomes such as the number of friends a person has, how often they go out, or other indices of 'outgoingness'. If the measure of interest does not correlate with the predicted outcomes, then it may not be a valid measure of that outcome. Measures of validity typically reveal lower correlations than those for reliability. A scale may satisfy Nunnally's (1978) criterion of a correlation of 0.7, but the relationship between a scale of extraversion and a person's number of friends may only be 0.4. That is, a scale can be deemed valid even though the correlation between the responses on the scale and responses on the phenomenon or phenomena of interest is fairly low. Social psychologists may also begin to examine the validity of their measures right from the beginning of scale development. Specifically, they will examine the items they have chosen for what is known as *face validity* – a qualitative appraisal of whether the scale measures the phenomenon or phenomena of interest. If the items have been developed from a particular theoretical perspective, then the researcher will qualitatively appraise the items for their *content validity* to determine whether all phenomena of importance to the theory have been covered.

Construct validity The association between a measure and an outcome that the measure is designed to predict.

Statistical significance

One of the most important aspects of quantitative social psychology is its test of **statistical significance**. When a researcher has a finding such as a predicted difference between two experimental conditions or a significant correlation between two variables, this is interesting, but is it meaningful? Is the finding of sufficient importance to be able to make conclusions about it? To answer these questions, quantitative social psychologists determine the statistical significance of their findings. This determines the probability that the finding of interest could have occurred by chance. The researcher sets the highest possible significance level – indicated by a probability out of 100 – they would be satisfied with. Convention in social psychology is that the probability (or p value) needs to be less than 0.05 (a chance of 1 in 20) or 0.01 (a chance of 1 in 100) for the result to be of statistical significance and therefore of social psychological significance.

Statistical significance The measure of the probability that a given finding could have occurred by chance.

We will not talk about the specific tests that social psychologists use to determine statistical significance because this is the realm of statistical textbooks. Suffice it to say, quantitative social psychologists use a range of statistical tests to establish the reliability of their findings. A significant finding typically occurs because of the size of the difference between experimental conditions, or the size of a correlation. However, the size of the sample also matters. For example, some very small correlations can be significant when the sample size is large. Statistical significance may not always be the best index of the actual importance of a research finding.

Basic and applied research

Basic research Focuses on fundamental questions about people's thoughts, feelings and behaviours.

Applied research Applies basic research to problems or social issues.

Interventions Used in applied social psychology, these are efforts to change people's behaviour.

Another key distinction in social psychological research is that of basic versus applied research. **Basic research** focuses on fundamental questions about people's thoughts, feelings and behaviours. For example, a social psychologist may investigate why people help others, what factors cause them to fall in and out of love, and what persuasive techniques are most effective. Such questions lie at the heart of human nature. Basic social psychology is typically oriented towards using the findings to develop further theoretical understanding on a topic. However, many social psychologists conduct **applied research**, which takes information that is learned from basic research and applies it to particular problems or issues, often with the aim of enhancing the quality of everyday life. Applied research typically focuses on areas such as health, business, law, the environment and politics. For example, applied social psychologists can help employers hire more suitable employees. They can also design interventions to address social problems, such as excess energy use, prejudice, smoking, criminal behaviour, or educational issues (see the Social psychology in the real world box).

Basic and applied psychology are closely related and there is a two-way relationship between the two. Specifically, basic research may mean that researchers develop theories that result in the development of **interventions** – efforts to change people's behaviour. One good example of this in social psychology is the work associated with the theory of planned behaviour, which is a theory about the link between attitudes and behaviour (Ajzen, 1985; see also Chapter 4). Much of the basic research associated with this theory identifies the various pathways in the theory, how attitudes become accessible and how (and when) attitudes predict what people do. However, the theory has been applied in many studies to the study of the relationships between beliefs, attitudes, behavioural intentions and behaviours in many applied fields, such as advertising and health (e.g., Albarracin, Johnson, Fishbein and Muellerleile, 2001; Ajzen, 1988; Armitage and Conner, 2001; Conner, Kirk, Cade and Barrett, 2003; Sheeran and Taylor, 1999). Basic research can, therefore, inform applied research that attempts to improve some aspect of people's lives. However, it is also the case that the results obtained from applied research can enable basic social psychologists to further develop theories. For example, practically testing the theory of planned behaviour in health settings gives researchers an idea of what aspects of the theory work and what aspects need to be modified. So, it is perhaps unsurprising that many social psychologists have both basic and applied interests.

SOCIAL PSYCHOLOGY IN THE REAL WORLD

Social psychology at work in the classroom

The work of social psychologist Carol Dweck has been influential in the field of education, helping practitioners to understand what kind of praise and criticism 'work' best for children to keep them motivated and focused on their learning. In particular, Dweck (1999) and Kamins and Dweck (1999) have argued that praise can be distinguished between comments that are aimed at evaluating a person's traits or the person as a whole (e.g., 'You are a clever girl') and comments that focus on the person's effort or strategies (e.g., 'You found a good way to do it'). Kamins and Dweck (1999) showed that praising a child in *person* terms after they succeed leads to helpless responses to subsequent failures more than when the feedback relates to the concrete *process* through which the success was reached. Comparing the two groups' responses on measures such as persistence on the task, self-esteem and motivation, the children who had been praised in process terms showed more positive outcomes than the children who had been praised in person terms.

Dweck and colleagues argued that 'person praise' leads children to interpret their achievements in trait terms and encourages a fixed mindset of success more so than 'process praise', which focuses more on effort and behaviour. Following person praise, failures may signal that outcomes are due to poor ability or negative traits, thus undermining performance evaluations, affect, motivation and leading to a helpless response. These findings are striking because the differences in the wording of the feedback are generally so small (e.g., 'You are a good drawer' versus 'You did a good job drawing') that the person giving the feedback may not even notice the difference. Further, even if teachers do notice the difference, they may not be aware that the different forms of feedback have contrasting implications. Based on these findings, it is unsurprising that the education sector strongly promotes process-related praise (rather than person-related) in interventions to improve students' performance (Rathvon, 2008). Many intervention programmes, such as the online interactive 'Brainology'

© PHOTODISC

program, apply the findings of Dweck's work in order to help students to develop a growth mindset of intelligence and help them deal with academic challenges.

Questions

1 We know the effects of 'person praise' and 'process praise'. What do you think the impact of giving students 'no praise' might be?

2 Can you think of other domains in which Dweck's work may be applied?

3 Do you think that a child's mindset can be changed?

4 Shortly, we will talk about research ethics and this research is a good way to start you thinking about ethical issues in social psychological research. Conducting research with children can sometimes be an ethical minefield and conducting work on praise and criticism of children creates a variety of ethical issues. For example, how did the experimenter ensure that the children in the 'person' condition did not continue to feel helpless after the experiment finished? Read one of Dweck's empirical articles and see how she dealt with such issues.

Cultural issues

Another important issue to consider in social psychology is the influence of culture. We have spent some time thus far discussing how the majority of social psychologists are interested in the 'universals' of human nature, of which there appear to be many. However, there are some key social psychological phenomena and processes on which cultures differ. For example, all cultures have norms and standards of behaviour, but these are not necessarily the same across cultures or are expressed differently across cultures. Gender roles differ across cultures (e.g., Dasgupta, 1998; Fischer, Rodriguez Mosquera, van Vianen and Manstead, 2004), as do nonverbal behaviours (e.g., Matsumoto, 2006). In general, cultures can have a strong influence on how people think about themselves and the social environment (Matsumoto and Yoo, 2006). Try the practical activity below before you read further.

Try it yourself Take a piece of paper and write down 10 things that define who you are. Do this before you read on.

After you have made your list, tally up the number of 'I'-related statements you used and how many of your self-descriptions relate to personal traits (e.g., 'I am friendly', 'I am a student'). Compare this with the number of times the self is defined in terms of collective aspects (e.g., 'sister', 'grandchild'). How do you think your responses are influenced by your cultural origins? If you come from a different culture to some of your friends, compare your responses to theirs. Is there a difference in the number of 'I' self-descriptions you use compared to your friends? This exercise can reveal how culture influences the self-concept – a key area in social psychology.

Individualist cultures Cultures where people see themselves as independent entities with independent characteristics and voluntary social bonds.

Collectivist cultures Cultures where people see themselves as dependent on others with characteristics that respond to social situations, and important and involuntary social bonds.

One of the most important features of culture that determines differences in social psychological phenomena is whether it is an **individualist culture** or a **collectivist culture** (Fiske, Kitayama, Markus and Nisbett, 1998; Hofstede, 1980; Markus and Kitayama, 1991, 1994; Triandis, 1989, 1995). Individualist cultures are characterized by their independence. People within individualist cultures see themselves as distinct social beings, separate from each other and having characteristics that make them distinct from others. Social relationships are important, but are seen as voluntary. Collectivist cultures, on the other hand, are characterized by their interconnectedness with others. People within collectivist cultures see themselves as social beings who are inextricably linked to others, and having characteristics that are responsive to the social situation. Social relationships are vital and involuntary – they are part of what makes a person who they are. You can probably guess which countries fit broadly into each category. Western cultures such as Britain, Australia, New Zealand and the USA are individualistic cultures, while Eastern cultures, such as China, Japan, Korea, and many Latin American cultures are more collectivist. The key differences between individualist and collectivist cultures are given in Table 1.1.

Given these differences, it is probably not surprising to learn that social psychological phenomena depend heavily on the cultural orientation of the people involved (see Figure 1.10). We discuss these differences in more detail throughout the book. For example, in

TABLE 1.1 Characteristics of individualist and collectivist cultures

Individualist	Collectivist
Uniqueness	Belonging
Expressing one's own views	Being aware of others' views
Promotion of one's own goals	Promotion of others' goals
Directness	Indirectness

Source: Markus and Kitayama, 1991. © 1991, APA. Adapted with permission

FIGURE 1.10 Individualist versus collectivist cultures Individualists frame the self more in terms of individual and unique characteristics, whereas collectivist cultures tend to use statements related to group membership or relationships.

Chapter 2, we discuss how people's concept of self differs across the two broad types of culture. In response to the question 'Who are you?', people from individualist cultures tend to respond with more 'I'-related statements (e.g., 'I am clever', 'I like reading books'), whereas participants from collectivist cultures tend to respond with statements related to group membership or relationships (e.g., 'I am a Muslim', 'I am a mother') (Dhawan, Roseman, Naidu and Rettek, 1995; Heine and Lehman, 1997; Kitayama, Markus, Matsumoto and Norasakkunkit, 1997; Trafimow, Triandis and Goto, 1991; Yik, Bond and Paulhus, 1998). This distinction begins early in life, with children at age six years displaying this cultural difference (Wang, 2006). This is just one example of social psychological evidence from one culture that may not automatically apply to all cultures.

Researchers need to examine theories and test hypotheses across different cultures and put away the assumption that people in different cultures all think and act the same way. A great deal of information can be missed if culture is not taken into account. As you read this book, you may justifiably criticize social psychology for being too 'Western'. Most of the studies you will read about are based on data collected in white, English-speaking countries (in particular the USA), and therefore a lot of social psychological knowledge we have is drawn from a relatively homogeneous group of participants. So, when we learn about 'universals' of human thought and behaviour, while many phenomena are probably universal, we can only ever really be sure that we know about 'universals' of white, American undergraduate students, unless hypotheses are tested more broadly. It is important to keep this issue at the back of your mind as you read about evidence drawn from social psychological studies.

Research ethics

Informed consent Participants need to indicate their willingness to participate in research after being fully informed about what the research involves.

Social psychologists carry out their research with human participants, or utilize data that have been provided by human participants. Thus, it is vital that research is carried out with the safety and privacy of participants firmly in mind. All social psychologists receive training in research ethics throughout the course of their studies, and so we begin with an overview of these important, basic ethical principles.

When conducting research with human participants, it is vital that they have given their **informed consent** to take part in the research. This principle ensures that participants know exactly what is going to happen in an experiment or study and then they give their consent. In other words, participants should only be asked to agree to take part after they have been fully informed about the purpose of the study and how it will be conducted. However, this principle is difficult to observe when research is conducted with children as participants, because it is not always possible to communicate the intentions and methods of research to children in a way they completely understand. In such cases, it is possible to gain the consent of parents and carers, who act in the children's best interests and make the informed decision about consenting to participate in the research.

Deception In social psychology, deception is a case where the participants are misled about the purpose of the research or some aspect of the research.

The principle of informed consent is further complicated by the use of **deception**, a methodological technique frequently used in social psychological research. Deception occurs when a participant is misled about some aspect or aspects of the research – typically something about the purpose of a particular feature of the research method – or is not made fully aware of the specific purpose of the study. Deception is an important feature of social psychological research and does not make the research unethical. In some cases, it is difficult to test a hypothesis unless deception is used. For example, social psychological research often makes use of **confederates** – members of the research team who pose as participants and follow a predetermined procedure set up by the experimenter – to test how people interact in specific situations. The participant is misled to think they are interacting with a real person when, in fact, they are not. However, this type of method allows experimenters to control specific aspects of the experiment and test the effect of only those that are of interest.

Confederate A member of the research team who poses as a real participant and is instructed to interact or respond in a predetermined way.

In such situations where the use of deception is crucial to test hypotheses, the deception can be deemed to be appropriate if the following conditions are met:

1 A non-deceptive method to study the same phenomenon does not exist.
2 The study has the possibility of making a significant contribution to scientific knowledge.
3 The deception is not expected to cause the participant any harm or significant emotional distress.

Ethics committee A committee that evaluates the ethicality of research proposals and judges whether they are appropriate to investigate.

These factors are typically judged by an **ethics committee**. You may also come across the term 'institutional review board', which is used in the USA and Canada to refer to ethics committees. Ethics committees closely examine research proposals and determine whether the proposed research is ethical. In a case where deception is proposed, the committee decides, according to the three criteria above, whether the deception is justified. If some aspect of the study is deemed to be overly detrimental to the participants, it will be refused ethical clearance. In such cases, the researcher needs to make changes to the procedure and then resubmit the proposal for further evaluation.

Exploring further Take a look at the British Psychological Society's ethical code of conduct for carrying out research with human participants. You will find this via the homepage of the British Psychological Society (http://www.bps.org.uk). Before you conduct any research involving human participants, you need to be familiar with these guidelines. It is also likely that you will need to apply for ethical approval to conduct your research.

Ethics committees do an important job. However, they did not always exist and many famous studies in social psychology were conducted without ethical clearance. In Chapter 9, for example, you will read about Stanley Milgram's obedience studies, where participants were told that their task was to deliver strong electrical shocks to another participant. The shocks were never given, but the participants were led to believe that the recipient (a confederate) was experiencing extreme pain. Many of the participants exhibited signs of emotional distress as a result of taking part in this procedure. One might speculate as to whether such an experiment would be granted ethical clearance today. This would indeed pose some serious questions for an ethics committee. However, even in such an extreme case, the committee would carefully consider the pros and cons of the study – does the knowledge that could potentially be gained from the study outweigh the negative aspects? In the case of Milgram's studies, one would have to say 'yes'. Much of what social psychologists now know about obedience and compliance come from Milgram's studies.

In any case, Milgram followed one other key principle of conducting ethical research – he fully **debriefed** his participants at the conclusion of the study. It is important to let research participants know the true nature of a study, its purpose and hypotheses so that they know exactly why they did what they did. Note that debriefing can also be important to ensure that participants have understood an experimental manipulation, so it serves the purpose of maintaining internal validity during the study as well as upholding ethical standards after the study. Participants are also free to withdraw their consent and have their personal responses removed from the study if they are unhappy with any aspect of the study. As mentioned earlier, these principles are in place to protect the participant from harm or emotional distress and protect their privacy. Following ethical guidelines also means that research participants are treated with respect.

Debrief Participants are informed about the purpose, aims and hypotheses of the research.

Social psychology and links to other disciplines

Social psychology is closely related to other branches of psychology, such as personality, clinical, cognitive, forensic and the rapidly emerging area of cyberpsychology. Social psychology is also closely related to academic disciplines outside psychology, such as biology, neuroscience, sociology, social anthropology and economics. In this section, we outline some of the ways in which social psychology has been influenced by these sub-disciplines and disciplines, as well as the impact that social psychology has had on them.

Personality psychology

Also referred to as the study of individual differences, personality psychology is a close relation of social psychology. Personality psychology is referred to as the study of how people come to be who they are (Murray and McAdams, 2007). The link between the two can be understood by the following quotation, taken from the website of the Society for Personality and Social Psychology (www.spsp.org):

> By exploring forces within the person (such as traits, attitudes, and goals) as well as forces within the situation (such as social norms and incentives), personality and social psychologists seek to unravel the mysteries of individual and social life in areas as wide-ranging as prejudice, romantic attraction, persuasion, friendship, helping, aggression, conformity, and group interaction. Although personality psychology has traditionally focused on aspects of the individual, and social psychology on aspects of the situation, the two perspectives are tightly interwoven in psychological explanations of human behaviour.

Indeed, as you learn more about social psychological research, you will notice that many of the prominent journals in the field, such as the *Journal of Personality and Social Psychology*, *Personality and Social Psychology Bulletin* and *Social Psychological and Personality Science*, publish research on both topics. Social psychologists are often interested in individual differences and psychologists who study personality and individual differences often link their work to the study of social psychological processes.

Clinical psychology

Clinical psychologists attempt to understand, prevent and relieve psychologically based problems and promote wellbeing. For example, clinical psychology focuses on understanding and helping people with psychological disorders, such as bipolar mood disorder, schizophrenia, depression and phobias. Social and clinical psychology are linked in many ways and the treatments used by clinical psychologists are often informed by social psychological findings. For example, social psychologists study the processes underlying addictive behaviours (e.g., Fishbein, 1982; Stroebe, 2000), eating disorders (e.g., Harrison, 2001; Stice, 2002), relationship satisfaction (e.g., Pearson, Watkins, Kuyken and Mullan, 2010; Vinokur, Price and Caplan, 1996) and the practice of safe sex (e.g., Armitage and Talibudeen, 2010; Sheeran, 2002). Treatment of various clinical disorders and promoting physical health are therefore informed by social psychological research.

Cognitive psychology

Cognitive psychology is concerned with the study of mental processes. More specifically, it is the study of how people perceive, remember, think, speak and how they solve problems. Cognitive psychology has close links to social psychology and, indeed, a sub-discipline called *social cognition*, which we discuss in some detail in Chapter 3 and throughout this book, is a combination of social and cognitive psychology. It is the study of how people think about themselves and the social world and, in particular, how they make decisions and judgements concerning the social world. One of the main elements of theories in social cognition is that social processes occur as a result of 'cognitive elements', such as stereotypes, that are represented in the brain. Social cognition applies many theories and paradigms from cognitive psychology, focusing on areas such as reasoning, attention and memory.

Forensic psychology

Forensic psychology is a sub-discipline that deals with both psychology and the legal system. It is a popular topic among students, thanks, in part, to fashionable television and cinematic portrayals of forensic psychologists, such as in *Cracker* and *Silence of the Lambs*. Forensic psychology is a rapidly developing scientific branch of applied psychology, drawing on clinical, cognitive and social psychology to address legal and criminal issues. One topic in which social psychology is closely linked to forensic psychology is in the study of eyewitness memory and the accuracy of eyewitness testimony. Researchers have investigated the effects of a wide range of social psychological factors on eyewitness testimony, such as the status of the interrogator, the status of the witness, and the nature of the communicative context (e.g., Ross, Read and Toglia, 1994; Sporer, Malpass and Koehnken, 1996). Further, research on criminal confessions has drawn upon social psychological knowledge on compliance and coercion (e.g., Kassin, 1997; Vennard, 1984). Forensic psychologists also apply knowledge on deception (e.g., Vrij, 2000) to detect lying in courtroom situations, and research on how people process social information to understand aggressive and violent behaviour (Crick and Dodge, 1994). Social psychological knowledge on sexist ideology has informed the study of rape proclivity among males (Abrams, Viki, Masser and Bohner, 2003). In summary, social psychology plays an important role in theories of criminal behaviour and therefore closely informs a great deal of research conducted in forensic psychology.

Cyberpsychology

Cyberpsychology is a rapidly developing sub-field of psychology, which deals with the psychological phenomena associated with emerging technology and human–technology interaction. Some key topics in cyberpsychology include the emergence and expression of identity online (Spears, Lea and Postmes, 2007), the development and maintenance of online relationships (Whitty, 2007, 2008), the use of support groups (Tanis, 2007), group dynamics in cyberspace (Brandon and Hollingshead, 2007; Postmes, 2007), discrimination and prejudice in online groups (Douglas, 2007), self and identity (Joinson and Paine, 2007; McKenna, 2007), and attitude change and social influence (Sassenberg and Jonas, 2007). The study of all such topics has been significantly influenced by social psychological theory and research. As a significant proportion of the world are now connected to the internet and communication technology is advancing so quickly, investigations of online social behaviour are becoming increasingly important and of interest to many social psychologists (e.g., Joinson et al., 2007; Konijn, Utz, Tanis and Barnes, 2008; Suler, 1996).

Biology and neuroscience

Biologists examine the nature, function and evolution of living things. They examine how genetic factors influence people and what they do. As such, there is a significant link between biology and social psychology. In particular, recent years have seen the rise in prominence of *evolutionary psychology*, which approaches the study of human behaviour based on the assumption that the things people do (and think about) are a result of human evolution and, therefore, are a result of human biology (e.g., Neuberg, Kenrick and Schaller, 2011). Put simply, social behaviour and social thinking have biological roots. Evolutionary psychologists attempt to describe which human psychological traits (e.g., aggression, altruism) and behaviours (e.g., sexual selection) are 'evolved adaptations', that is, if such traits and behaviours are the result of natural selection over generations, or a result of sexual selection. The general argument underlying evolutionary psychology is that traits and behaviours have evolved to help humans solve recurrent problems in ancestral contexts.

In recent years, social psychologists have also become interested in the parts of the brain that are associated with various social psychological phenomena such as emotions and problem solving (e.g., Damasio, Grabowski, Bechara et al., 2000; Heatherton, Macrae and Kelly, 2004; Panksepp, 1998). In part, this has been due to the rise of evolutionary psychology. Social psychologists use neuroimaging techniques to examine where in the brain various social processes occur. Some of these techniques include positron emission tomography, event-related potentials (ERPs) using electroencephalography (EEG), and transcranial magnetic stimulation.

Much used in recent research, **functional magnetic resonance imaging (fMRI)** detects the changes in blood flow related to neural activity in the brain during specific tasks (see Figure 1.11). Blood flows to parts of the brain when they are active, so changes in blood flow following particular tasks can be inferred to be a result of those tasks. In a typical study that uses this type of neuroimaging, a participant is asked to lie still within a large, tubular scanner and perform a task. An example might be a task that involves a person solving problems, or experiencing different emotions. The fMRI takes pictures of the brain at different times and enables social psychologists to determine which parts of the brain are active as a result of social psychological tasks. The technique has the advantage of being accurate – sometimes as good as within 1 mm in pinpointing an area of the brain – and can measure activity *within* the brain, which provides an advantage over other techniques such as EEG, which record activity at the cortical *surface*.

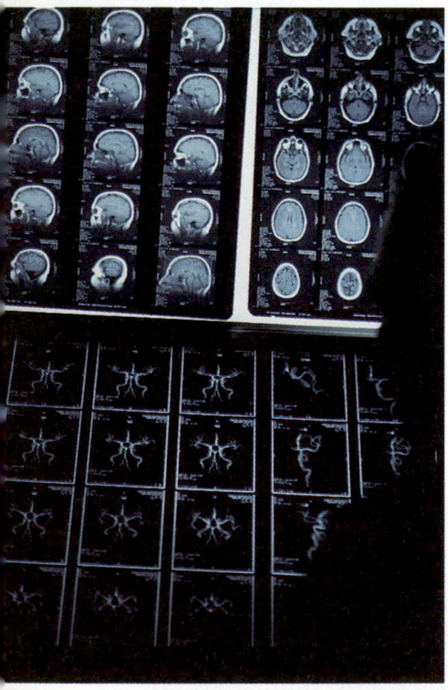

Social cognitive neuroscience – the study of social processes in the brain that allows people to understand themselves and others, and to successfully navigate the social world (Ochsner and Lieberman, 2001) – is a fast-growing sub-discipline of social psychology. It is a relatively recent area of study, beginning in the 1990s when researchers such as John Kihlstrom, Stanley Klein and John Cacioppo began to use methods such as ERPs to examine normal social cognitive processes. Instead of using questionnaires and reaction time measures, these social psychologists used neural measures to examine the origins of social processes (Lieberman, 2007; Oschner and Lieberman, 2001). The use of fMRI in social psychological research has exploded since 2000, and social psychologists now have a great deal of knowledge about things such as how people react to social rejection (e.g., Eisenberger, Lieberman and Williams, 2003), how people understand the self (e.g., Kelley, Macrae, Wyland et al., 2002), reactions to social interactions (e.g., Iacoboni, Lieberman, Knowlton et al., 2004), and social cognitive processing (e.g., Amodio and Frith, 2006). We will discuss some of these findings in social cognitive neuroscience throughout this book. The important thing to note about this area of social psychology is that although it is in its infancy, it has provided valuable insights into social processes and goes beyond simply describing which parts of the brain 'light up' following different social tasks. It provides a useful (although sometimes expensive) complement to behavioural and self-report measures.

Functional magnetic resonance imaging (fMRI)
A type of neuroimaging scan used by social psychologists to measure the change in blood flow that occurs in the brain during social tasks.

Social cognitive neuroscience
Study of processes in the brain that allows people to understand others and themselves, and to successfully navigate the social world.

© IMAGE 100

FIGURE 1.11 fMRI scans of the brain fMRI is a technique used widely in social neuroscience research to isolate parts of the brain associated with social psychological processes.

Sociology and social anthropology

Social psychologists address many of the same issues as sociologists and social anthropologists. For example, all three disciplines study the effects of culture, group membership, language and intergroup behaviour. However, these topics are approached in different ways. Specifically, while social psychologists typically focus on the effects of culture, groups and so on on individual members of a group (or indeed the individual's effect on cultures and groups), sociologists and anthropologists typically focus on the group or culture as a whole – how they are organized and how they function and change. The insights gained from sociology and social anthropology influence the theories and research of social psychology, and vice versa.

Economics

Social psychological principles are being used increasingly in the study of economics. Economics is often concerned with how people make trade-offs between various resources and options. For example, an economist may study how people choose to save versus spend their earnings or how they take risks in order to make monetary gains. Social psychological research on decision-making processes is applicable to these sorts of economic questions. Of particular interest to social psychology, economists study why people make choices that are not always best for them. For example, why do people donate to charity when it is not in their own financial interests? The field of *behavioural economics* uses insights gained from psychology (including social psychology) to understand how people make such economic decisions. In 2002, psychologist Professor Daniel Kahneman was awarded the Nobel Prize in economics, largely due to his focus on issues relevant to both psychology and economics, such as fairness in the marketplace. Together with Amos Tversky, Kahneman developed prospect theory, which describes decisions between alternatives when the choice involves risk or uncertain outcomes. The theory describes how people evaluate potential gains and losses in making decisions such as financial decisions.

Dissemination of social psychology

The primary means by which social psychologists communicate their findings to the scientific community is through publishing their work in scientific journals. As you progress through your studies, you will become familiar with all the major journals (and many others) – there has been a marked increase in the number of social psychological journals in recent years.

As mentioned earlier, many of the major journals publish work on personality and social psychology alongside each other, again reflecting the closeness of these two disciplines. Examples of such journals are the *Journal of Personality and Social Psychology*, *Social Psychology Quarterly*, *Personality and Social Psychology Bulletin* and *Social Psychological and Personality Science*. Other journals focus specifically on social psychology, such as the *Journal of Experimental Social*

Psychology, the *European Journal of Social Psychology* and the *British Journal of Social Psychology*. Other journals and volumes publish reviews of social psychological research, where authors consider the state of the art on a particular topic of research. Examples of such outlets are *Advances in Experimental Social Psychology* and *Personality and Social Psychology Review*. Finally, some journals focus on specific aspects of social psychology such as *Group Processes and Intergroup Relations, Social Influence, Law and Human Behaviour, Social Cognition* and *Sex Roles*. Qualitative research is published in journals such as *Discourse Studies, Feminism and Psychology* and *Qualitative Research in Psychology*, and some of the more 'mainstream' journals such as the *British Journal of Social Psychology* frequently publish qualitative research. Social psychologists also publish their work in multidisciplinary, applied, clinical, educational, biological and experimental journals, such as *Psychological Review, Psychological Science* and *Journal of Experimental Psychology: General*, reflecting the importance of social psychology across psychology as a whole.

Exploring further As an exercise, log in to ISI Web of Knowledge and go to the Social Sciences Journal Citation Reports. Select 'Psychology – Social' from the list of areas and take a look at the range of social psychology journals in which social psychologists publish their research. If your learning institution does not subscribe to ISI Web of Knowledge, try an internet search of 'journals in social psychology'.

Social psychologists often disseminate their research within book chapters. Also, with the growing use of the internet and social networking, social psychologists are increasingly making use of tools such as Facebook, Twitter, Academia.edu, LinkedIn, Google+, and other tools such as blogs, in order to share their research and insights. The British Psychological Society runs a brilliant research digest (BPS Research Digest), providing a monthly highlight of some of the most interesting papers in psychology, many of which are social psychology papers. In summary, social psychology has a significant presence within psychology, across other disciplines, and within the general public.

Chapter summary

This chapter provided a broad introduction to the discipline of social psychology, outlining its history, topics and methods. You will have learned that:

- Social psychology is the study of how people think about, influence and relate to each other. It aims to further knowledge about the relationships between people and the social world, focusing on how people are influenced by the actual or implied presence of others.
- The majority of social psychologists adopt the scientific method, empirically putting theories to the test to make discoveries and refine theories. Critical social psychologists challenge the scientific approach, arguing that there are no universals of human nature.

- Social psychology is a relatively recent discipline, having emerged in its own right in the late 1800s and early 1900s. Early work was influenced by behaviourism, focusing on the impact of positive and negative events on behaviour.
- Social psychology has also been deeply influenced by social events such as the Holocaust, and this continues to this day. Also, the social backgrounds of the scholars themselves have strongly influenced the development of social psychology.
- Much of social psychology focuses on real-world questions and issues. Because of this, many social psychological findings are seen as 'common sense' – a result of what is known as the hindsight bias or the 'I knew it all along' effect. Perhaps also because social psychological findings can be

intuitive, people see themselves as 'lay social psychologists'. The key difference between laypeople and social psychologists is that the latter devise theories to answer questions scientifically. Doing social psychology requires the generation of research questions and hypotheses that are tested using a variety of methods and critical thinking.

- Although most social psychologists adopt the scientific method, others have argued that hypothesis testing leads researchers to think less about the social context and so social psychology becomes less about social issues. In the 1970s, what was viewed as a 'crisis' in social psychology led some researchers to put the 'social' back into the discipline. This led to the development of critical social psychology, which gives more attention to social contexts and people's interactions with others.
- Social psychologists have a wide variety of research 'tools' or methods at their disposal. Once they have formulated a research question, they need to choose whether to conduct a quantitative investigation, a qualitative study, or to use both methods. Quantitative methods include surveys and questionnaires, and experiments. Qualitative methods include thematic analysis, conversational analysis, narrative analysis, discourse analysis and interpretative phenomenological analysis. Methods common to both approaches include observations, case studies and archival studies.
- There are several issues to consider in social psychological research. For example, how participants are sampled is important and, ideally, samples should be random in experimental research. A measure should be reliable, such that it brings about consistent results. Also, it should be valid, in that it measures what it is supposed to be measuring. When conducting a study, it is also important to consider if the findings are statistically significant, or determining the probability that the finding of interest could have occurred by chance.
- Another key distinction in social psychological research is that between basic research (focusing on fundamental questions at the heart of human nature), and applied research (applying social psychological findings to social problems or issues).
- Cultural issues are important in social psychology and it cannot be assumed that all people think and act in the same way. 'Western' social psychology often ignores key cultural differences between people – such as individualism and collectivism – that determine social outcomes.
- Social psychologists must also conduct their work ethically, that is, they must carry out their research with the safety and privacy of participants in mind.
- Social psychology has close links with many other sub-disciplines of psychology, such as cognitive, clinical and personality psychology. It also has close relationships with disciplines outside psychology, such as biology, neuroscience, sociology, social anthropology and economics.
- Social psychologists disseminate their research primarily through publications in scientific journals. However, they also publish book chapters, present their work in talks, and are making increasing use of social networking opportunities.

In Chapter 2, we begin our journey into the specific topic areas of social psychology, starting with the social self – the study of how people understand who they are.

Essay questions

At the beginning of the chapter, we asked you to consider these questions:

1 In the midst of the riots in England during August 2011, British Prime Minister David Cameron argued that: 'This is criminality pure and simple, and it must be confronted and defeated.' Many other media reports labelled the incidents as 'mindless violence'. Was this a fair assessment of the situation?
2 A social psychologist is interested in how media representations of gender roles have changed over the past 30 years. What research method(s) would enable the researcher to examine this question and what are the advantages and disadvantages of each?
3 At a party, a social psychologist tells a friend about their research, explaining that most of their findings come from studies where the participants were undergraduates. The friend says that the findings cannot tell us anything about humans in general. Is the friend correct?

Having read this chapter, these questions could also be framed as the following essay questions, which you can attempt in preparation for your examinations:

1 Critical thinking and weighing up evidence is crucial to social psychology. Explain, with examples, why this is the case.
2 Imagine that you are designing a study to examine media representations of gender roles over the past 30 years. Design a study that would enable you to do so and explain and justify your choice of research methods.
3 Sampling is a crucial issue in social psychology. Explain, with examples, why in some situations it is acceptable to test hypotheses using white undergraduate participants, and why sometimes it is not.

Some further reading

Allport, G.W. (1954). The historical background of modern social psychology. In G. Lindzey (ed.) *Handbook of Social Psychology* (vol. 1, pp. 3–56). Reading, MA: Addison-Wesley. For those of you who like to read the classics, this is Allport's history of social psychology, covering work up to the early 1950s.

Forshaw, M. (2012) *Critical Thinking for Psychology*. London: Wiley Blackwell. Introduces one of the key skills we have highlighted in this chapter: critical thinking. Explains what is expected from students, how to construct critical arguments and, using exercises, highlights the importance of critical thinking in psychology.

Judd, C.M. and Kenny, D.A. (2010) Data analysis in social psychology: Recent and recurring issues. In S.T. Fiske, D.T. Gilbert and G. Lindzey (eds) *Handbook of Social Psychology* (5th edn, vol. 1, pp. 115–42). Hoboken, NJ: John Wiley and Sons. Discusses some of the challenges that social psychologists face when they design studies and analyse data.

Reis, H.T. and Gosling, S.D. (2010) Social psychological methods outside the laboratory. In S.T. Fiske, D.T. Gilbert and G. Lindzey (eds) *Handbook of Social Psychology* (vol. 1, pp. 82–114). Hoboken, NJ: John Wiley & Sons. Goes into more depth on some of the alternative methods to studying social behaviour in laboratory settings.

Ross, L., Lepper, M. and Ward, A. (2010) History of social psychology: Insights, challenges, and contributions to theory and application. In S.T. Fiske, D.T. Gilbert and G. Lindzey (eds) *Handbook of Social Psychology* (vol. 1, pp. 3–50). Hoboken, NJ: John Wiley & Sons. Readable summary of the history of social psychology, highlighting some of the key challenges that have faced the discipline over the years.

Stainton Rogers, W. (2011) *Social Psychology*. Milton Keynes: Open University Press. A unique textbook because it presents a strong emphasis on critical social psychology and qualitative research. Stainton Rogers is known as one of the 'founding mothers' of critical psychology.

Wilson, T.D., Aronson, E. and Carlsmith, K. (2010) The art of laboratory experimentation. In S.T. Fiske, D.T. Gilbert and G. Lindzey (eds) *Handbook of Social Psychology* (vol. 1, pp. 51–81). Hoboken, NJ: John Wiley & Sons. Comprehensive overview and discussion of the art of conducting social psychological work in laboratory experiments.

 Visit the companion website at www.palgrave.com/psychology/suttondouglas for access to a wide range of resources to help you get to grips with this chapter.

Applying social psychology

Pets and psychological wellbeing: a critical thinking exercise

This exercise is based on the following article:

Herzog, H. (2011) The impact of pets on human health and psychological wellbeing: Fact, fiction or hypothesis? *Current Directions in Psychological Science*, 20, 236–9.

Herzog argues that extensive media coverage and books with titles such as *The Healing Power of Pets* have led to the widespread belief that pets are good for people's health, psychological wellbeing and life expectancy. Together, these ideas are commonly known as the 'pet effect' (Allen, 2003). Most pet owners agree that this effect exists. When asked why they own pets, people typically respond that their furry

companions are good for them. However, as you know from reading this chapter, personal opinions and convictions do not constitute evidence. To draw the conclusion that pets are good for people, scientific research must be conducted in the same way as medical, psychiatric or pharmaceutical investigations are conducted to examine the effectiveness of medical treatments and interventions.

A great deal of research has investigated the veracity of the claim that pets are good for people. As Herzog argues, this research question has intrigued psychologists for over 30 years. Interestingly, however, research investigating the pet effect is inconclusive. Some researchers have shown that pet owners are indeed happier and healthier than non-pet owners. For example, Friedmann, Katcher, Lynch et al. (1980) demonstrated that in a group of 92 heart attack victims, 28 per cent of pet owners survived for a year, while only 6 per cent of non-pet owners survived for the same period of time. Allen, Shykoff and Izzo (2001) showed that hypertensive stockbrokers who were assigned to a pet ownership condition showed lower levels of blood pressure six months later than a non-pet ownership group. Also, studies have shown a link between pet ownership and self-esteem, positive mood, life satisfaction and physical fitness (El-Alayli, Lystad, Webb et al., 2006; Headey and Grabka, 2011).

However, others studies have shown that pet owners fare no better than non-pet owners, and sometimes they are even less healthy and less happy. For example, Parker, Gayed, Owen et al. (2010) demonstrated in a study of 425 heart attack victims that pet owners were more (not less) likely than non-pet owners to die in the year following their heart attack. Other studies have shown that pet ownership has little effect in reducing hypertension (e.g., Wright, Kritz-Silverstein, Morton et al., 2007). Other research suggests that pet owners are no happier (Herzog, 2010) or less lonely than non-pet owners (Gilbey, McNicholas and Collis, 2007) and in another study, older individuals who were attached to their pets displayed higher levels of depression than those who were less attached (Miltiades and Shearer, 2011).

Why is the research inconclusive? Herzog offers some possible reasons. In particular, Ioannidis (2005) argued that conflicting results are prevalent in areas of science where samples are small and homogeneous, and research designs are varied. Further, 'hot' research topics that are associated with a great deal of pre-existing opinions and attitudes are often prone to problems concerning replication and inconclusive results. The study of the pet effect fulfils these criteria and this exercise will hopefully allow you to think of more issues concerning this area of research. Herzog's article is an excellent example of critical thinking and appraisal of available research evidence. Based on what you have read above, attempt to answer the following questions. Perhaps after you have done so, you can read the article for more information.

1 One key difference between studies showing the positive effects of pet ownership and those that show no effect is that the former tend not to use true experiments where participants are randomly assigned to 'pet' and 'non-pet' groups. How might this be one reason for the existence of conflicting results?

2 Many studies of the effects of pet ownership are based on self-report data, that is, pet owners report their health and happiness and so on. How might this influence the results?

3 A common problem in scientific research is known as the 'file drawer effect', in which researchers tend not to publish negative findings – they end up in the 'file drawer' never to be seen. Do you think this could be a problem in this area of research? Why/why not?

4 To what extent do you think personal opinions and vested interest could influence research on the effects of pet ownership?

Student project

Socially desirable responding

Harry Musson studied as an undergraduate student at the University of Kent and his dissertation supervisor was Dr Robbie Sutton. His research examined socially desirable responding – the tendency not to be entirely truthful or accurate in surveys for fear of looking bad, or in an effort to look good, which we discussed in this chapter. In particular, he was interested in how socially desirable responding can affect men and women differently when they answer rather sensitive questions about their sexual preferences. In Chapter 7, we will consider the debate about whether genetic evolution has shaped men and women's sexual desires in different directions. Harry's research is directly relevant to that debate.

My topic and aims

My study examined the role of socially desirable responding in men and women's reports of their sexual preferences. Sexual preferences can refer to what people want from 'short-term mating', that is, relatively casual sexual activity without any long-term commitment. Your short-term mating preferences can include how many partners you would ideally like to have, and how long you would prefer to know them before being happy to have sex with them. You can also have long-term mating preferences, such as the physical characteristics, personality traits and social status you would prefer in a lifelong partner. Previous self-report studies had found that men desire more sexual variety than women in short-term mating. Also, in long-term mating, men reported that they valued physical attractiveness in women, while women valued status in men. Since more or less the same findings are observed worldwide, this has been interpreted as evidence that genetic evolution has shaped men and women's sexual preferences differently.

In my experiment, I wanted to explore the influence of social desirability bias on these findings, that is, that men and women were not being honest in their responses due to social pressure. Going into it, I thought that perhaps women, more than men, experience social pressure to downplay their desire for sexual variety, such as the number of sexual partners they would ideally like to have. Further, men and women may experience some pressure to report 'traditional' long-term mating preferences – leading women to downplay the importance of a partner's attractiveness to them, or men to downplay the importance of a partner's social status. If men and women distort their responses in gendered ways in an effort to look good – or to avoid looking bad – then perhaps the gender differences that have been so often observed are not to be trusted.

My methods

Two hundred male and female undergraduates completed a questionnaire, which asked about their short- and long-term mating preferences. Questions about short-term mating preferences measured the number of partners participants desired in various time frames, the time they would need to know a partner they found attractive before consenting to intercourse and the extent to which they were currently seeking short-term partners. Questions about long-term mating preferences measured the extent to which participants were currently seeking a long-term partner, and the characteristics they would value most in a long-term mate.

The key manipulation was that half the participants were asked to be honest in their responses, and half were instructed to 'fake good', that is, to cast themselves in the best possible light. Participants were randomly assigned to one of these conditions. The other independent variable was participants' gender. Since participants' gender cannot be experimentally manipulated, the design of my study was technically quasi-experimental.

My findings and their implications

Results indicated similar gender differences in mating preferences as has been demonstrated in previous research. For example, compared to women, men reported a higher desire for sexual variety, wanting significantly more partners, and being prepared to have sex with people after knowing them for significantly less time.

Going against predictions, these gender differences were not more marked when participants were faking good. So, socially desirable responding, at least in my study, does not appear to be responsible for the gender difference that has been observed in many studies.

The 'faking good' manipulation did have one effect. It caused both men and women to report being less willing to have sex with people they knew for only a brief length of time (a few hours or days).

Typical long-term trait preferences were observed (regardless of the manipulation) and it was also found that women desired a partner who wanted children more than men, which could suggest that female participants' desire for reproduction was stronger than men's.

My journey

Since graduating, I have been working as an English teacher in Oxford and Málaga, Spain. I am now pursuing a career working in the travel industry. I have used experience from my psychology degree in my teaching, and I also hope to return to academia in the future.

I learned how to be disciplined and self-sufficient. I learned about the considerable amount of research, preparation and effort that goes into planning and completing a project. I learned that demand characteristics can affect any self-report measure, especially on a subject as loaded as the one I chose. I appreciated the value of completing an extended project under my own steam, with helpful advice and suggestions from my supervisor of course.

These skills have made me appreciate the value of determination, drive and hard work in life, and the satisfaction that can be gained from seeing a lengthy project to fruition.

My advice

Choose something that fires your imagination. You may face challenges and setbacks along the way and it is trickier to motivate yourself to overcome them if you are not very interested in your hypothesis. Also, don't be afraid to work alone, as it can be a rewarding experience to complete research under your own steam. Having said this, pose questions to your supervisor, peers and postgraduates in order to make sure you are heading in the right direction. Pick a good supervisor.

Part

1 Thinking and feeling

The social self: understanding ourselves

In this chapter, we cover the important social psychological concept of the self. We outline what the self is, what it is for, and how it defines what we think, feel and do. We discuss the key social psychological theories of the self, the motives that influence how we see ourselves, and some of the cross-cultural differences in the self-concept. By the end of this chapter, you will have a comprehensive understanding of this key topic in social psychology.

Topics covered in this chapter

- Self-knowledge and the self-concept
- Self-awareness
- Theories of self
- Self-esteem
- Self-presentation
- Motivated cognition regarding the self
- Culture and the self

Key features

Critical focus Ego depletion

Ethics and research methods Why social psychologists cannot just ask people why they do things

Social psychology in the real world The narcissism epidemic and its consequences

Applying social psychology Encouraging healthy eating in a school

Blind spot in social psychology Narcissistic leaders and their effects on decision making

Student project The effect of specific modes of feedback on learning in an HE setting

Questions to consider

1 Millie gossiped to someone about something a close friend told her in confidence. Millie instantly felt terrible about what she had done and although her friend never found out, Millie ruminated about what she had done. She could not help thinking what a horrible friend she must be to speak ill of a friend behind their back. How might you explain Millie's feelings? What consequences might there be for Millie?

2 Despite slight pangs of jealousy, James is genuinely happy for his friend Mark, who gets a place to study at Oxford University. However, he cannot say the same for one of his other classmates, Brian, who also got a place. What social psychological processes differentiate these two different responses to essentially the same event?

3 Antonia and Marvin are having an argument and Antonia says to Marvin: 'I know you better than you know yourself.' To what extent (and why) might this statement be true?

© PHOTODISC

Who are you? If someone asks you this question, you will be able to generate a long list of traits and identities that define how you see yourself. For example, you may say that you are a female, university student, politically liberal, a daughter, or a Muslim, among many other characteristics that together make you who you are. You may think about where you live or where you are from and consider yourself to be British, Irish or Australian. You may think about your daily activities and define yourself as a musician, feminist, or someone who likes sport. The list is endless and yet each of these aspects of the self is crucial to our sense of who we are. Further, at some point, you will think about who you *think* you are. Most people ask themselves questions like: 'I think I am a musician (or a feminist or someone who likes sport), but how confident am I about that?' Humans have a capacity to reflect on their own thinking (Lea and Kiley-Worthington, 1996), and this ability means that people are perpetually rethinking and redefining themselves.

The self is a fundamental aspect of being human and it is not only personal, but also intrinsically and intensely social. This is why the self is such an important topic in social psychology and has been a key focus of research for many years. The concept of the self is social because understanding the self is crucial to social life. Knowing who we are allows us to know what we should think, how we should feel and how we should behave. It helps us to interact with others, organize our experiences, promote our interests and regulate our behaviour. Our sense of self therefore defines not only what we think of ourselves, but also much of our social behaviour.

There is another sense in which the self is social: we have a social relationship with the self, that is, we have beliefs about our traits, relationships, strengths and weaknesses, much as we have beliefs about other people. We like or dislike aspects of ourselves, much as we like or dislike aspects of other people. Further, as we shall see, we can help or handicap ourselves by doing things that boost or sabotage our chances of success. We punish ourselves when we feel we have done something wrong (e.g., Bastian, Jetten and Fasoli, 2011; Nelissen, 2012) and we sometimes view ourselves as if from the outside – as if we were another person.

The complex, social nature of the self was one of the earliest insights of social psychology. James (1890) wrote that selfhood is characterized by a fundamental duality such that a person experiences being both 'I' and 'me'. In 'I' mode, they are an experiencing, acting subject, and as 'me', they are the object of their own perceptions. Cooley (1902) took this insight further by proposing the notion of the 'looking-glass self'. For Cooley and other **symbolic interactionists** (e.g. Blumer, 1969; Mead, 1934), a basic task of social life is to see ourselves from the outside, more or less as others see us, so that a person's developing sense of 'me' is attuned to the beliefs, expectancies and needs of others. Mead (1934) argued that when we evaluate ourselves, we normally adopt the perspective of the 'generalized other' – a nonspecific person who embodies the norms of our society and of those who matter to us. This view of ourselves helps us to be guided by social norms, to help

Symbolic interactionism
Researchers from this perspective investigate how people create meaning through social interaction, how they construct and represent the self and how they define situations when they are with others.

us so we can influence others and avoid being punished or banished. For the symbolic interactionists, therefore, being aware of ourselves is a crucial part of being able to control ourselves.

The symbolic interactionists did not typically frame their ideas in ways that were easily tested using scientific methods. However, their ideas have been hugely influential in the social psychological study of the self, including most of the research we explore in this chapter. They have been translated into testable ideas, and have largely held up in the century or so since they were first conceived. But how do people become self-aware? How does this awareness help people to evaluate the self in order to reflect on who they are and how to change? What are its emotional consequences? These are the more specific questions we will be setting out to answer in this chapter. We focus first on what is known as the 'self-concept'. Here, we consider what the self is made up of, what it is for and how our concept of self influences what we do. Then, we consider core theories concerning how the self-concept is formed and how people become self-aware. Next, we consider the construct of 'self-esteem' and how our feelings about ourselves influence how we cope with life situations. Moving on, we then discuss the role of motivations in how we perceive ourselves, in particular focusing on the core motivation to enhance and feel good about the self. We also consider some of the cultural differences in the study of self. By the end of this chapter, you will have a clear understanding of what the self is and what it is for.

Self-knowledge and the self-concept

Self-concept The complete set of beliefs people have about themselves.

The **self-concept** is defined as the complete set of beliefs that people have about themselves, which form their understanding of who they are (Markus, 1977; Markus, Hamill and Sentis, 1987). For example, one may see oneself as feminine, sensitive, introverted, hard-working, creative, talkative and so on. The self-concept has many distinct components for each individual and these components, which together form a person's overall self-concept, are known as **self-schemas** or different *dimensions* of the self. Of course, people's self-schemas are different and therefore people's overall self-concepts are unique – not everyone thinks of themselves as feminine, sensitive or introverted, for example. People are different and perceive themselves as such. Also, some self-schemas are particularly important to people and others are not. Markus (1977) argued that if people feel that a particular dimension is important to them, think that they are higher or lower than most people on that dimension, and are certain that the opposite is not true of them, they can be described as *self-schematic* on that dimension. For example, if a person feels that they are extroverted, are positive that they are not introverted, and being extroverted is important to them, then they are self-schematic on the dimension of extroversion. If a dimension is unimportant to a person's sense of self, the person is said to be *self-aschematic* on that dimension. Thus, people have a complex set of important schemas that form their overall self-concept.

Self-schemas Beliefs about oneself that help people process self-relevant information.

Self-schemas are important guiding factors that determine how people *think* they should think, feel and act in specific situations (Markus, 1977). Different contexts activate different aspects of the self. For example, for a person who is self-schematic on extroversion, that schema is likely to determine how they believe they should think, feel or behave at a social gathering – and these perceptions will be different for people who have the self-schema that they are introverted. A person who is aschematic on this dimension may be different yet again. This function of self-schemas was illustrated in a study by Markus (1977), who asked participants first to rate themselves on the traits of dependence and independence. From these ratings, participants were identified as either self-schematic for dependence or independence, or aschematic on both traits. Participants were then asked to complete a reaction time task where they read words on a screen. The words were either associated with independence (e.g., 'assertive', 'self-confident') or dependence (e.g., 'conforming', 'cautious') and participants were asked to press a button for 'me' or 'not me', depending on whether or not they felt that the trait was characteristic of them. Findings revealed that participants who were self-schematic on independence or dependence more quickly identified the words associated with their schemas, compared to those who were aschematic on both dimensions (Figure 2.1). Those who were self-schematic on one of the dimensions were also more able to recall experiences that demonstrated their dependence or independence. Participants' self-schemas were, therefore, useful in guiding their thoughts about themselves.

Self-schemas can influence aspects of one's daily life too. People who are weight conscious are a good example of this (Markus et al., 1987). Such people, for whom body weight is a significant daily concern, may experience visits to the supermarket, reading fashion magazines and shopping for clothing differently than those who are aschematic on that dimension. Such activities may trigger thoughts about the self in schematic individuals but be of little consequence for those who are aschematic. Such a self-schema can lead to body image preoccupations, in which people excessively monitor their weight and appearance, and even evaluate their worth according to their body shape (Altabe and Thompson, 1996: see also the concept of contingent self-esteem, below). This is a particular concern for women, who are more, although not uniquely, prone to body image concerns. Eating disorders are an extreme, but all too common manifestation of these concerns (Strelan and Hargreaves, 2005; Strelan and Mehaffy, 2003). This illustrates how self-schemas' ability to organize thought and motivate action means that they can become all-consuming and lead to counterproductive behaviours.

People even have schemas of their potential future self (Markus and Nurius, 1986; Markus and Sentis, 1982). These reflect our desired selves (e.g., happy,

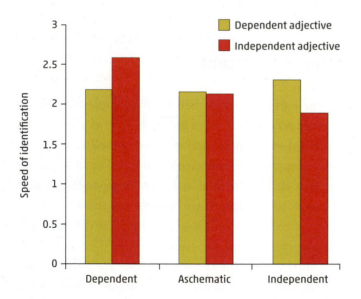

FIGURE 2.1 Self-schematic versus aschematic individuals Participants who are self-schematic on a trait (in this case, independence or dependence) more quickly identified the words that were characteristic of them, compared to participants who were aschematic on both dimensions.

Source: Data from Markus, 1977

successful) and feared selves (e.g., unhappy, unsuccessful) and highlight the importance of self-schemas in determining how we feel about ourselves – if one self-schema makes us feel unhappy, then we might focus more on self-schemas that make us feel good. For example, if we feel self-schematic for being disorganized and find this aspect of the self disappointing, then we may choose to focus instead on our conception of self as being creative, because this makes us feel better and compensates for aspects of the self we think are lacking (Linville, 1985, 1987). It is important, therefore, that people have multiple self-schemas so that there are always 'spare' schemas to focus on when they feel they fall short on other dimensions. Indeed, Linville (1985) found that low self-complexity (not many roles, more overlap) predicts illness, whereas high self-complexity (lots of roles, little overlap) does not. High self-complexity can therefore act as a buffer for stress.

Try it yourself Think of your own self-schemas. What dimensions are important to you? What dimension are you extreme on? Write down a list of schematic and aschematic dimensions. Put everything together and get an overall idea of your self-concept. Compare your self-concept with that of a friend's. How are your self-concepts similar? How are they different? Which of the traits and features you have listed most clearly define 'who you are'?

Multiple role theory Theory asserting that it is beneficial for a person's health and wellbeing to have multiple self-identities.

This claim is at the heart of **multiple role theory** (e.g., Powell and Greenhaus, 2010; Thoits, 1983), according to which it is psychologically beneficial for people to have multiple identities (e.g., sibling, student, friend, sports team member). Each role opens up new experiences, opportunities for social interaction, pleasure and personal growth, but also the risk of failure and frustration (see Figure 2.2). When one identity is creating negative feelings, having other identities enables a person to continue to grow and enjoy life. At the same time, however, self-schemas that are too well partitioned or too extreme can be problematic. For example, if some self-schemas are very positive and others are very negative, **priming** the schemas can have extreme effects on mood. Sometimes, it may be best to have less compartmentalized or more moderate self-schemas, so that priming them will not lead to extreme mood swings.

Priming Exposure to stimuli that activate a mental representation of a particular concept, value, goal or object.

It is also important that people attach positive meaning to these schemas. Some research on multiple role theory suggests that the *quality* (in terms of happiness, satisfaction and optimism) rather than the *quantity* of roles is important for psychological wellbeing (Baruch and Barnett, 1986). When people experience conflict between roles or self-schemas, they tend to experience distress (Burke, 1991; Meyer, 2003). It may be difficult, for example, for many women to see themselves both as a great mother and a dedicated worker. If people's schemas can be aligned with each other, for example if working women think of themselves as a positive role model for their children, they are likely to prosper (Greenhaus and Powell, 2006; Powell and Greenhaus, 2010).

FIGURE 2.2 **Multiple role theory** According to multiple role theory, it is beneficial for people to have multiple identities. If particular self-schemas can be aligned with each other, people are likely to prosper. However, when self-schemas are seen as being in conflict with each other, as is often the case for working mothers, people can experience distress.

Self-concept clarity The extent to which self-schemas are clearly and confidently defined, consistent with each other, and stable across time.

The need for the various parts of the self-concept to 'gel' is at the heart of **self-concept clarity** (Campbell, Trapnell, Heine et al., 1996). Self-concept clarity refers to the extent to which self-schemas are clearly and confidently defined, consistent with each other, and stable across time. It is important that one's self-beliefs and identities are clearly defined in one's own mind, that they cohere, rather than clash with each other, and that they do not change rapidly or unpredictably. Self-concept clarity enables people to see themselves as having many facets, but also as individuals, with a strong, unified self. Many of the projects in our lives are long term – as in our closest friendships and romantic relationships, or our careers. To succeed in these projects, we need to act consistently. It is not helpful if people's perceptions of their strengths, values, priorities and goals change from day to day, or are inconsistent with each other.

One of the benefits of self-concept clarity is that it bolsters self-esteem (Campbell, 1990; Campbell et al., 1996). It is also related to subjective wellbeing – a blanket term for the experience of psychological wellness, incorporating variables such as satisfaction with life, freedom from anxiety and sadness, and the experience of positive mood (Campbell et al., 1996). Correlational research suggests that self-concept clarity helps people deal with daily negative events (Lavallee and Campbell, 1995), being treated unjustly by others (de Cremer and Sedikides, 2005) and relationship breakups (Slotter, Gardner and Finkel, 2010).

There is also experimental evidence that self-concept clarity not only correlates with psychological wellbeing, but also actively bolsters it. For example, Lewandowski, Nardone and Raines (2010) manipulated self-concept clarity. They had participants undergo a procedure that either strengthened or weakened self-concept clarity. Participants assigned to the 'self-concept clarity condition' were asked to list the times they acted in ways that were consistent with three adjectives they had earlier indicated were descriptive of them. For example, if they had earlier said they were 'introverted', they were asked to describe times they had acted in an introverted way. In contrast, participants assigned to the 'self-concept confusion' condition were asked to list the times they had acted in ways that were consistent with adjectives they had already indicated were *not* descriptive of them. For example, if they said they were not open-minded, they were asked to recount the times they had acted in an open-minded way. Participants in the clarity condition, compared to the confusion condition, reported increased satisfaction with and commitment to their romantic relationships. Unfortunately, there was no baseline condition in which participants' self-concepts were not manipulated; therefore we can't say whether an increase in clarity, compared to baseline levels, was beneficial to relationship satisfaction and commitment, or whether an increase in confusion was harmful to it. Either way, research results like this highlight the social function of the self. Having a clear, coherent understanding of ourselves (versus a confused one) helps us cope more effectively with the stresses, injustices and rejections thrown up by our social lives. It also gives us the confidence and motivation to commit to, and enjoy, our relationships with others.

Where does self-concept clarity come from? The experiment by Lewandowski et al. (2010) shows that self-concept clarity is not only a personality variable. It is true that, averaged over time, you will generally have higher self-concept clarity than some people and lower self-concept clarity than others. Nonetheless, your self-concept clarity may also change somewhat from day to day, in response to situational factors. Research has cast a good deal of light on the sources of self-concept clarity. In a **diary study**, Nezlek and Plesko (2001) had over 100 participants complete the self-concept clarity scale developed by Campbell et al. (1996), twice a week, for up to 10 weeks. They found that self-concept clarity fluctuated from day to day. On some days, participants had a clearer, more coherent understanding of who they were than on other days. In particular, they found that the self-concept was notably less clear on days in which participants experienced bad events. This finding was mediated by negative mood and reduced self-esteem. Ritchie, Sedikides, Wildschut et al. (2011) also found that stressful events reduced self-concept clarity, which in turn was associated with negative changes to psychological wellbeing. Thus, self-concept clarity may help explain why stressful events can be so damaging to mental health: namely, by undermining the clarity with which you understand who you are. When we put all these studies on self-concept clarity together, the relationship between self-concept clarity and self-esteem appears to be bidirectional. It is easier to feel good about yourself when you are clear about who you are – it is also easier to feel that you know who you are when you feel good about yourself.

Diary study A research method that requires participants to keep track of their daily activities or events for a particular period of time.

Try it yourself First, complete the Campbell et al. (1996) scale of self-concept clarity in the table below. At the end of the task, you will need to calculate your total score for the 12 items. This is where it gets a bit more complicated. You will notice that some of the items are marked with an asterisk (*), indicating they will need to be **reverse scored**. Social psychologists do this in their scales to make sure that participants think about their responses. If all items indicated higher levels of self-concept clarity, for example, participants might not think properly about their responses and so respond similarly every time. Reverse scored items are a feature of a good scale. For example, you might be asked to rate your agreement with the following statements:

Social psychology is:

| Boring | 1 | 2 | 3 | 4 | 5 | Interesting |
| Relevant | 1 | 2 | 3 | 4 | 5 | Irrelevant |

An answer of 5 to both questions probably means that the participant did not properly read or think about the questions. If the participant has responded appropriately, reverse scoring the second item means that, together, the participant's mean response is an index of how positively they feel about social psychology.

Reverse coding means that the number the participant answers simply becomes its reverse, that is, a score of 1 becomes a 5, a score of 2 becomes a 4 and so on. You can do this for a 5-point scale like this one by simply subtracting the number you scored from 6. Reversing the items that would otherwise indicate low self-concept clarity (e.g., 'My beliefs about myself often conflict with one another') means that all items indicate increasing levels of self-concept clarity. In Campbell et al.'s (1996) study, the mean total was approximately 40. What is your score? If you score more than 40, then your self-concept is clearer that most.

Reverse scoring A technique used in questionnaires to ensure that participants think about their responses.

	Strongly disagree				Strongly agree
My beliefs about myself often conflict with one another. *	1	2	3	4	5
On one day I might have one opinion of myself and on another day I might have a different opinion. *	1	2	3	4	5
I spend a lot of time wondering about what kind of person I really am. *	1	2	3	4	5
Sometimes I feel that I am not really the person I appear to be. *	1	2	3	4	5
When I think about the kind of person I have been in the past, I'm not sure what I was really like. *	1	2	3	4	5
I seldom experience conflict between the different aspects of my personality.	1	2	3	4	5
Sometimes I think I know other people better than I know myself. *	1	2	3	4	5
My beliefs about myself seem to change frequently. *	1	2	3	4	5
If I were asked to describe my personality, my description might end up being different from one day to another. *	1	2	3	4	5
Even if I wanted to, I don't think I would tell someone what I'm really like. *	1	2	3	4	5
In general, I have a clear sense of who I am and what I am.	1	2	3	4	5
It is often hard for me to make up my mind about things because I don't really know what I want. *	1	2	3	4	5

Source: Cambell et al., 1996. © 1996 the American Psychological Association. Reproduced with permission

Self-awareness

Self-awareness The psychological state of being aware of one's characteristics, feelings and behaviours.

The self is a fundamental aspect of people's lives and, as we mentioned earlier, people constantly redefine themselves as they consider what they think, feel and do. However, this is not to say that people are constantly thinking about the self, that is, we are not always aware of 'who we are'. **Self-awareness** is the psychological state of being aware of one's characteristics, feelings and behaviours, or the awareness of oneself as unique. In this section, we will discuss how an awareness of self develops, the different types of self-awareness, and the neurological basis of self-awareness.

Development of self-awareness

Awareness of the self is not something people are born with. Instead, it develops throughout infancy and childhood, appearing to begin at around age 18 months. In one study demonstrating the development of self-awareness, Lewis and Brooks-Gunn (1978) placed a spot of rouge (red makeup) on the noses of infants aged between 9–12 months and sat them in front of a mirror. These young babies looked at their mirror image with no recognition and no effort to touch the rouge on their own noses. The authors argued that this was because the babies were not aware that the image in the mirror was their own, and they had no concept of self-awareness. However, children around 18 months of age who performed the same task made a concerted effort to rub the rouge from their own noses. It was argued that they did so because they had developed the understanding that the image in the mirror was their own and they understood that the rouge was on their own faces. Thus, they were in the process of developing a sense of self-awareness.

Humans are not the only animals who can recognize themselves in the mirror. For example, Reiss and Marino (2001) demonstrated that dolphins stopped by a mirror for longer if they had a black spot on their noses. Further, Gallup (1977) showed that great apes (gorillas, orang-utans and chimpanzees) were capable of self-recognition, using mirrors to help groom themselves, make faces and pick food from their teeth. More recent research suggests that rhesus monkeys can also recognize themselves in a mirror, despite it being long thought they were unable to do this (Rajala, Reininger, Lancaster and Populin, 2010). Thus, while people are predisposed to develop self-recognition at an early age, many animals also seem to have a sense of self.

Time to reflect The 'mirror test' of self-awareness has had its critics (e.g., Bekoff, 2003; de Veer and van den Bos, 1999). What do you think might be its shortcomings? It may help to break this general question down into two parts. First, does failing the mirror test really show that a person or animal lacks self-awareness? For example, can you think of reasons, other than a lack of self-awareness, why a person or animal might 'fail' the mirror test? Second, does passing the mirror test really show that a child or animal has a fully developed sense of self-awareness? Monkeys and apes can pass it – so what do 'we' normally have that 'they' probably lack?

Public and private self-awareness

It is generally understood that there are two types of self-awareness, depending on whether the person is aware of aspects of the self that are public or more aware of aspects of the self that are private. First, **public self-awareness** occurs when a person becomes aware of the public aspects of the self and how they could be judged by other people (Buss, 1980; Carver and Scheier, 1981; Duval and Wicklund, 1972). For example, think of a time when you were concerned about what others thought of you – maybe giving a presentation at university, singing to an audience or playing sport in front of a crowd. In such situations, your public self-awareness was activated. In these contexts, people are sometimes concerned about what others think because they are apprehensive about being judged or evaluated (Prentice-Dunn and Rogers, 1982). Nobody wants to be evaluated negatively by other people because this can lead to lowered levels of self-esteem and increased nervousness in future social interactions (e.g., Brockner, 1979; Leary and Kowalski, 1990). Therefore, public self-awareness can sometimes be debilitating and lead people to be too concerned with their outward behaviours. On the upside, however, it is public self-awareness that leads people to adhere to norms and societal standards of behaviour in specific situations. For example, if others are watching and a person needs to dispose of rubbish, they are more likely to do so in an appropriate way because their public self-awareness leads to concerns about being evaluated by onlookers who might not be so impressed by littering (e.g., Froming, Allen and Jensen, 1985; Prentice-Dunn and Rogers, 1982).

This state of public self-awareness is usually temporary. That is, people become more publicly self-aware because of a specific situation they are in. However, it is also the case that some people are more publicly self-aware than others in a chronic or dispositional sense. Specifically, people who are high in what is known as **public self-consciousness** are more chronically concerned about how they look

Public self-awareness
Awareness of the public aspects of the self and how these aspects may be seen by others.

Public self-consciousness
Chronic public self-awareness and concern about how one looks and is evaluated by others.

and how they are evaluated by others (Fenigstein, Scheier and Buss, 1975). Such people are more generally inclined to follow rules and norms for fear of being negatively evaluated by others if they deviate from these standards of behaviour (Prentice-Dunn and Rogers, 1982). Also, publicly self-conscious individuals are more likely to be concerned with their physical appearance and are more likely to judge others on their looks (e.g., Fenigstein, 1979; Fenigstein et al., 1975; Miller, Murphy and Buss, 1981; Striegel-Moore, Silberstein and Rodin, 1993).

These context-specific and more general concerns about public evaluation are echoed in the private sphere. Specifically, **private self-awareness** refers to the psychological state where an individual is aware of the private, personal aspects of the self (Buss, 1980; Carver and Scheier, 1981; Duval and Wicklund, 1972). For example, a person may think about a time when they helped a friend who was in trouble. Contemplating this situation may make them become privately self-aware of their kindness. Or, a person may think of a time when they stole something and felt shameful and aware of their deceit. Being privately self-aware can have positive and negative consequences for people's feelings about themselves. Also, if a person feels good at the time, reflecting on the self may increase the extent to which they focus on positive aspects, thus further improving their feeling of positivity (Scheier and Carver, 1977). On the downside, however, if a person does not feel good to begin with, reflecting on the self may increase the extent to which they focus on the more negative or problematic aspects of the self. This potentially depresses mood further (Mor and Winquist, 2002; Scheier and Carver, 1977).

Private self-awareness
Awareness of private, personal aspects of the self.

FIGURE 2.3 The effect of private self-awareness on emotional responses to reading positive and negative statements Emotional responses become exaggerated (more positive/more negative) under conditions where participants are asked to perform the experimental task while looking in a mirror.

Source: Data from Scheier and Carver, 1977

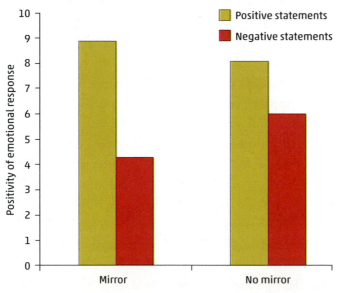

In a classic study, Scheier and Carver (1977) uncovered evidence of this tendency. They asked research participants to read a series of positive statements (e.g., 'I feel happy') out loud, while in another condition, people read out negative statements (e.g., 'I feel empty'). Reading positive statements about themselves led to feelings of happiness, whereas reading negative statements had the opposite effect, leading to feelings of sadness. Crucially, participants who looked at their image in a mirror while performing the task (a manipulation of private self-awareness) became more extreme in their emotional responses to the task than participants who were not asked to look at themselves in the mirror (see Figure 2.3).

Time to reflect It is perfectly plausible that being in front of a mirror increases your self-awareness. But why else might it amplify your emotional reactions to reading out statements like 'I feel happy', or 'I feel empty'? Hint: think about the facial expressions that most people would pull while reading out such statements. It might help to write a list of, say, five positive statements like 'I feel happy'. Say them in front of a mirror, and while not in front of a mirror. What differences can you observe?

FIGURE 2.4 Stealing sweets Beaman et al. (1979) demonstrated that unsupervised children were less likely to steal sweets if they were made privately self-aware by being placed in front of a mirror.

Boundary condition A level of a third variable under which an otherwise observed effect is no longer observed. For example, being insulted by a stranger does not cause the usual annoyance if one is wearing earphones and cannot hear them. A boundary condition means we can expect an interaction effect – the relationship between two variables depends on the level of a third variable.

Other studies have shown that private self-awareness can be activated in situations that are emotionally arousing. For example, Scheier and Carver (1980) asked participants to write an essay while either being placed in front of a mirror or not. The essay was to be written in such a way that was inconsistent with the participants' pre-existing attitudes (a counterattitudinal essay). This is a manipulation that is commonly used to generate a state of negative arousal – the rationale being that writing an essay that goes against one's attitudes means that one's behaviours are inconsistent with these attitudes. This creates a state of *cognitive dissonance* (see Chapter 4) and people often try to resolve the inconsistency by changing their attitudes. However, findings from Scheier and Carver's study revealed that the participants who were placed in front of a mirror – and were therefore more privately self-aware – exhibited less attitude change in their essays than the participants who were not placed in front of a mirror. Awareness of one's attitudes made participants adhere to them more rather than changing their minds. In essence, they were 'true' to themselves.

The ability of mirrors to arouse private self-awareness has another striking implication – being in front of a mirror can make us more moral. In one demonstration of this effect, Diener and Wallbom (1976) had participants take a test of cognitive ability in which they had to solve anagrams (e.g., 'cop go shyly' is an anagram of 'psychology'). Each participant was left in a room to solve anagrams and was given strict instructions that, although they were unsupervised, they should stop after the allotted time and await the return of the experimenter. In the self-awareness condition, participants were facing a free-standing mirror and, to crank up private self-awareness, were also played a tape recording of their own voice. In the control condition, participants sat to the side of the mirror and listened to a tape of someone else's voice. The dependent variable was whether participants elected to cheat, continuing to work after their allotted time was over. As predicted, participants in the self-aware condition were significantly less likely to cheat (see also Vallacher and Solodky, 1979).

This finding is consistent with the idea that private self-awareness makes our personal values salient. Feeling that cheating is wrong, we are less likely to cheat when we can observe ourselves doing so. As we shall see in Chapter 10, a lack of self-awareness has been blamed for the mob mentality that contributes to rioting, looting and intergroup atrocities such as lynchings. As the crowd gets bigger, all else being equal, so the personal moral standards of each individual become less salient. As a result, so does the severity of the violence meted out to victims and the incidents of antisocial behaviour. Of course, many other factors contribute to behaviours such as riots and crowd behaviour, as we will learn in Chapter 10 when we discuss the concept of deindividuation, but the mirror study of Diener and Wallbom (1976), in its small way, creates a situation that is diametrically opposed to a lynch mob.

This basic finding has been replicated and extended in several subsequent studies. For example, Beaman, Klentz, Diener and Svanum (1979) found that unsupervised children were less likely to steal extra sweets when placed in front of a mirror (see Figure 2.4). More recently, an interesting **boundary condition** has been observed by Heine, Takemoto, Moskalenko et al. (2008). They replicated the finding that North American participants were less likely to cheat in front of a mirror, but also found that putting a mirror in front of Japanese participants made no difference to their behaviour. Heine et al. reasoned that in an interdependent or 'collectivist' culture like Japan (see later in this chapter for a discussion of culture and self), people are more accustomed to seeing themselves as others see them. Thus, people in such cultures, to a greater degree than people from independent or 'individualistic' cultures, effectively carry a 'mirror in their heads' in which they can see how they appear to others.

Time to reflect Can you think of other consequences of having such a mirror in the head? Heine et al.'s study focused on the effects of culture on responses to the mirror task – can you think of other factors that might influence how people respond to this task?

Private self-consciousness
Chronic private self-awareness and concern about private aspects of the self.

Like public self-awareness, some people are more privately self-aware in a chronic sense. People who are high in **private self-consciousness** are more likely to be consistent in their attitudes, are likely to experience more intense emotions, and are more accurate in their self-perceptions (Fenigstein, Sheier and Buss, 1975). And, like public self-consciousness, private self-consciousness also has positive and negative consequences. For example, it has been found that because privately self-conscious individuals are more aware of changes in their physiology, they are less likely to suffer stress-related illnesses because they notice health problems sooner (Mullen and Suls, 1982). However, because of this heightened self-awareness, people high in private self-consciousness are also more likely to suffer from depression than others because they are more likely to dwell on negative feelings (Mor and Winquist, 2002; Smith and Greenberg, 1981).

Time to reflect To help you understand the different types of self-awareness and self-consciousness, draw up a table like the one below and list some examples of the positive and negative consequences of being high in each concept.

Concept	Positive consequences	Negative consequences
Public self-awareness		
Private self-awareness		
Public self-consciousness		
Private self-consciousness		

The biological basis of self-awareness

Evidence suggests that a specific part of the brain called the 'anterior cingulate cortex' (Figure 2.5) is responsible for controlling and monitoring intentional behaviour among other complex social cognitive processes such as processing information about the self (Kelley, Macrae, Wyland et al., 2002). This area, in the frontal lobe of the cerebral cortex, appears to be activated when people become self-aware (Kjaer, Nowak and Lou, 2002). Although this is probably not the only area associated with self-awareness, evidence that spindle cells in this part of the brain develop rapidly around 18 months of age also lends support to the importance of the anterior cingulate cortex in self-awareness. On the other hand, chronic

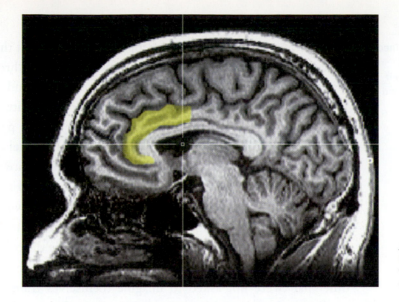

FIGURE 2.5 The anterior cingulate cortex The anterior cingulate cortex in the frontal lobe is thought to be responsible for processing information about the self.

Source: Geoff B Hall, from http://en.wikipedia.org/wiki/File:MRI_anterior_cingulate.png.

self-awareness, enduring through time rather than being produced by a situation, appears to be associated with a different region of the brain, the medial frontoparietal networks, which are normally activated when people are engaged in self-focused, effortful processes (Eisenberger, Lieberman and Satpute, 2005). Thus, so far we lack a clear picture of whether different regions of the brain are specialized in self-awareness. To our knowledge, no study has yet been published attempting to distinguish brain regions associated with public versus private self-awareness.

Question to consider Knowing what you now know about some of the processes related to the self-concept, reread question 1 at the start of the chapter. What do you think of Millie's situation and the potential consequences for her? How can you explain her feelings?

Theories of self

Now that we know how people develop a sense of self-awareness, what types of self-awareness exist, and something about the 'location' of self-awareness within the brain, we move on to consider some of the core theories of self. These theories address why people perceive themselves the way they do. As you read, you will notice that all these theories argue that people define the self in comparison to some standard. For example, self-perception theory argues that people learn about themselves through examining their own thoughts, feelings and behaviours. Self-discrepancy theory and the control theory of self-regulation argue that people can improve their self-concept by comparing it to their internal goals and standards. Regulatory focus theory proposes that people have distinct self-regulatory systems that are associated with their goals. Social comparison theory involves viewing the self compared to other people or the self at another time. Finally, the self-evaluation maintenance model explains how people are able to maintain positive self-esteem when they compare themselves to others. We now discuss these six theories.

Self-perception theory

Self-perception theory Theory that people learn about the self by examining their own thoughts, feelings and behaviours.

Self-perception theory argues that people may learn about themselves by examining their own thoughts, feelings and behaviours. Of these three, behaviours are most important, however, because they are more objective and observable. Bem (1967, 1972) argued that people become aware of their own attitudes (and in a sense, who they are) by looking at what they do. In other words, people look at their own behaviours and infer aspects of the self from those behaviours; for example, a person may reflect on their behaviour of studying hard for an exam and, as a result, they may view themselves as hard-working and studious. Self-perception effects like this can also occur by just imagining behaving in a certain way. For example, van Gyn, Wenger and Gaul (1990) split a sample of runners into two groups. One group trained on exercise bikes, while the other did not. Further, half the participants in each group were asked to imagine themselves training and the other half were not asked to imagine themselves training. Results revealed, as predicted, that the subsequent performance of groups who had trained on the exercise bikes was superior. However, those who had simply imagined themselves training did better than those who did not. Van Gyn et al. argued that imagining themselves training had influenced participants' self-concept, which then influenced their behaviour to be more consistent with the self-concept.

Self-discrepancy theory

Self-discrepancy theory Theory that focuses on people's perceptions of the discrepancies between their actual self and their perceived and ought selves. The theory examines emotional responses to these discrepancies.

Actual self How a person is at the present time.

Ideal self How a person would like to be.

Ought self How a person thinks they should be.

Self-discrepancy theory focuses on people's awareness of discrepancies between how they are, how they would like to be, and how they think they ought to be (Higgins, 1987). It also focuses on how people react, emotionally, to these discrepancies. According to Higgins, there are three aspects of the self-concept:

1 the **actual self**: how a person sees the self at the present time
2 the **ideal self**: how a person would like to see the self
3 the **ought self**: how a person thinks they ought to be, based on ideals of duty and responsibility.

According to the theory, people strive to make sure that their actual self is as close as possible to the ideal and ought selves, which both act as benchmarks to help guide behaviour (see Figure 2.6). If significant discrepancies exist between the actual, ideal and ought selves, this results in psychological discomfort. For example, if a person is studying dentistry at university but would really rather be a musician, and their parents would like them to join the family retail business, there are significant discrepancies between the actual, ideal and ought selves and the person will probably experience some psychological uneasiness.

According to the theory, different discrepancies are associated with different responses. Specifically, if there is a discrepancy between the actual and ought selves, this is said to lead to emotional reactions such as frustration and annoyance (Higgins, Bond, Klein and Strauman, 1986). The dentistry student who visits their parents during the university vacation will be acutely aware of the fact that their parents would rather they joined the family business. The student is not therefore

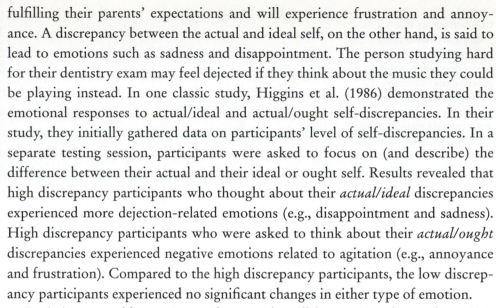

FIGURE 2.6 Self-discrepancy theory According to self-discrepancy theory, there are emotional consequences for people when the actual, ideal and ought selves are discrepant. For example, if the actual and ideal self do not match, this can lead to sadness and disappointment.

Self-regulation The attempt to match behaviour with an ideal or ought standard of the self.

fulfilling their parents' expectations and will experience frustration and annoyance. A discrepancy between the actual and ideal self, on the other hand, is said to lead to emotions such as sadness and disappointment. The person studying hard for their dentistry exam may feel dejected if they think about the music they could be playing instead. In one classic study, Higgins et al. (1986) demonstrated the emotional responses to actual/ideal and actual/ought self-discrepancies. In their study, they initially gathered data on participants' level of self-discrepancies. In a separate testing session, participants were asked to focus on (and describe) the difference between their actual and their ideal or ought self. Results revealed that high discrepancy participants who thought about their *actual/ideal* discrepancies experienced more dejection-related emotions (e.g., disappointment and sadness). High discrepancy participants who were asked to think about their *actual/ought* discrepancies experienced negative emotions related to agitation (e.g., annoyance and frustration). Compared to the high discrepancy participants, the low discrepancy participants experienced no significant changes in either type of emotion.

So, it is reasonable to assume that people will be motivated to reduce their self-discrepancies in order to eliminate, or at least attenuate, the experience of negative emotions. They may change aspects of their behaviour in order for their actual self to become more in line with the ideal, therefore engaging in a process of **self-regulation**. However, people may not necessarily display this adaptive response. Instead, negative emotions can sometimes get in the way of self-regulation and the ability to make changes. Feeling sad, frustrated or annoyed can lead people to look for 'quick fix' solutions that make them feel better in the short term rather than helping them reach a long-term solution. One common example often used to describe this type of outcome relates to how people manage their weight. A person on a diet might be able to manage what they eat, but being reminded that they are still not as thin as they would like may lead them to opt for a quick fix solution to their unhappiness. Thus, they may head to the nearest fridge for a chocolate bar. Similarly, you may know people who engage in 'retail therapy' to make themselves feel better. However, such behaviour does not assist the individual in reaching a long-term goal.

Exploring further We have just linked binge eating and consumerism, or 'retail therapy', to self-discrepancy. Can you find articles that, at least going by the titles and abstracts, seem to provide evidence for this? What other problematic behaviours have been linked to self-discrepancy? Use internet search engines or research databases to find out. For example, you could go onto the internet and use Google Scholar to find articles. Alternatively, if your university library has access to PsycINFO or a similar psychology-specific database, use search terms to try to find relevant articles. Try searching a combination of terms such as 'self discrepancy' (remember to put quote marks around the phrase, to be clear you are searching this as a phrase and not two separate words) and 'addiction'.

Regulatory focus theory

Higgins (1997, 1998) built on self-discrepancy theory to create **regulatory focus theory**, which proposes that people have two distinct self-regulatory systems – promotion and prevention – that are related to different types of goals. People who tend to be more focused on *promotion* will actively go out to seek ways to

Regulatory focus theory
Theory asserting that people have two distinct self-regulatory systems – promotion, which makes people more approach oriented in constructing the self, and prevention, which makes people more cautious and avoidant in constructing the self.

achieve their ideal, but people focused on *prevention* tend to think more about what they ought to be and the obligations they have. There is some evidence to suggest that there are individual differences in this construct. In other words, some people are generally promotion focused and others are more generally prevention focused. Higgins and Silberman (1998) argued that this difference emerges during childhood. In particular, promotion-focused adults tend to have more childhood experiences based on the presence or absence of positive adult responses (e.g., praised for being good and criticized for being bad). In contrast, prevention-focused adults tend to have more childhood experiences based on the presence or absence of negative adult responses (e.g., criticized for being bad and praised for being good).

The promotion system is related to people's achievements towards their ideal self. For example, they may focus on achieving a high grade and study harder to do so. They may, in general, show a focus on challenges as things to move towards and to achieve. Research suggests that promotion-focused people tend to remember information related to the pursuit of success, whereas prevention-focused people tend to focus on failures (Higgins and Tykocinski, 1992). Further, promotion-focused individuals tend to focus on tasks described as gains or non-gains, whereas prevention-oriented individuals appear to focus more on tasks described as potential losses or non-losses (Shah, Higgins and Friedman, 1998).

Although there are individual differences in regulatory focus, the same person can switch from promotion to prevention, and from prevention to promotion, depending on the situation. When people are presented with the possibility of losses, they become prevention focused, and when presented with the possibility of gains, they become promotion focused (e.g., Eiser, Eiser and Greco, 2004). Mood is another temporary factor that can influence regulatory focus, and was the topic of a **meta-analysis** by Baas, de Dreu and Nijstad (2008). Previous research had revealed mixed findings about the relationship between mood and creativity – some studies showed that positive mood states can enhance creativity, whereas others showed that people are more creative when in a negative mood. Analysing all these results together, Baas et al. found that regardless of their positivity or negativity, mood states associated with prevention focus (e.g., relaxed, anxious) were also associated with reduced creativity. Positive moods associated with promotion focus (e.g., happiness) were correlated with creativity, while negative moods were not related to decreases in creativity, so long as they were promotion oriented (e.g., sadness). A meta-analysis such as this is a good way of teasing apart discrepant findings but also relies on a good level of critical thinking. Baas et al.'s application of regulatory focus theory allowed them to solve the puzzle of the effects of mood on creativity.

Meta-analysis A technique in which the results of many studies are combined and analysed together.

The benefits of promotion focus for creativity and the adverse effects of prevention focus were also demonstrated in an experiment by Friedman and Förster (2001, Study 1). They elicited a temporary regulatory focus with a manipulation in which participants had to solve a maze. A mouse was depicted in the middle of the maze, and in the promotion-focus condition, a tasty-looking piece of Swiss cheese was outside the maze, while in the prevention-focus condition, a nasty-looking hawk was hovering over the maze. In solving the maze, participants were either promoting the mouse's pursuit of the cheese or preventing the mouse from being eaten. After completing the maze, participants were asked to complete a range of creativity tasks. Those who had completed the 'cheesy' maze were significantly more creative than those who had completed the 'hawky' maze.

Try it yourself One of the tests of creativity used by Friedman and Förster is as follows. First, get a pen and piece of paper and a timing device and set it for one minute (or ask a friend to time you). Then write down as many uses for a brick as you can in 60 seconds. Count how many uses you came up with. The average participant in these studies comes up with around six or seven. The second one is to evaluate how creative these responses are. Rate each one on the following scale:

0	1	2	3	4	5	6	7	8	9
very uncreative			neither creative nor uncreative					very creative	

This is the dependent measure of 'creativity' used in Friedman and Förster's (2001) study, which has been used quite widely elsewhere. Normally, of course, participants do not rate their own creativity – it is rated by a coder (or, more typically, several coders) who does not know the identity of the participants, nor what condition of the experiment they were in. There are no specific guidelines for judging creativity. Friedman and Förster (2001) asked an independent group of 12 coders to rate the creativity of the responses using the question above and scores were averaged to provide a mean score of creativity for each participant. An example of a creative solution was 'to crush it and use it to draw pictures on the sidewalk' and an example of an uncreative response was 'to build a house with it'.

How did you get on? You can try this out on your friends. Of course, this is not really a test of how creative you are as a person. The whole point of Friedman and Förster's (2001) experiment is that this measure of creativity can change as a result of a situational variable, such as cues that encourage promotion versus prevention focus in the environment. It is a task that seems to capture at least some aspects of creativity. How else do you think creativity could be measured?

Control theory of self-regulation

Control theory of self-regulation Theory of the self proposing that people test the self against private standards and regulate their behaviours to meet these standards.

The **control theory of self-regulation**, devised by Carver and Scheier (1981, 1998), argues that people compare themselves with internal or private standards for the self. However, in contrast with other theories, it proposes that people engage in a cognitive feedback loop of self-regulation that involves four steps: test, operate, test and exit. It looks a bit like a flowchart (see Figure 2.7). In the initial *test* phase, the individual compares the self with one of two standards. As we saw earlier, self-awareness involves both public and private awareness, so according to this theory, individuals may compare themselves to a public (e.g., group norm) or private standard (e.g., value) for the self. If this test reveals a discrepancy, that is, the self does not meet the ideal, then the individual addresses the problem by going into the *operate* phase of the loop. In this phase, the individual will endeavour to change some aspect of the self (usually a behaviour) to try to more closely match the standard they would like to meet. Naturally, at some later time, they will think

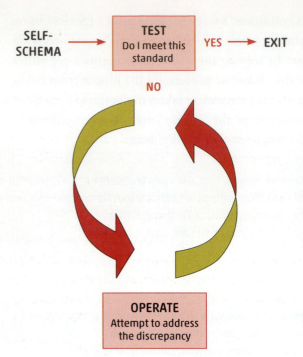

FIGURE 2.7 Carver and Scheier's (1981) control theory of self-regulation

Ego depletion The notion that self-control and willpower are a finite resource that can be used up.

Strength model of self-control Theory arguing that self-control cannot be maintained for an unlimited period of time and needs to be replenished.

about this aspect of the self again and, in doing so, they re-enter the test phase and reassess the extent to which their behaviour meets the standard or ideal. If no discrepancy is detected, then the process ends and the individual exits the feedback loop. However, until this standard is met, the individual will remain in the loop, changing their behaviour and retesting until the discrepancy has been resolved.

According to the control theory of self-regulation, people can make improvements to the self by self-appraisal and self-regulation. Indeed, there is some evidence to suggest that this may work in efforts to prevent relapse among sex offenders (e.g., Ward, 2000) and in people's efforts to pursue their goals (e.g., Emmons, 1996). However, this is not always the case. For example, Baumeister, Bratslavsky, Muraven and Tice (1998) demonstrated that carefully regulating an aspect of the self can actually make it more difficult to regulate other aspects of the self. Participants volunteered for a study ostensibly about taste perception. They were asked not to eat for some time before they participated in the study. When they came to the laboratory, they found that it smelled of chocolate cookies that had just been freshly baked. Participants were then seated behind a desk with a bowl of chocolate cookies on one side of the desk and a bowl of radishes on the other. Participants were placed in one of two possible conditions – in one they were asked to eat two/three radishes and in the other, they were asked to eat two/three cookies. Baumeister et al. reasoned that participants in the radishes condition would have to self-regulate, in other words, they would have to stop themselves from eating the cookies. Essentially, participants were in either a self-regulation condition or a condition where they were free to pursue their desired behaviour. After completing the task, participants were asked to help the experimenter on a second task, where they were asked to complete a virtually impossible problem and to take their time doing so. Those who had participated in the self-regulation condition (the radishes group) persisted to solve the difficult puzzle, on average, for only 8 minutes compared to participants in the other condition (the cookies group) who persisted, on average, for 19 minutes. Baumeister et al. argued that the first group of participants struggled because they had to self-regulate on the earlier task. This creates a problem because people do not possess endless cognitive resources to cope when self-regulation is required. The cognitively depleted participants therefore struggled to self-regulate on a second task, even when it had nothing to do with the original task.

Known as **ego depletion**, this effect has been widely demonstrated (for a meta-analysis of 83 studies, see Hagger, Wood, Stiff and Chatzisarantis, 2010), and is expected by the **strength model of self-control** proposed by Baumeister et al. (1998). According to this model, self-control is akin to physical exercise. Just as we get tired after exercising for a certain period of time and can no longer continue effectively, we are not able to exert effortful control for an unlimited period of time. After a rest, the ability to self-control returns (Tyler and Burns, 2009). People who regularly engage in self-control over a long period of time slowly become less susceptible to ego depletion, just as exercising regularly over a period of months makes people physically fitter (Gailliot, Plant, Butz and Baumeister, 2007).

CRITICAL FOCUS

Ego depletion: mind over matter, or matter over mind?

The concept of ego depletion is based on a metaphor that ultimately stems from the writings of Freud and other psychodynamic theorists. These theorists saw human beings as affected by mental energies. When people think and attempt to control themselves, they draw on a limited reservoir of mental energy that is eventually exhausted. Although intuitively appealing, this kind of metaphor is shaky ground for a scientific theory, no matter how brilliant the insights and how practically important the findings it helps to uncover. Further, there is a concern that ego depletion may not really depend on the fact that people are *really* consuming a limited resource but that they *think* that self-control consumes energy and they cannot keep it up forever (Landau, Meier and Keefer, 2010). Indeed, Job, Dweck and Walton (2010) found that only participants who believed that self-control is tiring and they cannot do it forever were actually susceptible to ego depletion. Those who believed that self-control is unlimited, or who were experimentally led to believe in limitless self-control, were not susceptible to ego depletion later.

However, the idea that self-control consumes energy may be more than just a metaphor. It appears that ego depletion may be underpinned by the consumption of blood sugar. The brain consumes much more glucose than its size would suggest. Ego depletion has been shown to be associated with decreases in blood glucose. Further, people are less prone to ego depletion if they consume sugar, for example in the form of sugary versus no-sugar, 'diet' lemonade (e.g., Dvorak and Simons, 2009; Masciampo and Baumeister, 2008). Who is right? Is ego depletion 'all in the mind' – a self-fulfilling prophecy, as suggested by the findings of Job et al. (2010), or is it a biological effect, in which self-control depletes our limited resources of blood sugar until they run out (e.g., Dvorak and Simons, 2009)?

This is an interesting question to consider, for two reasons. First, it is a good example of how recent findings appear simply to contradict each other, and the reasons why have not yet been identified. Each set of findings is supported by theories that are logical and plausible – we know that people's beliefs about behaviour can be self-fulfilling (see Chapter 3 for a discussion of self-fulfilling prophecies), and we know that intensive mental processes like self-control consume blood sugar. Our job as social psychologists is ultimately to offer reasonably simple, consistent theories which can account for all or most of the available evidence, and that have been tested thoroughly. This allows us to understand human behaviour with some confidence, and to turn our insights into useful interventions. In this case, social psychology has the potential to help people exercise greater self-control.

Second, the debate about self-control is interesting theoretically, because it is speaks to a much wider debate in contemporary social psychology (e.g., Niedenthal, 2007; Schubert and Semin, 2009). Is human behaviour principally driven by schemas (like the belief that self-control cannot go on forever), or is it dependent, in a more straightforward way, on situational and bodily factors (such as the exhaustion of blood sugars)? In Chapter 4, we will discuss the intimate relationship between the body and the mind in more detail, under the heading Embodied social cognition.

Further research is needed to determine which side of the debate will win out. Each set of experiments has problems and is therefore open to alternative interpretations, which need to be ruled out by further research. For example, in Job et al.'s (2010) research, perhaps people who are low in self-control justify themselves by saying that self-control is tiring. Perhaps, participants just want to be consistent – if they say they can self-control for a long time, they will not want to succumb to temptation very early when actually put to the test. As for the research by Masciampo and Baumeister (2008), perhaps participants can taste the difference between drinks sweetened by sugar versus artificial sweeteners.

Quite probably, the two processes work hand in hand, to create a genuinely psychosomatic effect. For example, perhaps your beliefs about self-control affect your responses to the bodily feelings that occur when blood sugar is running low – such as feeling tired. If you think that self-control is not tiring, you may not attribute the feeling of being tired to the fact that you have been engaging in self-control. Also, you will probably not see those tired feelings as being an obstacle to engaging in more self-control. But if you think self-control is tiring, you may be more likely to think that self-control has made you tired, and you are too tired to exercise more of it. This interplay between our bodily experiences and beliefs has been demonstrated many times before. For example, a well-known study by Dutton and Aron (1974) showed that heterosexual men found a female experimenter more attractive when they met her on a high, wobbly bridge. Apparently, they attributed their physical arousal, caused by being on the bridge, partly to the experimenter, and so concluded that she must be attractive. This type of psychosomatic interplay between our bodies and minds is yet to be examined in research on self-control.

Questions

1 Do you think self-control is limited by our biologies, our beliefs about self-control, or both? More generally, do you think we are primarily controlled by our bodies or our minds?
2 If you were to design a study on this topic, what would you do?
3 How would you rule out the possibility that participants can taste the difference between diet and sugary drinks, as in the Masciampo and Baumeister (2009) study?
4 How would you rule out the alternative interpretations of Job et al.'s (2010) study that we have suggested?
5 How would you begin to test the idea that our beliefs about self-control interact with our blood sugar levels in the way we have suggested?

Social comparison theory

In addition to observing their own behaviour and comparing their actual self with other internal standards of the self, people also look to others for important information about the self. Specifically, they compare themselves with other people – both those who they see as 'better' and those they view as 'worse' on various dimensions – to learn important information about themselves. This is quite different to the process of comparing oneself with various internal standards of the self. After all, a person's values, beliefs, attitudes and behaviours are subjective and cannot be validated against an objective source. When a person defines the self against their ideal self, for example, they are comparing themselves with an ideal that cannot be externally validated. Comparing oneself with others, on the other hand, allows the individual to compare the self with a source that can be externally validated. Comparing oneself with others provides an external and objective anchor against which one can compare one's values, beliefs, attitudes and behaviours.

Time to reflect List five people you compare yourself to from time to time. Once you have done this, read the rest of our coverage of social comparison theory, and return to this exercise.

Did you pick people who are largely upward comparators or downward comparators? Or are they much the same? What dimensions do you compare each of them to yourself on (e.g., interests, style, values, popularity, social skills, or ability, effort, achievement in work, study, sports or some other achievement domain)? Do you really measure yourself against each of these people or do you look to them as examples of what (not) to do? How well do you think social comparison theory applies to you?

Social comparison theory
Theory of the self arguing that to learn about, and define, the self, people compare themselves with other people.

Social comparison theory (Festinger, 1954) is specific about how people make these comparisons and why they do so. According to this theory, people learn information about themselves and how to perceive themselves by comparing themselves with other people. It is important for people to feel confident in their perceptions of themselves and in the absence of objectively valid information about the self, people tend to base their evaluations of themselves on comparisons with others. In making these comparisons, people often compare themselves with others who are similar to the self. This makes sense because people want to validate their sense of self and often look to the closest others to do so. However, it is often more useful (and sometimes even unavoidable) to compare the self with others who are 'better' than the self on whatever dimension. This **upward social comparison** – comparing oneself with someone who is perceived to be better than the self – can have a negative impact on self-esteem (Blanton, Crocker and Miller, 1999; Collins, 1996; Wood, 1989). However, there are strategies to deal with this, as we will discuss in the next section. It does not feel nice when one falls short compared to another person.

Upward social comparison
The act of comparing oneself with someone who is perceived to be better on the relevant dimension.

It is also possible to compare the self with others who are 'worse' than the self in a specific domain and this is known as **downward social comparison**. Of course, this type of comparison makes a person feel good. It is always nice to compare favourably to another person and, indeed, this has positive effects for the self-concept (Wills, 1981). However, to be able to make accurate judgements about the self, a person needs to engage in both upward and downward social comparisons. Think of a particular sporting ability, for example. People learn how good they really are at a particular sport by comparing themselves with a broad range of others, both those who do better and those who perform worse than themselves.

Downward social comparison
The act of comparing oneself with someone who is perceived to be worse on the relevant dimension.

Just as people compare themselves to others, they also compare themselves as they are now to themselves as they have been in the past. These are known as **temporal comparisons** (Albert, 1977). Like social comparisons, temporal comparisons can be upward (e.g., 'I used to be more relaxed') or downward (e.g., 'I am wiser now than I was'). Albert (1977) argued that these temporal comparisons behave in much the same way as social comparisons – downward social comparisons make us feel better about ourselves as we are now, whereas upward social comparisons may help us determine how to improve (e.g., recover lost ground). Subsequent research shows that people engage in temporal comparison at least as often as they engage in social comparisons. However, people are especially likely to engage in temporal comparisons – typically downward temporal comparisons – when they are interested in feeling good about themselves. When people want to improve, they are more likely to engage in social comparisons (Wilson and Ross, 2000).

Temporal comparison
The act of comparing oneself with the way one was in the past, or with an anticipated future self.

In a follow-up paper, Wilson and Ross (2001) reported that people boost their current self-esteem by denigrating their past selves, who then provide a convenient downward comparison. Wilson and Ross asked psychology students to rate themselves on a series of traits (e.g., narrow-minded, immature, naive, self-confident, self-motivated, socially skilled) about two weeks into their first year. Some two months later, the same students rated themselves a second time, and were also asked

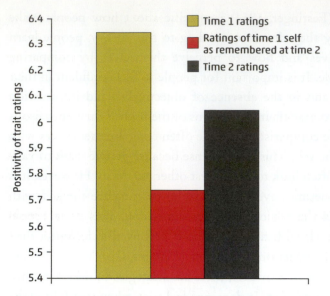

FIGURE 2.8 Students self ratings over time First-year students in psychology were asked to rate themselves at time 1 (two weeks into their first term), and then again at time 2 (two months later). At time 2, they were also asked to rate themselves as they had been at time 1. Results show that these students denigrated their past selves. In essence, people create a disadvantaged past self who is the basis for downward temporal comparison.

Source: Data from Wilson and Ross, 2001

to rate themselves as they were when they completed the questionnaire the first time. Results show that participants systematically denigrated their past selves, rating themselves more harshly in retrospect than they did at the time. This retrospective self-denigration allowed participants to convince themselves that they were better now than they had been two months earlier (see Figure 2.8). However, they actually seemed to see themselves somewhat less favourably at time 2 than they had at time 1 (the reason for this is unknown, but perhaps the excitement and anticipation of starting university provides a temporary boost to self-evaluation, which wears off within a couple of months).

It seems paradoxical that, at one level, people would want to preserve their self-esteem, but denigrate their past selves to achieve it. It would appear that the value of the past self is expendable in the pursuit to esteem the present self. However, this result may be less paradoxical than it seems. Different brain regions – the medial prefrontal cortex and the right inferior parietal cortex respectively – appear to be associated with thinking about the present self and the past (or future) selves (D'Argembeau, Stawarczyk, Majerus et al., 2010). Versions of oneself that are distant in time may be perceived to be rather unlike the 'me' of the present day, and their full humanity, relative to one's present self, may be less salient (Haslam and Bain, 2007).

Research has also shown that people maintain a similar 'illusion of improvement' with regard to their relationships. For example, Sprecher (1999) found that when asked to indicate how satisfied they were with their long-term romantic relationship a year ago, people remembered being less satisfied than they were at the time. Their actual relationship satisfaction did not change, but the retrospective denigration of their relationship as it had been allowed them to perceive that they were growing more satisfied with their relationship.

Self-evaluation maintenance model

Imagine you are a footballer who is constantly outscored by a particular teammate, or a student whose brother or sister always performs better at university. You are unlikely to feel particularly good about these things. After all, you are constantly in a situation where you are compared with someone 'better', in other words, you are constantly faced with an upward social comparison. Sometimes, comparing the self with others can make people good, and sometimes it may not. Ultimately, however, people want to feel good about themselves and maintain positive self-esteem. The **self-evaluation maintenance model** (Tesser, 1988) explains how people are able to do this in the case of upward social comparisons. Specifically, when people compare themselves with individuals whose achievements outshine their own, this model explains how they are able to maintain their self-esteem.

Self-evaluation maintenance model Theory explaining how people are able to maintain their self-esteem in situations where they engage in upward social comparisons.

As we learned earlier, people often engage in upward social comparisons. Knowing someone who is successful or a high achiever can naturally invoke an upward social comparison. This may be especially the case when the domain is *important* or *relevant* to the individual's self-concept. For example, a footballer will see their teammate as a relevant anchor for comparing the self, and their success may therefore be threatening to the self-concept, undermining the view of the self as successful. Another factor that may lead to social comparison is *uncertainty* about one's own abilities in the specific domain. For example, a footballer who is uncertain of their ability as a striker may be more likely to engage in upward comparisons with other strikers and may especially feel challenged when confronted with a high achiever. This uncertainty can lead to a cycle where the individual becomes less certain of their abilities and feels more threatened. Both factors are likely to adversely influence feelings about the self.

According to the self-evaluation maintenance model, people adopt specific strategies to deal with such situations so that they are able to maintain a positive sense of self (Table 2.1):

1 *Exaggerate the ability of the 'better' person:* Your football teammate may just be a freak or some kind of genius whom any person would struggle to surpass. In doing so, it is still possible to think of the self as good because the comparison other is in an entirely different league and is an unrealistic target to aspire to (e.g., Alicke, LoSchiavo, Zerbst and Zhang, 1997).

2 *Engage in downward social comparison:* While people are thinking of the person who is better, they can cope by also thinking of someone worse. You may think of your poor football friend on the bench who never gets the opportunity to play. Comparing the self with less favourable others is good for self-esteem.

3 *Avoid the comparison person:* One might avoid speaking to the football teammate, which makes one feel better because the person is not constantly visible, making obvious the gap in ability.

4 *Devalue the dimension on which the other person is better:* For example, you may say to yourself that football is not that important anyway – it is not the be all and end all – so it does not matter that your teammate is better.

TABLE 2.1 The self-evaluation maintenance model

Strategy	Example
The comparison other is exceptional and therefore an unreasonable comparison	They are a freak and it is ridiculous to compare myself with such a person. How can I ever be expected to be that good?
Think of other people with whom one can compare oneself downwards	The football teammate may be better but other teammates are not as good as me. It's better to compare myself with them
Remove oneself from situations where one compares oneself with the comparison other	Avoid the annoyingly high-achieving teammate
Devalue the comparison dimension	While they may be excellent at scoring goals, they don't have many friends off the field, unlike me

Source: Tesser, 1988. © 1988, reprinted with permission from Elsevier

However, people do not always engage in upward social comparison in such situations and so do not always need to resort to one of the self-esteem maintaining strategies. You can probably remember a time when a sibling, family member or close friend did well or achieved something good, but rather than feeling anxious and unhappy (and therefore needing to engage in self-repair), you felt proud and happy. How does this come about? Instead of engaging in a process of social comparison, people sometimes engage in **social reflection**, where they are able to derive their self-esteem from the success and achievements of close others, without thinking about their own achievement on a particular domain (e.g., Tesser, 1991; Tesser and Collins, 1988). For example, if we like a person, we are more likely to feel positive about their achievements, and we are also likely to have a positive response if we see the person as particularly deserving (Ortony, Clore and Collins, 1988). We also do this on a group level. For example, we have a tendency to 'bask' in the reflected glory of the sports team we support (see Figure 2.9) – it makes us feel good to associate ourselves with success (e.g., Cialdini, Borden, Thorne et al., 1976). According to the model, people may do so, but only if one of two conditions are met:

Social reflection Ability to derive self-esteem from the successes and achievements of close others, without thinking about one's own achievement on a particular domain.

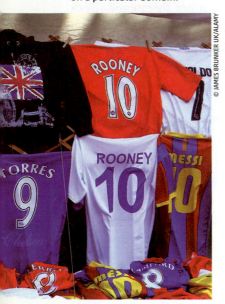

FIGURE 2.9 Replica football shirts The healthy market for these replica football shirts illustrates the appeal of 'basking' in the associated glory of highly successful people (Cialdini et al., 1976). Lockwood and Kunda's (1997) research shows that talismanic celebrities can be inspiring if people think they can improve and emulate something like their success, but can be deflating if they do not perceive they can improve.

1 The domain on which the high-performing person is successful may be *irrelevant*. For example, one may not consider it an important part of the self-concept to be a good singer. So, if one's close friend is a successful vocalist, this does not challenge our own self-concept. If this is the case, we can be happy for the person because it adds something to the self (e.g., we know someone successful) without feeling threatened.
2 We may be less threatened by a high-performing individual if we are confident that we too are exceptional in this particular domain. For example, if a person is a successful vocalist whose best friend on their course is also enjoying some success, threat to the self-concept is less of a problem. Again, the other person's success is likely to add something to our self-concept because it reminds us that we are surrounded by successful people, and that feels good.

In a similar vein, Lockwood and Kunda (1997) found that thinking about 'superstars' in self-relevant domains such as sport and the arts led to self-deflation when people felt their own abilities were fixed, or that similar achievements were unattainable for them. If people felt they were young and able enough to have a chance to emulate their superstars, then thinking about them actually produced inspiration. In later studies, Lockwood and Kunda (1999) found that superstars, while normally seen as inspiring role models, produced deflation if people had already been primed to think of the best aspects of themselves as they currently are. Apparently, superstars are inspiring in that they help us see how we might improve ourselves. If we don't think there's much scope for us to improve, then superstars are intimidating social comparators.

Question to consider Now you know more about social comparisons, reread question 2 at the start of the chapter. Can you explain James's different reactions to his two classmates going to Oxford University?

Self-esteem

From the theories covered in this chapter so far, you will now be in no doubt that people spend a lot of time thinking about themselves, comparing themselves with others and thinking about how they fare. We have also mentioned the term 'self-esteem' a few times already. As laypeople, we all know more or less what this concept means, and we know that our self-esteem can have significant implications for how we function psychologically. In this section we focus on the scientific study of self-esteem.

Self-esteem A person's subjective appraisal of the self as intrinsically positive or negative.

Self-esteem is defined in the literature as people's subjective appraisal of themselves as intrinsically positive or negative (Rosenberg, 1968; Sedikides and Gregg, 2003). A person's self-esteem can vary quite a bit depending on the situation. For example, it can be particularly high when we achieve success or when something good happens to us, or it can be particularly low when we fail at something important or if something bad happens. However, thinking of your friends, family and acquaintances, you can probably call to mind examples of people who generally have high self-esteem and those who have lower self-esteem. While there are situational fluctuations in self-esteem, there is evidence to suggest that there are chronic individual differences in self-esteem. We discuss these individual differences here, but to understand these differences, we must first understand the origins of self-esteem.

Exploring further Psychologists have measured self-esteem in many different ways. Use an internet search engine to find articles that have introduced different measures of self-esteem. Look back to the previous Exploring further exercise for some more specific suggestions about where to begin. Try, for example, combining the phrase 'self-esteem' and 'test', or 'scale'. See if you can find, and complete, at least two online measures (sometimes these are described in full in the article, but sometimes you need to find them in online lectures or demonstrations). Compare yourself to the reported means, and reflect on the similarities and differences between the measures.

Developing self-esteem

Theorists argue that the way children are raised is a strong determinant of their self-esteem (e.g., Baumeister, Campbell, Krueger and Vohs, 2003; Baumrind, 1991). Specifically, it is argued that there are three parenting styles that differ in terms of how demanding (e.g., controlling, punishing) and responsive (e.g., warm, supporting) the parent is to the child. Findings suggest that the following parental styles can affect self-esteem:

1 *Authoritarian:* Children with parents who are authoritarian (more demanding and less responsive) tend to have lower self-esteem. Such parents are often too strict with their children, leading children to feel less confident in their own abilities.
2 *Permissive:* Children whose parents are overly permissive (less demanding and more responsive) also have lower levels of self-esteem (e.g., DeHart, Pelham and Tennen, 2006).

3 *Authoritative:* Children with the highest self-esteem tend to have parents who are both demanding and responsive. Such parents seem to strike the right balance between strictness and punishment when children do things wrong, and being supporting and warm with their children.

There is some evidence to suggest that children develop a stable sense of self-esteem from their childhood experiences. However, it is also the case that self-esteem changes over the course of the life span. For example, a meta-analysis on self-esteem by Robins, Trzesniewski, Tracy et al. (2002) found that self-esteem among children (aged 6–11) was fairly unstable, arguably because children's self-concepts are in a process of development. It was found that among adults in their twenties, self-esteem was more stable than in the young children and that this remained into later adulthood. The authors argued that this is because adults have a more defined self-concept that is more resistant to life events. The authors also found, however, that people's self-esteem becomes less stable again around age 60. They argued that this might be because of the many life changes that occur during this period of life – people retire, their health may fail and they may experience the death of close others.

Time to reflect The question of how to parent is an ideological battlefield. Everything from antisocial behaviour, aggression and welfare dependency is popularly blamed on bad parenting. People do not always agree on what is good and bad parenting. Amy Chua's (2011) book, *Battle Hymn of the Tiger Mother*, highlights what she perceived as differences between Eastern and Western styles of parenting. The concept of the tiger mother refers to the style of traditional Chinese parenting, typically much stricter than Western parenting. The book generated mixed responses from parents and commentators. Many argued that Chua's approach could help encourage all children to reach their potential and the world would see less 'brats'. Others argued that children need to have a fun childhood in which they can explore and express themselves without strict parental control. Knowing what you know about the development of self-esteem, do you think tiger mothering is a good idea? What is the role of culture in this example?

Sources of self-esteem

Some sources of self-esteem are internal to the person. For example, Pelham and Swann (1989) found that people who tend to experience mostly positive emotions and rarely experience negative emotions have high self-esteem. People who have specific, positive self-schemas (e.g., a good friend, a hard worker, devoted mother) also experience higher self-esteem, especially if they are relatively certain of their positive self-evaluation on these specific dimensions, and if they attach importance to them. People who are abstract and flexible in the way they evaluate themselves on these schemas also have more robust self-esteem (Updegraff, Emanuel, Suh and Gallagher, 2010). For example, if you evaluate how good a friend you are strictly on the basis of how quickly you return texts and emails, your self-esteem may take a downward turn at times where you are too busy or distracted to reply to your friends' messages. In contrast, your self-esteem will be more resilient if you also bear in mind the other respects in which you are actually a good friend, such as the times you have helped your friend through a crisis.

Some sources of self-esteem come from outside the person. Social acceptance by others helps to boost self-esteem (e.g., Leary, Cottrell and Phillips, 2001; Leary, Tambor, Terdal and Downs, 1995). This is consistent with the symbolic interactionists' idea that the self is a social construct that serves social purposes. Leary et al. (1995, 2001) argue that self-esteem is a kind of internal barometer of the extent to which the person is being included versus excluded by other people. The more you are socially excluded, the lower your self-esteem; the more you are included, the higher your self-esteem. Thus, Leary et al. refer to self-esteem as a *sociometer*. High self-esteem is a pleasant state, whereas low self-esteem is aversive, so people are generally motivated to maintain high levels of self-esteem. According to **sociometer theory**, this motivation serves an important purpose. It drives us to behave in ways that increase self-esteem, which means that it motivates us to ensure that we are socially included by behaving in ways that are acceptable and rewarding for others. Conversely, it deters us from risking harm to our self-esteem by acting in ways that are likely to lead to rejection. Thus, self-esteem is part of a system in which we monitor our social environment for signs of inclusion or rejection, and modify our behaviour in order to ensure that we are socially included (see later in this chapter for the importance of inclusion, or 'belonging', in human life).

Leary et al. (1995) uncovered early evidence for their theory in a set of five studies. They showed that self-esteem was highly correlated with people's assumptions about whether they are likely to be accepted or rejected by other people. Denissen, Penke, Schmitt and van Aken (2008) compared the average self-esteem levels of citizens of a number of developed countries. These countries were members of the Organization for Economic Cooperation and Development (OECD), and hailed from all continents except Africa. They found that countries whose citizens regularly spend time with friends enjoyed higher levels of self-esteem. This finding held, even controlling for the overall happiness, wealth and anxiety levels of each country.

Other studies have dealt with the problems of interpreting correlational findings in cross-sectional research designs such as those used by Leary et al. That is, does *a cause b*, or does *b cause a*? In a longitudinal study, Srivastava and Beer (2005) showed that being liked by others predicted subsequent increases in self-esteem, precisely as sociometer theory suggests. Having high self-esteem did not predict being liked by others later. Similarly, in a study of German citizens, Denissen et al. (2008) found that the quality of interactions with friends and family members predicted self-esteem later in the same day. However, self-esteem did not predict interaction quality later in the day. Again, the direction of causality seems to point in the direction suggested by sociometer theory – from inclusive social interactions to self-esteem, and not vice versa (Figure 2.10).

Sociometer theory Theory of self-esteem arguing that people are motivated to maintain high levels of self-esteem and do this by ensuring they are socially included.

FIGURE 2.10 Causal sequence suggested by the sociometer theory of self-esteem Self-esteem acts as an internal 'barometer' of social inclusion. When there are signs of social exclusion (e.g., a rebuff from a friend, a party that one is not invited to), self-esteem is reduced, triggering negative emotions. To escape these negative emotions, people act in ways they think will result in their social reinclusion (e.g., making a renewed effort to strengthen the friendship).

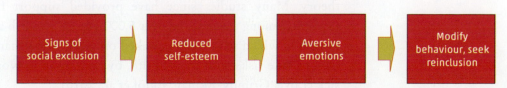

Signs of social exclusion → Reduced self-esteem → Aversive emotions → Modify behaviour, seek reinclusion

Sociometer theory is able to cast light on some of the specific sources of self-esteem. Anthony, Holmes and Wood's research (2007) found that self-esteem is most strongly connected to self-evaluations on traits that help gain social acceptance. For their participants (Canadian undergraduate students), this was typically appearance and popularity. Thus, self-esteem was most strongly correlated with these traits. However, when people are in roles where others depend on them, traits such as kindness and understanding may be more important in being accepted. For example, if you are in a close personal relationship, being kind and understanding is important in being accepted by the person whose acceptance of you presumably matters most – your partner.

Like other widely discussed theories, sociometer theory has had its critics. Notably, Pyszczynski, Greenberg, Solomon et al. (2004) point out that sociometer theory is less convincing about how people react to signs of social exclusion. Frequently, people react to rejections of romantic overtures, or social exclusion, by withdrawing further from social contact (Baumeister, Wotman and Stillwell, 1993), or even by being aggressive (Twenge, Baumeister, Tice and Stucke, 2001). If self-esteem really is part of a system designed to motivate people to seek social inclusion, they argue, people would respond to social rejection with lowered self-esteem, followed by efforts to be reincluded. It is difficult to explain why they would effectively exclude themselves further from social life following rejection. Interested readers might like to check out Leary's (2004) reply to this and other criticisms by Pyszczynski et al. (2004). Also of interest, a recent meta-analysis of 192 studies suggests that the experience of being rejected by others may not lower self-esteem. Instead, it produces a kind of emotional numbness in which people experience neither positive nor negative mood (Blackhart, Nelson, Knowles and Baumeister, 2010), although this may depend on precisely in what form the rejection is experienced (see Chapter 9 for a discussion of ostracism and its effects).

Contingent self-esteem

Sources of self-esteem vary from person to person. Some people base their self-esteem primarily on their appearance, others on social approval, others on how virtuous they are, and yet others on their successes. Crocker and Wolfe (2001) and Crocker and Park (2004) termed these the 'contingencies' of self-worth. They also developed a contingent self-esteem scale to measure differences between people in what is important to their sense of self-worth. They found that people who base their self-esteem on a narrow range of sources tend to experience lower levels of psychological wellbeing than those who stake their self-esteem on a broad range of sources. This finding is consistent with multiple role theory. Many studies since have provided support for its predictions. For example, among a sample of over 5,000 young Swedish adults, a contingent self-esteem in which self-worth is staked on work performance led both women and men to take risks with their health, by coming in to work even when they were sick (Löve, Grimby-Ekman, Eklöf et al., 2010).

Consequences of self-esteem

Why does it matter to have a high self-esteem? What happens to people who have lower self-esteem? Many social psychologists have attempted to answer these questions, identifying the consequences of having relatively high and lower levels of self-esteem (e.g., Baumeister, Tice and Hutton, 1989; Bushman and Baumeister, 1998). Here, we discuss some of the ways in which a person's level of self-esteem influences how they deal with life events.

Mood regulation

Some research has shown that people who have lower levels of self-esteem are less likely to make the effort to make themselves feel better (e.g., Heimpel, Wood, Marshall and Brown, 2002; Wood, Heimpel and Michela, 2003). For example, Wood et al. (2003) examined people's recollections of positive life events. They found that people with lower levels of self-esteem (compared to people with higher levels) were more likely to downplay the positive feelings they experienced in the event. They also showed a tendency to make themselves feel less positive and distract themselves from the positive feelings. Other findings have shown that people with lower levels of self-esteem also deal differently with negative life events. For example Heimpel et al. (2002) asked people who had reported a negative event (a failure) to make a list of their immediate plans and the reasons behind them. Results revealed that participants with higher levels of self-esteem (compared to people with lower levels) were more likely to report goals to deal with the setback and improve their mood. These findings together suggest that people who have higher levels of self-esteem make better efforts to regulate their mood. They are more likely to focus on the positive aspects of positive life events and show a more adaptive response to life's setbacks. In contrast, people with lower levels of self-esteem perhaps display a maladaptive response in dealing with life events.

Protection from the terror of death

According to terror management theory (Pyszczynski, Greenberg and Solomon, 1999; Solomon, Greenberg and Pyszczynski, 1991), the most profound anxiety we confront as human beings stems from the knowledge that one day, we must die. Much of our social cognition and behaviour is motivated by the desire to escape this anxiety. The effects of awareness of mortality are often tested by confronting participants with the inevitability of their death, for example by asking people to write about what will happen to their bodies when they die (versus, say, watching TV). Consistent with terror management theory, this so-called **mortality salience** induction has a range of effects on thoughts, feelings and actions that are consistent with the desire to escape or somehow transcend the inevitability of one's demise. For example, young adults who have just gone through a mortality salience induction report that they want to have more children than control participants – children being an obvious way to leave something of one's self in the world after one's demise (Fritsche, Jonas, Fischer et al., 2007; Wisman and Goldenberg, 2005).

Mortality salience The awareness of one's own inevitable death.

Self-esteem is an important buffer against the anxiety of death, according to this theory. The logic is as follows. To protect themselves against the anxiety of death, individuals collaborate to construct a cultural worldview – a shared set of assumptions about the world that impart meaning, permanence and stability to life. This cultural worldview entails agreed upon standards by which people may be evaluated, and if they live up to these standards of value, they have some hope of literally transcending death (e.g., by entering an afterlife), or symbolically doing so (e.g., being commemorated by one's community after one has died). In terror management theory, self-esteem is acquired by believing that one is living up to these standards of value (see also sociometer theory). Thus, self-esteem is a tremendous buffer against the anxiety elicited by awareness of mortality. If I am a good person according to my community's cultural worldview, then I feel that in some sense I am able to transcend death. Indeed, there is good evidence for this prediction. Participants who have chronically high self-esteem or whose self-esteem is temporarily boosted by an experimental procedure are less prone to the effects of mortality salience. Whereas low self-esteem participants respond quite strongly to mortality salience in various ways including defending their cultural worldview by derogating people with conflicting views, high self-esteem participants are less prone to doing this (Harmon-Jones, Simon, Greenberg et al., 1997). Recent research suggests that **implicit self-esteem** – the unconscious conviction that one is a person of worth – may be a more effective buffer than explicit self-esteem (Schmeichel, Gailliot, Filardo et al., 2009).

Implicit self-esteem
Unconscious, spontaneous or automatic evaluation of the self.

Aggression

Many researchers suggest that people with lower levels of self-esteem are more prone to antisocial acts such as murder (Kirschner, 1992), violent behaviour in gangs (Anderson, 1994), robbery (MacDonald, 1975) and domestic violence (Renzetti, 1992). However, the evidence to support these claims is mixed. Certainly, low levels of serotonin may be associated with both low self-esteem and aggression, as we shall see in Chapter 13. Some studies have shown that low levels of self-esteem are related to high levels of aggression (e.g., Donnellan, Trzesniewski, Robins et al., 2005). However, it is not clear whether aggression is really caused by low self-esteem. Narcissism, a variable that is positively associated with normal self-esteem but is decidedly not the same thing, may be more important.

Narcissism

What about people who have extremely high levels of self-esteem? Much of the literature points to the negative influence of lower levels of self-esteem, but until fairly recently, researchers have been less concerned with the effects of extreme levels of high self-esteem and exaggerated feelings of importance and superiority. Such **narcissistic** individuals, lying at the upper extremity of self-esteem, do not enjoy a stable sense of their self-worth and instead need the validation of others to maintain their self-concept (Kernis and Paradise, 2002). Indeed, some research suggests that narcissists, while professing positive evaluations of themselves, have unconscious doubts about their worth, which are accessible using a procedure known as the Implicit Association Test (Jordan, Spencer, Zanna et al., 2003; but for a critique and alternative findings, see Campbell, Bosson, Goheen et al., 2007). Therefore, having an extremely high self-esteem is not as good as one might expect it to be. Research also shows that narcissists can become aggressive in the face of criticism or any other perceived threat to their insecure image (Baumeister, Smart and Boden, 1996; Bushman and Baumeister, 1998).

However, putting aside their tendency to be more aggressive, narcissists tend to be psychologically healthy. Specifically, narcissism is negatively related to sadness, depression, anxiety and loneliness, and positively related to happiness and satisfaction. The reason narcissism is positively associated with psychological wellbeing is not that it is good for you, but that it is associated with normal or high self-esteem, which, as we have seen, *is* good for you (Sedikides, Rudich, Gregg et al., 2004). The relationship between narcissism and psychological wellbeing is, therefore, a classic example of a **spurious correlation** produced by their mutual relation to self-esteem. However, although the relationship is spurious, it nonetheless tells you that the average narcissist is likely to enjoy better psychological health than the average person who is not a narcissist. There is no need to feel sorry for them.

Narcissism Individual differences variable characterized by extremely high but insecure levels of self-esteem.

Spurious correlation When two variables have no direct connection but it is wrongly inferred they do, because of coincidence or the presence of a third (unseen) factor.

SOCIAL PSYCHOLOGY IN THE REAL WORLD

The narcissism 'epidemic' and its consequences

Narcissism, or excessive love of oneself, is said to be rife in US culture, according to social psychologists Jean Twenge and Keith Campbell (2009), who argue that narcissistic personality traits (e.g., overconfidence, vanity, materialism, lack of consideration for others) are turning America into a nation of egomaniacs, with potentially disastrous consequences.

© CHAOSS/FOTOLIA.COM

What are the causes of this epidemic? Twenge and Campbell argue that one of the main influences is parenting. For example, parents often tell their children they are the 'best' and they are 'special', which leads to overinflated feelings of self-worth. Children are also given more power in the home, such as what they have for dinner and what time they go to bed, than in previous generations. They also argue that celebrity culture has played an important role in the narcissism epidemic. For example, TV programmes such as *Big Brother* seem to be a vehicle for narcissistic personalities to get noticed for doing very little. Next, they target social networking sites and the media. People can strategically present themselves in a positive light on sites like Facebook, showing only pictures where they look 'hot' and concealing less positive aspects of the self, such as unflattering photographs. Social networking also allows users to 'show off' and favourably present themselves by displaying particular aspects of their identity such as their favourite bands, fashion shops and activities. Teenagers and adolescents use social networking sites so the narcissism epidemic may get to people very young. Finally, Twenge and Campbell argue that being able to obtain credit easily means that people can get a 'quick fix' and feel better off than they really are, at least until they have to pay off the credit card.

What are the consequences of narcissism? Narcissists are generally overconfident, think they are smarter than others and have a sense of entitlement. This has some positive consequences: narcissists are more likely to emerge as leaders from initially leaderless groups (Brunell, Gentry, Campbell et al., 2008), and even to head large organizations (Chatterjee and Hambrick, 2007). One possible reason for this is that narcissists may be charismatic and especially adept at convincing people to share their inflated opinion of themselves. Although narcissists are not necessarily more creative, they are seen as more creative by others (as well as themselves, of course), largely because they pitch their ideas with more enthusiasm. Indeed, narcissists' enthusiasm and charisma means that, up to a point, groups containing narcissists produce more creative ideas (Goncalo, Flynn and Kim, 2010). Thus, narcissism may, in some sense, have social value, despite the unpleasant and selfish behaviour with which it is associated.

On the downside, the overrepresentation of narcissists as CEOs does lead to an important and largely unexamined question. This is whether narcissism may have contributed to some of the spectacular and disastrous corporate failures we have witnessed globally in the 2000s. Because narcissists are unwilling to listen to dissenting opinions or heed warnings, and have an inflated sense of their abilities, it is reasonable to guess that narcissistic leadership has had something to do with recent disasters in the oil and banking industries (Chatterjee and Hambrick, 2007). Also, Twenge and Campbell argue that if narcissism continues to grow in US society, people will become more and more individualistic, focus only on themselves and harm other people in the process of achieving their own success.

Questions

1 Most of the arguments relate to narcissism in America, but are we any different in the UK?

2 Do you think any of the other social ills of our age – excessive debt, corruption, street crime – may have anything to do with the narcissism epidemic?

Self-presentation

The self we know is not always the self we present to others. Because what others think of us depends on the self we project, we often try to manage the impression we present to others. Also, the way we see ourselves is often constructed and influenced

Impression management
People manage the self they
present to others, so that they
appear to others in the best
possible light.

Self-monitoring People
control how they present
themselves, depending
on the person (individual
differences) and the situation.

Self-presentation People
make deliberate efforts
to create an impression
(usually favourable) of
themselves to others.

by interacting with other people. People constantly monitor their presentation of self in their interactions with others. This process is called **impression management** (Goffman, 1959). Specifically, people vary in the degree to which they engage in **self-monitoring** – how much they engage in **self-presentation** to others (Snyder, 1974). Research suggests that people who are high self-monitors tend to shape their behaviour to project the self they think is appropriate to their audience or situation. They are, therefore, *strategic* in their self-presentation. On the other hand, low self-monitors are less sensitive to situational demands and do not shape their behaviour in this way. Instead, they tend to be more *expressive* and less concerned with the perceived expectations of the audience. More generally, people also vary their impression management strategies depending on the situation they are in. For example, evidence suggests that people use different strategies to present the self, depending on whether they are in a public or private situation (e.g., Leary, 1995).

There are several motives that drive strategic self-presentation (e.g., Jones and Pittman, 1982):

1 to be seen as competent in the eyes of others (we talk more about enhancing self-image in the next section)
2 in an attempt to be liked by others
3 to make people believe we are dangerous, in order to keep them away
4 to be seen as morally respectable
5 to be seen as helpless and in need of sympathy, in order to gain others' pity.

Often, these strategies are effective (as we will see in Chapter 6 on persuasion) and other times they are not – specifically, ingratiation in the form of flattery can make people seem less trustworthy and sometimes insincere and 'slimy' (Vonk, 1998). However, much of strategic self-presentation is geared towards managing the impressions of others.

Expressive self-presentation, on the other hand, is more about managing our impressions of ourselves (Schlenker, 1980). People behave towards others in ways that help them validate their perceptions of self. This may be reflected in who we choose as friends. For example, if you think of yourself as outgoing and sociable, it helps to have friends who think the same of you. Expressive self-presentation is important because it provides external confirmation about how one sees oneself.

Expressive self-presentation can also help people to change their behaviour. For example, Tice (1992) found that public behaviour is internalized more into the self-concept than behaviour performed privately. Tice asked participants to act as if they were emotionally stable or unstable. They were asked to do so in either a public or private context. It was found that people internalized the stable or unstable behaviour as part of the self more when the behaviour was performed publicly (Figure 2.11), indicating that the way we are seen by others is an important determinant in how we see ourselves – and also influences how our self-concept changes. Self-presenting as a good person makes us privately feel better about ourselves (Gergen, 1965), and pretending to be more sociable than we are makes us behave more sociably later (Schlenker et al., 1994).

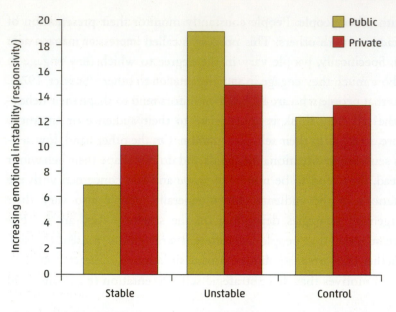

FIGURE 2.11 **Public versus private self-presentation and the self-concept** If behaviour is performed publicly (in front of other people) rather than privately, it is internalized more into the self-concept. Participants asked to act as if they were emotionally stable later rated themselves as more stable (that is, less unstable) than those who had acted as if they were emotionally unstable. However, this tendency was stronger among participants whose performance was public, rather than private. There was no public/private difference in the control condition.

Source: Data from Tice, 1992

This process largely works through the processes specified by self-perception theory, which we came across earlier in this chapter. Just as we learn about others from observing behaviour, we learn about ourselves. It has an important application in counselling and clinical psychology, according to Kelly (2000). Kelly argues that a crucial goal in therapy is to construct a new, healthier self. In doing so, clients should engage in positive self-presentations, which can be reinforced by the therapist. Controversially, Kelly (2000) argues that clients should therefore withhold information from their therapists if it too seriously undermines their effort to present themselves in a positive light. This might mean, for example, that they should conceal their dissatisfaction with the therapy, or even information about extremely unpleasant behaviours in which they have engaged that may have contributed to their current problems. Presenting a positive image to a therapist enables the therapist to reinforce a positive self-image.

Kelly's (2000) conclusions have been hotly disputed by other researchers in social and clinical psychology (e.g., Arkin and Hermann, 2000). One reason for this is not just that honesty and openness have historically been regarded as essential for clients of psychotherapy, counselling and clinical psychology, but that clients may be mistaken about what constitutes shameful and stigmatizing behaviour. One way in which therapists can help clients to develop a more positive understanding of themselves is to help them see that their own actions and circumstances need not be shameful or stigmatizing – and to help them act differently in the future (Hill, Gelso and Mohr, 2000). However, there is some evidence that at least circumstantially supports some of Kelly's (2000) arguments. For example, Braginsky and Braginsky (1967) found that institutionalized schizophrenics presented themselves as mentally healthy in interviews with psychiatrists if they thought the interview was designed to determine their suitability for a less secure ward with more facilities and freedom. In contrast, they presented themselves as mentally unhealthy if they thought the interview was about whether they should continue to be hospitalized (generally, this client group preferred to stay in the institution rather than confront life outside). Furthermore, the psychiatrists 'bought' these self-presentations, assessing clients' mental health according to whether they presented themselves as well or unwell. There is also evidence that presenting one's self as mentally healthy or unhealthy can be self-fulfilling, especially if one's self-presentations are confirmed by experts (McKillop and Schlenker, 1988). There are also studies showing that the number of self-disclosures a client makes during therapy is negatively associated with outcomes such as the smoothness of the session and even recovery (Shapiro and Firth, 1987; Strassberg, Roback, Anchor and Abramowitz, 1975), whereas keeping secrets from therapists may be associated with quicker recovery (Kelly, 1998). Even if we do not accept Kelly's (2000) conclusion that keeping secrets is a good idea for clients, at the very least her analysis points to the importance of self-presentational processes in the context of psychotherapy.

How accurate is our self-knowledge?

Thus far, we have learned much about the self. One of the key lessons from social psychological research is that it is useful to endeavour to take others' perspectives on ourselves. When we view ourselves as if from the outside, we are better able to regulate ourselves and meet the demands of social situations. Our self-esteem responds to being liked and included, or disliked and rejected, by others, acting much like an internal mirror of ourselves. But exactly how well do we really know ourselves? Of course, in many senses you know more about yourself than anybody else does. You will be able to recall many facts about yourself, many of the places you have been and experiences you enjoy, more than anybody else. But how well do you really understand yourself? Just how reliable are your insights into your personality traits, your fears and desires, the reasons you do things, and the things you will do in the future? Social psychologists have amassed a vast body of evidence suggesting that our self-knowledge is surprisingly weak and unreliable. There appear to be two major sources of error in our self-knowledge: we are unable and, for various reasons, unwilling to know ourselves completely.

The limits of self-awareness

In an influential paper, Nisbett and Wilson (1977) argued that people have surprisingly poor self-knowledge and, in particular, no direct introspective access to their mental processes. So, when asked: 'Why do you like him?', 'How did you solve this problem' and 'Why did you take that job', people will typically answer quite freely. However, for Nisbett and Wilson (1977), it is doubtful that their answers will be any more reliable than those of an informed third party, that is, a person who has access to the same biographical facts. They cite a number of striking demonstrations of this lack of introspective awareness of our own thought processes:

- *People appear not to notice when, or why, their attitudes change:* Bem and McConnell (1970) showed that after writing an essay contrary to their own attitudes (that students should have no choice in their academic curriculum) their attitudes changed, as if they had persuaded themselves. But when asked what their attitudes had been before they wrote the essays, students incorrectly indicated that their previous attitudes had been the same as their new, more anti-choice ones. This basic finding has been replicated time and time again. For example, Douglas and Sutton (2004) gave anti-gun control and anti-environmentalist messages to their participants. Participants were influenced by these messages, but incorrectly guessed that their pre-message attitudes, which had been assessed two weeks before, were the same as their new ones.

- *People appear not to understand how situational factors affect their behaviour:* Latané and Darley (1970, p. 124) found that people were less likely to help a suffering stranger when they were in the company of other people. They reported that: 'We asked this question every way we know how: subtly, directly, tactfully, bluntly. Always we got the same answer. Subjects persistently claimed that their behaviour was not influenced by the other people present. This denial occurred in the face of results showing that the presence of others did inhibit helping.'

- *People appear not to understand why they like things:* Nisbett and Wilson arranged nightgowns and stockings on a display within a retail store. Participants, who were told they were participating in a consumer survey, were asked to indicate which item was the best quality and why. Participants were heavily biased towards the items on the right, seeing them as the best quality, perhaps because attention is biased towards the right (Carruthers, 2010). However, when explaining why they picked out a given item of clothing as the highest quality, not one participant spontaneously mentioned its position within the display. When asked directly whether they may have preferred it because of its left/right position, all participants denied it.

- *People believe their behaviour is influenced by factors that, in fact, do not influence it:* Nisbett and Wilson found that an experimental group of participants wrongly thought that their enjoyment of a film was ruined by the noise of a power saw outside. In fact, their ratings of the film were the same as a control group who watched the film without the distracting noise in the background. A recent study makes much the same point. Have you ever been annoyed when someone lets slip what is going to happen at the end, and so ruins what would have been a suspenseful story? It seems that your annoyance may be misplaced. Leavitt and Christenfeld (2011) found that these 'spoilers' did not, in fact, reduce people's enjoyment of stories. In fact, quite the opposite was true: people enjoyed the 'spoiled' version of unfamiliar stories where the ending was revealed early, rather than the 'unspoiled' version of stories in which the ending was not revealed until, well, the end. In other words, people appear to enjoy stories more when they know what is coming. Nonetheless, we tend to believe, erroneously, that we will enjoy stories less under such conditions.

Subsequent research, much of which we will encounter later in this book, demonstrates the surprising inaccuracy of judgements about the self. We appear to be unable to make especially accurate predictions about ourselves. For example, we appear to be worse, not better, than others at judging how long our romantic relationships will last. In a bias known as the **affective forecasting error**, we appear to overestimate the emotional impact that positive and negative life events will have on us. This may be connected to our inability to understand our own personality traits accurately. According to results obtained by Spain, Eaton and Funder (2000), for example, your own ratings of how neurotic you are predict your emotional

Affective forecasting error
The tendency for people to overestimate the emotional impact that positive and negative events will have on them.

reactions to future events *less* well than others' ratings of your neuroticism. We also appear to be unable to explain or even accurately identify our previous behaviour. As you will see in Chapter 11, when asked to indicate how they had felt over the past few weeks, women indicated that they were particularly irritable before menstruation, in keeping with the notion of 'premenstrual syndrome'. However, daily records of their mood showed no such thing – mood was not significantly affected by the menstrual cycle (McFarlane, Martin and Williams, 1988).

Another interesting line of research suggests that we may be wrong about something very fundamental about ourselves – the extent to which we have free will. Wegner (2002) argues that our conscious thoughts do not drive our behaviour. Instead, our behaviour is shaped by unconscious or automatic responses to the environment. Wegner argues that the experience of free will arises because our conscious thoughts about our actions are typically consistent with our actions, occur shortly before our actions, and in the absence of evidence that something other than our free choice could have caused us to act. Thus, it naturally feels to us that we are making conscious choices, even if we are actually deciding things unconsciously.

Wegner and Wheatley (1999) conducted an ingenious study to test this notion that free will is an illusion. They set up an Ouija-type board (the flat lettered board often used as part of a game to 'contact the spirit world') on top of a computer mouse. The participant and a confederate put their hands on top of the board and were instructed to use it together to move the mouse around the screen, stopping every 30 seconds or so. The participant and the confederate wore headphones, through which participants heard the name of one of the objects on the screen (e.g., 'swan'), either 30 seconds, 5 seconds or 1 second before, or 1 second after, the mouse had stopped. On some trials, the participants genuinely had control over where the mouse stopped. On other trials, unbeknown to participants, the confederate was instructed to stop on a certain object, meaning that, on these trials, the participant did not control where the mouse stopped (Figure 2.12).

Of most interest is the extent to which participants thought they had intentionally stopped the mouse on the named object, even in the trials in which they exerted no influence on when the mouse stopped. Reasonably enough, they tended not to think they had intentionally stopped the mouse on the named object when it was primed 30 seconds previously. But if it was named shortly before the mouse stopped – 5 or 1 seconds previously – the majority of participants indicated they had intentionally

FIGURE 2.12 Illustration of the logic behind Wegner and Wheatley's (1999) experiment Hearing the word 'swan' triggered conscious thoughts about the object. When the confederate stopped the mouse at the picture of the swan on the screen a few seconds later, participants wrongly inferred that they themselves had intentionally done so. According to Wegner and Wheatley, this 'illusion of free will' mirrors everyday life. We consciously intend to do things, but our actions are driven largely by automatic psychological processes we are not conscious of. We think we have done things intentionally because our intentions tend to precede our actions, but, in reality, we are akin to a pilot who thinks they are in charge of a plane that is operating on autopilot.

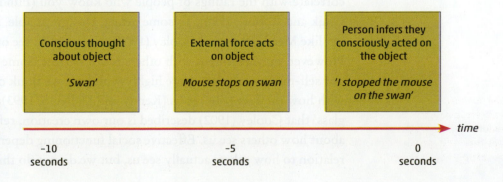

stopped the mouse. If they heard the object being named after the mouse stopped, they tended not to indicate they had consciously chosen to stop the mouse there. This experiment seems to suggest that people can be 'tricked' into believing they are exerting free will. Consistent with Wegner's theory of illusory conscious will, participants did not believe they had consciously chosen to stop the mouse when it rested on an object whose name they had not heard. It happened when what they heard triggered conscious thoughts about the object of their apparent action (the swan), shortly before they observed the mouse stop on that object.

This classic study has generated many experiments on the illusion of conscious choice, which have largely supported the claim that people can be 'tricked', or rather trick themselves, into believing their actions were the result of conscious choices. For Wegner, the upshot of this research is that our actions are largely decided unconsciously – or automatically. Conscious thoughts accompany and precede our actions, to be sure, but these thoughts are not necessarily causally responsible for our actions. This is entirely consistent with the behaviourist tradition of psychology. For Watson, Skinner and other behaviourists, conscious thoughts were not responsible for our behaviour. Nonetheless, modern social psychologists, unlike the behaviourists, regard conscious thoughts as important and amenable to scientific study, and as we shall see in many of the chapters in this book, notably Chapters 3 and 4, our conscious thoughts and deliberations affect our emotional reactions to events. Over time, they can affect our automatic decision-making processes (in Chapter 12, we will see how, if people are consciously determined to be less racist, they can change even their unconscious or implicit racism). Consciously held, long-term plans and intentions also reliably (although not perfectly) predict our later behaviour. It is just that our conscious intentions do not always seem to drive our immediate behavioural choices in day-to-day life. Instead, unconscious responses, beliefs and even goals appear to drive much of our behaviour (Custers and Aarts, 2010).

Time to reflect Wegner and Wheatley's (1999) study highlights a case where people think they've intentionally done something, whereas in fact they haven't. Does this really show that in the normal course of our everyday lives, we are wrong to suppose that our conscious intentions aren't responsible for our behaviour? Do you think perhaps their experiment simply hijacks or 'tricks' a process that normally leads us to correctly infer we have intentionally done things?

All this is not to say that people have no knowledge of themselves. There is a good chance that your ratings of your own personality (e.g., how extraverted you are) or behaviour (e.g., how often you tell jokes to lighten a tense moment) will correlate with the ratings of people who know you (Funder, 1995; Gosling, John, Craik and Robins, 1998). To some extent, we appear able, as symbolic interactionists like Mead (1934) and Cooley (1902) suggested, to see ourselves as others see us. However, our agreement with others is not perfect. Some studies have found that our self-ratings correlate more highly with how we think others see us, rather than with how they actually see us (Kenny and DePaulo, 1993). The mirror or 'looking glass' that Cooley (1902) described is our own creation, reflecting our assumptions about how others see us. Effective social functioning depends on this bearing some relation to how others actually see us, but we do not do this perfectly.

The key issue is not whether our self-knowledge is perfect, but where it comes from. By and large, there is surprisingly little evidence that we have special insight into our traits or motivations. We learn and make inferences about ourselves much as we do about people. As self-perception theory points out, we rely on the same observations of behaviour (Carruthers, 2010). If we are more expert on our own behaviour, motivations and preferences than others, it is probably because we have access to more facts about, and observations of, ourselves.

Question to consider   Now that you know about the limits of our own self-knowledge, reread question 3 at the start of the chapter. Could it really be the case that Antonia knows Marvin better than he knows himself?

ETHICS AND RESEARCH METHODS

Why social psychologists cannot just ask people why they do things

Nisbett and Wilson's (1977) findings have profound implications for how social psychological research needs to be conducted. As you read this textbook, you will notice all sorts of clever experiments designed to find out why people do things. You will see subtle measures of attitudes, especially in Chapter 4, that avoid asking people directly what they think about themselves, others or social issues, or why they think that way. When social psychologists do ask people why they do things, it is not normally because they want to find out the real reasons why they did them. It is because they are interested in why people come up with certain reasons for their own behaviour, and what effect their explanations of their behaviour has on the way they think, feel and behave (see Chapter 3). There is a fundamental distrust in social psychology of the validity of self-reports and, in particular, self-reported reasons for behaviour.

It is worth reflecting on this. Social psychology would be a lot simpler if we could just ask people why they do things. There would be no need for expensive, difficult to design, time-consuming experiments. But, social psychologists' distrust of people's insights into their own behaviour is not shared by most people. In everyday life, people still tend to ask each other what led them to make interesting or important choices in their lives. We (your authors) do some consultancy work on social psychological aspects of environmental issues, and are constantly amazed at clients' willingness to rely on survey and focus group results in which people are asked questions like: 'What kind of message would get you to

reduce your energy use?' We keep trying to convince our clients that people simply cannot give accurate answers to questions like this; indeed, in a later chapter, we will encounter research by Nolan, Schultz, Cialdini and Griskevicius (2008) that shows that people are completely wrong about what kind of energy use campaign would influence them.

However, this distrust in the accuracy of people's self-reports does not mean that they or people's experience and self-understanding more generally should be dismissed. Many of the mainstream experimental findings we review in this chapter reveal just how important people's accounts of their behaviour are to their psychological health and relationships. Entire qualitative research methods are devoted to uncovering the content and structure of everyday experience, and the meaning of the narratives they produce (e.g., Smith, Flowers and Larkin, 2009). Generally speaking, however, these methods are premised on a radical degree of scepticism about the extent to which people's accounts are accurate records of the psychological processes underlying their behaviour. What people say is assumed to reflect what they are experiencing, or perhaps how they are trying to present and justify themselves to others (Potter and Wetherell, 1987). It is not supposed to reflect introspective insight into the 'real' causes of their behaviour.

Questions

1   In what domains might self-report responses be appropriate and when might they be inappropriate?

2   Think of some of the core topics in social psychology. In which of these would self-report responses be likely to yield dishonest or misleading responses?

Motivated social cognition and the self

Motivated social cognition
Acquisition, processing and storage of information that is motivated and affected by goals (Kunda, 1990). A person's goal may be simply to be accurate, and motivated social cognition leads them to unbiased conclusions. However, the term 'motivated social cognition' normally refers to social cognition that is biased by goals. In other words, it refers to the processes by which 'people are capable of believing what they want to believe' (Jost, Glaser, Kruglanski and Sulloway, 2003).

Thus far, we have seen how important the self is. It organizes our experience, allows us to interact meaningfully with others, and shapes our emotions and behaviour. We have seen that some types of self-concept are more useful than others. For example, by and large, we are able to feel and function better if our self-esteem is reasonably high rather than low. In short, people have a vested interest in their self-concepts. It is not surprising, therefore, that people are strategic in the way they seek out, pay attention to, process, and remember information about themselves. In short, people engage in **motivated social cognition** about themselves. We return to motivated social cognition more generally in Chapter 3, but for now, it is useful to familiarize yourself with four of the motivations that influence social cognition (Baumeister, 1998; Kruglanski, 1990; Kunda, 1990):

1 To find out more about a topic, so as to increase our ability to understand, predict and control the world we live in.

2 To protect or enhance our self-esteem.

3 To ensure cognitive consistency – that our beliefs are consistent with each other and with facts about the world as we know them.

4 To feel that we are in control of the world in which we live (Table 2.2).

TABLE 2.2 Four key goals in motivated social cognition, as they apply to the self

Motivation	When the topic is the self	Example of process	Example of outcome
Accuracy motivation	Self-assessment	Completing online personality tests; seeking honest feedback from friends	Finding out more about yourself
Self-esteem motivation	Self-enhancement	Thinking you are better than average – the above-average effect	Having unduly positive views of yourself – the above-average effect
Cognitive consistency	Self-verification	Choosing friends whose behaviour towards you is consistent with your high (or low) self-esteem	Reinforcing your previous self-view; avoiding disconfirming feedback
Affirming control	Illusion of control	Attributing random or uncontrollable events to your own actions	Confidence, but also disaster

Self-assessment

Self-assessment The motivation to know objectively who we are.

First, we are motivated to know objectively and accurately who we are. This is the motive of **self-assessment** (Trope, 1986). This motive is important because having an accurate understanding of the self can enable an individual to be certain of their abilities and how they might act or perform in specific situations. For example, you may like to complete online personality and intelligence tests. In doing so, you are fulfilling your motive of self-assessment, and as a result – depending on the quality of the test – you have a greater understanding of yourself. It does not matter if the information we learn about ourselves is favourable or unfavourable. The key is that we have accurate and valid information about the self.

Self-verification

Self-verification The motivation to seek out information that confirms one's view of the self.

Another motive regarding the self is to confirm what we believe to be true about ourselves. This motivation is called **self-verification** (e.g., Kwang and Swann, 2010;

Swann, 1997) and people seek to do this, again, irrespective of whether the views about the self are positive or negative. We seek information that verifies our beliefs about ourselves. If we find it, we feel reassured that our perception of our self is consistent with our experience, in other words, that we have achieved cognitive consistency (e.g., Swann, Rentfrow and Guinn, 2003). This leads to some surprising and even disturbing outcomes for people who have low self-esteem (for a review, see Chang and Swann, 2012). For example, in their quest to verify their negative views of themselves, they will actually prefer the company of people who have a low (rather than high) opinion of them (Swann, Stein-Seroussi and Giesler, 1992), will become less committed to their marriage if praised by their spouse (Swann, Hixon and De La Rhonde, 1992), will be upset by their successes (Wood, Heimpel, Newby-Clark and Ross, 2005), show signs of cardiovascular stress if praised (Ayduk, Mendes, Akinola and Gyurak, 2008), and will be more likely to be absent from work after being effusively praised by their boss (Wiesenfeld, Swann, Brockner and Bartel, 2007). Finally, Wood, Perunovic and Lee (2010) found that people will even be saddened by saying positive things about themselves, such as 'I am a lovable person', and thus they conclude that, tragically, the popular technique of affirmation – boosting self-esteem by saying positive things about oneself – is likely to backfire for the very people who need it most.

Self-enhancement

Self-enhancement The motivation to seek out information that allows one to see one's self in a positive light.

Arguably the most important motive is to search for information that allows us to see the self positively. This motive is called **self-enhancement** (Kunda, 1990). People seek new, positive information about the self and they also seek ways to alter existing negative views of the self. There are various strategies that people use to enhance the self. An important means of enhancing is 'behavioural self-handicapping' (Jones and Berglas, 1978). Failure at a task presents some evidence that you are not much not good at it. To protect themselves from this conclusion, people sometimes act in ways that sabotage their own chances of success. If you stayed up late partying before that test, and go on to fail the test, you can conclude that your bad preparation, rather than low ability, is to blame. If you manage to do well on the test, you can convince yourself that you are especially clever, because you did so despite the late night (Rhodewalt, Morf, Hazlett and Fairfield, 1991). Research shows that self-handicapping does protect self-views (McCrea and Hirt, 2001), but comes at a price. Naturally enough, self-handicapping harms people's actual performance (Zuckerman and Tsai, 2005). There are many other manifestations of self-enhancement. To give you just a sample, we have put together a list:

Self-serving attribution bias Self-other bias, whereby people make internal attributions for positive aspects of the self but external attributions for negative aspects of the self.

- People evaluate feedback about the self less critically, and accept it more readily, when it is positive rather than negative. This applies to IQ tests (Wyer and Frey, 1983) and medical diagnoses (e.g., Ditto, Munro, Apanovitch et al., 2003).
- People take credit for their successes and deflect blame for their failures, in the **self-serving attribution bias** (Arkin, Cooper and Kolditz, 1980; Zuckerman, 1979). For example, after car accidents, people frequently make absurdly self-serving attributions such as: 'the tree came up and obstructed my view of the road' (Stewart, 2005).

- People recognize themselves in photographs more readily if their image is morphed to make them more attractive, rather than less attractive (Epley and Whitchurch, 2008).

- People in countries as diverse as Australia, Germany, Japan and Israel see themselves as not only better people, but more human, than the average person (Loughnan, Leidner, Doron et al., 2010).

- People generally evaluate themselves more favourably than others evaluate them. This applies to anything from ratings of their personality traits (Alicke, 1985), to the popularity and attractiveness of their profiles on online dating services (Preuss and Alicke, 2009).

- Logically, fewer than 50% of the population can be better than average at something. Yet, a study by Svenson (1981) showed that 69% of a sample of Swedish drivers and 93% of American drivers thought they were better drivers than usual. Similar results have been found with many other dimensions of value aside from driving behaviour. Williams and Gilovich (2008) found that this is not just a matter of bragging. Participants were willing to bet real money that they had scored better than average on a personality test.

These motives are all important in guiding how people behave. But which is the most important? Of course, if self-esteem is high, and warranted, these motives are compatible with each other. But often, the truth hurts. And when self-esteem is low, self-verification is completely at odds with self-enhancement. Some studies suggest that self-enhancement is the most important motive, but that self-verification is also a genuine social motive (e.g., Sedikides, 1993). However, comprehensive recent reviews suggest that self-verification is as or more important than self-enhancement (Kwang and Swann, 2010; van Dellen, Campbell, Hoyle and Bradfield, 2011). There has been a productive debate about the primacy of the self-verification and self-enhancement motives for some years, and the jury is still out.

Illusion of control

© PHOTODISC/GETTY IMAGES

Can you remember a situation in your life in which you felt you had no control over what was happening to you? Chances are, the feeling of a lack of control induced anxiety, even if the experience was essentially positive. Human beings appear to have a strong desire, and even a need, for control. People with an *internal locus of control* feel they are in charge of events in their lives, and experience higher levels of wellbeing than people with an *external locus of control*, who think events are not strongly controlled by them. Field experiments have shown that residents of care homes for the elderly are happier, more functional and may even live longer when given a higher degree of control over their schedules and the day-to-day events in their lives (Langer and Rodin, 1976).

We appear to uphold our beliefs in our control over events by overestimating the extent to which we have control over events. Langer (1975), for example, showed that people prefer to roll a dice rather than have someone roll it for them, as if they could exercise control over the outcome. We have already encountered one social cognitive process that helps produce this illusion of control. Remember how Wegner and Wheatley (1999) showed that people thought they were responsible for stopping the mouse on an object like a swan in their 'Ouija board' experiment, because they were made to think about the swan shortly before the confederate stopped the mouse. As we will see in Chapter 3, this same bias can cause people to think they may have hurt someone via a voodoo hex, or influenced the outcome of a sports match they are watching on TV (Pronin, Wegner, McCarthy and Rodriguez, 2006). As we shall also see in Chapter 3, depriving people of control causes them to restore a sense of control in surprising ways. For example, they start to see patterns that are not there (Whitson and Galinsky, 2008), and become more convinced that God influences events in day-to-day lives, even if they are not religious (Kay, Gaucher, Napier et al., 2008). If you lack control, you are motivated to think you can gain a kind of second-hand control by discerning order, regularity and control in the environment (Kay, Whitson, Gaucher and Galinsky, 2009).

Exploring further Why do human beings have such a need to control, or at least to feel like they are controlling, the environment? Is it culturally universal? Try using Google Scholar or a similar search engine as we have previously suggested. For example, you might like to try combining the term 'illusion of control' (remember to put quotation marks around a phrase, or if using advanced search options, indicate you are searching the exact phrase), and 'culture' in one search, and 'evolution' in another search. What can you find out about the origins of the need for control?

Culture and the self

As we have seen in this chapter, the self is a unique aspect of every individual. However, it is also the case that there are cultural differences in people's self-concept. In particular, researchers have focused on differences in the self-concept depending on whether individuals come from individualist or collectivist cultures, and whether people belong to one or more cultures.

Individualist and collectivist cultures

Individualist cultures, such as in Western and Northern Europe and some of the countries they colonized (e.g., Australia and the USA), emphasize personal achievement and uniqueness of the self. In such cultures, children from an early age are encouraged to think of themselves as distinct and unique individuals, focusing on the aspects of themselves such as their inner thoughts and feelings that make them different from other people. On the other hand, collectivist cultures, such as in many Eastern European and Asian countries, place more emphasis on groups and families. From a young age, children are encouraged to follow societal norms and be loyal and obedient to their parents. This more interdependent conception of the self is based on one's relationships with others and one's connection with families and social groups. The way people see the self is therefore different in these two different types of cultures. Specifically, individualist cultures have a more individual-oriented sense of self, whereas the self is defined in collectivist cultures more in line with group memberships (Gaertner, Sedikides and Graetz, 1999; Markus and Kitayama, 1991; Vignoles, Chryssouchoou and Breakwell, 2000).

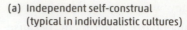

(a) Independent self-construal
(typical in individualistic cultures)

(b) Interdependent self-construal
(typical in collectivistic cultures)

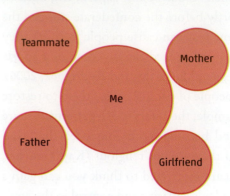

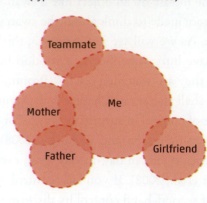

FIGURE 2.13 Independent and interdependent self-construals These self-construals might be typical of male students in an individualistic culture versus a collectivist culture.

This can be seen in Figure 2.13. A male student from an individualistic culture, such as Norway, the UK, France or Australia, will typically see himself as close to, but separate from, significant others in his life (Figure 2.13a). On the other hand, his counterpart in a collectivist culture, such as southern Italy, Portugal and Greece, or an Indigenous Australian, will partly define himself in terms of his relationships with others (Figure 2.13b). In an important sense, these people are part of him. He will even attribute their personality traits to himself (Markus and Kitayama, 1991). It is important not to overemphasize this cultural difference; it is a reliable, but not necessarily a large difference (Nisbett et al., 2001). Individuals within cultures differ as much, if not more, as cultures differ from each other in the extent to which independent versus interdependent self-construals are adopted. Nonetheless, this is one important way to understand cultural differences (e.g., Vauclair and Fischer, 2011).

The differences in the self-concept have been demonstrated widely by social psychologists and cross-cultural psychologists. For example, Trafimow, Triandis and Goto (1991) asked participants from the USA and China to write down 20 descriptions of themselves. They found that US participants wrote down many more individual-related descriptions (e.g., 'I am an intelligent person) than the participants from China, who tended to write about the self more in relation to group memberships (e.g., 'I am a Christian'). Similar studies exist comparing Japanese and Canadian participants (Heine and Lehman, 1997), Hong Kong Chinese and Americans (Yik, Bond and Paulhus, 1998) and others comparing Japanese and Americans (Regan, Snyder and Kassin, 1995).

In a way, people raised in individualist cultures learn that life involves many opportunities for self-enhancement, whereas for people raised in collectivist cultures, life provides opportunities for self-improvement (Kitayama, Markus, Matsumoto and Norasakkunkit, 1997). It is interesting to note, for example, that in Japanese, the word for 'self' (*jibun*) means 'one's portion of the shared space' (Hamaguchi, 1985).

Research has also demonstrated that people's self-descriptions vary as a function of the culture, the situation and the interaction between the two (Kanagawa, Cross and Markus, 2001). As in other research, Kanagawa et al. demonstrated significant differences in the ways in which Japanese and US students described themselves. Japanese students were more likely to express a self-critical orientation and a motivation for self-improvement (e.g., 'I get tense in public', 'I am not able to play a musical instrument'). The US students, on the other hand, were more likely to express unique and positive aspects of the self that are stable over time and across situations (e.g., 'I am good at maths', 'I am considered good at sports'). However, Japanese participants were more likely to describe themselves with specific reference to their appearance, activities, the immediate situation and their possessions, than their US counterparts.

Insights on the different nature of self across cultures have also been gained from qualitative studies of individual experiences. For example, Kondo, an ethnically Japanese woman born and raised in the USA, reports an interaction with her land-lady when she was later working in Japan (cited in Wetherell and Maybin, 1996). The landlady reflected on the Japanese treating themselves as individuals as less impor-tant than the collective, doing things for the sake of social relationships. This struck Kondo as a 'profoundly different way of thinking about relationships between selves and the social world' (Kondo, cited in Wetherell and Maybin, 1996, p. 272).

The cultural differences in how people perceive the self are also reflected in different cultural values between individualist and collectivist cultures. For example, Gardner, Gabriel and Lee (1999) investigated the link between how people see the self and their values. In one study, they asked participants from the USA to read a story which either primed individualist aspects of the self (by including words like 'I' and 'me') or more collectivist aspects (by including words like 'us' and 'we'). After reading the story, participants were asked to write 20 self-descriptions and then rate the values that were important to them. Findings revealed that participants in the individualist prime condition wrote more individual-oriented self-descriptions and more strongly endorsed individualist values like personal freedom and inde-pendence. On the other hand, the participants who were in the collectivist prime condition wrote more group-oriented self-descriptions and more strongly endorsed collectivist values like family and obedience. The significant differences in endorse-ment of individual and collectivist values are presented in Figure 2.14.

Bicultural individuals are an interesting case of cultural influences on the self-concept. Such individuals are able to deal with two different cultures at once – the host culture where they live, and their original (immigrant or heritage) culture where they are from (Phinney, Lochner and Murphy, 1990). Often, the two cultures vary significantly in terms of values, attitudes and norms. For example, a person from China who now lives in the USA may be considered bicultural if they are able to integrate aspects of both cultures into their self-concept. Of course, not everyone can do this. Some individuals maintain a strong heritage culture despite living among a different culture for most of their lives. However, many people are able to integrate two cultures into their self-concept. Yamada and Singelis (1999) argue that people are able to do this when they alternate their cultural orientation depending on the situation. Specifically, an individual is able to deal with

Bicultural individuals
Individuals who are able to deal with the presence of two cultural identities (heritage and host cultural identities) at the same time.

FIGURE 2.14 Collectivists and individualists compared
Participants primed with individualist concepts endorsed individualist values rather than collectivist values, while those primed with collectivist concepts endorsed more collectivist values than individualist values.
Source: Data from Gardner et al., 1999

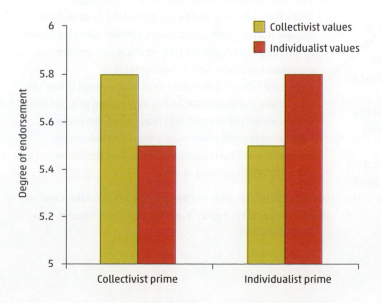

two identifies at once when they understand the ways in which each culture guides behaviour and uses this knowledge to think and behave accordingly in different situations. In a demonstration of how this works, Hong, Morris, Chiu and Benet-Martinez (2000) found that Chinese/American bicultural individuals changed their behaviour depending on whether they were primed with Western or Asian cues. Indeed, there are benefits to being able to integrate two cultures. For example, successful bicultural individuals are thought to have better mental health (Rogler, Cortes and Malgady, 1991) and higher self-esteem than monocultural individuals. They also less likely to report interethnic conflict or experience racial tension (Schwarzer, Bowler and Rauch, 1985).

Chapter summary

In this chapter, we have outlined how social psychologists have approached the study of the self. We have discussed what the self is, what the self is for, and how the self defines and influences what we think, feel and do. The key points to take away from this chapter are as follows:

- The self-concept is the complete set of beliefs that people have about themselves. It comprises self-schemas, or different aspects of the self.
- Schemas help determine how people think, feel and behave in specific situations. Different schemas are activated in different contexts, and people may be chronically schematic or aschematic on a particular dimension.
- According to multiple role theory, it is beneficial for people to have multiple identities. But also, self-concept clarity, that is, a clear sense of a strongly defined self, bolsters self-esteem and helps people deal with negative events.
- Self-awareness is the psychological state of being aware of one's characteristics, feelings and behaviours, or the awareness of oneself as unique. Public-self-awareness occurs when people become aware of how they could be judged by others. Public self-consciousness is a more chronic state of being concerned about being evaluated by others. Private self-awareness refers to the state where an individual is aware of the private, personal aspects of the self. This too can be chronic in the case of private self-consciousness.
- There is a biological basis of self-awareness. Regions of the frontal lobe are activated during tasks where participants process information about the self.
- Several theories address the self and its functions, including self-perception theory, self-discrepancy theory, regulatory focus theory, the control theory of self-regulation, the strength model theory of self-control, and social comparison theory.
- Self-esteem is the subjective evaluation of the self as positive or negative, and develops in childhood. Self-

esteem is affected by factors from within the self (e.g., positive self-schemas) or outside others (e.g., acceptance or inclusion by others).

- Having high self-esteem can have positive consequences. It helps people to regulate their mood. Self-esteem buffers people against the anxiety of death. This is particularly strong if people are implicitly aware of their own self-worth. Higher levels of self-esteem also make people less aggressive. However, exceedingly high levels of self-esteem (narcissism) can entail insecurity about the self, but narcissists are generally psychologically healthier than people with lower levels of self-esteem.
- People often try to manage the impression they present to others, through a process known as impression management.
- Self-knowledge is often inaccurate. For many reasons, people appear both unable and unwilling to know themselves completely. They also tend to overestimate the emotional impact that positive and negative life events will have, through the affective forecasting error.
- The self-concept is an important guiding principle in motivating what we do. We are motivated to accurately know ourselves (self-assessment), confirm what we believe to be true about ourselves (self-verification) and see ourselves positively (self-enhancement).
- Important cultural differences exist with respect to the self. Specifically, individualist cultures express the independent, unique aspects of the self, whereas collectivist cultures emphasize the self in terms of groups and belonging. Bicultural individuals successfully manage their membership of two different cultures at once.

Our focus in this chapter has been on people's understanding of who they are. In Chapter 3, we focus on how people understand others.

Essay questions

At the beginning of the chapter, we asked you to consider these questions:

1 Millie gossiped to someone about something a close friend told her in confidence. Millie instantly felt terrible about what she had done and although her friend never found out, Millie ruminated about what she had done. She could not help thinking what a horrible friend she must be to speak ill of a friend behind their back. How might you explain Millie's feelings? What consequences might there be for Millie?

2 Despite slight pangs of jealousy, James is genuinely happy for his friend Mark, who gets a place to study at Oxford University. However, he cannot say the same for one of his other classmates, Brian, who also got a place. What social psychological processes differentiate these two different responses to essentially the same event?

3 Antonia and Marvin are having an argument and Antonia says to Marvin: 'I know you better than you know yourself.' To what extent (and why) might this statement be true?

Having read this chapter, these questions could also be framed as the following essay questions, which you can attempt in preparation for your examinations:

1 What are the consequences (both positive and negative) of the different types of self-awareness and self-consciousness?

2 How do people cope when they don't 'stack up' compared to someone else? Answer with reference to research on social comparisons.

3 How well do we really know ourselves?

Some further reading

Baumeister, R.F. (1999) *The Self in Social Psychology*. Philadelphia, PA: Psychology Press. Presents an overview of the research on the self, centring on a series of key publications on the self.

Leary, M.R. (2007) Motivation and emotional aspects of the self. *Annual Review of Social Psychology*, 58, 317–44. Covers recent theory and research on the self-related motives covered in this chapter (e.g., self-enhancement, self-verification) and self-related emotions, with a focus on the self and social wellbeing.

Markus, H.R. and Kitayama, S. (1991) Culture and the self: Implications for cognition, emotion and motivation. *Psychological Bulletin*, 98, 224–53. Influential article discussing the different ways in which people construe the self dependent on their culture.

Sedikides, C. and Spencer, S.J. (eds) (2007) *The Self*. New York: Psychology Press. Two of the world's leading researchers on the self provide a comprehensive and up-to-date review of the literature.

Twenge, J.M. and Campbell, W.K. (2009) *The Narcissism Epidemic: Living in the Age of Entitlement*. Free Press: New York. Relates to the Social psychology in the real world box in this chapter, discussing the rise and rise of narcissism in modern US society.

 Visit the companion website at www.palgrave.com/psychology/suttondouglas for access to a wide range of resources to help you get to grips with this chapter.

Applying social psychology

Encouraging healthy eating in a school

Imagine you work for a school that is trying to encourage kids to eat in a more healthy way. Your school has a 'tuck shop' that sells meals and snacks to children. Children at your school tend to buy salty, fatty and sweet snacks rather than fruits and other healthy alternatives.

1 Your head teacher suggests that you survey the children and ask them why they buy the foods they do. Based on the material you have read in this chapter (e.g., in the Ethics and research methods box), what do you think you can and can't learn by following this approach? What approaches would you suggest?

2 Some children report that they would really like to buy healthier foods, but by the time they go to buy their food, they are already feeling tired and find it difficult to stick to their resolve to make the right choices. What psychological processes in this chapter may help to explain their difficulty? And what solutions might you be able to propose, based on these principles?

3 Like most schools, yours has a variety of children, ranging from those who are healthy and athletic and eat well, and those who fall a long way short of these standards. Your head teacher would like to highlight especially healthy children, recognizing their choices at assemblies, and so use them as 'role models' for the other children. Based on what you've read about processes such as social comparison, what are the merits and dangers of this approach? If your school were to go ahead with such a role model scheme, what steps would you take to enhance the likelihood that it will succeed, rather than backfire?

4 One possible approach to helping children make the right choices might involve simply mounting small mirrors among the shelves in the tuck shop, so that children can 'see themselves' as they make their choices. Why might this help, and why might it backfire? (See, for example, the section on self-awareness in this chapter, and the Social psychology in the real world box on 'nudge theory' in Chapter 15).

Blind spot in social psychology

Narcissistic leaders and their effects on decision making

In this chapter, we saw how narcissists are overrepresented in the top echelons of business (Chatterjee and Hambrick, 2007). This may not be a bad thing. Narcissists are often enthusiastic and charismatic individuals, and groups containing narcissists may, as a result, produce somewhat more creative ideas (Goncalo et al., 2010). However, Chatterjee and Hambrick argue that narcissistic leaders may be unwilling to tolerate criticism and alternative ideas to their own, or to heed warnings. Indeed, they suggest that narcissistic leadership may have contributed to disastrous corporate mismanagement, as in the *Exxon Valdez* scandal and those that led to the global financial crisis of 2008 onwards. Are they right? This idea has not been empirically tested.

1 Chatterjee and Hambrick's arguments suggest that narcissistic leaders may be more likely to preside over groups that engage in groupthink (Chapter 8), a rigid, closed-minded style of decision making in which groups do not consider alternative viewpoints or the disasters their plans might result in. How would you test this idea experimentally? Keep it simple: think of a simple experiment in which narcissists are, or are not, assigned to leadership positions. It may help you to read about group decision making and leadership studies in Chapter 8.

2 Building on this basic design, can you think of a way to test whether groups led by narcissists actually make more disastrous mistakes than those that are not?

Student project

The effect of specific modes of feedback on learning in an HE setting

Suzy Clarkson studied as an undergraduate student at Bangor University, and her final-year dissertation supervisor was Dr Fay Short. Her research on how students respond to feedback speaks to motivated social cognition about the self (e.g., the desire to learn about oneself versus protect one's self-esteem), a subject we have discussed in this chapter.

My topic and aims

The purpose of my study was to examine the effect of specific modes of feedback – positive, negative, mixed and no feedback – on learning in a higher education (HE) setting.

I became interested in examining feedback within HE when I read about the threefold rise in university fees in the UK beginning in 2012. This rise in fees has positioned universities in the role of business/supplier and students in the role of customer. This role change has put new pressures on universities in the competition to gain and retain students. Further, over the past seven years, the National Union of Students has reported that the feedback provided by university tutors ranks extremely low on their quality satisfaction scores. Feedback within HE is therefore an important topic to investigate.

My methods

We recruited our participants on an opportunity sampling basis, from a population of undergraduate psychology students. The 58 undergraduates were randomly assigned to one of the four feedback conditions – positive, negative, mixed and no feedback – and all participants attended three weekly testing sessions. The participants were required to observe a podcast during the initial session. The podcast explained APA referencing and was used to ensure that all participants received the same instructions. Assignments were supplied at all three sessions. The assignments directed each participant to create a reference list of five journal articles and two books that were supplied. In sessions 2 and 3, prior to the new assignments being distributed, participants received their work from the previous session and their feedback depending on condition. The feedback was supplied on a marking criteria and comment sheet (the no feedback group did not receive a sheet). The positive feedback group received ticks next to correct answers and blanks next to errors/omissions and a concluding standardized positive comment related to their grade. The negative feedback group received crosses next to errors/omissions and blanks next to correct answers and a concluding standardized constructive criticism comment related to their grade. The mixed feedback group received both ticks and crosses and both forms of comment. Measures of learning (e.g., the assignment mark) were taken and compared across the conditions to examine the impact of the different types of feedback on learning.

My findings and their implications

The results did not support my hypothesis that participants receiving feedback would, in general, demonstrate an increase in learning when compared to the no feedback condition. Further, although learning occurred, there were no significant differences in learning across conditions. Therefore, it appeared that the amount of learning was not dependent on the mode of feedback given (positive, negative, mixed or none).

The results imply that the mode of feedback may not significantly determine learning as is generally thought. The study also brings in to question a tutor's presumed power to influence a student's learning by the provision of feedback. The research also raises the question of whether receiving no feedback instils an emotional state of uncertainty, and whether this motivates an individual to devise strategies to reduce the uncertainty. Further research and a heightened understanding of feedback are required before HE tutors can attempt to improve feedback.

My journey

I am presently working on a 10-week research placement for the Centre for Evidence Based Early Interventions at Bangor University. The placement has involved undertaking research and writing a literature review that examines the effectiveness and evidence base of family/parenting interventions for adolescents with behavioural and emotional problems. Also, I am continuing to work for my dissertation supervisor on my study, with the intention of submitting a piece of work for publication. Subsequent to my placement, I aim to continue with my studies and complete a Masters degree in research, with the aspiration of progressing to a doctorate in education or research.

The knowledge and the confidence I have gained during my project has been and will be invaluable to me in the future. Being involved in the design, research and completion of my project has facilitated my development and understanding of project design, the manipulation and recording of data, interpretation skills and the importance of ethical considerations. The project has permitted me to work as a member of team, collaborate with staff, such as my supervisor and the Bangor technology team (in the production of a podcast), and become confident in my ability to problem solve and make decisions independently. I believe that I have become extremely proficient at researching articles and databases on the internet, and the research I have read and discussed has helped me improve my critical and analytical thinking and writing skills. The project has enhanced my skills and provided me with the confidence I require to continue with my studies.

My advice

The most important piece of knowledge I have gained from completing my project was that research and planning are paramount. Before beginning the design of the project, a thorough examination of the topic area must be conducted and when this has been achieved to the supervisor's satisfaction, the student must consider the simplest and most logical path to demonstrate and reveal the results. I believe that careful consideration is necessary to ensure issues are not too complicated, which can be an easy pitfall, and was one of mine. Designing a simple, clear project takes thought, planning and a full understanding of the research question, a skill that develops over the course of the project.

3

The social perceiver: understanding the social world

In this chapter, we consider two key social cognitive processes – how people explain events in their lives (causal attribution), and how they form impressions of other people (person perception). We discuss some common errors in social cognition and then consider the nature (and 'social nature') of social cognition. By the end of this chapter, you will have an understanding of people's capacities and limitations in social cognition and social thinking.

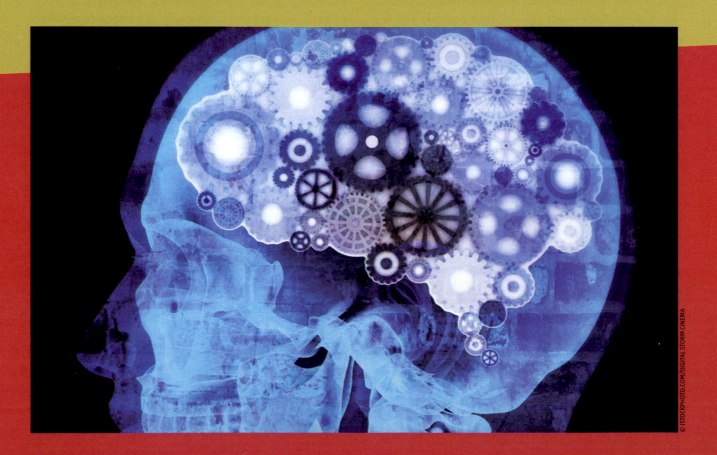

Topics covered in this chapter

- Causal attributions
- The naive scientist approach
- Two famous 'errors' in attribution
- Applications of attribution theory
- Person perception
- Heuristics and biases in social cognition
- Other biases and errors in social cognition
- The nature of social cognition

Key features

Critical focus The conjunction fallacy

Ethics and research methods Experimental control and replication

Social psychology in the real world 'Gaydar', politics and the importance of judging a book by its cover

Applying social psychology Applying social cognition to business problems

Blind spot in social psychology Why are morning people morning people?

Student project Victim blame in stranger and acquaintance rape

Questions to consider

1 Louisa really wants to be elected as the president of the psychology society at her university. She is required to give a speech to the group. Would she be best to present all her positive attributes or just a few of the most positive? What other factors might she take into account?

2 Ray meets Alan at a party and takes an instant dislike to him. He is unable put his finger on it exactly, but he does not like Alan. What social psychological processes can account for this instant dislike?

3 Jamie tells his friends he is studying social psychology and shares with them the findings of his final-year dissertation. His friends laugh and say the results were predictable and obvious. What could you say about this?

Computers are our creations, but they can already do many things we cannot. They can perform billions of calculations a second. The most powerful computers are capable of beating any human being at chess. They can simulate and predict the movements of the stars through the heavens, and the entire world's climate. They can calculate pi (π) to hundreds of decimal places. Even the relatively humble, average desktop computer can easily store more facts and figures than are contained in the world's most comprehensive sets of encyclopedias, and as long as it functions properly, it will never 'forget' them. In contrast, many, if not most of us struggle to multiply or divide numbers greater than a couple of digits long, or to remember nine- or ten-digit numbers.

So, are we being overshadowed by our creations? Are we less capable than we think we are? In our defence, the human brain is the most complex structure in the known universe (Edelman, 1993). It is capable of things that psychologists, working as we do in a relatively young science, are only beginning to understand. Despite the dazzling power of computers, they are inadequate at performing some of the tasks most of us can do effortlessly, day after day. For example, it is only recently that computer-controlled robots have begun to be able to walk up and down stairs, or recognize faces and voices. It is going to be a long time before any computer system can do more than one of these things at the same time.

One of the most vivid illustrations of our superiority to computers is their complete failure, thus far, to pass a deceptively simple test of artificial intelligence. This test was designed by Alan Turing, the brilliant mathematician, whose code-breaking work at Bletchley Park was instrumental in the defeat of Nazi Germany in the Second World War. Turing (1950) argued that we could judge a computer to be truly intelligent if people, after conversing by text with a remote computer for a few minutes, could not tell whether it was a computer or a human being. In the intervening six decades, no computer has got anywhere near passing the Turing test. This is not for lack of trying. The Loebner Prize is an annual competition in which programs have been put through their paces (Saygin, Cicekli and Akman, 2000). Although computers have been getting roughly twice as powerful every 18 months or so, it appears to be some way off before any will be 'clever' enough to pass this test.

The fact that holding a simple conversation is something that super-computers find impossible, but we generally find easy, illustrates the enormous social cognitive complexity that underpins successful social interaction. Although most of us experience awkwardness in some social situations, we generally find tasks such as holding a basic conversation to be so effortless that we rarely, if ever, stop to think about how we are doing it. Crucially, even if we did, it is unlikely we would be able to work out exactly how we are achieving the marvellous trick of social interaction. This is because, as we shall see in this chapter, many of the psychological processes that make social interactions possible are performed outside conscious awareness.

© MACMILLAN EDUCATION

Try it yourself Go online and try a Turing test – chat online with a computer. We recommend you chat to Jabberwock, winner of the 2003 Loebner Prize, which still seems to be the most sophisticated Turing robot available. Search for 'Jabberwock' and 'Turing' and you'll soon find it (it can speak to you in either German or English). How long in your conversation does it take to work out that you are not conversing with a human being? What tricks does it look like Jabberwock is using to come up with responses to your statements? How do these tricks differ from what a human being would do? If you find this interesting, you might also like to find out about the life story of Alan Turing by searching for him, and even read his 1950 paper 'Computing machinery and intelligence', which is widely posted online, and remains interesting and easy to read.

Fortunately, we do not have to rely simply on introspection to understand how our social minds work. A variety of ingenious scientific methodologies have been developed to identify the enormous extent, and the limits, of our insights into other people's minds and personalities, and our powers of interpretation, memory and predictors of their behaviour. Some of these studies have revealed ever more stunning powers of social cognition by ordinary people who, in other respects, are so inferior to computers. For example, later in this chapter we will learn how people of ordinary intelligence can judge significantly better than chance, just by looking at a complete stranger for a few seconds, or even milliseconds, whether they are likeable, attractive, trustworthy, extraverted, or whether they have a personality disorder. To a surprising degree, and with amazing, effortless speed, people appear to be able to judge a book by its cover.

As interesting and inspiring as it is to discover the fabulous powers possessed by the average person, doing so does not necessarily tell us how they do it. Advances by social psychologists over the past few decades have begun to unravel the psychological mechanisms that make our social lives possible. Understanding these powers does not make them any less fabulous, but it does make them less mysterious. A critical part of this research process has been to show that as remarkable as people's talents are, they are also fallible. Working out when and why people get things wrong provides vital clues to understand how it is they are able to get so many things right.

The case of 'Clever Hans' illustrates particularly well how it is possible to work out how a person is making sophisticated judgements by determining the conditions under which they fail to make those judgements. Clever Hans could do basic arithmetic problems, and toured Germany at the turn of the 20th century showcasing this talent. The reason Clever Hans's abilities caused a sensation was that he was not a human being, but a horse. His trainers would read him arithmetic problems, such as 'fifteen divided by three', and Clever Hans would tap the correct number of times (five in this case, although we hope you were not wondering). Clever Hans attracted the attention of many sceptics who wanted to work out how he was doing it. One of the first possibilities to be eliminated was that his handlers were somehow cheating by secretly communicating to Hans when he should stop. It was determined that Hans appeared to be able to do these sums even when his handlers were not around. Various other possibilities were eliminated one by one until the answer was found. If everyone around Hans was hidden from his view behind a screen, Hans lost his apparent mathematical powers. It was clear that Clever Hans was sensitive to the subtle shifts in body language that people unconsciously displayed as he approached the correct answer. When he was no longer able to read people's body language as he hit the correct number, he was no longer able to identify that number as correct. What made Hans clever was not his ability to understand spoken German, or do arithmetic, but his acute sensitivity to body language. Only by creating a situation in which Hans failed could people find out why he was normally so successful (Pfungst, 1911).

Social cognition The study of the cognitive underpinnings of social thought and social behaviour.

Social cognition – the study of the cognitive underpinnings of social thought and social behaviour – has, to a large extent, been about understanding how people's social skills and everyday powers of reasoning normally work, by creating situations in which they do not work. It has been dominated, therefore, by demonstrations of error. Borrowing techniques and experimental methods used in cognitive psychology, it has been possible to test the limits of human thought and by understanding when and why people make mistakes, social psychologists can understand why they are so clever. However, in their endeavours, social psychologists have uncovered a range of illogical, erroneous and irrational habits of thought. This is the yin and yang of social cognition, and of social psychology more generally – people are capable of such brilliance, and yet such stupidity. Since our understanding of our social environment is such an important determinant of our wellbeing, productivity and relationships with people and groups, social cognition is a prominent topic in social psychology, dominant throughout the 1980s and still active and vibrant now (Devine and Sharp, 2009; Fiske and Taylor, 2008; Hamilton, Stroessner and Driscoll, 1994).

In the first half of this chapter, we introduce you to people's capacities and limitations, in the context of two of the classic questions about social cognition. We consider how people explain the events in their lives (causal attribution), and how they form impressions of other people (person perception). We look at some other errors and biases in social cognition. We then turn to research and theory on the fundamental nature of social cognition. How important are conscious and automatic processes? To what degree can we separate our minds from our bodies? How 'social' is social cognition?

Causal attributions

Whenever you confront a problem in your life such as your car breaking down, it is important that you understand the cause of the problem. For example, if your car's battery is flat, it is not going to help you to invest in a new transmission because the car is still not going to start. Dealing successfully with the breakdown and getting your car on the road will depend on you making the correct **causal attribution** – assigning the correct cause to the event. In this case, to proceed

Causal attribution The process of assigning a cause to an event or behaviour.

successfully, you must attribute the car's breakdown to its flat battery. Likewise, it is important to understand the causes of our own and other people's behaviours, so that we can repeat or emulate them (or not) in the future. Causal attributions have tremendous social importance. Whenever we assign blame or credit, and so determine who should be punished and who should be rewarded, we are engaging in causal attribution. Causal attributions also contribute to our feelings about ourselves and other people. For example, if we blame ourselves for disappointing outcomes and attribute our successes to luck, our self-esteem will probably be lower than if we take credit for successes and blame our failures on adverse circumstances (Weiner, 1985; see also Chapter 2 for a discussion of self-esteem). Causal attributions are also powerful bases for predicting and controlling events and behaviours (Försterling and Rudolph, 1988). If we know what causes something, we may be more likely to allow or prevent it happening in future.

For these reasons, the study of causal attributions has been central to social psychology. Throughout this book, you will see how important attributions are to our lives. Some of the founders of social psychology, such as Lewin (1936) and Heider (1958a), wrote extensively about the perception of cause and effect. For these theorists and especially Heider (1958a), people engage in causal attribution not only to guide their behaviour (e.g., fixing the car), but also to make sense of the stream of events that make up their everyday lives. Heider (1958a) was influenced by the German movement of **Gestalt psychology**, which suggests that people seek to tie together apparently diverse sensory data into meaningful wholes or 'Gestalts' (see Chapter 1). To relate diverse events into a simpler, more holistic understanding, people seek to explain the events they can observe in terms of underlying causes they may not be able to see directly. For Heider (1958a), a person's intentions are an example of such an underlying cause that can explain diverse behaviours. Imagine that someone gets their credit card out and spends some time on a computer; some weeks later they take their cat to a stranger's house and leave it there, buy sun cream and insect repellent at a local shop, pack these with clothes and a tourist guide to Turkey into a case, and get on the telephone to order a taxi to the airport. Although these behaviours have little or nothing in common from a purely physical point of view, we can effortlessly infer they intend to travel to Turkey. This inference allows us to explain all their behaviours and tie them into a single Gestalt.

Such is the explanatory power of intentions that we are prone to overrelying on them as explanations. This tendency was powerfully demonstrated in classic experiments by Heider and Simmel (1944). They presented participants with a film animation in which simple geometric shapes moved around on the screen. When participants were asked to account for what they observed, they typically fabricated elaborate stories that granted intentionality to the shapes. For example, the circle and small triangle were supposed to be in love, and the large triangle was said to have been thwarted in an attempt to steal the circle from its lover. Similarly, Michotte (1962) found that participants would describe the behaviour of two balls on a screen in intentional terms, such as: 'The big ball is chasing the

Gestalt psychology Approach proposing that objects are viewed in a holistic sense. Relevant to attributions, people attempt to understand events or behaviours as a whole by understanding their underlying causes.

little ball, but the little ball wants to get away.' Intentionality is a powerful explanatory principle that people prefer even when other types of explanations are more objectively appropriate.

Try it yourself Use an internet search engine to search for animated demonstrations of the stimuli used by Heider and Simmel's (1944) experiment, and also those by Michotte (1962). Try, for example, the combination 'Heider Simmel demonstration' and 'Michotte demonstration'. You can see these animations for yourself and even try them on friends or relatives. How do they explain the behaviour of the objects on the screen?

The naive scientist approach

By arguing that people seek to explain apparently diverse behaviour in terms of simpler, underlying causes, Heider (1958a) suggested that they are much like scientists. They construct meaning by devising causal theories of events and human behaviour, and these theories resemble scientific theories. As such, people are **naive** (lay, or intuitive) **scientists** who seek **parsimonious** explanations for complex social puzzles. Achieving simplicity and unity of understanding is one of the most fundamental goals of science, and is for laypeople too. Indeed, all the theories you will discover in this book are scientific attempts to account for the complex phenomena of human beings' social lives in terms of relatively simple, underlying causes.

Heider argued that people often attribute causality to situations (e.g., social pressure, social context) and make external attributions for people's behaviours. At other times, they construct explanations that attribute cause to personal factors (e.g., personality) and make internal attributions. But because people seek causal explanations in order to be able to predict and control their social world, they tend to look more towards stable properties of the social world, and therefore prefer internal attributions such as explanations related to personality and ability. For example, if a person is rude to you, you are more likely to attribute their behaviour to something about them (e.g., they are rude), rather than to something about the situation (e.g., they had a bad day).

Jones and Davis (1965) developed **correspondent inference theory** to explain why and how people make these attributions. This theory is based on the observation that people attempt to infer whether a person's action is caused by internal dispositions and they do this by looking at factors related to the action, that is, they make **correspondent inferences**. This theory suggests that three factors influence the extent to which people make dispositional or situational inferences for a person's behaviour:

1 They think about the extent to which the person had the choice to engage in the action.
2 They ask whether the behaviour is expected, based on the situation or social role of the actor.
3 People consider the intended consequences of the actor's behaviour.

Naive scientist Heider (1958a) argued that ordinary people are scientific, rational thinkers who make causal attributions using similar processes to those of scientists.

Parsimony Also known as simplicity, this is the extent to which an explanation is simple rather than complex. Simpler explanations are preferred in science, because as explanations contain more parts, the chances that one part is false increase (see also the conjunction fallacy, which we discuss later in this chapter).

Correspondent inference theory Theory arguing that people attempt to infer whether a person's action is caused by internal dispositions and they do so by looking at factors related to the action.

Correspondent inference The attribution of a personality trait that corresponds to an observed behaviour.

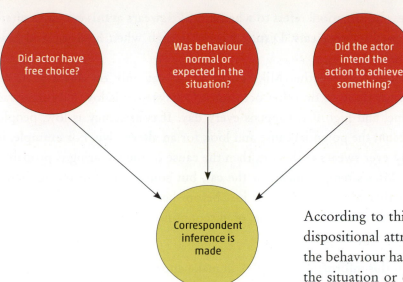

FIGURE 3.1 Correspondent inference theory People are more likely to infer that a person has traits that correspond to their behaviour (e.g., they're opinionated because they started an argument) when these three conditions are met. Subsequent research on correspondence bias (covered later in this chapter) suggests that people often do not pay much attention to whether the actor had a choice, or whether the behaviour was normal in the situation.

According to this theory, people are most able to make dispositional attributions for a person's behaviour when the behaviour has been freely chosen, is not a function of the situation or expected roles, and if intentionality can be clearly inferred (see Figure 3.1).

Covariation model Kelley's (1967) model of causal attribution, which argues that people typically attribute the cause of behaviour to a factor that covaries most clearly with the behaviour.

Covariation principle The attribution of events to conditions that tend to be present when the event happens, and absent when the event does not happen.

This point was picked up in the **covariation model**, the most influential and well-known model of causal attribution, put forward by Kelley (1967). Kelley explicitly argued that ordinary people are naive scientists, who make causal attributions in much the same way as professional scientists do. For Kelley (1967), the **covariation principle** lies at the heart of the causal attribution process for both professional and naive scientists and forms the basis of the covariation model. The covariation principle states that we attribute events to conditions that tend to be present when the event happens, and absent when the event does not happen. For example, we might attribute a headache to stress because we know we are more likely to get headaches when we are stressed than when we are not stressed. Similarly, we are more likely to attribute an argument between two housemates to the first house-mate, if we have noticed that there tend to be more arguments when they are around. In doing this, we are behaving much as professional scientists would do. As we saw in Chapter 1, we can infer that an independent variable (e.g., caffeine) causes irritability if those who we have given coffee are more likely to display irritable behaviour than those who have drunk a decaffeinated, 'placebo' coffee.

Kelley (1967) turned the covariation principle into a model of causal attribution made in social situations. The typical social situation has three key components. It has a *person* who displays a particular behaviour, an object or *stimulus* towards which the behaviour is directed, and occurs at a particular time or occasion. For example, consider the situation: 'Mike swore at a neighbourhood cat on Friday.' Something about any of these three components, the person (Mike), the stimulus (the cat) and the occasion (that particular Friday) might explain the effect (swearing). Applying the covariation principle, an observer can infer the most appropriate causal explanation by drawing on three dimensions of information about covariation:

Consensus Information about the extent to which other people react in the same way to a particular stimulus.

1 **Consensus** information: refers to whether Mike is more prone than other people to swearing at the cat. Consensus is low when he is, and high when other people swear at the cat just as much as he does.

Distinctiveness Information about the extent to which a person reacts in a particular way to a particular stimulus or reacts the same way to many other stimuli.

Consistency Information about the extent to which a person reacts in the same way to a stimulus on many other occasions.

Discounting If there is seemingly no relationship between a specific cause and a specific behaviour, the cause is discounted in favour of another.

2 **Distinctiveness** information: refers to whether Mike swears at this cat more often than he swears at other cats. Distinctiveness is high when he does, and low when he does not.

3 **Consistency**: refers to whether Mike swore at his cat only on this Friday, or whether he has done so on other occasions. Consistency is low if Friday was the first time, and high if it happens every day. If consistency is low, people tend to **discount** the potential cause and look for an alternative. For example, if Mike hardly ever swears at this cat, then the cause of the swearing is probably not due to Mike's temperament, or the cat, but some other covarying factor such as whether Mike tripped over just before he saw the cat (see McClure, 1998). We will return to the issue of discounting when we discuss person perception later in this chapter.

Armed with this information, people can make appropriate causal attributions. If consensus is low, but distinctiveness is low and consistency is high, then Mike is only one of three possible causes that covaries with swearing. There does not seem to be anything about the cat, nor the Friday in question that promotes swearing. Thus, it is appropriate to attribute the swearing to Mike. Conversely, if distinctiveness is high, consensus high and consistency also high, then the cat is the factor that tends to be around when swearing happens, and absent when it does not. It would appear that we are dealing with a bad cat that deserves to be the focus of causal attribution. Finally, if consistency is low, consensus high and distinctiveness low, then it would seem that there was something about that Friday that caused Mike to swear at the cat, because everyone appeared to swear more, regardless of who they were talking to. Perhaps it was a hot and difficult day. Kelley's model is often known as the ANOVA model because the procedure is similar to the statistical technique of analysis of variance. People make attributions for events (and predictions of future events) based on a careful weighing up of the information they have and how it all pieces together. The terminology may seem complex, but the ideas are elegant and simple. We use the example of Mike and the cat to illustrate Kelley's model further in Figure 3.2.

Extending Kelley's naive scientist approach

Many studies have essentially supported Kelley's (1967) model of causal attribution (e.g., Försterling, 1989; McArthur, 1972; Orvis, Cunningham and Kelley, 1975; Pruitt and Insko, 1980; Sutton and McClure, 2001). People generally make the causal attributions that Kelley predicted when presented with combinations of consensus, distinctiveness and consistency information. More generally, studies have shown that, everything being equal, people generally adhere to the covariation principle, attributing events to covarying causes – those that are present when similar events happen and absent when they do not happen. Where modifications and complementary models have been put forward, they have been largely in keeping with the idea that people approach causal attribution in ways that mirror scientific theories and explanations. Three key extensions of the naive scientist model are worth exploring here.

Covariation information that implicates **Mike**

Consensus is low: Only **Mike** swears at the cat		Distinctiveness is low: **Mike** swears at other cats		Consistency is high: **Mike** often swears at the cat	
Mike	Other people	The cat	Other cats	This Friday	Other days
&@%*!		&@%*!	&@%*!	&@%*!	&@%*!

Covariation information that implicates the **cat**

Consensus is high: Other people swear at the cat		Distinctiveness is high: Mike only swears at **this cat**		Consistency is high: Mike often swears at the cat	
Mike	Other people	The cat	Other stimuli	This Friday	Other days
&@%*!	&@%*!	&@%*!		&@%*!	&@%*!

Covariation information that implicates the **occasion**

Consensus is high: Other people swear at the cat		Distinctiveness is low: Mike swears at other cats		Consistency is low: Mike only swore at the cat **this Friday**	
Mike	Other people	The cat	Other stimuli	This Friday	Other days
&@%*!	&@%*!	&@%*!	&@%*!	&@%*!	

FIGURE 3.2 Kelley's (1967) covariation model of social attribution Is Mike prone to swearing in general, or did he have a bad day? Or is the cat just no good? The answer suggested by Kelley's theory (Mike, the cat, or the occasion) is in bold text.

Improved analysis of covariation between events, persons, stimuli and occasions

Early tests of Kelley's (1967) model of causal attribution generally supported it, but appeared to reveal a systematic mistake in the way that people used covariation information. People appeared to overattribute events to the person (McArthur, 1972). Thus, even when consensus information was high, suggesting (in our example) that everyone swears at the neighbourhood cat, people would often indicate that something about Mike was the cause of his swearing. This finding appeared to be consistent with the correspondence bias (also known as the fundamental attribution error), which we will review shortly, wherein people appear to infer from a person's behaviour that they must have a corresponding disposition, such as a short temper. However, it turns out that Kelley (1967; also McArthur, 1972) had made a subtle but important mistake in how he operationalized the covariation principle (e.g., Cheng and Novick, 1990; Försterling, 1989). If you want to know whether Mike covaries with swearing, you need to know whether he swears more than other people in general – not just whether he swears at the cat more. But this information is missing (Figure 3.2). Similarly, distinctiveness information, as Kelley formulated it, doesn't tell you whether other people swear at this particular cat more than other cats. Consistency information doesn't tell you about how other people behaved on the occasion, nor how Mike behaved in relation to other cats. More recent studies have shown that when participants are provided with complete information, they follow the covariation principle without systematic errors (e.g., Cheng and Novick, 1990; Försterling, 1989).

Beyond the covariation principle

In Chapter 1, we discussed an important truism – that correlation, by itself, does not entail causation. Just because two factors, A and B, are correlated, in other words, they covary, does not mean that one causes the other. A problem for Kelley's (1967) covariation principle is that it assumes that people will be content with covariation information alone. In order to be convinced that there is a causal relationship between A and B, scientists, at a minimum, want to understand that other possible causes have been controlled for. More recent research has shown that the same is true of ordinary, non-scientific folk. They are more likely to make a causal attribution to a factor such as Mike when they know there are no 'third causes' that might be responsible for his covariation with swearing (e.g., there is no one in the neighbourhood waging a vendetta against Mike by throwing the cat at him). Only under these circumstances will they grant 'causal power' to Mike (Cheng, 1997).

Causal mechanism The mechanism, or explanation for one variable causing another.

In order to be convinced that A is causing B, at least in the absence of a lot of robust evidence from controlled experiments, scientists also want to know that there is some plausible explanation of how A causes B. This is known as a **causal mechanism**. Ahn, Kalish, Medin and Gelman (1995) showed that causal mechanisms are important for laypeople too. In their studies, they asked participants to explain events such as a car accident. Even when they knew that the driver had a previously impeccable driving record – the driver did not covary with accidents – they attributed the accident to them if they knew they had been drinking, or were short-sighted and were not wearing their glasses at the time of the accident. Participants did this even when they knew that the other driver involved in the accident had been involved in several crashes before (see Figure 3.3). In these cases, armed with causal mechanism information about how the driver in question might have caused the accident, participants attached less weight to covariation information (see also White, 1995).

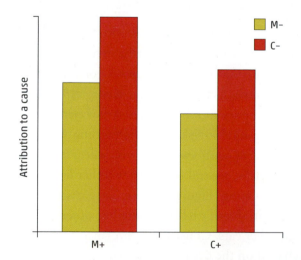

FIGURE 3.3 Covariation and mechanism information compared Ratings of the extent to which a given possible cause (e.g., the driver) was blamed for an event (e.g., a car crash), when covariation (C) and mechanism information (M) suggest different explanations. M+ means that causal mechanism information points to the driver (e.g., they were drunk). M– means that it points away from the driver (e.g., they are a careful person). C+ and C– means that covariation information points to and away from the driver, respectively (e.g., they have had many/few accidents). The pattern of results shows that participants gave greater weight to mechanism than to covariation information when they were rating explanations of the event. The cause is rated as more important when mechanism information, as opposed to covariation information, points to it (M+ compared to C+). The cause is rated as less important when mechanism information, as opposed to covariation information, suggests that it may not be responsible for the event (M– compared to C–).
Source: Data from Ahn et al., 1995

Beyond persons, stimuli and occasions

Another problem for Kelley's (1967) original model is that it is not very specific about the causal attributions that people make. Although assigning blame and credit are important, we are not usually satisfied with causal attributions such as: 'Something about Mike caused him to swear.' They seem more like preliminary attributions made early in a process of enquiry, and leave open the obvious question: 'Well, *what* about Mike caused him to swear?' In everyday life, we are more likely to blame Mike's behaviour on something specific about him: 'That Mike, he is always in a terrible mood', 'He must hate cats', 'A cat killed his pet hamster last year' and so on. This problem is compounded by the fact that it is sometimes difficult to pin down whether a given attribution is really about the person. If we are to say, 'Mike swore at the cat because he had a bad upbringing', is this really something about Mike? Or is it about something external to Mike – the way he was treated as a child? It is difficult to pin down some specific causal attributions and categorize them according to Kelley's (1967) scheme of person, stimulus and occasion (White, 1991).

In light of these problems, researchers have examined what kinds of more specific attributions people make, and how they make them. In doing so, they have returned to Heider's (1958a) insight that perceived intentions are central to explanations of people's behaviour. Malle, Knobe and Nelson (2007) have shown that people have a sophisticated theoretical understanding of intentional behaviour that, once again, resembles some of the concepts scientific psychologists would use. They explain behaviours in terms of concepts such as people's intentions, beliefs and desires, and causal history factors that explain how people came to have them.

This is not to say that the covariation principle is not important. Imagine that you are one of the few people to visit a particular lake. When the lake is fouled by pollution and surrounded by ugly factories, what makes you unusual is your desire to visit the lake for a holiday. Thus, people will explain your behaviour in terms of your unusual desire, and the personality quirks or your childhood history that made you like stinky, polluted lakes. However, if the lake is gorgeous but completely inaccessible unless you charter a plane at great cost, people are more likely to explain your visit in terms of your unusual ability to get to the lake – you are rich enough to visit it (McClure and Hilton, 1997; Sutton and McClure, 2001). It is this factor that makes you stand out, and explains why you went to the lake when so many others have not.

Two famous 'errors' in attribution

Thus far we have examined the cleverness, accuracy and sophistication of the causal attributions that ordinary people can make, even though they typically lack formal training in logic or statistics. It is for good reason that social psychologists have bestowed such people with the tag 'naive scientist', even if the naive part seems to be patronizing. Indeed, recent research suggests that, in some respects, the social cognition done by ordinary people has been more accurate and sophisticated than social psychologists have given it credit for. Nevertheless, many researchers and textbook writers have alleged that laypeople are prone to two key mistakes when they make causal attributions. These are the fundamental attribution error, and the actor–observer bias. These so-called 'errors' are related, and we will review each one in turn.

As we briefly mentioned earlier, the **fundamental attribution error** is the tendency to attribute behaviour – stable, underlying personality traits or dispositions – to the person when there is insufficient evidence to support such an attribution, and even when there is evidence that something about the situation is likely to have caused the behaviour (Gilbert and Malone, 1995; Jones, 1979). It was demonstrated in a classic study by Jones and Harris (1967). In the Cold War environment of the 1960s, they presented university students with essays, apparently written by other students at their own university, which expressed either positive or negative views towards Fidel Castro, the Communist leader of Cuba and bête noir of American politics. They were later asked to indicate the extent to which the writers were pro- or anti-Castro. Crucially, before they made this judgement, participants were told that either their fellow essay-writing students had expressed these opinions freely, or they had been told what to write (and so, presumably, were merely expressing the opinions they had been told to express). Of course, and quite appropriately, participants inferred that authors who had freely chosen to write pro-Castro essays must really be more pro-Castro than authors who had chosen to write an anti-Castro essay. However, quite remarkably, participants also made similar inferences even when they were told that writers were instructed to write a pro- or anti-Castro essay. Thus, even when they knew the essay writers were influenced by a strong situational factor – being told what kind of essay to write – observers still inferred that the essays reflected the writers' underlying beliefs (see Figure 3.4).

Later findings suggested that this attribution bias is perhaps dependent on too many factors to be truly described as 'fundamental'. For example, it is stronger in Western cultures, where the individual is seen as paramount and people tend not to think holistically about all the elements in a situation that might have caused the behaviour (Nisbett, Peng, Choi and Norenzayan, 2001). Further, the fundamental attribution error depends on age. In the West, young children explain behaviour in terms of specific factors within the situation (e.g., 'he cried because it was hot') and only later begin to show a tendency to favour personality attributions (e.g., 'he cried because he is a crybaby') (see White, 1988). In other cultures, children do not necessarily move towards the fundamental attribution error as they develop (e.g., Miller, 1984). These findings suggest that Western children are learning to conform to a culture-specific style of attributions. Also, for reasons we shall explore in more depth later in this chapter, the fundamental attribution error occurs principally when people are distracted or otherwise lack the cognitive resources to properly think through their attributions (Gilbert, 2002).

Correspondence bias (or fundamental attribution error) People's tendency to overattribute causes to a person and infer that if a person behaves in a particular way, it must be because of some underlying trait.

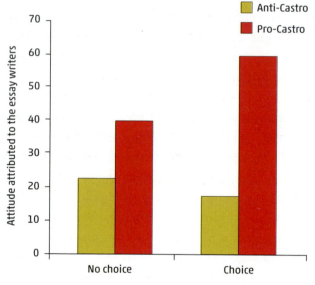

FIGURE 3.4 Demonstration of correspondence bias Participants who freely chose to write a pro- or anti-Castro essay were attributed with pro- or anti-Castro attitudes respectively. Unexpectedly, the same pattern emerged even when the essay writers had no choice. This demonstrates the correspondence bias – the tendency for people to attribute behaviours to underlying dispositions.
Source: Data from Jones and Harris, 1967

Thought experiment The process of thinking about a principle and its consequences.

If we can say that the so-called 'fundamental attribution error' is not 'fundamental', what can we say about whether it is an 'error'? As we saw in our coverage of Kelley's (1967) model of attribution, sometimes the mistakes that participants seem to be making are really quite rational responses to mistakes and oversights made by social psychologists. Were Jones and Harris's (1967) participants really wrong to say that people who wrote pro-Castro essays were somewhat pro-Castro? Here's a **thought experiment** that might help. Imagine that Jones and Harris (1967) had told participants to shoot their fellow students. If you were asked to explain the behaviour of a participant who complied with this instruction, would you be happy merely to say that 'someone told them to do it', or would you think that their compliance with this instruction says something about the kind of person they are? Obedience to such instructions is surely unthinkable for most people, violating as it does some of our most deeply felt moral convictions (but see Chapter 9, where we outline Milgram's obedience studies).

Returning to the Jones and Harris (1967) study, participants may have believed that truly anti-Castro students would refuse to go along with the instruction to write an essay in praise of him. The fact that essay writers obeyed the instruction suggests that they cannot have been *very* anti-Castro. Indeed, when Morris and Larrick (1995) took these kinds of beliefs into account, the fundamental attribution error disappeared. Participants who thought the instruction would be enough to make anybody write such an essay, regardless of the writer's opinions, did not attribute the essay to the writer's attitudes. As brilliant and elegant as their study was, Jones and Harris had simply not counted on the fact that their participants may not see the instruction as enough to produce the behaviour. More recent research suggests that when people have sufficient time, concentration, information and motivation, they do not irrationally overlook situational causes of behaviour and zero in on personality characteristics (Gilbert and Malone, 1995; McClure, 1998). For this reason, the tendency to infer that people have traits that correspond to their behaviour is now called the *correspondence bias* rather than the fundamental attribution error. We shall return to this bias later in this chapter.

Actor-observer bias The tendency for actors to attribute their own behaviours to the situation and for observers to explain behaviours in terms of personality traits.

The second so-called 'bias' that warrants closer investigation is the **actor-observer bias**, which has been found in several studies and widely claimed to be a robust and established finding (Malle, 2006). The actor-observer bias can be described as follows. As actors explaining our own behaviour, we tend to cite the situational factors that led us to act. As observers, we tend to explain the behaviour of other people in terms of personality factors. There have been two main theoretical explanations for the effect. One is perceptual – as an actor, you generally gaze from your perspective at the stimuli affecting your behaviour and you do not look at yourself. As an observer, on the other hand, you generally watch the person at least as much, and usually more, than the other factors in the situation (Malle and Pearce, 2001). Thus, as an actor, the attributions that come most easily to mind are the features of the situation you are looking at, whereas as an observer, the attributions that spring to mind are those concerned with the person who is the focus of your attention (Jones and Nisbett, 1971; Malle and Knobe, 1997).

Storms (1973) found support for this explanation in a series of studies in which participants were asked to have a conversation with another person while the conversation was being videoed. Some students watched the conversation from their own perspective (that is, they watched the other person and their behaviour), and some watched the conversation from the other student's perspective (that is, they watched their own behaviour). Participants were then asked how much they attributed their own behaviour and the other student's behaviour to situational (versus dispositional) factors. Of course, seeing yourself on video reverses your perspective, so that suddenly you look at yourself as an observer would do. Thus, we would expect the actor–observer effect to be reversed in conditions where their perspective was switched by the use of video technology. Indeed, this is what happened. Observers watching the scene unfold from the actor's perspective were less likely to make personality attributions than actors watching the scene from the observer's perspective (see Figure 3.5). A later study by Arkin and Duval (1975) suggested that actors do not necessarily have to watch the video in order to change the way they explain their own behaviour. The mere presence of video cameras caused them to explain their own behaviour in personality terms, apparently because they elicited the state of private self-awareness (see Chapter 2).

Although the actor–observer effect was observed in several early studies, contradictory findings soon emerged. In a meta-analysis of the results of 173 studies, Malle (2006) found that, on average, there was little or no actor–observer effect. Under some conditions, however, the actor–observer effect is significant. For example, when explaining *negative* behaviour such as cheating or mistakes, people invoke the situation for themselves and personality characteristics for others. But when explaining their own *positive* behaviour, people refer to internal causes, and when explaining others' positive behaviour, people refer to external causes. Clearly, people are motivated to take credit and deflect blame. It is this, rather than some fundamental shift in perspective, that leads people to explain their own and others' behaviour differently. Even when Malle (2006) considered all six studies that had examined the effect of perspective taking (through video cameras), he found that although reversing participants' perspective produced a pattern opposite to the actor–observer bias, the bias itself was not significant, on average, across the control conditions in which actors and observers viewed the scene from their normal perspectives.

This is not to say that actors and observers make exactly the same attributions for behaviour. Recent research shows, for example, that guided by their understanding of intentional behaviour, actors are more likely than observers to describe their behaviour in terms of *reasons* – the desires and beliefs that motivated them. This is partly because actors have some degree of inside knowledge – more than

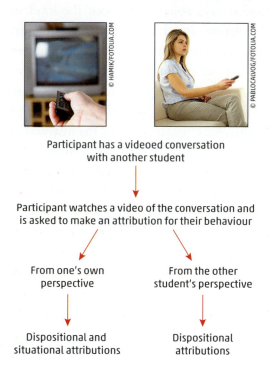

Participant has a videoed conversation with another student

↓

Participant watches a video of the conversation and is asked to make an attribution for their behaviour

From one's own perspective → Dispositional and situational attributions

From the other student's perspective → Dispositional attributions

FIGURE 3.5 The actor–observer effect Storms (1973) demonstrated that when participants watch themselves from another person's perspective, they are more likely to make a dispositional inference, thus reversing the actor–observer effect.

observers, they know what thoughts were going through their minds before they acted (Malle et al., 2007).

Other biases and errors

Attention to the motives underlying attributions and the errors that people sometimes make has shifted researchers' perspective away from the naive scientist model advocated by Heider and Kelley, and more towards a conceptualization of people as **motivated tacticians**, where attributions and judgements are said to be determined by personal motives. In particular, people are motivated to take the least cognitively demanding approach to the attributions they make, so that they tend to use **cognitive shortcuts** (or **heuristics**) to make attributions (Taylor, 1981, 1998), and can therefore be characterized as **cognitive misers** (Nisbett and Ross, 1980; Taylor, 1981). Sometimes, the choice of shortcut is influenced by personal motivations, and as we saw in Chapter 2, one of the primary motivations we have as human beings is to view the self positively – the so-called 'self-enhancement motive'.

As a consequence of this self-enhancement motive, people are prone to errors when they judge themselves and others. In particular, people seek new, positive information about the self and they also seek ways to alter existing negative views of the self. In Chapter 2, we discussed the phenomenon of *behavioural self-handicapping*, where people compensate for their failure at a task by sometimes acting in ways that sabotage their own chance of success (Berglas and Jones, 1978; Rhodewalt, Morf, Hazlett and Fairfield, 1991). Another example of attribution bias related to the motive of self-enhancement is the **self-serving attribution bias** (Arkin, Cooper and Kolditz, 1980; Zuckerman, 1979). People attribute the causes of negative events to aspects that deflect blame from the self (e.g., having a car accident that came about because a tree 'came out of nowhere'), or positive events that attribute success to the self (Stewart, 2005).

Yet another example are more general **self-serving beliefs** that lead to **self-serving biases**. As we saw in Chapter 2, people generally see themselves as 'better than average' in a wide variety of different ways, and less likely to experience negative outcomes. For example, people view themselves as less likely (10 per cent) than others (50 per cent) to be hurt in a terrorist attack (Lerner, Gonzalez, Small and Fischhoff, 2003). This **unrealistic optimism** can also cloud people's attributions for their own and others' behaviours. In particular, people tend to take credit for their successes (internal attribution) and deflect their failures (external attribution) in order to enhance and protect the self respectively. These dispositional and situational attributions tend to become more pronounced as children develop (Berger and Calabrese, 1975). Also, the tendency to commit these attributional biases seems to be consistent across many different cultures (Fletcher and Ward, 1988). In addition to motivational factors, there may also be cognitive factors associated with this type of bias. Specifically, Miller and Ross (1975) argued that people generally accept responsibility for their success because they expect to succeed. If they work hard to succeed, they may overinflate the correlation between their effort and their success, so they feel that they controlled their success more than

Motivated tactician Social cognitive approach that characterizes people as having various cognitive strategies to choose from – they choose on the basis of personal motives, needs and goals.

Cognitive shortcuts (heuristics) Because they are cognitive misers, people take shortcuts that provide mostly accurate information most of the time.

Cognitive miser Social cognitive approach, which argues that people will take the least cognitively demanding approach to attributions and social judgements.

Self-serving attribution bias Motivated by self-enhancement motives, this is the tendency for people to attribute events to causes that serve the self.

Self-serving beliefs The tendency for people to see themselves more positively (and experience more positive outcomes) than others.

Self-serving bias Attributional biases that favour the self in order to enhance or protect the self.

Unrealistic optimism The tendency for people to see themselves as more likely than others to experience good things, and less likely than others to experience bad things.

Illusion of control The belief that we have more control over the social world than we actually do.

False consensus effect The tendency for people to see their own behaviours, attitudes and opinions as more typical than they are.

False uniqueness effect The tendency for people to see themselves as more likely to perform positive behaviours than others.

they actually did. These types of biases may generally result from the **illusion of control** – the belief that we have more control over the world and the things that happen to us than we actually do (Langer, 1975).

Yet another bias related to self-enhancement is the **false consensus effect**. This is the tendency for people to view their own behaviours, attitudes and opinions as more typical (that is, shared by others) than they really are (Ross, Greene and House, 1977). For example, Ross et al. (1977) asked students on an American university campus to wear a sandwich board saying 'Eat at Joe's' for half an hour. Exactly half the participants agreed to do this. They were then asked what percentage of students had agreed to wear the sign. Those who had agreed to wear the sign estimated that the majority of students (68 per cent) would also agree and those who had refused to wear the sign also believed that the majority would have done as they did (77 per cent). This is a robust effect, and is self-enhancing because it allows people to justify negative events in their lives. If they feel that others would have behaved the same (e.g., performed poorly on a test of 'social sensitivity', as in Alicke and Largo, 1995), this illusion of consensus allows people to feel that their skills and abilities are normal. However, the **false uniqueness effect** refers to the tendency for people to see themselves as more likely to perform positive behaviours than others and to see themselves as less biased than others (Ehrlinger, Gilovich and Ross, 2005). This is said to occur in part because people underestimate the number of people who do positive things (e.g., giving to charity) and overestimate the number of people who do bad things such as stealing (Monin and Norton, 2003).

Applications of attribution theory

Although people are normally capable of making appropriate causal attributions so long as they have enough information, motivation and cognitive resources, the attribution process can go wrong. As Heider (1958a) observed, making incorrect attributions can lead to unhelpful decisions, with disastrous consequences for behaviour. It can also have profoundly negative consequences for mood. Research has shown that attributions can have these consequences in many aspects of people's lives. Below we illustrate some studies on some other topics that attribution theory has been applied to:

- *Mental health:* People with depression tend to have an 'attributional style' (Abramson, Metalsky and Alloy, 1989), in which they attribute negative events in their lives to internal, global and stable causes. For example, an attribution such as 'I failed the test because I'm stupid' is internal because the cause resides within you, global because being stupid is going to affect many areas of your life, and stable because if you are stupid now, there is a good chance you are always going to be stupid (whereas, say, being tired is a temporary condition that a good night's sleep will rectify). The dimensions of *internality*, *globality* and *stability* are consistent with Kelley's (1967) theory that attributions are made to the person (high internality), to the stimulus (low globality) or to the occasion (low stability). *Controllability* is another important dimension of attributions – people with depression and anxiety tend to attribute outcomes to events outside their control (e.g., physical attractiveness) rather than within their control (e.g., the way they dress). One of the cornerstones of modern approaches to psychotherapy, such as cognitive-behavioural therapy, is training people to stop explaining events in their lives in an overly pessimistic, self-defeating way (Beck, Rush, Shaw and Emery, 1979).

- *Aggression:* Aggressive people are prone to the *hostile* attribution bias, seeing innocent or ambiguous behaviours by other people (e.g., bumping into them) as deliberate acts of provocation (Orobio de Castro, Veerman, Koops et al., 2002; Pornari and Wood, 2010). Longitudinal studies have shown that if children at age five are predisposed to interpreting ambiguous behaviours in this way, they are more likely to be aggressive 12 years later (Lansford, Malone, Dodge et al., 2006).

- *Emotions:* Valins and Nisbett (1971) designed an intervention to be used in therapeutic situations that would transform negative emotions into positive emotions. For example, encouraging anxious people to attribute their anxiety to external factors rather than internal factors should reduce the extent to which people feel anxious about the self. This has met with some success, but tends to be restricted to laboratory settings and also tends to be short-lived (Parkinson, 1985).

- *Close relationships:* People who attribute their spouse's negative behaviour to internal, stable and global factors (e.g., 'they are demanding') are subsequently less forgiving and less satisfied with their marriage (Fincham, Paleari and Regalia, 2002).

- *Intergroup relations:* Becker, Wagner and Christ (2011) asked a representative sample of German participants to explain the global financial crisis of 2008. Those who blamed the crisis on the actions of bankers and speculators subsequently showed increases in anti-Semitism, since Jewish people are stereotypically associated with global finance. Those who blamed the crisis on immigrants showed increases in ethnic prejudice. Those who were encouraged to blame the crisis on the global financial system did not show any increases in prejudice towards outgroups. Intergroup attributions tend to be characterized by ethnocentrism, that is, the expectation that our own groups tend to do positive things and other groups tend to do negative things, and therefore resemble the self-serving biases discussed earlier (Hewstone and Jaspers, 1982). This type of bias is known as the **ultimate attribution error**.

Ultimate attribution error
Tendency to attribute positive ingroup and negative outgroup behaviours dispositionally, and positive outgroup and negative ingroups behaviours situationally.

- *Educational achievement:* A study of over 5,000 high school students in New Zealand showed that students achieve higher marks when they take credit for their best marks and deflect blame for their worst marks (McClure, Meyer, Garisch et al., 2011). Training people to avoid explaining their educational performance in terms of their ability, but in terms of changeable factors such as their effort, can reap results. Haynes, Daniels, Stupnisky et al. (2008) did this with first-year university students and found their grades improved over the following year. Their attributional retraining intervention helped by making students more motivated to learn (mastery motivation), rather than by making them more motivated to achieve high grades (performance motivation).

Culture and attribution

Although there appear to be some universals when it comes to attributions, research suggests that people of different cultures often make different types of attributions for the same behaviours. As we saw earlier, the correspondence bias is more pronounced in Western cultures. More generally, studies have shown that members of individualistic cultures are more prone to make dispositional attributions for their own and others' behaviours, whereas people in collectivistic cultures are more likely to make situational attributions. For example, Morris and Peng (1994) asked Chinese and American students to read brief summary accounts of two murder cases. In general, the Chinese students tended to place more blame on situational factors (e.g., media glorification of violence, economic recession), whereas the American students blamed the perpetrator (e.g., mental imbalance and personality problems). Findings such as these can be explained by the view of personality as changeable, which is more common in collectivistic than individualistic cultures (Choi, Nisbett and Norenzayan, 1999). In particular, people from collectivistic cultures are less likely to agree that 'someone's personality is something that cannot be changed'.

Another explanation is the effect of distraction on attributions. Knowles, Morris, Chiu and Hong (2001) asked student participants from the USA and Hong Kong to read a speech by another student who had supposedly been asked to advocate a particular position. Participants were asked to rate how much they thought the speech reflected the student's actual attitude. Crucially, some of the participants were distracted – they were asked to perform another task on the computer while listening to the speech. Findings revealed that the US students made more dispositional attributions when they were distracted than when they were not. However, the participants from Hong Kong did not respond to distraction in the same way, making few dispositional inferences in both conditions (see Figure 3.6).

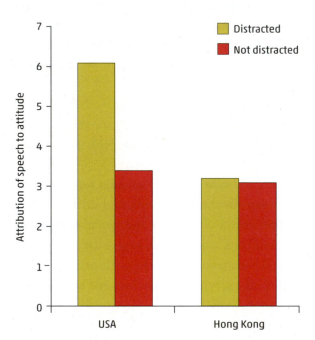

FIGURE 3.6 **The effect of distraction on attributions** Distraction leads to stronger dispositional attributions among US students but did not have the same effect on students from Hong Kong. *Source:* Data from Knowles et al., 2001

Another explanation for cultural differences in attribution is that people in individualistic cultures tend to pay less attention to the impact of the situation on behaviour than people from collectivistic cultures, who show a greater tendency to explain events with reference to the context (see Figure 3.7). Individualistic cultures are therefore less likely than collectivistic cultures to see connections

FIGURE 3.7 **People from different cultures make different attributions for the same behaviour** When asked to make observations about an aquarium scene in Masuda and Nisbett's (2001) study, Japanese participants tended to include more contextual information than US participants, demonstrating cultural differences in attribution between individualistic and collectivistic cultures.

between objects and events (Nisbett et al., 2001; Norenzayan and Nisbett, 2000). In one study demonstrating this effect, Masuda and Nisbett (2001) asked Japanese and US students to observe aquarium scenes that included various items such as fish, rocks and plants. They were asked to describe what they saw. In a later recognition test, they were shown some of the previously seen aquarium objects along with some new objects. Both the original and new objects were shown either in their original context or in a different context. Participants were asked to judge whether they had seen the objects. In a second study, participants performed the same task with photographs of wildlife. Masuda and Nisbett found that the Japanese participants made more statements about contextual information (e.g., the fish were near the seaweed, near the shells) than the US students, and also made more mention of relationships between the objects. Further, the Japanese participants recognized previously seen objects with more accuracy when they saw them in their original settings, whereas this had little effect on the US participants. These findings demonstrated that the Japanese participants were more likely to see things in relation to context than their US counterparts, and are consistent with other findings (e.g., Ji, Peng and Nisbett, 2000) demonstrating that US participants made fewer mistakes on a different task that required decoupling objects from a background. Thus, it appears that people from Eastern cultures may be more 'holistic' thinkers than those from Western cultures. When it comes to making attributions for events, they attend more to the 'bigger picture' and the whole situation rather than the agency of a particular target.

Time to reflect Findings such as those of Masuda and Nisbett (2001, p. 933) suggest that the 'Japanese may simply see more of the world than do Americans'. However, they may also suggest that East Asians find it difficult to separate objects from their contexts. What might be some of the implications of these findings? Could they be an important factor in determining other cultural differences in social psychology?

Person perception

Your safety, success and enjoyment in life depend not only on the attributions you make for your own and others' behaviours, but more generally on your ability to make accurate judgements about people. Who can you trust? Who is fun to be around? Who is needy or manipulative? Who will be able to help you with a task? People who struggle to make these judgements are more prone to a range of psychological disorders, including depression (Coyne, 1976; Lane and DePaulo, 1999; Russell, Stokes, Jones et al., 1993). How do we make these important judgements? This is the question at the heart of the study of **person perception** (also known as **impression formation**).

Person perception/impression formation The study of how people make judgements about others, and the information used to make these judgements.

Configural model of person perception

Early theoretical frameworks, like those in attribution theory, were influenced by Gestalt psychology and the notion that laypeople think like scientists. Asch's

Configural model of person perception Asch's model of person perception, which argues that central traits play a greater role in determining the final impression.

Central traits Traits that have greater influence on how people configure their impressions of others.

Peripheral traits Traits that have lesser influence on how people configure their impressions of others.

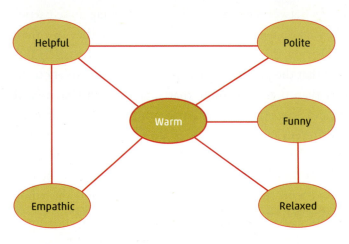

FIGURE 3.8 A configuration of traits as described by Asch's (1946) configural theory Here, the trait 'warm' is central, being correlated with all the other traits. Each of the other traits is more peripheral, being associated with only two of the other traits. If you know that someone is warm, you have information about a lot of their traits. This is the basis of a holistic or 'Gestalt' representation about the person.

(1946) **configural model of person perception** suggested that we form a holistic impression of people that integrates a small number of important cues (Figure 3.8). Some cues, known as **central traits**, have a lot of influence over the impressions we form of people, whereas others, known as **peripheral traits**, have less influence.

To test this model, Asch (1946) asked participants to read a list of attributes about a fictitious person (e.g., energetic, assured, talkative, cold, ironical, inquisitive, persuasive). There were two lists that different only slightly – specifically, the list given to one set of participants contained the word 'warm' and the list given to the remaining participants contained the word 'cold'. Participants were asked to rate the fictitious person on a list of bipolar dimensions such as happy/unhappy and reliable/unreliable. It was found that participants who were given the list containing the word 'warm' rated the person much more favourably than the participants who had the list containing the word 'cold'. From these results, Asch argued that being warm or cold is a central trait that has a strong influence on overall impression formation. He found that when the words 'warm' and 'cold' were replaced by 'polite' and 'blunt', the differences in the impressions formed was less striking.

Kelley (1950) tested the configural theory in a naturalistic setting. He introduced a visiting lecturer to several class groups – for half of the groups, the introduction included the trait 'cold' and for the other half, the introduction described the lecturer as 'warm'. The students were then later asked to evaluate the lecturer and, as predicted, student evaluations were more positive when the lecturer had been described as 'warm' rather than 'cold'. Interestingly, Kelley also observed that students were more likely to ask questions and interact with the lecturer who had been described as 'warm'. More recent research points to the centrality of warmth as a trait – so much so that the experience of warmth influences our social judgements. As we shall see in Chapter 4, Williams and Bargh (2008) found that participants who held a cup of hot (versus cold) coffee judged a target person as having a 'warm' personality, such as being generous or caring. Apparently, 'warmth' as a trait really is a deep-seated metaphor based on the physical sensation of warmth.

Time to reflect Why do you think warmth is such a central trait? Aside from warmth, what other traits would you say are central? How central would you say these traits are, compared to warmth?

Algebraic model

Another model proposes that observers assign 'scores' to people on their traits and characteristics. When a person forms an impression of another person, they average out the scores to form an overall evaluation (Anderson, 1965, 1996). This

Cognitive algebra Approach to the study of person perception proposing that people assign positive and negative valence to various person attributes and combine them to form a general evaluation of a person.

process is known as **cognitive algebra** – people assign positive and negative valence to various person attributes and combine them to be able to form a general evaluation of a person. For example, consider the two people in Table 3.1 who have been evaluated along various dimensions on a scale from –3 to +3 from least positive to most positive (e.g., Anderson, 1974). Each person has a 'score' on the first six traits (intelligent, hard-working, interesting, honest, friendly and funny). Based on the sums of their scores on these six traits, Kat comes out ahead, with a total of two, compared to 1.83 for James. Impressions of Kat should therefore be slightly more favourable.

TABLE 3.1 Information integration (Anderson, 1974)

	Kat	James	Analyst weighting	Kat (analyst)	James (analyst)	Holiday rep weighting	Kat (rep)	James (rep)
Intelligent	3	1	3	9	3	0	0	0
Hard-working	3	–1	3	9	–3	1	3	–1
Interesting	2	2	0	0	0	2	4	4
Honest	2	2	2	4	4	1	2	2
Friendly	1	3	1	1	3	3	3	9
Funny	1	3	0	0	0	3	3	9
Total	12	9		23	7		15	23
Average	2	1.83		3.83	1.17		2.5	3.83
Athletic	1	–	The figures on the left reveal what happens if you were to gain enough information about Kat to form impressions of these traits. According to the most basic version of the algebraic model, your overall impression of Kat becomes more positive, because the new trait information is positive. But according to the averaging model, your overall impression becomes less positive, because the 6 new traits score less high, on average, than the first 6. In this example, your impression of Kat based on 12 traits is now less positive than your impression of James, based on 6.					
Healthy	1	–						
Polite	1	–						
Relaxed	0	–						
Popular	0	–						
Respected	1	–						
Total	16	–						
Average	1.67	–						

Summation Model of cognitive algebra assuming that the overall impression that is formed is the total valence of all the pieces of information.

However, not all traits are equal all of the time. The example above describes the principal model of cognitive algebra that is based on **summation**. Here, the overall impression is simply the total valence (that is, the net positive or negative nature) of all the pieces of information. Using this principle, a person wanting to make a positive first impression might want to conceal their lack of honesty and interestingness in favour of the traits where they score well. In this model of cognitive algebra, every small piece of positive information adds to the overall positive evaluation that can be formed.

Averaging Model of cognitive algebra assuming that the overall impression is the average of all the traits on display.

The model of **averaging** assumes that people's overall impression is formed by calculating the arithmetic mean of all the traits on display. Using the averaging principle rather than summation can make a real difference, as Table 3.1 shows. For example, if you already have a positive impression of someone, and learn new information that is still positive, then according to the summing principle, your impression becomes even more positive. In our example, the total 'score' for Kat, taking into account the six additional traits we have learned about, goes up from

12 to 16. However, according to the averaging principle, our impression of Kat becomes less positive. This is because the new trait information, while positive, is less positive than the first six traits. We divide the new total of 16 by twelve traits, whereas we had divided the old total of 12 by just six traits. In fact, knowing all twelve of these traits about Kat will lead to a less positive impression of her than that of James, based on the first six traits. Thus, one implication of the averaging model is that the positive impression a person projects may be diluted if more information is presented. It may therefore be wise to present only a small number of the most positive attributes one possesses so that the perceiver receives the best possible overall impression.

This simple model of averaging is not without limitations either. It does not take into account the importance of different traits in different circumstances. For example, in judging a person's worthiness as a comedian, it would be typical to assign more importance to the trait of humour than honesty. Or, honesty and intelligence might be the most important traits in judging a politician. The model of **weighted averaging** takes into account the relative importance of traits in different circumstances. Using the example in Table 3.1, let us say you are evaluating the two people for a job as an analyst in an insurance company versus a holiday rep. Traits like intelligence and industriousness are important for the first job, while traits like being funny and friendly are important for the other. Taking into account how we might therefore weight the different traits, Kat comes out ahead as the insurance analyst, but James comes out ahead as the holiday rep.

However, it is a common finding that negative information is generally weighted more heavily than positive information. This is called the **negativity bias** (e.g., Kanouse and Hanson, 1972; Skowronski and Carlston, 1989; Smith and Collins, 2009), so even using the weighted averaging model, a person wishing to create a positive impression of themselves would be wise to conceal their most negative traits from the perceiver. Interestingly, for reasons that are not understood, the negativity bias changes over the life span. Older adults appear to be biased towards positive trait information. For whatever reason, our neural activity seems to be less responsive to negative information as we age, but does not become less responsive to positive information (Kisley, Wood and Burrows, 2007).

Weighted averaging Model of cognitive algebra assuming that people assign weights of importance to different traits in different contexts and form an overall impression of a person based on a weighted average.

Negativity bias The common finding that negative traits are weighted more heavily than positive traits.

Time to reflect Think of some of the people you know and your impressions of them. How are they influenced by the context in which you interact with them? Come up with your own table of traits and work out how people might be perceived differently depending on the summation, averaging and weighted averaging processes of cognitive algebra.

The weighted average model of person perception has gained a good deal of support from research evidence, and is still influential today (Singh and Simons, 2010). While it is a good model of how an overall impression of a person is built up from impressions of their personality traits, it does not attempt to explain how we form impressions of their specific traits in the first place. It also does not take into account the order in which we learn about their positive and negative traits. Trait impressions are formed quickly, and they have to be. If it takes you too long to identify a criminal, your bank account might be cleared out. If it takes you too long to work out that a potential match is not only physically attractive but also has desirable personality traits, your competition may already have pounced. In the next few pages, we review the human ability to form first impressions quickly, with little apparent effort, and the ongoing importance of those first impressions.

Question to consider Now that you know more about person perception, reread question 1 at the start of the chapter. What would be your advice to Louisa?

The power of first impressions

The study of person perception has produced two striking and consistent findings. First, impressions are formed extremely quickly, with a surprising degree of accuracy. Second, these first impressions, even when they are wrong, carry a lot of weight. Having made a good first impression, you are more likely to be able to 'get away' with doing bad or stupid things without too much damage to your reputation. And if you make a bad first impression, it is difficult to overcome it. Just how quickly do we form impressions, and how do we do it? One way we do it is to judge a book by its cover, relying on visible and superficial cues that are presented by people's appearance and demeanour. For example, consider the three pictures in Figure 3.9. Which of these men do you think would be most likely to go to a Star Trek convention? Which one might be a banker? Which one might like gangster rap? We think you could make these decisions very quickly.

FIGURE 3.9 First impressions On this type of task, people generally agree on the likely activities (sci-fi conventions, banking, gangster rap) of these three individuals. This demonstrates that we form impressions of people quickly even though we know very little about them.

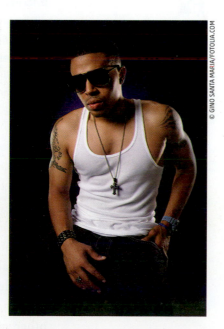

Research has explored two ways in which people judge a book by its cover. First, they extract a lot of information about people by observing brief, 'thin slices' of their behaviour. Some traits, such as extraversion, intelligence and conscientiousness, can be determined after five seconds of watching a video of another person. It can take longer to determine how neurotic, open to experience, and agreeable a person is, but in general the optimal trade-off between accuracy and speed is reached at about 60 seconds (Carney, Colvin and Hall, 2007). It appears to take 30 seconds for ordinary people to be able to spot whether others have a personality disorder (Friedman, Oltmanns and Turkheimer, 2007), and to tell how effective they would be as salespeople (Ambady, Krabbenhoft and Hogan, 2006). In general, for reasons that are not entirely clear, women appear to be somewhat better at judging a book by its cover than men (Ambady, Hallahan and Rosenthal, 1995).

It is by no means clear exactly how people – and especially women – manage to do this. However, it appears to be important to 'go with your instincts' – thinking in a deliberate way seems to actually impair performance on the ability to make quick but accurate judgements about others. As a result, sad and depressed people tend to be worse at this task, precisely because they try to think about it rather than doing it instinctively (Ambady and Gray, 2002; Ambady and Rosenthal, 1992). People who are impaired in other ways (e.g., alcoholic and psychiatric patients) also tend to have poorer 'thin slice vision' compared to normal samples (Rosenthal, Hall, DiMatteo et al., 1979). Also, there is little to no relationship between people's confidence in their judgements and their accuracy (Ames, Kammrath, Suppes and Bolger, 2010). This suggests that whatever techniques people are using, they do not have conscious access to them. Putting this all together suggests that we can thank automatic processes, occurring outside our awareness, for our extraordinary skills in person perception. We return to these unconscious processes later in the chapter.

Exploring further Use the internet to find other traits that ordinary, untrained people can judge by using 'thin slices' of behaviour or, even more minimally, photographs. Try searching terms like 'thin slice judgement' (you can try both British and American spellings), 'impressions' and 'traits'. Much of the research on judgements of personality from photographs uses the key phrase 'zero acquaintance'. Can you find any clues as to how people might be pulling off this trick?

Question to consider Now, reread question 2 at the start of the chapter. Why do you think Ray's first impression of Alan was so powerful?

Another way that people judge a book by its cover is to use an even more minimal source of information – people's physical appearance, as revealed, for example, by photographs. Traits that people appear to be able to determine, better than chance, merely by looking at head and shoulder photographs stripped of all other cues include intelligence (Zebrowitz, Hall, Murphy and Rhodes, 2002), extraversion (how outgoing someone is), neuroticism (how anxious they tend to be) and psychoticism (how loose and dissociated their thinking is) (e.g., Shevlin, Walker, Davies et al., 2003). Viewing a still photograph of a stranger for as little as 50 milliseconds – one-twentieth of a second – can be enough to allow people to judge whether they are extraverted (Borkenau, Brecke, Möttig and Paelecke,

2009). A person's conscientiousness (Albright et al., 1988), honesty (Bond, Berry and Omar, 1994) and aggression (Berry and Brownlow, 1989) can also be determined, to some extent, by strangers merely on the basis of photographs.

SOCIAL PSYCHOLOGY IN THE REAL WORLD

'Gaydar', politics and the importance of judging a book by its cover

© JAVIER BROSCH/FOTOLIA.COM

You may have heard of the popular notion of 'gaydar' – the ability of people, especially gay people, to judge at a glance whether a stranger is gay. There is controlled experimental evidence that heterosexuals are able to make this judgement fairly accurately based solely on a set of eight photographs, and that gay men and women are still more accurate (Ambady, Hallahan and Conner, 1999). Using photographs of straight and gay men taken from personal advertisements, recent research suggests that a 50 ms glance at a head and shoulders photograph of a man is enough for people to guess, at above-chance levels, whether he is gay (Rule and Ambady, 2008). The existence of a 'gaydar' makes eminent evolutionary sense, as Rule and Ambady point out. Successful mating has always depended on being able to size up opportunities, quickly. There is no point pursuing people who are not available to you. However, although it is easy to tell a story about why people are so good at it, research is yet to determine exactly how people do it.

Moving from 'gaydar' to politics, Todorov, Mandisodza, Goren and Hall (2005) demonstrated how quickly people can form consensual impressions of others and how much these impressions can matter. They asked participants to look at pairs of unfamiliar faces for only one second. The faces were those of politicians contesting the US elections in 2004. Participants were given one second only to rate the competency, intelligence, leadership, honesty, trustworthiness, charisma and likeability. They found that ratings of the individuals were highly differentiated into three clusters (competence, trust and likeability) – participants were rating the faces according to meaningful patterns. Interestingly too, judgements of competence predicted actual electoral success. Candidates who were rated as more competent were elected approximately 68 per cent of the time. Seemingly, election results were influenced by people's automatic judgements of a candidate's competence.

Questions

1 A wealth of research evidence suggests that people make reasonably accurate judgements about people based on very little information. Can you find an example of a research study that found the opposite? What was different about this study from those you have read about so far in this chapter?

2 Aside from evolutionary explanations, what other reasons might there be for people's skills at judging books by their covers?

3 Can you speculate on some explanations for *how* people are able to make such accurate judgements based on very little information? What does the literature tell you about this?

Given that we are not entirely sure how people can judge each others' characteristics from observing thin slices of their behaviour, it may not surprise you to learn that we do not understand how they do it from photographs, either. But this new line of research is already producing some intriguing clues. Engell, Haxby and Todorov (2007) presented a set of faces to Princeton University undergraduates, and asked them to rate them for trustworthiness. While they were doing this, they were inside a functional magnetic resonance imager (fMRI) – a machine that can track changes in blood flow within the brain as it engages in different tasks, commonly used in social neuroscience studies (see Chapter 15). Of particular interest was increases in blood flow to the amygdala (see Figure 3.10), a structure at the rear of the brain that is associated with judgements of trustworthiness (Adolphs, Tranel and Damasio, 1998; Winston, Strange, O'Doherty and Dolan, 2002), among other functions associated with the processing of emotional information. They predicted, and found, that as a participant found a face less trustworthy, activity in their amygdala would increase. However, something startling happened when the researchers controlled statistically for how trustworthy all the participants had found each face, on average. Each participant's amygdala response was better predicted by this consensual rating of the faces than by their own rating. Apparently, the human amygdala is capable of putting faces into boxes – faces that are generally agreed to be trustworthy or untrustworthy – independently of the conscious decision of its 'owner'. In other words, the amygdala 'lights up' in response to trustworthy and untrustworthy features of stimulus faces that are there for everybody to see, and not as a result of the individual decision of the perceiver. Here, then, is evidence that strongly suggests that our brains have learned, or are hard-wired, to detect personality traits based on features of people's faces.

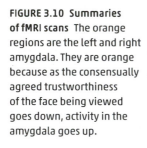

FIGURE 3.10 Summaries of fMRI scans The orange regions are the left and right amygdala. They are orange because as the consensually agreed trustworthiness of the face being viewed goes down, activity in the amygdala goes up.

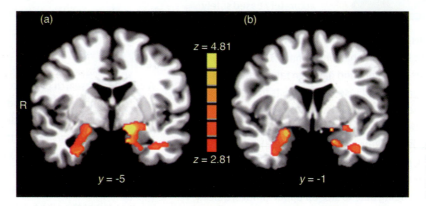

Source: Engell et al., 2007. Reprinted by permission of MIT Press Journals

But what features are important in judgements of trustworthiness and untrustworthiness? In a sophisticated set of studies blending experimentation with computer modelling, Oosterhof and Todorov (2008) found that high perceived trustworthiness is associated with happy expressions, and low perceived trustworthiness is associated with angry expressions. Look a little happy, and you will be more likely to appear trustworthy; look a little angry, and you will not. Although stimulus faces are generally pretested to ensure they are emotionally neutral, some people just have faces that look a little bit angry or a little bit happy most of the time. Engell, Todorov and Haxby (2010) suggest that to judge a trait like trustworthiness from these kinds of subtle emotional expression cues may not be accurate. Rather, angry people (like untrustworthy people) are to be avoided, and happy people (like trustworthy people) may be approached. Common brain systems may be involved in the evaluation of emotions and personality characteristics that suggest people should also be approached or avoided.

Using some facial cues *is* likely to lead to accurate judgements. The wider your face (width-to-height ratio), the higher your exposure to testosterone as you were developing, and the more likely you are to be aggressive in laboratory experiments or during professional sports (Carré and McCormick, 2008). Even more fascinatingly, others can tell – people with wider faces are seen as more aggressive (Carré, Morrissey, Mondloch and McCormick, 2010). It is worth pausing to consider the use of one facial cue that does not lead to accurate judgements – attractiveness. A person's physical appearance (and most notably their attractiveness) can influence the impression they make, but this may not reflect who they actually are.

In one study demonstrating the influence of appearance, Dion, Berscheid and Walster (1972) told participants they were participating in a study of the accuracy of social perception. They were to look at photos of actual people whose characteristics were purportedly being measured in another longitudinal study. Thus, participants thought that their responses would be compared to 'expert' ratings of the targets. The targets were preselected for different levels of physical attractiveness as judged by a set of independent raters. Thus, participants were presented with one attractive face, one face of average attractiveness and one unattractive face. Some striking results were found (see Figure 3.11). Specifically, attractive people were perceived to have the most socially desirable personality, higher marital competence and a more desirable occupational status. Thus, being attractive is seen to be associated with more desirable personality characteristics and life outcomes. Research suggests that this belief is wrong – although attractive people are seen as nicer, they are not actually nicer. However, it might be that nicer (more agreeable and extroverted) people take care more over their appearance in day-to-day life (Meier, Robinson, Carter and Hinsz, 2010).

There are many other effects associated with physical attractiveness. For example, teachers excuse the misbehaviours of attractive children but blame children who are unattractive (Dion, 1972). Attractive men receive higher starting salaries than unattractive men and this continues over the course of their career (Frieze, Olsen and Russell, 1991). Also, physically attractive defendants in court tend to be set lower bails (Downs and Lyons, 1991). It seems that people associate better success and better outcomes with being attractive, so that attractive people tend to be perceived positively across a variety of domains.

However, as Heilman and Stopeck (1985) found, this is further influenced by gender. In their study, they asked male and female MBA students to participate in

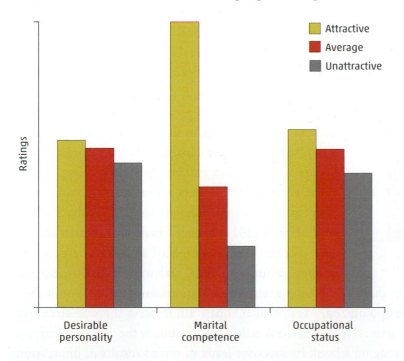

FIGURE 3.11 The influence of appearance on ratings of stimulus people Attractive people are rated as having a more socially desirable personality, greater marital competence and higher occupational status.

Source: Data from Dion et al., 1972

a study of 'personnel decision making'. Participants looked at pictures of various male and female targets and read their employee profiles. The first independent variable was the type of job (managerial or clerical), the second was the gender of the employee (male or female) and, finally, the experimenters manipulated the targets' attractiveness (more or less attractive). The dependent variables were performance evaluation and advancement potential. Heilman and Stopeck found that, for male employees, being attractive or unattractive did not matter, whether in a clerical or managerial position. However, for female employees, attractiveness was seen as an asset in a clerical position but not in a managerial position. The researchers argued that this occurred because of a lack of fit between the categories. Specifically, being attractive and female does not fit with the characteristics of being a good manager.

Recent research is also revealing how being good-looking can be a double-edged sword. In particular, although it normally encourages members of the 'other' sex to assign positive personality characteristics to you, it can have quite the opposite effect on members of the same sex. For example, Agthe, Sporrle and Maner (2011) had undergraduate students rate rival candidates for a job, whose applications included a photograph. Both male and female participants rated more attractive 'other-sex' candidates as more qualified for the job (even though, photos aside, the CVs and applications were identical). However, they also rated more attractive 'same-sex' candidates as *less* qualified for the job (see Figure 3.12). This suggests, of course, that attractive, same-sex people may be derogated because they are seen as a threat. The results of a second study by Agthe et al. supported this idea. High self-esteem participants, who were presumably secure in themselves and less prone to feeling threatened, were biased towards, rather than against, attractive same-sex candidates. In another study, Phillips and Hranek (2011) showed male and female university students a photograph of an attractive or unattractive woman student, and were asked to imagine the student letting them down on a group presentation assignment. Would they forgive her, if she apologized? 'Yes', said the male students, if she was attractive rather than unattractive. 'No', said the female students, under the same conditions.

It is clear that judging a book by its cover leads to mixed results in impression formation. But this is not the only way we form impressions of people quickly. Another much studied process that underpins the rapid formation of first impressions is *correspondent inference*, which we have already discussed with respect to attribution. When we see someone act in a greedy, hostile, kind or intelligent way, we automatically, and rapidly, infer that they must be greedy, hostile, kind or intelligent, accordingly. If you are cut up by a motorist driving aggressively, you are less likely to think, 'They must be in a hurry', than 'They are a bad driver' (or

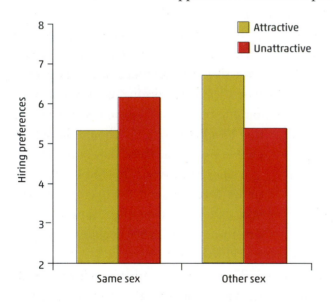

FIGURE 3.12 Hiring other-sex or same-sex candidates Male and female participants alike (in Germany) preferred to hire other-sex candidates if they were attractive (vs. unattractive), and same-sex candidates if they were unattractive (vs. attractive).

Source: Data from Agthe et al., 2011

worse). Many studies show that we do this, even when we are not asked to make such inferences (e.g., Carlston and Skowronski, 1994).

Todorov and Uleman (2003) used a clever methodology to uncover these 'spontaneous trait inferences'. They showed participants 60 pairs of photos of strangers with sentences describing the people doing things, such as 'Alice solved the mystery halfway through the book'. Later, they showed photos of the same people, with captions of the trait that was implied by their behaviour (in this case, 'clever'). They were asked to indicate whether this word appeared in the sentence they had read earlier. Of course, it had not; nonetheless, participants tended to falsely recognize the word, especially when they saw the initial sentences for a short period of time, when they were not thinking about the sentence deeply (e.g., when they were counting nouns), and when their minds were on another task they had been asked to do by the experimenter.

These findings reinforce a point made some years before in a study by Gilbert and Osborne (1989). They showed participants a video of a young female confederate, minus sound, who appeared to be acting very nervously (e.g., fidgeting with her hair, biting her nails, moving around in her seat). One group of participants was told that she was being asked to talk about positive or neutral topics (such as travel or books). In this experimental condition, participants have no good reason to suspect that despite her behaviour, the confederate is not a nervous person. In contrast, another group of participants was told that she was discussing nerve-wracking topics (imagine being asked to discuss your fears and phobias, or painful childhood memories on video). In this condition, according to classic models of person perception and causal attribution, we should engage in the process of *discounting* that we touched on earlier. Her nervous behaviour should be discounted in light of the information about the situation – any normal person would be nervous talking about their painful childhood experiences on video. Thus, the normal correspondent inference – she is acting nervously, therefore she is a nervous person – should be tempered.

This happened, so long as participants had sufficient thinking powers, or cognitive resources, free. When Gilbert and Osborne (1989) gave some of the participants something else to do – a task in which they had to memorize a list of words being read out to them while watching the video – the topic the woman was ostensibly discussing made no difference. Under this **cognitive load** manipulation, participants found it impossible to disregard the visible behaviour of the woman and so correspondent inferences dominated. For Gilbert and Osborne, this was evidence that people automatically make correspondent inferences. They will fall prey to the correspondence bias we discussed earlier – the tendency to ascribe correspondent traits to people even though the situation is more likely to have caused their behaviour – except when they are sufficiently motivated and able to correct for their first, biased impression.

Cognitive load Condition in which a task demands a person's attention and thinking capacity, leaving little left for another task. This is often manipulated by experimenters to determine whether a second task requires conscious thought and control.

Exploring further How else can cognitive load be manipulated? What other effects does cognitive load have? What does this tell us about the nature of social cognition?

More recently, a team of researchers (van Duynslaeger, Sterken, van Overwalle and Verstraeten, 2008) used electroencephalograms (EEGs) to measure brain activity. The EEGs showed that a unique brain response is associated with the reading of trait words that are consistent, rather than inconsistent, with the trait implied by earlier sentences describing behaviours. To go back to our earlier example, 'clever' is consistent and 'stupid' inconsistent with solving a mystery. This same brain response (a P300 in the parietal area of the brain) is also associated with the ability to remember the original behavioural sentence (about solving the mystery) when prompted on the screen with the correspondent trait (clever).

As we mentioned, first impressions are not only made quickly, but they are hard to shake. People tend to assign greater importance to the traits they observe first. It is common wisdom that first impressions are important, and indeed this is often true. For example, Asch (1946) asked participants to form an impression of a person after reading a list of adjectives. Crucially, for half the participants, the positive traits appeared first (e.g., intelligent) and for the other half, the negative traits appeared first (e.g., impulsive). Participants' impressions were influenced by the information that appeared first, such that the first group of participants formed more positive impressions of the target person than the second group. The traits presented first had a greater influence on the overall impression that was formed. This **primacy effect** implies that people may be wise to 'put their best foot forward' because social perceivers tend to pay more attention to information that is observed first.

Primacy effect Bias in person perception such that people remember (and assign the most importance to) the traits they observe first.

Time to reflect Why do you think first impressions count? Read the rest of this chapter and see if you can find at least two social cognitive principles that help to explain why the first information we receive about a person is so important.

Recency effect Bias in person perception such that people remember (and assign the most importance to) traits they observe most recently.

People sometimes pay more attention to information that is observed most recently. This is called the **recency effect** (Anderson, 1971; Dreben, Fiske and Hastie, 1979; Mayo and Crockett, 1964). Although primacy effects are most commonly observed, it is important to consider that people may be more likely, at least in demanding situations, to attend to information that is most recently presented. An underlying explanation for both primacy and recency effects is motivational, and found support in an experiment by Richter and Kruglanski (1998). People, especially when they are high in the desire to form a definite, clear, unambiguous impression of others, tend to 'seize' on the most easily accessible information they have. If you have the goal to form an impression of a person when you first meet them, which, as we have seen, seems to be the case normally, then you are likely to 'seize' on the first piece of information you receive about them. If, on the other hand, you have a goal of forming an impression of a person after you have known them for a while, the last piece of information you learned about them may be the most accessible.

Person memory

How much do we remember about people? How do we organize the information we learn about people? To answer these questions, social psychologists have

Associative network Memory model whereby ideas or nodes are connected by associative links.

turned to cognitive psychological theories of memory and, in particular, the notion of **associative networks** (Anderson, 1990). This type of memory model assumes that people store propositions, which consist of ideas or nodes that are linked by the associations between them. For example, various propositions (e.g., seeing a person is kicking a ball, the ball is a football, the person is wearing a football kit) have various nodes (e.g., person, kicking, ball, football kit), which are related to, or associated with, each other. In this type of memory model, some links between nodes are stronger than others but links can become stronger the more they are rehearsed. In other words, the more people think about people kicking balls, footballs and football wear, the stronger these attributes and events become linked together. Memories are also more likely to be recalled if there are multiple memory routes, or more ways to retrieve the memory. Recalling involves the activation of nodes and the subsequent activation of related nodes along associative links. If someone recalls a person kicking a ball, they are also likely to think of football because these nodes are strongly associated.

This type of associative network model can explain specific processes related to person memory. For example, if we have a strong impression of a person, we tend to remember information that is consistent with our impression (Fiske and Neuberg, 1990). Perhaps counterintuitively, however, people tend to more successfully recall information about a person if it is *inconsistent* with their general impression of the person. For example, we might be more likely to recall that a person likes sewing if we know they are also a professional wrestler. Social psychologists argue this is often the case, because information that is inconsistent with impressions demands more attention, generates more thought, and thus strengthens the links between nodes. This may reflect people's increased effort to reconcile information with their beliefs (Hastie, 1988; Srull and Wyer, 1989).

What does person memory consist of and how do we use it?

Theorists generally assume that person memory is organized so that positive and negative features are clustered together. More specifically, Schneider, Hastorf and Ellsworth (1979) argued that trait information is typically organized around the dimensions of competencies (e.g., intelligence) and socially desirable characteristics (e.g., friendliness). Trait inferences about a person are a result of complex processes of assigning causal attributions for people's behaviours. Memory for appearance is typically based on observable information (e.g., Lydia has brown eyes) and is stored like a 'picture in the mind'. Memory for behaviours is typically organized with respect to the person's goal in performing a behaviour (e.g., Mike swore at the cat because he was in a hurry and the cat was in his way) (Hoffman, Mischel and Mazze, 1981).

Typically, people remember others as a cluster of traits, appearances and behaviours, especially if they know them well, as is the case for close friends and family. According to Sedikides and Ostrom (1988), this produces more accurate person memories that are easily recalled. However, when we first encounter an individual, we may not be familiar enough with their traits to be able to organize a set of useful information about them. Instead, we may organize our impression of that person by judgements we make based on their group membership. As we will discuss later in this chapter, people heavily rely on information about groups – namely stereotypes – in order to make social judgements. But to what extent do people use person memory? Interestingly, not very much at all. Based on a review of a large number of findings, Hastie and Park (1986) concluded that people tend to form impressions in a more online fashion, that is, they rely disproportionately on information that comes in through the process of communication and impression formation rather than what is stored in memory.

Heuristics and biases in social cognition

We are by no means perfect scientists. We lack the time, information and sheer processing power to always make perfect judgements. Thus, we are prone to using certain *heuristics*. Heuristics are rules of thumb that can be used to make judgements that are not 100 per cent reliable, but which give an approximately accurate answer in most situations. In a set of studies that helped Daniel Kahneman later win the Nobel Prize for economics, he and his colleague Amos Tversky (Kahneman and Tversky, 1973; Tversky and Kahneman, 1974) discovered that people use three key heuristics to guide their decision making in everyday situations – the representativeness heuristic, the availability heuristic, and the anchoring and adjustment heuristic. We discuss these heuristics in turn and then discuss some other biases that affect our social cognition.

The representativeness heuristic

One of the most basic tasks in social cognition is categorization – essentially deciding which social categories people belong to. Categorizing in a reliable way requires a lot of information and complex reasoning processes that may not be within our reach. In order to get the job done, we often take a shortcut – we put people into a category simply on the basis that their attributes seem similar to, that is, representative of, other members of that category – the **representativeness heuristic**. For example, suppose you begin to get to know Tony, a neighbour in his thirties, who is shy, quietly spoken, very neat, helpful and always reading. If you were to guess his occupation, you might say that he is a librarian; certainly this occupation feels like a more likely guess than, say, a tradesman. This guess may often turn out to be right, and so the heuristic often serves us well. However, it is unreliable and can lead us into error. It can dangerously ignore so-called **base rates**; for example, the fact that there are many more managers than librarians and Tony is therefore much more likely to be a manager than a librarian. If you knew absolutely nothing about Tony except that he was a man in his thirties, and were still asked to guess his occupation, you would be much more likely to say he is a manager than a librarian.

The tendency to pay insufficient regard to base rates because of the representativeness heuristic is illustrated by the **conjunction fallacy**. Here is an example of the

Representativeness heuristic A cognitive shortcut where people are placed in categories based on their similarity or resemblance to the category.

Base rates Factual information about people and categories.

Conjunction fallacy The tendency to pay insufficient regard to base rates due to the representativeness heuristic.

conjunction fallacy – let us say that, after a while, you also notice that your neighbour Tony uses a hemp bag and cycles everywhere rather than driving. This, on top of everything else you know about him, is likely to tempt you into thinking he is not only a librarian but also an environmentalist. This is because he appears to be representative of both categories. Indeed, Tversky and Kahneman (1983) showed that when equipped with this kind of information, people indicated that conjunctions (that is, statements that suggest that people are a member of two categories), such as 'Tony is an environmentalist librarian', were judged more likely than either of the single statements, 'Tony is a librarian', or 'Tony is an environmentalist'. Logically, however, this cannot be correct. Each statement might be wrong, and if either is wrong, then the conjunction is wrong. If Tony is not an environmentalist, *or* he is not a librarian, then he is not an environmentalist librarian. Thus, the probability of the joint statement being correct can only ever be as high as the probability of the less likely single judgement, and it will be lower so long as the other statement is not 100 per cent guaranteed to be accurate.

FIGURE 3.13 The conjunction fallacy related to chronotype People are highly prone to the conjunction fallacy, but Bodenhausen (1990) demonstrated that this also depends on whether they are asked at their 'time of day', that is, whether they are a morning or evening person. Participants in their 'wrong' time of day were more likely to commit the fallacy than those in their 'right' time of day.

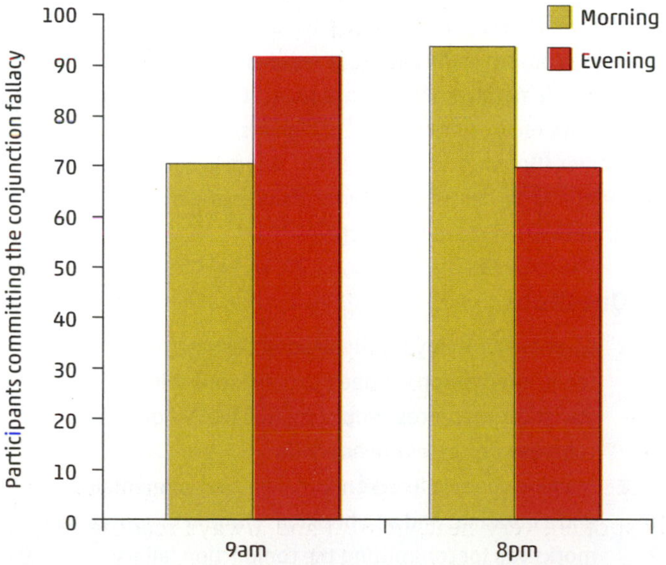

Bodenhausen (1990) obtained results that are consistent with the notion that we use heuristics especially when we lack the cognitive resources to think through our judgements thoroughly. He asked participants a set of standard questions to determine their chronotype, in other words, whether they are a 'morning' person who is at their most alert and clear-minded in the earlier part of the day, or an 'evening' person who is at their peak later in the day. He then put them through a test of the conjunction fallacy in the morning or afternoon, where participants were asked to make judgements based on information such as that given above in the example of Tony. Consistent with previous research, the majority of participants committed the error. However, participants were more likely to do it when they were not at their best time of day (e.g., 'evening' people taking part at 9am), and less likely to do it when the time of day suited them (e.g., 'evening' people taking part at 8pm). In a second experiment, Bodenhausen (1990) found that participants, at their 'wrong' time of day, were also more likely to rely on ethnic stereotypes when judging the guilt or innocence of a suspect (Figure 3.13). Under some circumstances, we may lean on stereotypes, just as we lean on the representativeness heuristic, when we do not have the cognitive resources to think more rationally. Bodenhausen's (1990) study also highlights the dependence of mind upon body – a major theme emerging in social psychology over the past few years.

Try it yourself Are you are morning or evening person? Run 'morningness-eveninginess questionnaire' through an internet search engine, and find out. There are free tests available online. You can also search for what your score means – what are the characteristics that are typical of morning vs. evening people?

CRITICAL FOCUS

The conjunction fallacy

As we discussed in Chapter 1, human beings are unlike other objects of scientific study – fruit flies or molecules, for example – in a very important respect, which is that they actively think about the experimental procedure they are undergoing, and tend to wonder why the experimenter is presenting them with the tasks and materials of the experiment. If you are a participant in a conjunction fallacy study, there is a good chance you will wonder, consciously or unconsciously, why the experimenter is telling you all this information that makes Tony look like both an environmentalist and a librarian. You are likely to infer they are making the case that Tony is both. Otherwise, the experimenter would seem to be breaking the rules of normal conversation by presenting you with irrelevant information. For example, if they do not want you to infer that Tony is an environmentalist, why are they telling you about his hemp bags and green transport habits?

Dulany and Hilton (1991) found evidence that the conjunction fallacy not only (or even necessarily) reveals something profound about the erroneous processing of probabilities. It also shows that participants follow normal conversational rules by inferring that the experimenter is suggesting to them that people (e.g., Tony) belong to both categories (e.g., environmentalist, librarian). Indeed, Slugoski and Wilson (1998) measured participants' conversational skills, reasoning that some people are better at understanding and following the rules of conversation than others. They found that those with better conversational skills were more prone to the conjunction fallacy and other apparent errors of judgement. Using good conversational logic and reading between the lines of what an expert is telling you about Tony may be a more effective, more social way to learn about your social environment than relying on base rate probabilities.

Other criticisms of the idea that people neglect base rates were put forward by Koehler (1996). One of Koehler's criticisms is that our social environment is full of rich and highly informative cues that sometimes tell us more than base rates ever could. Some of the cues in the conjunction fallacy are also so strong that they change the way the logic of probability should be applied. Let us say that Tony gives you two business cards. One is for his job as a librarian, the other for his role as an advocate in an environmentalist organization. You then have reasonably certain information that Tony is, indeed, both an environmentalist and a librarian. It is now less likely he is an environmentalist but not a librarian, because this would mean he is lying to you, and has gone to the trouble of giving you an invalid business card. Although the cues we considered before (e.g., the hemp bag, the cycling, the librarian-like demeanour) may be less certain than, say, business cards, if you have enough of them, you can become increasingly convinced that it is more likely that Tony belongs to both categories and not just one of them. In sum, the representativeness heuristic may be more reliable, in everyday life, than the use of base rates, which Tversky and Kahneman (1983) supposed to be more rational. However, it seems relatively clear that participants do not have such rich information in studies like Tversky and Kahneman's (1983). Thus, in these studies, it is reasonable to describe their judgement that Tony must be an environmentalist and a librarian as a fallacy, based on the apparent representativeness of Tony as a member of both categories. Even participants' reliance on the normal logic of conversation in such studies (Dulany and Hilton, 1991; Slugoski and Wilson, 1998) can be described as a normally useful but sometimes misleading heuristic.

Questions

1 Given that in everyday life we don't always have access to the information we need to make robust logical or statistical inferences, would you say that all our social cognitive processes are heuristic?

2 Imagine you say: 'I reckon Tony's an environmentalist and a librarian', and an obnoxious student in your class mocks you for committing the conjunction fallacy. Instead, they say: 'Tony's a librarian, but not an environmentalist.' Is their statement any more likely to be true than yours? Is their statement really any different from a conjunction fallacy?

3 If you can access the article by Koehler through your library website or the internet, and if you have time, read it and take a look at the open peer commentary. What criticisms did you find of Koehler's (1996) position?

The availability heuristic

Availability heuristic
Cognitive shortcut where the likelihood of an event is based on how quickly knowledge or ideas come to mind.

The **availability heuristic** is based on how available certain knowledge or ideas are to us when we make judgements – how fluently they come to mind. It is also known as the *ease-of-use heuristic*. A good illustration of the availability heuristic is to be seen in the aftereffects of seeing a good, scary film. People often enjoy 'freaking out' their friends after such films by playing tricks on them – jumping out of doorways at them and so on. Our readiness to interpret normally innocent stimuli such as strange or sudden noises, shadows and so on after seeing scary films is, in part, because scary interpretations of these stimuli are more mentally available to us. Thus, 'it's a monster' and other ideas – normally so far-fetched that they never occur to us – are much more at the forefront of our minds. Partly because the idea of monsters is so readily available, we assume, probably unconsciously, that it is plausible.

Schwarz, Bless, Strack et al. (1991) conducted one of the most well-known and compelling demonstrations of how the availability heuristic influences our thinking. To help you really get inside the logic of their experiment, we invite you to do the Try it yourself exercise below. It's worth the effort. Once you are finished, read on.

Try it yourself On a blank screen or piece of paper, write down 6 times you have been friendly, then 12 times you have been assertive. After doing this task, how friendly would you say you are? And how assertive?

Did you notice how difficult it is? The first few examples of assertiveness probably came easily, and then it became increasingly difficult. It would be understandable if you gave up at some point without generating all 12 examples. Schwarz et al. (1991) ensured that all their participants generated exactly the number of examples as they were instructed. Fortunately for *some* of their participants, they were not asked to generate as many as 12. Instead, they only had to generate 6. The number of examples (6 or 12) was the key independent variable in these experiments. The dependent variable was simple – participants were asked to rate how assertive they are. Intuitively, you might think that after generating 12 rather than only 6 examples of being assertive, participants would see themselves as more assertive. After all, they have just produced twice as much evidence of their assertiveness. But, in fact, participants saw themselves as less assertive after generating 12, rather than 6, examples of their assertiveness. Similarly, participants who were asked to recall 12 (versus 6) unassertive behaviours rated themselves as less unassertive.

These results appear to show that people were led to believe they were unassertive (or assertive) because they had found it difficult to remember occasions in which they had acted accordingly. In another of Schwarz et al.'s (1991) studies, participants were convinced that their childhood was less happy after being asked to recall more, rather than less, happy memories. This is exactly in keeping with the availability heuristic. If evidence for an idea is difficult to bring to mind, people infer that the idea is less plausible. This is, essentially, a *causal attribution* as we have been discussing throughout this chapter, that is: 'It's hard to remember times I was assertive because I'm not an assertive person.'

One of Schwarz et al.'s (1991) experiments provided clear evidence for the attributional processes underlying the availability heuristic. In addition to asking participants to generate either 6 or 12 assertive or unassertive behaviours, they were told either that most participants in a previous task had found this task difficult or easy. The rationale for this manipulation was participants should read more into their ease or difficulty of retrieval if they think it is unusual. If they think everyone finds the task similarly easy or difficult, then the effort they're expending probably won't seem to say anything about their assertiveness. The diagnostic condition provides participants with an alternative attribution for their difficulty in recalling many examples of being assertive, that is: 'It's not because I'm unassertive: others found this a difficult task too.' Under these conditions, participants who were asked to generate 12 examples of being assertive no longer assumed they were less assertive. If anything, the findings suggested that the more examples you listed, the more assertive you saw yourself as (see Figure 3.14).

FIGURE 3.14 Attributional processes underlying the availability heuristic Participants placed in a condition where ease of recall was perceived to be low (a) were able to attribute their failure to the difficult task rather than their lack of assertiveness. When ease of recall was high (b), participants attributed their difficulty in generating examples to their assertiveness.

Source: Data from Schwarz et al., 1991

(a) Ease of recall described as low (that is, difficult) for most other participants

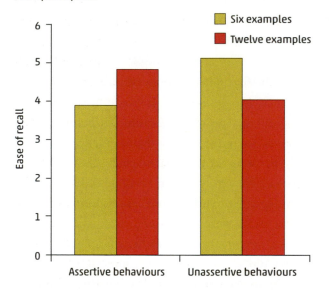

(b) Ease of recall described as high (e.g., easy) for most other participants

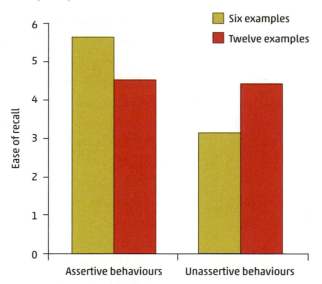

Exploring further The trick of manipulating the availability heuristic has been used widely in research to influence people's beliefs about a range of topics. Can you find any more examples? You could use Google Scholar or another database (Scopus, Web of Science) to find articles that have cited the paper by Schwarz et al. (1991). Search through the titles and abstracts until you find papers that have used their methodology. Alternatively, you could search for combinations of terms like 'availability heuristic', 'recall' and 'number of instances'.

The anchoring and adjustment heuristic

As we have seen, people have an amazing, although not infallible, ability to make quick, reasonably accurate, initial judgements on the basis of very little informa-

Anchoring and adjustment heuristic Cognitive shortcut where inferences are influenced by initial knowledge or information.

tion. According to Tversky and Kahneman (1974), we use these initial judgements as an anchor for our later judgements – the **anchoring and adjustment heuristic**. In other words, our first judgement is the one that, to a large extent, we stick with, making adjustments on the basis of later information. Let us say the first time you visit London, the streets are full of rubbish, and you do not visit some of the most attractive, well-kept areas of the city. Having made this first impression, it is hard to shake it off, even if you later come across lots of pieces of information suggesting that London really is a reasonably tidy place. Perhaps the refuse collectors had been on strike that day, and it had been one of the busiest shopping days of the year. Even if you see some statistics that support the idea that London is not an especially dirty city, it is likely that you are going to stick, somewhat, with your initial impression (Gilovich, Medvec and Savitsky, 2000).

This heuristic is often exploited by retailers. Imagine, for example, that you are on holiday and see a coat in a store that you really like, priced at €200. It is just a little more than you can afford, so, reluctantly, you put it back on the rack and walk out. You visit another store and see the same coat priced at €150. Seems like a good buy, right? There is every chance that you will now buy it. However, if the first store had been charging €100 for the coat, you would feel that the €150 price is excessive. This is because the first price you came across for the coat – either €100 or €200, is the *anchor* by which you judge other information. It is only slowly, through multiple experiences, that you would revise your impression of how much the coat is really worth. It is possible to apply these principles to a cause other than pure profit. One can manipulate the price people are willing to pay for an environmental cause using the logic of anchoring and adjustment. If led to believe that a large investment was necessary, then people are more willing later to pay a lesser, although still large, amount (Knetsch, 2010).

This also has a clear application to negotiation (Pruitt, 1981; Rubin and Brown, 1975). If you want to obtain a good price, start with a low, even insulting offer. So long as the vendor does not immediately walk away from the deal having taken offence, this initial low offer will advantage you by serving as the 'anchor' by which subsequent prices are judged. The adjustments made to the starting price will result in a better deal, for you, than if a higher offer were later adjusted (Benton, Kelley and Liebling, 1972; Northcraft and Neale, 1987; Ritov, 1996).

Other biases and errors in social cognition

Heuristics illustrate the duality of human beings discussed in the opening to this chapter. Human beings are very clever, in the sense that they use reasoning strategies that generally get them through the many social cognitive challenges of their everyday lives, but they are also not so clever, in that these strategies can seriously let them down. There are a number of other social cognitive errors that reflect this duality. People are prone to any number of biases and errors, because they use strategies that make a certain kind of sense, or help them cope with the demands of their lives. Creative thinking by experimental social psychologists exposes these strategies by catching participants in the act of making major, and sometimes amusing, errors.

Negativity bias

As we mentioned earlier, the valence (positivity or negativity) of information is important, and in particular, negative information tends to hold more weight in person perception than positive information (Fiske, 1980). Again, it is assumed that this is the case because negative information is more attention-grabbing. In particular, negative information may appear more distinctive or extreme and therefore attract more attention (e.g., Skowronski and Carlston, 1989). Negative information therefore tends to be more *diagnostic* of the target than positive information. Unfortunately, once negative information has been presented and this influences the overall impression that is formed, it is difficult to defuse the negative information. Even presenting a multitude of positive information may not be enough to reverse a negative impression (e.g., Hamilton and Zanna, 1974). Therefore, information valence is an important feature in impression formation. The bias towards negative information is pervasive, and makes a certain kind of sense. Being predisposed to see the worst in people, animals and other objects has always helped us to avoid disease, poisoning, being killed or eaten. Whether fortunately or unfortunately, it also helps people to protect their cultural norms and values by sanctioning and removing the 'bad apples' who threaten them. According to one review, negative things, be they people, events or traits, are seen as more contagious than good things (Rozin and Royzman, 2001).

Hindsight bias: the things that happened had to have happened

You may remember an occasion when you heard the result of a sporting match, election or some other competitive event. After hearing what happened, you said to yourself: 'Well, that was predictable!' But was it predictable, or is what you experienced the result of another common social psychological bias? In such a case, it is likely that the experience is an example of the **hindsight bias** – the tendency for people to exaggerate how much they could have predicted an outcome after it happened, which we discussed briefly in Chapter 1 with respect to people's perceptions of the predictability of social psychological findings (Choi and Nisbett, 2000; Fischhoff, 1975; Richard, Bond and Stokes-Zoota, 2001; Slovic and Fischhoff, 1977; Werth, Strack and Förster, 2002). Also known as the 'I knew it all along' phenomenon, the hindsight bias means that outcomes can seem inevitable and predictable once the outcome is known. In particular, people see the outcome as having been in line with their expectations, no matter what the outcome was. In other words, a completely different outcome would also be interpreted as being in line with one's expectations (Hawkins and Hastie, 1990).

Many studies have documented the hindsight bias. For example, Arkes, Wortman, Saville and Harkness (1981) showed that doctors were more likely to indicate they knew an uncommon diagnosis to be correct if told they were correct than if they were not. The bias has also been shown in legal settings (e.g., Casper,

Hindsight bias The tendency for people to exaggerate how much they could have predicted the outcome after it happened.

Benedict and Perry 1989; Harley, 2007). A study by Carli (1999) demonstrated the potential power of the hindsight bias. In this study, student participants read about a dating scenario between a pair called Barbara and Jack that ended in one of two ways – either with a marriage proposal or with a rape. The stories were identical in every respect except for the final line. Nevertheless, people saw the ending – based on the details of the story – as predictable in both situations. Two weeks later, the participants were also more likely to rate sentences as having been part of the story (when they were not), to the extent that the statement was consistent with the outcome of the story. For example, people were more likely to agree that statements such as 'Jack was a drinker' appeared in the rape story rather than the marriage proposal story. Likewise, they were more likely to agree that statements such as 'Jack gave Barbara roses' appeared in the marriage proposal story rather than the rape story. Therefore, people's tendency to process information in this biased manner may influence how they understand and interpret important events.

As we mentioned earlier, the hindsight bias also influences how people perceive real events. For example, Bryant and Guilbault (2002) examined people's predictions about whether US President Clinton would be convicted in his impeachment trial in 1999. After the trial, where he was found not guilty, participants reported that they knew all along what would happen. This judgement was made even though before the announcement of the acquittal, participants reported feeling that a conviction was likely. Thus, even when people report being unsure beforehand, they still report that they knew what would 'happen all along' when they know the outcome.

Various factors have been found to influence the hindsight bias. For example, Roese and Olson (1996) showed that hindsight biases are more likely to occur for negative outcomes than positive outcomes. They argued that this is the case because negative events tend to trigger more sense-making cognitions such as **counterfactual thinking** (imagining alternatives to reality, or how things might have been different) and causal attributions. Other researchers have found that it is possible to attenuate the hindsight bias under certain conditions. For example, Arkes, Faust, Guilmette and Hart (1988) showed that people succumbed to the hindsight bias less if they were asked to provide at least one reason for the event. Arguably, if people are asked to provide concrete reasons, perhaps they have to rely less on 'filling the gaps'. Casper, Benedict and Perry (1989) observed hindsight biases in jury decision making and found that pre-existing attitudes also influence the extent to which people succumb to the hindsight bias (see also Harley, 2007).

What causes the hindsight bias? Hoffrage, Hertwig and Gigerenzer (2000) argued that the bias may be adaptive. Specifically, after receiving feedback about an event, people update their knowledge, which leads them to exaggerate the extent to which they knew the result. For example, after finding out that her boyfriend cheated on her, a young woman has learned something about her boyfriend – that he is not terribly faithful. Armed with this new and unfortunate knowledge, his cheating on her does not seem to be so surprising (see Figure 3.15).

Counterfactual thinking
Imagining alternatives to reality.

FIGURE 3.15 The cheating boyfriend When this woman finds out that her boyfriend has been cheating on her, to what extent will she see this as expected?

In another series of studies, Nestler, Blank and von Collani (2008) found that people who were under conditions of high cognitive load were more likely to commit hindsight bias, suggesting that the psychological processes required to make accurate, non-biased judgements about outcomes require effort. Other researchers have argued that motivations may affect hindsight bias. People want to feel that events, especially negative events, are within their control, so that they can obtain some sense of optimism about the future. Thus, they tend to be less prone to hindsight bias following negative rather than positive events (Pezzo and Beckstead, 2008; Pezzo and Pezzo, 2007).

Exploring further There may be other causes of hindsight bias. Use an internet search engine or psychology articles database to see if you can identify other reasons why it may be useful to have 'known it all along'.

Question to consider Reread question 3 at the start of the chapter. Why do you think people often say that social psychology findings are 'obvious'? As an exercise, think of a classic study in social psychology and make some arguments for why the findings were not predictable.

Confirmation bias

Confirmation bias The tendency to notice or search for information that confirms one's beliefs and not notice (or even ignore) information that disconfirms one's beliefs.

People tend to seek and to notice information that confirms their beliefs more than information that disconfirms their beliefs. They will even go so far as to ignore information that disconfirms their beliefs. This tendency is called the **confirmation bias** (Trope and Thompson, 1997). Alternatively, they may ask questions designed to confirm expectations. For example, if you meet a person from France for the first time, you might ask them about their love of cheese and red wine, or if you meet someone from Australia, you might ask them questions about going to the beach. Restricting the amount of information a person is able to provide enables expectations and stereotypes to be confirmed. Perceivers can therefore seek out information that confirms what they think.

Research by Westen, Blagov, Harenski et al. (2006) demonstrated that people interpret information about others in ways that confirm their political leanings. During the 2004 presidential election in the USA, participants from both the Democrat and Republican 'sides' were shown multiple statements about the Democratic candidate John Kerry, the Republican candidate George W. Bush, or a neutral public figure. Sometimes, these seemed to expose contradictions in what these politicians had said. For example, Mr Bush was reported as saying that Ken

Lay, the CEO of Enron, was a great friend of his, but later, after the scandalous collapse of Enron, he denied knowing him. The researchers found that the contradictory information was evaluated differently depending on the pre-existing political leanings of the participants. Specifically, participants were much more likely to interpret statements as genuinely revealing a contradictory stance by the politician concerned if they were personally opposed to them. In this way, participants interpreted information in ways that confirmed their original beliefs. A further aspect of this study is that participants' evaluations were carried out while they were in an MRI scanner, which monitors brain activity. As participants rated apparently contradictory statements about their preferred candidate (but not an opposing candidate), emotional centres in the brain were aroused. The authors concluded that their results capture an active, emotion-laden process of dealing with information that is contradictory to one's beliefs.

Evaluation by association

As we have seen, people use associations between things to learn about causal relationships in their environment – if X and Y co-occur, there is a chance that X is causing Y. Indeed, this associative reasoning is the essence of how animals learn, and has been recognized by psychologists since Pavlov conceived the principles of classical conditioning in the 19th century. The human mind is largely associative – people who associate with each other are seen as having similar properties, and positive or negative perceptions of one stimulus can 'rub off' onto our impressions of another stimulus that is associated with it in our minds. Our associative minds, of course, are gleefully exploited by advertisers, who seek to pair a product or brand with positive associations, such as attractive models, values or lifestyles. Our associative minds can also lead us to like or dislike people by the mere fact of association. For example, relatives and friends of mentally ill or overweight people experience **stigma by association**, being devalued because of their association with a stigmatized individual. This happens among children as well as adults (Latner, Roseall and Simmonds, 2007), and can have negative consequences for the psychological health of the targets of stigma by association (Östman and Kjellin, 2002). It may be that sometimes there is a logic behind stigma by association. People who are related to stigmatized individuals, or who choose to spend time in their company, really may be more likely to share some of their characteristics. However, stigma by association is, sometimes, simply unfounded. Hebl and Mannix (2003), for example, found that male job applicants were denigrated simply because they were seated next to an overweight (vs. normal weight) woman while waiting to be interviewed. This 'mere proximity' version of stigma by association was found regardless of whether participants had anti-fat attitudes, whether they thought they knew them, or whether they were described as a highly intelligent, award-winning student.

The associative nature of impression formation has an important implication – be careful what you say about others. Mud sticks, but it sticks to the person throwing the mud, as well as the person getting hit by it. Building on their earlier work on spontaneous inference (Carlston and Skowronski, 1994), Skowronski,

Stigma by association The tendency for people to devalue someone because of their association with a stigmatized individual.

Carlston, Mae and Crawford (1998) introduced an ingenious twist. In their new experiments, participants were presented with a photograph of a person, with a caption indicating how they described the behaviour of someone else. For example, imagine one of the photos was of you, describing something one of your friends did. Later, people associated the trait implied by the behaviours with the person who had described them – not only with the person who had done them. They labelled this phenomenon *spontaneous trait transference*. This is another social cognitive bias that happens automatically – it is dependent on 'linking' things together associatively, rather than 'thinking' about them consciously and logically. Sometimes, therefore, what you say about others says something – to others – about you (see also Douglas and Sutton, 2006).

Projection and false consensus

Projection The process whereby people attribute their own characteristics (e.g., attitudes, emotions) to others.

It is difficult to know what others are thinking or feeling, or to predict what they are going to do. One of the tricks we have up our sleeves is projection. **Projection** is the process by which we attribute our own characteristics (be they attitudes, emotions, habits or traits) to other people. This concept made its way into social psychology through the writings of Freud, who saw projection as a defence mechanism – a way of denying that one has unwanted needs or desires by attributing them to other people. However, social psychologists do not use the term in this way any more. It is used as a way of solving a social cognitive problem – working other people out on the basis of limited information – rather than a way of denying one's own nature.

To illustrate, Douglas and Sutton (2011) asked British undergraduates to evaluate 17 conspiracy theories, such as the theory that the Apollo moon landings were faked, or that Princess Diana was murdered. The more highly participants had earlier scored on a measure of the trait of Machiavellianism – an amoral willingness to exploit others – the more they were inclined to endorse these conspiracy theories (seeing them as true, plausible, coherent, interesting and worth considering). The relationship between Machiavellianism and endorsement of these conspiracy theories was mediated or driven by personal willingness to conspire. In short, Machiavellian participants were more likely to indicate that they would personally play a part in conspiracies such as the murder of Princess Diana, and, for this reason, were more likely to see conspiracy theories as believable. In a second study, Douglas and Sutton asked half their participants to recall a time when they had helped another person out. The intention was to make these participants feel a little more moral and thus less willing to conspire than the control group. As predicted, participants who recalled helping someone out were less willing to take part in conspiracies and, as a result, were less likely to find conspiracy theories to be true, plausible, coherent and so on (see Figure 3.16).

FIGURE 3.16 To conspire or not conspire?

Magical thinking

Magical thinking Thinking based on non-rational assumptions about the ability of events to affect each other in ways that cannot be accounted for by the known laws of physics.

Research suggests that people are susceptible to what is known as **magical thinking** – thinking based on assumptions that are not rational, but are still compelling (Rozin and Nemeroff, 1990). For example, many hold the belief that when two objects touch each other, they pass on properties to each other (law of contagion). Also, many believe that objects that resemble each other share fundamental properties (law of similarity). Thinking about social events can, therefore, be susceptible to magical thinking. Rozin, Millman and Nemeroff (1986) demonstrated how people's behaviour is influenced by these laws of magical thinking – also known as *sympathetic magic*. For example, they showed that laundered shirts previously worn by a disliked person were less desirable than those previously worn by a neutral or liked person. Rozin et al. also demonstrated that people are less accurate at throwing darts at photographs of liked (versus disliked) individuals.

Also, as we saw in Chapter 2, people's need for control means that they sometimes see connections between events, even if these connections seem rather magical and unrealistic. Sometimes, these cognitions are related to person perception. For example, Pronin, Wegner, McCarthy and Rodriguez (2006) had participants perceive that they had harmed another person using a voodoo hex. The connection between the hex and the harm caused to the other person was seen as stronger if the participant had first been induced to harbour evil thoughts towards the victim. Thus, magical thinking and superstition play a part in how we view others and the social world.

Exploring further 'Harry Potter films "boost magical thinking" in children', according to Subbotsky, Hysted and Jones (2010). They found that children who watched extracts from these films were more creative, solving problems more easily and creatively (e.g., 'I would fly away on my broomstick') than children who did not view the extracts (e.g., 'I would run away'). Perhaps try to find the article in your own time and think about some of the possible implications of these findings for social cognition in children.

The nature of social cognition

As we have seen in this chapter and also Chapter 2, there are plenty of reasons to doubt the view that people are always rational, conscious thinkers. In this section, we consider research showing that much of our social cognition seems to happen outside our conscious awareness. Second, much of our social cognition seems to happen outside the self altogether. Further, social cognition is not only done individually, but also collectively. It is therefore important to outline what is 'social' about social cognition.

Automatic versus controlled social cognition

Historically, people have been thought to be largely in control of their behaviour, making conscious decisions about what to do. But as we saw in Chapter 2, people's thoughts, feelings and behaviours are often influenced by factors they are unaware of (Nisbett and Wilson, 1977), people erroneously think their behaviour is influenced by things that do not affect it (e.g, Leavitt and Christenfeld, 2011), and are prone to thinking they intentionally did things they didn't do (Wegner and Wheatley, 1999). Over the centuries, the importance of unconscious thoughts, feelings and decisions has been highlighted by religion and literature. However, Freud was the first to place the unconscious centre stage in psychology. Freud's ideas largely fell out of favour in experimental psychology and, with it, mainstream social psychology. However, since the 1970s, researchers have paid increasing attention to the aspects of people's mental and social lives that happen outside their awareness. Now, as we shall see throughout this book, many findings highlight the importance of the unconscious on our social lives – on topics as diverse as aggression, persuasion, intergroup relations, and the environment.

A number of theories in social psychology have distinguished between *controlled processing* – thoughts, feelings and emotions we would describe as conscious in the traditional sense – and *automatic processing*, which we would not. There are four features that, together, define whether a psychological process is automatic or controlled:

1 *Awareness:* People are often unaware of stimuli that are influencing them. As we shall read below, people can be influenced by visual stimuli or subliminal primes on a computer screen, that is, those they did not consciously notice. In other instances, they may be aware of a stimulus, but unaware that it is influencing their behaviour (remember in Chapter 2 how Nisbett and Wilson's shoppers preferred items on the right of a display, but did not realize it).

2 *Intention:* Some psychological processes may happen without us intending to start them. For example, studies have shown that sitting behind an impressive desk causes people to pursue power over others, without being aware of their goal (Chen, Lee-Chai and Bargh, 2001).

3 *Controllability:* Some psychological processes are difficult for people to stop or prevent. Sometimes, this is simply because they are unaware of those processes. But in other cases, such as when they engage in unwanted stereotyping of other groups, people find it difficult to stop, as we shall see in Chapter 12 (Devine, 1989).

4 *Efficiency:* An automatic process does not require conscious attention, whereas a controlled process does. Think back to Gilbert and Osborne's (1989) study of the correspondence bias, encountered earlier in the chapter. People were prone to the bias only when under cognitive load – when their conscious attention was consumed by another task. When their attention was free to focus on forming an impression of stimulus persons, they were not prone to the bias. This suggested that the processes that led to the correspondence bias are automatic, and the processes that correct the bias are controlled.

Theories that distinguish between automatic and controlled processes are known as *dual process theories*. However, it is important to note that the distinc-

FIGURE 3.17 Bargh's (1994) four horsemen of automaticity When people are unaware of a psychological process, did not intend to start it, cannot control when they stop it, and when the process is efficient, in the sense that it does not consume people's limited attentional resources, it can be said to be fully automatic. Most psychological processes of interest to social psychologists satisfy some but not all these criteria, so can be said to have automatic and controlled features.

tion is not as sharp as you might think. Bargh (1994) described awareness, intention, controllability and efficiency as the four jointly sufficient conditions – or the four horsemen – of automaticity (see Figure 3.17). He also noted that there are few, if any, cases in which interesting social psychological processes meet all four criteria for automaticity (see also Kahneman and Treisman, 1984). You may intend to form an impression of another person, for example, but be unaware of how you do it. Walking down the street is an efficient process, in the sense that it is so learned that you do not need to consciously think about it most of the time, but at the same time you can control it, that is, you can stop it if you want to. Thus, most psychological processes can be said to have both automatic and controlled features.

That said, there are some truly remarkable demonstrations of automaticity in social psychology. Studies using the technique of *priming* – activating associations in memory – give social psychologists insight into how our thoughts can influence other thoughts, and even our behaviours. One well-known example is a study by Bargh, Chen and Burrows (1996), who asked participants to complete a sentence containing words such as 'retired', 'wrinkle' and 'sentimental'. After doing so, the experimenters observed participants walking down the corridor as they left the laboratory and found that those who had been primed with age-related words moved more slowly. In another study, Chen and Bargh (1997) presented photographed faces of Black men to White university students so quickly (13 ms) that the participants did not notice them. Later, these participants behaved in a more hostile way towards an interaction partner while playing a collaborative game. The rationale is that a 'Black men are hostile' stereotype, current in the USA, activated the concept of hostility and so caused participants to behave in a hostile way. Indeed, much of our thinking and behaving is influenced by events or observations of which we are not aware, and, as such, much of our social cognition is implicit rather than explicit.

ETHICS AND RESEARCH METHODS

Experimental control and replication

The classic studies by Bargh, Chen and Burrows (1996) produced some of the most widely cited and striking results in social psychology in recent decades. However, relatively few direct replications of these results have been published. Recently, a Belgian team of researchers published the results of two attempts to replicate the Bargh et al. (1996) study, in which participants had walked more slowly after being primed with an elderly stereotype (Doyen, Klein, Pichon and Cleeremans, 2012). Closely following the method of the original study, they observed no effect. However, in their second study, they did observe the original effect when the research assistant running the study was led to expect that participants would walk slower after being exposed to the elderly stereotype. They concluded that unconscious priming effects were likely to explain Bargh et al.'s original effects, but not in the way that Bargh et al. thought. Participants appeared to walk more slowly, because they had unconsciously been influenced by the expectations of the experimenter, *not* by the elderly prime. If Doyen et al. are right, the participants in their study (and perhaps Bargh et al.'s) were remarkably similar to Clever Hans – picking up and conforming to subtle cues in the experimenter's behaviour. This is a classic case of a 'demand characteristic' in experimental social psychology (see Chapter 1). Further research is required to determine whether the original studies of Bargh et al. (1996) are replicable without such instructions to the experimenter, and, indeed, whether the findings of Doyen et al. (2012) are themselves replicable.

This points to a couple of problems inherent in mainstream social psychology. The first is that without careful experimental control, experimenters' biases may subtly influence the results of their research, even when they are setting out to collect data in a scrupulously honest and professional way. Researchers, like participants themselves, are prone to automatic social thought, emotion and behaviour that can influence their findings. More generally, in principle, there is always – or almost always – another way to explain a given finding than that put forward by the researchers who obtained it. The second problem is that biases in the publication process, combined with the way researchers use statistics to test their ideas, can lead to overconfidence in the results of published findings. As noted in Chapter 1, every finding could arise from chance alone – so, in principle, the results of Bargh et al.'s studies, like those of any other studies, could have been a 'fluke'.

In sciences like social psychology, researchers try to reduce the risk of making false conclusions by subjecting their results to *significance testing*, which determines how likely it is that a given result could have emerged by chance alone. Generally speaking, the results are seen as signifying a 'real' effect rather than a 'fluke' if $p < .05$, that is, if there is less than a 5 per cent or 1 in 20 possibility that the results could have happened by chance. The problem is, run a study 20 times over, and even if there is no 'real effect', chances are you will observe a significant result, $p < .05$, at some point. In general, it is hard to publish 'null effects', where the difference between conditions or the relationship between variables is not statistically significant. One reason for this is that journals want to

showcase new and eye-catching findings; another is that null effects can be hard to interpret (was the idea wrong? were the methods inappropriate?). Yet another reason is that when a finding has been shown to be significant before, a failed attempt to replicate that finding can be especially troubling and hard to understand, and so is less likely to be accepted by the scientific community. Thus, instead of seeing the light of day, these findings tend to languish, unpublished, in the 'file drawers' of researchers. This file drawer problem is a major issue in sciences like social psychology that rely on significance testing. The more unpublished null effects there are, the less confident we can be in the published tip of the iceberg. The significant published effects need to be seen in the context of the number of studies that have failed to replicate them – and this number is generally unknown. The published effects are increasingly likely to have emerged either by chance or because of some unreported aspect of the way the original study was done; for example, Doyen et al.'s results suggest that the experimenter running the studies reported by Bargh et al. may not have been as 'blind' to conditions as was suggested by their written account of the methods.

Also, meta-analytic investigations help, where the researchers ask their peers to provide them with unpublished data, allowing published results to be considered in the context of unpublished attempts to replicate them. Continued replication is crucial, so that null effects can see the light of day. At the time of writing, several of our colleagues are embarking on a programme of research to attempt to replicate key findings in social psychology.

Questions

1   The article by Doyen et al. (2012) is published in *PLOS ONE*, an online, open access journal. Use an internet search engine to find and read it (it's brief). If you have access to the original article by Bargh et al. (1996), also read it. What differences in method do you see? How exact is the replication?

2   Find out about the programme of research in which scientists are attempting to replicate major findings from social psychology. Search the term 'Reproducibility Project'. What advantages and disadvantages are presented by this project for the discipline of social psychology?

This distinction between automatic and controlled processes is often described using other terms – you will often read about implicit vs. explicit, conscious vs. conscious, or heuristic vs. systematic processes. For example, in Chapter 4, you will read about the heuristic-systematic model of persuasion, which separates the different social cognitive processes that occur when people encounter persuasive stimuli. On the one hand, there are the systematic (or controlled) processes that involve careful reasoning and close attention to information, and on the other, there are the heuristic processes where people do not consciously attend to information but use heuristics to process what they see (Chaiken, 1987; Chaiken, Liberman and Eagly, 1989). The notion of implicit and explicit processes runs throughout the study of social cognition as researchers attempt to understand what people can and cannot control about their thinking, feeling and acting.

One interesting development in the study of the unconscious side of social cognition is the finding that actions often influence thought. For example, a growing body of research suggests that the physical movements people engage in while they are evaluating stimuli (e.g., objects, people) determine how the stimuli are judged. Specifically, engaging in behaviours that typically accompany positive attitudes tend to lead people to evaluate stimuli favourably, whereas engaging in behaviours that typically accompany negative attitudes tends to lead people to rate the stimuli less favourably. For example, Strack, Martin and Stepper (1988) asked participants to either hold a pen between their teeth (an action that facilitates the use of muscles typically associated with smiling), or between their lips (an action that inhibits the use of muscles typically associated with smiling). They were then asked to watch a series of cartoons. It was found that participants who watched the cartoons under conditions that facilitate the smiling muscles rated the cartoons as more humorous than those in the inhibiting condition. This kind of effect has come to be known as 'embodiment' or 'embodied social cognition'. We discuss embodiment and associated research in more detail in Chapter 4.

The social nature of social cognition

What exactly is social about social cognition? Social cognition assumes that 'real-world' social issues and problems (e.g., prejudice) can be understood with respect to basic cognitive processes. Thus, the core topic of study for social cognition researchers is people, specifically how people think about themselves and other people. The discipline is therefore different from cognitive psychology, in that it focuses on how people see themselves within their social world, and not just how they perceive other 'things' such as inanimate objects. Understanding the 'social' in social cognition relies on the distinction between people and things. People perceive their environment and are perceived by others within it. People intentionally interact and influence those around them. Crucially, much of social cognition is *shared*. For example, we read about stereotypes earlier in this chapter – generalizations about groups and the characteristics of members of groups – and these beliefs are shared among many people. The sharedness of social cognition makes it inherently social.

By applying cognitive psychology to social phenomena, social cognition offers a powerful way to understand such phenomena. However, one drawback is that early social cognition neglected many social and emotional aspects of social experiences and it therefore became isolated from other research being carried out in social psychology. Many critics of social cognition argued that the area was overly reductionist, that is, it reduced complex social phenomena down to their most basic cognitive level and there was very little left that was truly social (Forgas, 1983; Markus and Zajonc, 1985; Moscovici, 1982; Zajonc, 1989). Markus and Zajonc (1985) went so far as to say that the restricted focus on cognition would be short-lived. It is true that social cognition has often dealt with social phenomena in a rather reductionist way, and recent developments in social neuroscience – the study of brain correlates of behaviour (see Chapters 1 and 15) – are even more reductionist. However, other areas of social cognition are much less reductionist and pay closer attention to the social context. For example, the way people think about and act towards social groups draws heavily on social cognitive theories such as social identity theory (Chapters 10 and 11). How and why people comply and conform demonstrates how thinking and behaviour is influenced by the social context (Chapter 9). Research on attitudes and persuasion shows how behaviour and individuals' attitudes are heavily influenced by social forces (Chapters 4 and 6). Social cognition also now pays closer attention to the emotions that people feel in social contexts (Chapter 4). These developments distinguish social cognition from cognitive psychology, and keep social cognition relevant to social psychology as a whole.

More recently, researchers have been paying increasing attention to how social cognition is 'social', in the sense that it is done collaboratively, and not just by individuals (e.g., Holtgraves and Kashima, 2008; Smith and Collins, 2009; Sutton, 2010). This is the notion of *distributed social cognition*. You engage in distributed social cognition all the time, even if you're not aware of it. When you are talking about a party or family occasion and ask someone to remind you of the name of the person who said something embarrassing, you are engaging in distributed memory (memory that is distributed across more than one person, within a social network). When you are gossiping (Chapter 5), you are effectively engaging in collective person perception, working together to decide who's clever, trustworthy or to be avoided. Stereotypes, group norms and cultural beliefs are all outcomes of distributed social cognition, which we will encounter several times throughout this book. To study social cognition does not entail a focus on the private mental processes of the individual mind.

Chapter summary

In this chapter, we considered two key social processes in social cognition – causal attribution and person perception – and discussed various errors that social perceivers can make while engaging in these processes. We also discussed the nature of social cognition. Throughout this chapter, you will have learned that:

- Social cognition is the study of the cognitive underpinnings of social thought and behaviour.
- Causal attribution – the process of assigning a cause to an event – is an important social process that can contribute to feelings about the self and others. In many respects, people are rational and scientific in the way they explain events, but sometimes they are prone to bias, especially when lacking time, motivation or information. This can affect all aspects of their life, such as their emotional wellbeing, relationships and educational performance.
- Two well-known 'errors' in attribution are the correspondence bias (the tendency to attribute behaviours to stable, underlying personality traits without sufficient evidence) and the actor-observer bias (the tendency for actors to attribute their own behaviour to the situation and for observers to explain behaviours in terms of personality traits).
- Other biases and errors include the self-serving attribution bias (the tendency for people to attribute the causes of negative events to aspects that deflect blame from the self), self-serving biases (seeing the self as better than average), unrealistic optimism (viewing outcomes for the self as better than outcomes for others), the illusion of control (belief that we have more control over the world and the things that happen than we actually do), the false consensus effect (the tendency to view one's own behaviours as more typical than they really are) and the false uniqueness effect (the tendency to see the self as more likely to perform positive behaviours and be less biased than others).
- The study of person perception (or impression formation) is the study of how people make judgements about others, and the information they use to make these judgements.
- Asch's configural model suggests that we form a holistic impression of people that integrates a small number of important cues. These are known as central and peripheral cues. The algebraic model suggests that people assign positive and negative valence to various person attributes and combine them to make a general evaluation of a person. It is generally accepted that people use a weighted average of traits to make the impression, but some information (especially negative information) tends to be weighted more heavily.

- First impressions are quick, accurate and powerful. Factors influencing person perception include a person's physical appearance (especially their attractiveness). Sometimes, traits people observe first tend to be assigned the greatest importance (the primacy effect), but they often give more attention to information that is observed most recently (the recency effect).
- The notion of associative networks allows social psychologists to explain how they integrate and organize information about people into memory.
- Because we often lack the processing power to make perfect judgements, we often rely on heuristics, or rules of thumb, that enable us to make approximate judgements. Examples of such heuristics are the representative heuristic (people are placed into categories based on their resemblance to the category), the availability heuristic (where the likelihood of an event is based on how quickly knowledge or ideas come to mind), the anchoring and adjustment heuristic (where inferences are influenced by initial knowledge or information), the negativity bias (the tendency to add more weight to negative information), the hindsight bias (the tendency for people to exaggerate how much they could have predicted an outcome after it happened), the confirmation bias (the tendency for people to notice information that confirms their beliefs and often ignore information that disconfirms them) and evaluation by association (assigning value to a person because of their association with another person).
- Other biases include projection (the attribution of our characteristics onto other people) and magical thinking (thinking based on non-rational assumptions). Emotions also strongly influence social cognition and behaviour.
- Much of our thinking and behaviour is influenced by events or observations of which we are not aware. Also, our thoughts are often influenced by our behaviours so that our cognition is 'embodied'.
- The 'social' in social cognition comes from the unique focus on how people think about themselves and other people. Social cognition may sometimes be too reductionist, but recent developments have attempted to reintroduce more of the 'social' in social cognition.

In this chapter, we have focused on how people understand the social world. In Chapter 4, we focus on how people judge and evaluate the social world. We discuss the core psychological topics of attitudes, emotions, social judgement and decision making.

Essay questions

At the beginning of the chapter, we asked you to consider these questions:

1 Louisa really wants to be elected as the president of the psychology society at her university. She is required to give a speech to the group. Would she be best to present all her positive attributes or just a few of the most positive? What other factors might she take into account?

2 Ray meets Alan at a party and takes an instant dislike to him. He can't put his finger on it exactly, but he does not like Alan. What social psychological processes can account for this instant dislike?

3 Jamie tells his friends he is studying social psychology and shares with them the findings of his final-year dissertation.

His friends laugh and say the results were predictable and obvious. What could you say about this?

Having read this chapter, these questions could also be framed as the following essay questions, which you can attempt in preparation for your examinations:

1 Describe and evaluate two different approaches to person perception.

2 How do people form first impressions and how accurate are they?

3 What is the hindsight bias, what causes it and what are some of its consequences?

Some further reading

Augoustinos, M., Walker, I. and Donaghue, N. (2006) *Social Cognition: An Integrated Introduction*. London: Sage. Alternative approaches to the study of social cognition (e.g., social representations and discourse analysis) are integrated with mainstream social cognition in this comprehensive volume.

Dijksterhuis, A. (2010) Automaticity and the unconscious. In S.T. Fiske, D.T. Gilbert and G. Lindzey (eds) *Handbook of Social Psychology* (5th edn, vol. 1, pp. 228–67). New York: Wiley. Up-to-date coverage of one of the key topics in social psychology: how social cognitive processes are often automatic.

Fiske, S.T. and Macrae, C.N. (2012) *The Sage Handbook of Social Cognition*. London: Sage. First handbook on social cognition, with contributions from 56 of the leading authors in the area.

Fiske, S.T. and Taylor, S.E. (2007) *Social Cognition: From Brains to Culture*. New York: McGraw-Hill. Comprehensive and detailed book on social cognition, highlighting cutting-edge research in

social neuropsychology, mainstream social cognition and cultural psychology.

Hilton, D.J. (2007) Causal explanation: From social perception to knowledge-based causal attribution. In A.W. Kruglanski and E.T. Higgins (eds) *Social Psychology: Handbook of Basic Principles* (pp. 232–53). New York: Guilford Press. Comprehensive review of the literature on social explanation and causal attribution.

McClure, J. (1991) *Explanations, Accounts, and Illusions: A Critical Analysis*. Cambridge: Cambridge University Press. Detailed analysis of research on social attribution and social thinking.

Trope, Y. and Gaunt, R. (2007) Attribution and person perception. In M.A. Hogg and J. Cooper (eds) *The Sage Handbook of Social Psychology: Concise Student Edition* (pp. 176–94). London: Sage. Detailed but readable overview of the literature on attribution and person perception.

 Visit the companion website at www.palgrave.com/psychology/suttondouglas for access to a wide range of resources to help you get to grips with this chapter.

Applying social psychology

Applying social cognition to business problems

Imagine you are a consultant employed by businesses and charities to advise on how they can apply psychological theories and findings.

1 One of your clients is in the property business and relies heavily on the ability to negotiate excellent prices for the properties it buys. Find three findings in this chapter and explain to the client how they could be used to help them negotiate good prices (write no more than 600 words in total).

2 Another client is a charity which, unfortunately, lost a lot of money when it invested in a fund that subsequently collapsed. A major media outlet has published an exposé blaming the loss on the management of the charity, arguing that the charity could and should have avoided the loss. This publicity is potentially damaging to the charity, as it is likely to deter donors from giving their money. It wants you to help it in preparing a response to the story. In particular, it is interested in the psychological biases that may lead people to assign blame incorrectly. What errors and biases from this chapter might have contributed to the heaping of blame on the charity by the media outlet?

3 An investment bank finds that its traders are particularly prone to the confirmation bias – once they decide a trade is a good one, they tend to ignore evidence to the contrary. Using internet search engines or databases, can you find how the confirmation bias can be counteracted, helping traders to make better and less risky trades?

Blind spot in social psychology

Why are morning people morning people?

1 Recall from the Critical focus box in Chapter 2 how the ego depletion effect may depend on people's belief that their self-control runs out after a while. People who think you run out of self-control, end up running out of self-control. Can you apply a similar argument to Bodenhausen's (1990) study? Might the increased use of stereotypes by 'evening people' in the morning depend on their belief that they can't think very well in the morning? Have a think about this and see if you can write down an argument for your position in three or fewer sentences.

2 Can you think of a way to measure people's beliefs in their own cognitive capacities at different times of the day? Propose a questionnaire of three or fewer items.

3 Can you think of a study using the measure you have developed? The aim of this study would be to test whether people's beliefs in their own cognitive capacities at different times of the day are correlated with their use of stereotypes. More generally, we are aiming to test whether morning people use stereotypes in the evening (and vice versa), just because they think they're not capable of processing information very well at the 'wrong' time of day. Assume that you can use exactly the same measure of stereotyping and chronotype as Bodenhausen (1990) used. We are interested here in how you use your new measure.

4 Can you think of a way to manipulate people's beliefs in their cognitive capacities? In other words, can you 'trick' a morning person into thinking they are clever and complex thinkers even in the evening?

5 Can you think of an experiment (or quasi-experiment) using the manipulation you have developed? In other words, can you manipulate people's beliefs in their own cognitive capacities at various times of the day, and show that this overrides their chronotype?

Student project

Victim blame in stranger and acquaintance rape

James Sims studied as an undergraduate student at the University of Kent and his dissertation supervisor was Dr Robbie Sutton. His research examined the attributions that people make in rape case scenarios. We covered the topic of attribution – how people explain events and behaviours – in this chapter.

My topic and aims

When I looked at the topic of stranger and acquaintance rape, I was shocked at how badly victims are treated, and wanted to explore why victims are treated as though they have committed the crime themselves.

The current research on rape attitudes highlights how people ascribe a lot of blame to victims when they know their attacker, as they are seen as 'leading them on' or acting in a manner that may suggest they are 'asking for it'. These shocking judgements run through society, and such views appear to have been normalized because of the existence of rape myths. These attitudes become an issue when a perpetrator is put on trial, as members of the jury are likely to have these common misconceptions and negative attitudes about the victim, which can affect their ability to give a fair and accurate judgement based on the evidence provided. It is hard to secure a conviction, as the only witnesses in the crime are the two people involved: the victim and the perpetrator. Acquaintance rapes are the most common type of rape, and the difficulty in securing a conviction is additionally hampered by the fact that consensual sex is more of a possibility between two people who are acquainted.

My study examined the issue of victim blame in stranger and acquaintance rape as a function of whether the rape was achieved or merely attempted. Higher blame for an achieved rape was predicted, as just world theory highlights that people are likely to struggle with the concept that a person has been a victim of a horrific crime for no reason, so tend to reach a conclusion that the victim must have done something to deserve the attack. In other words, that she must have 'led him on' or was 'asking for it'.

My methods

Participants were given questionnaires containing a short, easy to understand scenario of an alleged rape. The questions that followed were quick to complete, and focused on victim and perpetrator blame, derogation, likeability and trust violation. ANOVA and mediation analyses were conducted to explore whether victims of rape are blamed after an attempted or an achieved rape.

The mediation analyses were challenging, as they had not been taught to us at undergraduate level. But having sought advice from my supervisor and read up on some articles about it, a full mediation analysis was conducted on trust violation, which helped explain the relationship between acquaintanceship and levels of victim blame.

My findings and their implications

Initial results indicated that victims were blamed more in a stranger rape scenario, and a mediation analysis indicated that violation of trust fully mediated the relationship between acquaintanceship and levels of victim blame. The analysis highlighted that because a victim is entitled to trust someone she knows, she is therefore blamed less as a result. This was an unexpected finding, which was contrary to current research findings. There were no significant effects found regarding rape outcome, which was the primary aim of the study.

The results have great repercussions for future research, as they highlight that there are some cases in which the traditional stranger/acquaintance effect can be reversed. Although this effect was not originally expected, it was an important finding, and I have been able to explore the effect in more detail for my MSc research this year. When you focus on the idea that a victim is entitled to trust someone she knows, then people are far more forgiving in their judgements towards her.

My journey

I am just completing my MSc thesis. I continued working with my supervisor to explore the effects that I found in my final-year project, and have explored how trust violation, relationship 'baggage', and behavioural signals can all contribute to flipping the stranger/acquaintance effect of victim blame. In other words, these factors worked in portraying the victim as less blameworthy at higher levels of acquaintanceship. So far, we have discovered that relationship 'baggage' aggravates how much a victim is blamed, and victims are likely to be blamed more when they are seen as having a previous relationship history with their attacker.

I have learned a lot from my research. You learn how important it is to stick to deadlines, and to seek support and guidance if you feel stuck. It teaches you how to work as a scientist, and massively extends your knowledge and understanding in the subject area. The findings have led to a successful and ground-breaking set of results in my MSc studies, which I also hope to publish in order to contribute to psychological research and improve rape victim support.

My advice

The final-year project can feel really daunting at first, and especially scary considering how much you need to write. But once you start collecting data, it's a really exciting experience. You feel like a true scientist collecting data for your own study, which has the potential to become a published paper and can make a real-world contribution. If you have concerns, just chat to your supervisor or other students. Pace yourself, set yourself targets and deadlines, and keep in close contact with supporting staff. And, most importantly, you are allowed to have fun with the process, so relax and enjoy.

4

The social judge: attitudes, emotions and behaviour

In this chapter, we begin by considering the nature of attitudes, values and ideologies. We then consider how and why attitudes form and change, and highlight different types of attitudes. Further, we consider the distinction between explicit and implicit attitudes and then turn our attention to the role of our bodies, and emotions, in our social judgements and behaviours. By the end of the chapter, you will have a clear understanding of the important roles played by attitudes and emotions in our daily social lives.

© PHOTODISC

Topics covered in this chapter

- What are attitudes?
- Attitude formation
- Implicit and explicit attitudes
- Attitudes and behaviour
- Cognitive dissonance
- Embodied social cognition
- Emotions and social judgement
- Decision making

Key features

Critical focus Embodied social cognition

Ethics and research methods The Implicit Association Test

Social psychology in the real world Political attitudes

Applying social psychology Implementation intentions: turning ideas into action

Blind spot in social psychology Embodied warmth

Student project Accurately predicting strangers' emotions in the laboratory predicts higher quality relationships in real life

Questions to consider

1 On Facebook, Lisbeth is a member of several activist groups such as Amnesty International, Greenpeace and the Humane Society. What reasons are there for Lisbeth to be a member of these groups? Why do this on Facebook where others can see her group memberships?

2 Dirk is having a discussion with a friend who says they are studying psychology and doing a project on attitudes towards healthy eating. Dirk says to his friend that attitudes are impossible to measure. Is this right?

3 Luann has been a smoker for nearly 20 years, having started in secondary school. She knows that smoking causes lung cancer and a whole host of other negative ailments. Also, her great aunt died of lung cancer when she was a child. And yet, Luann still refuses to quit. What social psychological process might help explain Luann's decision?

4 When asked about a government proposal to raise tuition fees, Kieran argues that it is 'disgusting'. Is it likely that Kieran really experiences the emotional response of disgust to this proposal, or is another emotion more likely?

© PHOTODISC

The poet E.E. Cummings wrote: 'Since feeling is first, who pays any attention to the syntax of things/will never wholly kiss you.' This is an eloquent, if offbeat, statement of the importance of feeling, passion and preference in the lives of human beings. Chapters 2 and 3 were largely devoted to the study of the knowledge people have of themselves and others. This chapter is devoted to people's preferences, emotions and gut-level reactions. It is about how people *feel* about their social world, much more than what they *know* or believe about it. The study of preferences, in particular – or 'attitudes' as they are called in social psychology – is perhaps the most central topic in our discipline. Although most of this chapter is concerned with attitudes, we will encounter attitudes in every single chapter in this book. The study of attitudes has increasingly been supplemented by the study of emotions, and in recent years, the study of how not just our brains but the rest of our bodies are implicated in our attitudes and emotions. The poet, perhaps, would approve of the focus on feelings and, increasingly, emotions in social psychology. And he appeared to anticipate research into the role of our bodies in our feelings when, later in the same poem, he wrote: 'my blood approves,/and kisses are a better fate than wisdom.'

We begin this chapter by considering what attitudes are, and their relation to broader concepts such as values and ideologies. We then consider how and why we form attitudes, and what can cause our attitudes to change. Next, we outline different types of attitudes, in particular, the important distinction between explicit and implicit attitudes – broadly speaking, those we can consciously articulate versus those we cannot. We then review recent work on the role of our bodies, and our emotions, in our social judgements and behaviours.

What are attitudes?

Attitudes People's evaluations of aspects of the social world.

Attitude object The thing an attitude is about.

Attitudes are typically defined as a person's evaluations of various aspects of their social world (Eagly and Chaiken, 1993; Tesser, 1993; Tesser and Martin, 1996). People have attitudes concerning just about everything. For example, people hold attitudes about other people, groups of people, food, the weather, education, marriage, ideas, books, films – the list is endless. The thing an attitude is about can be described as an **attitude object**. In general, where an evaluation of an object, concept or otherwise can be formed, an attitude will emerge. Of course, such evaluations can vary in the extent to which they are favourable or unfavourable. For example, we may have a positive attitude towards one group of people but a negative attitude towards others. Another way of describing attitudes is that they are *preferences*. Seen this way, we can understand that attitudes are not exclusively possessed by human beings. However, human beings appear to be unique in the content of their attitudes, and how they can reflect on and express their attitudes. As Banaji and Heiphetz (2010, p. 353) put it:

Bundles of preferences characterize every living organism; without them, plants would not turn toward the Sun and cockroaches would not run away from it.

In us, preferences exist not only in these built-in forms shared with other living beings but in distinctly human ways, such as the consciously molded attitudes we convey through artistic expression, the moral codes by which we judge our worth and failings, or the words we craft to describe imagined utopias.

Time to reflect Look up the *Oxford English Dictionary* online or in hard copy, or use a search engine to search 'attitude definition'. Apart from the psychological meaning of the word 'attitude', what other meaning does the word have? This reveals that the psychological meaning of 'attitude' is another example of the use of metaphors borrowed from the physical sciences. Bear this in mind later in this chapter when we discuss embodied social cognition – the relationship between body and mind.

Ambivalent attitudes
Attitudes that are mixed, being both positive and negative.

Attitudes are not always straightforwardly positive or negative – they can sometimes be mixed or **ambivalent** (e.g., Glick and Fiske, 1996; Priester and Petty, 2001). For example, we might perceive chocolate cake to be both tasty and bad for us, so our attitudes are at once positive and negative. Attitude ambivalence is an important and wide-reaching concept in social psychology. As we saw in Chapter 2, many people are narcissistic, meaning they have ambivalent attitudes towards themselves – at once positive and negative – which can lead them to be defensive, constantly seeking praise and validation from others, and reacting aggressively to criticism or rejection. As we shall see in Chapter 11, people often have ambivalent attitudes towards groups of people, with both negative and positive aspects, which can profoundly affect relationships between groups. These are just two examples of how attitudes can have important emotional, behavioural and social consequences (Ajzen and Fishbein, 1980; Petty and Krosnick, 1995).

Values Enduring beliefs about important aspects of life that go beyond specific situations.

Attitudes can be distinguished from other, related concepts in social psychology. **Values** are enduring, evaluative beliefs about general aspects of life that go beyond specific objects and situations (Maio, 2010; Rokeach, 1973). For instance, 'equality' and 'happiness' are examples of personal values that generally transcend specific events. Values are organized along a hierarchy from those that are most important to those that are least important to the self (Ball-Rokeach, Rockeach and Grube, 1984). Rokeach (1973) suggested that values are higher order concepts than attitudes; and values that are particularly important to people influence and organize their attitudes. For instance, if a person strongly values health and fitness, this is likely to influence attitudes to various attitude objects such as exercise, diet and drinking alcohol. A person who has positive attitudes towards exercise, dietary restraint and drinking in moderation is more likely to engage in these behaviours (e.g., Homer and Kahle, 1988). Thus, a person's values can indirectly influence behaviour through their influence on attitudes. In a similar fashion, knowing something about a person's values can help us predict their opinions about justice in the world (Feather, 1991). Bardi and Schwarz (2003) found that people's values (e.g., traditional values) were correlated with participants' self-reported behaviour (e.g., following traditions).

The study of values has revealed important cultural differences. Some cultures value conformity, whereas others value self-expression. Roughly, this corresponds to the individualism–collectivism dimension encountered in Chapter 2. Also, people from some cultures value tradition more strongly, whereas in other cultures, rational, secular, 'modern' ideas are more valued (Esmer and Petterson, 2007). These are important differences, with implications for whether cultures will adopt democratic systems of government. For example, countries with autocratic (non-democratic) governments tend to become democratic if their population endorses values that are more self-expressive, rational and secular than their current system of government would suggest (Inglehart and Welzel, 2005). However, recent research has also revealed an apparent human universal – across cultures, there appear to be 10 key values (see Figure 4.1). Further, although these are endorsed to varying degrees in different cultures, their relationship to each other is the same across cultures. In other words, values that are positively (or negatively) associated in one culture also tend to be positively (or negatively) associated in other cultures (Schwartz, 1992, 2011).

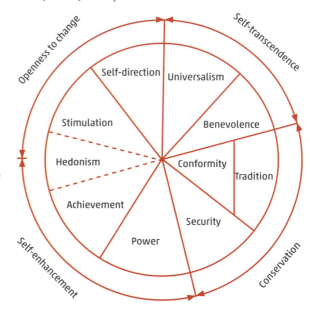

FIGURE 4.1 The Schwartz value circumplex (or 'wheel') This model of values has been widely tested worldwide and seems to offer a model of how values are organized in all human societies. Values that are positively associated are close together on the circumplex (e.g., security and power). Thus, people who endorse one value strongly will also tend to endorse neighbouring values strongly. Conversely, values that are opposite to each other on the wheel are negatively associated (once participants' tendency to agree with all the values is controlled for). Thus, people who strongly endorse security tend not to endorse self-direction so strongly. Different segments of the wheel loosely correspond to overall orientations. For example, self-direction and stimulation correspond to openness to change, whereas achievement and power correspond to self-enhancement (the desire to achieve high status, even at the expense of others if necessary).

Source: Borg et al., 2011. Used with permission from *Journal of Personnel Psychology*, 10(1), 1–12

Try it yourself Can you find which cultures highly value conformity and which highly value self-expression (individuality)? Try an internet search for the 'World Values Survey'. This global research project publishes an excellent pdf brochure online that summarizes its findings for a public audience, and locates different countries and regions of the world in terms of their values (Inglehart and Welzel, 2011). You might also want to find, and complete, the 21-item version of the Schwartz Values Survey by means of an internet search. This instrument is often used in cross-cultural studies of values and is probably the best example of how values are currently measured.

As well as being more general, values differ from attitudes in other ways. For example, people have often thought hard about their attitudes and have come to adopt attitudes after much consideration. As we shall see in Chapter 6, attitude change following persuasion is often longer lasting and more profound when people have really thought about the arguments presented to them. However, people find it difficult to articulate the reasoning behind their values. People simply have the experience of holding certain values dear without always knowing why. Maio and Olson (1995) demonstrated this in a series of studies where they asked participants to think about the reasons why they hold certain values. Performing this task changed their values. If people already had well-thought-out reasons for their values, we would not expect them to change as a result of a few minutes' thought. Thus, Maio and Olson (1995; also see Bernard, Maio and Olson, 2003a, 2003b; Maio, 2010) argued that values are 'truisms' or self-evident and hardly worth mentioning.

Ideologies Interrelated and widely shared sets of beliefs that typically relate to social or political contexts.

Ideologies, like values, are more general than attitudes. Whereas values refer to the importance one attaches to various aspects of life, ideologies refer to an inter-related and widely shared set of beliefs that serve to explain social realities (Thompson, 1990). Ideologies typically refer to social, economic or political systems, and contain ideas that not only explain those systems but also suggest how they should be run (Jost, 2006). They can influence values, attitudes and intentions to commit behaviours (Crandall, 1994). For example, sexist ideology, as we shall see in Chapter 11, is a set of beliefs about the roles that men and women occupy, and should occupy, within society. It is associated with attitudes to any number of attitude objects, including rape victims, career women, abortion, cosmetic surgery, and women's lifestyle choices during pregnancy. Ideologies are important to people because they offer them a way to agree on an understanding of the world and what actions they should take (Jost, Ledgerwood and Hardin, 2008). But, they are often hotly contested – as in the battles between sexism and feminism, left-wing and right-wing ideology, and so-called 'fundamentalist' and secular ideology (Jost, 2006). For more insight into the importance of ideologies in everyday life, and their relation to attitudes, see the Social psychology in real life box below on political conservatism (Chapters 11 and 14 also deal at length with ideologies).

SOCIAL PSYCHOLOGY IN THE REAL WORLD

Political attitudes

© CHRISHARVEY/FOTOLIA.COM

The ideology of political conservatism (also known as right-wing political orientation) has been widely studied by social psychologists in the past decade or two. Conservatism takes different forms in different countries, but two essential attitudes have been identified as characteristic of conservatism, wherever it is found (Jost, Glaser, Kruglanski and Sulloway, 2003). One is a relatively positive attitude to income inequality. Conservatives 'consider people as inherently unequal and due unequal rewards' (Erikson, Luttberg and Tedin, 1988, p. 75). Another is a relatively negative attitude towards social change, as compared to tradition and the status quo. Attitudes, then, are fundamental to politics. What drives people to adopt this conservative cluster of attitudes? Generally speaking, the results of research into this question do not make for pleasant reading if you happen to be a conservative/right-winger (but may delight you if you are a liberal/left-winger). But they are worth reading, because they reveal a good deal about where attitudes and ideologies come from and the purposes they serve.

One source of conservative ideology appears to be fear and anxiety - those to the right of the political spectrum fear threat, loss and death more than those on the left (Jost, Federico and Napier, 2009). They also tend to see the world as a more dangerous place (Duckitt, 2001). Further, they are more 'closed-minded' – less tolerant of ambiguity, and more inclined to prefer simple, straightforward, quickly obtained and apparently certain answers and explanations. For this reason they are less inclined to poetry, travel and foreign films (Jost et al., 2003; see also Calogero, Bardi and Sutton, 2009, who showed that closed-mindedness is associated with 'conservation' values on the Schwartz value circumplex). The argument is that right-wing ideology relieves fear and anxiety by affirming the social order and hierarchy that is contained in the status quo (Banaji and Heiphetz, 2010; Jost et al., 2003). Indeed, some research suggests that despite their underlying anxieties, conservatives are actually happier than liberals (Napier and Jost, 2008; van Heil and Brebels, 2011 – but for different findings, see Choma, Busseri and Sadava, 2009; Duriez, Klimstra, Luyckz et al., in press).

Much of this research is correlational and therefore hard to interpret in causal terms. Perhaps conservative ideology causes a disdain for 'foreign' things, and does not spring from closed-mindedness, for example. However, there is some longitudinal and experimental research that makes for even worse reading for conservatives. In analyses of data from national surveys of 15,000 British citizens born either in 1958 or 1970, Hodson and Busseri (2012) found that children with lower IQs were more likely to grow up to be politically conservative. Partly for this reason, they also grew up to be more racist. Eidelman, Crandall, Goodman and Blanchar (2012) found other evidence that reduced capacity to engage in high-level thought also increases political conservatism. In one of their studies, they went into a bar, and found that the more drunk the bar patrons, the more right-wing their attitudes became. In subsequent experiments, the same authors found that placing participants under cognitive load or time pressure also made them more conservative.

The picture that emerges from this research into political conservatism seems to be that it is an ideology adopted by those who are wracked with fear and less able to devote effortful, sophisticated thought to political information. It is not a flattering picture. However, some upsides to political conservatism have been suggested – apart from the possibility that they are happier, they are informed by moral principles that are of less interest to liberals, including loyalty, respect for authority and purity (Graham, Haidt and Nosek, 2009). They are also more likely to judge people according to moral principles (Haidt and Hersh, 2001). You may not necessarily agree with these moral principles or the use of morality to judge people. Nonetheless, it is clear that, in some respects, morality is more important to conservatives.

Questions

1 Can science tell us about the rights and wrongs of different political positions?

2 Most social psychologists, like most social scientists (Cardiff and Klein, 2005; Klein and Stern, 2005), identify as liberal/left wing. Few identify as conservative/right wing. A show of hands in a room full of roughly 1,000 researchers at the 2011 meeting of the Society for Personality and Social Psychology – the world's leading annual meeting of social psychologists – uncovered some 800 liberals and 3 conservatives (Tierney, 2011). Do you think the tendency for research to be unflattering about political conservatism might stem from the biased representation of left-wingers/liberals in social psychology? (Bear in mind that with rare exceptions, scientists do not falsify their results.) If so, how?

3 The research on the relationship between political conservatism and happiness is correlational. Can you find any experimental evidence that political conservatism affects mood or wellbeing? If not, do you think it is possible to design such an experiment?

Thus far, we have seen that attitudes are essentially evaluations of specific objects and entities in people's social worlds. This definition, however, does not tell us much about an important aspect of what attitudes are, that is, how they are structured. Much research into attitudes has focused on this question of *structure* – what components attitudes have and how they are related. Up until the 1990s, this research was dominated by a **tripartite model of attitudes** (see Figure 4.2). In this model, attitudes are seen as having three facets (e.g., Breckler, 1984; Smith, Bruner and White, 1956):

Tripartite model of attitudes
A model of the structure of attitudes which assumed that attitudes have three components: cognitive, affective (emotional) and behavioural.

1 *cognitive:* we can think about the positive and negative aspects of an attitude object
2 *affective:* we can feel positive or negative emotions towards an attitude object
3 *behavioural:* we can behave *favourably* towards an attitude object (typically by seeking it out or approaching it) or *unfavourably* (typically by avoiding it).

Thus, if you like dogs (in preference to, say, cats), you will probably think that dogs have positive attributes, for example they are playful, loyal and friendly. You will also have warm feelings towards dogs, and you will be more likely to choose to have a dog as a pet or interact with dogs you meet.

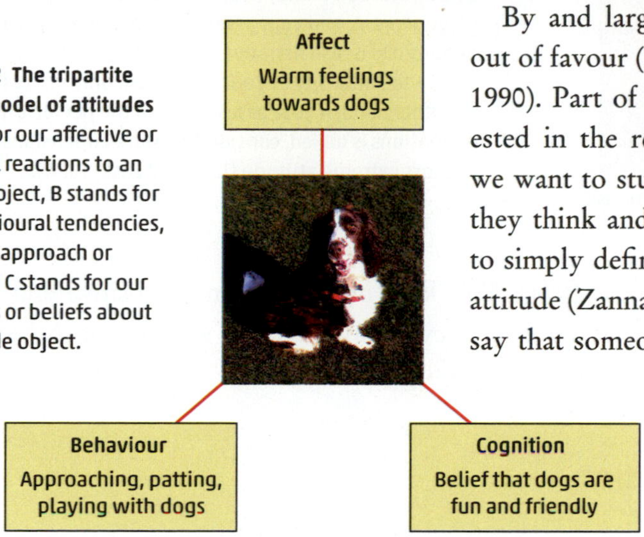

FIGURE 4.2 The tripartite (or ABC) model of attitudes A stands for our affective or emotional reactions to an attitude object, B stands for our behavioural tendencies, especially approach or avoid, and C stands for our cognitions or beliefs about the attitude object.

Affect
Warm feelings towards dogs

Behaviour
Approaching, patting, playing with dogs

Cognition
Belief that dogs are fun and friendly

By and large, this tripartite view of attitudes has fallen out of favour (Banaji and Heiphetz, 2010; Tesser and Shaffer, 1990). Part of the reason for this is that since we are interested in the relationship between attitudes and behaviour, we want to study how people's behaviour is related to how they think and feel about attitude objects. We do not want to simply define their behaviour as an inherent part of their attitude (Zanna and Rempel, 1988). To take an example, let us say that someone believes in all the tenets of a major world religion, such as Islam, and associates positive emotions with that religion. However, they do not behave in accordance with their beliefs and emotions. Should we say they are not religious, or they do not have very religious attitudes? Surely, it is more accurate to say they do not behave in accordance with their attitudes? Indeed, behaving in ways that are discrepant with one's attitudes has interesting causes and effects in its own right, as we shall see throughout this chapter, for example when we read about cognitive dissonance.

Attitude complexity The number of dimensions along which an attitude object is evaluated.

Other research has focused on the **complexity** of attitudes. We can see attitudes as comprising sets of evaluative beliefs about an attitude object. Your attitude towards dogs can be *simple*, in that it is based on only a small number of aspects or *dimensions* of dogs, for example how sociable they are. Another person's attitudes may be more *complex*, for example they may think about other dimensions, such as the way they smell, the mess they make and the way they look. Specific evaluations of an attitude object can be *consistent*, that is, they may all have the same valence. For example, 'dogs look cute', 'they are friendly' and 'I like that doggy smell' are all positive. However, they may be evaluatively *inconsistent*, as in 'dogs are friendly', 'dogs look cute', but 'I hate the way they smell'. Research suggests that attitudes become stronger – more extremely positive or negative – if they are both complex and evaluatively consistent. If attitudes are evaluatively inconsistent, they become weaker or more moderate as they become more complex (Judd and Lusk, 1984) (see Figure 4.3). Complex and inconsistent attitudes may be especially likely to lead to a moderate position on a topic when people have thought actively about the inconsistency and attempted to integrate their various beliefs (e.g., 'dogs smell bad, but that is partly because they are so much fun and love to

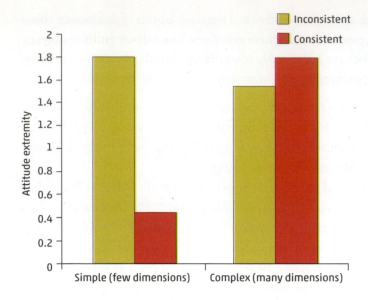

FIGURE 4.3 Attitude extremity as an outcome of complexity and consistency If your attitudes to a person are mixed or inconsistent, then the more dimensions you evaluate someone on, the less extreme your attitudes become. On the other hand, if your attitudes to an object are consistent, then your attitudes will become more extreme as the number of dimensions on which you evaluate the attitude object increases. For example, if you don't like the way someone looks or who their friends are, you will have a negative overall attitude to them. And if you add more dimensions of judgement, and your assessment of the person on these dimensions is also negative – their values, intelligence and so on – the intensity of your dislike will only increase. On the other hand, if your assessment of the person on these dimensions is mixed, considering more dimensions will lead to a less extreme attitude (Judd and Lusk, 1984).

play outside') (Tetlock, 1984). This kind of integration of positive and negative beliefs is probably what we mean in everyday life when we say that someone has a 'balanced and considered view' on a topic.

Attitude formation

Since attitudes are such an important and wide-reaching aspect of social psychology, it is important to understand where they come from. If a person likes dogs, why do they like dogs? If a person has a positive attitude towards their country's leader, how did this attitude form? Does it even make sense to say that a person 'likes dogs', or are attitudes highly unstable across time and responsive to situational forces? Most social psychologists argue that attitudes are learned from others. However, some argue that attitudes come about due to mere exposure, while others argue for a genetic component to attitudes. We will discuss each approach in this section.

Why do we form attitudes?

Attitude function The study of why people have attitudes.

Before we consider the details of *how* people form attitudes, it is useful to understand *why* they do so. The study of **attitude function** is the study of why we have attitudes. It is a special case of the study of motivated social cognition, which we encountered in Chapter 3. In a landmark paper, Katz (1960) defined four functions of attitudes:

Schema A cognitive structure that represents information about a concept, its attributes and its relationship to other concepts.

1 *The knowledge function:* Attitudes work as useful **schemas** or mental guides that help people make sense of many different kinds of information within a complex social world. Attitudes help us form opinions about factors related to the attitude object, so that thinking about the social world gets a little bit easier (Katz, 1960). Another way of looking at this is that attitudes perform a knowledge function that helps people focus on the important characteristics of an

attitude object so that they know how best to deal with it quickly and effectively. Thus, it is important to people that they feel confident in the accuracy and legitimacy of their attitudes (although as we saw in the Social psychology in the real world box earlier, this need is stronger in some people than others). Also, it is important to people that attitudes appear to be consistent with each other, so that they feel they are in possession of a coherent set of knowledge, beliefs and feelings about the world. This is one reason we are more likely to form attitudes that are consistent with our other attitudes (as we shall see in the coverage of balance theory and the APE model of attitudes later in this chapter). So, you will make choices more easily, quickly and with a greater sense of confidence if you feel your attitudes to alternatives (different jobs, different election candidates, different houses) are consistent and informed.

2 *The utilitarian function:* Attitudes can help us obtain rewards and avoid punishments. By having the 'right' attitudes, people might think that others will look favourably on them, so that expressing attitudes can perform an impression management function (Chaiken, Giner-Sorolla and Chen, 1996; Cialdini, Petty and Cacioppo, 1981; Jellison and Arkin, 1977; Nienhuis, Mansted and Spears, 2001; Snyder and Swann, 1976). For example, some cultures frown on prejudice towards certain groups (e.g., blind people), but actively endorse prejudice towards certain other groups (e.g., pregnant women who drink alcohol) (Crandall, Eshleman and O'Brien, 2002). Expressing positive attitudes to the right groups and negative attitudes to widely disliked groups is a way of affirming membership of the group, being valued and liked by others, and avoiding others' disapproval.

3 *The value expressive function:* Attitudes may allow individuals to express their deep-seated values. If equality is an important value to you, there is a good chance you will be motivated not to harbour negative feelings and thoughts about disadvantaged social groups (Monteith, Ashburn-Nardo, Voils and Czopp, 2002). Attitudes that express values are often the most resistant to change (Maio and Olson, 2000) and, as we shall see, are more likely to inspire commitment to attitude-consistent behaviours such as volunteering (e.g., Murray, Haddock and Zanna, 1996).

4 *The ego defensive function:* Attitudes can protect us from psychological threats. As we saw in Chapter 2, having a positive attitude to ourselves – high self-esteem – appears to make us less anxious and defensive when confronted with the inevitability of our own death, which is perhaps the supreme psychological threat (Greenberg, Solomon and Pyszczynski, 1997).

Thus, your attitudes can help you feel that you understand the world and your place in it, can help you win friends and avoid making enemies, can help you express your deepest values, and can help protect your psychological equilibrium from ideas and realities that threaten and perturb you. These functions of attitudes influence the attitudes we form. Now, we consider the specific psychological processes that affect attitude formation.

Mere exposure

Sometimes, simply being exposed repeatedly to a person or object can cause people to form more positive attitudes towards them. Zajonc (1968) termed this the **mere exposure effect**. In other words, merely being exposed to something often enough makes us like it. For example, you may see a particular cat on your way to university every day and develop a soft spot for that cat when you do not particularly like other cats. You may watch a particular news programme on TV because your friends like to watch it and you are more likely to switch over to this programme in future. The mere exposure effect does not require a person to take any action towards the attitude object. For example, Zajonc (1968, 1970) found that people were more likely to say that familiar nonsense words or characters (ones they had been exposed to earlier in the experiment) meant something positive (see Figures 4.4 and 4.5). Harmon-Jones and Allen (2001) found that people smiled more when they saw familiar faces rather than unfamiliar faces. As we will discuss in Chapter 7, the mere exposure effect is a strong determinant of the extent to which we are attracted to other people. The more we see them, the more we tend to develop positive attitudes towards them.

Mere exposure effect The more exposure we have to a stimulus, the more we tend to like it.

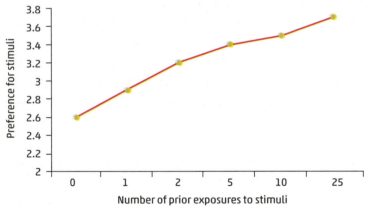

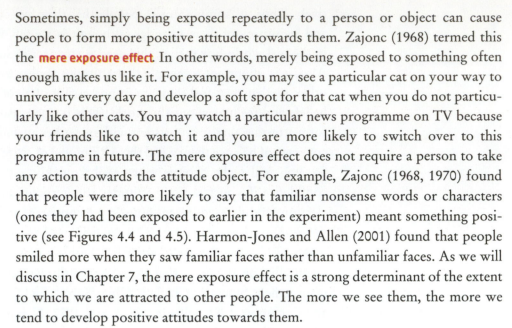

FIGURE 4.4 **Mere exposure effect** As participants were more exposed to a stimulus, in this case Chinese-like symbols, the more they evaluated them positively.
Source: Data from Zajonc, 1968

The mere exposure effect seems to say something startling and profound about the way our attitudes are formed. For Zajonc (1968, 1970), it suggested that 'preferences need no inferences', that is, we can form positive or negative attitudes without any thoughts about the object. Our psychological makeup appears to be such that our attitudes are shaped entirely by the objective features of our environment – in this case, how common and visible the attitude object is. Thus, the mere exposure effect provided an important, early line of evidence that attitudes and cognition are largely automatic and informed by factors that people are not aware of (Chapters 2 and 3).

However, the meaning of the mere exposure effect may not be so straightforward. In a major meta-analysis of the mere exposure effect, Bornstein (1989) found that it was larger in experiments where stimuli were presented only very briefly. In a subsequent set of experiments, Bornstein and D'Agostino (1992) presented stimuli such as photographs and geometric shapes either subliminally (5 ms exposures – just 1/200th of a second) or supraliminally (500 ms exposures – fully half a second). The mere exposure effect was more pronounced when shapes had earlier been presented subliminally. On the back of the meta-analytic findings (Bornstein, 1989) and their own experimental results, Bornstein and D'Agostino (1992) argued that mere exposure to a stimulus happens because of the operation of two processes. First, familiar objects are perceived more fluently – after being exposed to a novel stimulus, our perceptual systems learn

FIGURE 4.5 Typical stimuli for mere exposure effect studies In Zajonc's (1968) original study, Chinese characters had been placed around the campus of a US university. Stimuli that had become familiar by being placed on notice boards were liked more than stimuli that were not.

about them so that subsequent exposures are easier and faster to process. Second, people do not make the correct attribution for this perceptual fluency. Rather than attributing the fluency to the object's familiarity, they assume that they like the object. This is why, they argue, people are more prone to the mere exposure effect after having been only subliminally exposed to stimulus objects before. They simply do not realize they have seen the objects before, and so cannot correct their erroneous judgement that their fluency is attributable to some property of the object, rather than its mere familiarity. Further support for this interpretation came from correlational analyses of their results. Specifically, the more participants recognized the stimuli as having been seen before, the less prone they were to liking them, although Hansen and Wänke (2009) later found that conscious recognition did not affect the mere exposure effect. In later experiments, Bornstein and D'Agostino (1994) found that the mere exposure effect was reduced when people were told they had seen familiar stimulus objects before, or were told that familiarity can increase liking. Thus, the more able people are to realize they have encountered familiar stimuli before, the less prone they are to the mere exposure effect.

Bornstein (1989) and Bornstein and D'Agostino's (1992, 1994) account establishes that with controlled processing, people are able to correct for the mere exposure effect. However, it is not yet clear whether their findings establish that preferences do need inferences; that is, that the mere exposure effect only happens when people make an incorrect inference or misattribution of perceptual fluency to something other than the mere familiarity of a stimulus. There is no direct evidence that people make these attributions in the first place. (Bear in mind that any such attributions are probably made unconsciously, so it is probably not useful to ask participants what attributions they are making.) However, more recent findings do suggest that people make inferences on the basis of familiarity. In particular, when stimuli are more fluent than people expect them to be, they appear to like them more (e.g., Dechêne, Stahl, Hansen and Wänke, 2009). It seems something like an inference is happening, presumably at an unconscious level, along the lines of: 'This stimuli was easier to look at than I would have expected it to be, so I must find it likeable.'

Time to reflect The mere exposure effect contradicts the proverbial wisdom that 'familiarity breeds contempt'. Why do you think familiar stimuli are liked more? In particular, can you think of an evolutionary explanation for this effect? In other words, what survival or reproductive advantage would be conferred on individuals if they prefer familiar to unfamiliar attitude objects? Can you think of a way to test your hypothesis?

Social learning

Social learning People acquire their attitudes (as well as behaviours) often from others.

Most social psychologists agree that our attitudes are largely learned from others. We observe others, we listen and we interact with others and naturally we learn about their attitudes. Many of our own attitudes are acquired this way. It is argued that this **social learning** occurs through the following processes.

Classical conditioning

Classical conditioning Simple form of learning where a stimulus eventually evokes positive or negative reactions through repeated pairing with another stimulus.

This basic psychological process (also known as evaluative conditioning) can facilitate attitude formation. During a typical **classical conditioning** study, a stimulus (usually neutral to begin with) called the 'conditioned stimulus' is repeatedly paired with another stimulus (the 'unconditioned stimulus') that already evokes a positive or a negative reaction (the unconditioned response). For example, in Pavlov's ([1927]1960) initial investigations of canine digestion, the same laboratory technician would feed the dogs routinely. Naturally, the dogs would salivate (the unconditioned response) when food arrived (the unconditioned stimulus), but after a while, the dogs would salivate at the sight of the laboratory technician (the conditioned stimulus). They had come to associate the technician with the food so that, eventually, the presence of the technician alone was enough to elicit the natural response. Pavlov tried pairing a bell with the delivery of food and the same effect occurred. After a while, the dogs would salivate at the sound of the bell.

Although this may seem like a basic psychological effect with very little relevance to attitudes, social psychologists argue that it is potentially important in determining the formation of attitudes. In particular, if a stimulus is associated with an object that elicits a negative response, then a negative attitude may reasonably form to that stimulus. On the other hand, if a stimulus is associated with an object that elicits a positive response, then a positive attitude may emerge. For example, a child may observe that every time their parent sees a disabled person, they display negative nonverbal responses. The negative nonverbal responses make the child feel upset, but initially, exposure to disabled persons does not elicit a negative or positive response. However, with repeated exposure to the pairing of the neutral stimulus (disabled persons) with the negative stimulus (negative nonverbal behaviours), the child may come to associate disabled persons with feeling upset and thus develop a negative attitude towards them. This attitude has therefore been directly learned from the parent by the process of classical conditioning (see de Houwer, Thomas and Baeyens, 2001; Zanna, Kiesler and Pilkonis, 1970).

Subliminal conditioning Classical conditioning that occurs outside the learner's conscious awareness.

There is evidence to suggest that this process more often than not occurs outside the awareness of the learner by a process known as **subliminal conditioning**. For example, Krosnick, Betz, Jussim and Lynn (1992) exposed student participants to photos of another person doing everyday things such as shopping for food. Prior to each photograph of this stimulus person, other photographs were presented very briefly (13 ms) – so briefly, in fact, they could not be consciously recognized. These photos were of highly pleasant or unpleasant stimuli (e.g., a couple on their wedding day, a pair of kittens and smiling friends playing rugby, versus a bloody shark, a face on fire and a bucket of snakes). The dependent variable was the participants' feelings towards the original person in the photos. Findings revealed that participants who had seen the positive photos paired with the person felt more positively towards the person than those who had been exposed to a negative pairing (Figure 4.6).

Like the mere exposure effect, evaluative conditioning studies have shown that attitude learning can occur at an unconscious level (Walther, 2002). Although the

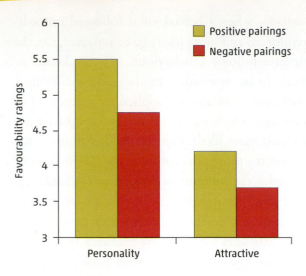

FIGURE 4.6 Subliminal conditioning The person paired with positive photographs was rated as having a better personality, and as more physically attractive, than the person paired with negative photographs. These results happened even when the positive and negative photographs were presented too briefly (13 ms) to be consciously noticed.

Source: Data from Krosnick et al., 1992

basic learning itself may be largely unconscious, research shows that consciousness does play an important role. For example, one study suggested that evaluative conditioning effects were wiped out when participants were placed under cognitive load, and so did not have conscious resources free to pay attention to the stimuli they were being exposed to (DeDonder, Corneille, Yzerbyt and Kuppens, 2010). Further, an experiment by Gast and Rothermund (2011) suggests that evaluative conditioning is stronger when participants are instructed to pay attention to how positive or negative the stimuli are. Thus, paying attention to stimuli pairings, and in particular whether they are desirable or undesirable, seems to allow associative learning to happen more strongly.

Thus far, findings are mixed on a final, important issue regarding the extent to which evaluative conditioning happens as a result of automatic or controlled processes. This concerns the role of conscious awareness that the attitude object is being systematically paired with negative or positive stimuli. Some findings suggest that awareness of this contingency enables people to *correct* the tendency to like objects paired with positive stimuli, and dislike objects paired with negative stimuli (Walther and Nagengast, 2006). Others suggest that a degree of awareness of the contingency between the attitude object and other stimuli is actually necessary for evaluative conditioning (Bar-Anan, De Houwer and Nosek, 2010). Thus, we still do not know for sure whether evaluative conditioning depends partly on an inference (e.g., 'this object is associated with other positive things, so I like it', rather like 'any friend of yours is a friend of mine'), or whether it happens automatically and is actually corrected (e.g., 'I have some positive feelings for this object, but this is only because it is paired with other positive things') (for a review, see Gawronski and Bodenhausen, 2011).

Whatever the precise mechanism that underpins evaluative conditioning, researchers are now widely using these implicit learning paradigms. Exposure to repeated pairings of self-related stimuli to positive stimuli in the laboratory has been shown to have the potential to increase self-esteem (Baccus, Baldwin and Packer, 2004; Ebert, Steffens, von Stülpnagel and Jelenec, 2009; Grumm, Nestler and Collani, 2009); as well as reduce the liking for chocolate (Ebert et al., 2009) and the craving for alcohol (Houben, Schoenmakers and Wiers, 2010). Olson and Fazio (2006) also managed to reduce racial prejudice among white participants by pairing white faces with negative stimuli and black faces with positive stimuli.

Instrumental conditioning

Being praised for doing or saying something is also a good way to learn. For example, your friends might praise your taste in wine so that the next time you are asked for your opinions about wine by other people, you are likely to articulate the response that was received favourably by others. This is an example of the

Instrumental conditioning
A form of learning whereby
a behaviour followed by a
positive response is more
likely to be repeated.

process called **instrumental conditioning** – when a behaviour is followed immediately by a positive outcome, it is reinforced and more likely to be repeated. On the other hand, when a negative response follows a behaviour, it is weakened or suppressed and is therefore less likely to be repeated. Like classical conditioning, the principle of instrumental conditioning can also be applied to attitudes. For example, if a child makes a statement that is followed by smiles and laughter from a parent, this positive response makes it more likely that the child will repeat the statement in future, in order to receive the same positive outcome. There is some evidence to suggest that adults' attitudes can be reinforced by positive feedback. For example, Insko (1965) showed that participants' responses to an attitude survey were influenced by positive feedback on the responses they gave a week earlier. In summary, reinforcing one's attitudes with positive feedback means that the attitudes are more likely to survive and be expressed on other occasions.

Observational learning

We also learn by simply observing others (Bandura, 1977), and this is another way in which people can form attitudes. For example, a child may overhear conversations between grownups or watch how they behave in specific situations. The child will often take on the information and it will influence the attitudes they develop. Similarly, observing people's behaviour on TV and in other forms of mass media can influence attitudes. There is some evidence to suggest that **observational learning** forms a significant role in attitude development. For example, children may express derogatory attitudes about particular ethnic groups but in reality they know very little about them – the attitude must have been learned by listening to or observing others (Aboud, 2005; Allport, 1954). Weisbuch, Pauker and Ambady (2009) found that characters in popular US television shows exhibited more negative facial expressions and body language to Black, versus White, characters (even when Black and White characters' social status was matched). Participants in their study viewed scenes in which this bias was evident. Although they did not consciously notice the bias, they were influenced by it, reporting more prejudiced attitudes on the Implicit Association Test, a measure to which we will return later in this chapter (see also Chapter 11). Observational learning can influence attitudes towards unfamiliar social groups. Findings show that people take on others' attitudes about groups when they do not have any experience or knowledge about the group themselves (e.g., Maio, Esses and Bell, 1994). This influence may be even stronger if, through the process of social comparison, we want our attitudes to be similar to those of others we admire. In Chapters 9 and 14, we return to the influence of group norms on our attitudes.

Observational learning
Individuals' attitudes (and
behaviours) are influenced by
observing others.

Innate factors

There is a growing body of evidence suggesting that genetic factors also play a role in attitude development. Unlike the social learning approach, this approach suggests that important features of attitude development occur because they are inherited (Arvey, Bouchard, Segal and Abraham, 1989; Keller, Bouchard, Arvey et

FIGURE 4.7 Genetic factors in attitude formation Playing chess is just one of the attitude objects towards which identical twins tend, more strongly, to have the same attitudes than non-identical twins (Olson et al., 2001).

al., 1992; Olson, Vernon, Harris and Jang, 2001). Much of this research centres around studies of identical and non-identical twins. As you know, identical (monozygotic) twins have exactly the same genetic makeup. In contrast, non-identical (dizygotic) twins, while having comparable life experiences, do not share the same amount of genetic material. Thus, if, on average, attitudes of identical twins are more strongly related than attitudes of non-identical twins, this is some evidence to suggest that attitudes can be inherited (see Figure 4.7). Indeed, findings show that these relationships are stronger for identical twins, for attitude objects as diverse as big parties, playing chess, roller coaster rides, abortion, the death penalty and capitalism (Olson et al., 2001).

Although diverse, these attitudes – towards novelty, risk and political beliefs – tend to be organized by political conservatism, as we saw earlier in this chapter. Political conservatism also seems to be heritable. Bouchard, Segal, Tellegen et al. (2003) found that conservative social attitudes are shared more strongly by monozygotic than dizygotic twins. This study focused on twins who were reared apart. In this case, similarities in upbringing cannot account for similarities in attitudes (Martin, Eaves, Heath et al., 1986; Waller, Kojetin, Bouchard et al., 1990). This is not to say that genetics accounts for all (or even most) of our attitude formation. On the contrary, evidence suggests that genetic effects are fairly small. Other research suggests that genetic factors do not strongly determine attitudes (e.g., Rozin and Millman, 1987; see also Chapter 13 for a critical evaluation of twin studies). However, it is intriguing to learn that the way we think, in addition to physical factors such as height and hair colour, appears to be influenced by our genetic makeup.

There is also some evidence to suggest that attitudes that are determined more by genetics are also more difficult to change (Crelia and Tesser, 1996), more important to people (Olson et al., 2001) and more likely to determine their behaviour (Crelia and Tesser, 1996; D'Onofrio, Eaves, Murrelle et al., 1999). Some researchers argue that these fascinating genetic effects are probably determined by general dispositions to be 'positive' or 'negative', which in turn influence how people evaluate aspects of the social world (e.g., George, 1990). Further research is required to determine whether the apparent heritability of political conservatism really means that our genes influence our political orientation per se, or instead affect some general psychological trait like optimism-pessimism, which in turn shapes our worldview.

Attitude consistency and balance

As we have seen, attitudes have a knowledge function, and so people prefer to have harmonious, consistent thoughts and feelings towards the people and objects in their lives. Heider (1958b), the influential social psychologist who founded attribution theory (Chapter 3), described this basic principle of harmony and consistency in terms of Gestalt psychology. When attitudes are consistent with each other, they are in a state of *balance* and form a coherent whole or *unit*. If we have a positive attitude to one object, we tend to form positive attitudes to

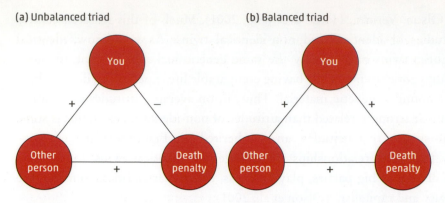

(a) Unbalanced triad

(b) Balanced triad

FIGURE 4.8 An unbalanced and a balanced triad In the unbalanced triad (a), you like another person and dislike the death penalty. The other person likes the death penalty. Since the multiplied signs are negative (there is one negative relation and two positive relations), the triad is not balanced, and the attitude relations do not form a coherent unit. When aware of this lack of balance, people tend to revise their attitudes. For example, they may revise your opinion of the death penalty. If you come to approve of the death penalty, a balanced triad (b) is formed.

other objects it is positively related to. The simplest and most cited example is in interpersonal relations and can be summed up with the proverbs, 'any friend of yours is a friend of mine' (when spoken to a friend), and 'my enemy's enemy is my friend'. Heider (1958b) asked his readers to imagine triads, involving two people and some attitude object (which might be another person). The attitude relation between each of the elements in the triad can be positive or negative. Let us say that you are opposed to the death penalty, but in discussions with one of your friends, it turns out that they are strongly in favour of it. In this case, your liking of your friend, their liking of the death penalty and your loathing of the death penalty form an *unbalanced triad* (see Figure 4.8). A likely response to this unbalanced triad is to change attitudes. Shocked to discover your friend's attitudes, you may now like them less. Alternatively, you may be motivated to listen carefully to your friend's opinion and revise your opinion on the death penalty. If you were to change your mind on the death penalty, your attitudes would then be balanced, and together, form a coherent unit – a *balanced triad*. Heider's (1958b) triads have an elegant property. They are balanced if multiplying the signs returns a positive value. Thus, three positive attitudes, or two negative attitudes and one positive attitude within a triad mean that attitudes are balanced. One negative attitude, or three negative attitudes, mean that they are unbalanced.

Many studies investigated Heider's (1958a) balance theory in the context of such triads and broadly supported it (e.g., Curry and Emerson, 1970; Insko, Songer and McGarvey, 1974; Monsour, Betty and Kurzweil, 1993; Newcomb, 1961; for a review, see Crandall, Silvia, N'Gbala et al., 2007). As predicted, attitudes are more likely to change if they are unbalanced. Balance theory also helps to predict attitude formation. Thus, if your friend, rather than someone you cannot stand, likes a film or performer you have not heard of, your initial attitude to that new attitude object is more likely to be positive, too. Balance theory continues to be influential in many areas of social psychology and related fields, including child development, marketing and group processes (e.g., Brusco and Steinley, 2010; Hummon and Doreian, 2003; Woodside and Chebat, 2001). It stands as the first model to embody the importance of the consistency of attitudes, which, as we saw earlier, is important to their knowledge function. Balance theory also brought attention to the social aspects of attitudes. It established that, over time, we tend to share the attitudes of people who are close to us. For example, this basic principle has been developed by researchers working on shared reality (Figure 4.9). In close relationships, typically within social groups, people often work together to achieve a self-consciously shared set of attitudes to the world (Echterhoff, Higgins and Levine, 2009; Hardin and Higgins, 1996; see Chapter 5

FIGURE 4.9 Applause as a 'shared reality' As members of an applauding audience, we communicate to each other that we share a positive attitude to the speaker's message (Harwood et al., 2000).

Social representations theory
Theory that beliefs about the social world are formed through processes of social interaction.

for more about the social construction of a shared reality through communication). This sense that 'we see things the same way', or 'we are on the same page' is exactly in keeping with Heider's (1958a) balance theory.

Social representations: the social formation of attitudes

The broad principle established by balance theory is that attitudes are not formed in a social vacuum. Our attitudes are influenced by other people and are often formed socially. **Social representations theory** (Moscovici, 1963, 1983, 1988) suggests that beliefs about the world – including evaluative beliefs, or attitudes – are built up by groups of people through processes of social interaction. Moscovici drew on Durkheim's ([1912]2001) notion of 'collective representation' – societally shared beliefs and attitudes – but abandoned the term 'collective' because he wanted to capture the notion that different representations of the same topic may be held by different sections of a society, or even by the same individual, at different points in time. Thus, Christian and Muslim students in the UK tended, in a study by Rafiq, Jobanuptra and Muncer (2006), to have different beliefs about the Iraq War. Although both groups shared generally negative attitudes to the war, and agreed on many of its causes, there was a notable difference, in that Muslim students were less likely to connect the war on Iraq to the so-called 'war on terror'. In another study by Liu and Hilton (2005), Māori (indigenous) and Pakeha (ethnically European descendants of settlers) were also found to have different social representations of New Zealand history. Notably, Pakeha had a generally negative view of their ancestors' behaviour during colonization, but to a lesser extent than Māori. Social representations are important because our attitudes are informed by our group and cultural memberships and are built up by social and cultural practices (discussions, media portrayals, art and science). They also demonstrate how we form attitudes to attitude objects that are outside the realm of our social experience. Thus, people living in overwhelmingly indigenous areas of their own country often harbour negative views of immigrant groups with whom they may have little or no contact, although social representations theory is not the only way to explain this (see, for example, Berg, 2009, and also Chapters 11 and 12 on intergroup contact).

Social representations theory has attracted many criticisms. One pithy critique came from Potter and Litton (1985, p. 82), who described it as 'a concept in search of a theory'. What they meant is that although the theory provides the appealing central concept of social representations, it does not offer a precise account of how social representations form, or how they affect other social psychological processes. As we saw in Chapter 1, one of the main jobs of theories in social psychology is to identify and explain causal relationships so that we can understand how and why social phenomena happen. Other criticisms of the theory attack the central concept itself, describing it as too vague and all-encompassing (Billig, 1988; Jahoda, 1988). Although Moscovici has offered definitions of social representations, it is not always clear what counts as a social representation, and ambiguity surrounds whether a social representation refers to the process by which people arrive at a common set of concepts, or the set of concepts itself (Wagner, 1998).

Defenders of social representations theory have responded to such criticisms with points that are both reassuring and worrying. Reassuringly, they point out that the relationship between social psychological phenomena is intimate and complicated, and we should not always expect to find simple or definitive accounts of social psychological phenomena (Marková, 2000; Voelklein and Howarth, 2005). Worryingly, they appear to use the complexity of social psychological phenomena to resist the pressure to provide clear definitions of concepts in the theory. Thus, talking about the phenomena of interest to social representations theory, Marková (2000, p. 430) wrote that 'attempts to provide an exhaustive definition of such phenomena are based on a misconception of their nature'. Voelklein and Howarth (2001, p. 437) suggest that 'Moscovici is keen not to apply a definition that is too restrictive as complex social phenomena cannot be reduced to simple propositions.' This reluctance to define terms precisely – in other words, the trend towards 'mysticism' – is worrying because any kind of academic enquiry needs to be clear and explicit. However, if we are prepared to suspend these worries, it is clear that social representations theory has inspired much research, which has generated discoveries about shared concepts, attitudes and behaviours, casting light on a range of topics, including how people collaborate to form attitudes to their history (Liu and Hilton, 2005; Sibley, Liu, Duckitt and Khan, 2008), political conflicts (Elcheroth, Doise and Reicher, 2011), political ideology (Corbetta, Cavazza and Roccato, 2009), technology (Devine-Wright and Devine-Wright, 2009), disease (Mayor, Eicher, Bangerter et al., in press) and the environment (Smith and Joffe, in press).

Exploring further In 2011, a special issue of the journal *Political Psychology* contained articles devoted to social representations theory. If you have access to this journal (some articles may be available to public readers on the internet), browse through the articles to get a sense of how the theory has developed. Some of the articles (e.g., Elcheroth et al., 2011) spend time explicitly defining and developing the theory. Do you think that social representations theory is now on a firmer scientific footing, offering clearer definitions and accounts of causal processes?

Question to consider Now that you know how attitudes form and why people have attitudes in the first place, reread question 1 at the start of the chapter. What social psychological reasons are there for Lisbeth to be part of these groups? Does Facebook facilitate any particular purpose?

Implicit and explicit attitudes

In Chapter 3, we encountered the important distinction between automatic and controlled social cognition. As we saw, we have more conscious awareness of, and control over, some aspects of our social cognition than others. Attitudes are no exception. A great deal of research has uncovered that far from having one attitude to an object we can consciously report, we have a mixture of unconscious (or implicit) and conscious (or explicit) attitudes. To understand this distinction, it is first necessary to have some idea of how attitudes are measured in social psychology. Thus, before exploring the different causes and functions of implicit and explicit attitudes, we briefly consider how attitudes are measured in social psychology. Sometimes, social psychologists simply ask people what their attitudes are, or observe their behaviour in order to gauge their attitudes. On the other hand, they may use less direct measures, using specific tests designed to tap into people's attitudes, or they may measure people's physical responses to attitude objects as an index of their attitudes.

Direct measures of attitudes

Attitudes are difficult to examine because unlike many physical objects, they cannot be observed. Thus, social psychologists often rely on people's own self-reports of their attitudes. The most common approach to doing this is simply to ask people to respond to questions about their attitudes, that is, ask them what they think. For example, you may have participated in a phone survey where a person asked you for your opinions about electronic goods, food, drink or something else. You may have completed a political opinion poll. In such cases, your attitudes are being measured. In studies of people's attitudes, social psychologists make use of **attitude scales**, a series of questions designed to measure specific attitudes. These scales are tested many times to ensure they are valid and reliable. A well-designed scale will measure the direction and strength of a person's attitudes on a particular topic (Dawes and Smith, 1985; Edwards, 1983; Likert, [1932]1974). For example, if you were asked to complete a scale concerning your attitudes surrounding popular conspiracy theories, you may be asked to rate your agreement with a set of statements, on a scale like this (from Douglas and Sutton, 2008, 2011; also Wood, Douglas and Sutton, 2012):

Attitude scale A series of questions designed to gauge a person's attitudes on a topic.

Princess Diana was murdered by rogue cells within MI6
Completely disagree   1   2   3   4   5   6   7   Completely agree

Your averaged responses inform a researcher whether or not you endorse conspiracy theories, and how much you endorse such theories. Measuring attitudes in this way is relatively easy and noninvasive, so it is not surprising this is the most popular way in which social psychologists tend to measure attitudes. However, social psychologists also observe people's behaviours in order to judge their attitudes. For example, a researcher may measure whether people volunteer to stuff envelopes for a campaign or give money to a charity in order to assess their attitudes towards the cause, or how those attitudes change in response to contextual changes (Deci, 1975; Jonas, Schimel, Greenberg and Pyszczynski, 2002; Wilson and Dunn, 1986). Observational studies are often used in organizational psychology to observe workers' attitudes to their co-workers and aspects of the workplace such as promotion decisions (Schwarzwald, Koslowsky and Shalit, 1992). Observing what people do is therefore a good technique for understanding their attitudes in a range of settings.

There are many advantages to these sorts of measures. In the case of attitude scales especially, the expense is relatively small and it is quick and easy to gauge people's attitudes. On the other hand, there are some drawbacks to using these methods. Most importantly, they rely on people being honest. Much of the time, people will say what they think and behave in ways that reflect their attitudes, so scale and observational methods can be effective. However, when topics are sensitive and people may feel embarrassed or afraid to say what they really think, self-report and observational measures may be less effective measures of people's actual attitudes. Social desirability is a powerful motivator, so sometimes researchers need to think of other ways to measure people's 'less desirable' attitudes.

One way to do this is to include a *lie scale* in the mix of the attitude scales of interest (e.g., Barrett and Eysenck, 1992; Reynolds and Richmond, 1979). Such scales were originally introduced into personality measures in order to detect whether people 'fake good' on scores of other scales, to make themselves look more socially desirable (O'Donovan, 1969). Lie scales are made up of items listing behaviours and issues that are either socially desirable but not frequently practised (e.g., 'I am always nice to everyone') or frequently practised but socially undesirable (e.g., 'I never say things I shouldn't'). From participants' responses, lying can be diagnosed when a set of desirable but infrequently performed behaviours are endorsed by the participant as being done frequently, and when frequently performed undesirable behaviours are denied by the participant. These responses can be statistically analysed alongside the attitude measures to compensate for social desirability concerns in attitude research. For example, in one study, Sutton and Farrall (2005) used a lie scale to demonstrate that men's attitudes towards crime (and specifically their fear of crime) were more marked than those of women, once lying was taken into account. In other words, men were more likely to be dishonest in expressing their feelings about crime, but using a lie scale allowed the researchers to show that men were actually more fearful of crime than women.

It is also possible to get around people's desire to look good simply by making their responses anonymous, so that their responses are not identifiable and they are not accountable for the views they express. However, social psychologists have also designed more indirect ways of examining attitudes that get around people's social desirability concerns. Some examples are discussed in the following section.

Indirect measures of attitudes

One such indirect measure is called the *bogus pipeline procedure*. Here, the participant is attached to a device known as the bogus pipeline (see Figure 4.10), and told it can detect their 'true' attitudes (Jones and Sigall, 1971; Quigley-Fernandez and Tedeschi, 1978; Roese and Jamieson, 1993). This is presumed to cause participants to fear that dishonest responses would be noticed, causing them to indicate their attitudes more honestly than usual. This technique has been used widely in areas such as the detection of substance abuse in teenagers (e.g., Murray and Perry, 1987), alcohol abuse among pregnant women (Lowe, Windsor, Adams et al., 1986), distorted thinking that supports offending among child molesters (Gannon,

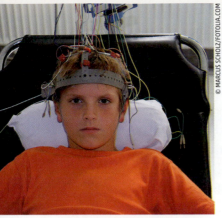

© MARCUS SCHOLZ/FOTOLIA.COM

FIGURE 4.10 The bogus pipeline procedure In the bogus pipeline paradigm, participants are led to believe that a device can read their 'true' attitudes. In the most robust version of this paradigm, participants are given a practice trial on the device, which displays 'answers' that match their attitudes which have been tested in an earlier session. This enhances the illusion that the device really has a mind-reading power. Participants typically express less socially desirable attitudes under these conditions than they do normally. The bogus pipeline, then, is one way that researchers can scratch beneath the surface of socially desirable responding when assessing participants' attitudes.

2006) and socially sensitive behaviours in surveys (Tourangeau, Rips and Rasinski, 2000; for a 20-year meta-analysis of bogus pipeline research examining studies up until the early 1990s, see Roese and Jamieson, 1993).

Social psychologists have also devised physiological measures to examine people's attitudes. For example, Cacioppo, Petty, Losch and Kim (1986) devised a measure that monitors muscular movements in the face to examine the direction and intensity of attitudes. The muscular movements are measured electronically through a process called electromyography (EMG), which specifically measures the electrical activity of the muscles. When people are happy or sad, different muscles in the face contract. Much of the time, this can be seen. For example, when someone is unhappy, their brow may contract into a frown, and when they are happy, the corners of their mouth will turn upwards. However, facial movements related to emotional or attitudinal experiences cannot always be seen. EMG allows researchers to examine subtle facial movements. Cacioppo and Petty (1979) used this technique to examine people's attitudes. They asked participants to listen to a speech that either opposed or supported their views on alcohol possession or university student housing visiting rules. Participants' EMG activity corresponded to the direction and intensity of their attitudes. Specifically, participants who opposed the speech showed more activity in the brow muscles associated with frowning and disapproval, whereas those in favour showed more activity in the muscles associated with smiling.

In recent years, advances in neuroscience have afforded researchers another way to measure attitudes – to observe the brain's responses to attitude objects. This is not a straightforward process. Attitudes are defined as evaluations or appraisals, and so are rather abstract concepts that may not translate into any particular psychological mechanism. If they do not, attempts to observe them in the brain may be misplaced (Amodio and Harmon-Jones, 2012). Nonetheless, some researchers have had success in capturing neural correlates of at least some aspects of attitudes. One approach to this is to use event-related potentials (ERPs), which can be observed using electroencephalogram equipment. As we saw in Chapter 1, this approach is particularly well suited to capturing rapid, short-term neural responses to stimuli. Crites and Cacioppo (1996) observed exaggerated P300 responses (associated with attention, arousal and updating of beliefs) in response to attitude objects that participants disliked. Cunningham, Espinet, DeYoung and Zelazo (2005) found that stimulus concepts rated as 'bad' (e.g., murder, terrorism, immigration) triggered these P300 responses in the right hemisphere of the brain, whereas objects rated as 'good' (e.g., love, babies, technology) triggered the same responses in the left hemisphere. These findings suggest the intriguing possibility that, to some extent, the brain hemispheres are specialized for positive and negative attitudes.

Another approach is functional magnetic resonance imaging (fMRI), a 'brain-mapping' technique that tracks which regions of the brain are being activated by monitoring changes in blood flow. In keeping with Amodio and Harmon-Jones's (2012) observation that attitudes are not psychological processes, many brain regions are activated in response to negative and positive attitude objects (Cunningham, Raye and Johnson, 2004). The amygdala, which is strongly associated with emotion, is activated when positively evaluated stimuli are presented (Zald, 2003), and still more strongly in the presence of negatively evaluated stimuli (LeDoux, 2000). Researchers have tried examining fMRI and ERP readings to explore the neuroscience of prejudice, and findings reveal that multiple areas of the brain are involved (Ibáñez, Haye, González et al., 2009). Perhaps the most interesting finding to emerge from this line of research is that neural responses associated with error recognition and cognitive control appear very quickly in response to other-race faces. This suggests that the inhibition of racial prejudice may be engrained in the brain and may occur even in the absence of a conscious effort to control the bias (Amodio, Harmon-Jones, Devine et al., 2004).

Although the use of neuroscience to assess attitudes is in its infancy and is beset by problems, there has been a lot of research on the use of performance measures to assess attitudes. Performance measures borrow from the techniques and concepts of cognitive psychology, and assess reaction time and accuracy of responding on computerized tasks (Gawronski and Bodenhausen, 2011). The two most commonly used performance measures of attitude have been the go/no-go association task or GNAT (Nosek and Banaji, 2001), and the **Implicit Association Test (IAT)** (Greenwald, McGhee and Schwartz, 1998). Of these two, the IAT is used most often, and is featured below in the Ethics and research methods box.

Implicit Association Test (IAT)
Reaction time test that measures the strengths of automatic associations between mental representations of objects (concepts) in memory.

ETHICS AND RESEARCH METHODS

The Implicit Association Test (IAT)

Participants in an IAT study typically sit behind a computer and are asked to press different keys to match concepts during a series of trials. For example, in the first trial, participants may be asked to tap a key on the left-hand side of the keyboard if they see a word they associate with 'good' and the right-hand key when they see a word that is associated with 'bad'. They do so for a series of words and their reaction time is measured. In the second trial, participants may be asked to perform a similar task but this time matching two different concepts. For example, they may be asked to tap left when they see a word they associate with 'me' and right when they see a word associated with 'them'. Again, their reaction time is measured. The third trial gets a little more complicated. Here, participants may be asked to tap left when they see a word associated with either 'me' or 'good' and right when they see a word associated with either 'them' or 'bad'. Their reaction times are again recorded by the experimenter. Finally, on the fourth trial, participants may be asked to tap left when they see a word associated with either 'me' or 'bad' and right when they see a word associated with either 'them' or 'good'. On which trial would you expect participants to be slowest? Research suggests that participants are typically slowest to respond on the final trial. Before reading on, think why this might happen. Why do you think participants are slowest on the trials when they are asked to respond when they see words associated with 'me' and 'bad' or 'them' and 'good'?

Greenwald et al. (1998) argue that the IAT tests people's automatic preference for some classes of stimuli over others. It is based on the idea that attitudes are associative mental networks and that associations are stronger if an attitude exists than when it does not. So, people will be able to more quickly link concepts that are related (for them) than those that are not. Thus, in the example above, 'me' or 'good' responses should be faster than 'me' or 'bad' responses – after all, people tend not to think of themselves as bad, so the association between 'me' and 'bad' should therefore be less accessible. On the other hand, 'them' and 'bad' associations are typically stronger, so people are often faster at responding to this pairing. To give another example, if a student dislikes university lecturers, they will be likely to respond 'yes' more quickly to words like 'nasty', and 'no' to words like 'nice' than if they had no negative attitude towards university lecturers. Many studies have used the IAT to examine implicit attitudes towards racial groups (e.g., McConnell and Liebold, 2001), gender attitudes (e.g., Greenwald, Nosek and Banaji, 2003) and homosexuality (e.g., Steffens and Buchner, 2003; see Greenwald, Poehlman, Uhlmann and Banaji, 2009 for a recent review). The popularity of the IAT even led to the publication of a tongue-in-cheek suggestion that since there are no people left alive who have not done the IAT, dead people should be exhumed and asked to do it (Bones and Johnson, 2007).

As well as satire, the IAT has attracted many serious criticisms. For example, some researchers have shown that responses to the IAT – said to be a measure of the extent to which a person endorses evaluative associations – do not correlate very well with other, more explicit attitude measures (e.g., Karpinski and Hilton, 2001). Perhaps, therefore, the IAT may be a better measure of the associations a person has been exposed to rather than the extent to which they endorse the associations themselves. However, this criticism may miss the basic point of dual attitude theories, in that implicit attitudes are *supposed* to be different from explicit attitudes (e.g., Bagenstos, 2007; Gawronski and Bodenhausen, 2011; Rydell, McConnell and Mackie, 2008). Further, the correlation is weak but statistically reliable, as we would expect (Greenwald et al., 2009). Another, perhaps more serious problem is that although the IAT is designed partly to circumvent the problem of socially desirable responding, with practice, people can fake it (Steffens, 2004). Finally, other social psychologists have criticized the IAT on a number of dimensions, such as the viability of the underlying association model itself, that is, the reasoning behind why IAT effects occur, and the difficulties in interpreting IAT scores (Fiedler, Messner and Bluemke, 2006; Mitchell and Tetlock, 2006). Nevertheless, the popularity of the IAT as a measure of implicit attitudes is remarkable. As of June 2012, the original article (Greenwald et al., 1998) had been cited 3,821 times in articles on Google Scholar.

Questions

1 Research on implicit prejudice inevitably has political repercussions. For example, some scholars have argued that the ubiquity of implicit prejudice uncovered by the IAT and similar measures highlights the need for affirmative action programmes in employment. Since unconscious bias against minority groups is everywhere, the argument goes, a deliberate bias towards them needs to be introduced to counteract it (Jolls and Sunstein, 2006; Kang and Banaji, 2006). It has also been seriously argued that as part of recruitment and hiring processes, employers should consider running applicants for jobs through the IAT (e.g., Ayres, 2001). What are the arguments for and against the use of the IAT in hiring decisions – is it legitimate not to hire someone because they come out as prejudiced on the IAT? Consider the ethical, scientific and logistical arguments for and against the use of this technology.

2 Use Google Scholar to find the article by Greenwald, McGhee and Schwartz (1998). How many times has it been cited now?

3 Use Google Scholar to find the article by Nosek and Banaji (2001) on the GNAT. Then find some summaries of the GNAT and arguments for and against its use (as opposed to, say, the IAT). Which, if any, is the better measure?

Try it yourself See what you think about the IAT. Try it yourself at Harvard University's Project Implicit website. You can try the GNAT here too.

Question to consider Now, reread question 2 at the start of the chapter. What would you say to Dirk, who thinks it is impossible to measure attitudes?

The relationship between explicit and implicit attitudes

Implicit and explicit attitudes tend, for the most part, to be positively correlated (Gawronski and Bodenhausen, 2011; Wilson, Lindsey and Schooler, 2002). For example, your attitudes to your best friends are likely (for the most part) to be positive whether they are measured on a self-report scale, or with a reaction time performance measure like the IAT, or even if we were to use measures from physiology and neuroscience. Nonetheless, they differ in many interesting ways (Rydell et al., 2008; Wilson, Lindsey and Schooler, 2002), which are displayed in Table 4.1. Broadly speaking, we can say that it is harder for people to deliberately change their own or others' implicit attitudes, as compared to their explicit attitudes, through appeals to logic and the other normal techniques of persuasion (e.g., Petty, Tormala, Briñol and Jarvis, 2006). However, implicit attitudes to new attitude objects may be formed more quickly than explicit ones. You may display a subtle negative or positive bias towards a person or group, for example, before you can report any negative thoughts or feelings towards them (Ashburn-Nardo, Voils and Monteith, 2001; Gregg, Seibt and Banaji, 2006). Although implicit attitudes are slower to change, they can be highly dependent on the situation. For example, given the widespread prejudice felt towards Roma Gypsies around Europe, a typical European might find negative appraisals like 'dishonest' quickly activated when they see a Gypsy in a shopping centre, but at the same time, positive appraisals like 'musical' at a folk festival (for a demonstration of the same logic with attitudes to Black people in the USA, see Barden, Maddux, Petty and Brewer, 2004). As we have seen, implicit attitudes are more likely to be socially or personally unacceptable than explicit attitudes (Degner and Wentura, 2008; Rudman and Kilianski, 2000), because people are reluctant to admit to others (Tourangeau and Yan, 2007) or themselves (von Hippel and Trivers, 2011) that they possess them. Another key difference is that implicit attitudes are more likely than explicit attitudes to influence our unplanned, spontaneous behaviours. For example, Dovidio, Kawakami and Gaertner (2002) found that implicit racial bias, as measured by the IAT, more strongly affected negative body language during interactions across racial boundaries. In another study by Hoffman and Friese (2008), female German university students with positive implicit attitudes to sweets were more likely to eat sweets in the laboratory, independent of their explicit attitudes. The effect of implicit attitudes was heightened when the students had consumed alcohol, suggesting that implicit attitudes are more likely to influence our behaviours when we are unable to devote controlled cognitive processes to 'stop them' from working on us.

Why are implicit and explicit attitudes different from each other? Probably the most influential current theoretical account of the implicit-explicit duality is Gawronski and Bodenhausen's (2006, 2007, 2011) **associative-propositional evaluation (APE) model**. According to this model, implicit and explicit attitudes are the behavioral outcomes of separate mental processes. Implicit attitudes spring from *associative processes*, such as evaluative conditioning. Associative processes can also be triggered by similarities between the stimulus and something in memory.

Associative-propositional evaluation (APE) model
Model asserting that implicit and explicit attitudes are the behavioural outcomes of separate mental processes.

TABLE 4.1 Differences between implicit and explicit attitudes

	Implicit attitudes	Explicit attitudes
How do they change?	Classical or associative conditioning (also known as evaluative conditioning)	As well as conditioning, explicit attitudes are affected by logic and evidence
How quickly do they change?	Implicit attitudes change slowly, but very different implicit attitudes can be temporarily activated by situations	Explicit attitudes can change quickly, but are somewhat less prone to strong temporary changes in a given situation
How much knowledge do they require?	Implicit attitudes can be almost instantly formed with little or no knowledge of an attitude object	Explicit attitudes are typically moderate or weak until people learn salient facts about an attitude object
How much do they conform to society's standards or norms?	Implicit attitudes do not necessarily respect society's standards or norms. However, if people internalize society's standards, they can condition their own implicit attitudes over time	Explicit attitudes are often strongly shaped by society's standards or norms. People are typically reluctant to express socially undesirable social attitudes, especially when they are accountable
What kind of behaviour do they primarily affect?	Spontaneous, unplanned behaviour such as body language	Planned decision making
What mental processes underlie them?	Associative processes	Propositional processes

Ever found yourself liking (or disliking) someone partly because they remind you of someone you used to know? This phenomenon was first noticed by Freud, who called it *transference*, and it is one of Freud's ideas to receive empirical support (e.g., Andersen, Reznik and Manzella, 1996). When these associations are activated in memory, an implicit evaluation will follow. On the other hand, the APE model holds that explicit attitudes spring from *propositional processes*. These are akin to beliefs or conclusions, and are defined as the validation of information that is implied by activated associations. Thus, for example, you might have a positive implicit attitude to a person simply because they have been paired with, or are similar to, another person who you value. This positive attitude might show up in an IAT, for example, or in some other indirect test of reaction time or accuracy. However, your implicit positive attitude may not necessarily lead you to draw the propositional conclusion that they really are a nice or attractive person. Whether you do so will depend partly on whether you think this conclusion is logically warranted, given what you know about them.

The APE model is relatively new, but evidence already suggests that it predicts and explains effects that are both interesting and useful. For example, consider two ways of reducing prejudiced attitudes towards disadvantaged outgroups – an important topic in social psychology, to which we return at great length in Chapter 12. One approach is to negate stereotypes (e.g., to practise repeatedly saying 'Gypsies are not thieves'). Another is to affirm counter-stereotypes (e.g., to repeatedly say 'Gypsies are honest'). Both techniques may work to reduce explicit prejudice – after doing this for long enough, people are likely to endorse prejudiced statements about Gypsies, since they are reminding themselves that many Gypsies are honest, that it is not warranted to label an entire group as thieves and so on. However, one technique is likely to have disastrous effects on implicit prejudice towards Gypsies. Which one, do you think? Since implicit attitudes are built up by associative processes including evaluative conditioning, the negation task has a cruelly ironic effect. It repeatedly pairs 'Gypsies' and 'thieves', so that in

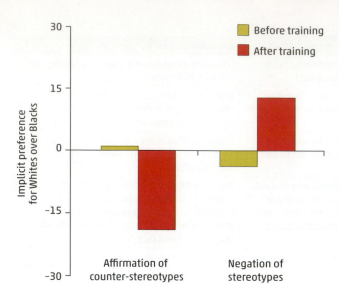

FIGURE 4.11 Effects of affirming versus negating stereotypes In an experiment by Gawronski et al. (2008), implicit racial bias was reduced when participants practised affirming counter-stereotypes (saying positive statements about an outgroup). However, it was increased when participants practised negating stereotypes (denying negative statements about an outgroup). This shows how prejudice reduction techniques can backfire if they are not informed by sound theory and evidence.

Source: Data from Gawronski et al., 2008. Copyright (2008), reprinted with permission from Elsevier

the very act of trying not to be prejudiced, a person who repeatedly says 'Gypsies are not thieves' is actually training their associative mental systems to produce an even stronger negative emotional reaction to Gypsies. Much the same logic, in relation to racial prejudice in the USA, was demonstrated in an experiment by Gawronski, Deutsch, Mbrikou et al. (2008) (see Figure 4.11).

Attitudes and behaviours

Attitudes are important to people. But to what extent do attitudes predict what people do? This question has occupied social psychologists for many years, and is central to the practical significance of attitudes. For example, are attitudes towards minority groups important if they have little effect on how people treat members of minority groups or influence what people say about them? The link between attitudes and behaviours is, therefore, an important issue to study. In a classic study, LaPiere (1934) demonstrated that attitudes do not necessarily determine what people do. At the time the study was conducted, psychologists generally agreed that attitudes were predispositions to behave in a certain manner (Allport, 1924), so they assumed that attitudes would be closely related to behaviour. LaPiere investigated if this link would exist in the study of prejudiced attitudes. Over the course of two years, he travelled around the USA with a young Chinese couple. In doing so, he stopped at 184 restaurants and 66 hotels. At all these establishments (with the exception of one), the Chinese couple were served courteously and politely. However, after this study, LaPiere contacted each establishment and asked the proprietors if they would serve Chinese clientele. Overwhelmingly, the business owners said that they would not serve Chinese visitors; out of 128 businesses that responded, a staggering 92 per cent said they would not. Thus, LaPiere's demonstration suggests that attitudes do not always predict people's behaviour. A more modern example might be how people respond to 'political correctness'. Negative attitudes have not necessarily disappeared, instead people monitor their behaviour so that it becomes more socially acceptable. Attitudes do not, therefore, always predict what people do.

Other research points to a tenuous link between attitudes and behaviours. For example, Wicker (1969) noted that the correlation between the two – based on a comparison between responses to questionnaires and actual behaviours – is typically lower than 0.3. This is relatively low considering that a perfect correlation is 1.0 and represents only a low or moderate effect size. These findings call into question the validity of questionnaire methods that examine people's attitudes. If there is little link between people's attitudes and what they actually do, then perhaps social psychologists are focusing too much time on a construct that means very little to social reality. From your own experience, you will probably be able to think of many instances where your attitudes do not match your behaviour. For example, you might think that your best friend's taste in music is awful but you do not tell them this because you do not want to jeopardize the friendship. Instead, you say nothing or compliment your friend's taste in music and so your attitude is inconsistent with your behaviour.

Further, there is a growing body of research demonstrating that automatic or spontaneous behaviour sometimes completely bypasses conscious attitudes. You may recall from Chapter 3 Bargh, Chen and Burrows' (1996) study in which participants walked more slowly after seeing words that were related to stereotypes of the elderly. This kind of automatic behaviour has been demonstrated in many other studies. For example, priming people with achievement goals leads them to persevere more with difficult tasks (Bargh, Gollwitzer, Lee-Chai et al., 2001). Priming people with French music in a market makes people buy more French wine and playing German music makes people buy more German wine (North, Hargreaves and McKendrick, 1999). Further, Dijksterhuis and van Knippenberg (1998) subliminally primed participants with the concept of either professors (educated, intellectual) or football hooligans (uneducated, non-intellectual). They found that participants who had been primed with the concept of professors performed better on a general knowledge test than participants who had been primed with football hooligans.

However, on many occasions, people's attitudes and behaviours are consistent with conscious attitudes. For example, you might hold strong left-wing political views and behave in support of these attitudes by becoming a member of progressive political parties and even participating in political rallies. People who hold negative attitudes about particular social and ethnic groups will often display prejudice towards those groups. It is therefore too pessimistic to say that attitudes are not important. Indeed, social psychologists agree that it is less of a question of whether attitudes determine behaviours *at all*, but *when* they do so. Social psychological research has focused more on this question in recent years. Specifically, while attitudes do indeed predict behaviour on many occasions (Bohner and Wänke, 2002; Kraus, 1995; Petty and Krosnick, 1995), the situation and aspects of the attitudes themselves are important. Other features such as values and habits also predict the extent to which attitudes and behaviours are linked.

Situational factors

It is not always possible to express or act on our attitudes. As in the above example, we often do not want to hurt people's feelings, so we cannot openly express negative attitudes to their ethnicity or their most recent haircut. Likewise, acting on our political beliefs can sometimes be offensive because not everybody holds the same beliefs. Forcing one's attitudes on others can have negative consequences, so much of the time people keep their attitudes to themselves. Thus, there are many situational constraints on the link between attitudes and behaviours. In many cases, situational constraints prevent the expression of attitudes (Ajzen and Fishbein, 1980; Fazio, Roskos-Ewoldsen and Powell, 1994). In most of these cases, these situational constraints relate to the strength of social norms and conventions.

On the other hand, many situational factors facilitate the expression of attitudes. For example, it becomes easier to express one's political attitudes in an online political forum or at a rally. Thus, perhaps unsurprisingly, people tend to seek out situations where they are able to express their attitudes (Snyder and Ickes, 1985) and, as a result, the attitudes can be strengthened (DeBono and Snyder, 1995). The expression of attitudes is often determined by situational factors but, at the same time, attitudes determine what situations people choose to find themselves in.

Attitudinal factors

Aspects of the attitudes themselves can determine the extent to which they are associated with behaviours. One factor is how the attitudes were formed in the first place. Some evidence suggests that attitudes formed on the basis of experiences are more strongly associated with behaviours than attitudes based on observation or other indirect ways (Fazio and Zanna, 1981; Haddock, Rothman, Reber and Schwarz, 1999). For example, Haddock et al. demonstrated that the strength of people's attitudes towards assisted suicide was influenced by people's experience of having a direct encounter with assisted suicide. In general, attitudes that have been formed through a direct experience are more closely related to actual behaviour (Doll and Ajzen 1992; Regan and Fazio, 1977).

The strength of the attitude is also important. In short, the stronger the attitudes, the more likely they influence behaviours (Holland, Verplanken and van Knippenberg, 2002; Petkova, Ajzen and Driver, 1995). Attitude strength is determined by three factors. First, the accessibility of the attitude is important, that is, how easily it comes to mind and how quickly it can be expressed (Eagly and Chaiken, 1998). Stronger attitudes tend to be more accessible and therefore exert a stronger influence on behaviour (Fazio, 1986). Fazio argues that accessible attitudes are more useful because they are quickly retrieved from memory and thus more easily help people make decisions. They can be automatically activated and have a stronger impact on behaviour (Fazio, Blascovich and Driscoll, 1992; Fazio and Powell, 1997). At the same time, highly accessible attitudes can be resistant to change and can hinder decision making in situations where attitude objects change (Fazio, Ledbetter and Towles-Schwen (2000). Second, the intensity of the attitude – or how strong an emotional reaction is evoked – influences attitude strength (Crano, 1995; Fishbein, 1967; Krosnick, 1988; Sivacek and Crano, 1982). Finally, the extent to which a person knows a lot about the issue or object in question influences attitude strength (Krosnick and Smith, 1994). These attitudinal factors all predict the correspondence between attitudes and behaviours (e.g., Holland, Verplanken and van Knippenberg, 2002).

Attitude–behaviour consistency is determined by the specificity, as well as the strength, of attitudes. Some attitudes are focused on specific objects or situations

and some are more general. For example, a person might be prejudiced against immigrants in general, or they may focus their negative attitudes on one specific immigrant group. Research suggests that the link between attitudes and behaviour is closest when the level of specificity is more closely matched (Ajzen and Fishbein, 1980, 2005; Fazio et al., 1994). Ajzen and Fishbein (1980) argued that one reason why many studies have failed to find a close correspondence between attitudes and behaviours is because researchers have tried to predict specific behaviours from general attitudes. To give an example, whether one helps a person of a specific immigrant group is more likely to be associated with their beliefs about that group in particular, rather than immigrants in general. A study by Davidson and Jaccard (1979) supports this argument. They found that women's general attitudes towards birth control did not predict their use of the contraceptive pill as well as more specific attitudes such as their attitudes towards using the contraceptive pill within the next two years. In summary, the more specific the attitude in question, the more closely it is likely to be linked to behaviour.

Values and ideology

Priming values also influences people's choices so they become more aligned with their values (Verplanken and Holland, 2002), such as when people are primed to think about the environment, they behave in a way that is friendly to the environment. Ideology is a similar construct to values. As we saw earlier, this concept refers to an interrelated and widely shared set of beliefs that serves to explain the social situation (Thompson, 1990). Ideologies typically refer to social or political contexts (e.g., sociopolitical and religious ideologies). They can influence values, attitudes and intentions to commit behaviours (Crandall, 1994).

Habits and individual differences

A person's habits can also predict their behaviour on future occasions. For example, if a woman gets into the habit of conducting breast self-examination every month, this will be a strong predictor of her intentions to continue doing so. In a study that supports this hypothesis, Trafimow (2000) found that university students who habitually used condoms during sex reported that they intended to do so in future sexual encounters and, specifically, on the next occasion. It has been argued that when behaviours are habitual, people do not need to think about their attitudes or whether their actions are appropriate. In some respects, the attitude-congruent behaviour becomes automatic (e.g., Norman and Conner, 2006).

Individual differences can also determine the link between attitudes and behaviours. For example, a person's consistency in answering questions about their personality is more likely to be higher in their behaviours on relevant dimensions (Bem and Allen, 1974). To give an example, a person who typically responds to an extraversion/introversion scale in the same way will typically behave in an extraverted or introverted manner in social interactions more so than someone whose responses are less consistent.

How do attitudes predict behaviours?

In addition to knowing the conditions under which attitudes predict behaviour, social psychologists are also interested in how it all happens. The **theory of planned behaviour** (and its predecessor, the **theory of reasoned action**) proposes that people make a decision to behave in a particular way as a result of a sequence of rational thought processes (Ajzen and Fishbein, 1980; Azjen, 1991). First, a person considers various behavioural options and their consequences and possible outcomes. These options are evaluated and a decision is made to perform a behaviour or not. This decision is then indicated by *behavioral intentions*, which are argued to be a key predictor of whether or not the behaviour is actually performed. These intentions are further influenced by a person's attitudes towards the behaviour (whether they think the behaviour will have positive or negative consequences), subjective norms (what people think others will think about the behaviour) and perceived behavioural control (whether or not a person thinks they can perform the behaviour).

The theory works as follows. If a person is considering an action such as joining a progressive political party, the question of whether or not they do so can be addressed by the theory of planned behaviour (see Figure 4.12). Specifically, the intention to join the political party depends on the person's intentions to do so, which are determined by their attitudes towards the behaviour (is joining the party a good thing to do?), subjective norms (do others think that joining the party is a good thing to do?) and perceived behavioural control (is it easy to join the party?). If these factors are satisfactory and intentions are strong, the person is more likely to join the political party. If, on the other hand, one of the determinants of intentions is not favourable (e.g., the person's closest friends abhor that particular political party), the chances of the person forming the intention and eventually performing the behaviour are reduced.

Research supports the principles of the theory. For example, Ajzen and Madden (1986) found that students' grades were only influenced by their own predictions when they took their own abilities into account. It is perhaps unsurprising that students wish to achieve good grades – after all, they are valued (attitudes). Also, subjective norms suggest that good grades are desirable in general. However, unless the issue of behavioural control is met, the predictive value of the attitude is diminished. In a study of nine behaviours that range from relatively easy to control (e.g., taking health supplements) or relatively difficult (e.g., getting a good night's sleep), Madden, Ellen and Ajzen (1992) found that perceived control influenced the predictive accuracy of intentions and actions. Further, the easier the behaviour was seen to be controllable, the more it predicted actual behaviour. The theory of planned behaviour has been applied extensively in health psychology,

Theory of planned behaviour
Theory concerning how attitudes predict behaviour. It argues that several factors, including subjective norms, attitudes towards the behaviour and perceived behavioural control, determine behavioural intentions concerning the behaviour, and, in turn, intentions strongly determine whether the behaviour is performed.

Theory of reasoned action
Predecessor to the theory of planned behaviour. It did not take perceived behavioural control into account as a predictor of intentions.

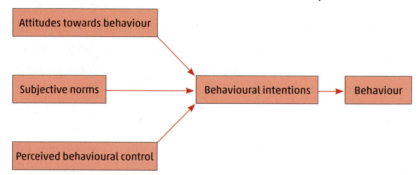

FIGURE 4.12 The theory of planned behaviour

such as in the study of safe sex behaviours (e.g., Sheeran and Taylor, 1999), smoking (Godin, Valois, Lepage and Desharnais, 1992) and alcohol consumption (e.g., Conner, Warren, Close and Sparks, 1999). It has also been applied to the study of driving behaviour (e.g., Parker, Manstead and Stradling, 1995). The theory has been found to be good at predicting what people do (for a review, see Armitage and Conner, 2001). In recent years, the theory of planned behaviour has been supplemented with Gollwitzer's (1993, 1999) concept of implementation intentions. If people not only form an intention to do or achieve something, but also specify exactly when and how they will do so, the link between intentions and behaviours becomes much stronger (see Applying social psychology at the end of the chapter for more details).

Unlike the theory of reasoned action and the theory of planned behaviour, the *attitude to behaviour process model* focuses on situations where a person does not have time to carefully reflect on different behaviours and their consequences. Many times, people need to react and perform a behaviour quickly. How do they do this? Fazio (1989) has argued that sometimes behaviours are determined by our attitudes in a more automatic manner. Encountering the attitude object, or a relevant cue to the object, may automatically activate your attitude (i.e., your evaluation) of that object. The extent to which your attitude is activated depends on the strength of the mental association between the object and its evaluation. Once these attitudes are activated, they will shape your perceptions of the object and the situation. Our awareness of social norms (what is generally acceptable and unacceptable) is also activated. Put together, and all happening very quickly, these factors influence our behaviour. So, for example, if a random person interrupts a private conversation you are having with a friend, this event triggers attitudes about people who interrupt. You are also likely to think of the general social norms surrounding conversations – one of which is that people generally know not to interrupt private talk between friends. You then quickly perceive the event (probably that this person is rude) and you are likely to behave accordingly by asking the person to leave you and your friend alone. So, this theory proposes that people behave rather spontaneously when their attitudes are activated.

Cognitive dissonance

So far, we have discussed the extent to which people's behaviours are consistent with their attitudes, when attitudes predict behaviours, and how this occurs. We know our attitudes do not always predict our behaviours, and this, of course, has consequences. Think of how it makes you feel when you comment positively on your friend's recent disastrous haircut. What emotions do you experience when you articulate an attitude you don't really mean? Most of us would agree that we feel uncomfortable. After all, we are not being true to ourselves. Another classic example is the fact that most people believe the evidence of a strong link between smoking and lung cancer, and yet a significant percentage of the population

Cognitive dissonance An unpleasant psychological state that occurs when people notice that their attitudes and behaviours (or their attitudes) are inconsistent with each other.

continues to smoke. People know they are not doing the right thing by their bodies, yet still continue with the behaviour. Social psychologists call this being in a state of **cognitive dissonance** (Festinger, 1957). Cognitive dissonance is defined as the unpleasant psychological state that occurs when people notice that their attitudes and behaviours (or their various attitudes) are inconsistent with each other. The study of cognitive dissonance has uncovered one of the most profound, surprising and important messages of social psychology – while our attitudes influence our behaviour, our behaviour also strongly influences our attitudes. What we do affects how we think and feel.

Cognitive dissonance was empirically demonstrated in a classic study by Festinger and Carlsmith (1959). They had people participate in a boring experiment where they were asked to perform repetitive tasks such as turning pegs on a board and removing the pegs one by one and then putting them all back. At the end of the study, the experimenter asked the participant for help. If they agreed to help, their task was to convince the next 'participant' (actually, a confederate) that the task was enjoyable and interesting. The payment for telling this lie was either $1 – obviously a measly sum for lying – or $20 – which in the late 1950s was a princely sum. Festinger and Carlsmith predicted that participants who agreed to describe the task as enjoyable to another participant would be put in a state of cognitive dissonance: they had volunteered to perform a behaviour that was inconsistent with their attitudes. Since $1 is not enough to justify lying, Festinger and Carlsmith predicted that participants' attitudes towards the experiment would change. Participants could not reasonably attribute their lie to the monetary reward, and so to resolve the inconsistency between their behaviour (saying the task was interesting) and attitudes (they found the task boring), they would have to revise their attitudes (so privately evaluate the task as less boring). Findings confirmed this hypothesis. As can be seen in Figure 4.13, participants in the $1 reward condition rated the experiment as less boring than control participants, who were not asked to convince the confederate that the task was interesting. Further, in a condition where participants were paid $20 to lie to the participants, they rated the experiment as relatively boring. Since $20 is a handsome reward for lying, participants could resolve the dissonance between their attitudes and behaviour by attributing their behaviour to the reward. This is striking finding: paying participants more to convince others that a task is interesting caused them to think they enjoyed it less.

This is a clear example of what happens to people's attitudes and behaviours when they experience cognitive dissonance. Festinger (1957) argued that people's motivation to reduce dissonance, rather than changing people's behaviours, can actually change their attitudes. In other words, to deal with dissonance, people often change the way they think rather than the way they behave. Cooper and

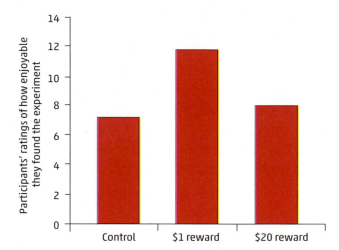

FIGURE 4.13 The phenomenon of cognitive dissonance Participants in a boring experiment rated the experiment as less boring when they were paid a measly $1 to tell the next participant they enjoyed the experiment. To deal with the attitude-behaviour inconsistency, they changed their attitudes about the boring experiment.

Source: Data from Festinger and Carlsmith, 1959

Fazio (1984) argued that four conditions need to be satisfied for dissonance to produce these types of effects:

1 *The individual has to realize that the inconsistency has negative consequences:* If the inconsistency has no negative consequences, it is unlikely that people will feel tension between the attitude and the behaviour. For example, if people reflect on the evidence that smoking causes ill health and the evidence is dismissed, no tension will occur. On the other hand, people who endorse the attitude that the behaviour (smoking) causes ill health are likely to experience cognitive dissonance (Cooper and Brehm, 1971).

2 *The individual has to take responsibility for the action:* Specifically, for dissonance to occur, the person needs to feel responsible for the attitude-incongruent behaviour. In the case of smoking, people need to think they are freely responsible for the decision to smoke. If people feel they have been told what to do, or coerced into performing the behaviour, the behaviour will not necessarily be inconsistent with their attitudes, so dissonance is unlikely to occur (Linder, Cooper and Jones, 1967).

3 *The individual has to experience physiological arousal:* Dissonance is an uncomfortable physical experience (Croyle and Cooper, 1983). For smokers, they probably feel unhappy or anxious that their smoking could cause them ill health.

4 *The individual has to attribute the feeling of physiological arousal to the action itself:* People need to be able to make the link between the feeling (e.g., being unhappy or anxious) and the behaviour (e.g., smoking) (Losch and Cacioppo, 1990).

These conditions produce a state of cognitive dissonance. Studies of cognitive dissonance suggest that people who are in a state of tension will change their attitudes to be more consistent with the behaviour they have performed. In many cases, the tension is fairly minimal. For example, it requires little commitment for a participant to tell another participant the white lie that a boring study is interesting. However, there is some evidence to suggest that the state of tension is especially strong when the inconsistencies are self-relevant, that is, they compromise people's positive sense of self (Baumeister, 1982; Steele, 1988). The need to reconcile inconsistent behaviours and attitudes therefore becomes stronger. For example, imagine putting up with an unhappy long-term relationship or working in a dead-end job. Because the feeling of dissonance is often chronically uncomfortable, people usually want to do something about it. According to dissonance theory (Aronson, 1968; Festinger, 1957), there are various ways in which people can reduce dissonance so that they feel better about what they are doing.

Reducing dissonance

First, people can approach the dissonance directly. In other words, they can focus on explicitly addressing the discrepancies between their attitudes and behaviours. There are various different ways to do this. First, people can change their attitudes so that they are more consistent with their behaviours. In the case of making comments about a friend's haircut, a person can attempt to change their attitude about the haircut by carefully evaluating it and convincing themselves that it is not such a bad haircut after all. A way of convincing oneself in this way is to find new information that supports the inconsistency with the behaviour. For example, similar haircuts might have been praised in the popular press or worn by a top model, supporting one's comments to the friend that the haircut is a good look. In short, a person can change their attitudes so that they closely match their behaviours. This everyday way of reducing cognitive dissonance is well supported in the literature. For example, Elliot and Devine (1994) showed that the discomfort experienced by attitude–behaviour inconsistency could be alleviated by attitude change.

Another way to reduce dissonance is simply by reducing the importance of the inconsistency. For example, we might decide that it is not such a bad thing to say one thing about a friend's haircut and mean something else. In other words, we might trivialize the discrepancy between our attitudes and behaviours. To do so, we may argue that the attitudes are not important in the first place, so if they are inconsistent with what we actually say or do, this is not really much of a problem. One study suggests that people do this with respect to cigarette smoking. In a study with an undergraduate student sample, Pervin and Yatko (1965) found that smokers reduced dissonance by minimizing the validity of anti-cancer research findings and the personal danger of smoking.

© BRAND X

Self-affirmation Restoring positive self-views when faced with cognitive dissonance.

Another approach is less direct. Instead of addressing the attitude–behaviour discrepancy explicitly, people may instead seek to reduce the discomfort associated with the discrepancy (Steele, 1988). Steele argues that the choice of such strategies occurs when attitudes are more important and we do not want to change them. For example, a person might hold strong views in support of one political party but compliment a friend's views in support of dubious opposing policies. This is likely to feel uncomfortable and one way to reduce the discomfort is to engage in a process of **self-affirmation**. Here, people reaffirm positive thoughts about themselves. In the above example, they may remember they attended a political rally the week before and they are an active campaigner for their party. By affirming their positive self-view and reminding themselves of the importance of their attitudes, people can reduce the discomfort created by dissonance (e.g., Elliot and Devine, 1994). Research also suggests that there are other ways in which people can reduce dissonance. For example, expressing positive affect can make people feel better (Cooper, Fazio and Rhodewalt, 1978) and consuming alcohol also helps (Steele, Southwick and Critchlow, 1981).

Thus, there are several options for people to reduce cognitive dissonance. However, it is also clear that people do not always seek to reduce dissonance. Think, for example, of smokers who know all the evidence of the dangers of smoking and yet still continue to smoke. Why do they do this? In many cases, the addiction to smoking prevents a person from dealing with the discrepancy between attitudes and behaviours. A smoker may know that smoking is harmful but they do not seek to reduce dissonance because the addiction overrides the need to do so. This also raises the question of just how negative the state of dissonance actually is. If people live with it relatively easily, can we necessarily say that it produces negative affect? The answer is yes. Harmon-Jones (2000) examined if dissonance makes people feel bad. He had participants write counterattitudinal essays (essays in which they were asked to express views contrary to their own) – in this case, they were asked to write that a boring paragraph was interesting. Some of the participants were asked to perform the task under conditions of low choice, that is, they were simply asked to argue that the boring paragraph was interesting. The remaining participants, however, were asked to do this under conditions of high choice, that is, they were told they could write what they wanted but it would be appreciated if they could write that the boring paragraph was interesting. In this condition only, dissonance was predicted because participants were expressing, of their own choice, attitudes inconsistent with their own beliefs. Findings confirmed this prediction. Participants in the high choice condition felt more discomfort and greater negative affect than participants in the low choice condition. This effect occurred despite the fact that participants threw their essays away afterwards. Thus, the negative feelings could not have been due to the concern that others may sanction them for their comments. In general, therefore, dissonance appears to make people feel uncomfortable (see Figure 4.14).

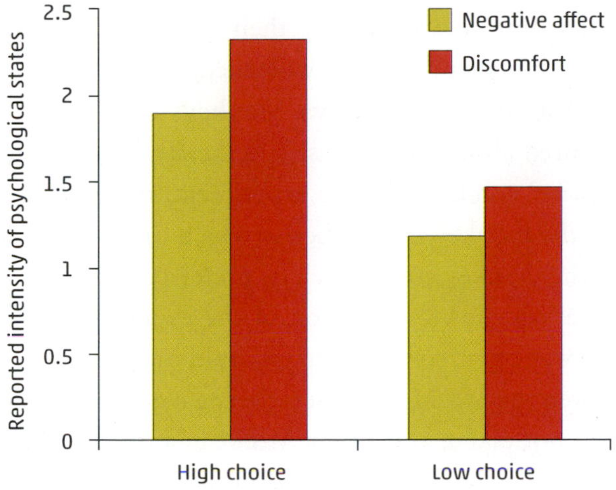

This feeling of discomfort is crucial to cognitive dissonance theory and separates it from a closely related theory that we briefly encountered in Chapter 2 – self-perception theory (Bem, 1967, 1972). Bem argued that since we do not have reliable knowledge of our own attitudes, we infer them from our behaviour. Thus, when we behave in a way that is inconsistent with our attitudes, we unconsciously infer that our attitude position cannot be very strong, after all. If we say we enjoyed a task when given a $1 reward, rather than a $20 reward, it is a reasonable inference that we must have enjoyed it at some level. In order to make this inference, we do not need to go through aversive psychological states, neither do we need to be motivated to escape them. However, research has shown that people do experience discomfort in cognitive dissonance experiments, much as Festinger's (1957) model predicted (Galinsky, Stone and Cooper, 2000; Kiesler and Pallak, 1976). And, as we have seen, the extent of this emotional discomfort is related to the extent of attitude change (Elliot and Devine, 1994).

FIGURE 4.14 The affect of cognitive dissonance
Participants who wrote counterattitudinal statements under voluntary conditions experienced more discomfort and negative affect than participants who had no choice but to write the statements.
Source: Data from Harmon-Jones, 2000

Question to consider Now, reread question 3 at the start of the chapter. Why does Luann still smoke and is there a way out of the addiction for her?

Biological vs. cultural influences on cognitive dissonance

From largely European and US-based studies, it cannot necessarily be concluded that all people experience dissonance. However, research does suggest that dissonance is common across cultures (Heine and Lehman, 2007). Not only is it universal among humans, it also seems that cognitive dissonance is experienced by other animals, too. We will illustrate this point by describing a delightful experiment by Egan, Santos and Bloom (2007) into post-decisional dissonance among monkeys. But first, you will need to understand what *post-decisional dissonance* is and how it relates to the theory of cognitive dissonance. The idea is that when you make a choice between two or more options, the fact that you have chosen one is dissonant with the fact that the other options also had appealing features. To resolve this dissonance, people need to change their attitudes by derogating the choice they did not make, and/or increasing their positive evaluation of their chosen option. Results of an early experiment by Brehm (1956) were true to this prediction. US consumers rated a variety of domestic appliances and were then allowed to choose between two they evaluated equally, to take home as a gift. After making their choice, participants' evaluation of their chosen appliance increased, while their impression of the other appliance worsened.

The setup of Egan et al.'s (2007) study was as follows. Monkeys were initially presented with two different coloured chocolate sweets (specifically, M&M's) in see-through cages. In the 'free choice' condition of the experiment, the cage was open in front of both M&M's, so the monkey could choose which one it wanted (the openings were placed so that the monkey could reach its preferred M&M, but not both at the same time). In the 'no choice' condition of the experiment, the opening to just one of the M&M's was open, so the monkey could only reach one of them. After the monkey had taken the M&M, the researchers gave the monkey a choice between the M&M it had not taken, and a new M&M in a third colour. The dependent measure was how often the monkey took the new, third M&M rather than the one they had not taken in the first trial. What would you predict would happen, on the basis of post-decisional dissonance? Well, cognitive dissonance theory suggests that in the free choice condition, monkeys would be more likely to reject the M&M they had not taken in the first trial. This is because the appealing qualities of the non-chosen M&M are dissonant with the fact that the monkey had chosen the other one. This leads to a revision of attitudes – specifically, to derogation of the non-chosen M&M. Thus, when given a choice between this M&M and a new one, they opt for the new one. On the other hand, monkeys in the no choice condition experience no dissonance and do not derogate the M&M they could not choose in the first trial. And what were the results? They supported these predictions. In the no choice condition, monkeys chose the M&M they could not take in the first trial around 60 per cent of the time. In the free choice condition, they chose the M&M they did not take in the first trial only 39 per cent of the time, preferring the new, third M&M instead.

Alert readers may have spotted a potential problem with this experimental paradigm – perhaps monkeys reject the non-chosen M&M in the second trial simply because they dislike it. If they dislike yellow M&M's, for example, they will not choose it in the first trial, nor will they choose it in the second. Hardly surprising, you might say. This is, in fact, a criticism of the 'free choice' paradigm in the study of post-decisional dissonance – positive attitudes to the chosen object and negative attitudes to the rejected object may not reflect post-decisional dissonance but simply pre-decisional preferences (Chen and Risen, 2010; Risen and Chen, 2010). Egan et al. (2007) attempted to control for this by carefully pretesting each monkey's preference for M&M's. They ensured that monkeys were given triads of M&M's that they had preferred equally in an earlier session. However, this does not guarantee that monkeys had not changed their minds since the time their preferences were initially tested (some days before), or that on the day of the main experiment, they simply liked some colours more than others.

Fortunately, a simple experiment suggests that although this alternative interpretation cannot be ruled out, the free choice paradigm does genuinely reveal that making a choice causes people to valorize the alternative they chose and derogate the alternative they did not choose. In a follow-up study, Egan, Bloom and Santos (2010) gave monkeys the *illusion* that they had chosen one of two sweets (this time, Skittles). They did this by showing monkeys two different Skittles, hiding them in a box in front of the monkey, but then covertly removing a Skittle. The monkey was then allowed to put its hand into the box, thinking that there were two Skittles, but in fact there was only one. After the monkey had taken the Skittle from the box, the experimenter pretended to remove the other Skittle from the box, to heighten the illusion that the monkey had made a free choice. In a second trial, the monkeys really did have a free choice, this time between the Skittle they had been led to believe they 'rejected' from the first trial and a second Skittle (see Figure 4.15). When they thought they had freely chosen not to take the Skittle in the first trial, they rejected it in the second trial, in favour of a new alternative, 60 per cent of the time. When they thought they had no choice the first time, they rejected it significantly less often – only 49 per cent of the time, which is how much you would expect them to reject it by chance.

The genius of this 'blind choice' paradigm is that the monkeys' choices in the first trial cannot reflect their preferences, since their free choice was an illusion. In other words, their attitudes could not have affected their behaviour. Their rejection of the second sweet in the following trial, compared to the control group who did not believe they had chosen, shows that choosing an option – or believing one has chosen an option – affects one's preferences. This is a clear case in which behaviour affects

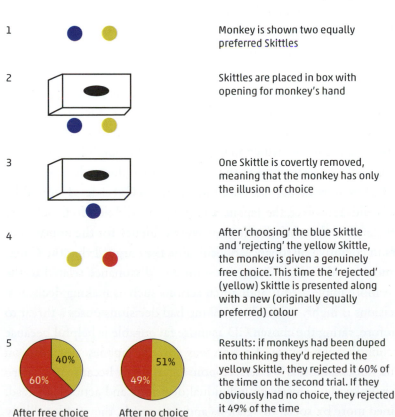

1 Monkey is shown two equally preferred Skittles

2 Skittles are placed in box with opening for monkey's hand

3 One Skittle is covertly removed, meaning that the monkey has only the illusion of choice

4 After 'choosing' the blue Skittle and 'rejecting' the yellow Skittle, the monkey is given a genuinely free choice. This time the 'rejected' (yellow) Skittle is presented along with a new (originally equally preferred) colour

5 40% 60% After free choice   51% 49% After no choice

Results: if monkeys had been duped into thinking they'd rejected the yellow Skittle, they rejected it 60% of the time on the second trial. If they obviously had no choice, they rejected it 49% of the time

FIGURE 4.15 Depiction of Egan et al.'s (2010) study

attitudes. Egan et al. (2010) obtained much the same results with a sample of human children. Also, Sharot, Velasquez and Dolan (2010) independently came up with another version of the blind choice paradigm and showed that adult humans respond in much the same way. Participants chose between two holiday packages, not knowing what the holiday destinations were. To give participants the illusion of informed choice, they were told that the holiday destinations associated with the two packages were flashing on the screen subliminally and that such information affects people's choices. In fact, only nonsense strings of characters (e.g., &^£(%^&) were appearing. After making their 'choice' between options A and B, participants were told, at random, that they had chosen a holiday to Greece over a holiday to Thailand (or vice versa). This caused participants to subsequently rate the holiday they thought they had chosen more favourably than the alternative holiday.

Thus, we can say that cognitive dissonance appears not to be unique to humans. It is not clear whether cognitive dissonance confers some kind of survival advantage, and therefore may have evolved, or whether it is a by-product of some other more universal cognitive and emotional machinery possessed by humans and other animals alike. For all animals, human or not, the knowledge function of attitudes means that a consistent set of attitudes about the world is likely to be advantageous, that is, there is some survival advantage in preserving a consistent set of knowledge about the world (McGregor, Nash, Mann and Phills, 2010).

This is not to say that culture is not important to cognitive dissonance, but rather than affecting the amount of cognitive dissonance that people experience, culture seems to affect the specific triggers that cause it. For example, Heine and Lehman (1997) asked Canadian and Japanese students to choose a set of 10 CDs from a bunch of 40. The participants were also asked to evaluate how much they would like to own each of the CDs they chose. After they had done so, participants were told they could have either the CD they rated fifth or the one they rated sixth. They were asked to choose and then rate the two CDs again. Results revealed that Canadian students rated the CDs further apart in terms of favourability than they did at the beginning of the experiment. In other words, they reduced dissonance by rating the chosen CD as more favourable (and the unchosen CD as less favourable) than they originally did. However, the Japanese participants did not do this. Heine and Lehman (1997) argued that their findings provide evidence for the importance of cultural factors in cognitive dissonance. Specifically, they argued that the Canadian students demonstrated a more Western response to dissonance related to the fact that the self is more implicated in individual actions such as making decisions. Making good decisions is highly valued but making bad decisions poses a threat to self-esteem. Therefore, rating the chosen CD as more favourable is helpful because it restores the feeling that the course of action was correct. Japanese students, on the other hand, did not exhibit this Western response – arguably because in Eastern cultures, the self is linked less closely to individual decisions and actions. Instead, these are determined more by social obligations and, as a result, they are less likely to experience dissonance in such situations.

Hypocrisy

Hypocrisy Publicly supporting an attitude or behaviour and yet behaving in a manner that is inconsistent with the attitude or behaviour.

When attitudes and behaviour are inconsistent, the discomfort that people experience can often be likened to **hypocrisy**. In particular, when people say they support a particular attitude or behaviour, but act in a way that is inconsistent with the attitude or behaviour, they look (and often feel) like a hypocrite. For example, a person may be a strong public advocate of limiting energy usage to reduce the impact of climate change, but may own a large home with many rooms and many appliances. Perhaps this person can 'talk the talk' but does not 'walk the walk'. One only has to think of the criticism faced by Al Gore, former US vice president and subject of the 2006 documentary *An Inconvenient Truth*, to see how detrimental this kind of hypocrisy – whether true or simply alleged – can be. However, feelings of hypocrisy like this can be useful. In particular, if people are aware they are publicly advocating an attitude or behaviour but behaving inconsistently, they can experience strong dissonance (e.g., Aronson, Fried and Stone, 1991). It is unlikely that the strong feelings of dissonance would be eliminated by the tactics we discussed earlier, such as self-affirmation and doing other positive things. Instead, the person may need to act in a way that directly removes the dissonance.

For example, Stone, Wiegand, Cooper and Aronson (1997) asked a set of participants to make a video where they advocated the use of condoms to promote safe sex. Afterwards, they were asked to think of reasons why they personally had not used condoms in the past, or reasons why people in general might not use condoms. At the end of the study, participants were asked if they would either like to buy condoms (a direct attempt at reducing dissonance), or make a donation to a homeless charity (indirect). The findings showed that when participants were asked to think of reasons why they personally had not used condoms in the past, they chose to buy condoms more so than in the condition where they were asked to think of people in general and their reasons for not practising safe sex. Stone et al. argued that the maximization of hypocrisy made people more motivated to reduce dissonance, and therefore they chose the most direct route to do so. In summary, feelings of hypocrisy can bring about positive behaviour change. When people are painfully aware that their behaviours do not match up to their own publicly stated standards and they have the means to rectify this discrepancy, it is likely they will change their behaviour to be more consistent.

Exploring further Use Google or another search engine to find some examples of famous hypocrites. What happened to them? Did they change their behaviours when made aware of their hypocrisy?

Embodied social cognition

Cognitive dissonance is not the only means by which our behaviour can affect our attitudes. A growing body of research suggests that people's attitudes are influenced by their physical actions, even at the most basic level. Early research in this area drew on self-perception theory (Bem, 1967, 1972), which asserts that people become aware of their own attitudes by looking at what they do. Thus, people look at their own behaviours and infer their attitudes from those behaviours. This may seem a bit strange – most people would think they always know their own attitudes – but there is some evidence that people infer their attitudes from their overt behaviours, and this is not only the case for weak or trivial attitudes. After writing counterattitudinal essays, arguing, for example, that students should have less control over what they learn, people come to believe that their attitudes were originally more in favour of their written position (Bem and McConnell, 1970). People inferred their attitude not from what they thought originally, but from what they had written.

As mentioned earlier, this happens at an even more basic level. For example, a growing body of research suggests that the physical movements people engage in while they are evaluating stimuli (e.g., objects, people) strongly determine how favourably the stimuli are evaluated. Specifically, engaging in behaviours that typically accompany positive attitudes tends to lead people to evaluate stimuli more positively, whereas engaging in behaviours that typically accompany negative attitudes has the opposite effect – people tend to rate the stimuli less favourably. This effect has come to be known as an example of **embodiment** or **embodied social cognition**.

Embodiment (embodied social cognition) An area of study where research shows broadly that bodily states influence attitudes, social perception and emotion.

For example, in one study, Wells and Petty (1980) asked participants to either nod their heads vertically (a behaviour associated with agreement) or shake their heads horizontally (a behaviour associated with disagreement) while listening to persuasive messages about a university-related topic. They found that the head movements later modulated participants' judgements of the message. Specifically, head nodding led to more positive attitudes towards the persuasive messages than head shaking (see also Tom, Pettersen, Law et al., 1991). In another study, Cacioppo, Priester and Berntson (1993) investigated the relationship between another attitude-relevant movement (arm flexion/extension) and a novel stimulus. Specifically, they demonstrated that novel Chinese ideographs presented during arm flexion, that is, pushing upwards from underneath a table – a behaviour associated with approach and positive attitudes – were later evaluated more favourably than ideographs presented during arm extension, that is, pushing downwards from the top of a table – a behaviour associated with avoidance and negative attitudes. In yet another striking study, Strack, Martin and Stepper (1988) asked participants to watch some funny cartoons while either holding a pen between their lips or their teeth (see Figure 4.16). Asking participants to hold the pen between the teeth facilitates the contraction of the zygomaticus (smiling muscle), whereas holding the pen between the lips inhibits the contraction of this muscle. Results from this study revealed that people rated the cartoons as funnier in the 'teeth' condition (see also Stepper and Strack, 1993).

To give another example, Schubert (2004) showed that making a fist can influence men's and women's automatic processing of words that are related to the notion of power. Many studies show similar findings, demonstrating that bodily postures and physical behaviours are related to positive and negative inclinations towards objects (e.g., Chen and Bargh, 1999; Epley and Gilovich, 2004; Friedman and Förster, 2000). Further, these inclinations influence attitudes towards the

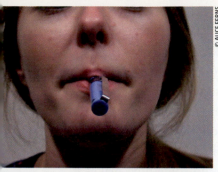

FIGURE 4.16 Investigating embodied social cognition Strack et al. (1988) asked people to view funny cartoons while holding a pen between their lips or teeth. Participants in the 'teeth' condition rated the cartoons as funny, arguably because this facial expression facilitates smiling compared to the 'lips' condition that inhibits smiling. This is an example of embodied social cognition.

Proprioception The perception of the body's position and movement.

objects. Therefore, attitudes seem to be determined (partly at least) by people's embodied responses (see Niedenthal, Barsalou, Winkielman et al., 2005).

Sometimes, objects do not need to be present to create an embodied response. For example, Förster and Strack (1997, 1998) conducted a study where participants were asked to generate the names of famous people and later classify them as people they liked, disliked or to whom they felt neutral. During the experiment, half the participants were asked to flex their arm upwards on a table (an approach behaviour) or to push down on the table (avoidance). Results revealed that participants who had performed the approach behaviour thought of more 'liked' famous people than disliked people. On the other hand, participants in the avoidance condition thought of more 'disliked' famous people than famous people they liked. Thus, variations in simple muscle movements in the arm caused people to recall completely different (evaluatively positive vs. negative) information from short-term memory.

These rather amazing research findings seem to show that our ability to perceive our bodily position and movement, or **proprioception**, plays a fundamental role in thoughts, feelings and actions that are logically irrelevant to what our bodies are doing. As we noted earlier, sometimes the body responds to attitude primes (e.g., Bargh et al., 1996). To give another example, generating words about pride and disappointment can influence a person's posture (Oosterwijk, Rotteveel, Fischer and Hess, 2009). People sit or stand tall when thinking about pride, and slump when thinking of disappointment. Findings like these suggest that the body is closely related to the processing of social information (Niedenthal et al., 2005). Theorists argue that cognitive representations (such as the mental 'building blocks' of attitudes) are closely related to their physical context. Specifically, cognition, or what we think, depends significantly on actual bodily states. To help understand this point, reflect on your behaviour during telephone conversations. You probably smile, frown, gesture, point and move around according to the content of your conversation, even though there is no communicative point in doing so, since you are talking to someone who can't see you. Our thoughts, feelings and bodily movements are so interconnected that it is difficult to 'turn off' our body language. As we shall shortly read, it may be more difficult to have certain thoughts or experience emotions when we cannot perform the body language normally associated with them.

Mimicry and imitation

Another line of research also suggests that our minds and bodies are intimately linked, with important consequences for attitudes and social behaviour. People often embody the behaviours of other people in their presence by imitating or mimicking their actions. For example, you can probably remember a time when you found yourself crossing your arms when somebody else crossed their arms, or smiling at a person who was smiling at you. For many years, researchers have argued for the importance of mimicry and imitation in social interaction (e.g., Bandura, 1977; Lipps, 1907). Indeed, mimicry and imitation are behaviours that humans engage in from birth. For example, babies imitate the behaviours of adults (Meltzoff and Moore, 1977, 1989). Mimicry remains important as humans become skilled communicators – when people talk, their rate of speech often matches each other's and they speak for a similar amount of time (e.g., Cappella and Planalp, 1981). Further, listeners tend to mimic speakers' gestures (e.g., Bavelas, Black, Chovil et al., 1988). In another interesting study by Chartrand and Bargh (1999), an experimenter rubbed their nose or shook their foot while they interacted with participants. Participants who observed the experimenter scratching their nose were more likely to do so themselves (rather than shaking their foot), whereas participants who had observed the experimenter shake their foot were more likely to do this (rather than scratching their nose). In other words, watching someone do something makes it more likely the person will also perform that action.

Why do people do this? Theorists argue that mimicry and imitation facilitate cooperation and empathy among people who interact (e.g., Hatfield, Cacioppo and Rapson, 1994; Neumann and Strack, 2000; Semin, 2000). Some additional research findings support this position. For example, higher levels of mimicry increase liking between partners and the perception that the interaction is going smoothly (Chartrand and Bargh, 1999). People who are close or like each other also tend to mimic each other more (e.g., van Baaren, Maddux, Chartrand et al., 2003). Research also suggests that imitation is driven by a specific neural mechanism. Specifically, Rizzolatti, Fadiga, Fogassi and Gallese (2002) observed that particular circuits involved in the production of motor behaviour also become active in response to *perceived* motor behaviour. Thus, watching someone running activates the same parts of your brain that you would need to run. *Mirror neurons* appear to be important in this phenomenon. When you watch someone performing an action, neurons that represent that action are activated in your premotor cortex – the part of the brain responsible for the same action (Iacoboni, 2009).

Although this hard-wired tendency to mimic may help us learn from others and increase liking (Hatfield et al., 1994), mimicry does not always pay. Kavanagh, Suhler, Churchland and Winkielman (2011) found that observers rated a confederate as less competent if they mimicked an unfriendly person, than if they mimicked a friendly person or did not mimic at all. Mimicry may be seen as inappropriate in some cases – a naive, misplaced attempt to be liked – and thus may cause damage to your reputation.

Embodiment of emotions

Emotions Brief, specific psychological and physical responses to an object or event.

There is growing evidence for the embodiment of **emotions** – brief, specific psychological and physical responses to objects and events. One line of evidence for this is sensitivity to others' facial expressions, which can cause us to mimic their emotional responses. Wicker, Keysers, Plailly et al. (2003) showed that the insula – a brain area responsible for processing somatosensory information – was activated when participants were exposed to disgusting smells. Crucially, however, it was also activated when they watched a film in which other people were displaying expressions of disgust. So, there is some evidence to suggest that people have an embodied response to emotions they perceive in others' body language. This response is similar to their own response. Mirror neurons appear to be able to influence our emotional as well as our motor behaviour.

Other research has demonstrated that people mimic others' emotional facial expressions (e.g., Bush, Barr, McHugo and Lanzetta, 1989; Dimberg, 1982). To give an example of how this works in the laboratory, Bavelas, Black, Lemery and Mullett (1986) asked a confederate to fake an injury and then grimace as if in pain. Participants who observed this behaviour were also more likely to grimace. They were more likely to do so if they could clearly see the actor's emotional expression. People's imitation of others' emotions seems, in many cases, to be automatic and sometimes even outside consciousness. For example, some research shows that people respond with positive and negative facial expressions to subliminal pictures of people smiling and frowning (Dimberg, Thunberg and Elmehed, 2000). Other findings have shown that people automatically mimic facial expressions in pictures as they are asked to categorize them into emotional expressions (Wallbott, 1991).

Being able to mimic also helps people to recognize emotions in others' faces. In one study, Niedenthal, Brauer, Halberstadt and Innes-Ker (2001) asked participants to view a series of facial expressions being morphed into different facial expressions. The participants' task was to detect the point at which the expression changed. Some participants were free to mimic the faces being shown to them, while others were prevented from mimicking by being asked to hold a pen between their teeth and lips. It was found that participants who were free to mimic were quicker at detecting the point at which the expression changed than participants who were prevented from mimicking (see also Niedenthal, Ric and Krauth-Gruber, 2002). These findings are important because they show that feedback from facial mimicry helps people to process emotional expressions. This can be quite helpful in social interaction; for instance, psychological processes like this may help people to better empathize with others. In a demonstration supporting this prediction, Zajonc, Adelmann, Murphy and Niedenthal (1987) showed that couples' facial similarity was closer after 25 years of marriage than at the beginning of the marriage. Couples grow to look more and more like each other. This makes sense, since couples are motivated to empathize with each other and will be more likely to mimic each other's emotional expressions. Over time, this mimicry causes permanent changes in facial structure.

Some other work suggests that people's emotional experiences can be directly related to their bodily movements. For example, Stepper and Strack (1993) asked participants to either sit upright or slumped in a chair while completing an achievement test. Participants were given bogus feedback about their performance – everyone was told they had done well. When participants were later asked to evaluate their own performance, participants who had sat upright expressed more pride in their performance than participants who had sat slumped in a chair. In another study, Riskind (1984) showed that adopting an upright posture and a smiling facial expression facilitated participants' retrieval of pleasant memories compared to unpleasant memories. Again, this is strong evidence that behavioural and emotional experiences are closely linked.

This point is reinforced by some work on the emotional consequences of Botox treatment – the injection of a strain of botulism into the skin in order to reduce the signs of ageing. The injection has the effect of partially paralysing facial muscles,

© ROBERT KNESCHKE/FOTOLIA.COM

FIGURE 4.17 Receiving a Botox injection The injection of Botox into the skin paralyses facial muscles and inflames tissues, leading not only to a temporarily more youthful appearance but also a reduced ability to express and therefore perceive and experience certain emotions.

which gives rise to the subtle appearance of emotional blankness in the faces of those who opt for the treatment. If proprioception is crucial to emotional experience, we might expect that Botox patients' reduced ability to express emotion with their facial muscles would interfere with their perception and experience of emotion. This does, in fact, seem to be the case. Havas, Glenberg, Gutowski et al. (2010) found that after undergoing Botox treatment, participants were slower to read sentences that referred to anger and sadness. The facial expressions of these emotions normally require the use of the newly paralysed muscle. Neal and Chartrand (2011) also found that Botox injections reduced people's ability to detect emotions on other people's faces. Davis, Senghas, Brandt and Oschner (2010) found that Botox patients, compared to those undergoing other cosmetic treatments, were less likely to report negative emotions such as inability, depression and anxiety. Being less able to express these emotions with facial muscles seems to cause people to be less likely to experience them (Figure 4.17).

Time to reflect Do you think the reduction in negative affect following Botox is fundamentally heart-warming or deeply scary? In Chapters 2 and 11, we explore the phenomenon of objectification – the tendency to reduce oneself or others to their physical appearance – which seems largely to give rise to cosmetic surgery (Calogero and Pina, 2010). Davis et al.'s findings (2010) seem to suggest that by altering our appearance in this particular way, people really do reduce their capacity to experience emotion, and in this sense take one step to reducing themselves from a fully experiencing 'subject' to a non-experiencing 'object'. Other forms of cosmetic surgery do not induce facial paralysis and so do not have these strange emotional effects.

CRITICAL FOCUS

Embodied social cognition

The surge in remarkable research findings linking the body and the mind has given rise to a movement known as 'embodied social cognition' or 'embodiment', which suggests that the body and its role in our attitudes, emotions and behaviours should be placed centre stage in social psychology (e.g., Barsalou, 1999; Marsh, Johnston, Richardson and Schmidt, 2009; Niedenthal, Winkielman, Mondillon and Vermeulen, 2009; Schubert and Semin, 2009; Winkielman and Kavanagh, 2012). The basic idea behind this movement is that the function of social cognition is to facilitate social action. Our brains and bodies have evolved together and constantly feed back to each other. Thus, it is a mistake to sharply separate mind and body (for a related view in clinical and cognitive psychology, see the engaging book by Damasio, 2006, called *Descartes' Error: Emotion, Reason, and the Human Brain*). Advocates of this view oppose the traditional idea in psychology that our behaviour is guided by mental representations, separated from our senses and movements. In its place, they argue that our mental representations are deeply embedded in specific sensory modalities and in our bodily experiences, postures and movements. Thus, in place of abstract mentalistic concepts like schemas, social psychology should be concentrating more on perception and action.

While the findings associated with this position are undeniably fascinating, as we have seen, there is controversy over whether they cumulatively show that our social minds are really 'embodied'. A lot of findings are taken to fall under this umbrella, but may not show that our bodily sensations and movements are taking the place of our minds, as we traditionally understand them (Fiedler, 2009). For example, people who are induced to sit or stand up straight, in a 'powerful' fashion, think in the same way as people who are really powerful (Carney, Cuddy and Yapp, 2010). This might implicate some special brain regions involving bodily experience, suggesting that the representation of power is embedded there. However, it might more simply suggest that sitting like this primes the concept of 'power', and so like any other prime, such as a power-related word on a computer screen, encourages people to think powerfully (Landau, Meier and Keefer, 2010). Similarly, a lot of research commonly understood to be concerned with 'embodiment' may not reveal the role of our bodies and senses in our decision making but rather that human beings have developed sophisticated metaphors linking abstract concepts to specific physical experiences (Lakoff and Johnson, 1980, 1999). For example, some researchers have found that experiencing physical warmth makes us see others as 'warmer', that is, friendly and approachable (e.g., Williams and Bargh, 2008). Others have found that notions like God and the devil, and good and evil, are associated with physical height (Meier, Hauser, Robinson et al., 2007). We can understand these results simply in terms of mental schemas, without having to rethink the fundamental basis of social psychology.

Questions

1 As you revise this chapter, think about the concept of embodied social cognition. How many of the findings you have been reading about can be explained in terms of basic bodily and perceptual processes? How many seem to require abstract mental thought?

2 What other criticisms of the concept of embodiment can you find, using Google Scholar or another academic database? Some useful articles include Fielder (2009), Goldman and de Vignemont (2009) and Zwaan (2009). This is a fast-moving research area and you can probably find later ones too.

3 Can you think up an experiment into embodied social cognition, along the lines of those you have read about in this chapter? Think of a gesture or posture, for example, that corresponds to a certain attitude or mindset. Can you covertly induce this posture, and test whether the bodily gesture can cause this? What dependent measure can you use?

Emotions and social judgement

Emotions help guide social judgement. Because many of the judgements and decisions people have to make are complex, they often rely on the way they feel about them to help them make judgements and come to decisions. For example, people may rely on a 'gut feeling' to decide whether or not to take a new job, whether to buy a new car, move house or move in with their boyfriend/girlfriend rather than dealing with the vast array of information associated with the issue. According to Schwarz and Clore (1983), people use emotions as pieces of information to guide social judgement. This **feelings-as-information perspective** proposes that emotions provide fast and reliable information about the issue that help shape what people do (Clore, 1992; Clore and Parrott, 1991; Schwarz and Clore, 1983). According to Forgas (1995, 2000), people tend to use emotions as information when they make complex rather than simple judgements.

In a study testing this theory, Schwarz and Clore (1983) studied the effects of the weather on people's emotions. They approached volunteer participants on the telephone on either a sunny or cloudy day and asked them – all things considered – how satisfied or dissatisfied they were with their lives. They were also asked to rate their general happiness. In one condition, participants were just asked to rate their life satisfaction and happiness, the researchers predicting that participants would generally show greater life satisfaction on sunny rather than cloudy days. In another condition, however, participants were first asked about the weather, the researchers reasoning that people would attribute their life satisfac-

Feelings-as-information perspective Theory proposing that people often rely on their feelings – often gut instincts – to guide important social judgements.

tion and happiness to the weather and therefore discount these feelings when making these ratings. The researchers found evidence to support their theory. When asked to rate their happiness and life satisfaction (without thinking about the weather), participants predictably rated these variables higher when they were tested on a sunny rather than a cloudy day. On the other hand, participants who had been asked first about the weather rated their happiness and life satisfaction at the same level on both sunny and cloudy days (see Figure 4.18).

There is a wealth of literature making a similar point. For example, the emotion of anger significantly influences social judgements. In many studies, researchers have shown that simply remembering a time in the past when they were angry leads participants to blame others for their problems and to assume that unfair things will happen to them in future events (e.g., DeSteno, Petty, Wegener and Rucker, 2000; Keltner, Ellsworth and Edwards, 1993; Lerner, Goldberg and Tetlock, 1998). Further, being in a bad mood often leads people to rate objects less favourably. For example, people in a bad mood are likely to rate products less favourably, but are also less likely to like politicians and economic policies (Forgas and Moylan, 1987). People who are experiencing a state of fear perceive danger and threat to a greater extent and are more pessimistic (e.g., Lerner and Keltner, 2001). In general, there is much evidence to support the supposition that emotions influence judgement.

Emotions also influence more complex reasoning processes. Specifically, being in a good or bad mood can influence the extent to which people rely on detailed situational information or stereotypes. For example, Bodenhausen, Sheppard and Kramer (1994) found that people who were experimentally induced to experience sadness were less likely to stereotype others than participants who had been induced to feel anger. This does not mean that stereotypes are bad, nor does it mean that being happy makes people take 'shortcuts' and rely on simpler types of information. Some research on creativity suggests that the emotion of happiness can make people think more flexibly and

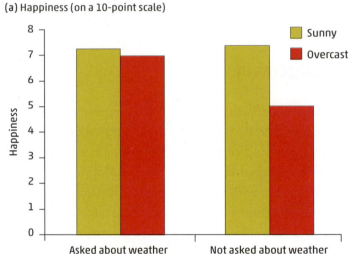

(a) Happiness (on a 10-point scale)

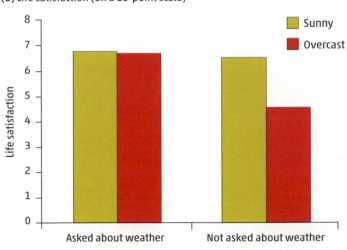

(b) Life satisfaction (on a 10-point scale)

FIGURE 4.18 Use of feelings as information in making social judgements Participants in this study predictably rated their happiness and life satisfaction higher on sunny rather than cloudy days. However, if first asked about the weather, participants were able attribute their feelings (positive or negative depending on the weather) to the weather and discount them when judging their overall happiness and life satisfaction. The result? Participants in this condition rated their happiness and life satisfaction equally on sunny and cloudy days.

Source: Data from Schwarz and Clore, 1983

creatively, coming up, for example, with more novel examples of categories (Isen, 1993; Isen, Daubman and Nowicki, 1987). Positive mood can therefore facilitate creativity and openness – characteristics that may be useful in domains such as the workplace; indeed, some findings suggest that mood plays a significant role in workplace creativity (Madjar, Oldham and Pratt, 2002). In general, social psychologists agree that positive mood broadens the way people think, which can have positive consequences for social interaction such as gaining knowledge from others, increasing empathy, building social networks and increasing the positivity of relations between groups (e.g., Fredrickson, 1998, 2001; Waugh and Fredrickson, 2006).

Emotions are also important in guiding our moral judgements. In one interesting study, Haidt (2001) showed how people use their emotions to judge whether things are right or wrong. He asked a sample of university students to read a story about a brother and sister who have sex once, while both using birth control. When asked whether the pair did something wrong, most of the participants immediately said 'yes' – a response typically associated with physical expressions of disgust. However, when asked why the behaviour was wrong, participants' responses became less assured. For example, many participants argued that it was wrong because breeding within families is dangerous for genetic reasons, but recall that both parties were said to have used birth control. Subsequently, many participants said that they just 'know that incest is wrong'. Haidt argues that, like many other types of social judgements, moral judgements are often based on gut feelings about what is right and wrong (Greene and Haidt, 2002; Haidt, 2003). People in Haidt's study 'just knew' that incest was wrong but could not necessarily recall or articulate reasons why they had come to this judgement. Instead, the emotional response of disgust probably guided participants' moral judgements about the situation. Emotions not only guide moral judgement, they can also guide moral behaviour. For example, people often experience shame and guilt for their immoral actions and consequently are more likely to want to make up for those actions (Tangney, Miller, Flicker and Barlow, 1996; Tangney, Wagner, Hill-Barlow et al., 1996). However, others experience these emotions to a lesser degree and are more likely to participate in criminal behaviour (e.g., Blair, Jones, Clark and Smith, 1997).

Many studies of emotions and moral judgements have been based on the study of anger and disgust; indeed, these are the most common emotions felt in response to moral violations. However, research has demonstrated that these emotions occur in different domains. Specifically, anger is experienced more in relation to moral violations about rights and freedoms (Rozin, Lowery, Imada and Haidt, 1999; Vasquez, Keltner, Ebenbach and Banaszynski, 2001), whereas disgust is typically related to impurity of body, mind or character (Haidt, Koller and Dias, 1993; Rozin et al., 1999). Interestingly, feelings of disgust (but not anger) strongly predict attitudes towards homosexuality as being immoral (e.g., Inbar, Pizarro, Knobe and Bloom, 2009; van de Ven, Bornholt and Bailey, 1996).

Question to consider Reread question 4 at the start of the chapter. Is it likely that Kieran was experiencing disgust, or a different emotional response? Why do you think people label these sorts of emotional responses as 'disgusting'?

Chapter summary

In this chapter, we considered the nature of attitudes, attitude formation and attitude change. We distinguished between explicit and implicit attitudes and, finally, we focused on the role of our bodies and emotions in determining our social judgements and behaviours. Specifically, you will have learned that:

- Attitudes are a person's evaluations of various aspects of their social world. They can be positive, negative or ambivalent. They can be distinguished from values and ideologies, but both can affect attitudes.
- Research suggests that attitude strength is determined by their complexity and consistency. Attitudes are formed as a result of four functions: the knowledge function (wanting to make sense of the social world), the utilitarian function (helping us gain rewards and avoid punishments), the value expressive function (allowing us to express our values) and the ego defensive function (protecting us from psychological threats).
- Mere exposure to a person or object can cause an attitude to form. Many attitudes are learned from others through various processes such as classical conditioning, instrumental conditioning and observational learning. Some evidence also suggests that genetic factors play a role in attitude development. Social representations theory asserts that people form attitudes through processes of social interaction.
- People prefer to have harmonious, consistent attitudes and seek to find balance.
- Implicit (unconscious) and explicit (conscious) attitudes can be measured in a variety of ways, such as directly via self-reports, or indirectly via procedures such as the bogus pipeline procedure, the Implicit Association Test, and physiological measures. Implicit and explicit attitudes tend to be correlated but differ in several important ways.
- Research is mixed on the ability of attitudes to predict behaviours, and situational factors play a pivotal role in the expression of attitudes (also attitude formation, specificity, values, habits and attitude strength).
- The theory of planned behaviour proposes that people make a decision to behave in a certain way based on a sequence of rational thought processes.
- Cognitive dissonance refers to the unpleasant psychological state that occurs when people notice that their attitudes and behaviours are inconsistent. This appears to be a universal phenomenon and can be likened to the feeling of hypocrisy. People attempt to reduce dissonance in a variety of ways.
- Research on embodied social cognition demonstrates that people's attitudes are influenced by their physical actions, even at the most basic level. People often embody the behaviours of others in their presence by mimicking their actions, which may be a way to facilitate cooperation and empathy.
- Emotions also help guide social judgements. Because many judgements are complex, people often rely on the way they feel in order to make them. Emotions are also important in guiding our moral judgements.

Our concern in this chapter has been on attitudes, emotions and behaviour. In Chapter 5, we turn our attention to the social psychology of communication.

Essay questions

At the beginning of the chapter, we asked you to consider these questions:

1 On Facebook, Lisbeth is a member of several activist groups such as Amnesty International, Greenpeace and the Humane Society. What reasons are there for Lisbeth to be a member of these groups? Why do this on Facebook where others can see her group memberships?

2 Dirk is having a discussion with a friend who says they are studying psychology and doing a project on attitudes towards healthy eating. Dirk says to his friend that attitudes are impossible to measure. Is this right?

3 Luann has been a smoker for nearly 20 years, having started in secondary school. She knows that smoking causes lung cancer and a whole host of other negative ailments. Also, her great aunt died of lung cancer when she was a child. And yet, Luann still refuses to quit. What social psychological process might help explain Luann's decision?

4 When asked about a government proposal to raise tuition fees, Kieran argues that it is 'disgusting'. Is it likely that Kieran really experiences the emotional response of disgust to this proposal, or is another emotion more likely?

Having read this chapter, these questions could also be framed as the following essay questions, which you can attempt in preparation for your examinations:

1 Discuss the reasons why people join groups.
2 Describe and evaluate the different methods that social psychologists use to measure attitudes.
3 Describe the concept of cognitive dissonance and, with reference to social psychological research, highlight the ways in which people reduce dissonance.
4 Discuss the role of emotions in making moral judgements.

Further reading

Albarracin, D. and Vargas, P. (2010) Attitudes and persuasion: From biology to social responses to persuasive intent. In S.T. Fiske, D.T. Gilbert and G. Lindzey (eds) *Handbook of Social Psychology* (5th edn, vol. 1, pp. 394–427). New York: Wiley. Provides a perspective on some of the neurological correlates of attitudes, in addition to a broad coverage of research on attitudes.

Banaji, M.R. and Heiphetz, L. (2010) Attitudes. In S.T. Fiske, D.T. Gilbert and G. Lindzey (eds) *Handbook of Social Psychology* (5th edn, vol. 1, pp. 353–93). New York: Wiley. Provides detailed, comprehensive and up-to-date coverage of research on attitudes.

Maio, G. and Haddock, G. (2010) *The Psychology of Attitudes and Attitude Change*. London: Sage. Describes how scientific methods have been used to understand attitudes and attitude change.

Niedenthal, P., Krauth-Gruber, S. and Ric, F. (2006) *Psychology of Emotion: Interpersonal, Experiential, and Cognitive Approaches*. New York: Psychology Press. Comprehensive look at the importance of emotions, including their measurement, conscious and unconscious processes, and situational and cultural influences.

Semin, G.R. and Smith, E.R. (2008) *Embodied Grounding: Social, Cognitive, Affective and Neuroscientific Approaches*. Cambridge: Cambridge University Press. Reviews current work on relations of the body to thought, language use, emotions and social relationships.

 Visit the companion website at www.palgrave.com/psychology/suttondouglas for access to a wide range of resources to help you get to grips with this chapter.

Applying social psychology

Implementation intentions: turning ideas into action

As we saw in this chapter, the link between attitudes and behaviour is statistically robust, but surprisingly weak. Although attitudes, under the right conditions, will cause us to form appropriate intentions, intentions account for only 20–30 per cent of the variance in behaviour. One of the main reasons for this is that people have good intentions, but fail to act on them (Orbell and Sheeran, 2000). In the past two decades, researchers have found a deceptively simple way to substantially increase the relationship between intentions and actions. This is of interest not only to researchers who are interested in the link between attitudes and behaviour, but also to anyone who wants to gain greater control of themselves and translate their best intentions into action. The technique is called *implementation intentions* (Gollwitzer, 1993, 1999).

Gollwitzer (1993, 1999) writes that when psychologists (and non-psychologists) think of intentions, they normally think of 'goal intentions'. These take the form 'I intend to reach X', where X is some desired end state. Thus, 'I intend to study hard for the forthcoming exam' is a classic goal intention. Implementation intentions are a subtype of these goal intentions. They specify when, where and how the goal will be reached. They take the form: 'When situation X arises, I will perform response Y.' For example: 'When my favourite TV show finishes on Monday night, I will take out my textbook and make notes from Chapter 4.' Theoretically, Gollwitzer expected that implementation intentions would help people achieve their goals in two main ways. First, by specifying a suitable situation in which the response is to be performed, they help a person notice and pay attention to the opportunity to act. Second, by specifying the response that is to be performed, they help people, when the time is right, to act more or less automatically. They do not have to consciously plan their behaviour in the moment, since when they earlier formed an implementation intention, they created a mental representation of the behaviour. In a nutshell, implementation intentions work by 'passing the control of one's behaviour on to the environment' (Gollwitzer, 1993, p. 173). In this way, they are supposed to ironically allow people to intentionally take advantage of the automaticity of human behaviour (which we reviewed in Chapter 3).

Do they work? The answer, in the many studies that have been conducted since then, is generally 'yes'. Implementation intentions have been found to increase goal achievement, sometimes dramatically, in many areas of life (for reviews, see Gollwitzer, 1999; Gollwitzer and Sheeran, 2006). These include intentions: to engage in exercise (Milne, Orbell and Sheeran, 2002; Prestwich, Lawton and Conner, 2003); have cervical cancer screening (Sheeran and Orbell, 2000); improve memory performance for older adults (Chasteen, Park and Schwarz, 2001); comply with speed limits (Elliot, Armitage and Baughan, 2003); reduce disgust reactions (Gallo, McCulloch and Gollwitzer, 2012); reduce implicit prejudice on measures such as a shooter task (see Chapter 11 for a description of this task), the IAT and the GNAT (Mendoza, Gollwitzer and Amodio, 2010; Stewart and Payne, 2008; Webb, Sheeran and Pepper, 2010); and reduce the effects of social anxiety (Webb, Obonaiye, Sheeran et al., 2010). Research has largely supported Gollwitzer's (1999) analysis of how implementation intentions work (e.g., Brandstätter, Lengfelder and Gollwitzer, 2001; Webb and Sheeran, 2007), and has uncovered additional mechanisms. For example, Webb and Sheeran (2007) found that implementation intentions helped participants overcome ego depletion (explored in Chapter 2). Achtziger, Gollwitzer and Sheeran (2008) found that implementation intentions helped shield participants' goals from unwanted thoughts and feelings. Koole and van't Spijker (2000) found that implementation intentions helped participants overcome the planning fallacy (Buehler, Griffin and Ross, 1994), the widespread tendency to underestimate the time it takes to complete a task. Ajzen, Czasch and Flood (2009) found that implementation intentions increased people's feeling of commitment to a task and their conscientious pursuit of its completion.

1   Turn the following goal intentions into implementation intentions that might be applicable in your life:

- 'I want to revise effectively for an upcoming assignment or exam.'
- 'I want to break an undesirable habit.'
- 'I want to get in contact with someone I feel I've been neglecting.'

2   Imagine you are working for *one* of the following:
- A health agency that wants to promote healthy eating among patients at risk of cardiovascular problems.
- An environmental agency that wants to promote changes to low-carbon behaviours such as taking shorter showers and using public transport.
- A charity that wants to increase self-examination behaviour for breast or testicular cancer.

Using Google Scholar or another academic database, find papers that review the literature on implementation intentions, and also one or more papers that report applications of implementation intentions to problems similar to the one you have chosen to address. In 400 words or fewer, describe implementation intentions, how they can be useful to the goals of the organization, and suggest how they could be specifically applied.

3   Using Google Scholar or another academic database, can you find any papers that suggest that implementation intentions are sometimes no better, or may even backfire, relative to goal intentions?

4   Using Google Scholar or another academic database, can you find papers that suggest how the benefits of implementation intentions can be increased?

Blind spot in social psychology

Embodied warmth

Ever since the pioneering study of Asch (1946), we have known that 'warmth' is a central trait in impression formation (see Chapter 3). If you think someone is warm, you will probably evaluate them positively on other dimensions too. It seems obvious, when we think about it, that the trait label 'warm' is a metaphor, meaning something like friendly and approachable. From the point of view of Lakoff and Johnson (1980, 1999), we might expect the metaphor to be based on our bodily experience. For example, it might be that in our early life, we learn an association between physical warmth and social intimacy through the experience of being cradled in adults' arms (Landau, Meier and Keefer, 2010).

If there is a metaphorical link between bodily and social warmth, we would expect physical feelings of warmth to cause us to rate people, and other objects, more positively, and in general to seek, or be conscious of, social intimacy. There is intriguing evidence for this. For example, Williams and Bargh (2008) found that when participants held a warm (versus cold) cup, they rated another person as more friendly. Ijzerman and Semin (2009, Experiment 1) used the same manipulation and found that it caused participants to rate themselves as socially closer to their friends and family members. In another study, Ijzerman and Semin (2009, Experiment 2) manipulated the temperature of the laboratory. In a physically warm (rather than cold) laboratory, participants felt socially closer to the experimenter. Other findings show that the metaphor works in the reverse direction, that is, thoughts about social isolation can make us feel colder. Zhong and Leonardelli (2008) asked participants to recall a time they had been socially excluded (Experiment 1) or exposed them to the experience of being isolated on a computer interaction (Experiment 2) (see Chapter 8 for more information on the study of ostracism). These manipulations caused participants to rate the laboratory as colder and to express a heightened desire for warm food and drinks. People do not rely only on warm food and drinks to warm themselves up, according to a recent study by Zhou, Wildschut, Sedikides et al. (2012). They also use the 'warm' emotion of nostalgia. Using a diary study methodology, Zhou et al. found that participants reported engaging more in nostalgic memories on colder days. Placing participants in a colder room also caused them to engage in more nostalgia.

How much, though, does social intimacy, friendliness or 'warmth' really have to do with our bodies? As we saw in this chapter, one of the key ambiguities surrounding the concept of 'embodied social cognition' concerns how much our bodies are really involved in our thoughts and emotions. It could be, simply, that having developed a cultural metaphor that equates physical and social warmth, any reminder of one kind of warmth affects perceptions of the other. Perhaps, then, all that these findings demonstrate is that priming concepts (see Chapter 3) work in intriguing and previously undreamt-of ways.

1   One way of priming the concept of warmth would be to display pictures of obviously warm scenes on a computer screen (e.g., steaming cups of coffee, the sun, a desert).
    • Can you think of any other ways to prime the concept of 'warmth', without placing participants in physically warm environments or allowing them to interact with physically warm stimuli?
    • If you did this, and asked participants to rate how friendly a target person is (e.g., the experimenter, or a stranger they read about), what would you expect to find based on the theory that embodied social cognition effects are driven largely by conceptual metaphors (e.g., Landau et al., 2010)? And what you would expect to find based on the theory that embodied social cognition effects are driven directly by bodily experiences?
    • This critical test between the two different theoretical views has not been run, to our knowledge, and certainly does not appear to have been published. What if both

views are right? In other words, what if the relationship between perceptions of physical and social warmth is driven by a metaphor and also by the bodily feeling of warmth being an intrinsic part of the way we think and feel? How would you test this? (Hint: you should think of experimental designs that include a control condition in which warmth is not primed, a condition in which the concept of warmth is primed, and a condition in which participants physically experience warmth.) Describe your method and your predictions – based on the idea that both the concept and the physical experience of warmth is important – in 300 words or less.

2   Thus far, research has established that social isolation makes people feel colder, and social inclusion and 'warm' memories make people feel warmer. However, the precise mechanism for this is not understood. Perhaps perceptions of friendliness and intimacy cause changes in blood flow, for example by activating the sympathetic nervous system (associated with approach and the activation of behaviour) rather than the parasympathetic nervous system (associated with avoidance and the inhibition of behaviour). In keeping with this possibility, Ekman, Levenson and Friesen (1983) found that emotions affect skin temperature. Indeed, several types of emotional arousal tend to make the skin warmer, including anger, happiness and surprise (Levenson, Ekman and Friesen, 1990). This leaves open two interesting possibilities regarding the idea that the metaphor 'warmth' is really rooted in immediate physical, bodily reality. First, people who are interpersonally 'warm' may actually be physically warm. Second, people and stimuli who are liked, and who arouse feelings of social closeness, may make us not only feel warmer subjectively, but objectively warmer. How would you test each of these possibilities? Outline your ideas in less than 300 words.

Student project

Accurately predicting strangers' emotions in the laboratory predicts higher quality relationships in real life

Argyro-Despoina Antypa studied as a Masters student at the University of Crete, supervised by Dr Konstantinos Kafetsios. In this chapter, we considered the importance of emotions in people's social lives. Argyro-Despoina's research investigates how well people are able to 'read' others' emotions.

My topic and aims

My study investigated how people process socioemotional information. Using laboratory experiments and naturalistic social cognitive methods, my project examined links between how accurately we perceive other people's facial emotion expressions (using a laboratory task) and emotion perception and experience in naturally occurring everyday interactions, also taking into account intrapersonal differences in both cases. The project was done for a laboratory course on social cognition and was part of a research collaboration between my supervisor Dr Kafetsios at the University of Crete and Professor

Ursula Hess at Humboldt University, Berlin, which looked at social factors in emotion perception.

The course on social cognition was part of a MSc degree, 'Brain and Mind', and much of the MSc concerned neuroscience topics. Being an interdisciplinary MSc (between medicine, psychology, sociology, neuroscience), it also included topics on social psychology. I was interested in social psychology and hence it was interesting (and challenging) to carry out a project that looked at how perceiving other people's facial emotion expressions affects actual social interactions using both laboratory and field methods.

My methods

The course provided hands-on training in experimental and naturalistic sociocognitive methods of emotion perception and both these methods were applied in my project. In the laboratory, we examined how accuracy and inaccuracy in perceiving facial emotion expressions, while people interact in a group, could be affected by how other people in a group express emotion and how they orient towards the person who is the target of emotion perception.

In the field, we collected participants' reports of how they affectively experienced their everyday, naturally occurring social interactions with other people, and how they perceived the other people with whom they interacted: friends, partners, family and others. Every time they met with another person for more than 10 minutes, participants recorded in a printed 'diary' how they felt and how they perceived the other person's emotions.

The project also included individual difference measures and controls, such as trait emotion regulation, emotional intelligence abilities, adult attachment orientations, positive and negative affectivity, and big five personality traits.

My findings and their implications

In the experimental emotion perception task, participants systematically recognized the emotion corresponding to the target expression as intended (e.g., sad, angry, happy). The levels of accuracy and inaccuracy in this task were independent of each other.

Interestingly, accuracy and inaccuracy in perceiving facial expressions in a group situation in the laboratory was associated with how people perceived their friends and relatives in real-life interactions.

Participants who perceived emotions more accurately in a group situation in the laboratory task reported a more positive interaction experience in everyday interactions, especially in social interactions with more close persons (close friends, partners, family), while participants who perceived emotions inaccurately in the laboratory task tended to have more negative interaction experiences. These associations continued to be significant even when we controlled for individual differences that may have accounted for emotion perception inaccuracies, such as insecure attachment, emotional intelligence abilities or trait level affect and emotion regulation.

From these findings, we concluded that accurately inferring the emotional expressions of other people when these expressions are embedded within a social context not only depends on how good one is at the task at hand, but also on social factors such as the presence of other people who are, at the same time, expressing emotions.

The combination of experimental and naturalistic methodologies for the description of emotion perception in social interaction indicated relationships between experimental and real-life experiences and these findings (and the methodological approach itself) are likely to be useful for further research.

My journey

At present, I am applying for further research work as I would like to continue working in research. I am applying for positions that meet my interests.

Because of my MSc project, I had the opportunity, along with the necessary time and appropriate supervision, to further study emotion theories and sociocognitive methodologies, and to be trained and conduct psychological experiments. In addition to the knowledge and skills this project offered me, I feel I have also gained a new perspective in psychology and its methods. As a psychologist completing a Masters-level degree in neuroscience, I was fascinated by the possibilities that a social psychological perspective can have and the project revived my interest in the field.

My advice

My personal recommendation would be to try to work on a topic you really want to learn more about, and something that seems really interesting to you.

Part

2 Relating

Chapter
5 Communication

This chapter will provide an overview of the social psychology of communication. It will outline the rules of language, and the important social functions of language for identity, culture, cognition, gender and stereotyping. The chapter will also provide an overview of the study of nonverbal communication, conversation and discourse, and will end with a focus on social behaviour in new communication media. By the end of the chapter, the reader will have a broad understanding of this important topic in social psychology.

© STOCKBYTE

Topics covered in this chapter

- Language and the 'rules' of language
- Language, culture and cognition
- Language, personality, identity and gender
- Language and stereotyping
- Nonverbal communication
- Conversation and discourse
- Communication and technology

Key features

Critical focus The evolution of facial expressions

Ethics and research methods The logic of conversation in survey design

Social psychology in the real world Nonverbal communication and the haka

Applying social psychology Training language use to reduce prejudice

Blind spot in social psychology Having something to talk about: the communicative logic of celebrity culture

Student project What kind of person self-discloses online?

Questions to consider

1 Siobhan emails her university lecturer to ask for some help with an essay. She simply writes: 'Where are the slides from the last lecture? I need them for my essay.' Outline some reasons why this might provoke an unhelpful response from the lecturer.

2 Carol thinks her partner has been cheating on her. She confronts him and asks him directly if he is having an affair. Will Carol be able to tell if her partner is telling her the truth?

3 Jake is angry with a situation at work and wants to complain to his boss. Would he be better to do this face to face or via email? What would be the advantages and disadvantages of using each medium?

Communication The transfer of information from one individual to another, or from one group to another.

A chapter like this one is quite often missing from social psychology textbooks. We think this is an unfortunate oversight for a number of reasons. In particular, **communication** – the transfer of information from individual to individual, or from group to group – is at the heart of social interaction. It is difficult to think of a social interaction that occurs without it. Also, a multitude of social psychological phenomena can be observed through communication. For example, it is through communicating with others that we express our emotions, our thoughts, our intentions and our identities. Communication is also fundamentally social. The development and use of language are strongly embedded in cultural and social systems, so there are many social antecedents and consequences of communication (Holtgraves, 2010). Communication is also vital to the study of social psychology because it is the primary means by which people influence (and are influenced by) others.

It is therefore surprising that communication has long been a neglected topic in social psychology. While topics such as social cognition, group processes, aggression and others have seen major theoretical and empirical advances over previous decades, advances in the study of communication have not been as plentiful (Fiedler, 2008). This is not to say that communication is completely ignored. For example, persuasive communication is a topic covered largely under the banner of social cognition (see Chapter 6) and self-presentation processes are mostly dealt with under the umbrella of the self (see Chapter 2). However, the study of communication is often missing from social psychological theorizing. It is perhaps for this reason that a chapter on communication is quite often missing from undergraduate social psychology textbooks.

In this chapter, we will underline why communication is such a vital topic in social psychology. We will examine how communication is shaped by our culture and how a language can influence what we think. We will talk about some of the ways in which our communication with others reveals important aspects of ourselves, our personalities and our identities. We will discuss how language can be characterized as a 'tool' to communicate beliefs and stereotypes. We will then devote some time to discussing the features of nonverbal communication, conversation and discourse. Finally, we turn to communication in the digital age and how new media shape our social interactions. The study of communication is extremely complex and draws on many different disciplines such as linguistics, sociolinguistics, sociology, cognitive psychology and literature. It not only encompasses the way people speak to each other but also how they communicate without words. To study communication, we must also attempt to understand what people intend to do or say, as well as the subtle aspects of communication that enable them to conceal their intentions and instrumental goals. Before we address these many issues, we need to know a bit about language and the 'rules' that govern our linguistic interactions with others.

Language and the 'rules' of language

Language A set of sounds that convey meaning because they are organized according to a set of rules.

Utterances Complete units of speech in spoken language.

Semantic rules Rules that determine the meaning of sounds and words.

Grammar Collection of morphological, syntactic and semantic rules that govern the production and comprehension of a language.

Grammatical gender Organization of nouns along masculine, feminine and neutral dimensions.

A **language** is simply a set of sounds (phonemes), structured into meaningful components (morphemes), which are then organized into meaningful units of words, sentences and complete statements or remarks. Within a language, words are the smallest unit of meaning and form the foundations of larger meaningful units such as sentences, paragraphs and whole conversations. The organization of a language depends on different sets of rules – morphological rules on how to structure sounds into words and syntactic rules about how communicators should organize words into sentences that make sense. Further, the meaning of our **utterances**, that is, complete units of speech, is further determined by a set of **semantic rules** so that we, as communicators, can generate language that makes sense to others. Together, these rules make up the **grammar** of a language. Shared knowledge of a language's grammar enables us to communicate meaning to others and understand others' meaning when they communicate with us. Language enables us to communicate about almost anything with anyone and is such a powerful social tool that we would be completely lost without it.

Of course, different languages vary in many ways, including their grammatical rules. For example, some languages have a system that uses **grammatical gender**, where nouns are classified along masculine, feminine and neutral dimensions, which are prefaced with appropriate gendered pronouns. Variations in linguistic features such as grammatical gender can influence the meaning of an utterance. For example, consider the noun 'papa' in Spanish – 'el papa' refers to the pope, 'la papa' refers to a potato, and 'papá' refers to one's father.

Despite these differences, all human cultures have languages with sophisticated rules of grammar. This obviously confers a massive survival advantage. Our use of language allows us to share and accumulate knowledge within families and communities, in ways that no other animal can. It allows us to collectively think about and solve important challenges. Human beings can strategize about fights with other groups, for example, before the fight happens, when there are no members of those groups physically present. Similarly, hunting, building, tool making and all sorts of other activities are greatly enhanced by the capacity that language gives us to pass on knowledge and collectively plan and organize ourselves. We pay a heavy biological price for this linguistic competence. The shape of our jaws and mouths, for example, has changed to enable us to produce a sophisticated array of sounds. To make room at the back of the mouth for these functions, our teeth have become crowded, which means that we, unlike other animals, are prone to problems with our wisdom teeth. Further, we are more prone than many animals to choking for much the same reason. Clearly, the survival advantage that language gives us outweighs these very real and tangible risks (Corballis, 2003; Pinker, 1994).

With these considerations in mind, some theorists, such as Chomsky (1957), have argued that there is an innate component to language or a *linguistic nativism*, such that the human brain contains a 'hard-wired' set of rules for organizing language (see also Pinker, 1994). It is said that this innate system enables children to learn the rules of language with amazing speed and efficiency. Indeed, it seems that the average two-year-old can produce and comprehend 500 words and a five-year-old as many as 3,000 words (Aitchison, 2003; Holtgraves, 2010). Advocates of this point of view note that it appears to be easy to learn language early in childhood – in the so-called 'critical learning period' – but hard to learn languages later in life, as if the brain were biologically prepared to learn language early on. There is evidence that isolated communities of young children will spontaneously create grammatical languages even when they grow up in the absence of any language. For example, Nicaraguan sign language appears to have been developed by deaf peasant children who had no exposure to sign language and were naturally deprived of language (Senghas and Coppola, 2001). Children who grow up in new territories where immigrants use pidgin – a simplified mixture of languages that lacks rigorous rules of grammar – typically create Creole languages, which retain a mixture of words from different languages but impose a strict grammatical system on them (e.g., Sandler, Meir, Padden and Aronoff, 2005). Of course, these very young children, often preschool or lacking formal schooling, have little or no formal training in grammar, and may be unable to articulate the grammatical rules they have invented.

However, other theorists argue against the universal grammar hypothesis. They argue that language has adapted to the structure of the human brain – if it's universal, or if people appear to be able to create grammatical languages, this is because language reflects the way our brains are programmed to think (Christiansen and Chater, 2008). These critics suggest that there are so many structural departures between languages that the concept of a universal grammar is unrealistic – languages are just too different (e.g., Lock, 1978, 1980). This perspective also asserts that most of the meaning in language is determined by social context. Despite this (as yet unresolved) debate, theorists generally agree there are some basic features of language that allow it to convey meaning. Of particular relevance to social psychology, linguistic researchers and philosophers, such as Austin, Searle and Grice (discussed in the next section), have identified some of the features of language that enable people to communicate meaning to others and also understand the meaning and intentions of others. After all, the primary function of communication is to transfer information to other people, so language needs to be set up to enable people to do so.

The features that enable the communication of social meaning are best understood by way of an example. Consider the statement: 'I'm here now.' How do we know what this means? At face value, this statement informs the listener about the physical presence of the person making the utterance, but is this always what the person really means? Clearly not – the meaning of an utterance is largely dependent on the context in which it is made and the speaker's intention. But how exactly do we understand what people say to us? How do we deal with the ambiguities of a person's language? Also, how do we convey our meaning and intentions to others? The study of these questions is called **pragmatics**.

Pragmatics The distinction between what a speaker's words literally mean and the speaker's intended meaning.

Exploring further Read about the arguments for and against a 'universal grammar'. What evidence is there to suggest the existence of this? What evidence suggests otherwise? An accessible introduction to this issue can be found in popular author Steven Pinker's 1994 book *The Language Instinct*; while those who want a more technical case can read the Christiansen and Chater (2008) article and the many replies by other scientists that follow in the same issue of *Behavioral and Brian Sciences*.

Pragmatics

Sometimes, we say things in ways that do not match their literal meaning. Using the above example, 'I'm here now' could be intended as an apology for being late, a reassurance to a sick friend, or a boastful announcement of arrival at a meeting. Despite this range of possibilities, listeners are skilled at being able to infer the speaker's intended meaning. Communicators are able to reflect on the context and relevance of utterances in order to understand their meaning and respond accordingly. These skills are obviously important for our everyday social interactions. For a conversation to be successful, communicators need to be able to understand each other.

Austin (1962) argued that people are able to separate literal meaning from intended meaning and work out what people intend to say because they have the ability to determine the actions performed by speech. In this **speech act theory**, Austin argued that all language is *performative*, in that it allows people to perform or achieve actions, so that in making statements, we intend something to happen. He argued that there are three characteristics of utterances that enable people to do this:

1 **locution**: the non-ambiguous or literal meaning of an utterance. In the case of the example 'I'm here now', the locution is that the person is physically present.
2 **illocution**: the action performed by the utterance. For example, this may be the apology or the reassurance and reflects the intention of the person making the utterance.
3 **perlocution**: the utterance may also have unintended consequences. For example, saying 'I'm here now' might make the addressee angry, especially if made in a context where the statement is perceived as boastful or unapologetic.

Austin argued that people are adept at understanding these possibilities but they are also able to accurately distinguish the speaker's meaning. Further developing speech act theory, Searle (1975) argued that it is sufficient to use **indirect language** to convey meaning, that is, people do not even need to say approximately what they mean to say for them to be understood. For example, if you have ever seen a sign stating 'This is a no smoking area', you are able to understand, even though it is an indirect statement, that you are not permitted to smoke there. In general, people are able to interpret the intentions of others despite the apparent indirectness of their speech (Figure 5.1). In most cases, when people have mastered a language, indirect speech acts are as effective as those that are direct. People search for meaning in utterances and are generally good at finding the correct,

Speech act theory Theory proposing that speakers use language to perform specific actions.

Locution Non-ambiguous (literal) meaning of an utterance.

Illocution The speech act that is performed by an utterance.

Perlocution The unintended effects of an utterance.

Indirect language Use of language in which the intended meaning is not stated explicitly yet is commonly understood.

FIGURE 5.1 The power of indirect language This signage has only two words, 'Private parking', and yet people know what they are not supposed to do in this area. The sign communicates meaning in an indirect but effective manner. The study of pragmatics helps us to understand how people are able to comprehend seemingly ambiguous combinations of words and indirect requests.

Theory of conversational implicature Grice's theory argues that people are able to understand each other and communicate effectively because they follow various 'rules' of conversation.

Cooperative principle The principle that people follow a set of rules that enable communication to function effectively.

intended meaning. But how exactly are recipients able to do this? How is it that people can distinguish between what is said and what is meant? Of course, the context is important; as we will discuss next, philosopher H. Paul Grice (1975, 1989) argued that communicators also follow certain cooperative 'rules' when they speak to one another.

Grice and the cooperative principle

Grice (1975) devised the **theory of conversational implicature,** in which he argued that speakers tend to be cooperative when they talk. Specifically, communicators mean more than they say because they mutually adhere to what is known as the **cooperative principle.** In Grice's words (1975, p. 45), speakers should aim to make their 'conversation contribution such as it is required, at the stage at which it occurs, by the accepted purpose or direction of the talk exchange in which you are engaged'. In other words, people should communicate in ways that are consistent with the context and topic being discussed – they need to follow rules that make it work and, in general, communicators do appear to follow the rules so that the communication meets its intended purpose. What are these 'rules'? Grice argued that there are four rules, which he called *maxims* of communication:

1 *Quantity:* communicators make their contribution to the conversation as informative as required for the current purpose of the exchange but do not make their contributions more informative than required.
2 *Quality:* communicators generally attempt to make their contributions true, do not say things they know to be false, and do not say things for which they lack adequate evidence.
3 *Relation:* communicators aim to only say things that are relevant.
4 *Manner:* communicators aim to be clear and straightforward and avoid ambiguity.

Grice argued that conversation generally works because people follow these basic rules of communication. We are able to understand others and others are able to understand us because we hold the same assumptions about the rational and efficient nature of talk. These principles guide our conversations with others and we can understand what people intend to say because we assume they also follow the Gricean rules of communication.

There are, however, always exceptions to the rule. Sometimes, people break the rules in a subtle fashion and at other times, they openly flout them. Crucially, people tend to mutually assume everyone will adhere to the cooperative principle and the four Gricean maxims, so this assumption assists the receiver to interpret the speaker's utterances. Specifically, they will assume that the communicator intended to be clear, relevant, truthful and informative, and interpret the meaning based on these principles. When a communicator violates the cooperative principle in some way, this influences the receiver's interpretation of what they say.

For example, Holtgraves (2010) highlights the example of a conversation between former US President Bill Clinton and an interviewer with ABC television in 2008. The interviewer asked Clinton if he felt that Obama was suitably qualified to be president:

Interviewer: You think he's completely qualified to be president?
Clinton: The constitution sets qualifications for the president, and then the people decide who they think would be the better president.

Perhaps because Clinton's comment was narrow and uninformative (so violating the maxim of quantity), it was interpreted by many as a less than convincing endorsement of the future president.

Consider also the example of a university student complaining about the work being too difficult, and receiving the lecturer's response: 'Well, this is a university.' This flouts the maximum of quantity (it is obviously a university, so it was not necessary for the lecturer to say this), but the meaning of this statement can be clearly understood despite the violation of the rule. In this case, flouting a Gricean maxim tells the student exactly what the lecturer means (that is, university work is meant to be difficult), with a slight touch of sarcasm. Indeed, flouting maxims can be a powerful way for communicators to convey implicit meaning in everyday social interactions.

Try it yourself Look at the examples below – can you identify which maxim is being violated in each example? Can you tell what the respondent was trying to communicate in each case? Examples like these demonstrate our ability to understand conversation that violates basic rules of communication.

A: What happened to that cheese I put on the table?
B: The dog looks happy.

A: I hear you went to a concert last night. How was the lead singer?
B: She produced a series of sounds corresponding closely to the score of the song 'Dancing Queen'.

A: I bought a new tie.
B: The scissors are in the drawer.

A: Have you seen my car keys?
B: I've seen them on the hook, next to the fridge and also in the door lock.

A: Where did you go today?
B: Somewhere nice.

ETHICS AND RESEARCH METHODS

The logic of conversation in survey design

Grice's theory has been influential in social psychology (see also *relevance theory:* Sperber and Wilson, 1986). Of particular relevance to social psychological research is how participants respond to self-report questionnaires. Social psychology studies involve communication between researchers and participants, and participants' responses occasionally reflect the pragmatics of the

▶

situation rather than the interpersonal or intergroup phenomena the studies are designed to test (Holtgraves, 2010). For example, if given a piece of information in an experiment, participants may use the information simply because they assume it is relevant – why would the experimenter have introduced it otherwise? However, in such experiments, the researcher may precisely be interested in whether or not the information is used and the conversational dynamics of the situation hinder the researcher's objective (see Hilton and Slugoski, 2001).

Schwarz, Groves and Schuman (1998) and Schwarz, Strack, Hilton and Naderer (1991) have further elaborated on this issue, arguing that surveys and questionnaires are like conversations between researchers and participants. Like other conversations, surveys are governed by the cooperative principle – respondents answer honestly, clearly and give as much detail as is required, and they expect that the researcher does the same. To give an example of the impact this can have, Schwarz, Knauper, Hippler et al. (1991) found that when asked how successful their lives had been, 34 per cent of respondents rated their lives as very successful when asked to respond on a scale from –5 to +5. However, only 13 per cent reported having very successful lives when the scale was from 1 to 10. It was argued that respondents' assumptions about what the numbers mean (e.g., that negative numbers must mean negative events) influence the responses. Participants were probably making the assumption in one case that the researcher wanted to know about the presence of negative events, but in the other that the researcher wanted to know only about the presence of positive events. Respondents therefore answered according to the assumptions they drew about the researcher's objectives. In another example, Schwarz, Strack and Mai (1991) showed that when a question about marital satisfaction appeared in a survey immediately before a question about life satisfaction, respondents' answers to the two questions were strongly correlated. However, these responses were not correlated when the two questions were set together as subordinate parts of one larger question. Schwarz et al. argued that in the first case, respondents assumed that the two answers ought to be related, whereas in the second case they assumed that the answers should be different so that the interviewer is not given redundant information.

Haberstroh, Oyserman, Schwarz et al. (2002) demonstrated that this type of effect also depends on the way in which people construe the self. In one experiment, participants were asked to complete what they thought was a language comprehension task. In fact, this was a priming task where one group of participants was primed with the concept of independence by reading words such as 'I' and 'me' and another group was primed with the concept of interdependence by reading words such as 'we' and 'our'. Participants were then asked to rate their happiness and life satisfaction. However, at this point, one group of participants answered both questions together at the end of one questionnaire, whereas the other group answered them in two separate questionnaires. Haberstroh et al. predicted that participants in the interdependence condition would be more sensitive to the redundancy of the happiness and satisfaction questions than those in the independence condition, because they would be more attuned to the requirement of cooperative conversational conduct. Specifically, because they have been primed as interdependent with others, they should pay closer attention to the common ground of the conversation. However, it was argued that this redundancy would only be noticed when both questions were presented closely together in the same questionnaire. Hence, interdependence-primed participants should provide different information in response to the two questions, resulting in a lower correlation between answers relative to the one-questionnaire condition. Independence-primed participants should not be as sensitive to the redundancy issue, and the correlations between their answers should be same in both conditions. Indeed, this is what the results revealed (Figure 5.2).

Questions

1 Imagine you were working for a market research company commissioned to do a customer satisfaction survey by a cosmetics company. These companies regularly provide results of such surveys in their advertisements (e.g., '80 per cent of women were satisfied with this product'). Imagine, also, that you had no moral scruples. How would you design questions to lead customers to provide apparently positive evaluations of the product?

2 Using an internet search engine or academic database, can you find a paper that criticizes a scale in social or personality psychology on the basis of Schwarz's analysis of survey design?

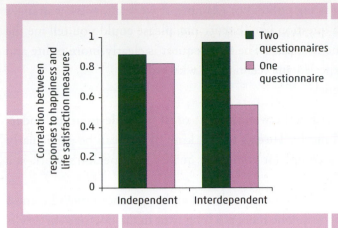

FIGURE 5.2 **Questionnaire design influences how participants respond** Self-construal level influences participants' attention to redundancy in questionnaires. When individuals are primed with interdependence, they are more likely to notice the redundancy in asking two similar questions and attempt to provide new information, perhaps because they think this is what the experimenter must want. So, when redundant questions appear close together in the questionnaire, the correlation between the answers is attenuated for interdependence-primed participants relative to participants primed with independence.

Source: Data from Haberstroh et al., 2002, Experiment 1

As we have seen, the rules of language are powerful in many different ways. However, breaking the rules can be powerful too. Another way we slightly break the rules of communication is in our conversations about 'delicate' matters, when we often adopt **politeness** strategies – phrasing utterances as a function of particular social concerns.

Politeness Processes by which communicators frame their conversations in order to save the face of their interlocutors.

Politeness

Some things are not easy to communicate. Imagine trying to tell a friend that they smell bad, or perhaps you can remember an occasion where you needed to confront someone you thought was telling a lie. These are not easy situations to deal with and a certain level of delicacy is often required. Indeed, in social interactions, what people say to others can make or break their relationships, so as communicators, it is important to know what and how to say things so that social relationships are maintained.

Time to reflect Spend a few moments thinking of some ways to let someone know that they smell bad, and to let them know that you think they are lying. Write down a few different examples and indicate which ones you would prefer. Why do you prefer these statements? Can you relate these examples back to our discussion about direct and indirect speech acts?

Brown and Levinson (1978, 1987) argued that people manage these types of situation through the use of politeness strategies. They devised a theory of politeness phenomena and argued that in communication, a great deal of difference between what is *said* and what is *implied* can be attributed to politeness. To explain, Brown and Levinson referred to the notion of **face** (Goffman, 1959). A person's face is like their self-esteem. You may have heard the expression 'to save face', referring to the basic human need to maintain a positive sense of how one is viewed by others. In everyday social situations, face is often put at risk. Even in basic social interactions where people respond to simple requests such as being asked for the time, face is put at risk because the person on the receiving side of the request has to go out of their way to do something for someone else. When we communicate such requests to other people, we typically attempt to compensate

Face People's concern about their value or standing in the eyes of others.

for these threats to face by being polite. For example, if we want to ask a stranger for the time, we may use a question like 'Excuse me, please could you tell me the time?' rather than 'Give me the time'. The first request is clearly more polite and saves the recipient from experiencing feelings of awkwardness.

Face comes in two varieties:

Positive face A person's wish to be liked.

1 **positive face:** a person's wish to be well thought of. It is the desire to be understood, liked and treated nicely. Threats to this kind of face can be particularly harmful. For example, a complaint about the quality of a person's work is a threat to their positive face.

Negative face A person's wish not to be bothered.

2 **negative face:** a person's wish not to be bothered and to go about one's business unimpeded. Thus, telling someone there is a long wait in the doctor's surgery is a threat to negative face.

Because these threats to face feel unpleasant, our utterances are often oriented to the positive or negative face of those we interact with. To counteract threats to positive face, we might use expressions of solidarity like 'Got the time, mate?', whereas to deal with threats to negative face, we might use expressions of restraint such as 'Could I perhaps just ask you what the time is?' Alternatively, we can go 'off record' and use indirect approaches such as 'Oh dear, I've left my watch at home!' These types of utterances can be just as powerful as direct language and some research has demonstrated that these strategies are often judged to be more polite than direct strategies (e.g., Francik and Clark, 1985; Gibbs, 1986; Holtgraves and Yang, 1990). Clearly, we have many options to deal with threats to face and you may be able to think of many different examples of how you use polite language in your everyday social interactions.

Time to reflect Think back to the examples you came up with to let your friend know that they smell and to confront your lying friend. Which examples do you think would work the best? Which were the most polite? Are the ones that you think would work the best also the most polite?

Brown and Levinson studied the languages of three different cultures, Tamil (southern India), Tzeltal (spoken by Mayan people in Mexico) and British/American English, and argued that there are distinct universals in politeness phenomena. It appears that, universally, communicators tend to assess the 'burden' of the request on the addressee and as the burden is increased, the level of politeness increases. However, the use of politeness strategies is not the same for every person we deal with. Our use of politeness strategies differs depending on the status differential in the interaction and what is expected. For example, research suggests that less powerful individuals are more likely to use negative politeness (indirect) strategies when they are making requests to more powerful individuals (Brown and Gilman, 1989; Holtgraves and Yang, 1990). Further, people in higher positions of power are less likely to display politeness in conversations (Holtgraves and Yang, 1990, 1992; Leichty and Applegate, 1991; Lim and Bowers, 1991) and this effect has been demonstrated cross-culturally (Ambady, Koo, Lee and Rosenthal, 1996; Holtgraves and Yang, 1992).

Further, the 'closeness' of the relationship between the addresser and the addressee can sometimes predict the use of politeness strategies – less politeness is used in closer relationships (Brown, 1993; Johnstone, Ferrara and Bean, 1992). However, one important boundary condition for politeness strategies to be used at all is that the relationship between the addresser and the addressee is generally positive (Slugoski and Turnbull, 1988). Statements are judged less polite when the dyadic (two-person) relationships are negative and in positive relationships, even indirect insults are interpreted as being more polite. Finally, people who are in sad moods tend to prefer greater politeness than people in happy moods (Forgas, 1999). Brown (1965) postulated a **universal norm** of politeness and formality in communication behaviour, which, in the intervening five decades, has not been contradicted by evidence. The universal norm is that we use more formal, polite forms of address when communicating with people higher than us in a social hierarchy, and those who we do not know very well. Thus, across human cultures, language appears to convey and reinforce social hierarchy and social distance.

Universal norm The culturally universal tendency to use more formal, polite language with people who are higher in status than ourselves, or higher in social distance from ourselves.

Question to consider Reread question 1 at the start of the chapter. Knowing what you know about the 'rules' of politeness, where did Siobhan go wrong and why?

In general, there is often a mismatch between the way a communication seems and how it is intended to be interpreted. Communicators are generally skilled at being aware of this mismatch and are able to work out what others actually intend to say and do. At the same time, there are some good reasons why utterances should not always be taken at face value. We use politeness strategies to 'soften the blow' in tricky social situations in order to maintain positive social relationships. Now that we know a bit more about language and the 'rules' of communication, and how people actively interpret what we say, we will move on to the effects our language can have on our own cognitions.

Language, culture and cognition

It has been argued that language has significant power over people's thoughts. This perspective on language was made famous by the anthropologist Benjamin Whorf (for a review, see Fiedler, 2008). In its extreme form, this argument posits that language entirely determines thought. As such, people who speak different languages see the world in different ways (Whorf, 1956). To give an example, the English language has a linear conception of time (e.g., days/hours/minutes) and any point in time is a point on a linear timeline, but the Native American Hopi language lacks a tense system. So do Hopi and English speakers have a different experience of time? Some research suggests they might. For example, Hong, Chiu and Kung (1997) exposed 'westernized' Hong Kong Chinese students either to images common in Chinese culture (e.g., dragons), or to neutral perspective drawings. After exposure to the Chinese drawings, participants were found to endorse traditional Chinese values to a greater extent and they also made more internal attributions than participants who viewed neutral pictures. It was argued that the drawings activated a cultural meaning system, which determined how the participants perceived the world around them. Similarly, Earle (1969) found that bilingual Chinese students were less dogmatic (on responses to a dogmatism scale) when they responded to the scale in English as opposed to when they responded in Chinese. Bond (1983) found that bilingual Hong Kong Chinese students endorsed 'Western' values more when they responded to a questionnaire in English than students who completed the questionnaire in Cantonese. Further, Ramírez-Esparza, Gosling, Benet-Martinez et al. (2006) demonstrated this **cultural frame switching** in relation to personality. They asked Spanish-English bilinguals to respond to a scale of the big five personality characteristics (openness, conscientiousness, extraversion, agreeableness and neuroticism) either in Spanish or English. They found that across three bilingual samples, extraversion scores were higher in English than in Spanish (see Figure 5.3). Similar findings were uncovered for the traits of agreeableness and conscientiousness. Wang, Shao and Li (2010) found that bilingual adolescents in Hong Kong were more collectivistic when answering questions in Chinese and more individualistic when answering questions in English (see Chapter 2).

Cultural frame switching
Because languages are learned in different cultural settings, different knowledge structures are learned and this influences thought.

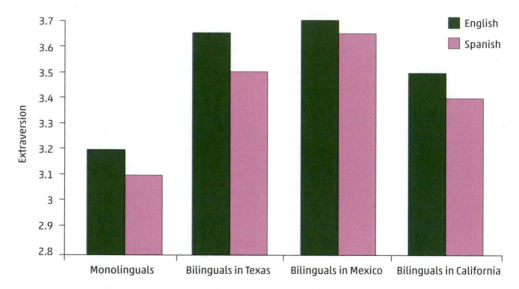

FIGURE 5.3 Cultural frame switching Findings demonstrate that Spanish-English bilinguals can show different personalities when using different languages. Here, participants scored higher on the trait of extraversion when they responded to a questionnaire in English than in Spanish.
Source: Data from Ramirez-Esparza et al., 2006

Another useful example can be seen in a study by Kashima and Kashima (2003), who distinguished between languages that use personal pronouns, such as English (e.g., 'I went out last night') and those in which pronouns are optional (e.g., 'Went out last night'), such as Japanese. The former is a linguistic practice consistent with the speaker's emphasis on the individual, whereas the latter is a practice more consistent with collectivism. Kashima and Kashima demonstrated that people from countries where pronouns were used scored higher on Hofstede's (1980) individualism scale than those from countries where pronouns are optional. Together, these findings support the idea that because different languages are learned in different settings, different cultural knowledge structures are learned and the use of the language influences thought and even personality.

Does language entirely determine thought? Most theorists would say not, taking a moderate perspective on the issue (e.g., Hoffman, Lau and Johnson, 1986). Instead of arguing that language entirely determines thought, theorists tend to argue that language allows people to communicate more easily about aspects of the world that are important (Krauss and Chiu, 1998). It is clear that people live in complex, continually changing environments and in order to survive in such environments, they need to act in a coordinated, cooperative way. To do this, people need a shared focus, when required, on a discrete subset of goal-relevant objects and events. This is where language becomes important. Like a 'lens', language directs the joint focus of senders' and recipients' attention, thought and memory. In this sense, it constrains the reality that people experience (Sutton, 2010).

The focusing, lens-like power of language is often obvious, as in the statement 'There's a car coming', which focuses the listener's attention. At other times, however, it is more subtle. **Masculine generic language** is a good example. Here, linguistic convention in English has long had it that masculine terms, such as 'man', 'his' and the collective noun 'man', can be used to represent people in general, irrespective of gender. Thus, our examples are supposed to refer to 'person', 'his or her' and 'humanity', respectively. Nonetheless, Ng (1990) showed that participants who had been presented with these masculine generic terms did not encode them in this gender-neutral way. Rather, a subsequent memory test showed that they had encoded the masculine generic as referring to men *and not women*. This result suggests that male individuals will tend to be seen as the ones who contribute 'manpower', who are responsible for the achievements of 'mankind' and so on. Technically, people should think of individuals of both genders when the masculine generic is used, but they do not. Of course, it is true that the masculine generic effect occurs partly because words like 'man' and 'his' are often used to refer only to males, and so acquire an association with male referents that is carried over even into other contexts. However, we see here the power of words to focus attention, memory and cognition, irrespective of the linguistic rules and conventions that are supposed to govern it.

Relations between other groups are also affected by this lens-like power of language. Of particular importance are the words that people use to denote groups. Of course, some of these verbal labels are derogatory, as in 'fags', whereas others are neutral or positive, as in 'gays' (Carnaghi and Maass, 2007). In this respect, the labels are like vessels with which positive and negative attitudes to a group are communicated. The complexity of group labels is also important (Leader, Mullen and Rice, 2009; Mullen, Calogero and Leader, 2007). Here, complexity is a property of a set of group labels, rather than any single group label. Each label indicates a particular means of categorizing the group, for example according to its territory, language or customs. A set of labels is simple if it tends to cluster within just one of these categories. It is complex if it is distributed across several categories, meaning that available group labels collectively indicate many facets of the group.

Leader et al. (2009) experimentally varied the complexity of labels for an outgroup – group insults known as *ethnophaulisms* – derogatory terms to describe

Masculine generic language
Use of masculine words such as 'man' and 'mankind' to represent people in general.

people of particular ethnic groups. Participants exposed only to simple sets of labels subsequently indicated negative attitudes and intentions towards the group, while those exposed to complex labels indicated more positive attitudes and intentions. Perhaps complex sets of labels call attention to and focus people's thoughts on the three-dimensional human character of groups, making negative attitudes and intentions difficult to justify.

Another way in which language shapes cognition is in the **saying is believing effect** (e.g., Echterhoff, Higgins and Levine, 2009; Hausmann, Levine and Higgins, 2008). This effect occurs when the act of describing persons or groups changes subsequent memory for them. For example, when you believe your audience does not like a group, you are more likely to describe the group in negative terms and subsequently remember them more negatively. The saying is believing effect tends to grow over time. Attributing negative traits to a group creates, in memory, an association between the group and those traits. If you have just made the negative comments, you will remember them clearly and realize that they contribute to your negative feelings about the group. If you made the comments some weeks ago, you are less likely to recall exactly what you said and why. Thus, the negative mental associations seem attributable to the group itself, rather than what you have said about it. The general point made by the saying is believing effect is crucial for understanding the language–cognition interface – our language changes how we, as well as our audiences, think (for reviews, see Fiedler, 2008; Hausmann et al., 2008; Holtgraves and Kashima, 2008).

Saying is believing effect
The tendency for a person's memory for individuals, groups or events to be influenced by what they have said about them.

Exploring further The saying is believing effect is closely linked to the phenomenon of audience tuning - the process of communicating a message in such a way that matches the audience's pre-existing beliefs on a particular issue. Findings suggest that once people have 'tuned' to their audience and are later asked to recall their attitudes, they recall attitudes that are more consistent with the audience's perspective, that is, the communicator believed what they said even if it was not what they believed before (for a review, see Echterhoff et al., 2009). The saying is believing effect is therefore relevant to a variety of social domains. Specifically, can you find any evidence of saying is believing effects in realms such as politics?

Language, personality, identity and gender

Language is a useful vessel to us for another reason – people can infer things about us from *what* we say. As discussed in the previous section, what people say can convey to recipients something about a speaker's thoughts and beliefs. However, *how* people say what they say can also be a useful source of information for receivers. In other words, our language use can convey 'clues' or **social markers** to receivers about who we are, what we are feeling and what we are thinking (Scherer and Giles, 1979).

Social markers Features of language use that convey information about a speaker's characteristics.

Personality

First, listeners often make inferences about a speaker's personality characteristics from their language use. A typical experiment to examine inferences about person-

Matched guise technique
Technique used to measure attitudes about a speaker based on the speaker's language use.

ality dimensions utilizes the **matched guise technique**, where speech characteristics are manipulated experimentally and participants are asked to evaluate the speaker along dimensions such as competence and sociability. Findings have generally shown that rapid speech rates are associated with high ratings of competence, sociability and trustworthiness, while long, silent pauses are associated with low ratings of competence. Utterance length is associated with ratings of dominance. Finally, elevated social pitch is associated with perceptions of deceit and emotional instability, but variability in vocal pitch is associated with perceived dynamism and extraversion (Scherer, 1979; for a review, see Krauss and Chiu, 1998). There is some evidence to suggest that differences in personality do indeed predict differences in speech style (e.g., Furnham, 1990), but little evidence that 'true' variations in language (due to personality traits) can be accurately detected by recipients.

Identity

Many researchers have investigated how language use can provide an indication of a person's social class and status. George Bernard Shaw popularized public awareness about this issue in his play *Pygmalion* (later adapted into the musical *My Fair Lady*), in which he depicted a young Cockney flower seller with 'kerbstone English' that would probably 'keep her in the gutter for the rest of her days' (Shaw, [1916]1951, p. 28). Indeed, Shaw was right in some ways – people can infer a lot about us from how we speak. Speakers know this and will often go to great lengths to change the way they speak and conceal their origins, as was the case for Eliza Doolittle in Shaw's play, who became a 'project' to a professor of phonetics.

The most significant indicator of social status is at the phonological level, that is, one's accent. Perceived class variations in accents seem to occur in most societies (Guy, 1988). Research demonstrates that varieties in speech communities can be ordered on a continuum of 'prestige' and that speakers' evaluations reflect this ordering (Bradac, 1990; Giles and Coupland, 1991). In the UK, for example, regional accents and those from urban areas, such as Birmingham's 'Brummie' accent and London's Cockney accent, tend to be associated with lower ratings of social class. In general, speakers who deviate from the more standard or **received pronunciation (RP)** accents tend to be judged less favourably than middle-class speakers (Giles, 1970; Giles and Powesland, 1975). People are able to rate socioeconomic status quickly and accurately. For example, Ellis (1967) asked participants to judge the social status of recorded voices and they were able to rate the speaker's socioeconomic status with remarkable accuracy. They could even do so based on hearing a speaker count from 1–10. The advent of new digital techniques for linguistic analysis has made it possible to examine the influence of various different linguistic markers on person perception. For example, Campbell-Kibler (2007) used the matched guise technique to examine the influence of using 'ing' in a spoken word (e.g., washing) or dropping the 'g' (e.g., washin). It was found that the use of 'ing' was associated with higher ratings of education and articulateness compared to when the 'g' was dropped. Typically, findings suggest that standard speakers are rated as more confident, competent and intelligent than non-standard

Received pronunciation (RP)
Standard, high status spoken accent.

speakers, but that non-standard speakers fare better on ratings of solidarity dimensions such as friendliness and generosity (Marlow and Giles, 2008; Ryan, Giles and Sebastian, 1982).

Exploring further Research suggests that regional and urban speakers may be rated less favourably on measures of social status. Can you find any evidence that this is not always the case? For example, how are people with regional and urban accents rated on dimensions such as friendliness and trustworthiness?

Although people's language use typically identifies them with a particular social or ethnic group, which may, in turn, have positive or negative consequences for how they are judged, language is one of the most significant and important markers of identity. Despite the potential consequences of being identified with a group through language, it is difficult for people to change the way they speak. Equally importantly, people may not *want* to do so. If an individual is proud of their ethnicity, they may be more motivated to maintain aspects of their language and linguistic style that mark this identity. For example, an Indian person who has lived in Britain for 20 years may still speak with a strong Indian accent, partly because it is difficult to change one's accent but partly because speaking with an ethnically marked accent means that the person can maintain an important identity and therefore also maintain their distinctiveness. Further, interactions between groups can influence linguistic behaviour. Giles, Bourhis and Taylor (1977) devised the concept of *ethnolinguistic vitality*, arguing that differences in group status and support for a language can determine the continued use and sometimes even the survival of a language in a particular social context. Sometimes, languages cease to be used among groups who live away from their first country. One example is third-generation Japanese people residing in Brazil, who have all but lost their Japanese linguistic culture (Kanazawa and Loveday, 1988). The Japanese language suffered in this context arguably because it had low ethnolinguistic vitality. However, in some cases, this lack of status and support can encourage the revival of dying languages. For example, Hebrew and Welsh have both seen a resurgence in recent years by speakers across the world (Fishman, 1989). Competence in the language is also an important predictor of its survival (Coupland, Bishop, Evans and Garrett, 2006).

It is the case, however, that people linguistically adapt to their environment. At a general level, people tend to adapt their speech style to the context in which they are placed. **Speech accommodation theory** asserts that people will make adjustments to their speech style based on who they are speaking to and the motives involved in the communication (Giles and Smith, 1979; Giles, Coupland and Coupland, 1991; Giles, Taylor and Bourhis, 1973). For example, try to remember a time when you spoke to someone who had a different accent. After a while you may have noticed your speech style changing and becoming more like your listener's, and their speech style may have been doing the same thing and becoming more like yours. This is an example of speech accommodation and can result from a variety of motives, such as trying to be better understood or wanting to be liked by the communication partner.

Speech accommodation theory Theory asserting that people modify their speech style in conversations to suit the context.

Speech convergence Speech-style shift towards that of the listener.

Speech divergence Speech-style shift away from that of the listener.

Communication accommodation theory Extension of speech accommodation theory, asserting that people modify their speech style and nonverbal behaviours in conversations to suit the context.

Occasionally, people will converge their speech to their listener's as in the above example. This process of **speech convergence** typically occurs when two friends converse. Speech convergence increases the extent to which the communication partners' speech styles are similar, and this increases interpersonal liking and approval (Bourhis, Giles and Lambert, 1975). In a similar way, lower status individuals may shift their speech style to be more like a higher status individual's (and vice versa) to equalize the conversation, again promoting liking. However, in other interactions, a different picture can emerge. For example, in a situation where two groups have a less than positive relationship, their speech patterns might diverge. This **speech divergence** can serve to maintain a group's distinctiveness from the other. This divergence is particularly prominent in situations where a lower status group has the perception that they can linguistically 'pass' for members of the high status group. While the former will attempt to converge to the higher status speech style, the latter will diverge in order to maintain its distinctiveness from the lower status group. However, in other cases where linguistic vitality is high (e.g., Welsh speakers in the UK), the minority group is likely to diverge to accentuate their distinctive and identity-rich accent (Bourhis and Giles, 1977; Giles and Coupland, 1991). This use of language is sometimes self-conscious, and is often contentious and political. Those speaking regional, distinctive accents often confront, and themselves generate, the criticism that 'We won't get ahead speaking like that!' People understand both the benefits, and the potential downsides, of speaking with distinctive minority accents that may not confer high status in wider society (Marlow and Giles, 2010).

There is widespread evidence for speech accommodation processes. Even Queen Elizabeth II's English accent has been found to change over the years, moving from an extremely upper-class RP accent to a more standard RP accent (Harrington, 2006). More recently, speech accommodation theory has been extended to include accommodation in nonverbal behaviours too. Renamed **communication accommodation theory** or sometimes just 'accommodation theory', it is argued that people converge and diverge on a range of behaviours associated with language (Coupland, 2010; Giles and Ogay, 2007; Giles, Mulac, Bradac and Johnson, 1987). We will talk more about nonverbal communication later in this chapter.

Exploring further Many factors influence the extent to which people either accommodate or diverge in their conversational speech patterns. See if you can find some research that identifies some of these factors.

Gender

Researchers have also been interested in speech differences related to gender. However, these are often quite complex and difficult to interpret. For example, there are significant differences in the vocal pitch of female and male speakers, but the extent to which this relates to anatomy or social factors is difficult to determine. However, within vocal register ranges, females tend to use the middle part of the register, whereas males favour the lower part of the register (Krauss and Chiu, 1998). Arguably, it is more socially desirable and stereotypical for men to speak with a 'deeper' voice. A study of Japanese women's speech over several years revealed another interesting finding. In general, Japanese women tend to favour the upper part of the speech register more than other cultures, but this has changed over the years and their voices have 'deepened'. The change coincides with changes in women's societal status, providing further indication that speech may be influenced by gender and gender roles (Kristof, 1995).

Try it yourself Interpreting the results of studies of vocal pitch and social change is difficult, partly because research has been essentially correlational (e.g., in Japan, there is a negative correlation between time and pitch of women's voices, which coincides with increasing gender equality in that society). Let us try a simple experiment to shed light on this 'blind spot' in social psychology. You will need to coopt two friends or family members for a simple, less controlled demonstration. Think of five powerful sentences, such as 'I am strong', 'Do what I tell you', and five powerless sentences, such as 'I am weak', 'I will do what you tell me'. Write them down. Have one person read these sentences out carefully and in as natural a style as possible. Have another person listen to each sentence and rate on a 10-point scale how high or low pitched the sentence was; it is crucial, of course, that neither the speaker nor the rater knows what you expect to find or what the independent variable is. Does the speaker use a higher pitch for the powerless sentences? Of course, a problem with this experiment is that the rater may have an implicit belief that powerlessness is associated with high pitch. Can you think of a simple solution to this problem? And can you think of more controlled experiments you could do, if you had the resources, to test the effects of gender roles and power on pitch of speech?

This raises interesting questions about language, gender and power, an issue Lakoff (1973, 1975) addressed directly. In addition to differences in vocal pitch, Lakoff argued that women display a female speech register in which speech differs to that of men's on different levels, indicating women's subordinate position in society. This is outlined in Table 5.1. Lakoff argued that women display distinctive characteristics of speech in their conversations and that this register serves as a marker for women's subordinate social status. Specifically, she argued that the female speech register reinforces attributions to stereotypes, such as incompetence and timidity, which can be damaging for women. This hypothesis is supported by findings related to other gender differences in language use, such as the finding that in conversations, women tend to interrupt less often than men (Ng and Bradac, 1993; Reid and Ng, 1999; Zimmerman and West, 1975). However, other findings support the idea that instead of this register being unique to women, it is characteristic of low status groups in general (Lind and O-Barr, 1979; McFadyen, 2011) and is therefore more likely to be a 'powerless' linguistic style (Blankenship and Holtgraves, 2005). However, it is also the case that the majority of this research has been carried out in the English language, so findings cannot necessarily be generalized to other cultures (Eckert and McConnell-Ginet, 1999). More recently, Leaper and Robnett (2011) conducted a meta-analysis of studies investigating gender and language style. They found that there was a small, but statistically significant effect in which women used more tentative language. However, this effect

TABLE 5.1 The female speech register

Level of variation	Examples
Lexical	Fewer expletives, e.g. 'Dear me!' instead of 'Oh s**t!' Empty adjectives, e.g. 'divine', 'adorable'
Syntactic	Tag questions, e.g. 'It's hot today, isn't it?'
Prosodic	Rising intonation in statements, e.g., 'Dinner will be ready at 6 o'clock?'
Pragmatic	More indirect speech acts, e.g. 'Would you mind terribly turning down the TV?'

was larger in longer conversations, which suggests that women's use of tentative speech style may reflect their greater sensitivity to their conversational partners, rather than lack of assertiveness.

Exploring further The BBC 'voices' project provides an interesting look at accents and language use across the UK. Find the 'voices' project online and listen to the different accents. You can learn about how they evolved and are changing over time. Read about words that are peculiar to particular parts of the UK. Is there a difference between a 'scally' and a 'ned'? Think about your own accent and the words you use. Does your language fit in with the place where you live, or does it make you stand out? To what extent do you see your language use as part of your identity?

Language and stereotyping

Through language, we also let others know what we think about our own and other groups. Of course, the simplest way in which language can transmit ideas about groups is for senders to explicitly assert them (e.g., 'Group A is amazing' or 'Group B is aggressive') (Sutton, Douglas, Elder and Tarrant, 2008). However, this type of explicit open statement can have its disadvantages. For example, in making such bold assertions, people run the risk of being seen as biased or even prejudiced. So, it is not surprising that language provides avenues to express ideas about groups more indirectly. For example, it is possible to transmit stereotypes of a group without explicitly referring to it. One can, for example, describe the behaviour of individual group members in biased ways (e.g., Fiedler, 2008; Lyons and Kashima, 2003; Maass, 1999; Wigboldus and Douglas, 2007).

Serial transmission

© IMAGESOURCE

An example of such a bias is when talking about a particular group or group members, a communicator can describe more behaviours that are consistent, versus inconsistent, with stereotypes. For example, Lyons and Kashima (2003) asked participants to retell a story that contained stereotype-consistent and inconsistent information about individual group members in serial communication chains. These chains are rather like the children's game sometimes called 'Chinese whispers'. Typically, playing this game shows that as the original story is told to a recipient who in turn tells it to another recipient and so on, it bears less and less resemblance to the original. Indeed, Lyons and Kashima found that by the time the story had reached the end of the chain, much of the stereotype-inconsistent information had disappeared, while significantly more of the stereotype-consistent information had survived. Imagine you were told a story about a working-class football fan who, among other things, drank a lot of beer and wrote a moving and eloquent poem to his boyfriend. You tell this story to another person, who passes it on to a third person, who passes it on to a fourth. The first piece of information, being stereotype consistent, is more likely to last to the end of this chain than the last. Crucially, Lyons and Kashima (2003) found that this bias was stronger when communicators were led to believe that the stereotype was widely shared by others in their community. It appears that people tend to reproduce stereotype-

Common ground Shared worldview between individuals.

consistent information because they think it is consistent with a shared worldview, or a **common ground,** and is therefore likely to be easily understood and accepted by recipients (Clark, 1996; Kashima, Klein and Clark, 2007; Klen, Clark and Lyone, 2010). In contrast, information that is inconsistent with widely shared stereotypes is less likely to result in successful communication. Instead, communicators may anticipate receiving puzzled or even argumentative responses.

This suggests that senders implicitly view their language as a *vessel* – a means to transmit information in the context of a shared set of assumptions about the world (Sutton, 2010). Ironically, they therefore withhold pieces of stereotype-inconsistent information, fearing that these would disrupt transmission. Apparently, how people think about language affects how they use language. This reflexivity gives language the power to do much more than transmit thought. The serial transmission paradigm illustrates why we can view cognition and language as 'two sides of the same integral whole' (Fiedler, 2008, p. 45), capable of creating and modifying reality as well as reproducing it.

Subsequent research has shown that the desire to be liked by one's conversation partner is important (Castelli, Pavan, Ferrari and Kashima, 2009). Telling people stories that contradict our shared beliefs about the world can be highly informative, but is a socially risky strategy, in part because it may lead to failures of communication. When people strongly want to be liked, they are more likely to withhold stereotype-inconsistent information (Clark and Kashima, 2007). Thus, driven by the temporary, small-scale, 'local' goals we have in conversation (to transmit information, to be liked), our actions inadvertently have the effect of reinforcing cultural assumptions, including stereotypes. Another line of research leads to a similar conclusion. Fast, Heath and Wu (2009) found more famous, familiar sports players are discussed more by fans, independently of how well they are actually performing. In this case, the desire to find 'common ground' in conversation trumps the actual quality of players, and reinforces the fame of players who are not necessarily any better. An interesting 'blind spot' in social psychological research is the possibility that the desire to find common ground in our everyday lives reinforces the often lamented 'celebrity culture' of recent years, in which obviously mediocre people achieve high levels of cultural prominence (Marshall, 2006) (see Blind spot in social psychology exercise at the end of the chapter).

Language abstraction

Linguistic intergroup bias (LIB) The tendency for people to describe ingroup positive and outgroup negative behaviours abstractly, but to describe ingroup negative and outgroup positive behaviours concretely.

Whereas the study of serial transmission is concerned with biases in *what* behaviours are described, much research has been devoted to biases in *how* they are described. A considerable body of research has examined how language may perpetuate and transmit stereotypes and prejudice in a process called the **linguistic intergroup bias (LIB)** (Maass, 1999; Wigboldus and Douglas, 2007). Informed by the linguistic category model, which asserts that descriptions of events can occur at varying levels of abstraction from concrete (e.g., verbs) to abstract (e.g., adjectives) (Semin and Fiedler, 1988), the LIB assumes that behavioural events can be described at different levels of abstraction, ranging from concrete verbs such as 'hit' or 'kissed' to adjectives such as 'violent' and 'affectionate' and also nouns (e.g, 'aggressor') (Carnaghi, Maass, Gresta et al., 2008). As language becomes more abstract, it conveys less about the situation and the specific form of the behaviour, implies longer duration, and conveys more about the characteristics of the person whose actions are described.

In the LIB, ingroup members' positive behaviours and outgroup members' negative behaviours are described in abstract terms, as if they reflected the underlying qualities of each group. In contrast, ingroup members' negative and outgroup members' positive behaviours are described in concrete terms, as if they were isolated events quite unrelated to how group members would normally behave (see Table 5.2). Therefore, even if an equal proportion of the positive and negative behaviours of each group were described, ingroup members' would be described more favourably. The LIB occurs in many intergroup contexts, in many countries, in several languages, and in naturally occurring settings as well as the laboratory (for a review, see Wigboldus and Douglas, 2007). In part, the linguistic bias reflects the impact of stereotypical expectancies on the way people encode social information. Having encoded a negative behaviour abstractly, perhaps because of ingroup bias, people are more likely to describe it in those terms (Ruscher, 1998). The transmission of information in more abstract terms also leads to more stereotypical impressions being formed by recipients (Karpinski and von Hippel, 1996; Wigboldus et al., 2000).

TABLE 5.2 Linguistic intergroup bias

	Ingroup	Outgroup
Positive	Abstract, e.g. caring, helpful	Concrete, e.g. cared, helped
Negative	Concrete, e.g. hit, hurt	Abstract, e.g. aggressive, violent

The LIB is affected not just by how communicators have encoded events. It may reflect a motivational tendency to protect one's social identity – it is heightened when communicators perceive an outgroup to be threatening, arguably because they are motivated to derogate it while bolstering the ingroup (Maass, 1999). The LIB is also greater for people who score high on the need for cognitive closure – a desire to possess a definitive answer to a topic (Webster, Kruglanski and Pattinson, 1997). It is also influenced by mood (Beukeboom and Semin, 2005, 2006), knowledge about the recipient (Fiedler, Bluemke, Friese and Hofmann, 2003), proprioceptive cues such as arm extension (Beukeboom and de Jong, 2008), contextual expectations such as legal and employment settings (Rubini and Menegatti, 2008; Schmid and Fiedler, 1996, 1998) and culture. With respect to culture, Kashima, Kashima, Kim and Gelfand (2006) found that South Korean speakers tend to use verbs to describe social objects, but English speakers tend to use adjectives (see also Maass, Karasawa, Politi and Suga, 2006). It is argued that this occurs because adjectives are more abstract and are therefore devoid of contextual referents. This decontextualizing linguistic process is less consistent with collectivistic cultural practices.

Further research suggests that under some circumstances, communication goals may even reverse the bias, which in interpersonal terms is called the **linguistic expectancy bias**. For example, the linguistic expectancy bias would normally imply that people describe their friends' positive and enemies' negative behaviours abstractly, and their friends' negative and enemies' positive behaviours concretely – because these descriptions correspond to what is expected. However, given a

Linguistic expectancy bias Interpersonal version of the linguistic intergroup bias, whereby people describe expected behaviours abstractly and unexpected behaviours concretely.

(a) Positive behaviours

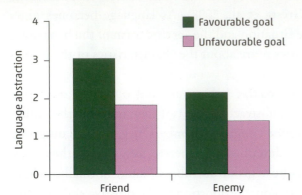

(b) Negative behaviours

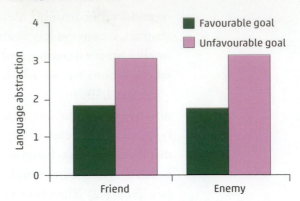

FIGURE 5.4 Reversal of the linguistic bias Although descriptions of others' behaviours are strongly influenced by interpersonal factors such as prior expectancies, this research demonstrates that the explicit goal to select a favourable or unfavourable description can reverse the typical linguistic bias. For example, for positive behaviours (a), participants described enemies' behaviours more abstractly if given a favourable rather than unfavourable goal. For negative behaviours (b), participants described friends' behaviours more abstractly if given an unfavourable rather than a favourable goal.

Source: Data from Douglas and Sutton, 2003, Experiment 1

temporary motivation to describe an enemy in positive terms, communicators tend to use abstract language to describe their positive behaviour and concrete language to describe their negative behaviour, reversing the normal bias (see Figure 5.4). The linguistic bias is also reversed for descriptions of friends, where, for negative behaviours, descriptions become more abstract with an instruction to describe the behaviour unfavourably (Douglas and Sutton, 2003; for a review, see Wigboldus and Douglas, 2007). Thus, the strategic use of abstract and concrete language may allow communicators to create impressions of ingroup and outgroup members that diverge from their own perceptions. Far from merely replicating biased mental representations (although this is in itself an extremely important function), the LIB may be used to create new ones.

Although communicators appear able to use linguistic bias strategically, they also appear to have limited power to inhibit bias when instructed to do so (Douglas, Sutton and Wilkin, 2008). As a result, even communicators with egalitarian intentions may be prone to the LIB, and so unwittingly contribute to intergroup bias (Maass, 1999). Sometimes, therefore, people will be unable to stop themselves from transmitting their stereotype when they communicate with others. Obviously, people rely on this vessel-like property of language to gain information about groups from people who have direct knowledge of the group. However, as Sutton (2010) argues, language is not a perfect vessel because its use not only transmits but also transforms information. People cannot always be unbiased in their communication, so the 'true' nature of information changes as it is passed on from person to person – stereotypes are changed, and new stereotypes are formed. In sum, language changes social information and transcribes it from psychological to societal media. Once made public, the information will impact on the psychological representations of many others.

Nonverbal communication

Nonverbal communication
Everything that communicates a message but does not include words.

The old saying goes that 'actions speak louder than words' and to examine the extent to which this is true, we now turn our attention to **nonverbal communication**. Nonverbal communication is everything that communicates a message but does not involve words. DePaulo and Friedman (1998, p. 4) define nonverbal communication as 'the dynamic, mostly face-to-face exchange of information through cues other than words' (see also Ambady and Weisbuch, 2010). When you think of nonverbal communication, you probably think of things like gestures, facial expressions and tone of voice. However, the term can be considered to be even more broad than this – when social psychologists think of nonverbal behaviours, they also think of things like dress style and tattoos, which communicate information about personality, identity, likes and dislikes without a person needing to utter a word. Nonverbal communication can also be something as simple as how furniture is arranged in a room. For example, picture a situation where you walk into a lecturer's office to find yourself immediately confronted by their desk – what are they trying to communicate to their visitors? Does this make the lecturer seem approachable? Clearly, it is not always necessary to use words to convey a message loud and clear (see Figure 5.5). People can communicate a great deal of information without using words (Ambady and Rosenthal, 1992, 1993; DePaulo and Friedman, 1998). Theorists have also argued that the ability to communicate nonverbally is at the core of our **social intellect** – the ability to infer others' motives, emotions, personality and intentions, and the communication of information about ourselves (Ambady and Weisbuch, 2010). It is surprising therefore that nonverbal communication has been relatively overlooked in mainstream social psychology compared to other topics.

Social intellect Set of skills involving the ability to infer people's emotions, motives, intentions and personality, and the ability to communicate the same information about the self.

FIGURE 5.5 Nonverbal communication is communication 'without words' People are skilled nonverbal communicators and are able to decode a vast number of nonverbal communicative actions. How many different forms of nonverbal communication can you think of?

Perhaps this is because it is often difficult to separate nonverbal communication from speech in everyday social interaction (Krauss and Chiu, 1998). Also, people are capable of such a wide variety of nonverbal behaviours, hundreds of thousands of facial expressions, gestures and movements in all (Pei, 1965), and when one or more behaviours are used in combination with others, *and* together with speech, it is difficult to break down and code distinct behaviours to try to understand their purposes and consequences. Although difficult to study, it is clear that nonverbal cues serve several purposes in communication. In particular, Patterson (1983) argued that nonverbal behaviour can help people communicate by enabling them to:

○ *express intimacy with others:* Close personal distance, touching, gaze and positive facial expressions enable a person to establish intimacy and the opposite would indicate a desire to keep social distance.

○ *establish dominance in conversations:* Threatening gestures in conversation are likely to lead the receiver to see the speaker as aggressive.

○ *facilitate the achievement of goals:* If a person wants something across the room, pointing to the object indicates the desired goal of the speaker.

○ *regulate conversation:* Behaviours such as gestures, gaze and expression can indicate a person's intention to speak or a desire to regulate turn-taking in conversation.

○ *provide information about one's thoughts and feelings:* A person's facial expressions, the way they move and the way they look at others can give observers a good idea of what that person is thinking. Likewise, a person's vocal pitch and speech rate (paralanguage) can lead observers to make inferences about a communicator's state of relaxation or anxiety.

Overall, nonverbal cues are a powerful tool for enhancing communication (see also Argyle, 1990).

The use of nonverbal cues helps us communicate information and messages above and beyond the simple use of words. Sometimes, we even use nonverbal cues that contradict what we say and this too can be powerful. For example, what might it mean to say to someone that you are happy while showing a big smile versus making the same statement with a frown or a sneer? From the first interaction, the recipient might believe that the smiling person is actually happy as they have stated, but a sneer or frown might be interpreted as dishonesty or sarcasm (Bugental, Love and Gianetto, 1971). Clearly, the nonverbal cues we use when we speak to others can add an extra dimension to our communication. Nonverbal cues are therefore a vital part of being able to communicate successfully. Also, we learn nonverbal communication like we learn a first language, without any formal training. Sometimes, we do not even know we are using it. In many ways, we take nonverbal communication for granted, so much so that we often underestimate its importance and impact.

There are many types of nonverbal communication and the following sections specifically cover some of the main types of nonverbal behaviours that accompany speech, such as touch, facial expressions, gestures and nonverbal information conveyed in speech. These are also known as **co-verbal behaviours**, because although they can occur without speech, they are the types of nonverbal behaviours that people exhibit when they converse with others. We examine how social psychologists study these behaviours, how people's nonverbal behaviours are influenced by the presence of others, and how people 'decode' others' nonverbal behaviours. Finally, we highlight the role of nonverbal behaviours in deception.

Co-verbal behaviours
Nonverbal behaviours that accompany speech and convey information to a receiver.

Exploring further In your spare time, observe a conversation between two people. What nonverbal behaviours do they use? If you cannot hear what they are saying, can you get the gist of the conversation from the nonverbal behaviour being exhibited?

Touch

At a basic level, we communicate with others through touch. For example, placing one's hand on another person's shoulder can be a way of communicating comfort to them when they are ill or upset. Alternatively, placing a hand on a person's chest can be a way to communicate that you want them to go away. Touch is therefore a powerful means of communicating with another person without the use of words. There are many different types of touch. Heslin and Patterson (1982) argued that there are five specific types of touch based on the objectives they are intended to achieve:

1 Professional/functional, for example a physician touching a patient
2 Social/polite, for example shaking someone's hand
3 Friendship/warmth, for example friendly touch such as hugging
4 Love and intimacy, for example kissing
5 Sexual, for example making love.

The meaning of the touch is therefore dependent on who is being touched (and where) and the context in which the touching occurs. For example, an affectionate touch between a romantic couple may be meant to communicate enduring love, whereas a similar touch between friends can be a gesture of friendship. Of course, touch is not always positive. People often use touch to assert dominance over others and induce compliance – sometimes these goals are achieved by aggressive touches such as shoves and slaps (Burgoon, Buller and Woodall, 1989).

There are also distinct gender differences in the effects of touch. For example, it appears that, in general, women like to be touched more than men but it depends on who is doing the touching (Burgoon et al., 1989; Heslin, 1978). For example, women report not liking touch from male strangers at all, whereas men do not mind the touch of a female stranger. Women are also more likely to read sexual messages into touch than are men (Heslin and Alper, 1983). In general, people are more likely to touch people of the opposite sex than the same sex, but men touch women more than women touch men (Henley, 1973). This later finding may reflect differences in status because it has also been found that people who 'make the first move' in touching another person are seen as higher status. In judging the pleasantness of being touched by another person, people could be influenced by sex differences related to status differences between men and women in society. There are also significant variations in touch across cultures. People from some cultures (e.g., Mediterranean, Middle Eastern and South American) use a lot of touch in their communication but others (e.g., British, American and Asian) do not (Argyle, 1990). Like gender differences in touching, these cultural differences have the capacity for misinterpretation and miscommunication.

In relation to touching parts of people's bodies, humans also show contextual preferences for the space that is maintained *between* people's bodies in communication. In other words, they are able to communicate with others through the **interpersonal distance** they keep from others. Keeping a larger interpersonal distance makes it possible for a person to conceal information from the person they are interacting with. For example, a large interpersonal distance might make it more difficult for a recipient to detect and read nonverbal communication cues, whereas being 'up close and personal' allows people to see more and also do more

Interpersonal distance The closeness between one person and another.

(e.g., touch). Therefore, people may vary their interpersonal distance from others as a way of maintaining privacy and intimacy. Hall (1966; see also Hall, 1984) conducted observational studies on interpersonal distance and observed four 'zones' of interpersonal distance. People use these zones of distance in interpersonal contact situations depending on the context and who is being spoken to (see Figure 5.6). These zones are as follows:

1 *Intimate zone:* this is the 'up close and personal' distance (up to 0.5 m) that allows people to read and detect the most subtle nonverbal cues. This distance also makes it easier to touch and detect other personal cues such as body temperature and smell. It is generally reserved for close intimate relationships such as romantic couples.

2 *Personal zone:* this distance is still close (typically 0.5–1 m) allowing touch to occur, but not so close that body temperature and smell can always be detected. It is generally observed between friends and close acquaintances.

3 *Social distance:* typically used in casual interactions with strangers, newer or more distant acquaintances, this distance (usually 1–4 m) does not typically allow touch to occur, but still allows people to maintain eye contact and observe other nonverbal cues such as facial expressions.

4 *Public distance:* this is the largest distance in social communication (over 4 m) and is typically used in professional situations to signal differences in status, power or the desire for interaction. For example, bosses may distance themselves in meetings by heading the table and keeping employees at an acceptable public distance.

Like touch in general, differences in interpersonal distance can be a powerful way to communicate with another person. Imagine interacting with an acquaintance who suddenly 'invades' your personal space. What are they trying to communicate to you? What do you think of them? Perhaps more importantly, what would you do? Argyle and Dean (1965) argued that people strongly protect their interpersonal distance and attempt to compensate for any threats to this distance. Because interpersonal distance is such a strong marker of intimacy, people will go to some lengths to protect themselves and maintain their desired level of intimacy. In particular, if our personal space is challenged in some way (e.g., by someone getting too close to us in conversation), we tend to adapt by making adjustments in other cues (e.g., by looking away). We also use inter-

Interpersonal distance zones

Intimate distance
Up to 0.5 m

Personal distance
0.5–1 m

Social distance
1–4 m

Public distance
Over 4 m

FIGURE 5.6 Levels of communication distance
People find different levels of distance to others appropriate depending on the social situation and the person being communicated with. Our most intimate zone is reserved for those with whom we have intimate relationships. Our most public distance is typically used in professional contexts.

personal distance to maintain differences in social status (Dean, Wills and Hewitt, 1975). Again, there are cultural differences in interpersonal distance. For example, some cultures think nothing of standing very close to one another during conversation, but it may make others feel uncomfortable (Hall, 1966).

Exploring further One very funny episode of the US TV programme *Seinfeld* shows a group of people struggling to cope with a 'close talker' – a man who, in conversation, constantly invades others' personal space by getting too close. If you can, watch this episode and observe how people react to this person. These sorts of behaviours often stand out to us because they violate social norms. Can you think of a time and place when this happened to you? How did you react?

Facial expressions

Facial expressions Voluntary or involuntary changes in the face that convey information to a recipient in conversation.

Perhaps the most studied mode of nonverbal communication is people's **facial expressions.** Facial expressions are changes in the face that can occur as an automatic response to an internal state (e.g., feeling or emotion) or as a voluntary response to a social situation (e.g., letting someone know a feeling or emotion). They can also be used to replace words, such as raising one's eyebrows to ask a question. Over the years, social psychologists have been most interested in discovering if facial expressions are consistent within specific emotions and also if facial expressions of emotion are effectively decoded by others. This has largely stemmed from Darwin's (1872) position that there is a small set of human emotions that are associated with a set of facial expressions. Indeed, later research has shown that there are six basic emotions (happiness, sadness, anger, fear, surprise and disgust) and that these are reflected in six basic emotional facial expressions (Ekman, 1982; Ekman and Friesen, 1975). These basic expressions are associated with distinguishable patterns of muscular activity.

Research suggests that people's facial expressions tend to match the emotion being expressed in their voices (Putnam and Krauss, 1991; Winton, Putnam and Krauss, 1984). Also, the facial expressions associated with the six basic emotions have been shown to be relatively universal (Ekman, 1971; Ekman and Friesen, 1971; Ekman, Friesen, O'Sullivan et al., 1987). In many studies, Paul Ekman and his colleagues showed people from many different countries a series of photos depicting the six basic emotions and found that people in a variety of Western, Asian and tribal cultures were very accurate in recognizing the six different emotions. Moreover, they were accurate in judging the expressions of faces from within their own culture and from other cultures. Thus, facial expressions of emotion appear to be largely consistent across cultures. Whether this reflects innate links between facial movements and emotional expression or universals in socialization processes (or both – see the Critical focus box later) is an interesting question, but while many other social psychological factors vary across cultures, facial expressions of basic emotions appear to be more or less universal.

The work of Ekman and his colleagues has been extremely influential; indeed, most investigations of emotional facial expressions use the photographs developed in his research. Some researchers have, however, criticized this method, arguing that the use of static, posed photographs cannot capture the dynamic nature of emotional expressions (e.g., Russell, Bachorowski and Fernandez-Dols, 2003). Other techniques have been developed to get around this issue, such as a technique devised by Krauss, Curran and Ferleger (1983), where research participants are asked to identify emotions from video footage. The findings using this technique, as well as the cross-cultural consistency of facial emotions, largely echo the findings from Ekman's research. Ekman's own work has led to the development of the Facial Action Coding System – a standardized way of measuring small muscle movements that can allow for the decoding of emotional facial expressions and comparisons of human expressions with animal (e.g., chimpanzees) expressions (Vick, Waller, Parr et al., 2007).

One important point to note is that although facial expressions appear to be consistent across cultures, there are some important cultural differences in the rules governing when the expressions can be displayed. In other words, while the basic expression of the emotion may be innate and therefore universal, the **display rules** for the emotion for a particular culture are not fixed and must be learned. For example, it appears to be less acceptable for men in Western cultures to show emotions than women (Argyle, 1990), so they must learn the display rules that are appropriate for their cultural context. Another example of appropriateness within the same culture dictates that people are not permitted to laugh at funerals, but laughing is more than appropriate with the same group of people in a different context (e.g., at the pub).

In light of examples like this, Ekman (1971) argued that the universals of language are restricted by cultural norms of acceptability. Research supports this argument. For example, Ekman (1973) found that when Japanese and American participants were asked to view an unpleasant video in private, both groups displayed facial expressions of negative emotions. However, when later talking about the video with an experimenter, the Japanese participants did not continue to display these expressions, unlike the American participants. Both groups adhered to their own cultural display rules for the expression of negative emotions. Another interesting example is that people tend to be better at recognizing facial expressions within their own race or ethnic group (Kitayama, Mesquita and Karasawa, 2006). Thus, while basic facial expressions might be the same across cultures, the subtleties of expressions (and subsequent decoding of these expressions) might be dependent on cultural differences in expressing emotions.

Display rules Cultural rules governing the appropriateness of expressing emotions in particular contexts.

Time to reflect Think about some social encounters you have had with people of different cultures. Did you ever experience a 'culture clash' in nonverbal behaviour? Could you always read each others' facial expressions?

Gestures

People communicate with their faces and they also communicate with their hands and arms in ways that are different from basic touching. For example, think about how you ask for the bill in a busy restaurant. Think about how you would communicate with a driver who disobeyed a road rule. It is likely you will think

Gestures Hand and arm movements that accompany verbal communication.

of some kind of expression that involves your hands and arms in order to deal with these social situations. The many common movements we use to communicate, both with and without verbal communication, are another kind of nonverbal communication known as **gestures** (Ekman and Friesen, 1972). Gestures are common in groups who do not speak (e.g., religious groups who have taken a vow of silence) and the hearing-impaired where specific languages of gestures (sign languages) facilitate communication. Also, gestural movements are common when people who do not speak the same language communicate with each other.

There are many different types of gestures and, again, some are universal. For example, imagine someone asks you for directions – you are likely to point your finger in the direction the person should go. If someone silently offers you the popcorn in the cinema, it is likely that you will either accept with a smile or decline with an appropriate hand gesture. Gestures go along with speech to help us say what we want to say but they can also replace speech when it is not possible. Some of these latter types of gestures are called **emblems** or **quotable gestures** and again many of these are widely understood across cultures, such as waving the hand to say hello. However, many gestures are culture specific. One example is the 'moutza' in Greece, in which the open palm of the hand with extended fingers is thrust towards the recipient, accompanied by an expletive or insult. This gesture is likely to have little impact on, or at least meet with some confusion from someone outside Greece. Also, the same gesture can mean different things in different cultures. For example, 'no' in the UK is signalled by shaking the head from left to right, but the same gesture in India means 'yes'.

Emblems (quotable gestures) Gestures that replace or substitute for verbal communication.

In cases such as this, cross-cultural miscommunication may arise. One must be careful not to offend people with gestures that can be highly offensive in some cultures. For example, the 'thumbs up' gesture can mean a job well done or other kind of positive response to a British, American or Australian person, but to someone in the Middle East, this is an insulting 'up yours!' Clearly, it is advisable to consult one's travel guide to avoid miscommunications while travelling. As an interesting aside, you may be familiar with HSBC advertisements that appear on TV and in international airports. In these adverts, the bank argues that its understanding and sensitivity to different cultural practices around the world makes it the 'world's local bank'. An awareness of cross-cultural differences in nonverbal communication is considered to be important for effective business practice.

Also, the cultural basis of gestures is reinforced by the fact that new gestures are formed regularly and some that have originated from the popular media have become commonplace, everyday gestures. For example, gesturing to make the letter 'L' on one's forehead to signify that the recipient is a 'loser' was apparently first used in the film *Ace Ventura: Pet Detective* in 1994.

Although gestures vary widely across cultures, they are used in all cultures; indeed, in our evolutionary history, gestures preceded speech as the main channel of communication (Corballis, 2003). The recent interest in embodied social cognition (Chapter 4) has seen an upsurge of interest in gestures and their function. Research shows that gestures are not merely an optional 'added extra' in thought and communication, but play a fundamental role. If you are speaking and cannot bring a word to mind, gesturing it helps you (Krauss, 1998). This finding has been used to help people who have difficulties after a stroke (Hadar, Wenkert-Olenik, Krauss and Soroker, 1998). Similarly, gesturing helps people comprehend words (Goldin-Meadow and Singer, 2003). Gesturing left, right, up and down helps speakers and listeners alike as they try to solve spatial problems (Hostetter and Alibali, 2008). Sitting or standing up straight, in the fashion of a powerful person, causes physiological changes that are indicative of power (Carney, Cuddy and Yap, 2010).

SOCIAL PSYCHOLOGY IN THE REAL WORLD

Nonverbal communication and the haka

Before each game, the New Zealand national rugby team (the 'All Blacks') perform a haka – a traditional Māori dance, characterized by vigorous synchronized movements, stamping and rhythmic shouting. The opponent team stands by watching the haka, which has become a traditional and respected part of the game. However, in 2005, the All Blacks introduced a new haka that offended players and viewers so much that it had to be withdrawn. What was wrong with it? It contained a throat-cutting gesture that many players and viewers saw as representing the 'slaughter' of opponents, and was perceived as an aggressive, insulting and unnecessary gesture.

When asked to comment on this, the coach of the All Blacks said it was intended to symbolize the 'cutting edge' of sport. The captain of the All Blacks said (*Tana Umanga*, *New Zealand Herald*, 23/11/05): 'We didn't really think it would cause as much reaction. We've stated what it means and if people don't understand it, then what can we do?' This incident shows the power of nonverbal communication but also (perhaps, we cannot know for

© MARTIN JONATHAN

sure) its tendency to be misinterpreted. Especially when different cultures are involved, nonverbal communication needs to be carefully managed.

Questions

1 Do you think the haka should have been withdrawn? Why/why not?

2 Explain how cultural values (on both sides) may have been challenged or compromised by the change in the haka.

Gaze

Gaze Looking at another person's eyes.

Eye contact (mutual gaze) When two people are looking at each other's eyes at the same time.

When a person communicates one on one with another person, they spend two-thirds of the time looking at the other person's eyes – a process known as **gaze** (Argyle and Ingham, 1972). Further, people also spend about a third of their time in conversations engaged in mutual eye contact with another person (**eye contact** or **mutual gaze**). Gaze is an important aspect of nonverbal behaviour. The amount of time a person spends gazing and the type of gazing can give a lot of information about what the person is feeling, their personal status and their intimacy with the person they are looking at. For example, just like interpersonal distance and touch, people tend to gaze more at people they like and people with whom they seek greater intimacy. People also like others who gaze more (Kleinke, 1986; Kleinke,

Bustos, Meeker and Staneski, 1973). Of course, gaze is not always positive. Unwanted eye contact from strangers or disliked individuals can be uncomfortable. As such, people will often explicitly avoid making eye contact with others and adopt special strategies (e.g., wearing sunglasses) to steer away from embarrassing social situations and maintain their privacy.

Time to reflect Think of some of the situations in your life when you have wanted to avoid eye contact with another person. Why did you want to do this? How exactly did you avoid the eye contact?

Again, there are some interesting gender differences in gaze in the use and interpretation of eye contact. For example, women have been shown to engage in more eye contact than men (Hall, 1984; Henley and Harmon, 1985). Also, the rules of gaze appear not to be universal. For example, while in Western cultures people tend to gaze more when they are listening than speaking (Argyle and Ingham, 1972), one study showed that a sample of African American communicators adopted the opposite pattern – they gazed more when speaking (LaFrance and Mayo, 1976; for two studies of cultural differences in gaze, see Adams, Franklin, Rule et al., 2010; Schofield, Parke, Casteñada and Coltrane, 2008). People tend to use gaze as a way of signalling intentions in conversation such as the intention to begin speaking, so different cultural patterns like this could be the source of confusion and miscommunication. As in all aspects of nonverbal communication, it is important to take into account cultural differences so that insulting and embarrassing situations can be avoided (Hall, 1966).

Nonverbal communication, self-presentation and influencing others

Like much of what we do, our nonverbal behaviours are influenced by the presence of others (see also Chapter 9). Simply sitting in a room with other people alters our facial expressions, gestures, gaze and posture so that they are different from how they would normally be if we were sitting alone in a room (DePaulo, 1992; LaFrance, 1979; Morris, 1977). Why do we do this? As with other types of self-presentational behaviours, it partly comes down to the human desire to be liked (Argyle, 1990). We change even the most basic nonverbal aspects of our behaviours in response to what others are doing and what we think others think (and what we would like them to think) about us.

Our nonverbal behaviour is influenced by the presence of others in a variety of ways. For example, we may 'mimic' other people's gestures, postures and pauses, our accents change, our gaze patterns more closely match those of the communication partner and, at a more general level, we take turns in conversation (Bush, Barr McHugo and Lanzetta, 1989; Hatfield, Cacioppo and Rapson, 1994; Provine, 1989, 1992; Stel and van Knippenberg, 2008). Argyle and Dean (1965) argued that people typically reach an equilibrium in conversations and maintain it by responding in compensatory ways to any changes in their conversational partner's behaviour. In other words, we make adjustments in the way we speak and in our nonverbal behaviours in response to what our conversation partners are doing.

© PHOTODISC/GETTY IMAGES

Also, people tend to use nonverbal cues differently when they are attracted to the person with whom they are talking. Specifically, a process of coordination occurs more when people like each other. Smiles and affectionate gazes are generally linked to liking, attachment and relationship satisfaction. Likewise, positive nonverbal expressions and coordination increase interpersonal rapport. However, just like positive feelings and satisfaction, hostility can also be reciprocated through nonverbal communication (Cappella, 1997).

Much of this behaviour is automatic (see Chapter 3). That is, many of our nonverbal communications are spontaneous and implicit responses to others and the context around us. Nevertheless, there is some evidence to suggest that communicators do have some awareness of, and control over, their nonverbal expressions and can use them to manage their image and influence other people (DePaulo, 1992). Think, for example, about the behaviours of politicians during their speeches. What we see is typically slick and controlled with respect to nonverbal behaviours. Such individuals sometimes hire coaches to help them eliminate confusing or deceptive nonverbal behaviours from their communication. While this may not always be perfect, it is clear that people do have some control over the image they present to the world via their nonverbal behaviours.

The nonverbal behaviour of others can also influence what people think. For example, Weisbuch and Ambady (2009) exposed female participants to a series of silent video clips featuring female actors of varying body sizes. As the actors' body sizes marginally increased, the participants received either increasingly positive nonverbal behaviour from others (pro-heavy condition) or increasingly negative behaviours (pro-slim condition). Results revealed that participants in the pro-slim condition reported desiring a slimmer figure and admiring slimmer women more than participants in the pro-heavy condition. This occurred despite the fact that the participants were unable to identify the patterns of clips, and even when they were given monetary reward for their participation. It therefore appears that indirect and nonverbal social influence can exert an automatic influence on people's preferences (see Table 5.3).

It is also interesting to note that people's nonverbal cues can sometimes determine the behaviours of others. In a recent study, Beukeboom (2009) showed that the nonverbal cues exhibited by listeners can influence our subsequent language. Beukeboom asked undergraduate students to watch a video about a kiosk owner and then describe the video to two other people. These people were confederates who were asked by the experimenter to display either a positive (e.g., smiling and nodding) or negative (e.g., unsmiling and frowning) listening style. When speaking to a positive listener, people tended to use more abstract, subjective language, whereas when speaking to a negative listener, people stuck to objective facts and concrete details through the use of concrete language. Further, the positive listeners elicited more comments about the thoughts and emotions of the target in the video, and partici-

TABLE 5.3 The power of nonverbal social influence

	Body ideal 10 = quite slim 90 = quite large	Attitudes to slim women 1 = least favourable 5 = most favourable
Pro-slim condition	28.8	4.5
Pro-heavy condition	34.1	3.9

Source: Data from Weisbuch and Ambady, 2009

pants in this condition also gave more of their own opinions. It is argued that the positive listening style acts as a sign of agreement and understanding, which encourages people to give a more interpretative account. On the other hand, a negative listening style makes the speaker more cautious and descriptive. Thus, the nonverbal cues of listeners could have a significant impact on what people communicate and therefore what information is passed on to others.

In general, the expectations of one person can sometimes determine the behaviour of another. For example, evidence suggests that the expectations of healthcare personnel can affect the outcomes of their patients' medications (DiMatteo, 1993; Roter and Hall, 1992; Whitcher and Fisher, 1979), biased interviewers can elicit expected or stereotypical responses from their interviewees (Fiske, 1998; Gilbert, 1998; Hyman, 1954; Weitz, 1972; Word, Zanna and Cooper, 1974) and teachers' expectations can influence students' academic performance (Ambady and Rosenthal, 1992, 1993; Harris and Rosenthal, 1985). Nonverbal cues such as touch, gaze and tone of voice undoubtedly play a significant role in these effects.

How well do people decode nonverbal behaviours?

Nonverbal sensitivity Ability to discern other people's thoughts, feelings and intentions from their nonverbal behaviour.

In studying some of the factors (such as age and gender) that might influence nonverbal communication, psychologists have examined people's general **nonverbal sensitivity** – their ability to discern other people's thoughts, feelings and intentions from their nonverbal behaviour. Using the profile of nonverbal sensitivity test (Rosenthal, Hall, DiMatteo et al., 1979), everyday life situations are performed by an actor and video clips are presented to participants in varying modalities (e.g., facial expressions, body movements and tone of voice). Participants are then asked to 'decode' the nonverbal behaviours in the test (e.g., what is the person in the scene thinking, doing and feeling?). Using this procedure, it is possible to measure individual differences in sensitivity to nonverbal cues and examine some of the consequences of these differences. Using this test, it has been found that people's nonverbal sensitivity generally improves with age and experience (Buck, 1984; DePaulo and Rosenthal, 1982; Rosenthal et al., 1979). Also, psychopathology sometimes compromises people's ability to understand nonverbal behaviour (Buck, 1984; Rosenthal et al., 1979). Further, women appear to be better at reading most facial expressions and other nonverbal cues than men. Using a newer test called the test of nonverbal cue knowledge (Rosip and Hall, 2004), it has been shown that women show a better knowledge of nonverbal cues, supporting the social psychological explanation that because of women's social roles (e.g., nurturing and child rearing), they are encouraged to be more expressive and emotionally responsive than men (Mansted, 1992).

Other, more complex relationships exist. For example, it has been found that doctors who are good at reading body cues tend to have more satisfied patients (DiMatteo, Hays and Prince, 1986). Also, students who score high on nonverbal sensitivity learn more than less sensitive students (Bernieri, 1991). Finally, nonverbal sensitivity is linked to competence and status in children (Feldman, Philippot and Custrini, 1991). So, there is some evidence for individual differences in sensitivity to nonverbal behaviour. It should be noted, however, that basic intelligence (Rosenthal et al., 1979) and the ability to recognize faces (Etcoff, 1989) do not correlate with nonverbal sensitivity.

Time to reflect People often refer to using a 'poker face' to conceal information from others. Before you read on and learn about the science of deceptive communication, do you think that people can always hide what they feel? How good do you think people are at reading others?

Nonverbal communication and deception

An interesting question that follows is whether nonverbal cues reveal the 'inner truths' that people may not want to reveal. Many talk shows introduce 'experts' who 'decode' body language to establish that a person is being dishonest. This echoes the popular belief that while people may be able to control what they *say* in order to hide their deceit, which is more often than not the case (Knapp, Hart and Dennis, 1974), they cannot control their nonverbal behaviour or may even overcompensate for their deceit, which makes matters worse. This is not always the case. In particular, research shows that facial expressions are not very helpful in aiding people to detect deception (Ekman and Friesen, 1974; Zuckerman, DePaulo and Rosenthal, 1981). Based on facial expressions, receivers' accuracy in detecting whether or not someone has lied is not much better than chance because, in general, it seems that people are able to exert some control over their facial expressions and adjust them in an attempt to hide deceit.

However, it appears that problems may arise when people place too much effort into controlling their facial expressions. In doing so they can forget that they are displaying cues to deception in other aspects of their nonverbal behaviour. For example, while people are focusing on their facial expressions, they may not be thinking about their elevated vocal pitch (Ekman, Friesen and Scherer, 1976), their excessive fiddling with objects (Knapp et al., 1974) or the number of times they touch their face (Ekman and Friesen, 1974). These other nonverbal channels can therefore become 'leaky' and receivers may perceive that something is up. Overall, though, receivers do not seem particularly adept at reading nonverbal deceptive cues (DePaulo, 1994). While people may experience a general feeling of suspicion, they cannot necessarily pinpoint exactly if and how they are being deceived (DePaulo and Rosenthal, 1979). Contrary to popular belief, women are no better at detecting lies through nonverbal cues than men (Rosenthal and DePaulo, 1979).

On the upside, however, people in professions that require them to detect lies are often better at doing so than the general population (Mann, Vrij and Bull, 2004; Vrij, Mann, Robbins and Robinson, 2006). Also, it has been found that nonverbal behaviours are most helpful to people in detecting deceit the more the 'liars' are motivated to hide their deceit. This **motivational impairment effect** means that people, in trying too hard to hide their deceit, actually make it easier for others to notice (DePaulo, Kirkendol, Tang and O'Brien, 1988). Further, other research suggests that women are more likely to show the motivational impairment effect

Motivational impairment effect The ironic tendency for the motivation to hide deceit to make concealing deceit less effective.

than men (DePaulo, Stone and Lassiter, 1985) and attractive people display the effect more than less attractive people (DePaulo et al., 1988). Further, when people try to simultaneously control all their verbal and nonverbal cues, their deceit is more likely to be detected by recipients (DePaulo et al., 1988). Finally, people appear to find it easier to detect deceptive emotional communication than deceptive unemotional communication (Warren, Schertler and Bull, 2009). In summary, it is not always the case that people can 'hide' their attempts to mislead others but at the same time, there are many variables that influence people's ability to conceal their deceit (see also DePaulo, Lindsay, Malone et al. 2003).

Exploring further Face expert Paul Ekman argues that people can be trained to read 'microexpressions' in others' faces. He argues that people often make these small 'slips' of gestures when they are deliberately trying to conceal something – people just need to know how to detect these subtle changes of behaviour. Read about Paul Ekman's work and learn more about the research associated with the study of microexpressions.

Time to reflect If a person from another culture violated a norm of nonverbal behaviour in your culture, should you tell them? Why/why not?

Question to consider Reread question 2 at the start of the chapter. How likely is it that Carol will be able to tell if her partner is telling her the truth about his suspected affair?

CRITICAL FOCUS

The evolution of facial expressions

To understand the functions of nonverbal behaviour, social psychologists often refer to a proposal made by Charles Darwin in 1872. In his work, *The Expression of the Emotions in Man and Animals*, Darwin asked why people's facial expressions of emotions take the forms they do. For example, why do we wrinkle up our noses when we feel disgusted about something? Why do we bare our teeth in anger? Darwin argued that people do these things because they are behaviours that earlier in our evolutionary history had specific and direct functions – most notably, they were useful for our survival. For example, baring one's teeth is a way of signalling an attack and wrinkling up one's nose is a way to avoid smelling unpleasant smells.

But if these behaviours are relics of our prehistoric age, why do we still do them? Do we still need them for some reason? It is not necessary for us to attack with our teeth anymore, so why do we still use the teeth-baring facial expression to express anger? According to later theorists (e.g., Hinde, 1972; Tinbergen, 1952), humans still display these expressions because over the course of their evolutionary history, the expressions have acquired value for communication. Specifically, they provide others with an indication of an individual's internal state. This is valuable social information and according to the evolutionary perspective, these are behaviours that have been selected for, even if they are no longer used for their original biological function.

Earlier in the chapter, we discussed the universality of emotional facial expressions. For example, the six primary emotions appear to be recognized consistently across cultures (Ekman, 1971; Ekman and Friesen, 1971; Ekman, Friesen, O'Sullivan et al., 1987). However, as we also discussed earlier, although facial expressions appear to be cross-culturally consistent, important cultural differences in display rules determine when the expressions can be displayed. Ekman (1971) argued that the universals of language are restricted by cultural norms of acceptability. Ekman's approach is therefore both universal and culture specific (Matsumoto, 2004).

What is more important, nature or nurture? Meta-analyses confirm that both universals and cultural factors are important in recognizing the six primary emotions (Elfenbein and Ambady, 2002; Russell, 1994) and also how they are experienced (Kitayama et al., 2006). Thus, scientific thinking at present suggests that the apparent universality of facial expressions reflects differences in socialization and an innate link between emotions and facial muscle activity. This can be represented as in Figure 5.7 for an example related to fear. When a person encounters an emotion-arousing stimulus, they appraise the stimulus, which activates an innate system of facial muscle movements in response. At that point, different facial display rules apply and determine the final emotional expression that is displayed. There is some evidence that the brain is specialized to process and respond to facial expression. For example, Wicker, Keysers, Plailly et al. (2003) found that watching a disgusted facial expression in another person's face activated the same areas of the brain as when

participants were disgusted themselves. However, this is not proof that facial expressions have a neurological basis. It could be that people learn which facial expressions correspond to disgust, which informs their own responses to these expressions.

Questions

1 If facial expressions provide information about communicators' internal states, why do you think people still use them when they are communicating on the phone?

2 How do you think the Darwinian argument might apply to other nonverbal behaviours? A special issue of the *Journal of Nonverbal Behaviour* (Patterson, 2003) explores the evolutionary bases of nonverbal behaviours such as mimicry, expressivity and laughter.

3 How easy is it to design an experiment to test the prediction that facial expressions are evolved? What variables might you manipulate, how would you do this and what would you measure?

4 Evolutionary psychologist Michael Corballis (1999, 2004) argues that hand gestures preceded our spoken language. He argues that as hominids evolved from the other apes, some of the early bipedal hominids began to use hand gestures, syntax was added to these gestures, and that speech now dominates gestures in human communication. Critically review this argument and the evidence that supports it.

FIGURE 5.7 The role of culture and innate factors in the display of emotional facial expressions Ekman (1971) argued that both innate (nature) and culture-specific display rules (nurture) influence expressions.

Conversation and discourse

Conversations Interactions between individuals encompassing both verbal and nonverbal communication.

Of course, in our everyday **conversations**, we communicate with words and nonverbal cues at the same time. For example, people use both verbal (e.g., words like 'hello', 'go ahead' and goodbye') and nonverbal (e.g., waving, pausing, looking away) cues to begin, take turns in, and end interactions with others. People are generally skilled in their use of verbal and nonverbal conversational cues and resist attempts to violate conversational norms such as interrupting when someone has not finished what they are saying (e.g., Ng and Bradac, 1993; Reid and Ng, 1999). Communicators also make use of **back channel communication** cues (e.g., 'uh huh', 'sure', nodding and so on) to allow the speaker to know they are listening. Following these 'rules' is important to make communication go smoothly and rule violations such as interrupting can be perceived as rude, or attempts to exert power in a conversation (Ng and Bradac, 1993). Further, the norms of communication differ depending on the context of the communication. For example, a conversation between a long-term romantic couple or between two close friends will probably include more instances of personal disclosure than conversations between more distant acquaintances, and the rules of turn-taking and reciprocity might be less important (Morton, 1978). A doctor–patient conversation may contain less reciprocity and turn-taking for an entirely different reason – the power difference between the interactants. Of course, to some extent, doctors need to take charge of the conversation because they need to diagnose the patient's illness. However, research demonstrates that doctors show a tendency to dominate conversations to a significant extent, often allowing little scope for patients to respond and ask questions of their own (West, 1984). Thus, the power imbalance in this particular interaction significantly influences the course of the conversation.

Back channel communication Cues that let the speaker know that a person is listening.

Time to reflect If doctors tend to dominate communication in the consultation room too much, what might be the implications of this for the effective diagnosis and treatment of illnesses?

Conversation analysis (CA) The study of talk in interactions, which attempts to describe the structure and patterns of conversation.

Patterns of communication can also be examined using a technique called **conversation analysis (CA)**, where researchers study talk in interactions. CA generally endeavours to describe the structure and patterns of interactions in everyday conversations (e.g., Drew, 2005; Heritage, 2005; Pomerantz and Mandelbaum, 2005; Sacks, Schegloff and Jefferson, 1974; Schegloff, 2007). Typically, a researcher devises a research question or problem and then collects data via video or audio-recorded conversations. The researcher does not intervene in the data collection so that the analysis examines natural talk in interactions. Once the data have been collected, a researcher transcribes the conversation and, based on an inductive data-driven analysis, examines patterns in the conversation. Thus, rather than an experiment or observational study where hypotheses are formulated prior to the study taking place, the outcomes and conclusions drawn from CA are driven by the data itself. Much of what we know about turn-taking in conversation is drawn from research using CA (e.g., Sacks et al., 1974). Using CA, researchers have identified that turn-taking is almost universal in conversation – communicators tend to talk one at a time, leaving little gaps and with little evidence of people talking at the same time.

Another approach adopted by social psychologists to analyse conversation is to conduct **discourse analysis (DA)**. DA refers to a number of methods used to analyse written texts (e.g., newspapers, articles), spoken language (e.g., conversations, speeches) or sign language use (see also Chapter 1). DA is based on the fact that conversations rarely take place in a neutral environment, so the context of the conversation is important. Specifically, what happens in discourse can be related to context, power and interaction. It is argued that mainstream methods in the social psychology of communication (e.g., artificially designing linguistic materials and speech) fail to capture the meaning of the communication. First, the content of conversations provides information about the people who are talking. For example, a teenager is likely to talk about completely different topics to someone in middle age. Second, the way in which people talk to one another (e.g., paralinguistic cues, nonverbal cues) can largely determine the meaning of the conversation. Therefore, isolating and examining specific features of communication can mean that researchers miss the meaning of the communication and can misunderstand how communication influences attitudes. Specifically, discourse analysts argue that language and non-linguistic cues are impossible to separate and that researchers should therefore examine the entire discourse in order to understand its meaning and influence (Billig, 1987; Edwards, 1997, 2005; Edwards and Potter, 1992, 2001; Giles, Coupland, Henwood et al., 1990; Potter, 1996; Potter and Wetherell, 1987; Wetherell and Potter, 1992).

Discourse analysts have developed discourse-based alternatives to the study of many mainstream topics in social psychology. For example, memory and causal attribution have been examined through everyday event reporting (Edwards and Potter, 1992, 1993; Middleton and Edwards, 1990). The role of emotions in relationships and actions has been studied through how people call upon emotional states in their personal narratives such as disputes and in counselling situations (Edwards, 1997, 1999). DA has also been used extensively in the study of prejudice (e.g., Condor, 1988; Potter and Wetherell, 1987; van Dijk, 1993) and in the study of crowds, collective action and protest (Drury and Reicher, 2005; Reicher, 2001, 2004). In general, discourse analysts argue that by examining an entire discourse, it is possible to see people doing the kinds of things for which psychology has a set of explanations and definitions (Edwards, 2005). This is the main point of departure between DA and mainstream social psychology. While mainstream social psychologists argue that the unit of analysis can be the individual, the group or a specific cognition (e.g., attitude, emotion and so on), discourse analysts argue that the basic unit of analysis should be the talk. The cognitions and psychological constructs that social psychologists investigate are assumed by some discourse analysts to exist only through talk (e.g., Edwards, 1997; Potter, 1996; Potter and

Discourse analysis (DA)
Analysis of an entire communicative event located in a particular sociohistoric context.

Wetherell, 1987). This view poses problems for mainstream social psychology, which is one reason why the DA approach is often critiqued and the two approaches are often perceived to be at odds with one another (Giles and Coupland, 1991). Perhaps more optimistically, mainstream and DA approaches may be able to inform each other to gain a clearer understanding of how social psychological processes occur and are brought about through communication.

Communication and technology

Recently, the market research company Student Monitor (2012) conducted a lifestyle and media survey, which revealed that the top five things that are 'in' on university campuses across the USA were drinking beer followed by using Facebook, text messaging, using iPods and drinking other types of alcohol. Thus, two of the top five activities among university students – at least according to this survey – involve communication via technologies that simply did not exist a few years ago. One important question for social psychologists is how these technologies influence our communication and social behaviour. Perhaps unsurprisingly, this is a growing area of research.

Computer-mediated communication

Computer-mediated communication (CMC)
Communication via the use of computer networks.

Most of the research on communication via new technology so far has focused on **computer-mediated communication (CMC)** and the differences between CMC and face-to-face communication. Of course, as other technologies develop (e.g., text messaging, social networking, microblogging), more research will emerge, but for now most of the research has been concerned with how people communicate via email and the internet. More specifically, many studies of CMC have focused on the capacity of CMC users to communicate anonymously and on the hypothesis that communication via computers is different from other modes of communication. This idea has been explored extensively in a variety of settings since the beginnings of CMC, such as work-related behaviour (e.g., Siegel, Dubrovsky, Kiesler and McGuire, 1986; Sproull and Kiesler, 1986), the development of online relationships (e.g., Lea and Spears, 1995; van Gelder, 1985) and the level of hostility in CMC (e.g., Douglas and McGarty, 2001, 2002; Kiesler, Siegel and McGuire, 1984; Lea, O'Shea, Fung and Spears, 1992). CMC is generally perceived to allow communicators the freedom to act in ways they normally would not, and liberate them from normal rules and standards of behaviour. The general argument that communication over the internet is disinhibited stems from the argument that anonymous behaviour releases people from constraints that would normally keep behaviour regulated and in line with societal norms and standards. This concept of *deindividuation* (Diener, 1980; Zimbardo, 1969) means that people are able to get away with bad behaviour because they do not need to answer for it. You will learn more about deindividuation in Chapter 10 on group behaviour. Generally, the concept of deindividuation is used to explain a variety of features of CMC, such as the higher levels of disclosure that are witnessed in CMC versus face-to-face interaction (Joinson, 2001), even if this is reasonably superficial (Attrill and Jalil, 2011), high levels of hostile, disinhibited or *flaming* behaviour witnessed over computer networks (e.g., Kiesler et al., 1984; Lea et al., 1992) and the tendency for hate groups to use the internet to transmit their views and recruit new members (see Douglas, McGarty, Bliuc and Lala, 2005; for overviews, see Douglas, 2007, 2008). Also, going back to the topic of lying and deceit, a recent study showed that people who were highly motivated to tell lies were better able to do so in a text-based communication medium than when communicating face to face (Hancock, Curry, Woodworth and Goorha, 2008). Thus, the complete elimination of nonverbal cues may provide the freedom to violate social norms and also pave the way for people who want to deceive others.

There is also some evidence of other negative phenomena existing in CMC. For example, research by Williams, Cheung and Choi (2000) and Zadro, Williams and Richardson (2004) has examined how people deal with being ostracized in a computer-mediated setting, such as when their emails are unanswered or they are ignored in a chat room. Using a unique program called the 'Cyberball' program, Zadro et al. (2004) showed that people have strong negative emotional reactions when they are ostracized in a CMC setting, even when they think they are only interacting with a computer. These reactions stem from an overarching need to belong and be socially included. However, the ambiguity of communicating with someone via a computer and the uncertainty concerning why they are being ignored (e.g., it could just be technological problems) does not attenuate the negative impact of ostracism (see Chapter 8). Also, there is evidence that people are often harassed, 'cyberstalked' and bullied when they communicate over the internet (Baruch, 2005; Khoo and Senn, 2004; Ybarra and Mitchell, 2004) and women and youths are the most common victims of these phenomena. Again, the most common explanation for these phenomena is that the medium is anonymous and therefore allows perpetrators to get away with negative behaviour. This may be the case, but it is unclear whether these phenomena actually occur more in CMC than in face-to-face communication.

Try it yourself Is too much internet use bad for you? Research using the generalized problematic internet use scale (Caplan, 2002) suggests that overuse and misuse of the internet can be associated with several psychosocial variables including depression, self-esteem, loneliness and shyness. In your own time, complete the scale below, but always bear in mind that correlation does not always entail causation (see Chapter 1), so there is no need to worry if it appears you might use the internet too much.

Rate the extent to which you agree/disagree with the following statements: 1 = strongly disagree, 5 = strongly agree.

I use the internet to talk to others when I feel isolated.	1	2	3	4	5
I seek others online when I feel isolated.	1	2	3	4	5
I use the internet to make myself feel better when I'm down.	1	2	3	4	5
I go online to make myself feel better when I'm down.	1	2	3	4	5
I am treated better online than in face-to-face relationships.	1	2	3	4	5
I feel safer relating to others online rather than face to face.	1	2	3	4	5

I am more confident socializing online than offline.	1	2	3	4	5
I am more comfortable with computers than people.	1	2	3	4	5
I am treated better online than offline.	1	2	3	4	5
I have got in trouble at work or school because I was online.	1	2	3	4	5
I have missed class or work because I was online.	1	2	3	4	5
I have missed a social event because of being online.	1	2	3	4	5
I have made unsuccessful attempts to control my internet use.	1	2	3	4	5
I feel worthless offline, but I am someone online.	1	2	3	4	5
I am unable to reduce my time online.	1	2	3	4	5
I feel guilty about the time I spend online.	1	2	3	4	5
I have tried to stop using the internet for long periods of time.	1	2	3	4	5
I lose track of time online.	1	2	3	4	5
I use the internet for longer times than I expect to.	1	2	3	4	5
I have spent a good deal of time online.	1	2	3	4	5
I often go online for longer time than I intended.	1	2	3	4	5
I am preoccupied with the internet if I can't connect for some time.	1	2	3	4	5
I miss being online if I can't go on it.	1	2	3	4	5
When not online, I wonder what is happening online.	1	2	3	4	5
I feel lost if I can't go online.	1	2	3	4	5
It is hard for me to stop thinking about what is waiting for me online.	1	2	3	4	5
I don't worry about how I look when socializing online.	1	2	3	4	5
I don't worry about relationship commitment when socializing online.	1	2	3	4	5
I have control over how others perceive me online.	1	2	3	4	5

Source: Caplan, 2002. Copyright (2002), reprinted with permission from Elsevier

Also, it is clearly the case that CMC is not always bad. One perspective proposes that what people do when they communicate via computers is governed more by group norms and standards than we might think. In particular, the social identity model of deindividuation effects (Reicher, Spears and Postmes, 1995; Spears and Lea, 1994), which we will revisit in Chapter 10, argues that anonymity can facilitate the enactment of social identity. Rather than proposing that anonymity always leads to chaos and deregulated behaviour, Spears and Lea (1994) proposed that anonymity of the self to a powerful audience may be liberating in another way – anonymous communicators need not feel pressured to conform to the norms and expectations of the group (see also Reicher and Levine, 1994a, 1994b), but may enact other aspects of their identity that the group would normally deem unacceptable. CMC can therefore equalize the context of communication to make it less constrained by communicators' status. In other situations, the presence of an ingroup audience can strengthen the salience of the group's norms and people will react more strongly in accordance with those norms rather than going against them (e.g., Douglas and McGarty, 2001, 2002; Postmes, Spears, Sakhel and de Groot, 2001; Sassenberg and Boos, 2003). Thus, there is more purpose to anonymous behaviour than previous theories might suggest. Overall, the internet provides people with a choice to either identify themselves or not, and this freedom may facilitate the expression of their identity to both opponents and like-minded individuals and groups.

People have also found neat ways to deal with the limited nonverbal cues present in CMC. You will all be familiar with the use of emoticons such as smiley faces made up of keyboard symbols to denote emotional reactions, such as :–) for happiness and :–(for sadness. Because of the limited nonverbal cues available to computer-mediated communicators, these tools have become a valuable way of expressing what would otherwise be lost (Derks, Bos and von Grumbkow, 2004; Walther and D'Addario, 2001). Interestingly, there is some evidence that women may make more use of emoticons than men (Wolf, 2000).

Question to consider Reread question 3 at the start of the chapter. Now you know about some of the features of computer-mediated communication and the differences between CMC and face-to-face interaction, which medium should Jake use to complain to his boss?

Other technologies

As mentioned earlier, less is known about the social psychological implications of other new technologies such as mobile phone communication. However, some theorists point to the potential for mobile phone communication to affect how we think and behave in significant ways. For example, Katz and Aakhus (2002) argue that while mobile phones increase the pace and efficiency of people's lives, they may 'rob' them of their leisure time. In always being accessible, people may never be released from their daily obligations. It may also be the case that the amount of time spent using mobile communication can decrease the amount of time people spend communicating face to face (Figure 5.8). This may have implications for how people interact with others and the quality of everyday social interactions. However, it may be the case that mobile telecommunications can actually bring people together, for both good and bad. For example, you may have heard the term 'flash mob' – these are groups of people who assemble suddenly in a public place for some specific purpose such as a demonstration, or for pure entertainment, and then quickly disperse (Duran, 2006). Such groups are typically organized through social networking, SMS messaging or viral emails. Clearly, such new technologies have the capacity to change the way people communicate in a variety of ways.

© BANANASTOCK

FIGURE 5.8 Plugged in, or off the hook? Does modern telecommunications technology make people more isolated or can it bring people together? (As you may know, Lady Gaga's hit song 'Telephone' is a colourful exploration of the irony that as we become more chronically connected, we may feel less inclined to be intimate with others.)

Chapter summary

This chapter has provided an overview of the social psychology of communication. We have discussed the rules of language, and the important social functions of language in identity, culture, cognition, gender and stereotyping. We have also discussed the study of nonverbal communication, conversation and discourse, and the social psychology of new communication media. You will have learned that:

- The organization of a language depends on a set of structural and semantic rules so that the communication makes sense. However, the meaning conveyed by language does not always match the literal meaning and as skilled communicators, people are able to distinguish what someone means from what they say.

- People tend to be cooperative when they talk and obey a series of further rules or maxims (quantity, quality, relation and manner) so that the communication meet its intended purpose. Breaking these rules can be a powerful way to make a point. People also observe rules of politeness, which mean that social interactions can run smoothly.

- Language influences the way we think. Language does not necessarily determine thought entirely but many findings suggest that language allows people to communicate more easily about aspects of the world that are important. Words can also influence what we think about groups and can influence our social interactions.

- Language contains important social markers, meaning that from language (and language use), communicators convey information about themselves. Language and its use can be a cue to our personality characteristics, social identities and our gender.

- People adjust the way they communicate to the context in which they are placed. In particular, people adjust aspects of their speech such as their accents to either converge with or diverge from their communication partners. In general, convergence occurs in positive, friendly interactions and people diverge to maintain their own identity or distance. This theory of speech accommodation has been broadened to include nonverbal communication in communication accommodation theory.

- There is some evidence to suggest that women and men speak differently. Women sometimes display the characteristics of a female speech register, which may or may not contribute to gender and power relationships in society.

- Language also enables people to communicate stereotypes. People can do this openly or more covertly through the use of verbs and adjectives varying in abstraction, or by only passing on stereotype-consistent information to others.

- Much of communication occurs through nonverbal channels such as facial expressions, touch and gestures. Some nonverbal behaviours are consistent across cultures but many are unique to specific cultures. We can influence (and be influenced by) others through nonverbal behaviours. Much of our nonverbal behaviour in social interaction is automatic or unconscious.

- Findings suggest that people are not particularly skilled at decoding facial expressions and there are many individual differences variables that predict how well people are able to decode nonverbal communication. Facial expressions are also not very helpful in aiding people to detect deception. However, people in legal professions are generally more skilled at detecting deception than the general population.

- The study of conversations examines both verbal and nonverbal communication. Conversation analysis studies talk in interactions to describe the structure and patterns of interactions in everyday conversations. Discourse analysis comprises a number of techniques to analyse written texts or sign language use. This method emphasizes the importance of conversational context.

- New technology influences communication in interesting ways. Many studies have focused on the effects of anonymous communication on behaviour, including increased disinhibition and hostility. However, digital communication such as communication on the internet can allow people to express important aspects of their identity.

Our concern in this chapter has been on communication and the importance of language and nonverbal behaviour in social interaction. In Chapter 6, we turn to the study of persuasion. When people try to persuade others, when are they successful and when do their efforts backfire? How do people understand persuasion processes?

Essay questions

At the beginning of the chapter, we asked you to consider these questions:

1 Siobhan emails her university lecturer to ask for some help with an essay. She simply writes: 'Where are the slides from the last lecture? I need them for my essay.' Outline some reasons why this might provoke an unhelpful response from the lecturer.

2 Carol thinks her partner has been cheating on her. She confronts him and asks him directly if he is having an affair. Will Carol be able to tell if her partner is telling her the truth?

3 Jake is angry with a situation at work and wants to complain to his boss. Would he be better to do this face to face or via email? What would be the advantages and disadvantages of using each medium?

Having read this chapter, these questions could also be framed as the following essay questions, which you can attempt in preparation for your examinations:

1 Critically overview Brown and Levinson's (1978, 1987) theory of politeness phenomena.

2 How good are people at being able to detect deception?

3 Critically discuss the advantages and disadvantages of face-to-face and computer-mediated communication.

Some further reading

Ambady, N. and Weisbuch, M. (2010) Nonverbal behavior. In S.T. Fiske, D.T. Gilbert and G. Lindzey (eds) *Handbook of Social Psychology* (5th edn, vol. 1, pp. 464–97). New York: McGraw-Hill. Up-to-date chapter on nonverbal behaviour, arguing that people's ability to communicate nonverbally is one of the fundamental aspects of functioning as a social being.

DePaulo, B.M. and Friedman, H.S. (1998) Nonverbal communication. In D.T. Gilbert, S.T. Fiske and G. Lindzey (eds) *The Handbook of Social Psychology* (4th edn, vol. 2, pp. 3–40). New York: McGraw-Hill. Classic chapter on nonverbal communication.

Fiedler, K. (ed.) (2007) *Social Communication*. London: Psychology Press. Edited by one of the leading researchers on the social psychology of communication, contains 16 chapters by leaders in the field on topics such as intergroup communication, sexism in language, and language abstraction.

Fitch, K.L. and Sanders, R.E (eds) (2005) *Handbook of Language and Social Interaction*. London: Lawrence Erlbaum. Good reference for scholars of language and communication, covering mainstream methods and qualitative approaches such as discourse analysis and conversation analysis.

Holtgraves, T. (2010) Social psychology and language: Words, utterances and conversations. In S.T. Fiske, D.T. Gilbert and G. Lindzey (eds) *Handbook of Social Psychology* (5th edn, vol. 1, pp. 1386–422). New York: McGraw-Hill. Detailed, up-to-date review of the literature on social psychology and language, arguing for the importance of investigations in social psychology that address language and communication.

Holtgraves, T.M. and Kashima, Y. (2008) Language, meaning, and social cognition. *Personality and Social Psychology Review*, 12, 73–94. Comprehensive review article on language and social cognition, arguing that the two are interconnected because language is the primary medium for developing, representing, retrieving and communicating social information.

Krauss, R.M. and Chiu, C.Y. (1998) Language and social behaviour. In D.T. Gilbert, S.T. Fiske and G. Lindzey (eds) *The Handbook of Social Psychology* (4th edn, vol. 2, pp. 41–88). New York: McGraw-Hill. Classic chapter reviewing the literature on language and social psychology.

 Visit the companion website at www.palgrave.com/psychology/suttondouglas for access to a wide range of resources to help you get to grips with this chapter.

Applying social psychology

Training language use to reduce prejudice

People tend to describe ingroup positive behaviours and outgroup negative behaviours more abstractly, and positive outgroup and negative ingroup behaviours more concretely, arguably because expressing events this way reflects enduring expectations and stereotypes about how groups behave (Maass, Ceccarelli and Rudin, 1996; Maass, Salvi, Acuri and Semin, 1989). Research investigating people's use of language abstraction in social contexts suggests that communicators are not conscious of their linguistic choices and find it difficult to control them (Franco and Maass, 1996, 1999). It is not surprising, therefore, that the use of language abstraction has been linked to the expression and perpetuation of stereotypes and prejudice (for an overview, see Wigboldus and Douglas, 2007).

However, other research indicates people's capacity to use language abstraction strategically. For example, people's linguistic choices are determined by threats to their own group (Maass et al., 1996) and communication goals (Douglas and Sutton, 2003). The fact that people's linguistic choices are receptive to motivational factors and communication goals suggests that language abstraction may not simply be a 'leaky' channel that betrays people and allows their stereotypes and prejudiced attitudes to seep through.

Imagine you work for a government organization that would like to develop a new prejudice reduction technique based on language use. Based on what you have read about language abstraction in this chapter, provide answers to the following questions:

1 What techniques might you suggest to make people aware of their use of language abstraction and its consequences? What are the merits and pitfalls of each and how easy would they be to introduce?
2 If you are able to make people aware of their linguistic choices and their consequences, how might you 'train' people to monitor the language they use when they talk about others?
3 How would you test the effectiveness of your intervention(s)?

Blind spot in social psychology

Having something to talk about: the communicative logic of celebrity culture

Many commentators, including some academics, bemoan the rise of *celebrity culture* – the apparently obsessive attention to the lives of people who are famous – even when there appears to be no particular talent behind the fame. Academics, participants in studies and members of the public often link celebrity culture to a variety of ills, including eating disorders (Fox-Kales, 2011), educational underachievement (Demie and Lewis, 2011) and criminality, as seen in the London riots (Reicher and Stott, 2011).

Theorizing about the underlying causes of celebrity culture is, to some extent, outside the scope of social psychology and belongs more naturally in the realms of history and sociology. Some thinkers have related it to the rise of social inequality – the worship of celebrities is supposed to enshrine the principle that some people are more valuable and noteworthy than others (e.g., Marsh, Hart, and Tindall, 2010; Moss, 2002).

Another, related possibility refers to another change in social structure in recent decades – people are less socially connected than they used to be. As people have become more mobile and busier in response to the demands of work and consumerism, they have ended up spending less time with friends and extended family than people a generation or two ago (Twenge, 2006). It is possible that the feeling that we know a lot about celebrities' lives, and even that we know them in some weirdly personal way, may be a kind of substitute for normal social connections. However, in this chapter, we saw some research by Fast et al. (2009) that suggests another function of celebrities – the very fact of their fame gives us something to talk about. In other words, they provide conversational common ground – a topic, like the weather, about which we feel we have shared knowledge and can talk freely about. When social connections become increasingly shallow and transient, perhaps celebrity culture plays an important role.

The study by Fast et al. (2009), however, was not about celebrities generally but specifically sports players. They found, you may recall, that the fame of sports players predicted who fans would talk about, independently of their merit as defined by their performance statistics. Fame, then, appears to be self-perpetuating, independent of objectively assessed worth.

1 Can you think of a way to adapt the methodology of Fast et al. (2009) to examine whether the degree of celebrities' fame predicts how much people are likely to talk about

them, over and above their independently assessed talent or merit? How would you pick celebrities? You will need to think of celebrities who vary in the extent to which they are famous and to which they are talented. You will then need to think of a way to check that your evaluation of their fame and merits is warranted. How can you do this? With sports stars, there are publicly available statistics that objectively assess performance. With other celebrities, there may not be. How, then, can you test how talented or merited they are? (Hint: this need not be entirely objective – it is probably enough to test how talented or worthy of merit people think the celebrities are.) And how would you measure the dependent variable, that is, the extent to which people talk about the celebrities in question? Outline your ideas briefly, in no more than three paragraphs.

2 Consider the idea that celebrity culture, and the tendency to talk about celebrities in particular, plugs the gap of loneliness in contemporary life. How can this be tested? What individual differences between participants would you assess as a function of the extent to which they talk about famous celebrities? Is it possible to experimentally make people feel lonely? (Hint: look in the Index of this book, or on the internet, for terms like 'social exclusion', 'ostracism' and 'loneliness'.) Outline your ideas, and provide references, in no more than two paragraphs.

3 Find another explanation for celebrity culture by using an internet search engine or academic database. In one or two paragraphs, outline the explanation and provide a reference. If you are able to locate the original article, describe and briefly evaluate the evidence for this explanation.

Student project

What kind of person self-discloses online?

Rahul Jalil studied as an undergraduate student at De Montfort University and his final-year dissertation was supervised by Dr Alison Attrill. Rahul's work extends research on computer-mediated communication considered in this chapter.

My topic and aims

My study explored the relationships between personal characteristics such as shyness and social anxiety, and attitudes towards forming relationships online. Literature suggests that shy and socially anxious individuals may have more favourable attitudes towards making friends and finding lovers online because online communication offers anonymity, reduced social cues, and asynchronous communication and so allows people to overcome inhibitions. Moreover, as self-disclosure is key to relationship closeness and intimacy, it was also predicted that those who are likely to engage in online communication, and have favourable attitudes towards relationship formation online, would show heightened self-disclosure online.

I am particularly interested in human attraction and how interpersonal attraction exists and extends from the internet to face-to-face encounters. How does interpersonal attraction develop and differ online and offline? Why do some relationships develop online and others not, and what factors drive possible online and offline differences? One particular

question that fascinated me was the possibility that individual characteristics could be central to predicting the inclination to form online relationships.

My methods

I chose a quantitative methodology, measuring correlations between variables. Established scales were used to measure the individual characteristics of shyness and social anxiety. A measure originally designed to assess self-disclosure in a clinical setting was adapted for use online. Given the absence of a robust scale in the literature to measure attitudes towards platonic and romantic relationship formation online, a pilot study was carried out to develop and test an 'attitude towards online relationship formation scale', now called the 'ATORF scale' in the literature. For the main study, 48 students and 48 non-students (equal numbers of males and females) were recruited, offering a broad representation of UK internet users.

My findings and their implications

The findings were mixed. Contrary to predictions, levels of shyness and social anxiety were not significantly associated with attitudes towards online relationship formation, nor were these two factors significantly associated with levels of self-disclosure online. Intriguingly, however, there was a significant positive relationship between levels of self-disclosure and attitudes towards online relationship formation. Further, positive attitudes towards online relationship formation significantly predicted levels of self-disclosure for certain types of self-information (personal matters and interests). This finding contributes to the literature because previous research has primarily focused on the amount of personal information shared online rather than what types of information people reveal about themselves.

Further, while previous research has largely focused on romantic relationships, this study offered the first rigorously developed tool to measure attitudes towards platonic and romantic relationships online. It also demonstrated that these attitudes not only appear to determine individuals' reported levels of self-disclosure, but different types of self-information exchanged during online relationship formation. In line with Altman and Taylor's (1973) social penetration theory, the study uniquely reported the disclosures of subtypes of self-information that could be considered to be of a hierarchical or categorical nature. The interplay between the subtypes of self-disclosure and ATORF scale scores suggested that different types of self-information may be more important to the initial stages of developing relationships online, rather than the initially postulated individual characteristics.

My journey

Since graduating, I completed a postgraduate course in forensic psychology at Nottingham Trent University. Following this, I secured a studentship from the University of Northampton along with a placement at St Andrews Healthcare to carry out research leading to the award of a PhD. My long-term goal is to become a clinical psychologist.

I took a lot of pride in my dissertation, because of the time and effort I invested in it, and developed a strong set of skills such as reviewing literature, being critical and evaluative in my approach, and working within ethical boundaries. I found that, aside from the obvious research skills, my studies helped me to develop a range of employability skills, such as interpersonal communication, problem solving, teamwork and academic integrity. I feel that my experience has made me more independent, and has given me the confidence to progress to doctoral-level research.

Some of the findings from my research formed the basis of a paper that focused on the ATORF scale development and associated online self-disclosure (Attrill and Jalil, 2011). This paper highlights how little is known about online self-disclosure and serves as a starting point for further research exploring self-disclosure online. The ATORF scale has also been translated and used in Chinese research, and has recently been subjected to more rigorous worldwide testing that has seen it reduced from a 15- to a 14-item scale (Attrill and Semper, 2012).

My advice

It would be a cliché to say 'do something that interests you' when thinking about what you would like to research for a dissertation. However, this couldn't be any more true for me. You will be working on your dissertation, unlike an assignment or essay, for a year. Your interest in the topic will ultimately be your driving force to get you through from the literature review and data collection to the write-up. During each of these stages, being organized, proactive and ensuring efficient and effective time management is also essential. And, yes, that does include taking a break and socializing with friends too (in moderation).

6 Persuasion

In this chapter, we turn our attention to the topic of persuasion. We outline some of the factors that determine when persuasion will be effective, the key models that explain persuasion, some of the techniques that people can use to be persuasive and, finally, how people are able to resist persuasion. By the end of this chapter, you will know when and how persuasion works and how persuasive techniques are used in advertising, marketing and everyday life.

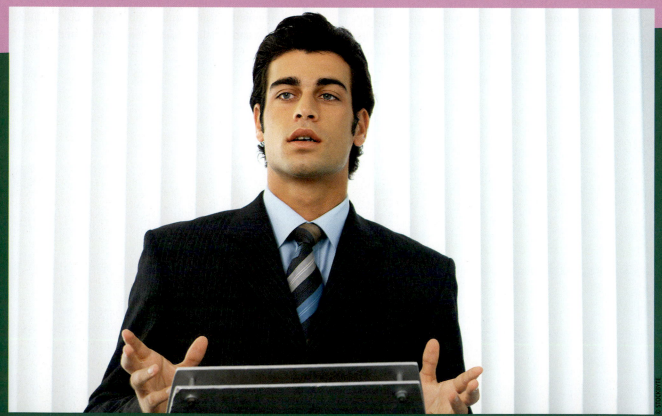

© STOCKBYTE

Topics covered in this chapter

- When does persuasion work?
- How does persuasion work?
- What can people do to persuade others?
- When persuasion does not work

Key features

Critical focus How do people understand persuasion?

Ethics and research methods Subliminal messages

Social psychology in the real world How to get people to stop smoking

Applying social psychology Persuading people to change their ways in order to avert or minimize climate change

Blind spot in social psychology What is the psychological profile of a persuasive communicator?

Student project The extent to which people tailor persuasion attempts to 'fit' their audience

Questions to consider

1 Ulrich has just bought a new iPod and wants to sell his old one on eBay. He is wondering how best to word his advertisement to maximize the appeal of the used iPod. What suggestions might you have for Ulrich to maximize his chances of making a sale?

2 Imogen asks Clare for some relationship advice. She has met a new man and cannot decide whether or not to go out with him. Clare offers her advice but then Imogen asks if she will go on a double date. What is the likelihood that Clare will agree to this? Would Imogen have been better off asking Clare directly in the first place?

3 Fern watches at her window as a salesman walks around her street with a clipboard. When he comes to her house, she listens to what he has to say but then politely declines to buy the product he is selling. Why do you think Fern was so easily able to resist the salesperson's persuasive attempt?

Why do car advertisements often depict attractive women in provocative poses draped over car bonnets? Why do famous celebrities promote perfume and beauty products? Why do politicians employ staff to write their speeches and help them with their campaigns? Try to imagine a day in your life when you are not confronted with commercial advertising designed to make you buy the latest fashions, phones and experiences. How would you decide what to buy? If political advertisements, speeches and propaganda did not exist, how would you decide who to vote for? We are persistently exposed to information attempting to influence what we buy, what we eat, who we vote for, what we look like, how we spend our free time – the list goes on. Indeed, persuading (and being persuaded) forms a vital part of our everyday life and it is impossible to imagine a world without persuasion. In this chapter, we turn our attention to this core topic in social psychology.

Persuasion The process by which a message changes a person's attitudes or behaviours.

Persuasion is the process by which a message changes a person's attitudes – how they evaluate an object – or changes their behaviours. Attempts at persuasion can be powerful. For example, in 1933, millions of people in Germany voted for the Nazi Party despite its radical policies, thanks, in no small part, to a highly efficient and persuasive propaganda machine. On the positive side, 'quit smoking' campaigns have had a significant impact on smoking habits in many countries. In Britain, for example, smoking fell to its lowest recorded level in 2007 when only 21 per cent of the population aged 16 and over were smokers (ONS, 2009). Similarly, casualities from road accidents involving illegal alcohol levels dropped significantly between 1986 and 1998, reflecting the success of long-standing drink driving campaigns. So, persuasion can have both positive and negative effects.

However, we must note that not all persuasive efforts are effective in changing people's attitudes and behaviour. For example, an attempt that persuades one person to quit smoking may not persuade another. Also, a persuasive political message that one person finds informative and useful, another may see as propaganda and therefore react negatively to it. Thus, persuasion is a complex and important process worthy of social psychologists' attention.

Exploring further The study of persuasion is a core aspect of social psychology; one reason being that it involves many other areas besides psychology, such as marketing, consumer studies, health and politics. Use a search engine such as Google Scholar or a database such as PsycINFO or Web of Science and key in the search term 'persuasion'. How many results do you find? How much social psychological research (roughly) can you see?

Accordingly, a great deal of research has investigated social psychological factors involved in persuasion processes (e.g., Cialdini, 2001; Petty and Cacioppo, 1986a, 1986b; Sagarin, Cialdini, Rice and Serna, 2002). In this chapter, we will provide an overview of research and theorizing on the social psychology of persuasion. We will begin by outlining some of the conditions that make persuasion work. Specifically, we focus on the features of the persuasive source, the message itself and the target of the persuasive effort that make the effort successful. We then turn to the social psychological theories that explain how persuasion works. Here, we pay specific attention to the psychological pathways or processes that have been theorized and shown empirically to make persuasion happen. We then talk about some of the specific techniques that people can adopt to reach their persuasive targets most effectively. Finally, we focus on the contexts and consequences when persuasion attempts 'backfire' or simply do not work.

When does persuasion work?

Before we begin to consider how persuasion works in general, it is useful to know about the 'ingredients' of successful persuasive efforts that have been identified in social psychology. That is, what elements need to be present for persuasion to happen? This section focuses on the three main features:

Source The origin of the persuasive effort – 'who'.

1 The **source** of the message: Who is trying to persuade? Perhaps a lecturer is attempting to get students to study, a cosmetics advertiser is promoting a new type of mascara, or a friend is trying to convince another friend to go to a party.

Message The content and method of the persuasive effort – 'what'.

2 The **message** itself: What is the point and how does the message make its point? For example, perhaps a lecturer sends a strongly worded email to their students to get them to study, or the cosmetics advertiser designs a slick magazine advertisement to promote a mascara. Perhaps a friend sends a friendly text message with a picture of everyone else having fun at a party.

Target The recipient or audience of the persuasive effort – 'to whom'.

3 The **target** or **audience** of the persuasive attempt: Who is receiving the message? In our examples, the relevant audiences are the students, the potential buyers of the mascara, and the friend sitting at home not attending the party.

Overall, the persuasion process can be characterized as the study of who says (or does) what, to whom, and what is the effect.

Yale approach to communication and persuasion Approach that considers the three factors that influence persuasion – message, source and audience.

This approach, which forms the basis of contemporary marketing and advertising to date, represents the **Yale approach to communication and persuasion**. Towards the end of the Second World War, Carl Hovland was contracted to work for the US War Department to examine how propaganda could be used to gain public support for the US war campaign. After the war, his research continued, which resulted in this well-known model of the factors involved in persuasion (Hovland, Janis and Kelley, 1953). The approach emphasizes the importance of examining the characteristics of the person (or persons) presenting the message, its contents, and the characteristics of the person (or persons) who receive it. In particular, Hovland et al. identified four steps in persuasion – attention, comprehension, acceptance and retention. The various outcomes (opinion change, perception change, emotion change and action change) depend on a complex interplay between the source, message and recipient. In the next section, we outline what social psychologists know about the contribution of the factors identified by the Yale approach.

The source

Imagine you are watching a debate about climate change on TV. On one side are climate change scientists who use scientific data to argue that climate change exists and puts the world in imminent danger. On the other side are representatives from a large oil company who argue that climate change is a myth, instead arguing that there have always been phases of heating and cooling in global temperatures. Regardless of your views on climate change, which side of the argument should be the most persuasive? To give another example, when choosing a new skin care product, would you be persuaded by an advertisement depicting an attractive or an unattractive celebrity? Clearly, the source of the message matters. Research has demonstrated that the source's attractiveness, likeability and similarity to the target, perceived credibility, expertise and trustworthiness are all important determinants of the success of a persuasive attempt.

Attractiveness, likeability, and similarity

Unsurprisingly, if a message source is perceived to be attractive, it will be more persuasive. The reason for this is quite logical – imagine looking at a skin care product featuring an attractive and healthy skinned model. When people look at such advertisements, they tend to imagine that if they themselves use the product, they will become more attractive just like the model. In a more general sense, attractiveness is persuasive. This effect was demonstrated experimentally by Eagly and Chaiken (1975), who asked attractive and unattractive people to walk around and request that students sign a petition. The attractive persuaders were effective 41 per cent of the time, but the unattractive persuaders were only successful 32 per cent of the time. It appears that people are also more persuaded by emotional arguments made by attractive rather than unattractive people (Chaiken, 1979; Dion and Stein, 1978).

Other findings suggest that likeable people are particularly effective in eliciting persuasion via video and audio messages. Chaiken and Eagly (1983) gave participants persuasive messages from communicators who seemed likeable or unlikeable. Likeability had been experimentally manipulated by means of another passage in which communicators said that they liked the University of Toronto – where the participants were studying – more or less than their former university, the University of British Columbia. (Of course, these statements made the communicator seem more and less likeable, respectively.) In two studies, they found that the unlikeable communicator was just as persuasive as the likeable communicator in writing, but much less persuasive in audio and video messages (see Figure 6.1). Why might this be the case? Chaiken and Eagly found that people thought less about the communicator in written communication, and more about them in the audio and video conditions. Thus, being able to hear and/or see the source can, to some extent, distract

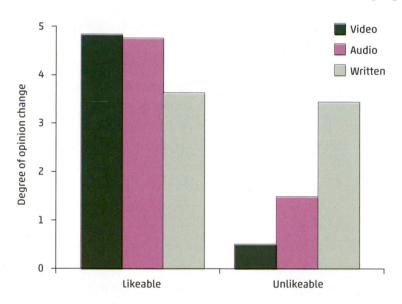

FIGURE 6.1 Attitude change (persuasion) achieved by likeable and unlikeable communicators

Source: Chaiken and Eagly, 1983. Copyright 1983 American Psychological Association. Reproduced with permission

us from the message and towards the characteristics of the source. Depending on the social context, then, communicator likeability can play a disproportionate role in determining how much a person will be persuaded.

Indeed, source attractiveness, be it physical or social attractiveness, appears to be a powerful persuasive technique and so, unsurprisingly, is one that advertisers are adept at exploiting (see also Chaiken, 1979; Chaiken and Eagly, 1983). One only needs to consider a few familiar advertisements on TV to understand the power of attractiveness in advertising (Figure 6.2). Attractive celebrities advertise anything from washing powder to cosmetics, to prestige cars. The assumption behind the use of such people in advertising campaigns is that attractive, likeable and popular examples are persuasive and so influence the extent to which consumers want to buy the product. Social psychological evidence suggests that this is indeed an effective technique (e.g., Chaiken, 1979; Chaiken and Eagly, 1983). It is so effective that everyday persuaders have a fairly good idea of how attractiveness can be exploited to persuade other people. For example, Vogel, Kutzner, Fiedler and Freytag (2010) demonstrated that people anticipate the success of a persuasive attempt largely based on the attractiveness of the persuader. They are also able to exploit attractiveness in attempts to persuade others.

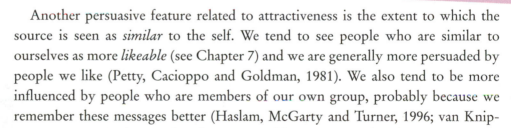

Exploring further Do you think that persuader attractiveness will have the same effect on all recipients? That is, will attractive people tend to persuade everyone? Later on in the chapter, we will discuss the notion of processing motivation – the extent to which people are motivated to process a message – and the influence of various different types of cues such as persuader attractiveness on different 'types' of persuasive targets. As in the previous Exploring further exercise, take a look at the literature and try to understand when attractiveness 'works' and when it might sometimes be a less effective tool of persuasion.

FIGURE 6.2 Attractiveness sells Research has demonstrated that attractive sources are generally more persuasive than unattractive sources. So, it is not surprising that advertisers exploit attractiveness in their campaigns.

Another persuasive feature related to attractiveness is the extent to which the source is seen as *similar* to the self. We tend to see people who are similar to ourselves as more *likeable* (see Chapter 7) and we are generally more persuaded by people we like (Petty, Cacioppo and Goldman, 1981). We also tend to be more influenced by people who are members of our own group, probably because we remember these messages better (Haslam, McGarty and Turner, 1996; van Knippenberg and Wilke, 1992; Wilder, 1990; Wood, 2000). For example, a study by Mackie, Gastardo-Conaco and Skelly (1992) asked student participants to read a persuasive speech about euthanasia or gun control. The speech was said to be from a student at their own university or another university. Results showed that the students were persuaded by the speech that supposedly came from a person within their own institution but were not persuaded when exactly the same speech was said to come from someone in a different institution. Familiarity – something that is strong within groups and weaker between groups – is persuasive. However, this is not to say that people will accept any old message as long as it comes from within one's own group. For example, Mackie, Worth and Asun-

© MIKHAIL LUKYANOV/FOTOLIA.COM

cion (1990) asked participants to read both weak and strong arguments from within the group and found the stronger messages to be more influential, suggesting that people do process the content and quality of messages from within the group. However, the same study demonstrated that participants were equally dissuaded by strong and weak messages from outside the group, suggesting they did not pay much attention to the content. Therefore, group familiarity appears to be an important predictor of persuasion. Other theorists have argued that the perceived validity of social information in general is largely determined by a perceiver's belief that it comes from a self-relevant group. Such a group is more likely to be a reliable and qualified source of information about social reality (Haslam, McGarty and Turner, 1996; Turner, Hogg, Oakes et al., 1987). This perspective can also explain the finding that persuasion tends to be strongest from within the group.

Further, people who act in a similar way to ourselves (e.g., similar gestures) or who mimic our own gestures tend to be more persuasive (e.g., Tanner, Ferraro, Chartrand et al., 2008). For example, van Baaren, Holland, Steenaert and van Knippenberg (2003) demonstrated that a confederate waitress received significantly larger tips when she mimicked her customers (e.g., by repeating their order to them verbatim) than when she did not (e.g., by paraphrasing). Thus, the waitress was arguably more persuasive in getting tips if she mimicked the customer. In another study, van Baaren, Holland, Kawakami and van Knippenberg (2004) found that participants who had been mimicked by the experimenter performed more prosocial acts such as picking up pens the experimenter had dropped, or giving to a charity suggested by the experimenter. Again, the sales industry is good at exploiting this knowledge. Salespeople are often trained to mirror and mimic their customers to increase the possibility they will make a sale. However, it should be noted that similarity does not always produce the most influence. Where matters of taste are concerned, people are more influenced by similar others, but when the issue is more about facts and being right, dissimilar sources can be more influential (Goethals and Nelson, 1973). So, if you were asked who was Britain's best prime minister, you would be more likely to be swayed by the input of a friend who shares your own political outlook and might be likely to respond like you. However, if you were asked how many prime ministers there had been, you might be more likely to listen to a dissimilar source.

Perceived credibility, expertise and trustworthiness

As has been demonstrated in a range of studies, sources who appear to be expert or competent are more persuasive than those who lack credibility (e.g., Chaiken and Maheswaran, 1994; Tormala, Briñol and Petty, 2006; Verplanken, 1991; Wu and Shaffer, 1987). You will notice that fitness professionals often advertise exercise equipment, dentists (and people with great teeth) advocate toothpaste and sportspeople advertise sporting goods. This kind of advertising works because people tend to see fitness professionals as qualified to endorse exercise products and so on. Because people are deemed to have the expertise to comment on certain products, we take their comments more seriously (see also Tormala and Clarkson, 2007).

Findings show that people are also more persuaded by others they perceive to be trustworthy. In particular, if we see someone as having an ulterior motive or perhaps suspect that they are actively attempting to manipulate us, we are less likely to be persuaded (e.g., Walster and Festinger, 1962). Related to this, we are also more likely to be persuaded when we see someone as acting against their own self-interests (Eagly, Wood and Chaiken, 1978; Wood and Eagly, 1981). We view such people as sincere and therefore more trustworthy. A study by Eagly et al. (1978) demonstrates this phenomenon. Participants were asked to listen to a political speech in which a person accused a large company of polluting a river. Some of the participants were told that the speaker was a pro-business candidate addressing a group of company supporters and some were told that the speaker was a pro-environmental candidate addressing an environmental protection group. Findings revealed that the pro-business candidate was more persuasive. Why? Eagly et al. argued that the candidate seemed the most sincere and trustworthy because he was perceived to be acting against his own interests.

Many other variables can influence how trustworthy a persuader appears. For example, Miller, Maruyama, Beaber and Valone (1976) found that people who talk quickly are judged to be more intelligent, trustworthy and credible and are therefore more persuasive. Also, recent exposure to a non-credible message increases people's susceptibility to more trustworthy persuasive sources (Tormala and Clarkson, 2007). In a twist on the 'mere exposure effect' discussed in Chapter 4, repeated exposure to a message can increase the perceived credibility of the source and thus the likelihood of being persuaded (Fragale and Heath, 2004). Repetition of a message can also make it appear more true (Arkes, Boehm and Xu, 1991; Moons, Mackie and Garcia-Marques, 2009), or make the brand name seem more 'famous' and therefore more credible (Campbell and Keller, 2003).

Although the credibility of the source is an important determinant of persuasion, the cause of non-credible communicators is not entirely lost. Over time, they may become persuasive. As time goes on, and it is harder to recall who presented the message, people's opinions may be less and less determined by source credibility. Instead, they are persuaded by the message itself. This phenomenon is called the **sleeper effect** (Pratkanis, Greenwald, Leippe and Baumgardner, 1988). For example, you may have read a piece of information in a down-market tabloid or weekly celebrity gossip magazine and immediately dismissed it because of its dubious source credibility. However, over time, you may forget where you read the information and instead be persuaded by its content. This effect was originally demonstrated by Hovland and Weiss (1951). They asked student participants to read an article arguing that nuclear submarines were safe. Half the participants were told the article was written by Robert Oppenheimer (the scientist in charge of developing the atomic bomb) and the other half were told the message source was the Soviet news agency Pravda. Bearing in mind the political tensions of the time, the second source was much less credible than the first. Unsurprisingly, the participants were immediately most convinced by the credible source. However, four weeks later, the partici-

Sleeper effect A message that is not persuasive at first (probably due to concerns about source credibility) becomes persuasive over time as the source is forgotten.

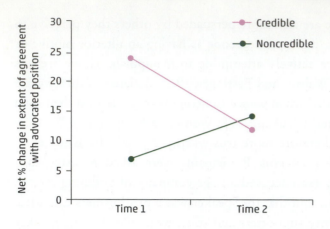

FIGURE 6.3 **The sleeper effect** People are most convinced by credible sources. However, over time, non-credible sources can be persuasive because people lose their memory for the source.
Source: Data from Hovland and Weiss, 1951

pants were tested again and the advantage for the credible source disappeared (see Figure 6.3). In particular, the participants in the non-credible source condition found the article as convincing as the participants in the credible source condition. The sleeper effect is a robust phenomenon, having been demonstrated in a wide variety of contexts and experiments (Crano and Prislin, 2006; Kumkale and Albarracin, 2004). However, if participants are reminded of the source before asking questions in the second phase of the study, the effect disappears (Kelman and Hovland, 1953).

Time to reflect Think about the public exposure related to the personal life of golfer Tiger Woods during 2010, when he was found to have had a number of extramarital affairs. Before the media frenzy, Tiger Woods held multi-million dollar advertising contracts with leading brands such as Nike. Many of these contracts were lost. Is he now less qualified to advertise these products?

The message

The source of the message matters, and what the message contains (and how it is presented) are also vital ingredients that determine the success of persuasion. First, there are many aspects of the message itself that affect its persuasiveness. Here, we will talk about the length of the message, its consistency with the audience's opinion, its repetition, the extent to which it arouses fear and whether it is factual or emotional.

Message length

It is not simply the case that longer or more detailed messages are more persuasive than shorter messages. Bigger is not necessarily better when it comes to persuasion. In many aspects of social psychology, the relationship between variables is complex, and the link between message length and persuasion is no exception to this rule. For instance, findings show that long messages are more effective if they are strong, but they are less effective if they are weak (Petty and Cacioppo, 1984; Wood, Kallgren and Preisler, 1985). Also, long, weak messages are less impactful than short, strong messages (Friedrich, Fetherstonhaugh, Casey and Gallagher, 1996). If a person is trying to influence another, they are perhaps best off writing a quick message with a few key, strong points rather than writing a longer message where the important details can easily get lost. All else being equal (understanding, complexity and familiarity), a 'strong' message typically includes objective facts that are central to an issue, whereas a 'weak' message provides information that is peripheral to the issue. Message strength can also be influenced by the source's likeability, credibility and consistency.

Consistency

The consistency between a persuasive message and the target's original attitude is also an important factor in determining the message's persuasive effectiveness. For example, it would be difficult to persuade an animal rights activist to endorse animal testing for cosmetics, or a committed Conservative Party supporter to vote for the Green Party. If a message is too distant from the audience's attitude, it is likely the message will be ignored. One demonstration of this effect comes from a study by Liberman and Chaiken (1992; see also Sherman, Nelson and Steele, 2000), who found that coffee drinkers were more likely to reject a message arguing for a link between caffeine consumption and ill-health than were non-coffee drinkers. The message was incompatible with participants' love of coffee, so perhaps participants simply did not want to know about it. This tendency to ignore messages that are inconsistent with our attitudes can have important consequences. For example, one consequence may be that people's attitudes become more extreme over time. If people ignore evidence that disconfirms their opinions but keep interacting with like-minded individuals (and thus accrue more information that is consistent with their attitudes), then original attitudes may strengthen (Pomerantz, Chaiken and Tordesillas, 1995).

A classic study by Lord, Ross and Lepper (1979) demonstrates this phenomenon. In this study, students who were either opposed to or in favour of the death penalty were asked to read about the results of two fictional studies. One study suggested that the death penalty reduces homicides and the other showed no reduction. After reading about the studies, participants rated how much their attitudes towards capital punishment had changed. Results showed that the participants who were against capital punishment at the beginning of the study became more opposed to capital punishment after reading the two articles. The participants who were originally in favour of capital punishment became more in favour. Their ratings of the articles' strength were also influenced by prior attitudes towards the topic (see Figure 6.4). Here, participants who were originally in favour of capital punishment rated the 'in favour' article as stronger than the 'against' article. On the other hand, participants who were originally against capital punishment rated the 'against' article as stronger than the 'in favour' article. This latter finding points to another interesting fact – viewing both sides of an argument does not always make people more impartial. People tend to think that arguments from their own 'side' are stronger, so reading or hearing arguments from the other 'side' is not always going to change people's minds.

FIGURE 6.4 Consistency of message with existing attitudes Participants tend to rate an article as more convincing when it is consistent with their original opinion.

Source: Data from Lord et al., 1979

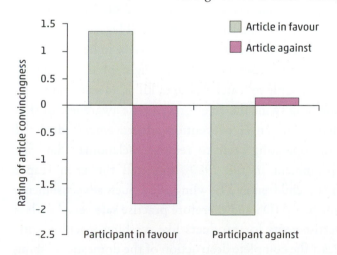

Repetition

When you are watching commercial TV, no doubt you get sick of seeing the same advertisements over and over again. However, there is good reason why they are shown so often. Evidence suggests that messages become more effective if they are repeated. For advertisers, the logic behind this is that people need to be exposed to messages on multiple occasions in order for them to be remembered and recalled. Of course, this does not mean that information needs to be repeated endlessly and indiscriminately. This would be expensive and would waste a lot of valuable advertising money and resources. However, it appears that advertisements are most effective when people are exposed to them two to three times per week (Tellis, 1987). This echoes other findings suggesting that the simple repetition of information can make it appear more true (Arkes et al., 1991).

However, the picture is a bit more complex than it originally seemed to be. Specifically, there is some evidence to suggest that repeated exposure to messages is most effective when people are already somewhat familiar with what is being advertised and have had an initially positive response to the advertisement (Campbell and Keller, 2003). Repeated advertising of a brand new product is not as effective. In this case, a certain level of familiarity is important if repeat advertising is going to work. Also, there is some evidence to suggest that the effects of advertisements can plateau or even 'wear out' with repeated exposure (Campbell and Keller, 2003; Craig, Sternthal and Leavitt, 1976; Hughes, 1992). Repetition is, therefore, more likely to be an effective persuasive technique when the repetition is carried out with some level of variety. Advertisers may need to change their advertisements, techniques or presentation periodically in order to maximize their chances of success.

Fear arousal

Messages can also be persuasive by making people feel bad. In particular, many persuasion attempts are designed to arouse fear in recipients. Readers in the UK will be familiar with 'stop smoking' advertisements featuring death-related images and graphic depictions of the hazards of cigarette smoking. By making people feel scared, vulnerable and aware of their own mortality, advertisers hope that people will quit smoking (see the Social psychology in the real world box) and most of the time this works (Leventhal, Watts and Pagano, 1967; O'Hegarty, Pederson, Nelson et al., 2007). Fear campaigns like this are used extensively in health-related advertising, for example. Health advertisements at the height of the swine flu outbreak in 2008/09 encouraged people to 'catch it, bin it, kill it' (a sneeze, that is) or else put others at risk of catching swine flu. In efforts to raise awareness of skin cancer, Australian government skin cancer prevention advertisements depicted people being cut open on the operating table to remove melanomas. Safe sex advertisements, especially prominent in the 1980s, depicted the grim reaper bowling down men, women and children in a bowling alley. Such advertisements were designed to make people fear AIDS and therefore practise safe sex. At a less extreme level, think of advertisements for products like washing machine anti-limescale tablets, which forecast the complete destruction of the domestic washing machine if this product is not used. Fear is a powerful tool of persuasion, and no doubt you can think of many other examples where fear is used in advertisements and more generally in everyday persuasion attempts.

But how much fear is enough to persuade people? Some research shows that the more fear people feel, the more persuaded they are by advertisements (de Hoog, Stroebe and de Wit, 2007; Leventhal et al., 1967). However, it is clear that fear-inducing advertisements do not always work. After all, people still smoke and engage in other risky or unhealthy behaviours. People still sunbathe and not everyone buys anti-limescale products for their washing machines. Aronson (1997) argued that fear is sometimes ineffective in persuasion because people often engage in *denial* when the problem seems unsolvable. Findings suggest that this denial can be avoided, and fear again becomes persuasive when a tangible solution to the problem is offered (Devos-Comby and Salovey, 2002; Witte, Berkowitz, Cameron and McKeon, 1998). For example, a person may be more likely to stop smoking if information about help and support is presented in the advertisement. Others have argued that an 'inverted-U' curve hypothesis may explain how much fear is most effective in persuasion attempts (see Figure 6.5). In particular, Janis (1967; see also McGuire, 1969) argued that a moderate amount of fear was most effective to induce attitude change. This is probably because people are simply not motivated to process the non-threatening message. Also, high levels of fear may lead people to be too anxious and therefore sink into denial, so again the persuasion attempt is ineffective. However, if people are moderately fearful, they are likely to be swayed by a message because there is a reasonable balance – people take notice of the message because it is moderately threatening, but not so threatening as to induce panic (see also Block and Keller, 1995). If the problem seems solvable, people will do something about it. More recent research (O'Neill and Nicholson-Cole, 2009) has demonstrated much the same point about advertising campaigns encouraging people to reduce their carbon footprint in order to mitigate the threat of climate change – a subject to which we return in Chapter 14.

FIGURE 6.5 Relationship between fear and attitude change 'Inverted-U' curve relationship between the amount of fear and the amount of attitude change. Moderate levels of fear are said to be optimal.

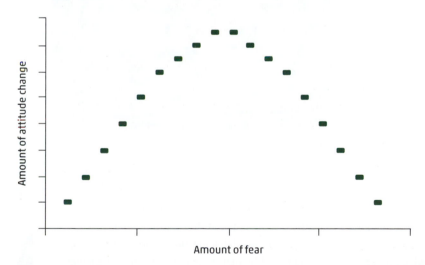

Exploring further In 2010, a UK government advertising campaign, called 'Act on CO$_2$', was withdrawn after many viewers complained that it exaggerated the risks associated with climate change. Use an internet search engine to find the campaign (try searching by combining the terms 'UK', 'climate change', 'advertising', '2010' and 'campaign'). You can view the advertisement and read about the story online (e.g., the BBC News website has a story online about it). This costly fiasco highlights another of the dangers of fear campaigns –they can risk a backlash, especially when the message being proposed is one that a vociferous minority of the population do not want to hear. Based on the findings in this chapter, how would you modify this campaign?

Scarcity technique A persuasive technique emphasizing (truthfully or not) the rareness of the item in question, thus increasing its attractiveness to the target.

A less extreme version of the fear technique is known as the **scarcity technique**, whereby the persuader makes the item of interest more attractive by convincing the target that the item is rare. You will no doubt be familiar with the common sales term 'while stocks last', or 'hurry, only one left at this price', based on which people rush to buy the product in question. There is evidence that this technique works. For example, Worchel, Lee and Adewole (1975) gave participants a choco-late chip cookie and asked them to taste and rate it on a number of scales. In one condition, there were only two cookies in the jar but in the other condition, the jar had 10 cookies. Therefore, in the first condition, the cookies were a scarce resource. Worchel et al. found that people rated the cookie as more desirable where they were asked to take a cookie from the two-cookie jar, that is, when the cookies were a scarce resource.

SOCIAL PSYCHOLOGY IN THE REAL WORLD

How to get people to stop smoking

Over the past 10 years, public health advertisements in the UK and elsewhere have increasingly featured morbid scenes of early graves for smokers and the grieving children of parents who have died of smoking-related health problems. More common perhaps are advertisements featuring scenes of clogged arteries, smokers being 'hooked' through the mouth by fishing lines and advertisements showing blood clots in smokers' dissected brains. These scare tactics are common features of health-related advertising and their effects are viewed as very powerful. The statistics also speak to the success of anti-smoking campaigns, with the lowest levels of smoking ever recorded in Britain in 2007.

One fairly recent innovation in the campaign against smoking is to place warnings on cigarette packets. In such warnings, smokers are notified in bold, block letters about the health risks associated with smoking. For example, smokers are told that 'smoking causes heart disease', 'smoking harms your unborn baby' and 'smoking causes impotence'. The rationale for using such warnings is that an immediate and explicit reminder of the hazards of smoking will encourage people not to light up. Does this work? As we noted earlier, smoking has definitely reduced over the past few years, but recent social psychological research provides an interesting twist. Hansen, Winzeler and Topolinski (2010) conducted an experiment where they first measured how important smoking was to the self-esteem of 39 student smokers. After this, the smokers were divided into two groups. One group was asked to

© COREPICS - FOTOLIA.COM

look at two cigarette packs that featured death-related warnings, while the other group was asked to look at cigarette packs that featured death-neutral warnings such as 'smoking makes you unattractive'. Next, all the participants rated their attitudes to smoking.

Findings showed that in students for whom smoking was important to their self-esteem, those who viewed packets with death-related warnings reported *more* (not less) positive attitudes to smoking compared with those who looked at neutral warnings. The opposite pattern of results was found in participants for whom smoking was not vital to their self-esteem. In other words, for some smokers, smoking makes them feel good – they may feel that it is an important aspect of their identity or they think it makes them look cool. For these people, death-related warnings do not have the intended effect and actually make them want to smoke more.

Questions

1   Can you think of reasons why the death-related warnings do not work for the smokers who derive a self-esteem 'boost' from smoking? (Hint: check out terror management theory by using the Index of this textbook or by looking online. The theory states that

self-esteem is a vital buffer against the fundamental fear of death.)

2   What kinds of messages might be more effective on these people?

3   What are the potential implications of these findings for anti-smoking campaigns? After all, many people who smoke genuinely enjoy it and are happy to be smokers.

Factual appeals versus emotional appeals

Sometimes, persuaders arm themselves with the objective facts in order to sway others. For example, advertisers may present a convincing set of statistics or a list of specifications and technical details. At other times, however, advertisers present their own or others' opinions which are more subjective. These two different types of persuasive messages are often termed **factual** and **evaluative advertising.** Both are effective, but which works best? Seemingly, the optimal approach depends on the target of the persuasive appeal. Research suggests that analytical and well-educated people are more persuaded by rational appeals (Cacioppo, Petty and Morris, 1983), while disinterested or disengaged audiences are more swayed by their liking for the persuader (Chaiken, 1980). The effectiveness of factual versus evaluative appeals also depends on how a person came to have their attitudes in the first place. Specifically, if an attitude was acquired through emotion, they can be changed by other appeals to emotion. However, attitudes acquired via facts and information are less likely to be changed by emotional appeals and more likely to be changed by factual appeals (Edwards, 1990; Fabrigar and Petty, 1999; Petty and Wegener, 1998).

Obviously, advertisers use both types of appeals and often use both in the same advertisement. Perhaps this intuitively takes into account the fact that different people are influenced by different types of appeals, but also that advertisers are covering all options. In other words, if an advertisement makes someone feel like the product is good and at the same time convinces people of the facts, how can it fail to persuade?

Factual advertising
Advertising that uses objective facts to persuade the consumer.

Evaluative advertising
Advertising that focuses more on subjective opinions and evaluations.

The method

Several features of the way in which the message is sent can influence its effectiveness. For example, whether an argument is presented as one-sided or two-sided is often important. Also, when the vital information is presented (first or last) can determine how much effect it has on people's attitudes and behaviours. Further, the channel of delivery is important. We will discuss each of these factors in turn.

Two-sided messages

People are often presented with more than one argument at once. For example, think of members of a jury who hear both the arguments of the prosecution and the defence and ultimately need to decide on the guilt or innocence of a defendant. Thus, persuaders need to know how to deal with competing arguments to enhance the effectiveness of their own messages. One way to do this is to present a two-sided argument; that is, persuaders can present information in favour of an idea, attitude or product, but at the same time present information that is against the intended persuasion attempt. Two-sided arguments are particularly effective if people are aware of opposing arguments (e.g., Jones and Brehm, 1970). For example, a study by Werner, Stoll, Birch and White (2002) demonstrated the effectiveness of a recycling campaign that used a prominent counterargument. On a university campus rubbish bin, students were asked not to dispose of aluminium cans but instead take them to a recycling bin located on an upstairs floor. When the message on the bin was accompanied by an acknowledgement of the major counterargument against taking the cans upstairs (that it was, of course, inconvenient to have to go upstairs to recycle the cans), recycling behaviour reached 80 per cent. This was a significant increase from a condition where no such message was given, and demonstrates that presenting people with a counterargument makes a persuasive attempt more effective. Similar effects occur in the court room where a defence case appears more credible if lawyers pre-empt some of the information that will be used by the prosecution (e.g., 'of course he has stolen cars in the past but he is a good man and there is no evidence that he committed this crime'). In presenting conflicting information before it is intended to do damage and therefore 'stealing the thunder' of the prosecution, the damage is somewhat controlled (Williams, Bourgeois and Croyle, 1993).

FIGURE 6.6 Effectiveness of two-sided arguments Werner et al. (2002) found that campaigns to promote recycling were most successful when arguments in favour of recycling were accompanied by an acknowledgement of the inconvenience of recycling.

© PHOTODISC

In a similar vein, the way in which a message is framed can influence its meaning, and therefore how it is received. For instance, if a message is framed as 'reverse discrimination', it is less likely to be accepted and is viewed less favourably than if it is presented as 'equal opportunities' (Bosveld, Koomen and Vogelaar, 1997). It is more effective, therefore, to promote minority presence in a particular profession by advertising that the employer values equal opportunities rather than advertising that they have a 'quota place' for a particular minority group. Also, if a message with positive outcomes is presented in terms of gain (e.g., gains in wellbeing through exercise), it will be more successful than if framed in negative terms (e.g., losing weight through exercise). Thus, the way a message is presented and framed influences its ability to persuade its target.

Question to consider You now know a lot about what makes a source and a message persuasive. Now, reread question 1 at the start of the chapter. How would you help Ulrich increase his appeal as a seller and the appeal of the used iPod?

Primacy and recency effects

Imagine you are competing in a talent contest and there are 20 performers in the line-up (Figure 6.7). Would your chances of winning be better if you performed near the beginning, in the middle, or closer to the end? Would people remember you better if you went first, would you be 'lost' if you went in the middle, or does being the most recent performance in the judges' minds give you the best chance of success? Social psychological research gives us some idea of what to expect.

Some research suggests that information presented first is most persuasive (Asch, 1946). For example, Asch showed that if a person is described as 'intelligent, industrious, impulsive, critical, stubborn and envious', people tend to form more positive impressions of them in comparison to when they are described as 'envious, stubborn, critical, impulsive, industrious and intelligent' (Asch, 1946). This is because, in the first description, the more positive information is presented first. In this case, the positive information benefits from a primacy effect: it is presented first, remembered better and therefore has the most influence on the recipient. On the other hand, the second example presents negative adjectives first and therefore these have the most influence.

Try it yourself Here is the list of traits used by Asch (1946). List 1 presents the positive traits first and list 2 presents the negative traits first. Asch found a primacy effect, such that participants reading list 1 liked the hypothetical person more than those who had read list 2. Try it on your friends. Ask, say, 20 friends to read one of the lists (10 for each list) and then ask them one question: How likeable do you think this person is on a scale of 1–7. Tally up and calculate a mean for each group. Did your results replicate the effect observed by Asch?

List 1	List 2
intelligent	envious
industrious	stubborn
impulsive	critical
critical	impulsive
stubborn	industrious
envious	intelligent

Source: Asch, 1946. This material as a whole is now in the public domain

FIGURE 6.7 **Do first or last impressions count?** If you are one of 20 performers in a line-up, would your performance stand out more if you went first or last?

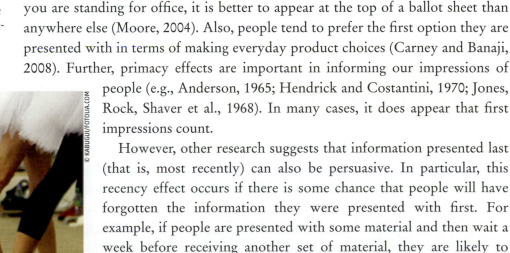

© KABUGUI/FOTOLIA.COM

This primacy effect has practical implications. First, people tend to side more with the arguments they hear first in speeches (Miller and Campbell, 1959), and if you are standing for office, it is better to appear at the top of a ballot sheet than anywhere else (Moore, 2004). Also, people tend to prefer the first option they are presented with in terms of making everyday product choices (Carney and Banaji, 2008). Further, primacy effects are important in informing our impressions of people (e.g., Anderson, 1965; Hendrick and Costantini, 1970; Jones, Rock, Shaver et al., 1968). In many cases, it does appear that first impressions count.

However, other research suggests that information presented last (that is, most recently) can also be persuasive. In particular, this recency effect occurs if there is some chance that people will have forgotten the information they were presented with first. For example, if people are presented with some material and then wait a week before receiving another set of material, they are likely to forget the first set of information and be influenced by the material presented most recently (Miller and Campbell, 1959). This effect was originally demonstrated by Luchins (1957), who found that participants remembered the information they were presented with first (primacy effect) in cases where all the information was presented in immediate succession. However, when there was a delay mid-way through presenting the information, participants remember the most recent information best (recency effect).

Of course, a complex set of factors influence whether we can expect a primacy or recency effect to occur. For example, primacy effects are more common, even after a delay, if the first set of information stimulates thinking (Haugtvedt and Wegener, 1994). It is thought that the primacy effect is also more common generally, because accommodating new information means changing one's initial impression – first impressions are strong and people are at their most attentive when making initial impressions (Anderson, 1975). However, if the recipients are asked to make a commitment straightaway after the most recent information is presented, then a recency effect is more likely to occur. Therefore, it is not easy to answer the questions posed at the beginning of this section unless we know more about the way in which the acts are performed in the talent contest. However, all things being equal, primacy effects are the most powerful and, therefore, most of the time, it seems that it is better to go first (you might want to read over the coverage of primacy and recency effects in impression formation in Chapter 3, where conclusions are largely similar).

Exploring further Look up the winners of a judged event (e.g., song or talent contest) over the past few years. Take, for example, the Eurovision Song Contest. If you search for 'Eurovision order 2012', for example, you can find the song order of the final, and if you search 'Eurovision results 2012', you can also find these results. If you search back a few years, does it look like contestants are more likely to win if they appear in the middle, or can you see evidence for primary and/or recency effects?

The channel

The mode through which the information is presented (e.g., face to face, video, TV advertisements, flyers and so on) is an important factor in determining the effectiveness of persuasive attempts. There is no denying that TV advertisements can be powerful. For example, in the US presidential primaries (the first stages of electing the president), the candidates who advertise the most tend to do much better than those who spend less on their TV advertising campaigns (Grush, 1980). As we saw earlier, repetition of a message can make it more powerful, so repeated presentation of the same TV advertisement is likely to have a significant effect on voting behaviour. However, more specific features of persuasive attempts can influence their impact. Chaiken and Eagly (1976) argued that for information that is difficult to comprehend, written information should be the most persuasive because this medium gives people the opportunity to carefully work through and consider the message at their own pace. To test this, they compared the influence of messages presented in written form, or via TV and audio channels (Chaiken and Eagly, 1983). In general, they found that video presentations were the most effective in bringing about attitude change. However, when the message was more complex or difficult to understand, written material had the most impact. So, although common wisdom may suggest that the visual impact of TV advertising is the most powerful, in fact a

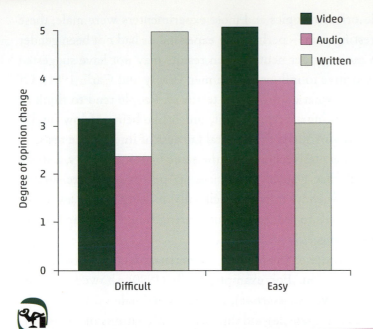

FIGURE 6.8 Attitude change for easy or difficult messages
The effectiveness of 'easy' messages is enhanced by video presentation but for 'difficult' messages, written presentation is the most persuasive.
Source: Chaiken and Eagly, 1983. Copyright 1983 American Psychological Association. Reproduced with permission

message's impact depends more on the type of information presented (see Figure 6.8). Advertisers can make good use of this information to increase the effectiveness of their campaigns. In particular, presenting an advertisement in video format takes away targets' opportunity to consider the message, and so they may rely more on simple cues presented in the message that are not part of the central argument. As we will see later, simple cues can often be persuasive in effecting attitude change.

Time to reflect Chaiken and Eagly's study was conducted in 1983. A lot has changed since then, and advertisers now have a wealth of new advertising media to use, such as websites, social networking sites and SMS messaging. Take a look Chaiken and Eagly's results. Do you think that 'easy' and 'difficult' messages would be differentially effective in these new media?

The target or audience

The effectiveness of a persuasive message is also strongly influenced by features of the target or audience at whom the persuasive attempt is aimed. For example, individual differences, such as gender, age, self-esteem and personality traits, can influence the effectiveness of persuasive messages. We will now briefly discuss some of these target features that influence persuasion processes.

Gender

Overall, research tends to suggest that women are more susceptible to persuasion than men. Some researchers argue that perhaps this is because women and men have different social roles. In particular, women are said to be more *cooperation focused*, whereas men are said to be more focused on *independence* in their interactions with others (Eagly and Carli, 1981; Eagly, Wood and Fishbaugh, 1981). Thus, women are perhaps more *socially sensitive* or receptive to the influence of others than men. Other researchers suggest that gender differences in persuasion are also dependent on the nature of the influence attempt (Guadagno and Cialdini, 2002). In particular, findings show that women tend to be more persuaded by face-to-face appeals than other types of written messages like emails, whereas men show no difference. Again, perhaps women's cooperation focus makes it more difficult to resist persuasive appeals that are made in person.

However, other findings suggest that women are only more influenced than men when the topic of discussion is something with which males are more familiar (Sistrunk and McDavid, 1971). Because most messages used in attitude research typically involved male-oriented topics and most experimenters were male, these findings raised an interesting point – perhaps the experiments had not been gender fair. If topics had been more gender neutral, then results may not have suggested that women are more sensitive to influence than men (Eagly and Carli, 1981). Of course, this treads into somewhat controversial territory. People tend to think of being 'easily persuaded' as being a negative trait, much like being of low intelligence. A lot of controversy surrounds the cultural fairness of intelligence tests, so perhaps considerations of persuasiveness suffer the same biases. Recently, a study by Eaton (2009) showed that gender differences in persuasion were largely dependent on the salience of gender norms. Specifically, making people aware, or 'priming' female sex roles, leads to reduced attitude strength in women and therefore openness to attitude change.

Also, to add more complexity to the picture, the persuasive context influences gender differences in persuasion. For example, Carli (1990) showed that the nature of the speaker (tentative vs. assertive), their gender (male vs. female), the nature of the audience (male vs. female) and different combinations of these variables influence message success. For example, in this experiment, when the speaker was female and tentative, male targets were more susceptible to persuasion than female targets. However, male speakers were equally influential, irrespective of how assertive or tentative they were. The relationships between gender and persuasion are quite complex and much about the link between gender and persuasion is still unknown.

Age

Research suggests that late adolescents and young adults are the most susceptible to persuasive messages, so it perhaps unsurprising that these groups are targeted heavily by TV advertisers (Krosnick and Alwin, 1989; Sears, 1986). It is argued that this demographic is more easily persuadable because, compared to adults, younger people have less stable attitudes and show less resistance to authority, so their attitudes and behaviours are easier to influence and change. Indeed, some countries ban advertising aimed at children, probably for this reason. They are seen to be in the 'impressionable years' and therefore more easily influenced (Sears, 1986). However, other research suggests a different developmental pattern of persuasion. Specifically, Visser and Krosnick (1998) found that people in early and late adulthood were more receptive to persuasive messages than those in middle adulthood. They argued that susceptibility to persuasion is high in early adulthood but decreases as people get older. Further, people become less susceptible to persuasion because their accumulated experiences increase their resistance. In early adulthood, core attitudes, values and beliefs are formed, and in later adulthood, people become more susceptible to persuasion again so that people are the least susceptible in middle adulthood. Finally, Visser and Krosnick argued that people are generally open to attitude change across the life span, but core attitudes and values (secured in early adulthood) tend to be resistant to change throughout the remainder of the life span.

There is evidence to support all these hypotheses to some extent (e.g., Tyler and Schuller, 1991; Visser and Krosnick, 1998). Again, however, the nature of the message also matters. For example, Fung and Carstensen (2003) showed that older adults were more influenced by messages that focused on meaningful goals (e.g., 'Capture the special moments'), but that younger adults showed no preference for such messages. Therefore, like gender, the relationships between age and persuasion are complex.

Personality and individual differences

Need for cognition (NFC) An individual's need to think, assessed by self-reports of how much they enjoy and derive fulfilment from thinking.

Research into the personality characteristics that influence how prone a person is to persuasion has also yielded quite complicated results. Indeed, many other social contextual variables can influence relationships between personality/individual differences variables and persuasion. However, one common factor that researchers have investigated is people's **need for cognition (NFC)** – the extent to which they derive fulfilment and enjoyment from thinking about things (Cacioppo and Petty, 1982; Haugtvedt and Petty, 1992; Jarvis and Petty, 1996). In general, people who have a greater need to evaluate information are more likely to express evaluative opinions when they look at new things (e.g., 'I would never wear that') and will also think more about the information presented. The likelihood that they will be influenced by a message will therefore depend on the strength of the message (Cacioppo, Petty and Morris, 1983). Weaker messages have lesser impact on people who score high on the need to evaluate information. Later in the chapter, we will talk more about how individual differences in thinking styles are related to persuasion. **Need for cognitive closure (NFCC)** also influences persuasion

Need for cognitive closure (NFCC) The extent to which an individual is closed-minded, desiring quick and/or certain answers to questions and resistant to ambiguity or disconfirmation.

(Kruglanski, Webster and Klem, 1993), with people who score higher on NFCC being generally less susceptible to influence, arguably because they are more cognitively closed-minded and essentially less persuadable simply because they have a predisposition to 'make their minds up' early on. Similarly, people who show a preference for consistency (Cialdini, Trost and Newsom, 1995) and show high attitude importance (Zuwerink and Devine, 1996) are less likely to be persuaded than people who score low on these variables.

Try it yourself This is a shortened version of the NFCC scale. Complete it for yourself. Are you high, medium or low in NFCC? Do you think of yourself as someone who is susceptible to influence and advertising?

	Strongly disagree					Strongly agree
I don't like situations that are uncertain.	1	2	3	4	5	6
I dislike questions that could be answered in many different ways.	1	2	3	4	5	6
I find that a well-ordered life with regular hours suits my temperament.	1	2	3	4	5	6
I feel uncomfortable when I don't understand the reason why an event occurred in my life.	1	2	3	4	5	6
I feel irritated when one person disagrees with what everyone else in a group believes.	1	2	3	4	5	6
When I have made a decision, I feel relieved.	1	2	3	4	5	6

	Strongly disagree					Strongly agree
When I am confronted with a problem, I'm dying to reach a solution quickly.	1	2	3	4	5	6
I would quickly become impatient and irritated if I could not find a solution to a problem immediately.	1	2	3	4	5	6
I don't like to be with people who are capable of unexpected actions.	1	2	3	4	5	6
I dislike it when a person's statement could mean many different things.	1	2	3	4	5	6
I find that establishing a consistent routine enables me to enjoy life more.	1	2	3	4	5	6
I enjoy having a clear and structured mode of life.	1	2	3	4	5	6
I do not usually consult many different opinions before forming my own view.	1	2	3	4	5	6
I dislike unpredictable situations.	1	2	3	4	5	6
I don't like going into a situation without knowing what I can expect from it.	1	2	3	4	5	6

Source: Roets and van Hiel, 2011. Copyright (2011), reprinted with permission from Elsevier

Mood

Messages can also be persuasive by making people feel good. Good feelings can promote persuasion partly because such feelings enhance positive thinking and positive thinking increases impulsive decision making (Bodenhausen, 1993; Mackie and Worth, 1991; Moons and Mackie, 2007). On the other hand, when people are in a good mood, they are also more likely to associate the message with positive feelings and this promotes influence. This effect was demonstrated in a study by Janis, Kaye and Kirschner (1965), who showed that people were more persuaded by a message they were reading if they were able to snack and consume a soft drink while they were reading. Other research reveals more complex effects. For example, Bless, Bohner, Schwarz and Strack (1990) found that participants put in a sad mood were influenced by counterattitudinal messages when they were strong (not weak), but that happy participants were equally influenced by strong and weak messages (see also Schwarz, Bless and Bohner, 1991; for a review, see Petty and Briñol, 2008). As we saw in Chapter 4, emotion affects cognition, and, in particular, being in a sad mood can make people more inclined to think rationally and reach accurate conclusions.

How does persuasion work?

Above, we highlighted some of the source, message and audience characteristics that make persuasion a likely outcome. These findings are useful and a whole range of individuals, groups and companies can use these techniques to maximize the impact of their persuasive attempts. However, as informative as these findings are, they tell us little about exactly *how* persuasion happens. That is, how are certain types of messages successful at influencing people? How does it come about that some people are more influenced than others? Researchers have attempted to uncover the psychological processes underlying persuasion by proposing and testing social psychological theories of persuasion.

Two of the most prominent models are the elaboration likelihood model (Petty and Cacioppo, 1986b; Petty and Wegener, 1999) and the heuristic-systematic model (Chaiken, 1980, 1987; Bohner, Moskowitz and Chaiken, 1995). Although these approaches differ in many respects, they both propose that persuasion occurs via two processes, which depend on the different types of persuasive cues that are given attention by the target – thus they are **dual process models**. Both models assert that the source of the message and the message itself play distinct roles in persuasion and that the outcome of a persuasive interaction also depends on the target or receiver's motivation and ability to process information. Note, however, that not all models of persuasion are dual process models. In particular, one recent model called the *unimodel* offers an alternative to the dual process models, asserting that the two processes proposed by the dual process models are functionally equivalent in the persuasion process (e.g., Kruglanski, Chen, Pierro et al., 2006; Kruglanski and Thompson, 1999). Although this model provides a competing perspective on persuasion, the dual process models still tend to dominate scientific thought.

The elaboration likelihood model (ELM)

The elaboration likelihood model (ELM) of persuasion asserts that variations in the nature of persuasion outcomes are dependent on the likelihood that recipients will engage in elaboration of (or thinking about) the arguments relevant to the issue. This model argues that people focus on different features of a persuasive message depending on the level of cognitive effort they give to the information relevant to the persuasive subject (Petty and Cacioppo, 1986b). Specifically, when people think carefully about a persuasive message and pay special attention to the argument quality, they are attending to the **central cues** of the message. Central cues are features of the message such as scientific arguments, consumer reports and expert arguments. For example, imagine you are booking a holiday abroad and you want to ensure you find a good hotel. You may consult a website such as Tripadvisor.com to browse numerous reviews of various hotels, comments from travel organizations and independent travellers' comments to make the most informed choice about where to stay. You think about the reviews in some depth, compare them to other reviews and keep a note of the pros and cons of your potential choices. You make your choice after careful consideration of the information you have. Central cues take a significant effort to process, so whether this route is successful depends on people's ability and motivation to process the cues (see Figure 6.9). When people are persuaded by such cues, they are said to be influenced via the **central route to persuasion**. The central route represents the persuasion process that occurs when elaboration of the persuasive message is high. Some research

Dual process model A model that advocates for two processes leading to a psychological outcome. For example, the elaboration likelihood model and heuristic-systematic model assert that there are two routes to persuasion.

Central cues Persuasive features of a message, such as message quality and scientific arguments, that require processing or elaboration by the target.

Central route to persuasion Processing of a message that occurs when people have the ability and motivation to attend to the message carefully and evaluate its arguments, leading to people being persuaded by central cues.

© COMSTOCK

FIGURE 6.9 The power of central cues Doing a lot of research for your upcoming holiday (e.g., checking customer reviews, hotel credentials and so on) means that you are being influenced by central cues involving a high level of elaboration according to the ELM.

suggests that a specific site in the brain is activated during the elaboration of expert arguments (Klucharev, Smidts and Fernández, 2008). Specifically, fMRI studies demonstrate that the caudate nucleus is activated, which is an area of the brain involved in trustful behaviour, reward processing and learning. More generally, 'feeling persuaded' has been associated with increased activity in specific regions of the temporal lobe and prefrontal cortex (Falk, Rameson, Berkman et al., 2010).

On the other hand, when people attend to the more superficial characteristics of a message instead of the argument quality, they are attending to the **peripheral cues** of the message. Consider the same example of booking a holiday. Here, being persuaded by peripheral cues means that you would be paying more attention to photographs of happy vacationers frolicking in the pool or images of relaxed people drinking cocktails in beachside bars rather than detailed written accounts of the quality of the breakfast buffet or the airport parking facilities. The slick graphical design on holiday websites is also likely to grab your attention. These cues do not take a great deal of cognitive effort (or motivation) to process, so they can be successful under the right conditions. Being persuaded by these types of cues involves the **peripheral route to persuasion**. The peripheral route represents the persuasion process that occurs when elaboration of the persuasive message is relatively low.

It is possible to see the difference between these approaches to persuasion in advertisements for a similar product. For example, some car advertisements feature arguments about the car's performance, speed and other specifications that give the potential buyer a good overview of the product they are going to get. Other car advertisements display attractive models draped over cars with breathtaking scenery in the background, or other more sophisticated imagery. Computer companies often opt for slick advertisements with lots of pictures of the product, while others focus more on the technical specifications. Clearly, both routes to persuasion are effective and this is why advertisers choose to adopt them in different forms and for different audiences (Figure 6.10).

Peripheral cues Persuasive features of a message, such as models, slogans and jingles, that do not require substantial processing.

Peripheral route to persuasion Processing of a message that occurs when people do not have the ability and motivation to attend to the message carefully and evaluate its arguments, leading to people being persuaded by peripheral cues.

FIGURE 6.10 The elaboration likelihood model According to this model, persuasion can occur through either of two routes. The central route involves the persuasive target considering the quality of the argument. The peripheral route involves reliance on superficial cues. The route to persuasion depends on the target's ability and motivation to process the persuasive message.

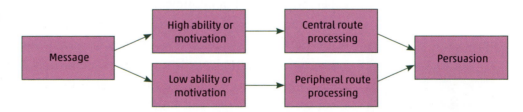

Systematic processing Processing of a persuasive message that occurs when people pay careful attention to a message.

Heuristic processing Processing of a persuasive message that occurs when people use heuristics or cognitive 'shortcuts'.

The heuristic-systematic model (HSM)

The heuristic-systematic model (HSM), while also arguing for two distinct processes to persuasion, puts things slightly differently. Instead of using the terms 'central' and peripheral', the HSM uses the terms 'heuristic' and 'systematic' to describe conceptually similar processes. According to this model, **systematic processing** occurs when targets actively scan and process the arguments put forward in a message. **Heuristic processing** occurs when people do not carefully consider the arguments. Instead, they resort to cognitive 'shortcuts' or heuristics to process the message. One reason to process a message through the heuristic rather than systematic route is because the task of processing a lot of information is just too difficult (Chaiken, 1987). Heuristics make the task simpler. For example, instead of listening carefully to a person make a detailed argument about the nuances and effects of gender differences and judging the argument's reliability, it is easier to resort to the truism that men and women are simply different and that gender differences are here to stay. That is, the reliability of the message is judged by applying a simple rule, or heuristic instead of attending carefully to the message itself.

So, while the ELM and HSM are slightly different in the way they see the two processes occurring during persuasion, they both argue for two distinct routes to persuasion – one involving more complex processing or elaboration of a message and the other involving a more instinctive, simplistic processing. People use the central/systematic route to persuasion when they attend thoughtfully to a message, but use the peripheral/heuristic route when they do not attend thoughtfully to a message or use simple cognitive shortcuts to deal with the message. We mentioned the 'unimodel of persuasion' earlier, which offers an alternative to the dual process models, asserting that the two processes proposed by the dual process models are functionally equivalent in the persuasion process (e.g., Kruglanski et al., 2006; Kruglanski and Thompson, 1999). It is proposed that in each route, receivers of messages try to reach conclusions about what views to hold, using any information available to them. Although the dual process models argue that different kinds of evidence are used in the two routes (peripheral cues and central cues), the unimodel asserts that there is just one process of reasoning involved. The processes may appear to be distinct because studies on the ELM and HSM have typically involved simple peripheral cues versus complex arguments, and are not therefore equalized with respect to complexity. Kruglanski and Thompson argue that if these cues are equalized, they will be seen to be processed in similar ways and there is no need to study persuasion as two separate processes. You are probably thinking this all sounds a bit complicated and, indeed, research is yet to clearly tease apart these different explanations. Thus, we maintain our focus on the ELM and HSM and will now consider how each of the proposed routes to persuasion (central/systematic and peripheral/heuristic) work and the factors that influence which route of persuasion people use.

Exploring further Spend some time on Google Scholar and find some research that relates to Kruglanski's unimodel of persuasion. What insights does it offer that are different from the dual process models?

Factors determining the processing route

The first key factor that determines the route to persuasion is the persuasive target's *ability to focus*. When a person is distracted, preoccupied, interrupted or under time pressure, it is difficult for them to concentrate on the central cues of persuasion because they require a significantly greater amount of processing than peripheral cues. As such, when people lack the ability to focus, they are more likely to attend to peripheral cues (Petty, Wells and Brock, 1976). Petty et al. (1976) empirically examined how the ability to focus can influence how people process a persuasive message. They exposed students to either a weak or a strong argument in favour of an increase in student fees. The strong message argued that an increase in fees would improve teaching by allowing the institution to hire better teachers; it would also make class sizes smaller. On the other hand, the weak message talked about the more aesthetic benefits of increased fees, such as being able to employ more gardening staff and making the campus more attractive. In addition to this manipulation, some students listened to the messages without any distractions, while others listened to the messages alongside performing a distracting task. Participants were then asked to rate their overall agreement with the increases in student fees. Results showed that the undistracted participants were more persuaded to agree with an increase in student fees after having listened to the strong arguments rather than those who had listened to the weak arguments. However, the distracted participants agreed approximately equally in the weak and strong message groups (see Figure 6.11). Petty et al. argued that the distraction manipulation works to inhibit the dominant cognitive response to a message. If a dominant response is to develop counterarguments (a negative response), distraction will enhance persuasiveness because the target will not be able to generate counterarguments. However, if the dominant response is to develop pro-arguments (a positive response), distraction will reduce its persuasive impact because people will not have the resources to develop pro-arguments. So, both favourable and unfavourable responses to a persuasive attempt can be disrupted by an inability to focus.

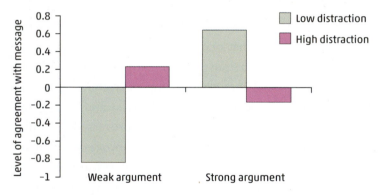

FIGURE 6.11 The effects of message strength and distraction on persuasion Participants who were not distracted were more persuaded by the strong arguments than the weak arguments. Participants who were distracted tended to be persuaded by both messages. Can you think of a way that advertisers might use these findings? *Source:* Data from Petty et al., 1976

Factors other than distraction can influence people's ability to process a message. For example, Petty et al. (1976) found that in a standing position, people were less persuaded by an argument in favour of increasing student fees than they were when they were lying down. They argued that a standing position enables resistance to persuasion by facilitating the generation of negative responses, while lying down promotes susceptibility to persuasion because it inhibits negative responses. Further, Cacioppo, Sandman and Walker (1978) found that participants who were conditioned to increase their heart rates were more resistant to persuasion. Arguably, increased heart rate facilitates message processing and enables targets to process and reject the message.

The second key determinant of the successful route to persuasion is whether the persuasive target has the *motivation to process*. Sometimes, people are just not involved in the message or are simply not interested in the issues relevant to the persuasion attempt. Without this motivation to process, findings show that people are more likely to rely on peripheral cues to persuasion such as a message's length or speed (Maheswaran and Chaiken, 1991; Smith and Shaffer, 1991). In general, as a person's level of involvement in the topic increases, the motivation to engage in central/systematic processing increases. The motivation to process a message can also be influenced by the recipients' level of need for cognition (NFC), which we briefly discussed earlier. NFC is an individual differences characteristic that reflects people's tendency to engage in and enjoy effortful thought (Briñol and Petty, 2005). People who display higher levels of NFC generally have a higher elaboration motivation and will therefore be more influenced through the central/systematic route to persuasion (Cacioppo and Petty, 1982; Cacioppo, Petty, Feinstein and Jarvis, 1996; Haddock, Maio, Arnold and Huskinson, 2008; Petty and Cacioppo, 1986b).

Try it yourself Like need for cognitive closure, a person's level of NFC is strongly associated with their susceptibility to persuasion. In your own time, complete the NFC scale (by rating your agreement with each statement) and see how you score. Do you see yourself as someone who is easily persuaded? What types of cues do you think you are most sensitive to? The items with an asterisk will need to be reverse scored (see Chapter 2 for how to do this). Once you have done this, tally up your score and you have your overall NFC score. The maximum score is +72 and the lowest score is –72.

	Strongly disagree								Strongly agree
I would prefer complex to simple problems.	-4	-3	-2	-1	0	1	2	3	4
I like to have the responsibility of handling a situation that requires a lot of thinking.	-4	-3	-2	-1	0	1	2	3	4
Thinking is not my idea of fun. *	-4	-3	-2	-1	0	1	2	3	4
I would rather do something that requires little thought than something that is sure to challenge my thinking abilities. *	-4	-3	-2	-1	0	1	2	3	4
I try to anticipate and avoid situations where there is likely a chance I will have to think in depth about something. *	-4	-3	-2	-1	0	1	2	3	4
I find satisfaction in deliberating hard and for long hours.	-4	-3	-2	-1	0	1	2	3	4
I only think as hard as I have to. *	-4	-3	-2	-1	0	1	2	3	4
I prefer to think about small, daily projects to long-term ones. *	-4	-3	-2	-1	0	1	2	3	4
I like tasks that require little thought once I have learned them. *	-4	-3	-2	-1	0	1	2	3	4
The idea of relying on thought to make my way to the top appeals to me.	-4	-3	-2	-1	0	1	2	3	4
I really enjoy a task that involves coming up with new solutions to problems.	-4	-3	-2	-1	0	1	2	3	4
Learning new ways to think doesn't excite me very much. *	-4	-3	-2	-1	0	1	2	3	4
The notion of thinking abstractly is appealing to me.	-4	-3	-2	-1	0	1	2	3	4
I would prefer a task that is intellectual, difficult and important to one that is somewhat important but does not require much thought.	-4	-3	-2	-1	0	1	2	3	4
I feel relief rather than satisfaction after completing a task that required a lot of mental effort. *	-4	-3	-2	-1	0	1	2	3	4
It's enough for me that something gets the job done; I don't care how or why it works. *	-4	-3	-2	-1	0	1	2	3	4
I usually end up deliberating about issues even when they do not affect me personally.	-4	-3	-2	-1	0	1	2	3	4
I prefer my life to be filled with puzzles that I must solve.	-4	-3	-2	-1	0	1	2	3	4

Source: Cacioppo, Petty and Kao, 1984. Reprinted by permission of Taylor & Francis Ltd, http://www.tandf.co.uk/journals

Other factors also determine how people deal with persuasive messages. For example, our mood at the time of a persuasive attempt can influence how the message is processed (see Mackie and Worth, 1989; Wegner, Petty and Smith, 1995). Sometimes, being in a sad mood can encourage a more peripheral/heuristic processing depending on the ambiguity of the information (Bohner, Chaiken and Hunyadi, 1994). Being in a good mood (e.g., by listening to nice music) can also enhance elaboration (Bruner, 1990; Gorn, 1982). The perceived credibility of the source is also an important factor, as is the perceived importance of the issue relevant to the persuasion attempt (Chaiken and Maheswaran, 1994).

It is also important to note that while both routes of persuasion are effective, they affect people in different ways in different situations. This may sound rather vague, but as you now know, persuasion is a complex phenomenon so it is not always easy to give straight answers. For example, a message concerning an issue that is important to an individual will be effective in persuading them so long as they have the time and resources to pay attention. It is also the case that the same cue can be processed in different ways depending on motivation and ability. For example, glossy hair on a shampoo advertisement, while typically being processed as a peripheral cue to attractiveness, can also be processed centrally because it contains information about how effective the shampoo is (so long as we are prepared to assume that the model has actually used it). More generally, persuasion via the peripheral/heuristic route is typically not as effective as the central/systematic route in changing attitudes and behaviours in the long term. Peripheral route persuasion often results in superficial or temporary attitude change, while central route persuasion leads to longer lasting attitudinal and behavioural change (Chaiken, 1980; Mackie, 1987; Petty, Haugtvedt and Smith, 1995).

Time to reflect Imagine you are an advertising executive and are involved in designing advertisements for perfume, cars, 'alcopops' and energy drinks. What would your advertisements look like for each of the different products and why? How do the features of your advertisements map onto the routes of persuasion identified by social psychologists?

What can people do to persuade others?

There are several tactics that people can use to be more effective persuaders. For example, they can ingratiate themselves to their target, make small requests before plunging in with a more substantial request, make a large and unrealistic request before making the intended smaller request, or 'lowball' targets with hidden costs to a persuasive request. All are effective in eliciting persuasion. We will discuss these interpersonal persuasive tactics briefly in turn.

Ingratiation and reciprocity

Ingratiation A persuasive technique that involves making the persuasive target like you in order to persuade them.

One way to persuade people to agree with you or do what you want them to do is to first make them like you. A person may **ingratiate** themselves to their persuasive target by agreeing with them, flattering them or simply being nice to them before making the persuasive attempt (Smith, Pruitt and Carnevale, 1982). This can be effective, but it may also backfire if the ingratiation is too obvious. Too much flattery, for example, can make people suspicious that the flatterer has ulterior motives. If indeed the flatterer intends to influence the target, then the target has good reason to be suspicious (Gordon, 1996). A similar technique is to use the **reciprocity principle** to one's advantage and rely on the accepted convention that people will treat others as they are treated themselves (Gouldner, 1960). In other words, if someone receives a favour from another person, they are likely to return that favour. This is a useful technique in persuasion because doing something nice for another person creates good relations and activates the reciprocity principle. People feel obliged to do something nice for the other person. The persuasive target is receptive to the idea of returning the favour and is therefore more likely to be persuaded when a request is made. Indeed, Regan (1971) showed that people were more likely to be persuaded if they had received a favour beforehand than if they had been given no favour (see also Whatley, Webster, Smith and Rhodes, 1999). Of course, failure to return a favour can result in heavy social penalties. For example, a person who does not abide by the reciprocity principle is likely to be deemed a 'freeloader' or a 'sponger' for taking a social favour but not paying it back (Cotterell, Eisenberger and Speicher, 1992). People generally want to avoid these sorts of labels and are also likely to feel guilty if they do not return a favour, so the norm of reciprocity is a powerful tool of persuasion (Carlsmith and Gross, 1969). We discuss the reciprocity principle further in Chapter 7 when we cover the topic of close relationships.

Reciprocity principle A persuasive technique that involves 'doing a favour' for a person before asking them to do something for you.

Door-in-the-face technique

Door-in-the-face technique A persuasive technique that involves the persuader making a large and unrealistic request before making a smaller, more realistic request that is likely to be successful.

The **door-in-the-face technique** is closely related to the reciprocity principle and involves the persuader making a large, unrealistic request, which is almost certainly refused, and then making a smaller, more realistic request (Cialdini, 1984). This technique works because the persuader makes a concession by accepting the target's refusal of the first request. The target then feels obliged to also make a concession and is therefore more likely to be persuaded by the smaller, more realistic influence attempt. For example, imagine a charity worker asks you to give a £50 donation to an appeal. You initially say 'no', feeling that this is a lot of money to part with out of the blue, but then concede to buying £5 worth of raffle tickets for the same appeal. This is known as the door-in-the-face technique because the persuasive target first slams the door in the face of the persuader but then opens it a tiny bit to concede to a smaller request (Reeves, Baker, Boyd and Cialdini, 1991).

Cialdini, Vincent, Lewis et al. (1975) demonstrated the strength of this technique in a study where university students were asked if they would like to chaperone a group of juvenile delinquents on a trip to the zoo. Unsurprisingly, 83 per cent of the students said 'no' to this request. However, for students who had first been asked if they would like to participate in an intensive counselling programme for juvenile delinquents lasting two years, 50 per cent agreed to chaperoning the juveniles on the zoo trip. The door-in-the-face phenomenon can therefore be a powerful technique of persuasion. Cialdini et al. (1975) also argued that this technique capitalizes on a contrast effect. The small request seems reasonable in contrast to the larger intrusive request, so it is seen as much more acceptable. You will notice this technique used extensively in sales contexts. For example, a salesperson may show a prospective TV purchaser a very expensive, top-of-the-range TV before showing them cheaper (but still expensive) models. The customer is likely to see the latter options as more reasonable than they normally would, because they appear to be a nice contrast to the wallet-busting options first presented. Note, however, that this technique only occurs if the second request is made by the same person as the original request. If two requests are made by two different people, the door-in-the-face technique will not work.

That's-not-all technique

That's-not-all technique
A persuasive technique that involves the persuader making a request but afterwards throwing in some 'added extras' to pressure the target to reciprocate.

The **that's-not-all technique** also capitalizes on the reciprocity principle and involves the persuader giving the person something that will further convince them to comply with the request. The technique involves offering a person a product at a high price, not allowing them to respond for a short while, and then offering them a better deal by offering another product or lowering the price. Using the example above, the TV salesperson might show the customer an expensive TV the customer is likely to refuse. However, if the salesperson later shows the customer a cheaper TV, or mentions that the TV also comes with a free satellite set-up and a Blu-ray DVD player, then the new TV probably seems better value, and perhaps the customer is also more likely to feel that they owe the salesperson something for 'throwing in' some extras. When this that's-not-all technique is used, people are more likely to be persuaded by the influence attempt (Burger, 1986).

Burger (1986) demonstrated that this procedure induces greater compliance than in a control condition where participants were given the better deal in the first place. However, research demonstrates that this effect is dependent on the size of the initial request. For example, Burger, Reed, DeCesare et al. (1999) found that, compared to a control group who received only the final request, participants who were presented with an initial request that was significantly larger than the final request were less likely to comply, whereas those who were presented with only a marginally smaller initial request were more likely to comply. Further, Pollock, Smith, Knowles and Bruce (1998) demonstrated that this technique only occurs when people consider an offer instinctively.

Foot-in-the-door technique

Foot-in-the-door technique
A persuasive technique in which a person makes a small and unobtrusive request before making the larger request of interest.

The **foot-in-the-door technique** involves persuaders first making a small and relatively unobtrusive request before making the intended (larger) request. The persuader gets their foot in the door with a reasonable appeal, making it more likely that they will succeed with the request they are most interested in. Freedman and Fraser (1966) demonstrated this effect by asking members of a community to display large ugly sandwich boards in their front gardens depicting the message 'Drive carefully'. Only 17 per cent of the targets agreed to do this, but for participants who had agreed to display a small 'Be a safe driver' sign in their windows two weeks earlier, 76 per cent agreed to the more obtrusive request. Again, we see a powerful tool of persuasion. Indeed, one review suggests that this technique can even persuade people to eventually comply with large requests such as becoming organ donors (Saks, 1978).

However, this technique does not always work. In particular, if the first request is too small and the second request is too large, the foot-in-the-door technique will not be effective because the link between the two requests is broken (Foss and Dempsey, 1979). One way around this is for the persuader to 'build up' to the larger request by beginning with a small request, making another (slightly larger) request and so on, until the large and intended request is made (Goldman, Creason and McCall, 1981). A good example of this is how many charities work. They may begin by asking for a signature on a petition, follow that up with a request for a small donation, then finish with the intended request of a monthly direct debit donation. The charity giver is likely to agree to this graded persuasive attempt.

Lowball tactic

Lowball tactic A persuasive technique that involves the persuader changing the terms of the agreement during the interaction by introducing hidden costs. The target accepts the change because they have already made a commitment to the action.

Using the **lowball tactic**, the persuader changes the terms of the agreement during the interaction by introducing hidden costs. For example, imagine you are shopping for a holiday at your local travel agency and you find the perfect getaway for what looks like a reasonable price. You are about to make the purchase but at the last minute the salesperson lets you know about a special 'sun tax' that will add £100 to the cost of your holiday. In this example, you have been lowballed. In other words, you were told about a hidden cost after you had committed to the holiday. What do you do? Research suggests that you would still go ahead and purchase the holiday. Specifically, once people are committed to an action, they are more likely to stick to their decision, accept the sunk cost and go ahead.

The power of this technique was demonstrated in a study by Cialdini, Cacioppo, Bassett and Miller (1978). In this experiment, half the participants were asked to participate in an experiment. If they agreed (56 per cent), they were told it began at 7am; 95 per cent turned up. The same request was made of a control group, although these participants were immediately told about the 7am start; only 24 per cent agreed to participate.

Question to consider In light of what you have learned so far, reread question 2 at the start of the chapter. What influence tactic is this an example of? Would Imogen have a better chance of convincing Clare to come out on a double date by using a more direct approach, or not?

When persuasion does not work

Even when the most powerful persuasive techniques are used, you can probably think of many occasions when persuasive attempts do not succeed. For example,

Reactance or negative attitude change A negative reaction to an influence attempt that threatens personal freedom. This reactance increases resistance to persuasion.

Boomerang effect Lay term for reactance.

most advertisements you see will not make you go out and buy a product, nor will the majority of political messages influence how you vote. In general, people are highly resistant to persuasion (Figure 6.12). If they were not, their attitudes (and behaviours) would be constantly changing, so it is just as well that people are able to resist most persuasion attempts. The next question to consider, therefore, is why are people so resistant to persuasion? Here, we will discuss a number of factors that enhance people's ability to stand firm in the face of even the most expert and accomplished efforts at persuasion.

Time to reflect Charities often employ fundraisers to approach people on the street and persuade them to sign up to monthly payments to the charity. These fundraisers have been nicknamed 'chuggers', or charity muggers, for their often insistent approach. Have you ever been stopped by a 'chugger' asking for a donation? What persuasive techniques did they use? Were you persuaded? How did it make you feel?

Reactance

FIGURE 6.12 Saying 'no' Persuasion attempts do not always work and people simply say 'no'. Many factors influence people's resistance to persuasion.

When people are confronted with a persistent influence attempt, they often become annoyed and resentful of the effort to change their attitudes. For instance, when a persuader really puts on the pressure, for example a 'hard sell' salesperson, the target of the influence may become increasingly irritated and resentful. The net result – the target reacts against the message and ultimately adopts the completely opposite attitude to that of the intended persuasion attempt. This is the process of **reactance**. People can react strongly like this against blatant or persistent influence attempts because such attempts are direct threats to personal freedom. For example, the 'hard sell' salesperson is pushing a person to buy a product. Nobody likes to be forced to do something, or to have their personal freedom compromised, so the natural reaction is to defy the persuader and go one's own way. Also, nobody likes to have their self-image of an independent person challenged, so blatant persuasive attempts are often doomed to failure. Research has widely documented this phenomenon (e.g., Brehm, 1966; Rhodewalt and Davison, 1983; Rhodewalt and Strube, 1985), which is sometimes also called **negative attitude change**. In this sense, the persuasive attempt can really backfire on the persuader, who find themselves confronting someone with a stronger attitude or a more defiant resistance to persuasion than before the influence attempt began (Tormala and Petty, 2002, 2004). Indeed, threats to personal freedom will often create a defiant response, sometimes known as a **boomerang effect** (Brehm and Brehm, 1981).

Time to reflect Henriksen, Dauphinee, Wang and Fortmann (2006) investigated the effectiveness of tobacco industry-sponsored anti-smoking advertisements (versus independent advertisements) on teenagers' intentions to smoke. They found no difference across the two types of advertisements in intentions to smoke, but found that the teenagers who had viewed the tobacco industry-sponsored advertisements had more favourable attitudes to the tobacco industry. Why do you think this might have occurred? What do you think some of the potential consequences might be? Could tobacco industry-sponsored anti-smoking advertisements perhaps do more harm than good?

Prior knowledge/forewarning

When we are aware of a persuasion attempt, are we more able to resist it? For example, when we watch a political speech, we know that the politician would like to have our vote, but does awareness of this fact mean that they will be less successful? When a salesperson walks up to us and hands us a brochure, are we less likely to be persuaded to purchase their product? Some research suggests that the answer is 'yes'. Specifically, if people are forewarned about a persuasive attempt, they are less likely to be persuaded by the attempt than if they have no prior knowledge of the attempt (Cialdini and Petty, 1979; Johnson, 1994). Why is this the case? People are more resistant to persuasion after **forewarning** because the advance knowledge of a persuasion attempt activates several cognitive processes that are important for persuasion.

For example, advance knowledge gives people the opportunity to develop counterarguments that render the attempt less successful. Also, people have more time to seek alternative facts and information that are counter to the persuasive message. The importance of the original attitude is also important (Krosnick, 1989; Petty and Cacioppo, 1979). That is, the benefits of forewarning are stronger when people consider the associated attitudes to be important than if the attitudes are seen as trivial. If a person has strong feelings about a topic, then being fore-warned of an attempt to change their minds will arm them with the accessibility of their own attitudes to counteract the persuasion attempt.

Counterarguing

People can actively resist persuasion attempts by addressing and arguing against attitude-incongruent arguments directly. By being proactive and counterarguing against the persuasive attempt, people are able to defuse persuasion attempts and, again, this renders such attempts less effective (e.g., Eagly, Chen, Chaiken and Shaw-Barnes, 1999).

In one study, Eagly, Kulesa, Brannon et al. (2000) asked students to listen to either 'pro-life' (anti-abortion) or 'pro-choice' (in favour of women's choice to have an abortion) messages delivered by a female commu-nicator. The messages were consistent or inconsistent with the participants' prior attitudes ('pro-life' or 'pro-choice'). After listening to the message, participants were asked to list their thoughts throughout the experiment. Results revealed that participants had more opposing thoughts towards counterattitudinal messages and more supportive thoughts during the attitude-consistent messages. So, participants generated counterarguments against the messages that were inconsistent with their attitudes, but supportive arguments for the message that was consistent with their existing attitudes (see Figure 6.13). Therefore, one way that people resist counterattitu-

Forewarning Prior knowledge of a persuasion attempt that often renders the persuasion attempt less effective.

FIGURE 6.13 Resisting persuasion by generating counterarguments Participants reported thinking of more supporting arguments than opposing arguments when exposed to a message that was consistent with their pre-existing attitudes. However, those who were exposed to a message that was inconsistent with their pre-existing attitudes reported thinking of more opposing arguments than supporting arguments.
Source: Data from Eagly et al., 2000

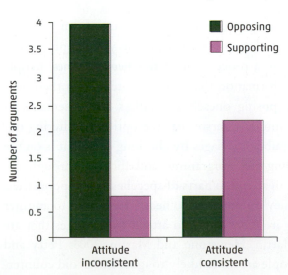

dinal messages is to actively process the arguments and argue against them. In doing so, they provide strong 'self-defence' against persuasion attempts.

Attitude inoculation

Attitude inoculation
Presenting people with weak attitude-inconsistent attacks prior to a stronger persuasive attempt helps people to resist the message. They are in a sense 'inoculated' against the stronger influence attempt.

In another important line of research, McGuire (1961, 1964) showed that it was possible to inoculate people against influence attempts by presenting them with weak counterattitudinal arguments before presenting them with a stronger influence attempt (e.g., a counterattitudinal message). In the same way that immunizations are designed to fight diseases, weaker arguments 'inoculate' people against stronger influence attempts. The individual is able to mount a defence and therefore becomes less susceptible to the persuasive attempt. McGuire demonstrated the effectiveness of **attitude inoculation** by presenting people with some cultural truisms (e.g., it is a good idea to brush one's teeth after every meal) and presenting a counterattitudinal message (e.g., experts say that too much brushing can damage one's gums). If no inoculation occurred, participants were persuaded by the attitude-incongruent message, but if participants had been first presented with a weak attack on their attitudes, they were much less persuaded. Also, if they were asked to write an essay refuting the mild attack, they were less susceptible to the stronger persuasive attempt.

McGuire and Papageorgis (1961) argued that this works because presenting targets with weak arguments helps them to generate counterarguments of their own, which in turn makes their attitudes more resistant to change. Another example was demonstrated by Bernard, Maio and Olson (2003), who found that people who were first asked to write and then refute reasons for opposing equal opportunities were more resistant to anti-equality messages at a later time. Of course, this is not perfect and attitude inoculation will not always work. One example of where the effect falls away is when people think that their resistance to persuasion has been weak. On such occasions, people can become more susceptible to follow-up influence attempts (Tormala, Clarkson and Petty, 2006).

Avoidance

Selective avoidance People's tendency to filter out information that is inconsistent with their pre-existing attitudes. This increases resistance to persuasion.

Another way to resist persuasion is simply to ignore or filter out information that is inconsistent with pre-existing attitudes, or information that you simply do not wish to engage with. By engaging in a process called **selective avoidance**, people direct their attention away from information that is inconsistent with their attitudes. For example, instead of exposing oneself to endless advertisements in between one's favourite TV programme, a person has the option of filtering out the unwanted advertisements and public messages by checking out what is on the other TV channels or by recording the programme and flicking through the advertisements. Likewise, people can attend to parts of speeches that support their attitudes and ignore the sections they do not wish to hear. This points to another interesting phenomenon – people are *more* likely to attend to messages that are consistent with their attitudes (Martin, Hewstone and Martin, 2003; Petty and Cacioppo, 1979). That is, while people are more likely to ignore or avoid counterattitudinal messages, they give pro-attitudinal messages more attention and thought. These two processes, in team with one another, help ensure the stability and strength of pre-existing attitudes.

Other means of resistance to persuasion

Attitude polarization People's tendency to evaluate mixed information in a way that strengthens pre-existing attitudes and makes them more extreme.

Biased assimilation People's tendency to evaluate counterattitudinal information as biased or unreliable.

Hostile media bias People's tendency to view counterattitudinal media as biased and untrustworthy.

Other factors influence people's resistance to persuasion. Briefly, **attitude polarization** is the tendency for people to evaluate mixed information or messages in a way that strengthens their original attitudes and makes them become more extreme (Pomerantz et al., 1995). Also, the process of **biased assimilation** is people's tendency to evaluate attitude-inconsistent information as unreliable and less convincing than attitude-consistent information (Lord et al., 1979). Like other means of resisting persuasion, attitude polarization and biased assimilation protect people's original attitudes from new information designed to change those attitudes. Further, people can protect their attitudes by questioning the source of the persuasive message if the attitude it presents is different from their own. For example, one common finding is that people accuse the media of being biased and therefore untrustworthy, particularly if they present a view contrary to their own. This **hostile media bias** increases resistance to persuasion and can mean that people reject even the strongest arguments (Duck, Terry and Hogg, 1998; Vallone, Ross and Lepper, 1985).

Question to consider Now that you know about the ways people are able to resist persuasion, reread question 3 at the start of the chapter. Why was it so easy for Fern to resist the persuasive attempt of the salesman?

CRITICAL FOCUS

How do people understand persuasion?

Social psychologists know a lot about how people can be persuaded, the models that explain persuasion and the features of individuals that lead them to be more persuaded. However, for all psychologists know about persuasion, they know less about the sense that people make of this important social phenomenon. What motives, thought processes and intuitive concepts affect observers' judgements of messages' persuasive power and, conversely, of people's susceptibility to persuasion? In other words, what commonsense representations do people have about persuasion? Do they have any conscious knowledge of the tools they use to persuade people and how they themselves are persuaded? This is an intriguing gap in the literature on persuasion and attitude change.

A good starting point to address this issue is research on the **third-person effect (TPE)**, which is the tendency for people to assume that persuasive attempts have more influence on others than they do on the self (Davison, 1983). People have a basic assumption that persuasion is experienced differently by themselves and others (see also Chapter 3). This applies in many different media domains such as politics and the news, political speeches and advertising (e.g., Cavazza and Mucchi-Faina, 2008; Douglas and Sutton, 2004; Duck, Terry and Hogg, 1995; Gibbon and Durkin, 1995; Gunther, 1995; Hoorens and Ruiter, 1996; Perloff, 1989; Reid, Byrne, Brundidge et al., 2007; Tal-Or, 2007). The TPE is said to reflect a self-serving bias; that is, people see themselves as less susceptible to persuasion than others because being 'gullible' is viewed as an undesirable trait. In a sense, people like comparing

Third-person effect (TPE) The tendency for people to assume that the media have a greater influence on others than on the self.

themselves downwards with people who are less fortunate or able than themselves. Supporting this account, the TPE tends to be stronger among individuals high in self-esteem (e.g., Perloff, 1989) and internal locus of control (e.g., Haridakis and Rubin, 2005).

However, in addition to arising from these self-serving processes, the TPE may also result from people's intuitive psychological understandings of persuasive processes. These **intuitive theories** of persuasion have not been examined before despite their potential impact on persuasion judgements and behaviours. At a general level, it is in the nature of human beings to engage in psychological theorizing. People constantly wonder about psychological states and traits, and invoke these psychological constructs in explanations of their own and others' behaviour (Heider, 1958a; Malle, 2004). In doing so, they make use of culturally shared assumptions and intuitive theories about human psychology (Fletcher, 1995; Levy, Chiu and Hong, 2006; Wegener and Petty, 1998). It is reasonable to hypothesize that people do the same to understand how persuasion works.

In some of our own research, we have addressed this issue, to try to gain more knowledge of how people understand persuasion. Specifically, if we want to know how people understand persuasion, we need to begin by focusing on what we, as social scientists, already know about persuasive processes. So, we focused on the elaboration likelihood model discussed earlier in this chapter. Based on research testing the principles of the ELM, we know that factors such as need for cognition (NFC) determine the extent to which people are influenced by different types of persuasive media (e.g., Cacioppo et al., 1996; Haddock et al., 2008). In particular, people who are high in NFC tend to be persuaded by central cues such as scientific evidence and strong arguments, whereas those who are low in NFC often appear to be more susceptible to peripheral cues – features of a message that do not typically provide logical or empirical grounds to accept the central argument of a message (Petty and Wegener, 1999). We investigated whether people's intuitive understanding of persuasion resembles the ELM in one key respect. Specifically, we investigated whether perceived NFC is negatively related to perceived susceptibility to persuasive advertisements that contain peripheral cues.

In the study (Douglas, Sutton and Stathi, 2010), we asked undergraduate participants how much each of several advertisements would affect themselves or other undergraduate students. These advertisements employed peripheral cues rather than direct arguments in favour of the advertised products. We used a between-groups design to determine whether the predicted TPE (lower perceived influence on the self than others) is influenced by perceived NFC. Specifically, we predicted that individuals would tend to rate themselves as higher than other undergraduates in NFC and that this difference would be able to account for the TPE. Results supported this hypothesis, demonstrating that people's intuitive understanding of persuasion resembles an established theoretical model of persuasion (the ELM) in a key respect. Specifically, perceived NFC is related to perceived resistance to persuasion by advertisements that rely on typically peripheral cues. This gives psychological and evaluative meaning to resistance and susceptibility to persuasion, helping explain why individuals are motivated to see themselves as less influenced than others. Of course, people may not necessarily be able to articulate their understanding of this link between NFC and persuasion. For example, it is unlikely that people would be able to invoke NFC as a construct in everyday life because it is probably not readily accessible, unlike features such as intelligence and critical thinking. This research provides the first evidence that people do indeed use their intuitive understanding of persuasion and the personal characteristics associated with persuasion to judge the extent to which persuasive attempts will be successful.

Questions

1   In this study, Douglas et al. (2010) only tested people's responses to glossy advertisements. What do you think might have happened if they had focused on advertisements containing strong arguments?
2   How do you think other models of persuasion (e.g., the HSM and unimodel) would account for these findings?
3   What might be some of the implications of these findings? For example, do you think that people could use their understanding of persuasion in their own attempts to achieve social influence?

Intuitive theories Theories people have about human thought and behaviour that arrive from 'intuition'. These are also called 'lay theories' because they relate to how everyday people think about thought and behaviour.

ETHICS AND RESEARCH METHODS

Subliminal messages

People are consciously aware of most messages that are designed to influence their attitudes and behaviours. However, using *subliminal stimuli*, advertisers sometimes attempt to influence people through an unconscious route. Subliminal ('below threshold'), unlike supraliminal ('above threshold'), stimuli are any type of sensory stimulation that occurs below an individual's absolute threshold for conscious perception. The idea of subliminal messages has caused some controversy over the years. For example, in 1985, two young men attempted suicide (one succeeded) and their families argued that it was because of the subliminal message 'do it' in the song 'Better by you, better than me' by British band Judas Priest. The families sought damages in the region of US$6 million and although the case was dropped, the judge ruled that the events would not have taken place if it were not for the 'power of suggestion'. A more recent example occurred in a US political TV advertisement run by the Republicans during the 2000 election, where the word 'RATS' was quickly flashed on screen during the advertisement. This was a subliminal message aimed to induce negative feelings about the Democratic Party and its policies. Subliminal messages such as these have been used in advertising for many years.

The results of some laboratory studies suggest that they work. For example, Krosnick, Betz, Jussim and Lynn (1992) showed participants pictures of people performing everyday tasks. Before looking at the pictures, the participants had been subliminally presented with pleasant (e.g., kittens) or unpleasant images (e.g., dead bodies). Krosnick et al. found that when paired with pleasant subliminal images, participants rated the target people more favourably than those for whom the pictures were paired with unpleasant images (see also Dijksterhuis, Aarts and Smith, 2005; Karremans, Stroebe and Claus, 2006; Strahan, Spencer and Zanna, 2002). However, outside the laboratory, there is little evidence that subliminal messages work. Specifically, there is no evidence that subliminal messages will induce people to go out and buy things they do not want to buy, or do things they do not want to do (DeFleur and Petranoff, 1959; Pratkanis, Eskenazi and Greenwald, 1994; Trappey, 1996).

So, is all the fuss over nothing? Perhaps, but whether subliminal messages are effective, marginally effective or not effective at all, they still present an ethical issue. Using such messages, advertisers are exposing people to material they are not consciously aware of. People are therefore being deceived about the intent of the advertisement. For this reason, subliminal messages are illegal in the UK and Australia.

Questions

1   Can you think of other ethical question marks over the issue of subliminal messages?
2   What factors would make a subliminal message more or less effective?
3   Can you see good reasons to use subliminal messages?

Exploring further Take some time to research the history of subliminal advertising. Why do you think its use is so controversial?

Chapter summary

In this chapter, we have focused on the topic of persuasion. We have outlined some of the factors that determine when persuasion will be effective, discussed the key models that explain persuasion, outlined some of the techniques that people can use to be persuasive, and finally, discussed how people are able to resist persuasion. Specifically, you will now know that:

- Persuasion is the process by which a message changes a person's attitudes or behaviours.
- Persuasion is a function of three features: the source, message and target.
- If a message source is seen as attractive, it will be more persuasive. Another persuasive feature is the extent to which the source is seen as similar to the self. Findings show that people are also more persuaded by others whom they perceive to be trustworthy.
- In terms of the message, longer messages are not always best and there is a complex interplay between the length and strength of a message. The consistency between a persuasive message and the target's original attitude is also an important factor in determining the message's persuasive effectiveness. Messages can also be persuasive by making people feel fearful, bad, or that the item of interest is scarce. Sometimes, persuaders arm themselves with the objective facts in order to persuade others. Two-sided arguments can also be effective. Further, information presented first (primacy effect) or last (recency effect) can be the most persuasive. Finally, it is important to consider the channel, or mode with which the information is presented.
- In terms of the target, the effectiveness of a persuasive message has been found to be influenced by gender, with women typically found to be more susceptible to persuasion than men, although findings are mixed. Age is also an important factor, with late adolescents and young adults being the most susceptible to persuasion. Many other social contextual variables and personality variables can influence persuasion, including a person's mood.
- Several models explain the processes involved in persuasion. The key models are dual process models, asserting that the source of the message and the message itself play distinct roles in persuasion and that the outcome of a persuasive interaction also depends on the target or receiver's motivation and ability to process information.
- The elaboration likelihood model (ELM) asserts that variations in the nature of persuasion outcomes are dependent on the likelihood that recipients will engage in elaboration of (or thinking about) the arguments relevant to the issue. When people think carefully and pay special attention to the argument quality, they are attending to the central cues of the message and are being influenced via the central route to persuasion. On the other hand, when people attend to the more superficial characteristics of a message instead of the argument quality, they are attending to the peripheral cues of the message and are being influenced via the peripheral route to persuasion.
- The heuristic-systematic model (HSM) argues that systematic processing occurs when targets actively scan and process the arguments put forward in a message. When heuristic processing occurs, they resort to cognitive 'shortcuts' to process the message.
- Various factors influence the processing route to persuasion. First, the persuasive target's ability to focus influences whether superficial or deep processing will occur. The second key determinant is whether the persuasive target has the motivation to process. This can be influenced by a recipient's need for cognition (NFC) – an individual differences characteristic that reflects a person's tendency to engage in effortful thought.
- There are several well-known techniques that people can adopt to persuade others. First, persuaders can be more effective if they make themselves likeable to the target, or reciprocate something for them. The door-in-the-face technique entails the persuader making a large and unreasonable request that is followed by the smaller (intentional) request. The that's-not-all technique entices the target with extra for their effort or money. The foot-in-the-door technique entails the persuader making a small request before moving in with the larger (intended) request. Finally, the lowball tactic involves the persuader changing the terms of the agreement during the interaction by introducing hidden costs.
- Sometimes, persuasion does not work. When the persuader really puts pressure on, the target can become irritated, resentful and can react against the persuasion attempt. Further, if people are warned about a persuasive attempt, they are less likely to succumb to it. People can also actively resist persuasion by addressing and arguing against attitude-incongruent arguments directly. The process of attitude inoculation demonstrates that weaker arguments inoculate people against later stronger influence attempts. Avoidance is another resistance tactic, where the target simply ignores or filters out information that is inconsistent with their pre-existing attitudes.

This chapter has covered persuasion. In Chapter 7, we turn our attention to close relationships.

Essay questions

At the beginning of the chapter, we asked you to consider these questions:

1 Ulrich has just bought a new iPod and wants to sell his old one on eBay. He is wondering how best to word his advertisement to maximize the appeal of the used iPod. What suggestions might you have for Ulrich to maximize his chances of making a sale?
2 Imogen asks Clare for some relationship advice. She has met a new man and cannot decide whether or not to go out with him. Clare offers her advice but then Imogen asks if she will go on a double date. What is the likelihood that Clare will agree to this? Would Imogen have been better off asking Clare directly in the first place?
3 Fern watches at her window as a salesman walks around her street with a clipboard. When he comes to her house, she listens to what he has to say but then politely declines to buy the product he is selling. Why do you think Fern was so easily able to resist the salesperson's persuasive attempt?

Having read this chapter, these questions could also be framed as the following essay questions, which you can attempt in preparation for your examinations:

1 What elements of persuasion does a person need to consider when they are trying to sell something (e.g., selling a used iPod on eBay)? Discuss the elements of the source, message and target that might end with a successful sale.
2 How can a person get another person to comply with a significant request? Discuss some of the persuasive tactics that people can use to get what they want.
3 What are some of the factors that enable people to resist persuasive attempts?

Some further reading

Bohner, G. and Wänke, M. (2002) *Attitudes and Attitude Change*. Hove: Psychology Press. Comprehensive and accessible introduction to the basic issues in the psychological study of attitudes, with a focus on both North American and European research.

Brock, T.C. and Green, M.C. (eds) (2005) *Persuasion: Psychological Insights and Perspectives* (2nd edn). London: Sage. Broad coverage of the area from experts in the field.

Eagly, A.H. and Chaiken, S. (1993) *The Psychology of Attitudes*. Forth Worth, TX: Harcourt Brace Jovanovich. Written by two of the most distinguished researchers in the field, provides comprehensive coverage of classic research.

Knowles, E.S. and Linn, J.A. (eds) (2004) *Resistance and Persuasion*. Mahwah, NJ: Erlbaum. Collection of chapters from leaders in the research field. Interesting look at resistance to persuasion, with a focus on how resistance can be reduced, overcome or used to promote persuasion.

Maio, G. and Haddock, G. (2009) *The Psychology of Attitudes and Attitude Change*. London: Sage. Comprehensive review of the literature on attitudes and attitude change, focusing on both basic and applied research.

Petty, R. and Wegener, D.T. (1998) Attitude change: Multiple roles for persuasion variables. In D.T. Gilbert, S.T. Fiske and G. Lindzey (eds) *The Handbook of Social Psychology* (4th edn, vol. 1, pp. 323–90). Boston: McGraw-Hill. Useful chapter providing a comparison of the ELM and HSM models of persuasion.

 Visit the companion website at www.palgrave.com/psychology/suttondouglas for access to a wide range of resources to help you get to grips with this chapter.

Applying social psychology

Persuading people to change their ways in order to avert or minimize climate change

Over 98 per cent of publishing climate scientists agree that human beings are causing the world to get warmer. To avert the negative consequences of increased warming in the future, behaviour change is required. However, a large minority of the public in many countries, particularly Western countries, is largely unconvinced that there's a problem.

1   Use an internet search engine or an academic database to find out what proportion of the public of your country, and around the world, are doubtful that human beings are affecting the world's climate.
2   Find an article that evaluates the use of fear campaigns to persuade people of the climate change hypothesis and the need for action. Are they effective?
3   What alternatives to fear campaigns have been used? Which appear to be among the most promising or successful?

4   A common intuition among environmentalists is that people resist environmental messages because of *defensiveness* related to their self-esteem. They feel bad or guilty about the possibility that they are part of the problem, and so refuse to believe the messages they are getting from climate sciences, governments and charities. Can you find any experimental evidence suggesting that this intuition may be right? (Hint: 2010 is a good year to look in.)
5   Find two examples of climate change advertising campaigns (be it TV, newspaper or radio advertising, the internet, social networks, or posters). Compare, contrast and evaluate them in light of what you have learned in this chapter. How could they be improved?
6   In light of what you learned about the relationship between attitudes and behaviour in Chapter 4, do you think it is more productive to attempt to persuade people that the world is warming because of us, or to give up on getting them to 'believe in' climate change, and focus instead on persuading them to alter their behaviour? Why?

Blind spot in social psychology

What is the psychological profile of a persuasive communicator?

In this chapter, we have reviewed a lot of research into the factors that make people prone to being persuaded. These included externally apparent aspects of a person such as their age and gender, but also features of their psychological makeup. Motives and personality characteristics such as self-esteem, and the needs for distinctiveness, (low) cognition and (high) cognitive closure have all been shown to shape how prone to persuasion people are likely to be.

As well as knowing who is prone to persuasion, we also know quite a bit about who is persuasive. As we have seen, research on 'source characteristics' has revealed that people who are seen by the audience to be attractive, expert, high in status or similar to themselves are more likely to be persuasive. The message is clear: if you want to persuade other people, then seek to develop these characteristics – or at least, seek to look like you've got them. If you want to recruit someone to persuade on your behalf, try to get hold of people with these attributes.

However, although we know a lot about the external attributes of persuasive people, very little research has addressed their psychological makeup. What motives and personality characteristics are likely to help people be

persuaded? In general, research has focused much more on how persuasive messages are processed by recipients, rather than on how they are produced. This is an important omission, since 'in every day life we are all practicing persuaders, and we must rely on verbal communication to get our way with others' (Forgas, 2007, p. 514).

For this exercise, imagine you are a psychological researcher contracted by a large recruitment company to advise on the personality characteristics that determine who is able to persuade others. The ultimate aim of this company is to propose a set of psychometric personality tests that can be used to help select effective communicators.

By all means, your own insights and intuitions may provide one source of inspiration for this task, but you should not try to rely solely on them.

One way to think in a psychologically informed way about the characteristics that make an effective persuader is to review the literature on the features of persuasive messages. People are persuasive to the extent that the messages they produce are persuasive. So, the effects of their personality characteristics on their ability to persuade people must be mediated by features of the messages they produce.

So, for example, what kinds of people are likely to use techniques such as the foot-in-the-door, or to produce consistent messages, or to use fear? Variables such as Machiavellianism and dogmatism may be important.

Another psychologically informed way to think about what kind of traits characterize persuasive people is to think about the personality variables that underpin social skills and the ability to influence others in general. In other chapters, you will find passages about variables such as *self-monitoring* and *narcissism*, which are relevant to skills such as being able to influence others and to monitor their reactions to your communication.

Your specific tasks are:

1 Propose at least one personality variable that may be related to effectiveness as a persuasive communicator. Explain what the variable is, with references, and explain how, specifically, it might be related to effective persuasion (e.g., what features of the messages will it be associated with).

2 Propose how you might test your hypothesis. You need to identify an existing measure of your personality variable, specific features of messages that need to be coded in a study, and a measure of how much an audience is persuaded.

Student project

The extent to which people tailor persuasion attempts to 'fit' their audience

Oliver Arnold (with the collaboration of two fellow students) conducted a research project in his second year of undergraduate studies at the University of Heidelberg, supervised by Dr Tobias Vogel. His research project explored how sophisticated ordinary people are when they attempt to persuade each other. Specifically, it explored the extent to which people tailor persuasion attempts to 'fit' their audience, in line with the elaboration likelihood model, which we discussed in this chapter.

My topic and aims

According to the ELM, people's need for cognition (NFC) (Cacioppo and Petty, 1982) determines what kinds of messages they will find persuasive. For instance, Putrevu (2008) showed that only among low NFC participants, products advertised by strong sex appeal were rated more positively than products advertised by low sex appeal. Conversely, participants high in NFC did not simply ignore the sexy 'peripheral cues' but even felt disturbed and ended up evaluating products more negatively. Building on current research on implicit persuasion theories (Vogel, Kutzner, Fiedler and Freytag, 2010), our research project examined whether people who have not had formal training in the ELM nonetheless follow its principles when trying to persuade others. That is, would they use peripheral, sexy cues when attempting to persuade people who are low in NFC, but more central, informative cues when communicating with those who are high in NFC?

My methods

Forty female students were asked to take the role of a marketer and to prepare a video clip that advertises a new yoghurt named 'fruit whirl'. They were informed that the product addressed a certain target audience, the description of which was derived from the NFC scale. Half the students were randomly assigned to a 'high NFC audience' condition, and were given descriptions of the audience that are consistent with high NFC (e.g., that concentrated thinking is their idea of fun). The other half were assigned to a 'low NFC' condition (in which they were told, for example, that concentrated thinking is not their audience's idea of fun). We then provided a pretested list of slogans transporting either relevant facts (e.g., 'Does not contain preservatives or artificial flavours') or a sexually appealing message (e.g., 'A single spoon is better than a kiss') and our participants chose slogans they would convey in the clip.

We were also interested in our participants' nonverbal persuasion behaviour. Thus, they were asked to choose gestures from a list, which were either rated as sober (e.g., 'Pointing towards the product') or flirtatious (e.g., 'Licking lips'). Upon returning their questionnaires, we asked if they were willing to actually cast the clip. Thirty-four participants agreed and were handed a camera, a cup of yoghurt and a spoon.

My findings and their implications

Participants targeting their advertisement at a high NFC audience exhibited a clear preference for slogans transporting facts and sober gestures, while participants with a low NFC target group selected a mixture of facts and sexually appealing messages and planned to mainly employ flirtatious gestures in the video clip. Further, independent raters (who did not know our hypotheses) rated participants as being more flirty (but not less serious) in advertisements designed for low NFC audiences. These results suggest that people do, indeed, seem to have a rather sophisticated, if unspoken knowledge of the principles of persuasion. Although they might not ever have heard of the ELM or NFC, they nonetheless use information about NFC to tailor their messages, exactly as the ELM suggests they should.

My journey

The most valuable thing I gained during my project was the motivation to become further involved in attitude and persuasion research. This was fuelled by the positive feedback we received for our work and the feeling of contributing to a hot and fascinating research field. I presented the results of the project on a poster at the Congress of the European Federation of Psychology Students' Associations (EFPSA) in 2009, winning the award for the best poster presentation. EFPSA is a great platform for undergraduate psychology students to become involved in international research, annually organizing a congress and featuring a peer review journal, the *Journal of European Psychology Students*.

The knowledge and skills I acquired came in handy when I started working as a student assistant in the social psychology department and during a research internship abroad. It also set the ground for my current work as a PhD student. I now employ an attitude research paradigm recently proposed by Kaiser, Byrka and Hartig (2010), that builds upon a formal rather than causal conception of the attitude–behaviour relationship. It describes individual behaviour as a function of a person's attitude level and the specific behavioural costs. I explore how environmental attitudes moderate the efficacy of information and technology interventions to reduce energy consumption in private households. Both intervention strategies usually do not result in the anticipated amounts of energy saved. A sufficient level of motivation to engage in environmental preservation and energy conservation might be a prerequisite for their efficiency.

My advice

Enjoy what you are doing. You are lucky to have the time on your hands to address your own research questions. Look around you: very likely there are a bunch of other dedicated young researchers and a faculty member offering a helping hand – all you have to do is to seize the opportunity and be creative. If you are bold enough to think out of the box while planning the project, there is a good chance you will have fun presenting your results afterwards – even if your hypotheses may not be supported.

7 Close relationships

In this chapter, we review the social psychological literature on close relationships, focusing primarily on romantic relationships, but also friendships. We outline the factors that determine when people are attracted to each other. We then review some of the key social psychological theories of attraction. Our focus then turns to love and romantic relationships more specifically and how romantic relationships are maintained. Finally, we focus on the often painful process of relationship breakdown.

© EKATERINA POKROVSKY/FOTOLIA.COM

Topics covered in this chapter

- Interpersonal attraction
- Theories of attraction
- Love and romantic relationships
- Attraction and bonding
- Maintaining relationships
- When relationships end

Key features

Critical focus Sexual strategies theory

Ethics and research methods Student samples in relationships research

Social psychology in the real world Same-sex relationships: 'the love that dare not speak its name'

Applying social psychology Abusive relationships

Blind spot in social psychology The politics of sexual variety

Student project Attachment style, disclosure and relationship quality

Questions to consider

1 What chances are there for average-looking Matt to have a romantic relationship with Melissa, the most beautiful girl in school? How might he be able to overcome the discrepancy in physical attractiveness?

2 Kay and Leigh live on different continents. They met one day on the internet and became friends. Ewan and Jai live in the same building. They met one day in the lift and likewise became friends. What is different about these two friendships? Do they have an equal chance of success?

3 Leila feels that her husband takes more than he gives, and that she does all the hard work to make their marriage a success. What social psychological theory can you link this situation to? What are the likely consequences of this relationship imbalance?

4 Once deeply in love, Jenna and Kate now argue constantly and both feel that their relationship is over. What factors will determine where they go from here?

Close relationships are at the very centre of human existence. Families love, support and bring joy to each other throughout life. Romantic partners enable people to feel nurtured, needed, important and special. Close friendships provide people with support and acceptance, shared interests and shared experiences. Having close relationships makes people feel good and as human beings, we have a fundamental need to affiliate and bond with others (Baumeister and Leary, 1995; Reis and Collins, 2004; Reis, Collins and Berscheid, 2000). Of course, we do not bond with everyone we meet. We like some people and can strongly dislike others. You may only need to think momentarily about your school days to remember how intensely you liked some of your classmates and the dislike you felt for others. Most of the time, the feelings were mutual. Interpersonal attraction is a powerful thing. So, it is probably not too surprising that a vast proportion of songs are about love, relationships and heartbreak. Close relationships are also one of the most common themes in movies, television and novels. Turn on the radio and it is likely that within a few minutes you will hear someone singing about love and relationships, uttering words like 'I need you' or 'you've got a friend'. Humans seem to be preoccupied with the idea of being 'in love' or in other kinds of close relationships.

This preoccupation makes sense. The loss or lack of close relationships can lead to negative outcomes such as depression, loneliness and alienation (Buckley, Winkel and Leary, 2004). People feel ostracized and sometimes become angry and aggressive when they are rejected by close others (Williams, Cheung and Choi, 2000). People feel deep sadness when relationships come to an end (Simpson, 1987). Close relationships are therefore necessary for survival and happiness and humans strive to seek and maintain these close social bonds with others. For example, we spend a lot of time and energy making ourselves attractive to prospective mates. We spend money on clothes, makeup and exercise equipment to maximize our physical appeal. We join groups to find others with whom we share interests. We do things that our friends also like to do. In short, we need to belong with others and will go to great lengths to make close relationships a core feature of life. Indeed, evolutionary psychologists have long argued that attraction, relationships and love are core to human survival and, as we will see in this chapter, basic principles of attraction have evolved to ensure the survival of the fittest (e.g., Barrett, Dunbar and Lycett, 2002; Buss, 1995, 2000, 2009).

In Part 3 of this book, we will focus on the many benefits that humans gain from being around other humans in groups, but in this chapter we focus on the formation and development of close relationships between individuals. Specifically, why and when people are drawn to each other in the first place, what this magical thing is that we call 'love', theories of close relationships, how we maintain them and how we end close relationships. Much of the research in this chapter relates to the development, maintenance and ending of *romantic* relationships, but we also discuss literature related to other close relationships such as friendships. As you will see, the factors that influence attraction and many other relationship factors are essentially the same for romantic relationships and close friendships.

Interpersonal attraction

We all know from personal experience that we tend to like some people, but not others. Indeed, it is possible to take an immediate like or dislike to someone when we first meet them. Sometimes, we can articulate the reason why we feel this reaction and at other times we are only aware of a 'gut' response to another person that influences whether or not we think they are likeable or attractive, and worth getting to know better. Social psychologists have identified several key factors that influence who we like, or are attracted to, and who we are not. Some are physical factors such as appearance and proximity. Others are psychological factors such as attitude similarity and mutual liking.

Physical determinants of attraction

Many of the reasons why we are drawn to others are simple things and they are often features of our daily lives we cannot control. For example, we may like people simply because they are close by (e.g., Festinger, Schachter and Back, 1950). People who we see a lot are familiar and so we like them more than people who we see less often, which can influence our friendships and romantic relationships. Also, we tend to like people who are similar to ourselves on basic features such as looks, and this is particularly important with respect to romantic relationships (e.g., Murstein, 1986; Sprecher, 1998). Such factors can be defined as the physical determinants of attraction – features of our environment or appearance that influence our liking for others. The key physical determinant of attraction is a person's physical appearance, which we discuss first.

Physical appearance

Probably the most important factor in determining judgements of attractiveness is a person's physical appearance. Like it or not, we judge others (and are likewise judged by them) based on looks. This fundamental effect was demonstrated in a study by Hatfield, Aronson, Abrahams and Rottman (1966), who asked undergraduate students to complete a range of personality and aptitude tests before matching them up randomly at a social dance. The experimenters also rated the physical attractiveness of each participant. The couples spent time together during the evening before evaluating their partner and the success of the date. Results showed that personality and aptitude factors were poor predictors of participants' ratings. For example, participants did not show preferences for partners with high self-esteem or low anxiety, as one might expect. Instead, only the physical attractiveness of the partner seemed to matter. In other words, the more attractive the partner, the more likely it was the participant liked them and wanted to go out on another date.

If a person is physically attractive, this is an asset in other facets of life (Langlois, Kalakanis, Rubenstein et al., 2000). For example, an attractive person is more likely to go out on dates (e.g., Berscheid, Dion, Walster and Walster, 1971; Rowatt, Cunningham and Druen, 1999), get better marks at university (Landy and Sigall,

1974), be successful in a job interview (Dipboye, Arvey and Terpstra, 1977; Mack and Rainey, 1990; Marvelle and Green, 1980) and earn more money once they have a job (French, 2002; Frieze, Olson and Russell, 1991; Mobius and Rosenblat, 2006; Umberson and Hughes, 1987). Attractive people are more likely to win elections (Poutvaara, Jordahl and Berggren, 2009), attractive university teachers get higher evaluations (Hamermesh and Parker, 2005), while attractive people are treated more leniently in the legal system (Downs and Lyons, 1991). An attractive person is also perceived by participants in studies as more likely to get married (Dion, Berscheid and Walster, 1972), to be more honest (Yarmouk, 2000) and to be happier (Dion et al., 1972). Research has further shown that small babies prefer to look at attractive faces than less attractive faces (Langlois, Roggman, Casey et al., 1987; Langlois et al., 2000). Further, children tend to prefer attractive children (Dion, 1973; Dion and Berscheid, 1974; Langlois et al., 2000), and adults tend to think that attractive children are more intelligent and more successful (Clifford and Walster, 1973). Clearly, it is good to be good-looking.

These findings show that people often attach positive qualities to attractive people. This is sometimes called the **physical attractiveness stereotype** – the tendency for people to assume that attractive people possess other socially desirable traits in addition to their looks (Dion et al., 1972; Moore, Graziano and Millar, 1987). To some extent, this is true. Some research shows that physically attractive people *are* more popular and outgoing (Langlois et al., 2000). However, these small differences may be due, in part, to self-fulfilling prophecies: because being physically attractive is socially desirable, attractive people may become more confident and outgoing and so may be more popular with others. The stereotype thus becomes self-fulfilling. Also, it is important to note that physical attractiveness has its drawbacks. In particular, more attractive people are often the subject of unwanted advances and resentment from less attractive individuals (Hatfield and Sprecher, 1986). Attractive celebrities are often the victims of stalking (Roberts, 2007). Also, attractive, popular adolescents are more likely to engage in aggressive, destructive and norm-breaking behaviours (Dijkstra, Lindenberg, Verhulst et al., 2009). Thus, being attractive is not always as favourable as it may seem. Nevertheless, attractiveness is a key variable in the study of relationships. What specific features make a person attractive to others?

Physical attractiveness stereotype The tendency for people to assume that physically attractive people possess other socially desirable traits such as warmth and intelligence.

What is attractive?

Naturally, there is wide variation in what specific features people view to be appealing. For example, some people think that tattoos and piercings are attractive but others do not. Some women adopt the 'thin ideal', whereas others would prefer to be more voluptuous. Some men wear facial hair and others prefer to be clean shaven. There are, of course, other reasons to adopt these aspects of one's appearance. For example, beards may be worn for religious purposes, a woman may need to be thin to be a model, and a person may need to have tattoos in order to be part of a gang. However, a lot of the time, people show preferences for physical features in themselves that they find attractive. The list of differences in personal preferences is endless (Perrett, 2010). Likewise, there is a lot of variation in people's preference to see these types of features (e.g., tattoos, beards) in others. However, despite these many differences, there is strong consensus both within and between cultures about attractiveness (Langlois et al., 2000). Specifically, when rating faces, people across the world seem to agree quite closely on who is attractive and who is not. For example, Langlois and Roggman (1990) asked participants to rate the physical attractiveness of a range of faces from different nationalities and ethnic groups. Participants' ratings agreed to a significant extent, with correlations between them reaching up to .93. Perhaps surprisingly, there seem to be universal standards of attractiveness.

Is there some kind of 'super person' who everyone finds attractive? The answer is no. Interestingly, the most attractive face tends to be the most 'average' face (Rhodes, 1996; Rhodes, Halberstadt, Jeffery and Palermo, 2005). For example, Winkielman, Halberstadt, Fazendeiro and Catty (2006) asked participants to view a series of faces. Some faces were normal (e.g., how the person actually looks) and others were digitized or combined multiple faces to produce 'mathematically average' or prototypical faces. Findings showed that, on average, people perceived the artificial prototypical faces to be more attractive than the actual faces. Winkielman et al. argued that this **averageness effect**, or preference for prototypical faces, occurs because average faces are closer to the mental prototype of a face. In other words, they are more 'face-like' and therefore more familiar. The authors further argued that this familiarity leads to higher ratings of attractiveness because the prototypical faces are easier to process. As people are exposed to more and more faces, a typical face prototype is developed and new faces are compared to this prototype. The closer a novel face is to the prototype, the more quickly it is processed and the more it is liked (see Figure 7.1). This is a case where **perceptual fluency** – the relative ease of mental operations – is high (Jacoby, 1983; Mandler, 1980; Schwarz, 1998). However, it can also be related to the mere exposure effect, which we discuss later in this chapter, where repeated exposure to a stimulus makes people like it more. In this case, the repeated exposure leads the person to create a prototype of 'face-like-ness', which is then used as a benchmark from which to judge the attractiveness of other faces.

Averageness effect The finding that people prefer average or prototypical faces to faces that have distinctive features.

Perceptual fluency The relative ease of mental operations.

Other studies have produced similar results. For example, Johnston (2000) created an average female face by combining 16 female Caucasian faces. He then subtly exaggerated the femininity of the faces by enhancing the features in which women and men typically differ (e.g., bigger eyes, fuller lips). Most people tend to find the composite female face to be more attractive and familiar

FIGURE 7.1 Original and manipulated photos The original photograph is on the left-hand side and the manipulated photo is on the right. In these types of studies, most people tend to agree that the manipulated photo is more attractive.

(see also Langlois and Roggman, 1990; Monin, 2003; Rhodes and Tremewan, 1996; Rhodes, Yoshikawa, Clark et al., 2001). Evolutionary theorists argue that this preference for prototypicality in faces has evolved because prototypicality is a signal for health and therefore for reproductive fitness (e.g., Symons, 1979; Thornhill and Gangestad, 1993).

It is also the case that averageness is not always best. Perrett, May and Yoshikawa (1994) made composite faces from groups of faces that had previously been rated as 'average' and another set of composite faces that had previously been rated as 'highly attractive'. A composite of the 'average' faces was constructed for both Japanese and Caucasian faces and the same was done for the 'highly attractive' faces, resulting in an average composite of each type of face and for each race. These were then shown to a group of participants who were asked to rate the attractiveness of the faces. Results revealed that the 'highly attractive' composites were rated as more attractive than the 'average' composites, as one might expect. Further, Japanese and British participants showed similar ratings to each other, for both race composites, suggesting again that there are universal aspects of attractiveness.

Another factor to consider is that composite or average faces tend to be more *symmetrical* and people tend to find symmetrical faces more attractive than asymmetrical faces (Halberstadt and Rhodes, 2000; Penton-Voak and Perrett, 2001; Rhodes, 1996, 2006; Rhodes, Sumich and Byatt, 1999). People also rate symmetrical faces as healthier, more dominant and more extroverted (Shackelford and Larsen, 1997). Within sets of identical twins, the twin with the most symmetrical face is rated the most attractive (Mealey, Bridgstock and Townsend, 1999).

Why is facial symmetry important? Some social psychologists have proposed that this preference for average and symmetrical faces has evolved; that is, throughout the course of our evolution, people have come to prefer certain dimensions in faces (Langlois et al., 2000; Langlois, Roggman and Musselman, 1994). It is argued that this preference comes about because a prototypical face is a good indicator of the biological quality of a potential partner. For example, people who have more average faces tend to have a more diverse gene pool. Such diversity means they are likely to be stronger and more able to fight off diseases. Thus, they are more reproductively fit and, essentially, a better choice of mate (Grammer and Thornhill, 1994). So, participants in experiments may tend to prefer composite faces because they do not have some of the atypical features that make faces asymmetrical. Interestingly, the averageness effect also extends to people's judgements of the attractiveness of dogs, watches, birds, cars and other non-human objects (e.g., Halberstadt and Rhodes, 2000, 2003). If a preference for prototypicality has evolved, then perhaps the averageness effect should only be seen for human faces.

Others argue that, in evolutionary terms, physical attractiveness signals that a person is young, healthy and fertile and this is why attractiveness is valued (e.g., Jokela, 2009; Swami, Furnham and Joshi, 2008). Evolutionary social psychologists also argue that there are biological reasons why heterosexual women tend to find high status men attractive and heterosexual men focus more on a woman's youth and beauty. For example, Buss (1989, 2003; see also Mathes and Kozak, 2008) argued that the characteristics preferred by men signal reproductive fitness and the characteristics sought by women in their men signal stability and the ability to provide for offspring.

Evolutionary psychologists have also explained why men almost universally prefer women whose waists are in a 30:70 proportion to their hips – this shape is associated with fertility, and events that affect fertility such as pregnancy and malnutrition also cause changes in shape (Singh, 1993; Singh and Young, 1995; but see also Swami, Gray and Furnham, 2007). Interestingly, women show similar effects, preferring more masculine features at the time they ovulate or during their fertile years of life than at other times (Gangstead, Simpson, Cousins et al., 2004; Jones, DeBruine, Perrett et al., 2008; Little, Saxton, Roberts et al., 2010; Macrae, Alnwick, Milne and Schloerscheidt, 2002). Incredibly, women prefer the smell of T-shirts worn by physically symmetrical men, a finding more pronounced at the time of ovulation (Gangstead and Simpson, 2000). Another striking finding is that strippers earn more tips when they are at the most fertile time in their menstrual cycle (Miller, Tybur and Jordon, 2007). However, this was only the case for women who were not taking the contraceptive pill; those who were on the pill (and therefore not ovulating, and presumably less interested in mating) did not show an increase in earnings via tips. Further, women are rated by men and also rate themselves as more attractive at the peak of their menstrual cycle (Röder, Brewer and Fink, 2009; Schwarz and Hassebrauck, 2008), while studies have also shown that women wear more provocative clothing at the time they are most fertile (e.g., Durante, Li and Haselton, 2008; Röder et al., 2009). All this is quite fascinating, but what does it mean? According to evolutionary psychologists, these findings mean that men prefer women who appear most fertile, and when women are at their most fertile, they prefer the 'fittest' men to mate with. Mating, like other fundamental needs, is driven somewhat by biological factors. Even considering some cultural variations – such as in foraging societies, where thinness is undesirable because it signifies malnutrition and fatness signifies wealth (e.g., Marlowe and Wetsman, 2001) – attractiveness seems to be a sign of reproductive fitness. The Critical focus box below presents an evolutionary perspective on mate selection and relationships.

Exploring further It is clear that the 'ideal female shape' has not always been the same. For example, compare the more voluptuous Marilyn Monroe from the 1950s with a super-slim catwalk model of today. What does this tell us about the factors that influence what we find attractive? Is it all down to evolution? Do you think that standards would differ for men and women? Find out more about the evolutionary perspective on attractiveness and consider what other features influence our view of what is attractive. Try to construct arguments for and against the evolutionary perspective on attractiveness, drawing on other examples such as changes in 'tanning' over the years.

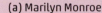

(a) Marilyn Monroe

(b) Today's super-slim catwalk model

Time to reflect In the UK, a novel take on the 'blind date' TV show formula invites participants to go on dates in the dark, supposedly taking the crucial factor of physical attractiveness out of the equation. 'Dating in the dark' forces contestants to get to know each other without this cue to attraction. At the end of the show, contestants are physically 'revealed' to each other and decide whether or not they want to go on further dates. Do you think this technique facilitates people's attraction to each other? Or, ultimately, does physical attractiveness always matter? What other factors might influence the success of the dates?

CRITICAL FOCUS

Sexual strategies theory

Evolutionary psychologists construe human attraction (and specifically their sexual preferences) as being part of a sexual strategy, designed by evolution to maximize people's chances of transmitting their genes. According to this perspective, this is why males and females show different preferences when choosing a long-term mate. *Sexual strategies theory* (Buss and Schmitt, 1993) purportedly explains why males show a preference for youth, physical health and attractiveness (cues to fertility and reproductive value) and why females show a preference for status, maturity and resources (cues related to the potential ability to provide for mother and child). It also attempts to explain why men tend to engage in short-term mating more than women. After all, men are able to 'pass on' more of their genes by mating with multiple females. If a man mates with many women, there is a good chance he will father more children. The same behaviour in women provides no evolutionary advantage. She can mate with many men but can only produce one child at a time. However, Buss and Schmitt (1993) argue that women can benefit from short-term mating if it gives them access to an exceptionally good male. An exceptionally good male may produce an exceptionally good child with good genes, thus suiting an evolutionary purpose for the woman. Successfully copying your genes is much more a matter of quality for women, since the quantity of offspring that women can have is limited.

According to sexual strategies theory, whether long- or short-term strategies are chosen depends on factors such as opportunity, personal 'market value', sex ratio available in the 'pool' and other cultural and social features. However, when short-term mating is opted for, it is predicted that:

1   Men will desire more sexual variety (more partners).

2   Men require less time to elapse before consenting to sex than women.

3   Men tend to actively seek more mates than women.

To test this theory, Schmitt, Alcalay, Alik et al. (2003) measured the desire for sexual variety of 16,000 participants in 52 countries. The measures looked like this:

Ideally, how many different sex partners would you like to have ...

In the next month
In the next six months
...
Your remaining lifetime

Schmitt et al. also measured the time required before an individual is willing to engage in sexual intercourse as follows:

If the conditions were right, would you consider sexual intercourse desirable if you had known that person for ...

1 hour   (definitely yes +3 + 2 +1 0 –1 –2 –3 definitely no)
...
5 years   (definitely yes +3 + 2 +1 0 –1 –2 –3 definitely no)

Finally, the researchers measured the degree to which the individual is actively seeking short-term mating partners:

Not at all   1 2 3 4 5 6 7   Strongly

The results were *winsorized*, which means that extreme outliers were removed. For example, anyone who said that they wanted more than 100 sexual partners was removed so as not to skew the results (for interest's sake, these were men).

The results concerning the 'number of partners' measure supported the first hypothesis, that across all regions of the world, men desired more partners. To test the second hypothesis, Schmitt et al. (2003) compared results for men and women's required time before consenting to sex. Again, there was a significant sex difference in all regions. By and large, men were happy to have intercourse with someone within a month of knowing them; women wanted to take longer. Finally, to test the third hypothesis, Schmitt et al. compared females and males on the 'actively seeking short-term mates' measure. Yet again, men were more likely to report actively searching for short-term mates, even when they were already in a relationship.

Schmitt et al. argued that their results provide evidence for the evolutionary basis of mate selection. Across cultures, males and females show different mating preferences, suggesting a deep-rooted biological basis for mate selection. The evidence seems compelling. However, like any piece of research, it is necessary to critically evaluate the claims made from the study:

1 The methods rely on self-report data, that is, people report their sexual preferences in a questionnaire. Arguably, this is not, therefore, an objective measure of actual sexual preferences. In particular, it may be socially desirable for men to appear 'macho' by reporting that they have (and desire) many mates. So, do participants' responses adequately represent reality? In defence of sexual strategies theory, Schmitt et al. (2003) argue that their results mirror those of other studies, which have used observational data. For example, the prevalence of adultery and use of pornography is higher in males than females.

2 The many student participants may not be representative of 'people in general' because there may be a student subculture across countries and cultures.

3 One key criticism of the evolutionary approach to human mating is that even if we accept that sex differences are real, is the evolutionary approach the only, or even the best explanation? Is it really scientifically viable?

Eagly and Wood (1999) offer the most thorough, concentrated criticism and constructive alternative. First, it is important to note that they accept biological differences. For example, men are bigger than women, as well as more physically powerful. Women are more invested in children. Because of the differences observed by Schmitt et al., men are more likely to have the role of hunter-gatherer and women are more likely to have the role of carer. The crucial difference between Eagly and Wood's approach and the evolutionary approach is that mate selection is determined by *social roles* and not inherent biological differences. There is no necessary or strong genetic influence on sexual preferences, which are socially determined. Both theories acknowledge social and genetic factors, but to a different extent. Debate about these issues is ongoing. One key issue is how to distinguish which theory is best to explain sexual preferences.

Questions

1 Can you think of other issues concerning the self-report method?

2 How do you think Schmitt et al. would argue against the criticism that student participants are an inappropriate sample?

3 Can you think of ways to distinguish between Schmitt et al. and Eagly and Wood's theories? What type of study might enable social psychologists to find out which is a better explanation for sexual preferences?

Try it yourself If you cannot quite believe these differences, try it out for yourself with some friends. Ask a group of friends the questions Schmitt et al. asked of their participants (described in the Critical focus box above). In other words, how many sexual partners do your friends want to have over the next month, the next six months and so on? Do you notice the gender difference?

With almost universal agreement about standards of attractiveness, readers may come to the conclusion that everyone seeks the same type of partner. While it may be the case that everyone wishes to have a great-looking partner, it is clear that this is not possible. Obviously, it is not possible for every heterosexual man to end up with an objectively attractive woman and, likewise, every heterosexual woman cannot pair up with a man who meets the culturally universal standards of attractiveness. In romantic relationships, what other factors determine who is attracted to whom?

The matching phenomenon

Matching phenomenon The tendency for individuals to choose as partners people who are a similar match to themselves in terms of their physical attractiveness.

One key mechanism that determines who people are attracted to is what social psychologists call the **matching phenomenon**. This is where people tend to be attracted to people who are about the same level of physical attractiveness as themselves. For example, many studies have found a strong association between the attractiveness of married and dating couples (Murstein, 1986; Sprecher, 1998). Further, other studies show that in dating-type scenarios, people tend to approach people whose attractiveness is fairly close to their own (Berscheid et al., 1971; Price and Vandenberg, 1979; Stroebe, Insko, Thompson and Layton, 1971; Taylor, Fiore, Mendelsohn and Cheshire, 2011). Also, people who are a close physical match tend to have more long-lasting relationships than those who are less closely matched (White, 1980).

Does this mean that people never date people who are 'out of their league'? Clearly not. This fantasy of dating people who are more attractive is another preoccupation that humans seem to have. It is a common theme in teenage movies and TV programmes to 'catch' the hottest boy or girl in school. Also, many songs and poems speak of coveted others who are out of reach, mainly because they are too beautiful or too handsome. Even though the matching phenomenon is powerful, this does not mean that people never have successful relationships with more or less physically attractive others.

Time to reflect Research suggests that people tend to be attracted to others who are their match with respect to physical attractiveness. Does this mean that people stop wanting 'more'? What do you think the processes might be that lead people to end up with their own physical matches? Is partner selection like the marketplace? We want something we simply cannot afford, so settle for something else instead?

In such cases, social psychologists argue that for less physically attractive people, *compensatory factors* often mean that they can make up for their looks and make themselves attractive in other areas. For example, they may be wealthy, intelligent and witty, or belong to an attractive social circle. These features are attractive. Such compensatory factors increase a person's appeal to others who may be more physically attractive but value these other attributes more than looks. In this respect, although it sounds strange, seeking a relationship can be compared to the process of going shopping. When we go shopping, we sometimes value an item's specifications over its aesthetic appeal. We weigh up what we value most and make a decision based on that process. For example, we might think that a phone is clunky and dull, but really value its high specification camera. We do the same in relationships and the value of the respective 'assets' generates an equal match. You will see this phenomenon in action on dating websites and personal advertisements. People offer their attributes and hope to meet others who share some similarities and complement them in other ways (Cicerello and Sheehan,

1995; Koestner and Wheeler, 1988). Or, they may seek people who value the traits they themselves possess. Interestingly, Morgan, Richards and VanNess (2010) explored the online personal advertisements of 294 heterosexual and homosexual women and men by comparing the narratives that participants generated about themselves and their preferred partner. The self and partner narratives were remarkably similar and even though there were some differences (e.g., homosexual individuals were more likely to list physical attributes than heterosexual advertisers), the study provides strong support for the matching phenomenon in dating websites rather than seeking complementary characteristics.

However, some research shows that there are some gender differences in what men and women offer and seek. Studies have shown that while women tend to offer looks and seek wealth and status (e.g., 'Attractive 28-year-old woman seeks professional man'), men tend to offer wealth and status while seeking looks (e.g., 'Professional 40-year-old man seeks attractive young woman') (Baise and Schroeder, 1995). This is sometimes called **asset matching** and allows people to exchange what they want from relationships. From an evolutionary perspective, this also makes sense. Women may seek high status in men so that they can provide for their offspring. On the other hand, men may seek the most sexually attractive female mate to increase their reproductive success (Buss and Schmitt, 1993).

Matching with similar others is not just about physical attractiveness either. As we will see later, people tend to seek relationships with others who are also similar in terms of attitudes, values and preferences. Thankfully, it is not all about looks, despite the powerful influence of physical attractiveness.

> **Asset matching** Seeking complementary 'assets' allows people to exchange what they want from relationships.

Question to consider Reread question 1 at the start of the chapter. What are the chances of Matt ending up with Melissa? From your own experience, think of friendships and romantic relationships between people of different attractiveness levels. What brought them together? Did they stay together? What social psychological phenomena can you see in practice?

Familiarity and proximity

> **Proximity/propinquity effect** Being or living close to others can facilitate attraction and relationship formation.

In addition to good looks, simply finding someone familiar or being in close **proximity** to others can facilitate attraction. Familiarity may even influence people's ratings of *physical* attractiveness. For example, Little and Perrett (2002) found that when participants rated the attractiveness of faces, they preferred the faces that were most similar to their own. Also, they rated a series of photos of the opposite sex – crucially, one of the faces had been 'morphed' with their own face. The participants rated this morphed, opposite-gender version of their own face as the most attractive. Thus, it seems that we like what we see as physically similar to us. Further, Little, Burt and Perrett (2006) demonstrated that if a person was said to possess a certain (desirable) personality characteristic that is familiar and important to the perceiver, the perceiver rated the face as more attractive.

Familiarity influences attraction in other ways. For example, in terms of friendships, we are often friendliest with the neighbours who live closest to us (see Figure 7.2). At school, we may have bonded with the child sitting next to us in class. Being close to others makes it more likely that we will form friendships or romantic relationships with them (Berscheid and Reis, 1998). This effect of proximity (sometimes also called the **propinquity effect**) was demonstrated in a classic study by Festinger et al. (1950), who found that, in a housing complex for married couples at a large US university, when people were asked to name their friends, they tended to name people in the same building even though the other buildings were only metres away. Also, within a building, people tended to choose friends who were living on the same floor as themselves, as opposed to those who were on other floors or in other buildings. Further, the location of key building features such as staircases and mailboxes also had an impact on friendships. In particular, people situated on different floors but directly next to a staircase were more likely to become friends than those situated on different floors and further away from the staircase. Likewise, the people closest to the staircases and mailboxes on the lower floor were more likely to have friends upstairs than those who were further away from the building's key features. These important features made people even more proximal; people close to the stairs and mailboxes were even more likely to come into contact with each other. As a result, they were also more likely to become friends. A similar effect was also demonstrated in a study by Back, Schmukle and Egloff (2008), who randomly assigned students to sit next to someone, or in the same row as that person, for one whole term during a psychology class. A year later, the researchers measured the students' liking for the person. Results revealed that the closer they sat to the person, the more they liked them.

Perhaps these findings seem quite logical. After all, it is easier to get to know someone who lives nearby and with whom you anticipate interacting in future. But why exactly does proximity make us like people more? Social psychologists argue that proximity is effective because we tend to like things (in this case, people) that are familiar to us. Further, repeated exposure to another person – particularly if the exposure is positive – is likely to lead to more favourable evaluations of that person. Even tiny babies tend to smile more at photos they have already seen before than those that are unfamiliar (Lewis and Brooks-Gunn, 1981). This is an example of the mere exposure effect. Zajonc (1968, 2001) argued that when we first encounter a stimulus, which can be anything from nonsense words to people's faces, we feel slightly uncomfortable. It is reasonable that we react this way because new and unfamiliar objects (and people) might cause us danger. Again, this makes evolutionary sense. To ensure survival, it is important to avoid things that may cause us danger.

However, as people are repeatedly exposed to a stimulus, it becomes more familiar. Further, if the stimulus has caused no harm, then feelings of uncertainty will dissipate and liking will increase. For example, Zajonc (1968, 1980) found that people were more likely to say that familiar nonsense words (ones they had been exposed to earlier in the experiment) meant something positive. Harmon-Jones and Allen (2001) found that people smiled more when they saw familiar faces rather than unfamiliar faces. In the Festinger et al. (1950) study, people were

FIGURE 7.2 Familiarity increases the likelihood of attraction These neighbours are more likely to form friendships with one another than with people who do not live so close to them. This is called the proximity/propinquity effect.

© ROB/FOTOLIA.COM

more likely to see people who were either close (on the same floor) or *functionally close* (near mailboxes and stairs) in the building. Thus, they became more familiar over time and from this familiarity, liking increased and friendships and relationships grew.

Time to reflect If you have ever lived in student accommodation, who did you consider to be your closest friends? Are there any patterns (e.g., proximity, familiarity and so on) similar to those observed in social psychological research?

The effect of repeated exposure on liking was also demonstrated in a study by Moreland and Beach (1992), set in the context of a US college course. In the study, one experimental assistant, posing as a student, attended the course 15 times, one attended 10 times, one attended 5 times and one did not attend at all. None of the assistants ever interacted with the students. At the end of the course, students in all the classes were shown photographs of all four individuals and were asked to indicate how much they liked each one. As can be seen in Figure 7.3, the more times an assistant attended the class, the more the students were attracted to them. Strikingly, without even interacting with a person, simply seeing them more often makes them more attractive to us.

Familiarity works on other interesting levels too. For example, we often associate names with positive experiences and other names with negative experiences. We may have met a Bob we really liked, or an Adam we did not like at all. A kind of stereotype emerges if we associate a particular name with positive attributes and this stereotype influences our future judgements about others who share the name (Macrae, Mitchell and Pendry, 2002). Sometimes, stereotypes about a name become shared, so that many people will associate a certain name with particular traits (Mehrabian and Piercy, 1993). Perhaps this is one good reason why most parents do not call their newborn baby boy Adolf or Osama, but at least in some parts of the world, Jesus is a relatively popular name. More generally, children's names tend to follow trends. For example, in 2011 the top three names for British newborn girls were Amelia, Olivia and Lily, and for boys, Harry, Oliver and Jack (ONS, 2011). Contrast these names to those that were most popular in 1904 for girls (Mary, Florence, Doris), and for boys (William, John, George). One reason for such trends is that familiar names from the media, sport and other areas are liked more and so more parents choose these names for their own children.

Proximity to others also increases the anticipation that we will interact with them in future. With this anticipation of future interaction, liking also increases (Berscheid, Graziano, Monson and Dermer, 1976; Darley and Berscheid, 1967). For example, Darley and Berscheid (1967) gave female students some vague information about two other women, one of whom the participant was supposed to

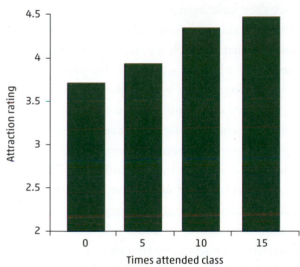

FIGURE 7.3 Repeated exposure effect The more times an assistant attended a class, the more they were liked by the course students.
Source: Data from Moreland and Beach, 1992

interact with immediately afterwards. When asked to rate how much they liked each woman, participants rated the woman they were supposed to interact with as more likeable. It is argued that this phenomenon helps people form positive relationships. If anticipating interaction with another person increases liking for them, then this *anticipatory liking* will increase the chance of the relationship's success (Klein and Kunda, 1992; Knight and Vallacher, 1981). This makes adaptive sense for us too. An old saying goes that 'you can choose your friends but not your family' – thankfully, the effect of anticipatory liking means that we are adapted to like those with whom we have regular contact. Thus, while we cannot necessarily choose our family, we are more or less 'programmed' to like them because we expect to see and interact with them often.

The effect of mere exposure can even occur outside the perceiver's awareness. For example, repeated exposure to subliminal stimuli (see Chapter 6) increases liking for the stimuli, which even generalizes to other similar stimuli (Monahan, Murphy and Zajonc, 2000). Sometimes, mere exposure has an even stronger effect on liking when people are not aware they have been exposed to a stimulus (Bornstein and D'Agostino, 1992). You may be able to remember a time when you 'just liked' or 'just didn't like' someone you met. In such a case, you may have been unaware that you already knew someone who was similar to this person – your judgements of the 'new' person were clouded by your exposure to the other person. Zajonc (1980) argued that, in such a case, emotions are often more instant than thinking. So your 'gut' reaction to a person, while being a result of some kind of exposure, is preceded by a strong emotional response. Again, this reaction has adaptive functions. We need to be aware when a new stimulus may cause us danger. On the other hand, an automatic negative evaluation of a person may explain the way that people occasionally react strongly and negatively to people who seem unfamiliar in terms of their skin colour or some other distinguishing feature. Such strong immediate reactions can potentially be a source of prejudice.

Thus, proximity and familiarity do not always lead to liking and attraction. For example, you can probably imagine that if a person lives close to an annoying neighbour with a dog that barks in the middle of the night, liking is more likely to *decrease* with proximity and familiarity. In general, when a person's initial reaction to a stimulus is negative, repeated exposure will have the opposite effect than when the initial reaction was positive and liking will decrease (Swap, 1977). Proximity can also sometimes lead to hostility. For example, many assaults and murders occur among close others. Domestic violence is a significant problem in the UK and in many other countries. An old saying goes that 'familiarity breeds contempt', and in some key respects this is true, with significant consequences. More often, however, proximity is associated with liking rather than disliking. We tend to associate and form close relationships with people we see on a regular basis, such as workmates, classmates and people who live in the same neighbourhood.

Some modern relationships are, of course, not dependant on physical proximity. Many of you will use social networking sites like Facebook or Google+ to continue friendships with people who have moved away, or to forge new friendships with people you have only briefly, or have never met in person. Some of you may have used dating websites like www.eharmony.co.uk or www.match.com to meet prospective romantic partners. Many of you will keep in touch via email and Skype. In such cases, people can be thousands of miles apart and yet still be attracted to one another (Chan and Cheng, 2004). They may see each other frequently, infrequently or never, and yet still be friends or develop long-lasting romantic relationships. People who meet in cyberspace may also meet in 'real life' or may never meet at all and yet a social bond can be very strong.

Computer-mediated communication and other electronic means of communication are, however, limited in some respects. For example, as we discussed in Chapter 5, people lack many of the social cues that are typical in face-to-face conversations (e.g., Bargh and McKenna, 2004; Tanis and Postmes, 2003; Whitty and Gavin, 2001). The absence of such social cues also provides scope for dishonesty and people may not, in fact, be all they seem (e.g., Whitty and Joinson, 2008). People can conceal aspects of their identity they do not like and instead enhance those features of themselves (their looks and personality) that they think will be appealing to others (see also Chapter 2 where we discuss the phenomenon of narcissism). Also, some findings suggest that people find it difficult to form friendships in cyberspace and increased time spent on the internet is associated with feelings of depression and loneliness (Kraut, Patterson, Lundmark et al., 1998). However, on the positive side, the growth of the internet allows people to communicate with others who they would not otherwise have had the opportunity to meet. People with similar interests can more easily find each other than once was the case, and some findings suggest that people do form lasting friendships with people they meet on the internet (e.g., Bargh, McKenna and Fitzsimons, 2002; McKenna and Bargh, 2000). People also tend to like people they first met on the internet more than those they have met in real life (McKenna, Green and Gleason, 2002). Crucially, electronic communication and forms of interaction such as internet dating are easy and inexpensive, and people are increasingly technologically savvy, so these new means of communication do not necessarily seem daunting.

Questions to consider Reread question 2 at the start of the chapter. How is Kay and Leigh's relationship, formed and maintained over the internet, different from Ewan and Jai's 'normal' relationship, which came about through everyday interaction? List the similarities and differences. Based on what you have read so far, which relationship has a greater chance of success?

Exploring further The reality film *Catfish* depicts the relationship between photographer Nev Schulman and a young girl called Abby who contacts him to ask permission to paint one of his photographs. As their online relationship unfolds via Facebook, Nev becomes involved with Abby's older sister Megan. However, as time goes on, it becomes clear that Abby and Megan are not all they seem to be. Nev goes to Michigan to meet Megan, Abby and their family and it is quite a surprise what he finds there. If you get a chance, watch *Catfish* and think about what questions it raises about the development and maintenance of relationships in the digital age.

Physiological arousal

Another situational factor that influences attraction is physiological arousal, which can lead to a process called **excitation transfer**. This occurs when the arousal caused by one stimulus is added to the arousal of another stimulus and the overall arousal felt is attributed incorrectly to the second stimulus. This phenomenon was demonstrated in a classic study by Dutton and Aron (1974). In this study, male participants completed a questionnaire and were then asked to cross either a shaky or stable bridge to pass the questionnaire to the experimenter (who was either male or female). The dependent variable in this study was whether the participants called the experimenter with any further queries about the study. While the participants were generally unlikely to call the male experimenter, the shakiness or stability of the bridge significantly influenced the likelihood that they would call the female experimenter (see Figure 7.4). Specifically, the participants were much more likely to call a female experimenter if they had crossed the shaky bridge than if they crossed the stable bridge. It was argued that the arousal felt by the participants who crossed the shaky bridge was transferred to the female experimenter, to whom the participants then felt more attracted. Several other studies have demonstrated the misattribution of other types of arousal for attraction (e.g., Allen, Kenrick, Linder and McCall, 1989; White, Fishbein and Rutsein, 1981; Zillman, 1972).

Excitation transfer A phenomenon that occurs when the arousal from one stimulus is added to the arousal of a second stimulus. The overall arousal is misattributed to the second stimulus.

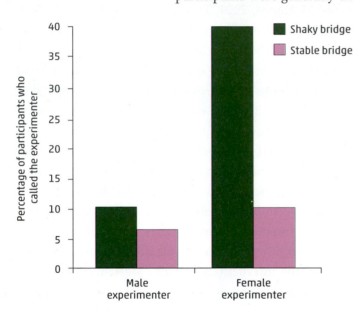

FIGURE 7.4 Excitation transfer Male participants were more attracted to a female experimenter when they had been put in the arousing situation of being asked to cross a shaky bridge.
Source: Data from Dutton and Aron, 1974, Study 1

Psychological determinants of attraction

Physical determinants of attraction are very powerful. However, in social psychology it is rare that one or two factors explain the whole picture. In this case, one's attraction to another person cannot solely be explained by their physical attractiveness, otherwise everyone would want to have relationships with the most attractive people and many would be left alone. Also, proximity alone cannot explain attraction, otherwise everyone would be best friends with their neighbours, which, of course, is not always the case. TV programmes such as *Neighbours from Hell* will certainly attest to this. Typically, a combination of factors is important in determining who is attracted to whom. This is where psychological factors also become important. First, we will consider how the basic human need to affiliate with others influences our attraction to others.

Need to affiliate

Need to affiliate The motive to seek and maintain relationships with others.

Psychologists argue that a desire to seek and maintain interpersonal relationships with others – that is, the **need to affiliate** – is as fundamental to our psychological wellbeing as food and water are to our physical wellbeing (Baumeister and Leary,

1995). Essentially, affiliation keeps us alive. Some evidence suggests that people respond to facial cues of satisfaction and dissatisfaction in others (Hassin and Trope, 2000) and even that we process faces and facial information differently from less biologically important stimuli (Ro, Russell and Lavie, 2001). Thus, we process others' reactions to us and even show a preference at an early age for faces over other stimuli (e.g., Valenza, Simion, Cassia and Umiltaa, 1996). Our attraction to others is driven by a psychological need to be involved in social relationships.

Of course, people differ in their need to affiliate. Like many other social psychological constructs, there are broad variations in the extent to which people seek out human contact. Some people are predisposed to want a higher level of affiliation than others (e.g., Craig, Koestner and Zuroff, 1994). For example, some people seek many relationships, whereas others would prefer to be alone for much of the time. There are also situational factors that influence the extent to which people seek relationships with others. For example, making people aware of the inevitability of their own death leads them to want to be around others more (Wisman and Koole, 2003). There is also a common wisdom that people like to be around others in times of trouble, especially when they are anxious or frightened. In a classic study, Schachter (1959) demonstrated that in a situation where experimental participants were expecting to be given electric shocks, the participants wanted to be around others who were also facing the situation rather than being alone. It is possible to consider examples of this phenomenon in everyday life. For example, people come together during major disasters. Recall the 33 trapped Chilean miners in August 2010 and the rallying of their families and the community to maintain the physical and psychological wellbeing of the men. Families also rally together after the passing of a loved one. One reason they do this is because being around others helps people to understand their feelings and compare them with people who are sharing the same experiences and feelings. Working from social comparison theory, Schachter argued that comparing one's feelings with those of others reduces anxiety and makes a person less fearful of events because their feelings are shared. There is often safety in numbers.

Therefore, affiliation satisfies some fundamental psychological needs. However, if people's need to affiliate is not satisfied, this can result in negative consequences, such as feelings of rejection, sadness and anger (Williams et al., 2000; see also the discussion of social ostracism in Chapter 8). At a more extreme level, an unsatisfied need to affiliate can result in less effective cognitive functioning (Baumeister, Twenge and Nuss, 2002). Studies of social deprivation, which we discuss later, allow us to better understand some of the consequences of an unfulfilled need for affiliation.

Try it yourself Below is a scale used to measure need for affiliation. It measures an individual's desire to spend time with others, a lack of desire to spend time with others, a desire to complete tasks alone and a desire to work with others to complete tasks. Have a go at doing the scale yourself. Read each statement and rate whether you strongly agree (SA), agree (A), disagree (D) or strongly disagree (SD) with each. Calculate your total score for need for affiliation by adding all the scores together. An average score is typically somewhere around 32.

	SA	A	D	SD
I like to go to places and settings with lots of people.	1	2	3	4
I would never want to live completely on my own.	1	2	3	4
In my leisure time, I prefer to do things together with others.	1	2	3	4
I cannot stand being alone.	1	2	3	4
I prefer to go my own way alone.	1	2	3	4
I really prefer to stay as short a time as possible at occasions where there are lots of people.	1	2	3	4
When on vacation, I avoid contact with other vacationers as much as possible.	1	2	3	4
It is not my thing to undertake something with a group of people.	1	2	3	4
It sounds awful to have a job in which you are alone.	1	2	3	4
I find it stressful to have people around me constantly.	1	2	3	4
I like to talk to others.	1	2	3	4
Even when I am in a relationship, I still have a strong need to be alone.	1	2	3	4
The ideal way to spend my leisure time is to do something on my own.	1	2	3	4
I like to be alone.	1	2	3	4
I love teamwork.	1	2	3	4
I don't like to undertake something totally on my own.	1	2	3	4

Source: Buunk, Zurriaga, Peiro et al., 2005

Emotions

Affect Emotional state consisting of feelings and moods.

Attraction to others is also influenced by **affect,** or emotions. Positive feelings lead people to evaluate others positively, and negative affect is more likely to lead to negative evaluations (Byrne, 1997). This effect can work very simply. For example, imagine if you met someone for the first time and that person complimented you on your new bag. You are much more likely to form a positive impression (and be attracted to) that person than another who said they thought your bag was hideous. Research suggests that we like people who make us feel good (e.g., Shapiro, Baumeister and Kessler, 1991). This effect can be explicit, as in the above example, or it can work in a less obvious way. Specifically, some research suggests that simply being around someone when something good happens to us can make us more attracted to that person (e.g., Olson and Fazio, 2001). Through a process like classical conditioning, we associate the positive feeling with the person who is present, which makes us like them more even though they have nothing to do with it. Perhaps you fondly remember people you met on holiday or at a music festival. Maybe the positive emotions you experienced at these events are somewhat responsible for the positive feelings you experience now. We will discuss this effect in more detail when we discuss the theories of attraction later in the chapter.

Similarity of attitudes, interests and values

Research suggests that people find others more attractive when they are similar to themselves in ways other than their level of physical attractiveness. In particular, one of the most important psychological determinants of attraction is similarity of attitudes, interests and values. Sir Francis Galton ([1870]1952) provided the first empirical evidence of this. He obtained correlational data from married couples, which indicated that the wives' and husbands' attitudes were quite similar. Additional findings suggest that these similarities are greater than would occur by chance (Hunt, 1935). Further, Newcomb (1956, 1961) asked a sample of male US college students to complete a series of questionnaires about their attitudes and values, in exchange for free accommodation. The students completed one set of questionnaires prior to their arrival at university and then throughout the year. They were also asked to rate the attractiveness of their fellow students. Newcomb found that early on in the year, proximity was the key predictor of attraction. Echoing Festinger et al.'s (1950) study, students tended to like their classmates who lived closest to them. However, after the initial settling-in period and as the academic year progressed, attraction was more closely related to similarity of attitudes and values, as measured before the students met each other (see also Gaunt, 2006; Lee and Bond, 1998; Luo and Klohnen, 2005).

The importance of attitude similarity was further reinforced by Byrne (1971), who argued that attraction towards a person is directly – and linearly – related to the proportion of attitudes that one shares with that person. This 'law of attraction' (Clore, 1976; Clore and Byrne, 1974) also works to reinforce existing attraction, such that the things people do can make them even more attractive. For example, imagine you have a friend you like because you share similar values and interests. If you then find out that your friend loves a particular music group (they are your absolute favourite group), you will probably find your friend even more attractive. People tend to match themselves with others who share interests such as these, as well as leisure activities (Sprecher, 1998). Of course, it is also the case that we often choose to be around people who have similar interests to ourselves in our basic everyday choices. For example, everyone in your class chose to study social psychology, so you all have some interests in common even before you begin to interact (see Figure 7.5). Thus, the effects of similarity can work in quite a subtle way – people seek out situations where they will be able to interact with similar others. However, even given these subtle effects, a significant body of research points to the importance of attitude similarity in determining attraction (e.g., Byrne, 1997; Byrne and Nelson, 1965; Condon and Crano, 1988; Koestner and Aube, 1995; Moreland and Zajonc, 1982).

Similarity may be important for a number of reasons. First, some theorists argue that similarity helps people find balance in relationships. According to **balance theory** (Heider, 1958a; Newcomb, 1961), people compare their attitudes with those of others and if they are similar in some key respect, then balance is achieved. Balance enhances positive feelings, which makes people attracted to each other. Attitude dissimilarity, on the other hand, causes imbalance. Such imbalance produces negative feelings and makes attraction less likely. In such a case, people are more likely to be indifferent to one another. In the first place, however, attitude similarity needs to mean something. Why does it matter that others' attitudes are similar to our own? The answer is perhaps social comparison (Festinger, 1954; see also Chapter 2). One way that people evaluate the validity of their own attitudes and beliefs is by comparing them to others' attitudes and beliefs. Finding out that other people share our beliefs means that the beliefs must have some basis, and this

© CORBIS

FIGURE 7.5 Attitude similarity and attraction Students of psychology all have something in common – an interest in psychology – and research findings have shown that attitude similarity increases attraction.

Balance theory People sharing similar attitudes are likely to reach balance – a positive emotional state. Attitude dissimilarity can lead to negative emotions, a need to restore the balance, or indifference between individuals.

makes us feel good. Of course, another reason for the importance of similarity, like proximity and familiarity, may be that, from an evolutionary perspective, it is adaptive to like similar others. Dissimilar others may present a danger to survival.

Exploring further The research we have discussed with respect to balance theory seems a bit old. What is new (if anything) for balance theory? Use this as a search term on Google Scholar to find new papers related to this theory from the 1950s. Write down one novel finding that has emerged in the past 10 years. Note that you may need to narrow the search by including additional search terms such as 'relationships'.

People who are similar in personality and interpersonal skills are also more likely to be attracted to one another (Sprecher, 1998; Stevens, Owens and Schaefer, 1990). For example, in a study of gay male relationships, Boyden, Carroll and Maier (1984) found that men sought men with similar personalities. Specifically, men who scored high on masculinity desired other men with masculine traits. On the other hand, men who scored high on femininity sought other men with more feminine traits. The same preference for similar personality traits applies in heterosexual romantic relationships and friendships (Acitelli, Kenny and Weiner, 2001). Even in children as young as three years old, similarity (e.g., on dimensions such as food preferences and toy preferences) predicts liking (Fawcett and Markson, 2010). Also, Sprecher (1998) found that personality factors such as warmth and kindness were more important to people in relationships than interests, values and attitudes.

Further, people who have a similar communication style are more compatible (Burleson and Samter, 1996), whereas those who have different interpersonal styles are less likely to have successful relationships (Burleson, 1994). Specifically, some people are more willing to disclose information about themselves than other people. This willingness – called **self-disclosure** – is an important factor in determining long-term relationship success. People tend to like people more who reveal more about themselves and their thoughts (Collins and Miller, 1994). Also, people tend to reveal more to the people they like and trust. Self-disclosure is important for building trust in a relationship and making people feel safe (Cvetkovich and Löfstedt, 1999). Self-disclosure also encourages the other person in the relationship to disclose information, which builds further trust and rapport (Joinson and Paine, 2007; Reis and Shaver, 1988). Mutual disclosure (or disclosure reciprocity) increases attraction and can deepen intimacy in an existing relationship (Baumeister and Bratslavsky, 1999). A relationship with mutual self-disclosure tends to be happy, satisfied and enduring (Sprecher, 1987).

People from similar backgrounds are also more likely to be attracted to one another (Watson, Klohnen, Casillas et al., 2004). In the study by Newcomb (1961) described earlier, men who were from similar demographic backgrounds (e.g., they were both from a rural area) were more likely to be friends. Also, findings show that people desire people of a similar level of attractiveness, and who are similar in other features such as wealth (Buston and Emlen, 2003). This basic effect of similarity is quite far-reaching. Findings in one study even showed that people were more attracted to others who had similar names to themselves, whose arbitrary experimental code numbers resembled their own birthday numbers, and whose surnames

Self-disclosure Willingness to share information about oneself and one's feelings with another person.

shared letters with their own surnames (Jones, Pelham, Carvallo and Mirenberg, 2004). Going back to what we said earlier about the matching hypothesis, it really does seem to be the case that people like others who are similar to themselves on some dimension, and not just the dimension of physical attractiveness.

Complementarity The idea that people seek out traits in potential relationship partners that complement, or add what is missing, to their own.

But, what about the popular saying 'opposites attract'? This is commonly portrayed in movies and on TV when seemingly polar opposites who think and behave completely differently pair off and walk away into the sunset. Does this really happen? Indeed, there are some interpersonal contexts in which **complementarity** leads to liking (e.g., Sadler and Woody, 2003). For example, in one study, Amodio and Showers (2005) found that when people wanted a stable, long-lasting relationship, similarity was important and people sought partners who were similar to themselves in key respects. However, when people were looking for a 'fling', dissimilarity was more important. Perhaps the adventure of being with someone completely different to oneself provides excitement in a short-term, low commitment relationship. However, on the whole, social psychological research suggests that rather than 'opposites attract', 'birds of a feather flock together'. When considering attitudes, values, intellect, ability and many minor preferences, similarity is a key predictor of attraction (Byrne, 1971). Of course, we may think of pairs who are 'opposites' in one important respect, but in general, these pairings are likely to be similar in many other fundamental respects. Similarity increases liking, and dissimilarity in attitudes, interests and preferences can lead to disliking and avoidance (Chen and Kenrick, 2002; Norton, Frost and Ariely, 2007; Singh and Ho, 2000; Tan and Singh, 1995). In particular, if people are dissimilar on key important attitudes and moral convictions, avoidance may be even stronger. You can probably think of many examples such as dislike for opposing political parties (Rosenbaum, 1986) or even people from different religious or ethnic backgrounds (Biernat, Vescio and Green, 1996).

Like judgements of attractiveness, the effect of similarity on liking seems to be consistent across cultures. For example, Brewer (1968) interviewed an extensive sample of people from African tribal groups and found that perceived similarity was a strong determinant of attraction between tribes. People tended to avoid contact with other tribes whose attitudes were thought to be different, but when attitudes were perceived to be similar, it was possible to have close contact with the other tribe.

Mutual liking

A person's attraction to another person is often determined by reciprocity. Does the other person like them too? This effect of *mutual liking* is also called the reciprocity principle. In general, we like people who like us and dislike people who dislike us. Dittes and Kelley (1956) demonstrated this effect in a now classic study. The researchers put student participants into small discussion groups and told them that their fellow group members either liked or disliked them. The students who thought that they were liked were more attracted to their group. Mutual liking can even overcome some important differences. In the previous section we discussed how

important similarity, especially similarity of attitudes, is in determining attraction. However, Gold, Ryckman and Mosley (1984) found that when a young woman expressed interest in male participants (by use of nonverbal cues such as attentive listening), she was liked more than when she expressed no interest – even when the male participants knew that she disagreed with them on central issues. The perception that a person likes us is therefore a significant determinant of our liking for them (Berscheid and Walster, 1987; Kenny and Nasby, 1980; Montoya and Insko, 2008). Discovering that someone likes you may also awaken romantic feelings that might not ordinarily have been apparent (Berscheid and Walster, 1987). Again, this is another common feature in popular films. Best friends, having difficulties in their current relationships, suddenly realize that they have loved each other all along. The mutual liking they had for each other awakened their underlying attraction.

However, it is not all good news. Eastwick, Finkel, Mochon and Ariely (2007) used a speed dating paradigm to study mutual liking. They found that people who were selective in their liking, that is, they did not like everyone, generally experienced more reciprocal liking. However, those who were unselective, that is, they wanted to date everyone, were perceived as less desirable partners. Therefore, the belief that a discerning person thinks that one is special can facilitate liking, but a less discerning person inhibits liking. This suggests that who likes us might be as important as whether we are liked at all. You can probably remember a time when someone liked you and you simply did not like them back. Stambush and Mattingly (2010) showed that people's self-esteem, mood and ratings of their own attractiveness can actually drop if they think that an unattractive person expressed interest in them. This effect was particularly marked for female participants. This reflects the complexity of mutual liking, and at this point, it is good to reflect back upon the 'beauty is good' stereotype we discussed earlier (Dion et al., 1972). It seems that attraction is influenced even by being liked by attractive others rather than those we find less appealing.

Culture

We have mentioned culture throughout this discussion and many of the findings discussed suggest that several aspects of attraction – in particular what is deemed physically attractive – are universal. In other words, there seems to be little variation across cultures in terms of what constitutes an attractive face. Also, there is a large set of personality traits that are, perhaps unsurprisingly, seen as universally attractive, such as friendliness, happiness and likeability (Wheeler and Kim, 1997).

However, this is not to say that culture is irrelevant in determining who is attracted to whom. This is far from the truth. For example, Liu, Campbell and Condie (1995) found that heterosexuals of four different ethnic groups in the USA (African, Asian, Latino and European) preferred to date within their own group, despite all groups rating European Americans as either more attractive or of higher status than members of their own group. Cultural similarity is therefore important. Further, it is possible that other social factors, such as the approval of one's family and friends, help determine who people are most attracted to. It is perhaps not surprising that even in multicultural societies, people tend to form romantic relationships more with people from their own culture. Preference for one's own culture when finding friends and partners tends to occur in the closest realms of society.

Theories of attraction

Now we know something about the physical and psychological factors that determine attraction, we move on to theories of interpersonal attraction that attempt to link these factors together. There are two key theories of attraction. The first – social exchange theory – is based on an economic approach to human behaviour, arguing that relationship satisfaction depends on the 'costs' and 'rewards' of the relationship. The second – equity theory – follows a similar line of logic, arguing that relationship satisfaction depends on the extent to which the outcomes that people receive from a relationship are proportional to their contributions. The key difference between the two is that social exchange theory argues that in relationships, people are after the most rewards for the least cost they have to put in. On the other hand, equity theory posits that people are not simply after rewards with little cost – they also need equity and fairness in relationships. We review these theories in turn. We also discuss less prominent theories of attraction arguing that attraction is based on reinforcement.

Social exchange theory

Generally speaking, it is rewarding to be in a relationship. For example, it is rewarding when someone validates our attitudes or shares our values. Also, it is nice to be liked by an attractive person who we like too. It follows that the more social rewards a person offers, the more we will be attracted to that person. On the other hand, if we perceive the *costs* as outweighing the benefits of being in a relationship with a person, then we will be less attracted to that person. In a way, this is like drawing up a mental 'pros and cons' list, which people often do when they make important life decisions. If the 'pros' outweigh the 'cons', the likelihood is that the relationship will be a success. If the opposite is the case, the relationship is less likely to succeed. You may remember friendships that were 'more give than take'. This can be unsatisfying and jeopardize the chances of the relationship's success.

The basic idea that relationships work like economic exchange, much like a marketplace, has been expanded by psychologists and sociologists to form complex theories of social exchange that mainly deal with close relationships such as romantic relationships (e.g., Homans, 1961; Kelley and Thibaut, 1978; Thibaut and Kelley, 1959). **Social exchange theory** posits that people's evaluation of such a relationship depends on their perception of:

1 the rewards they gain from the relationship
2 the costs they incur from the relationship
3 the relationship they deserve and the likelihood that they could have a better relationship with another person.

Social exchange theory
How we feel about our relationships depends on our perception of the rewards we gain from the relationship and costs we incur. We also evaluate whether or not we could have a 'better' relationship.

FIGURE 7.6 Social exchange theory Social exchange theory argues that people's evaluation of their relationships depends on the perception of what they 'get' from the relationship, their perception of what they 'give' and their perception of the relationship as 'worthy' of them, that is, could they get someone better?

Comparison level People's expectations about the level of costs and rewards based on previous relationships.

Comparison level for alternatives People's expectations about the costs and benefits they might receive if they were in a different relationship.

People are sensitive to the rewards and costs of their relationship. The relationship 'marketplace' is all about maximizing profits and minimizing losses, so we want to interact with people who offer the best profit. That is, people evaluate their relationship and judge whether or not this is the best they could have. Are they getting adequate reward for what they put in? Is there something better to compare it to? However, there is another person in the relationship, so there is an *exchange* of rewards and costs, as the name of the theory suggests. The other person in the relationship is also making their own cost–reward analysis of the relationship, which may be similar to – or completely different than – their partner's. Thus, social exchange theory proposes that the outcomes for the two people in the relationship are jointly dependent on their actions. This kind of exchange occurs constantly in relationships and sometimes people do not even realize that social exchanges are being made. For example, we might put up with a partner's bad habits (e.g., talking with their mouth full of food, leaving worn socks around the house – most definitely costs) because they are kind and loving (a benefit). Likewise, our partners may put up with our bad habits and awkward friends (costs) because we are incredibly good-looking, have a lot of money and have a good sense of humour (benefits). Thus, there are many different types of costs and rewards and many levels on which exchanges are made (Foa and Foa, 1975). Many are trivial and short-lived but some are exchanges that have long-term, important consequences. Whatever the exchange, we can think of the outcome of a relationship as being determined by a mathematical formula: outcomes = rewards – costs.

Relationship satisfaction also depends on one's **comparison level**. Specifically, over the years, people have plenty of relationships with others, so they have come to expect certain costs and benefits of being in a relationship. From these expectations, people have an idea of what their future relationships will be like (Kelley and Thibaut, 1978; Thibaut and Kelley, 1959). Some people expect more rewards than costs from relationships, and if a relationship fails to meet their expected high standards, they will be disappointed. On the other hand, some people expect fewer rewards and more costs and they may be pleased with less rewarding relationship because at least it is what they expect.

It is important to note that people may also have a **comparison level for alternatives**. In other words, they may have the perception that they could be in a better relationship than the one they are currently in. This concern with alternatives – or the idea that there are indeed 'plenty of fish in the sea' – may mean that people leave relationships because they feel there is something better out there. On the other hand, people who expect that the alternatives could be worse than they already have, that is, they have a low comparison level for alternatives, may be more likely to stay in a costly relationship (Simpson, 1987). For such people, it may be a case of 'better the devil you know'. It is also important to consider that what is a cost for one person may not seem so costly to another. Further, what is seen as rewarding for one person may not be so rewarding to others. Social exchange theory therefore allows for quite a bit of variation in relationships.

Social exchange theory has gained much support in social psychological research. For example, Le and Agnew (2003) conducted a meta-analysis of over 50 studies demonstrating that relationship breakdown is strongly related to a lack of commitment. Over time, relationship partners become interdependent (Rusbult and van Lange, 2003), fulfilling the needs of each other (Le and Agnew, 2003). Rewards, costs and comparison levels are crucial in determining relationship satisfaction and commitment (Rusbult, Martz and Agnew, 1998).

Try it yourself Choose two of your past relationships – either friendships or romantic relationships – that you no longer have. Make a list of the rewards you gained from the relationship. Make another list of the costs and sacrifices you had to make as part of the relationship. Did the costs outweigh the benefits? Or did you get a sense that you overbenefited from the relationship? In any case, how did you feel about the situation you were in? Are there other reasons why these relationships are no longer a part of your life?

Now take a few minutes to think of a current relationship. How does your relationship fare on the following scale?

+3	I am getting a much better deal
+2	I am getting a moderately better deal
+1	I am getting a slightly better deal
0	We are both getting an equally good or bad deal
−1	They are getting a slightly better deal
−2	They are getting a moderately better deal
−3	They are getting a much better deal

This is a scale often used to measure relationship equity, which you will read about in the next section.

Equity theory

Equity theory The theory that people are most satisfied with relationships in which the cost-reward ratio is approximately the same for both parties.

Perhaps social exchange theory does not quite capture an essential factor in determining relationship success – the notion of equity or fairness. **Equity theory** posits that people are not simply after the most rewards and the least costs. They also need equity and fairness. In other words, the cost–reward 'payoff' should be approximately the same for both parties in the relationship (Adams, 1965; Hatfield, Walster and Berscheid, 1978). In a similar way to social exchange, equity can be seen as a mathematical formula (Adams, 1965). Equity exists when: (A's rewards – costs) ÷ A's inputs = (B's rewards – costs) ÷ B's inputs. When a relationship is equitable, the party's outcomes (rewards – costs) are roughly equal to the other person's. In this respect, distributive justice (Homans, 1961) has been reached and outcomes are fair, based on what both parties have put in and what they have got out.

According to equity theory, people are happiest in equal relationships. Equitable relationships are also the most stable. On the other hand, some relationships suffer an imbalance in the cost–reward ratio for each party. One person may take more than they give; the other may give more than they take. This can lead to tension and dissatisfaction. For example, Schafer and Keith (1980) surveyed a sample of married couples across a wide age range, taking note of those who felt that their relationships were unfair (e.g., one spouse did not contribute enough to the cleaning or cooking). Findings revealed that people who perceived their relationships to be inequitable felt more unhappy and distressed.

Underbenefited partners will seek to restore balance to the relationship so that they no longer feel like the relationship is too costly. Alternatively, they may attempt to restructure their perceptions of their own costs and rewards so that the ratios do not feel inequitable. If a balance cannot be reached, the relationship is less likely to succeed (Adams, 1965). However, perhaps surprisingly, overbenefited partners also typically seek to restore equity. Why do they do this? Social exchange theory is less able to describe why low-cost, high-gain partners also attempt to rebalance inequitable relationships. Instead, theorists explain this effect as a result of a powerful social norm prioritizing equity. Even the most profitable partners will eventually come to feel guilty for taking too much away from a relationship. Equity is a pervasive social norm and deviations from such norms, where situations are unfair, make everyone feel uncomfortable. Having said this, research shows that restoring equity is more of a concern for partners who benefit less from relationships (Buunk and Schaufeli, 1999; Sprecher, 2001; Sprecher and Schwartz, 1994; van Yperen and Buunk, 1990). Also, people may not always prefer an equity norm (Deutsch, 1975). Further, men prefer an equity norm more than women. Instead, women tend to prefer an *equality* norm, where everyone receives the same no matter what (Major and Adams, 1983; Major and Deaux, 1982), to an equity norm where outcomes are equal based on costs. It is important to note that people do not go about their daily business calculating what they have done for others and what they have received in return (Clark, 1986). In most close relationships, people do not always keep score of their costs and rewards – this would be time-consuming and perhaps a bit sad – and, indeed, many relationships succeed with one selfless partner (Buunk and van Yperen, 1991). However, there is generally a strong norm of equity in close relationships. Another key norm in relationships is the **norm of reciprocity** – to receive, we must also give.

Norm of reciprocity In relationships, this is the norm that if people are to take, they must also give.

Question to consider Reread question 3 at the start of the chapter. What is the likelihood of Leila's marriage being a success? What might each party have to do (or concede) to make things work?

Reinforcement and rewards

Other approaches propose that attraction is a result of direct reinforcement. As we mentioned earlier, we sometimes like people who are present when something good happens to us, even though they sometimes have no relation to the reward (Lott and Lott, 1972). In particular, instant reinforcement is powerful. For example, Lott, Aponte, Lott and McGinley (1969) found that children liked a person who they saw after immediately receiving a reward, rather than after a few seconds' delay. In a variation of the reinforcement model, Byrne and Clore's (1970) **reinforcement affect model** posits that people can be liked (or disliked) depending on their association with positive (or negative) feelings. To illustrate this effect, Lewicki (1985) asked an experimenter to be unfriendly to a sample of participants. At the

Reinforcement affect model This model of attraction posits that we like people who are present when we experience positive feelings.

end of the study, participants were asked to hand their responses to one of two experimenters: one who looked like the unfriendly experimenter and one who did not. Overwhelmingly, the participants chose the person who did not resemble the original unfriendly experimenter. In an opposite condition, the experimenter was friendly. In this case, the students chose the person who resembled the experimenter. In a more recent study, Berk and Andersen (2000) asked participants (perceivers) to interact with a naive target who either did or did not appear to resemble the perceiver's own (positively or negatively regarded) significant other. Independent judges rated the positive affect expressed in the targets' behaviours. It was found that the targets expressed more positive affective behaviours when they resembled the perceiver's own positively valued significant other rather than when the significant other was negatively valued. This suggests that the positive feelings of the perceiver transferred to the naive target, suggesting a means by which present relationships may resemble past relationships.

Further, Clore and Byrne (1974) argued that people associate others with features of the environment. If the features are positive, this evokes positive emotions and a positive response (liking) is likely to emerge. However, if the features are negative, this evokes negative emotions and a negative response (disliking) is more likely. This type of effect is sometimes called *liking by association*, or the *reward theory of attraction*.

Other experiments confirm that reinforcement is important in determining liking. For example, Griffitt (1970) asked students to evaluate a person while either sitting in a pleasant, comfortable room or an unpleasant, hot room. As above, people rated others more positively if they were in a pleasant environment (Maslow and Mintz, 1956). One message from these findings is that it is good for relationships to be associated with positive experiences such as romantic candlelit dinners and holidays (Hatfield and Walster, 1981). The findings also help explain why, in general, people are attracted to warm and trustworthy individuals (Fletcher, Simpson, Thomas and Giles, 1999; Wojciszke, Bazinska and Jaworski, 1998). The rewards are rather pleasant.

Love and romantic relationships

Love A grouping of emotions, behaviours and cognitions that a person can experience in intimate relationships.

Thus far, our discussion has been about the factors that influence people's attraction for each other. Much of this is related to *liking*. Although many people believe in 'love at first sight', many would argue that attraction is what immediately draws a person to another, or what makes them like the other person. In this section, we distinguish the process of attraction and liking from that of *loving*. Many would agree that loving someone is quite different to simply liking them. We may not be able to work out exactly how to express it, but we know that **love** is something *more* than liking and is not simply a matter of quality. Social psychologists have taken great strides in understanding what love is, and how close, loving relationships work (e.g., Dion and Dion, 1988). Studying love is difficult. For example, it is not possible to experimentally manipulate love in the laboratory, as it is to manipulate variables such as proximity and good looks. However, through survey and interview methods, social scientists are learning more about love.

So, what is love? Is love really just a lot of liking? Is romantic love just a lot of liking, but with sexual attraction? Unsurprisingly, it is difficult to define love. Love is often seen as an inexplicable and magical thing and something that is difficult for people to articulate. Sometimes love is desperately passionate, giddy and overwhelming and sometimes love just makes us feel warm and contented. What is it? Are there different kinds of love?

Researchers have distinguished liking as being different from loving. In particular, Rubin (1970) developed two questionnaires to measure what he argued to be two different constructs. He asked 198 undergraduate students to complete questions related to what he theorized to be about liking (e.g., 'I feel that _____ is a very stable person', 'I have confidence in _____'s opinions') and others that measured loving (e.g., 'I feel strong feelings of possessiveness towards _____', 'I would do almost anything for _____'). Crucially, Rubin asked participants to complete the scale based on how they felt about their romantic partner and a good friend. The results showed that good friends scored highly on the liking scale, but only romantic partners rated highly on the items related to loving. Also, analyses of different kinds of love, such as familial and romantic love, have distinguished between two distinct types of love that entail a combination of emotions that occur in intimate relationships: passionate and companionate love (Fehr, 1994; Hatfield and Walster, 1981). We focus first on the differences between these two types of love, with a primary focus on romantic relationships because this is what most of the research is about.

Passionate and companionate love

The love that people have for their friends and family members is obviously different from the love that people have for a romantic partner. However, even within romantic relationships, love can appear and feel different. Think of your close friends and you will see examples of people passionately in love and completely absorbed with each other. On the other hand, if you consider many elderly people, such as your grandparents, the passionate, all-consuming love has typically given way to a calmer, more stable and secure kind of love. Although both are referred to as *love*, they are clearly different (Berscheid and Meyers, 1996; Fehr and Russell, 1991; Vohs and Baumeister, 2004). Psychologists call the first type 'passionate love' and the second 'companionate love' (Hatfield, 1987; Hatfield and Sprecher, 1986) (see Figure 7.7).

Passionate love Love characterized by intense emotional and physical feelings for another person.

Passionate love is the type of love that involves intense feelings, uncontrollable thoughts and deep longing for another person. Passionate love often involves physical arousal, a rapid beating heart and shortness of breath among other physiological 'symptoms'. You will be familiar with the notion of love as a 'drug' in songs, or a 'bug' that affects people and makes them do silly things. They are referring to what social psychologists call 'passionate love'. In the presence of the object of affection, a person experiencing passionate love will feel happy and elated if the affection is reciprocated, but sad, desperate and jealous if the feelings are not returned (Fisher, 2004; Hatfield, 1987; Hatfield and Sprecher, 1986; Regan and Berscheid, 1999). Passionate love is the feeling of loving someone but also being 'in love' (Berscheid, 1994). Passionate love is heightened by physiological arousal. For example, physical exercise, watching horror films and going on scary rides increase our romantic responses to people we find attractive (Foster, Witcher, Campbell and Green, 1998). Aron, Fisher, Mashek et al. (2005) have found that passionate love involves a strong biological element. Specifically, being in love engages dopamine-rich areas of the brain that are generally associated with reward. There is also a lot of evidence demonstrating the role of the hormone oxytocin in love and desire (e.g., Carter, 1998; Diamond, 2003, 2004; Gonzaga, Turner, Keltner et al., 2006; Porges, 1998). Also, fMRI studies have shown that viewing pictures of romantic love activates parts of the brain's reward system that coincide with areas rich in oxytocin and vasopressin receptors (Bartels and Zeki, 2004). These overlap with, but are also different to, the regions of the brain that are activated when mothers view pictures of their children. Both types of relationships (romantic and maternal) deactivated regions of the brain associated with negative emotions.

Companionate love Love characterized by a deep caring and affection for another person.

On the other hand, **companionate love** involves deep, secure feelings that are not accompanied by the frenzied, passionate and physical feelings that are associated with passionate love (Hatfield, 1987). Theorists argue that this kind of love is common in relationships that once were passionate, such as marriages that last a long time. The partners may still be in a sexual relationship but without experiencing the level of intensity or 'spark' they once had (Argyle and Henderson, 1985). Even in the closest, most loving relationships, the spark does not necessarily last and some findings support this idea; for example, long-term married couples express affection much less than newlyweds (Hustin and Chorost, 1994). Romantic relationships that last seem to depend more on the secure, stable, loving feelings that people have towards one another rather than the intense feelings experienced during the fiery first stages of a relationship. Findings show that

(a) Passionate love

(b) Companionate love

FIGURE 7.7 Passionate and companionate love Theorists distinguish between (a) passionate love, the all-consuming giddy love that people typically experience at the beginning of relationships, and (b) companionate, or more secure and stable love.

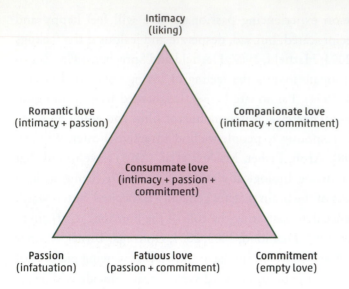

Intimacy
(liking)

Romantic love
(intimacy + passion)

Companionate love
(intimacy + commitment)

Consummate love
(intimacy + passion +
commitment)

Passion
(infatuation)

Fatuous love
(passion + commitment)

Commitment
(empty love)

FIGURE 7.8 Triangular theory of love Sternberg argues that love is a combination of passion, intimacy and commitment and that combinations of each result in different kinds of love.

Source: Sternberg, 1988. Copyright © 1988 by Yale University Press. Reproduced with permission

companionate love activates different areas of the brain (Aron et al., 2005). Also, outside romantic relationships, companionate love is characteristic of non-sexual close friendships. The key characteristic of companionate love is a deep caring and affection for the other person – the kind of love that makes us feel warm, happy and nurtured.

Sternberg (1988) argued for a slightly more complex conceptualization of love based on three key factors: passion, intimacy and commitment, and that the type of love can be mapped onto a triangle of these factors, as in Figure 7.8.

Other research has distinguished even more specifically between several different kinds of love in romantic relationships (Hendrick and Hendrick, 1995). Six love styles were identified by Lee (1973, 1976), who referred to these love styles as 'colours of love' (see Table 7.1). Findings suggest that there are gender differences in who displays the different types of love, with men scoring higher on eros and ludus than women, who were more pragmatic, storgic and manic (Hendrick, Hendrick, Foote and Slapion-Foote, 1984). Findings also suggest that there are cross-cultural differences in attitudes related to love. In particular, the factors of pragma, storge and ludus, which arguably involve social rules and norms, are dependent on cultural influences, whereas the factors of mania, eros and agape, which arguably involve strong personal feelings, are relatively free of cultural influences (Neto, Deschamps, Barros et al., 2000).

TABLE 7.1 The six types of love

Name	Style of love	Characteristics
Eros	Passionate love	Love is all-consuming. Sex is important. The feeling of 'love at first sight' is common
Ludus	Game-playing love	Love is a game. Lovers are more interested in quantity of relationships than quality. Sex is sport. Commitment is a trap. Infidelity is common
Storge	Friendship/companionate love	Love grows from friendship. Commitment is important. Sex is less important. Intimacy without passion
Mania	Possessive love	Love is intense. Lovers are possessive, jealous, anxious and insecure. Sex is reassurance of love
Agape	Selfless love	Generous love. Lovers are unconditionally faithful, loving and caring. Sex is viewed as a gift
Pragma	Logical love	Practical and realistic love. Lovers think rationally and realistically about their partner. Sex is a means of reward and procreation

Source: Based on Hendrick and Hendrick, 1995; Lee, 1973, 1976

Time to reflect Think of the different types of love identified by Hendrick and Hendrick (1995) and Lee (1973, 1976). We know there are gender differences, in that men tend to score higher on ludus and eros than women. Complex cultural influences are also important. Can you think of any explanations why these differences might exist? What might an evolutionary social psychologist infer from these gender differences?

FIGURE 7.9 Arranged marriages Research suggests that while 'love' marriages start off happier than arranged marriages, the love begins to decline after a few years. On the other hand, the love experienced in arranged marriages increases.

Romantic love and culture

As is the case for attraction, some aspects of love are fairly universal. For example, it seems that most cultures have a conception of passionate or romantic love, as indicated by behaviours such as flirting and feelings such as physiological arousal, and the idea that love is a condition for marriage (Jankowiak and Fischer, 1992). However, cultures also differ on this dimension, as can be seen in the example of arranged marriages (see Figure 7.9). In such cases, love is not viewed as a precondition for marriage, instead, love is seen as something that grows once people are married (Dion and Dion, 1993). A study by Gupta and Singh (1982) demonstrates the difference in reported love over time between 'love' marriages and arranged marriages in an Indian sample. The researchers asked 50 couples to complete Rubin's (1970) love scale, where they were asked to answer questions about their partner such as 'I would do anything for _____' (see earlier) and found that respondents who married for love reported decreased love over the years. On the other hand, respondents from arranged marriages reported increased love (see Figure 7.10).

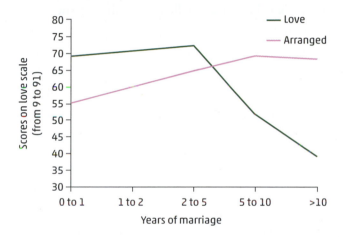

FIGURE 7.10 Reported love over time in arranged and 'love' marriages 'Love' marriages decreased in reported love over the years of marriage. While beginning at a lower level of love, arranged marriages increased in reported love over the years of marriage.

Source: Data from Gupta and Singh, 1982

Divorce rates differ across countries. For example, in August 2011, the USA had the highest divorce rate in the world (4.95 per 1,000 people), with the UK (3.08) and Australia (2.52) not far behind. On the other hand, in China, the divorce rate was only 0.79 per 1,000 people, it was 0.37 in Turkey and 0.15 in Sri Lanka (data from www.nationmaster.com). Some theorists argue that this is due to cultural differences in the focus on personal feelings versus the focus on the more practical aspects of a relationship. It may also relate to individualist versus collectivist perspectives on obligations and duties. Specifically, US samples have been shown to focus on the former, while Asian cultures are generally more focused on the latter (Dion and Dion, 1988; Sprecher and Toro-Morn, 2002) and are less individualistic (Dion and Dion, 1991), which may also be a factor in increasing Western divorce rates.

Love and gender

There is some evidence to suggest that women and men experience passionate love differently. Perhaps surprisingly, men tend to fall in love more quickly than women (Dion and Dion, 1985). Men are also less likely to initiate breakups. On the other hand, women are more likely to focus on emotional rather than physical intimacy and are typically more emotionally invested in a relationship than men (Hendrick and Hendrick, 1995). As we mentioned earlier, women and men also rate the experience of love quite differently, as evidenced by their different love styles. As we saw earlier in the Critical focus box, it seems that women and men even approach the basics of mate selection quite differently. According to popular thinking and some popular writers, men are from Mars and women are from Venus (Gray, 1992), but evidence suggests that this is overexaggerated and cultural differences in perceptions of romantic love are more powerful than gender differences within cultures (Sprecher and Toro-Morn, 2002).

Attachment and bonding

As we discussed earlier, the need for affiliation is a fundamental human requirement for psychological wellbeing. Studies of social deprivation in infants provide some indication of the consequences of an unfulfilled need for affiliation. In a series of controversial studies in the 1950s and 60s, Harlow separated rhesus monkeys from their mothers and placed them in isolation chambers for a period of up to 24 months. Social isolation caused the monkeys both psychological and physiological stress, suggesting that early maternal contact is vital to wellbeing (Harlow, 1958; Harlow and Harlow, 1965). Similar effects occur in humans. For example, Bowlby (1969) observed the behaviours of infants and their mothers. When separated, infants would seek to be reunited with their mothers and would use a variety of behaviours (crying, smiling) to reunite with the mother, or other behaviours (e.g., clinging) to stay close to her. Bowlby argued that these **attachment behaviours** are all indicators of the fundamental need to affiliate. Deprived of affiliation with others, children often become fearful, withdrawn and silent (Bowlby, 1980). Bowlby argued that intimate attachment to others is a necessary means of drawing strength and enjoyment from life. Further, Bowlby argued that attachment behaviours are not confined to child–carer interactions, but continue throughout the life span in different types of relationships. In other words, the nature of attachment in babies and children is similar to the attachments people display in later life with friends, family members and in romantic relationships.

Attachment behaviours The behaviours an infant will exhibit to stay close to, or be reunited with, a primary carer.

Theorists have argued that people's relationship experiences later in life are determined by their experiences with parents or carers during childhood and infancy (e.g., Feeney and Noller, 1990; Hazan and Shaver, 1994; Shaver and Hazan, 1993). That is, good and stable adult relationships are likely to be a consequence of early experiences, specifically with carers (Berscheid, 1994). Relationships between children and carers are important because these typically form the first contact with another person. Babies come into the world and immediately begin interacting with others. Of course, there are differences in the ways that carers interact with their children and differences in infants' own preferences for interaction.

Attachment styles
Expectations that people develop about their relationships, based on relationships with carers as infants and children.

Strange situation Procedure designed to observe attachment relationships between carer and child.

These differences appear to have important implications for relationships with others – family relationships, friendships and romantic relationships alike – later in life. This research focuses on **attachment styles** (Ainsworth, Blehar, Waters and Wall, 1978; Bowlby, 1969, 1973, 1988). People can be classified as exhibiting one of three main attachment styles in their relationships.

To examine attachment styles, Mary Ainsworth (1973, 1979) set up a paradigm known as the **strange situation**. In the strange situation, a child is observed playing for 20 minutes while their carer leaves and re-enters the room. The rationale is that the situation varies in the extent to which it is stressful to the child and the child's different ways of coping can be observed and used as an index of their attachment to their carers. The child experiences the following events:

1 The carer and infant enter the room.
2 The carer and infant are alone. The carer does not participate but the infant explores the room.
3 The stranger enters, talks to the carer, and then approaches the infant. The carer leaves inconspicuously.
4 The carer and child are now separated. The stranger's behaviour is geared to that of the infant.
5 The carer re-enters the room. S/he greets and comforts the infant, then leaves again.
6 The carer and child are therefore separated again. This time, the infant is left alone.
7 The separation episode continues. The stranger enters and gears their behaviour to that of the infant.
8 The carer re-enters the room. S/he greets and picks up the infant. The stranger leaves inconspicuously.

Four aspects of the child's behaviour are observed:

1 The amount of exploration (e.g., playing with new toys) throughout the situation.
2 The child's reactions to the departure of their carer.
3 The stranger anxiety (when the baby is alone with the stranger).
4 The child's reunion behaviour with their carer.

Secure attachment style
Attachment style distinguished by trust, less concern about being left alone and a secure feeling of being worthy and liked.

Using this procedure, results reveal that somewhere between 55–70 per cent of infants (and adults) display a **secure attachment style** (Hazan and Shaver, 1987; Jones and Cunningham, 1996). Beginning in infancy, when placed in the strange situation, securely attached infants play with their carer and are happy to explore the environment. When the carer leaves, the child becomes distressed and is comforted when the carer returns. After the carer returns, the child begins to explore and play again (Ainsworth, 1973, 1979). This secure attachment style is characterized by trust, high self-esteem and a secure feeling of being loved (see Table 7.2). Theorists argue that this attachment style is the basis of secure adult relationships, characterized by commitment and trust. Specifically, during difficult times such as separation or conflict, the underlying trust helps maintain the relationship (Miller and Rempel, 2004). Research also demonstrates that secure attachment leads to satisfying and enduring relationships (Collins and Read, 1990; Feeney and Noller, 1990).

Avoidant attachment style
Attachment style distinguished by low trust and avoidance of relationships.

Anxious/ambivalent attachment style Attachment style distinguished by anxiety and concern that feelings are not reciprocated.

Infants displaying an **avoidant attachment style** show little distress when being separated from a carer and also have little reaction to the carer returning to the room after separation. People exhibiting an avoidant attachment style in adulthood tend to avoid close relationships altogether or become involved in unhappy relationships. They are also less likely to be invested in relationships and are more likely to leave them. They are also likely to have more one night stands and sexual relationships without love (Tidwell, Reis and Shaver, 1996). In general, it appears that avoidant individuals have a less positive perception of others than of themselves.

Finally, in the strange situation, an **anxious/ambivalent** infant will cling closely to the carer. When they leave the room and return, the infant may be indifferent or even hostile towards the carer. In adulthood, this attachment style is characterized by possessiveness, jealousy and a lack of trust. Anxious/ambivalent adults tend to become emotional and angry in conflicts (Cassidy, 2000; Feeney and Noller, 1990). In general, such people seek close relationships but are fearful they will eventually be rejected; that is, they have a positive perception of others but a rather negative view of themselves.

There is some additional research to support the argument that infant–carer attachments are associated with the nature of attachments in adult relationships. For example, Rholes, Simpson and Blakel (1995) studied the relationship between a mother's feelings towards her children and her own attachment style in her adult relationships. It was found that mothers who were avoidant in their close adult relationships were less close to their children than securely attached mothers. Further, studies show that secure individuals are often paired with other secure people (Feeney, 1994), demonstrating that attachment styles during childhood do seem to have an influence on later relationships. Also, attachment seems to be a key feature of relationships across the life span. In particular, relationship quality is often determined by adult attachment style, with securely attached adults having better quality relationships and enjoyment of affection, compared to avoidant adults who have difficulty forming relationships, and anxious adults who fall in love easily but generally feel unhappy (Brennan and Shaver, 1995). It is important to note that attachment levels can change (Kirkpatrick and Hazan, 1994), but that a secure attachment style provides the best hopes for relationship success. Hazan, Gur-Yaish and Campa (2004) argued that, in general, early attachment experiences shape the ways in which people think about relationships. Sensitive, trustworthy carers encourage a sense of trust in their offspring and this example helps mould the way people view their own relationships with others later in life.

TABLE 7.2 Attachment styles

Style of adult relationship	Approximate percentage of people	Background and characteristics
Secure	56	Carer was responsive and positive. People feel well liked and are able to trust others in close relationships
Avoidant	25	Carer was aloof and distant. People have difficulty forming intimate relationships for fear of rejection
Anxious/ ambivalent	19	Carer was inconsistent and overbearing. People are anxious and concerned that feelings are not reciprocated

Source: Data from Hazen and Shaver, 1987

Try it yourself You may wish to complete this adult attachment scale for yourself. AV stands for items that relate to avoidant attachment style, S for secure, and AX for anxious. There are six items for each. Once you have finished, tally up your scores for the three different attachment styles. Are you more secure than avoidant? More anxious than secure? Knowing what you know about attachment styles and relationships, what might your scores mean for your own relationships?

	Not at all						Very
I find it difficult to allow myself to depend on others (AV)	1	2	3	4	5	6	7
People are never there when you need them (AV)	1	2	3	4	5	6	7
I am comfortable depending on others (S)	1	2	3	4	5	6	7
I know that others will be there when I need them (S)	1	2	3	4	5	6	7
I find it difficult to trust others completely (AV)	1	2	3	4	5	6	7
I am not sure that I can always depend on others to be there when I need them (AX)	1	2	3	4	5	6	7
I do not often worry about being abandoned (S)	1	2	3	4	5	6	7
I often worry that my partner does not really love me (AX)	1	2	3	4	5	6	7
I find others are reluctant to get as close as I would like (AX)	1	2	3	4	5	6	7
I often worry that my partner will not want to stay with me (AX)	1	2	3	4	5	6	7
I want to merge completely with another person (AX)	1	2	3	4	5	6	7
My desire to merge sometimes scares people away (AX)	1	2	3	4	5	6	7
I find it relatively easy to get close to others (S)	1	2	3	4	5	6	7
I do not often worry about someone getting close to me (S)	1	2	3	4	5	6	7
I am somewhat uncomfortable being close to others (AV)	1	2	3	4	5	6	7
I am nervous when anyone gets too close (AV)	1	2	3	4	5	6	7
I am comfortable having others depend on me (S)	1	2	3	4	5	6	7
Often, love partners want me to be more intimate than I feel comfortable being (AV)	1	2	3	4	5	6	7

Note: Collins and Read's (1990) adult attachment scale was designed to measure three components of attachment that underlie attachment styles. These are known as 'comfort with closeness', 'comfort with dependency', and 'anxiety about being abandoned or rejected'. The scale was not designed to capture secure, avoidant and anxious/ambivalent attachment styles. Nonetheless, since each item was taken from descriptions of these attachment styles as labelled here, the average of your responses will give an informative estimate of your secure, avoidant and anxious/ambivalent tendencies.

Source: Collins, 1996; Collins and Read, 1990. Copyright © 1990 by the American Psychological Association. Reproduced with permission

Other family relationships

So far, we have focused on how early experiences with a primary carer can influence romantic relationships later in life. In studies, this primary carer is typically the mother. However, some work suggests that interactions with other family members (e.g., fathers and grandparents) are also important in shaping future relationships (Lin and Harwood, 2003) and can compensate for shortcomings in the relationship with the primary carer (Clark, Konchanska and Ready, 2000).

Relationships with siblings are also important (Dunn and McGuire, 1992). For example, some research suggests that having siblings makes children more liked by their peers in school, presumably because interacting with other children helps children understand the rules of social interaction (Kitzmann, Cohen and Lockwood, 2002). On the whole, siblings tend to get along well, especially if the parents also get along (McGuire, McHale and Updegraff, 1996). Siblings who relate well to each other, especially those who share an even closer bond such as identical twins, are more likely to maintain a strong relationship through adolescence and into adulthood. However, if the relationship with the sibling is not so good, this may have consequences in later life. People judge their relationships with others compared to their sibling relationships, and the positive or negative feelings associated with a sibling relationship are likely to influence interactions with others. For example, one study showed that school bullies are more likely to have had a negative relationship with a sibling or siblings (Bowers, Smith and Binney, 1994).

Maintaining relationships

Relationships often go through rough patches and there are many factors that can influence relationship satisfaction. For example, many relationships experience conflict and married couples report an average of two to three arguments per month (McGonagle, Kessler and Schilling, 1992). How people handle conflict is a strong predictor of relationship satisfaction. Jealousy is a common problem in relationships because people are predisposed to be wary of any threats (e.g., Parrott and Smith, 1993). How do people keep their relationships strong in the face of trouble? How do people stay satisfied with their relationships? Research suggests that several factors are important. Perhaps the most important is commitment.

Commitment is defined as a person's wish or intention to stay in a relationship. A person's level of commitment to a relationship is primarily dependent on their attraction to the partner and the perceived negative consequences of exiting the relationship (Johnson, 1991). More specifically, Adams and Jones (1997) noted that there are three factors that motivate people to stay in a relationship. First, a person's dedication to the partner is important. If they have a positive attraction to their partner and the relationship, they are more likely to be committed. Second, many factors make is costly to exit a relationship. For example, there may not be many attractive alternatives available. Third, the longer a relationship continues, the more likely people are to share friends, money and property – ties that are difficult to break (Kurdek, 1998). According to Rusbult's investment model of commitment (Figure 7.11), people's commitment to a relationship is not only predicted by the level of investment they feel they have put into the relationship, but also what they feel they would lose if they left the relationship.

Commitment The wish or intention of a person to stay in a relationship.

FIGURE 7.11 Rusbult's investment model of commitment People's commitment to a relationship and the ultimate stability of the relationship is determined by perceived costs, rewards and comparison level for alternatives.

Source: Rusbult, 1983. Copyright © 1983 by the American Psychological Association. Reproduced with permission

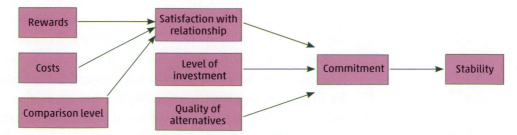

However, a person's values are also important. Specifically, the extent to which people have a moral commitment to the relationship influences their motivation to maintain the relationship (Adams and Jones, 1997). For example, religious values may encourage people not to leave a partner, or people may simply feel an obligation to keep a promise, especially in the case of marriage where a legal contract has been made.

The higher the commitment, the more likely a couple will stay together (Adams and Jones, 1997). Commitment also predicts marital satisfaction and trust (Kurdek, 2000; Wieselquist, Rusbult, Foster and Agnew, 1999). In turn, trust also predicts relationship success. As we mentioned earlier, an insecure attachment style is associated with a lack of trust.

Other factors help maintain relationships. For example, forgiving a partner's transgressions can keep a potentially difficult relationship going (McCullough, Worthington and Rachal, 1997) and provides an alternative to breaking up. Also, some research suggests that people use cognitive strategies to maintain relationships. Specifically, when a relationship is less ideal, people can lower their expectations to more closely match the benefits they gain from their partner (Fletcher, Simpson and Thomas, 2000). People can also think more about the positive aspects of their partner and less about their faults (Murray and Holmes, 1999). Another alternative is to directly act upon the partner to make them a closer match to the ideal. Specifically, Overall, Fletcher and Simpson (2006) argued that people can engage in **partner regulation**, where they actively attempt to change the partner to be closer to what they would like. For example, if a partner is not living up to one's expectations in terms of their earnings, one way might be to suggest that they go back to university and train to get a better job. Overall, Fletcher, Simpson and Sibley (2009) examined the success of different communication strategies that partners used when trying to produce changes in each other. Partners were videoed while trying to bring about changes in the partner and were later asked about the success of their attempts, both immediately and at three-month intervals in the following year. Results revealed that direct strategies (positive and negative) were not perceived as immediately successful but predicted increased change over the following 12 months. On the other hand, indirect strategies (especially those that were positive) were immediately rated as successful but did not predict later change. In summary, people can attempt to mould their partner to be what they want them to be and some communication strategies can be more effective than others.

Partner regulation Actively attempting to change one's partner to make them closer to one's ideal.

Time to reflect Knowing what you know about similarity, attraction and relationship success, what do you think might be the advantages and pitfalls of trying to 'mould' a relationship partner to make them who you want them to be?

SOCIAL PSYCHOLOGY IN THE REAL WORLD

Same-sex relationships: 'the love that dare not speak its name'

© NASTYNEGS/FOTOLIA.COM

You may be wondering what social psychologists have to say about homosexual relationships. Do they differ from heterosexual relationships in any way? To date, there is little research concerning how gay and lesbian relationships form, are maintained and how they break up. Of course, this has much to do with the social stigma that has historically been associated with homosexual relationships. After all, until relatively recently in human history, homosexuality was illegal. But as society is changing and homosexual relationships are legally recognized in many countries, more researchers are studying homosexual relationships. For example, Peplau and Fingerhut (2007) reviewed the current empirical work on same-sex couples in the USA. They found many similarities between homosexual and heterosexual relationships, but also some differences.

What is similar between gay and straight relationships?

- Both value affection, dependability, shared interests and similarity of religious beliefs.
- Relationship satisfaction is largely driven by similarity in backgrounds, attitudes and values.

- For men, physical attractiveness is of key importance, whereas women place more emphasis on personality.
- Relationships commonly form through proximity and familiarity (e.g., knowing friends or being in the same neighbourhood).
- The internet is a key tool for establishing new relationships.
- High emphasis on equity within the relationship.
- Commitment is a strong predictor of relationship success.

What is different?

- Lesbian relationships are more likely to originate from pre-existing friendships.
- Gay and lesbian couples are more likely to stay friends after relationship breakup.
- Division of labour within the household is more equitable.
- Controlling for demographic variables, homosexual relationships are more likely to break up.

Questions

1 One common perception of homosexual relationships is that they are less happy and more dysfunctional than heterosexual relationships. What do you think? As an exercise, find out what research suggests about this issue.

2 One key difference between homosexual and heterosexual relationships is the presence of children (although this, too, is changing). What impact might the lack of children have on relationships?

3 To what extent do you think that prejudice and discrimination put stress on homosexual relationships?

When relationships end

Not all relationships stand the test of time. In 2010, there were 119,589 recorded divorces in England and Wales (ONS, 2010). The consequences of relationship breakdown can be alarming, even for people who are not part of the relationship. For example, Tucker, Friedman, Schwartz et al. (1997) found that adults who had experienced their parents breaking up were more likely to be involved in marital breakups themselves. In Figure 7.12, you will see the reasons people cite on their divorce papers. Most people report that 'falling out of love' is the key reason for

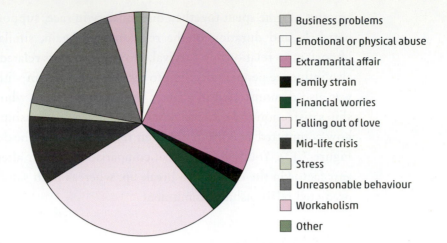

Business problems
Emotional or physical abuse
Extramarital affair
Family strain
Financial worries
Falling out of love
Mid-life crisis
Stress
Unreasonable behaviour
Workaholism
Other

FIGURE 7.12 Reasons for divorce in the UK in 2010

Source: Thornton, 2011. Grant Thorton, 2011. Reproduced with permission

the breakup. How do things go so wrong that people choose to end their relationships? In this section, we discuss the process of relationship breakdown, again with a specific focus on romantic relationships.

Factors influencing relationship breakdown

People who enter into relationships with the view that the relationship should be long-lasting tend to have more satisfying and enduring relationships (Arriaga and Agnew, 2001). Further, feelings of obligation to a relationship, as well as a lack of consideration of alternatives, can keep a relationship together (Adams and Jones, 1997). This may also be influenced by culture, as norms of obligation and commitment differ across individualist and collectivist societies. As we saw earlier, divorce rates differ significantly across countries and there seems to be a general trend for high divorce rates within individualist cultures and lower rates in collectivist cultures (Triandis, 1994). Perhaps individualists tend to expect relationships to provide more fulfillment for the self, including passion, which exists to a lesser extent in collectivist cultures where the focus is more on the concerns of others (Dion and Dion, 1993).

Relationships also tend to last longer if the individuals share similar backgrounds and experiences. For example, couples of a similar education level, age and religious commitment are more likely to stay together (Fergusson, Horwood and Shannon, 1984). If factors such as these are absent, relationships have a lower likelihood of success. Another important factor seems to be the extent to which partners are similar in terms of their love attitudes, disclosure, investment, commitment and relationship satisfaction (Hendrick, Hendrick and Adler, 1988). This is not to say that relationships are doomed if people do not have these specific factors in common. However, from other research discussed in this chapter, we know that similarity and common experiences are important. They are important for attraction in the first place, and they are also important for relationship survival.

Felmlee, Sprecher and Bassin (1990) demonstrated a range of factors associated with relationship breakdown, such as comparison level for alternatives, the amount of time spent together, dissimilarity in race, support from partners' social network, and duration of the relationship. Again, similarity in many ways is important to relationship survival. However, factors related to social exchange can also influence people's decision to terminate or remain within a relationship. This was also demonstrated in a study by Rusbult (1983), who showed that relationship satisfaction and the level of investment in a relationship significantly predicted how committed a person felt to their relationship and the decision to break up (see Figure 7.13). You will notice that comparison level for alternatives was the strongest factor in the decision to break up, whereas both satisfaction and investment predicted relationship commitment.

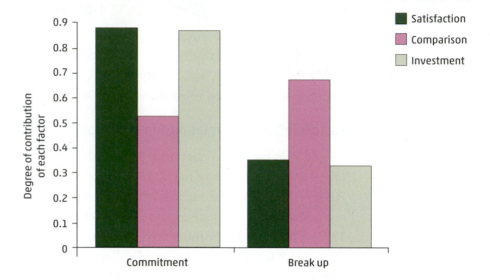

FIGURE 7.13 Factors determining commitment and breakup The same three factors, relationship satisfaction, comparison for alternatives and level of investment, predict both relationship commitment and the decision to end relationships.

Source: Data from Rusbult, 1983

In general, research suggests that people are likely to feel that a relationship is coming to an end if there is a lack of commitment to the relationship (Levinger, 1980). Also, people may begin to consider alternative partners (Arriaga and Agnew, 2001) and expect that the relationship is going to fail.

How do people end relationships?

Once a decision has been made that a relationship is ending, people can choose to react in several different ways. For example, Rusbult and Zembrodt (1983) argued that people can react actively or passively to the crisis. In other words, they can either work at improving the relationship and remain loyal to their partner (constructive) or choose to end it (destructive). Alternatively, they can wait for the relationship to improve (constructive) or simply ignore the situation and hope that things will get better (destructive) (see also the additional work of Rusbult, Johnson and Morrow, 1986; Rusbult, Morrow and Johnson, 1987; Rusbult et al., 1998, 2001).

If a person chooses to actively detach from the relationship, this is not an easy process. Severing ties with a close other takes time, and even removing emotional factors from the equation, there are many practical factors to consider, such as children, property and other binding factors. Some theorists (e.g., Baxter, 1984; Duck, 1998; Hazan and Shaver, 1994; Rollie and Duck, 2006), argue that the process of detachment from a long-term relationship follows a series of stages, including the following types of events:

- An individual thinks about the problems in the relationship. They hope to repair the relationship and often seek advice from others about how to do so. The focus is largely on the partner's behaviour and an evaluation of their 'performance' in the relationship. The pros and cons of staying in the relationship are considered.

- The two parties discuss their differences and potentially argue about who is responsible for the differences. They negotiate with each other and consider breaking up or reconciliation. At this stage, it is possible for the partners to talk through their problems and repair the relationship. If only one person wishes to end the relationship, they can differ in their strategy (compassionate vs. non-compassionate) to do so (Sprecher, Zimmerman and Abrahams, 2010; see also Fehr and Sprecher, 2009).

- If the two parties are not able to solve their problems, they acknowledge that the relationship is coming to an end. Each party seeks social support and validation of their position. Each party tries to save 'face' to others.

- The two parties separate and perform the functional aspects of the breakup including dividing property and agreeing custody arrangements. Social support is again important, as well as presenting a positive 'face' to others. The two parties attempt to 'get over' each other, return to normal life and gain a renewed sense of self, ready for new relationships.

In general, the process of relationship breakup is fraught and, depending on the length of the relationship and the level of intimacy involved, can cause a great deal of pain and sadness, distress and trouble with coping (Fine and Harvey, 2006; Orbuch, 1992; Simpson, 1987; Sprecher and Fehr, 1998; Vangelisti and Perlman, 2006). Feelings of guilt can be powerful for people who leave relationships (Baumeister and Wotman, 1992). However, for many people, the benefits of leaving a relationship outweigh the costs and so divorce rates remain high. If a relationship is characterized by disagreement, criticism and conflict, then people are unhappy and, perhaps unsurprisingly, they are also more likely to break up (Noller and Fitzpatrick, 1990). Successful relationships are less likely to be characterized by these types of destructive behaviours within relationships (Notarius and Markman, 1993; Yovetich and Rusbult, 1994). This is not to say that successful couples do not fight – they do – but there is evidence to suggest that successful couples are able to reconcile their differences and find a balance between conflict and affection (Gottman, 1998).

Question to consider Reread question 4 at the start of the chapter. Is the future bright for Jenna and Kate?

Exploring further Sprecher et al. (2010) demonstrated that people differ in their choice of strategy to end romantic relationships. Some strategies are compassionate (e.g., honestly conveying one's wishes to a partner, finding time to talk face to face) and some are less so (e.g., asking a third party to break the news, breaking up via text or email). Of course, this depends on the length of the relationship and various other factors, but take some time to reflect on the different consequences of using these diverse strategies to end relationships. Do you think women and men might choose different strategies? Find a copy of Sprecher et al.'s paper to find out more.

ETHICS AND RESEARCH METHODS

Student samples in relationships research

Many studies of relationship breakup, as well as other aspects of close relationships, have been conducted with university students as participants. This is a practical choice for the most part – students in many institutions are required to participate in research to earn credit for their course, and this presents an easy source of participants for researchers.

In many cases of social psychological research, student samples are appropriate. For example, there is no reason to believe that basic social cognitive processes like many of those we discussed in Chapter 3 would vary between people of different ages or levels of education. However, the choice of sample may be important in other aspects of social psychology. In the questions below, we would like you to consider the study of close relationships and whether (and when) student participation is appropriate.

As a researcher, it is important to consider the research question being asked and the type of study being conducted. When reflecting on the suitability of a sample, and especially when criticizing a study or area of research based on choice of sample, it is important to go beyond the criticism that 'this sample was not representative of society'. It is important to be clear about why it is not representative, how the sample may differ systematically from the population as a whole, and specifically, how results may have been affected.

© BANANASTOCK

Questions

1 Do you think that relying on student samples to study relationship phenomena is a problem?
2 Can you find any evidence that undergraduates' and non-students' relationships are different? If so, in what ways are they different?
3 How might any differences influence the study of relationships?
4 On balance, are students a suitable sample to study relationships? Why/why not? This final question is something you can ask in most chapters of this textbook and will help you understand more about sampling in social psychology.

Chapter summary

In this chapter, we have focused on the physical and psychological determinants of attraction and have outlined the major theories of attraction. We have outlined what social psychologists know about love and romantic relationships and their link to attachment processes in childhood. We have discussed how people maintain relationships and, finally, how people end relationships. You will now know that:

- The most important factor in determining judgements of attractiveness is a person's physical appearance.
- There is strong consensus both within and between cultures about what features are attractive.
- One key mechanism that determines attraction is called the matching phenomenon – people tend to be attracted to others who are about the same level of physical attractiveness as themselves. However, less attractive individuals can compensate by making themselves attractive in other areas.
- In addition to good looks, people are attracted to others who are familiar, or those who are close by. Proximity is effective because we tend to like things that are familiar to us. Repeated (positive) exposure to another person is likely to lead to more favourable evaluations. This is called the mere exposure effect.
- Attraction is also determined by psychological factors, key to which is the need to affiliate – the motive to seek and maintain interpersonal relationships with others.
- Attraction to others is also influenced by emotions.
- Attraction is also influenced by similarity of attitudes, interests and values. People who are similar in personality, interpersonal skills and communication style are also more likely to be attracted to one another.
- People from similar social backgrounds are more likely to be attracted to one another.
- A person's attraction to another person is also determined by reciprocity – does the other person like them too?
- Social exchange theory argues that the more social rewards a person offers, the more we will be attracted to that person. People weigh up the rewards and costs to determine whether to enter into a relationship. They also consider their relationship alternatives.
- Equity theory proposes that people are not simply after the most rewards and the least costs. They also need equity and fairness so that the cost-reward payoff is the same for both parties in the relationship.
- Other approaches propose that attraction is a result of direct reinforcement or reward.
- Passionate love is the type of love that involves intense feelings, uncontrollable thoughts and deep longing for another person. There are physiological 'symptoms' to passionate love.
- Consummate love involves deep, secure feelings that are not accompanied with the physiological arousal of passionate love.
- People's experiences of love and relationships in later life are determined by their attachment experiences with parents or carers in childhood and infancy.
- Maintenance of relationships is largely driven by the level of commitment – a person's wish or intention to stay in the relationship. The higher the commitment, the more likely a couple will stay together. Similarity and common experiences are also important.
- The process of ending a relationship is said to progress through a series of stages and is determined by a variety of factors, such as the length of the relationship and the level of intimacy involved.

In this chapter, we have focused on the close, intimate relationships that are formed between individuals. In Chapter 8, we turn our focus to the broader relationships and commitments that people make to their groups.

Essay questions

At the beginning of the chapter, we asked you to consider these questions:

1 What chances are there for average-looking Matt to have a romantic relationship with Melissa, the most beautiful girl in school? How might he be able to overcome the discrepancy in physical attractiveness?
2 Kay and Leigh live on different continents. They met one day on the internet and became friends. Ewan and Jai live in the same building. They met one day in the lift and likewise became friends. What is different about these two friendships? Do they have an equal chance of success?
3 Leila feels that her husband takes more than he gives, and that she does all the hard work to make their marriage a success. What social psychological theory can you link this situation to? What are the likely consequences of this relationship imbalance?
4 Once deeply in love, Jenna and Kate now argue constantly and both feel that their relationship is over. What factors will determine where they go from here?

Having read this chapter, these questions could also be framed as the following essay questions, which you can attempt in preparation for your examinations:

1 Outline the factors that influence attraction and discuss, with reference to social psychological research, the factors that influence the likelihood of a person entering a relationship with a more attractive individual.

2 Evaluate the research suggesting that physical proximity is a strong determinant of attraction. In your answer, consider the implications of new information communication technology.

3 Outline social exchange theory and its major alternatives. Which theory best describes why people form relationships?

4 Describe the process of relationship dissolution. At each stage, discuss the factors that influence people's decision to stay with or end their relationships.

Further reading

Baumeister, R.F. and Bratslavsky, E. (1999) How is friendship different from love? Passion, intimacy, and time: Passionate love as a function of change in intimacy. *Personality and Social Psychology Review*, 3, 49–67. Interesting review article discussing the differences between friendship and love.

Berscheid, E. and Reis, H.T. (1998) Attraction and close relationships. In D.T. Gilbert, S.T. Fiske, and G. Lindzey (eds) *The Handbook of Social Psychology* (4th edn, vol. 2, pp. 193–281). New York: McGraw-Hill. Overview of the research on attraction and close relationships, discussing in more detail some of the topics covered in this chapter.

Duck, S. (2007) *Human Relationships* (4th edn). Thousand Oaks, CA: Sage. Introduction to the study and understanding of human relationships, with up-to-date coverage of the research from social, personality and developmental psychology, as well as other disciplines such as family studies and sociology.

Fehr, B. (1996) *Friendship Processes*. Thousand Oaks, CA: Sage. A look at friendships from one of the leading researchers in the field.

Fitness, J., Fletcher, G. and Overall, N. (2003) Interpersonal attraction and intimate relationships. In M.A. Hogg and J. Cooper (eds) *The Sage Handbook of Social Psychology* (pp. 258–78). London: Sage. Discusses emotions in relationships and some of the evolutionary origins of attraction and relationships.

Hendrick, C.A. and Hendrick, S.S. (eds) (2000) *Close Relationships: A Sourcebook*. Thousand Oaks, CA: Sage. A varied view on close relationships research, with examples from current literature, research and practical applications.

 Visit the companion website at www.palgrave.com/psychology/suttondouglas for access to a wide range of resources to help you get to grips with this chapter.

Applying social psychology

Abusive relationships

We have spent little time on the 'dark side' of close relationships in this chapter. But relationships can go disastrously wrong. For most people, relationships are a source of love, support and strength, but for all too many, they are primarily a venue of danger, abuse and dominance. What does social psychology have to say about why relationships become abusive, and how the problem of abuse and violence within close relationships might be addressed? To think about these questions, it is necessary to read beyond just this chapter, and to tie together different strands of social psychology. In answering these questions, keep an eye out for material in other chapters.

1 What causes some people to be abusive in relationships? (Hint: check out the chapters on aggression, intergroup relations and justice.)

2 Why do so many people who find themselves being abused fail to leave the relationship?

3 Apart from physical or sexual violence, what other, more subtle forms might abuse within close relationships take?

4 Do you think that self-verification theory (Chapter 2) may play a role in intergenerational cycles of violence? Consider why people who were raised in the context of abusive relationships between parents may be more likely to find themselves abused in relationships as an adult.

Blind spot in social psychology

The politics of sexual variety

In the Critical focus box in this chapter (see also the Student project below), we encountered the research of Schmitt et al. (2003), who investigated worldwide gender differences in sexual preferences. Their key finding was that men, compared to women, report wanting more sexual partners, requiring less time to know a person before being prepared to have sex with them, and more actively pursuing short-term mating opportunities.

Schmitt et al. (2003) interpret their findings as evidence for sexual strategies theory – over millennia, men and women have evolved different mating strategies. However, as we have seen, others have suggested different interpretations of such results (e.g., Eagly and Wood, 1999). These alternative interpretations often surround the gender roles and norms that have developed among human cultures.

One variable that could be associated with sexual preference is political conservatism (recall the Social psychology in real life box in Chapter 4). Politically conservative people tend to have more traditional preferences for long-term partners. Conservative, rather than left-wing, women are more likely to desire high status men, for example, whereas liberal, rather than right-wing, men are more likely to desire younger, attractive but not necessarily high status women. Heterosexual couples comprising an older, higher status man and a younger woman symbolize traditional gender ideals associated with political conservatism (see Doosje, Rojahn and Fischer, 1999; Johannesen-Schmidt and Eagly, 2002).

What about the number of partners desired? One could argue that the well-known sexual double standard, by which promiscuity is more acceptable among men than women, is associated with traditional views of gender, in which chastity and sexual prudence are valued more among women than men. Thus, men who report wanting several partners and women who want fewer partners may, to some extent, be playing out the traditional status quo and, in so doing, reaffirming a conservative worldview.

1   Propose a study to test whether conservatism is indeed associated with the traditional sexual double standard, whereby sexual promiscuity is perceived to be more acceptable for men than it is for women. Outline it in 300 words or so. How would you measure (or manipulate) political conservatism? How would you measure the perceived acceptability of promiscuity for men and women?

2   Propose a second study to test whether the gender differences in the desire for sexual variety observed by Schmitt et al. (2003) are moderated by political orientation. In particular, is the gender difference larger among conservatives than liberals? If findings showed that political orientation was indeed shown to be associated with the gender gap in the desire for sexual variety, what would this mean for Schmitt et al.'s (2003) evolutionary 'sexual strategies theory'? Would this theory be falsified?

Student project

Attachment style, disclosure and relationship quality

Rosabel Tan studied as an honours year student at the University of Auckland, supervised by Dr Nickola Overall. Her research on attachment style, relationship quality, and communication between intimate partners touches on many of the issues we considered in this chapter.

My topic and aims

My research examined the links between attachment style, disclosure during 'normal' or routine discussions in relationships, and relationship quality over time.

My interest in attachment theory was sparked when we covered it at undergraduate level. I had a lot of fun secretly analysing my friends' (and my own) relationships. In the summer before my final year, I completed a studentship with Dr Nickola Overall, which involved coding video-recorded interactions of couples discussing everyday events over their past week. These discussions were the warm-up exercise for a series of interactions examining conflict and support behaviour.

Nearly all prior research examining the impact of attachment insecurity focused on the destructive behaviours enacted by people during threatening relationship events, such as hostility or withdrawal during conflict. We hypothesized that attachment anxiety and avoidance would also influence the way people related and disclosed during more routine interactions. We thought that how couples behaved in 'normal' interactions would be just as important as how people resolve conflict, and would shape relationship quality over time.

My methods

My project was part of a larger study involving observational and longitudinal data. Couples completed questionnaires assessing attachment anxiety and avoidance and relationship quality, and took part in a series of videotaped discussions. They also reported their relationship quality one year later.

I coded the warm-up exercise where couples discussed recent events. This was done with another student to ensure our coding was reliable. We rated (a) the degree to which people disclosed to their partners, (b) how intimate these disclosures were, and (c) whether their discussions were self-focused or relationship-focused. This built on prior research conducted by Bradford, Feeney and Campbell (2002) that examined the links between attachment insecurity and these two types of disclosure as assessed using self-report measures. We also coded general behaviours, like how warm and responsive partners were.

My findings and their implications

I made predictions based on attachment theory – for instance, because highly anxious people are driven by a desire to create and maintain high levels of intimacy, I expected them to talk to their partner more about themselves and their relationship. I also expected this would have a positive impact on relationships one year later, since disclosure has been found to increase intimacy and commitment. I expected attachment avoidance to predict the opposite since avoidant people are motivated to maintain their autonomy and independence.

The predictions were partially supported. First, more anxious people engaged in more relationship-focused disclosure, and this type of disclosure was associated with better quality relationships over time. This is interesting because prior research has focused mostly on the destructive behaviours that result from anxious attachment, and here we found a positive effect.

Second, avoidant people were less likely to disclose about their relationship, and they experienced declines in relationship quality over time. This suggests that one of the reasons avoidance is associated with less stable relationships is because avoidant people are generally less involved in their relationships.

These patterns show that talking about your relationship during routine interactions plays an important role in maintaining your relationship. Therefore, relationship research shouldn't just focus on the tough interactions, like conflict resolution, but pay attention to how couples are talking to each other day to day.

My journey

My work was accepted in 2011 for publication and published in 2012 (Tan, Overall and Taylor, 2012).

After my honours year I went on to do two Masters degrees – one in psychology at The University of Auckland, focusing on the psychological benefits of reading fiction, and the other in creative writing at the International Institute of Modern Letters, where I wrote a collection of short stories.

Afterwards, I was offered a two-year contract at the Liggins Institute as a research assistant within their education network, which is where I am now. It's a great job with a lot of variety, which is ideal for someone like me with such different interests.

I found honours to be a steep learning curve. For the first time in my academic life I found myself struggling with the workload, and as a result I had to figure out how to manage it all. I'd never worked on a big project before, so I had to break down this huge task into smaller tasks to ensure I stayed on track – and this was a huge help in my Masters and for life in general.

I also learned a number of valuable research skills during my project – from coding observational data to using structural equation modelling to writing everything up in journal article format. These are all skills that I've been able to apply in my current career, where I'm designing and executing studies in a completely different field.

My advice

Don't expect to change the world with your first research project – the value of this project lies in developing skills that are essential for a researcher and which you might not have had the opportunity to develop before. Keep your focus small. You don't have much time to do it and you need to be realistic about what you can achieve in that time. Make the most of it – ask questions, be proactive in learning the skills you need to learn, and manage your time well. Make sure you're doing something you're genuinely interested in – otherwise it won't be a fun ride. Be prepared for disappointment. If your findings aren't in line with your hypotheses, don't despair – this is a natural part of research and the important thing at this point is to learn from it. Back up your work regularly.

8 The social group

This chapter explains why groups are so important to people. We outline how and why groups form and what they mean to the individuals who belong to them. We also discuss how the norms or 'rules' of group behaviour develop, and the consequences of violating group norms. We outline some of the negative aspects of group membership, such as when groups break up, and the negative consequences for people who are left out of groups. By the end of this chapter, you will have an understanding of why groups are central to human existence.

© GETTY

Topics covered in this chapter

- What is a group?
- Formation of groups
- Group structure
- Fitting in to groups
- What do groups do for us?

Key features

Critical focus Gender roles: a minefield of science and politics

Ethics and research methods Ethical considerations in ostracism research

Social psychology in the real world Imposters within groups

Applying social psychology Multiple social identities and coping

Blind spot in social psychology The upsides of social ostracism

Student project Social categories and person perception

Questions to consider

1 Juma wants to join an exclusive gang of boys at his school. As part of his 'initiation', Juma is asked to walk down the high street wearing nothing but his underpants. After he has completed the task, do you think Juma will be happy to be a member of this gang? Would he be happier if the gang just let him in without initiation?

2 Cerys visits the pub with her friends every Friday night. She has a reputation for 'sitting' on the last drop of her pint, waiting for someone to buy the next round. She rarely buys a round herself. What is Cerys's behaviour an example of? How is it likely to be received by her friends (and why)?

3 Ed is an ex-army man who served during the Falklands War. He is an active member of an ex-servicemen's group in his local town. He organizes the local Remembrance Day functions. One year it is revealed that Ed never engaged in active combat and was an army catering official during the war. How do you think his ex-servicemen's group would react to this news?

Groups are a central part of human existence. We are members of a wide variety of groups in almost every facet of life, from our daily work (e.g., project teams, research groups) to our social lives (e.g., peer groups, sports clubs) and our personal lives (e.g., the family unit). Our groups define who we are. We often refer to ourselves in terms of our group memberships, such as 'I am a woman', 'I am Chinese' or 'I am a member of the hockey club', so that when we think about ourselves, we think about the social groups that come together to make us who we are. But groups not only define who we are, they also influence how we live. The groups we belong to determine some of the most basic aspects of our lives, such as our attitudes and beliefs, our cultural practices and the language we use to talk to one another. Our groups can also determine where we live and who we know. Groups influence what we do in specific situations too. As we will see throughout Part 3, groups can influence our behaviour in a variety of ways, both good and bad. Even the groups we are *not* part of can influence what we do. In general, it appears that groups have a strong power over us and we cannot function properly without them.

But why is this the case? Why do people need groups? In this chapter, we will explain why group membership is important to humans as social beings. We will examine how and why groups form, what groups mean to individuals' sense of their own identity and feelings of self worth, how the norms or 'rules' of group behaviour develop, and what happens when people violate these rules. Finally, we will turn to the often distressing processes of group breakup or division, and how being left out of, or rejected from, groups can be painful, psychologically and physically. In short, we will explain why people cannot live without groups.

What is a group?

'What is a group?' may seem to be a simple question, but it is more complex than you think. Groups are so diverse that we need to have ways of describing how they differ, as well as a core definition that can encompass groups of all types. Among many other dimensions of groups, researchers have differentiated between them according to whether they are big or small, structured or unstructured, specific and general, physically close or scattered (Deaux, Reid, Mizrahi and Ethier, 1995). For example, it is easy to differentiate between groups that are big (e.g., religious groups) and small (e.g., families). Although such groups may share features in common – for example, a family group may share the same religion – they are easily distinguishable because of their sheer size. In a similar way, an online self-help group for people who wish to lose weight can be distinguished from a weight loss group that meets at the local village hall every week – this difference relates to physical proximity. You can probably think of many dimensions on which groups can differ.

Groups are also distinguished in terms of their **entitativity** – the degree to which they appear to be a distinct unit that is bound together in some way (Campbell, 1958; Castano, Yzerbyt, Paladino and Sacchi, 2002; Gaertner and Schopler, 1998;

Entitativity The feature of a group that makes it appear a distinct unit that is bound together.

Hamilton and Sherman, 1996; Hamilton, Sherman and Lickel, 1998). Groups that are highly entitative tend to be homogeneous, with a clear structure, purpose or boundaries, whereas groups that are less entitative tend to be more heterogeneous and unstructured. Lickel, Hamilton, Wieczorkowska et al. (2000) argued that entitativity is highest for **intimacy groups**, such as family groups, and lower for **task groups**, such as those brought together temporarily to achieve a particular goal. Lickel et al. also argued that groups are less entitative if they are simply determined by social category memberships, such as religions, or if they are transitory, such as a group of people waiting for a train.

There are other ways to distinguish groups. For example, some social psychologists separate groups into those based on groupings of similarity between members, and those that are interaction based (e.g., Arrow, McGrath and Berdahl, 2000; McGrath, Arrow and Berdahl, 2000). Others categorize groups as either **common bond groups**, which depend on attachment among group members, or **common identity groups**, which depend on members' direct attachment to the group itself (Postmes and Spears, 2000; Prentice, Miller and Lightdale, 1994; Sassenberg, 2002). Any social group can be described by a variety of features that define it and set it apart from other groups. But what are the common features that define groups? To understand groups and group life, we first need to understand what a group is. We know what makes groups different from each other, but what makes them the same thing? What are the typical characteristics of groups? Can we isolate particular qualities that are common to all groups? This is not a straightforward task.

Intimacy groups Groups that are closely tied together (e.g., family groups).

Task groups Groups that come together temporarily to achieve a specific goal.

Common bond group Groups in which the members have close personal bonds within the group.

Common identity group Groups in which the members have close personal ties to the group itself.

Time to reflect There are many ways to distinguish between groups. Make a list of some of these for yourself. In real life, what dimensions do you think people might focus on the most? In other words, what makes different groups really different from each other?

At face value, the question 'What is a group?' looks simple. After all, everyone can think of many examples of groups they belong to and can describe them very well. We think we know what groups are. However, it is difficult to define what a group is. Specifically, it is not easy to tease apart the common features of groups that separate them from collectives that look like groups but in fact are not. Indeed, you may find that what you consider to be a group does not fit with a social psychological definition of a group (see Figure 8.1). For example, are students in a lecture theatre a group? Is a pair of jogging partners a group? Do all people who have blonde hair qualify as a group? Most social psychologists would say not. These examples would perhaps be better classified as instances of **collectives** or **aggregates** but not groups. This is because they are not related, *psychologically*, in any particular way. They have things in common but there is nothing uniquely psychological that binds them together. For example, they may simply be in the same place at the same time, doing similar things. They may share a physical characteristic that makes them look different to others who do not have that characteristic. They are collectives without necessarily being groups. Even so,

Collectives and aggregates People who share some connection, but there is no psychological value to the connection.

FIGURE 8.1 Is this a group? Is a group of students in a lecture theatre a group? Most social psychologists would say not.

it is often difficult to define what distinguishes such collectives from groups themselves and thus one clear definition of a group is difficult to find.

According to some theorists, group members must feel that they have a *common fate* (Lewin, 1948; Campbell, 1958; Rabbie and Horwitz, 1988). Using this definition, Jewish people in Nazi Germany would be considered a group because they shared the same tragic fate of stigmatization and genocide – so long as they felt that their likely fate as individuals was shared by other group members (Brown, 2000). For other social psychologists, groups must have a defined and accepted social structure consisting of status hierarchies and social roles (e.g., Sherif and Sherif, 1969). A company with a CEO, managers and workers is a good example of this. However, for others, groups must interact face to face to qualify as groups (e.g., Bales, 1950). Johnson and Johnson (1987, p. 8) provided a definition encompassing these features and thus produced an account of what many social psychologists would agree makes up a group:

> two or more individuals in face-to-face interaction, each aware of his or her membership in the group, each aware of the others who belong to the group, and each aware of their positive interdependence as they strive to achieve mutual goals.

According to this perspective, groups possess several key features. In particular, group members are said to be interdependent, follow norms or rules of behaviour, and typically join together to meet a common objective. This makes good sense for the small groups we are used to in everyday life, such as work teams, families and friendship groups. However, the utility of this kind of definition is significantly compromised when we consider *large* groups. We mentioned the example of Jewish people in Nazi Germany as a group, but using the definition above they would not qualify as a group. They do not all interact face to face for a start. Many large groups such as gender, religious, social class and ethnic groups do not interact face to face. Nor do they necessarily have a joint need or goal. But are they still groups? Do people need these features to feel part of a group? Many social psychologists argue that they do not. Indeed, as we will see in Chapters 9–12, larger group memberships can influence people's behaviours as much, if not more than the smallest, most powerful, face-to-face group. People do not even need to be in the presence of other members of the group to be influenced by it – the group still strongly defines who the person is, how they live, who they associate with and what they do. Thus, even the most accepted definitions of group membership are limited.

This issue has led some theorists to propose a more general definition of the group to include larger groups. According to Turner (1982, p. 15), a group exists when: 'two or more individuals … perceive themselves to be members of the same social category'. The key to this definition, then, is the extent to which people *identify* with groups. This concept is at the heart of social identity theory (Tajfel and Turner, 1986), to which we shall return later in this chapter (also see Chapter 11). The utility of this definition lies in its inclusiveness. Indeed, it is difficult to think of a group whose members, at least at some point in time, have not classified themselves as belonging to the group. Nevertheless, Brown (2000) thinks that the inclusiveness of the description is also its main problem. He argues that an important feature of groups is that others who are not members still *recognize* them as groups. Brown argues that social psychologists would have little interest in people who secretly decide to define themselves as a group when the group's existence remains hidden to everyone else. To understand groups and group behaviour, it is important to consider groups in relation to other groups. Therefore, Brown (2000, p. 3) extended the definition of groups, stating that a group: 'exists when two or more people define themselves as members of it and when its existence is recognized by at least one other'.

Adding slightly to this definition, we draw on Turner's argument that groups perceive themselves as 'us' compared to 'them'. In seeing themselves as a group, people naturally compare themselves to groups they are not a part of. Thus, a **group** can be defined as:

> two or more people who define themselves, and are recognized by others, as a group and have a sense of 'us', which can be compared to 'them'.

This is the definition we use in the remainder of this chapter and beyond. You will also notice that we use the terms **ingroup** and **outgroup** throughout the book. Here, we are using the social psychological convention to differentiate between and name groups we are members of (ingroups) and groups to which we do not belong (outgroups).

Group Two or more people who define themselves as a group (having a sense of 'us') and who are also recognized by at least one other person.

Ingroup Term used to describe groups we belong to.

Outgroup Term used to describe groups we do not belong to.

Time to reflect Does the above definition concur with your intuitive understanding of what a group is? Are there any more features of groups that you would add to this definition and why?

Try it yourself Make a list of 10 groups you currently belong to (e.g., family, sports, religious, national). Which are the most entitative? Which influence you the most? Can they be classified as one of the types of group we have discussed above (e.g., intimacy group, common identity group)? Now, make a list of 10 groups you do not belong to. Which of these are the most entitative and which of them influence you?

Formation of groups

You will be able to think of many different kinds of groups that make up who you are. Obviously, many of your group memberships are chosen for you by birth. However, one common feature of many groups is that you can *choose* to join them. Likewise, you can choose to leave them. For example, if you do not like your hockey club or project group, you are more often than not free to leave. So, groups can be flexible, dynamic structures where people come and go. The movements of others and the makeup of the group at any given time can influence the nature of the group. Likewise, the group can influence its members, as we will see throughout Part 3. However, it is surprising that this aspect of groups is given little attention in social psychology. Social psychological examinations of group phenomena and intergroup relations deal with a wide range of processes and influences but the effects of time are often neglected (Levine and Moreland, 1990; Tuckman, 1965; Worchel, 1996).

Nevertheless, Tuckman proposed a well-known stage model of the development of groups over time. Tuckman (1965) recognized the distinct phases that groups go through and argued that groups need to experience each stage (up to stage four at least) before they can achieve maximum effectiveness. The stages are as follows:

1 *Forming:* Here, individuals hope to be accepted by others and avoid conflict or controversy. People focus on busying themselves with routines such as group organization, structure and roles. Individuals learn about each other and their task. Little gets done in this stage, which is mainly concerned with orientation and gathering information.

2 *Storming:* Everyone in the group now knows one another and so the group begins to address issues (see Figure 8.2). This phase is characterized by conflict. Group members question the role of the work of the group and the roles/ responsibilities within the group. Some group members will wish to retain the security of phase 1. Conflict in the group may be suppressed in the interests of harmony and the group task, or will be addressed in this phase.

3 *Norming:* The rules of engagement are established, roles and responsibilities are agreed and conflict has been addressed. People in the group understand each other better and can appreciate the skills and experience that others bring to the group. This stage is characterized by listening, support and flexibility. People feel they are part of a cohesive, effective group. A common sense of identity and purpose emerges.

FIGURE 8.2 A group may need to 'storm' before it can perform

4 *Performing:* This stage is characterized by a state of interdependence and flexibility. Not all groups reach this phase. Here, everyone in the group knows each other well enough to trust one another and work together or independently. Roles and responsibilities change according to needs in a flexible and harmonious manner. People feel comfortable and have good morale. Because relations within the group are good, the group can be directed towards the task.

5 *Adjourning:* This phase was added later (Tuckman and Jensen, 1977). Here, the group completes the task and disengages. People in the group come to terms with the task having been completed and the group now ends. Sometimes, adjourning can occur if group members lose interest or motivation and the group dissolves (van Vugt and Hart, 2004).

© BANANASTOCK

Group socialization

Group socialization The process of groups as a whole and group members coming together to meet each other's needs and accomplish goals over time.

Moreland and Levine devised a model of **group socialization** to describe and explain the dynamic nature of the group over time (Levine and Moreland, 1994; Moreland and Levine, 1982, 1984, 2001). In this model, the *inter*relationships between the group and its individual members are important. Specifically, group members come together to meet each other's needs and accomplish goals. Thus, group socialization is not simply a one-way process in which groups influence what individuals do. Members coming into (and leaving) a dynamic and changing group can be a powerful source of influence on the group itself and may change the way the group communicates and functions.

According to Moreland and Levine's model, individuals and the group are constantly evaluating one another to determine how rewarding or worthwhile the interrelationships are. These evaluations bring about feelings of commitment that can change (go up and down) over time. If the changes are significant, the group may cross a 'decision criterion', bringing about role transition. In other words, individuals within the group can occupy different roles within the group at different times. More specifically, Moreland and Levine argue that there are five membership phases, as shown in Figure 8.3. These are:

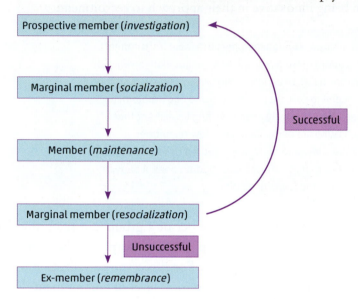

FIGURE 8.3 Model of group socialization
Source: Moreland and Levine, 1982

1 *Investigation:* Here, an individual is a prospective member of the group. The individual engages in reconnaissance and the group engages in recruitment. If an 'entry criterion' or level of commitment is met by both the group and the individual, the individual enters the group and socialization begins. There are many forms of investigation in everyday life. If you are looking for work (and are therefore a potential new member of an organization), you will examine employment advertisements and investigate – if you can afford to be choosy – whether the company looks good to work for. If the company is looking for new members, it will typically advertise a job, and will then scrutinize the CV and the character of applicants. The processes in friendship, special interest and political groups may look different but they have the same basic structure of reconnaissance by new members and recruitment and scrutiny by the group. In an interesting study of clubs on university campuses, Cini, Moreland and Levine (1993) found that clubs' recruitment behaviour changed markedly depending on whether they already had enough, too many or too few members. Groups who were understaffed – who lacked members – were more interested in recruitment, were more likely to allow people to join their group at any time, and were less fussy about who could join the group. Thus, the logic of supply and demand can influence investigation – groups that already have more members, and prospec-

tive group members who have more choices, may be choosy and use more elaborate investigation techniques than those who have fewer. Surprisingly, groups who were understaffed used *fewer*, not more, recruitment methods. Cini et al. (1993) noted that this finding may reflect the practical or emotional effect of understaffing on groups – the stress of being overworked and overlooked, and the sheer lack of time for group members who are working hard to keep the group functioning, may cause groups to stick rigidly to a small set of procedures they know, rather than being innovative in their approach to recruitment.

Time to reflect Cini et al. (1993) showed that groups who do not have enough members use fewer recruitment methods. They suggest that being understaffed causes groups to adopt more restricted, less imaginative recruitment procedures. But could it be the other way around – could the historical lack of variety in recruitment practices simply cause the groups to be understaffed? What kind of research is needed to sort out this chicken and egg problem, to work out whether staffing levels mostly affect recruitment or recruitment mostly affects staffing levels? Another interesting possibility is suggested by this research. Just as groups who are understaffed use few recruitment methods, perhaps because they lack the resources to be innovative, individuals who are accepted by relatively few groups may tend not to undergo enough reconnaissance behaviours, or may choose inappropriate ones. A paper by Pavelchak, Moreland and Levine (1986) explores some of these issues and is worth reading.

2 *Socialization:* The individual is now a new member of a group and the group attempts to assimilate the person into the group. During this phase, the group member attempts to accommodate to the group. For successful socialization to occur, the individual and group need to reach a critical level of commitment. If so, the 'acceptance criterion' is reached and acceptance occurs. The maintenance phase of group membership begins. This phase was investigated by Ashforth, Sluss and Saks (2007), in a survey of business and engineering graduates in their first seven months of work. They found that the more companies invested in proactive, formal socialization (e.g., special occasions to welcome and train new employees), *and* the more new employees acted independently to socialize themselves, the better the outcome. When the company and the employee both committed like this to socialization, the employees learned more, they were better psychologically adjusted, and indicated more desire to stay with the group (that is, not to leave the company). Importantly, joining the group does not necessarily mean losing one's original identity. Groups that try to strip away too much of an individual's previous identity – a process called *divestiture* – risk exposing individuals to stress and uncertainty. On the other hand, groups that embrace and value their employees' previous identities – a process called *investiture* – may create a sense of 'psychological safety' (Edmondson, 2004). In their study, Ashforth et al. (2007) found that investiture did not affect employees' learning but helped boost their wellbeing and commitment to the group.

© RUBYSOHO/FOTOLIA.COM

FIGURE 8.4 The investigation phase of group socialization Employment is a classic case of the investigation phase of group socialization. Both parties – groups (companies and other organizations) and prospective members (prospective employees) – are engaged in processes that lead to the mutual selection of groups by individuals, and individuals by groups. The results of Cini et al.'s (1993) study suggests that vicious cycles may emerge, in which groups that are short of members may recruit in less effective ways. The same thing may be true of individuals who tend to be accepted by relatively few groups.

Exploring further   Stanley Kubrick's classic 1987 war film *Full Metal Jacket* is an interesting exploration of –
among other things –the socialization stage. It portrays a brutal system of socialization in the US Marine Corps at the
time of the Vietnam War. Trainee soldiers are encouraged to forget their previous identities and undergo a series of
tough, deindividuating training drills. This practice seems to have risks. Some soldiers thrive on it and are spurred to
learn quickly. For others, the loss of their original identity is disorienting. This film is worth watching as a case study
in group socialization processes.

3 *Maintenance:* The individual is now an accepted member of the group. Role
   negotiation occurs between the individual and the group regarding the specific
   duties the individual might engage in, such as leadership, for rewards. The
   maintenance phase can last for a long time but sometimes commitment on both
   sides can fall. For example, the individual may not agree on their assigned role,
   or may deviate from what is expected of group members. In one study, workers
   identified several kinds of deviance in the workplace, including theft, destruction of property, misuse of information, time or other resources, unsafe behaviour, poor attendance, poor work quality, abuse of alcohol or drugs, and bad or
   hostile language (Gruys and Sackett, 2003). On the other hand, groups may fail
   to value or invest in their members properly. Some group members may be
   unfairly favoured over others by the leadership of the group (Kacmar and
   Baron, 1999). If these kinds of failures occur on either side, the 'divergence
   criterion' is reached and the group member becomes marginalized. The process
   of resocialization begins.

4 *Resocialization:* The group makes efforts to reassimilate the individual and the
   individual attempts to accommodate to the group. If this process is successful,
   commitment increases and convergence may occur (the reverse of divergence). If
   not, and commitment falls further, the 'exit criterion' may be met and the individual exits the group. The individual becomes an ex-member and the process of
   remembrance (5) begins. Processes of resocialization of established group
   members are often harsher and less forgiving than those of socialization of new
   members, as was demonstrated in a set of experiments by Pinto, Marques,
   Levine and Abrams (2010). Portuguese high school and university students
   evaluated full members more harshly than new members of their student group
   when they deviated from its norms (e.g., by saying 'I think university students
   are not mature enough to know what's best for them'). They were also more
   strongly in favour of harsh responses to full members (e.g., forcing or threatening them to adopt the group's normal perspective). In contrast, they were
   more willing to adopt gentle persuasion with new members (e.g., using rational
   arguments to convince them of the merit of the group's position). Apparently,
   more is expected of full than new members. Thus, if you break the normative
   'rules' of a group you've just joined, the socialization processes may be relatively
   gentle and educative. Resocialization may be less pleasant (but is not always
   harsh or punitive; for a review, see Moreland and Levine, 2001).

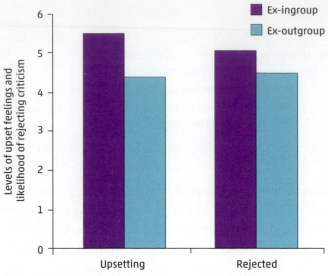

FIGURE 8.5 Psychological importance of the 'remembrance' phase of group socialization
Participants were more upset by, and more likely to reject, criticism of their former group's work when it came from other members of their former group, rather than members of other groups. The ties that bind groups together continue to influence people, even after they are formally cut.
Source: Data from Moreland and McGinn, 1999

5 *Remembrance:* The individual reminisces about being a member of the group and the group remembers the individual as part of its tradition. Levels of commitment eventually become low for both the individual and the group. Although the individual has left the group, there are continued feelings of obligation and loyalty. Moreland and McGinn (1999) demonstrated this point by having groups of students work together on an art poster. The groups were then dissolved. Participants were later exposed to criticism of the poster their group had made. This was rated as more upsetting, and was more likely to be rejected, when participants believed it came from former members of their group than former members of another group (Figure 8.5).

Similar theories from a communication perspective argue for slightly different stages of socialization. For example, Anderson, Riddle and Martin (1999) proposed that socialization goes through a series of stages:

- *antecedent phase:* people share their beliefs and attitudes
- *anticipatory phase:* individuals decide what they want from the group and any pre-existing group norms influence individuals
- *encounter phase:* individuals come together to establish group goals and roles
- *assimilation phase:* involves new group members accepting the established group culture and beginning to identify with the group. Successful assimilation occurs when group members see their own values and interests coinciding with those of the group (but fails when they do not)
- *exit phase:* the task comes to an end and the group diffuses.

Although it is argued that these basic processes are common to most groups, they can mean different things for different groups. Take, for example, the divergence that occurs in Moreland and Levine's model. This may be unexpected, such as when someone within a group is dissatisfied with their role and chooses to leave. Resocialization might be possible in such a case if the individual and the group can reconcile their differences and negotiate a new role for the individual. But, sometimes divergence is not entirely expected. For example, a student leaves school to enter university. This is a case of role transition, and the process of resocialization into the current group (school) is not possible. Indeed, role transitions such as this are important aspects of group life. Brinthaupt, Moreland and Levine (1991) and Moreland and Levine (1989) have investigated these sorts of role transitions in some detail. These transitions can often become ritualized events, rites of passage, and occasionally involve *initiation rites*. They can be pleasant and marked with ceremony and gifts (e.g., a wedding), but can often be unpleasant and involve humiliation (e.g., the associated 'stag do'). Such events, although sometimes painful, can serve to publicly recognize the role transition, help individuals become accustomed to their new role, and enhance commitment to the new group. Social psychologists explain people's acceptance of unpleasant initiation rituals in terms of cognitive dissonance (Festinger, 1957) (see also Chapter 4). An unpleasant initiation creates dissonance – feeling unpleasant about undergoing an embarrassing initiation rite, and feeling negative about the group – which can be reduced by focusing on the positive rather than the negative aspects of the group. This is a way of maintaining loyalty towards the group.

Question to consider At this point, reread question 1 at the start of the chapter. Do you think that Juma would be more committed to the group if he was asked to complete the unpleasant task as part of his initiation into the group, or if he was not asked to perform any task?

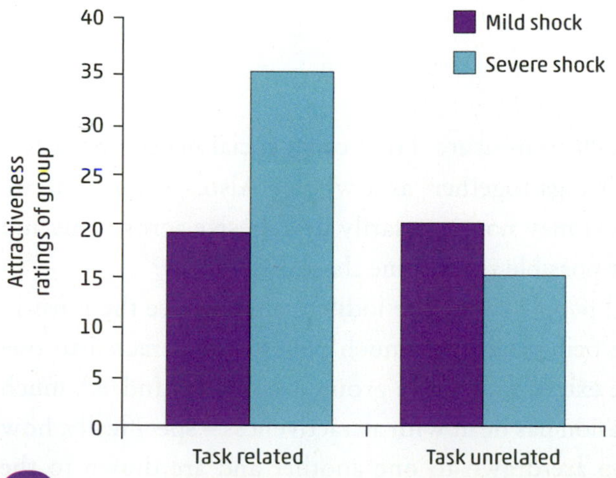

FIGURE 8.6 Initiation tasks and cognitive dissonance
When an unpleasant task (severe electric shock) is perceived to be an initiation into a group, the group is seen as more attractive than when the task is perceived to be unrelated to the group. Compared to participants who received only a mild shock, the participants who received a severe shock rated the group as much more attractive, arguably as a result of cognitive dissonance.

Source: Data from Gerard and Mathewson, 1966

This cognitive dissonance effect was demonstrated in a study by Aronson and Mills (1959). The researchers recruited female participants to take part in a group discussion about the psychology of sex. They were about to join the discussion but were first asked to read a boring excerpt of the discussion. Participants were then divided into three groups. One group performed a mild initiation task to read out five words with vague sexual meaning. One group performed a much more embarrassing initiation task to read out sexually explicit passages. Finally, a control group had no task. Results revealed that the group asked to perform the extreme initiation rated the discussion as much more interesting than the other two groups. Arguably, the embarrassing and uncomfortable task of reading out sexually explicit passages created a state of dissonance, increasing commitment to the group discussion. Interestingly, this effect seems to be specific to situations where the unpleasant task is perceived to be an initiation. Gerard and Mathewson (1966) replicated Aronson and Mills' study, including a condition where the more unpleasant task (receiving a severe electric shock in this case, compared to only a mild shock) was perceived to be unrelated to the later task. Evaluation of the group was not affected in this condition, arguably because the task was independent of the group task. However, the unpleasant experience enhanced the evaluation of the group (compared to the less unpleasant experience) when it was perceived to be an initiation for the group (see Figure 8.6).

Attractiveness ratings of group

■ Mild shock
■ Severe shock

Task related — Task unrelated

Exploring further Use the internet to read more about different types of initiation rites or 'rites of passage' from around the world. Notice how they vary in severity and degree of embarrassment for the initiated person.

Socialization outcomes These
relate to how members of
the group feel about how
they functioned to reach
the group's purpose. The
most prominent outcome
is group cohesion.

Group cohesion The extent
to which a group holds
people to one another (and
the group as a whole), which
gives the group a sense of
unity and commonality.

Groups can therefore benefit from positive socialization. **Socialization outcomes** describe how members and the group as a whole feel about how they functioned to reach the group objective. The most prominent of these outcomes, for social psychology, is group cohesion.

Group cohesion

Once a group is operating, one of its main features is **group cohesion** – the degree to which it holds together as an entity. A group's level of cohesion depends on group members' mutual support for one another and consistency of conduct or behaviour. As such, it is similar to the concept of entitativity discussed earlier, where entitative groups appear to be coherent and 'bound' together as a unit. Of course, cohesion differs between groups. Some groups are not at all cohesive and from the outside, some groups can look very little like groups. On the other hand, some groups are highly cohesive and appear almost impenetrable from the outside. So, what makes a group cohesive? What psychological processes draw people together to form cohesive units?

Festinger, Schachter and Back (1950) argued that the key ingredients determining a group's level of cohesion are its attractiveness (both of the group and its members) and how much the group satisfies individual goals. These forces are depicted in Figure 8.7.

**FIGURE 8.7 Festinger et
al.'s (1950) model of group
cohesion (from Hogg, 1992)**
Forces act on the individual
to make the group cohesive.
Group cohesion then
determines individual
adherence to group standards.

Source: Hogg, 1992.
Reproduced with permission
from Michael Hogg

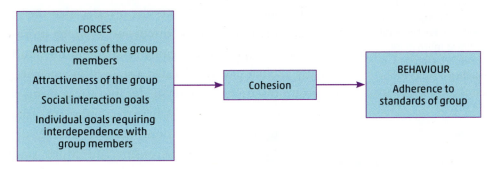

Cohesion is, however, difficult to measure. How can a social psychologist test the degree to which a group 'hangs together' as a whole? Also, groups that are cohesive in one time and context may not necessarily be cohesive across time and in different contexts. How is it possible to examine these differences?

Festinger et al. (1950) asked people to list the individuals they see the most in social contexts – the rationale being that how much people are attracted to one another largely determines the extent to which a group is cohesive. Indeed, much of the research examining cohesion has dealt with attractiveness – specifically, how much people within the group are drawn to one another and are drawn to the group (for a review, see Dion, 2000). However, others argue that quantifying group cohesion by measuring attractiveness is not always appropriate. Specifically, some theorists argue that if social psychologists measure individual-level attractiveness, they are not capturing a process that is unique to groups (Hogg, 1992; Turner, 1984, 1985). They are simply examining interpersonal attraction. These researchers argued and, indeed, found that group-level variables such as group prototypicality and norms are significantly related to group-based social attraction but not individual-based social attraction (e.g., Hogg and Hardie, 1991). Thus, some of the basic structural features of groups, and not simply interpersonal attraction, can determine how groups hang together to form a cohesive unit. We examine some of these structural features of groups in the next section.

Time to reflect Think of your most important social groups. How cohesive are they? Can you think of some of the differences between your cohesive and less cohesive groups?

Group structure

As we mentioned earlier, groups vary in many simple ways, such as in their size and composition. Groups also exist for many different purposes. Subsequently, they tend to have organizational systems that enable them to meet their objectives. Here, we discuss some of the structural features of groups that enable them to perform their purposes. We outline the important role of norms in defining group structure and determining group members' behaviour. We also discuss how social roles and social status shape the nature of groups.

Norms

Have you ever been in a situation where you unintentionally (or intentionally) offended someone with your behaviour? Perhaps you laughed at a funeral or shouted in a library. Perhaps you pushed into a long queue at your local supermarket. On your travels, you may have said or done something that angered someone from another country. What happened in these situations? How did you feel? These are examples of basic social norm violations, which can often have disastrous effects. Indeed, sometimes when we violate social norms, we are shunned by and excluded from the group, as we will see later (Marques, Abrams and Serodio, 2001).

Social norms Uniformities of behaviour and attitudes that determine, organize and differentiate groups from other groups.

Social norms such as these are strong determinants of our behaviours. Norms are defined as the uniformities of behaviour and attitudes that determine, organize and differentiate groups from other groups. They are the formal or informal rules unique to specific groups, which are adopted to regulate its members' behaviours. Some norms are basic rules that everyone is supposed to obey (e.g., being quiet in a cinema) and others are dependent on the culture of the group (e.g., what colour clothing is appropriate to wear at a funeral). Much of the time, social norms are written, formalized or spoken openly and indeed this is often effective. A study by Cialdini, Reno and Kallgren (1990) demonstrates how the open expression of expected behaviour has a strong influence on people's actions. Cialdini et al. placed flyers on the windows of cars parked in a university car park. Some flyers expressed a clear anti-littering message: 'April is Keep Arizona Beautiful Month. Please Do Not Litter', while others carried a message irrelevant to littering: 'April is Arizona's Fine Arts Month. Please Visit Your Local Art Museum'. The researchers observed the car owners' behaviour and counted the number of each type of flyer that had been thrown on the ground. They found that 25 per cent of people who had received an irrelevant message threw the flyer away before getting into their cars, compared with only 10 per cent of those who had received the anti-littering norm message (see also Chapter 9). Thus, direct communication of norms can be effective.

However, some norms are more subtle and seldom explicitly stated; but these implicit or 'hidden' norms still have a powerful influence on people's behaviour. Even when we violate the most implicit and unspoken of norms, we often find out when we have transgressed. Garfinkel (1967) developed a technique called **ethnomethodology** to uncover and understand some of these hidden norms. Ethnomethodology is the study of the everyday methods that people use for the production of social order. It is done by documenting the methods and practices through which people make sense of their social world (Garfinkel, 2002). One of the techniques involves people violating social norms (e.g., norms of familial inter-actions) so that attention is drawn to them. It is intended that the violation of the norm would uncover the true norm underneath. This technique is commonly known as a **breaching experiment**, in that it seeks to examine people's reactions to the breaching of common social norms or rules. Indeed, in Garfinkel's original work, students who were asked to behave differently than they normally would at home (e.g., to behave like polite, formal boarding students instead of their parents' children) were met with shock and surprise from their parents. Here, it was argued that the normative conduct of behaviour had been revealed and its violation elic-ited a strong reaction from the parents. Another example can be found in a study conducted on the New York subway in the 1970s. In this study, Milgram asked able-bodied graduate students (posing as passengers) to board a train and ask able-bodied and seated passengers, without explanation, to give up their seats. As you will learn in Chapter 9, people quite easily comply with such requests and, in this case, 68 per cent of passengers gave up their seat willingly. However, the students making the requests felt deeply uncomfortable doing so (Luo, 2004). One student reported that she felt like she was going to throw up. Milgram said in an interview for *Psychology Today* in 1974 that even he 'froze' when he attempted to make the request himself. These reactions point to the power of social norms in guiding our behaviour. These often invisible rules of social behaviour help maintain social order but go largely unnoticed until they are violated (see Blass, 2004).

Further, norms do not have to be explicit in order to influence our behaviour. In another study, Cialdini et al. (1990) placed participants in either a clean or dirty (littered) setting and observed the participants' littering behaviour. More people littered the dirty environment. Also, it was found that the percentage of people who littered was highest when participants saw someone littering in an already dirty environment but lowest when people saw someone litter a clean environment. Cialdini et al. explained this apparent contradiction in terms of *norm accessibility* – the littering person's behaviour drew the participant's atten-

Ethnomethodology A method used for understanding 'hidden' social norms by analysing people's accounts and descriptions of their day-to-day activities.

Breaching experiment A technique used in ethnomethodology that seeks to examine people's reactions to violations of common social norms.

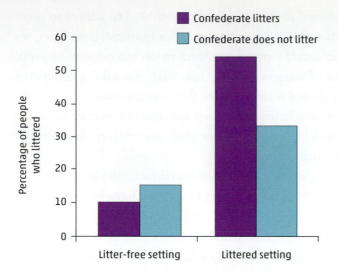

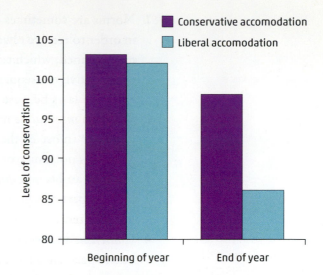

FIGURE 8.8 The effects of norms on littering In a litter-free setting, a confederate who litters draws attention to the implicit norm to keep the place clean and so people tend to litter less. On the other hand, a confederate seen littering an already dirty environment activates a norm of untidiness and people tend to litter more often.
Source: Data from Cialdini et al., 1990

FIGURE 8.9 The effects of social norms on attitudes US college students were randomly assigned to conservative (sorority) accommodation or liberal (dormitory) lodgings. After a year at the college and having been exposed to the different norms, the dormitory students became significantly more liberal in their attitudes.
Source: Data from Siegel and Siegel, 1957

Frames of reference The range of possible positions/attitudes/behaviours that people could adopt in a given situation. People use these frames of reference to guide their own thoughts and actions.

tion to the norm (to litter or not to litter), which subsequently influenced their behaviour (see Figure 8.8). In another condition where only one piece of rubbish was visible, people littered even less, supporting the idea that implicit and environmental cues lead people to really think about what behaviours are normative and anti-normative.

As we will see in Chapter 9, norms strongly influence our behaviour. In particular, they can determine what we say and do when we are unsure of how to behave. In this respect, they can provide us with useful **frames of reference** from which to judge (and recalibrate) our own behaviour (Sherif, 1935, 1937; Jacobs and Campbell, 1961). By establishing the normative behaviour of others in the group, we obtain a useful guide for our own responses.

However, group norms can also change what we do and what we think even when we have already established our own internal frame of reference. Siegel and Siegel (1957) randomly assigned students entering a US college to different types of student residences. Some were assigned to sorority accommodation (where a conservative culture was dominant) and others were assigned to dormitory accommodation where they were exposed to more liberally minded norms. Siegel and Siegel measured students' levels of conservatism at the beginning of the year and again at the end of the year. In Figure 8.9, you can see that although the attitudes of both groups were similar at the beginning of the year, exposure to liberal norms significantly reduced conservatism at the end of the year.

As we can see, norms are powerful. But why do they work so well? Why do norms guide people's behaviour so strongly? Going back to Cialdini et al.'s littering example, it is possible to highlight several reasons:

1 Norms are sometimes *enforced* so that people are motivated to adhere to them in order to receive rewards and avoid punishments. For example, if we litter, we may be fined, which is unpleasant – putting rubbish in the bin helps us to avoid the negative consequences of norm violation. Likewise, we adhere to written rules and laws because we do not want to suffer the consequences.

2 We often *internalize* norms and believe that they are right. For example, we do not litter (most of the time) because we know that throwing rubbish on the ground is not a nice or prosocial thing to do.

3 Norms can become *fixed* during the process of socialization so that when we become part of a group, its norms become part of us – we have been socialized not to litter.

4 *Consensus* influences the power of norms to determine our behaviour. Seeing others perform a particular behaviour makes the behaviour look like the appropriate thing to do. If people consistently behave in a normative manner, you will also know that they expect you to do the same. As we saw in Cialdini et al.'s (1990) study, watching other people litter made people more likely to do the same. Likewise, if others are doing something normative, they will *support* you in the face of threats from people who do not share the same norms.

5 Norms are often *activated*. The more we interact with members of the group, the more we are exposed to group norms. Just being reminded of our group membership makes us think about the group and its norms.

6 Norms act as useful *heuristics* that make our lives easier. When we are busy or in a complex situation, awareness of group norms gives us something to fall back on so that we know how to behave.

Question to consider   Knowing what you know about norms, reread question 2 at the start of the chapter. How do you think you would react if you were Cerys's friend? Where did Cerys go wrong?

Norms are also useful to the group's overall function and can often help a group achieve its purpose. This is particularly useful in organizations, as a study by Coch and French (1948) demonstrated. In this study, the researchers compared pyjama factory workers' responses to three different ways of changing production routines. In this factory, the female workers were paid a set amount of money per unit of work they completed and any changes to the working routine would have an impact on their income. Workers in a control group were simply informed that new routines had to be adopted and were told about corresponding changes to their pay scheme. A second group were given the same information but were also told why the changes were being made and were given the freedom to choose who would teach them the new routines. The third group received the same information as the second, but this time each participant was given the freedom to establish for themselves the best way to learn the new practices and was also allowed to establish their own norm of what was an acceptable productivity level. Which group had the best productivity? Which group do you think was the happiest? Results showed that the productivity of the final group, after immediately drop-

© GETTY

ping slightly, became 15 per cent better than before the changes were introduced. Their morale also remained high. In fact, people who did not adopt the norm were often ostracized or had their work sabotaged by other group members. Thus, the norm became strong and people deviating from the norm were seriously dealt with. There are often significant consequences for people who violate norms, and we will discuss some of these consequences with respect to group deviance and ostracism later in the chapter. Going back to the factory study, it was not surprising that the first group responded most negatively to the changes. In this group, morale dropped and workers even started to leave the factory. A study by Marks, Mirvis, Hackett and Grady (1986) demonstrated similar results – here, members of small work groups in a factory were more productive and were absent from work less than a comparison group. Generally, research findings suggest that norm formation with respect to goal setting in organizations has positive consequences for productivity, work rates and satisfaction.

Permitting groups to form their own norms is one useful way to increase the effectiveness of a group. This practice has been successfully adopted in many different contexts, and countries such as Japan have long used techniques such as participative decision making and *quality circles* (small groups who meet regularly to discuss productivity) to increase efficiency in industries. Likewise, Swedish car companies such as Saab and Volvo have utilized cooperative work groups and have a strong reputation for high-quality cars. The positive effects of permitting group members to form their own norms can last even after people have left the group. For example, a self-help group for weight loss can assist an individual to develop their own norms of healthy living. In fact, allowing groups the freedom to produce their own norms might be a way to facilitate important social change. For example, if people in a neighbourhood establish norms encouraging pro-environmental behaviour (e.g., recycling, lower energy use), how might these norms influence surrounding neighbourhoods? Could this type of norm formation potentially establish a more far-reaching positive norm of pro-environmental behaviour?

In general, norms provide the standards for group behaviour and guiding principles for group attitudes. It is through norms that groups exert their influence on individual group members. We spend more time discussing the power of norms in Chapter 9, when we discuss the core topic of social influence and the power of the group above and beyond the norms and standards of the individual. We discuss how norms form and develop in the first place, and highlight more of the important ways that norms influence our social behaviour.

Roles and status

Social roles Expectations shared by group members about how particular people in the group are supposed to behave.

In addition to social norms, many groups have well-defined **social roles**, or shared expectations of how particular people are supposed to behave in groups. The distinction between norms and roles is fairly simple. Whereas norms determine how all groups members should (or do) act, roles specify how people who hold *particular positions* within a group should behave. For example, a work team will usually consist of a boss or line manager and workers. These roles have clearly defined standards of behaviour and a line manager and their workers are expected to behave in different ways to make the group function appropriately. Likewise, students working on a collaborative group project will often establish clear roles such as assigning one person to write the introduction, one person to write the method and so on. Each group member therefore has a prescribed role that helps the group meet its purpose. Roles emerge in groups so that members have a clear idea of what they need to do, how they should behave, and what their place is within the group. In general, findings suggest that when people in a group stick to a set of well-defined roles, they are more satisfied and perform better (Barley and Bechky, 1994; Bettencourt and Sheldon, 2001).

However, clearly defined social roles are not always a good thing. As we will see in Chapter 9, being too embedded in social roles can sometimes have seriously negative consequences. In particular, you will read about the Stanford Prison Experiment where young men were assigned to the role of prisoner or guard in a simulated prison environment at Stanford University (Haney, Banks and Zimbardo, 1973). In this study, the guards became embedded in their roles and performed role-consistent behaviour – such as brutality and intimidation towards the prisoners – to such an extent that the study had to be ended prematurely. Rigid adherence to roles can have other types of negative consequences. Gersick and Hackman (1990) describe the example of an Air Florida pilot (arguably accustomed to typically warm weather) automatically responding 'yes' to his team member's routine question 'anti-ice off?' despite the snowy weather at Washington DC airport. Nobody checked and the plane crashed shortly after take-off, resulting in the death of crew and passengers. Do social roles sometimes 'take over' our personal identities and make us lose sight of some of the things we would normally do? We examine this issue in more detail in the Critical focus box in Chapter 9. Social roles might also become problematic when they are, or seem, illegitimate or arbitrary. In the Critical focus box below, we examine the case of gender roles.

CRITICAL FOCUS

Gender roles: a minefield of science and politics

Gender roles are often raised as examples of roles that do not always make logical sense. Many cultural groups have expectations about how women and men ought to behave. For example, it is often the case that women are expected to rear children and maintain a household at the expense of having a career, while men are supposed to work and earn money for the family (Wood and Eagly, 2010). Associated with these gender roles is a pattern of basic male dominance or *patriarchy*, in which men have more status and power than women. Men generally have more status and power in all contemporary human cultures; for example, having more access to high-paying jobs, being paid more for doing the same jobs, and being more represented in the highest levels of leadership in politics, religion and business (López-Claros and Zahidi, 2005). Gender roles are interesting to social psychologists. They touch all our lives on a daily basis – perhaps no system of social categorization and specialization is so

Gender roles Shared expectations about how women and men are supposed to behave.

universal and potent – and the study of gender roles requires us to think about stereotypes (Chapter 11), ideologies such as sexism (Chapter 4), and the biological bases of our behaviour. Although there are many interesting scientific questions we can ask about gender roles, one of the most central questions is whether current gender roles, and particularly the disproportionate assignment of women to domestic, nurturing roles and men to competitive, economically valued roles, are an inevitable feature of human life.

Here is where disagreements begin. For some researchers, male dominance or patriarchy has evolved to become an intrinsic part of human nature. In this model, early humans evolved in hunter-gatherer bands in which men were given the economically valuable role of hunting, and needed to control women in order to be sure that the children they were investing in were really theirs (Kaplan and Robson, 2002; Sidanius and Pratto, 1999). However, other researchers dispute this. Evolutionary arguments like this tend to involve speculation about how early humans lived, often in the absence of archeological evidence. Some evidence now suggests that matriarchy was important in early human societies, with female alliances forming to look after children, meaning that women did not depend on men as much as has been suggested (Opie and Power, 2008).

Since the study of 'race' and racial superiority faded in the aftermath of the Second World War, arguments about nature versus nurture are never more politically loaded than when they touch on gender roles (Wood and Eagly, 2010). If gender roles arise from societal conditions, they presumably can be changed, reversed or eliminated as society sees fit, but if they are (to some extent) instilled in us by evolution, then complete gender equality may be an impossible dream. The clear political danger of putting forward evolutionary arguments for gender roles is to imply that gender roles cannot – and perhaps should not – be entirely revised. This political concern, especially with reference to gender, has left some social psychologists uneasy about evolutionary social psychology. Thus, Reicher (2011, p. 353) writes that evolutionary social psychology can lead us to 'reify all the imperfections and inequalities of our contemporary world'.

Despite this unease, even if we were to scientifically establish that gender roles have evolved, this does not necessarily mean they are right or appropriate for contemporary society. Evolutionary researchers argue against committing the 'naturalistic fallacy' – to show that a certain behavioural tendency has evolved does not mean that it is right or should be approved of. Conditions have changed, and it is possible that we have inherited psychological dispositions that are no longer right for us. Indeed, Dawkins (1976) points out that genes have evolved in order to replicate themselves and do not necessarily have our interests at heart, so sometimes it is appropriate to seek to counteract their influence on us, or, in other words, 'fight the replicators'. Also, few social psychologists would wish scientists to be censored, or even to censor themselves, on political grounds. Our job is to discover truths, even if these truths are not always comfortable or palatable to us.

Nonetheless, progress on gender inequality is frustratingly slow. For example, traditional stereotypes of men and women persist. Women are paid less than men for doing the same jobs, and inequality of pay is changing only slowly despite legislation and policy. In heterosexual couples in which the man and woman do the same amount of paid work, she will spend 50 per cent more of her time looking after the children, and doing domestic chores, than he will (for a review, see Wood and Eagly, 2010). Some changes present women with a double-edged sword, since they are now under pressure to build a career and fulfil their gender roles (e.g., Brislin, 1993). There is evidence of a 'backlash' against recent advances in gender equality, such that women (and men) who do not live up to old-fashioned gender types are derogated, especially when their deviance from gender types is of a kind that threatens male dominance. Underpinning many of these gender role attitudes is precisely the belief, held widely by members of the public, that gender differences are biologically ordained – that men and women are inevitably different, and will inhabit different roles because of their biology. This is called 'essentialism'. When people believe, or are led to believe, that there are fundamental, psychologically important biological differences between men and women, they are more likely to endorse gender inequality and oppose efforts to change it. The clear danger in putting forward evolutionary explanations of gender role specialization is to reinforce current gender roles and make gender equality more difficult to achieve. This is a heavy responsibility, and demands that scientists exercise high standards of skill in designing and conducting their research and caution in interpreting the results.

Questions

1 Using the internet, can you find any gender equality statistics for your country? For example, how large is the 'pay gap' in your country, and how overrepresented are men in political and business leadership?

2 Do you think that scientists' political persuasion may influence the scientific models they use? For example, do you think that more conservative, traditional or right-wing scientists may be drawn to evolutionary

social psychological explanations of gender roles, whereas more feminist, left-wing scientists may be drawn to accounts of gender roles that emphasize socialization and culture? How would you test this possibility in a study?

3 Using the internet, find media coverage of studies of gender differences. Do these tend to favour nature (biology, hormones, evolution) or nurture (socialization and culture) explanations?

Exploring further It is widely believed (and probably rightly so) that gender roles are particularly restrictive for women. However, it is also important to consider how gender roles can present challenges for men. Using an internet search engine or database such as PsycINFO, can you find studies that have examined the effects of male gender roles, or expectations of what men should be like? What did these studies show?

Thus, social roles can often cause us conflict. Interestingly too, they can change who we are. A study by Twenge demonstrates how changing gender roles can influence our personalities. Twenge (2001) tracked women's social status in the USA between 1931 and 1993. She compared this with women's own reports of their assertiveness. In general, women's self-ratings of assertiveness followed the same pattern as their social status. For example, with the improvements in social status between 1931 and 1945 (e.g., more women gaining university degrees and more women in the workforce), women reported feeling more assertive. Likewise, after 1968, when the feminist movement took hold and women's social status improved, they again reported greater levels of assertiveness. The period in between (1946–67), where more women stayed at home and less went to university, was marked by a decrease in self-reports of assertiveness. This striking effect is shown in Figure 8.10. In general, the roles that people occupy in groups (and society) are powerful in forming their behaviour, feelings and even their personality (Eagly and Steffen, 2000; Wood, Christensen, Hebl and Rothgerber, 1997).

FIGURE 8.10 The influence of changing gender roles on personality Women's self-reported assertiveness mirrors trends in their social status. Prewar improvements in rated assertiveness mirrored similar improvements in their status. Postwar movements to more traditional social roles were associated with lower ratings of assertiveness. However, women's social status recovered with the feminist movement and self-ratings of assertiveness again increased.

Source: Adapted from Twenge, 2001. Copyright © 2001 by the American Psychological Association. Adapted with permission

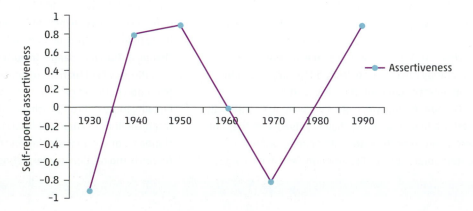

Status Shared evaluations of the 'prestige' of roles within a group, the members of the group, or the group as a whole.

Of course, roles are often closely linked to one's **status** in general and the above example shows how gender roles and women's status in society are similar. Gender roles mean that women and men are not always treated equally. In many other groups too, the roles that people occupy are not equal. Thus, our discussion of roles naturally leads us into the issue of status.

Some roles within a group are more valued than other roles and are associated with higher status. Generally, the leader of a group is accepted as the highest status position, but within groups we often see a hierarchy of roles, and subsequently a 'ranking' of the people who occupy the roles, which tends to be accepted by others both within and outside the group. Indeed, for a group role or individual member in a group to be seen to have status, the perception of status needs to be shared by others. There is little point in assuming that one has status if nobody around recognizes it.

Exploring further In the 1993 film *The Age of Innocence* directed by Martin Scorsese, a young lawyer in 19th-century, New York high society (Daniel Day-Lewis) falls in love with a woman who is separated from her husband (Michelle Pfeiffer). However, the lawyer is engaged to the woman's cousin. The film gives an insight into the norms, status roles and gender roles of a society and what may happen to individuals if those norms are violated.

Group members who are seen to have status within a group display a tendency to initiate activities and suggest ideas – these suggestions are more likely than others' suggestions to be taken up by the group. For example, a person chairing a meeting may be more likely to make a suggestion that is agreed upon by the rest of the group because they are seen as having a certain level of standing or authority. However, a person's status within the group is not set forever and status differentials within a group can change over time. For example, a person chairing a meeting may not always do so and duties such as these may be shared between members of the group over time. Similarly, the head of an academic department at a university will typically serve a set amount of time before someone else is elected to do the job. One's status within a group can also differ across contexts. For example, an academic department head will have less status in a university-level meeting than in a departmental meeting. While they are 'in charge' in one context, they may be a regular group member in others.

How do status differentials emerge within groups? One explanation comes from Festinger's social comparison theory (Festinger, 1954). According to this account, status hierarchies reflect social comparisons within the group. Being in groups presents people with relevant others with whom to compare themselves. We look at others, their opinions and their abilities and 'place' ourselves within the group according to certain valuable characteristics. Sometimes, this process happens quite naturally and everyone in a group is happy with their position. Frequently, however, status in a group is contested. One example is group leadership, a role that is often toughly contested (Figure 8.11). A group role such as this is a high status and desirable one because it brings with it a lot of power and influence. Thus, the process of social comparison with others is often competitive and

© BRAND X PICTURES

FIGURE 8.11 Leadership is a highly coveted and contested role within a group

role assignment is dependent on how people compare with others on status-relevant dimensions. One prospective leader may run a stronger and more convincing election campaign. Another candidate may simply impress their group with a demonstrated capacity to take the group forward. Obviously, not everyone can become the leader, so once the allocation of status is resolved within a group, people must be content with their own position. This is one way that status becomes a shared or consensual phenomenon within the group – people who do not win and become followers naturally feel – in some way – inferior to the emergent leader. In short, they have to learn to deal with it and one way to do this is to legitimize the status-relevant differences between themselves and the leader. In doing so, the prestige of the high status position is reinforced and perpetuated over time and as new leaders emerge or are elected. These types of processes also occur between groups when one group is perceived as having higher status than the others. We will cover this topic in more detail in Chapter 11 on intergroup relations.

Sometimes, people simply accept that other people in a group are of a higher status than themselves. Some research by Strodtbeck, James and Hawkins (1957) demonstrated this *status institutionalization* in newly formed status hierarchies. They established mock juries whose role was to read transcripts of actual trials and produce verdicts based on the transcripts. They found that the high status role of jury 'foreman' was typically assigned to a person with higher status in real life. More specifically, the groups awarded the higher status positions in the experiment to people who held occupations outside the experiment such as teachers and other professionals rather than people who occupied working-class occupations like cleaners or mechanics. It may be that people simply expect some individuals to be associated with higher status roles in general because they occupy a high status role (or roles) in society. Such **diffuse status characteristics** may not be directly associated with the group task at hand but they are generally positively evaluated and therefore generate favourable expectations. For example, a professional individual such as a doctor or lawyer may know very little about making quality judgements about music (a **specific status characteristic**). Nevertheless, they may be more likely to be chosen as a band manager because they are seen as having status in another domain (Berger, Fisek, Norman and Zelditch, 1997; Ridgeway and Berger, 1986).

As we will see in Chapters 11 and 14, the legitimization of status differences *between* groups means that people often support systems that are unfair to them personally. **System justification theory** (Jost and Banaji, 2004) posits that people depend on social systems for wealth and security and are therefore motivated to justify those social systems, seeing them as fair and functional. When they come across inequality or unfairness, low status group members tend to internalize the negative stereotypes of their group that serve to justify their low status position, to believe

Diffuse status characteristics Attributes not directly relevant to the group task but positively valued in society.

Specific status characteristics Attributes directly relevant to the group task.

System justification theory Theory that people's dependence on social systems for wealth and security motivates them to justify these social systems and see them as fair.

that authorities act in their interests, and that economic inequality is legitimate or even necessary (Jost, Pelham, Sheldon and Sullivan, 2003). In Chapter 14, we discuss how this system-justifying tendency of low status group members influences women's feelings of their own entitlements in employment settings (Bylsma and Major, 1994; Callahan-Levy and Meese, 1979), and for people to endorse inequality in their own society (Kay, Whitson, Gaucher and Galinsky, 2009).

People's expectations about ability and status can explain how status roles emerge within groups. These expectations may help people to deal with their position within the group if they are not the leader. People may not always simply 'deal with it' though. Often, the process of losing out on an important status dimension can make people feel uncomfortable and unhappy. People can deal with this dissatisfaction in other ways besides simply accepting or internalizing the idea that they are inferior. They may choose to emphasize the things they are good at and downplay the features on which they fall short. Again, these processes occur between groups too and group members often redefine the important features of their group on which they prefer to be evaluated. Dimensions that favour the ingroup (e.g. 'we are good at sport'), rather than disfavour the group (e.g., 'we are a poor country'), tend to be the preferred means of comparison for low status groups, especially if alternative groups (high status groups) are impermeable. This process, called **social creativity**, serves to maintain group members' self-esteem (Tajfel and Turner, 1979). By engaging in comparisons on unorthodox dimensions that tend to favour their own group, people are able to feel good about their group even if they are low status on other dimensions (see also Haslam, 2001).

Social creativity Strategies that group members engage in to maintain the esteem of the group.

Further, research from the system justification theory perspective suggests that people justify a system – regardless of their own position in the system – using complementary stereotyping. The idea is that if people are 'poor', they may be okay because they are probably 'happy'. On the other hand, the 'rich' may be 'miserable'. This line of reasoning implies that low status has its rewards and high status has its drawbacks (Kay and Jost, 2003). Also, if people think they can improve their status by leaving the group, they will do so, whereas if they cannot leave the group, they will seek to improve its status (see the discussion of social identity and intergroup relations in Chapter 11). It is clear that people will not always simply accept an inferior status position, or if they do, they have system-justifying mechanisms to make themselves feel reasonably good about it.

Time to reflect   Think about a specific group you belong to. Can you identify some of the norms of the group? Are there specific roles within the group? Is status a factor in this group?

Fitting in to groups

Norms, roles and status are important features that determine how individuals behave within groups. But what happens to people who violate these norms and behave in ways that are contradictory to their roles and status? Here, we discuss what happens to individuals when they deviate from group standards, when they do not quite fit the prototype of the group, and when they are seen as 'impostors' within a group. We will consider the effects that such marginal group members can have on the group as a whole. We also consider how group deviance can sometimes lead to 'breakoff' groups being formed within the larger group.

Marginal group members ('deviants')

Marginal group members ('deviants') People who deviate too far from prototypical group members and group norms.

Black sheep effect Derogation of deviant or marginal ingroup members.

People who do not embody the group's most important attributes or who 'deviate' too far from prototypical group members are known as **marginal group members** or **deviants**. Whereas some group members have the capacity to exert influence over the group, deviants typically do not. On the contrary, they are often seriously disliked by the group. Research on the **black sheep effect** demonstrates how strongly groups can react to marginal group members (Abrams, Rutland, Cameron and Ferrell, 2007; Castano, Paladino, Coull, and Yzerbyt, 2002; Doosje and Branscombe, 2003; Marques, Yzerbyt and Leyens, 1988; Pinto et al., 2010; Shin, Freda and Yi, 1999). We are all familiar with the term 'black sheep' – a person who goes against the standards of their family (or other important group) and is subsequently shunned by the group in some way. In an early study of this effect, Marques and Yzerbyt (1988) presented Belgian law students with taped speeches that had allegedly been made by other students. One of these speeches was good, and the other was truly bad. In the 'ingroup' conditions of the experiment, the law students were told that the speech was by another law student. In the 'outgroup' conditions, they were told that it was by a philosophy student. Participants rated the speeches, and the speaker (e.g., 'In your opinion, this person's capability to express ideas is …') (1 = weak, 7 = strong). As one might expect, the apparently competent speaker was rated more favourably when they were a member of the ingroup, that is, another law student (Figure 8.12). This is standard ingroup favouritism – in general, we tend to be biased towards our own 'kind' (see also Chapter 11). However, Marques and Yzerbyt found that if the speech was bad, the ingroup speaker was apparently rated *less* favourably than the outgroup speaker.

FIGURE 8.12 The black sheep effect Participants were presented with good or bad speeches, and told these were made either by an ingroup or an outgroup member. In keeping with the usual tendency to favour the ingroup, good speeches were rated more favourably when participants believed they were made by an ingroup, rather than outgroup, member. Bad speeches, however, were rated similarly, or even worse, when participants believed they came from an ingroup rather than an outgroup speaker.
Source: Data from Marques and Yzerbyt, 1988, Study 1

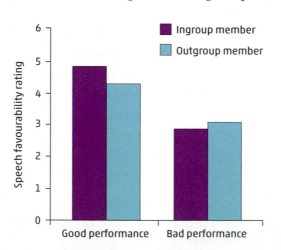

Exploring further   Note that the interaction effect (see Chapter 1) reported by Marques and Yzerbyt (1988) is statistically significant – the good or bad quality of the speeches moderated the effect of speakers' apparent group membership on how they were evaluated. However, the researchers did not report whether or not the tendency to rate bad ingroup speeches more negatively than bad outgroup speeches was statistically significant. Readers who are confident in their statistics might want to run a basic paired-samples t-test to see if it was (n = 26, a within-participants design, M (ingroup) = 2.82, SD = 1.01, M (outgroup) = 3.08, SD = 1.07). Readers who are not as confident may want to search the internet for a basic formula to work out a t-test based on means (M), standard deviations (SD) and sample sizes (n). Try searching for other black sheep studies (you might want to use a database like Google Scholar or Web of Science) to see if you can find cases where responses to an ingroup deviant are indeed significantly harsher than responses to an equivalent outgroup deviant.

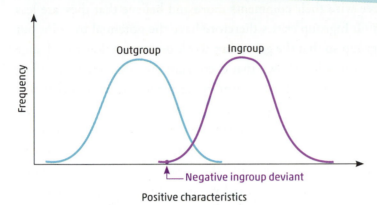

FIGURE 8.13 Subjective group dynamics model According to the subjective group dynamics model (Marques et al., 2001), ingroup members who flout the norms of desirable behaviour are derogated by the group because they threaten the perceived superiority of their group to the outgroup. This figure plots the number of people from the ingroup and outgroup who are perceived to possess a given level of positive characteristics. An ingroup member who does not live up to the perceived standards of the ingroup is effectively like an outgroup member, and so dilutes the perceived superiority of the ingroup.

Intergroup sensitivity effect
The tendency to prefer criticism to come from within the group than from an outsider.

Why do you think this happens? Marques et al.'s explanation is that deviant ingroup members are threatening to the positive image of the ingroup (Marques et al., 2001). As we see later in this chapter when we consider social identity theory, people want to perceive their group in positive terms. In particular, they value its positive distinctiveness – its superiority, on valued dimensions of judgement, to other groups. A group member who deviates from the perceived high standards of the group threatens this perception of ingroup superiority. This threat causes ingroup members to treat such ingroup deviants harshly. The theoretical model that Marques et al. (2001) developed to explain the black sheep effect, based on the principles of social identity and self-categorization theories, is termed 'subjective group dynamics'.

Research generally supports the subjective group dynamics model. Marques et al. (2001) showed that when participants felt certain about the superiority of their group on the dimension in question, they did not derogate ingroup deviants any more than outgroup equivalents. Apparently, under these conditions, they did not find the ingroup deviant to be threatening to the positive image of the ingroup. Only when they felt uncertain about the superiority of the group – and thus found the ingroup deviant disturbed it – did they exhibit the black sheep effect. Abrams et al. (2007), in a study of British school children attending a summer school, provided further evidence of subjective group dynamics. Participants who were accountable to the ingroup – who thought their responses would be seen and discussed by other summer schools – were more likely to derogate deviant ingroup members and valorize ingroup members who followed the norms. One of the functions of the derogation of ingroup members, then, seems to be to ensure that ingroup members 'stay in line' by adhering to group norms, and that other ingroup members play their part in enforcing group norms.

This can sometimes be unfortunate for the group. Specifically, deviance from group norms can often be useful in pointing out things that are wrong within the group (Packer, 2008; Packer and Chasteen, 2010). Indeed, deviants can be important to the group in bringing about positive social change and allowing the group to grow and change. In Chapter 9, you will read more about special cases of minorities holding different views from the majority who are able to make positive social changes. A good example of this from social psychological research comes from the body of work on the **intergroup sensitivity effect** that we will revisit in Chapter 9. Hornsey, Oppes and Svensson (2002; see also Hornsey and Imani, 2004) have shown that people are more ready to accept criticism from within the group than from outside the group. Ingroup critics are naturally 'deviant' members of the group because they are speaking ill of their own kind. However, because they are perceived to be constructive, at least compared to outgroup members, ingroup members agree with their comments more and believe that they are less threatening and harmful. Ingroup critics therefore have the potential to point out problems within the group so that the group can work on its mistakes and change for the better. Other research has shown that even from outside the group, when people have no vested interest in the criticism being made, ingroup criticism is seen as more acceptable (Douglas and Sutton, 2011; Sutton, Elder and Douglas, 2006). The deviant ingroup critic is therefore viewed as more constructive than an outgroup critic even from an impartial observer's perspective. Of course, in real-life situations, the ingroup critic may not find their task very easy. Voicing one's negative opinions about the group can be risky, especially if the group sees the critic as a deviant member. Sometimes, it may be necessary for the critic to find like-minded others and form a minority group within the group. As we will see in Chapter 9, minority groups often show great capacity to influence larger groups.

Exploring further In the research on the black sheep effect, ingroup deviants are derogated and often shunned by the group. However, work on group criticism shows that ingroup critics' comments are accepted by the group with little or no sensitivity. Are these findings at odds with one another? Why/why not? Why do you think deviant group members are rejected in one paradigm but accepted in the other? Read more about the theoretical arguments underlying the black sheep effect and intergroup sensitivity effect to find out.

Impostors

We now know that group members often deal harshly with people who deviate from group norms. The need to protect the identity and integrity of the group is indeed powerful. There is another interesting case of deviant group membership we have not yet dealt with – occasionally members of a group 'pose' as legitimate group members when they are not. Instead, they fail to fulfil important criteria for group membership. How groups deal with these group members – called **impostors** – is a fairly new area of enquiry in social psychology. In the laboratory, several studies examined group members' reactions to people who pose as legitimate members of the group (Hornsey and Jetten, 2003; Jetten, Summerville, Hornsey and Mewse, 2005; Warner, Hornsey and Jetten, 2007).

Impostors People who threaten the group by fraudulently claiming to be members.

Question to consider Reread question 3 at the start of the chapter. How would you react to Ed if you knew that he had not actively served in the war?

In one study, Jetten et al. (2005) presented vegetarians (ingroup members) and meat eaters (outgroup members) with a person claiming to be a vegetarian, but caught eating meat. It was found that ingroup members were more displeased with the target than outgroup members. Ingroup members also derogated the target more than outgroup members. This impostor threatens the distinctiveness of the

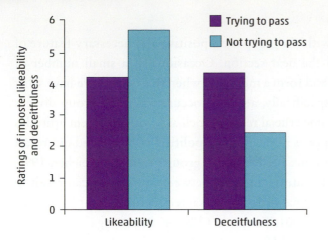

Trying to pass
Not trying to pass

FIGURE 8.14 Perceptions of impostors within groups Participants rated an older adult trying to 'pass' as younger to be less likeable and more deceitful than an older adult not attempting to 'pass'. This study demonstrates the general disdain for people who are seen as imposters to a group.

Source: Data from Schoemann and Branscombe, 2011

group by claiming to be a member and is, like deviant ingroup members, dealt with harshly. Indeed, the negative reactions towards the impostor were greatest when people perceived vegetarians and non-vegetarians to be highly distinctive groups. It also appears that vegetarians who 'eat meat occasionally' are harshly perceived by ingroup members (Hornsey and Jetten, 2003). In another study, Schoemann and Branscombe (2011) asked younger adults what they felt about an older adult target who was attempting to look younger. Participants read a description of a person who was (or was not) trying to 'pass' as younger and were asked to rate them on several dimensions such as likeability and deceitfulness. Following the logic of Jetten et al.'s research, it was predicted that participants would like an older adult attempting to look young less than an older adult who does not attempt to look young. This is exactly what they found (see Figure 8.14). Participants rated an older person trying to 'pass' as younger as less likeable and more deceitful than an older person not attempting to 'pass'.

SOCIAL PSYCHOLOGY IN THE REAL WORLD

Impostors within groups

In Australia, several cases of fraud have recently been uncovered where men living as war heroes were found to be impostors who had never engaged in active service. Sometimes, these men had never even been employed by the armed forces. One example has been presented of a man who masqueraded as a colonel and wore Order of Australia and active service medals. He was, in fact, an accountant who never served in the army or went to war. He was convicted by a Sydney court of falsely posing as a returned soldier. Similarly, in the USA, a man was recently convicted of posing as a decorated Vietnam War veteran and was required to pay a fine. He was also asked to carry out community service. The man was convicted under the 2006 Stolen Valor Act – a federal law that makes it illegal to falsely claim war hero status and military decorations.

These examples demonstrate how strongly people can react to impostors who, like deviant group members, threaten the integrity and image of a valued group.

Questions

1 Think of examples of impostors from your own experience. Are there any specific groups, like war veterans, where impostorism is particularly frowned upon? What are the characteristics of these groups?

2 Are impostors always harmful to the group? Can you think of examples where impostors may actually help the group?

3 Why is it so important to us to protect the integrity of our groups?

Schism and subgroups

Sometimes, smaller factions within a group are a positive and necessary feature of group life, as we will see in the next section. Occasionally, a small number of ingroup members 'break off' and form a minority; when this occurs, we have what is known as a **schism**. More specifically, a schism occurs when the group divides into **subgroups** that differ in some crucial respect, such as having different attitudes or values. This sometimes happens in religious or political contexts and can result in extreme and destructive conflict for the larger group (Sani and Reicher, 1998, 2000). Also, in organizational contexts, mergers between companies can result in two subgroups coming together that differ and disagree on fundamental issues or values (Terry, Carey and Callan, 2001; Terry and O'Brien, 2001). Again, as we will see in Chapter 9, active minorities within a group can sometimes be valuable additions to the group that can exert positive social change.

Smaller groups within a large group can, of course, also occur without a schism. Natural subgroups occur in many groups simply because of the group's structure. For example, companies are divided into different departments that have different functions to perform. One part of the company might be responsible for finance, one for production, one for human resources and so on. Also, within a national Olympic team, there are separate teams for swimming, gymnastics, athletics and so on. Even smaller and more specialized groups can exist within groups that are ultimately part of a larger group. For example, an Olympic team is made up of the various different sporting groups but even within the sporting groups there are smaller divisions for specific purposes such as the 'track' athletes and the 'field' athletes. Further still, **cross-cutting categories** are subgroups that represent categories that have members outside the immediate larger group (Crisp and Hewstone, 2007). For example, a group of athletes may belong to a national Olympic team but also to an international association for athletics. Many groups have complex structures of nested groups and cross-cutting categories but nevertheless define themselves ultimately as one large group.

Subgroups can significantly influence the dynamics within the larger group. As we will see in Chapter 11, subgroups often engage in competition and conflict that can be harmful for the larger group. One obvious example is the conflict between the Catholic and Protestant groups in Northern Ireland (Hewstone, Cairns, Voci et al., 2006). Intense conflict and rivalry between these subgroups contribute to extremely negative intergroup dynamics in society.

What do groups do for us?

Now that we know what groups are, how they are structured and how people 'fit in' to groups, we turn our attention to the functions of group membership. Of course, the purpose of belonging to groups and the meaning of group memberships differ depending on whether or not people have the *choice* to join groups. In many of our social groups such as our race and gender, we cannot simply opt in

Schism A group divides into subgroups that differ usually in terms of their attitudes or values.

Subgroups Smaller groups nested within a larger group.

Cross-cutting categories Subgroups that represent categories that have members outside the immediate larger group.

and out, whereas in other groups we are free to come and go as we please. It is likely that the question 'what do groups do for us?' is not the same, say, for our ethnic group (where we might learn norms and customs of behaviour) and our student union group (where we have the opportunity to air our opinions about important student matters). However, even when we cannot opt out of a group such as our ethnic group, we can nevertheless determine what this group membership *means* to us. For example, we have a choice about what norms we follow and we can decide the extent to which we adopt our ethnic customs and rituals. Thus, even when we cannot choose our group memberships, we can still control what our group membership implies for us as individuals. But, there are several reasons why people belong to groups, and we will now outline these reasons, beginning with interdependence.

Interdependence

Groups allow people to achieve more and sometimes better things than individuals would be able to do on their own. At a simple level, some tasks depend upon people working interdependently and to get these tasks done, people join groups. For example, one person could not have built Stonehenge or the Great Wall of China. The task and outcome depended on the contributions of many people working together. Also, how groups do things is often quite different from how individuals perform tasks on their own. People are influenced by their interactions with other group members, causing them to form goals and behave differently than they would alone. In short, coordinated group action allows people to achieve things that would not be possible by an individual acting alone. Many social psychologists argue that interpersonal interdependence is the essential defining feature of groups (e.g., Rabbie and Horwitz, 1988; Thibaut and Kelley, 1959).

Similarity, support and the need for affiliation

Opinion-based groups
Groups that are formed around shared opinions.

Others join groups when they find people who share their attitudes and opinions. For example, many political and activist groups centre around specific opinions or attitudes. In social psychology, these groups are often known as **opinion-based groups**. Membership of such groups can allow people to achieve the things they want to achieve. For example, Bliuc, McGarty, Reynolds and Muntele (2007) demonstrated that when people identify with opinion-based groups, they are more likely to display intentions for political action. For the groups we already belong to, such as our ethnic group, we share a wide range of customs, norms and beliefs. Thus, we tend to share a lot of important features of 'who we are' with members of our most important groups. Also, at an even more basic level, people tend to join together with, and have more liking for, people who are in close proximity with themselves (Festinger et al., 1950).

From their group memberships, people can also receive social support. In times of hardship or stress, groups can provide a foundation for individuals and insulate them from the harmful effects of stress (Cohen and Wills, 1985). Indeed, people often actively seek support groups for their specific problems. One good example is Alcoholics Anonymous groups that provide people with social support and encouragement to beat alcohol addiction.

By being in groups people satisfy their basic need for affiliation and to belong. According to sociometer theory (Baumeister and Leary, 1995; Leary and Baumeister, 2000), it is adaptive for people to be included in groups and build relationships with others because social inclusion enhances our self-esteem (see our review of sociometer theory in Chapter 2). In support of this view, Leary, Tambor, Terdal and Downs (1995) demonstrated that people's self-esteem was higher in situations where they felt themselves to be included than when they felt excluded (where levels of self-esteem were depressed). Leary et al. argue that self-esteem is therefore a measure of the effectiveness of our social relationships. If self-esteem is high, this means that our group memberships are stable; but if it is low, we seek ways to improve it such as attempting to improve our inclusion in groups. Ultimately, we do not want to be excluded from desirable groups, or be left to feel lonely, so we attempt to 'repair' our group memberships to enhance our personal self-esteem.

Terror management

Terror management theory
Theory proposing that human awareness of death creates a constant source of 'existential anguish' that must be dealt with.

Another social psychological reason for people to affiliate with others derives from **terror management theory** (Greenberg, Pyszczynski and Solomon, 1986; Pyszczynski, Greenberg, Solomon et al., 2004). According to this theory, human awareness of the inevitability of one's own death (mortality salience) creates a continuous source of 'existential anguish'. People therefore attempt to reduce this terror by organizing, structuring and giving meaning to their lives. They can do this in a variety of ways, as we discussed in Chapter 2, and the central mechanism for managing this terror of death appears to be one's self-esteem. According to this account, joining with others and being in groups raises one's self-esteem and feelings of self-worth. Our views are validated and our anxiety about death is reduced. In short, we feel good (and sometimes even immortal) when we affiliate with others and this helps us manage the idea, always in the back of our minds, that our lives are finite.

Greenberg, Pyszczynski, Solomon et al. (1990) demonstrated how this makes us feel about people in general. They found that when people are reminded of their own death, their feelings of attraction to people to consensually validate their own beliefs increases and their attraction to those who threaten their beliefs decreases. Thus, mortality salience may not only enhance our desire to affiliate and join groups but may also mean that we develop a strong preference for our own groups and, in particular, our larger 'ideological' groups (Hogg, Hohman and Rivera, 2008). This may also have implications for how ingroup members deal with deviants who do not uphold the values of the group. It may also influence how we feel about other groups, therefore having implications for ingroup favouritism, prejudice and intolerance. We discuss some of these aspects in more detail in Chapter 11 on intergroup relations.

Research by Wisman and Koole (2003) highlights quite another response to mortality salience. Students from two Dutch universities were exposed to a

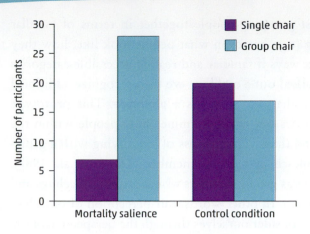

FIGURE 8.15 Mortality salience and the need to belong This shows the number of participants choosing to sit with other participants (group chair) or by themselves (single chair) under mortality salience vs. control conditions. These effects were the same regardless of whether participants were led to believe that other members of their discussion group opposed or supported their worldview.

Source: Wisman and Koole, 2003. Copyright © 2003 by the American Psychological Association. Adapted with permission.

Social identity The aspect of our self/identity that is determined by our group memberships.

Social identity theory The theory of group membership and intergroup relations arguing that personal identities and group memberships complete people's sense of self.

standard manipulation of mortality salience, being asked to describe the emotions they feel when thinking about their own death, and what happens to them when they physically die. In the control group, participants were asked much the same questions about watching TV, with no mention of mortality. After this manipulation, students were invited to take a seat, and told that other students were about to join them in a discussion group. These (fictional) students did not necessarily share participants' own worldview: half the participants were told that the other students opposed Dutch values such as tolerance and democracy. Regardless of whether participants believed other students opposed or supported their own worldviews, participants were more likely to sit in a clustered chair, rather than an isolated chair, following the mortality salience manipulation (see Figure 8.15). Thus, it would seem that under threat of mortality, people do not want to be alone; they prefer company. As we have seen, groups provide us not only with a shared worldview, but also satisfy our deep human need to belong. As we shall see in Chapter 11, one of the functions of a shared worldview may be precisely to satisfy our need to belong, since it provides us with a common understanding of the world within which we can relate to each other. Wisman and Koole's (2003) findings suggest that when the two needs are placed in conflict, the need to belong may sometimes actually override the need to validate our worldviews.

The need for social identity

Another function that groups perform is to provide us with a **social identity**. According to **social identity theory** (Tajfel and Turner, 1979; Turner, Hogg, Oakes et al., 1987), there are two broader types of identities that make up the self. These are one's personal identity (defined by one's personal characteristics and relationships) and one's social identity (defined by one's group memberships). While personal identity is associated with our own personal behaviour and close personal relationships, social identity is associated with our behaviour within (and between) groups. As we saw in Chapter 2 our personal identity is important to our self-concept. However, our social identities are also important to us. For example, we often label ourselves and identify strongly with our national groups, our peer groups and our sporting groups. Therefore, according to this perspective, we need to be part of groups to complete our definition of who we are. In different circumstances, we see ourselves in terms of our personal and social identities to the extent that one is more salient than the other. For example, in a meeting on gender relations in the workplace, we might be more likely to consider ourselves as a man or a woman, but when watching a cricket match, we might be strongly aware of our national identity.

We identify groups as 'fuzzy' sets of characteristics and attributes that define what one group is and differentiate it from other groups. We can do this in many different ways, perhaps by first grouping people together in terms of familiar categories that we use regularly (e.g., based on what people look like, how they behave) and then more complex ways if familiar and readily accessible categories do not work. Once we have worked out a category, we then recognize additional information about the category that we 'store' as a **prototype**. This prototype describes the group's characteristics but also determines how people within the group are expected to behave and think. The process of identifying with a group involves **self-categorization** of oneself as a group member (Turner et al., 1987). Once we do this, we see ourselves as group members whose attitudes, feelings and behaviours are driven by the group. In other words, our perception of ourselves becomes depersonalized and we consider ourselves through the perspective of the group prototype and its associated behaviours and attitudes. It has been argued that categorization as a group member is a precondition for determining group membership itself and that interdependence is a product of the process of social categorization (Platow, Grace and Smithson, 2012). Social categorization is also argued to be a necessary precondition for any affective feelings that go with group membership (McGarty, 1999).

The content of the prototype also determines how we feel about ourselves personally. When we identify with a group, we identify with the characteristics of that group, including its values, prestige and status. It is therefore in our interests to categorize ourselves as members of esteemed groups because if our self-concept derives in part from our social identities, then so too may our self-esteem (Abrams and Hogg, 1988; Long and Spears, 1997). We will all be able to remember times when we felt good about our favourite sports team winning a major competition – being associated with positively valued groups makes us feel good. It is also in our interests to protect or enhance the esteem of the groups we belong to and cannot leave (e.g., our gender or ethnicity). In general, we need to feel good about ourselves and one way to do this is to feel good about the groups we belong to. As we will see in Chapter 11, people's motivation to derive positive self-esteem from being members of groups is an important factor in determining ingroup favouritism. Showing a preference for the ingroup is a way of feeling good about the group and also a way of feeling good about the self. For example, it has been found that people who are given the opportunity to discriminate against an outgroup show higher levels of self-esteem (Lemyre and Smith, 1985). In summary, groups are self-defining and determine important aspects of our self-concept. Social identity is implicated in a wide range of social psychological phenomena and so we will revisit social identity theory many times throughout this book.

A related idea about what groups can do for us also derives from social identity theory. This argument proposes that group membership delivers people from a state of **subjective uncertainty**. Too much uncertainty about who we are and what we are supposed to do can feel uncomfortable (Hogg, Hohman and Rivera, 2008). Because identifying with groups tells us a lot about who we are and how we are supposed to behave, group memberships remove a lot of uncertainty from our everyday lives (Hogg, 2007). We then know how to behave and we can also predict

Prototype 'Fuzzy' sets of characteristics that define a group and distinguish it from other groups.

Self-categorization Cognitive process of categorizing oneself as a group member.

Subjective uncertainty Uncertainty about who we are and what we are supposed to do, which is alleviated by identification with groups.

how people are likely to behave towards us. Hogg, Sherman, Dierselhuis et al. (2007) found that people identify with groups when they feel themselves in a state of uncertainty and the group is able to reduce that uncertainty, as may be the case for highly entitative groups.

Try it yourself Below is a commonly used scale of group identification adapted from Brown, Condor, Mathews et al. (1986). The name of the group (in this case 'university students') is altered depending on the group membership of interest. Complete the scale for yourself and examine your level of identification with university students. Also, substitute another group membership in place of 'university students' and repeat the scale. How does your level of identification change with the nature of the group?

I identify with other university students.

| not at all | 1 | 2 | 3 | 4 | 5 | very much |

I am a worthy member of the university student community.

| not at all | 1 | 2 | 3 | 4 | 5 | very much |

In general, being a university student has little to do with the way I see myself.

| not at all | 1 | 2 | 3 | 4 | 5 | very much |

The fact that I am a university student is an important part of who I am.

| not at all | 1 | 2 | 3 | 4 | 5 | very much |

In general, I am pleased that I am a university student.

| not at all | 1 | 2 | 3 | 4 | 5 | very much |

Source: Adapted from Brown et al., 1986

Optimal distinctiveness

Optimal distinctiveness
People like to feel unique as individuals but at the same time they feel the need to affiliate with others. They need to find the optimal balance between these needs.

Identifying with groups can make people feel positive about themselves even when the groups do not help relieve uncertainty. Also, the groups do not have to be positive. This is partly because we do not just want to achieve a positive view of ourselves, but also a clear, coherent view of ourselves as a person who is distinct from others (e.g., see self-concept clarity in Chapter 2). The idea of **optimal distinctiveness** is that people generally like to distinguish themselves from others and see themselves as unique individuals. At the same time, they also feel the need to affiliate with others. Group membership helps people meet both these needs. People can distinguish themselves from others who belong to different groups, and they are also connected or affiliated with others who are similar to themselves (Brewer, 1991). Finding this optimal distinctiveness satisfies two fundamental needs.

Following optimal distinctiveness theory and deriving ideas from social identity theory, Hornsey and Jetten (2004) identified eight strategies that people can adopt in order to meet the balance between the need to be different and the need to belong:

1 *Identify with a numerically distinct group:* Small groups tend to command more loyalty because they satisfy the need for belonging and affiliation/inclusion without sacrificing a person's sense of distinctiveness. This is the basic argument formed from optimal distinctiveness theory (Brewer, 1991, 1993; Brewer and Weber, 1994). The assumption here is that smaller groups (e.g., minority

political parties, smaller work groups) will offer more distinctiveness than larger groups but still satisfy people's need to belong.

2 *Identify with a subgroup:* Sometimes we identify with subgroups and subcategories in order to achieve numerical distinctiveness. For example, political parties often contain formalized subgroups or factions that reflect different opinions or ideologies within the overarching ethos of the party (e.g., moderate and hard-line Republican groups).

3 *Identify with a 'non-mainstream' group:* Some groups pride themselves on being 'different' from the mainstream group. People can join these types of groups to maintain their sense of belonging to a group while keeping their distinctiveness from other groups. An example of this might be the punk movement in the 1970s. People looked different, behaved differently and had different attitudes from the mainstream – even though they shared these things in common (so in some ways they were less distinctive than they thought), they still maintained their distinctiveness from the mainstream.

4 *Enhance the distinctiveness of one's group:* People can maintain the distinctiveness of the group by perceptually enhancing the group's distinctiveness. This strategy draws on social identity theory and the notion that people are motivated to accentuate the similarities within their group and the differences between their group and other groups (Tajfel and Wilkes, 1963; Turner et al., 1987).

5 *Differentiate oneself within a group through roles:* People can achieve distinctiveness within a group by adopting a specific role. Having a specific role within a group (e.g., mother in a family, IT specialist in a small company) means that the need for distinctiveness is met while the person still feels that they belong in a group.

6 *Identify with a group that prescribes individualism:* Many groups are characterized by norms of individualism and independence (e.g., national groups such as being British). In this case, what it means to conform to the group's norms is changed, so that the conformity essentially becomes an expression of distinctiveness or differentiation.

7 *See oneself as loyal but not conformist:* Using this strategy, people rationalize their own conformist behaviour. Instead of seeing one's behaviour as conformist, it is possible to see the behaviour as the actions of a loyal group member. In doing so, they feel part of the group but also maintain their need to be independent.

8 *See oneself as more normative than other group members:* People show a general tendency to consider themselves to be more normative or typical than other group members. For example, when cooperativeness is considered to be group normative, people see themselves as more cooperative than other group members (Codol, 1975, 1984). This bias reflects an attempt to maintain the unique self while still being a part of a group and behaving in a manner that is socially acceptable to the group.

Recently, Spears, Ellemers and Doosje (2009) demonstrated another process that helps people balance their need for distinctiveness with their need for connection with others. They showed that people tend to like a majority to share their ideological opinions (e.g., on the importance of the environment), but prefer to be a member of a minority with respect to matters of taste, such as preferences for TV channels. Thus, sharing one's opinions with others helps people to feel they belong and have social support, but sharing tastes with a smaller number of others helps people to maintain an optimal level of distinctiveness from others.

Time to reflect Again, think of a social group that you belong to. What is your primary reason for being a part of it? Does it satisfy certain psychological needs for you?

Ostracism and social exclusion

Social ostracism Being excluded from a group by the consensus of the group.

So far we have discussed mostly positive aspects of group life. However, another significant drive to our need for groups is that we simply do not want to be left out. When we are not part of a desired group, we feel lonely, are deprived of social interaction, miss out on achieving important goals, lose a sense of how we should behave and of who we are. Social psychological research on **social ostracism** demonstrates some of the negative consequences we suffer when we are left out of groups.

Exploring further Many US high school comedies and dramas depict the phenomenon of 'cliques' and how being left out of cliques and ostracized by particular groups can be painful. Some recent examples are *Mean Girls* (2004), *Never Been Kissed* (1999), *10 Things I Hate About You* (1999) and *American Pie* (1999).

In a significant body of research, Kip Williams and colleagues have investigated the many ways in which social ostracism can affect people (Gonsalkorale and Williams, 2007; Smith and Williams, 2004; Williams, 2009; Williams, Cheung and Choi, 2000; Williams, Govan, Croker et al., 2002; Williams and Sommer, 1997; Zadro, Williams and Richardson, 2004). Many of these studies have used a unique computer program (the Cyberball program) to simulate a ball-tossing game. In a typical experiment, a person sits behind a computer where they believe themselves to be playing a ball-tossing game with two other participants. In fact, these supposed other participants are not 'real' participants but are created by the program. The participant starts playing the game and at first the ball throwing is equitable – everyone has the ball thrown to them an equal number of times. However, after a few trials, the experiment changes and participants might find themselves in a condition where they are no longer thrown the ball. In this condition, they are ostensibly being ostracized from the game by the other two participants. How does this make them feel? Williams' findings suggest that people who are ostracized feel sad, angry and psychologically distressed. These responses are similar to the effects of physical ostracism or when someone gives us the 'cold shoulder' or 'silent treatment' in real life. Interestingly, ostracism seems to hurt even when it comes from a despised outgroup. For example, Gonsalkorale and Williams (2007) showed that people felt the negative effects of social ostracism even when people who were supposedly members of the Ku Klux Klan would not involve them in the Cyberball game.

ETHICS AND RESEARCH METHODS

Ethical considerations in ostracism research

Research on ostracism demonstrates that there are some seriously negative consequences suffered by people who are left out of groups. Carrying out ostracism work in the laboratory does, however, present some thorny issues. If people feel so bad about being ostracized, how do researchers ensure that the effects of the experiment are not long-lasting?

Given the variables that ostracism researchers study (e.g., mood, self-esteem), it is important to ensure that people return to a normal state after participating in the experiment. Researchers make this happen by using the procedure of informed consent and following ethical guidelines for working with human participants. At the beginning of an experiment, research participants would be informed about the types of questions they would answer so that they know what they are going to do. Most importantly, however, at the conclusion of the experiment, research participants would be fully debriefed about the purpose of the experiment. In the studies on ostracism, participants would have been informed about the nature of the study and that the experimenters were manipulating feelings of ostracism. Participants would also have been told that they were not really being ostracized by other people. In some studies (e.g., Zadro et al., 2004), participants were given the opportunity to discuss their experiences in the experiment. By following these types of procedures, experimenters ensure that participants do not leave the experiment with any ill effects from having participated in the research.

Questions

1 Can you think of any other ethical issues presented by ostracism research? How would you deal with them?
2 How much do you think laboratory experiments on ostracism can tell us about the effects of long-term ostracism that people experience in their everyday lives?

© PHOTODISC

FIGURE 8.16 Being ostracized is painful

Further, ostracism has also been found to cause us physical pain. In a study where participants played the Cyberball game while lying in an MRI scanner, Eisenberger, Lieberman and Williams (2003) showed that the dorsal anterior cingulate cortex – a region of the brain activated when physical pain is experienced – was activated during Cyberball ostracism. Further, activation of this brain region was significantly related to later self-reports of psychological distress. These studies demonstrate that the psychological pain people experience when they are ostracized is closely related to real physical pain. MacDonald and Leary (2005) offer a theoretical perspective concerning the pain of social exclusion and argue that social exclusion is perceived as painful because the way people react to rejection is directly influenced by aspects of the physical pain system.

Exploring further Williams and his colleagues' research is intriguing because it shows that people feel bad even when they are ostracized in the most minimal of senses (e.g., by a computer) and by groups they hate (e.g., the KKK). Why do you think that this 'cold shoulder' is so powerful? What psychological needs are not being met when we are ostracized and why does it not matter who/how ostracism occurs? Take a closer look at the research on social ostracism and map out some of the reasons why it is so powerful.

Chapter summary

In this chapter, we have explored why groups are so important to people. We have explained how and why groups form and what they mean to individuals who belong to them. We have also discussed how the norms or 'rules' of group behaviour develop, and the consequences of violating group norms. We have also outlined some of the negative aspects of group membership, such as when groups break up and the negative consequences for people who are left out of groups. Specifically, you will have learned that:

- There are many different definitions of a group. However, it is generally agreed that the minimum requirement for a group to exist is that people perceive themselves to be part of the group. However, we have also argued that groups can only really exist if they can be compared to other groups. So, with a sense of 'us-ness' (our ingroups) there must also be a sense of 'them-ness' (our outgroups).
- There are many different types of groups and groups vary on several dimensions, such as being big, small, structured and unstructured. They may be cohesive or 'bound together' as a unit, or they may not. They may form differently – some groups may be a part of our self from birth (e.g., our ethnicity) or we may join a group to get a specific task done. These latter groups are said to go through stages of development or socialization over time so that they achieve maximum effectiveness. However, despite these differences between groups, a common feature of groups is that they determine important features of our selves. Our groups determine who we are, how we behave and our attitudes and beliefs.
- One key feature of groups is that they almost always have a set of rules or norms that specify how group members are supposed to be behave. These may be implicit or explicit. They may be enforced or not enforced. Either way, norms are strong determinants of our behaviours. They can also influence or even change what we think.
- In addition to social norms, groups often have well-defined social roles or shared expectations of how particular individuals in the group are supposed to behave. Like norms,

these are powerful determinants of our behaviour. Sometimes, roles are good for the group – they keep people focused on the task and a division of labour is established that helps the group function to its potential. However, sometimes people can be 'locked' inside a role and its rigid behaviour, which can have negative consequences and cause us conflict.

- We have also discussed what happens to people when they do not quite fit into groups. Deviant or marginal group members who stray too far from group norms are often disliked and shunned by the group. These people can become 'black sheep', who are disliked more by their own groups even than outgroup members. Likewise, impostors who illegitimately claim ingroup status are rejected and spurned by the group. Sometimes, however, breakoff groups can emerge via a process of schism, or natural subgroups can exist effectively under the umbrella of a larger group.
- Finally, we discussed what groups do for us. First, groups help us to achieve things that we would struggle to achieve without others – interdependence is often a key to success. People also join or identify with groups to satisfy their needs for social support and affiliation. Group memberships are also helpful to us in coping with the inevitability of our own death. Groups provide us with a social identity. They also help us balance our need to be distinctive or different with our basic human need to belong. As we saw from the research on ostracism, being excluded from groups, and therefore being deprived of the opportunity to fulfil those needs, can have negative social and even physical consequences. In short, it is clear that people need groups to satisfy some basic needs.

Our concern in this chapter has been on the nature of the group and the relationship between the individual and the group. In Chapter 9, we turn to the study of how groups are able to exert influence on the behaviour of the individuals who belong to them. How do people respond to influence from their groups? How can groups change the attitudes and behaviours of their members?

Essay questions

At the beginning of the chapter, we asked you to consider these questions:

1 Juma wants to join an exclusive gang of boys at his school. As part of his 'initiation', Juma is asked to walk down the high street wearing nothing but his underpants. After he has

completed the task, do you think that Juma will be happy to be a member of this gang? Would he be happier if the gang just let him in without initiation?

2 Cerys visits the pub with her friends every Friday night. She has a reputation for 'sitting' on the last drop of her pint,

waiting for someone to buy the next round. She rarely buys a round herself. What is Cerys's behaviour an example of? How is it likely to be received by her friends (and why)?

3 Ed is an ex-army man who served during the Falklands War. He is an active member of an ex-servicemen's group in his local town. He organizes the local Remembrance Day functions. One year it is revealed that Ed never engaged in active combat and was an army catering official during the war. How do you think his ex-servicemen's group would react to this news?

Having read this chapter, these questions could also be framed as the following essay questions, which you can attempt in preparation for your examinations:

1 How do people react to initiation rites and what social psychological process(es) can account for these reactions?
2 Drawing on social psychological research on norm violation, explain why norms are so powerful.
3 How do people react to 'imposters' within groups? Refer to social psychological research in your answer.

Some further reading

Brown, R.J. (2000) *Group Processes* (2nd edn). Oxford: Blackwell. Covers a wide range of issues in the study of group processes, including detailed coverage of the nature of groups.

Hogg, M.A. and Tindale, R.S. (eds) (2001) *Blackwell Handbook of Social Psychology: Group Processes*. Oxford: Blackwell. Collection of chapters by leading scholars in the field. Relevant to this chapter, it contains chapters on social categorization, group socialization, norms and status.

Levine, J.M. (ed.) (2012) *Group Processes*. New York: Psychology Press. Brings together chapters from experts in the field who provide a comprehensive outline of classic and contemporary research on phenomena related to social group membership.

Levine, J.M. and Moreland, R.L. (eds) (2006) *Small Groups*. New York: Psychology Press. Collection of key articles that have been published on the social psychology of groups. Prefaced by a discussion of what a group is, the history of group research, and how group research is done.

Williams, K.D. (2001) *Ostracism: The Power of Silence*. New York: Guilford Press. Comprehensive examination of social ostracism, exploring the short- and long-term consequences for people who are ignored or excluded.

 Visit the companion website at www.palgrave.com/psychology/suttondouglas for access to a wide range of resources to help you get to grips with this chapter.

Applying social psychology

Multiple social identities and coping

In this chapter, we have seen how belonging to groups, and identifying with them, helps us meet several needs – the need for self-esteem, to belong, and yet to be distinctive. Groups also provide us with opportunities for successful social interaction, by helping put us in contact with other people with whom we have a shared identity and a shared set of values and understandings. Recently, researchers have been examining the consequences of social identity for our physical health. In so

doing, they are working at the overlapping boundaries of social psychology and health psychology. Findings reveal that social identity brings with it a range of significant health benefits (Haslam, Jetten, Postmes and Haslam, 2009).

Traditionally, social identity theory (and self-categorization theory) have been concerned with simple identities – what happens to us as a result of belonging to a single group? For the first two or three decades of research in this tradition, researchers paid little attention to the fact that each person belongs to multiple social groups. Indeed, the theories tended to assume that, psychologically speaking, only one group membership can be prominent in our minds at any given time. This claim, known as *functional antagonism*, holds that being aware of one group membership tends to suppress awareness of the other groups to which one belongs. Thus, in a given moment, our social world is reduced to the people, history, norms, values and traits of the ingroup versus the outgroup. However, over time, this claim became less plausible, and increasingly out of touch with several meaningful and important effects that were emerging in the study of social identity and intergroup relations. For example, as we shall see in Chapter 12, one of the most promising and often-tested methods of reducing prejudice involves making people aware of more than one group identity. For example, ethnic prejudice may be reduced when people are aware that they do not just belong to a given ethnic group, but also to another group such as the identity 'university student'. On balance, intergroup relations appear to be improved when people have a multifaceted, complex social identity.

A recent line of research explores the importance of having multiple social identities on our ability to cope with stress and illness. The theoretical idea behind this research is that since it boosts the clarity and value of our self-concept, social identity is a psychological resource that boosts our resilience in the face of stress and adversity. In a longitudinal study, Iyer, Jetten, Tsivrikos et al. (2009) found that British students coped better with the transition to university when they started out with more social identities – when they could recount, in other words, a higher number of groups to which they belonged. In a study of patients at a hospital in Devon, Jones, Williams, Jetten et al. (2012) found that patients were less likely to develop post-traumatic stress symptoms after a brain injury if they formed new group memberships at the time of their injury.

While these studies are longitudinal, and therefore are able to suggest that multiple social identities lead to improved coping rather than the other way around, it is always desirable to run experiments to gain a more convincing picture of cause and effect relationships. This was precisely the aim of Jones and Jetten (2011), who asked Australian students to categorize themselves in terms of one, three or five social group memberships. They were then asked to do the cold pressor task – to submerge their nondominant hand in a bucket of ice-cold water and keep it in there for as long as they could stand it. By the way, this task hurts. And it is not to be tried at home, since there is a risk of injury if not professionally conducted and supervised (Mitchell, MacDonald and Brodie, 2004). Results showed that participants in the latter group, who defined themselves in terms of five group membership, were able to keep their hands in water for roughly twice as long (44.5 seconds) as those who had defined themselves in terms of one

group membership (22.9 seconds). The experimental findings offer striking support for the idea that being aware of our multiple social identities helps us to cope with life's challenges. These are clearly important results from the point of view of the theory of social identity and its application to wellbeing.

1. Imagine that you work for a school or university facing severe budget cuts. It is proposed that funding for social and club activities should be cut, since this is less important than the core academic curriculum. Using the findings described above, write an argument for the value of the social and club activities of your school/university (max. 300 words).

2. In a major study (Barber, Eccles and Stone, 2001; Eccles and Barber, 1999; Eccles, Barber, Stone and Hunt, 2003), it was found that children who were involved in team sports tended to go on to like school more, gain higher grades in their final year of school, attend university, stay at university for longer, and then get a job that gave them autonomy and a meaningful career path. (On the risky flipside, they tended to binge drink more, no doubt because of the drinking culture often associated with team sports.) On the basis of the studies you have read about in this section, do you think these benefits would apply, to the same extent, for individual sports or other extracurricular activities? Finally, how do you think team sports might be beneficial to wellbeing, leaving aside the fact that belonging to a team gives you an additional social identity? In other words, how else might team sports boost your wellbeing?

3. Jones and Jetten (2011) note that apart from providing us with social identity, groups do us good in other ways. For example, many groups provide friendship networks and social support. Jones and Jetten (2011, p. 242) were interested in the 'mere salience of an increasing number of groups', rather than these additional benefits. Thus, they deliberately asked people to categorize themselves in terms of memberships of social categories, rather than list the friendship, family and other more intimate social groups that they belong to. But going further, if their argument is right – and belonging to many groups gives us a purely existential identity boost that is independent of other benefits that groups bring – then we would expect variables such as 'self-evaluations, and/or self-knowledge' (p. 243) to mediate their effects. That is, listing a higher number of groups helps us cope because it increases variables such as self-esteem and self-concept clarity (see Chapter 2). However, by their own admission, they did not test for this pattern of mediation. So, it remains unclear why awareness of multiple group membership is a boon to coping. If you were replicating their study, but wanted to measure variables that might mediate their effects, what would you measure? As well as self-esteem and self-concept clarity,

what variables might you include? Can you find measures of perceived social support, for example, and perceived social inclusion? In no more than 400 words, describe your study.

4 There was no control condition in Jones and Jetten's (2011) study; that is, no group of participants just did the cold pressor task without first having answered any questions

about their social identity. Does this matter? Do we know, for example, whether listing five group memberships really boosts resilience to levels that are higher than normal, or whether listing just one group membership might actually reduce resilience?

Blind spot in social psychology

The upsides of social ostracism

Kip Williams and colleagues have shown that being ostracized by others can affect us in many different ways – from making us feel sad, angry and isolated to making us experience real physical pain. Ostracism feels particularly bad when we are aware that it is happening and can see that we are being ignored. Although it has devastating effects on the individual, does ostracism have some function for the group?

1 Using an academic database or search engine, can you find research that suggests that social outcomes, such as willingness to cooperate rather than act selfishly, are improved when people are aware that they may be ostracized as a result of their behaviour? (Note: 'social exclusion' is another phrase often used in place of ostracism.)

2 In Chapter 14, we examine the human need for justice at some length. People do not like to see bad deeds go unpunished. Can you imagine situations in which you would want to see a person ostracized from a group as a result of their behaviour? Can you imagine a situation in which you or others would be annoyed if a person were not ostracized?

3 Using an internet search engine, see if you can find fictional or real stories in which people express a desire for another person to be ostracized as a result of their behaviour.

4 Design a basic experiment to simulate one of the situations you read about or imagined above. What independent variable and what dependent variable do you need to test to discover whether people sometimes find it unfair and upsetting to think that wrongdoers are not ostracized from the group?

Student project

Social categories and person perception

Laura Crookston studied as an undergraduate student at the University of York and her dissertation supervisor was Dr Julian Oldmeadow. In this chapter, we considered how our perceptions and evaluations of people – including ourselves – do not always take their unique individual characteristics into account. Instead, we often see ourselves and others in terms of social categories. Laura's project explored the extent to which people's perceptions of weight are categorical.

My topic and aims

Body image is a key interest of mine, especially after having done a lot of work with eating disorders through volunteering for the charity Beat. I believe everyone at some point has seen someone walking down the street and either thought or said out loud that they thought the person was too skinny or overweight. I wanted to examine if people just used these two categories or instead judged people's weight on a continuum. Women's weight is a much more salient cultural concern than men's, and women are much more accustomed to thinking about weight. I was therefore interested in whether men and women are judged differently, and whether male and female observers judge weight differently.

My methods

To examine whether body size was perceived in terms of categories, I adapted a method used by cognitive psychologists to assess categorical perception, which is when a continuous dimension, like the colour spectrum, is perceived as consisting of categories, like 'green' and 'blue'. To adapt this method for body size, images of two male and two female bodies were morphed so that they ranged on 11 points from apparently lightest to heaviest. On a computer, participants were shown one body on its own and then two bodies that were 20 per cent different in size. Participants had to identify which of the two images matched the one shown on its own. Categorical perception would be indicated if participants were more accurate at choosing between bodies perceived as belonging to different size categories than when choosing between bodies perceived to belong to the same size category.

Two further tasks were administered. In the first, participants were shown each image one at a time and had to classify each as 'overweight' or 'not overweight'. In the second, the largest and smallest bodies were shown on either side of the screen and in the centre one of the remaining nine bodies was shown. Participants had to indicate whether the central body looked most like the large or small body. These tasks measured the size at which male and female bodies were judged to be overweight, allowing us to assess whether female bodies were held to stricter standards than male bodies.

My findings and their implications

Categorical perception was found for male but not for female bodies. That is, participants were better able to discriminate male bodies on the border between overweight and not overweight, relative to male bodies that were more clearly overweight or not. This was not found for female bodies. These results suggest that male bodies are perceived in terms of simple categories, as either overweight or not overweight, whereas female bodes are perceived as varying along a continuum. Another finding was that female bodies were judged as 'overweight' sooner than male bodies, suggesting female bodies are held to stricter criteria. There were no significant differences between results from the male and female participants.

The differences in the way male and female bodies are perceived may be due to the way society treats male and female bodies differently. For instance, male clothes sizes are generally 'small', 'medium' and 'large', whereas women's clothes are sized in a much more gradual way. A greater focus on women's bodies relative to men's may lead to more detailed cognitive representations of female bodies, and stricter standards. On the other hand, that male bodies were perceived categorically suggests overweight men may be more prone to being stereotyped. Further research is needed to explore these possibilities, but the results of this study suggest that the way society perceives male and female bodies may influence the way individuals perceive them at a fundamental level.

My journey

Doing my project taught me that when you are studying something that really interests you, putting the work in is a lot easier. I really enjoyed managing my own time and workload, and it made me realize that I would like to use this skill in a future career. Although I love working in a team, I felt a lot more motivated and productive in this situation. I found it quite challenging and overwhelming at times, particularly as I wanted to make it perfect, but I realized how proud I was of the work I did at the end. It made me realize that having to work hard on something that can be challenging can make you more proud of the end result.

I currently work as a nursing assistant on a rehabilitation ward for females. This is giving me a lot of experience with mental health issues and it is very rewarding seeing the improvements of individuals in our care over time. My aim for the future is to do further training in order to become a psychological wellbeing practitioner or a mental health nurse.

My advice

Find a topic that you are eager to learn more about. It can be a bit overwhelming having to decide on a topic, especially as psychology is such a wide-ranging subject. However, as you spend around a year working on your project, it is important for it to keep your interest throughout. Also, make sure you give yourself plenty of time to complete the work. It is such an important part of your degree that you will regret it if you end up rushing it at the end and not achieving your full potential.

Chapter

9   Social influence

In this chapter, you will learn about social influence – the effect that others have on our thoughts, feelings and behaviours. Through an analysis of classic research, you will learn how people respond to social influence in different ways depending on their own personal characteristics and the characteristics of the situation. You will learn about the ways in which people resist social influence, and how minorities are able to influence majorities. By the end of the chapter, you will have a comprehensive understanding of this core topic in social psychology.

© SUPERSTOCK

Topics covered in this chapter

- What is social influence?
- Classic studies of social influence
- When are people influenced?
- Why are people influenced?
- Who is influenced?
- Resisting social influence
- Minority social influence

Key features

Critical focus The Stanford Prison Experiment and the psychology of 'evil'

Ethics and research methods Ethics and the Milgram studies

Social psychology in the real world The suffragette movement

Applying social psychology Can conformity decrease antisocial behaviour?

Blind spot in social psychology Referent informational influence

Student project Social influence and prejudice

Questions to consider

1 Imagine you are in a room with 10 of your peers, voting on who will be the next president of the tennis club. Everyone before you votes for Jo but you really want Malika to get the job. Who will you vote for? What conditions would make it easier for you to vote for Malika?

2 How would you explain the actions of an RAF pilot who, when asked to drop bombs on an Iraqi village, does so without question?

3 A small political party holds only 5 per cent of the seats in Parliament. It has a strong position on environmental issues and its main agenda is to influence governmental policy on these matters. What options are open to this party to achieve its goal?

Social influence The effects that other people can have on our thoughts, feelings and behaviours.

No doubt in your recreational reading, watching TV or chatting with your friends, you have come across a tale or two about **social influence** – the effect that others have on our thoughts, feelings and behaviours. There is a good chance that some of these tales were cautionary, for example about the evils of peer pressure or the perils of falling in with 'the wrong crowd'. People in Western countries are accustomed to seeing social influence as a bad thing, partly because of the value they place on the independence and freedom of the individual (McAuliffe, Jetten, Hornsey and Hogg, 2003). Indeed, social influence clearly leads people to harm themselves or others, and academics, policy makers and law enforcers have recently become interested in **radicalization**, a special type of social influence in which people are encouraged to strike out at a society they are led to believe is fundamentally wrong or immoral (e.g., Ryan, 2007).

Radicalization Type of social influence where people are encouraged to strike out at a society that they are led to believe is fundamentally wrong or immoral.

Although social influence can be harmful, it is easy to think of any number of cases in which social influence is beneficial. Through social influence processes such as conformity, compliance and obedience, human beings adhere to social norms that make peaceful coexistence and cooperation possible (see Chapter 8). Imagine what the drive to university or work would be like if everybody completely ignored the rules of the road, or getting your lunch at a busy cafeteria if no one had any respect for queues. One of the reasons these social norms are adhered to is that people enforce them. People are inclined to criticize and punish those whom they see violating the norms of the group (e.g., Marques, Yzerbyt and Leyens, 1988; Rucker, Polifronti, Tetlock and Scott, 2004). It is no coincidence therefore that many violent crimes occur in places that cannot be surveilled by members of the public, such as poorly lit streets, large crowds and, indeed, private homes. Just as they dislike and punish deviants, people are inclined to like and reward those who behave prosocially and thus enhance the lives of others (e.g., Wedekind and Milinski, 2000).

Conformity The convergence of one's thoughts, feelings and behaviours with an external standard.

Compliance The process of doing as one is asked or as one is required by regulations.

Obedience The process of doing as one is told by an authority figure.

Conformity is the most widely studied and general form of social influence. **Conformity** is defined as the convergence of one's thoughts, feelings and behaviours with an external standard. One form of conformity is **compliance**, where people do as they are *asked* and as they are *required* to act by formal regulations. For example, everyone tends to pay their taxes.

Another type of conformity is **obedience**, where people do as they are *told* by a powerful or authoritative figure. For example, children tend to do things when instructed to do so by their parents. However, conformity is possible when no one is around to ask or tell you what to do, to give you orders or scrutinize what you are doing. Specifically, people often conform to norms, which allow others to influence them even when those others are not present in the here and now. Most important are the **injunctive norms** of the group – the norms that are perceived as being approved of by other people. These norms prescribe what we should do and proscribe what we should not do (see Chapter 8).

Injunctive norms Norms that are perceived as being approved of by other people.

Much of our understanding of social influence has developed from a number of classic 20th-century studies. These studies demonstrate the power of norms to guide behaviour and the command that groups have over individuals' thoughts and actions. We will begin by outlining some of the important findings from these studies and consider some of the key elements of social influence. We will then discuss when, why and how social influence takes place and outline the processes that occur when people resist social influence. Finally, we will consider the unique case of minority social influence, where small groups or individuals bring about social change against the odds.

Classic studies of social influence

Sherif's studies of emergent group norms

Sherif (1935, 1937) provided one of the first compelling demonstrations of social influence in his study of the emergence of social norms. Sherif investigated the emergence of social norms in now classic laboratory experiments. He argued that because people have a basic need to feel that they are thinking and acting appropriately in social situations, they will probably use other people as *frames of reference* to guide their own thoughts and actions. In particular, people use others as social comparators under conditions of uncertainty or ambiguity; that is, when they are unsure how to respond, they will look to others for examples, information and guidance. Because they do this, people also have a tendency to prefer moderate or 'average' positions because they are the most frequent and are hence perceived as the most appropriate or correct. Sherif argued that this basic preference for moderateness explains how norms emerge in groups and how the convergence of group members to the emergent norms can intensify consensus within groups. If people use others as a frame of reference, their behaviours should converge over time and people will also use that information to guide future behaviours and judgements.

Sherif (1935) carried out experiments in which he asked two or three participants to sit in a darkened room and observe a pinpoint of light. A visual illusion called the *autokinetic effect* makes the light look as though it is moving in the dark – this illusion is a result of eye movements occurring when physical objects are not present to act as frames of reference. At this point in the study, the light suddenly disappeared and participants (who were unaware of the visual illusion) were asked to estimate how much the light had moved. Using this technique, Sherif capitalized on the fact that participants would be uncertain about their judgements and would need to establish their own internal frame of reference. Over 100 trials, Sherif discovered that participants did just that – as time passed, their estimates converged to a small range of responses, so that each participant adopted their own personal frame of reference.

Later, Sherif (1935) asked participants to perform the same task, but instead of making their estimates on their own, they were asked to call out their responses in a group of two or three other participants. Here, the results showed that participants quickly started to agree with each other, and responses converged, so that a *group normative* estimate evolved after only a short number of trials. By the third and fourth testing session, a strong group norm had developed and everyone's estimates had become similar (see Figure 9.1a). Sherif argued that in this task, the group members questioned the internal frame of reference they had developed earlier and instead used each others' estimates to guide their own responses. So, gradually, a *joint* frame of reference was established, which informed future judgements. Indeed, further testing demonstrated that this norm persisted over time, even when participants were asked again to provide their own individual estimates. After three group testing phases, participants' individual responses relied strongly on the group normative estimates that had been established earlier (see Figure 9.1b). When the participants saw how others had responded, they modified their responses and, as a group, converged on a consistent answer.

Time to reflect Sherif's work demonstrates that people use the attitudes and behaviours of others to guide their own responses. In particular, people tend to do this when they are unsure of their own position. Can you think of a time when this happened to you? Was this a good or bad thing?

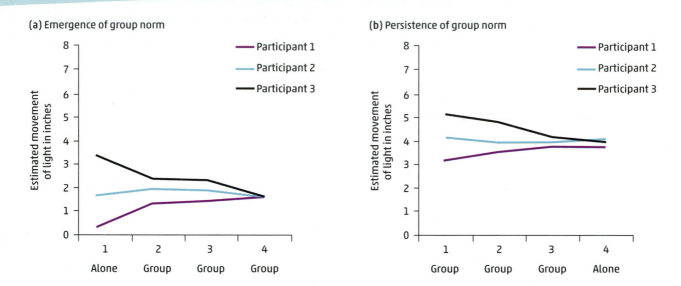

FIGURE 9.1 Emergence and persistence of group norms In (a), participants were asked to call out their estimates of how much a pinpoint of light moved in the dark. Doing so alone, their responses were quite varied but when they called their estimates out loud in a group, over repeated phases a group norm emerged and the variation in responses all but disappeared. In (b), we see how the norms persisted – after three group phases of the same task, participants relied on the group norm when giving their responses individually.

Subsequent investigations corroborated Sherif's findings. For example, Jacobs and Campbell (1961) conducted the same experiment but this time used only one participant. The other group members in the study were confederates who had been asked to respond in a predetermined (and often extreme) manner. Again, results revealed that the majority norm influenced individual participants' estimates (see also MacNeil and Sherif, 1976). Rohrer, Baron, Hoffman and Swander (1954) demonstrated that people retested individually a year later were still influenced by the group norm. Overall, these experiments provide a cogent demonstration of the power of the group to influence individuals' judgements, even when those judgements are trivial, meaningless and even false. In these studies, conformity to the group's norm was a rational response to ambiguity. The norm provided a framework for individuals to judge the most appropriate response when they were unsure of their own individual judgements. The norm also guided behaviour even in the absence of the group (see Turner, 1991). In essence, the

FIGURE 9.2 **New norms of behaviour** New norms of behaviour form all the time. For example, it is now normal to use a smartphone to text, email and social network even while physically hanging out with friends and family.

norm was contagious. There are many real-life examples of norm formation and contagion. For example, some behaviours become more socially acceptable over time, such as talking on a mobile phone while using public transport. Also, think of the language and symbols you use to email and text message your friends. Accepted ways of expressing emotion such as the use of emoticons have emerged among users and these have caught on in such a big way that most users are familiar with these norms of communication and use them (see Chapter 5). For new users who are uncertain how to communicate using these methods, the norms help guide their own behaviour.

Try it yourself When you are next in a busy place (e.g., like a shopping centre), take some time out to observe people's behaviour. What social norms can you see in action? Can you see any examples of norm violation and, if so, did anything happen when someone violated the norm? This is a fun observational task to give you an idea of the depth and persistence of social norms and their importance in guiding social behaviour.

Time to reflect In your everyday university, work or family life, what other examples of norm formation can you think of?

Asch's studies of conformity

Asch argued, along a similar vein to Sherif, that people look to others to help them decide how to act themselves, and that it is logical to do so in ambiguous situations when they are uncertain about how to behave. However, Sherif argued that when people are confident that their own judgements and behaviours are appropriate, they should not necessarily be affected by the norms of a group. In particular, when the appropriate judgement is *unambiguous* and one would expect no disagreement in judgement, individuals should resist group influence.

Asch (1951, 1952, 1956) invited a group of male participants to take part in what was said to be a perceptual judgement task. They were seated around a table in a group of seven or nine. Only one man was a true participant; the rest were confederates who, as in Jacobs and Campbell's (1961) study, had been asked to respond in a predetermined manner. The group was presented with a diagram of a standard line (see the left of Figure 9.3) and three comparison lines (see the right of Figure 9.3). The participants' task was to choose which comparison line matched the standard line. Confederates and the participant were asked to call out their answers to the rest of the group, and the participant

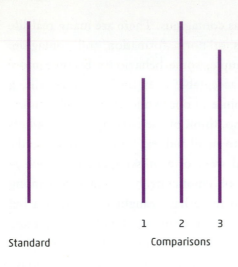

FIGURE 9.3 Line judgement task from Asch (1951)

was asked to respond second to last in the group. In the first trial, the judgement was easy – it was obvious which one was the correct line and everyone agreed. The participant took his turn and confidently gave the correct response. In the second trial, everyone was again able to correctly identify the line that matched the target line. However, something more interesting happened on the third trial. As in the previous trials, it was obvious which one was the correct line, but this time all the confederates responded incorrectly. It was then the participant's turn and he was faced with a confusing situation. How should he respond? He knew his peers were wrong but responding differently would make him stand out from the crowd. There were 18 trials altogether and the confederates were asked to give an incorrect response on 12 trials. There was also a control condition in which participants gave their responses privately, as individuals.

Results revealed that, in the control group, where everyone gave their responses individually, 99 per cent of participants chose the correct line. This task was easy and unambiguous, and so there was no reason to expect that the norm formation observed by Sherif would occur. However, in the experimental group, where participants made their judgements alongside a group who gave clearly incorrect responses, approximately half the participants conformed to the group's incorrect judgements in 6 or more of the crucial trials. Further, approximately 5 per cent of the participants conformed to the erroneous group decision in all 12 key trials. Indeed, the 'average' conformity rate across participants and trials was around 32 per cent, and only one-quarter of participants showed no conformity at all. Asch (1955, p. 6) concluded:

> That we have found the tendency to conformity in our society so strong that reasonably intelligent and well-meaning young people are willing to call white black is a matter of concern. It raises questions about our ways of education and about the values that guide our conduct.

Such is the power of the group over the individual.

Question to consider Knowing what you now know about group influence, reread question 1 at the start of the chapter. Who do you think you would vote for, Jo or Malika? Why?

On the face of it, the participants in Asch's experiments were under no obvious pressure to conform; that is, there were no consequences for conforming, being sensitive to group norms or for dissenting against them. Team players and individuals alike were not rewarded or punished for what they did. As such, these results are quite fascinating. In a situation where the consequences for participants' actions are minimal, they should make their own choices, should they not? When participants in Asch's studies were asked about how they felt, they reported experiencing self-doubt and uncertainty. They reported a variety of feelings and reasons for conforming, such as fear of disapproval, not wanting to stand out and feeling anxious. However, because the task itself was relatively trivial, researchers questioned the power of the findings to explain behaviour in more meaningful situations. In particular, if people react to such a trivial task in this way, how might they behave in a task that *does* have important consequences associated with the decision to conform or dissent? Also, if people conform so clearly on such a trivial task, how might they respond to an authority figure who is directly trying to coerce them? Are people blindly obedient to the orders of others, even when they are asked to perform cruel acts? Stanley Milgram wanted to know more about these processes. He sought to investigate specifically what happens if the social pressure to conform conflicts with the pressures of conscience.

Milgram's studies of obedience

Milgram (1965, 1974) was deeply concerned about the psychological properties of people who commit atrocities. Specifically, he was influenced by the 1961 trial of Adolf Eichmann (Arendt, 1963), who, as one of Hilter's primary officers during the Second World War, sent millions of Jewish people to their death in Nazi concentration camps. Contrary to public expectation, Eichmann did not display the characteristics of an evil, cruel 'monster' when on trial. Instead, he presented as a normal, everyday, perhaps even boring, family man. When questioned about his actions, he stated that he had nothing in particular against Jewish people, he was merely 'following orders'. The question raised by Eichmann's trial is intriguing and addresses one of the fundamental aspects of human nature – if placed in a situation where the behaviour you were being asked to perform went against your conscience, how would you behave? If you were asked to hurt another human being, would you simply follow the order?

These questions inspired Milgram to conduct some of psychology's most famous and controversial experiments (Blass, 1992, 2004). To begin his programme of research, Milgram placed an advertisement in a newspaper for male participants aged 20–50 to participate in a scientific study on memory and learning at Yale University. Once they arrived in the laboratory, they were informed that their task was to teach another person (the 'student') a series of paired words, and then test their memory for those words. The student was, in fact, a confederate who was trained to respond in a predetermined manner. If their partner made any errors, participants ('teachers') were required to punish them by giving electrical shocks. At this point, it is important to emphasize that no shocks were *actually* given to the students. The crucial aspect of this experiment is that the teachers all *believed* that they were going to administer painful shocks to students when they responded incorrectly.

To begin, the teacher watched as the student was strapped into a chair and had paste and an electrode attached to his wrist (Figure 9.4a). The experimenter explained that the paste was to prevent blistering and burning. The experimenter also explained that although the shocks are painful, they would cause no permanent tissue damage. At this point in the experiment, the student explained to the experimenter that he

FIGURE 9.4 Stanley Milgram's famous experiment on obedience

Source: From the film *Obedience* (c) 1968 by Stanley Milgram, copyright renewed 1993 by Alexandra Milgram and distributed by Penn State Media Sales

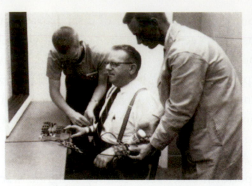

(a) The confederate 'student' is strapped to the machine that will supposedly deliver him painful shocks

(b) The shock generator

had a slight heart condition. Then the teacher was separated from the student and was seated in a room in front of a machine called the 'shock generator' (see Figure 9.4b), while the experimenter was seated at a desk behind the teacher.

The shock generator consisted of 30 switches, each incrementally rising by 15 volts; so, voltage labels ranged from 15v ('slight shock'), 75v ('moderate shock'), 135v ('strong shock'), right through to 450v ('XXX'). Underneath each voltage value and label was a push-down button that allowed the experimenter to administer the shocks. The teacher was given a small (real) sample shock of 45v, and the experiment began. The teacher began to teach the words to the student and then test their memory for the pairs. For each error, the teacher was instructed to administer the next level of shock to the student. The first error was 'punished' with a shock of 15v, the second with a shock of 30v and so on. If the 450v mark was reached, the teacher was asked to keep administering this shock every time the student made an error.

As mentioned earlier, the student was a confederate, and so he was asked to respond in the same scheduled manner for every experimental participant. This is an important aspect of the study as it means that every participant had as close to the same experience of the experiment as possible. The script he was asked to follow is presented in Figure 9.5. He got some of the answers correct, but also made some incorrect responses, which were punished at a higher level of shock every time. After receiving a shock of 75v, he grunted 'Ugh!' At 180v he shouted that he could take no more and continued to cry with pain after each shock until he screamed with agony at 270v and then ceased to respond at all after 330v. The teacher was instructed to treat this non-response as an incorrect answer and keep flicking the switch to punish the student.

Unsurprisingly, this was an extremely uncomfortable situation for the teachers and this was reflected in their behaviours. They often asked to stop the experiment and check that the student was okay. However, in response, the experimenter, like the confederate student, responded with a scripted set of four responses starting with 'please continue', followed by (after a further request to stop the experiment) 'the experiment requires that you continue' and then, 'it is absolutely essential that you continue', and finally the most coercive instruction, 'you have no other choice,

FIGURE 9.5 The confederate schedule in Milgram's study
Source: Milgram, 1974, pp. 56–7

75 volts	Ugh!
90 volts	Ugh!
105 volts	(*loud*) Ugh!
120 volts	Ugh! Hey, this really hurts
135 volts	(*loud*) Ugh!
150 volts	(*loud*) Ugh! Experimenter! That's all. Get me out of here. I told you I had heart trouble. My heart's starting to bother me now. Get me out of here, please. My heart's starting to bother me. I refuse to go on. Let me out.
165 volts	(*shouting*) Ugh! Let me out!
180 volts	(*shouting*) Ugh! I can't stand the pain. Let me out of here!
195 volts	Ugh! Let me out of here. Let me out of here. My heart's bothering me. Let me out of here. You have no right to keep me here! Let me out! Let me out of here! Let me out! Let me out of here! My heart's bothering me. Let me out! Let me out!
210 volts	Ugh! Experimenter! Get me out of here. I've had enough. I won't be in the experiment any more.
225 volts	Ugh!
240 volts	Ugh!
255 volts	Ugh! Get me out of here.
270 volts	(*Agonizing scream*) Let me out of here. Let me out of here. Let me out of here. Let me out. Do you hear? Let me out of here.
285 volts	(*Agonizing scream*)
300 volts	(*Agonizing scream*) I absolutely refuse to answer any more. Get me out of here. You can't hold me here. Get me out. Get me out of here.
315 volts	(*Intense agonizing scream*) I told you I refuse to answer. I'm no longer part of this experiment.
330 volts	(*Intense and prolonged agonizing scream*) Let me out of here. Let me out of here. My heart's bothering me. Let me out. I tell you. (Hysterical) Let me out of here. Let me out of here. You have no right to hold me here. Let me out! Let me out! Let me out! Let me out of here! Let me out! Let me out!
Then silence...	

FIGURE 9.6 Actual vs. predicted conformity in Milgram's obedience experiment Experts predicted that most people would disobey at around 135v but, in reality, the majority of participants persisted with the experiment until the end.
Source: Data from Milgram, 1965

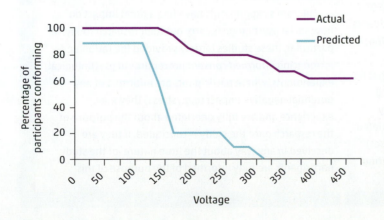

you must go on'. Milgram described his experiment to psychiatrists, middle-class adults and students, and asked them to predict how far people would be prepared to go in this experiment. What shock level would they go up to? People in all three groups thought they themselves would disobey at about 135v. None predicted that they would go above 300v. Similarly, people predicted that normal everyday people in general would never reach the XXX mark on the shock generator. The experts also agreed that probably only around 10 per cent of normal people would ever exceed 180v and that virtually nobody would persist to the conclusion of 450v (XXX) – maybe about one in a thousand people might do so. But were they correct? As can be seen from Figure 9.6, the reality differed significantly from the experts' and others' predictions. As predicted, obedience decreased as shock intensity increased. However, 63 per cent of teachers went up to and beyond the 450v XXX maximum shock level. Even after the four prompts to continue the experiment, some participants continued to punish the student and eventually the experimenter had to stop the participant from continuing with the study.

These results are significant for many reasons. First, we must remember that people were administering what they thought were extremely dangerous and painful shocks to another human being who had been screaming with pain to be let out and had complained that his heart was bothering him. This is surprising behaviour by any standards. Participants' persistence with the task is even more surprising, given the obvious distress they were under. Many of the participants pleaded to stop the experiment, trembled, stuttered when they spoke, laughed nervously and even offered to take the student's place.

Exploring further There are several demonstrations of Milgram's experiment online, including an example shown on the BBC in 2009. Take some time to watch an example and note the participants' response to the task. You will notice that some were deeply uncomfortable with their task, so why did they continue?

Milgram's results are also significant because they suggest that people's attitudes often fail to determine their behaviour, especially when external influences override them. In this case, the experimental context, on the whole, had a greater influence on participants' behaviour than their own wishes to go no further.

ETHICS AND RESEARCH METHODS

Ethics and the Milgram studies

For obvious reasons, Milgram's studies sparked a great deal of debate about the ethics of conducting studies with the potential to cause psychological distress to participants; so much so that his application to join the American Psychological Association was delayed for a year (for coverage of the ethical debate, see Baumrind, 1964, 1985; Marcus, 1974; Miller, 1986, 2009). After all, it is not every day that participants in university research believe they are administering painful shocks to other people. In particular, critics pointed out that the participants experienced severe distress and that this distress could have lasting effects beyond leaving the laboratory. Further, they argued that the nature of the debrief, revealing that the participants had been the subjects of a huge hoax, could have a significant impact on participants' self-esteem and future trust in others (Baumrind, 1964; Schlenker and Forsyth, 1977).

In response to these criticisms, Milgram argued that he was concerned about the welfare of his experimental participants. He argued that his debrief was carefully constructed and delivered and that upon being debriefed, participants were actually relieved (not angry or upset) when they discovered that they had not been delivering painful shocks to another person. Further, in follow-up interviews and questionnaires administered to over 1,000 experimental participants, Milgram found that over 83 per cent of participants said they were glad to have taken part, while just over 1 per cent were sorry to have taken part; 15 per cent reported neutral feelings (Milgram, 1992, 2009). Interviews conducted with the aide of a psychiatrist indicated that there were no psychological ill effects for the participants. However, some critics have argued that these data are not enough to establish that his studies were ethical. If no participants suffered enduring distress, this may be a matter of good luck more than good management. The point is, these critics argue that Milgram took risks with the welfare of his participants that may not have been warranted.

Milgram's experiments have had a great impact on how social psychologists carry out their research today. In particular, these studies largely provided the rationale for introducing *informed consent* procedures in psychological experiments, where participants are informed of any potential negative impact (e.g., stress) they may experience and are fully debriefed about the purpose of the research once the study is concluded. If they are deceived in any way about the 'true nature' of the study, participants are fully informed of the purpose of this deception. *Codes of ethics* are in place to protect research participants from undue harm in doing psychological experiments. A discussion of research ethics in social psychology is presented in Chapter 1.

Despite the controversy about ethics, we know much about conformity based on Milgram's work and the classic studies of conformity. It is important to note that the experimental settings designed by Milgram, Asch and Sherif are very different from many real-life contexts requiring conformity (Darley, 1992). It is unclear whether obedience in Milgram's laboratory task will extend to real-life situations. Context matters, as we will see. For this reason, some have argued that continued replication of Milgram's studies is needed (Burger, 2009; Miller, 2009). A specific unanswered question about Milgram's research, for example, is whether the group memberships, or *social identities*, of the experimenter, teacher and victim influence obedience. Would there be even more obedience if the victim was a member of a disliked outgroup – as was the case in the Nazi atrocities that the Milgram studies were designed, in part, to simulate? For these reasons, Burger (2009) replicated the Milgram studies, with an important modification. He capped the shocks that could be delivered at 150 volts. He found that obedience up to this level was comparable to that observed by Milgram. The 150 volt level is important, since the majority of participants who disobeyed the experimenter in the original studies tended to do so at this point (Miller, 2009; Packer, 2008). At the same time, at the 150 volt level, the teacher does not necessarily think they are delivering a dangerous, even lethal, dose of electricity to the student. Thus, many of the ethical difficulties surrounding the original Milgram study were averted. Overall, the depressing conclusion is that we have no compelling reason to suppose that obedience levels would have declined in the decades separating us from Milgram's studies. And in Burger's (2009) results, we have evidence to suggest that they have not declined.

Questions

1   There are two crucial questions to ask: Do you think Milgram's study should have been conducted? Does the information gained outweigh the potential stress caused by the participants? This is one of the main considerations for people who are asked to review research ethics applications. Write down some points to justify your answer. There is plenty of commentary on the ethics of the Milgram studies, on the internet and in academic journals. Locate these sources by following the references cited in this section (eg., Miller, 2009), and also try searching for 'Milgram ethics'. How do your views compare with those expressed by others?

2   Imagine that Milgram had found – as his panel of bystanders had predicted – that few, if any, participants had obeyed the experimenter's instructions. Do you think that people would be as likely to view the experiment as unethical?

3   By today's standards, Milgram's procedure was rather extreme. For ethical reasons, it is unlikely that a researcher today would be permitted to conduct a study where participants believe themselves to be administering dangerous shocks to another person (but for partial replications, see Burger, 2009; and for a replication in a virtual reality environment, see Slater, Antley, Davison et al., 2006). What other methods might an experimenter use to elicit conformity? Reading further in this chapter where we discuss some of the factors that influence conformity may help you answer this question.

Importantly, the classic studies of social influence show that conformity often predominates over common sense. In the case of Milgram's studies, conformity also clashes with the demands of conscience. These results have had a significant impact on many areas of social psychology and have provided the foundations for the study of social influence. However, before we turn our attention to some of the mechanisms underlying conformity, we need to discuss one last study that has significantly shaped how we view social influence.

Question to consider   Reread question 2 at the start of the chapter. Knowing what you know about obedience, how would you explain the action of the RAF pilot?

Try it yourself It is difficult to come to terms with Milgram's findings. In lectures, we often show original footage of the Milgram study and students watch with muted giggles. We ask them what they think they would have done themselves if in the same situation and most respond with answers such as 'I would never do that', or 'I could never give someone electric shocks'. It is difficult to believe that this behaviour is possible. But the reality is that many of them would do exactly what Milgram's participants did. It is easy to demonstrate the powerful norm of obedience. For example, try standing by a doorway at university and tell students who try to go through the door that they cannot use it (you do not need to say any more than this). Count how many people turn away and find a different door, simply because they are told to do so. How does the number you counted map onto the figures observed by Milgram? Can you think of other demonstrations of conformity?

The Stanford Prison Experiment

Perhaps the results of Milgram's experiments are not enough to shake your faith in the decency of ordinary men and women. After all, the participants in these experiments were only doing as they were told and they did not appear to enjoy it. Certainly, no participant went above and beyond the call of duty by, say, administering stronger than instructed shocks, or taunting their victims. Surely, we should not expect a group of ordinary people to engage in wilful, extensive and improvised tyranny while at close quarters with their victims? Well, they did, according to a famous study by Philip Zimbardo and his colleagues (Haney, Banks and Zimbardo, 1973). In the summer of 1971, this group of researchers posted a newspaper advertisement asking for male university students to participate in a 'psychological study of prison life' for a period of one to two weeks. The study was to take place in Stanford University, situated in the San Francisco Bay area; ironically, well known as an unusually liberal region of the USA. Respondents were screened to ensure they were free of medical or psychological problems and did not have a criminal or violent past. The 24 eligible respondents were assigned randomly into 'prisoner' or 'guard' roles.

A few days later, the 'prisoners' were surprised to find themselves arrested on criminal charges by officers from the local police force. Much like 'real' suspects, they were cuffed, searched, read their rights, bundled into a police car and taken to the police station for processing. The prisoners were then taken to the prison, which had been constructed in the basement of the psychology department. Here, they were extensively searched, stripped naked and sprayed with insecticide, again much as 'real' prisoners would be. They were further humiliated by virtue of being clothed in smocks – that is, uniforms that looked like dresses – as well as noisy, uncomfortable ankle chains and stockings on their heads meant to approximate the head-shaving that was often imposed on prisoners. Each prisoner was assigned a number, to be used in place of their name throughout their time in the prison. The guards were briefed by Zimbardo, who played the role of superintendent of the prison, and his co-researchers, who played warden and lieutenant roles. They were dressed in a khaki-coloured uniform, carried a truncheon and wore mirrored sunglasses, which were meant to **deindividuate** them (see Chapter 10 for more on this topic). They were given no specific training for the roles, but were charged with maintaining law and order in the prison. They made up a set of prison rules and were responsible for enforcing them.

Deindividuation The tendency for people in groups, or people who are anonymous in some way, to abandon normal constraints on their behaviour and behave in a deregulated manner.

The first day of the prison simulation passed without major incident, but a prisoner rebellion unexpectedly broke out the next day. This rebellion provoked a sharp and immediate lurch towards authoritarianism. Guards stripped prisoners of their privileges and, indeed, their clothes. This marked the beginning of an orchestrated campaign of harassment, degradation and intimidation visited by the guards upon the prisoners, although by no means all the guards played an enthusiastic role in this campaign. Prisoners were even denied the use of the toilet facilities at night, being forced to urinate and defecate into buckets. They were also forced to clean the toilets with their bare hands. Eerily reminiscent of the abuse that was to occur over 30 years later in the US-run Abu Ghraib prison for Iraqi POWs, prisoners were also forced to simulate homosexual acts. Conditions became so filthy, oppressive and distressing that the experiment had to be stopped after only six days. By that stage, one prisoner had already left after suffering acute psychological distress, becoming irrational, incoherent and paranoid.

Time to reflect Accounts of US military abuse and torture of prisoners held at Abu Ghraib prison in Iraq arose in 2004 after the release of photographs that appalled people around the world. How can Zimbardo's Stanford Prison Experiment help us to understand these events?

It is rare to find a study in which so much care has been taken to create an emotionally impactful situation, one that seems real to participants and involves them completely. It is also rare to find a study that produced such incendiary and important results. Milgram had already shown that, in the right circumstances – indeed, circumstances that mimic the settings of many historical atrocities – ordinary people can do extraordinarily appalling things. In contrast to the reluctant, morally conflicted obedience of Milgram's participants, Zimbardo's guards applied initiative, creativity and even some enthusiasm to the tasks demanded by the roles they had been given.

Exploring further It is worth watching the 2007 film *Die Welle* (*The Wave*), where we see the influence of Milgram's and Zimbardo's work on the power of the situation. In this film, a high school teacher runs an experiment with his class to demonstrate to his students what life would be like under a dictatorship. The students become gripped by the new 'fascist' social order and the experiment spirals out of control.

CRITICAL FOCUS

The Stanford Prison Experiment and the psychology of 'evil'

Arguably, the Stanford Prison Experiment and Milgram's studies are among the most important in social psychology. Their impact has been felt well beyond the disciplinary boundary of social psychology. In his recent book about the life and legacy of Milgram, Thomas Blass (2004) refers to him as the 'man who shocked the world'. The media regularly mention Milgram's work, and 'rediscover' the studies periodically in response to topical examples of social influence and obedience. Many professions have taken note of his work – for example the US army teaches Milgram's findings to officers in training in order to educate them about issues surrounding obedience (Persaud, 2005). Political scientists, sociologists and historians have drawn on Milgram's and Zimbardo's findings in their accounts of the appalling conflicts of the 20th century and beyond (e.g., Browning, 1992). These experiments have also had an effect on the popular imagination. Some films are actually about fictional versions of these experiments, such as the German films *Das Experiment* (*The Experiment*) and *Die Welle* (*The Wave*). Milgram and Zimbardo's influence can also be seen in the successful TV series, *Lost*, in which survivors of a plane crash are stranded on an remote and uncharted island and appear to be unwitting participants in a vast psychological experiment. Here, the power of the experiment over social behaviour and perception appears literally to be magical.

For most social psychologists, including Zimbardo and Milgram themselves, their experiments showed that evil arises from the *power of the situation*. According to the general form of this idea, if you want to explain social behaviour, you are more likely to find the answers in the situations that people find themselves in, rather than in their personality profiles. More specifically, some situations are 'evil', placing normative pressure on people to perform evil deeds. In these situations, people enter a psychological state in which moral judgement and personal responsibility are suspended in favour of conformity, whether to the commands of a leader or the norms of the group. Zimbardo (2007), in a book of the same title, calls this the 'Lucifer effect' and argues that the power of the situation is sufficient to cause good people to do bad things.

Along similar lines, historian Hannah Arendt (1963) coined the term 'the banality of evil'. For Arendt, even the most atrocious historical evils are banal, meaning that they are committed by individuals without malice, but also without reflection. Arendt was inspired by attending the trial of Adolf Eichmann – the apparently normal, timid, rather dull, but spectacularly murderous official who had been responsible for the administration of the Nazis' 'final solution', in which millions of European Jewish people were killed. Recently, however, historians have questioned the banality of evil. Later in Eichmann's trial (interestingly, after Arendt had left), some witnesses testified that far from being mild-mannered, he was a fanatical bully who expressed vehement hatred for Jewish people (Cesarani, 2005). These historians argued that far

from being led into evil by the Nazi regime, as if sliding down a slippery slope (Haslam and Reicher, 2008), people like Eichmann strived towards increasingly evil objectives in pursuit of their careers, their ideology and the extreme prejudices that ensued. They were, in the words of the Holocaust archivist Yaacov Lozowick (2003, p. 279), the 'alpinists of evil'.

The key point that Lozowick and other critical historians make is that evil does not arise only from situations. This same essential point underlies some of the recent criticisms by social psychologists of the standard interpretation of Milgram's and Zimbardo's studies. One such critique is that it is not normally the case that people are randomly allocated to situations. People seek out situations that suit them, that speak to their values and preferences (Ickes, Snyder and Garcia, 1997; Larsen, Diener and Emmons, 1986). It is difficult to blame a situation entirely for the behaviour of people who have chosen to put themselves in that situation (Blass, 1991).

Carnahan and McFarland (2007) ran a study that elegantly demonstrated the relevance of this point to Zimbardo's prison experiment. In the campus newspapers of several universities in southern USA, they posted one of two advertisements for a psychological study. The 'experimental' advertisement was modelled closely on the original from the Stanford Prison Experiment, asking for male college students to participate in a 'psychological study of prison life'. The 'control' advertisement was largely identical except the last three words – 'of prison life' – were deleted. The first thing that Carnahan and McFarland found was that many fewer students volunteered for the 'prison life' than the 'control' study. It was even necessary to rerun the 'prison life' version of the advertisement just to get the numbers up to an acceptable minimum. Finally, after screening participants for criminality and health problems, as Zimbardo and his colleagues had done, they ended up with 30 volunteers for the 'prison life' study and 61 for the 'control' study. Apart from the difference in numbers, the young men were also psychologically different. Specifically, they were more aggressive, authoritarian, Machiavellian, narcissistic, higher in social dominance orientation, less empathic and less altruistic. This is quite a list of traits, all related to the kinds of abuse and tyranny observed in the Stanford Prison Experiment. Thus, although Carnahan and McFarland did not go on to replicate the Stanford Prison

Experiment, there is reason to believe that its findings might be explained, in part, by the characteristics of those who volunteered to take part in it.

There are other reasons to doubt that the bulk of the blame for evil actions can be laid at the feet of 'evil situations'. As well as choosing what situations to place themselves in, people create and modify these situations. Indeed, both Milgram and Zimbardo carefully constructed the situations in which their participants were placed. In other words, the situations that promoted evil behaviour in these experiments were human creations, designed precisely to give evil every chance to flourish. Of course, the 'evil situations' that one encounters in the real world – concentration camps, organized death squads and shadowy interrogation centres – are similarly designed precisely to facilitate acts that we would normally call 'evil', such as torture and murder. Purely situational explanations for evil actions leave the creation of evil situations unexplained.

Evil situations are not only designed by people, they are typically commanded by people who have been granted or who assume a leadership role. Milgram's studies of obedience were designed to explain the psychology of those who follow, rather than give, orders. In contrast, Zimbardo's study seemed to show that people would act in evil ways even in the absence of orders to do so. Certainly, the specific forms of tyranny exercised by guards were not explicitly ordered, such as the frequent demand that prisoners do press-ups, the confinement to cells or forcing prisoners to clean toilets with their bare hands. But Haslam and Reicher (2007) point out a telling passage in Zimbardo's instructions to the guards at the beginning of the experiment:

> We can create in the prisoners feelings of boredom, a sense of fear to some degree, we can create a notion of arbitrariness that their life is totally controlled by us, by the system, you, me … They'll have no freedom of action, they can do nothing, or say nothing that we don't permit. We're going to take away their individuality in various ways. In general what all this leads to is a sense of powerlessness. (Zimbardo, 2007, p. 55)

It is clear from this passage that the guards had been provided with a set of general instructions that we would normally call 'evil', being extremely authoritarian, creating a strong sense of 'us' and 'them' and thus tending to motivate and legitimize the kinds of behaviours that

the guards went on to perform. As Haslam and Reicher (2007) point out, in many cases of real-world tyranny, not least in the Nazi Holocaust, orders are often in this general, strategic form. Those on the front lines are responsible for interpreting these orders and working out how to implement them. This often requires considerable initiative and ingenuity. They are seldom given orders in a step-by-step form that they could mindlessly follow as if they were machines.

There is other evidence that the experimenter and his assistants – who also played leadership roles inside the prison environment – actively contributed to the tyrannical climate of the prison. In their report on the Stanford Prison Experiment, Haney et al. (1973, p. 78) admit that 'over time, the experimenters became more personally involved … and were not as distant and objective as they should have been'. What does this mean? Further insight is to be found on the excellent, official website of the Stanford Prison Experiment. Here, Zimbardo recounts how Gordon Bower, his friend, former college roommate and eminent psychologist in his own right, dropped by to see the experiment in progress (http://www.prisonexp.org/psychology/27):

> I briefly described what we were up to, and Gordon asked me a very simple question: 'Say, what's the independent variable in this study?'
>
> To my surprise, I got really angry at him. Here I had a prison break on my hands. The security of my men and the stability of my prison was at stake, and now, I had to deal with this bleeding-heart, liberal, academic, effete dingdong who was concerned about the independent variable! It wasn't until much later that I realized how far into my prison role I was at that point – that I was thinking like a prison superintendent rather than a research psychologist.

Thus, Zimbardo and his colleagues, by their own tacit admission, had a role – a leadership role – in the events that transpired in their prison. One way of thinking about this limitation of their research is that the experiment is rife with *demand characteristics* (Banuazizi and Movahedi, 1975). While true, this point may not completely undermine the value of this particular experiment, given the surprising level of brutality that emerged. After all, as Thayer and Saarni (1975) pointed out, what are demand characteristics but a form of social pressure – much like the pressures that might be expected in many real-life prisons?

The most telling point about these demand characteristics is not that the brutality that occurred is somehow unrepresentative of violence and brutality in 'real' prisons and other oppressive institutions. Rather, the crucial point is that the brutality of the Stanford Prison Experiment may not have been an inevitable outcome of the guards conforming to their role. Further, it may not have occurred without the moral support and active encouragement of the experimenter and his assistants who played a leadership role.

Haslam and Reicher (2006a, 2006b, 2007, 2008) demonstrated this point in their replication of the Stanford Prison Experiment. This was funded and broadcast by the BBC in 2002, in a series called *The Experiment*, now known as the BBC Prison Study. Just like the original Stanford Prison Experiment, this has its own website (http://www.bbcprisonstudy.org/). In this version of the experiment, the experimenters did not give the prisoners and guards the same authoritarian instructions. They did not play an internal role in the prison, such as 'superintendent', as Zimbardo had. Much like the original experiment, the BBC Prison Study had to be stopped short because of concerns about the wellbeing of the participants. But these concerns were not aroused by the tyranny of the guards on hapless prisoners. In fact, the prisoners had instigated a revolution, and at one point had effectively taken over the prison. No clear leadership had emerged among the guards and their sense of identity and cohesion as guards had declined through the first few days of the experiment. In contrast, the prisoners tended to have clear leadership structure, provided by a dominant personality in the prison and a trade union negotiator who had been introduced by Haslam and Reicher (2006a, 2006b, 2007, 2008), precisely to provide leadership and promote cohesion. This strong and effective leadership appeared to bolster the social identity of the prisoners and gave them the capacity to outmanoeuvre the divided and ineffective guards. After the 'revolution', the participants experimented with a liberal, egalitarian commune in which the prison/guard distinction was erased. However, this social structure did not appear to be effective and at the time the experiment terminated, the climate was becoming increasingly authoritarian.

In sum, the value of Milgram's and Zimbardo's studies is undeniable, and they deservedly rank among the most important social psychological studies of all time. They remind us that evil actions such as mass murder are not the exclusive preserve of mentally disturbed or psychopathic individuals who come out of the woodwork when the opportunity arises. Their 'moral' is incredibly important – we should be careful not to complacently assume that we ourselves, or those we love, would refrain from evil actions when ordered or pressured to do so. However, we should not overdo the extent to which we blame the evils that these studies documented, and those in history, on the situation. People create, command and change situations, just as they themselves may be changed by them (Haslam and Reicher, 2006a, 2006b, 2007, 2008). The greatest acts of evil arise from these interactions between people and situations (Carnahan and McFarland, 2007; Haslam and Reicher, 2007).

Questions

1 As we saw in Chapter 1, *experimenter bias* – effects observed in experiments because of the expectations and behaviours of the experimenter – can be powerful and operate without the consciousness of either experimenters or participants. Of course, researchers can also influence their results by setting up experiments in ways that favour their hypotheses. Based on your reading here and, if possible, your reading of the original papers, to what extent do you think that each side may have obtained results they 'wanted' to obtain? (Note: it is crucial to point out there is absolutely no suggestion that these biases operated consciously or that the researchers had any intention of obtaining misleading findings.) What reasons are there to believe that the effects are not entirely due to experimenter bias?

2 In the Ethics and research methods box in Chapter 3, we considered the importance of replication in social psychology and the Reproducibility Project. To what extent do you think a risk confronting this project is that null findings may emerge from these replications because, at some level, the researchers 'want' to obtain them?

Exploring further Another film related to the concept of 'the power of the situation' is *The Reader* (2008), in which Kate Winslet plays an ex-Nazi guard in a concentration camp. She is facing trial for war crimes and is forced to face the atrocities in which she participated and her own personal responsibility in these situations. The film explores the ambiguities surrounding the notion of the banality of evil. Watch the film, and consider where you stand in relation to Kate Winslet's character, given what you have learned in these pages. To what extent is she evil or blameless? Can you find other films related to the themes of Milgram's and Zimbardo's experiments?

But why exactly do people conform? What specific psychological mechanisms are at play? What specific features of people and situations can breed this sort of unlikely behaviour? Thinking specifically about Milgram's studies, the fact that participants were so uncomfortable about their predicament makes it unlikely that they conformed because they were cruel people. Perhaps the power of the situation and the power of the instructions were more influential. Perhaps Zimbardo's results may create a cloudier picture, suggesting the importance of an interaction between the person and the situation. In the sections that follow, we break down these issues to examine when people conform, why, and if certain people are more likely to do so.

When are people influenced?

Milgram ran many different variations on his conformity experiments. Likewise, social psychologists have used different variations of Asch's paradigm to further examine the psychological antecedents and consequences of conformity. Unsurprisingly, Zimbardo's work has only been replicated on a couple of occasions, including the BBC Prison Study. However, from replications of studies using a similar paradigm to Milgram and Asch, social psychologists have a clearer understanding of the factors that influence when people conform and when they do not. These appear to fall under two broad headings – *contextual* factors and *group-related* factors.

Contextual factors

In one version of his experiment, Milgram manipulated the *proximity of the experimenter*, or authority figure, to the teacher and found that obedience to authority dropped significantly the further away the experimenter was from the participant. For example, if instructions were delivered by phone, obedience dropped to 21 per cent (Milgram, 1974). When no instructions were given at all, only 2.5 per cent of participants continued with the experiment until the end, although this is still surprising, given that participants were completely free to do as they wished. Studies in other domains suggest that the closer the person making the request is to the subject, the more likely the subject is to conform. For example, in field studies, Kleinke (1977) showed that people are more likely to conform to requests on the street if the requester looks at them and touches them.

Milgram also manipulated the *proximity of the student* to the teacher. In one condition, the teacher could not see the student and was unable to hear his cries of pain. Instead, the student could only be heard pounding on the wall at 300v and 315v, then falling silent. In this condition, nearly all participants shocked the student up to 255v and 65 per cent of participants went up to, and beyond, the maximum voltage. In another condition where the teacher was also unable to hear the student's pounding, nearly 100 per cent of teachers were obedient and continued to the maximum voltage and beyond. On the other hand, obedience dropped significantly when the student was closer to the teacher. For example, in one condition where the teacher was in the same room as the student, obedience dropped to 40 per cent. In yet another condition where the teacher was asked to force the student's hand down onto an electrode, obedience was reduced (but was still high) at 30 per cent. Thus, the *immediacy* or *emotional distance* of the victim was an important predictor of compliance in Milgram's experiment. This is consistent with research on the moral dilemma commonly known as the 'trolley problem' (Greene, Sommerville, Nystrom et al., 2001). In this task, people are asked to save the lives of five people lying on train tracks, and findings show that people are less willing to do so by actively pushing someone onto the tracks to stop the train than by pulling a switch that diverts the train to another track on which one person is lying. As in the case of Milgram's participants, the immediacy of the victim was a key determinant of the participants' behaviour. It is easier to pull a switch to end someone's life than throw them directly to their death.

This immediacy effect may have something to do with the fact that being physically closer to someone makes us more aware of their humanity – being apart from them makes it less possible to hear their cries or witness their emotional expressions. Being closer to someone also allows us to empathize with them. These ideas relate to the concept of **dehumanization**, which you will come across again in Chapter 11. This is the phenomenon whereby groups are sometimes seen as less than human, typically by being described with an animal metaphor (Haslam, 2006). Research has shown that dehumanizing a group and stripping them of their humanity allows people to justify atrocities against them (Haslam, 2006; Haslam, Loughnan, Kashima and Bain, 2008). In Milgram's and Zimbardo's studies, perhaps the distance created between the 'teacher' and 'student', or the 'guard' and 'prisoner' made participants feel that they were dealing with someone less than human, thus justifying extra levels of shock, or prison brutality.

Everyday life examples demonstrate that it is easier to be cruel to someone if they are emotionally distant. For example, orders for pilots to bomb cities during wartime are rarely disobeyed. At a less cruel but still significant level, people often feel little empathy towards the victims of large-scale disasters in faraway countries, but feel more compassionate when the disaster happens on their own doorstep. In these situations, the victims are perhaps dehumanized to some degree, and it is therefore easier to forget that they feel pain like everyone else.

Further, the perceived *authority of the situation* can influence compliance. You will remember that the original Milgram experiments were carried out in a labora-

Dehumanization Describing a group as less than human – typically with an animal or machine metaphor.

tory at the prestigious Yale University. Likewise, the Stanford Prison Experiment was conducted under the auspices of the renowned university bearing the same name. For everyday people, these are situations that command authority and respect for status. When Milgram reran his experiment in the much less prestigious setting of a modest office building, compliance dropped significantly, but was still high at 48 per cent. Similarly, the perceived *authority* or *status of the experimenter* is important in inducing compliance or not. People are sensitive to the legitimacy of the authority figure and use this information to determine whether or not it is the right thing to conform. In one rather alarming study, 22 nurses were called by an unknown physician to administer an obvious drug overdose to a patient (Hofling, Brotzman, Dairymple et al., 1966). All but one of the nurses did as they were told, until they were intercepted en route to the patient. Another group of similar nurses said that they would never do such a thing. Again, you will remember that the experimenter in Milgram's original studies was dressed in a white lab coat, looking very much the authoritative and knowledgeable scientist. In another condition where an ordinary person was giving the orders, compliance dropped significantly to around 20 per cent (Milgram, 1974). These results illustrate the power of status in predicting conformity. In general, higher status people tend to elicit more conformity (Driskell and Mullen, 1990). People will sometimes

FIGURE 9.7 The 'power' of uniforms Patients are reassured by the doctor's white coat and stethoscope, seeing them as symbols of the knowledge needed to make them better.

© CORBIS

go so far as to openly reject the influence of lower status or stigmatized individuals (Swim, Ferguson and Hyers, 1999). These results also demonstrate the influence of everyday symbols and situations that people use to guide their behaviour. Authority figures wear uniforms to encourage adherence to rules and regulations. Doctors often wear lab coats and carry stethoscopes so that we appreciate their position and knowledge of medical matters (Figure 9.7). Universities bear crests to display their established status as centres of knowledge. Even the neatness of a person's appearance affects their power to influence others. For example, in one study, people were more likely to accept the opportunity to take a survey from a well-dressed person on the street than someone who was dressed poorly (Walker, Harriman and Costello, 1980). It is also not surprising that Zimbardo chose to dress his guards in uniforms reflecting their 'job'. These types of symbols of authority and status for both people and institutions are important in promoting compliance. Authority is challenged when these important markers are not present.

Group-related factors

In another version of his classic experiment, Milgram found that *group pressure* was an important predictor of conformity. In particular, if two disobedient peers were present in the experiment, who refused to go past a certain voltage point on the shock generator, complete compliance to the task was reduced to a much lower 10 per cent. On the other hand, two obedient peers raised complete obedience to 92.5 per cent. Presumably, the presence of obedient and disobedient others provides people with a frame of reference to judge the legitimacy of going along with the experimenter's instructions. If others around them are obeying the instructions, then it feels like this is the legitimate and appropriate thing to do. On the other hand, if others have ceased administering the shocks, then this is probably perceived to be the most acceptable course of action. Similarly, Asch (1955) demonstrated the importance of the *unanimity* of the group. He found that unanimous groups breed conformity, whereas if just one person in the group dissents, conformity only occurs one-fourth as often.

Time to reflect Can you remember a time when you were asked to do something you thought was wrong? What did you do? What contextual factors influenced your behaviour? Can you see parallels between your experiences and the social psychological research on social influence? Can you think of other factors (not discussed in this chapter) that may determine whether people are influenced?

Unanimity was also shattered when the dissenter was more obviously incorrect than the majority, when they were undecided and changed their mind (Shaw, Rothschild and Strickland, 1957) and this was even the case when they said that they could not see properly (Allen and Levine, 1971). In general, a single dissenter can drastically reduce conformity, but it is difficult for individuals to dissent when the group is unanimous (see also Nemeth and Chiles, 1988). In a similar vein, group cohesion, or the extent to which people feel like they are bound together as a group, also influences the extent to which people conform. Specifically, the more cohesive a group is, and the more group members are attracted to each other, the more power the group has over its individual members. For example, people who are attracted to their group are more likely to be influenced by it than those who are less attracted to the group (Berkowitz, 1954). In general, groups who are unanimous and closely bound together are difficult to resist. But why might this be the case? Why is it so difficult to go one's own way in the face of a unanimous and cohesive group?

Exploring further Think about this question with respect to the British system of trial by jury. Are twelve heads really better than one? Are their judgements really independent? This is what Richard Dawkins (1997) has to say on the topic: 'There is also strong pressure to conform to a unanimous verdict, which further undermines the principle of independent data. Increasing the number of jurors doesn't help, or not much (and not at all in strict principle). What you have to increase is the number of independent verdict-reaching units.'

One obvious explanation of the power of unanimous groups is that group members risk *group disapproval* by dissenting. Fear of this disapproval can force people to go along with decisions they would not normally agree with, and perform behaviours they would not normally endorse. As we briefly mentioned earlier, Asch questioned participants as to why they conformed to the group when they obviously knew that the group's judgements were wrong. Overwhelmingly, compliant participants reported that they feared the group's disapproval and did not wish to stand out. This fear of social disapproval is very powerful. Indeed, Asch (1951) demonstrated in another experiment – where 16 participants faced one erroneously responding confederate – that participants openly mocked and laughed at this single dissenting individual. The desire to avoid such ridicule and discomfort is one explanation for Asch's findings. In another experiment Asch asked participants to write their own responses privately after hearing the incorrect judgements of the group. In this study, conformity decreased significantly, to 12.5 per cent. The fear of disapproval is therefore very potent but the presence of dissenting others can empower people with the moral courage to be independent. It is much easier to stand up for oneself and one's opinions in private than in front of a group.

However, once a person has made a *prior commitment* to a decision or response, the presence of the group will rarely make them change their mind. In other words, people are much less likely to succumb to the pressure of a group if they have already vocalized a response (Deutsch and Gerard, 1955). How many times have you seen a football referee change their mind after issuing a yellow card to a player? Probably none (see Figure 9.8). People rarely go back on their decisions even when they are under pressure to do so (Saltzstein and Sandberg, 1979). This is more than just plain stubbornness. After making a commitment to a particular course of action, people lose face by reversing their decision to conform to a majority decision, even if they lose out by keeping to their original choice (Fox and Hoffman, 2002). So, more often than not, they accept the 'sunk cost' and move on. In a way, this is a means of avoiding another form of disapproval from the group – that of being perceived as weak or easily pushed around. Of course, in the example of the football referee, this issue may be enhanced by the status of the referee as the main authority in the game. If they lost authority, the entire match could seriously collapse. This responsibility alone may make it difficult for the referee to change their mind. However, it is interesting to note that even though people tend to stick to their public commitment, they may still moderate their judgements in later situations, so that they are more aligned with the group. For example, the referee may be reluctant to issue a yellow card next time, and a judge of a scored sporting event such as gymnastics may provide more moderate scores after noticing that their own scores are misaligned with the scores of the other judges.

As we discussed in Chapter 6, people tend to like others with whom they share similar characteristics (Byrne, 1971). This similarity–attraction link can explain why people tend to conform more in settings where they like others within their group, or if they like the group as a whole. For example, when people within the group are similar (Abrams, Wetherell, Cochrane et al., 1990), and when there are friends within the group (e.g., Thibaut and Strickland, 1956), conformity increases. *Perceived interdependence* is another determinant of conformity. Specifically, when people perceive that their fates depend upon other people (and others' fates likewise depend upon them), and that they need to work together to reach a common goal, then conformity increases (Allen, 1965; Deutsch and Gerard, 1955). This works in a similar way to group performance effects that we will discuss in Chapter 10. Specifically, people will exert more effort on the part of a group if they perceive that their own and others' contributions to the group are important and indispensable (Karau and Williams, 1993). We also know from Sherif and Sherif's (1953) work that interdependence can increase cooperation within groups.

FIGURE 9.8 Will the referee change his mind? Referees will rarely change their decisions once they have issued them. Once a person has made a prior commitment, the pressure of the group will rarely make them change their mind.

Group size is also important in predicting whether or not someone will conform, but a group does not need to be large to have a significant effect. For example, Asch (1955) found in variations of his experiments that participants who were confronted with groups of three to five people conformed more rather than when just one or two other people were present. On the other hand, Milgram, Bickman and Berkowitz (1969) ran an interesting experiment where they had a crowd of varying size (either 1, 2, 3, 5, 10 or 15 people) pause on a busy New York City street and look up. What did passers-by do? Results revealed that the percentage of people passing by who also looked up increased with the size of the stimulus crowd. However, compliance only increased up to a stimulus crowd of five. Groups of five or more individuals tend made no difference to conformity, as illustrated in Figure 9.9.

Wilder (1977) argued that the effect of group size has less to do with the number of people present and more with the number of perceived independent sources of influence within the group. For example, you may come across four people who all express the same opinion, but who do so independently. Or, you may come across the same four people who together convey one collective opinion. Findings suggest that a group perceived to be a single information source is less influential than a group in which the sources of information are perceived to be independent. Further, Campbell and Fairey (1989) argued that group size influences conformity differently depending on the person's motivations and the type of judgement being made. Specifically, with matters of taste, group size has a linear effect, that is, as group size gets bigger, people conform more. This may be because on matters of taste, there is no objective standard and deviating from the group means not 'fitting in'. On the other hand, on judgement tasks where there is an objectively correct response, smaller group sizes are enough. More voices agreeing does not increase confidence or influence decision making.

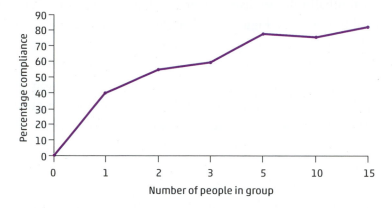

FIGURE 9.9 The effect of group size on conformity Individual conformity appears to increase steadily as a person is confronted with a group of increasing size, but after reaching about five members, a group becomes no more influential as members are added.

Source: Data from Milgram et al., 1969

Why are people influenced?

Now that we have a clearer understanding of the conditions under which people are more likely to conform, we can begin to consider *why* people conform. When people behave differently than they 'normally' would, why do they do it? Social psychologists argue that there are two general reasons why people fold under group pressure. First, they sometimes conform to avoid rejection and second, they often conform in order to be correct and accurate. Deutsch and Gerard (1955) named these factors normative influence and informational influence.

Normative influence is akin to 'going along with the crowd'. It is the pressure to conform to the positive expectations of other people, and the perceived 'norms' of

Normative influence Social influence that comes about because people wish to gain the social approval (or avoid disapproval) from others.

the group (Deutsch and Gerard, 1955; Kelley, 1952). Individuals have a general need to gain the approval of others and, at the same time, avoid their disapproval. When normative influence is at play, people more often than not actually disagree with the influence attempt, they may not change their mind, or any influence that takes place may be short-lived (Nail, 1986). However, people suppress their disagreement so that they will be liked (and avoid being disliked) by others. Thus, in general, normative influence is the public agreement or compliance with an influence attempt, when private views *do not* change. An important requirement for normative influence is that the individual believes that they are being watched or monitored by a powerful group. The group has the power to hand out rewards and punishments, so it is important for the individual to display commitment to the group and not stand out with a nonconformist opinion or behaviour. Going back to the classic studies discussed earlier, it is reasonable to assume that normative influence was at play in Asch's (1955) experiments. Participants' behaviours were being observed by the group, eliciting the pressure for them to avoid the group's disapproval. Further, we know that people conformed less readily in Asch studies when they were asked to make their responses in private. Presumably, normative influence is not as strong when individual behaviour is not being monitored by the group, and individuals are then more at liberty to make their own decisions about how to behave.

Informational influence
Social influence that comes about because people wish to be correct and accurate and therefore accept information from others.

On the other hand, **informational influence** is the type of influence that comes from the desire to be correct. This type of influence typically occurs when a task is ambiguous and people are uncertain about how they should respond. It can also occur when there is disagreement among a group about the correct response or behaviour. To resolve this uncertainty or ambiguity, people look to others as a useful source of information, and compare themselves with others to learn the most appropriate way to act (Festinger, 1950). Because they are uncertain, people therefore rate the judgements of others as more credible and superior to their own judgements, which can lead people to accept that the majority view is correct and accurate. As such, informational influence is akin to 'conversion' or 'acceptance', where people come to accept the influence attempt and not simply go along with it – that is, their private views *do* change. With regard to the classic studies discussed earlier, informational influence was probably at play in Sherif's (1935, 1937) studies involving the autokinetic effect. The task was ambiguous – the light did not, in fact, move at all and so there was no means of participants knowing what the 'correct' response ought to be. Participants therefore compared their responses with those of others and responses converged upon a group norm so that participants 'informationally influenced' one another. Alexander, Zucker and Brody (1970) followed up Sherif's study but instead informed participants that the autokinetic effect was a visual illusion. Interestingly, compliance did not occur, probably because others' responses were no longer useful as benchmarks for the correct response. The reality was that there was no correct response, so people had no reason not to believe their own responses above those of others. Thus, informational influence was not effective (see also Levine, Higgins and Choi, 2000).

Deutsch and Gerard (1955) attempted to eliminate both normative and informational influence in order to identify how much people will comply when there is very little pressure to do so. They argued that if a task is unambiguous, the participant responds privately (and anonymously) and they are not being monitored by the group in any way, there is no reason to conform to an erroneous decision. If there is no apparent reason to comply, then why should anyone do it? Deutsch and Gerard ran an experiment where, in the first condition, a participant was placed face to face with three other people. These people were confederates who had been asked to make unanimous (incorrect) judgements of the length of lines in focal trials – in much the same manner as in Asch's original studies. As you have probably gathered by now, confederates are used quite a lot in this type of research. In the second condition, the participant was asked to provide responses privately and anonymously. In a third condition, the participant remained face to face with the confederates but was given the group goal to try and be as accurate as possible. Thus, in one condition group pressure was minimized and in the latter condition it was maximized. Deutsch and Gerard also manipulated the participants' uncertainty surrounding the task. For this manipulation, half the participants responded while the stimuli were visible, and for the other half the stimuli were removed before participants made their judgements. As expected, when uncertainty decreased, so did conformity (see Figure 9.10). Also, when participants were allowed to give their responses privately and anonymously, they conformed less than when they were face to face with the group, which in turn invoked less conformity than the same face-to-face interaction with the added pressure of a group goal. However, when both certainty and group pressure were largely eliminated, people still conformed on over 20 per cent of responses.

This raises an interesting question. Why was conformity not completely eliminated when both normative and informational influence were kept to a minimum? Perhaps there is another 'type' of social influence that needs to be considered, which goes beyond the 'desire to be liked' (normative influence) and the 'desire to be right' (informational influence). Do we need a different perspective that uniquely describes conformity within groups? Social identity theorists have attempted to provide such a perspective.

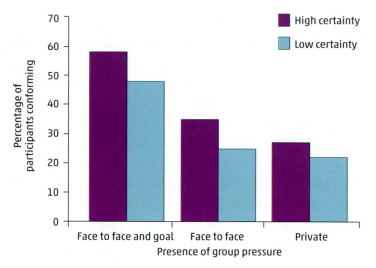

FIGURE 9.10 Influences on conformity Conformity is influenced by the perceived goal of the task (to be as accurate as possible), the degree of group pressure and the degree of uncertainty in the judgements. While conformity was lowest when there was no group pressure and the task was ambiguous (low certainty), many participants still conformed.

Source: Data from Deutsch and Gerard, 1955

Social identity theory and referent informational influence

Social identity researchers (e.g., Tajfel and Turner, 1979; see also Chapter 8) argue that the basic distinction between normative and informational influence, which Turner (1991) refers to as a *dual process dependency model of social influence*, is inadequate for explaining social influence within groups. In particular, social identity theorists have challenged this type of model because, they argue, it underplays the crucial importance of belonging to groups and the importance of belongingness in predicting adherence to the norms and standards of the group. That is, we adhere to the norms of the group because we feel that the group is part of us (see also David and Turner, 2001). To address this issue, Turner coined the term **referent informational influence**, where he argued that people conform to the group norm simply because they are group members. This is the only precondition necessary. More specifically, people are not looking for information from others in order to be correct. Nor are they striving to gain the approval (or avoid the disapproval) of the group. In fact, they are not conforming to other individuals at all – they are conforming to a group norm and can do so when they are not even being monitored by the group. People conform because they have *internalized* the group norm as the appropriate way to act as a member of that group.

The utility of referent informational influence to explain conformity in groups has found support within the social identity tradition (e.g., Abrams et al., 1990; Hogg and Smith, 2007; Turner and Oakes, 1989) and in studies of crowd behaviour (e.g., Reicher, 1984a, 1984b). It has also been nicely demonstrated in a study by Platow, Voudouris, Coulson et al. (2007). Platow et al. – in this case, several of his undergraduate students – were interested in how referent informational responses might influence the way we react to physical pain.

Referent informational influence Social influence to conform to a group norm because adherence to the group norm defines the person as a group member.

Time to reflect Before you read on, consider this question. How might a researcher elicit pain ethically and safely in the laboratory? Try to think of three or four different ways and then read on to learn about how Platow et al. did this.

Platow et al. used the cold pressor task, in which participants were asked to immerse their hand in a bucket of ice-cold water and keep it there for as long as they can. After a while, this really begins to hurt. Incidentally, this is in the 'don't try this at home' category, because after too long, it can actually be dangerous. Platow measured participants' physiological response to pain using the galvanic skin response (GSR). This involved placing electrodes on the participants' skin (not the submerged part). The more each participant sweats – a measure of physiological arousal – the more their skin conducts electricity, which is what GSR captures. An advantage of this technique is that it is non-reactive, that is, it is hard for participants to deliberately alter how much they sweat.

After the participants had done the cold pressor task once, they were asked to dry their hands and wait to do it again. At this point, a confederate appeared, posing as another participant who had already done the study and was returning a form. This confederate reassured the participant: 'Well, don't worry, the second time's much easier.' You will remember the terms *ingroup* and *outgroup* from Chapter 8 – the independent variable in this experiment was whether this confederate posed as an ingroup member (a science student) or an outgroup member (an arts student). To achieve this manipulation, separate boxes were placed in the laboratory for arts and science students. The confederate conspicuously placed their form in one of these two boxes. The upshot is, if participants thought the reassuring confederate was an ingroup rather than an outgroup member, they showed a significantly less dramatic physiological response to the pain of having their hand immersed in cold water. The reassurance of the outgroup member had no effect on GSR. This was the same as in a control condition where no reassurance was given by anybody.

The principle of referent normative influence is also consistent with the intergroup sensitivity effect, first shown by Hornsey, Oppes and Svennson (2002; see also O'Dwyer, Berkowitz and Alfeld-Johnson, 2002). The intergroup sensitivity effect is the tendency, when confronted with criticism of one's group, to express relatively low levels of emotional sensitivity and high levels of agreement and goodwill towards the critic – if the critic belongs to your ingroup. If the critic is an outsider, chances are you will be more sensitive, less liable to agree, and less charitable in your assessment of the critic's character. This effect holds even when the criticism is identical, word for word (Hornsey, Trembath and Gunthorpe, 2004). Apparently, the views of insiders are more influential than outsiders, even when they are expressing critical views of their group. In further support of the concept of referent informational influence, insiders who criticize the group are especially influential when they have a history of adherence to the group's norms (Tarrant and Campbell, 2007). If a person seems to embody the group's norms, then they are likely to seem like a good candidate to develop a shared sense of social reality with.

However, there is also evidence that the intergroup sensitivity effect can occur in the absence of referent informational influence. We respond more favourably to a critic who belongs to the group they are talking about, even if we do not belong to the group ourselves. For example, British participants express more agreement, less sensitivity and more favourable evaluations of a critic who voices negative opinions of Australians if they are an Australian (Sutton, Elder and Douglas, 2006). Likewise, British participants prefer criticisms of Chinese people that are voiced by Chinese critics, and Spanish people by Spanish critics (Sutton, Douglas, Elder and Tarrant, 2007). People also prefer criticism of the mentally ill – a typically stigmatized group – to come from within the group (Douglas and Sutton, 2011). Apparently, reactions to criticism of groups are informed not just by referent informational influence but by social 'codes of conduct' that determine who can say what about whom.

Exploring further In the literature, can you think of other factors that might determine people's preference for criticism to come from 'inside' a group? Are there particular social psychological factors that you have read about in this text so far?

Who is influenced?

Personality

Many social psychologists have attempted to understand whether there are certain 'types' of people who are more likely to conform than others. Such investigations have been largely prompted by the existence of vast individual differences in conformity and have focused on *personality characteristics* as factors that make people more susceptible (or open) to social influence. However, there is little research to support the proposal that personality factors predict conformity. In particular, there are only weak associations between specific acts of conformity and personality characteristics (Mischel, 1969). Indeed, Milgram (1974, p. 205) himself concluded: 'I am certain that there is a complex personality basis to obedience and disobedience. But I know we have not yet found it.'

© GETTY

In some studies, however, a handful of individual differences have been linked to conformity behaviours (Elms and Milgram, 1966). Indeed, going back to Milgram's studies, he found that the person who was the recipient of the request responded differently depending on their *status*. 'Blue-collar' workers were more influenced by the experimenter than 'professional' participants in his experiment, arguably because they felt less able to express themselves in the presence of the higher status individual. Also, an *authoritarian personality* profile displaying traits such as conventionalism, submission to authority and aggression (Adorno, Frenkel-Brunswik, Levinson and Sanford, 1950) has been linked to higher levels of conformity (Elms and Milgram, 1966). In Chapter 11 we will explore this same personality type as a predictor of prejudice towards social groups. However, many contradictory findings bring into question the presence of a meaningful link between individual differences, personality characteristics and conformity. People often conform in one situation but not in another. It is likely that the issue of whether or not a person conforms is more about contextual rather than personality factors. Further, theorists are generally in agreement that while internal factors (e.g., attitudes and traits) sometimes predict behaviour, they seem to be better predictors of a person's *average* tendency to behave in a certain way across different situations rather than how they will behave in a specific situation. In other words, personality factors may predict susceptibility or openness to social influence across a variety of different situations, but not be so good at predicting how a person will respond in a specific experiment. It is also the case that personality is a better predictor of behaviour when social influences are weak. One could argue that personality has little effect on behaviour in the Milgram studies because the social influence to conform was strong.

Try it yourself Mehrabian and Stefl (1995) devised a scale to measure individual differences in conformity. Are some people more predisposed to conform than others? Complete the scale for yourself. Here, conformity is measured on a nine-point scale from –4 (very strong disagreement) to +4 (very strong agreement). A total score is computed by summing participants' responses to seven positively worded items measuring higher tendency to conform (+) and by subtracting this value from the sum of responses to four negatively worded items indicating lower tendency to conform (–). Higher values indicate a greater disposition towards conformity. Responses on this scale have been used in investigations to measure relationships between conformity and variables such as societal standards of attractiveness (Vartanian and Hopkinson, 2010), acceptance of cosmetic surgery (Swami, Chamorro-Premuzic, Bridges and Furnham, 2009) and belief in extraterrestrial life (Swami, Pietschnig, Stieger and Voracek, 2011).

	Very strong disagreement			Neutral				Very strong agreement	
	-4	-3	-2	-1	0	1	2	3	4
I often rely on, and act upon, the advice of others. (+)									
I would be the last one to change my opinion in a heated argument on a controversial topic. (–)									
Generally, I'd rather give in and go along for the sake of peace than struggle to have my way. (+)									
I tend to follow family tradition in making political decisions. (+)									
Basically, my friends are the ones who decide what we do together. (+)									
A charismatic and eloquent speaker can easily influence and change my ideas. (+)									
I am more independent than conforming in my ways. (–)									
If someone is very persuasive, I tend to change my opinion and go along with them. (+)									
I don't give in to others easily. (–)									
I often rely on others when I have to make an important decision quickly. (+)									
I prefer to make my own way in life rather than find a group I can follow. (–)									

Source: Mehrabian and Stefl, 1995. Copyright held by Society for Personality Research. Reproduced with permission

Gender

Research findings are also inconclusive with respect to gender differences in conformity. On average, studies into gender differences tend to reveal that women are somewhat more susceptible or open to conformity than men. However, Milgram (1974) found little evidence for this in his own work. He found that the same percentage of women obeyed as men. Further studies (e.g., Eagly, 1987; Eagly and Carli, 1981) also found no gender differences in conformity. It has since been argued that the experimental task is important in predicting female and male conformity behaviour. Many conformity tasks may be more familiar to men than women, meaning that women may be more uncertain about the task, and hence may conform more because of the increased importance of informational influence for them. This could be a simple explanation for why women on average conform more than men. To test this idea, Sistrunk and McDavid (1971) ran an experiment in which the type of conformity task was manipulated. In this task, women and men were subjected to group pressure while being asked to rate their agreement with a series of traditionally feminine items (e.g., family, fashion), masculine items (e.g., mathematics, mechanics) or neutral issues. Results revealed that women conformed more to group pressure for the traditionally masculine issues, whereas men conformed more on the traditionally feminine issues. There was no difference on the neutral trials. These results suggest that even gender differences in conformity are context specific and that expertise and uncertainty are more likely to be the proximal predictors of conformity than gender.

However, it should be noted that women do tend to conform more than men in public settings such as experiments utilizing the Asch paradigm. Eagly (1978) argued that this may occur because women are more concerned with maintaining agreement within the group than men, but a further study by Eagly, Wood and Fishbaugh (1981) found evidence contrary to this argument. If interpersonal concerns explain gender differences in conformity, then women's greater conformity ought to be limited to circumstances in which they believe that their opinions are being monitored by others. Only under these conditions should conformity influence interpersonal relations. In this experiment, a pretest was conducted to obtain participants' opinions on various university campus issues. Participants were then asked to take part – in groups of two males and two females – in a study supposedly about impression formation in groups. The participants interacted with each other while seated individually in cubicles and for each of four issues they:

- read the opinions supposedly indicated by the other three group members
- gave their impressions of the others' knowledgeability
- gave their own opinions on the issues.

To make participants believe that their responses were being monitored, their names were indicated on their answer sheets, which were ostensibly distributed to the other group members. In the no surveillance condition, participants were told that their responses would not be distributed. The results were consistent with the hypothesis that women would conform more than men under surveillance conditions. However, Eagly and Wood (1985) also found that men were particularly resistant to influence in public settings, and argued that, for males, public nonconformity may be perceived to be a way of winning social approval.

Culture

Examinations of cultural differences have revealed fairly robust and significant differences in conformity. In particular, studies have shown that conformity (as measured using variations of the Asch paradigm) tends to be higher in 'tight' cultures such as those displaying strong traditions (Huang and Harris, 1973; Meade and Barnard, 1973), communal social organization (Boldt, 1976) or authoritarian structure (Chandra, 1973). Further, more sedentary, agricultural groups appear to exhibit higher levels of conformity than other cultures where there are heavy punishments for nonconformity (Whittaker and Meade, 1967). Also, a meta-analytical study has shown that individualistic cultures, such as Britain, Australia and the USA, tend to show lower levels of conformity than collectivistic cultures, such as Asian and non-Western cultures (Bond and Smith, 1996). In a study of 133 replications of the Asch experiment across 17 countries, Bond and Smith showed that participants who scored high on the collectivism scale, measuring the degree to which individuals are integrated into groups (Hofstede, 1980), conformed more than people who scored low on this scale. In general, conformity was highest among collectivistic cultures than individualistic cultures such as the USA and northern Europe (Smith, Bond and Kağıtçıbaşı, 2006).

Markus and Kitayama (1991) argue that these findings point to the fact that conformity acts as a kind of 'social glue' that binds a culture together. In collectivistic or interdependent cultures, this closeness is important and social norms and relations govern behaviour. This is less important for individualistic cultures, so this is another reason why we perhaps see less conformity in individualistic cultures where the individual self is the primary guide to behaviour (see also Heine and Ruby, 2010; Oyserman, Coon and Kemmelmeier, 2002; Vignoles, Chryssochoou and Breakwell, 2000). Markus and Kitayama's argument also brings into question how different cultures view conformity and what it means to be 'conformist'. In collectivistic cultures, conformity is seen as a positive factor promoting cohesion and harmony within the group, whereas individualistic cultures value independence and making one's own behavioural choices, and so conformity is often viewed as sheep-like behaviour to be avoided. Who is right? Of course, both conformity and independence are important. Following the majority is essential for social cohesion. On the other hand, resisting the majority is crucial for innovation and social change. We now turn our discussion to situations when people resist social pressure to conform.

Resisting social influence

Obviously, we do not always conform to social pressures. In fact, we often react strongly to attempts to influence our opinions and behaviours and deliberately (but sometimes also unconsciously) react in the opposite direction to the influence. This kind of negative reaction occurs in particular when influence attempts are blatant or obvious. In such situations, we feel that our personal freedom is being violated or challenged, so we react against the attempt in order to protect our freedom. People in general do not like to be manipulated. **Reactance** against influence is a way to maintain our uniqueness, uphold our own opinion, or behave in a way that we want rather than what someone else wishes to impose on us (Brehm, 1966). Reactance can lead to acts of rebellion, for example a child who is ordered to tidy their room may react by doing the opposite and making an even bigger mess. A young teenager warned about the effects of smoking may smoke simply to defy parents or guardians (Figure 9.11). When our freedoms are challenged, we often defy convention and do the opposite (see also Chapter 6).

Ironically, reactance against blatant attempts to limit our personal freedom can be used against us. For example, some persuasive sales methods capitalize on reactance by manipulating a consumer into choosing a product they might ordinarily not have chosen, or might have casually overlooked. One neat example of this was in the successful launch campaign of South African *Destiny* magazine, where the professional female target audience was encouraged not to buy the magazine because of its 'dangerous content'. In lay terms, this process is referred to as 'reverse psychology', which can often be an effective technique. Another everyday example is how parents sometimes attempt to persuade their noncompliant children. Parents would probably agree that one way to get a child to eat their broccoli might be to tell them: 'Whatever you do, *do not* eat your broccoli.' In an act of defiance, the child may do the opposite, at least on some occasions.

Reactance Deliberately reacting against an influence attempt.

FIGURE 9.11 Teenage smoking: reactance or defiance? This teenage girl knows she is not supposed to smoke. Is she reacting against social norms, or perhaps defying the advice of others?

Another way to resist social influence is by *asserting uniqueness*. It is clear that people feel uncomfortable when they stand out from everyone else, but they also feel uncomfortable when they see themselves as too similar to others. Snyder and Fromkin (1980) found that people like to find a happy medium, that is, they like to feel moderately unique. They ran an experiment demonstrating how asserting uniqueness is one way to resist social influence. They led university student participants to believe that their attitudes were either nearly identical to or distinct from the attitudes of a group of other students. Participants then participated in a conformity experiment. Results revealed that participants whose feeling of uniqueness was threatened were less likely to conform. In this way, they were able to reclaim their individuality that had been previously lost. In a recent study, Imhoff and Erb (2009) presented participants with a message that was said to be either a majority viewpoint (that is, most people agree with it) or a minority view-point (that is, very few people agree with it). They also manipulated participants' *need for uniqueness* by issuing a personality test and informing one-third of the participants that they were 'average' and one-third that they were 'different'. There was also a control condition with no manipulation of uniqueness. Results revealed that, in the control condition, participants showed a preference for the majority message, as did participants who were informed they were 'different'. However, participants whose uniqueness was threatened showed a strong prefer-ence for the minority message. Imhoff and Erb argued that people seek out a level of uniqueness from others, and one way to restore that uniqueness when it is threatened is to express a preference for a message that is endorsed by a smaller group of people. An everyday non-experimental example of how people assert their uniqueness is in their personal dress style. For example, if everyone wore a white T-shirt and jeans every day, it would not only be a dull world to live in, but people would also feel uncomfortable with their lack of uniqueness.

Time to reflect Can you think of social psychological reasons why people might *not* wish to assert their uniqueness?

As we discussed earlier, features of the situation can also enable people to resist social pressure. For example, conformity in the Asch paradigm is drastically reduced with the addition of just one dissenting participant. Perhaps this gives people the social support they require to resist influence. In other words, the addition of an individual sharing an isolated person's viewpoint helps them resist the majority's influence and present their own opinion or behaviour and there is less risk of negative consequences. However, when a person is a minority voice within a group and stands alone, it is difficult for them to dissent. This might lead to the assumption that it is even more difficult for the lone or minority voice to attempt to convince the unyielding majority that they are wrong, yet this type of social influence does occur. Many instances in history demonstrate that an individual with unique views, behaviours or perspectives (e.g., Galileo, Sigmund Freud) or a numerical minority (e.g., the suffragette movement) can influence majority opinion and bring about significant social change. Indeed, social change would be impossible without the innovations of such people and groups. Everyone would yield to the majority's views and practices and society would be practically homogeneous and static. But how do minorities execute this innovation? How do they bring about social change? These questions are answered in the next section (see also the section in Chapter 10 on leadership).

Minority social influence

Minority social influence
Social influence processes whereby a minority group (in terms of numbers or power) changes the attitudes of a majority group.

The possibility that small and/or seemingly powerless minorities can influence large and/or powerful majorities was not investigated until the 1960s, when Moscovici began his work on **minority social influence**. Can a minority in a group bring about changes in the opinions of a majority? As we know from our earlier discussions, this is a difficult task. One person or a small group of people against a large and cohesive majority can be a daunting and intimidating position to occupy. Indeed, as discussed earlier, Asch (1951) exposed a large group of participants to one erroneously responding confederate – these participants openly mocked and laughed at him. Thus, the minority faces the prospect of some harsh treatment from the group if they choose to air their opposing views. It is also the case that groups try to socialize and include people who deviate from the group in order to maintain power and unanimity (e.g., Levine and Moreland, 1994). However, single people and minority groups are not completely powerless. It is clearly the case that small minorities influence larger groups. Indeed, Asch also showed that a larger minority (nine) of erroneously responding confederates against a correct

majority of eleven participants was no longer openly mocked. The majority did not conform but as a cohesive group, the minority was a more serious force to be reckoned with. At the very least, minorities can force majorities to stop and think. They can raise questions about what the group is about. If they are influential enough, they will cause others to 'break off' from the majority group, orchestrating a schism (e.g., Sani and Reicher, 1999). But how can they achieve these things?

FIGURE 9.12 How do smaller minorities influence majorities?

© GUNNAR3000/FOTOLIA.COM

How can minorities be influential?

How can minorities exert more influence than they realistically ought to? The study of minority social influence was advanced significantly by the work of Moscovici and his colleagues. He argued that the influence of minorities cannot be accounted for by the same principles that explain majority influence (Moscovici, 1976). After all, they are but a few people, and they have little control compared to the majority. Instead, he argued that the impact of minority groups lies in their *behavioural style*. In particular, they must propose a clear position from the outset, stick to it, and resist social pressure to change it. In short, they must be *consistent* to exert influence over the majority. Moscovici broke this down into two components:

1 *diachronic consistency:* they must display *intra*individual consistency (that is, each individual must not waver in their opinion) and therefore show stability over time.

2 *synchronic consistency:* they must display *inter*individual consistency (that is, individuals within the minority should show the same opinion) and therefore show stability across the group.

Moscovici and colleagues ran experiments to test this idea.

In one study, Moscovici, Lage and Naffrechoux (1969) showed groups of six participants 36 coloured slides. The slides were all blue and only differed in their intensity. Participants were asked to state aloud what the colour of each slide was. Moscovici et al. manipulated the *consistency* of a minority within the group. In the consistent condition, two confederates always answered 'green' so that they were both diachronically and synchronically consistent. In the inconsistent condition, the confederates answered 'blue' on 12 trials and 'green' on 24 trials (the inconsistent condition). There was also a control condition where there were no confederates. Results revealed that participants committed practically no errors in the control condition and almost always correctly identified the slides as blue or green. In the inconsistent minority condition, only 1.25 per cent of participants gave an incorrect answer, which was only marginally higher than the control condition. However, in the consistent minority condition, 8.42 per cent of participants gave an incorrect answer (see Figure 9.13). Although not a huge increase in influence, this is significant considering the minority status of the confederates. The fact that they were consistent in their responding was enough to convince some people some of the time.

FIGURE 9.13 Agreement with consistent or inconsistent minorities When minorities are inconsistent, people are much less likely to agree compared to when they are consistent. Moscovici et al. argued that one of the keys to minority group success was a minority's consistency.

Data from Moscovici et al., 1969

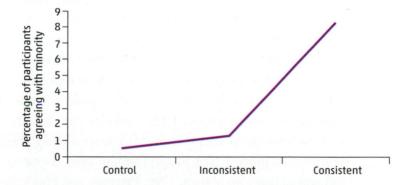

In a refinement of Moscovici et al.'s study, Nemeth, Swedlund and Kanki (1974) included two additional conditions where confederates responded 'green' on half the trials and 'green-blue' on the other half. The confederates either responded 'green' or 'green-blue' randomly, or 'green' on the brighter of the slides and 'green-blue' on the duller slides – the latter condition being the consistent minority condition – consistent because there was a logical pattern to their responses. In this study, the random condition had no effect. However, the consistent condition led to 21 per cent of responses being aligned with the influence attempt. Interestingly, results did not replicate Moscovici et al.'s (1969) 'green minority' condition. Nemeth et al. argued that this was probably because their participants were permitted to respond with more than one colour. In Moscovici et al.'s study, the minority showed no *flexibility* when the context clearly allowed it. Perhaps they did not influence the group because they were perceived as rigid and unrealistic (see also Mugny and Papastamou, 1982). Other research shows that people often interpret the actions of minorities in terms of psychological peculiarities (Papastamou and Mugny, 1990). Consistency within the minority is therefore important but a minority's influence is also dependent on how their consistency is interpreted by the majority.

Time to reflect Have you ever found yourself in a situation where you needed to change the opinions or behaviours of a majority group? What did you do? If you were with other people, what did they do? Was the attempt successful? Thinking about Moscovici's work on minority influence, did the minority do the right things in order to influence the majority?

Majority and minority influence

Moscovici believed that minorities do not exert influence in the same way as majorities, and the influence mechanisms are not the same. In particular, he argued that it is less likely that minorities induce normative influence because there is no normative pressure from the majority to conform to the minority position. Also, minorities are sometimes disliked (Moscovici and Lage, 1976), so why would the majority want to follow them? Further, Moscovici argued that minorities influence majorities in a different way, that is, the influence that occurs is quite different. Instead of the influence occurring on a public, surface level, he argued that minorities exert their influence at a more private, deeper level. Majority influence, according to Moscovici, activates a social comparison process where the participant compares their response to that of others without attending very much to the issue itself. They therefore conform to the normative response of the group and any private acceptance will be short-lived. Minorities, on the other hand, he argued, evoke a *validation process*. Here, the participant attempts to understand why the minority consistently holds its position. This process leads the participant to think more closely about the issue (process the information more systematically) and, in turn, they may become more privately influenced (see also Martin, 1996; Peterson and Nemeth, 1996). The processes of minority influence are depicted in Figure 9.14. However, this puts the participant in an awkward position – do they publicly change their mind, or keep it to themselves? Moscovici believed that people will often do the latter. In other words, even when the majority pressure may prevent people from showing their attitude (or behaviour) change openly, they may still privately accept the position of the minority. Thus, Moscovici and others have argued that majorities are more likely to induce compliance with no acceptance, but that minorities are more likely to achieve acceptance with no compliance. This is the basic tenet of **conversion theory** (Moscovici, 1980) and much research has supported this posi-

Conversion theory Moscovici's cognitive account of how members of the majority process minority messages.

tion (see also Maass and Clark, 1984, 1986; Nemeth and Wachtler, 1974). Using a slightly different argument, Nemeth (1986, 1995) also argued that minority (but not majority) influence allows divergent thinking and innovation. According to this account, the stress that is induced when people realize that they disagree with the majority restricts divergent thinking compared to the realization that one agrees with the minority. Social identity theory offers a perspective on minority influence too. Here, it is argued that the minority will be most influential if they can somehow frame themselves as part of the ingroup (David and Turner, 2001). In particular, a shared ingroup allows people to consider the minority as part of the group and think closely about their qualifications and credentials. Research supports this view. For example, David and Turner (1996, 1999) demonstrated that ingroup minorities achieved greater attitude change among a majority than outgroup minorities.

FIGURE 9.14 Mechanisms of minority influence, as explained by Moscovici's (1980) conversion theory Minorities can influence majorities if they are consistent and produce relevant evidence that encourages systematic processing. Such systematic processing will lead to private acceptance.

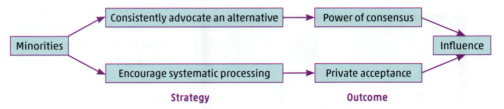

These perspectives argue for a *dual process* approach to social influence. Minorities and majorities exert their influence in different ways. However, Latané and Wolf (1981) proposed that a *single process* model can explain both minority and majority influence. They argued that influence is a unitary process regardless of its source (minority or majority). They proposed that *social impact* is a multiplicative function of the strength (power, expertise), immediacy (proximity in space and time) and size (number) of the source. In particular, impact decreases with each additional input. For example, the 20th person in a group will make less of a difference than the 19th person. Further, influence is divided across targets. This is why, they argue, minorities have less influence than majorities. They are smaller in number and their power is diffused across many targets. There is an ongoing debate between proponents of these two perspectives. Some theorists argue that the two perspectives can be integrated into a common theoretical framework. For example, de Dreu and de Vries (1996) offered a *differential processing model of persuasion*, arguing that stable attitude shift, regardless of the source, will occur if arguments are perceived to be convincing, people have the ability to process information and they are also motivated to process information.

Other studies have shed more light on the conditions under which minorities and majorities are influential, enabling us to better understand the different processes that might be at work for majorities and minorities to exert their influence. For example Erb, Bohner, Hewstone et al. (2006) showed that actual consensus within the minority is an important predictor of influence. But this also depends on the consensus that group members *perceive* to exist. In particular, Erb et al.

found that telling people there was 20 per cent consensus among a minority had more influence if this was more than expected (e.g., if participants expected only 10 per cent consensus), but less if actual consensus was less than expected (e.g., if participants expected 30 per cent consensus). Thus, it is not only the actual features of the minority that are important, but also how people see it (see also Erb and Bohner, 2007). Overall, it is clear that minorities can be influential just like majorities, but social psychologists agree less on the exact processes that make this happen (see de Dreu and de Vries, 1996; for reviews of minority influence, see Martin and Hewstone, 2008; Martin, Hewstone, Martin and Gardikiotis, 2008).

SOCIAL PSYCHOLOGY IN THE REAL WORLD

The suffragette movement

Until the early 20th century, British women were not permitted to vote. Members of Parliament believed that women would not understand how Parliament functioned and should therefore take no part in electoral procedures. A minority group of women disagreed. Founded in 1903 by Emmeline Pankhurst, the Women's Social and Political Union (aka the 'suffragettes') began their fight for social change. Their task was not easy – they needed to convince a large and established majority to change the law. How did they do this? The suffragettes are a classic example of minority influence in action. Consistent and unwavering in their commitment to the cause, they were prepared to

perform extreme acts, go to prison and risk their lives to earn women the vote. Slowly, the suffragettes forced Parliament to reconsider their views. After the First World War, the Representation of the People Act was passed in 1918 by Parliament, giving the right to vote to women of property over the age of 30. All women over the age of 21 were granted the right to vote in 1928.

Questions

1 Many assume that the success of the suffragette movement was a 'reward' for the vital work done by women during the First World War. However, women in France (who were also instrumental in the war effort) were not similarly rewarded. Do you think this is a good explanation?
2 What might be another reason for their success?
3 Many of the suffragettes' activities were violent (e.g., arson, vandalism). Thinking about how minorities are influential, would these activities have helped or hindered their cause?
4 What other influences might the suffragettes have had? Think also about our discussion of status and roles in Chapter 8.

Exploring further   Consider a protest or minority lobby group that interests you. Research it on the internet. Do you think that public reaction to the group fits the pattern predicted by conversion theory? What advice would you give to this group about achieving influence? Do you think it is currently adopting effective strategies?

Chapter summary

In this chapter, we have learned that people respond to social influence in different ways depending on who they are and the situation in which they find themselves. People are sometimes influenced because they do not want to stand apart from the group and risk rejection, ridicule and other negative responses from the group. Sometimes, however, this social influence can have negative consequences, as is often the case when people 'blindly' follow rules and orders. Here is a brief summary of the points covered in this chapter:

- Several conditions increase the likelihood of social influence, such as being confronted with an authority figure, experiencing group pressure and fearing disapproval from the group. Cultural factors also affect social influence, with some cultures showing greater levels of conformity than others.

- People are not always easily influenced and some conditions will actually reduce the likelihood of social influence occurring. For example, being in a group that is not unanimous or having made a prior commitment to a decision will make an individual less likely to be influenced by the group.

- There are said to be two different types of social influence. Normative influence occurs when people are influenced without changing their attitudes. Informational influence occurs when people are outwardly influenced and their attitudes also change. Research findings suggest that our attitudes and behaviours are more likely to be influenced by the groups we belong to – a process called referent informational influence.

- Of course, people often resist social pressure because they want to be unique or uphold their own opinions. People can react against group conventions or assert their uniqueness in other ways such as dressing or talking differently to other members of the group.

- Finally, minorities (individuals and group) can innovate and change people's attitudes and behaviours in order to force social change. They can do so by being consistent, clear and unwavering in their attempts to influence the majority.

Our concern in this chapter has been how social groups can exert an influence on the behaviour of the individuals who belong to them. In Chapter 10, we turn to how individuals can exert an influence on the behaviour of the groups they belong to. Individuals often collaborate in ways that mean they are effectively thinking, feeling and acting as a unit. How do they work together to solve problems, identify and pursue common goals, and even experience emotions?

Essay questions

At the beginning of the chapter, we asked you to consider these questions:

1 Imagine you are in a room with 10 of your peers, voting on who will be the next president of the tennis club. Everyone before you votes for Jo but you really want Malika to get the job. Who will you vote for? What conditions would make it easier for you to vote for Malika?

2 How would you explain the actions of an RAF pilot who, when asked to drop bombs on an Iraqi village, does so without question?

3 A small political party holds only 5 per cent of the seats in Parliament. It has a strong position on environmental issues and its main agenda is to influence governmental policy on these matters. What options are open to this party to achieve its goal?

Having read this chapter, these questions could also be framed as the following essay questions, which you can attempt in preparation for your examinations:

1 What are the factors that influence conformity within groups? Discuss with reference to relevant research on social influence processes.

2 Everyone is capable of 'evil' – it all depends on the situation. Do you agree with this statement? Why/why not?

3 With reference to relevant research, explain how minorities can influence majorities.

Some further reading

Brown, R.J. (2000) *Group Processes* (2nd edn). Oxford: Blackwell. Covers a wide range of issues in the study of group processes, including coverage of social influence processes within groups.

Cialdini, R.B. and Trost, M.R. (1998) Social influence: Social norms, conformity and compliance. In D. Gilbert, S.T. Fiske and G. Lindzey (eds) *The Handbook of Social Psychology* (4th edn, vol. 2, pp. 151–92). New York: McGraw-Hill. Comprehensive chapter on social influence which takes a particularly close look at persuasion and social norms.

Hogg, M.A. (2010) Influence and leadership. In S.T. Fiske, D.T. Gilbert and G. Lindzey (eds) *Handbook of Social Psychology* (5th edn, vol. 2, pp. 1166–207). New York: Wiley. Provides a detailed and current look at research on social influence and detailed coverage of work on minority influence.

Mugny, G. and Pérez, J.A. (1991) *The Social Psychology of Minority Influence*. Cambridge: Cambridge University Press. Overview of social influence research with a particularly European focus and comprehensive coverage of minority influence.

Pratkanis, A.R. (ed.) (2007) *The Science of Social Influence: Advances and Future Progress*. New York: Psychology Press. Collection of chapters on key topics related to social influence by experts in the field.

Social Influence. Journal published four times a year, airs cutting-edge research on topics covered in this chapter, including special issues on specific topics.

Turner, J.C. (1991) *Social Influence*. Buckingham: Open University Press. Theoretical text on social influence that takes a European and social identity focused approach.

 Visit the companion website at **www.palgrave.com/psychology/suttondouglas** for access to a wide range of resources to help you get to grips with this chapter.

Applying social psychology

Can conformity decrease antisocial behaviour?

Have you ever walked down the streets of a big city and wondered how to stop people throwing their litter all over the place? Well, making people aware of social norms is one way of reducing such antisocial behaviour. For example, seeing another person pick up litter in a car park reduces the percentage of people who throw leaflets from their car's windscreen onto the ground (Kallgren, Reno and Cialdini, 2000). Also, Reno, Cialdini and Kallgren (1993) ran a study in a dirty car park that had litter strewn all over the place. A confederate walked by and either threw litter on the ground, or picked up and appropriately disposed of some litter. There was also a control condition where there was no confederate. In each case, the experimenters had put a leaflet on people's cars and observed their behaviour when they got back to their car. The results revealed that in the control condition, 38 per cent of the car owners threw the leaflet onto the ground. In the condition where the confederate littered, 30 per cent of car owners littered too. However, in the condition where the confederate disposed of their litter, only 4 per cent of observed car owners littered. These studies demonstrate that making people aware of prosocial norms may be a useful technique for decreasing littering behaviour.

In this exercise, we would like you to think of another example of a common antisocial behaviour and devise an intervention against this behaviour. Base your intervention on the concept of norm awareness and write down the following things:

1 A statement of the problem.
2 A description of the intervention you would introduce (e.g., what would you manipulate?) and the theoretical basis for this intervention.
3 An outline of how you will measure the outcomes. In other words, how will you know if your intervention has worked?

Blind spot in social psychology

Referent informational influence

Several studies have shown that people are more likely to laugh at TV comedies that are accompanied by prerecorded or 'canned' laughter (e.g., Cialdini, 1993). Platow, Haslam, Both et al. (2005) built on these findings to design a clever experimental test of the concept of referent informational influence. They had participants watch, alone, a stand-up comedy routine on video. The tape either contained no laughter, or canned laughter inserted after each joke. Participants were led to believe that the audience comprised either ingroup members – fellow students at La Trobe University in Australia – or outgroup members, in this case members of an Australian far-right political party. The results were

- ingroup audience and canned laughter: participants laughed for an average of 3.92 minutes
- ingroup audience with no laughter: participants laughed for 0.90 minutes
- outgroup audience and canned laughter: participants laughed for 0.94 minutes
- outgroup audience with no laughter: participants laughed for 0.79 seconds.

1 What independent variable(s) are there in this experiment, and what are their levels?
2 What is the dependent variable in this experiment?
3 What hypotheses for this study can you draw from the concept of referent informational influence?
4 Plot the average time spent laughing in a graph, formatting according to APA style (or the style preferred by your institution, if different). Use a software package such as Microsoft Word, Excel, SPSS or Google Documents.
5 Your figure should show a large difference between the time spent laughing in the 'ingroup laughter' condition and the other three conditions. Assume this difference is statistically significant, and the other three conditions are not significantly different from each other. Are the results consistent with referent informational influence? Do they support the hypotheses you drew up in question 3?
6 What other dependent variables might have been used in this experiment to assess the effects of ingroup and outgroup laughter? What advantages would they offer?
7 The 'outgroup' in this study was a far-right political party in Australia known as One Nation. These people are likely to have radically different values and worldviews than your average, relatively liberal, psychology student at La Trobe

University in Melbourne. Imagine if participants had been told that the audience had comprised an outgroup that shared the same basic beliefs and values as the ingroup. Can you think of an example of such an outgroup? In this case, do you think that participants would have been indifferent to whether the outgroup was laughing? Why/why not? (Back up your answer with examples from the chapter.)
8 In light of your answers to question 7, how convincing do you think this experiment is as a demonstration of referent informational influence?
9 Now that you have completed this exercise, think about a potential application of the logic of this experiment on referent informational influence. Recently, there has been controversy over sexist and racist humour. According to some people, a joke is a joke, and people should not worry too much about racist and sexist jokes. According to others, humour and our reactions to humour are important, partly because they define social norms about the acceptability of representations of social groups. There is some support for the latter, pessimistic view of humour. Male participants exposed to sexist jokes subsequently show increases in rape proclivity – the self-reported willingness to rape (Romero-Sánchez, Durán, Carretero-Dios et al., 2010). However, this effect was moderated by how unpleasant (aversive) these jokes were perceived to be. Men who found sexist jokes to be highly aversive did not show any increase in rape proclivity. The experiment by Platow et al. (2005) suggests that the emotional reactions of the audience – especially an ingroup audience – will affect a man's emotional reactions to sexist humour. The worst combination of circumstances we can imagine is a large audience of people laughing at sexist jokes, which may lead men to find jokes less aversive than they would when alone. This has led to media debate on the rise of 'rape humour' by stand-up comedians such as Ricky Gervais and Jimmy Carr. Indeed, a show by Carr was called *Rapier Wit*, apparently in a gruesome pun (see, e.g., Logan, 2010). Design an experiment to examine this blind spot. What kind of study would you conduct to examine whether men do find sexist jokes less aversive when there is an audience laughing than when either alone or when an outgroup audience laughs, and whether this has knock-on effects on rape proclivity. You might want to research briefly how rape proclivity is measured using internet search engines or academic databases.

Student project

Social influence and prejudice

Nikita Woodcock studied as an undergraduate student at Sheffield University, and her final-year dissertation supervisor was Dr Thomas Webb. Her work is an innovative extension of the research on social influence as a function of who the source of influence is. As a study of implicit prejudice, it also speaks to many of the issues we consider in Chapters 4 and 11.

My topic and aims

Prejudice cannot be measured simply by asking people about their attitudes towards particular social groups (e.g., Do you like Asian people?). Although a number of measures of implicit prejudice exist, such as the Implicit Association Test (IAT) (Greenwald, McGhee and Schwartz, 1998), they tend to reflect people's attitudes, rather than their actions. The main focus of my project was on designing an unobtrusive measure that was better able to predict prejudiced behaviour.

I selected this area of research due to my personal experience that most people seem to identify themselves as non-prejudiced. It logically follows that prejudiced attitudes and behaviours should be declining. However, there is of course still a significant amount of prejudice and discrimination in society. I was interested to find out whether people are aware that they hold prejudiced views, and whether these beliefs influence people's behaviour.

My methods

Participants undertook two measures of implicit prejudice, the first being the IAT. They then completed an advice-taking task which was the new measure of prejudice. The advice-taking task is a computer task in which participants have to find tokens hidden in either a blue or red box. Before they select a box, however, a face appears on the screen offering advice (e.g., 'choose the red box!'). There were six Asian faces and 12 White faces – a total of 54 trials with each face offering advice three times – twice correct and once incorrect. We compared the proportion of advice taken from White versus Asian advice-givers.

To measure discriminatory behaviour, participants received an incorrectly addressed email one week after taking part in the computer tasks (a technique borrowed from Stern and Faber,

1997). The 'lost email' was addressed to Irfan Patel (a typically Asian name) and referred to coursework which had been incorrectly submitted and required resubmission within 24 hours or they would be penalized. I measured whether participants replied to this email or not.

My findings and their implications

We found that the proportion of advice taken from Asian and White faces correlated with the results of the IAT, suggesting that responses to the advice-taking task reflected implicit prejudice. However, only the advice-taking measure predicted whether participants responded to the lost email they received. Around 90 per cent of participants explicitly stated that race would have no impact on whether they would take advice or not, suggesting that they were unaware of any racial discrimination during the advice-taking task, and, thus, that the task was unobtrusive.

The results highlight that not only do we have attitudes we may be unaware of, but these attitudes can influence our behaviour in a way contrary to how we believe we would behave. This has implications for understanding why, despite self-reported prejudice declining, there is still prejudice and discrimination in society. It is not that people are lying about being prejudiced but that they may hold prejudiced attitudes at an unconscious level and it is these which can influence actions towards others.

My journey

I am currently working as a GCSE, AS and A2 psychology teacher in Kent. This allows me to continue to learn about psychology and, hopefully, enthuse young people about psychology. I enjoy teaching and have found my understanding of human behaviour very beneficial in this career. I have to deal with a wide variety of different students with a range of different needs and I frequently find myself drawing on my knowledge of psychology to help me with this. I always saw myself moving into educational psychology and this is still an option for the future. However, at the moment, I am enjoying my job too much to consider moving on.

Through undertaking my research project, I learned a substantial amount about the challenges that researchers face and exactly what goes into completing psychological research. I also learned a lot about myself and what I am able to achieve when I put my mind to it. I developed confidence in my ability to undertake a challenge and succeed at it. I found it daunting at first but remember immersing myself in the project, spending hours in the labs and the library not just because I had a deadline, but because I enjoyed it. One of the most useful skills that I gained in terms of my current career was time management. With a relatively short timeframe to complete the project, I learned to prioritize and manage my time efficiently, a skill that is vital for teaching.

The data and findings from my research project formed part of a paper written by my supervisor. The paper consisted of four experiments developing the advice-taking task as an unobtrusive measure of prejudice. My data are described in Experiment 3.

My advice

My advice for anyone embarking on a research project is first and foremost to select an area that you are truly interested in. The project will consume a lot of your time and if it is not something you are interested in, you will struggle to give it the dedication it requires. Students should also remember that their supervisor is there to help and offer guidance and support. It is a big challenge and one which any student would struggle to undertake alone. Be organized, and finally, enjoy it.

10 Group behaviour

In this chapter, we consider the factors that facilitate and hinder collective human behaviour. We examine how group members are influenced by each other through the processes of social facilitation, social loafing and deindividuation. We also discuss how groups make decisions and how they cooperate, experience conflict and avoid conflict. Finally, we discuss leadership in groups. By the end of this chapter, you will have learned about the factors that facilitate and obstruct collective human achievement.

© BRAND X PICTURES

Topics covered in this chapter

- Social facilitation
- Social loafing
- Deindividuation
- Group decision making
- Leadership

Key features

Critical focus Emergent norm theory

Ethics and research methods Studying groupthink

Social psychology in the real world Road rage

Applying social psychology Women in leadership: the glass cliff

Blind spot in social psychology Race and leadership

Student project Civic disengagement and belief in conspiracy theories

Questions to consider

1 Diana is learning to tap dance and has been practising for a forthcoming recital. She practises in front of a mirror and makes all the right moves. However, when the recital comes along, she makes many mistakes and cannot understand why she messed up so badly. All her family and friends were watching her. How might we explain this?

2 Faiza is working with a group on an assignment about stereotypes of the British. Everyone has agreed to collect five references on the topic for the group to share. Faiza does not try very hard and only provides two references, letting the group down. What social psychological processes (intentional and unintentional) might lead Faiza to do this?

3 Ben is at a concert. It is his favourite band and he is very excited. The audience is huge and everyone is dancing. Quite spontaneously, Ben moves up to a female stranger in the audience and grabs her by the wrist. Why would he do such a thing?

Groups do great and terrible things that individuals cannot. Our everyday language reflects the wisdom that groups do things. For example, we effortlessly speak of how the Ancient Egyptians built the pyramids of Giza, Ancient Britons Stonehenge and Ancient Chinese the Great Wall. We also talk of the wrongs perpetrated by one group upon another – how one group suppresses, tyrannizes or even commits genocide upon another. Thus, we appear to assume that groups are capable of bearing collective responsibility for their actions (Branscombe and Doosje, 2004). Sometimes, they are even punished collectively, as when countries are forced to pay reparations, or companies are sued for their wrongdoings. Groups are perceived to be more than merely the sum of their parts.

In this chapter, our focus is on group behaviour and, in particular, how groups do things. In so doing, it is important to think about what it means to say that groups do things. When we say 'group X did something', we do not mean exactly the same thing as when we say 'person X did something'. For one thing, although a person may sometimes have conflicting goals, and selfhood may not be quite as unitary as we normally imagine (see Chapter 2), a person is clearly a moral unit in a way that a group is not. A given member of group X may have contributed nothing to its actions, and may even have tried to obstruct them (Lewis, 1948). For example, women may have achieved the right to vote despite many barriers, even from within their own group. A member of group X may not have even been born when it committed atrocities (van den Beld, 2002). For example, although Germans committed many atrocities during the Second World War, most Germans alive today were not alive when these events occurred. It is a much debated point whether such people should receive any blame (or credit) or accept any responsibility for their group's actions. In contrast, we cannot choose to punish or reward only part of a person for their actions. An interesting example is how serial killers such as Ted Bundy use as their defence the argument that they have multiple personalities and that just one personality was responsible for the murders. How does one punish a personality?

Another important point is that the human brain is the most complex structure in the known universe (see Chapter 3). Having one makes it possible for individuals to form aspirations and goals, experience emotions, have thoughts and memories, and plan and execute behaviour. Of course, groups also have means of storing and processing information, as in books, public archives, through information sharing and discussion. But these are nowhere near as sophisticated as the operations permitted by the human brain. Even if we were to allow that groups can have a mental life – an idea scotched by many scholars – it would be a much simpler and less coherent life than that experienced by individuals. Thus, when we speak of groups' mental, emotional and motivational states, we are either talking metaphorically or about states that are widely shared by their members. The behaviour of a group cannot be spurred by its mental states in the same way that a person's can.

Group behaviour Behaviour displayed by people who are acting within, and as, a group.

Nonetheless, when we refer to many **group behaviours**, as in 'The Ancient Chinese built the Great Wall', we are not just saying that a number of individuals from this group built it. We are saying that those individuals were influenced by their interactions with other group members, causing them to form goals and act differently than if they were alone. In particular, these group members adopted common goals and worked together in a coordinated fashion in order to achieve them. This coordinated **group action** is the kind of group behaviour we are most interested in here. It is what allows human beings to achieve together what they cannot do alone. In this chapter, we will consider the factors that facilitate and obstruct collective human achievement. In particular, we shall examine how groups influence their members through the processes of social facilitation, social loafing, deindividuation, decision making, cooperation, conflict and leadership.

Group action Behaviour by group members that is coordinated in order to achieve a common goal.

© PHOTODISC

Social facilitation

One way in which groups can achieve more than the sum of their individual parts is by influencing the efforts and achievements of their members. Gordon Allport (1954, p. 46) asked: 'What changes in an individual's normal solitary performance occur when people are present?' In other words, how does the group influence the individual? Does the group help or hinder individual performance? Triplett (1898) was the first to investigate these sorts of questions. He observed that cyclists' racing times were faster when racing against the clock than when racing without being timed. However, he also found that cyclists made better time when racing alongside other cyclists than when racing alone against the clock. Intrigued by this observation, he set out to examine the phenomenon experimentally, where he asked children, either alone or **co-present** with others, to wind string onto a fishing reel as quickly as possible. He found that the children who worked alongside others wound faster than the children who completed the task alone.

Why did this happen? Why would children perform this task better in the presence of others rather than when they acted alone? Triplett thought that competing with others 'energizes' people and enhances their task performance. Many other experiments followed Triplett's studies, demonstrating that the co-presence of individuals improves the speed with which people perform simple mathematical and motor tasks. To this day, social scientists investigate how the presence of others improves performance on tasks such as solving anagrams and puzzles (Flynn and Amanatullah, 2012); and Gardner and Knowles (2008) demonstrated that the person present does not even need to be real – being in the 'presence' of a fictional TV character can facilitate performance on simple tasks.

Floyd Allport (1920) called this phenomenon **social facilitation** – the process by which the presence of others can facilitate behaviour. However, unlike Triplett, Allport did not assume that the context needed to be competitive. Instead, he argued that the **mere presence** of others could facilitate behaviour. In other words, all that is necessary is that other people are around, either doing the same thing (as **co-actors**) or simply watching passively. Allport also argued that this phenomenon is not just present in human beings, and research suggests he was right. Studies have demonstrated examples of social facilitation in other animal species,

Co-presence Performing a task in the presence of other people.

Social facilitation The process by which the presence of others can facilitate behaviour.

Mere presence Social facilitation effects need not necessarily be competitive. The simple presence of others is enough to facilitate behaviour.

Co-actors People performing the same task at the same time but not performing the task collectively.

specifically in the feeding behaviour of rats (Harlow, 1932), dogs (James, 1953) and chicks (Tolman, 1964). Other studies have demonstrated that a variety of creatures such as kangaroos, monkeys and horses eat more and run faster and perform other behaviours better when other members of their species are doing the same thing (Dindo, Whiten and de Waal, 2009; Pays, Dubot, Jarman et al., 2009; van Dierendonck, de Vries and Schilder, 1995).

However, not all studies demonstrated results that were consistent with the idea of social facilitation. Shortly after the initial discovery of the social facilitation effect, some studies showed that the presence of others actually impairs performance, for both animals and humans (for a review, see Bond and Titus, 1983). The presence of others can sometimes be so inhibiting that the phenomenon can actually become a case of **social inhibition** rather than social facilitation. For example, men take longer to urinate when someone is standing immediately beside them at a urinal than when they are alone (Middlemist, Knowles and Matter, 1976). Other findings have shown that people who are asked to perform a complex task, such as typing their name backwards, do so more slowly in the presence of other people than when they are alone (Schmitt, Gilovich, Goore and Joseph, 1986). The presence of others can sometimes be helpful but at other times is a hindrance. So, what kind of social presence is important and for what kind of task?

Social inhibition The process by which the presence of others can hinder behaviour.

Zajonc (1965) argued that the presence of others makes people alert and sometimes anxious (see Mullen, Bryant and Driskell, 1997). Drawing on a well-established principle from experimental psychology research, Zajonc argued that this arousal enhances whatever response tendency is the dominant one – in particular, when people are anxious, they tend to do better on easy tasks (tasks they are already good at) and worse on difficult ones (tasks where they may normally struggle). Zajonc argued that this phenomenon enables us to understand why the presence of others is sometimes helpful but sometimes harmful to task performance. For example, when they are being watched, people perform well on simple mathematical tasks because they are easy, whereas by comparison, they do poorly on complex mathematical tasks because they are difficult. Whether social facilitation or inhibition occurs for people depends on the nature of the task they are doing (see Figure 10.1).

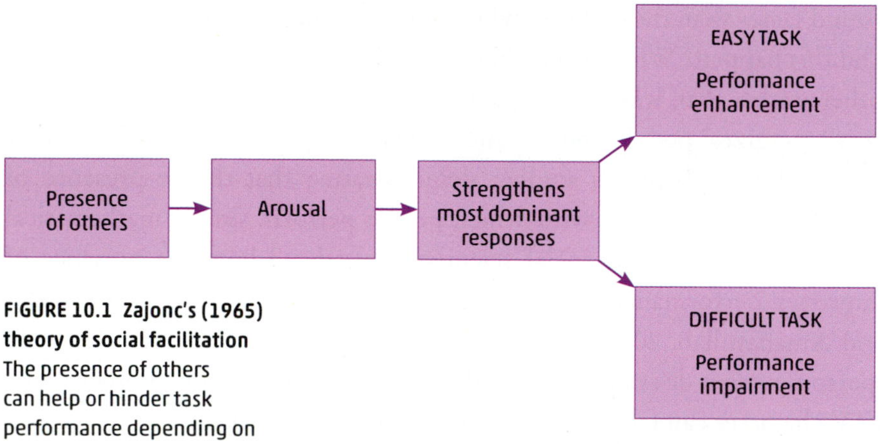

| Presence of others | → | Arousal | → | Strengthens most dominant responses |

EASY TASK Performance enhancement

DIFFICULT TASK Performance impairment

FIGURE 10.1 Zajonc's (1965) theory of social facilitation The presence of others can help or hinder task performance depending on task difficulty.

Question to consider Reread question 1 at the start of the chapter. Why do you think Diana performed her dance so poorly in the presence of others?

Tasks such as learning mazes are naturally difficult for people, so being watched does not help – it makes people anxious and they perform worse. On the other hand, completing a simple addition is easy and the presence of others energizes people to do well on these easy tasks. They look good in front of others and therefore feel good. Thinking back to our earlier example, if you were learning how to perform a difficult task like play the piano, it would probably help not to be aroused by the presence of watchful eyes. This is likely to make you feel anxious and perform badly. However, if you were an experienced pianist, the arousal produced by the presence of others is likely to be exhilarating and performance enhancing. In sports, the presence of an audience may provide athletes with that extra something to perform to their best, or beyond their ability. For the less skilled athlete, however, this may trigger a 'choking under pressure' response.

Try it yourself Try to design a simple study to test Zajonc's principles of social facilitation. For example, ask friends to complete either a simple or complex crossword in a room with other students, or watch them do it by themselves. Do they complete the task more quickly in a group if the task is simple? Perhaps you can think of other tasks where the findings would be different. This is a good exercise in designing a study to test a hypothesis.

Exploring further Look on the internet for examples of so-called 'choking' in sporting events. For example, what happened to Rory McIlroy in the Masters golf tournament in the USA in Augusta in 2011 when his skills seemed to abandon him? Why did John Terry slip on the penalty spot and miss his shot in the 2008 Champions League final? Write down a list of 5–10 of these events and think about how they display some of the characteristics of social inhibition. Is this something that also affects teams of people rather than just individuals within groups? Was the highly favoured US women's soccer team loss to Japan in the 2011 World Cup an example of social inhibition?

Later studies have supported Zajonc's theory. To give one interesting example, Michaels, Blommel, Brocato et al. (1982) studied the performance of pool players in a student union. They found that skilled pool players (who made over 70 per cent of successful shots while being observed secretly) performed better (performance increased to 80 per cent) when four observers came to watch them. On the other hand, poor players (averaging less than 40 per cent of shots under normal conditions) performed worse (making only a quarter of their shots) when they were being watched. For skilled players, the dominant response was to successfully sink the balls and the presence of others facilitated their performance (Figure 10.2). However, for the less skilled players, the dominant response was to fail (they failed most of the time), so the scrutiny of others made them even worse. Other examples are plentiful. People and cockroaches learn simple mazes quicker in the presence of others but learn complex mazes more slowly (e.g., Zajonc, Heingartner and Herman, 1969).

More recently, Blascovich, Mendes, Hunter and Solomon (1999) found physiological evidence supporting Zajonc's theory. Here, the presence of others triggered arousal in people who were performing a task and heart rate patterns were consistent with findings of improved performance on familiar tasks and impaired performance on unfamiliar tasks. There are other interesting effects too. For example, gambling intensity (among people who already gamble) is intensified when people think they are in the presence of others (Rockloff and Dyer, 2007). In other words, people gamble more and lose more money when they think they are not gambling alone. Some researchers have also shown that there are individual differences in receptivity to the presence of others. For example, some research suggests that people who are extraverted and have high self-esteem are more likely to be facilitated when behaving alone rather than in the presence of others. Further, a meta-analysis by Oviatt and Iso-Ahola (2008) found that the presence of others generally has moderate effects on many different kinds of motor behaviours.

But why does this happen? Why are we aroused when others are present? It was generally assumed that the presence of others increases **drive**, which facilitates more dominant responses, but the finer grained processes were less clearly articulated. Research evidence suggests that there are three possible ways in which the presence of others can influence our behaviour. These are mere presence, evaluation apprehension and distraction.

Drive A negative state of tension associated with an unsatisfied need and motivates efforts to satisfy the need.

Exploring further Zajonc's work has been influential in social psychology in many areas other than the study of social facilitation. Read more about his life and work. A good starting point may be *The Selected Works of Robert Zajonc* (2003).

Mere presence

Zajonc argued that nothing else about the presence of others was necessary to influence behaviour – simply the mere company of others is enough to increase drive and facilitate or hinder behaviour. This seems plausible in some examples. Specifically, why do joggers run faster in the presence of others when there is no direct competition or evaluation? They appear to be energized by the mere situation of performing their task in the presence of others. Indeed, people choose to jog with others because they know it helps their behaviour. Also, on tasks where there are no 'right' and 'wrong' answers, people make stronger judgements in the presence of others rather than when they act alone. For example, people show stronger colour preferences when they are with other people (Goldman, 1967) – merely being with others makes a difference on such simple, trivial tasks.

However, in some situations, the presence of others comes with additional features such as competition and evaluation. For example, sports are often played with others in competitive contexts and an audience is often present too, watching players' every move. Other social psychologists have therefore argued that the mere presence of others, while being important in some situations, cannot fully explain how behaviour changes in other situations. The picture is much more complex. The research we have discussed so far also does not explain exactly how the presence of others makes a difference to people's behaviours. The concept of evaluation apprehension helps to explain this further.

© STOCKBYTE

FIGURE 10.2 Being watched improves the performance of skilled pool players Michaels et al. (1982) found that skilled pool players performed even better in the presence of others but poor players did not.

Evaluation apprehension

Cottrell, Wack, Sekerak and Rittle (1968) observed that the enhancement of dominant responses is strongest when people think they are being watched. In an experiment, they asked participants to complete three tasks they had practised and therefore generally performed well, that is, the dominant response would be successful task performance. They were asked to complete the tasks in front of an audience who were either blindfolded, co-present but inattentive, or fully attentive. Results revealed that the fully attentive audience produced the strongest social facilitation effect. People performed best when the members of the audience were paying close attention.

Cottrell et al. (1968) argued that this occurred because the participants were concerned about how the audience were evaluating their performance. The blindfolded and inattentive audience made no difference to performance presumably because their presence did not make the participants anxious – the audience were not scrutinizing their performance so their presence mattered little. On the other hand, the attentive audience were closely watching and this made the participants apprehensive about their performance. Wanting to perform well for their audience, this **evaluation apprehension** worked in their favour and they performed even better. Thus, evaluation apprehension can be invigorating and a positive influence on task performance. In general, the evaluation apprehension hypothesis argues that performance is determined directly by how people think they are being *evaluated* rather than the fact that others are there. For example, if you are a talented piano student, you may still be worried that your teacher, family or friends will laugh at you or tell others that you are a hopeless case. At this point, however, your dominant performance will prevail and you are likely to perform at your best, facilitated by the observation of others (Butler and Baumeister, 1998; Kors, Linden and Gerin, 1997; Wallace, Baumeister and Vohs, 2005).

The evaluation apprehension hypothesis can explain other findings too. For example, it has been found that the people who are most concerned about what others think (and therefore are dispositionally more concerned about evaluation) are most influenced by the presence of others (Geen, 1983, 1991; Geen and Gange, 1983). Also, people perform better on tasks when they are co-present with someone they perceive as superior to themselves (Muller, Atzeni and Butera, 2004), arguably because they are predisposed to compare themselves with people who perform slightly better than themselves (Festinger, 1954). Thus, the self-consciousness we feel in the presence of others can sometimes be our friend.

Of course, evaluation apprehension is not always our friend. Some research has shown that when people are performing tasks, the presence of others can, unfortunately, become their enemy. For example, Markus (1978) asked participants to perform the task of undressing and dressing in their own clothes or undressing and dressing in unfamiliar clothes. Participants performed this task alone, in the presence of an inattentive audience, or in the presence of an attentive audience. Markus found that social facilitation only occurred when the task was easy (participants

Evaluation apprehension
Concern about being evaluated by observers when performing a task.

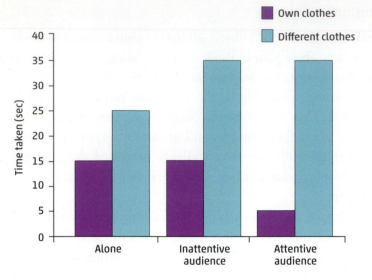

Own clothes
Different clothes

FIGURE 10.3 How the presence of others influences performance The time taken for people to dress in familiar and unfamiliar clothes as a function of audience attentiveness. An attentive audience was detrimental to performance on the unfamiliar task, demonstrating that evaluation apprehension is sometimes detrimental to performance.

Source: Data from Markus, 1978

dressed in their own clothes). In the presence of an attentive audience, participants performed this task faster than in the presence of an inattentive audience or when they were alone. On the other hand, when the task was difficult (dressing in unfamiliar clothes), the presence of any kind of audience was detrimental to behaviour (see Figure 10.3).

In another study, de Vet and de Dreu (2007) found that thinking aloud can hinder creativity and the generation of ideas – a finding that was particularly pronounced for individuals who are highly sensitive to what others think of them and have a lower ability to adapt to others' expectations. Further, Schmitt et al. (1986) asked participants to type either their name or a code backwards on the computer. The mere presence of others made people perform the simple task quicker and the difficult task slower. The introduction of an evaluation apprehension condition (an attentive audience, as in Markus's study) made little difference to participants' typing speed. From these findings, it seems that evaluation apprehension is sometimes helpful but sometimes not necessary for social facilitation. Even more interesting, evaluation apprehension can sometimes be harmful.

Distraction

Further expanding on these findings, Sanders, Baron and Moore (1978; see also Baron, 1986) argued that self-conscious evaluation apprehension facilitates behaviour on simple tasks but hinders performance on complex tasks because people become *too concerned* about what others are doing and how these others are evaluating their behaviour. As such, people become distracted and perform worse. This is more likely on difficult or unfamiliar tasks than simple or familiar tasks because when people are distracted, drive occurs and, as we know, drive facilitates performance on simpler tasks rather than complex activities.

Sanders et al. (1978) ran an experiment in which participants performed either an easy or difficult digit task. They did so either alone or with someone who was performing the same or a different task. Distraction was therefore operationalized by what the co-actor was doing. Sanders et al. argued that people should be more distracted by the presence of someone else if they are doing the same as themselves. They will be busy watching what the other person is doing and comparing the person's behaviour to their own. People should perform worse on the same difficult task because the potential for distraction to become a problem is maximized. Indeed, this is exactly what happened. People performed worse when someone else was doing the same thing as them. Other studies support Sanders et al.'s theory. For example, compared to more experienced drivers, younger drivers tend to have more accidents when they have passengers in the car than when they are driving alone (Chen, Baker, Braver and Li, 2000).

It is important to note that these kinds of effects can arise not only from the presence of others. Sanders (1981) showed that nonhuman distractors such as bursts of light can have similar effects on social facilitation. Thus, it could be argued that there is nothing uniquely 'social' about social facilitation. Distraction effects can also explain social facilitation in animals when the evaluation apprehension explanation is not as plausible. For example, it is plausible to argue that animals are distracted in the presence of other animals and that this simple distraction affects their behaviour rather than something 'social' about the presence of other animals.

Other explanations for social facilitation

Not all explanations of social facilitation involve the notion of arousal. For example, the concept of self-awareness (Carver and Scheier, 1981; Duval and Wicklund, 1972) has been suggested as another mechanism. Specifically, if people compare their actual performance on a task with their ideal performance (how they would like to do), there will be a small discrepancy for easy, well-practised tasks. On the other hand, the discrepancy will inevitably be larger for difficult or non-learned tasks. For example, people will generally perform as well as they would like to perform on an easy maths task but may fall short of what they would like to achieve on a complex or difficult maths task. This self-discrepancy (Higgins, 1987) can motivate people to perform better, but only if the discrepancy is small. If it is too large, motivation will decrease – people will simply give up because they cannot attain their ideal. Being watched by others can increase awareness of self-discrepancy. This is another explanation for why performance on easy tasks improves but performance on difficult tasks actually gets worse. You can probably think of examples from your own experience – when performing slightly below your standard, you may feel energized and try harder. However, when you fall short of your desired standard, perhaps you give up and move onto something else.

Interestingly, drawing attention to the self and making a person self-conscious can also interfere with behaviours that people perform automatically. For example, Mullen and Baumeister (1987) found that basketball players who are asked to monitor their body movements were more likely to miss than those who were not asked to do so. Thus, even in the case of well-practised (although still difficult) behaviours, attention to the self is not always a good thing. It has been argued that the embarrassment caused by failing in front of others impairs performance (Bond, 1982). Because people are generally worried about how they appear in front of others, the anticipation of failure, especially on difficult tasks, can be a hindrance to performance.

Another explanation for social facilitation phenomena is the notion that people feel 'overloaded' in the presence of an audience and this distracts them from cues they need to attend to (Baron, 1986; Mansted and Semin, 1980). This does not matter much for simple tasks and can be advantageous because attention is narrowed to a small set of cues, thus minimizing distraction. On the other hand, performance on difficult tasks – where broader attention is required – is impaired.

Of course, these are quite varied explanations for social facilitation. Because findings are varied too, it is clear that there is no one 'true' explanation for why

TABLE 10.1 Classification of group tasks

Divisible or unitary?	*Divisible:* work is divided within the group and people perform different tasks, e.g. playing in a football team
	Unitary: work cannot be divided into different tasks and everyone must do the same, e.g. tug-of-war
Maximizing or optimizing?	*Maximizing:* do as much as possible (quantity), e.g. generating many answers to a problem
	Optimizing: do the best job possible (quality), e.g. generating the best answers to a problem
How are individual's inputs related to the outcome?	*Additive:* the outcome is the sum of all group members' efforts, e.g. tug-of-war
	Compensatory: the outcome is the average of all group members' efforts, e.g. group assignment at university
	Conjunctive: the outcome is determined by the level of performance of the weakest member because every member of the group must perform, e.g. four-person relay race
	Disjunctive: the outcome depends on how well the most talented member performs, e.g., a brainstorming group may opt for the best suggestion
	Discretionary: the group decides on the actions it will take, e.g. choosing to vote on the best answer to a problem

Source: Steiner, 1972, 1976

this phenomenon occurs – many factors may be at play. It is likely that all these factors contribute to the impact that the presence of others has on our behaviour. Bond and Titus (1983) conducted a meta-analysis of 241 studies on social facilitation, enabling them to examine the key factors in driving social facilitation effects. They found that the mere presence of individuals in these experiments accounted for only small variations in behaviour, so many other factors are probably responsible for social facilitation phenomena (see also Uziel, 2007). In particular, instead of drawing the simple distinction between 'easy' and 'difficult' tasks determining social facilitation phenomena, it has been proposed that researchers should pay closer attention to the *nature* of the task itself. Steiner (1972, 1976) attempted to devise a 'list' or taxonomy of types of group tasks, highlighting how people performing different types of tasks may respond differently to the presence of co-actors and audiences (Table 10.1).

Classifying tasks on these dimensions allows us to take a closer look at how the presence of others might influence behaviour. Steiner believed that group performance is naturally worse than the sum of a group's individual potential. This *process loss*, or deterioration of group performance, is said to occur because of various factors, such as the time taken to coordinate the group, distractors and the presence of dominant group members. However, using the taxonomy given in Table 10.1, one can see that groups will arguably perform better on some tasks than on others. In particular, social facilitation occurs when people work towards goals individually and when their effort can be individually evaluated.

But what happens in other kinds of tasks where people 'pool' their efforts towards a common goal and where individual effort cannot be evaluated? For example, in a tug-of-war (a unitary, maximizing and additive task), will everyone pull as hard as they can? On a group assignment where four students are working on a psychology report and each member of the group will receive the same grade, will everyone work as hard as they can? Steiner thought not. He suggested that instead of many hands making light work, or strength in unity, certain tasks would promote laziness and decreased effort as people lose motivation to perform.

Time to reflect Think of some examples of social facilitation. Which explanation of the phenomenon works best for each example and why? Before you read on, can you think of any examples where people might 'slack off' in groups? Why do you think they might do this? You can use your own experiences to answer this question.

Social loafing

Ringelmann (1913) investigated how efficient people are in performing tasks in different group sizes (Kravitz and Martin, 1986). In one task, he asked people to pull horizontally on a rope (in a similar way to a tug-of-war) while the rope was attached to a device measuring the force of the pull of the participants. Participants performed the task either alone or in groups. Ringelmann found that the amount of pull exerted by participants decreased as the size of the group increased. In larger groups, individuals exerted the least amount of force to pull the rope, such that the collective effort of the group was around half the sum of the potential individual efforts (Figure 10.4). This is known as the **Ringelmann effect**.

Ringelmann effect The observation that as group size increases, individual effort on the task decreases.

Why does it occur? Perhaps people are not coordinating their efforts optimally when they are in a group. For example, process loss could occur because people pull on the rope differently and their efforts are therefore occasionally antagonistic. Or, perhaps there is not enough room for people to pull to their full strength. Maybe their timing is slightly off. On the other hand, it might be the case that people 'slack off' when they know they are not accountable for their own individual performance. In other words, they somehow lose the motivation to do their best. To test these explanations, Ingham, Levinger, Graves and Peckham (1974) conducted an experiment. In one condition, they blindfolded participants and put them in the front position of the tug-of-war. The crucial aspect of this condition is that participants believed that other people were doing the task with them, but they were in fact the only person doing the pulling. Ingham et al. made participants think that others were pulling on the rope by introducing confederates standing close by who made exertion noises as if they were physically pulling on the rope. In the second condition, the groups were real. Participants were pulling and the other members of the group were doing the same. Participants performed the task either alone or in groups.

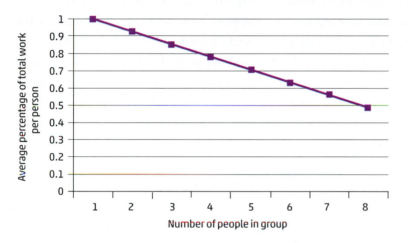

FIGURE 10.4 The Ringelmann effect The work exerted by individuals pulling on a rope as a function of the number of individuals in the group. Individual performance decreased as group size increased.

Source: Data from Kravitz and Martin, 1986

Results revealed that in the artificial groups, individuals showed a significant decrease in performance as group size increased. Remember, there were no coordination difficulties because no other people were pulling on the rope. Thus, decreases in effort could not be due to problems associated with pulling, shoving and bad timing. Instead, these decreases appear to be down to a loss of motivation. The real groups showed a further deficit in individual performance due to coordination loss, but this experiment was the first to show the real effect produced by a loss of motivation within the group. So, do many hands make light work? It appears not.

Social loafing The tendency for people's performance to decrease in a group when they are not individually responsible for their actions.

This phenomenon has been named **social loafing** and is defined as the tendency for people to put in less effort when they pool their efforts towards a group goal

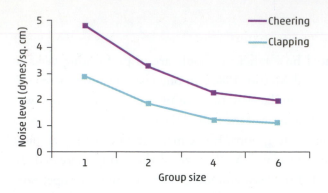

FIGURE 10.5 The social loafing effect As group size increased, the level of noise produced by people cheering and clapping was significantly reduced. This is a classic demonstration of the social loafing effect – the tendency for people to exert less effort when they pool their efforts towards the group than when they act alone.

Source: Data from Latané et al., 1979

than when they are individually accountable for their efforts. This is a form of group behaviour, where the group produces *less* than the sum of its individual parts. Latané, Williams and Harkins (1979) examined social loafing in different ways, for example demonstrating that the noise produced by six people shouting or clapping (with an instruction to do so as loud as they could) was less than three times the noise produced by one individual alone. In a condition where participants were asked to complete the tasks in groups of six, the amount of noise produced per person was reduced by a staggering 60 per cent. However, this could also be due in part to coordination loss. To examine the effects of motivation loss above and beyond this general group inefficiency, Latané et al. ran the experiment in a similar way to Ingham et al.'s (1974) study. Here, they blindfolded six people and sat them in a semi-circle. They wore headphones and listened to loud clapping and shouting. On a number of trials, the participants were asked to clap and shout as loud as they could, either alone or with the group. The results were similar to Ingham et al.'s. There was a significant reduction in effort for participants in the artificial groups, with an extra significant decrease (coordination loss) for real groups (see Figure 10.5).

Thus, social loafing is a general tendency for people to take a 'free ride' when they feel that others in the group are taking on some of the task too. It has been demonstrated, even in recent years, in many domains such as in technology-supported groups (e.g., Alnuaimi, Robert and Maruping, 2010), work teams (e.g., van Dick, Tissington and Hertel, 2009), undergraduate classrooms (e.g., Jassawalla, Sashittal and Malshe, 2009) and handball team performance (Høigaard, Fuglestad, Peters et al., 2010). Social loafing is also related to another phenomenon known as the **free rider effect**, where a person takes advantage of a shared resource without making their due contribution to the resource (Kerr, 1983; Kerr and Brunn, 1983). For example, someone who cheats the taxation system is a free rider because they enjoy the benefits of society without having paid any of the costs. The main difference between a loafer and a free rider, however, is that the loafer does put in *some* effort – just not as much as they should. The free rider completely exploits a situation without making any effort at all. Interestingly, the participants in Latané et al.'s (1979) experiment did not think they had been loafing – they thought they had put in the same effort in both conditions. This points to another difference between the loafer and the free rider. The loafer may lose motivation without really realizing it, but the free rider knows exactly what they are doing.

Free rider effect The tendency for people to take advantage of a shared resource without having made an appropriate contribution.

Question to consider Reread question 2 at the start of the chapter. What is Faiza's behaviour an example of? Would people react to her behaviour differently if they saw it as intentional or unintentional?

In a meta-analysis of social loafing studies, Karau and Williams (1993) found it to be a robust phenomenon, occurring in over 80 per cent of the investigations. It happens in a range of experimental tasks from laughing and clapping, generation of ideas, cheerleading, swimming, maze learning and evaluative tasks such as rating poems. It is also a phenomenon that occurs across many different cultures, although see later for some key cultural differences. But why does it happen? We know from the studies on social facilitation that the presence of others can often energize us to perform better. So what is going on here? Why does the presence of other people sometimes mean that we 'slack off' and perform below our abilities?

The main explanation for social loafing is an interesting variation on evaluation apprehension – the predominant explanation for social facilitation. Instead of increasing evaluation apprehension, the tasks associated with social loafing actually *decrease* evaluation apprehension. In social loafing experiments, individuals believe that their efforts are only being judged when they perform alone. Specifically, in group tasks, people are not accountable for their efforts and therefore concerns about being scrutinized decrease. Also, individuals find it difficult to monitor or evaluate their own efforts. Taking both factors into account, it is easy to see how responsibility is diffused across all group members and how social loafing occurs. In general, any situation where being in the presence of others *increases* evaluation apprehension, *social facilitation* will occur. On the other hand, if being in the presence of others *decreases* evaluation apprehension, *social loafing* will occur (Jackson and Harkins, 1985; Sanna, 1992; see also Harkins and Szymanski, 1987) (see Figure 10.6).

FIGURE 10.6 Social facilitation and social loafing compared Which one will happen? Typically, when the presence of others increases evaluation apprehension, social facilitation is more likely to occur, but when the presence of others does not increase (or reduces) evaluation apprehension, social loafing is more likely.

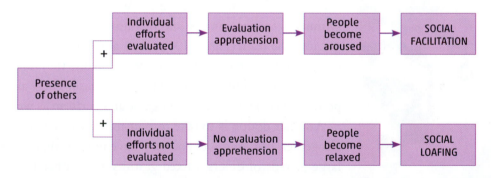

However, the picture is more complex, as the difficulty of the task must also be taken into account. When the presence of others increases evaluation concerns, performance on easy tasks will be enhanced and performance on difficult tasks will be impaired. When the presence of others decreases evaluation concerns, performance on easy tasks may be impaired because the individual is demotivated or uninspired, whereas performance on difficult tasks may be enhanced because of the social support provided by others (e.g., Karau and Williams, 1993; Lea, Spears and Rogers, 2003).

There are other explanations for social loafing that implicate different psychological processes. For example, people may generally feel that others loaf in social tasks and if they do not do so too, they will feel like a 'sucker'. This **output equity** explanation is also about motivation – when people learn that others are not pulling their weight, they too can lose motivation and put less effort into tasks. For example, if people perceive that a working relationship is unjust, this can influence the extent to which social loafing occurs (e.g., Murphy, Wayne, Liden and Erdogan, 2003). Perhaps you can think of a time when you worked with someone who did not sufficiently contribute to a task. Perhaps you felt so annoyed by this that you withheld your full participation from the task. Nobody would blame you because nobody likes being taken advantage of. Sometimes, people might loaf because they have no clear standard to work with – they simply do not know how hard they need to work. The presence of a clear standard should reduce social loafing, and findings suggest this is the case (Geen, 1991; Harkins and Szymanski, 1987; Szymanski and Harkins, 1987).

Whatever the exact mechanism (or combination of mechanisms) responsible for social loafing, one obvious strategy to combat it is to make individual group performances identifiable. This increases evaluation apprehension, makes everyone's output transparent and makes the standard clear. Indeed, it has been found that swimmers perform faster in relay races when someone closely monitors and announces their individual times (Williams, Nida, Baca and Latané, 1989). The swimmers are accountable and therefore responsible for the amount of effort they put into the team (Figure 10.7). They also know what the general standard is from the performances of their teammates. Finally, they know how much effort other members of their team are putting into the task. These all mean good things for team performance. People raise their game and perform as well as they possibly can.

Another option is to take responsibility and accountability out of the equation altogether. For example, you may have noticed that many restaurants now charge large groups of diners a fixed gratuity rate rather than allowing everyone to tip individually. Presumably, this strategy has been put in place because it is expected that diners in a large group will engage in social loafing and tip disappointingly (Boyes, Mounts and Sowell, 2004).

Evidence suggests that people will also loaf less when the tasks themselves are challenging, appealing or involving (Karau and Williams, 1993). When tasks are challenging, people may feel that their own individual efforts are indispensable. Also, if they feel that others are not putting in the required amount of effort, people may even *compensate* for their shortcomings by putting in even more effort to make up the gap (Williams and Karau, 1991). Further, if a task is appealing and there is the possibility of a reward in exchange for effort, people tend to work harder (Harkins and Szymanski, 1987; Shepperd and Taylor, 1999). It therefore makes a lot of sense that social loafing is not a big problem in high-level competitive team sports. The task is too engaging and the outcome too

Output equity People like everyone to pull their weight on tasks but generally perceive that others loaf.

FIGURE 10.7 How fast will they swim? Will these swimmers swim faster when they are accountable for their times? Research on the influence of accountability on social loafing effects suggests they will.

important to loaf. Thinking back to the example of the swimmers, there are many reasons for high-level athletes to strive for excellence rather than pure accountability for their performance.

Values, personality, gender and culture

Research has also demonstrated that people loaf less when they value the group with whom they are interacting. In particular, loafing is reduced when group members are friendly with or identify with one another (Karau and Williams, 1997; Worchel, Rothgerber, Day et al., 1998). Thus, perhaps one way to ensure that a university group assignment runs as smoothly as possible would be to work with friends, or at least with people who share things in common. This example parallels findings demonstrating that people work harder when there is a general spirit of commitment to the 'team' (Hackman, 1986). Other interesting findings have emerged in relation to values and personality differences. For example, Smrt and Karau (2011) have recently shown that social loafing is moderated by participants' level of Protestant work ethic (PWE). The researchers pretested participants' PWE and then asked them to work either coactively (in the presence of others, but independently) or collectively on a task of generating ideas. It was found that the higher participants were in PWE, the less likely they were to loaf when working collectively. This suggests that people who have a strong personal work ethic are less likely to engage in social loafing. Other findings suggest that people who score high on conscientiousness and feelings of responsibility are less likely to loaf (Hoon and Tan, 2008). Social loafing is also influenced by narcissism. In particular, Woodman, Roberts, Hardy et al. (2011) showed that high narcissists were less likely to loaf, especially when their behaviour was being explicitly monitored. Presumably, the narcissists put in more effort when they knew their performance was going to be identified and they would be personally credited for their contribution.

There are also cultural differences in social loafing phenomena. Some studies have demonstrated the cultural generality of social loafing after conducting studies in countries such as Japan, Thailand and India (e.g., Gabreyna, Wang and Latané, 1985). However, many later studies have shown that Western cultures (e.g., the UK, the USA, Australia) tend to show more social loafing in laboratory tasks than Eastern cultures (e.g., China, Japan) (Karau and Williams, 1993; Kugihara, 1999). In an organizational setting too, Earley (1989) asked American and Chinese management trainees to perform a task under conditions of low or high accountability and low or high responsibility. It was found that the Chinese sample exhibited less social loafing than the American sample. Perhaps these results are not surprising if we consider the importance of social bonds and social cohesion in collectivist versus individualist cultures. Letting one's friends and family down is simply not part of the mindset of collectivist cultures, so it stands to reason that less 'slacking off' might be witnessed in such cultures.

With respect to gender, women generally tend to exhibit social loafing less than men (Karau and Williams, 1993; Kugihara, 1999). Gabrenya et al. (1985) found consistent gender differences – with women exhibiting lower social loafing than men – in both Chinese and American samples. They also found that while males tended to increase their tendency to loaf as they got older, females' social loafing remained constant. Thus, while loafing appears to exist in both genders, it is lower for women, and for men, the tendency may be dependent on the situation. It is argued that this difference occurs because women are generally more collectivist than men (e.g., Earley, 1989, 1993) and therefore social loafing is against their values, at least compared to men (Gabrenya et al., 1985).

To sum up our discussion of social loafing, groups sometimes perform poorly compared to individuals, but this is not always the case. If the conditions are right, group task performance can be ideal. In an open, accountable group engaging in a challenging, appealing and involving task, groups can be arousing and exciting and will often outperform individuals. In such a case, the group really does function effectively. But let us now consider another common situation for groups. From the social loafing research, we know about the importance of accountability within groups for completing tasks effectively. We also know from the social facilitation research that groups can arouse people. What happens when both these features of group interaction are put together? For example, how do people behave in crowds when they are often in an intense situation with a large number of people? How might people behave with the reduced level of accountability experienced when they communicate on the internet? We now turn our discussion to the phenomenon of deindividuation.

Try it yourself If you talk to people about social loafing, most will say they have been at the receiving end of it but few will admit to being responsible for it themselves. This is an example of a classic self–other bias discussed in Chapter 3. Of course, everyone has, at some time, 'slacked off' in a group task. The existence of social loafing can be demonstrated in a simple task you can try on your friends. Ask a group of friends to divide into two groups of four/ five people and get each group to sit in a tight circle so that they cannot see or hear what the other group is doing or being told. Give each person in each group a copy of something mundane to copy down, such as entries from a phone book. Each person also receives a number of slips of paper and a pen. Tell each group they have 10 minutes to write down as many entries as possible. At this point, the group task differs. One of the groups is to hand their completed slips into the middle and the group's number will be counted – no individual tallies will be known to the group (group condition). The other group's members are to keep their own personal slips, which will be tallied at the end, so that each person is accountable to the group for the number of responses they produce (individual condition). It is important that each group is not aware of the instructions given to the other group. At the end of the task, you would expect participants in the individual condition to have produced more slips than those in the group condition, as evidence of social loafing occurring when group members are not accountable for their input. Did this happen? How did your friends feel if they found out that they were, indeed, social loafers? (Note: this task was adapted from the Everton social loafing task, http://siopwiki.wetpaint.com.)

Deindividuation

Crowd behaviour

The first ideas generated about groups, accountability and selfhood came through a consideration of crowd behaviour. It was thought that crowds were a unique kind

FIGURE 10.8 Large group behaviour What are some of the common features of large group behaviour? The study of deindividuation examines how people behave in arousing situations where personal responsibility is diffused.

Contagion Le Bon argued that this process leads to ideas being 'spread' unpredictably and rapidly through crowds.

of group that arouse people (the same as other groups) but at the same time diffuse people's sense of responsibility. Putting these aspects together, what might be the consequences? The outlook could appear to be quite grim. Many examples of crowd behaviour come immediately to mind that help us think about this issue. Looting, rioting, lynching and bystander apathy are all examples of crowd behaviour. Why would people do such things? Why do people think it is appropriate to act in these negative ways when they are part of a large group or crowd? No doubt some of the features of human aggression (as we will discuss in Chapter 13) come to play in such situations. But is there something fundamental about groups that can bring about this kind of behaviour? Also, it is important to note that we should not focus only on the bad things that crowds do, even though this is largely the focus of research on deindividuation. Indeed, gentle protests and demonstrations, festivals and celebrations are also examples of large group behaviour. Why do people do these sorts of things? What is the common theme shared by all these behaviours?

One of the earliest theories of crowd behaviour, or collective behaviour, was proposed by French researchers Gabriel Tarde (1890) and, more notably, Gustave Le Bon ([1908]1986). Le Bon's ideas have been instrumental in the formation of the theories of crowd and collective behaviour that we know today (e.g., Reicher, 1987, 1996, 2001; Reicher, Spears and Postmes, 1995). Le Bon observed and read stories of revolutionary crowds in the 1848 revolution in France and during the Paris Commune of 1871. He was deeply disturbed by the seemingly primitive behaviour of these crowds, akin to the instinctive behaviour of animals and the antisocial behaviour of barbarians. Le Bon argued that people in crowds behave in a primitive, base manner because they are anonymous and in being anonymous, they lose personal responsibility for their actions. Further, through a process known as **contagion**, ideas spread unpredictably (and quickly) through the crowd. Finally, Le Bon argued that while everyone has antisocial motives at some stage, much of the time they remain in the unconscious, but, unleashed by a process of suggestion (similar to hypnosis), these antisocial tendencies are expressed in the crowd. Freud took this last idea further by proposing that the crowd unlocks the unconscious and that a powerful leader can become a 'hypnotist', controlling people's unconscious impulses and turning them into a horde of savages. Similar ideas were put forward by McDougall (1920), who argued that the crowd was suggestible and easily swayed by emotional impulses such as fear and anger.

More recently, social psychologists have drawn upon Le Bon and McDougall's ideas to devise a theory to explain the unrestrained and deregulated behaviour that occurs within groups. Relying less on emotional explanations, much of social psychological thinking about collective behaviour focuses on the loss of accountability presented by the group situation. According to this perspective, being 'lost' in a group means a loosening of constraints on behaviour. Festinger, Pepitone and Newcomb (1952) argued that when people behave one way in groups and another way as individuals, they do so because they are in a state of deindividuation. This state is defined as the tendency for people in groups to abandon normal constraints on their behaviour, lose a sense of their individuality and responsibility, and

Individuation The process of differentiating between people. This is essentially the opposite of deindividuation.

consequently behave in ways they normally would not. The term 'deindividuation' implies that this kind of behaviour is the opposite of **individuation** or the process of differentiation between people. People lose their sense of self or their identity and succumb to other influences.

Zimbardo (1970) further developed the concept of deindividuation. He focused on the effects of the so-called 'cloak of anonymity' provided by the group. He argued that being shielded by this cloak takes away individuals' responsibility for their actions. They lose a sense of their identity and also lose their concern for social evaluation. This state of deindividuation leads them to behave in impulsive and deregulated ways; that is, they behave differently within the group than how they would act alone.

Research suggests that large groups elicit more deindividuated behaviour than smaller groups. Mullen and colleagues' research on lynch mob atrocities is a good example of this. Mullen (1986) examined newspaper accounts of 60 lynchings of African American people occurring between 1899 and 1946. He found that as the lynch mob got larger, the more willing its members became to commit the worst kinds of atrocities against their victims. Leader, Mullen and Abrams (2007) also demonstrated that as the size of the group increases, so does its level of violence. In a different vein, Mann (1981) found that when a crowd gathers to watch a person threatening to jump off a building, the crowd are more likely to jeer and taunt the individual and yell 'jump!' when the crowd is larger – a disturbing finding indeed. Interestingly, this phenomenon is intensified at night-time when people are made more anonymous by the darkness. Apart from being immersed in a group, what specific factors influence this state of deindividuation? According to Prentice-Dunn and Rogers (1982, 1983), there are two types of environmental cues that contribute to this state. These are attentional cues and accountability cues.

Exploring further *Les Miserables* is a 1998 film directed by Bille August and based on the novel by Victor Hugo. It tells the story of Jen Valjean who, after being convicted for stealing bread, spends his life on the run from the police officer Javert. This pursuit consumes the lives of both men and Valjean becomes involved in the student revolutionary crowds in early 19th-century France. Take a look at how the crowds were depicted in this film for an interesting take on crowd behaviour. Similarly, Emile Zola's masterpiece *Germinal*, written in 1885, tells the story of a coalminer's strike in France in the 1860s. Angered by poverty and frustration, the miners and their families are driven into a violent riot. The crowds are eventually confronted by the police and the workers return to the mine. *Germinal* provides another example of people's behaviour in crowds.

Attentional cues

Attentional cues Features of the environment that draw attention away from the self.

The first kind of cue identified by Prentice-Dunn and Rogers (1982, 1983) are **attentional cues** – features of the environment that draw attention away from the self. Drawing on Duval and Wicklund's (1972) theory of objective self-awareness (awareness of the self as an object of attention), Diener (1980) argued that features of the environment that shift attention away from the self are deindividuating. When people's self-awareness is reduced, they find themselves in a 'deindividuated state', where they respond less to established standards of conduct and instead react to the immediate situation (Diener, 1980). Normal standards slip and people act on impulse. So, in a crowd, for example, people may become absorbed in the environment and attend less to themselves and their behaviour within it. As we have noted, this impulsive behaviour need not always be negative, but, according to this perspective, deindividuation does make the path clear for antisocial behaviour.

A good example of an attentional cue is intense environmental stimulation. Studies have shown experimentally that groups of people who were placed in highly stimulating environments (with features such as loud music and colourful video games) were more extreme, disinhibited and aggressive in their actions (Diener, 1979; Prentice-Dunn and Rogers, 1980; Spivey and Prentice-Dunn, 1990). Such features are often present in crowds, so it is easy to link this perspective to crowd behaviour.

Time to reflect Can you remember a time when you felt 'swept away' by a situation? What were the characteristics of that situation and can you map them onto some of the situations characteristic of deindividuated contexts?

An alternative way to look at deindividuation and self-awareness is to distinguish between two kinds of self-awareness: public (how one wants others to view the self) and private (attitudes, thoughts, emotions and other private features of the self) (see Carver and Scheier, 1981; Scheier and Carver, 1981). Using this perspective, a loss of both aspects of self-awareness will lead to a state of deindividuation. So, for example, becoming less concerned with one's appearance to others in a crowd and becoming less aware of one's own attitudes may influence behaviour. However, antisocial behaviour is more likely to emerge when public self-awareness is lowered and people become less aware of social norms of conduct. A loss of private self-awareness need not lead to antisocial behaviour unless the salient norm is to behave antisocially.

Accountability cues

Accountability cues Factors that determine what behaviours people can 'get away with' in a social context.

Accountability cues may determine what people think they are able to get away with. When accountability is low, people may choose to engage in behaviours that are gratifying but would normally be inhibited. The most studied effect on deindividuation is *anonymity*. Imagine that you are allowed to be invisible for a day. What would you do? When a group of US college students were asked to answer this question anonymously, most responses involved criminal activities and the most common response was to 'rob a bank' (Dodd, 1985).

Try it yourself Sometimes it is difficult to believe findings such as those of Dodd (1985). Would people really want to rob a bank if they were invisible for a day? Perhaps people would respond differently if they were asked to indicate their identity instead of responding anonymously. You can try this for yourself. The next time you are in a large group of friends or acquaintances, ask them to write down, on a piece of paper, what they would do if they were invisible for 24 hours. On half of the pieces of paper, tell your friends that their responses will be completely anonymous. On the other half, ask your friends to write down their name alongside their answer. Take the pieces of paper and read out your friends' answers. This is like a game – your friends will laugh when they hear what others have to say. So, what did they say? Were the responses largely related to antisocial activities? Did the anonymous responses differ from the identifiable responses? How does this map onto the findings of deindividuation research?

Exploring further To give a real-life example, you may like to read about the Heysel Stadium disaster in 1985. Think about the features of the situation, the people and the environmental cues that brought about this disaster. Events such as these have significantly impacted on how we now deal with football hooliganism.

Other research highlights the effects of anonymity on deindividuation. For example, Festinger et al. (1952) found that participants made more negative comments about their parents when they were placed in a dim room and were asked to wear grey lab coats than those in a control condition. Further, when placed in similar clothing (and so were unidentifiable), participants in a study by Singer, Brush and Lublin (1965) used more indecent language to discuss erotic literature than did identifiable individuals. Zimbardo (1970) investigated this effect further. He ran a series of experiments where participants were asked to wear cloaks and hoods (similar to the Ku Klux Klan) in a deindividuated condition, or normal clothing in a control condition. In one study, female participants were asked to administer shocks to a female confederate in a paired associate learning task. The deindividuated participants delivered shocks that were twice the duration of participants in the control condition. Note again, just as in the Milgram study, that the shocks were not real, but the importance of the findings is that the participants *thought* they were real. Zimbardo also ran the now infamous Stanford Prison Experiment featured in Chapter 9 (Zimbardo et al., 1982). Importantly for our discussion of deindividuation, the prison guards were protected, to some extent, by their uniforms. This anonymity was arguably the major contributor to their behaviour – the guards were physically brutal to their prisoners who were also deindividuated.

In another novel study, Diener, Fraser, Beaman and Kelem (1976) demonstrated the effects of being in a group *and* being anonymous at the same time. At Halloween, they observed children trick-or-treating in Seattle, USA. The children (either alone or in groups) approached homes where they were asked to take *one* of the sweets. The experimenter then left the room and a hidden camera observed how many sweets the children took. Results revealed that children in groups were twice as likely to break the rules by taking more than one sweet than children who were alone. This effect was further enhanced when the children's identity was unknown versus when the experimenter asked the children their names and where they lived (see Figure 10.9).

However, the loss of personal identity does not always lead to antisocial behaviour, suggesting that anonymity may interact with other features of the environment – sometimes this will lead to bad behaviour and sometimes it will not. For example, Zimbardo (1970) used his deindividuation paradigm with participants who were Belgian soldiers. Here, he found that the soldiers gave

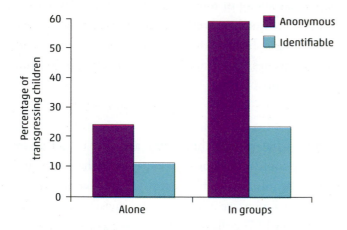

FIGURE 10.9 Two principles of deindividuation: groups and accountability Children transgressed more when they were in groups than when they were alone but even more when they were anonymous. This study demonstrates two principles of deindividuation – it is fostered in the presence of others (group) and when people lack accountability.
Source: Data from Diener et al., 1976

shocks of shorter duration when dressed in cloaks and hoods than when dressed in uniform. Zimbardo argued that the group was already deindividuated because they were wearing uniforms, and the addition of the cloak and hood had the counterintuitive effect of reducing deindividuation. Other studies, however, suggest an alternative explanation. In particular, a study by Johnson and Downing (1979) demonstrated how being anonymous can sometimes make people act more prosocially. In their experiment, half the female participants were dressed in clothing similar to that worn by members of the Ku Klux Klan, while the other half were dressed in nurses uniforms. Within each group, half were personally identifiable and half were anonymous. They were then asked to increase or decrease the intensity of electric shocks given to another female participant who had previously behaved obnoxiously. Results revealed that participants in the Ku Klux Klan clothing increased the shock level, regardless of whether they were anonymous or identifiable. On the other hand, participants dressed as nurses decreased shock intensity four times more often when they were anonymous (Figure 10.10).

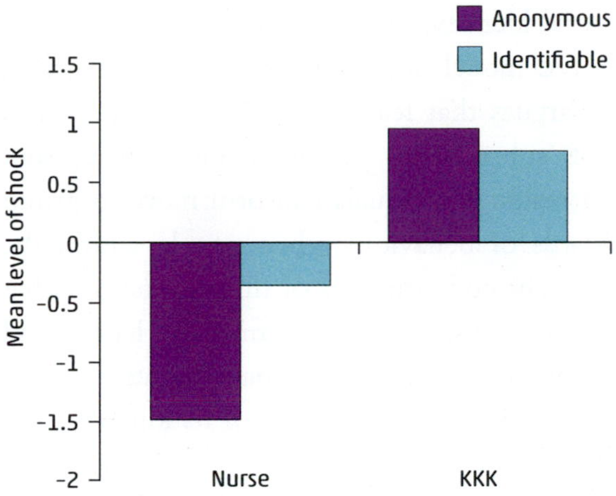

These findings are interesting because they demonstrate that sometimes being unaccountable or less self-aware can have positive consequences. Apart from bringing out people's less desirable tendencies, unaccountability can make people more sensitive to the needs of others. It has been argued that exactly how a person reacts to their lack of accountability depends on the norms of the group that directly surround the individual. Taking Johnson and Downing's (1979) example, one might expect generally high levels of aggressive behaviour from people wearing Ku Klux Klan outfits because aggression arguably fits the norm for Ku Klux Klan members. On the other hand, this norm is inconsistent with expectations of nurses, who are expected to be kind and caring. Thus, it makes sense that people who are immersed in the role of nurse would perform prosocially and decrease the level of electric shock. This account also explains why the Belgian soldiers in Zimbardo's study were more aggressive in uniform, where it is arguably normative for them to be aggressive.

FIGURE 10.10 **Effects of anonymity and costume on antisocial behaviour** Participants dressed in Ku Klux Klan-style outfits shocked their target regardless of their identifiability, but anonymous participants dressed as nurses decreased their shocks (possible range of −3 to +3). Why do you think this happened? Try to answer before reading on.
Source: Data from Johnson and Downing, 1979

Deindividuation: necessarily a process of loss?

Now that you have read about the various different accounts of deindividuation, read the Critical focus box below on **emergent norm theory** – a prominent theory of crowd behaviour (Turner and Killian, 1987). This theory has been influential in social psychologists' efforts to understand crowd behaviour, and deindividuated behaviour more generally, and argues that rather than being driven by randomness, crowd behaviour is driven by norms. The view of the 'random' crowd is less commonly held among social psychologists and sociologists nowadays as they more fully consider the motivations for crowd formation and crowd behaviour.

Emergent norm theory
Theory of crowd behaviour which argues that rather than being a product of randomness and process loss, behaviour in crowds is a result of social norms.

Social identity model of deindividuation effects (SIDE)
Theory of deindividuation phenomena arguing that such phenomena are largely a result of increased group focus rather than a loss of individual focus.

Related to this point, another common feature of the deindividuation accounts discussed so far is that they each explain deindividuation as a result of losing an important aspect of the self. For example, people lose a sense of their individuality when they are in a crowd. They lose self-awareness. They lose a sense of their own identity, which leads to a loss of rational behaviour. However, Johnson and Downing's (1979) findings above suggest something different. Specifically, the norms associated with a particular context might matter. The **social identity model of deindividuation effects (SIDE)** takes these findings further and argues for a different perspective on deindividuation (Klein, Spears and Reicher, 2007; Reicher, Spears and Postmes, 1995). SIDE argues that all the focus on 'loss' restricts the kinds of behaviours that social psychologists can explain. Instead, the focus should be on *change* from personal identity to social identity, or even *increased norm awareness*, or *group consciousness*. The SIDE model draws on principles from social identity theory (see Chapter 8) and argues that features of the context such as anonymity have the consequence of 'submerging' people within a group and enhancing their social identity. As a result, individuals conform more to group norms rather than individual standards of behaviour when people within the group are anonymous to one another. The consequences of this depend on what the norms are. If, for example, a group's sense of 'us' is defined by hatred and prejudice towards another group, then deindividuation will have negative consequences. On the other hand, if a group defines itself in terms of its kindness and charity, then the outcome will be positive.

Therefore, according to emergent norm theory and the SIDE model, deindividuation is not all bad – it depends entirely on the context and standards of the group. Much research supports this position. In particular, a meta-analysis of 60 studies by Postmes and Spears (1998) supports the argument that being anonymous makes people more focused on the group than the self, and people become more responsive to the norms of the group. Whether the norms are positive or negative will determine the outcome. We discussed research investigating the principles of the SIDE model in relation to communication in Chapter 5.

Question to consider Reread question 3 at the start of the chapter. Perhaps you could jot down a few points based on the previous section that help explain Ben's behaviour at the concert.

Time to reflect You may recall some of the media commentary on the London riots of August 2011. The looters and rioters were said to be performing 'mindless' acts of violence and criminality. Is this fair? What would different theorists say about the rioters' behaviours? You may wish to read the perspectives of social psychologists Clifford Stott and Stephen Reicher, who wrote a commentary in *The Psychologist* in October 2011, and also the perspective of British police officer Karyn McCluskey in the same issue.

CRITICAL FOCUS

Emergent norm theory: a theory of crowd behaviour

Throughout history, crowds have been seen as dangerous, unpredictable, chaotic, threatening and inhuman. In the 19th century, industrialization and urbanization gave the masses more chances to congregate. Scholars such as Le Bon continued to emphasize the irrational and chaotic aspects of crowd behaviour. However, in the 20th century, scholars realized that there was a method to crowds' apparent madness. The behaviour of even violent crowds is seldom entirely random. Turner and Killian's emergent norm theory was one of the most important theories to elaborate on this idea. Turner and Killian (1987) assumed that instead of being determined by randomness, social behaviour is driven by norms. Specifically, they suggested that in extraordinary circumstances, such as in certain types of crowds, the mundane norms that govern the course of our everyday lives no longer apply. New norms are created by the crowd. Initial uncertainty is reduced as people get together and develop a shared understanding of the situation. Second, individuals make positive suggestions for action and these suggestions are likely to be accepted if they converge with the predispositions of a large part of the crowd. For example, if many people in the crowd are angry, aggressive individuals are more likely to have an influence. As a result of this process, the crowd arrives at a consensual understanding of what is right and wrong in the situation arrived at. The crowd now appears to behave with some logic and purpose, and to be capable of enforcing its new norm. Thus, via processes of *normative influence*, participants begin to experience pressure to conform to the implicit norm they perceive to be taking shape. By conforming to this new norm, crowd members influence those around them, who infer from their conformity that the norm is widely accepted.

However, this does not mean that the crowd is unanimous. Contrary to popular thinking about crowds, there is no 'group mind' in emergent norm theory. However, as the situation unfolds, individuals feel different, act differently and participate for different reasons. This is crucial to emergent norm theory and distinguishes it from earlier accounts of crowd behaviour. Some people are more committed to action than others, some are concerned but still uncertain about the correct course of action, others are curious spectators, and still others are simply present to capitalize on the situation, perhaps for the thrill of violence or destruction. However passive and disengaged are curious spectators, and mercenary are exploiters, their presence and failure to intervene are likely to be seen as a sign of approval by the active participants. In this way they contribute to the growing illusion of unanimity among the crowd.

A problem many critics have had with this theory is that too often it tends to *describe* rather than genuinely *explain* crowd behaviour. For example, the theory identifies certain people who take on roles within the crowd (e.g., observers and exploiters) but it does not specify what causes different people to adopt these roles. Turner and Killian (1987) argue that 'distinctive' individuals and behaviours are likely to shape the emergent norm, but do not propose specific or principled criteria for distinctiveness. More generally, critics have alleged that the theory is not specific about how crowds form and are organized. Where emergent norm theory does make clear predictions, empirical support is mixed. For example, according to the theory, rumour is central to the formation of crowds. However, field studies of crowd events, such as the Detroit riots of 1967, showed that more participants heard about it through the mass media than by rumour. Empirical studies of crowds have produced other problems for emergent norm theory. For example, the theory predicts that conformity to crowd behaviour should be strongest when crowd members are identifiable: participants perceive that the crowd will reward compliance and punish deviance. But most relevant research findings suggest that people are more susceptible to crowd influence when they are anonymous rather than identifiable, and lacking in rather than high in self-awareness. These findings are consistent with deindividuation accounts of crowd behaviour.

Other critiques have centred on the extent to which the long-standing norms of the group and the societies in which they are embedded are left behind when crowds form, requiring entirely new norms to emerge. Critics from various perspectives have asked whether there really is a radical discontinuity between the norms that govern our everyday lives and the norms that govern crowd situations. Research by Stephen Reicher and his colleagues shows that the ongoing social identities and associated normative codes of crowd members, whether as environmental protestors, anarchists or police, have been shown to have a profound effect on their behaviour in crowd situations. According to the SIDE model, the creative potential of crowds lies in the ability of its participants to discover group norms that may not have been apparent to them before, and to transform and adapt group norms in light of the new situation. Finally, critics have pointed out that it is not clear in what sense the so-called 'collective behaviour' of crowds is different from the aggregated behaviour of the individuals who comprise the crowd. For example, while psychological states such as 'uncertainty' and 'urgency' can be ascribed to individual crowd members, it is not clear they can be ascribed to the collective, at least not without resurrecting the 'group mind' hypothesis.

Despite the many criticisms that have been levelled at emergent norm theory, even its critics acknowledge the many valuable insights it contributes to the study of crowds. In particular, the point that crowds have an energizing and creative potential, but nonetheless behave in rational, systematic and normative ways has been highly influential. We may or may not have cause to fear the crowd, but it is clear that we should no longer regard crowds as lacking in all human reason or constraint.

Questions

1 Think of the different motivations that people might have to be part of a crowd. What behaviours might we witness from so-called 'exploiters', who are simply present to capitalize on the situation?

2 There is a body of work by Clifford Stott on the behaviour of football hooligans in crowds. In your own time, read some of this work, which develops an understanding of 'unruly' football-related crowd behaviour from a social identity perspective.

3 Reicher (1996) developed the elaborated social identity model of crowd behaviour, which focuses on the emergence and development of crowd conflict (see also Drury, Reicher and Stott, 2012). According to this perspective, crowd conflict is argued to be meaningful, but can bring about social and psychological change because this meaning may be contested. How can this be linked to the ideas of emergent norm theory?

SOCIAL PSYCHOLOGY IN THE REAL WORLD

Road rage: losing it behind the wheel

© THESUPE87/FOTOLIA.COM

In 1950, Disney released an animated short, *Motor Mania*. In it, Goofy 'plays' a decent, mild-mannered chap called Mr Walker, who considers himself to be a good driver. But when Mr Walker gets behind the wheel of his car, he morphs into 'Mr Wheeler', an abominable creature of limitless competitiveness, impatience and rage. (The film is easy to find on the internet, and apart from the cars and some male-centric language, it hasn't aged a day.) The film captures a truth about motoring that is all too recognizable even now, over 60 years later: people seem to undergo some kind of personality transformation when they drive. They appear to be more prone to antisocial behaviour, risk taking and anger, doing, saying and gesturing things that they would never normally contemplate. We've all seen it, and many of us have done it. In its most extreme form, it is known as 'road rage' (e.g., Ayar, 2006; Byrne, 2000).

The remarkable transformation that driving seems to cause in some people is interesting from a social psychological perspective, since it seems to illustrate *the power of the situation* to override personality and shape our behaviour. But what is it about the driving situation, specifically, that seems to give it such power? One key answer that has often been advanced is that road rage and other forms of antisocial driving stem from deindividuation (Ayar, 2006; Byrne, 2000; Dula, 2011; Ellison-Potter, Bell and Deffenbacher, 2001; Novaco, 1998). In a car, you are surrounded by others, meaning that you are, in a sense, in the presence of a group, but nonetheless you are largely anonymous and physically cut off from them in the metal and glass shell of your car. As we have seen, this meets the two key conditions for deindividuation effects, in which people feel less inhibited about aggression.

However plausible it seems, direct evidence for the deindividuating explanation is scarce. About the best experimental demonstration comes from Ellison-Potter et al. (2001). They manipulated anonymity and showed that participants drove more aggressively in the 'anonymous' than in the 'identifiable' condition of their experiment. However, their drivers were in a simulator, not actually on a road (for obvious ethical and practical reasons). Also, anonymity was manipulated merely by asking participants to imagine that other drivers could, or could not, identify them. So, there is much doubt about whether the results really show that anonymity makes people drive more aggressively, or merely whether they think it does, and acted out their own expectations in the experiment.

A fascinating study by Parkinson (2001) uncovered some important factors apart from deindividuation. Parkinson asked British participants questions about the last time they had been angry while driving and while not driving, and compared the answers. As might be expected, people reported more intense experiences of anger, associated with stronger levels of other-blame, when they were driving. This seems to be due to some social psychological aspects of driving. Participants indicated that while driving (vs. not driving), complete strangers were much more likely to be the targets of their anger. Given that driving interactions are relatively simple and we haven't met most of our fellow drivers before, there's little room for complicated emotions, or to find some kind of historical fault with one's own behaviour. Another key factor was uncovered in Parkinson's study: in driving situations, participants reported being less able to communicate their anger to others and to see their anger being acknowledged. You can gesture, wave and swear as much as you like, but the other driver may not notice or may speed into the distance before you've seen their reaction. This failure of communication tends to frustrate and anger people even more.

Further, although situational factors are important, we should not overestimate the extent to which our behaviour behind the wheel is completely divorced from our day-to-day behaviour. People who are aggressive or stressed when not driving are more likely to be prone to aggression behind the wheel (Gulian, Matthews, Glendon et al. 1989; Lowenstein, 1997). People who try to present an intimidating image of themselves to the world in their everyday lives are also more likely to experience road rage (Bassett, Cate and Dabbs, 2002). Deindividuation may be a factor in road rage, but it does not tell the whole story.

Questions

1   Thinking about the methods of manipulating deindividuation you have been reading about, what else do you think they may be manipulating? Specifically, how do they interfere with communication between people? Does this represent a confound, and what does it mean for the evidence cited in favour of the concept of deindividuation?

2   What do you think the SIDE model would have to say about the idea that road rage emerges because of the deindividuating aspects of the driving situation? According to this model, when might driver aggression increase, and when might it decrease, in response to the anonymous conditions of driving?

3   According to Halpern (1998), a good critical thinking skill is to think of two improvements that could be made to an experiment (see Chapter 15). Based on the description of the study by Ellison-Potter et al. (2001), what improvements do you think you could make? (Note: if you would like further information, look up this article in the References section of this book, and see if your institution's library holds the journal in which it was published.)

Group decision making

Now, we turn our discussion to how people in groups make decisions and solve problems. Thus far, we have discussed many ways in which group behaviour can differ from the behaviour of solitary individuals. Research on how groups arrive at decisions and deal with problems is no exception. Of particular importance here are the following questions. Does interaction with people in groups intensify our decisions? Do groups generally make 'good' or 'bad' decisions? How does real group decision making compare with folk wisdom suggesting that groups are more conservative than individuals in decision making and that they err towards caution? How do groups solve problems differently than individuals acting alone?

Group polarization

When people discuss important issues, they often do so with people who already think the same way. We generally speak more often with people who share the same opinions and attitudes and go to meetings with like-minded others and so on. Does this kind of interaction make our attitudes stronger? Findings suggest that the answer is yes and that groups may not be more conservative in their decisions at all. Stoner (1961) tested this folk wisdom by presenting participants with scenarios (e.g., a person planning to write a book) and asking them to advise the person in the scenario how much risk they should take (e.g., based on the probability of the book's success). For example, participants might be asked to rate the *lowest* probability of success that the book should have before considering it acceptable to recommend that the author should write it (the lower the probability, the riskier the advice). After responding to a series of items privately, people would get together in groups and reach agreement on each item. Rather than providing more moderate decisions in groups, findings showed that the group decisions became riskier. This was dubbed the risky shift phenomenon and was replicated in a variety of different settings (see also Wallach, Kogan and Bem, 1962).

However, this shift is not universal and is not necessarily best characterized as 'risky'. Subsequent research has demonstrated that groups sometimes make less risky decisions than the individuals on average. Overall, it depends on the initial leanings of the group. As Moscovici and Zavalloni (1969) stated, discussion typically strengthens the average inclination of group members. This phenomenon is called group polarization (see Figure 10.11). Moscovici and Zavalloni found that group discussion enhanced French students' (already) positive attitudes towards their president and enhanced their (already) negative attitudes towards Americans.

This finding has been replicated in a number of different settings. For example, Brauer, Judd and Jacquelin (2001) found that when students shared their mutual dislike for other people, their negative attitudes of these people were even stronger. After discussing a traffic case, Isozaki (1984) found that students gave stronger judgements of

Risky shift The finding that groups seem to make riskier decisions than individuals.

Group polarization Group interaction strengthens the initial leanings of group members so that attitudes (and decisions) become polarized.

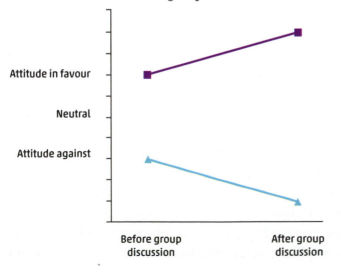

FIGURE 10.11 **The group polarization hypothesis** Group interaction enhances the initial attitudes of group members.
Source: Moscovici and Zavalloni, 1969. Copyright © 1969 by the American Psychological Association. Adapted with permission.

'guilty' than beforehand. Further, Myers and Bishop (1970) organized groups of students who were high and low in prejudice and asked them to respond to various indicators of racial attitudes before and after discussing their attitudes with their group. Again, the discussions enhanced the initial leanings of the group; that is, the high prejudiced groups became more prejudiced and the low prejudiced groups became less prejudiced. Group polarization effects have been demonstrated more recently in settings such as in computer-mediated communication (Sia, Tan and Wei, 2002; Spears, Lea and Lee, 1990), efforts to reduce conflict (e.g., Paluck, 2010), choice dilemmas (e.g., Krizan and Baron, 2007) and even on social networking sites such as Twitter (e.g., Yardi and Boyd, 2010).

© BRAND X

Group polarization is a robust phenomenon in experiments – run an experiment and there is a good chance you will observe the effect. But what does it mean for everyday life? As mentioned earlier, we are most likely to associate with people who share similar attitudes to us. The research on group polarization suggests that our attitudes are likely to become even stronger after interacting with these like-minded people. Indeed, research in real-life situations suggests this does occur. What is commonly known as 'terrorism' is a good example. As people come together to share their grievances in a given social situation, they often interact in isolation from potentially moderating people and groups. Unsurprisingly, they become more extreme over time and individuals can perform violent acts that would not have occurred in the absence of the group (McCauley and Segal, 1987). Indeed, the 9/11 attacks on the World Trade Center in 2001 were arguably the result of a long process of interaction between like-minded people and the strong polarizing effect of group interaction.

Another good example is how children develop gender roles. When they are young, children typically play in larger, mixed-gender groups but as they grow older, they self-segregate into all-female and all-male groups. Eleanor Maccoby (2002) argued that this has the polarizing effect of accentuating gender-typical behaviour and gender roles. As girls interact more with other girls, they become more 'girly' and relationship oriented. As boys interact more with other boys, they become more 'boyish' and competitive. This polarization is a robust consequence of group interaction, which can have both positive and negative consequences. But why exactly does it happen? Why do groups typically adopt decisions and attitudes that are significant exaggerations of the average opinions of their members? There are two main reasons: normative influence and informational influence (see also Chapter 9).

Time to reflect Can you think of other examples of group polarization? What might be some of the consequences of group polarization?

First, group polarization may occur because when we interact with others, we naturally compare ourselves with them. You will remember from Chapter 8 that Festinger (1954) argued in his theory of *social comparison* that people are motivated to evaluate their opinions and abilities. Thus, one way to evaluate one's own attitudes is to compare them with others' attitudes. If we find that others share our views, we may express stronger attitudes because we want the like-minded people to like us. In general, we are most persuaded by people who are like us – our 'reference groups' and people with whom we identify (Abrams, Wetherell, Cochrane et al., 1990) – so it stands to reason that if we find out that people are indeed like us, we will want to be viewed favourably by them. On the other hand, group discussion might reveal that our attitudes are not shared by the group, in which case, we may endeavour to avoid the disapproval of the group. This is an example of *normative influence* – the tendency to conform to the perceived norms of the group.

Group discussion is therefore good for dispelling what is known as **pluralistic ignorance**. This is when we often do not really know what people are thinking because they keep their attitudes to themselves (Miller and McFarland, 1987; Prentice and Miller, 1993). People may be wary of introducing their attitudes for fear they will be rejected. So, we may think our own attitudes stand out. However, group discussion makes others' attitudes clear, paving the way for people to express their true attitudes if these are indeed shared by the group. On the other hand, if people find that their attitudes are not shared by the group, they can conceal their attitudes, or even adopt the desirable attitude by jumping on the bandwagon (the *bandwagon effect*; see Codol, 1975). Because they want to be seen in a positive light by the group, they may compete to express the most extreme opinion at the desirable end of the pole, even if this is not their attitude at all.

However, people may also be genuinely swayed by the opinions of the group and find them persuasive. Thus, group polarization can also be a result of *informational influence*, in which when the correct attitude or behaviour is unclear, people look to others for guidance. It is argued here that through group discussion, people's ideas are pooled. Most of the ideas may support the dominant opinion and occasionally group members will introduce new arguments that members of the group had not previously considered. The pooling of familiar ideas and new persuasive arguments may sway group members' opinions further and cause their opinions to become more extreme (Burnstein and Vinokur, 1977; Vinokur and Burnstein, 1974). As a result, the group as a whole becomes polarized. To give an example, someone who is against abortion is likely to become even less in favour of abortion after a discussion with like-minded individuals who introduce new arguments against abortion. It is important to note here that active participation in the group is important. Verbalizing one's opinions to the group has the effect of reinforcing attitudes. So, the more group members discuss and repeat their shared ideas, the more they are validated (Brauer, Judd and Gliner, 1995). But even simply anticipating a discussion with a person holding an opposing view can motivate people to prepare their arguments and express them more strongly (Fitzpatrick and Eagly, 1981).

Self-categorization theorists (see also Chapter 8) have proposed a third account that treats polarization as a process of social conformity (Turner and Oakes, 1989). Specifically, it is argued that people in groups form a representation of the group

Pluralistic ignorance A situation where a majority of group members privately reject a norm, but assume (incorrectly) that most others accept it.

norm from the opinions expressed by others in the group compared to those opinions assumed (or known) to be held by outgroups. The process that is responsible for identification with a group (known as *self-categorization*) produces conformity to the group norm. If the group norm is polarized, then group polarization will occur. If the norm is not polarized, people will adopt the mean group position. The important feature of this argument is that for polarization to occur, the initial group leanings need to be perceived as a norm (Abrams et al., 1990; Mackie and Cooper, 1984; McGarty, Turner, Hogg et al., 1992; Turner, Wetherell and Hogg, 1989; see also Spears, Lea, Postmes and Wolbert, 2011).

Groupthink

We now know that groups do not necessarily err towards caution. They often express their opinions more extremely than their individual members would do alone. But what is the impact of groups on the quality of the decisions they make? Janis (1971, 1982) questioned why groups have sometimes been known to make disastrous decisions. In particular, he wanted to explain how group decision-making processes explain some significant international disasters, such as the US failure to anticipate the Japanese attack on Pearl Harbor in 1941 and the botched invasion of Cuba at the Bay of Pigs in 1961. According to Janis, these events shared some important features. In particular, Janis believed that in each case, the decision-making groups suppressed dissent in order to maintain group harmony. Unfortunately, a dissenting opinion would have gone a long way. Janis believed that these events were also characterized by three main features:

Groupthink The mode of thinking that groups engage in when cohesion seems more important than making the right decision and considering alternatives.

1 a cohesive group where people come from similar backgrounds
2 the group is isolated from outside opinions
3 there are no clear rules that guide decision making.

TABLE 10.2 Symptoms of groupthink

Illusion of invulnerability	Excessive optimism that encourages the group to take risks and not consider the dangers
Belief in morality of the group	The group assumes its inherent rightness and ignores challenges or concerns about the consequences of its decisions
Collective rationalization	The group explains and justifies its assumptions and decisions as a way of discounting challenges
Stereotyped view of the outgroup	The group has a negative view of the other group, or 'enemy', which makes conflict resolution difficult
Pressure for dissenters to conform	Group members who raise doubts about the group's decision are put under pressure to conform
Self-censorship	Group members withhold opinions that deviate from the group's consensus
Illusion of unanimity	The consensus opinion within the group is assumed to be unanimous
Self-appointed 'mindguards'	Group members who protect the group's decision and the group's leader from opposition

Janis (1971, p. 43) argued that these features of groups lead to bad decisions and he defined **groupthink** as: 'The mode of thinking that persons engage in when concurrence-seeking becomes so dominant in a cohesive in-group that it tends to override realistic appraisal of alternative courses of action.' According to Janis, there are several 'symptoms' of groupthink, which help group members maintain faith in their decision under difficult circumstances (see Table 10.2). As a result of these features, Janis argued that people do not seek or discuss alternative possibilities to their planned decision, they do not assess the risks involved in the group decision, and they do not make contingency plans in case the group fails. The outcomes, as we have seen, can be fatal.

Janis (1982) recommended that groups should take several factors into account in order to prevent groupthink. He based these on examples of unsuccessful decision-making processes, including the Kennedy administration's handling of the USSR's deployment of medium-range ballistic missiles in Cuba in 1962. These are:

1 Groups, and especially leaders of groups, need to be impartial and not endorse any one position from the outset.
2 Groups should assign someone the role of critical evaluator or 'devil's advocate', who will critically evaluate the group's decisions, question assumptions and plans, and encourage the group to consider alternative options.
3 Everyone within the group should be encouraged to critically think about the decisions being made.
4 It is useful to divide groups, encourage members to seek advice from trusted outsiders, and then reunite them to discuss any differences.
5 Groups should regularly invite critiques from outside experts who will challenge the group's decisions.
6 Before implementing the final decision, groups should spend time discussing lingering issues or doubts and considering the dangers and consequences of their decisions.

Many of these principles are being taught in training programmes, such as those for airline flight crews, where flawed group dynamics are often responsible for plane accidents (Helmrich, 1997). Academic research has contributed to efforts designed to prevent groupthink among high-level policy making (Hart, 1998).

However, although Janis's theory has received much attention, not all researchers are convinced by his analysis. The main problem seems to be that much of the evidence for groupthink has been retrospective. Some findings support the theory (e.g., Hart, 1990; McCauley, 1989; Tetlock, 1979), but others are inconsistent with the basic principles of groupthink. In particular, group cohesiveness will not always lead to groupthink. The norms of a cohesive group can actually produce favourable decisions so long as the norms favour critical evaluation (Postmes, Spears and Cihangir, 2001). Further, after an examination of many different events, Tetlock, Petersen, McGuire et al. (1992) concluded that even good decision-making processes can lead to bad decisions. Experimental work has not always supported groupthink, in particular with respect to cohesiveness, where sometimes there is an association between cohesiveness and groupthink and sometimes there is not, largely dependent on the conditions of the experiment (e.g., Bernthal and Insko, 1993; Flowers, 1977; Rovio, Eskola, Kozub et al., 2009; Turner, Pratkanis, Probasco and Leve, 1992). Other researchers have argued that cohesiveness itself should be more clearly defined before we can fully understand how it influences good decision making. Its influence may be quite different if we think of cohesiveness in terms of liking, friendship or interpersonal attraction; indeed, findings suggest this is the case (Hogg and Hains, 1998; McCauley, 1989; see also McCauley, 1998). Nevertheless, the concept of groupthink has influenced how social psychologists understand the processes underlying good and bad decisions. Clearly, two heads are not always better than one.

ETHICS AND RESEARCH METHODS

Studying groupthink

© BANANASTOCK

As we have discussed, one important criticism of groupthink is that the evidence for the phenomenon has been retrospective case studies of group decision making. For example, scholars have looked to events like the space shuttle *Challenger* disaster and Pearl Harbor to link bad group decisions with faulty group processes in each example. However, this approach is not without problems. For instance, it is relatively easy in hindsight to find specific examples that support a theory. Applying a theory to specific examples may also mean that the researcher misses other potentially important factors. Further, the researcher has no control over the variables of interest. For example, if a researcher wants to investigate the role of cohesion in promoting groupthink, historical examples can only tell us if cohesion (in a general sense) may have had an influence on the decision. It can tell us very little about how different degrees of cohesion may influence group decisions.

One way to answer this criticism and test the effects of variables related to groupthink is to take investigations into the laboratory and conduct experiments. There have been some attempts to do this, although results have been mixed and sometimes contradictory. For example, Flowers (1977) manipulated group cohesion (high and low) and presented participants with a crisis problem to solve. In addition to this manipulation, the groups operated with leaders who either adopted an open or closed leadership style. Flowers found that the open leadership style produced the most suggested solutions and promoted more complete use of the information than the closed leadership style. In this study, levels of cohesion

had no effect, which is contrary to the theory of groupthink. However, Turner, Pratkanis, Probasco and Leve (1992) manipulated group cohesion slightly differently and found that in addition to self-esteem threat, cohesion had an independent effect on decision making, such that decisions resulting from highly cohesive groups were poorer than those resulting from less cohesive groups. This provides some support for the theory. In another study, Callaway and Esser (1984) found that intermediate cohesiveness (not low as the theory may suggest) produces the best decisions. Thus, the results from studies that have explicitly investigated groupthink – especially the effects of group cohesion on group decision making – have been mixed. This presents challenges for the theory. As you will know from your social psychology studies so far, theories face difficulties if they are not supported by empirical findings.

What might the problem be? One issue may be the way the experiments have been conducted. For example, Park (1990) criticized efforts to empirically test the principles of groupthink because they tend to include only one variable (or a small number) at a time. It is therefore difficult to know how various factors such as leadership and cohesion work in combination with each other to produce groupthink phenomena. In statistical terminology, there may be interactions between variables that are missed in studies that only investigate single variables. Further, as Rose (2011) has recently noted, despite 40 years of groupthink theory, experimental studies are extremely limited, with only a small number of all the model's variables being adequately tested. As a result, many scholars now see groupthink as a myth, while others remain committed to the theory. Of course, another consideration is that the theory may be incomplete and may need to be revised. In general, research on groupthink has not yielded a consistent picture that either supports or undermines the theory.

Questions

1   One interesting thing to note about groupthink is that despite contradictory findings and difficulties in carrying out conclusive experimental studies testing the theory, it still enjoys a great deal of attention. For example, management training programmes often focus on the prevention of groupthink. Groupthink has

been applied to many different domains where decisions are made, such as juries and sporting teams. Why do you think the theory is so influential?

2 Would it be possible to test the full model of groupthink? Take a look at the literature to see if this has been done. What are the difficulties in testing such a large social psychological model?

3 Can you think of a study to test one of Janis's recommendations for reducing groupthink?

Exploring further In the 1957 film *Twelve Angry Men*, directed by Sidney Lumet and starring Henry Fonda, the jury members begin their deliberations in a capital murder case where an 18-year-old man is accused of killing his father. The film follows the decision-making processes of the jury, riddled with errors, misconceptions and prejudices akin to the phenomenon of groupthink. One juror attempts to convince the jury of the defendant's innocence. If you get a chance, take a look at the film and think about Janis's groupthink principles. How did the group overcome its problems? Also think about our discussion of minority influence in Chapter 9.

Group problem solving

We now consider how individuals versus groups solve problems. The predominant conclusion from research is that two (or more) heads *are*, more often than not, better than one. On various intellectual tasks, people perform better in groups than they do alone. For example, Laughlin and Adamopoulos (1980) presented participants with analogy problems and found that participants' answers were more accurate after discussion than when answering alone. Also, it is clear that when groups rely on expertise within the group when solving problems, the group performs better (Brodbeck and Greitemeyer, 2000; Davis and Harless, 1996). In eyewitness testimony, group accounts are much more accurate than individual reports (Warnick and Sanders, 1980). Further, when groups get together and critique each other's ideas, they have been found to come up with better quality ideas (McGlynn, Tubbs and Holzhausen, 1995; McGlynn, McGurk, Effland et al., 2004).

Brainstorming Process of groups getting together and discussing a problem openly, allowing (many) ideas to flow freely.

This may explain why **brainstorming** can sometimes be an effective technique in group problem solving, at least if groups follow certain principles identified by Brown and Paulus (2002):

- combine group brainstorming with individual brainstorming
- have group members interact with one another in writing (see also Mullen, Johnson and Salas, 1991)
- make use of electronic communication technology (see also Gallupe, Cooper, Grisé and Bastianutti, 1994; Gallupe, Dennis, Cooper et al., 1992).

It has also been suggested that brainstorming groups are more effective if they are small rather than large, and if the experimenter is not present to monitor the process (Mullen et al., 1991). If ideas are allowed to flow in an efficient manner, working in groups to solve problems can be effective. On the other hand, there is evidence to suggest that if only simple group brainstorming is used with no break-out input from individuals, solitary efforts are typically better than those of the group (Diehl and Stroebe, 1987; Paulus, Larey and Ortega, 1995). People may feel good about taking part and feel that they have worked productively even if they may not have done so (Stroebe and Diehl, 1994).

Leadership

One question we have not addressed so far is the role of the leader in group decision making. Also, what makes a great leader? Do leaders need a particular combination of personality traits to be effective? Or do leaders simply have to be in the right place at the right time? In this section, we consider research on leadership in the context of group decision making.

What makes a good leader?

Great person theory Theory of leadership asserting that leaders have an ideal combination of personality traits that enables them to be effective.

The **great person theory** of leadership asserts that good leaders have an ideal combination of personality traits that enable them to lead effectively, regardless of the situation. Originating in the 19th century and linked to the work of historian Thomas Carlyle, it is argued that a leader is someone who is gifted with unique qualities that capture people's imaginations. Some people are born with the necessary characteristics to set them apart from others and it is these characteristics that determine their place in positions of power and authority. However, the great person theory is not well supported by research. Studies have generally found only weak correlations between personality traits and leadership ability. Some patterns have emerged; for example, leaders tend to be more intelligent, more extraverted, socially skilled, confident, driven by a desire for power, more charismatic and less neurotic than non-leaders (Albright and Forziati, 1995; Hogan, Curphy and Hogan, 1994; Judge, Bono, Ilies and Gerhardt, 2002). There is also some research suggesting that leadership may be heritable; for example, twins tend to display similar leadership behaviour (Arvey, Rotundo, Johnson et al., 2006; Arvey, Zhang, Avolio and Krueger, 2007). However, in general, relationships appear fairly modest so it seems unlikely that people are 'born leaders'. Other factors must contribute to leadership success (for reviews, see Judge, Bono, Iles and Gerhardt, 2002; Lord, DeVader and Alliger, 1986).

Theorists have examined the possibility that particular combinations of personality traits may be right for certain *contexts*. In other words, perhaps personality traits alone cannot explain leadership ability, but considering personality traits in particular situations may provide a clearer picture of when certain people may be good leaders and when they may not. Several theories of leadership have examined the characteristics of leaders themselves, and also their followers and the characteristics of situations (Hollander, 1961; Sternberg and Vroom, 2002). One such theory is the **contingency theory of leadership**. This theory argues that leadership success is dependent on how *task related* or *relationship oriented* the leader is, and

Contingency theory of leadership Theory arguing that leadership success is dependent on how task related or relationship oriented the leader is, and the amount of influence they have over the group.

the amount of influence they have over the group (Fiedler, 1967, 1978). Thus, two types of leader are assumed to exist. It is argued that task-oriented leaders focus more on the task at hand and getting the job done, and less on followers' feelings and relationships. On the other hand, relationship-oriented leaders focus more on followers' feelings and relationships and less on getting the task completed.

Central to this theory is that neither leader type is best across the board. Instead, the type of leader that is optimal depends on the context and, more specifically, the amount of influence the leader has over their group. In *high control* contexts, the leader has strong interpersonal relationships with the group, a strong position in the organization or group, and the work to be done is well structured and clear. In *low control* contexts, the leader has poorer relationships with the group and the tasks are less clearly defined. Fiedler argued that task-oriented leaders are likely to be more effective in high control contexts (where everything is running smoothly, everyone is happy and the leader can focus on the task) or low control contexts (where the leader takes charge and imposes order). Indeed, research has shown that specific, challenging goals and the monitoring of achievement by progress goals helps improve work outcomes (Locke and Latham, 1990, 2009; Latham, Stajkovic and Locke, 2010). On the other hand, relationship-oriented leaders are likely to be most effective in conditions of moderate control. In such a context, things are generally running smoothly but the relationship-oriented leader can step in when necessary to resolve relationship difficulties that may reduce overall group effectiveness (see Figure 10.12). Research reveals that this kind of leadership is good for morale, increases group cohesion, and people feel more satisfied with their situation (Spector, 1986; Tabernero, Chambel, Curral and Arana, 2009). In a democratic environment, people also become more motivated to achieve (Burger, 1987) and rate the outcomes more positively (van den Bos and Spruijt, 2002).

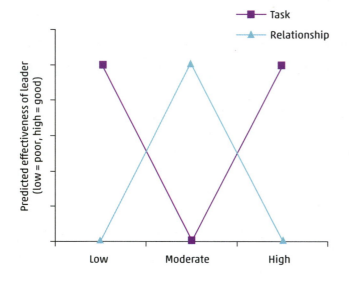

FIGURE 10.12 Fiedler's contingency theory of leadership Task-oriented leaders are likely to be more effective in high control contexts or low control contexts, whereas relationship-oriented leaders are likely to be more effective in moderate control contexts.

Source: Adapted from Chemers, Hays, Rhodewalt and Wysocki, 1985

Leadership effectiveness can also be viewed as a process of minority influence (see Chapter 9). For example, some research has demonstrated that leaders, like minorities, can inspire and influence people because they are consistent in their views and goals and exhibit self-confidence (Bennis, 1984; House and Singh, 1987). They gain the trust of their group by communicating their clear and consistent view to others.

Exploring further Draw up a short list of leaders you either know personally, or prominent world leaders. Using the principles you have read about so far, what type of leader are they? How is their leadership influenced by the context?

Culture and leadership

Increasing globalization has created a need to understand the role of culture in leader behaviour and performance. According to House, Hanges, Javidan et al. (2004), there are some aspects of desirable leaders that appear to be universal. For example, the GLOBE (Global Leadership and Organizational Behavior Effectiveness) project identified a list of leadership attributes endorsed by 17,000 people across 62 countries, and isolated 22 universal positive attributes (see Table 10.3). The project also identified 8 attributes universally regarded as negative, such as being egocentric, dictatorial and ruthless.

TABLE 10.3 Universal leadership attributes

Trustworthy	Arouses motives	Skilled administrator
Just	Motivator	Coordinator
Honest	Dependable	Team builder
Foresight	Intelligent	Excellence oriented
Forward plans	Decisive	Informed
Encouraging	Effective bargainer	Dynamic
Positive	Win-win problem solver	Communicative
	Builds confidence	

Source: Adapted from House et al., 2004

However, there are also some key differences in leadership behaviour across cultures. For example, the GLOBE project revealed that while countries in Latin America, the Middle East and Southern Asia scored high on ingroup collectivist leader behaviour such as promoting loyalty and joint interests, Western countries scored much lower. Also, while Western countries scored higher on uncertainty avoidance and future orientation, other regions scored lower. Thus there are clear cross-cultural differences in leadership orientation.

Increasing globalization has also made it necessary to know more about how leaders can best function in cross-cultural working environments. Adler and Batholomew (1992) argued that leaders need to develop five attributes in order to work effectively as global leaders:

1 An understanding of business, political and cultural environments in relevant domains
2 An understanding of the perspectives, trends and technologies of other cultures
3 An ability to work with people of different cultures
4 An ability to adapt to other cultures
5 An ability to relate to other cultures as equals.

An appreciation of cultural differences, and the ability to adapt to these differences, strongly influences leader behaviour in cross-cultural contexts.

Try it yourself Below is an excerpt from the dimensions of culture scale (House et al., 2004) which was used to identify cultural differences in leader behaviour across cultures. It was adapted from Hofstede's culture in the workplace questionnaire and identifies the different aspects of leader behaviour. Take a look at the scale and complete it yourself. If you have time, perhaps ask friends from other countries to complete the scale and compare your results. Do you notice any trends?

Uncertainty avoidance

In this society, orderliness and consistency are stressed, even at the expense of experimentation and innovation.

strongly disagree   1   2   3   4   5   6   7   strongly agree

In this society, societal requirements and instructions are spelled out in detail so citizens know what they are expected to do.

strongly disagree   1   2   3   4   5   6   7   strongly agree

Power distance

In this society, followers are expected to:

Question their leaders   1   2   3   4   5   6   7   Obey their leaders when in disagreement without question

In this society, power is:

Shared throughout the society   1   2   3   4   5   6   7   Concentrated at the top

Institutional collectivism

In this society, leaders encourage group loyalty even if individual goals suffer.

strongly disagree   1   2   3   4   5   6   7   strongly agree

The economic system in this society is designed to maximize:

Individual interests   1   2   3   4   5   6   7   Collective interests

Ingroup collectivism

In this society, children take pride in the individual accomplishments of their parents.

strongly disagree   1   2   3   4   5   6   7   strongly agree

In this society, parents take pride in the individual accomplishments of their children.

strongly disagree   1   2   3   4   5   6   7   strongly agree

Gender egalitarianism

In this society, boys are encouraged more than girls to attain a higher education.

strongly disagree   1   2   3   4   5   6   7   strongly agree

In this society, who is more likely to serve in a position of high office?

Men   1   2   3   4   5   6   7   Women

Assertiveness

In this society, people are generally:

Nonassertive   1   2   3   4   5   6   7   Assertive

In this society, people are generally:

Tender   1   2   3   4   5   6   7   Tough

Future orientation

In this society the accepted norm is to:

Accept the status quo   1   2   3   4   5   6   7   Plan for the future

In this society, people place more emphasis on:

Solving current problems   1   2   3   4   5   6   7   Planning for the future

Performance orientation

In this society, students are encouraged to strive for continuously improved performance.

strongly disagree   1   2   3   4   5   6   7   strongly agree

In this society, people are rewarded for excellent performance.

strongly disagree   1   2   3   4   5   6   7   strongly agree

Humane orientation

In this society, people are generally:

Not at all concerned about others   1   2   3   4   5   6   7   Very concerned about others

In this society, people are generally:

Not at all sensitive to others   1   2   3   4   5   6   7   Very sensitive towards others

Gender and leadership

How do female and male leaders compare to one another? How does the gender of a leader influence group processes? It is commonly believed that women need to work much harder than men from the beginning to achieve the same level of status. Also, everyday experience would suggest that female leaders are evaluated differently than male leaders who do exactly the same job. For example, a confident kind of leader may be perceived as bossy or 'mannish' if she is female. Research supports this common wisdom (Biernat, Crandall, Young et al., 1998). For example, Eagly, Makhijani and Klonsky (1992) found that if a female leader adopts a typically male leadership style, she is evaluated more negatively than a male leader behaving in the same manner. Further, this is especially the case if the people making the evaluations are male. In another study, Butler and Geis (1990) showed that group members react differently to assertive leaders depending on whether the leaders are female or male. Participants in this study (especially males) reacted more negatively to the assertive female leader.

Does this mean that female leaders will be more effective if they adopt a typically 'female' style? Are women who are more *communal* (helpful, kind and concerned about others) more successful in gaining the respect of their group and promoting positive group processes, while males who are *agentic* (assertive and self-confident) make better leaders? Research suggests that women find themselves in a catch-22 situation. If they behave in a communal way, they are perceived as having low leadership potential because good leaders are supposed to be agentic. On the other hand, if they behave counter-stereotypically and lead in an agentic manner, they are evaluated negatively (Carli and Eagly, 1999; Eagly and Karau, 2002; Eagly, Karau and Makhijani, 1995). In this case, their behaviour goes against how women are 'supposed' to behave. These factors pose significant problems for female leaders and compromise their effectiveness. It is not surprising that in 2006 only 8.5 per cent of CEOs in Europe were female (European Professional Women's Network, 2006). The picture for women leaders becomes even more bleak when we consider that they are consistently paid less than men for doing the same work (Kulich, Ryan and Haslam, 2007) and that they are more likely to be appointed to risky or 'doomed to failure' leadership positions than men (known as the glass cliff effect) (Ryan and Haslam, 2005). Perhaps more optimistically, some evidence suggests that people have become more tolerant of women who violate stereotypically female behaviour norms (Twenge, 1997) and it is generally accepted that leaders must display both communal and agentic behaviours in order to get the most from their group (Eagly and Karau, 2002).

Time to reflect Think about gender and leadership in the context of gender roles as we discussed in Chapter 8. How much do you think people's ideas about women leaders have changed? Have things changed enough? What other challenges still face aspiring female leaders?

Chapter summary

In this chapter, we have learned that being a member of a group significantly influences what we do. Groups allow people to do things together that they would not be able to do alone. Sometimes group behaviour is good and sometimes it is not. In this chapter, you have learned that:

- The phenomenon of social facilitation suggests that working alongside others can energize people to work faster, better and to reach their individual potential.
- The arousal experienced in the presence of others enhances whichever response tendency is dominant, so whether social facilitation (or its opposite – social inhibition) occurs depends on the nature of the task. This is primarily due to the process of evaluation apprehension – people become concerned about the evaluation of others and their performance on 'easy' tasks is facilitated, whereas their performance on 'difficult' tasks is inhibited. People can also be distracted by the evaluation of others.
- Research on social loafing suggests that people will often 'slack off' when working in a group, in particular when their own contribution is not being monitored. This occurs when evaluation apprehension is low – typically when people are not accountable for their input. Social loafing can be reduced by making tasks challenging, appealing or involving.
- It is sometimes possible to see the dark side of humanity when people are deindividuated in crowds or bear no accountability for their actions. People can perform acts they would not normally do, such as looting, rioting and other forms of antisocial behaviour. Large groups tend to display more deindividuated behaviour than smaller groups. It is argued that being deindividuated draws attention away

from the self, such that people become less self-aware and less aware of how they would normally behave.
- More recent theories of deindividuation argue that it is not a case of loss of identity or self-awareness, but increasing awareness of social identity or group norms. Deindividuated behaviour is not therefore always antisocial.
- Groups can facilitate decision making and problem solving such that – more often than not – people solve problems more accurately when they work with others than when they work alone. Research on group polarization suggests that group decisions enhance initial leanings of the group, through processes of normative and informational influence.
- However, not all groups make good decisions. When we examine the group decision-making processes that preceded some major world catastrophes, we can see symptoms of 'groupthink', which arguably led to disastrous outcomes.
- Working under an effective leader can drive a group to success and accomplishment in many ways. There are several theories to describe effective leadership behaviour and an emerging body of literature describing the challenges facing female leaders.

Groups are complex and dynamic. Nevertheless, people need groups and cannot live without them. Groups allow people to achieve together what they cannot do alone. Understanding group behaviour is therefore a topic of great importance to social psychologists. Our concern in this chapter has been on how people behave in groups. In Chapter 11, we turn to the study of how people in different groups behave towards one another. In the study of intergroup relations, social psychologists attempt to understand how groups react to and influence one another in positive and negative ways.

Essay questions

At the beginning of the chapter, we asked you to consider these questions:

1 Diana is learning to tap dance and has been practising for an forthcoming recital. She practises in front of a mirror and makes all the right moves. However, when the recital comes along she makes many mistakes and cannot understand why she messed up so badly. All her family and friends were watching her. How might we explain this?
2 Faiza is working with a group on an assignment about stereotypes of the British. Everyone has agreed to collect five references on the topic for the group to share. Faiza does not

try very hard and only provides two references, letting the group down. What social psychological processes (intentional and unintentional) might lead Faiza to do this?
3 Ben is at a concert. It is his favourite band and he is very excited. The audience is huge and everyone is dancing. Quite spontaneously, Ben moves up to a female stranger in the audience and grabs her by the wrist. Why would he do such a thing?

Having read this chapter, these questions could also be framed as the following essay questions, which you can attempt in preparation for your examinations:

1 What is social facilitation? Draw on evidence from social psychology to explain when social facilitation is likely (versus unlikely) to occur.

2 Drawing on theory and research, provide an overview of the antecedents and consequences of social loafing.

3 Is deindividuation a result of a 'loss of self'? Explain with reference to various theories of deindividuation, and associated research.

Further reading

Baron, R.S. and Kerr, N. (2003) *Group Processes, Group Decision, Group Action* (2nd edn). Buckingham: Open University Press. Comprehensive overview of the literature on group decision making and other processes occurring within groups.

Janis, I.L. (1982) *Groupthink: Psychological Studies of Policy Decisions and Fiascoes.* New York: Houghton Mifflin. Rather than reading a second-hand review, read Janis's original formulation of the theory of groupthink.

Karau, S.J. and Williams, K.D. (1993) Social loafing: A meta-analytic review and theoretical integration. *Journal of Personality and Social Psychology*, 65, 681–706. Although published in 1993, still an excellent, must-read paper on the phenomenon of social loafing.

Kramer, R.M., Tenbrunsel, A.E. and Bazerman, M.H. (eds) (2010) *Social Decision Making: Social Dilemmas, Social Values and Ethical Judgements*. New York: Psychology Press. Collection of chapters from experts in the field, providing a

comprehensive overview of research on both social decision making and social dilemmas.

Reicher, S., Spears, R. and Postmes, T. (1995) A social identity model of deindividuation phenomena. *European Review of Social Psychology*, 6, 161–98. Comprehensive review of older deindividuation research, including classic theory and research on deindividuation. Introduces the SIDE model of deindividuation phenomena. Some discussion of crowd behaviour.

Williams, K.D., Harkins, S.G. and Karau, S.J. (2003) Social performance. In M.A. Hogg and J. Cooper (eds) *The Sage Handbook of Social Psychology* (pp. 327–46). London: Sage. Review of the literature on how being in a group influences various aspects of people's performance.

Yukl, G. (2002) *Leadership in Organizations* (5th edn). Upper Saddle River, NJ: Prentice Hall. First published in 1981 by one of the experts in the field of management and leadership, focuses on the study of leadership in organizations.

Applying social psychology

Women in leadership: the glass cliff

1 According to Ryan and Haslam's (2007) glass cliff effect, women are assigned to precarious leadership roles, such as when an organization is likely to experience hardship or failure in the near future. In the run-up to the 2008 US presidential election, it was clear that the presidency would be a precarious position. America was beset by the gathering clouds of two frustrating and seemingly intractable wars, the spectre of domestic and international terrorism, declining international prestige, the threat of climate change and the economic and political difficulties of

mitigating this threat, and rapidly bursting 'bubbles' in the housing and financial sectors. However, American Democrats opted for Barack Obama, the leading male candidate, rather than Senator Hillary Clinton, the leading woman, to run in the election. How would you reconcile this electoral outcome with the glass cliff effect?

2 If men and women were equally likely to win election to the presidency of the USA, approximately how many presidents ought to have been female? Is the running total of female presidents, which is none, significantly less than would be expected by chance?

 Visit the companion website at www.palgrave.com/psychology/suttondouglas for access to a wide range of resources to help you get to grips with this chapter.

Blind spot in social psychology

Race and leadership

Researchers know something about the principles that influence women's appointment to, and success in, precarious leadership roles, but what about people of minority racial groups? Is there a 'glass cliff' for members of minority racial or ethnic groups? In other words, are racial minority members more likely to be appointed to precarious leadership positions?

1 Can you find theoretical grounds to hypothesize that racial minority members, like women, may be subject to the glass cliff effect? (Hint: it might be useful to examine the social

identity model of leadership. We have not covered this in this chapter but several of the key readings are available publicly or widely held by university libraries; e.g., Ashforth and Mael, 1989; Hogg, 2001). According to this theory, leaders are endorsed and therefore succeed to the extent that they embody the norms and values of a group. In other words, effective and popular leaders tend to be prototypical. Perhaps a person's minority racial background might raise questions in the minds of some about their prototypicality?

2 Can you design a study to test whether racial minority members are subject to a glass cliff effect?

Student project

Civic disengagement and belief in conspiracy theories

Robert Brotherton studied as an undergraduate student at the University of Kent and his dissertation supervisor was Dr Karen Douglas. His research investigated whether civic disengagement predicts the extent to which people believe in conspiracy theories – alternative theories for significant events that are often associated with mistrust within groups. Conspiracy theories present a challenge to group cohesion and leadership, which are factors discussed in this chapter.

My topic and aims

My study examined whether civic disengagement – a lack of participation in positive civic behaviours like voting, protesting and recycling – predicts the extent to which people believe in conspiracy theories. I argued that people who are disengaged or disenfranchised from society may be more accepting of negative claims about significant events that happen around them, such as the claim that important events are controlled from behind the scenes by a nefarious conspiracy.

I was interested more broadly in the slightly weird areas of psychology like false memories, magical thinking, superstitions, belief in the paranormal, and how they inform our understanding of belief formation in general. When I discovered there was a member of staff researching conspiracy theories I thought that was perfect. Understanding how people can come

to hold beliefs in unsubstantiated, implausible, and sometimes damaging conspiracy theories might tell us a lot about how we come to believe anything at all.

My methods

I used an experimental design, aiming to manipulate how civically engaged our participants would see themselves, and then to test the impact of this civic engagement manipulation on beliefs in a variety of conspiracy theories. Participants completed a questionnaire asking about their civic intentions and behaviours (e.g., 'How often do you vote?' 'Do you intend to vote in the next election?'). Afterwards, I gave participants false feedback about their answers, randomly telling half the participants that they scored pretty high in comparison to their peer group (high civic engagement), and the other half that they scored pretty low (low civic engagement). Then I asked them to complete a questionnaire assessing their beliefs about various conspiracy theories, such as the idea that climate change is a scientific fraud, Princess Diana is not dead, and the American moon landings were faked.

My findings and their implications

Our data did not support our hypothesis. The two experimental groups did not differ in their endorsement of conspiracy theories. However, a manipulation check revealed that the false feedback manipulation simply had no effect on participants' beliefs about their own level of civic engagement. That is, self-reported civic engagement was no different whether we told the participant they were high or low compared to their peers. They just didn't buy it. Unfortunately, this meant that a fair test of our hypothesis was not possible.

Therefore, I still don't know whether civic disengagement leads to susceptibility to conspiracy theories. Further research will be necessary to answer that question. I did personally learn the importance of including a manipulation check in a study like this. Without the manipulation check, I might have concluded that the data showed no effect of civic engagement on conspiracy beliefs, when in fact it was the manipulation that was ineffective.

My journey

I am now doing a PhD at Goldsmiths, University of London. The topic of my thesis is why people believe in conspiracy theories. Most of all I learned the value of building a project around whatever you happen to find most interesting. Psychology is an extremely broad subject – the scope for what you can choose to research is almost never-ending. However, if you can find something you think is important and interesting, it's going to motivate you, sustain your interest and, ultimately, come across in the quality of your work.

My advice

Give yourself as much time as possible to think about which questions in psychology interest you the most. Read as widely as you can, both academic articles and pop psychology books where relevant, and find out what research is going on in your department. But don't worry if you aren't completely sure when the time comes. If you begin with just a vague interest you might find that it grows into enthusiastic intrigue, which grows into zealous fascination – unless that's just me.

11 Intergroup relations

In this chapter we review the bases of stereotypes, prejudice and discrimination. We consider how these phenomena play out in relations between different groups, such as those differentiated on the basis of gender, race, religion and age. Finally, we consider some of the vicious cycles in intergroup relations. By the end of this chapter, you will have learned about the fundamental social psychological processes that occur between groups of people.

Topics covered in this chapter

- Bases of stereotypes, prejudice and discrimination
- Stereotyping, prejudice and discrimination in different intergroup contexts
- Vicious cycles in intergroup relations

Key features

Critical focus The minimal group paradigm

Ethics and research methods Ageism and cardiovascular health

Social psychology in the real world Homophobia

Applying social psychology Understanding and improving boys' academic achievement

Blind spot in social psychology The contested nature of social identity

Student project Marginalizing prejudice

Questions to consider

1 You may have heard of various homophobic hate groups that have a strong presence on the internet. Members of these groups stage homophobic demonstrations and, in one specific case, picketed memorials for soldiers killed in the Iraq War, taking the view that these soldiers' deaths are a form of punishment against the USA for its tolerance of homosexuality. Which of the social psychological processes described in this chapter may be contributing to the behaviour of these groups?

2 Mark, a manager for a large bank, genuinely feels very warm towards women. He thinks that men should cherish, protect and revere women. Do Mark's attitudes mean that he is less likely than other male managers to discriminate against women, for example to oversee unequal pay?

3 Many countries invest a lot of effort and money into counteracting racism. Why is racism so resistant to eradication?

4 What common principle might be illustrated by these two scenarios? 1. Suriya is in her sixties but has not aged well and has health problems one would normally associate with someone significantly older. 2. Danni does quite well in mathematics in class but gets a poor mark whenever she sits a mathematics exam.

You have probably noticed that people often resist being categorized. Try to impose a group label on someone – be it 'English', 'British', 'smoker', 'bisexual', 'feminist' or 'left-winger', to name a few – and there is a decent chance they will object. 'Don't pigeonhole me', 'don't label me' are familiar refrains. This phenomenon is not much studied by social psychologists, and we are inclined to think of it as a 'blind spot' in research as it stands (see the Blind spot in social psychology exercise at the end of this chapter). One of the reasons for this wariness about being slotted into a category probably relates to the desire for a distinctive personal identity (Brewer, 1991) (see Chapter 8). One does not want to be seen merely as a member of a given group but also as an individual with unique qualities. This suggests that people have an intuitive awareness of some of the social dangers inherent in being categorized. One danger stems from the existence of **stereotypes** – simplified but widely shared beliefs about the characteristics of groups and their members. Thus, you may find yourself being *stereotyped*, meaning that people will assume you must have the characteristics that are stereotypically associated with your group, even if they know nothing else about you. Further, and worse, you may find yourself the target of **prejudice**, a negative affective reaction to your group, so called because it can cause people to prejudge you. Finally, if people are prejudiced against you – and, as we shall see, even if they are not – you may find yourself a victim of **discrimination**, meaning that others treat you less well because of the group to which you belong.

Stereotypes, prejudice and discrimination are the most often studied forms of intergroup relations. This is not to say that they are the most common forms of relations between groups. Children and adults, women and men, and members of different occupational groups generally live, work and play together with few problems. It is the job of social psychologists, like other scientists, to understand and help solve problems, so it is not surprising that their research gravitates towards the negative end of intergroup relations. In this chapter, we will review the bases of stereotypes, prejudice and discrimination. We then consider how these phenomena play out in relations between different groups, such as those differentiated on the basis of gender, race, religion and age. Finally, we consider some of the vicious cycles in intergroup relations.

Stereotype A simplified but widely shared belief about a characteristic of a group and its members.

Prejudice A negative, affective prejudgement about a group and its individual members.

Discrimination Negative treatment of a group member simply because of their group membership.

Bases of stereotypes, prejudice and discrimination

Cognitive limitations and faults

One of the oldest theoretical perspectives on stereotyping and prejudice arose from the so-called 'cognitive revolution' of the 1950s and 60s. Informed by models of behaviour that gave great weight to cognitive processes, theorists speculated that stereotypes and prejudice may arise from the limitations of human beings as information processors. Stereotypes were seen as necessarily impoverished, simplistic understandings of groups and their members. In this perspective, one reason that stereotypes arise is that human beings have limited cognitive resources.

People are seen as cognitive misers (Fiske and Taylor, 1991; see also Chapter 3). There is just not enough space, particularly in working memory, for observers to take in each person, and each group, fully as they come. Instead of incorporating all the ambiguous, idiosyncratic and apparently contradictory information that is available, it is easier and more realistic for observers to take certain shortcuts known as heuristics (see Chapter 3). For example, noticing a trend for a group to have certain characteristics, such as friendliness and warmth, individuals may save a lot of time and effort by assuming the trait is probably possessed by a new acquaintance – 'Luigi is Italian; Italians are warm and friendly; therefore I can expect Luigi to be warm and friendly.'

This idea is supported by many studies in which individuals are shown to draw upon stereotypes in order to furnish them with rich, elaborate knowledge about individuals they barely know (e.g., Dijker and Koomen, 1996; Gilbert and Hixon, 1991). It is also supported by studies that examine when people do, and do not, apply stereotypes. For example, Stephan, Berscheid and Hatfield (1971) demonstrated that female undergraduate students were less prone to committing basic social cognitive errors when thinking about a potential dating partner than about a man they thought they would never meet. Apparently, being 'outcome dependent' on another person motivates people to expend more of their limited and precious cognitive resources, with dramatic effects on accuracy. Similarly, Pendry and Macrae (1994) showed that people are less prone to stereotyping others upon whom they depend – but only if they have the cognitive resources free to do so.

© GETTY

In one of their experiments, Pendry and Macrae (1994) led undergraduate participants to believe that they would work with an elderly woman named 'Hilda' on a problem-solving task. They were also told that the best problem solvers in the experiment would be eligible for a £20 prize. In the outcome-dependent condition of the experiment, participants were told that they would work together with Hilda to jointly produce solutions, and would both receive the £20 prize if they were the most successful pair. In the outcome-independent condition, participants were told that they and Hilda would each produce their own solutions, and the £20 would go to the best performing student and the best performing non-student partner. Participants read a personal profile of Hilda, half of which was consistent with stereotypes of elderly women and the other half inconsistent. As predicted, participants who expected to depend on Hilda, being motivated to expend more cognitive resources in order to paint an accurate mental picture of her, later evaluated her in more accurate, less stereotypical terms than participants who did not. But this advantage disappeared among participants who were also required to mentally rehearse an eight-digit number while reading Hilda's profile. In this case, participants are 'motivated but thwarted tacticians' (Pendry and Macrae, 1994, p. 303), who have good reason to spend time and effort in forming an impression of Hilda but are unable to do so. In fact, in support of a cognitive miser view, you can see in Figure 11.1 that participants who were dependent on Hilda but made cognitively 'busy' relied more than any other group on stereotypes.

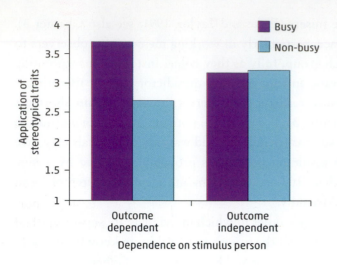

FIGURE 11.1 Cognitive busyness leads to greater use of stereotypes Effect of outcome dependence and cognitive busyness on ratings of the stimulus person, 'Hilda', on stereotype-consistent traits (in this study, 'intolerant, prudish, and critical').

Source: Data from Pendry and Macrae, 1994

Illusory correlation bias An exaggerated perception of a correlation between two variables. In intergroup relations, the perception that a behaviour is more frequently displayed by a minority than a majority group, when the behaviour is displayed equally by both groups, in proportional terms.

The cognitive miser perspective holds that stereotypes and prejudice may stem from a human insufficiency of thought and memory – there is simply not enough of it to ensure a subtle, authentic representation of people and groups. But stereotypes and prejudice may also stem from faults in human thought and memory. In this view, people are like 'faulty computers' (Nisbett and Ross, 1980). Ironically, many of these flaws may have evolved as hard-wired shortcuts designed to compensate for the miserliness that is required because of human limitations in raw processing speed and power (Gilbert, 1999). The upshot is, however, that if one's thought processes are inherently flawed, it does not necessarily help to expend more time thinking about a group and its members. One such flaw in human thinking appears to be the illusory correlation bias (Hamilton and Gifford, 1976).

Illusory correlation

Typically, we have much less contact with minorities and outgroups than we do with majorities and our own groups. Thus, we have fewer opportunities to observe or learn about instances of behaviour by members of such groups. This relative lack of information can lead us to commit a crucial cognitive error. Let us take an example. Imagine that you live near the ground of Hometown Football Club. Whenever this team is playing at home, you see the procession of its fans walking to and from the ground. Once a year, this team has a home fixture with Neighbourtown Football Club. So you see this team's fans much less often. Each team has a minority of fans, let us say five per cent, who are hooligans – drunken, aggressive and loutish fans who make spectacles of themselves and are occasionally involved in violence. If asked, would you indicate, correctly, that hooliganism is as frequent, proportionately speaking, in the two groups (see Table 11.1)? According to over 100 published demonstrations of the **illusory correlation bias**, the answer is probably no (Fiedler, 2004). In such cases, where a minority and a majority group are equally prone to an undesirable behaviour, this trick of the mind leads people to believe that the behaviour is actually more common among the minority group.

The illusory correlation bias can be used to explain, in part, why certain undesirable behaviours are unfairly perceived to be more characteristic of real-life minority groups. Even if we allow that many stereotypes contain a 'kernel of truth', such that there are real differences between groups, we can expect any correlation to seem larger than it really is (McGarty, Haslam, Turner and Oakes, 1993). If you reflect for a few moments, we are sure you could think of a few possible examples of this phenomenon in real-life groups (see Figure 11.2).

TABLE 11.1 Observed instances of hooligan and civilized behaviour

	Hooligan behaviour	Civilized behaviour
Hometown FC	100	1,900
Neighbourtown FC	5	95

FIGURE 11.2 Illusory correlation bias Illusory correlation bias might make you think that hooliganism is more common among smaller groups, for example fans of the 'away' team versus the 'home' team, even when the same proportion of their fans are hooligans.

How can we explain the illusory correlation effect? Several psychological mechanisms would appear to underpin it, as we might expect for an effect that is so robust, that is, likely to be obtained each time a study is repeated. For example, Fiedler (1991) showed that imperfections in human learning and memory may help produce the illusory correlation effect. Memory for events is faulty, so people do not perfectly encode the actual ratio of positive to negative behaviours for each group. As time goes by, their estimate of this ratio shifts in the direction of a 50:50 split. This causes them to underestimate the proportion of good behaviours, and overestimate the proportion of bad ones, since bad behaviours are more rare. In our example in Table 11.1, the ratio was 5 per cent bad, 95 per cent good behaviour.

Why is this bias more pronounced for the behaviours of the minority group? According to Fiedler (1991), observers are exposed to fewer instances of their behaviour, thus their memory is weaker to begin with; and memory for the frequency of their behaviour shifts still further towards the 50:50 split. The result of this larger shift is that the ratio of negative to positive behaviours will seem higher for the minority than the majority group – the illusory correlation effect. Consistent with this explanation, Eder, Fiedler and Hamm-Eder (2011) found that the illusory correlation bias was higher among participants who had a lower working memory capacity. Also, when they temporarily reduced participants' working memory with a *cognitive load* manipulation, the illusory correlation bias increased relative to a control group.

Rothbart's (1981) explanation of the illusory correlation bias also emphasized the accessibility of information at the time of retrieval. Positive behaviours by the majority are the most common (1,900 in our example – far more than all the other types of behaviour combined). Thus, they are the most accessible in memory. As a result, the majority group are seen more favourably than the minority group whose positive behaviours are fewer and therefore less accessible. In this view, the illusory correlation effect is driven by positivity towards the majority group, rather than negativity towards the minority. In a later model (based on a general model of memory proposed by Hintzman, 1986), Smith (1991) suggested that the absolute number of positive and negative behaviours, rather than the ratio between them, is more likely to be remembered. The majority group is therefore likely to be evaluated more favourably because the absolute difference between positive and negative behaviours is larger (in our example, 1,800 for Hometown FC, versus 90 for Neighbourtown FC).

The most well-known explanation of the illusory correlation effect refers to the tendency for distinctive behaviours to capture our attention and receive the most elaborate processing (Hamilton and Gifford, 1976). Distinctiveness is a tricky concept to pin down; indeed, this is one of the criticisms of this approach to the illusory correlation bias (e.g., McGarty and de la Haye, 1997; van Rooy, van Overwalle, Vanhoomissen et al., 2003). However, it is possible to define it in terms of mere statistical rarity. In this sense, minority behaviours are, by definition, distinctive relative to majority behaviours. Also, undesirable behaviours are rarer and thus more distinctive than desirable ones. So, undesirable behaviours by the minority group are distinctive on two counts: they seize the most attention, and carry the most weight (see also Sherman, Kruschke, Sherman et al., 2009).

The illusory correlation bias is a vivid, robust and well-explained bias, which would appear to underpin processes of stereotyping and prejudice. It may lead to unduly harsh perceptions of minority groups or of outgroups with whom people have little direct experience. Certainly, it highlights how a little knowledge of an outgroup can be a dangerous thing. That said, no one is pretending that illusory correlations are enough to explain all forms of stereotyping and prejudice. In order to do this, one has to consider other processes, and especially the emotions and motivations that go along with belonging to groups. Further, some have questioned the sense in which an illusory correlation always deserves to be called a 'bias'. It may be legitimate to evaluate a group according to the sum total of good things it does, rather than the proportion (Berndsen, McGarty, van der Pligt and Spears, 2001; McGarty et al., 1993).

Category accentuation

The illusory correlation effect refers to a cognitive error that can occur when people have more information about one group than another. A still more basic error is *category accentuation*, in which the *mere act of categorization* can distort the way people think about members of groups and the groups themselves. Placing objects into categories changes the way they are perceived, such that differences between categories are maximized and differences within categories are minimized (Tajfel, 1959). This was demonstrated in a classic study by Tajfel and Wilkes

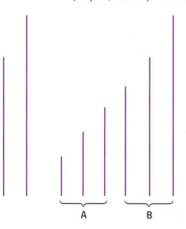

(1963). Participants were presented with an array of lines of varying lengths. In one condition, the lines were unlabelled. In another condition, shorter lines were labelled, with the letter A, whereas longer lines were labelled B (see Figure 11.3). Thus, Tajfel and Wilkes had created two categories, A and B, tending to comprise short and long lines respectively. When lines were categorized in this way, the difference between the shortest and longer line in the whole array was perceived to be larger, even though the objective difference was identical in the unlabelled condition.

FIGURE 11.3 Illustration of Tajfel and Wilkes's (1963) study The labels caused participants to perceive the lines in group A as similar to each other, the lines in group B as similar to each other, and to perceive larger differences between the line groups.

Tajfel and Wilkes (1963) found much the same differences when observers made judgements about people. Many researchers have since found that differences among people between categories, and similarities among people within categories, are accentuated (e.g., Corneille and Judd, 1999; McGarty and Penny, 1988; Queller, Schell and Mason, 2006). The effect extends beyond judgements about individuals. When asked to make judgements about the categories themselves, people also make a similar mistake. For example, Krueger, Rothbart and Siriam (1989) told participants that sprinters

© PHOTODISC/GETTY IMAGES

generally weigh more than marathon runners and, in a 'category learning' phase, presented them with the body weights of a number of individuals who, by and large, conformed to this rule. In a later 'category change' phase, participants were presented with more body weight information, this time about people who either confirmed (heavy sprinters, featherweight marathon runners) or bucked (lithe sprinters, bulky marathoners) the trend. Participants' estimates of the average weight of these two groups changed more in the first condition than in the second, that is, when the new category members tended to accentuate, rather than to minimize, the difference between categories. Apparently, people attend to and remember more easily people who confirm, rather than disconfirm, category-based expectations (see also Krueger and Rothbart, 1990).

Cognitive motivations: dogmatism, closed-mindedness

Stereotypes and prejudice stem not only from limitations in how people are *able* to think. It is also important to consider how they *want* to think. As we considered in Chapter 3, human beings share a desire to understand their environment, and a general aversion to uncertainty or ambiguity about matters that are important to them. A number of social psychologists have linked this *epistemic* (knowledge) need with intergroup perceptions. This epistemic need can engender stereotypes and prejudice by causing people to seek haste, simplicity and clarity in the way they process information. Stereotypes meet these needs because they provide explanations for real or imagined patterns in behaviour. They are a type of social knowledge that helps us feel that we can understand our social environment in relatively simple terms. Similarly, prejudice can be seen as a natural reaction to groups who seem to threaten our understanding of the world. For example, one way of feeling that we understand our social environment is to classify behaviours into 'right' and 'wrong'. Prejudice can be seen as a response to groups of people whose values and behaviour seem to contradict our sense of right and wrong, and therefore the beliefs and values we use to understand the world (Duckitt, 2006).

Most tests of this approach have focused on individual differences. The reasoning behind these tests is that some people experience these epistemic needs more acutely than others, and those people should be the most prone to stereotyping and prejudice. Rokeach (1956, 1960) was among the first to take this approach. According to Rokeach, individuals with high levels of antipathy towards outgroups were likely to share a trait he termed **dogmatism**. Dogmatism is the tendency to be able to tolerate mutually inconsistent beliefs by isolating them from each other in memory. This rigid cognitive structure tends to be resistant to change. Rokeach (1960) developed a measure of dogmatism and found some evidence that it is related to prejudice towards various groups. However, the measure he designed seemed to measure not only dogmatism but also some rather specific ideological and personality variables. It seemed to overlap with a variable we shall review shortly called authoritarianism (Adorno, Frenkel-Brunswik, Levinson and Sanford, 1950) – sharing its concern with personal inadequacy,

Dogmatism The tendency for people to be able to tolerate mutually inconsistent beliefs by isolating them from each other in memory.

power and status (Webster and Kruglanski, 1994; for a review of the historical relationship between dogmatism and authoritarianism, see Brown, 1995).

Personal need for structure (PNS) A person's preference for structure and clarity in most situations, and level of annoyance experienced by ambiguity.

The **personal need for structure (PNS)** is a construct that addresses human beings' epistemic concerns in a more direct way (Neuberg and Newsom, 1993). People who score highly on this variable – indicating a preference for structure in most situations – tend to stereotype others more. For example, Neuberg and Newsom (1993) presented participants with one of two descriptions of an undergraduate student. These descriptions were identical except that the student was called either 'Richard' or 'Michelle'. Sure enough, participants who were high in PNS assigned more stereotypically 'female', negative traits such as irrationality and gullibility to Michelle than to Richard. Participants who were low in PNS did not do this (see Figure 11.4) (see also Schaller, Boyd, Yohannes and O'Brien, 1995).

Still another construct is the need for cognitive closure (NFCC) (Kruglanski, 2006; Webster and Kruglanski, 1994). This is defined as a general desire to seek 'an answer on a given topic, any answer … compared to confusion and ambiguity' (Kruglanski, 1990, p. 377). This latent desire is viewed as being expressed in five facets: the desire for predictability, a preference for order and structure, discomfort with ambiguity, decisiveness, and closed-mindedness (discussed in Chapter 6 in relation to persuasion). Like the need for structure, it has been shown to be associated with prejudice and stereotyping. For example, Dijksterhuis, van Knippenberg, Kruglanski and Schaper (1996) found that participants who scored highly on a measure of NFCC tended to recall more stereotype-consistent information about a group of football hooligans, whereas participants who were low in NFCC recalled relatively more stereotype-inconsistent information.

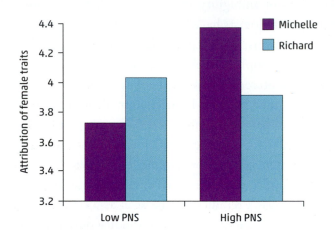

FIGURE 11.4 Personal need for structure and stereotyping Participants who were high in PNS may be more likely to stereotype others in ambiguous situations (by assigning more 'feminine' traits to female targets) than those low in PNS.

Source: Data from Neuberg and Newsom, 1993

In sum, research supports the basic idea that the more an individual is motivated to understand the world in simple, highly structured terms, the more they are likely to rely on stereotypes and be prejudiced. Epistemic concerns may also shape stereotyping and especially prejudice in an indirect or *mediated* way. It is related to variables that themselves have been shown to predict prejudice towards certain groups that are perceived either as a threat to the social order or as deserving of their lowly position in the social status quo. These variables include political conservatism (Jost, Glaser, Kruglanski and Sulloway, 2003) and certain values such as security, conformity and tradition (Calogero, Bardi and Sutton, 2009). It is to these variables, associated with preferences or ideologies surrounding how society should ideally be ordered, that we now turn.

Try it yourself Below is the personal need for structure scale (Thompson, Naccarato and Parker, 1989). Complete it for yourself and determine whether you are high, low or moderate in personal need for structure. The items marked with an asterisk need to be reverse scored before you can tally your results and calculate your mean. Once you have calculated your mean, a score from 1–26 is deemed to be low in PNS, a score of 27–37 is below average, 38–46 is average, 47–57 is above average, and 58–72 is high. Knowing what you know about social psychological research, do your results mean that you will be more or less likely to stereotype and be prejudiced?

Read each of the following statements and decide how much you agree with each according to your attitudes, beliefs and experiences. It is important for you to realize that there are no right or wrong answers to these questions. People are different, and we are interested in how you feel. Please respond according to the scale: 1 = strongly disagree to 6 = strongly agree.

1 It upsets me to go into a situation without knowing what I can expect from it.
2 I'm not bothered by things that interrupt my daily routine. *
3 I enjoy having a clear and structured mode of life.
4 I like to have a place for everything and everything in its place.
5 I enjoy being spontaneous.*
6 I find that a well-ordered life with regular hours makes my life tedious. *
7 I don't like situations that are uncertain.
8 I hate to change my plans at the last minute.
9 I hate to be with people who are unpredictable. *
10 I find that a consistent routine enables me to enjoy life more.
11 I enjoy the exhilaration of being in unpredictable situations.*
12 I become uncomfortable when the rules in a situation are not clear.

Source: Thompson et al., 1989

Ideologies

The study of the role of ideology in intergroup relations has a long history in social psychology. Arguably, the person who has had the most profound, far-reaching impact on the study of intergroup relations is Karl Marx, with his collaborator Friedrich Engels. Marx and Engels ([1848]1998) were especially interested in conflicts between the social classes. For Marx, social classes arise from excess production in an economy. When agriculture or industry are efficient enough to produce more than is required for survival at a subsistence level, the *ruling classes* emerge who own the means of production (land, factories). The ruling classes dominate the *working classes* who supply the labour required to operate the means of production. In economies based largely on agriculture, the most fundamental classes are landowners and peasants. The bourgeoisie (or capitalists) and the proletariat (or working class) are the most basic and familiar of the classes in industrialized economies based on mass production (for a more fine-grained analysis of social class, see Giddens, 1981).

For Marx, these classes have inherently different, and conflicting, interests. Class conflict stems from the fact that it is in the interests of the ruling class to retain control of the means of production and to perpetuate their exploitation of the working class. For their part, it is in the interests of the working class to overthrow this exploitation and share in the profits that stem from ownership of the means of production. Two key concepts developed by Marx have a strongly social psychological flavour. For Marx, the unequal class system is preserved by 'false consciousness'. The working classes are distracted from awareness of their disadvantaged position in the class system, their common interests with fellow working-class people, and their competing interests with the ruling class. Ideologies, such as the Protestant work ethic and religious notions of providence (that people's position in society is divinely ordained), play a key role in keeping people in a state of false consciousness. In contrast, 'class consciousness' emerges when the fog is lifted and people become aware of the implications of social class.

In their general form, some of Marx's key ideas are incorporated in all the approaches we are about to consider, including authoritarianism, social dominance orientation, realistic conflict theory and social identity theory. These are:

1 Groups have unequal levels of status in society.
2 Individuals within these groups tend to have interests in common.
3 These groups tend to have conflicting interests.
4 Members of these groups are not fully aware of their interests and hence fail to act on them.
5 Awareness is hampered by ideologies that obscure status inequalities, justify them, or make them seem unchangeable.

Authoritarianism

Authoritarianism A form of social organization characterized by preference for, and submission to, authority.

Adorno et al. (1950) were the first to link the preference for hierarchy to prejudice. Their research, like Milgram's (1961) studies of obedience (see Chapter 9), was largely an attempt to make some sense of the Holocaust of the 1940s. The key difference is that whereas Milgram (1961) linked evil intergroup behaviour to the power of the situation, Adorno et al. looked for a cause in the personalities of the wrongdoers and their supporters. The result was the concept of the 'authoritarian personality'. Adorno et al. were able to show that people with this type of personality were indeed more prejudiced. However, the scale they deployed, known as the F-scale (F for fascism), was not reliable or valid (Altemeyer, 1981). Also, their concept seemed to resonate with politically right-wing rather than left-wing forms of **authoritarianism** (Rokeach, 1960). Thus, it tended to account better for prejudice towards groups that right-wingers, rather than left-wingers, seem to dislike (e.g., the poor, as opposed to the aristocracy).

Exploring further Locate and read the excellent biographical entry on Theodor Adorno on Wikipedia. Adorno was a brilliant individual, who, in addition to his social scientific work, was a public intellectual and a music composer. Like several eminent social psychologists in the second half of the 20th century, Adorno was Jewish and emigrated from Germany in the 1930s, although unlike many others, he returned to Germany after the Second World War. What other major Jewish social psychologists can you find who lived through the Holocaust? How do you think this experience influenced their thinking?

Right-wing authoritarianism An individual differences variable characterized by authoritarian submission, authoritarian aggression and conventionalism.

Adorno's ideas and methods were refined by Altemeyer (1981, 1998), who put forward the concept of **right-wing authoritarianism** and developed a much improved scale to measure it. This scale measures the three components of this concept:

1 *conventionalism:* the desire for adherence to traditional social values and mores
2 *authoritarian aggression:* the desire to aggress against or punish those who defy these social conventions
3 *authoritarian submission:* the tendency to yield to authority.

Altemeyer (1998) found that right-wing authoritarians are more prejudiced towards a range of groups, particularly those who are traditionally low in status (e.g., Black people) or who seem to flout traditional values (e.g., gay people).

Exploring further Look for research on *left-wing* authoritarianism, using Google Scholar or another research database. Compare and contrast this variable with right-wing authoritarianism. Why do you think relatively little research has been done on this topic? Does it suggest that social psychologists tend to be rather left-wing and are thus more eager to demonstrate the shortcomings of right-wing ideology? Or is it because left-wing authoritarianism is simply less powerful and wide-reaching in its effects?

Although Altemeyer's (1998) results are clear and compelling, debate surrounds how they should be interpreted. Altemeyer explained them in terms of personality processes, arguing that something about the psychological makeup of authoritarian people creates a need to be prejudiced. However, others see right-wing authoritarianism as more like an ideology than a facet of someone's character. In support of this view, authoritarianism turns out to be more strongly related to attitudes and values than to deep-seated personality dimensions (Heaven and Connors, 2001; Saucier, 2000). Further, right-wing authoritarianism changes in response to situational forces. For example, when the social order is threatened, people become more authoritarian (Duckitt and Fisher, 2003). This does not seem to be compatible with the view that right-wing authoritarianism is wired into people's character by their genes or childhood experiences.

Time to reflect Do you think that authoritarianism is always a bad thing? What might be some of the benefits of authoritarianism? Can you think of ways to test your ideas?

Social dominance orientation

Social dominance orientation An individual differences variable that measures people's preference for hierarchy within any social system.

The relationship between ideology and intergroup relations is addressed more squarely by another key concept in social psychology – **social dominance orientation** (Sidanius and Pratto, 1999). Like right-wing authoritarianism, this concept is 'multidimensional', in that it comprises more than one component:

1 a general preference for hierarchical, as opposed to equal, relations between groups
2 a desire for one's own group to dominate or be superior to other groups.

And, like right-wing authoritarianism, it enjoys a good deal of research support. For example, Pratto, Sidanius, Stallworth and Malle (1994) found that individuals who scored highly on social dominance orientation tended to be prejudiced towards a range of social groups, such as Black people and gay people, and opposed social policy measures designed to enhance the welfare and esteem of these groups. They also tended to endorse beliefs that legitimized the unequal status of different groups, such as the belief that in America, everyone has an equal opportunity to succeed regardless of the ethnic group they were born into (for more detail on the legitimization of the status quo, see Chapter 14).

As illustrated by right-wing authoritarianism and social dominance orientation, the development of new concepts inspires research that uncovers valuable insights into the causes of prejudice and other social behaviours. But there is a danger inherent in this creative process – we can end up with too many variables, each claiming to explain the same phenomenon. A key aim of science is parsimony – the explanation of the complex phenomena of the world in simple and understandable terms (Chapter 1). As Occam pointed out in the 14th century, when making sense of the world, we should try to posit the existence of as few things as we can. Each time we posit a variable, we increase the chances that the variable does not exist and therefore that our understanding is wrong. Thus, it is important to consider whether right-wing authoritarianism and social dominance orientation really are different, having different effects on intergroup relations, instead of just being superficially different ways of describing the same basic processes.

Fortunately, it turns out they *are* different. Duckitt (2006) measured his participants' right-wing authoritarianism as well as their social dominance orientation. He found that high scores on right-wing authoritarianism were correlated with prejudice towards groups perceived to pose a threat to the social order, as measured on items such as: 'They seem to reject moral values that are important to me.' In contrast, social dominance orientation was positively correlated with prejudice towards groups that seem to be in competition with the ingroup (e.g., 'If they make economic gains, people like me will be worse off'). These results highlight the essential difference between the two variables. Right-wing authoritarianism is associated with perceiving the world as a dangerous place, and striving to preserve society from threats to its shared values, cohesion and safety. Social dominance orientation involves the perception of the world as a competitive jungle in which dog eats dog, and is concerned with preserving a clear hierarchy within which one's group is highly placed (for other differences between these variables, see Duriez and van Hiel, 2002; Heaven and Connors, 2001).

Ethnocentrism and the struggle for superiority

As we have seen, social dominance orientation is ideological insofar as it reflects a preference for a clear status hierarchy, or 'pecking order', in society. However, its second component is not ideological, equating instead to the desire for 'us' to dominate 'them'. More generally, people seem to want their own social group to be superior in some sense to others. This desire may ultimately stem from what people want for themselves.

For example, many social groups, such as teams, companies, political movements and armies, work collaboratively in the face of competition from other groups. Individuals within these groups are better off if their group functions as a collective. This basic pattern of relationships – cooperation within groups, competition between groups – is a common feature of human experience. The competitive nature of relations between groups can easily spill over into prejudice and intergroup conflict. This is especially so in 'zero-sum' situations where resources can only be gained by one group at the expense of the other (e.g., there is only so much land in central Europe that can be claimed as territory; similarly, there can be only one winner of the Eurovision song contest). This approach to intergroup relations can be traced back to Marx's ideas about class conflict, and is exemplified by **realistic group conflict theory** (Sherif, 1966).

Realistic group conflict theory Theory of intergroup conflict that explains intergroup behaviour with respect to the need to secure scarce resources.

The quest for the superiority of the ingroup is not all about material welfare, however. As we saw in Chapter 2, individuals strive to achieve a positive and coherent identity. As we saw in Chapter 8, a positive image of the self depends on a positive image of the groups to which one belongs, which, in turn, depends on seeing one's group in positive terms relative to other groups. This approach to intergroup relations is exemplified by social identity theory (see also Chapter 8). Some of the different emphases between these two theories are shown in Table 11.2.

TABLE 11.2 Characteristics of realistic group conflict theory and social identity theory

	Realistic group conflict theory	Social identity theory
Groups are principally	Collectives working to achieve common goals	Social categories
Prejudice and intergroup conflict stem primarily from	Competition over finite resources	The desire to feel positively about the ingroup
The most important resources are	Material and political, e.g., territory, money and power	Symbolic, e.g., markers of esteem and prestige
Groups strive for	Absolute resources – groups strive to maximize how many resources they control in absolute terms, more than in relation to others	Relative resources – superiority in comparison with others is more important than absolute level of resources
Individual-level motivation	Material security, affiliation with ingroup members	Self-esteem, sense of meaning and understanding

In general, realistic group conflict theory and social identity theory emphasize different aspects of intergroup relations. Whereas realistic group conflict theory highlights the need to secure scarce resources for the ingroup, social identity theory focuses on the need to view the ingroup positively. Other differences in emphasis are shown in Table 11.2, and are highlighted by probably the most famous and archetypal tests inspired by each approach to intergroup relations: Sherif, Harvey, White et al.'s ([1954]1961) 'Robbers Cave' study, and the first 'minimal group paradigm' pioneered by Tajfel, Billig, Bundy and Flament (1971).

Although realistic group conflict theory and social identity theory emphasize different strategic priorities, they share an essential feature that differentiates them from the cognitive, personality and ideological approaches considered so far. In explaining relations between groups, their focus moves beyond the processes inside an individual, although these remain important, to include processes occurring at the group level. Intergroup contexts cause people to identify themselves and others with the groups to which they belong. They then interact with each other *as members of groups*. They start to see their own group as better than its rivals, in a mindset known as **ethnocentrism**, and start to pursue strategic objectives on behalf of their group.

Ethnocentrism Preference for one's own group, and features of one's own group, over others.

The Robbers Cave study

Sherif et al. ([1954]1961) devised a vivid test of their ideas about how prejudice and conflict spring from a mix of intragroup cooperation and intergroup competition. Inspired by Golding's 1954 novel *The Lord of the Flies*, they decided to take children, whose behaviour may be more malleable than adults, out of their normal environment to an isolated locale, where, free from the civilizing influences that normally constrain them, the development of conflict and prejudice could be studied. They created a summer camp they called the 'Robbers Cave' for 11-year-old boys in rural Oklahoma. The subsequent field experiment unfolded in three key phases:

- *Phase 1 – group attachment:* The boys arrived and were divided into separate groups, staying at opposite ends of the camp in cabins located far apart. For a week, they engaged in fun, recreational activities like swimming, sports and walking, in blissful ignorance of the other group's existence. They chose names for their groups – the 'Rattlers' and the 'Eagles', respectively – along with group symbols, flags and even T-shirts.

- *Phase 2 – intergroup competition:* Having established the kind of ingroup attachment and cooperation that is supposed to underlie prejudice and inter-group conflict, the experimenters then introduced the other theoretically important ingredient: competition between groups. They brought the two groups together to compete in a series of contests. Not only would the winning group receive a trophy, but its members would receive desirable prizes such as pocket knives. So, the interests of individuals were strongly aligned with the interests of their group. Almost immediately, there were signs of ethnocentrism – boys saw their own group as superior to the other. Similarly, conflicts arose between the groups almost straightaway. These were initially confined to taunts and name calling, but then shifted up a gear to include symbolic acts of intergroup violence; for example, one group burned the other's flag. These triggered a familiar tit-for-tat pattern of aggression and retaliation between groups. Groups raided each others' cabins and stole property, and used increasingly hostile language to describe each other, and displayed ever more intense ethnocentrism. It is worth noting that the Robbers Cave study was run three times, with different groups of boys in different summers. On two of these runs, the situation became so hostile and stressful that the study had to be abandoned on ethical grounds. (You may recall from Chapter 9 that the same fate befell the Stanford Prison Experiment and the BBC Prison Study.) On just the final run, the study proceeded to the final phase.

- *Phase 3 – intergroup reconciliation:* In this phase of the study, the experimenters attempted to douse the flames of conflict they had fanned so effectively. One technique they tried was to increase the amount of contact between the groups, for example by having them eat together. Consistent with much work on the **contact hypothesis**, which we will discuss in more detail in Chapter 12, merely increasing contact between the groups did not work and, if anything, worsened the situation. For example, shared mealtimes were treated less as an opportunity to iron out differences than to throw food at members of the rival group. In contrast, what really worked was the introduction of shared or **superordinate goals**. Each group retained a separate identity, but was posed challenges that could only be solved in cooperation with the other group. In one case, the experimenters secretly sabotaged the camp's water supply and had all the boys

Contact hypothesis Theory of prejudice reduction, which proposes that prejudice and conflict between groups can be reduced by bringing them together.

Superordinate goal A goal that two (or more) groups can aspire to but that can only be achieved by working together in cooperation.

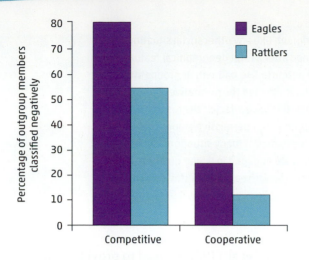

FIGURE 11.5 Superordinate goals reduce ethnocentrism
In the Robbers Cave study, the introduction of superordinate goals significantly reduced ethnocentrism. For example, the percentage of outgroup members who were classified negatively after cooperation was much lower than the percentage of outgroup members who were classified negatively after competition.
Source: Data from Sherif et al, [1954]1961

work together to repair it. On another occasion, the boys all had to work together to pull a broken-down truck out of some mud – using a rope that had earlier featured in a competitive game of tug-of-war. The effect of working together was to reduce the ethnocentrism and intergroup hostility that had so dominated life in the camp before. For example, the percentage of outgroup members who were rated negatively after cooperation was significantly lower than the amount classified negatively after competition (see Figure 11.5). Some boys even struck up friendships with members of the other group.

The essential findings of the Robbers Cave study have been widely replicated (Fisher, 1990). The study has been highly influential in social psychology, especially as the flagship for realistic group conflict theory and its descendants (e.g., Stephan and Stephan, 1985). Its influence also extends far beyond social psychology. Although we hope you have not had an experience as aversive as the Robbers Cave, there is a good chance that you have undergone some of the 'team-building' exercises that it and similar studies have inspired. These are widely used by organizations such as schools, sports clubs and corporations to foster ingroup cooperation and prevent or defuse intergroup conflict. Although they may sometimes feel forced and 'cheesy', the evidence suggests that they are generally effective in enhancing relations within groups (Blake and Mouton, 1961; Klein, DiazGranados, Salas et al., 2009).

One of the great strengths of the Robbers Cave study, like many of the iconic studies in social psychology, is its resemblance to the real-life situations from which spring many problematic social behaviours. The boys were immersed in an unfolding situation that engaged a range of intense emotions and motivations, and fostered dynamic social relationships (see Figure 11.6). This richness is invaluable but comes at a price – it is difficult to tease out the influence of any given causal factor. Which of the many conditions of the Robbers Cave field experiment were necessary, and which if any were sufficient (that is, enough on their own), to bring about the various forms of conflict and ethnocentrism that arose? In particular, the Robbers Cave study left an important question unanswered – can socially significant displays of prejudice and ethnocentrism arise even when groups are not locked into a zero-sum, competitive situation? Is it enough simply for people to be in an intergroup context?

© MACMILLAN AUSTRALIA

FIGURE 11.6 Robbers Cave study of intergroup relations Sherif et al.'s Robbers Cave study demonstrated how prejudice and conflict can arise from the creation of a competitive environment.

Time to reflect The normative climate of a social psychological experiment, like any other social situation, is affected by language. Sherif et al. told the boys that their camp was named after a local geographical feature, but in fact there was no Robbers Cave in the vicinity. The boys chose, and were permitted, to name their groups after predatory animals – rattle snakes and eagles. How might these choices have affected the normative climate of the camp? What other kinds of names might have been chosen and how might this have affected the results of this experiment? Can we see the experimenters' choice of name for the camp, and their permissive stance to the boys' choices of group names, as a 'demand characteristic'? Finally, reflect on the names of many situations, systems and groups in real life. For example, many countries in the West claim that they are engaged in a 'war on drugs', army units are often given names like 'the Desert Rats' and so on. To what extent can we see these as strategic choices designed to affect the behaviour of people in these situations?

The minimal group paradigm

The classic minimal group study by Tajfel et al. (1971) seemed to provide an answer to the question left open by Sherif et al.'s Robbers Cave study. The main aim of the study was to examine whether merely placing people into different social categories can generate ethnocentrism and problematic intergroup relations. A further aim of the study was to re-examine whether prejudice and conflict are necessarily motivated by the desire to procure as many resources for the ingroup as possible. Tajfel et al. asked a sample of British schoolboys to evaluate unfamiliar and unattributed paintings, and then divided them into two groups. One group was told that they had preferred paintings by the artist Kandinsky, whereas the other was told that their preference was for Klee. In fact, participants' assignment to these groups was entirely random and had nothing to do with their evaluations of the paintings. The participants knew that everybody had been categorized, but did not know which of the other boys belonged to the Kandinsky or the Klee groups.

Thus, Tajfel et al. (1971) had created *minimal groups*, based on an apparently trivial (in fact, bogus) difference, lacking history, common goals or indeed any prospect of a common future, and independent of interpersonal friendships. To test whether the boys would discriminate even on the basis of this minimal group basis, Tajfel et al. told them that they were to participate in a decision-making task. Each boy was given several opportunities to assign points to two other boys, on the understanding that the points would be converted into real money at the end of the experiment. These two boys were known only by their code number and group membership: one was always in the Kandinsky and one in the Klee group. The decision maker was asked to choose from a matrix of allocations.

The first key finding was that boys assigned more points to ingroup than to outgroup members. This seemed to show that merely belonging to a group is, indeed, enough to produce ingroup favouritism. The second key finding was that in their striving to favour ingroup members in *relative* terms, participants were prepared to sacrifice some of the points they assigned to the ingroup in *absolute* terms. For example, imagine that a boy can choose to either give 17 points to the ingroup and 21 to the outgroup member, or 18 to the ingroup and 23 to the outgroup member. Neither of these choices is attractive because they entail giving less to the ingroup member. But the first choice is less unattractive, because the ingroup

Minimal group paradigm
Experimental manipulation that tests the effects of mere categorization on behaviour.

member is relatively worse off by only 4 points, rather than 5. Typically, participants will opt for this allocation, even though it gives the ingroup member 1 less point in absolute terms. To paraphrase a familiar expression, people will cut off their own group's nose to spite another group's face. Figure 11.7 provides an illustration of the possible allocations that can be made in the minimal group paradigm.

In a typical study using the minimal group paradigm, participants are asked to circle the numbers on each line to indicate the resources they would like to allocate to the ingroup and the resources they would like to allocate to the outgroup. The numbers typically signify money. The numbers vary from matrix to matrix and different matrices are used in different studies, but this is an example:

Ingroup member	1	2	3	4	5	6	7	8	9	10	11	12	13	14
Outgroup member	14	13	12	11	10	9	8	7	6	5	4	3	2	1

From an analysis of how participants distribute points across a number of different matrices like the one above, it is possible to determine which of the following is a participant's preferred strategy in allocating resources:

- F – fairness: the most equal allocation
- MD – maximum difference: the most ingroup-biased allocation which makes the ingroup member most well off relative to the outgroup member, regardless of the absolute number of points they receive
- MIP – maximum ingroup profit: the allocation which gives the ingroup member most points, regardless of how much the outgroup member receives
- MJP – maximum joint profit: the allocation that awards the highest number of points (regardless of the difference between the groups)
- FAV – favouritism: employment of MIP and MD

FIGURE 11.7 The possible allocations in the minimal group paradigm

This study has been replicated hundreds of times with variations across many settings (Diehl, 1990). Its key finding seems to give strong support for the social identity approach to intergroup relations, especially to discrimination. Specifically, participants in these studies do not always seem to be interested in maximizing resources for their ingroup as realistic group conflict theory would suggest. Instead, they will often expend the resources of their group to ensure that it comes out ahead of other groups in relative terms. Just as social identity theory predicts, people seem to be pursuing the symbolic superiority of their group and are prepared to spend material resources in doing so. It is important to note that the minimal group paradigm is not a zero-sum situation – participants are not forced to divide a fixed total between two groups, but can choose allocations that involve a higher or lower total (in our example above, the first option entails a total of 38 points, and the second 41 points). In contrast, a zero-sum situation means that one cannot give relatively less to the outgroup without also giving absolutely more to the ingroup. Thus, it is impossible in these situations, unlike Tajfel et al.'s (1971) study, to disentangle the two motives. This is a great strength of the minimal group paradigm and probably mirrors many real-life situations in which groups stand to make mutual gains if they can find ways to cooperate with each other. Now, read the Critical focus box that further explores the minimal group paradigm.

Question to consider Reread question 1 at the start of the chapter. What social psychological processes may lead to such extreme homophobic beliefs?

CRITICAL FOCUS

The minimal group paradigm

Despite its success, the minimal group paradigm has been critiqued on a number of grounds.

1 *Is the minimal group paradigm too minimal?*
An obvious critique of the minimal group paradigm is that it is different from most everyday group contexts, and therefore lacks ecological validity (see Chapter 1). Real groups tend to have a history and a future, tend to feature bonds between their members that are created by ongoing interactions, or are based on within-group similarities and between-group differences that appear to be meaningful to participants. The stakes are generally much lower in the minimal group studies, where participants typically allocate tokens or tasks, than in real-life situations where intergroup relations have enduring and often profound consequences.

These charges cannot be denied, but the question is how important they are. The point of the minimal group paradigm was precisely to create an experimentally controlled situation in which the effects of merely being categorized could be studied in isolation from other factors. This scientific requirement means that the experiments must necessarily be different from many real-life situations in which the various aspects of group life go hand in hand. And, it is always important when evaluating a particular methodology to compare the results it produces with those from other types of research. If other studies, which do not share the limitations of the research in question, produce similar results, then we have converging evidence for its conclusions. In this case, experiments with groups that have an enduring history have revealed much the same pattern of ingroup-favouring allocations as in Tajfel et al.'s (1971) study (e.g., Amancio, 1989; Mullen, Brown and Smith, 1992). Brown's (1978) field study also showed that in real-life wage negotiations, groups of workers were prepared to reduce their own wage settlements in order to ensure that other groups did not receive more. Each of these studies may be criticized on various grounds, but together, precisely because they have different strengths and weaknesses, the similar results they have produced are rather compelling.

2 *Is the minimal group paradigm not minimal enough?*
Another, less intuitive critique of the minimal group paradigm is that it is not sufficiently minimal: participants may imagine that their assignment into categories reflects some underlying psychological characteristic. For example, our preference for different artists may seem to say something about how open-minded, conservative and sensation-seeking we are. In many minimal group studies, participants are even instructed that a range of unspecified psychological differences distinguishes people from the two groups (e.g., Elder, Douglas and Sutton, 2006). This raises the possibility that observed patterns of intergroup relations in these experiments do not stem from the mere fact of categorization but also require that these categories are seen to have some deeper meaning. However, anticipating this criticism, researchers have created groups that are yet more minimal, in which groups are merely called 'X' or 'Y' and participants are explicitly told that their assignment to groups is entirely random. Even under these conditions, ingroup favouritism is to be found (e.g., Billig and Tajfel, 1973).

3 *Is the minimal group paradigm subject to demand characteristics?*
Another criticism of the minimal group paradigm refers to the ever present danger of demand characteristics (see Chapter 1). Critics such as Gerard and Hoyt (1974) point out that participants are likely to be aware that the experimenters are dividing them into groups with the clear expectation that this will affect their behaviour. They argue that, specifically, participants are likely to infer that they are expected to behave in a discriminatory way, given that groups are stereotypically expected to be competitive along 'us' and 'them' lines (rather like the 'group' heuristic below). The argument goes, participants are merely doing what they believe to be expected of them.

There are several things that can be said about this criticism. First, in some studies, the experimenters make their expectations explicit by telling participants that the norm in this situation is either cooperative or competitive. In these studies, there is little evidence that participants adhere to the norms that are presented to them (e.g., Billig, 1973). Second, recent studies have shown that categorization in minimal groups causes people to exhibit apparently automatic forms of intergroup favouritism that they find difficult, if not impossible, to control. For example, Ashburn-Nardo, Voils and Monteith (2001) demonstrated ethnocentrism following a minimal group manipulation in the Implicit Association Test – reaction times revealed that

▶

they associated negative words more readily with the outgroup and positive words with the ingroup. Performance on a task like this is less likely to be affected by demand characteristics than the explicit assignment of resources to ingroup versus outgroup members.

4 The group heuristic: they will scratch my back, so I am scratching theirs

Yamagishi and colleagues (Foddy, Platow and Yamagishi, 2009; Karp, Jin, Yamagishi and Shinotsuka, 1993; Yamagishi and Kiyonari, 2000; Yamagishi, Makimura, Foddy et al., 2005) have proposed an alternative to the social identity explanation of ingroup favouritism in the allocation of resources. In this 'group heuristic' account, participants' allocation of resources to ingroup members simply reflects their intuitive understanding of how groups work – not necessarily the desire to enhance their social identity. As we have noted, cooperation within groups and competition between groups is a common feature of human life, so much so that it would be surprising if people did not acquire some intuitive appreciation that people are generally helpful and fair within group boundaries, and relatively cutthroat across them. Further, human beings have lived in this way throughout most of their evolutionary history, so it is possible that they are biologically prepared to expect intragroup cooperation and intergroup competition (Cosmides, 1989; Cosmides and Tooby, 1992). Thus, people may give more to ingroup than to outgroup members because they have a generalized expectation that this is how people behave.

This interpretation was tested in a study by Karp et al. (1993). In the original study by Tajfel et al. (1971), participants were told that the people to whom they allocated resources would not be given an opportunity to reciprocate. However, they were led to believe that they would receive allocations from *other* ingroup and outgroup members. Karp et al. (1993) reasoned that, based on the group heuristic, participants would expect to receive more from ingroup than from outgroup members. Thus, they give more to ingroup members as a way of reciprocating the favourable allocations they expect to receive: a kind of 'thank you in advance'. In support of this idea, when Karp et al. (1993) made it clear to participants that their own reward would not be determined by other participants, ingroup favouritism disappeared: participants gave equally to ingroup and outgroup members. Here, there was no ingroup favouritism to expect and therefore to reciprocate.

If ingroup favouritism is based on a generalized principle of reciprocity, it also ought to disappear when people do not believe that their group identity is known to others. Your fellow group members cannot treat you especially well if they do not know that you belong to their group, so, as in the study by Karp et al. (1993), there is no favouritism to reciprocate. Indeed, when participants know others' group identity, but are told that their own group identity is unknown to others, ingroup favouritism disappears (Yamagishi et al., 2005). This alternative model poses a powerful challenge to the traditional interpretation of Tajfel et al.'s (1971) famous study and its many replications. However, it is too early to reject the social identity account of the minimal group paradigm altogether. One problem is that there is currently no direct evidence of the existence of the group heuristic. People behave *as if* they believed that generalized reciprocity is the norm within the ingroup, but there is no other, more direct evidence that they have this belief (Yamagishi et al., 2005).

Indeed, when St Claire and Turner (1982) asked participants to guess the results of minimal group studies, they significantly underestimated the extent of group bias. This raises doubts about whether people have a full heuristic appreciation that ingroupers will be more generous to them. That said, St Claire and Turner's (1982) participants were not actually in a minimal group situation. Instead, they were bystanders who merely had such a situation described to them. Given the low stakes, they may not have expended the same level of cognitive resources as people who find themselves in a real minimal group context (as we saw earlier in this chapter with Pendry and Macrae, 1994). This may have prevented them from fully understanding how people are likely to treat each other in such a context.

5 Dominance or identity? Some concluding notes

Both realistic group conflict theory and social identity theory can claim to be extensively supported by experiments in the laboratory and the field. Nonetheless, there are important questions about how the results of many of these experiments should be interpreted, and it is probably impossible to tell whether a winner has yet, will ever, or ought to emerge. This is partly because there is a lot of overlap and agreement between these two approaches to intergroup relations. As we have noted, both theories are strongly social, specifying how intergroup relations are affected by the social contexts in which people find themselves. Both theories are also concerned with the pursuit of groups' material as well as symbolic welfare, even if they emphasize them differently. This is not surprising: after all, the material welfare of a group and the esteem in which it is held are strongly linked. Material wealth is often considered to be a marker of esteem – groups that are doing well for themselves materially tend to be held in high esteem, as we shall see elsewhere (Chapter 14). Conversely, when a group is well regarded, it tends to prosper: its members are unlikely to be discriminated against and ingroup members show greater loyalty to it and a willingness to make sacrifices in its interests (van Vugt and Hart, 2004).

Questions

1   Using Google Scholar, or an academic database such as the Web of Science or PsycINFO, how many replications of the minimal group paradigm can you find?

2   Can you think of examples where groups have engaged in conflicts in which huge sacrifices appear to have been made by each group in a contest for a trivial prize?

3   Sacrificing resources for merely relative superiority – getting less overall to ensure that one gets more than an outgroup – would, on the face of it, seem to be counterproductive. However, is there a possibility that participants are playing 'a long game' – being prepared to pay a short-term price in order to accrue later rewards? What benefits might flow from ensuring the group gets more resources than the outgroup, even if it gets less resources in absolute terms?

4   Yamagishi et al. (2005) wrote that: 'The existence of the group heuristic … cannot be directly tested.' Is this true? Can you briefly outline a way in which it could be tested?

Stereotyping, prejudice and discrimination in different intergroup contexts

Relations between groups have, historically, taken different forms depending on the nature of the groups involved. For example, slavery has been a feature of race relations, but not relations between people of different age groups. Genocide has featured in relationships between religious as well as racial groups, but not in gender relations. Although the theories we have reviewed thus far in this chapter were not designed with any particular groups in mind, they nonetheless have much to say about the experiences of the many different groups who have confronted grievous forms of prejudice through the ages. But, additional theoretical assumptions are sometimes required to understand the particular forms of prejudice and discrimination that different types of groups have encountered. We now consider relations between gender, age and racial groups as examples.

Gender

It is possible to argue that gender is the most important of all intergroup contexts. All over the world, men and women are constantly interacting. Gender is always apparent, not only by virtue of the physical differences between men and women but also because of the different ways in which they speak, dress and act. The very survival of the species depends on successful cooperation between men and women, but relationships between these two groups are not always cooperative. And as both men and women – but especially women – recognize, women have generally been at the wrong end of the 'battle of the sexes' (Sutton, Douglas, Wilkin et al.,

2008). Worldwide, women are socially and economically disadvantaged relative to men on indices such as earnings, career and educational opportunities, freedom of dress and movement, victimization in sexual and domestic violence, and representation in political, business and religious leadership (e.g., López-Claros and Zahidi, 2005; Rhode, 1989). Nonetheless, they are generally seen as nicer than men, and are liked more, in a 'women are wonderful' stereotype (Eagly and Mladinic, 1994; see also Fiske, Cuddy, Glick and Xu, 2002). This apparent paradox – that women seem to experience less prejudice but more discrimination than men – is possibly the most distinctive feature of gender relations. It also illustrates that prejudice and discrimination do not always go hand in hand.

One reason that relations between gender groups differ from relations between other social groups is that they have been deeply affected by **sexism**. Sexism refers to beliefs about differences between men and women and the roles they perform. Typically, sexism not only includes beliefs about differences in the way men and women think, feel and act, but also includes beliefs about the appropriateness of these differences. Put differently, sexism does not just tell you *how* the genders differ, it also purports to tell you how they *ought* to differ. Thus, sexism, like, say, right-wing authoritarianism, is an ideology. However, sexism differs from the ideologies we have considered thus far, in that it is often rooted in ancient religious and cultural practices (Harris, 1991; Rhode, 1989; Stockard and Johnson, 1992), and is specific to relationships between genders, even if it is often correlated with other ideologies and social practices that have nothing directly to do with gender (e.g., Pratto et al., 1994).

There are different types of sexism, and much has been learned in recent years since the advent of the distinction between hostile and benevolent sexism, first made by Glick and Fiske (1996):

- **Hostile sexism** is a negative view of women characterized by the belief that they pose a threat to men's position.
- **Benevolent sexism** is an apparently positive view of women, in which they are seen as necessary for men's happiness, and, indeed, superior to men in many ways, especially morally (e.g., as more kind and pure).
- **Ambivalent sexism** contains both positive and negative attitudes to women.

Research on ambivalent sexism has shown that the distinction between benevolent and hostile sexism holds across many countries in many parts of the globe. Indeed, Glick and 30 colleagues (2000) ran a large-scale global survey and found that, across countries, hostile and benevolent sexism were generally positively correlated, but nonetheless emerged as separate variables when factor analyses were performed. In most countries, men endorsed hostile sexism more than women. Across countries, hostile but not benevolent sexism predicted negative stereotypes of women, suggesting that these variables are indeed functionally different. However, differences between men and women on benevolent sexism seemed to differ across countries. As shown in Figure 11.8, in countries where gender inequalities are especially strong according to UN figures, women endorsed

Sexism Beliefs about differences between men and women, the roles they perform, and beliefs concerning the appropriateness of these differences.

Hostile sexism Traditionally sexist view of women that is characterized by the belief that they pose a threat to men's position.

Benevolent sexism Apparently positive view of women in which they are seen as necessary for men's happiness, and superior in a number of ways (e.g., morality).

Ambivalent sexism Reconceptualization of sexism to take into account the fact that sexism can include both positive and negative attitudes at the same time.

benevolent sexism more strongly than men (e.g., Cuba, South Africa and Turkey). In countries where these gender inequalities are not so pronounced, men and women endorsed benevolent sexism roughly as equally (e.g., Australia and the Netherlands). This finding seems to support a key prediction of social identity theory – where status differences between genders are marked and stable, members of low status groups will engage in **social creativity** – that is, preserving a positive self-image by identifying and giving weight to dimensions on which they are superior to the high status group (Jetten and Spears, 2003; Oakes, Haslam and Turner, 1994).

Social creativity Preserving a positive self-image by identifying and giving weight to dimensions on which they are superior to the high status group.

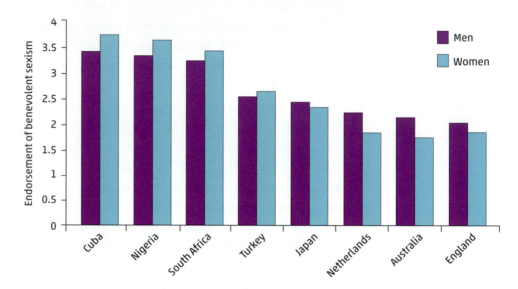

FIGURE 11.8 Endorsement of benevolent sexism in a selection of countries In most countries, men endorsed hostile sexism more than women, but in countries were gender inequalities are especially strong, women endorsed benevolent sexism more strongly than men.

Source: Data from Glick et al., 2000

As you've been reading this, you may be wondering, what's the problem? Surely benevolent sexism is a quaint, perhaps old-fashioned, but ultimately harmless view of women? Alternatively, you may be thinking, 'it is sexism – so what's 'benevolent' about it?' As Glick and Fiske (1996 p. 491) noted: 'some readers might view ... *benevolent sexism* as oxymoronic'. It is important to note that they were arguing that benevolent sexism is associated with overtly positive responses to women, not that it is good for them. Indeed, for Glick and Fiske (1996; Glick et al., 2000), benevolent sexism tends to justify women's consignment to a subordinate role. For example, if women are kind, pure and sensitive, they are presumably well equipped for nurturing roles and poorly equipped for the kinds of competitive and status-driven roles that are so richly rewarded. Thus, benevolent sexism tends to justify the status quo. As a result, women who endorse this ideology are less likely to try to change it.

A study conducted by Jost and Kay (2005) supports precisely this contention. Moving away from the correlational approach of Glick and his colleagues (e.g., Glick and Fiske, 1996; Glick et al., 2000), Jost and Kay adopted a priming procedure in which participants were experimentally presented with benevolent sexism items from Glick and Fiske's (1996) scale – specifically, items 8, 13, 19 and 22 (see *Try it yourself* later). Participants either indicated their agreement with each item or rated how ambiguously each item was worded (results showed that it did not

FIGURE 11.9 **Benevolent sexism** The belief that women need to be protected and revered by men is part of the concept of benevolent sexism.

matter which). This exposure to benevolent sexism caused women to endorse the status quo, indicating that society is fair, more than women who had been exposed to positive, but non-stereotypical statements about women (e.g., 'Men are less creative than women'). In fact, women exposed to benevolent sexism endorsed the status quo as much as men, whereas they normally endorse it much less than men. Exposure to hostile sexism had no effects on women's endorsement of the status quo. As Jost and Kay (2005, p. 504) note, their findings suggest that 'when it comes to maintaining inequality, honey is typically more effective than vinegar'. For their part, men were unaffected by exposure to any kind of sexism, tending to view the social status quo as being fine as it is (see also Sutton et al., 2008).

Exploring further Society routinely exposes people, and young children, to benevolent stereotypes of women. You may be interested to read about the ongoing debate concerning sexism in Disney films. Of course, the female characters in these films are generally pleasant, but they are also – almost without exception – subordinate to male characters. As an exercise, choose a Disney film (e.g., *Cinderella*, *The Little Mermaid*) and think about what happens in the film. What was the main female character like? What happened to her? What relationships did she have with the male characters? Knowing what you now know about sexism, are these depictions sexist? What might the consequences of these depictions be?

Research has revealed several other pitfalls of benevolent sexism for women. Moya, Glick, Exposito et al. (2007) found that Spanish women who were high in benevolent sexism found it more acceptable for husbands to give orders to their wives, as long as these orders had a protective justification (e.g., 'you should not drive, because it will stress you out'). Dardenne, Dumont and Bollier (2007) found that a sample of Belgian women became literally less intelligent immediately after being primed with benevolent sexism. Sutton, Douglas and McClellan (2011) found that benevolent sexists in the UK were more likely to indicate that they would refuse to serve pregnant women alcohol, cheese or even tap water. These results suggested that benevolent sexism may underlie the cultural impulse to restrict the freedoms of pregnant women in ways that may not be warranted by medical evidence. Abrams, Viki, Masser and Bohner (2003) found that individuals (whether men or women) who were higher in benevolent sexism were more likely to blame the victims of acquaintance or 'date' rape. Viki and Abrams (2002) found that benevolent sexists were especially likely to blame married women who were raped while on a date with another man, that is, whose infidelity violated positive, so-called 'benevolent' expectations of women. Rudman and Glick (2001) found that female job candidates who present themselves as highly agentic – ambitious and competent, for example – may suffer a *backlash* as a result of defying the kind, generous, nurturing stereotypes associated with benevolent sexism. As a result, such women tend to be rated as less warm and less likely to work well in a team.

Time to reflect The United Nations Development Programme annually reports statistics that provide an index of gender equality across the world. The gender empowerment measure (GEM) examines the degree to which women have achieved positions of status and power within a nation (e.g., women in government, managers of businesses). In cross-national comparisons, Glick et al. (2000, 2004) have shown that average benevolent sexism scores are negatively associated with the GEM. The same occurs for hostile sexism, and both effects are present irrespective of respondent gender. So, it seems that women have less status and power in nations where people score highest in benevolent and hostile sexism. Data from Glick et al. (2000) are presented in Figure 11.10 below. These are the results from 19 countries. Although not all significant, the correlations are high, suggesting that approximately 15–25 per cent of the variance is shared by sexism and objective gender inequality. Why do you think these relationships are so strong? What are the functions of hostile and benevolent sexism in maintaining, or reducing resistance to, inequality?

HS = hostile sexism
BS = benevolent sexism

FIGURE 11.10 Gender inequality across countries is significantly correlated with hostile sexism (HS) and benevolent sexism (BS)

Source: Data from Glick et al., 2000

Try it yourself Below are some example items from Glick and Fiske's ambivalent sexism inventory. This contains 11 items measuring benevolent sexism, and 11 for hostile sexism. The response scale for each item runs from 1 = disagree strongly, to 7 = agree strongly.

Three items measuring benevolent sexism are:

1 A good woman should be set on a pedestal by her man.
2 In a disaster, women ought not necessarily to be rescued before men (this item is reverse scored).
3 Women, as compared to men, tend to have a more refined sense of culture and good taste.

Three items measuring hostile sexism are:

1 Once a woman gets a man to commit to her, she usually tries to put him on a tight leash.
2 Feminists are not seeking for women to have more power than men.
3 Women are too easily offended.

The ambivalent sexism inventory is available online (and is included in an appendix to Glick and Fiske, 1996). Locate it, and complete it. Calculate your mean hostile and benevolent sexism score. Remember to reverse score the appropriate items where disagreement indicates higher sexism. In these cases, change 5 to 0, 4 to 1, 3 to 2, 2 to 3, 1 to 4, and 0 to 5. Find means for hostile and benevolent sexism from at least one study. How do your scores compare? What does this say about you? Do you think your results on this test would be different if you had no idea what the test was about?

Source: Glick and Fiske, 1996. Reproduced with permission from Peter Glick and Susan Fiske

As well as providing ideas about how the genders ought to differ, sexism also suggests *why* they differ. Like the racist ideologies we are about to encounter, sexism tends to appeal to biology to explain the characteristics of each gender, especially women. In Western thought, women have long been associated with nature and their behaviour attributed to bodily rather than purely mental processes, in contrast to men who are seen to have transcended their biology through the powers of reason and self-control. For example, the term *hysteria* (from the Greek, *hystera*, meaning womb), used to describe an extreme and irrational state of emotional distress, originated from the ancient idea that madness in women was caused by the womb wandering about the body.

Arguably, this ancient idea has a modern equivalent in exaggerated popular stereotypes about the influence of the menstrual cycle on women's mood (Chrisler and Levy, 1990; Walker, 1995). Stereotypically, women are irascible and irrational for a few days prior to menstruation. This 'premenstrual syndrome' has even been used as a legal defence by women facing criminal charges (Chrisler, 2002). But for women, the downside of this notion of premenstrual syndrome is that they are likely to be taken less seriously. And it even shapes the way that women see themselves, as McFarlane, Martin and Williams (1988) have shown. In their diary study, women were asked to report on their mood for 70 days. These concurrent, daily reports did not show a significant deterioration in mood at that time of the month. However, at the end of the study, they were again asked to indicate what their moods had been over that time – without access to their concurrent reports. These retrospective estimates were not terribly accurate; in particular, women wrongly 'remembered' being in a negative mood at the premenstrual phase of their monthly cycle. As we saw in Chapter 2, our self-knowledge, especially when we are making retrospective guesses about our thoughts, feelings and intentions, is not very reliable (Nisbett and Wilson, 1977; Ericsson and Simon, 1980). In place of reliable memories, we make inferences about ourselves based partly on our expectations – in this case, stereotypes about the menstrual cycle. In memory, therefore, stereotypes have the capacity to *seem* to be accurate even when they are not.

Objectification The view of women as being represented by their bodies.

The sexist tendency to equate women with their bodies is also apparent in an extensive research literature on **objectification**. Objectification occurs when women are viewed as if their bodies are capable of representing them (Frederickson and Roberts, 1997), that is, as if women were their bodies. One manifestation of objectification is 'face-ism': the tendency for women's faces to be less prominent than men's, and their bodies to be more prominent than men's, on TV and in print media like newspapers and magazines (Archer, Iritani, Kimes and Barrios, 1983). Objectification of women changes the way they are evaluated and treated. In a striking example, Heflick and Goldenberg (2009) had participants write about Sarah Palin, John McCain's running mate in the US presidential election of 2008. Participants were asked to describe either the positive and negative traits of 'this person' (in the control condition), or 'this person's appearance' (in the experimental, 'objectification' condition). Participants led to objectify Sarah Palin in this way rated her as less competent and even reported a reduced intention to vote for the McCain/Palin combination in the coming election. This manipulation had a similar effect on ratings of the Hollywood actress Angelina Jolie, although she is not (at least, not yet) running for office – so Heflick and Goldenberg did not ask participants whether they intended to vote for her.

Question to consider Reread question 2 at the start of the chapter. Despite Mark's positive feeling about women, is he less likely or more likely to discriminate against them?

© IMAGE SOURCE

According to objectification theory (Fredrickson and Roberts, 1997), objectification not only changes the way women are treated by others, but also changes the way women themselves think, feel and act. Women frequently experience objectification, for example when they are the object of a prolonged gaze by a male observer, or are flattered on the basis of their appearance. This chronic experience can cause them to engage in self-objectification, that is, to monitor their appearance, anticipating that this will be a major factor in how they are seen by others (Calogero, 2004). Although men engage in self-objectification too (e.g., Strelan and Hargreaves, 2005), the sexist tendency to objectify women more often means that women are likely to do it more often, and with more adverse consequences. For example, Fredrickson, Roberts, Noll et al. (1998) had women try on either a swimsuit or a sweater. As predicted, wearing the swimsuit elicited higher levels of self-objectification, with the result that women in this experimental condition experienced more shame about their appearance, restrained their eating, and did worse on a test of mathematical ability. Self-objectification has also been linked to the severity of striving for thinness among young women in eating disorder clinics (Calogero, Davis and Thompson, 2005). A study of English university students found that when women were primed with benevolent sexism, they became more accepting of the status quo between men and women, which in turn caused them to objectify themselves (Calogero and Jost, 2011).

Race and ethnicity

Relations between people of different racial or ethnic backgrounds have always had a different nature from gender relations. In part, this is no doubt because racial or ethnic groups are not necessarily in contact with each other, and do not need to cooperate with each other on the same daily basis as the gender groups. Not only is contact between different racial groups less frequent but it is often more recent, historically speaking. Indeed, much of the early contact between different ethnicities and racial groups arose from exploration, invasion and mass migration, which tends to bring people into the kinds of competition for resources described by realistic group conflict theory (Sherif, 1966). Ethnocentrism in its strongest sense is often a feature at least in the early history of relations between racial and ethnic groups. Those who look, dress and act very differently, who have different ideas about what is morally acceptable and what is disgusting, and who speak an unintelligible language may seem less than fully human (Sumner, 1906).

This dehumanization of racial groups tends to legitimate even the worst actions against them (e.g., Haslam, 2006). Thus, relations between racial groups have been characterized by outbursts of organized, large-scale violence seen elsewhere only in some conflicts between religious groups. You are probably familiar with the expressions 'ethnic cleansing', where attempts are made to forcibly move whole peoples from an area, and 'genocide', where attempts are made to eliminate them altogether. Slavery has also been a recurrent feature of relations between racial groups. You may have read H.G. Wells' famous 1898 novel, *The War of the Worlds*, or seen a film adaptation of it. Quite astoundingly, the following appears on the first page of Chapter 1:

> And before we judge them [the Martians] too harshly, we must remember what ruthless and utter destruction our own species has wrought, not only upon animals, such as the vanished Bison and the Dodo, but upon its own inferior races. The Tasmanians, *in spite of their human likeness*, were entirely swept out of existence in a war of extermination waged by European immigrants, in the space of fifty years. Are we such apostles of mercy as to complain if the Martians warred in the same spirit? [emphasis added]

Even in this book, which was meant as a critical parody of British colonialism, we see voiced the quintessentially racist idea that some races are superior to others, and more striking, that some races are not fully human, possessing only a 'human likeness'. And we see documented the fact that these people, seen not fully as people, were exterminated by European settlers – the last 'full-blooded' member of this group died in 1876 (Ryan, 1996).

Historically, racism has been underpinned by the belief that not only are people of different races different, especially in terms of their intelligence, but that these differences are underpinned by genetic differences. For a long time, researchers, especially in Britain and Europe, looked for physiological differences between racial groups, for example in cranial capacity, and even the number of folds in the cortex of the brain (see Gould, 1996). These tests proved inconclusive, but the hold of the eugenics movement, which advocated that differences in intelligence and behaviour between groups (such as the races and the social classes), over the popular imagination remained strong – nowhere more so than in Nazi Germany, where it contributed to the policy of extermination of Jews, Gypsies, people with learning disabilities and some Slavic people.

For much of the 20th century, over much of the world, overtly racist ideas and policies predominated. In some countries, most famously South Africa and many US states, there was a policy of forced racial segregation, where people of colour were excluded from restaurants, public facilities and even residential areas. In other countries, such as Australia, people were excluded from the vote on the basis of race, and mixed-race children were forcibly removed from indigenous families in order to be raised in a white cultural milieu. Such racist policies are at odds with the egalitarianism that these same countries' laws and even constitutions have been based upon. If 'all men are created equal', as stated in the 1776 US Declaration of Independence, then how is race-based slavery and segregation possible? This ambivalence and tension has always been a defining feature of racism (Allport, 1954; Walker, 2001). One way of resolving the tension is to suppress, inhibit or control racism (Devine, 1989). There is extensive evidence that people who do not consciously endorse or possess racist attitudes nonetheless display unconscious or implicit racism.

Another way to resolve the tension between egalitarianism and racism is to find a way to justify distinctly unegalitarian policies – as did the racist, eugenic notions that some races are inferior to others and therefore worthy of inferior opportunities. As we shall see in Chapter 14, there are a number of social psychological mechanisms available to human beings in order to help then justify behaviours, beliefs and social systems that conflict with their cherished notions of what is right and wrong (e.g., Jost and Banaji, 1994; Lerner, 1980).

One can also resolve the tension between racism and fair-mindedness in the way that one talks. As we saw in Chapter 1, discourse analysis (Billig, 1997; Potter, 1996) is a qualitative research method designed precisely to illuminate how people use talk strategically. Potter and Wetherell (1987) employed this method in their study of racism in the context of relationships between Pakeha (people descended from European settlers) and Māori (the indigenous people) in New Zealand. In the following extracts, a Pakeha interviewee expresses rather egalitarian, anti-racist sentiments:

- and [in my class] I had this child who said 'What would happen if you got a whole lot of Maoris living next to you?' and I said to him 'that's a very racist remark and I don't like it'
- I don't like them [racist jokes] I don't find them amusing
- The extended family situation's brilliant, they've got this lovely idea that a child born out of wedlock would have to be the best sort of child because it was obviously born in love … I think their way with children is wonderful … They've got a lot to show us I think.

But, interviewees did not always express such noble views, as shown in the following extracts:

- the ridiculous thing is that, if you really want to be nasty about it, and go back, um, the Europeans really did take over New Zealand shore, and I mean that Maoris killed off the Morioris beforehand, I mean it wasn't exactly their land to start with, I mean it's a bit ridiculous. I think we bend over backwards a bit too much. [The notion that Maoris killed off an earlier indigenous population of Morioris on mainland New Zealand is a fiction, once taught in New Zealand schools, that seemed to justify European colonialism. In fact, Morioris were based on the distant Chatham Islands.]

And this is the part that I think is wrong with, a bit wrong with the Maoris as well there, the problems they have, they're not willing, I mean it's a European society here and they've got to learn to get in and work, otherwise it's, I mean you can't tell them to go back to where they came from.

Now, you may be surprised to learn that *all* the extracts presented here – the first few anti-racist ones and the latter two more apparently racist and defensive quotes – were taken from *the same interviewee*, in *the same interview*. This illustrates how inconsistent people will be as they embed potentially racist statements in anti-racist talk, allowing them to express racist views while defusing the charge that they are racist.

Recent experimental work has similarly shown that people express more prejudice after **moral credentialing** – that is, having an opportunity to demonstrate that they are not prejudiced. In one study, Monin and Miller (2001) gave Princeton undergraduates a chance to select a candidate for a position in a hypothetical consulting firm. When the standout candidate was either a Black person or a woman, Monin and Miller (2001) reasoned, then participants had been given a chance to 'hire' this person and thus to display their moral credentials, 'proving' that they are not prejudiced. Later, these participants, compared to control participants whose 'star' candidate had not been a minority group member, were *less* likely to hire a fictional Black applicant for a job as a police officer. Having 'proved' themselves to be non-prejudiced, participants appeared to be more willing to discriminate against another Black candidate. It is notable that participants were more willing to discriminate against Black candidates for the police position after hiring a Black *or* a female candidate. They seemed to feel that hiring any sort of minority candidate is sufficient to show that their later hiring decision is not racist. In a subsequent study, Monin and Miller showed that people were more willing to reject a minority job applicant even when their earlier decision to hire a minority candidate for a different position was unknown to others. Apparently, moral credentialing has this effect because people want to prove to themselves, rather than to other people, that they are not prejudiced (see also Harber, Stafford and Kennedy, 2010).

The kind of moral unease about racism illustrated by Monin and Miller's (2001) findings appears to be one of its defining features. It is also entirely consistent with theories of **modern racism** (Dovidio and Gaertner, 1998). According to this theory, the growing unacceptability of racism has not caused racism to disappear but has driven it underground. In place of 'old', overt racism, a modern, subtle variant has appeared, in which racism is expressed in forms and in situations that make it appear to be socially acceptable and consistent with the prevailing sense of fair play. For example, instead of advocating that all ethnic migrants should be deported to their countries of origin, modern racists will agree that ethnic migrants *who have committed serious crimes* should be deported. This qualifier deflects the charge that their opinion is racially motivated (Meertens and Pettigrew, 1997). Ironically, from their review of research, Gaertner and Dovidio (1986) conclude

Moral credentialing
Demonstrating one's credentials (e.g., to be not prejudiced) often means that people will express more prejudice.

© STOCKBYTE

Modern racism Subtle and less aggressive form of prejudice based on race.

Aversive racism Inner conflict between an egalitarian view and racist impulses can be aversive, such that people avoid contact with specific racial groups.

that White people in the USA may find the inner conflict between their egalitarian values and racist impulses to be aversive – causing them to avoid interactions with Black people for fear of experiencing discomfort and unease. This **aversive racism** can be seen as an example of the intergroup anxiety that people experience in their dealings with outgroup members.

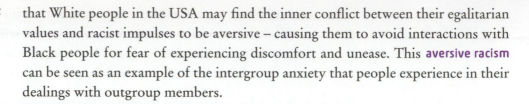

Question to consider Now, reread question 3 at the start of the chapter. Why do you think racism is so difficult to eradicate? This is a good question to consider before reading Chapter 12.

Exploring further Think of some films you have seen that have involved the theme of racism. Have more films dealt with old-fashioned racism than modern racism or vice versa? Why do you think this might be?

Age

Ageism Prejudiced attitudes about a person or group because of their age.

Ageism is a widespread form of prejudice and older people face many forms of negative stereotyping, discrimination and ridicule (Age Concern, 2006; Nelson, 2002). It is an intriguing form of prejudice because the perceiver is bound to become a member of the target group – barring some disaster (Nelson, 2005). This allows it to be self-fulfilling in a unique way: it can negatively affect the ageing process itself, causing the perceiver to be weaker, more infirm and more dependent as they age. Thus, if a perceiver is ageist, they are ultimately more likely to become a prototypical example of their negative view of the elderly. This hypothesis may seem like a long shot, but the evidence in favour of it is surprisingly abundant and compelling. Ageism may be as bad for you as smoking. Combating ageism may not only be a matter of social justice but also public health.

Consider a study by Levy, Zonderman, Slade and Ferrucci (2009). These researchers drew on data from the Baltimore Longitudinal Study of Aging, which started in 1968 and tracks a large and renewing sample of adults from adulthood into old age. Levy et al. considered only those respondents who were less than 50 years old at baseline, who had not experienced a cardiovascular event (e.g., heart attack or stroke), and who completed a measure of ageist stereotypes as they entered the study. This widely used, reliable and valid measure included items such as 'old people are helpless' (Tuckman and Lorge, 1953). Results were startling in their support for the 'ageism is bad for you' hypothesis. Levy et al. compared the health outcomes of participants who entered the study endorsing ageist stereotypes more than average with those who endorsed them less than average. Fully 25 per cent of the first group, who endorsed ageist stereotypes, turned out to have a cardiovascular event in the subsequent 30 years. In comparison, only 13 per cent of the second group of participants, who did not endorse these stereotypes as strongly, experienced a cardiovascular event. If you are thinking like an experimentalist, you may have been thinking: 'Probably the people who originally

FIGURE 11.11 Association between age stereotypes and time until people experience an initial cardiovascular event The percentage of people who had not experienced a cardiovascular event over time was related to the positive and negative age stereotypes held by the respondents. In particular, participants who held positive age stereotypes were less likely to experience cardiovascular events.

Source: Data from Levy et al., 2009

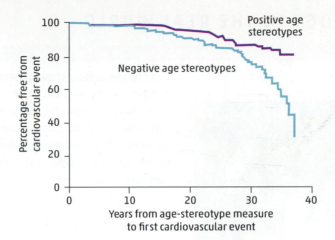

endorsed ageist stereotypes of ageing were different, perhaps less educated and less healthy, from those who did not endorse them.' Of course, correlation does not entail causation. But Levy et al. (2009) controlled for these and a host of other factors, including age, body mass index and family history, obtaining the same results (see Figure 11.11).

ETHICS AND RESEARCH METHODS

Ageist stereotypes and cardiovascular events

Although Levy et al. (2009) controlled carefully for third causes, and employed a longitudinal design, it is difficult to infer that ageist stereotypes really caused the cardiovascular events because the study was correlational. Can you think of experimental approaches to this problem? In other words, how can you try to affect people's stereotypes about ageing and the aged, in order to observe effects of these stereotypes on health outcomes?

An effective manipulation might not just be a way to test theory; it might also be an extremely helpful intervention that, if widely implemented, could improve the health and wellbeing of thousands, if not millions, of people.

- You will need a control group: what kind of control would be best?
- You will need an experimental group.
- What ethical and scientific issues are raised by attempts to increase participants' ageism; and decrease participants' ageism?
- What are the most effective ways to get stereotypes to change?

Have a go at doing this yourself. You might want to consult Chapter 13 on the reduction and mitigation of prejudice, and Chapter 6 on persuasion techniques. What are the best dependent measures? Is it necessary to measure cardiovascular events, or are you also interested in measures such as blood pressure, exercise behaviours, dietary behaviours and so on? What can your choice of measures tell you about *why* ageism is linked to negative health outcomes?

SOCIAL PSYCHOLOGY IN THE REAL WORLD

Homophobia

© PHOTODISC

Thus far, we have talked about sexism, ageism and racism as specific forms of prejudice. Another significant form is prejudice against homosexuals. *Homophobia* has not always been a problem in society. Indeed, the Romans were tolerant of different sexual orientations and other civilizations and cultures have been permissive of non-heterosexual orientations over the years. However, few would disagree that prejudice against homosexuals is pervasive in many societies today – one reason perhaps being the rise of Christianity and the development of different norms regarding sexual behaviour. It is also interesting to note that it was as late as 1973 that the American Psychiatric Association removed homosexuality as a psychiatric disorder from its listing.

Of course, attitudes have generally become more positive over the years but significant anti-gay sentiments still exist. For example, the recent introduction of the Civil Partnership Act in 2004, which gave same-sex couples in the UK the rights and responsibilities identical to civil marriage, met with general opposition from the public – 86 per cent of respondents to a Northern Ireland consultation document on the Civil Partnership Act opposed the introduction of the Act (Office of Law Reform, 2004).

It is important to consider some of the antecedents and consequences of anti-gay prejudice.

Questions

1 Anti-gay prejudice is associated with stronger Christian attitudes (e.g., Batson, Schoenrade and Ventis, 1993). What other variables do you think anti-gay prejudice would be correlated with?

2 What impact do you think the AIDS virus has had on attitudes towards gay men?

3 Take some time to search the literature on homophobia. Is anti-gay prejudice against same-sex male couples the same as against same-sex female couples? What are the similarities and differences?

4 List some of the consequences of anti-gay prejudice. How are they similar or different to racism, ageism and sexism?

Vicious cycles in intergroup relations

In Chapter 12, we will deal at length with how relations between groups can be improved, reducing unwanted phenomena such as prejudice, discrimination and intergroup conflict. We think it is useful to close this chapter by considering why these phenomena are so intractable, in order to highlight just how immense and important is the challenge that confronts social psychologists. Of particular interest is something you may have noticed while reading through this chapter: stereotyping, prejudice, discrimination and other undesirable intergroup dynamics appear to have a remarkable ability to perpetuate themselves.

Vicious cycles in social cognition

One way stereotypes and prejudice perpetuate themselves is by affecting – we might even say 'hijacking' – the way people process social information. Stereotypes can affect the way we think so that the information we are receiving from the environment *seems* to confirm them, even when it does not, objectively speaking. In Chapter 3, we covered the *correspondence bias* – the tendency to infer that a person who acts a certain way must possess the trait that is associated with that behaviour (as opposed to seeing the behaviour as a product of the situation, for example). One manifestation of this bias is **spontaneous trait inference**, shown when people take longer to correctly decide they have not seen a trait (e.g., 'kind') in a set of sentences presented earlier (e.g., 'Leigh donated money to charity'). Wigboldus, Dijksterhuis and van Knippenberg (2003) showed that when sentences convey stereotype-inconsistent information (e.g., 'the girl hits the saleswoman'), people made much weaker spontaneous trait inferences than when the sentences were consistent with stereotypes. In a subtle but pervasive way, it seems, stereotypes perpetuate themselves by causing us to attribute stereotype-consistent traits to people more than stereotype-inconsistent traits. Dunning and Sherman (1997) went so far as to describe stereotypes as 'inferential prisons', which constrain our perceptions so that we are condemned to experiencing a world in which even completely unwarranted stereotypes seem to be true.

Researchers have also uncovered a rather cruel way in which prejudice can gain a kind of self-perpetuating momentum. Groups who experience prejudice, discrimination and oppression come, over time, to be associated with prejudice, discrimination and oppression. Uhlmann, Brescoll and Paluck (2006) used the Implicit Association Test (IAT) and showed that African Americans were mentally associated (by a sample of White Americans) with oppression (the words were *oppressed*, *brutalized*, *dominant* and *powerful*). The more strongly participants associated African Americans with oppression, the more implicit prejudice they showed against this group on another IAT. Uhlmann et al. followed up this correlational study with experiments in which participants viewed pairings of the name of a fictional group, the 'Noffians', with words related to either oppression or privilege. Participants who had learned to associate Noffians with oppression were, as a result, more prejudiced towards them in a later test of implicit prejudice. Even people who appraise the negative experiences of a group in an egalitarian way – seeing them as symptoms of oppression – may, as a result, associate this group with oppression and thus unconsciously devalue them. As the saying goes, mud sticks. In a supreme irony, thinking that mud has been thrown unfairly at a group may foster prejudice towards that group.

Exploring further Srull and Wyer (1979) reported perhaps the most famous demonstration of the power of stereotypes to influence social judgement, in ways that make them 'seem' true. Using Google Scholar or a similar database, find the full reference for this article, and obtain a list of the many papers that have since cited it. Many of these papers will investigate how stereotypes distort people's thinking in ways that make incoming information appear to 'fit' or support the stereotype. Identify three different ways in which this happens.

Vicious cycles in social emotion

Just as people experience emotions such as fear and anger towards each other, group members can experience emotions towards other groups (Smith, 1993,

Spontaneous trait inference
People sometimes spontaneously infer others' traits from their behaviour without intending to, or being aware.

1999). According to intergroup emotions theory (Mackie and Smith, 2002), the precise nature of these intergroup emotions will depend on factors such as the relative power and status of the groups. For example, Mackie, Devos and Smith (2000) found that when people perceive their ingroup to be powerful, they are more likely to experience anger towards an outgroup. On the other hand, if they perceive their group to be relatively weak, they are more likely to fear outgroups. People who experience anger rather than fear are more likely to take offensive actions against an outgroup, whereas those who experience fear rather than anger are more likely to attempt to avoid the outgroup. Intergroup emotions have the capacity to dampen intergroup aggression and conflict. For example, Maitner, Mackie and Smith (2007) found that the experience of intergroup guilt about acts of aggression by the ingroup reduced support for further acts of aggression.

However, they also have the capacity to play an important role in irrational cycles of tit-for-tat aggression between groups. In the same studies, Maitner et al. found that the experience of *satisfaction* after acts of aggression by the ingroup led to increased support for further acts of aggression. Further, it does not require great powers of deduction to realize that from the perspective of the victim group, the experience of anger in response to being attacked is likely to motivate retaliatory aggression, especially if the victim group feels powerful enough to strike back (Mackie et al., 2000).

Exploring further Using Google Scholar, PsycINFO or Web of Science, find papers on 'collective guilt' (social psychological work on this topic began with Doosje, Branscombe, Spears and Manstead, 1998). A quick survey of the abstracts of these papers should give you a feel for the helpful and harmful role this intergroup emotion can play.

Anxiety is one of the most important types of intergroup emotion and also plays a crucial role in perpetuating unhealthy, conflictual relationships between groups. Its role in intergroup relations was highlighted by Stephan and Stephan's (1985) **intergroup anxiety model**. This model was originally formulated with racial or ethnic groups in mind, but could in principle be applied to many other intergroup contexts as well. According to this model, people expect negative outcomes when they interact with, or even anticipate interacting with, outgroup members. Specifically, they may expect:

Intergroup anxiety model
Model arguing that people expect negative outcomes when they interact with, or anticipate interaction with, outgroups.

1 Negative psychological consequences, such as feeling embarrassed or uncomfortable
2 Negative behavioural consequences, such as being exploited or dominated by outgroup members
3 Negative evaluations by outgroup members, for example a White person may fear being seen as racist, a Black person may fear confirming widespread prejudices
4 Negative evaluations by ingroup members, for example being seen as disloyal or too friendly to the outgroup.

These negative expectations represent threats, and these threats elicit anxiety. The threats and hence anxiety may be exaggerated when people have strongly stereotypic views of the outgroup (Allen, 1996), perceive that the outgroup poses a threat to the ingroup (Stephan, Boniecki, Ybarra et al., 2002), lack knowledge about the outgroup (Britt, Boniecki, Vescio et al., 1996) or have little previous experience of interaction with its members (Stephan, Diaz-Loving and Duran, 2000).

Anxiety is not 'all bad' and may have some positive effects on intergroup relations. For example, it may cause people to attend closely and with interest to their interaction partner. The fear of being seen as racist may sometimes motivate people to act in a more friendly, positive way (Harber, 1998; Littleford, O'Dougherty Wright and Sayoc-Parial, 2005). However, anxiety is not 'all good' either and can be expected to have several negative effects on the interaction and its downstream consequences.

For one thing, even when anxiety may have motivated people to behave in a friendly, positive way, the effort is stressful (Ickes, 1984), reduces their enjoyment of the interaction (Shelton, 2003), and may impair their effectiveness as communicators (Stephan and Stephan, 1985). Anxiety may also energize and heighten any negative thoughts and feelings towards the outgroup (Stephan, Stephan and Gudykunst, 1999). Also, as we have seen, when members of minority groups fear confirming negative stereotypes of their group, their task performance tends to suffer (Steele and Aronson, 1995). Another downside of anxiety is that it can interfere with self-control (Easterbrook, 1959; Stephan and Stephan, 1985). Alas, as we shall see in Chapter 12, some kind of self-control seems essential in the reduction of prejudice. Thus, the anxiety arising from interactions with outgroup members may make people unable to stop themselves from exhibiting prejudiced responses.

To test this last idea, Amodio (2009) had White American participants talk about race with either a White or a Black interviewer (see also Lambert, Millimet and Slottje, 2003). Later, their saliva was sampled to obtain a measure of cortisol, a hormone associated with anxiety. Also, they completed a measure of race bias known as the *weapon identification task* (Payne, 2001). In each trial of this task, participants were presented with a Black or White face on a computer screen, then a picture of a gun or a tool. The task was to identify the object. In this task, pairings of Black faces with weapons and White faces with tools are stereotype congruent; pairings of White faces with guns and Black faces with tools are stereotype incongruent. Given a congruent pairing, both automatic race bias and the motivation to control prejudice should lead participants to respond accurately. That is, they should correctly identify guns after seeing them primed with Black faces, and correctly identify tools after White faces. In contrast, incongruent pairings cause controlled processing and automatic race bias to pull participants in opposite directions. For example, an automatic race bias might lead participants to wrongly indicate 'gun' after they have seen the pairing of a Black face with a tool. On the other hand, the motivation to control prejudice will tend to lead them to correctly indicate 'tool'.

Results showed that among participants who had been in the interracial interview, increased levels of cortisol were indeed associated with reduced ability to control race bias. In contrast, cortisol did not affect performance in the weapon identification task by participants who had dealt with a same-race (White) inter-viewer. This finding supports the predictions of the intergroup anxiety model – anxiety, as indexed by cortisol, would appear to disrupt attempts to control biased responding. On the other hand, self-reported anxiety was not related to race bias. Thus, the physiological rather than the phenomenological aspects of intergroup anxiety appear to be most responsible for the disruption of people's ability to control race bias.

Time to reflect Do social neuroscience methods such as those used by Amodio (2009) enable researchers to pin down a causal pathway where self-report measures fail? What are some of their weaknesses?

Vicious cycles in social behaviour

Stereotypes need not be false. As you have been reading about stereotypes, preju-dice and so on, it may have occurred to you that many stereotypes contain at least a kernel of truth. Indeed, research shows that they do. For example, the 'women are wonderful' stereotype may overstate the case, but studies do show that, on average, and in many (but not all) situations, women are somewhat more consci-entious, less egocentric and more nurturing (e.g., Andreoni and Vesterlund, 2001; Feingold, 1994; Hoffman, 1977). These findings are not necessarily comfortable to contemplate. But, putting aside our political preferences, it is of vital importance for any scientist to be honest, with others and with themselves, about what the data show. Equally, it is important to examine *why* stereotypes sometimes contain a kernel of truth. Do gender or racial groups sometimes behave differently because of innate biological differences? Or do political and social psychological factors contribute to these differences (Campbell, 1967)?

This is where the self-perpetuating properties of stereotypes are so important. Stereotypes have the power to change people's behaviour in ways that seem to verify the stereotypes. One of the most powerful, striking and cruelly poetic cases of this power has been uncovered by research on the **stereotype threat** phenomenon (Steele, 1997). Ironically, when people's performance is being tested, and they belong to a group that is stereotypically not expected to do well, they become anxious that they may confirm the stereotype. This anxiety interferes with their performance – causing them to fall precisely into the trap that they were so anxious to avoid. Thus, girls do worse in maths tests when they are made aware of the stereotype that girls are not as good at maths as boys (Keller, 2002; Spencer, Steele and Quinn, 1999; Steele, 1997). Black students do worse in scholastic aptitude and IQ tests when they are made aware of their supposed academic inferiority (Steele and Aronson, 1995). Older adults' cognitive performance declines when reminded of ageist stereotypes (Abrams, Eller and Bryant, 2006), and the scholastic aptitude of students from poorer backgrounds declines when they are reminded of their socioeconomic background (Croizet and Claire, 1998).

Stereotype threat Fear of being judged in terms of a stereotype and negatively fulfilling the stereotype. Stereotype threat leads to poorer performance on a task.

FIGURE 11.12 **Will this girl pass her maths test?** If this girl is told that boys are better at maths than girls, how well will she do on a maths test? The concept of stereotype threat suggests that she will perform even worse when made aware of this threatening expectation.

Stereotype lift The reverse of stereotype threat. Fulfilling a positive stereotype leads to enhanced performance.

Just as stereotypes stand in the way of success for groups that are not expected to do well, they give a boost to groups that are expected to succeed. Thus, if individuals are made aware of a negatively stereotyped outgroup, their own test performance is actually enhanced, in a phenomenon that Walton and Cohen (2003) called **stereotype lift**. Further, as we have seen in Chapter 3, racist stereotypes about the alleged hostility of Black people (in the USA) have the potential to become self-fulfilling, because the activation of these stereotypes can cause people to act in a more hostile way, with the result that the people they interact with become more hostile (Bargh, Chen and Burrows, 1996). Further, people are conscious of the 'backlash' that is often experienced by people who buck stereotypical expectations, such as women who act in assertive and fearless ways (Rudman and Fairchild, 2004). This consciousness motivates people to conform to expectations, and so appear to confirm the stereotype. Thus women may portray fearfulness, and men fearlessness, because they want to be evaluated positively (e.g., Sutton and Farrall, 2005, 2008).

Question to consider Now that you know about stereotype threat, reread question 4 at the start of the chapter. Jot down some reasons for the women's behaviour. How did it work in each specific situation? What were the stereotypes and what impaired the women's performance?

Chapter summary

In this chapter we have covered the bases of stereotypes, prejudice and discrimination. We have considered how these phenomena play out in relations between different groups, such as those differentiated on the basis of gender, race, religion and age. Finally, we have considered some of the vicious cycles in intergroup relations. Specifically, we have learned that:

- Stereotypes are simplified, but widely shared beliefs about the characteristics of groups and their members. Prejudice is a negative affective reaction to a group. Discrimination is the negative treatment of a person based on their group membership.
- The cognitive miser approach argues that people use stereotypes as shortcuts because they have limited memory resources to deal with everyone as an individual. Also, stereotypes and prejudice may stem from faults in human thought and memory.
- Typically, people have less contact with minorities and outgroups than they do with majorities and their own groups. Because they have fewer opportunities to learn about such groups, this leads to an overestimation of the

undesirable behaviours of minority group members. This is called the illusory correlation bias.
- The mere act of categorization can also distort the way people think about members of groups and the groups themselves. Placing objects into categories changes the way they are perceived, such that differences between categories are maximized and differences within categories are minimized.
- However, stereotypes stem not only from human limitations, but also from what people want to think. Dogmatic individuals (those with the tendency to be able to tolerate mutually inconsistent beliefs by isolating them from each other in memory) tend to be more prejudiced. Likewise, people with high personal need for structure (indicating a preference for structure in most situations) and those high in need for cognitive closure (indicating a desire for definitive answers to questions) stereotype more.
- Ideology also plays a part in stereotyping and prejudice. Further, people who possess an authoritarian personality and score high in right wing-authoritarianism tend to be more prejudiced.

- Social dominance orientation (a preference for hierarchy and for one's own group to be dominant) is associated with higher levels of stereotyping.
- Two theories of intergroup relations – social identity theory and realistic group conflict theory – differ from the cognitive, personality and ideological approaches to the study of intergroup relations by focusing on processes that occur at the group level.
- Stereotyping, prejudice and discrimination occur in a vast array of intergroup contexts. One example is gender, where attitudes towards women contain ambivalent (hostile and benevolent) stereotypes. Further, women are objectified, or viewed as if their bodies are capable of representing them. Such objectification changes the way that women think, feel and act.
- Another example is race, where members of different racial groups are often dehumanized, or stripped of their human qualities. Such dehumanization legitimizes negative actions towards racial groups. There are different forms of racism and more traditional (hostile) racism has given way to a more subtle (modern) racism.

- Ageism is a widespread form of prejudice and older people face many forms of negative stereotyping, discrimination and ridicule. Another example of prejudice that we discussed in this chapter is homophobia.
- We then discussed some of the vicious cycles in intergroup relations. Specifically, stereotypes can affect the way people think so that the information people receive from the environment seems to confirm them, even when it does not. People experience strong emotions towards others groups and, in particular, anxiety plays a crucial role in perpetuating unhealthy, conflictual relationships between groups.
- Stereotypes may not always be false and may contain a 'kernel of truth'. Such stereotypes are powerful and the process of stereotype threat, awareness of a stereotype, and anxiety about fulfilling the stereotype may lead to impaired performance.

We now know about the factors that contribute to stereotyping, prejudice and discrimination. We also know about the consequences of these important social psychological processes of intergroup relations. In Chapter 12, we focus on improving intergroup relations.

Essay questions

At the beginning of the chapter, we asked you to consider these questions:

1 You may have heard of various homophobic hate groups that have a strong presence on the internet. Members of these groups stage homophobic demonstrations and, in one specific case, picketed memorials for soldiers killed in the Iraq War, taking the view that these soldiers' deaths are a form of punishment against the US for its tolerance of homosexuality. Which of the social psychological processes described in this chapter may be contributing to the behaviour of these groups?

2 Mark, a manager for a large bank, genuinely feels very warm towards women. He thinks that men should cherish, protect and revere women. Do Mark's attitudes mean that he is less likely than other male managers to discriminate against women, for example to oversee unequal pay?

3 Many countries invest a lot of effort and money into counteracting racism. Why is racism so resistant to eradication?

4 What common principle might be illustrated by these two scenarios? 1. Suriya is in her sixties but has not aged well and has health problems one would normally associate with someone significantly older. 2. Danni does quite well in mathematics in class but gets a poor mark whenever she sits a mathematics exam.

Having read this chapter, these questions could also be framed as the following essay questions, which you can attempt in preparation for your examinations:

1 Discuss some of the social psychological processes that can explain the behaviour of hate groups.

2 Overview the theory of ambivalent sexism and, referring to research evidence, describe some of the consequences of hostile and benevolent sexism.

3 With reference to social psychological theory and research, explain how racism is resistant to eradication. What do we know about prejudice reduction from social psychology?

4 Overview the research to date on stereotype threat and stereotype lift phenomena. What are the consequences of each and when are each more likely to occur?

Further reading

Brewer, M.B. (2007) The social psychology of intergroup relations: Social categorization, ingroup bias, and outgroup prejudice. In A.W. Kruglanski and E.T. Higgins (eds) *Social Psychology: Handbook of Basic Principles* (2nd edn). New York: Guilford Press. Extensive coverage of research on intergroup relations, prejudice and discrimination.

Brown, R.J. (1995) *Prejudice: Its Psychology* (2nd edn). Oxford: Blackwell. Comprehensive coverage of the topic of prejudice, including the major theoretical approaches and analyses of recent research developments.

Brown, R.J. (2000) *Group Processes* (2nd edn). Oxford: Blackwell. Clear and engaging introduction to the study of relationships between and within groups.

Dovidio, J.F., Hewstone, M., Glick, P. and Esses, V.M. (eds) (2010) *The Sage Handbook of Prejudice, Stereotyping and Discrimination*. London: Sage. Multidisciplinary and cutting-edge set of chapters on the state of research and future avenues for research on prejudice, stereotyping and discrimination.

Oakes, P.J., Haslam, S.A. and Turner, J.C. (1994) *Stereotyping and Social Reality*. Oxford: Blackwell. Scholarly, comprehensive review of social psychological theories and research on stereotyping. Outlines the authors' own research programme in this area, from a social identity perspective.

Spears, R., Oakes, P.J., Ellemers, N. and Haslam, S.A. (1996) *The Social Psychology of Stereotyping and Group Life*. Oxford: Blackwell. Comprehensive overview of major theories and research on stereotyping and intergroup relations.

Yzerbyt, V. and Demoulin, S. (2010) Intergroup relations. In S.T. Fiske, D.T. Gilbert and G. Lindzey (eds) *Handbook of Social Psychology* (5th edn, vol. 2, pp. 1024–83). New York: Wiley. Up-to-date overview of the area of intergroup relations.

 Visit the companion website at www.palgrave.com/psychology/suttondouglas for access to a wide range of resources to help you get to grips with this chapter.

Applying social psychology

Understanding and improving boys' academic achievement

In this chapter we reviewed quite a lot of literature on sexist stereotypes and gender role attitudes, with particular attention to their negative consequences for women. However, women are by no means alone in being adversely affected by social understandings of gender.

One context in which men and boys appear to be suffering is in educational achievement. There is overwhelming evidence that, globally, girls outperform boys academically. Girls have narrowed, closed and reversed the historical gender gap in academic performance within school settings (e.g., DfES, 2007; van Houtte, 2004; West, 1999).

One such study was conducted by the Organisation for Economic Co-operation and Development (OECD, 2010). Under the auspices of its Programme for International Student Assessment, it assessed the educational outcomes of 15-year-old children in the 34 OECD countries, including the USA, Canada, Australia, the UK, France, Spain, Germany and Italy, as well as 41 partner countries. Although boys outperformed girls in maths by an average of 12 points, girls significantly outperformed boys in reading in every participating country by an average of 39 points, which is the equivalent of an average school year's progress (OECD, 2010). Thus, boys' advantage in maths is considerably smaller than their disadvantage in other core subjects.

Further, in some countries, there is evidence that boys are disadvantaged even in maths and science. For example, throughout elementary, middle and high school in the USA, girls obtain higher grades than boys in all major subjects, including maths and science (AAUW Educational Foundation, 1998;

Pomerantz, Altermatt and Saxon, 2002). Similarly, recent statistics from England's Department for Education (DfE) reveal that girls outperformed boys on reading, writing, maths and science at Key Stage 1 (age 5–7) through to GCSE stage (age 16), where 58.8 per cent of girls achieved five or more A*–C grades (including English and Maths) compared to 51.1 per cent of boys (DfE, 2010a, 2010b).

In addition to obtaining higher grades, research suggests that girls receive more referrals to gifted programmes (Bianco, Harris, Garrison-Wade and Leech, 2011), are more self-disciplined, and overall progress better scholastically than boys (Duckworth and Seligman, 2006; Mathews, Morrison and Ponitz, 2009). Girls also go on to outnumber men in university degree programmes. For example, women outnumber men 58:42 in UK universities (Higher Education Statistics Agency, 2011), and 57:43 in the USA (Snyder and Dillow, 2011). In contrast, boys represent the majority of referrals to special education services, as well as suspensions and expulsions from school (DfE, 2009, 2011).

Imagine that you have been asked to provide psychological consultancy on the causes and possible remedies of this problem. How can boys' performance be improved, without negatively impacting on girls' performance? In particular, your brief is to suggest causes and solutions that have not yet been identified in the literature.

There are many possible solutions to this problem, but let us focus on one that is directly relevant to some of the important social psychological principles we have been discussing in this chapter. In particular, we discussed how stereotypes can be self-fulfilling. Recall that stereotype threat – the anxiety that one's performance will be viewed through the lens of adverse stereotypes – undermines the academic performance of Black people, older adults, children from poorer economic backgrounds. Although these are all relatively disadvantaged or even stigmatized groups, stereotype threat can also affect relatively high status groups. This applies when such groups are the target of specific stereotypes suggesting they are inferior at a particular task. For example, White participants underperform in athletics when the task is said to reflect natural athletic ability (Stone, Lynch, Sjomeling and Darley, 1999). Also, men underperform on social sensitivity and affective processing tasks when they are reminded that women outperform them in this domain (Koenig and Eagly, 2005; Leyens, Desert, Croizet and Darcis, 2000).

We saw in the chapter that stereotype threat has been successfully applied to study women and girls' performance in maths and science, which is held by traditional and probably outdated stereotypes to be inferior (e.g., Keller, 2002; Spencer, Steele and Quinn, 1999; Steele, 1997). Has it been applied to study boys' academic performance? Is this a promising

approach, and how could it be achieved? If stereotype threat does contribute to boys' academic underachievement, how could this inform interventions to boost their performance?

1 *Search the literature: Has this idea been tested before?* How many articles can you find that have examined how stereotype threat can worsen women and girls' academic performance? How many have examined stereotype threat effects on men and boys' academic performance? Is stereotype threat really a new possible explanation of boys' academic underachievement? (Remember your clients have asked you to explore causes and remedies that have not been investigated before.)

2 *Search the literature: Are boys stereotypically inferior to girls academically?* Stereotype threat happens when people feel that their performance might be viewed through the lens of unfavourable stereotypes. Thus, in order for stereotype threat to afflict boys, it is necessary for there to be a stereotype that boys are in some sense academically inferior to girls. Is there any evidence of such a stereotype in the research literature? Bear in mind that evidence that boys are *actually* underachieving does not count. What you need is evidence that boys are *perceived to be* underachieving.

3 *Search the literature: Are boys aware of such a stereotype?* Not only stereotypes but also meta-stereotypes are required for stereotype threat to occur. This is because people must be aware that they may be viewed through the lens of unfavourable stereotypes.

4 *Sketch studies* If you did not find studies in questions 1, 2, or 3, then think about how you might design studies to address these 'blind spots' in knowledge. Take a look at the coverage of stereotypes, meta-stereotypes and stereotype threat in the chapter, and look up some articles to see how the studies are done. Outline each of your studies in no more than 150 words, plus references.

5 *Think about interventions* Assuming stereotype threat does turn out to contribute to boys' academic performance, how might stereotype threat be reduced? Can you find studies that reduce or eliminate stereotype threat effects for other groups, and borrow their ideas? Or are there other interventions in this chapter that you can adapt to reduce stereotyping, meta-stereotyping and other forms of intergroup anxiety that you can adapt? Outline your ideas in no more than 300 words, plus references where appropriate.

Blind spot in social psychology

The contested nature of social identity

A great deal of research and theory on intergroup relations assumes that individuals are identified with social groups; that is, they are placed into social categories by themselves and others. This is seen as a necessary condition for stereotyping, prejudice, discrimination and other forms of intergroup relations. Once we see ourselves as a member of a social group, it is then possible for us to identify ourselves with that group, to act in its interests, and, where it seems necessary, to act against the interests of other groups. Therefore, most studies on intergroup relations create contexts in which it is clear and uncontroversial, to all involved, what groups participants belong and do not belong to.

However, as we suggested at the start of this chapter, real life may not always be like that. People may actively resist categorization – into a particular group, or into any group. People may not agree on categorization. I may see myself as a feminist, but some of my friends may see me as a sexist. As we know, people often preface apparently racist marks with classic disclaimers such as 'I'm not a racist, but ...', as if they were aware of, and attempting to obstruct, the potential that they would be categorized as a racist. Many, if not all, social categorizations tend to be rather subjective in nature and are *socially constructed* by processes of enactment, display and negotiation that sometimes do, and sometimes do not, result in consensus (Dixon and Durrheim, 2000; Howard, 2000). We would like you to draw on your intuition and life experience to think about this issue and come up with some suggested answers to the following questions. The more suggestions you can think of, the better. Then, it is possible to search the literature to see which of your ideas have been acknowledged in the literature and which remain relatively unexplored.

1   We each belong, or can be seen to belong, to a huge number of social categories. On a sheet of paper, list 10 categories to which you would see yourself as belonging. Start each line with 'I am a ...' or 'I am an ...'. On a second sheet of paper, write 10 statements about yourself that describe some of your qualities as you see them. Start each line with 'I am' and do not place yourself into categories with 'a' or 'an'. Which task took you longer? Which made you feel more anxious? Finally, can you think of any categorical boxes that you think others might want to place you into, but with which you would you not necessarily agree. Start each line with 'Others may see me as a/an ...'. What is it that makes you uncomfortable about being categorized in these ways?

2   Why are people sometimes reluctant to accept categorization? You might want to think about categories such as 'English', 'British', 'White', 'Black', 'smokers', 'bisexuals', 'feminists', or 'left-wingers'.

3   Imagine that you are a participant in a minimal group paradigm experiment. Participants in this experiment are assigned, at random, either to the 'blue group' or the 'red group'. Participants are told that 'blue groupers' are tolerant, whereas 'red groupers' are intolerant. Do you see yourself as a tolerant or intolerant person? Which categorization would you therefore be more willing to accept? And which you would you be more likely to reject? Why?

4   Imagine that Said is the son of North African migrants to the Netherlands. He is devoutly Islamic, a big supporter of Feyernoord Football Club, and talks at length to like-minded friends about the corrupt and tyrannical foreign and domestic policies of Western nations and how these might be violently overturned. What possible social categories could Said be categorized as, based on this minimal information? What kinds of people might want to place him into each category and, in doing so, what might they be trying to do, consciously or unconsciously?

Student project

Marginalizing prejudice

Brad Carron-Arthur studied as an honours student at the Australian National University, under the supervision of Professor Michael Platow. His research explores a newly identified type of prejudice called 'marginalizing prejudice'.

My topic and aims

My project investigated the psychological processes underpinning the phenomenon of marginalizing prejudice. Marginalizing prejudice occurs when a person treats a fellow ingroup member as if they are included in the group, but are not truly 'in' because they lack some essential feature of the group. This feature could be a particular ethnicity or place of birth. For example, a person might be considered Australian because they are a citizen, but not fully Australian since they are not of European ancestry, or were not born in Australia. In contrast to traditional conceptions of prejudice, such as old-fashioned racism, which simply involve discriminatory exclusion, marginalizing prejudice is a dualistic prejudice – one in which inclusion and group membership are promised with one hand and at the same time withdrawn by the other.

Marginalizing prejudice is a relatively understudied phenomenon and the aim of my project was to identify some broad factors that may provide a plausible explanation for its occurrence. One cognitive factor (a framing effect) and one motivational factor (a manipulation of procedural fairness) were chosen for this task.

When my supervisor first described marginalizing prejudice to me, I was particularly excited by the thought of working on something that no one else had studied before. Research really grabs you when you can conceptualize a phenomenon and you get the sense that it really exists, only you don't have any proof so it is up to you to demonstrate its existence through empirical research.

My methods

Participants in this study were Anglo Australian-born citizens. Their task was to judge whether to include 24 targets within the group 'Australians'. The targets, who were all Australian citizens, varied systematically on four factors (ethnicity, country of birth, gender and intellectual prestige of occupation). To judge their inclusion in the group, participants were asked to indicate which targets they would like to see included in an Australian citizens' assembly. Two variables were manipulated in the study. Some of the participants were instructed to select those targets they would like to see included, while others were instructed to select the targets who they would exclude. Orthogonal to this, some of the participants were told that the citizens' assembly would be instrumental in making changes to the nation, while others were told that its opinion would be heard but would not be instrumental.

My findings and their implications

Theoretically, inclusion and exclusion judgements should yield complimentary sets. That is, those who were not included should also have been excluded. Psychologically, however, this does not necessarily hold true. The main finding of this experiment was that some of the applicants were often neither included when participants were asked who they would include and nor were they excluded when participants were asked who they would exclude. That is, they are not truly 'in' the group but they are not 'out' either. In effect, they are being subjected to marginalizing prejudice.

Interestingly, this finding was also dependent upon the other experimental factors. For example, citizens who were not born in Australia were simply 'out' rather than being marginalized, but only if they were also non-Anglo and the assembly was non-instrumental – this reflects overt discrimination (e.g., old-fashioned racism).

This research has important theoretical implications. Previous conceptions of groups have held that group boundaries are either permeable or impermeable to new group members, but not both. This study demonstrates that it is possible for a person's psychological representation of a group to be simultaneously open to new group members in the sense that they are not actively excluded, but nor are they truly accepted in the sense that they are not actively included either. They are relegated to the margins of the group.

The project was presented by my supervisor at the Society of Australasian Social Psychologists conference in Adelaide in April 2012.

My journey

After completing my honours in psychology, I took the following year off to run across Australia (5,000 km) Forrest Gump style. It took four months and I raised over $35,000 for mental health research. At the time of writing, I have just returned home and I am currently applying for a scholarship to undertake postgraduate study overseas in a similar field to the current research.

In order to take the step up to conducting research of the scope that is expected in your honours year, it is necessary to engage with the literature on the theoretical level. Reading vast amounts of literature and reducing it into your own study is incredibly daunting if you can't see the (theoretical) wood for the trees (details). This is a skill that my supervisor helped foster in me and I am glad because I now see the ideas behind the words in anything I deal with rather than getting bogged down in the details.

My advice

In the lead-up to your thesis, read widely, not just what you are required to. Fascination, inspiration and novel solutions to problems puzzling psychologists come from a breadth of knowledge and experience. Once you have picked a topic that most interests you, read with depth. Read everything in that area until you even understand the full historical progression of research and where everything fits into the field. You will see all the gaps in understanding. Coming up with solutions will take both breadth and depth of understanding.

Part

4 Applying

Improving intergroup relations is a primary concern for social psychologists. In this chapter we consider the major strategies to do so, from changing the way individuals from different groups are treated, intergroup contact, strategies based on categorization, strategies based on values, and media and communication. Finally, we consider political strategies for improving intergroup relations, such as intergroup apologies, reparations, communication and negotiation. By the end of this chapter, you will have a comprehensive knowledge of social psychologists' progress on this important issue.

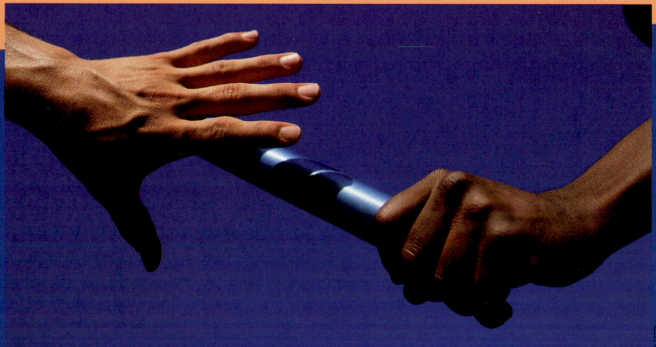

© GETTY

Topics covered in this chapter

- Tokenism and affirmative action
- Intergroup contact
- Categorization-based approaches
- Values-based approaches
- The media and real-world conflict
- Intergroup apology and forgiveness
- Communication and negotiation
- Collective action

Key features

Critical focus Reservations and unanswered questions about contact

Ethics and research methods Reducing real-world intergroup conflict

Social psychology in the real world Tokenism and the election of Barack Obama

Applying social psychology Intergroup emotions

Blind spot in social psychology Intergroup apologies

Student project The effectiveness of imagined contact

Questions to consider

1 Lisa asks her boss why her co-worker, Bill, has been promoted and she has not. She suspects that Bill (who has the same qualifications and experience) is being favoured because he is male. Lisa's boss argues that gender is not an issue in their company, which includes two females in senior roles and one who has recently been promoted. What social psychological phenomenon could this be an example of? What might be the future prospects for Lisa working with her current boss?

2 Fred has no Asian friends but his friend Jake has many Asian friends. Are Fred's attitudes towards Asians likely to be better or worse for knowing his friend Jake?

3 In a conversation about racism and prejudice, Sharon argues that these phenomena would disappear if everyone forgot about colour, cultural differences and what makes people different, and focused instead on what everyone has in common. Is this likely to work?

4 Jarek believes that an apology can solve any conflict. Is he right?

As we saw in Chapter 11, relations between social groups are fraught with problems. But social groups cannot live in perfect isolation. Trade, invasion, colonization and immigration have always been features of human life that have brought people from different tribal, ethnic and cultural groups together. As recent centuries and decades have passed, economic, technological and political forces have accelerated this process. At the time of writing, Marseille, France's second city, was predicted to become the first Muslim-majority city in Western Europe (Dickey, 2012). However, this prediction overlooks the fact that until the territories of modern Spain were recovered by Christian armies, cities such as Cordoba and Granada were inhabited mostly by Muslims. Faced with the historical inevitability, the present fact and the future increase of diversity, how are we to avoid conflict and inequality between social groups? More positively, how can social groups be encouraged to join forces, to work together to solve common problems, and even to capitalize on their diversity (Crisp and Meleady, 2012; Crisp and Turner, 2011)?

In this chapter we consider the major strategies for improving intergroup relations that have been considered by social psychologists:

1 Change the way individuals from different groups are treated. This is the essence of techniques known as tokenism and affirmative action.
2 Increase the extent and manage the nature of contact between individuals from different groups.
3 Change individuals' perceptions of the boundaries between groups and the meaning of group differences. This is the basic idea behind categorization- and cooperation-based approaches.
4 Change the values and ideologies that underpin intergroup relations, so that diversity and tolerance are embraced as positive values, and prejudice is seen as a bad thing.
5 Encourage strategies for reducing intergroup conflict at a political level by the joint action of different groups. This involves truth and reconciliation, intergroup apologies and reparations, negotiations and treaties.
6 Collective action by the disadvantaged groups in society to improve their position. This strategy does not assume that increases in goodwill and cooperation are always required for improvements in intergroup relations, but focuses on the elimination of inequality and disadvantage.

Tokenism and affirmative action

The causes of social inequality are often much too old, deep-rooted and large scale for any individual, organization or even government to hope to deal with in one fell swoop. However, it is within everyone's power to make small gestures that are of help to individual members of disadvantaged groups. For example, if you are an employer taking on a new staff member, perhaps you can try to give a job to a minority group member ahead of other, similarly qualified applicants.

FIGURE 12.1 An example of tokenism? Has the employer 'proved' they are not prejudiced by hiring this woman? How would she feel if she knew she was being hired because of her gender?

Tokenism Performing positive actions towards members of minority or disadvantaged groups as a reaction to the discrimination they suffer. Tokenism may be a genuine attempt to counteract prejudice, or an attempt to deflect the charge of prejudice.

If you are a teacher, perhaps you can make a special attempt and go out of your way to give more pleasant, less critical feedback to minority group members (Harber, 1998). This process of favouring a member of a minority group over a member of a majority group in isolated episodes is the essence of **tokenism** (see Figure 12.1).

On the surface, this may look like a promising attempt to reduce prejudice. After all, a person is consciously going out of their way to provide a positive outcome for someone within a minority group. However, one problem with tokenism is that it can be used, consciously or unconsciously, as a means to disguise one's prejudices. This makes it easier, psychologically, to engage in subsequent acts of discrimination. This point was made clearly in studies conducted by Monin and Miller (2001). In these studies, participants who were given the opportunity to hire well-qualified Black applicants for fictional jobs were more willing to discriminate against women or Black people in subsequent hiring decisions, having already 'proved' that they are not prejudiced. Interestingly, it did not matter whether participants thought anybody else knew they had previously hired a Black job applicant. Participants who had 'proved' to themselves, but no one else, that they were not prejudiced were more willing later to discriminate when it seemed legitimate to do so. These findings suggest that tokenism can be motivated purely by the desire for people to prove *to themselves* that they are decent, fair-minded and unprejudiced people. Thus we can see tokenism as an example of the desire to self-enhance, as we explored in more depth in Chapter 2. This effect is known as moral credentialing (Monin and Miller, 2001). If an individual displays a good track record of egalitarianism, they can establish an unconscious ethical or moral licence that actually increases their likelihood of making less egalitarian decisions later (Figure 12.2). Recently, Kouchaki (2011) demonstrated that the moral credentialing effect occurs even when people have observed a member of their own ingroup being egalitarian, that is, they display a vicarious moral licensing effect. Here, participants who had seen a member of their own ingroup displaying non-prejudiced hiring behaviour were more likely to reject another minority group member (in this case, an African American man) for a job that was stereotypically suited for majority members.

FIGURE 12.2 Moral credentialing A study by Monin and Miller (2001) suggests that people who have been given the opportunity to 'prove' to themselves that they are not prejudiced were more likely to discriminate against minorities in subsequent situations. This moral credentialing occurs even when others do not know about the individual's egalitarian track record.

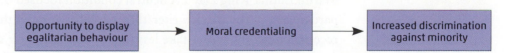

| Opportunity to display egalitarian behaviour | → | Moral credentialing | → | Increased discrimination against minority |

A good deal of research has centred on whether tokenism is helpful, even to the individuals who directly receive its apparent benefits. One downside of

Affirmative action A collective name for policies designed to promote the employment of people from disadvantaged minority groups.

tokenism is clear – people are perceived as less competent by their colleagues if it is known that they were hired as part of an **affirmative action** policy (Heilman, Block and Lucas, 1992). Such policies, which include employment 'quotas' where organizations are required to hire a certain percentage of minority members, are forms of tokenism because they involve granting positive outcomes to minority members. Employment quotas are now illegal in many countries. Such policies may also mean that organizations fail to take more important steps towards equal opportunities. Having 'made the effort', leaders of organizations may feel there is nothing else that needs to be done. Findings also suggest that another downside of affirmative action policies is that the employees suffer reduced self-esteem, motivation and job satisfaction if they perceive they are 'tokens', who have been hired because of their group membership such as their race or gender (Chacko, 1982). Clearly, tokenism can be harmful both to the organization, which may ultimately fail to be progressive, and its employees, who ironically feel worse because of the organization's efforts.

Another harmful face of tokenism may be close to home for you as a student in higher education. Studies have shown that teachers may mark identical work more highly and make fewer critical comments if they believe it is by a Black as opposed to a White student (Fajardo, 1985; Harber, 1998). At first glance, this so-called **positive feedback bias** may not look like a big problem; surely, positive feedback is nice? However, the problem is that bias can harm minority students' education. Specifically, it can cause students to misdirect their efforts at improvement (Massey, Scott and Dornbusch, 1975), and it can demoralize them, by suggesting that praise reflects their race rather than their achievement (Crocker, Voelkl, Testa and Major, 1991). The risk, then, is that students feel patronized and are deprived of the critical feedback that all students need to realize their potential.

Positive feedback bias The process of giving more positive feedback (or less critical feedback) on work believed to have been performed by a minority group member rather than a majority group member.

Like Monin and Miller (2001), Harber, Stafford and Kennedy (2010) were interested in whether this form of tokenism was motivated by teachers' desire to prove to themselves, or to others, that they are not prejudiced. They gave White trainee teachers the opportunity to give feedback on a poorly written essay that had supposedly been authored by either a Black or a White student. The participants then provided feedback to the supposed student. Crucially, participants privately completed one of three versions of the Social Issues Survey as employed by Monin and Miller (2001). In an 'egalitarian boost' condition designed to reinforce pro-minority views, participants were asked to rate their agreement on items such as 'Government offices should be closed on Martin Luther King Day'. An 'egalitarian threat' condition, designed to express opinions that are unfavourable to minorities, included items such as 'It should be legal for businesses to open on Martin Luther King Day'. A neutral condition focused on shopping. As predicted, participants in the Black writer/threat condition rated the essay more favourably, recommended the writer take less time to develop their skills, and provided more favourable comments. Participants in the Black writer/boost condition provided feedback that was no different to feedback provided by participants in the White writer conditions, both of which were unaffected by the threat/boost manipula-

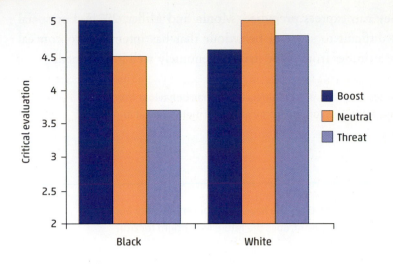

FIGURE 12.3 Positive feedback bias Participants rated work that had supposedly been written by a Black student less critically if their self-image as egalitarian had been threatened. Ratings of work that had supposedly been written by a White student were unaffected. This research demonstrates the positive feedback bias and suggests that it may be a reflection of people's desire to prove their moral credentials.

Source: Data from Harber et al., 2010

Reverse discrimination
Sometimes, people will attempt to deflect accusations of prejudice by being openly or publicly prejudiced towards people in minority groups.

tion (see Figure 12.3). Thus, it seems that the positive feedback bias is probably a reflection of teachers' desire to prove their moral credentials.

In light of these research findings, it is clear why tokenism is so often discussed as a harmful strategy. It is widely considered this way even by the authors of social psychological textbooks. For example, Baron and Byrne (2003, p. 215) wrote that 'tokenism is one subtle form of discrimination worth preventing'. However, tokenism need not be seen as an entirely bad thing. Tokenism may sometimes be Machiavellian or deceitful, but, equally, it may sometimes be a noble attempt to counteract inequality and injustice. Whatever the motives for tokenism, it may reduce prejudice by placing competent minority members in prestigious, powerful positions, and so 'proving' that their group membership does not make them incompetent or untrustworthy (Plant, Devine, Cox et al., 2009: see the Social psychology in the real world box on Barack Obama's election). Further, although affirmative action policies can reduce the self-esteem of those who are explicitly told that is why they got their job, it can actually increase the self-esteem of minority group members who are *not* told this. Under these conditions, 'tokens' are free to think that they got where they are because of their own achievements (Unzueta, Guttierez and Ghavami, 2010).

Perhaps a more extreme version of tokenism can be seen in what is known as **reverse discrimination**. For people who harbour negative attitudes towards particular minority groups, openly displaying pro-minority behaviour, or public behaviour that favours the minority, is a way to deflect accusations of prejudice. Dutton and Lake (1973) asked 40 White male and female undergraduate students, who had rated themselves as unprejudiced and in favour of equality, to participate in a study ostensibly about involuntary control of autonomic behaviour. Participants in a high-threat condition were led to believe that they had displayed physiological responses indicative of prejudice, while participants in a low-threat condition were led to believe that their response indicated no prejudice. Following the manipulation, participants were approached by either a Black or White confederate who was begging for money. As the researchers predicted, the Black confederate received more money from participants in the high-threat condition than from participants in the low-threat condition. Contributions to the White confederate were unaffected by the threat manipulation. Like other forms of tokenism, it is argued that reverse discrimination can have positive short-term effects but, ultimately, the practice is not good for minority groups. There is no evidence that the practice improves the attitudes of the person displaying the reverse discrimination. It may seem to be egalitarian, but may mask underlying prejudice or ambivalence about groups (Gaertner and Dovidio, 1986), and provide people with the moral credentials to feel that they can express prejudice (Monin and Miller, 2001). For social psychologists, it is difficult to separate behaviour that has intentions to conceal underlying negative attitudes from those that are genuinely well intentioned.

Exploring further How might a social psychologist attempt to separate genuinely egalitarian behaviour from behaviour that is intended to conceal underlying negative attitudes? Consider some empirical methods that might be able to tease these behaviours apart.

Question to consider Reread question 1 at the start of the chapter. Does Lisa have a fair concern that her boss's promotion decision may have been sexist? If this is an example of tokenism, does the future look bright for Lisa?

SOCIAL PSYCHOLOGY IN THE REAL WORLD

Tokenism and the election of Barack Obama

In an exercise in Chapter 10, we considered the possibility that the election in 2008 of Barack Obama, the first Black president of the USA, might be considered a manifestation of the 'glass cliff effect', whereby people from a group who are underrepresented as leaders are given leadership positions precisely when those positions are precarious, that is, likely to lead to failure because of the extraordinarily difficult circumstances.

It is worth pausing to reflect on whether Obama's election was a case of tokenism. A classic sign of tokenism is that the positive outcome granted to a minority group member is cited as disproof of prejudice. Even before Obama was elected, the fact that his election merely looked likely was being cited as evidence that racism was a thing of the past:

> Win or lose, Obama has proved (if more proof were needed) that although many Blacks are still mired in poverty – a legacy of our racist history – contemporary White racism has been driven to the fringes and is no longer a serious impediment to Black advancement. (Taylor, 2008)

Social psychology provides methods and concepts to determine whether Obama's election exhibits some of the hallmarks of tokenism, as demonstrated in a 2009 issue of the *Journal of Experimental Social Psychology*. Here, several papers reported results that seemed to be

more consistent with this rather pessimistic view than with the halcyon optimism that surrounded the event in the media. For example, Effron, Cameron and Monin (2009) found that White participants who endorsed Obama were subsequently more likely to discriminate in favour of White people. They explained their results in terms of moral credentialing theory; that is, acts of tokenism display an individual's credentials as a decent, non-prejudiced person, thus making it easier for them to engage in subsequent acts of discrimination without feelings of guilt or shame (Monin and Miller, 2001). Kaiser, Drury, Spalding et al. (2009) found that White Americans' support for egalitarian social policies designed to reduce racial injustice actually declined after Obama's election. This decline was associated with reductions in the perception that racism is a pressing social problem in America.

These findings seem to show that, consistent with tokenism, people cite Obama's election as 'proof' that White Americans, individually and collectively, are no longer racist – ironically making them feel more free to engage in discrimination and less obliged to support measures to counter racism.

These consequences of Obama's election are disturbing enough, but what about the antecedents or causes of Obama's election? Is it possible to view Obama's election as being, in part, a tactic designed to prove that racism in America is no longer a big deal? Yes, according to Knowles, Lowery and Schaumberg (2009). They found that social dominance orientation – an anti-egalitarian ideology that entails the continuing dominance of White over Black people (see Chapter 11) – made some people more, rather than less, likely to vote for Obama. Which people? Those who thought that Obama's election would 'prove' that racism is no longer a problem in America. This study provides impressive but perhaps rather depressing evidence that some people who voted for Obama were engaging in tokenism in its worst sense – an act designed to mask the reality of racism and thus legitimize the ongoing disadvantages experienced by Black people in America.

Nonetheless, Plant et al. (2009) provided some evidence for the benefits of Obama's election to office, even if it can be seen as a case of tokenism. They found that White Americans' levels of unconscious or 'implicit' prejudice and stereotyping of Black people reduced after Obama's election. It is possible to see tokenism as a double-edged sword in terms of its effects on majority attitudes; on one hand, it tends to lead majorities to deny or downplay the existence of prejudice, but on the other, it may actually reduce the prejudice they feel – at least in cases such as Obama where the token is generally seen as competent and likeable.

Another potential benefit of tokenism is that it can inspire minorities to aspire to succeed, believing that success is possible. According to Marx, Ko and Friedman (2009), Black people's performance on academic tests showed a subtle but statistically significant increase after the Obama election result. For Marx et al., the presence of a salient, positive role model can have a beneficial effect on minority groups. However, their conclusions were challenged by Aronson, Jannone, McGlone and Johnson-Campbell (2009), who conducted an experiment in which no improvement was found in Black people's test performance after they had been reminded of Obama's election (compared to a control group). The jury is still out, therefore, on whether this case of tokenism – if indeed it is tokenism – has the effect of helping disadvantaged people to lift themselves up by their own bootstraps.

In sum, social psychological research has been able to cast light on whether Obama's election can be seen as a case of tokenism, and has also highlighted some of the pitfalls and potential merits of tokenism. It is premature to dismiss tokenism, and related social policies such as affirmative action, as altogether a bad thing. The causes of poverty, prejudice and disadvantage are deep-rooted. Addressing these is beyond the power of one person or organization. Nonetheless, individuals and organizations are often in a position to grant positive outcomes to single members of disadvantaged minority groups. Further research and theorizing are required to determine if, when and how tokenism should be considered.

Questions

1 What has been the gender, religious and ethnic makeup of leaders of your country? Have there been any 'minority' leaders elected? Do you see any signs of tokenism in the election of your country's leaders?

2 Barack Obama is a highly educated, accomplished and articulate man who had many credentials as a leader. If he was White, there would be no discussion of whether or not he was a token. To what extent is it appropriate to ask whether he is a token? Is this counterproductive, harmful or even offensive?

3 Of course, Obama was re-elected in 2012. What implications does this fact have for the notion that Obama's original election in 2008 was tokenism. Is it plausible to say that his election and re-election are both cases of tokenism?

Intergroup contact

We, the authors of this book, are old enough to remember 'the Troubles' – a long period of violence in Northern Ireland – which, with tragic monotony, featured in the evening news while we were growing up. Riots, shootings, bombings and killings took place largely between the nationalist community (who sought the independence of Northern Ireland from the UK and generally envisage a merger with the Irish Republic, and were largely from the Roman Catholic minority), and the unionist community (who sought for Northern Ireland to remain part of the UK, and were largely from the Protestant majority). The violence also spilled over these group boundaries and involved security forces from the British mainland, and terrorist attacks on English cities including London, Birmingham and Manchester, largely by the Irish Republican Army (IRA). With great political will, the flames of this conflict were doused by a period of negotiations culminating in the 'Good Friday Agreement' of 1998.

Although sporadic violence and a good deal of prejudice and mistrust survive, this extraordinary reduction in violence deserves to be seen as one of the most inspirational examples of intergroup reconciliation in living memory. A striking feature of this peace process is that it was not associated with increasing contact between the nationalist and unionist communities. On the contrary, schools and housing developments became increasingly segregated throughout the Troubles and this process of segregation appears to continue. In some parts of the country and in Belfast in particular, the communities became starkly divided by so-called 'peace walls' that were designed as a means of defusing sectarian tensions. Most are still standing today (see Figure 12.4). In recent years, 'peace gates' have been opened to allow nationalist and unionist communities to interact more freely and to foster greater links between them, but the barriers set up during the Troubles are taking a while to come down completely.

Does this mean that contact between groups is harmful, and that to resolve conflict, groups should be separated? Certainly, some degree of contact is necessary for groups to engage in conflict with each other – no matter how much groups may hate each other, the range of harms they can do to each other is limited if they cannot reach each other. Some thinkers have regarded contact between groups as fuel to the flames of hatred, suspicion, fear and resentment (e.g., Baker, 1934). But across hundreds of studies, the evidence suggests that contact between groups tends to douse, rather than fuel, the fires of intergroup conflict (Pettigrew and Tropp, 2006, 2008). Perhaps more accurately, research shows that contact generally has the effect of reducing the *prejudice* that individuals feel towards outgroups. Indeed, contact has become the most studied method for reducing prejudice.

FIGURE 12.4 Cupar Way peace wall The extensive Cupar Way peace wall divides the Protestant Shankill Road from the Catholic Falls Road area of west Belfast.

When and why does contact work?

Research on when and why contact works was placed on a systematic theoretical foundation, since labelled **contact theory**, by Allport (1954) in his book *The Nature of Prejudice*. (As an aside, contact theory was only one of the foundational insights on prejudice to be published in that book; others included early statements about dehumanization, moral exclusion, and the importance of categorization for prejudice. It remains recommended reading for those planning higher study in social psychology.) The basic tenet of contact theory is that bringing members of opposing groups together should improve intergroup relations, and reduce prejudice and discrimination. For Allport, contact between groups could reduce prejudice, especially if four optimal conditions were met:

1 *Equality of status:* The groups must have roughly equal status in the situation. If group members do not meet as equals, there is every chance that the inequality will be exploited by those who find themselves at an advantage and resented by everybody else. Of course, groups often differ in status, as is the case in Northern Ireland where the unionist community is larger and more affluent than the nationalist community, and this inequality can erode the value of a contact situation (Brewer and Kramer, 1985; Foster and Finchilescu, 1986). Thankfully, however, research suggests that most important is the *perception* of equal status *in the situation* (Cohen, 1982; Riordan and Ruggiero, 1980; Robinson and Preston, 1976). As long as this condition is met, the contact situation can be successful, even if the groups went into the situation with different levels of status (Patchen, 1982; Schofield and Eurich-Fulcer, 2001).

2 *Common goals:* The people in the situation should be working towards a goal that both groups share. Participation in mixed-race sports teams is a good example – whatever the racial background of the players, they share the goal of victory for their team (Patchen, 1982), with the effect of reducing racial prejudice.

3 *Intergroup cooperation:* The two groups' pursuit of common goals should be based on cooperation, rather than competition, between their members. Recall, for instance, the peace-making effect of having boys from the Rattlers and the Eagles work together in the Robbers Cave experiment (Sherif et al., [1954]1961) (see Chapter 11).

4 *The support of authorities, law or custom*: This stamps legitimacy on the contact situation, and establishes that acceptance between groups is the norm. As we shall soon see, perceived social norms appear to have a strong impact on the expression of prejudice (Crandall, Eshleman and O'Brien, 2002). It may be especially important in gaining the positive attitudes that may develop between individuals to generalize beyond the contact situation, and beyond those people who were not personally present in a contact situation – which has been one of the defining challenges in research on contact. The importance of the support of an authority has been shown in field studies of contact interventions in real-life settings, such as the military (Landis, Hope and Day, 1984), a credit card company (Morrison and Herlihy, 1992) and a church (Parker, 1968).

Pettigrew and Tropp's (2006) extensive meta-analysis of 515 articles examined the effectiveness of contact in the presence and absence of Allport's (1954) optimal conditions. The results confirmed that even when the optimal conditions are not all present, contact generally works. Contact reduced prejudice not only between the racial and ethnic groups it was originally designed for. It also reduced prejudice based on age, disability, mental illness and sexual orientation. These effect sizes are not large – contact, as an independent variable, generally explained around 7 per cent of the variance in prejudice, as the dependent variable. But they are in the right direction, and highly statistically significant, when considered across the studies. And in support of Allport's (1954) contact theory, the effect of contact increased when the four optimal conditions were present. The benefits of these optimal conditions are clearest when they are together as a package. Thus, it would appear that these conditions combine to create the right atmosphere for contact, rather than adding up incrementally, increasing the effectiveness of contact one by one. So, for example, it may not help to work cooperatively in the pursuit of common goals unless groups do this as equals, with the sanction of authority.

Exploring further Take some time to research a specific example in society where contact has been used as a prejudice reduction technique. How did it fulfil the optimal conditions specified in Allport's contact theory? Did contact produce positive outcomes in this example? Relate this to a well-known example of effective contact pioneered by Aronson, Blaney, Stephan et al. (1978). Aronson et al. adapted the optimal principles of contact in a widely used and successful classroom intervention called the 'jigsaw classroom'. In this intervention, teachers bring children from different social groups together to work cooperatively, as equals, towards common goals. Using search terms such as 'jigsaw classroom' and the 'jigsaw technique', find, and read, educational websites and academic references on this technique. Familiarize yourself with the technique and make sure you understand how it relates to the principles of contact theory.

What if contact is not possible?

There is a serious problem that limits the applicability of contact theory to many cases of prejudice and intergroup conflict. Specifically, it can be difficult and expensive to arrange suitably controlled contact situations. Even if the resources are available, groups may live in separate territories, so that meetings can involve long or dangerous journeys. Prejudice may be too intense, and the wounds of intergroup conflict too fresh and too raw to stage controlled contact between groups (Staub, 1996; Stephan and Stephan, 1984). Therefore, researchers have investigated ways in which people can benefit from the idea of contact, even when they are unable to directly experience it.

Extended contact effect
Finding that people are less prejudiced if they are friends with an ingroup member who they know to have good friendships with outgroup members.

One method of benefiting from contact without directly experiencing it is known as the **extended contact effect** (Wright, Aron, McLaughlin-Volpe and Ropp, 1997). You have extended contact with an outgroup if you know that one of your ingroup friends has good friendships with outgroup members. Wright et al. found that people are less prejudiced if their friends have high-quality contact with an outgroup, even if their own contact with the outgroup is limited. Their findings were replicated in Northern Ireland by Paolini, Hewstone, Cairns and Voci (2004). Thus, Catholics were less prejudiced towards Protestants if they knew that at least one of their Catholic friends was good friends with at least one Protestant. It seems that being able to include the other in the self (Wright, Aron and Tropp, 2002), or to experience others as themselves, reduces dislike for those others.

Of course, these studies of extended contact were largely correlational. Having friends with people who enjoy excellent contact with an outgroup was associated with lower personal levels of prejudice towards the group. This begs the question, does having extended contact lead to lower prejudice, or does lower prejudice lead to having extended contact? Intuitively, if you have positive attitudes to an outgroup, you are more likely to have friends who are also low in prejudice. However, there is also good experimental evidence for the extended contact hypothesis. For example, Liebkind and McAlister (1999) exposed adolescents to an unknown ingroup member who was good friends with an outgroup member, with the effect of lowering their prejudice relative to a control group of adolescents. The prejudice of British school children towards refugees (Cameron, Rutland, Brown and Douch, 2006) and the disabled (Cameron and Rutland, 2006) was reduced by implementing intervention techniques derived from the extended contact hypothesis (for further research on the effectiveness of extended contact, see also Islam and Hewstone, 1993; Turner, Hewstone, Voci and Vonofakou, 2008).

Time to reflect Do you think that demand characteristics could be responsible for these effects? How serious a problem might this be and how can it be countered?

Question to consider Reread question 2 at the start of the chapter. With your knowledge of the extended contact hypothesis, explain the likely impact on Fred's attitudes towards Asians of having Jake as a friend.

Another form of indirect contact seems even more ephemeral than the vicarious experience of extended contact, but is also showing signs of promise as a weapon in the fight against prejudice. Specifically, prejudice may be reduced, at least temporarily, by imagining a positive episode of contact with an outgroup member (Crisp and Turner, 2009). Imagine, for example, you are on a busy train and you get talking to the person sitting next to you about the novel they are reading. You end up having a conversation ranging over many topics, from where you live, to what your children enjoy doing, sports and films. Time flies and before you know it, your train arrives at your stop. If this person is an outgroup member (e.g., someone of a different race, religion, age group or sexuality), chances are that merely imagining this encounter will make you feel better about their group. This is named the **imagined contact effect**.

Imagined contact effect
Merely imagining positive encounters with people of minority groups will make people feel more positive towards that group.

Turner, Crisp and Lambert (2007) asked young British participants to imagine this kind of contact with older adults, and heterosexual men to imagine (non-sexual) contact with gay men. Impressively, none of the participants in these studies were able to guess the aims of the experiment, which tends to rule out the interpretation that participants were merely responding to demand characteristics.

Further, Turner and Crisp (2010) showed that imagining contact with outgroups reduced implicit prejudice, measured on the Implicit Association Test (IAT). Although the IAT is not entirely resistant, it is clearly much harder to fake than answers to straightforward questions about how prejudiced one is. This is another reason, then, to doubt that the effects of imagined contact can be dismissed as a mere demand characteristic (for arguments against other alternative interpretations of the imagined contact effect, see Crisp and Turner, 2009).

Imagined contact has other subtle and intriguing effects, which suggest the promise of this approach. Previous research had shown that older adults are prone to stereotype threat effects on intellectual performance – reminded of negative stereotypes of the elderly, their performance declines (Abrams, Eller and Bryant, 2006). Recent research suggests that if older adults imagine positive contact with younger people, they are subsequently less susceptible to this stereotype threat effect (Abrams, Crisp, Marques et al., 2008). Further, Stathi and Crisp (2008) found that majority or *mestizo* Mexicans who imagined contact with indigenous or Amerindian Mexicans were later more prone to projecting their own positive traits to the outgroup. For example, a participant who sees themselves as entertaining would be more likely to see indigenous Mexicans in the same way, after imagining contact with them. This process of projection is likely to reflect a sense that the outgroup may not, after all, be so very different from oneself (Ames, 2004; Jones, 2004). It is also likely to contribute to a more positive general feeling towards the outgroup, that is, less prejudiced (Brown and Hewstone, 2005). However, research is yet to test whether prejudice is reduced by projection from the self to the outgroup. Further, some recent research (West, Holmes and Hewstone, 2011) discovered a complicating factor of imagined outgroup contact. Specifically, it revealed that if individuals imagine contact with a threatening or challenging group (e.g., schizophrenics), prejudices can be heightened. Imagining contact with such a group can amplify pre-existing tensions and negative associations rather than reduce them. This effect can be reduced, however, if participants are asked to integrate positive features into these images.

Time to reflect As a prejudice reduction technique, imagined contact holds a lot of promise and does not appear to be subject to typical demand characteristics. How long-lasting do you think the effects of imagined contact might be? Can you find evidence to support your answer?

CRITICAL FOCUS

Reservations and unanswered questions about contact

It is clear there are many success stories associated with intergroup contact. But a number of important criticisms have been levelled at contact theory, which leaves question marks over its applicability to many settings (e.g., Amir, 1965; Forbes, 1997, 2004; Ford, 1986; Hopkins, Reicher and Levine, 1997). Many of these criticisms were gathered together and eloquently put forward in a review by Dixon, Durrheim and Tredoux (2005) and we outline them here.

1   Are the conditions for contact too many?

One of Dixon et al.'s (2005) key criticisms follows from the fact that much of theory and research has focused on the ideal conditions for contact (e.g., Brewer and Miller, 1984; Brown and Zagefka, 2005; Hewstone and Brown, 1986; Schofield and Eurich-Fulcer, 2001). Of course, this makes sense if we want to use research to inform how to engineer meetings between group members under conditions that can be tightly controlled. But this focus has led to two key problems. First, research and theory led to the identification of so many conditions that, in the colourful words of Stephan (1987, p. 17), intergroup contact came to resemble 'a bag lady who is so encumbered by excess baggage she can hardly move'. In addition to the four originally proposed by Allport (1954), Dixon et al. (2005) list some other ideal conditions for contact that have been identified by researchers:

- Contact should be regular and frequent
- Contact should occur across a variety of social settings and situations
- Contact should involve interaction with a counter-stereotypic member of another group
- Contact should be free of anxiety or other negative emotions
- Contact should involve a balanced ratio of ingroup and outgroup members
- And several more.

Thus, so many conditions are specified that designing the 'optimal' contact situation can be a fiddly and difficult task, if one wishes to take them all seriously. There is also a suspicion that the growth in the number of supposed conditions for *when* contact works has not been checked because social psychologists have not been able to agree on a simple or parsimonious theory of *why* contact works. If we know exactly what social psychological mechanisms are involved, we presumably do not have to rely on a shopping list of conditions. Instead, we are likely to use our understanding of the processes involved in contact to work out which of a small set of conditions might be needed in a particular setting. As it stands, there are several competing theories and some are rather complex, invoking a range of different emotional and cognitive variables (for some of the leading examples of theories of contact, see Brown, 1995; Dovidio, Gaertner and Kawakami, 2003; Kenworthy, Turner, Hewstone and Voci, 2005; Pettigrew, 1998).

In defence of the contact literature – and it should be borne in mind that despite their criticisms, Dixon et al. (2005) are explicit that they are 'broadly sympathetic' (p. 697) to it, and regard it as 'one of the most successful ideas in the history of social psychology' (p. 698) – the profusion of conditions for contact has been slowed and even reversed recently. As we have seen, Pettigrew and Tropp's (2006) meta-analysis focused only on Allport's (1954) four original conditions. Further, their analysis suggested that these conditions are best considered together, as a kind of package, rather than separately. Recent work has also brought some theoretical simplicity and clarity about why contact works. For example, in a second meta-analysis of the literature, Pettigrew and Tropp (2008) found that the effect of contact on prejudice was mediated by two key processes. First, contact between groups increases people's willingness to empathize with outgroup members and take their perspective (e.g., Aberson and Haag, 2007). Second, contact between groups reduces intergroup anxiety, especially anxiety about contact itself (e.g., Blascovich, Mendes, Hunter et al., 2001; Stephan, Stephan and Gudykunst, 1999). Contact also increases knowledge of the outgroup, which helps to reduce prejudice, but, according to Pettigrew and Tropp's (2008) meta-analysis, to a lesser extent than the changes in intergroup emotion (anxiety and empathy) that contact brings.

2   Are the optimal conditions for contact realistic?

Let us say that researchers are able to whittle down the ideal conditions to a package of four or fewer and that theorists are able to agree on why contact reduces prejudice. Clearly, this would be progress. However, an important question remains. In the majority of studies in the intergroup literature, researchers have examined the impact of experimental contact situations that have been carefully engineered to produce a good outcome. However, the vast majority of contact situations occur in the much less controlled conditions of real life, where members of different groups live close together and go to the same places for their work, education and recreation. In these conditions, there is no guarantee that the contact is of good quality. This requires us to do two things when considering the applicability of experimental findings.

First, we should not automatically generalize to real-life settings from studies of contact in carefully controlled settings, be they in the field or the laboratory. These experiments may be a good model for interventions in

▶

classrooms or community halls, which bring people together in a positive and supervised way for a specified period. But they may not be a good model for the everyday contact that happens in our playgrounds, streets and other public spaces. Thus, while we can assume that well-designed, controlled encounters between groups can reduce prejudice, we cannot assume that prejudice will be reduced if people from different groups live, work, study and play in the same places. In general, findings from the contact literature do not automatically justify policies of desegregation in housing or education, although there may be many other grounds for backing such policies (Brewer and Miller, 1984).

Second, we should try to find out how well experiments actually model the contact that happens in naturally occurring situations. Of course, there is always a worry that, in principle, experiments cannot be generalized to real life (as we saw in Chapter 1). But in practice, the extent to which the generalizability of experiments is limited depends on exactly what differences exist between experiments and specific real-life situations, and what effect these differences have on behaviour. Recent research has cast a good deal of light on specific differences between contact, as it unfolds in many experiments, versus real life. In an observational study, Dixon and Durrheim (2003) watched relations between Black and White people on a beach in post-apartheid South Africa. They found that a mix of races (mostly Black people, with a significant minority of White people and those of other racial backgrounds) used the beach. This desegregation, impossible in the appalling days of apartheid where different areas of beach were reserved for those of a different racial background, clearly constitutes a kind of minimal contact. But how did this contact play out in practice? The essential finding was that direct interaction between the racial groups was rare. Different racial groups tended to cluster together in different areas of the beach. When members of different groups were in close proximity, they tended to construct racially exclusive territories with strategically positioned sun umbrellas (see Figure 12.5). Racial groups also segregated themselves with 'temporal processes of flux and withdrawal' (Dixon et al., 2005, p. 704). For example, if a large number of Black holidaymakers arrived at a beach, White people tended to leave.

Lee (2003) carried out a qualitative study in which Black shoppers were asked about their experience of shopping in predominantly White and Black

FIGURE 12.5 Groups tend to self-segregate In an observational study, Dixon et al. (2005) found that Black and White people on a South African beach would segregate themselves from each other with the use of barriers such as strategically placed sun umbrellas. Contact is said to be a key to improving intergroup relations, but what if people do not want to be in contact?

neighbourhoods in the USA. Again, the lived experience of this kind of contact differed radically from those taking place in carefully engineered contact situations. Black shoppers reported feeling watched and distrusted (e.g., being watched covertly by store detectives), leading some of them to avoid contact while shopping in White areas or to avoid shopping. Others took care to wear expensive clothes and accessories so as to avoid being stereotyped as poor and potentially criminal because of their race.

Of course, none of this is to say that contact theory is wrong. It has never said that *any* type of contact will reduce prejudice. What it does show, however, is that the lived experience of groups who work, study or play together does not necessarily include actual interaction with outgroup members, in the style of carefully designed contact interventions. Arguably, then, a key challenge for social psychologists is to understand how groups interact with each other when sharing physical spaces and how to improve the quality of that contact. In our view, this means there should be greater dialogue between contact theorists and scientists from other disciplines, including environmental psychologists, who study the impact of physical environments on human behaviour, and political psychologists, who are concerned among other things with the effect of the political environment on behaviour (see Chapter 14). In this way, there is a greater chance that everyday experiences of contact will be improved by insights from the contact literature.

3 *There is more to life than prejudice, and more to intergroup relations than prejudice reduction*

The final criticism of research on contact is that the vast majority of it has focused on reductions of prejudice, that is, it has sought to improve the attitudes of individual participants to the outgroup (Dixon et al., 2005; Forbes, 1997, 2004). Of course, this is an important and desirable outcome, but does not mean that contact improves all aspects of intergroup relations. Increasing contact in everyday life brings opportunities for positive contact, but also new opportunities for acts of intergroup aggression (see Chapter 13), disrespect, suspicion and fear (Amir, 1965). Forbes (1997, 2004), for example, argues that increased contact in everyday life may heighten perceptions of threat. Individuals who are directly in contact with the outgroup may experience reductions in prejudice, but those in the wider community who see more outgroup members around but are not in contact with them may feel threatened – the effect being a net increase in threatened and negative feelings across the group overall.

Although Forbes' arguments are yet to be directly tested, there is recent evidence of another potential downside of contact. Saguy, Tausch, Dovidio and Pratto (2009) found one problem with contact is that, among members of disadvantaged minority groups, it may breed an unrealistic expectation that the majority group will start to treat them in a fair and equal way. Ironically, this unrealistic optimism seems only to emerge after high-quality contact, that is, contact that is perceived as positive or is focused on what groups have in common rather than what makes them different. It is as if minorities think, 'now that they've met us and seen we're not so different, they'll treat us right'. In the first of the two studies they published, Saguy et al. (2009, Study 1) conducted 35 sessions in which a total of 210 participants were divided into two minimal groups of three members. Each group gave itself a name and wore the same coloured T-shirts as a kind of uniform. One group was placed in an advantaged position over the other, being empowered to decide the rewards the two groups would receive. These rewards were research credits (course credits awarded to students in exchange for participating in studies). Meeting the 'advantaged' group and talking about what they had in common tended to cause the 'disadvantaged' group to be more optimistic about how many credits they would receive from them. However, it did not affect the number of credits they actually got from the advantaged group. Consequently, high-quality contact caused disadvantaged

groups to develop unrealistically optimistic expectations about how they would be treated: they imagined they would get more from the advantaged group than they actually got (Figure 12.6).

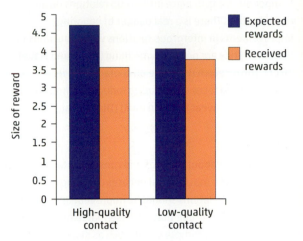

FIGURE 12.6 The ironically widened gap between expected and received rewards after high-quality contact For disadvantaged groups, high-quality contact (vs. low-quality contact) created unrealistic expectations about the distribution of rewards. Participants in a high-quality contact condition believed they would receive more rewards than they actually received from the advantaged group.
Source: Data from Saguy et al., 2009

Saguy et al. (2009, Study 2) followed this up with a correlational study of Israeli Arabs' perception of how they would be treated by Israeli Jews. In this second study, they found that Arabs who indicated they had more Jewish friends and acquaintances expressed less prejudice towards Jews. This, of course, is the classical effect of contact. Alongside this finding came greater trust that Jews intend to treat Arabs fairly – similar to the expectation of just treatment that contact fostered in the minimal groups of Saguy et al.'s first study. This expectation of just treatment appeared to lead Arabs who enjoyed positive contact with Jews to express lower support for social changes in Israel that might lead to more equal relations between groups. Unlike the first, minimal group study, the second study had no measure of whether Arabs' expectations of just treatment were right or wrong, realistic or unrealistic. However, what the two studies have in common is that groups who are relatively powerless or disadvantaged in a given social setting are led by positive contact to expect better treatment from the powerful or advantaged groups. This expectation can be unrealistic (Study 1), or can undermine the support of the powerless and disadvantaged for policies that would improve their lot (Study 2). For Saguy et al., this is the 'irony of harmony'. Yes, contact can reduce prejudice, but at the same time, it may have other effects which might hamper attempts to place intergroup relations on an equal footing. There is a real danger of equating improvements in intergroup relations with reductions in prejudice. They are not the same thing (Tropp and Mallett, 2011). The research literature on contact, with its overwhelming focus on prejudice reduction, should be read with this caveat firmly in mind (Dixon et al., 2005).

Questions

1 Controversy about the pros and cons of contact touches on one of the most topical debates about how intergroup relations should be improved. On one hand, many scholars argue that it is essential to reduce prejudice and promote values such as diversity and tolerance. On the other hand, some scholars argue that the key is to facilitate collective action by disadvantaged groups. Can you find articles published in 2012 and later that discuss this debate?

2 In the Social psychology in real life box in Chapter 4, we saw in Hodson and Busseri's (2012) study how less intelligent people tend to become more prejudiced. One of the reasons this happened is that less intelligent people adopt right-wing or 'conservative' political ideologies that are associated with prejudice. What was the other mediator, though? Use an academic database like Google Scholar to find the abstract, or the article itself.

3 In a recent theoretical review, Crisp and Turner (2011) argue that experiences of diversity, such as intergroup contact, may increase the capacity for creative and complex thought. What do you think this adds to the debate about the contact hypothesis?

Time to reflect We have spent some time critiquing the contact hypothesis, but as you read on, consider the extent to which similar criticisms could be levelled at research and theory on other approaches to improving intergroup relations.

The concept of intergroup contact has sparked a great deal of research interest and debate in social psychology. As in the earlier example of Northern Ireland, it is worrying that a lack of contact reflects and potentially fuels prejudice. However, it is also important to note that laboratory studies of contact are not about living side by side. What we may think of as 'contact' in everyday life is different from the programmed, structured, legitimized meetings between people that are typical of modern studies of contact. The wider, everyday meaning of contact also requires the input of political scientists, sociologists and human geographers.

Categorization-based approaches

As we saw in Chapter 11, ever since Allport's (1954) pioneering work, social psychologists have known that a vital precondition for stereotyping, prejudice and discrimination is the human tendency to place themselves and others into categories. Even a minimal categorization into 'us' and 'them' appears to be enough to elicit certain forms of stereotyping and prejudice (Ashburn-Nardo, Voils and Monteith, 2001). However, theory and research over the past two decades have suggested that categorization does not necessarily lead to ingroup bias. In fact, social categories can be used as a tool to reduce prejudice. The key insight underlying these developments is that a minimal categorization into 'us' and 'them' is *especially* likely to lead to intergroup bias. If people can be encouraged to categorize in more inclusive and complex ways, there is a good chance that biases can be eliminated.

One option is to go through a process of **decategorization** (or personalization), where personal rather than group identity becomes the focus (Miller and Brewer, 1984). Thus, people regard one another as 'me' and 'you' rather than 'we' and 'they', which is said to reduce intergroup bias by undermining the validity of outgroup stereotypes (Brewer and Miller, 1984; Miller, 2002; Miller, Brewer and Edwards, 1985). This process has been shown to be effective in reducing intergroup conflict in the laboratory. For example, Miller et al. (1985) showed that intergroup conflict that permits more personalized interactions (e.g., being more person focused than task focused) elicits more positive attitudes to outgroup members who are both present and not present.

However, in the real world, this kind of avoidance of group boundaries is not always going to be possible. An alternative categorization-based approach to reducing prejudice is offered by the **common ingroup identity model**, which suggests that if members of rival or opposing groups are encouraged to **recategorize** themselves as members of the same ingroup, intergroup attitudes will improve, or perceived differences may even disappear (Gaertner and Dovidio, 2000; Gaertner, Mann, Murrell and Dovidio, 1989). In part, this model emerged from research on the contact hypothesis, which, since Allport (1954), has emphasized the importance of having common goals and working cooperatively towards them. In their experiments, Gaertner et al. (1989) assigned participants to small work teams of three people. They brought two such teams together and encouraged them to represent themselves as one big team encompassing six people, rather than two separate teams of three. To do this, they used techniques such as manipulating seating arrangements so that teams had to sit together rather than apart, giving them common rather than unique team names, and ensuring that participants' success or failure was linked to that of members of the other team of three people, as well as the members of their own team. Under these conditions, which encouraged participants to form a common ingroup identity, bias between the teams was eliminated or at least reduced. Other research has demonstrated that common ingroup identity may be achieved by increasing the salience of existing common superordinate identities (e.g., schools) or categories (e.g., students) (Gómez, Dovidio, Huici et al., 2008), or by introducing factors such as a common goal or fate that is perceived to be shared by the group memberships (Gaertner, Dovidio, Rust et al., 1999).

Results of field surveys have also supported the common ingroup identity model. Gaertner, Rust, Dovidio et al. (1994) asked students at a multiracial school in the USA to circle which of several racial, ethnic and national labels applied to them. Participants who circled inclusive labels that included several racial and ethnic groups (e.g., American) reported lower levels of racial and ethnic prejudice. Once again, a common identity appears to be able to reduce negative feelings

Decategorization Group members emphasize individual (personal) differences rather than group identity.

Common ingroup identity model Categorization-based approach to prejudice reduction asserting that a common ingroup identity will improve intergroup attitudes.

Recategorization Group members emphasize a common ingroup.

© PHOTODISC

between groups. Interestingly, bias was reduced still further when participants did not just indicate a common (or 'superordinate') identity, but also classified themselves into a unique (or 'subordinate') identity, such as Black, White or Asian (Gaertner et al., 1994). Many studies have since echoed this finding that simultaneously identifying with both subordinate and superordinate categories leads to the most effective reductions in intergroup bias (e.g., Hornsey and Hogg, 2000; Huo, Smith, Tyler and Lind, 1996; Smith and Tyler, 1996). We need not throw away our identification with smaller, more distinct groups. Instead, it is possible, and better, to complement our group identification with higher level identification with superordinate identities.

For the common ingroup identity model, there are two good reasons why this kind of simultaneous identification reduces prejudice. First, it can be seen as a form of **crossed categorization** (Crisp, Walsh and Hewstone, 2006; Hewstone, Islam and Judd, 1993). If you categorize yourself along one dimension (e.g., French), you are likely to perceive fewer differences between yourself and a person of another nationality (e.g., British) if you simultaneously perceive that person and yourself to share membership of another category (e.g., you are both Asian). This is because you will perceive similarities between yourself and that person because of your common racial identity, and not just differences because of your distinctive national identity. The two category accentuation processes (see Chapter 11) are at odds, with the result that overall bias is reduced compared to the situation where you were only aware of your different nationalities. Second, if people retain distinctive as well as superordinate identities while working with people from other groups, they are more likely to be able to show reduced prejudice in other settings. For example, if a French participant is thinking, 'we are no longer Asian or White, but we are all French', they may be less well equipped to show reduced bias in later encounters with French members of racial outgroups. The experience is more likely to generalize if they are aware of racial identities at the same time, so that they are really learning, for example, that 'those White people are not so bad' (Gaertner and Dovidio, 2000).

However, the common ingroup identity model is not the only account of why it is beneficial for people to acknowledge both superordinate and subordinate identities. According to the **mutual differentiation model** (Crisp, 2005; Hewstone, 1996; Hewstone and Brown, 1986), people are often very committed to subordinate groups. As social identity theory has made clear, commitment to their social identities is a strong, characteristic feature of human nature and people strive to maintain the positive distinctiveness of their social identity (Tajfel and Turner, 1986).

Further, relatively small, distinctive groups often satisfy people's need for identity and belonging more completely than large, inclusive groups (Brewer, 1991; Hornsey and Jetten, 2004). Thus, in the mutual differentiation model, people are prone to 'distinctiveness threat' when a superordinate identity looks like it might swallow up, and replace, more distinctive subordinate groups. This feeling of threat can undermine the gains that might be made by reducing category accentuation effects.

Crossed categorization
Categorizing oneself or someone else on more than one dimension at the same time can decrease the perception of differences between groups.

Mutual differentiation model
Model arguing that people are committed to some subordinate groups and experience 'distinctiveness threat' when a superordinate identity looks as though it may replace distinctive subordinate groups.

How can we differentiate between the common ingroup identity model and the mutual differentiation model? They both make many of the same predictions. But differentiating between the models is important, because it is crucial that professionals and policy makers are guided by a correct understanding of how people are going to respond to their interventions. According to the mutual differentiation model, attempts to get people to simply identify with superordinate groups, in place of meaningful subordinate groups, can actually backfire, producing increased prejudice. Why? Because the threat of losing a cherished and distinctive identity can make people defensive. People are motivated to reassert the uniqueness and, indeed, the superiority of their group. What better way to do this than to discriminate and express prejudice towards the outgroup? This prediction is not made by the common ingroup identity model, because it does not acknowledge that the loss of subordinate identity can be threatening. Several studies have now produced clear support for this unique prediction of the mutual differentiation model. For example, Hornsey and Hogg (2000) had participants – university students in Queensland, Australia – complete a problem-solving task while different aspects of their identity were made salient. The conditions were:

FIGURE 12.7 Different types of identification affect ingroup bias Ingroup bias was greatest in the superordinate category condition than in the other three conditions (individual, subordinate or simultaneous), suggesting that imposing a superordinate identity without preserving subordinate identities can actually increase prejudice.

Source: Data from Hornsey and Hogg, 2000

1 *Individual identity salience:* Participants were told that ordinary individuals could solve problems in ways that trained professionals could not.

2 *Superordinate identity salience:* Participants were told that university students could solve problems in ways that trained professionals could not.

3 *Subordinate identity salience:* Participants were told that the problem solving of humanities students and maths/science students would be compared.

4 *Simultaneous identity salience:* Participants were told that university students could solve problems in ways that trained professionals could not, and that the performance of humanities and maths/science students would be compared.

After completing the task, participants were told they would solve a similar problem again, but this time in groups. They were asked how much they would like working with members of their own, versus the other, subordinate group (humanities or maths/sciences). This was taken as a measure of ingroup bias. Results revealed that ingroup bias was higher in the superordinate condition than in the other three conditions (see Figure 12.7). Indeed, it appears that prejudice between groups can be made worse by imposing a superordinate identity without preserving the subordinate identities at the same time (see also Kenworthy et al., 2005).

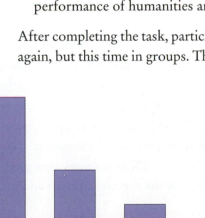

Question to consider Reread question 3 at the start of the chapter. Is Sharon's strategy for reducing prejudice likely to work? What qualifications to this strategy might make it more effective?

If you identify strongly with a relatively small, distinctive group, there is a good chance you will feel especially threatened if you perceive that it stands to be replaced with some larger, more inclusive social category. Thus, it is all the more likely that you will react to this threat with increased prejudice towards the other groups with which your group may be merged. Indeed, this is what Crisp and Beck (2005) and Crisp, Stone and Hall (2006) have found. They had British people imagine what life would be like in a United States of Europe, where being British would no longer have any special relevance. They then had participants complete measures of prejudice towards a European outgroup (the French). Participants who had a low (below median) level of identification – that is, a weak sense of being 'British' – responded to the superordinate identification with lower levels of implicit prejudice towards the French. High identifiers (above median) responded with *increased* levels of prejudice, relative to a baseline condition.

Exploring further Can you identify the different category-based approaches we have discussed from the diagrams below? Try to identify (a) the common ingroup identity model in its simplest sense, (b) crossed categorization, and (c) the mutual differentiation model. Each letter ('A', 'B' and so on) denotes different groups, which are sometimes separated (in a distinct circle) within the greater circle. Which results in the least prejudice and why?

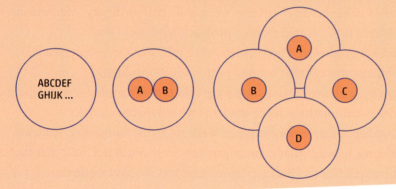

The common ingroup identity model and the mutual differentiation model are concerned with how people think about the relationship between ingroup and outgroup categories. Are they entirely separate with nothing in common? Can the boundaries between them be dismantled? A promising new model of the role of categorization in prejudice, and prejudice reduction, is concerned exclusively with how people think about their own social categories. This model of **social identity complexity** (Roccas and Brewer, 2002) assumes that people have many ingroups (see also Crisp, 2005). Try out the exercise below and you will see what we mean.

Social identity complexity The extent to which a person's important social identities or group memberships overlap with each other.

Try it yourself We would like you to try this social identity complexity exercise. People belong to any number of social groups; for example, they can classify themselves according to their gender, sexuality, religion, ethnicity, nationality, interests, occupation and the organizations to which they belong. On a sheet of paper, list four important social categories you belong to.

1 _____   3 _____

2 _____   4 _____

Now, think about the overlap between these social categories. In each pairing below, write how much each pair of the categories overlap. Use a scale from 1 to 10. For example, write '1' if you think 'very few' people who belong to the first category in each pair also belong to the second category, 5 if you think 'about half' of them do, and 10 if you think all of them do.

Of persons who belong to category 1, how many also belong to category 2? _____
Of persons who belong to category 1, how many also belong to category 3? _____
Of persons who belong to category 1, how many also belong to category 4? _____
Of persons who belong to category 2, how many also belong to category 3? _____
Of persons who belong to category 2, how many also belong to category 4? _____
Of persons who belong to category 3, how many also belong to category 4? _____

Source: Roccas and Brewer, 2002. Copyright © 2002. Reprinted by permission of Sage Publications

Now, add the six numbers up. Subtract your total from 60, to 'reverse score' it. For example, if your total is 26, then your reverse scored total is 60 – 26, which equals 34. This score is one measure of your social identity complexity, and is calculated very much as in the first study that Roccas and Brewer (2002) reported. The higher your score, the more complex your social identity. This means that you perceive there to be little overlap between your various important social identities. You think of yourself as belonging to a range of different, rather dissimilar, groups. The lower your score, the more simple your social identity. This means that you perceive your important social identities as overlapping to a high extent. Thus, it is as though they are facets of a single social identity. Perhaps have some friends or family do this exercise and compare results.

According to some provisional findings published by Roccas and Brewer (2002), the more complex your social identity, the less you value personal power, the more you value tolerance and other 'universalist' values, and the more positive you are about outgroups. As you may remember from Chapter 5, Mullen, Calogero and Leader (2007) obtained further support for this idea in their archival studies of intergroup conflict. Tribal groups, and urban gangs, who used more complex (non-overlapping) sets of labels to describe themselves, committed fewer atrocities against other groups. For Roccas and Brewer (2002), complex social identity works by making people less closed-minded and equipping them with greater cognitive flexibility, as a result of experiencing life from multiple perspectives (see Figure 12.8). Further, if your social identities are largely separate, it is likely that threats to one of your identities are going to be easier to cope with, because your entire identity is not under attack.

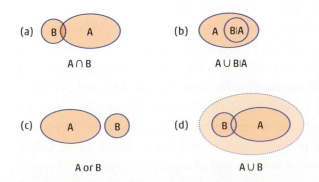

FIGURE 12.8 Social identity complexity

Source: Roccas and Brewer, 2002. Copyright © 2002. Reprinted by permission of Sage Publications

Consider the two social categories, A and B. One way that an individual can recognize more than one social identity and maintain a single ingroup representation is to define the ingroup at the *intersection* of multiple group memberships (a). For example, a female lawyer can define her primary social identity in terms of the compound combination of her gender and her profession, which is an identity shared only with other female lawyers. Another way of representing group membership is *dominance* (b). A female lawyer may see herself overwhelmingly as a lawyer (group A). Although she recognizes she is a female lawyer (group B within A), she does not feel kinship with other women, only with other lawyers. Another mental model of group membership is *compartmentalization* (c). A female lawyer may see her gender and professional identity as completely independent, and so will think, feel and act 'as' a woman in some settings, and 'as' a lawyer in others. Finally, she may see her gender and legal identities as *merged* (d), so will feel a strong sense of commonality and solidarity with women (whether or not they are lawyers) and with lawyers (whether or not they are women); she doesn't see anything special about female lawyers.

Values-based approaches

As we have seen, the contact and categorization approaches to improving inter-group relations have had many successes. It is clear they can be applied in class-rooms and communities to reduce prejudice between groups. They do not always work and sometimes may even backfire, but research has identified many of the conditions in which this happens and thus it is possible to reduce the risks. However, because the approaches do not always work, it is sensible to look for other approaches to achieving harmony between groups.

Many approaches to understanding how relations between groups may be improved have concerned themselves with values. Values such as tolerance, multi-culturalism and egalitarianism may encourage positive attitudes and behaviours towards outgroups and discourage hateful or competitive attitudes and behaviours (Crandall and Eshleman, 2003). If these values can be strengthened or if people can be made mindful of them, there is a good chance they will relate to outgroups in a more positive way. They can also defuse the harmful effect of values such as social dominance and ideologies such as right-wing authoritarianism, which can contribute to prejudice and conflict, as we saw in Chapter 11. A major strength of this approach is that the effect of values may be felt far beyond prejudice. Values have the potential to provide a common moral language, which means that not just prejudice but any harmful, negative action towards an outgroup is likely to be disapproved of, whereas acts of conciliation and consideration towards outgroups may be highly prized (Roccas and Brewer, 2002; Schwarz, 1994).

To some extent, we can view the 20th century as a kind of giant, naturalistic experiment. Throughout that century, values concerning intergroup relations changed dramatically. As we saw in Chapter 11, at the beginning of the century, many forms of prejudice, including racism, sexism and homophobia, were seldom-questioned norms. Although the principles of equality and freedom were already enshrined in the constitutions of many Western nations, numerous groups were routinely excluded from this noble tradition. However, values were transformed by the traumas and immense social changes of the century. In particular, the new horrors of industrialized genocide were brought to people's attention with ever increasing rapidity by the mass media. This brought to people's living rooms indelible and visceral proof of where irrational hatred and feelings of superiority can lead. Globalization brought different ethnic, cultural and religious groups into close contact and demanded that they learn at least to tolerate each other. The racist doctrines of their early 20th-century predecessors were discredited by biolo-gists and social scientists (e.g., Gould, 1996). Social scientific terminology like 'prejudice', 'racism' and 'homophobia' entered popular consciousness. To openly discriminate or express blatant prejudice was to risk being fined, fired, jailed, mocked and ostracized. The century saw the end of legally enforced racial segre-gation and discrimination in many countries, including the USA, South Africa and Australia. Blatant, open forms of prejudice declined dramatically. For example, Dovidio, Brigham, Johnson and Gaertner (1996) conducted a meta-analysis of the

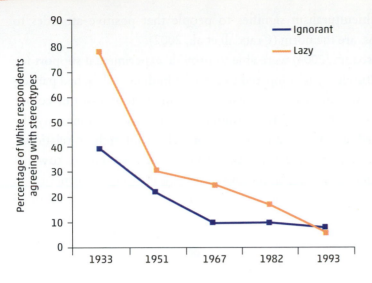

FIGURE 12.9 Decrease in negative stereotypes against Black people in the USA The overt expression of negative stereotypes against Black people in the USA has significantly declined in the 60-year period 1933-93.

Source: Data from Dovidio et al., 1996

Multiculturalism The ideology that diversity in a society should be acknowledged and celebrated.

Assimilationism/ integrationism/colour blindness The idea that diversity in a society should be downplayed and attempts should be made to downplay differences between groups.

literature on White people's stereotypes, prejudice and discrimination against Black people in the USA and found that the extent to which they selected derogatory terms to describe Black people (e.g., lazy, ignorant) had significantly decreased since 1933 (Figure 12.9).

Clearly, the changes in values in the last century were accompanied by massive improvements in many aspects of intergroup relations. This should be recognized as a phenomenal victory for human decency and dignity. But it is by no means a complete victory. In many countries, massive disparities in power, status, health and wealth exist between racial groups, even in the absence of legally enforced disadvantage. War, terrorism and hate crimes are by no means extinguished. If anything, some tensions, such as that between people of Christian and Muslim faiths, seem to have worsened. Further, how can we be sure that reductions in racism, homophobia and the like can be attributed to the new value priorities of tolerance and equality? Theory and evidence are needed to establish what the link is between these two.

Multiculturalism

Multiculturalism is the ideology that diversity should be acknowledged and celebrated (Takaki, 1993; Yinger, 1994). Different groups are seen as having equal value but being able to make unique contributions and offer unique perspectives to society. This ideology envisions a society that is more dynamic, creative and ultimately harmonious as a result of the coexistence of different peoples. It can be contrasted with ideologies that stress the importance of downplaying differences between groups, variously known as **assimilationism, integrationism** and **colour blindness**.

The 'melting pot' ideology of colour blindness has obvious intuitive appeal; indeed, it is widely favoured by teachers and administrators in US schools (e.g., Schofield and Eurich-Fulcer, 2001). Would we all get along better if we did not obsess, or even notice, each other's differences? But a good deal of evidence suggests that multiculturalism is the better policy for reductions in bias. One reason for this is clear after reading the categorization literature – multiculturalism provides a framework that acknowledges differences between groups but also suggests that these groups combine to create a new, superordinate, emergent identity. Thus, it encourages the simultaneous identification with superordinate and subordinate groups, which, as we have seen, tends to be beneficial for intergroup relations (Crisp, 2005; Gaertner et al., 1999; Hornsey and Hogg, 2000). Conversely, colour blindness may threaten people's cherished subordinate identities (Crisp et al., 2006; Hornsey and Hogg, 2000). Further, when group differences are acknowledged, it is easier for people to notice, and remedy, instances of injustice and disharmony between groups (Banks, Cookson, Gay et al., 2001). Also, the ideological nature of multiculturalism signifies to people that positive attitudes to diversity, to outgroups, are the norm (Crandall et al., 2002).

Richeson and Nussbaum (2004) were able to provide experimental support for the merits of multiculturalism, as compared to colour blindness. They had participants read a one-page statement that endorsed either multiculturalism or colour blindness, and then asked them to write a summary of five key reasons why the ideology they had read about was 'a positive approach to interethnic relations'. Afterwards, participants completed the classic IAT for implicit racism towards Black people, and then rated Black, White and other ethnic groups in America on a **feeling thermometer**. The multiculturalism induction led to declines in all these indices of racial bias (Figure 12.10).

Feeling thermometer A rating scale (resembling a thermometer) designed to measure feelings of 'warmth' or 'coldness' towards people of different groups.

FIGURE 12.10 Multiculturalism, compared to colour blindness, reduces bias People displayed less implicit and explicit intergroup bias in an experimental condition where multiculturalism was emphasized in contrast to a condition where colour blindness was emphasized.

Source: Data from Richeson and Nussbaum, 2004

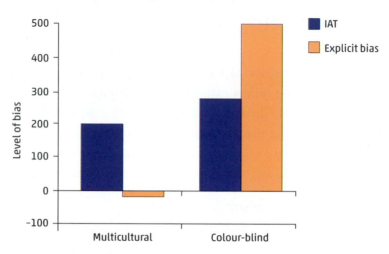

Exploring further Richeson and Nussbaum (2004) observed a clear difference between the multicultural and colour-blind prime. Can you tell from their results whether the multicultural prime had the effect of reducing prejudice? Why/why not? (Hint: think about the experimental design they used.)

Time to reflect 'Imagine there's no countries/It isn't hard to do.' In his song 'Imagine', can you recognize the technique of improving intergroup harmony that John Lennon was advocating?

Suppression of prejudice

As we saw in Chapter 11, many forms of prejudice and discrimination, including racism and sexism, have always been at odds with sincerely held values of liberalism and equality. Thus, people in avowedly liberal and democratic countries have experienced a dilemma – on one hand they are prejudiced, but on the other they subscribe to values suggesting that human beings are of equal worth regardless of race, religion, gender or creed. These two opposing pressures have long been recognized by social psychologists. Myrdal (1944), for example, wrote of the 'American dilemma', one of its horns being racism and the other the ideology of opportunity for all. Allport (1954) claimed that although some White Americans are bigots who are at ease with their prejudices, the majority experience compunction (moral guilt). More recently, as we saw in Chapter 11, people who are squeezed between these opposing forces are prone to modern racism (McConahay, 1986) and automatic prejudice (Devine, 1989). According to these theories, the mounting emphasis throughout the 20th century on values such as 'liberalism, egalitarianism, sympathy for the underdog … and humanitarian values' (Crandall and Eshleman, 2003, p. 415) has increasingly motivated people to suppress prejudice and the impulse to discriminate. These values have translated into social norms that suggest it is no longer acceptable to express overt prejudice towards many groups. These norms are extremely powerful, as some recent findings suggest.

Crandall et al. (2002, p. 363) asked 150 US undergraduate students to rate how acceptable prejudice was towards each of 105 groups, according to the 'predominant social norm'. Each group earned a mean prejudice acceptability score between 0 and 2, which ranged from 0.047 for blind people and women who stay home to raise kids, to 1.967 for rapists and child molesters. They then asked a separate sample of 121 US undergraduate students to rate how they felt about each of these 105 groups on a feeling thermometer from 0 = 'cold/not positive' to 100 = 'hot/ very positive'. This was later reverse scored (e.g., a score of 20 would be translated to 80, and a score of 90 would be translated to 10), so that the higher the score, the more the participants were prejudiced towards each group.

As Figure 12.11 shows, the more participants in the first group perceived prejudice towards each group to be socially acceptable, the more participants in the second group expressed prejudice towards each group. Indeed, this correlation was extraordinarily high at $r = .96$, just shy of the maximum, perfect correlation of 1.0. For reassurance that this whopping correlation was not a fluke, see Graziano, Bruce, Tobin and Sheese (2007) who found something similar ($r = .94$). To put the correlation obtained by Crandall et al. (2002) into context, the typical correlation between contact and (lower) prejudice is around $r = .27$ (Pettigrew and Tropp, 2006). It is tempting to say, therefore, that the effect of social norms is nearly four times as large as the effect of contact. However, this is a serious understatement. To get an idea of how the proportion of the ups and downs in one variable (prejudice) overlap with another variable (contact, or perceived social norms), you should square the correlation coefficient to obtain r^2. Squaring .27, we get a little over .07, or 7 per cent of the variance in common between contact and prejudice. Squaring .96, we get .92, or 92 per cent of the variance in common.

In an experiment reported in the same article and inspired by Asch's (1951) famous experiments on conformity, Crandall et al. (2002) had a confederate express prejudice. This had the effect of increasing the prejudice that participants themselves expressed towards the same group. This provides some evidence that norms, be they societal norms or the local norms among small groups of people

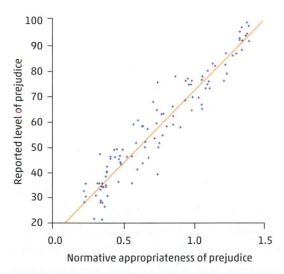

FIGURE 12.11 Correlation between level and appropriateness of prejudice
The correlation between the norm of acceptability of prejudice towards various social groups is strongly associated with the prejudice that is expressed.

Source: Crandall et al., 2002. Copyright © 2002 by the American Psychological Association. Reproduced with permission

gathered in a laboratory, genuinely have the power to influence, and do not merely reflect, the prejudices people are willing to express. Norms can motivate people to suppress prejudice in different ways. For example, if you are comfortable with your own prejudices but suppress them because you think others will disapprove, you are extrinsically motivated. On the other hand, if you dislike your prejudices and suppress them for this reason, irrespective of how you are viewed by others, you are intrinsically motivated. People may start out being extrinsically motivated to suppress prejudice, but, over time, internalize anti-prejudice norms and thus become intrinsically motivated (Crandall et al., 2002).

Evidence suggests that the intrinsic motivation to suppress prejudice may be more effective. One reason for this is that intrinsically motivated people experience genuine emotions, especially guilt, when they fail to live up to their own non-prejudiced standards. Plant and Devine (1998) attempted to disentangle the motivation to respond without prejudice by distinguishing between external/social (extrinsic) and internal/personal (intrinsic) motivation. They developed scales to measure both types of motivations to respond without prejudice towards Black people. Intrinsic motivation referred to internalized and personally important non-prejudiced standards, whereas extrinsic motivation referred to the social pressure to conform to non-prejudiced norms. Plant and Devine (1998) found that intrinsic motivation to respond without prejudice was associated with lower racism (self-reported racism scores), whereas extrinsic motivation was related to higher self-reported racism scores.

In another series of experiments, Monteith (1993) had participants decide whether a hypothetical applicant should get a place to study in law school. The applicant was weak and was duly rejected by all but 11 participants. Half the participants had been told at the outset that the applicant was gay, and were also led to believe they had discriminated against the applicant because of it. The other half had been told the applicant was heterosexual. Participants who were low in homophobia according to tests run before the experiment had thus been tricked into thinking they had violated their own moral standards. Following this, all participants read an essay about stereotyping and prejudice, ostensibly written by Monteith. Pretending she was seeking feedback on her ideas, she asked participants for their thoughts about it. What she was really interested in was whether participants mentioned their own prejudices, and whether they mentioned any discrepancies between their egalitarian principles and their behaviour. Results showed that after being led to believe they had discriminated against a gay person, low homophobia participants showed increased negative thoughts about themselves and took longer to read the essay on stereotyping and prejudice. They also thought more about themselves and the discrepancies between their ideal standards and their actual behaviour. The awareness manipulation had no significant effect on participants who scored high in homophobia (Figure 12.12).

Theoretically, these guilty reactions should help people exert self-control, because they bring the self into focus, motivating people to think carefully about controlling their future behaviour. Indeed, in a subsequent experiment, Monteith

(1993) led low homophobia individuals to believe they had acted in a manner discrepant with their standards. This led them to rate derogatory jokes about gays as less funny, witty and creative. In a later series of studies, Monteith, Ashburn-Nardo, Voils and Czopp (2002) found that, to some extent, practice makes perfect. The more people suppress prejudice over time, the more certain psychological cues such as the experience of guilt and self-reflection help them control prejudice.

Time to reflect Monteith (1993) excluded from the study the 11 participants who accepted the applicant into law school. Why?

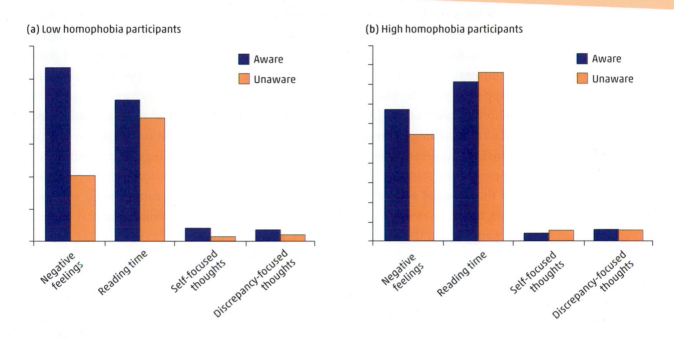

FIGURE 12.12 What happens when low prejudiced people are aware of having discriminated Low homophobia participants (a) who were made aware (versus not made aware) of their discriminatory hiring decision reported more negative affect, spent more time reading about prejudice, and experienced more self- and discrepancy-related thoughts. This awareness manipulation had no effect on homophobic participants (b), for whom a discriminatory hiring decision would not necessarily violate their moral standards.

Source: Data from Monteith, 1993

Can suppression backfire?

The findings we have been reviewing are impressive and cause for hope. Apparently, we have the power to control our own prejudices, at least if we really want to. Or not? In a classic experiment, Macrae, Bodenhausen, Milne and Jetten (1994, Experiment 2) explored the limits of the human ability to suppress their attitudes towards an outgroup. They showed Welsh participants a photograph of a male skinhead, and asked them to spend five minutes writing about a typical day in his life. Half the participants were assigned, at random, to the suppression condition. These participants were told that our perceptions of others are often based on stereotypic preconditions, and were asked to try to avoid thinking about the skinhead in a stereotyped way while writing their stories. The remaining participants were assigned to the control condition, and were merely asked to write the story without any such condition.

The manipulation was successful. Participants managed to suppress stereotypes while writing the stories. Those in the suppression condition wrote stories that were rated by independent coders (who were blind to conditions, which means that they did not know the instructions each participant had been given) as significantly less stereotypical than the controls. But of greater interest to Macrae et al. (1994) was what happened after participants had finished the stories and were no longer required to suppress the stereotypes. At this point, the experimenter told participants that they were about to meet the skinhead they had just written about. The experimenter led each participant to a neighbouring room containing a row of eight chairs. A denim jacket and bag, apparently belonging to the skinhead, were slung on a chair at one end of this row. The experimenter explained that the skinhead had left the room temporarily, and invited the participant to have a seat. The dependent variable in this study was how far away from the skinhead's belongings the participants chose to sit, from 1 (the next chair) to 7 (the furthermost chair).

What would you expect to happen? It would make sense to predict that those in the suppression condition would sit closer to the skinhead's belongings, right? Presumably, they have put their negative feelings aside and thus would feel more comfortable anticipating being close to the skinhead. But the exact opposite happened – those who had suppressed stereotypes sat *further away* than those who had been allowed to make their stories as stereotypical as they liked. Why? Macrae's findings reveal something about mental regulation. Once you have finished suppressing an unwanted set of thoughts or feelings, it can 'rebound', coming back stronger than ever. According to the leading theoretical explanation of this **rebound effect of thought suppression**, it happens because thought suppression relies on two types of mental machinery. The first monitors mental content for any sign of the unwanted thought, and alerts the second system that is responsible for eliminating or replacing it. Ironically, the monitoring machinery *activates* the unwanted thought (see Chapter 2 for coverage of the concept of activation). Thus, when participants give up trying to control the unwanted thought, it is left highly activated but is no longer being dealt with. So, in a rush and quite unchecked, it enters consciousness (see Figure 12.13). This theoretical process is known as **ironic monitoring** (Wegner, 2009).

Rebound effect of thought suppression The finding that after suppressing an unwanted thought, it can come back stronger than before.

Ironic monitoring The idea that monitoring mental content for signs of unwanted thoughts can ironically activate the unwanted thought.

Time to reflect Monteith's and Macrae's ideas can be linked to philosophical models of humanity. The Enlightenment model sees human beings as functioning best when irrational and unwanted impulses are kept in check. The Romantic model suggests that human nature is warped, with harmful consequences when people try to control their deepest impulses and desires. Whose ideas map onto the conception of Enlightenment and whose are Romantic? (If this is not immediately clear, it may help to look up 'Enlightenment' and 'Romantic' philosophy on the internet.)

This research shows that attempts to suppress stereotypes can rebound. Should we conclude that suppression is too risky a strategy for the reduction of prejudice, and look instead to other techniques for improving intergroup relations? This would be a sad conclusion, casting doubt as it does on the efforts of human beings worldwide to improve themselves in this important respect – to turn their backs on messages of hatred, intolerance and group-based inferiority in favour of a humane appreciation of equality. Fortunately, we have evidence that suppression can work in other circumstances (Monteith, Sherman and Devine, 1998). In the Wales of the early 1990s, there were few if any social rules that said to people that

© CREATAS

FIGURE 12.13 Can you avoid thinking about white bears? Wegner's (1994, 2009) research suggests that you may not. He instructed participants *not* to think of white bears. People were able to follow this instruction quite well, until the instruction lapsed. When permitted to think what they wanted, participants reported extraordinarily frequent and intense thoughts of white bears, compared to a control group.

it was not okay to stereotype skinheads. This was not and still isn't a group that is normatively 'protected' from prejudice (Crandall et al., 2002). As a result, participants were not used to suppressing stereotyped thoughts about skinheads. As we have seen, practice appears to make perfect (Monteith et al., 2002). Indeed, research suggests that if people are motivated over a period of years to think of groups as equals, they are unable to control even unconscious forms of stereotyping and prejudice in their thinking (Moskowitz, Gollwitzer, Wasel and Schaal, 1999). As we saw in Chapter 4, these unconscious, automatic or implicit forms of stereotyping and prejudice are commonly thought to be the most resistant to change.

The media and real-world conflict

One recent development in prejudice reduction research involves the role of the mass media in reducing conflict. Paluck (2009) argued that, for many years, psychological research has attempted to reduce prejudice and intergroup conflict with various methods, but that scholars still know relatively little about what interventions have been shown to reduce prejudice and conflict in real-world settings (Paluck and Green, 2009). Paluck argued that a largely ignored source of knowledge may lie in the mass media's role in shaping beliefs and behaviours, especially those related to prejudice. After the two world wars, social psychologists were interested in the role of propaganda in improving intergroup attitudes and reducing conflict and prejudice (e.g., Doob, 1935; Cooper and Jahoda, 1947), but this interest waned over the years as researchers became more focused on other methods of conflict reduction, and contact in particular.

Paluck (2009) focused on the central African country of Rwanda, in which 10 per cent of the population (and 75 per cent of the Tutsi ethnic minority population) were killed in an act of genocide during a three-month period of intense conflict in 1994. Radio communication was instrumental in fuelling the conflict as it is the most important form of mass media in Rwanda. It is well documented that radio communication was culpable in the genocide of 1994 (e.g., Article 19, 1996; Li, 2004; Thompson, 2007) and is specifically relevant to intergroup conflict as, just as in other parts of the developing world, Rwandan people gather together to listen to the radio (Bourgault, 1995; Hendy, 2000). Ten years after the conflict, a nongovernmental organization produced an 'education entertainment' soap opera specifically designed to promote reconciliation between the ethnic groups in Rwanda. The programme contained messages designed to address the mistrust, lack of communication and interaction, and the trauma remaining from the genocide. It contained educational messages designed to influence listeners' beliefs about the origins and prevention of prejudice, as well as paths to healing. It also contained information about norms – demonstrations of what listeners' peers do (descriptive norms) and should do (prescriptive norms) in everyday situations.

Paluck (2009) conducted a year-long field study to examine the effect of the programme on people's beliefs, perception of social norms, and behaviours.

Specifically, Paluck attempted to answer three questions. First, do the mass media have the capacity to influence personal beliefs about prejudice, violence and trauma? Second, can the media influence perceptions of social norms? Third, can the media influence behaviour? Communities were randomly assigned to a treatment condition (they listened to the radio programme), or a control condition (they listened to a radio programme about health and were asked not to listen to the other programme which was publicly available). Results revealed that the reconciliation programme did not significantly influence listeners' personal beliefs, but it did significantly influence listeners' perceptions of social norms. Further, normative perceptions were realized by actual behaviours such as active negotiation, open expression about sensitive topics, and cooperation. Thus, Paluck argued that in order to change prejudiced behaviour, a useful technique may be to target social norms rather than personal beliefs, and the mass media are a useful way to do so. This suggestion presents a challenge to other prejudice reduction techniques, which typically target personal beliefs and cognitive processes as the main source of prejudice.

However, this approach also has some limitations. Perhaps, the results are specific to the Rwandan culture and context. Perhaps, it does not consider the influence of age, particularly the possibility that younger listeners tend to be more influenced by the media (Paluck, 2007) and their beliefs are more flexible than older people's beliefs (Krosnick and Alwin, 1989). Also, although media exposure may lead to less bigotry and prejudice (Stephan and Stephan, 2001), if people are exposed to other sources of prejudice or negative stereotypes in the media or elsewhere, anti-prejudice interventions will have limited effect. It also raises some questions, such as how durable the effects are and how exactly the media work to influence perceptions of norms and thus prejudiced behaviour. Such issues may be addressed by longitudinal research, which would enable researchers to examine the social, political or individual processes that change over time to influence the perception of social norms. The Ethics and research methods box below looks at reducing real-world intergroup conflict.

ETHICS AND RESEARCH METHODS

Reducing real-world intergroup conflict

A great deal of research on prejudice reduction tests various techniques within controlled laboratory settings. In such *laboratory experiments*, units of observation (e.g., people, school classrooms) are randomly assigned to either a 'treatment' condition, which involves the specific prejudice reduction intervention of interest, or to a 'control' condition, where no intervention is implemented or the participants complete an irrelevant task. While there are significant advantages to this approach, Paluck and Green (2009) suggest there are some significant limitations of laboratory studies when it comes to making conclusions about prejudice reduction in real-world contexts.

Paluck and Green (2009, p. 349) argue that with the drive for simplification and experimental control, laboratory experiments may 'eliminate elements of their intervention environments, and theories that are critical to the external validity of their lessons for real-world prejudice reduction'. Perhaps most importantly, the situations engineered in laboratory experiments often lack correspondence with regular contexts of conflict. How can the results of laboratory experiments realistically be applied to real-world situations of conflict, with all their history and complexity?

Further, Paluck and Green (2009) argue that laboratory experiments test 'quick fixes'; for example, prejudice is measured, intervened upon and reassessed within the scope of a brief study typically taking less than one hour. As we alluded to earlier, how can researchers know if the effects of the intervention last much longer than the study period? Also, many of the prejudice reduction techniques tested in the laboratory are subtle and often minimal – for example, people might be asked to wear the same colour T-shirt or sit near each other. In contrast, real-world situations involve more significant impositions such as citizenship requirements and economic sanctions. Laboratory interventions also pay little attention to the roles of power and authority that typically exist in real-world conflict situations and significantly influence the perceptions of roles, norms and stereotypes. Further, the reliance on predominantly US college students to test prejudice interventions arguably limits the scope of the findings' applicability, since they tend to report less prejudice than the average person (Judd, Park, Ryan et al., 1995) and are more aware of the social proscriptions

against the expression of prejudice (Crandall et al., 2002). Paluck and Green outline several other key problems with the laboratory-based experimental approach to studying prejudice reduction.

They argue that *field experiments* – randomized experiments that test the effects of real-world interventions (e.g., like the radio programme we described above) in naturalistic settings (e.g., communities) – are a more effective way of studying prejudice reduction. They posit that the strength of field experiments rests on their ability to assess causal relationships and their ability to examine whether an intervention is effective – and persistent – among a vast array of real-world influences, including political climate, economic changes, social pressures and distractions.

Questions

1 Paluck and Green's (2009) analysis makes a strong argument for the inclusion of more field experiments in the area of prejudice reduction. However, there are some obvious barriers to conducting such studies. Write down some of these barriers and potential limitations and then read Paluck and Green's (2009) review for further insights and perspectives. Why do social psychologists favour experimental laboratory approaches over field experiments?

2 How might the field experimental approach contribute to theory on prejudice reduction?

Exploring further Another prejudice reduction technique is to allow the subjects to experience prejudice for themselves. Jane Elliott, an Iowa school teacher, pioneered this technique in her own classroom in the 1960s and became known globally for her anti-racism demonstration. She divided her classroom into children who had brown eyes and those with blue (and other coloured) eyes. Blue-eyed children were first designated as the 'superior' group. Elliot asked the brown-eyed children to wear collars as a way of identifying the minority group. The blue-eyed children were given special privileges, sat in the front of the classroom (while the brown-eyed children sat at the back), and drank from special water fountains that the brown-eyed children were not allowed to drink from. She singled out the brown-eyed children and referred to them with stereotypes such as being lazy and sloppy. Immediately, Elliott noticed changes in the behaviour of both groups and how they interacted with each other – the 'superior' group becoming bossy and arrogant and the 'inferior' group becoming submissive and timid. The next day, the exercise was reversed, making the brown-eyed group superior to the blue-eyed group. What do you think happened? In your own time, learn more about Jane Elliott's demonstration and what can be learned from it. Consider the ethical implications of asking children to participate in such an exercise.

Intergroup apology and forgiveness

As we saw in Chapter 10, it is possible to see groups as agents, whose members do not just act as individuals but together act as a collective. This means that it is possible for groups to acquire a kind of collective moral responsibility for their actions. For some thinkers, this means that when one group has transgressed against another, it is morally obliged to consider offering an apology (Brooks, 1999; Philpot and Hornsey, 2008). Perhaps the moral obligation to apologize is more pressing if it can be shown that the apology benefits the group that has been wronged. However, to date, social psychologists have not turned their attention to this question. It is a 'blind spot' in research that we think leaves open the opportunity to do much intellectually exciting and important research over the next few years (see the Blind spot in social psychology exercise at the end of the chapter). Another intended function of apology, however, is to allow the perpetrator and victim groups to reconcile with each other. What makes a good intergroup apology? Blatz, Schumann and Ross (2009) identified 10 elements of government apologies that theory and research suggest should make them satisfactory so far as the victim group is concerned (see Table 12.1).

TABLE 12.1 Ten elements of government apologies that should make them satisfactory to victim groups

Desirable elements of collective (government) apologies	Plain English examples
1 Show remorse	'We are sorry'
2 Accept responsibility	'It's our fault'
3 Admit injustice or wrong	'What we did was wrong'
4 Acknowledge harm or suffering	'We know we hurt you'
5 Promise to act better	'We will not do it again'
6 Offer reparation	'We will compensate you'
7 Address identity concerns	'We now appreciate and value you'
8 Minimize resistance from own group	'We are better now'
9 Praise current system	'This is a good country'
10 Dissociate from the past	'This would never happen now'

Source: Blatz et al., 2009. Copyright © 2009, reproduced with permission from Wiley

The first six elements had already been studied in research on apologies between individuals. The last four were specific to intergroup contexts and based mostly on theory rather than research findings. Blatz et al. (2009) found some of these elements present in all governmental apologies, such as in the South African premier's apology to Black people for apartheid, and the Queen's apology to New Zealand Māori for the illegitimate seizure of their lands. However, they were all present in only one apology. This will surprise many Australian readers, because, according to Blatz et al. (2009), the only apology that scored 10 out of 10 was an apology they attributed to Australian Prime Minister John Howard in 1999, regarding the forcible removal of a 'stolen generation' of Aboriginal children from their families. This certainly came as news to us in researching this textbook, as we knew that John Howard had spent many years after 1999 refusing to apologize, and that Kevin Rudd, his successor, had delivered what seems to most Australians to have been the first such apology. John Howard, no longer in office, criticized Kevin Rudd's apology as a mistake. This case raises a number of questions about what counts as an apology, how subjective the perception of an apology and its elements might be and thus how it might differ from person to person, and also, just possibly, the striking phenomenon of collective amnesia for apologies (see the Blind spot in psychology exercise at the end of chapter). Research by Giner-Sorolla, Castano, Espinosa and Brown (2008) adds another element to the mix.

They studied the importance of the emotions an outgroup member expresses in the process of making apologies and offering reparations. They found that ingroup members can be offended and feel insulted if apologies and offers of reparations are offered without emotion or with guilt. Only shame, a self-conscious emotion associated with low self-esteem and self-abasement, was enough to defuse the feeling of insult.

Exploring further Blatz et al. (2009) have helpfully posted the full texts of the government apologies they coded. Using Google Chrome, try to find this list by including search terms such as 'Political apologies and reparations'. Take a look at the list. Do you agree with the authors about the elements that each apology contains?

Do intergroup apologies, whatever positive effects they might have, elicit the forgiveness of the group by its victims, as the apologizers presumably intend? Intergroup forgiveness is a relatively new area of research and the signs are not good (for a review, see Blatz and Philpot, 2010). McLernon, Cairns, Hewstone and Smith (2004), studying a Northern Irish sample, found participants to be less forgiving of outgroups than people usually are in studies of interpersonal forgiveness. Philpot and Hornsey (2008) found that although good apologies convinced recipients that the outgroup felt remorse for what they had done, and would sometimes lead them to forgive the person doing the apologizing for the actions of their group, they did not affect recipients' willingness to forgive the outgroup as a whole for what it had done. Further, Philpot and Hornsey (2011) asked people whether the Japanese government had apologized for their aggression during the Second World War. Participants were more likely to believe (incorrectly) that they had not apologized than to believe (correctly) that they had. Although participants in Philpot and Hornsey's studies were slightly more forgiving if they felt that an apology had been issued, memory for apology was generally so poor so that it is difficult to fully appreciate how apology may influence forgiveness. Recently, Wohl, Hornsey and Bennett (2012) argued that one reason why apologies may not be terribly effective in eliciting forgiveness is because people view the outgroup as less able to experience complex, uniquely human emotions such as remorse. In support of this idea, they found that Canadian participants forgave Afghanis for a friendly fire incident to the extent that they perceived Afghanis as able to experience emotions such as anguish. The role of apology in the reconciliation process becomes more complex still if the victim group refuses to accept the apology. Harth, Hornsey and Barlow (2011) reminded participants about an ingroup transgression and were told that their ingroup had apologized to the target group. Participants were then placed into one of two conditions – one where the target group accepted the apology, or another where the group rejected it – and were asked to rate the target group. Results revealed that when the target rejected the apology, they were met with a strong emotional backlash and were rated with higher levels of racism. Participants also expressed reduced willingness to financially compensate the target group.

Facilitating intergroup forgiveness is a major challenge confronting researchers. The early signs are that apologies may not be a fruitful route to this goal (Wohl,

Hornsey and Philpot, 2011). However, recent research points to the fact that the dehumanization of the apologizer may be partly responsible for a lack of evidence linking apology and forgiveness. If victim groups view the apologizing group as capable of experiencing complex emotions such as remorse, forgiveness increases. Further, an ingroup proxy apologizer can eliminate the negative influence of dehumanization (Wohl et al., 2012). When an ingroup member relays the apology, trust and forgiveness become more likely. The message and tone of the apology may be important too. For example, empathic messages may improve attitudes towards an apologizing group, if trust in the group is high (Nadler and Livitian, 2006). The path to reconciliation via apology may therefore be possible if the right conditions are met.

Question to consider Reread question 4 at the start of the chapter. How effective are apologies as a means of defusing intergroup conflict? Is Jarek right in believing that an apology can solve any conflict?

Communication and negotiation

More often than not, communication enables people to cooperate and overcome conflict (Bornstein, Rapoport, Kerpel and Katz, 1989). Especially in the case of social dilemmas, when conflicting parties communicate with each other, they approach the issue as a common problem that needs to be dealt with in the interests of everyone. Communication can be particularly effective if conducted face to face, as it encourages people (or maybe even forces them) to follow established norms and adhere to certain expectations (Bouas and Komorita, 1996; Kerr and Kaufman-Gilliland, 1994). Three main elements make communication work as a method of conflict reduction and resolution. These are bargaining, mediation and arbitration:

Bargaining Conflicting parties seek an end to the conflict through a process of negotiation.

1 **Bargaining:** When both groups are fighting over something, one thing they can do to resolve the conflict is to attempt to bargain their way out of the problem. Specifically, one group can offer something and the other group either accepts it or communicates a counter offer. One question is whether it is best to drive a 'hard bargain' and go into the communication with a strong offer, or to attempt to resolve the conflict with a more reasonable, conciliatory offer. Some research suggests that tough bargaining may be effective because it reduces the other party's expectations, making them willing to accept less for themselves (Yukl, 1974). However, too much inflexibility can present conflicting parties with a situation where both lose out. Consider some serious world conflicts that have led to war, for example. Arguably, conflict escalated as a result of neither side being willing to negotiate a reasonable solution for all involved. As we discussed in Chapter 5, 'saving face' is a primary concern for humans (Goffman, 1955), and conceding more than one wants to concede, or backing down on a conflict from which a hard bargain is being driven, can mean a serious loss of face.

Mediation Conflicting parties seek an end to the conflict by negotiating with the aid of a third (independent) party.

2 **Mediation:** Sometimes, it is not possible to solve a problem without a third (independent) party stepping in to help. Using a mediator usually means that

the parties are both prepared to make concessions and if the concessions are made with the aid of another person, it is possible for face to be saved (Pruitt, 1998). Neither party is seen as weak if they both concede equally, with the help of another person. How does mediation work? Specifically, mediators help resolve conflicts by helping conflicting parties to rethink the situation and gain information about each other's perspective. This perspective-taking technique has been found to decrease stereotyping of a target (Esses and Dovidio, 2002; Galinsky and Moskowitz, 2000; Thompson, 1990). However, sometimes it is difficult to achieve (Carroll, Bazerman and Maury, 1988; Galinsky and Mussweiler, 2001), especially in intercultural contexts, which are common in political conflict (e.g., Bond and Smith, 1996). Likewise, learning information about someone can overcome reliance on stereotypes (Crawford, Jussim, Madon et al., 2011; Locksley, Borgida, Brekke and Hepburn, 1980). These processes allow the mediator to turn the situation into one where both parties can win. Indeed, Thompson (1990) found that with experience, mediators become more skilled at making losing situations into winning ones. A key factor that a mediator needs to build between groups is trust (Ross and Ward, 1995) and this begins by building trust with the mediator themselves. Then, through a process of negotiation, perspective-taking and explicit statement of a group's concerns, the conflict can be overcome (e.g., Kelman, 1997; Staub, Pearlman and Miller, 2003; Staub, Pearlman, Gubin and Hagengimana, 2005).

Arbitration Conflicting parties seek an end to the conflict with the aid of a third (independent) party who studies the situation and imposes a settlement.

Arbitration: Occasionally, the conflict may be too intense or the underlying interests of the groups may be too different for negotiation to work, even with the aid of a mediator. In such a case, it may be necessary for a third-party arbitrator to actually impose a settlement on both groups. As you can imagine, this is a difficult task – the arbitrator needs to carefully study each group's history, current position, concerns, interests and so on and devise a resolution that is mutually beneficial, or as beneficial for both groups as it can possibly be. This is also a risky option for conflicting parties to take. How can each group be sure that the arbitrator will do what is best for them? It is for this reason that groups tend to prefer to bargain or go through a mediator than have a conflict resolved for them through arbitration (McGillicuddy, Welton and Pruitt, 1987).

Real-world examples attest to the effectiveness of these techniques. For example, a successful mediation process was instrumental in resolving the Israel–Egypt conflict in the late 1970s. US President Jimmy Carter brought Egyptian President Anwar Sadat and Israel's Prime Minister Menachem Begin together and after 13 days of mediation, an agreement was reached that ended the long-standing conflict. A classic example of how bargaining may have helped resolve conflict can be seen in the media communication between US President George Bush (senior) and Saddam Hussein over the Iraqi invasion of Kuwait in 1990. A hard line was driven between the two groups when Bush promised to 'kick Saddam's ass' and Hussein promised to make the 'infidel' Americans 'swim in their own blood' and sadly there was no going back from there.

Graduated and reciprocated initiatives in tension reduction (GRIT) A conflict reduction technique that relies on both groups reciprocating a series of de-escalating actions.

Unfortunately, communication processes may be completely ineffective when conflicting parties are so suspicious of each other. In such instances, a process advocated by Osgood (1962) may be effective. This **graduated and reciprocated initiatives in tension reduction (GRIT)** approach works on the principle that one side in the conflict initiates a few small de-escalatory actions after declaring a desire to de-escalate conflict. Often, this intention is made public so that the pressure is on the other group to reciprocate the efforts of the other side. If done voluntarily, the technique may promote a series of conciliatory actions that lead to de-escalation of the conflict. There is some evidence to suggest this works. For example, in the laboratory, social dilemmas have been found to be resolvable through a bit of 'give and take', where conflicting parties match each others' efforts (e.g., van Lange and Visser, 1999). However, this strategy can easily fall apart if one group refuses to be cooperative (e.g., Lindskold, 1981).

Collective action

Sometimes, the most effective way to improve intergroup relations may not be to try to improve the way groups feel about each other, nor to bring them together in collaborative processes such as bargaining and reconciliation. The most problematic intergroup relations tend to involve entrenched inequality and conflicts of interest. In these conditions, ill feeling is a less important problem to solve than the material disadvantages that are built into the relationship between groups. Also, it is less likely in such circumstances that groups will approach each other with a sincere spirit of collaboration and reconciliation. Thus, the most effective way to improve intergroup relations may be collective action (Blumer, 1939; Major, 1994; Olson, 1965; Turner and Killian, 1993). In its general sense, **collective action** can be defined as the pursuit of goals by more than one person. It is a type of group behaviour, which was our focus throughout Chapter 10. However, in the social psychological study of intergroup relations, the term is a shorthand for the coordinated actions of disadvantaged group members in order to change intergroup relations.

Collective action The pursuit of goals by more than one person. Specifically, it is the coordinated actions of disadvantaged group members in order to change intergroup relations.

Sometimes, collective action is not taken by group members on their own behalf, but in the wider cause of justice and in response to the needs of other groups (Thomas, McGarty and Mavor, 2009a). On 15 February 2003, in the cold of an English winter, hundreds of thousands of British people descended on London's streets to protest against the forthcoming invasion of Iraq. For several years from 1998, many thousands of non-Indigenous Australians circumvented their government's refusal to apologize for historical wrongs against Indigenous Australians by signing a 'sorry book' that contained a collective apology (Leach, Iyer and Pederson, 2006). However, since people are more likely to take action en masse on behalf of their own group, research has focused mostly on this type of collective action (see Figure 12.14). Overwhelmingly, the study of collective action is focused on protest (e.g., van Stekelenburg and Klandermans, 2012; van Zomeren,

© PHOTODISC

FIGURE 12.14 Protest: the most studied form of collective action

Postmes and Spears, 2008), but other forms of collective action may include lobbying, organized charity and volunteering (Thomas, McGarty and Mavor, 2009b). Some famous examples of collective action have led to material advances in the welfare of the group and for wider intergroup relations. These include the velvet revolutions of the late 1980s and early 1990s in Europe, which led to the overthrow of Communist regimes throughout central and Eastern Europe, the civil rights movement in America, and the feminist and gay rights movements of the 1960s to the present day. Other examples of collective action have failed owing to crushing counteractions by authorities and advantaged groups, exemplified in the Tiananmen Square massacre of student protestors in 1989 in China. At the time of writing, other examples of collective action are ongoing and are meeting both success and failure, as in the Arab Spring pro-democracy protests and insurgencies in North Africa and the Middle East.

What motivates people to take collective action to improve their group's situation? After meta-analysis of many studies of collective action, van Zomeren, Postmes et al. (2008) concluded that three interrelated variables are of crucial importance. In their integrative *social identity model of collective action* (SIMCA), identity is central. People who are highly identified with their group are more likely to coordinate with others and act on its behalf. As we saw in Chapters 8 and 11, strong identifiers are more willing to make personal sacrifices in the interests of their group, more likely to trust and feel close to other members of their group, and more likely to share their emotional reactions to situations (Mackie, Smith and Ray, 2008). Thus, it is not surprising that identification straightforwardly promotes collective action.

The relationship between identification and collective action is not only direct, however. It is also mediated by two other variables, which themselves affect the likelihood of collective action. One of these is perceived injustice. The more people perceive intergroup relations to be unjust, the more motivated they are to take collective action to repair the injustice. As we shall see in Chapter 14, justice is important to people, and under the right conditions, they will go to considerable lengths to correct injustices. In particular, feelings of relative deprivation are important (we shall learn more about this concept in Chapter 13). Relative deprivation is the sense that one, or one's group, is deprived of benefits that others enjoy. Feeling relative deprivation as individuals, people often respond in counterproductive ways, including with aggression. But when they share with others a sense that their group is relatively deprived – a feeling known as fraternal, or group-based relative deprivation, they are likely to take collective action (Dubé-Simard and Guimond, 1986; Runciman, 1966; van Zomeren, Spears and Leach, 2008). The more strongly people identify with their disadvantaged group, the more they tend to perceive its situation as unjust. Finally, an important variable is the perceived efficacy of the group to change its situation. When collective action seems destined to fail, or to achieve only small gains, people are less likely to engage. People who

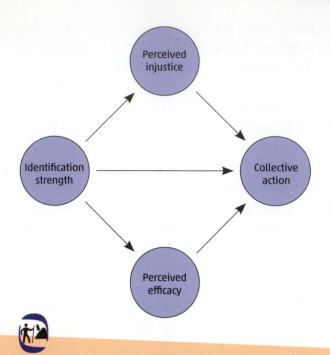

strongly identify with their disadvantaged group are more likely to perceive that it has the power to make a difference to its own situation (Mummendey, Kessler, Klinke and Mielke, 1999) (see Figure 12.15). Other models of collective action are broadly similar to the SIMCA model, but some emphasize other factors such as intergroup emotions, including anger (van Stekelenburg and Klandermans, 2012).

FIGURE 12.15 The SIMCA model of group identification Collective action is promoted by perceptions that a group's position is unjust, and the group is able to unify to improve its position. The strength of members' identification with the group also promotes collective action, both directly and by serving as the 'bridge' between perceptions of injustice and efficacy. Thus, identification has direct and mediated effects on collective action.

Source: van Zomeren, Postmes et al., 2008. Copyright © 2008 by the American Psychological Association. Reproduced with permission

Exploring further In 2009, the *Journal of Social Issues* published an excellent special issue on collective action (volume 65, issue 4), containing articles by several leading researchers. Locate this and read through the abstracts to get a flavour of developments in this field. Another excellent read is the article by Dixon, Levine, Reicher and Durrheim (in press) in *Behavior and Brain Sciences*, which is published along with several commentaries from peers. This reading will give you an excellent insight into the known facts, the untapped potential and the limits of collective action as a basis of improving intergroup relations.

Chapter summary

Improving intergroup relations is a primary concern for social psychologists. In this chapter we considered the major strategies to do so. Specifically, you have learned that:

- One method of prejudice reduction is to favour minority groups over majorities in isolated episodes. This is called tokenism, and although it may be well intentioned, one problem is that it can be used unconsciously as a means to disguise one's prejudices. Other specific forms of tokenism are affirmative action and the positive feedback bias.

- A more extreme version of tokenism is reverse discrimination, where people who harbour negative attitudes towards particular minority groups display pro-minority behaviour or public behaviour that favours the minority, as a way to deflect accusations of prejudice. A challenge for social psychologists is to separate well-intentioned behaviour from behaviour that has intentions to conceal underlying negative attitudes.

- Intergroup contact has become the most studied method of reducing prejudice. The basic tenet of contact theory is that

bringing together members of opposing groups should improve intergroup relations and reduce prejudice and discrimination, if certain optimal conditions are met (equality of status, common goals, intergroup cooperation and the support of authorities, law or custom). Research suggests that contact is generally effective in reducing prejudice.

- When contact is not possible, research shows that participants who are asked to think about vicarious contact – contact that friends or acquaintances have with minorities – show reduced prejudice. This is called extended contact. Simply imagining positive contact with an outgroup member can reduce prejudice in laboratory settings.

- Techniques based on the cognitive process of categorization have also been used to reduce prejudice. For example, the common ingroup identity model suggests that if members of opposing groups are encouraged to recategorize themselves as members of the same ingroup, intergroup attitudes will improve. However, it may be counterproductive to ignore identification with smaller, more distinct groups. It is best to complement this identification with superordinate identities that can include other groups. Another model – the social identity complexity model – argues that the more complex a person's social identity, that is, the less their group memberships overlap or are related to each other, the more positive they are likely to feel about the outgroup.

- Other approaches have been concerned with values such as tolerance, multiculturalism and egalitarianism, which may encourage positive attitudes and behaviours towards outgroups. In particular, multiculturalism – the ideology that diversity should be acknowledged and celebrated – is successful compared to approaches that downplay differences between groups (e.g., colour blindness).
- Social psychologists have investigated the extent to which people are able to suppress prejudice. Social norms suggest it is no longer acceptable to express overt prejudice towards many groups. Suppression, however, can sometimes backfire as in the case of stereotype rebound – once a person has finished suppressing an unwanted thought, it can come back stronger than ever.
- Another approach that is more directly related to real-world conflict is the role of the media in shaping (and potentially changing for the better) people's beliefs and behaviours. It

is argued that using the media overcomes many of the limitations of laboratory experimentation.

- Apology is seen as an obligation of a group that has transgressed against another group. There are said to be several features that make a good apology.
- Direct communication and negotiation may be a useful way to reduce intergroup tensions, through processes of bargaining, mediation and arbitration.
- Another way of improving intergroup relations is to take collective action. Here, group members work together to promote a common cause. This cause may be the interests of their own group, or wider causes such as justice, peace and equality. Social identity, perceived injustice and the perceived efficacy of the group in being able to bring about positive changes are important to collective action. Intergroup emotions may also play a key role. Collective action is often aimed at eliminating inequality and injustice, rather than creating goodwill or reducing prejudice.

In this chapter, you have acquired a comprehensive knowledge of social psychologists' progress on the important issue of reducing intergroup conflict. We have outlined a wide range of strategies that continue to change (and new techniques emerge) as social psychologists get to grips with the complexities of intergroup conflict. In Chapter 13, we focus on yet another dark side of human behaviour – human aggression.

Essay questions

At the beginning of the chapter, we asked you to consider these questions:

1 Lisa asks her boss why her co-worker, Bill, has been promoted and she has not. She suspects that Bill (who has the same qualifications and experience) is being favoured because he is male. Lisa's boss argues that gender is not an issue in their company, which includes two females in senior roles and one who has recently been promoted. What social psychological phenomenon could this be an example of? What might be the future prospects for Lisa working with her current boss?

2 Fred has no Asian friends but his friend Jake has many Asian friends. Are Fred's attitudes towards Asians likely to be better or worse for knowing his friend Jake?

3 In a conversation about racism and prejudice, Sharon argues that these phenomena would disappear if everyone forgot about colour, cultural differences and what makes people different, and focused instead on what everyone has in common. Is this likely to work?

4 Jarek believes that an apology can solve any conflict. Is he right?

Having read this chapter, these questions could also be framed as the following essay questions, which you can attempt in preparation for your examinations:

1 Outline the advantages and disadvantages of tokenism, affirmative action and positive discrimination.

2 What is the extended contact hypothesis and what does associated research demonstrate about its effectiveness as a prejudice reduction technique?

3 Is colour blindness an effective way to improve intergroup relations? Explain your answer with respect to the common ingroup identity model and the mutual differentiation model.

4 How effective are intergroup apologies in resolving intergroup differences?

Further reading

Brown, R.J. and Hewstone, M. (2005) An integrative theory of intergroup contact. *Advances in Experimental Social Psychology*, 37, 255–343. Critical overview of research on the contact hypothesis.

De Dreu, C.K.W. (2010) Social conflict: The emergence and consequences of struggle and negotiation. In S.T. Fiske, D.T. Gilbert and G. Lindzey (eds) *Handbook of Social Psychology* (5th edn, vol. 2, pp. 983–1023). New York: Wiley. Detailed discussion of the role of negotiation in resolving conflict between groups.

Dovidio, J.F. and Gaertner, S.L. (2010) Intergroup bias. In S.T. Fiske, D.T. Gilbert and G. Lindzey (eds) *Handbook of Social Psychology* (5th edn, vol. 2, pp. 1084–121). New York: Wiley. Provides a section on the various strategies that social psychologists have proposed to reduce intergroup conflict.

Dixon, J., Durrheim, K. and Tredoux, K. (2005) Beyond the optimal contact strategy: A reality check for the contact hypothesis. *American Psychologist*, 60, 697–711. Critical review of the contact hypothesis that expands on some of the points made in the Critical focus box.

Forbes, H.D. (2004) Ethnic conflict and the contact hypothesis. In Y.T. Lee, C. McAuley, F. Moghaddam and S. Worchel (eds) *The Psychology of Ethnic and Cultural Conflict* (pp. 69–88). Westport: Praeger. Critical look at the contact hypothesis in the context of ethnic conflict. In particular, how is it possible that higher levels of intergroup contact are associated with increases and decreases in ethnic antagonism?

Kenworthy, J.B., Turner, R.N., Hewstone, M. and Voci, A. (2005) Intergroup contact: When does it work, and why? In J.F. Dovidio, P. Glick and L.A. Rudman (eds) *On the Nature of Prejudice: Fifty Years After Allport* (pp. 278–92). Malden: Blackwell. Provides an overview of Allport's contact hypothesis, developments since Allport's original ideas, a comprehensive overview of how contact works, and some suggestions for future directions.

Thompson, L.L. (2009) *The Mind and Heart of the Negotiator* (4th edn). Upper Saddle River, NJ: Prentice Hall. Clear and comprehensive overview of the psychology of negotiation.

 Visit the companion website at www.palgrave.com/psychology/suttondouglas for access to a wide range of resources to help you get to grips with this chapter.

Applying social psychology

Intergroup emotions approach

In the past decade or so, researchers have begun to look beyond simple prejudice – a negative emotional reaction or attitude to an outgroup – and have explored more textured, nuanced emotions towards other groups (Iyer, 2008; Mackie and Smith, 2004; Mackie et al., 2008; Thomas et al., 2009a). We can experience a range of negative emotions such as anger, fear, disgust and envy towards other groups. When people's social categorization is salient, they are more likely to share these emotions with other members of their group, meaning that it makes sense to say that emotions are experienced collectively (Rydell, Mackie, Maitner et al., 2008). These specific emotions are often more important than a general feeling of negativity towards groups in predicting support for intergroup actions and policies. For example, Cottrell, Richards and Nichols (2010) found that the emotion of disgust towards gay people was more important than overall prejudice towards them in predicting people's support for gay rights, and pity towards Mexican migrants to the USA was more important than prejudice in predicting support for caps on immigration. In the context of Northern Ireland, Tam, Hewstone, Cairns et al. (2007) found that anger towards the outgroup predicted decreased forgiveness – and that this anger could be reduced by intergroup contact.

Intergroup emotions and intergroup behaviour are involved in a complex interplay. This is consistent with contemporary theories of emotion, which stress that emotions have important functions and are not just by-products of our experience. For evolutionary theorists, emotions function to control our responses to threats and opportunities in the environment (Levenson, 1994; Tooby and Cosmides, 1990). Emotions also serve to resolve problems in relationships

(Keltner and Haidt, 1999). From this functional perspective, we would expect emotions to be related to specific action tendencies towards outgroups. From intergroup anger, but not necessarily disgust, for example, we would expect intergroup aggression to follow. Indeed, when groups are unable to respond with aggression to an outgroup that has angered them, intergroup anger intensifies, and when groups have the opportunity to aggress successfully, the emotion dissipates (Maitner, Mackie and Smith, 2006).

Collective guilt is an important intergroup emotion, which can motivate perpetrator groups to make amends for their behaviour and seek reconciliation with victim groups (Wohl, Branscombe and Klar, 2006). In two longitudinal studies, Brown, González, Zagefka et al. (2008) found that non-indigenous Chileans who felt guilty about their group's actions towards indigenous Chileans (the Mapuche) throughout colonial history were later more likely to support reparation. Ironically, the atrocities committed against the ingroup can reduce feelings of guilt about the harmful aspects of its own behaviour. For example, Wohl and Branscombe (2008) found that Jewish participants, when reminded of the Holocaust, felt less guilty about Israeli treatment of Palestinians. Sometimes, people feel angry about the perceived transgressions of their group. This feeling of ingroup-directed anger, over and above guilt, predicts non-Indigenous Australians' willingness to engage in political action to improve the lot of Indigenous Australians (Leach et al., 2006). British people who felt angry about their country's participation in the war against Iraq were more likely to want to compensate Iraq, to confront people seen as responsible for the war, such as Tony Blair, and to withdraw British troops from Iraq (Iyer, Schmader and Lickel, 2007).

This approach to understanding intergroup relations may suggest ways in which intergroup relations can improve. If we pay attention not just to the relatively coarse outcome of generalized prejudice, but also to the specific emotions that people feel towards their own and other groups, we may be able to improve intergroup relations.

1 An interesting intergroup emotion is *Schadenfreude* – defined as a feeling of joy derived from the misfortunes of others. Using Google Scholar or a similar database, find social psychological research on Schadenfreude. What effects does Schadenfreude appear to have on subsequent intergroup relations? What conditions increase Schadenfreude, and what conditions decrease it?

2 In light of what you have read in this chapter, should victim groups let go of anger? What are the advantages and disadvantages of intergroup anger for victim groups? You might want to read an interesting piece by Thomas, McGarty and Mavor (2009a) to help you.

3 Can you find any intervention specifically targeting an intergroup emotion in order to effect some improvement in intergroup relations? If not, do you think such an intervention manipulation is possible? Consider, for example, some of the embodied emotion manipulations of Chapter 4.

Blind spot in social psychology

Intergroup apology

As we have seen, research thus far has been unable to demonstrate a consistent, substantial benefit of intergroup apology (Páez, 2010). There have been some studies in which an apology from a perpetrator group seems to promote forgiveness from members of the victim group (Brown, Wohl and Exline, 2008), but more that appear to show that intergroup apologies fail to elicit forgiveness (Philpot and Hornsey, 2008, 2011). Indeed, when the victim group appears to reject an apology, members of the perpetrator group may react with adverse intergroup emotions including anger, as well as a reduced desire to compensate victim groups (Harth et al., 2011). This is not to say that there is not a strong moral case for groups to apologize. The rights and wrongs of apology may not reduce, in a utilitarian way, to the costs and benefits of apology (Barkan, 2000; Blatz and Philpot, 2010; Wohl et al., 2011). Still, the case for making intergroup apologies would be stronger if we had evidence for positive effects. As Philpot and Hornsey (2008, p. 486) put it, 'the time is ripe for a systematic exploration of what effects intergroup apologies have'. There are reasons to suggest that intergroup apologies may have some or all of the following benefits to the victim group, which remain largely neglected by research thus far. Specifically, intergroup apologies may:

1 Boost the collective self-esteem of the victim group. Research on interpersonal apologies suggests they may enhance the dignity or 'face' of both perpetrator and victim (Gonzales, 1992; Hodgins and Liebeskind, 2003). Receiving an apology may enhance victim group members' perceptions of the worth of the group, and may help them feel that their group is valued by others. This is known as *private* and *public* collective self-esteem, respectively.

2   Encourage the victim group to take collective action on its own behalf. Research on intergroup apology thus far has been rooted, more or less, in the prejudice reduction tradition of improving intergroup relations. In other words, the aim of an intergroup apology has been seen to foster reconciliation and reduce ill feeling between groups. But perhaps intergroup apologies help mobilize victim groups to help themselves by acting cohesively to promote their own interests. This can work by:

- Increasing the *self-esteem* of the victim group, providing the foundation for collective action.
- Increasing the *self-efficacy* of the victim group. Victim groups may expect apologies to signify that the perpetrator group is ready to change its behaviour (Philpot, Balvin, Mellor and Bretherton, 2011). This may translate into optimism that efforts to gain concessions from the perpetrator group will be successful.

- Strengthening the *identification* of members of the victim group. An intergroup apology acknowledges the reality of transgression and confirms a dichotomous categorization of groups. It acknowledges that the offence was not perpetrated by individuals against individuals, but groups against groups. A strong sense of identification is key to collective action.

Design an experiment to test one of these possible effects of intergroup apology. Find an intergroup transgression that interests you and where an apology would make sense. Your experiment should include an experimental condition in which an apology is offered, and a control condition in which no apology is offered (or there is no information about whether or not an apology is offered). What dependent measures would you use? Outline your study in no more than 400 words.

Student project

The effectiveness of imagined contact

Zara Christie studied as an undergraduate student at the University of Leeds and her final-year dissertation was supervised by Dr Rhiannon Turner. Her research investigated the effectiveness of imagined contact – an innovative way to reduce prejudice which we considered in this chapter.

My topic and aims

My study examined whether imagined contact (that is, imagining a social interaction) with an asylum seeker would reduce prejudice towards asylum seekers.

I volunteered with Student Action for Refugees (STAR) throughout my degree, teaching English and providing support to asylum seekers and refugees. Asylum seekers are a stigmatized group and through my volunteering I met many who had experienced prejudice in the UK. After reading about imagined contact and discussing my ideas with my supervisor, I was able to design a research proposal using this paradigm to explore the attitudes of British teenagers towards asylum seekers. At the time, neither teenagers nor asylum seekers had been used in research exploring the efficacy of imagined contact.

My methods

I used the imagined contact paradigm, which is the mental simulation of a social interaction with a member of another social group. Eighty-two 16- and 17-year-olds were randomly allocated to one of three conditions: an interaction with an asylum seeker, an interaction with an asylum seeker with reciprocal disclosure of personal information, or a control condition where participants imagined an interaction with an ingroup stranger.

Prior to receiving the instructions, participants read a few neutral facts about asylum seekers. Participants in the control condition were given this factual information after their imagination task. To reinforce the effect of the imagination tasks, all participants were instructed to write down details of the scenario they had imagined. Following this, participants completed a multiple choice questionnaire which assessed intergroup bias, specifically measuring intergroup anxiety, intergroup trust, outgroup attitudes, approach behavioural tendencies, and outgroup stereotypes.

My findings and their implications

Participants in both the imagined contact conditions reported significantly more positive attitudes towards asylum seekers than those in the control condition. No significant differences were found between the three conditions on outgroup stereotypes.

Participants who imagined interacting with an asylum seeker, compared to those who imagined self-disclosing information to an asylum seeker or interacting with an ingroup stranger, reported significantly higher levels of intergroup trust, were significantly more likely to report wanting to approach an asylum seeker, and also reported significantly lower levels of intergroup anxiety. Therefore, imagined contact proved to be a better intervention than imagined self-disclosure.

Furthermore, the effect of imagined contact on approach behavioural tendencies was mediated by increased intergroup trust. This novel finding is valuable as it highlights the importance of intergroup trust as well as the possibility of imagined contact increasing future intergroup contact.

My research project was successful in strengthening the imagined contact paradigm and further reinforcing the paradigm as a prejudice reduction mechanism. Furthermore, it demonstrated that imagined contact can successfully reduce prejudice within a school environment, suggesting that policy makers and educators should implement such interventions to promote harmony and tolerance within schools.

My research has also identified a new mediator – intergroup trust – which significantly increased the likelihood of wanting to interact with an outgroup member. My work has been accepted for publication (Turner, West and Christie, in press).

My journey

After graduating, I worked as a research assistant with my project supervisor, before volunteering in Indonesia teaching English to survivors of the 2004 Boxing Day tsunami and spending a few months travelling around Southeast Asia. On my return to the UK, I volunteered in the audit and evaluation team in the Medical Foundation for the Care of Victims of Torture in London. Following this I was employed by the NHS in Ayrshire as a research assistant participating in quantitative and qualitative research in psychosocial oncology. After this I worked as an assistant psychologist in Oxford and was involved in a national craniofacial audit. I have two further publications (Snowden et al., 2011, 2012). Recently, I started a doctorate in clinical psychology at the University of Glasgow and I am currently on an adult mental health placement. I hope to be able to work with refugees and asylum seekers during my training and once I qualify.

In choosing my student research project, I learned that it was possible to combine different issues I was passionate about: working with refugees, and social psychology. While conducting my research, I became efficient in managing my time and working to personally set deadlines. For example I collected my data very early on in the process which gave me more time to focus on my analysis and write-up. Time management is an invaluable skill and allows me to combine my current work as a trainee clinical psychologist with attending classes, conducting audits, and undertaking assessments.

My advice

I believe that it is important to choose a research area you are really interested in. You will have to read a lot of articles on the subject and if you are genuinely interested in it, you will enjoy the process and get more out of your research. I worked as a research assistant the summer before my final year. I would recommend this, as it gives you the opportunity to conduct research and enables you to think more concretely about your project. I would also advise you to be organized – plan different stages of your research (e.g. design, data collection, analysis, write-up) and not to leave things to the last minute.

13 Understanding and controlling aggression

In this chapter, we outline the causes of aggression and discuss the means by which aggression may be reduced. We outline the basic types of aggression that researchers have studied. We discuss the biological, social and cultural roots of aggressive behaviour, and consider the intergroup as well as the interpersonal aspects of aggression. At the end of this chapter, you will have learned about the key theories and perspectives in the study of aggression.

Topics covered in this chapter

- The human animal: biological bases of aggression
- The social animal: social causes of aggression
- The tribal animal: the group dimension of aggression

Key features

Critical focus Violence against women

Ethics and research methods Measuring aggression in the laboratory

Social psychology in the real world Alcohol and aggression

Applying social psychology Bullying interventions

Blind spot in social psychology Ideology, sport and war

Student project Policing of crowd behaviour and violence

Questions to consider

1 Your friend has a punch bag and lets the bag have it whenever someone really annoys them. They say it's a good way to let off steam and stops them from doing or saying aggressive things to people. Is this coping strategy a good idea?

2 Johnny plays a lot of violent video games. Should his parents worry that this will make him aggressive?

3 You are discussing the latest war and one of your female friends says: 'Why are men always so aggressive? If the world were run by women, there would be fewer wars!' Is she right?

Wherever you go in the world, you will encounter human aggression. At whatever time of human history (not to mention prehistory) you care to examine, you will also find evidence of human aggression. Since time immemorial, people have beaten, clubbed, stabbed, choked, hung, shot and tortured each other, applying not just their animal strength but also their human ingenuity to the problem of how to hurt other people. Indeed, for philosophers such as Hobbes ([1651] 2007), extreme levels of aggression are natural for human beings. Hobbes argued that a stable infrastructure of laws, institutions and governments is required to keep human aggression in check; without it, human life is 'nasty, brutish, and short'.

As we shall see in this chapter, there are all sorts of reasons why human beings are so aggressive. To some extent, evolution appears to have hard-wired aggression into our biology, as it has all animals whose survival has depended on the ability to fight and kill. Matters are not helped by our ability to feel deprived relative to others, to experience injustice keenly, to attribute responsibility and intentionality to the annoying or frustrating behaviour of others, and to experience anger when we do so. Finally, many of the social processes that begin when we gather in groups also seem to lead to aggression.

Realistically, human beings will always display some aggression, although many of our instincts and aspirations are much more noble, as other philosophers such as Dryden (see Scott, 1883) and Rousseau ([1749]1998) have pointed out. The hope motivating research on aggression is that by understanding its causes, we can begin to reduce the terrible toll it takes on the lives of people worldwide. Social psychology is well placed to do this. With its commitment to scientific methods, it can add evidence and discovery to the insights of philosophers such as Hobbes. There is hope, then, that we may be able to alleviate the problem of humanity's inhumanity to humanity.

What is aggression? This is a difficult question and you will encounter different definitions in the literature. At first, you might think of it as doing harm to others. However, if you think about it for a while, you will realize that doing harm is not a necessary component of aggression. You might try to hit someone, and miss, so you have not hurt them – but your act was surely aggressive. Neither is hurt sufficient for aggression. If you make the mistake of going to the dentist, there is a good chance they will hurt you. But not all dentists are bad people, and their goal is not necessarily to hurt you. Most researchers now think that the intention to hurt is a key component of aggression (e.g., Geen, 1990). Thus, a decent working definition for **aggression** is behaviour primarily intended to harm another living being. Note that 'harm' is a broad term and this is deliberate. Although **physical aggression** is probably the form of aggression that comes most easily to mind, and is discussed the most in this chapter, much aggression does not involve physical harm. Insults, malicious gossip, ostracism and hate speech are all acts of **social aggression** that are intended to harm, but will not break your bones or directly cause you any kind of physical damage.

Among nonhuman animals, it is also useful to distinguish two types of aggression. *Hostile aggression* occurs between members of the same species, is accompa-

Aggression Behaviour primarily intended to harm another living being.

Physical aggression Behaviour intended to cause physical harm to another living being.

Social aggression Behaviour intended to cause harm to another person's emotional or social wellbeing without inflicting physical injury.

nied by displays of anger and is often triggered by competition over resources such as food, mates or status. *Instrumental* (or 'silent') *aggression* occurs between animals of different species, such as predator–prey pairs, and is not accompanied by displays of anger (Bushman and Anderson, 1998; Renfrew, 1993). This distinction has often been applied to human aggression, too. In humans, hostile aggression (also known as 'impulsive', 'affective', or 'angry' aggression) is said to be accompanied and motivated by angry feelings, typically impulsive rather than thought out, and motivated entirely to hurt someone. In contrast, instrumental aggression is premeditated, rather more coolly calculated behaviour that is motivated to hurt someone, but in the service of some other goal, such as for money or revenge. However, its application to human beings has been heavily criticized, largely on the basis that many acts of human aggression have hostile and instrumental components. Premeditated murder is often motivated by anger, and impulsive acts of aggression may be triggered by threats to one's status or a sense of injustice (Bushman and Anderson, 2001). Thus, we will not distinguish between these forms of aggression in this chapter.

The human animal: biological bases of aggression

Although human beings' approach to aggression is uniquely diverse, clever and technological, many thinkers have seen our willingness to aggress as part of our animal heritage. In their view, human beings, like other animals, have been equipped by evolution with a biology that predisposes us to aggress. The most thorough and influential statement of this biological view of aggression was made by Lorenz (1966), an Austrian **ethologist** who was awarded the Nobel Prize for his work.

Ethology The study of animal behaviour.

Biological drive theories of aggression

Lorenz's analysis of aggression was heavily influenced by two great thinkers. From Freud ([1930]2004), he got the idea that human behaviour is instinctive and affected by the *psychodynamic* build-up and release of energies within the individual. From Darwin ([1859]1996), he got the idea that instincts are acquired through natural selection, and that natural selection is driven by struggle between rivals. For Lorenz (1966, p. 27), it is 'always favourable for the species if the stronger of two rivals takes possession of the territory or of the desired female'. As a result of this evolutionary pressure, human beings and most other animals have developed a 'fighting instinct', causing them to aggress against members of the same species. This fighting instinct drives our behaviour in much the same way as our instinctive desire to eat, drink and have sex – all activities that are central to our ability to pass on our genes to our descendants. Lorenz (1966) argued that in much the same way as hunger and thirst, the desire to aggress is a kind of energy that builds up within the organism, getting stronger and stronger. It is released when external circumstances, such as the annoying or provocative behaviour of another person, allow the organism to 'consummate' its desire to aggress.

Lorenz's analysis has two important and rather depressing implications for human aggression. First, it implies that aggression is inevitable, being caused by a biologically programmed, hormonally regulated build-up of aggressive energy that needs to find some release. Second, it implies that in much the same way as hungry people go looking for food, people whose aggressive energy has built up to uncomfortable levels will seek out opportunities to aggress – to pick fights and look for trouble. Is this level of pessimism warranted? This depends on how well Lorenz's theory stacks up conceptually, and whether it is supported by evidence. Although it is important that we treat theories and findings on their scientific merits (as we saw in Chapter 3, people are inclined to wishful thinking, being sceptical of strong science that contradicts their cherished beliefs, and uncritically accepting of weak science that reinforces their preconceptions), it is perhaps fortunate that there are some important reasons to be sceptical about the pessimistic implications of Lorenz's theory.

For one thing, his analysis was built on a flawed understanding of evolutionary theory. You will note that Lorenz (1966) argued that aggression is 'favourable for the species', but natural selection is not driven by the survival of the species. Evolution is driven much more strongly by what is good for individuals and their families than what is good for larger groups – especially groups as large as an entire species (Dawkins, 1976; Dunbar, 1993, 1998). And although it is clear that aggression has been an important part of the success of individual human beings and the species as a whole, it is not clear that aggression is always a good thing for perpetrators. In human societies, at least, individuals who are overly or inappropriately aggressive, even if they manage to avoid incurring serious injury or death in the process, often find themselves punished and excluded by the group (e.g., Barner-Barry, 1986). This is scarcely a recipe for reproductive success. Thus, it would seem unlikely that there would be any advantage in having a hard-wired need to aggress that gets stronger the longer it is pent up.

Another major problem for Lorenz's theory arises from one of its most central ideas. For Lorenz, the build-up of aggressive energy within an individual may not lead to disastrous acts of aggression if it is released in a process known as **catharsis**. This is the familiar idea that if you can harmlessly release pent-up feelings of anger and frustration, you are less likely to actually take them out on someone else. As the idea goes, if you whack a punch bag, burn an effigy of your lecturer or even engage in revenge fantasies, your aggressive energy will dissipate. You may not be restored to a Zen-like calm, but at least you will be less likely to hurt people. Lorenz's thinking on catharsis was similar to, and no doubt influenced by, Freud's. Freud attributed human aggression to *thanatos*, a death instinct he thought was activated when *eros*, the innate desire to survive and to foster life, was frustrated (although Freud did not himself use the term thanatos, which was later introduced by his secretary, Paul Federn). Rather than aggress against themselves, people displace their aggressive energy and aggress towards others. Civilized societies are able to manage aggression by providing opportunities for catharsis: viewing aggressive or blood sports, for example, and expressing anger in milder forms.

Catharsis The release of pent-up aggressive energy through vicarious or symbolic acts of aggression.

The problem with the idea of catharsis, as plausible and in tune with our intuitions as it may be, is that it appears to be wrong. Many studies have been conducted examining whether catharsis reduces aggression. Cathartic techniques that have been studied include using verbal rather than physical aggression to a provocateur (Mallick and McCandless, 1966), watching violent films (Siegel, 1956), taking out one's aggressive energy on other people (Konecni and Doob, 1972) or engaging in vigorous physical exercise or contact sports (Frinter and Rubinson, 1993). The clear majority of studies show that these attempts to cathartically release aggressive impulses do not work (Bushman, Baumeister and Phillips, 2001; Geen and Quanty, 1977). Catharsis tends either to have no effect or actually makes matters worse, increasing the likelihood of aggression. One reason for this may be that precisely because catharsis feels good, it is rewarding. Thus, when people engage in cathartic release by watching other people aggress, or engaging in symbolic substitutes for aggression, they risk teaching themselves, subtly and unconsciously, that aggression is rewarding (see the material on social learning theory, below).

So why is the notion of catharsis so intuitively appealing? This is an interesting question that, as far as we can tell, has not been researched. Indeed, this 'blind spot' in social psychology might make an interesting student research project. Probably, we have all found it rewarding to engage in some kind of cathartic activity. If the activity is physically demanding, exciting or rewarding, then the flood of hormones such as adrenaline and endorphins is likely to have an immediate, short-term, positive effect on our sense of wellbeing. Indeed, Bushman et al. (2001) found that people engage in cathartic acts of aggression in order to improve their mood. For example, if they were told that a pill they had just taken as part of the experiment had the effect of freezing their mood, they no longer engaged in cathartic aggression. If something feels good, we may be inclined to feel that it is good for us in other ways, such as releasing our aggressive feelings. The fact that we are effectively training ourselves to be aggressive when we engage in cathartic feelings is less likely to be available to conscious awareness.

Another interesting possibility is suggested by the 'embodied social cognition' perspective we considered in Chapter 4. Lakoff and Johnson (1999) argue that people's understanding of the world is often based on their bodily experiences. Because anger and frustration lead to muscular tension and rising blood pressure (e.g., Kamarck, Shiffman, Smithline et al., 1998), we experience a bodily feeling of heat and pressure. As a result, we talk about anger in terms of related physical metaphors (Eatough and Smith, 2006). Very angry people are 'at boiling point', and need to 'vent' or 'let off steam', otherwise they will 'blow their top', and so on. The notion of catharsis makes sense to us because, arguably, it corresponds to the metaphorical sense we make of anger and aggression. In this case, we are perhaps misled by our metaphors. Those who believe that catharsis is effective may be drawn to the very behaviours that will make their aggression worse. Indeed, a study of participants in nonaggressive and aggressive sports found that participants who believed in catharsis were more likely to engage heavily in aggressive sport (Wann, Carlson, Holland et al., 1999). As we shall see later in this chapter, engaging in aggressive physical sports is a highly counterproductive way to reduce off-field aggression.

Exploring further You can do a quick informal test to highlight the intuitive appeal of drive theories and catharsis in the popular understanding of aggression. Referring to question 1 at the start of the chapter, ask some friends this question, without mentioning the 'letting off steam' part. Get them to explain their answer. Without you prompting them with these ideas, do they spontaneously talk about anger and aggression in terms of energy, pressure, heat, release, cooling down and venting? Scientists rely partly on metaphor and intuition when building theories (Fletcher, 1995). Do you think that theorists such as Lorenz (1966) may have been informed by commonsense metaphors of anger and aggression when they postulated that catharsis is an effective means of defusing aggressive tendencies?

There are some final points worth making about catharsis. First, there are some instances where being able to aggress works, as if there were indeed a cathartic release of energy. In a set of studies conducted in the 1960s, Hokanson (1974) found that being able to retaliate against an aggressor allowed people's blood pressure to return more quickly to normal. However, this only happened when participants could retaliate against the original wrongdoer, when the retaliation was seen as justifiable, and when the wrongdoer was not intimidating. This looks less like the mechanical release of energy than satisfaction that justice has finally been done (see Chapter 14) – 'I've given this person what they deserve, and it's over now'.

The second point about catharsis is that its failure to work does not disconfirm the biological approach to aggression. It simply disconfirms aspects of some biological theories of aggression, such as Lorenz's (1966). As we shall see in the rest of this chapter, there is plenty of evidence that aggression is influenced by biological factors, including our genes, our brain chemistry and our brain structure.

Question to consider Now that you have read the material on the notion of catharsis, reread question 1 at the start of the chapter. Do you think your friend's aggression levels are likely to drop by using the punch bag?

Genetic influences on aggression

The core of the biological approach to aggression is that the predisposition to aggress, under some circumstances, must have been of survival value to our ancestors and therefore must have been shaped by evolution. If so, we should expect to see some evidence that the tendency to aggress can be inherited. The answer seems to be clearly yes, at least in studies of nonhuman animals. In a striking study, Swedish researchers Lagerspetz and Lagerspetz (1971; Lagerspetz, 1979) isolated mice that appeared to be aggressive from those that displayed low levels of aggression, breeding these mice in two separate bloodlines. After 26 generations, they had created a race of aggressive, territorial, difficult to handle 'warrior mice', and another race of 'pacifist' mice.

In a larger scale study conducted in Siberia, the biologists Belyaev (1979) and Trut (1999) bred from a semi-wild population of Russian silver foxes. When the breeding programme started in 1959, the vast majority of these foxes behaved as we would expect wild animals to behave. They displayed intense fear when human beings approached them and would often try to bite the handlers. Belyaev and Trut selected those foxes that were least wild and bred from them, for generation after generation. Each generation became successively tamer, showing less fear and more willingness to be handled. After a few generations, foxes with an 'elite' level of domestication began to appear. These foxes did more than tolerate their human handlers, indeed, they actively sought out contact with humans and displayed affectionate, friendly behaviours towards them, much as a domestic dog would normally do. Although these animals were a small minority even after 10 generations of breeding for tameness, they comprised over two-thirds of the population after 30 or so generations of breeding (see Figure 13.1).

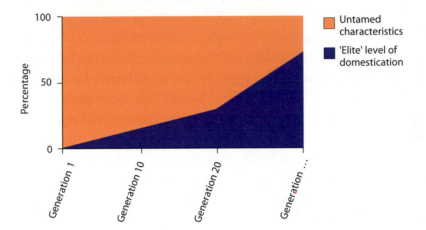

FIGURE 13.1 Proportion of foxes showing highly domesticated versus untamed characteristics
Source: Data from Trut, 1979

Notably, these behavioural characteristics were accompanied by some striking physical changes. Much more often than in the first, wild generation, the later, tame generations tended to have tails that were short or rolled in a circle and to have floppy ears. Most particularly, they displayed changes in their colour (that is, pigmentation). They tended to be more mottled, have a higher incidence of grey hairs and to show a white (depigmented) 'star' pattern on their face. The researchers point out that this pattern of depigmentation is common to many breeds of domestic dog. Indeed, large white patches are common to many domesticated animals, and relatively rare in the wild. It seems that the genes controlling aggression in many animals are also responsible for a number of physical characteristics. For biologists like Belyaev (1979) and Trut (1999), this makes sense – behaviour, aggression included, is regulated by hormones and neurochemicals, so selecting for tameness and against aggression amounts to selecting animals according to their **endocrinology**. These biochemical features regulate not just behaviour but all sorts of physical characteristics as the animal grows.

The Siberian silver fox experiment, like Lagerspetz's (1979) 'warrior mice' study, provides a controlled demonstration of commonsense wisdom about animals. Wild animals tend to be born wild and cannot be tamed. Some species are more aggressive than others. Some breeds within species are more aggressive than others, which is why certain dogs, such as the American pit bull, are banned in

Endocrinology The manufacture, storage, chemistry and biological function of hormones within the body.

several countries (e.g., DEFRA, 2009). Indeed, these experiments can be seen merely as accelerated simulations of the selective breeding to which people have been subjecting their animals for millennia, giving us the array of domesticated animals we see today. This seems to provide compelling evidence that the level of aggression shown by nonhuman animals, and potentially ourselves, is indeed influenced by genes.

Time to reflect A central plank of evolutionary psychology is that important aspects of our behaviour are controlled by our genes. Are the silver fox and warrior mice studies definitive evidence that this point is right?

Twin studies Quasi-experimental studies in which similarities in the behaviour of monozygotic (identical) twins are compared to those between other siblings such as dizygotic (non-identical) twins. Behaviours can be seen as heritable if they are shared significantly more among monozygotic twins. Stronger evidence of a genetic component comes from studies of twins reared apart.

For obvious ethical and practical reasons, there has not been a study on human beings to determine whether levels of aggression can be affected by breeding. One hopes there never will be. In the absence of controlled experimental evidence that aggression is heritable, researchers have instead relied on two main types of research to determine whether our genes can help to cause us become aggressive.

The first is a type of correlational study known as a **twin study**. Monozygotic or 'identical' twins have exactly the same genetic makeup because they are the product of the splitting of a single fertilized egg. If aggression is caused partly by genetic variations, then we would expect to find a close relationship between the aggression levels of monozygotic twins. This relationship should be less strong between dizygotic twins and between other siblings, who share less genetic material in common (see Figure 13.2). For example, Raine (1993) studied twins of convicted criminals in the USA. Half of convicts' identical twins but only one-fifth of their non-identical twins also had criminal records. Thus, the more genes that twins of convicts have in common, the more likely they are to share their criminality. Many studies produce similarly stronger relationships between the aggression levels of monozygotic twins than dizygotic twins (e.g., Tuvblad, Raine, Zheng and Baker, 2009). A study of 234 Canadian six-year-old twins suggested that physical but not social forms of aggression may have a genetic basis (Brendgen, Dionne, Girard et al., 2005).

Twin studies suggest that roughly 50 per cent of the variation in human aggression is attributable to our genes (Miles and Carey, 1997). However, this methodology has a number of weaknesses. First, it is hard to pin down cause and effect because twin studies are essentially correlational, relating naturally occurring genetic and behavioural variations to each other. The obvious potential confound or 'third cause' in this research is that genetic similarities normally go hand in hand with environmental similarities. Siblings not only share genetic material but are normally raised in the same households. Identical twins may share exactly the same genetic makeup but also are often treated and even dressed more similarly than other siblings. Although researchers normally attempt some control over these variables, it is difficult and probably impossible in practice to measure and control for all the complex environmental variables that affect our aggression levels as we grow up.

Some studies attempt to deal with this problem by focusing on twins who were separated at, or soon after, birth. Obviously, twins reared apart may have

FIGURE 13.2 Twin studies
Twin studies aim to determine whether aggression has a genetic basis.

© STUART MONK/FOTOLIA.COM

quite different environments even if they are genetically identical. These studies, too, suggest that the aggression levels of monozygotic twins are more similar than those of less closely related, dizygotic twins. In an early example of such a study, Tellegen, Lykken, Bouchard et al. (1988) not only observed this result, but also found that the relationship between the self-reported aggression levels of monozygotic twins was equally as strong when they were raised apart as when raised together (see Figure 13.3). They concluded that the environment alone cannot explain aggression. However, these studies also have their problems. Twins reared apart developed in the same womb, within which hormonal exposure to chemicals such as testosterone may have lasting effects on aggression (Ramirez, 2003). Their physical similarity, for example their size and level of physical attractiveness, is likely to mean that they will still be treated more similarly than other sibling pairs (you may recall the effects of physical attractiveness on social judgements in Chapter 3). Also, some meta-analyses have suggested that the apparent effect of genetics is strong in self-reports of aggression, as in questionnaires, but small or nonexistent when aggressive behaviour is observed in the laboratory (Miles and Carey, 1997).

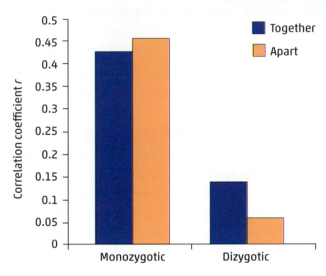

FIGURE 13.3 Strength of correlation between aggression levels in monozygotic and dizygotic twins raised together and apart

Source: Data from Tellegen et al., 1988

Generally, studies that have attempted to link genes to human behaviour produce mixed results (Ebstein, 2006). Even if we are prepared to accept that our behaviour is affected by our genes, the relationship is bound to be complicated, normally involving more than one gene, and certainly involving a raft of environmental factors that shape the way our genetics are expressed. But there is some direct evidence of a genetic component of aggression in human beings. For example, women with a mutation on a gene known as AP-2 have been found to show increased rates of indirect or social aggression (Damberg, 2005). These findings come from a second type of correlational research, which looks for relationships between genes and behaviours.

Mutations in a gene called monoamine oxidase A (MAO-A), located on the X chromosome, have received considerable research attention as a possible cause of aggression. This makes some sense because MAO-A acts to effectively 'switch off' neurotransmitters, including serotonin, which control many aspects of our mood and behaviour. For this reason, MAO-A has been found to be related to depression (Yu, Tsi, Hong et al., 2005). Crucially, as we shall see, low levels of serotonin are associated with increased rates of aggression. Indeed, variations in MAO-A levels in the brain have been linked to increased aggression and delinquency rates in teenagers and young adults (Guo, Ou, Roettger and Shih, 2008).

Although there is some evidence for genetic involvement in aggression, the relationship between genes and human behaviour is generally complicated, rather weak and dependent on a number of environmental factors. Thus, we should not expect genes to have a strong or straightforward effect on our behaviour. They may have no impact whatsoever, until an environmental trigger comes along (Ebstein, 2006). Some findings suggest that the MAO-A gene interacts with environmental factors to shape human aggression, and authors have even suggested that it may play a role in aggravating the 'cycle of violence', by which maltreated children themselves grow up to be more aggressive adults. In one study, a specific variation in the MAO-A gene was found to elevate the chance that maltreated children would go on to develop **psychopathy** (Caspi, McClay, Moffitt et al., 2002). Psychopathy is a personality disorder featuring reduced empathy and conscience, and is associated with an increased willingness to exploit and aggress against others. This finding led Gibbons (2004) to label the mutated MAO-A as the **warrior gene**. However, Caspi et al. were only able to find this effect of MAO-A among ethnically European participants, and not among other ethnic groups (Crampton and Parkin, 2007).

Some controversies surrounding MAO-A research illustrate the social and political implications of explaining human behaviour in terms of genetic influences. The labelling of a specific mutation as 'the warrior gene' is a striking example of how scientific concepts are sometimes 'branded' in vivid ways that capture public attention but overstate their importance. Fully 34 per cent of ethnically white participants have the 'warrior gene' (Caspi et al., 2002), of whom only a small proportion could, presumably, be termed 'warriors'. Nonetheless, this concept has been used successfully to reduce the sentence of a convicted murderer. In the American state of Tennessee, Bradley Waldroup attempted to kill his estranged wife with a machete and shot dead her friend. The defence argued that because Waldroup had the warrior gene, he should be held less responsible for his crimes. The jury agreed and commuted his sentence from death to 32 years' imprisonment (Barber, 2010). Whatever one thinks about the rights and wrongs of the death penalty, it is remarkable that a jury perceived this man to be less responsible for his crime because he possessed a gene linked so weakly to aggressive behaviour.

There has also been considerable controversy regarding ethnic differences in the incidence of the so-called 'warrior gene'. For example, this gene is more common among the indigenous Māori of New Zealand. In a conference presentation, some researchers commented on this finding and suggested that it might be because of the increased adaptive value of warrior-like behaviour among the Māori as they migrated across the Pacific and established new colonies (Lea, Hall, Green and Chambers, 2005, cited in Lea and Chambers,

Psychopathy A personality disorder characterized by impaired moral conscience, lack of empathy for others, and sensitivity to fearful and negative stimuli.

'Warrior gene' A gene responsible for regulating the manufacture of monoamine oxidase A (MAO-A). Some 34 per cent of the population carry this gene, which has been associated with a heightened incidence of psychopathy and aggression among ethnically European samples.

© PHOTOALTO

FIGURE 13.4 Who has the 'warrior gene'? Most if not all the people in this crowd are white. We can therefore expect roughly a third of them to possess the MAO-A gene (Caspi et al., 2002). Yet, there is no evidence in this photograph that members of this crowd are hacking each other to pieces. The extremely high frequency of this gene suggests that it does not deserve to be labelled the 'warrior gene'. Relationships between genes and behaviour are generally inconsistent and dependent upon environmental triggers.

2007). The argument is that the aggression encoded by the 'warrior gene' might have become more common among the Māori because those who were more warlike were more likely to survive, and pass on their genes, under these circumstances. This theorizing was based on a sample that included only 46 Māori participants. Unfortunately, this argument was picked up by the media and some politicians as an 'explanation' of elevated offending rates among Māori (Crampton and Parkin, 2007). There is no evidence that links MAO-A mutations to offending rates among Māori (Merriman and Cameron, 2007), and as we have seen, the relationship between these mutations and aggression in other ethnic groups is weak and dependent on environmental factors. The tendency to explain ethnic differences in behaviour in terms of differences in genetic makeup is disturbingly reminiscent of the old-fashioned racism that has been so damaging in world history, as we saw in Chapter 11.

Biochemical influences on aggression

Serotonin

Serotonin A monoamine neurotransmitter found in the gut, blood and central nervous systems of humans and other animals. It is involved in the regulation of sleep, appetite and mood. Depressed levels or function of serotonin are associated with increased levels of aggression.

The biological approach assumes not only that behaviour is heritable but that it is controlled by chemical processes within the brain and the wider body. Indeed, it turns out that aggression is influenced by endocrinological processes. Deficits in the levels or the neural uptake of **serotonin**, a key neurochemical, have been repeatedly linked to aggression in both animals and humans. Correlational studies examining levels of chemicals in the blood, urine or cerebrospinal fluid show that human beings who have chronically low levels of serotonin activity are more prone to aggression (Berman, Tracy and Coccaro, 1997; Moore, Scarpa and Raine, 2002). Evidence of causality is provided by experiments. For example, tryptophan is an amino acid found in protein-rich foods such as cheese, soya beans, sesame and sunflower seeds, which is used by the body to manufacture serotonin. If people are deprived of dietary sources of tryptophan, their serotonin levels drop, causing them to be more aggressive (Bjork, Dougherty, Moeller et al., 1999; Bond, Wingrove and Critchlow, 2001).

Drugs that affect serotonin also have an immediate impact on aggressive behaviour. Berman, McCloskey, Fanning et al. (2009) gave groups of previously aggressive and nonaggressive participants either a placebo or a dose of paroxetine, a drug that increases serotonin activity. Participants in both groups were provoked by a fictitious confederate who gave them increasingly intense electric shocks as part of a competitive reaction time game. Later, participants were given an opportunity to retaliate by delivering shocks back to the confederate. The drug had little effect on participants who did not have a history of significant aggression in their lives – these participants seldom retaliated, so there was no scope for the drug to make a difference. However, among those with a previous history of aggression, the paroxetine had a dramatic effect. Those who received the paroxetine dose were much less likely to retaliate, giving fewer than one-third as many shocks at the end of the experiment than those given the placebo. Intriguingly, a low status or

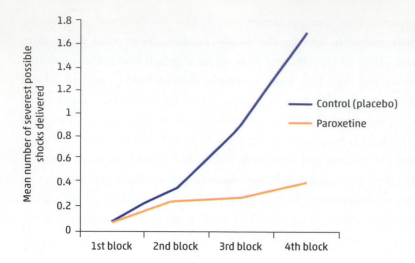

FIGURE 13.5 Serotonin activity and aggression The mean number of times participants administered the severest possible shock to a confederate who had been shocking them with increasing intensity over blocks of trials is shown as a function of the capsule that participants had taken. It contained either paroxetine, a drug that activates serotonin activity and is theoretically expected to inhibit aggressive responding, or no psychoactive components. These results were obtained from participants who were already prone to aggression at baseline. The provocation did not elicit aggressive responses from participants who were not already aggressive so it was impossible to test whether paroxetine inhibits aggression among such people.

Source: Berman et al., 2009

'subdominant' social position seems to reduce serotonin activity, in both animals and humans (Manuck, Flory, Ferrell and Muldoon, 2004). Serotonin depletion may therefore be a kind of signal that there's little to lose, that it is worth taking a risk by aggressing in order to try to improve one's position (see Figure 13.5).

Testosterone

Testosterone A steroid hormone found in both sexes of many animals, but in amounts roughly 10 times higher in men than in women. It is associated with increased bone and muscle mass. Studies suggest it may be associated with increased risk taking, selfishness and aggression.

Men are more likely to engage in acts of serious physical aggression than women (Björkqvist, 1994), and have much higher levels of **testosterone**. Research suggests that this could be more than coincidence – aggression really can be heightened, if not literally 'fuelled', by this chemical (Archer, 1991). Individuals who are chronically high in testosterone report stronger feelings of tension and agitation, are more aggressive, and are more likely to be in prison for unprovoked violent crimes (Book, Starzyk and Quinsey, 2001). However, the perennial question – does X cause Y, or Y cause X – is posed by a number of studies that suggest that aggression is associated with testosterone.

One line of studies shows that levels of testosterone rise when men win competitive encounters, and drop when they lose. Mazur and Lamb (1980) found that testosterone levels rose in men as a result of winning a doubles tennis match, and receiving a university degree. Similar results were observed in further studies of men (e.g., Booth, Shelley, Mazur et al., 1989) and other animals engaging in competitive encounters, including sparrows (Wingfield, 1985), mice (Leshner, 1983), fish (Hannes, Franck and Liemann, 1984) and monkeys (Bernstein, Rose, Gordon and Grady, 2006). However, research also suggests that among humans, who have higher cognitive capacities than other animals, the link between winning and elevated testosterone is not a direct one. Gonzalez-Bono, Salvador, Serrano and Ricarte (1999) found that after a match between two professional basketball teams, testosterone only increased if the winners made internal attributions for their victory, assigning credit to themselves rather than to external circumstances.

Experimental research on animals has shown that if testosterone levels are artificially increased under controlled conditions, increases in aggression will follow (e.g., Bronson and Desjardins, 1968; DeBold and Miczek, 1985). However, the case is less clear with humans. Abusers of anabolic steroids offer uncontrolled but naturally occurring experiments – steroids mimic the function of testosterone and users report increases in aggressive feelings (Perry, Anderson and Yates, 1990). However, people have expectations about the drugs they are taking, which can result in placebo effects. Björkqvist, Nygren, Björkland and Björkqvist (1994) found that men given testosterone over a one-week period showed no increase in feelings of anger, irritation, impulsivity or frustration relative to a group given placebo pills.

As always, it is hard to interpret experimental results that are null (show no effects) or inconsistent. We should not necessarily conclude that testosterone does not cause aggression in people. It is possible that testosterone is already at such a level in males that introducing more testosterone does not make much of a difference (Anderson, Bancroft and Wu, 1992). Indeed, it is possible that administering testosterone to men experimentally causes their bodies to produce less testosterone, undermining the attempt to experimentally alter levels of testosterone in the body (Björkqvist et al., 1994). Alternatively, it may be that testosterone affects aggression by changing the development of the nervous system over the long term (Bronson and Desjardins, 1968), more than by inducing immediate behavioural effects.

Although the jury is out on the role testosterone plays in aggression, it is often cited as a factor that may cause gender differences in aggression (Archer, 1991, 2009). Meta-analyses of hundreds of studies show that men and boys are more likely to engage in physical aggression than women and girls (e.g., Card, Stucky, Sawalani and Little, 2008). Roughly 10 times more murders are committed by men than by women (Bjorkqvist, Lagerspetz and Osterman, 2002). Approximately 97 per cent of murders in which offender and victim are the same sex involve men, meaning that only 3 per cent involve women (Daly and Wilson, 1990). However, men and boys do not appear to be any more prone than women to social aggression (Card et al., 2008). Also, the role of testosterone in higher rates of male physical aggression is unclear (Archer, 1991). Other factors such as men's greater strength, impulsivity and social understandings of gender roles may also play a role. For example, Crick, Bigbee and Howes (1996) found that children viewed physical aggression as normal outlets of anger among boys, but social aggression as a normal outlet for girls.

Time to reflect The Y chromosome is possessed by roughly one half of the human population (that is, males). Research has shown that males are more prone to aggression than females, therefore the Y chromosome is clearly related to aggression. Compare this to the much weaker relationship between aggression and possession of the MAO-A or 'warrior gene' on the X chromosome that we read about earlier. Should we call the Y chromosome the 'warrior chromosome'? Should men being tried for murder be able to plead diminished responsibility because they possess the Y chromosome? If you are interested in reading more about this topic, we recommend you search the internet with the key terms 'genetic determinism' and 'responsibility'.

Neuroanatomical influences on aggression

Another line of evidence that biology matters comes from studies on the structure of the brain. If it is possible to show that structures in the brain are specialized for aggression, then there is evidence that humans and other animals have been hard-wired with a propensity to aggress. In a series of studies conducted during the 1950s and 60s, Yale University researcher José Delgado used electrical stimulation of specific brain regions (usually the hypothalamus) to achieve more and more refined control over the aggressive responses of monkeys and cats. By the mid-1960s, Delgado (1967) had successfully created what might be termed 'remote-controlled monkeys', whose aggressive and defensive responses could be controlled by means of remote-controlled electrodes in their brains. It even seemed that monkeys could control each other – a small monkey, for example, was able to 'turn off' a larger animal when it began to display aggressive tendencies. In a notorious, showman-like demonstration of the power of brain stimulation, Delgado put himself in a ring with a charging bull and stopped its charge with one of his remote-controlled devices.

Exploring further Delgado pulled off his bullfighting stunt in 1963. Use the internet to find out more about it and to see still and moving image files.

People are not immune from this technique of brain control (Blank, 2005). A psychiatrist narrowly escaped injury after his client became enraged and smashed her guitar after she had received painless electrical stimulation in the amygdala (Moyer, 1976). However, more recently evolved brain structures such as the prefrontal cortex can sometimes step in, saving us from enacting the aggressive impulses being suggested by brainstem and limbic systems deep in our brains. Notably, studies using positron emission tomography scanning suggest that the prefrontal cortex is significantly less active in murderers and other violent offenders than in the general population (e.g., Davidson, Putnam and Larson, 2000; Raine, Buchsbaum and LaCasse, 1997).

SOCIAL PSYCHOLOGY IN THE REAL WORLD

Alcohol and aggression

In many countries over the past decade or two, a blaze of publicity has surrounded the problem of alcohol-fuelled aggression in town centres. How real is this concern? Well, if you are looking for a statistically powerful cause of aggression, look no further than alcohol. Here are some statistics that are staggering in more than one sense of the word. According to the best estimates of many studies, at least two-thirds of all murders are committed under the influence of alcohol, at least half of sexual offences, and around half of all domestic violence offences perpetrated by men against their spouses (e.g., Bègue and Subra, 2008; Roizen, 1997). This is not just correlation, it is also causation – any number of experimental studies have shown that having participants drink alcohol makes them more aggressive (e.g., Taylor and Gammon, 1975). If we were to eliminate the consumption of alcohol, therefore, it is clear that undreamt-of reductions in violence would follow. If we were to limit or control its consumption more

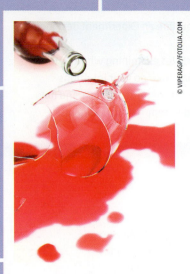

© VIPERAGP/FOTOLIA.COM

effectively, it is clear that substantial reductions could also be achieved. Ideally, campaigns to reduce alcohol consumption should be targeted at those most at risk of aggressing. Those who are aggressive even when they are sober are more likely to drink heavily (Gustafson, 1994). And when they do drink, alcohol has an especially powerful effect on their aggression (Bailey and Taylor, 1991). Unfortunately, big men, who are capable of doing the most damage to others, are also most prone to becoming aggressive when they drink. A recent pair of experiments showed that smaller men's aggression levels are less affected by the consumption of alcohol. So, watch out for the 'big, the bad, and the boozed-up', as the researchers colourfully put it (DeWall, Bushman, Giancola and Webster, 2010).

How does alcohol exert such a massive effect on aggression? It is a complex drug and works in many ways. It seems to interact with testosterone – mice and human beings with high testosterone levels are especially prone to the effects of alcohol (deBold and Miczek, 1985). It can also interact with other drugs, such as the party drug flunitrazepam – mice and rats given combinations of alcohol and this drug were especially aggressive (de Almeida, Saft, Rosa and Miczek, 2010). Alcohol also works to impair the function of the prefrontal cortex, meaning that people fall victim to 'alcohol myopia' (Steele and Josephs, 1990). This is an inability to control their behaviour, linked to a failure of imagination – people cannot foresee the consequences of their behaviour. Undoubtedly, there are biochemical pathways, meaning that we can see the influence of alcohol on aggression as being consistent with the biological approach. However, this is not quite the whole story.

For one thing, it is not always necessary to actually drink alcohol; sometimes, it is enough merely to think that one has drunk it. There is a small but apparently significant placebo effect across studies – if people take a drink that contains no alcohol but are told it is alcoholic, they will tend to be more aggressive (Exum, 2006). This effect may be larger when experiments are carefully designed to disentangle the effect of real and 'pretend' alcohol. In a recent study, Bègue, Subra, Arvers et al. (2009) gave one-third of male participants a non-alcoholic drink, one-third a moderately alcoholic drink and one-third a highly alcoholic drink. Within each of these experimental conditions, one-third of participants were told they were drinking a non-alcoholic drink that tasted alcoholic, one-third were told they were drinking a moderately alcoholic drink, and the rest were told they were drinking a highly alcoholic drink. In the placebo (no-alcohol) conditions, the rims of the glasses were sprayed with a trace of alcohol to ensure that all drinks tasted alcoholic. As in several previous studies, aggression was measured by the amount of hot spice and salt that participants gave to a confederate as part of a taste test. In this set-up, aggression was affected by what participants believed they had drunk, not what they had actually consumed. Thus, the beliefs, and the culture, that surround alcohol seem to be an important determinant of its effects on behaviour. Indeed, being primed with alcohol-related words on a computer screen appears to activate the concept of aggression, making aggression-related words easier to identify (Bartholow and Heinz, 2006). Even showing alcohol-related imagery to children who have not yet consumed alcohol increases the likelihood that they will subsequently aggress in a laboratory task (Brown, Coyne, Barlow and Qualter, 2010).

All this means that it will not be enough merely to control the consumption of alcohol, although this must be an important part of the story. It is also going to be necessary to change the way that people think about alcohol and its effects. A big problem is that people associate alcohol with aggression. Indeed, qualitative interviews of untreated heavy drinkers in the West Midlands repeatedly showed that these 'problem' drinkers thought that alcohol was very much to blame for violent conduct (Rolfe, Dalton, Krishnan et al., 2006). Another qualitative study, this time involving men who had been involved in violence in pubs and bars in England, also revealed a strong cultural equation of alcohol and violence. In the words of one participant in the study: 'It feels like you're drinking testosterone by the glass, liquid strength or something. You just feel invincible when you're really hammered or drunk, I guess' (Graham and Wells, 2003, p. 551).

Questions

1 Many public campaigns designed to reduce problem drinking among young people link alcohol to violence. See if you can find an example by searching 'alcohol' and 'violence' using Google or a similar search engine. Do you think these campaigns might backfire? How?

2 In a few sentences, outline an experiment designed to test your idea.

3 See if you can find articles examining whether these campaigns do backfire. How do your intuitions compare with the results of these studies? And how similar were the studies reported to your own?

Try it yourself What are your alcohol expectancies? Complete Fromme, Stroot and Kaplan's (1993) measure of alcohol expectancy, called CEOA (short for Comprehensive Effects of Alcohol). Have a friend or family member complete it too, and compare your responses. This scale has seven subscales. Items 1–7 refer to sociability, 8–10 tension reduction, 11–15 liquid courage, 16–19 sexuality, 20–28 impairment, 29–33 risk and aggression, 34–37 self-perception. Calculate your mean for each subscale (add up the scores for each item, and divide by the number of items in each subscale). How do they compare to those of others? Although Fromme et al. (1993) do not report means of each subscale, you could find out what means arise from studies that have since used it (if you are interested, use a search engine or database).

If I were under the influence of drinking alcohol:

1 I would act sociably	disagree	1	2	3	4	agree
2 It would be easier to talk to people	disagree	1	2	3	4	agree
3 I would be friendly	disagree	1	2	3	4	agree
4 I would be talkative	disagree	1	2	3	4	agree
5 I would be outgoing	disagree	1	2	3	4	agree
6 It would be easier to express feelings	disagree	1	2	3	4	agree
7 I would be energetic	disagree	1	2	3	4	agree
8 I would feel calm	disagree	1	2	3	4	agree
9 I would feel peaceful	disagree	1	2	3	4	agree
10 My body would feel relaxed	disagree	1	2	3	4	agree
11 I would feel courageous	disagree	1	2	3	4	agree
12 I would feel brave and daring	disagree	1	2	3	4	agree
13 I would feel unafraid	disagree	1	2	3	4	agree
14 I would feel powerful	disagree	1	2	3	4	agree
15 I would feel creative	disagree	1	2	3	4	agree
16 I would be a better lover	disagree	1	2	3	4	agree
17 I would enjoy sex more	disagree	1	2	3	4	agree
18 I would feel sexy	disagree	1	2	3	4	agree
19 It would be easier to act out my fantasies	disagree	1	2	3	4	agree
20 I would be clumsy	disagree	1	2	3	4	agree
21 I would feel dizzy	disagree	1	2	3	4	agree
22 My head would feel fuzzy	disagree	1	2	3	4	agree
23 My responses would be slow	disagree	1	2	3	4	agree
24 I would have difficulty thinking	disagree	1	2	3	4	agree
25 My writing would be impaired	disagree	1	2	3	4	agree

26 I would feel shaky or jittery the next day	disagree	1	2	3	4	agree
27 My senses would be dulled	disagree	1	2	3	4	agree
28 I would neglect my obligations	disagree	1	2	3	4	agree
29 I would take risks	disagree	1	2	3	4	agree
30 I would act aggressively	disagree	1	2	3	4	agree
31 I would be loud, boisterous, or noisy	disagree	1	2	3	4	agree
32 I would act tough	disagree	1	2	3	4	agree
33 I would feel dominant	disagree	1	2	3	4	agree
34 I would feel moody	disagree	1	2	3	4	agree
35 I would feel guilty	disagree	1	2	3	4	agree
36 I would feel self-critical	disagree	1	2	3	4	agree
37 My problems would seem worse	disagree	1	2	3	4	agree

Note: The CEOA also asks participants to evaluate each of these effects (on a five-point scale, where 1 = bad, 3 = neutral, 5 = good). This feature of the CEOA is not found in other measures of alcohol expectancies. For the sake of brevity, we have not included it here.

Source: Fromme et al., 1993. Copyright © 1993 by the American Psychological Association. Reproduced with permission

The social animal: social causes of aggression

It is clear by now that human biology plays an important role in aggression. However, researchers studying aggression from a biological perspective would seldom argue that biology is the only important dimension. Social factors – variables that arise from our social relationships with others and the social situations in which we find ourselves – are also important. Some of the social factors we are about to consider are also experienced by other animals (e.g., frustration, heat, crowding and pain), whereas others appear to be unique to humans (e.g., the perception of relative deprivation and injustice).

Self-esteem and narcissism

As we saw in Chapter 2, self-esteem can be considered a social rather than a purely personality variable. It reflects and is affected by the quality of our relationships with other people. Findings of correlational studies attempting to link self-esteem to aggression have been mixed (Bushman and Baumeister, 1998). Different facets of self-esteem, which are themselves positively related to each other precisely because they are dimensions of self-esteem, may have opposite effects on aggression.

This point was demonstrated by Kirkpatrick, Waugh, Valencia and Webster (2002). They examined two aspects of self-esteem: self-perceived superiority (feeling better than others) and social inclusion (number of positive social relationships). Participants high in self-perceived superiority were more likely to aggress against a confederate who had marked their essay harshly. Participants high in social inclusion were less likely to aggress against the confederate. These opposing effects of the two aspects of self-esteem could be detected when each was considered separately. However, no relation between overall self-esteem and aggression was found, because the different aspects of self-esteem were effectively cancelling each other out. Interestingly, Kirkpatrick et al. found that the relationship of the different aspects of self-esteem to aggression occurred over and above the effects of narcissism, which was also measured in their study. Finally, the relationship between self-esteem and aggression may be different among different people. For example, Taylor, Davis-Kean and Malanchuk (2007) found that although low self-esteem (specifically relating to achievement at school) was related to aggression among most of the children in their study, a minority of the children showed aggression in response to threats to high self-esteem.

In recent decades, some researchers have argued that we can expect to find only weak or mixed relationships between normal self-esteem and aggression. For these researchers, what really matters is a particularly elevated but insecure form of self-esteem known as narcissism (e.g., Baumeister, Smart and Boden, 1996). Narcissists display a positive, even boastful self-image but tend to have implicit doubts about their worth. As a result, they go to great lengths to obtain positive feedback from others and respond to criticism or other threats to their self-image with hostility.

Bushman and Baumeister (1998) did indeed find that participants who scored highly on a measure of narcissism were more likely to aggress. Participants wrote a pro-life or pro-choice essay on the topic of abortion. They were then given negative feedback, ostensibly from another participant, such as: 'This is one of the worst essays I have read!' Later, they were asked to deliver blasts of noise to the person they thought had given them this negative feedback, or another participant – whoever was slower to answer a series of questions. Crucially, the participant was able to adjust the level of the noise, between 60 dB and 105 dB. The latter level of noise is very unpleasant indeed, although short bursts are not dangerous. Narcissistic participants gave the person they thought had criticized their essay louder bursts of noise. They did not give the other participant louder bursts of noise any more than non-narcissistic participants. This suggests that narcissism leads to aggression that is directed squarely at people who threaten the self-image, and does not lead to **displaced aggression**. However, this experiment gave participants a clear choice to vent their aggression either at the person who had slighted them or an innocent third party. More recent findings suggest that narcissists will indeed be more likely to aggress against innocent people when they are unable to retaliate against the person who provoked them (Reidy, Foster and Zeichner, 2010). Also, Martinez, Zeichner, Reidy and Miller (2008) found that narcissists would deliver stronger shocks to innocent confederates after having received negative feedback on their writing skills by a computer. Indeed, such participants were especially likely to deliver shocks to innocent confederates when they were expecting to receive feedback from the computer but did not know what it contained. Apparently, narcissists may use aggression to boost their self-image when it is threatened, even against people who have not insulted them, and even when they only *anticipate* that they *might* be insulted. Research also suggests that people can be narcissistic about their groups, as well as themselves, and respond aggressively to threats to the positive image of their group (Golec de Zavala, Cichocka, Eidelson and Jayawickreme, 2009).

Displaced aggression
Aggression that is aroused by one source but directed at another.

Cues in the social environment

Frustration An aversive state that is triggered when individuals are prevented from achieving a goal they are pursuing.

One of the earliest and simplest accounts of human aggression is the frustration-aggression hypothesis. **Frustration** occurs when an individual is prevented from achieving a goal they are pursuing. For Dollard, Doob, Miller et al. (1939), who pioneered this hypothesis, 'frustration always leads to some form of aggression', and conversely, all acts of aggression stem from the frustration of a goal. If you have read Chapter 1, scientific alarm bells should already be ringing – any psychological principle that does not allow for exceptions is setting itself up for a fall. Nonetheless, there is plenty of evidence that frustration does facilitate aggression, especially if one or more of the following applies (Miller, 1941):

1 The individual anticipated that they would feel satisfied when they achieved the goal that was eventually frustrated.
2 The frustration is total, so that all hope of achieving the goal is lost.
3 The individual is frustrated more than once.
4 The individual was frustrated when they had nearly achieved their goal.

© PHOTOALTO

Later research allowed scientists to better predict when frustration does, and does not, cause aggression. As is so often the case with people, causal attribution – the perceived cause of the frustration, in this case – is of central importance. This was demonstrated in a classic experiment by Burnstein and Worschel (1962). They had participants work together to solve problems in groups. Eventually, a male confederate planted in the group caused it to fail the task because he had not taken in some important information. Whether or not aggression followed depended on the ostensible cause for the confederate's frustrating behaviour – it did, if he 'wasn't paying attention', and it did not, if his 'hearing aid failed'. What seemed to matter was whether the person's frustrating behaviour was controllable.

Aversive condition Any condition that an organism finds unpleasant and seeks to avoid, modify or escape where possible. An array of aversive conditions have been shown to trigger aggressive responses.

Still later, other research suggested why frustration so often triggers aggression – it is unpleasant to be frustrated. Technically, frustration can be described as an **aversive condition,** and any number of 'aversive conditions' have been linked to aggression. These include uncomfortable levels of heat, the feeling of being crowded, and physical pain (Berkowitz, 1982). These will cause animals and humans to lash out. For example, Berkowitz (1982) had an experimental group of participants keep their hand in cold water, which, after a while, becomes very painful. Compared to the luckier control participants who had their hands in lukewarm water, they were more prone to subject confederates who annoyed them to loud blasts of noise. Also, the effect of heat on aggression is rather powerful. Extrapolating from the results of earlier experiments (Anderson, Deuser and DeNeve, 1995), Anderson, Bushman and Groom (1997) calculated that predicted increases in temperature due to global warming would result in more than 100,000 extra serious assaults per year in the USA alone by 2050.

Why does practically any aversive condition appear to have the power to elicit aggression? We have already touched upon one reason – it makes some evolutionary sense (Malamuth and Addison, 2001). To survive and thrive, organisms need to be able to escape from or transform dire situations; fighting their way out of them may be an appropriate response. Another reason was presented by Berkowitz's (1990) cognitive neoassociation model. For Berkowitz (1990), aversive conditions will trigger aggression when they help make people angry. This emotion is associated in people's minds with aggression, and makes the possibility of aggressive responses more salient to them. Thus, they are more prone to aggress, without necessarily thinking through the consequences. This is a form of automatic social cognition, with potentially disastrous effects.

Indeed, some research suggests that the mere cognitive availability of aggressive responses can make people more prone to aggress. In a famous but controversial study, Berkowitz and LePage (1967) found that the presence of a gun in a room can make people more aggressive. In a later study, Berkowitz (1988) showed boys a clip of a violent ice hockey game (as if there were any other type), in which some of the players were wearing toy radios. Boys were subsequently more aggressive if a similar walkie-talkie was in the room with them. The object appeared to cue the possibility of violence akin to that the boys had just seen.

Exploring further Do an internet search of 'Berkowitz and LePage' and 'critique'. Can you find any of the criticisms that were made of this study?

Hostile attribution bias

In Chapter 3 we encountered attribution theory, an influential model of social cognition, which suggests that our emotional and behavioural reactions to events are determined by the causes we perceive to underlie them. From this perspective, Dodge (1986) and Crick and Dodge (1994) argued that errors in attribution may underpin much aggressive behaviour. According to their model, responding appropriately to people's behaviour requires an effective attribution process. When someone knocks into you, there is a good chance it is an accident. When someone pulls a face, it may have nothing to do with you. If you interpret these ambiguous situations as evidence that their intentions are hostile, there's a much greater chance that you will form the intention to retaliate. Indeed, many studies show that aggressive people are prone to the *hostile attribution bias*, seeing innocent or ambiguous behaviours by other people (e.g., bumping into you) as deliberate acts of provocation (Orobio de Castro, Veerman, Koops et al., 2002; Pornari and Wood, 2010). Longitudinal studies have shown that if children at age five are predisposed to interpreting ambiguous behaviours in this way, they are more likely to be aggressive 12 years after (Lansford, Malone, Castellino et al., 2006). Although findings are mixed, a meta-analysis of many studies found that the effect is reliable, and is bigger in studies where participants are in an actual social interaction rather than reflecting on a hypothetical situation (Orobio de Castro et al., 2002).

Try it yourself The following scenario is adapted from a study of hostile attribution bias in French youths by Bègue and Muller (2006). Read it and complete the questions. You might also want to try it on family or friends you think are relatively placid or aggressive. You could also create your own scenarios.

You are about to sit down on a spare seat at a table in the university café to eat some lunch. As you do so, someone at the table says: 'You can't sit here, that seat is taken.'

1 On a scale from 0 (not at all likely) to 10 (extremely likely), how likely is it that what the person said is false – that the seat really isn't taken?

2 On the same scale, how likely is it that the person's intention towards you was hostile?

The higher your scores, the more you might be prone to the hostile attribution bias. Of course, this is a hypothetical task. As we have just seen, the correlation between aggression and the hostile attribution bias is stronger when people are confronted with actual ambiguous situations. Why do you think this is? Read the paper by Orobio de Castro et al. (2002) and related works on the hostile attribution bias in real-life situations to find out why.

Relative deprivation and perceived injustice

Relative deprivation The perception that, relative to others, one is not receiving good treatment or experiencing desired outcomes.

Another powerful social trigger of aggression is **relative deprivation** – the perception that, relative to others, one is not receiving good treatment or experiencing desired outcomes (Crosby, 1976; Smith and Kim, 2007). Relative deprivation is especially aversive when it is perceived as unjust. Although there is surprisingly little experimental research into the effects of relative deprivation on interpersonal aggression, it is widely linked by social scientists to the incidence of crime and forms of intergroup aggression such as terrorism, as we shall see (Moghaddam, 2005). Relative deprivation is also linked to increases in behaviours such as theft (Hennigan, Del Rosario, Heath et al., 1982) and gambling (Callan et al., 2008), which may, like aggression, appear to present a 'way out' of disadvantage.

Ironically, the human love of justice often provides a powerful motive to aggress. Legal punishments such as fines and imprisonments can be seen as acts of aggression, in that they are acts designed to harm offenders. Indeed, people seem to be most satisfied with legal punishments that are seen as 'just deserts' for those who have done wrong, in keeping with the biblical proverb 'An eye for an eye' (Darley, Carlsmith and Robinson, 2000). Similarly, those who murder, assault or verbally abuse others often appear to have been motivated, in part, to punish them for their wrongdoing (Tedeschi and Quigley, 1996). People who are chronically concerned with justice and who react with negative emotions to injustice are also more prone to aggress against people they perceive to be wrongdoers (Gollwitzer, Rothmund, Pfeiffer and Ensenbach, 2009). Justice-driven aggression is not necessarily motivated simply by the desire to see the wrongdoer suffer for their sins, however. It is perhaps more important that wrongdoers get the message and understand why they are being punished. Seeing victims get the message is more satisfying than seeing them suffer (Gollwitzer and Denzler, 2009).

Learning aggression from others

Aggression is not just triggered by cues in the environment but can be learned from observation of others. Bandura's highly influential social learning theory offered the first explanation of this phenomenon. This theory emerged as the so-called 'cognitive revolution' was moving psychology away from a behaviourist period to take into account mental processes. For Bandura, a key concept was vicarious conditioning – we learn not only by being rewarded and punished for our behaviour, but also by observing others being rewarded and punished for theirs. Thus, if a person appears to enjoy themselves while committing aggressive acts, or is otherwise rewarded for doing so, and if they escape punishment, observers learn that it might also be safe and rewarding to aggress themselves. Bandura, Ross and Ross (1961) illustrated this point with a set of studies in which children watched an adult pound an inflatable 'Bobo' doll with their fists, feet and weapons. When children were later frustrated and given access to a similar doll, they copied the aggressive behaviour they had just seen. Not only did watching the aggression make the children more aggressive, but they frequently copied the specific forms and 'catchphrases' of the aggressive model, who in some conditions had verbally taunted the unfortunate doll during the aggressive acts.

These studies have been criticized on various grounds, most tellingly by Tedeschi and Quigley (1996), who pointed out that as far as the children were concerned, they might well have been engaging in harmless play. If they do not intend to commit harm, their behaviour does not count as aggression. However, these studies and Bandura's theoretical edifice called attention to the point that aggression is all too often learned and copied from others. Indeed, children who witness domestic violence between their parents are more likely to assault their own partners when they grow up (Foshee, Bauman and Fletcher, 1999). Oliver Stone's 1994 film *Natural Born Killers* has been the target of a lawsuit after it was apparently the basis of a 'copycat' killing (Boyle, 2001). Two 18-year-olds from Oklahoma, Sarah Edmondson and Ben Darrus, went out with a .38 calibre handgun and shot two strangers after having repeatedly watched the film while high on LSD. This is but one case of many that has been attributed to learned, copycat violence (Kunich, 2000).

Of course, it is impossible to explain, with any certainty, individual cases of copycat violence in terms of social learning theory. These cases almost certainly were caused by additional factors. Berkowitz's (1990) cognitive neoassociation model, for example, would suggest that violence simply becomes more salient to people as a possible response when they have witnessed it repeatedly. People may be more prone to the hostile attribution bias – seeing aggressive intent when it is not there – when they have seen many instances of deliberate violence (Crick and Dodge, 1994). However, some findings do provide additional support for social learning theory. For example, Perry, Perry and Rasmussen (1986) found that more aggressive children reported that they felt able to engage in aggression and that it would bring them rewards. Some of the findings we will encounter soon about the effect of sporting outcomes on violence among spectators also provide some support for social learning theory.

Time to reflect Are the findings of Perry et al. (1986) consistent only with social learning theory? What else would be needed for this study to provide strong support for social learning theory?

ETHICS AND RESEARCH METHODS

Measuring aggression in the laboratory

As we have just seen, Bandura et al.'s (1961) Bobo doll studies have been heavily criticized for measuring aggression in an unrealistic and invalid way. For the most part, researchers of aggression are attempting to explain real-world cases of physical or social aggression that have real and important consequences. But for ethical reasons, it is difficult and perhaps impossible to allow participants to really hurt each other, or risk really hurting each other, in the laboratory. You will not find laboratory experiments in which the dependent measure is the number of punches that participants throw at each other. The importance of ensuring that participants do not come to serious harm is one factor that prevents researchers from accurately simulating real-life forms of aggression.

Another obstacle to the realistic study of aggression in the laboratory is that 'normal' participants are often reluctant to aggress unless features of the situation clearly make aggression seem an available and acceptable response. Many laboratory studies are set up so that participants are not only allowed but actually required to deliver some aversive stimulus to the targets of aggression. Very often, the set-up is that the participant is supposed to 'train' the target of aggression by punishing them with an aversive stimulus when they give a wrong answer. The participants are often given access to some apparatus that is expressly designed to deliver these aversive stimuli. These include the delivery of electric shocks, loud noises and hot chilli sauces of mild to severe intensity. The measure of aggression is effectively a measure of participants' willingness to inflict nastier experiences than necessary on a person in their fulfilment of a role that already requires them to impose some nasty experiences.

This lack of realism casts a pall over laboratory studies of aggression. Some laboratory studies get around the problem by measuring angry feelings, intentions or physiological responses that are known 'precursors of aggression'. These studies are clever and important, but the question that must hang over them is whether the laboratory simulations would translate into violence in

© IMAGESOURCE

everyday life. As in all areas of social psychology, but perhaps more so than some, the experimental study of aggression is only viable when it is done as part of a wider research programme that includes other research methods, including observational and archival studies, field experiments and surveys. As we shall see, the study of media violence is an excellent example of how many methods have been used to obtain findings that have pointed in the same direction – exposure to media violence is both related to and causes aggression.

Questions

1 Using a search engine or database, find an example of an article that reports experiments using each of these dependent variables in the study of aggression: electric shocks, loud noises, and chilli sauce.
2 Find an example of an experiment cited in this chapter that uses measures of angry feelings and/or physiological arousal.
3 Propose a measure of aggression, suitable for use in a laboratory, that is ethically acceptable but has not been used in a study before. It might help you to think of how you would measure aggression if freed from all ethical constraints, and then to think about how you could capture the essence of that measure in an ethically acceptable way – one in which participants are not at risk of harm.

Media effects

One of the hottest debates in popular culture over the past 50 years or so has been the link between media violence and aggression. Does exposure to media violence really lead to increased levels of violence? Although the debate rages on TV, in the press and the blogosphere, and academics from some other fields of enquiry remain sceptical (e.g., Trend, 2007), social psychological research has uncovered abundant evidence for a causal relationship (Bushman and Anderson, 2001). In their review of the literature, Bushman and Anderson point out that the observed link between media violence and aggression, in meta-analytic studies, is two to three times as strong as the link between homework and academic achievement, and exposure to lead and IQ scores in children. One study estimated that, at the end of the 1980s, the average 13-year-old American child had witnessed 100,000 violent acts on TV (Huston, Donnerstein, Fairchild et al., 1992). The relationship between exposure to violent media material and violent behaviour appears to be getting stronger, perhaps in part because of the advent of increasingly realistic special effects in films and computer games (Bushman and Cantor, 2003). Further, although correlations are always to be questioned – violent kids may gravitate to violent films and games, for example – there are any number of experiments showing that exposure to media violence causes increases in aggressive behaviour (Bushman and Cantor, 2003).

Thus, 'research has shifted from whether media priming exists to how media priming works' (Roskos-Ewoldsen, Roskos-Ewoldsen and Carpentier, 2002, p. 97). Meta-analyses show that the effect linking the consumption of media violence to aggression is larger than many of the effects that grip the public imagination, such as the effect of homework on academic achievement, or passive smoking in the workplace and lung cancer (Bushman and Huesmann, 2006; Huesmann, 2007) (see Figure 13.6).

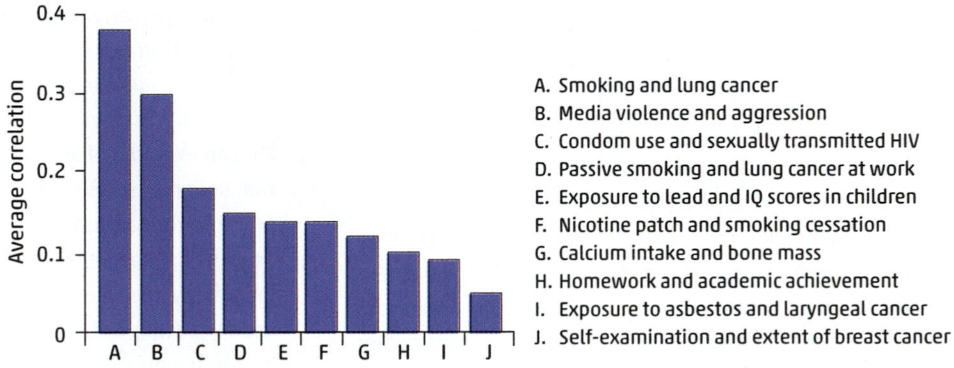

FIGURE 13.6 A comparison of media violence-aggressive behaviour correlations with other correlations

Source: Huesmann, 2007. Copyright 2007, reprinted with permission from Elsevier

A. Smoking and lung cancer
B. Media violence and aggression
C. Condom use and sexually transmitted HIV
D. Passive smoking and lung cancer at work
E. Exposure to lead and IQ scores in children
F. Nicotine patch and smoking cessation
G. Calcium intake and bone mass
H. Homework and academic achievement
I. Exposure to asbestos and laryngeal cancer
J. Self-examination and extent of breast cancer

This link is explained by several major social psychological theories of aggression. We have just touched on three of the causal mechanisms that can link media consumption to violence – encountering violence in the mass media makes it a more cognitively salient response possibility (social cognitive theory), may make it seem safe and rewarding (social learning theory), and may contribute to the hostile attribution bias by leading people to believe that violent, antisocial intentions are more common than they really are.

This last point is echoed by the claim that excessive consumption of mass media results in a **mean world syndrome**, in which ordinary citizens become paranoid about the risk of crime (Gerbner, Gross, Eleey et al., 1977). Ironically, this paranoia may

Mean world syndrome
Exaggerated perceptions of the frequency of violence and antisocial behaviour that may follow from the consumption of violent media material.

make crime actually more likely, as law-abiding people withdraw from public space and become less engaged in society (Putnam, 2000). This effect of television viewing on trust and civic engagement has been questioned by some authors, such as Uslaner (2002). Uslaner found that when he controlled for Americans' optimism about the future, the relationship between television viewing and decreased trust and civic engagement disappeared. Uslaner (2002, p. 467) concludes that 'it is not television that makes people less trusting, but optimism for the future that makes people more trusting'. However, his analysis does not exclude the possibility that declining optimism mediates the relationship between television viewing and trust. Using similar measures with a Flemish sample, Hooghe (2002) found robust relationships between watching television, and especially entertainment shows and commercial channels, and reduced civic engagement.

Desensitization Reductions in negative emotions to violence that ensue from repeated exposure to violent stimuli. Because negative emotions help deter people from aggression, desensitization can lead to increased levels of aggression.

Another way in which media violence may promote aggression is that repeated viewing may reduce the fearful, negative reactions to violence that people normally experience. This process is termed **desensitization** (Bandura, 1978). It is essentially an example of normal associative learning processes. Whereas in real life, aggression is normally paired with fear and danger, in violent media, aggression is often paired with fun, laughter and bad characters getting their comeuppance. Thus, violent media can cause people to unlearn the normal negative emotional associations of violence (Bushman and Huesmann, 2006). The theory is that when people contemplate aggressive responses or 'scripts' in real-life situations, they are normally deterred by their strong, negative emotional associations. If the prospect of aggressive responses arouses less fear and anxiety, they will seem more attractive (Huesmann, 1998). Although there is little direct evidence linking desensitization to aggressive behaviour, there is plenty of evidence showing that exposure to violence in films (Linz, Donnerstein and Adams, 1989; Thomas, Horton, Lippincott and Drabman, 1977) and video games (Carnagey, Anderson and Bartholow, 2007) reduces physiological responses to real-life violence.

In the past decade, research has uncovered a neurological mechanism by which desensitization may occur and lead to increased violence. A structure called the anterior cingulate cortex (ACC), located in the frontal lobe, has been linked to aggressive behaviour (Sterzer, Stadler, Krebs et al., 2003). It is associated with links between cognition and emotion, and inhibition of part of the ACC may be indicative of the suppression of emotional information processing (Bush, Luu and Posner, 2000). In other words, it may play a part in the suppression of emotional reactions to violence, or desensitization (Carnagey et al., 2007). In one study of adolescents diagnosed with a clinical disorder but who were not necessarily violent or disruptive, participants who reported consuming a great deal of violent media showed reduced ACC activity compared to those who did not. In fact, high consumers of violent media showed the same lowering of ACC activity as a group of adolescents with antisocial conduct disorders (Matthews, Kronenberger, Want et al., 2005). An fMRI study by Weber, Ritterfeld and Mathiak (2006) analysed patterns of brain activation frame by frame and revealed modified ACC activity at the moment of violent actions in the game.

Time to reflect We first encountered the ACC in Chapter 2, where it was associated with self-awareness. It is often the case that the same part of the brain can be associated with many functions. If you search 'functions of the amygdala' on the internet, you will find a long list. It is worth considering whether this means that specific brain regions really have a multitude of precisely identified functions, or whether specific brain regions affect many different aspects of our psychology, but in ways that are not precisely understood. With regard to the present findings, perhaps desensitization works by causing people to think less about themselves, and perhaps less about their moral standards, when encountering violence. It could be seen as a neurological parallel of 'moral disengagement' or 'deindividuation'. You can read about these topics in Chapter 14 and Chapter 9 respectively.

General aggression model (GAM) Model describing the situational and personality variables that combine to produce human aggression.

In sum, media violence affects violent behaviour in real life in many ways. Watching violent material or playing violent games can cause people to develop more positive attitudes towards aggression (e.g., as described by social learning theory), can desensitize them, can cause them to be more likely to perceive aggression in the environment (e.g., as described by hostile attribution bias), can lead them to be more likely to expect aggression from others or themselves, and can make aggressive 'scripts' more cognitively available to people as viable response options. All these mechanisms are incorporated in Anderson and Bushman's (2002) **general aggression model (GAM)**. This model describes the situational and personality variables that combine to produce human aggression (see Figure 13.7). Use of violent media changes people's personality, over time. The GAM also suggests that these personality factors along with situational factors, such as pain, provocation, drugs and incentives to aggress, affect the social encounters that people experience. They may seek more aggressive social encounters. They may also respond to identical social encounters differently. Specifically, they may respond with higher levels of arousal, more negative, angry emotions, and more aggressive thoughts. In turn, these responses affect their decisions, for example whether to engage in a thoughtful or an impulsive action. People's actions change the social encounters they are in, for example by provoking or frightening others. Thus, people's behaviour affects their personality and the situations in which they find themselves.

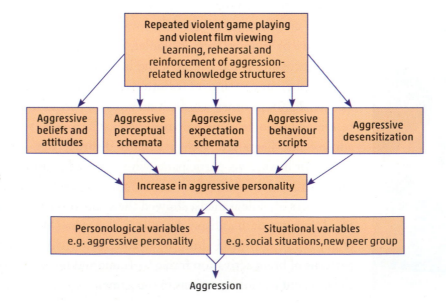

FIGURE 13.7 The many paths linking use of violent media to heightened aggression in real life

Source: Anderson and Bushman, 2002. Republished with permission of *Annual Reviews*, permission conveyed through Copyright Clearance Center, Inc.

Sometimes, violent media may interplay with people's personalities in a kind of vicious cycle. Recall the commonly held belief that aggressive energy builds up inside people over time, or as they are provoked, and that it can be released by catharsis. People who hold these 'catharsis beliefs' particularly strongly are more likely to play violent video games when they are angered (Bushman and Whitaker, 2010). Unfortunately, this attempt to expunge angry feelings and aggressive impulses is more likely to make them stronger.

Question to consider Having read the material on media effects, reread question 2 at the start of the chapter. Do you think there is a good chance Johnny is more likely to be aggressive as a result of playing video games?

Sport and aggression

The media are an important cultural source of ideas about aggression that can shape our behaviour. Sport is another, but its relationship with aggression is complex. Of course, sports vary widely in the extent to which they allow physical contact between players and hence behaviours that, in other contexts, would be regarded as straightforwardly aggressive (e.g., pushing, hitting and knocking to the ground). They also vary in the extent to which, outside the rules, aggressive conduct takes place. Theories of the function of sport have characterized it as a symbolic equivalent of war, in that sportspeople, like military personnel, engage in competitive, physically strenuous activity in order to win prestige for the wider national or regional groups they are representing. One line of thought portrays sport as a substitute or alternative to war. Writing from a psychodynamic perspective under the influence of Freud, Fenichel (1945, p. 558) claimed that sport is a kind of 'substitute discharge' of aggressive energy that might otherwise be devoted to making war. This is clearly related to the notion that aggression can be released by means of catharsis. Indeed, Lorenz (1966, p. 271), who is most closely associated with the catharsis model, claimed that 'the main function of sport today lies in the cathartic discharge of aggressive urge' and argued that, in particular, it provided an alternative outlet for 'collective militant enthusiasm' (p. 273). Another line of thought portrays sport as a complement to war. For Lüschen (1970, p. 9), for example, 'sports are not only representative of societal norms and values … [but] socialize toward such patterns'. Thus, cultures that valorize group-based aggression and physical competition (that is, see these as good things), which are norms that might predict support for war, are more likely to engage in aggressive contact sports.

These two theoretical views of the relationship between sport and aggression generate different predictions. If sport is a cathartic outlet for aggressive energy that would otherwise lead to war (Fenichel, 1945; Lorenz, 1966), we would expect a negative relationship between sport and war at the societal level. Thus, we would expect more warlike societies to engage in fewer aggressive contact sports, and we might also expect that, during times of war, a given society will engage in such sports with lower intensity. This is because aggressive energy can be 'released' by either sport or war, and if one is present, there is no need for the other. On the

FIGURE 13.8 Two models of the relationship between aggressive contact sports and war The left-hand 'catharsis' model suggests that sport provides a release of aggressive energy, and so reduces the inclination to go to war (which would otherwise be required to release aggressive energy). The more aggressive contact sports that are played, the less aggressive energy there is, and so the less war there is (it also suggests that since war is an outlet for aggressive energy, warlike cultures would have little spare aggressive energy to vent by means of sport). The right-hand 'norms' model suggests that sport and war both reinforce a cultural norm of aggression. The more aggressive contact sports are played, the more aggression is seen as appropriate, and thus the more warlike a culture will be (likewise, the more war is waged, the more aggressive norms are reinforced, and these norms will be increasingly expressed in aggressive contact sports). So, there will be a positive rather than a negative relation between aggressive contact sports and war. Research supports the latter, norms model, dealing another blow to the notion of catharsis.

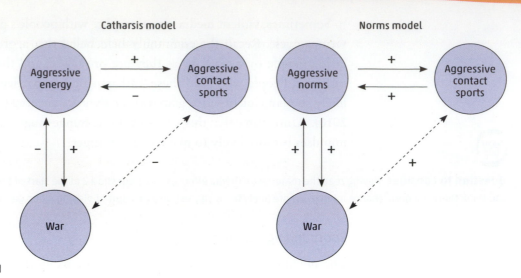

other hand, if sport is the symbolic 'acting out' of cultural norms and values that can lead to war, we would expect exactly the opposite relationship: that aggressive sporting activity will be more common in warlike cultures and at times of war (see Figure 13.8).

When Sipes (1973) examined data from a number of anthropological studies, he found that 87 per cent of warlike cultures featured aggressive contact sports, whereas only 11 per cent of cultures not classified as warlike did so. Similarly, when Sipes analysed sporting activity in the USA in the middle part of the 20th century, he found that sports such as hunting and football showed modest increases during the Second World War and the Korean War. In contrast, baseball did not show such an increase. Far from being a cathartic outlet for collective aggression that makes war less likely, aggressive, physical sports seem to be part and parcel of a cultural mindset that underpins war.

Possibly, this cultural mindset is captured by the concept of *social dominance orientation* (SDO) (Pratto et al., 1994), the opposition to inequality and desire for group-based dominance that we encountered in Chapter 11. Although there is no evidence linking SDO to aggressive sports, there is abundant evidence associating it with support for war, as we shall see later. This 'blind spot' in knowledge is one that could be addressed with student research projects (see the Blind spot in social psychology exercise at the end of the chapter).

The fact that physical contact and struggle is inherent in some sports led Fields, Collins and Comstock (2007) to argue that researchers should not overlook the fact that some sports are inherently aggressive and so should not focus exclusively on illegal acts when they study aggression within sports (e.g., Fields, Collins and Comstock, 2010). Nonetheless, these same researchers (Collins, Fields and Comstock, 2008) found that illegal acts of aggressive cheating make a disproportionate contribution to sporting injuries. Some 6.4 per cent of nearly 100,000 sporting injuries included in their survey came from foul play, with a third of these afflicting the head or face and a quarter leading to concussion. An earlier study of injuries among British rugby players found that up to 31 per cent of reported injuries were attributable to foul play (Davies and Gibson, 1978). Foul play, along with reckless play, was cited as the most common cause of sporting injuries among Irish school children (Watson, 1994).

Given the number of sporting injuries that arise from foul play, it is important to examine its causes. Research has uncovered several situational and personality factors that underpin aggression on the sports field. By and large, the best predictor of aggressiveness on the field is aggressiveness off the field – much the same factors predict aggression in sport elsewhere (e.g., Maxwell and Visek, 2009). But also, a recurring finding, from both qualitative and quantitative research, is that participants in physical sports regard aggression on the field as more normal and acceptable than in everyday life (Traclet, Rascle, Souchon et al., 2009). Just as we saw with alcohol, we should not see sport as an automatic trigger of violent conduct. The cultural meaning that people attach to sport is important and guides their expectancies and motivation (Russell, 2008).

Frank and Gilovich (1988) uncovered a surprising influence on aggression among sportspeople. They reasoned that since black is associated across many cultures with evil and death (for experimental evidence of this association, see Meier, Robinson and Clore, 2004; Sherman and Clore, 2009), teams who wear black jerseys may be penalized more for foul play. To test this idea, they first conducted an archival study of penalty rates in professional American football and ice hockey leagues. This revealed that teams wearing black were among the most penalized. When these teams changed their colours, for example when they wore their away strip, they were penalized less often. These findings are upheld by more a recent archival investigation of ice hockey matches (Webster, Urland and Correll, 2012). They are also consistent with other findings that support the notion of 'enclothed cognition' – what we wear profoundly influences how we think and act (Adam and Galinsky, 2012). Adam and Galinsky found, for example, that people paid more attention and made fewer errors on experimental tasks when wearing a white coat, as worn by doctors and scientists.

Frank and Gilovich (1988) also reasoned that the associative connotations of the colour black can affect penalty rates in two ways. First, it may cause referees to be quicker to penalize teams wearing black than some other colour, because the team kit almost literally colours the way they perceive the teams' play. Second, it may cause the players themselves to change their behaviour. Wearing black may subtly influence their self-image and motivation, causing them to be more prone to foul play. In a pair of experiments, Frank and Gilovich found support for both mechanisms. In the first of these experiments, participants watching videos of identical sequences of play were more likely to hypothetically penalize a player wearing black (rather than white) team kit. In the second, participants wearing black (rather than white) were more likely to choose to play aggressive games (e.g., 'dart gun duel' as opposed to 'stacking blocks'). Donning a black team kit caused the experimental group to choose these games more than when they were wearing no team kit, whereas the white kit had no effect on their choices. Black kit, then, appears to be a bad influence, but white does not improve people's morality on the sports field. Of course, this last experiment does not exactly replicate on-field aggression, so its external validity is open to question. However, in tandem with Frank and Gilovich's archival findings, it is more convincing: we have converging evidence that wearing black worsens conduct in sport.

Time to reflect It seems to be clear that the colour of the clothing people wear on the sports field can affect their aggression. Can you think of examples where this might happen off the sports field? Do you think certain kinds of clothing worn on the street might trigger aggression – either by changing the psychology of the person wearing the clothes, or by changing other people's reactions to those clothes? You might want to conduct a database or Google Scholar search of terms like 'clothing' and 'aggression' to see if there is any support for your intuitions.

© IMAGE SOURCE

FIGURE 13.9 Aggressive clothing, aggressive behaviour? In the UK, this kind of clothing is stereotypically associated with aggressive behaviour. On the basis of the effects of wearing black on the sports field, this kind of clothing might affect aggression on the streets.

Sport elicits aggression not only in players but also in spectators. One of the biggest global sporting events is the American football Super Bowl final. Sachs and Chu (2000, p. 1192) found that domestic violence calls to the local police and emergency admissions of women spiked after the final, leading them to conclude that 'Super Bowl Sunday is often the biggest day of the year for domestic violence'. Following Welsh international rugby and football matches between 1995 and 2002, emergency admissions to Cardiff hospitals also increased (Sivarajasingam, Moore and Shepherd, 2005). Findings like these cause charities to brace themselves for increases in violence after major sporting events such as the Rugby World Cup (e.g., New Zealand Women's Refuge, 2011).

The effect of the outcome of sporting events is of key theoretical interest. Consider the predictions of social learning theory and the frustration-aggression model. Which one predicts more spectator violence among the supporters of the winning team, and which one predicts more spectator violence among the losing teams' fans? Losing is frustrating, and should generate more aggression among spectators according to the latter model. Conversely, to the extent that the sports match entails some kind of aggression, watching your team win amounts to watching it being rewarded for aggression. Social learning theory therefore predicts that more violence will be perpetrated by winning rather than losing fans. Studies that have analysed the effect of the outcome of matches on aggression point consistently in the direction of social learning theory. In their study, Sivarajasingam et al. (2005) found that Cardiff hospital admissions were higher after the Welsh team had won rather than lost. Earlier, White, Katz and Scarborough (1992) found that aggravated assaults of women increased in Washington, DC, after the Washington Redskins, the local ice hockey team, won. When the team lost, this type of violence was the same as on non-match days.

Here, as always, it is important to consider alternative explanations for these correlations. Can you think of any? A clear possibility is the consumption of alcohol, which we have already seen to be a major contributing factor to aggression. Intuitively, we might guess that supporters stay out for longer, and drink more, after their team has won, because they are in a happy, celebratory mood – but go home with their tail between their legs if their team loses.

However, research by Moore, Shepherd, Ede and Sivarajasingam (2007) suggests that this increase in alcohol consumption is not responsible for the effect of victory on spectators' aggression. Moore et al. (2007) sampled from male fans attending rugby union matches at the Millennium Stadium in Cardiff, Wales. Some (115) were sampled before the match started, and served as a baseline against which the responses of the remaining (87) participants, who were sampled after the match, could be compared. Results showed that men whose team had just won reported feeling more aggressive than the baseline, pre-match group. Losing had no effect on their aggressive feelings. Interestingly, men's happiness did not increase when their team won – although losing decreased their happiness. Further, men who were happy were no more likely to indicate that they planned to drink. These findings suggest that men were not likely to stay out drinking because they were in an especially celebratory mood. While the intention to drink was not correlated with happiness, it was correlated with aggressive feelings. The more aggressive men were feeling, the more they wanted to drink. It would seem that we cannot use alcohol to explain away the effect of winning on aggression. If anything, alcohol may magnify the effect, by seeming especially attractive to those who have developed aggressive feelings. It seems that the cultural equation of alcohol and aggression discussed earlier (see the Social psychology in the real world box) plays an important part in the social consequences of sporting wins.

The tribal animal: the group dimension of aggression

Group processes and aggression

The amazing sociality of human beings – our ability to form coalitions, identify with groups and act together – has been the secret of our extraordinary successes, and has also, very often, been our downfall. In the colourful terminology of Brewer (1999), 'ingroup love' is all too often accompanied by 'outgroup hate', with sometimes terrible impacts on our behaviour. As we saw in Chapter 10, there are powerful *social facilitation* effects on aggression. Recall, for example, Mullen's (1986) research into lynchings, the appalling violence inflicted on African American victims by Whites in southern parts of the USA. The more ingroup members (White lynchers) present, compared to outgroup members (the Black victims), the more horrific and degrading the lynchings became.

   The southern part of the USA has been the venue for another important breakthrough in the scientific understanding of how group processes can facilitate aggression. Social facilitation is normally defined as the effects of the mere presence of others on our behaviour, but the norms, values and cultures that groups of people create are also important. The southern part of the USA has historically been more violent than the North (Fischer, 1989). We have already seen that heat is a trigger for aggression – but it is not that Southerners are more aggressive in every which way. Rather, they are more aggressive than Northerners specifically in situations where they are required to defend themselves and their reputation, and when they are insulted (Nisbett, 1993). This led Cohen and Nisbett (1994) to suggest that the American South is characterized by a **culture of honour** – a particular concern for honour and reputation, and the belief that violence is justified and sometimes even

Culture of honour A culture in which honour and reputation, especially of men, is held to be important, and in which violence is seen as a justified means of defending one's honour.

required to defend it. For Cohen and Nisbett, this culture emerged because, for many years, the South was populated by herders who were left vulnerable to crimes such as banditry and cattle theft due to insufficient law enforcement. In this environment, it became important for men to establish a reputation that meant would-be criminals would not mess with them. Thus, in a vacuum of official law enforcement, it became normal to use violence in order to punish and deter wrongdoers.

Manifestations of this culture have been cleverly explored by this group of researchers. Cohen, Nisbett, Bowdle and Schwartz (1996) brought men from the North and South into the laboratory to complete a study. While they thought they were waiting to participate, a man bumped into them, adding a verbal insult while he was at it, and kept walking down the hall. Unbeknown to the participants, this man was, of course, a confederate of the experimenters. Compared to the Northerners, the Southerners subsequently displayed a spectacular array of aggressive responses, and cognitive and physiological precursors of aggression. The stress hormone cortisol increased, as did testosterone. They were more likely to believe that the confederate had harmed their reputation as a 'real man', were more likely to be rude to the experimenter, behaved more aggressively in an experimental game and wrote more aggressive stories.

In a subsequent field experiment, Cohen and Nisbett (1997) wrote unsolicited and fictional job applications to hundreds of retail shops in different parts of the USA. In the letter, the applicant (a 27-year-old, apparently local man) disclosed that he had been convicted of a crime. This was either a car theft or a crime of passion, in which he had hit a man with a pipe, because he had taunted him in a bar, in front of his friends, about sleeping with his fiancée. The taunter died of his injuries, resulting in a manslaughter conviction for the applicant. He asked the managers to send him an application form, to invite him to drop by, or to give him the name of a contact person. Responses to the 'motor vehicle theft' letter were the same across different regions of the USA. But responses to the 'murder' condition were markedly different in the South and West (which had inherited a culture of honour from their colonial past) than in the North. In the North, return letters were much colder in tone (as rated by coders who did not know where the businesses were located) and much less likely to comply with the applicant's requests. It seems that in a culture of honour, it is okay to meet insult with injury (see Figure 13.10).

FIGURE 13.10 Findings from the field experiment in which letters were sent to employers in different areas of the USA The findings show that the 'honour' letter, in which the fictional job applicant confessed to having killed a man who taunted him about sleeping with his fiancée, tended to receive more sympathetic treatment in the North than in the South and West of the USA. There were no significant regional differences in response to the 'control' letter, in which the job applicant confessed to having stolen a car.

Source: Cohen and Nisbett, 1997

(a) Control letter (motor vehicle theft)

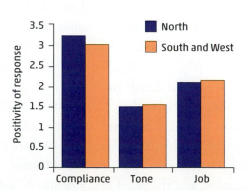

(b) Honour letter (killed rival for lover)

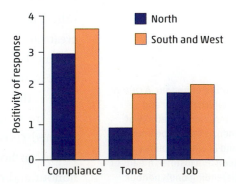

It is important to note, however, that the honour motivation is not restricted to highly patriarchal 'honour' cultures. Subcultures exist in many places in which aggression is deemed an acceptable way to resolve disputes, have fun and win honour. A qualitative investigation of pub brawls in England revealed that male honour played a big part in participants' accounts of their own aggressive behaviour. For example, one young male accounted for his violent reaction to a perceived provocation by saying: 'because I don't want some guy pushing me around, that's normal for me … I'm not going to let some guy do that, then I'm not a real man right, if some guy can tell me who I can talk to and not, right' (Graham and Wells, 2003, p. 557).

Intergroup violence: hate crimes

Lynching, the horrific form of violence investigated by Mullen (1986), not only illustrates a social facilitation effect, it also exemplifies the intergroup nature of much human aggression. Frequently, people do violence to each other not because of their individual qualities but because of their social identities. Intergroup violence, therefore, can be seen as one manifestation of prejudice – the innate dislike of other groups. When individuals are attacked because of their membership of a disliked group, the offence is known legally as a **hate crime** (McDevitt, Levin and Bennett, 2002). In several countries including the UK, hate crimes attract harsher penalties in law, so that the group-based nature of violent crimes is treated as an aggravating circumstance (Bleich, 2011). Verbal aggression, in which hatred and insults towards groups are expressed, is described as 'hate speech' and is also outlawed in many countries (Josey, 2010). Hate speech and hate crimes have been shown to create a raft of mental and physical health problems both for people who are directly its victims and other members of the stigmatized groups (Boeckmann and Turpin-Petrosino, 2002; Meyer, 2003).

Although hate crimes are officially disapproved of, some research suggests that unofficial attitudes to hate crimes may be more ambivalent (Craig and Waldo, 1996; Lyons, 2006). For example, Lieberman, Arndt, Personius and Cook (1999) conducted two studies investigating people's attitudes to hate crimes from a *terror management theory* (TMT) perspective. In TMT, awareness of our own mortality encourages us to symbolically seek immortality. In particular, TMT suggests that people respond to the fear of death by affirming cultural worldviews that promise to outlive them. Lieberman et al. reasoned that this may have a double-edged

Hate crime An aggressive and illegal act against a person or persons that is motivated by prejudice towards the group to which they belong.

effect on attitudes to hate crime. On one hand, the perpetrators of hate crimes violate cherished social norms against violence and prejudice, and so threaten culturally shared worldviews. And in Lieberman et al.'s first study, participants were indeed more likely to support legislation targeting hate crimes after their own mortality had been made salient. On the other hand, the targets of hate crimes may themselves be perceived as a threat to culturally shared worldviews. For example, in homophobic cultures, gay men and women are perceived as a threat to 'normal' marriage and family life. In Lieberman et al.'s second study, participants were presented with descriptions of specific hate crimes, against either a Jewish or a homosexual victim. They were then asked to set a 'bail' amount that the perpetrator would have to pay to avoid being detained in prison while awaiting trial. Participants whose mortality had recently been made salient set lower bail amounts. Putting the two studies together, mortality salience seems to encourage opposition to hate crimes in the abstract, when a specific victim is not mentioned. However, when victims represent worldviews that are perceived to be different from their own, mortality salience may cause people to be relatively condoning of hate crimes.

CRITICAL FOCUS

Violence against women

Imagine that one group in society brutalizes another group in a modern Western society like the UK, murdering hundreds of its people, severely beating and raping thousands more. Associated with this violence, the perpetrator group tends to endorse a set of hostile stereotypes and ideologies about the group it is victimizing that consign the group to a relatively powerless, subordinate social position (Glick and Fiske, 1996). Well, there is actually no need to use your imagination, because we are referring to the violence that is actually perpetrated by men against women.

Admittedly, we are being provocative, but this is a factually accurate description of what happens in the UK, and elsewhere. According to official statistics (Walby and Allen, 2004), twice as many women than men in the UK (21% compared to 10%) have been subject to domestic violence as an adult. The domestic abuse inflicted by men upon women tends to be much more severe than the other way around – women comprise 89% of the population of those who are subject to repeated and serious physical abuse in which injuries are inflicted. For women in their reproductive years, being murdered by a current or former partner is one of the leading causes of death, and has been estimated to be roughly as common a killer as cancer (Garcia-Moreno, Heise, Jansen et al., 2005; World Bank, 1993). Seventeen per cent of women and 2% of men have been subjected to sexual victimization in their adulthood. And although our opening here is a little provocative, it is nothing compared to Brownmiller's (1975) landmark feminist treatise of the 1970s. Brownmiller (1975, p. 15) claimed that rape, perhaps the most salient of all forms of violence, is 'nothing more or less than a conscious process of intimidation by which all men keep all women in a state of fear'.

What are we to make of this claim? It has all sorts of problems if we treat it literally as a scientific hypothesis – and you can explore these for yourself in the Applying social psychology exercise at the end of the chapter. But the statistics we have quoted and the role that sexism seems to play in violence towards women (see, e.g., Abrams, Viki, Masser and Bohner, 2003) suggest that Brownmiller may have had a point. The point is that violence by men against women has an intergroup dimension, even though it generally occurs interpersonally, between individual men and women. It is much more frequent and serious than violence by women against men, it is supported by and associated with men's prejudice towards women and ideologies about women's role, and, in turn, it has detrimental and restrictive effects on women, even those who have not themselves been directly raped or assaulted.

If we read Brownmiller's (1975) claim in this way, there is extensive research support for it. Women are more afraid of crime than men (Hale, 1996). In large part, this is because women are much more afraid of being raped, which means that other crimes, such as burglary and robbery, take on a much more sinister meaning for them (Warr and Stafford, 1983). This fear of crime is accompanied by feelings of vulnerability, meaning that women perceive themselves as more likely to be the victim of an unprovoked attack, and less likely to be able to defend themselves (Jackson, 2009; Riger and Gordon, 1981; Smith and Torstensson, 1997). Fear of crime generally and rape in particular deters women from using public spaces, especially by themselves and especially at night (e.g., Riger and Gordon, 1981). After reading newspaper reports of rape, women who have not themselves been raped experience reduced self-esteem, and tend to be more likely to endorse a subordinate social role for women (e.g., Bohner, Weisbrod, Raymond et al., 1993; Schwarz and Brand, 1983). In a cruel irony, the moral burden for the victimization of women tends to fall on women, who are expected to be the guardians of their sexuality and are often blamed when they are raped (e.g., Viki and Abrams, 2002). Recent research also suggests that women experience pressure to be fearful and cautious, and are judged more favourably if they are fearful (Sutton, Robinson and Farrall, 2011). According to research and theory, then, the fear of crime disempowers women in several ways – it deters them from activities perceived to increase the risk of victimization, it causes them to internalize ideologies and prejudices that are detrimental to their gender group, and it imposes on them a perceived duty to be cautious and even fearful.

We therefore think – although you may disagree – that we should view the violence that men do to women, in the social and ideological context in which it happens, as a form of intergroup violence. It is not an easy or comfortable position to take, and it is debatable. But it is worth taking seriously. The way we opened this section was crafted not just to provoke this consideration but also to encourage you to look at this aspect of gender relations with fresh eyes. As we saw in Chapter 5 on communication, we often 'normalize' or take for granted the status quo between the genders. Thus, we accept sexist language such as the masculine generic when we would not accept similarly racist language; for example, 'Throughout man's history, there has been violent intergroup conflict' does not read as oddly and unacceptably as 'Through whites' history, there has been violent intergroup conflict', because we are accustomed to it and it is supported by gender ideologies we unconsciously accept. There is a real possibility that we have taken for granted, if not quite accepted, gendered violence in much the same way.

Questions

1 Brownmiller's claim is often attacked as either implausible or too vague to be tested scientifically. What is wrong with it? Take a careful look, for example, at some of the key words – 'all' men keep 'all' women down. Do you think this is true? And do you think keeping women in their place in this way is something that men do 'consciously'? Can you find research in this textbook or on the internet to support your view?

2 Using an internet search engine, find research on 'domestic violence' or 'partner violence'. Do you think it could be explained in the same way as Brownmiller explains rape, that is, it serves to keep women in their place generally (not just its direct victims)?

Hate crimes are a manifestation of prejudice. However, intergroup violence can happen even in the absence of prejudice – sometimes, mere stereotypes are enough. In research on the 'weapons effect', Payne (2001; Payne, Lambert and Jacoby, 2002) presented American participants with a picture of either a Black or a White face, sometimes subliminally, that is, so fast that people were unable to consciously identify what they had just seen. Immediately afterwards, they were presented with a picture of either a handgun or a hand tool (e.g., a screwdriver) (see Figure

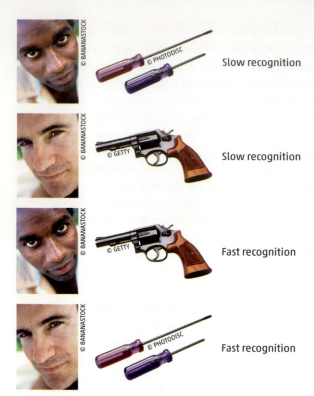

Slow recognition

Slow recognition

Fast recognition

Fast recognition

FIGURE 13.11 The weapons effect In the weapons effect, participants are slower to correctly recognize weapons than innocent hand tools if they have first seen a White face, but faster to recognize weapons than hand tools if they have seen a Black face. This is thought to be due to the stereotypical association of Black people with violence and weapons.

13.11). If they had just seen a Black face, participants were quicker to correctly identify the handguns; if they had just seen a White face, they were quicker to correctly identify the hand tools. One reason this might have happened is that in America, Black people are stereotypically associated with crime and violence, because of race biases in the objective incidence of crime and, perhaps especially, in media portrayals of crime. Even participants who do not have an emotional aversion to Black people have been exposed, many times, to this stereotype.

In support of this interpretation of the weapons effect, Judd, Blair and Chapleau (2004) presented Black and White faces in a similar way, but in their experiment, followed these with pictures of positive and negative stimuli that were not stereotypically associated with Black people, such as fruit and insects, respectively. Exposure to Black faces had no effect on the time taken to recognize these objects. If a generally negative attitude towards Black people was the driving force in Payne's (2001) study, we would expect people to be subsequently quicker to identify insects (the negative stimuli) than fruit (the positive stimuli). Another important finding, making the same point, was that exposure to Black faces not only facilitated recognition of handguns, it also facilitated recognition of sports equipment (e.g., American footballs). These are *positively* valued stimuli that are also stereotypically associated with Black people in the USA.

Why might this weapons effect matter? What if you were a police officer working in poor visibility and you saw a Black person emerge, appearing to carry something that might be a gun? Having cottoned on to the potential for this bias to result in disaster, researchers have begun to employ computerized 'shooting games'; ingroup or outgroup members appear suddenly on the screen and the participants' job is to 'shoot' them by depressing a computer key – if they are armed. In the USA, participants are more likely to mistakenly shoot unarmed targets if they are Black (rather than White), and are also less likely to mistakenly fail to shoot armed Black targets (Correll, Park, Judd and Wittenbrink, 2002).

A recent study confirmed that, once again, stereotypes, rather than prejudice, appear to be largely responsible for this effect. When Australian participants were exposed to a mood induction procedure that put them in a good mood, they were more likely to show an intergroup bias, being especially prone to shooting targets wearing Muslim headdress (Unkelbach, Forgas and Denson, 2008). When placed in a negative mood, they were less likely to show this bias. Previous research shows that positive mood increases reliance on stereotypes, because people are less motivated to be careful or accurate in their decision making (Forgas, 1998). In contrast, negative mood states encourage caution and accuracy. The pattern of results makes sense from a stereotyping perspective – Muslim headdress is stereotypically associated with aggression and thus elicits biased responses when people are in a good mood. If prejudice was the key to the shooting bias, we would expect, if anything, the negative mood to heighten it.

It is reassuring, in a sense, that intergroup violence is not always due to out and out prejudice. Biases may stem from innocent mistakes triggered only by widely known, shared stereotypes. However, this is a double-edged sword – it suggests that intergroup aggression can erupt even when groups do not hate each other. In the next section, we shall see how large-scale forms of intergroup aggression emerge from conflicts over resources and the fear of coming last.

Corporate intergroup aggression: when aggression is a group behaviour

A strong feature of human aggression is that it is often a coordinated, group-level activity. Groups, as well as individuals, aggress against each other. War is one mode of intergroup aggression, in which groups act collectively to do harm to each other, by means of military personnel and specialized military technology. Terrorism is another mode of intergroup aggression in which members of one group carry out aggressive actions designed to inflict fear on another group in order to achieve some political objective. Genocide occurs when members of one group attempt to systematically remove or eliminate another group.

As we saw in Chapter 11, we have known since Sherif et al.'s Robbers Cave study ([1954]1961) that intergroup conflict, including acts of verbal and physical aggression, is often triggered by conflicts over resources. Large-scale conflicts such as war and genocide are often triggered by the competing demands of rival groups for land, power or other resources. In a crude economic sense, these conflicts, setting aside the moral questions and the appalling suffering they inflict, may make sense. In a zero-sum game, groups benefit if they can grab resources. However, there is plenty of theory and evidence to suggest that these kinds of conflicts are not coolly calculated. Groups will sometimes engage in mutually destructive conflicts over resources that could never be valuable enough to replace those being expended, even leaving moral questions aside (Sidanius and Pratto, 1999).

One reason they do this appears to be the desire to ensure that whatever happens, the ingroup comes out ahead of, or at least not behind, the outgroup in relative terms. So, people acting on behalf of their group sometimes make what has been called 'Vladimir's choice' – a decision that amounts to sacrificing the wellbeing of the ingroup in an effort to ensure that the outgroup does even worse (Wildschut, Insko and Gaertner, 2002). Thus, when playing intergroup social dilemma games (there is more on social dilemmas in Chapter 14), people prefer to secure, say, 90 credits for the ingroup in order to ensure that the outgroup gets less (say, 80), rather than secure 120 credits for the ingroup and risk the outgroup getting still more. This has been linked to social dominance orientation (SDO). In one study, participants who were higher in SDO were more likely to make Vladimir's choice in a social dilemma (Sidanius, Prato and Levin, 2006).

As is often the case, social comparison processes are important. It is not so much what we have, as what we have relative to others. When groups find themselves relatively worse off, the situation they strive so hard to avoid, aggression often follows. A sense of relative deprivation may be important in triggering individuals to be aggressive, but appears to be even more important in triggering groups to be aggressive. A sense of relative deprivation has been found to be an important trigger, blamed for actions as diverse as riots, terrorism (Moghaddam, 2005), international aggression and genocide (Staub, 2000).

Different forms of intergroup violence, such as war, terrorism and genocide, may have different social psychological underpinnings. Although war and terrorism are both ways of securing symbolic victories for the ingroup over the outgroup, they may appeal to different groups for different reasons. War, for example, may be the method of choice for economically and politically dominant groups, who perceive that they have the means to protect and reinforce their dominant position. Terrorism, on the other hand, may be favoured by groups that are economically and politically weaker, who may perceive acts of terror as a means of 'freedom fighting', that is, counteracting the dominance they feel other groups exert over them (Bueno de Mesquita and Dickson, 2007; White, 1991).

This analysis was supported by an intriguing study of support for war and terrorism in the Middle East conflict by Henry, Sidanius, Levin and Pratto (2005). Among an American sample, both SDO and right-wing authoritarianism (RWA) were positively correlated with support for military action by the USA and its allies against Afghanistan and Islamist terrorists. Thus, Americans who were high in either SDO or RWA agreed more strongly with statements such as 'Afghanistan should be invaded or bombed until they surrender bin Laden'. These results contrasted with a Lebanese sample, who were asked whether they supported anti-Western violence that would traditionally be labelled as terrorism. Lebanese participants who were high in SDO were *less* likely to endorse this type of anti-Western aggression, and so tended to agree *less* strongly with statements such as 'The attack on the World Trade Center was justified'. Even so, just as RWA was positively correlated with support for warlike actions among American participants, it was also positively correlated with support for terrorist actions among Lebanese participants (see Figure 13.12). RWA is associated with adherence to traditional values and deference to authority, so can be expected to lead to support for aggressive actions, sanctioned by ingroup authority figures, against an outgroup that appears to have different values. However, SDO is associated with a preference for hierarchical, dominance-based intergroup relations. The different patterns observed on the two sides of the Middle East conflict suggest that, at least in this context, intergroup aggression in the form of military action, for Americans, serves the purpose of dominance. On the other hand, for Lebanese, intergroup aggression in the form of terrorism serves the purpose of counteracting group-based dominance.

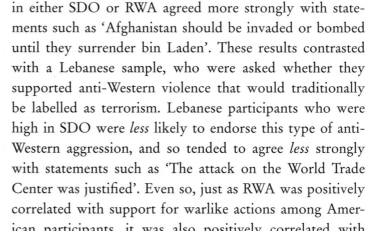
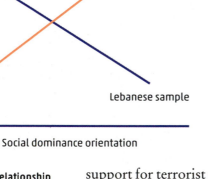

American sample

Lebanese sample

Support for intergroup aggression

Social dominance orientation

FIGURE 13.12 Relationship between social dominance orientation and support for intergroup violence Terrorist actions against Western targets, in the case of the Lebanese sample, and military action against Middle Eastern targets, in the case of the American sample, serve the purpose of counteracting group-based dominance.

Source: Henry et al., 2005

Evolutionary bases of intergroup violence

We started this chapter by considering whether, as many thinkers have argued, human beings' biological heritage has hard-wired aggressive responses into them (e.g., Lorenz, 1966). For other scholars, the extent and nature of aggression is primarily, or entirely, a matter of culture – what we learn and observe from others and the responses that are readily available to us (Bandura, 1978). A recent manifestation of this fundamental debate between evolutionary social psychologists and scholars from other theoretical perspectives has surrounded the topic of gender differences in support for intergroup aggression.

Of course, males *are* more likely to be active participants in armed conflicts, but this could be explained purely in terms of gender role specialization: men are physically bigger and stronger on average and so, in a way, it makes sense to 'give' them this role (Eagly and Wood, 1999). However, recent findings have been used to suggest that evolutionary processes have predisposed males towards warfare. The argument is that competition between males is a feature of any species in which they are the sex that invests less in parenting (Trivers, 1972). In such species, males are the bigger sex, mature later, take more risks, vie for mates and show higher levels of intra-sex aggression. Evolutionary anthropologists have argued that males who are successful warriors have privileged access to women. For example, one estimate based on studies of the Y chromosome suggests that 16 million men worldwide and up to 8 per cent of Asian men are descended from Genghis Khan (Zerjal, Xue, Bertorelle et al., 2003). For evolutionary psychologists, war is a manifestation of a tendency to compete with each other, ultimately for access to mates, that has been built into men by these evolutionary forces (e.g., van Vugt, de Cremer and Janssen, 2007).

In an attempt to test this idea, van Vugt et al. (2007) had undergraduate students in an English university play a social dilemma game. We will discuss social dilemmas further in Chapter 14, but the basic structure of these games is that participants are allocated money, which they can either keep for themselves or donate to their group. Each individual participant is always better off if they keep their own money, but, overall, everyone in the group benefits if participants are willing to sacrifice some of their money for the good of the group. The twist in this study was that an experimental group of participants were led to believe there was an intergroup dimension to the social dilemma. Specifically, they were told that groups of students from other English universities were playing the game too, and that the aim of the task was to compare how well students at different universities did the task. In the control, 'individual' condition, participants were told that the purpose of the experiment was to compare how well different individuals did the task. In this 'individual' control condition, men were less willing than women to donate their money to the group cause. However, in the intergroup condition, when participants thought they were collectively competing against other universities, men were much more willing to donate their money to the group cause, and in fact donated more money than women.

The male warrior hypothesis
The argument that men who are effective warriors have had an advantage in accessing mates and thus passing on their genes. As a result, through evolutionary processes, men have acquired a psychological makeup that predisposes them to warlike behaviour.

Van Vugt et al. (2007) argued that their experiments reveal how in times of intergroup conflict, men are predisposed to sacrifice their personal interests for the sake of the ingroup. They term this idea the **male warrior hypothesis**. The extent to which you accept this label should depend on whether the experiments are really an accurate model of the choices confronting men at times of war. There is no physical aggression displayed in these studies, and no overt reference to war or aggression is made in the experiments. There is no animosity towards the outgroups. The experiment is also open to other interpretations. Perhaps male participants were more motivated simply to be competitive and thus responded to the instructions more sensitively than women. Thus, when they were led to believe they could 'win' as individuals, they hoarded their money, and when they thought they were trying to ensure their group would 'win', they donated to the group. On the basis of this experiment alone, the 'male warrior', like the 'warrior gene' before it, may turn out to be a good example of scientific marketing that does not necessarily reflect empirical findings.

However, other studies also appear to provide some support for the evolutionary argument that males are predisposed towards war. In a series of experiments with Chinese participants, Chang, Lu, Li and Li (2011) assessed male and female heterosexual participants' expressed support for warlike statements, and their attentional bias towards warlike stimuli such as soldiers and tanks. All participants had first been shown photos of attractive, opposite-sex stimulus persons. When these faces were attractive, male participants later expressed more support for war and responded more quickly to warlike stimuli. Female participants were not affected by the attractiveness of the stimulus photos. Chang et al. (2011) argued that these findings reflect the effect of mating goals in promoting warlike behaviour in men. They appeal poetically to the notion that Helen of Troy was the 'face that launched a thousand ships' in the Trojan War – that female beauty inspires warlike behaviour. An alternative interpretation might be precisely that there is a widespread cultural idea that there is something chivalrous or sexually glamorous about war. In other words, perhaps we inherit entirely from our culture, and not from our biological heritage, the idea that warlike activity is a way for men to win the favour of attractive women.

Still more evidence gives reason to think that perhaps there could be a culturally universal male orientation towards war and other forms of intergroup aggression. As we have noted, men tend to be higher in social dominance orientation than women. However, this finding may emerge simply because men tend to occupy a dominant position in society. Sidanius, Pratto and Bobo (1994) found that men reported higher SDO scores than women when their cultural, demographic or political persuasion was held constant. That is, among participants of the same cultural, demographic and/or political persuasion, men tended to be higher in SDO than women. Sidanius et al. interpreted this finding as support for the notion that SDO should be expected to be higher in men than women across cultures. Social dominance theory attempts to integrate evolutionary and cultural analyses of masculinity and warfare. It suggests that the selective evolutionary pressures in favour of male aggression have contributed to cultural ideologies that venerate male dominance and aggression.

A single sample of Los Angeles residents such as in Sidanius et al.'s study is not enough to provide convincing support for the claim that men are universally higher in SDO than women. The fact remains that within any group in society, matched on other variables, men will also be members of the higher status group. It is difficult, if not impossible, to rule out the possibility that they are higher in SDO simply because of their relatively dominant position. In fact, a recent article by Batalha, Reynolds and Newbigin (2011) suggests that this social, rather than evolutionary, explanation for the gender difference might be more likely. In one of their studies, Batalha et al. found that men endorsed SDO more than women in Australia but not in Sweden – the latter being a more egalitarian society in which social hierarchies between women and men are less marked. In another study, they found a significant gender difference in SDO when participants were assigned to low status but not high status groups. They divided Australian undergraduate students into small groups of men and women and got each group to solve anagram tasks. In a bogus feedback manipulation, each small group was told that they were either doing much better (high status) or much worse (low status) than the opposite gender group. When assigned to low status groups, men reported higher SDO than women, but when assigned to high status groups, the gender difference in SDO was no longer significant.

Try it yourself Complete the social dominance orientation scale and compare your mean to that of established studies.

Which of the following objects or statements do you have a positive or negative feeling towards? Beside each statement, place a number from 1 = very negative to 7 = very positive.

1. Some groups of people are simply inferior to other groups.
2. In getting what you want, it is sometimes necessary to use force against other groups.
3. It's OK if some groups have more of a chance in life than others.
4. To get ahead in life, it is sometimes necessary to step on other groups.
5. If certain groups stayed in their place, we would have fewer problems.
6. It's probably a good thing that certain groups are at the top and other groups are at the bottom.
7. Inferior groups should stay in their place.
8. Sometimes other groups must be kept in their place.
9. It would be good if groups could be equal.
10. Group equality should be our ideal.
11. All groups should be given an equal chance in life.
12. We should do what we can to equalize conditions for different groups.
13. Increased social inequality is beneficial to society.
14. We would have fewer problems if we treated people more equally.
15. We should strive to make incomes as equal as possible.
16. No one group should dominate in society.

Source: Pratto et al. 1994. Copyright © 1994 by the American Psychological Association. Reproduced with permission

This is the scale developed by Pratto et al. (1994). It, or shorter versions, have been widely used in subsequent studies. You can add up and then calculate the mean of your 16 responses. Items 9–16 should be reverse scored: 7s should become 1s, 6s become 2s, and so on, because they reflect negative reactions to social dominance. Note how abstract the scale is – it takes care not to refer to specific groups or specific aspects of intergroup relations.

If nothing else, the study by Batalha et al. (2011) shows that men are not always significantly more oriented to social dominance than women. However, it has to be said that in each of their studies, there was always a 'main effect' of gender – meaning that averaging across all the experimental conditions, men's SDO was significantly higher than women's. Also, even in the conditions where the gender difference was no longer significant, the trend was for men to report higher SDO – their mean was higher, but not significantly so, than women's. Finally, it is not clear why men's SDO should have been higher when they were told they were doing worse (the low status condition) than women in the anagram group rather than better (the high status condition). A control group in which men and women were of equal status – simulating the relatively egalitarian social conditions of Sweden, in their first study – would have been useful.

All in all, it appears that men are generally, if not always, higher in SDO (Sidanius et al., 1994; Batalha et al., 2011) and are more likely to act like traditional warriors. Exposure to attractive women appears to heighten their interest in war (Chang et al., 2011), and involvement in intergroup competition seems to enhance their willingness to sacrifice their interests to the group (van Vugt et al., 2007). But these conclusions are based on just a handful of articles, and much more research is needed before we can generalize across cultures and make claims about human universality. In principle, it is going to be difficult to tease apart any evolutionary mechanisms from culture in explaining these effects. Sex role specialization, in which men take on physically risky and combative roles, appears to be a more or less universal feature of human cultures. Whether this is simply because of men's greater size and strength (Eagly and Wood, 1999) or evolved differences in men and women's psychology is difficult to determine, no matter how many research findings we have at our disposal.

Question to consider   Now that you have read about gender differences in warlike ideology and behaviour, and the material earlier on gender differences in aggression, reread question 3 at the start of the chapter. Do you think your friend was right to say there would be fewer wars if women had greater control over world events?

This recent debate is but one aspect of the still more general conundrum – is human aggression hard-wired, and does culture do much more than merely shape the form it takes? In this chapter, we have seen evidence that in other animals, levels of aggression can be inherited, so much so that it is possible to breed aggressive and nonaggressive strains. In humans as in other animals, specific brain structures and chemistries seem to play a role in aggressive behaviour. Humans, like other animals, respond with predictably heightened aggression when confronted with aversive conditions like heat, overcrowding and frustration. Aggression between individuals and groups appears to feature in all known human societies. However, the level and the form of aggression appear to change radically between cultures. Norms, values, the media and recreational drugs play a unique role in shaping human levels of aggression. Aggressive responses in the aftermath of the use of alcohol or violent media content appear to depend on the cultural meaning attached to these cues – if people expect them to lead to aggression, their expectancies tend to become self-fulfilling. Clearly, human aggression is the joint product of biological and cultural evolution. Major questions about the interplay between these two forces, and the extent to which biological evolution has shaped much more than the basic tendency to aggress, remain for new generations of researchers to answer.

Chapter summary

In this chapter, we have outlined how social psychologists, and scientists from other disciplines such as biology, have approached the problem of aggression. We have discussed the forms and the causes of human aggression. In particular, we have discussed the ways in which biological, social and cultural forces interact to produce aggressive behaviour. The key points to take away from this chapter are as follows:

- Aggression is behaviour intended to harm another. The intended harm may be social or physical.
- Philosophers and biologists have argued that aggression is hard-wired into human beings, like other animals, because of its evolutionary value in competition for resources.
- Some biological approaches to aggression have suggested that humans and other animals are subject to an aggressive drive or energy that requires release by means of aggressive behaviour. However, there is little support for this notion that catharsis reduces aggressive energy. If anything, attempting to reduce aggression by means of catharsis is counterproductive.
- However, there is plenty of evidence that aggression does have a biological basis in humans and other animals. Aggression has been experimentally bred into, and out of, mammalian species. Twin studies have some profound methodological problems but suggest that the more genetically related two people are, the more similar their levels of aggression will be. Specific chemicals and structures in the brain have been linked to aggressive behaviour. Thus far, there is no compelling evidence linking specific genes to aggressive behaviour.
- Alcohol is a major cause of aggression in humans, but its effects are not purely biological. They also depend on cultural beliefs about alcohol and its effects.
- Social forces are important in human aggression. When people are narcissistic (have inflated but insecure views of themselves), they require others to bolster their self-view and react aggressively when their self-image is threatened by others. People respond to frustration, the feeling of relative deprivation and the modelling of aggression by

others. Their aggression also depends on whether they perceive others' intentions to be hostile.
- Mass entertainments, such as the media and sport, have a powerful role in shaping aggressive behaviour. Consumption of violent media material and participation in and viewing of aggressive sports contribute to aggressive behaviour. This is especially so when the aggression in sport and media is rewarding, consistent with major social psychological theories such as social learning theory. Repeated exposure to violence in the media also desensitizes people to aggression: they become less sympathetic to victims and respond to aggression with lower levels of negative emotion.
- Culture affects aggression. For example, aggression is more common in cultures of honour, in which reputation and honour (especially of men) are highly prized. Also, the cultural metaphors that people have about aggression can contribute to aggressive behaviour. For example, the notion that anger is a kind of heat or pressure can lead people to try to control their emotions and aggressive tendencies by engaging in aggression.
- Many forms of aggression are not directed solely at individuals but also at the groups to which they belong. These can be termed 'hate crimes'. Examples include lynching, genocide and, arguably, rape.
- Aggressive behaviour is fostered when cues in the environment bring the possibility of aggressive responses to the forefront of people's minds. Thus, the presence of guns or other weapons may elicit aggressive responses. This has an intergroup dimension: people from certain cultural backgrounds may experience outgroup clothing, such as religious headdress, as a prime that reminds them of aggression. Black sports kit may also prime aggression.
- Some catastrophic forms of human aggression are perpetrated not only by individuals but also by social groups – individuals from one group acting in concert against another. War, terrorism and genocide are examples of this 'corporate' aspect of human aggression.

- Human beings, and men in particular, may have evolved to engage in this kind of corporate intergroup aggression. However, the experimental evidence for this argument is currently weak and controversial.

Our focus in this chapter has been on one of the darkest aspects of human behaviour. In Chapter 14, we consider nobler features of human nature – a love of justice, the willingness to cooperate with each other and preserve the environment.

Essay questions

At the beginning of the chapter, we asked you to consider these questions:

1 Your friend has a punch bag and lets the bag have it whenever someone really annoys them. They say it's a good way to let off steam and stops them from doing or saying aggressive things to people. Is this coping strategy a good idea?

2 Johnny plays a lot of violent video games. Should his parents be worried about this making him aggressive?

3 You are discussing the latest war and one of your female friends says: 'Why are men always so aggressive? If the world were run by women, there would be fewer wars!' Is she right?

Having read this chapter, these questions could also be framed as the following essay questions, which you can attempt in preparation for your examinations:

1 Evaluate the claim that aggression can be reduced by means of catharsis.

2 How does consumption of violent media material, such as violent video games, contribute to real-life aggression?

3 Evaluate theory and research findings suggesting that men are more aggressive in interpersonal and intergroup relations.

Some further reading

Anderson, C.A., Gentile, D.A. and Buckley, K.E. (2007) *Violent Video Game Effects on Children and Adolescents: Theory, Research, and Public Policy.* New York: Oxford University Press. The authors discuss the trend in which the effects of violent media on real-life violence appear to be getting stronger over time. They argue that this effect may be due to the increasing intensity and realism of violent content in video games, in which people are not merely witnesses but active participants.

Brownmiller, S. (1975) *Against our Will: Men, Women and Rape.* London: Pelican. Susan Brownmiller's work has been extremely influential in the social psychological study of gendered violence. Written in the heyday of the feminist movement in the 1970s, the writing remains fresh and controversial.

Graham, K. and Homel, R. (2008) *Raising the Bar: Preventing Aggression in and around Bars, Pubs and Clubs.* Cullompton: Willan. Readable book that applies the lessons of social psychology, sociology, policing and criminology to the problem of reducing aggression in the real-life context of pubs and clubs.

Malley-Morrison, K., McCarthy, S. and Hines, D. (eds) (2012) *International Handbook of War, Torture, and Terrorism.* New York: Springer. Comprehensive, interdisciplinary collection of essays from leading international experts on the psychology of war and intergroup aggression. Will broaden and deepen your understanding of the social psychology of international conflict, and reveals how social psychological insights and discoveries dovetail with developments in other academic disciplines.

Pinker, S. (2011) *The Better Angels of our Nature: The Decline of Violence in History and its Causes.* London: Penguin. Steven Pinker is an engaging writer. He presents a strong case that violence has become much less frequent through history, as a result of increases in the rule of law, education and cosmopolitanism. He suggests that these historical forces have reduced aggression principally by helping people to empathize with others and to see aggression as wrong. In this respect, he is a modern-day descendant of Hobbes, who, you may recall, discussed how modern civilization has rescued human beings from the barbarous state of nature.

 Visit the companion website at www.palgrave.com/psychology/suttondouglas for access to a wide range of resources to help you get to grips with this chapter.

Applying social psychology

Bullying interventions

Bullying is a common and problematic form of aggression, which features repeated acts of aggression against people who cannot easily defend themselves (Olweus, 1993; Salmivalli, Kaukiainen and Voeten, 2005). It is a pattern of behaviour that exploits and widens a power imbalance between bully and victim, and is associated with bad outcomes for victim and bully. Although bullying can involve physical and social acts of aggression, its overall flavour is social, as its principal aim seems to be to do emotional and social harm to the victim (Merrell, Gueldner, Ross and Isava, 2008).

Imagine that, as a social psychology consultant, you have been asked by a local school to advise it as it designs an intervention to try to reduce bullying in the school. In consultancies like this, your first job is normally to search the psychological literature for theory and evidence on the topic. You would then make recommendations for an intervention based on what appears to be the most promising and effective principles of intervention. The exercises below are designed to provide an approximate simulation of this process.

1 Do an internet search using a database such as Google Scholar to find at least three anti-bullying interventions designed in the past 20 years. Note the full citations in APA format. Also note how often each has been cited in academic and other sources (this information is provided by most databases along with the title and abstract). This gives you some idea of how influential and widely applied the intervention has been, although newer papers will have been cited less often. Good search terms would include 'bullying' and 'intervention'.

2 There are many such interventions, and articles outlining and testing interventions will be available to you for free through your institution's library or on publicly accessible websites. Retrieve three of these articles. They should be original empirical papers describing and outlining a single intervention with method and results sections, rather than review articles. Write a paragraph on each aspect of each paper:
   - Interventions are informed by a theoretical understanding of the causes of the problem. What theoretical assumptions does each article make about the causes of bullying?
   - What are the key features of each intervention? How thoroughly described are they and how do they relate to the underlying theoretical assumption?

   - How was the effectiveness of the manipulation tested? What outcomes were assessed, how, and with what results?

3 In addition to original empirical papers, meta-analyses and other reviews of the literature (literature reviews that do not include a meta-analysis are sometimes called *qualitative reviews*) are useful sources in consultancies like this. They typically compare and contrast different theories, interventions and methods for testing the effectiveness of interventions. Thus, they provide you with an excellent overview of the research literature and also help you find empirical articles that may have escaped your attention. Find at least one review article published within the past 10 years on bullying interventions.

4 Write down the full citation of the review paper you have found, and summarize its key conclusions in one or two paragraphs. Notably, how effective generally do bullying interventions seem to be? Which type of intervention seems to be most effective? What outcomes are most likely to be affected by bullying interventions? Note that some interventions do not affect actual rates of bullying behaviour, and may not be designed to do so: instead, some bullying interventions target attitudes to bullying.

5 Finally, restrict the search you did in exercise 1 above to the past two years, to find a new bullying intervention. This will help give you some idea of the 'state of the art' in the field. Note down the full citation and summarize as you did in 2 above.

6 Now, write a brief summary of the report you would provide for the school. This should fit on two sides of an A4 page. Your report summary should include:
   - a title
   - a definition of bullying and a summary of its consequences for school children
   - major theoretical accounts of bullying
   - an evaluation of different approaches to intervention – which is most likely to be effective?
   - recommendations for steps that the school should take to reduce bullying
   - recommendations for how the school should test the success of its intervention
   - a reference list (citations should be made in text, in APA format).

Blind spot in social psychology

Ideology, sport and war

As we saw in this chapter, there is no research on the ideological nature of aggressive contact sports. However, several theorists have described sport as a kind of symbolic substitute for war, with many of the same elements of physical struggle and a quest for dominance. Thus, it is reasonable to expect that enjoyment and approval of aggressive contact sports will be positively associated with positive attitudes to warfare. It is also possible that personality and ideological variables like SDO, which underpin support for war, are also related to aggressive contact sports. However, these ideas have not been directly tested, as far as we can tell.

1 Design a project that assesses whether positive attitudes to aggressive contact sports are correlated with positive attitudes to warfare and also with SDO. The SDO scale is included in the chapter, but you will need to adapt or develop scales to measure attitudes to sport and war. Usually, it is best to try to adapt tried and tested scales from published articles. That way, you do not have to worry about

the scales you have developed being unreliable or invalid, and it will be easier to interpret your results. Using databases or search engines such as Google Scholar, try to find reliable and valid scales. (In the chapter, we have also cited papers that assess attitudes to war and participation and enjoyment of aggressive sports.) If you cannot find them, then develop the scales. Write a structured abstract of no more than 500 words for your project. This should include the following headings: background, aims, participants, measures and hypotheses. Also include a copy of your proposed questionnaire in an appendix.

2 If the competitive, dominance-oriented worldview is reinforced by aggressive contact sports, we might expect that SDO, and support for war, would be increased immediately after watching or participating in such sports. In no more than 250 words, outline an experimental or quasi-experimental study to test this hypothesis. You can use the same measure of attitudes to war that you employed in the first study.

Student project

Policing of crowd behaviour and violence

Jade Norris studied as an undergraduate student at Aberystwyth University, and her final-year dissertation was supervised by Dr Gareth Hall. In this chapter, we spent some time discussing the problem of violence among sport followers. Jade's research explores aspects of the policing of crowd behaviour and violence. It is also relevant to group behaviour (Chapter 10) and us/them thinking in intergroup relations (Chapter 11).

My topic and aims

My research examined whether police discourse regarding public order policing (e.g., protest policing and police presence at football matches) reflects outdated perceptions of crowd behaviour. I also asked whether police officers' discourse changes over time – for example, does discourse change after training as a special constable?

'Outdated' perceptions of crowd behaviour refer to the ideas of Le Bon (1896) and Allport (1924) towards crowds as inherently barbaric and dangerous, with a tendency to be easily led by a violent minority. My study aimed to assess the impact of such perceptions on practical policing tactics, media coverage and accountability. It is possible that the unnecessary use of indiscriminate force and physical tactics is perpetuated by outdated perceptions of crowds. This is applicable to tragic incidents such as the death of Ian Tomlinson in 2009, which sparked debate in the UK about a seemingly deteriorating relationship between the police and the public.

In 2010, I began training as a special constable with Dyfed-Powys police. The training materials and delivery methods intrigued me. In particular, I was keen to understand to what extent training discourse can impact perceptions, and how these perceptions can potentially influence behaviour. At around this time, the student protests and London riots occurred. As the media began to place blame on either the rioters or the police, I was keen to investigate how these perceptions of accountability, crowd behaviour, and the efficacy of tactics could influence practical application of public order policing.

My methods

My project used a longitudinal design and qualitative methods. Semi-structured interviews were conducted with four trainee police constables before and after their six-month training period. The longitudinal design accounted for any perceptual changes after receiving training, and the pre-training interviews allowed for perceptions minimally influenced by immersion within the police institution. All interviews were transcribed, and were analysed using discourse analysis. This method was utilized to investigate the ways in which different constructions of blame and accountability were used, to create a picture of the interviewee's perceptions of crowd behaviour, and to understand their perceptions of the efficacy of public order policing tactics.

My findings and their implications

It was found that both before and after the training period, the interviewees constructed the crowd in terms of 'outdated' attitudes. For example, they provided examples of 'mob mentality' and its implications for the behaviour of the crowd as a whole. These examples tended to increase in frequency throughout the constructions at post-training, suggesting that the institutional discourse may reflect outdated perceptions. This would imply that institutional discourse has not shifted towards more recent theories of crowd behaviour, such as social identity theories. It was concluded that these outdated perceptions could be harmful when mixed with the practical application of public order tactics, in that the assumption that a crowd is inherently dangerous could lead to increased use of indiscriminate force, and perhaps create a self-fulfilling prophecy. Practical limitations of the study were acknowledged – in particular, it is difficult during a public order situation to utilize discriminate force (that is, target each individual breaking the law separately, without using controversial tactics such as kettling, that detain ordinary bystanders as well as law breakers).

Although previous literature had examined the use of tactics fuelled by outdated perceptions of crowd behaviour, few had undertaken a qualitative analysis of these perceptions within the police service. Stott and Reicher (1998) introduced the police perspective by interviewing public order trained officers. However, the current study interviewed the trainees both before and after training, which allowed for the investigation of perceptions of crowds from the 'public' perspective before training. The analysis suggests that pre-training constructions of crowds were only further solidified throughout training, suggesting that outdated perceptions of crowd behaviour could be more commonly held than simply within the police service. The interviewees did not receive any formal public order training, which suggests that the perceptions talked about during interview reflect institutional everyday discourse. My dissertation concluded by acknowledging the need for explicit introduction of newer theories of crowd behaviour, and reduced reliance on Le Bonian literature within training materials.

My journey

I am starting a PhD in September. I intend to work within academia, continuing with research and also teaching.

My project opened my eyes to complicated methods of policing, but also to the value of qualitative analysis. My interviewing skills have been enhanced by the experience, and my flexibility and open-mindedness in terms of analysis have increased. As a whole, conducting the research increased my self-confidence, not only in research and writing skills, but in professional self-presentation. This was achieved through integration with other institutions leading to the effective management of data collection.

My advice

My advice would be to start on your project early, gather up key articles both old and new, and always try to take a critical approach to the literature you use. Look for a 'gap' in the literature which you could address through your research project to ensure you have a relatively 'new' idea. I think it is also important that the project could be applicable in the real world, and that your findings could be useful in terms of practical application.

14 Altruism and justice

In this chapter, we examine some of the positive aspects of social behaviour, considering what leads people to perform acts of kindness and generosity towards others. First, we consider how people make sacrifices for the benefit of others (altruism), but also whether this can, in part, fulfil selfish motives. We consider how people respond to social dilemmas and how cooperative behaviour can be encouraged. We then outline why people defend justice and how the importance of social justice influences the way people think, feel and act towards others. By the end of this chapter, you will have a good understanding of altruism and justice.

© GETTY

Topics covered in this chapter

- Altruism
- Social dilemmas
- Encouraging cooperation
- The social psychology of justice

Key features

Critical focus The Kitty Genovese case

Ethics and research methods Eliciting distress in studies of the 'just world'

Social psychology in the real world Economic inequality and economic crisis

Applying social psychology Encouraging energy saving among students

Blind spot in social psychology Changing social value orientation: Can people be made more prosocial?

Student project The psychology of 'retail therapy'

Questions to consider

1 You are out one evening and while walking through the city streets, you notice a heated argument between a man and a woman. The man is shouting and looks like he is about to hit the woman, who is clearly distressed. Rather than helping, everyone appears to be walking past, ignoring the woman's plight. Is this unusual, and why is it happening? Under what conditions are people more likely to help?

2 Ziva describes why she gives to a charity in support of famine victims. 'Once I saw those starving children on TV, I just knew I'd feel awful if I didn't do something. I feel much better now that I've given a bit of money away.' Was Ziva's donation a selfless act of charity, or was she being selfish?

3 Jane is working in a competition between two teams and discovers that one of her own teammates is cheating in order to win the competition. Risking her own fate in the competition, she tells the organizer about her teammate's dishonesty. What social psychological processes might help explain Jane's behaviour?

4 A university teacher asks her students to write down their expected income after they graduate. She compares what males think they might earn with what the female students think they would earn and finds a significant difference – the males think they will earn more; or looked at differently – the female students think they would earn less. What social psychological theory might help explain this finding?

Much of this book has been concerned with the worst in human nature – the defective thinking, self-centredness, mindlessness, parochialism, cruelty and violence of which we, as a species, are so capable. In doing so, the focus of this book simply reflects that of the discipline of social psychology, which has always been concerned with finding solutions to social problems such as aggression and prejudice. As we saw in Chapter 9, much of the impetus for experimental social psychology was provided by the Holocaust that took place during the Second World War. While Milgram, Asch and Sherif built up a theoretical and empirical edifice to try to explain the horrors of the Holocaust, Oliner and Oliner (1988) set out to document, and explain, the extraordinary acts of kindness that occurred during this darkest period of human history. In their estimate, between 50,000 and 500,000 non-Jewish people risked their own and their families' lives in Nazi-occupied Europe in order to shelter Jewish people from the death camps. For every one of these people, Oliner and Oliner estimated that some 10 more risked their lives to help indirectly, for example by donating food or transmitting messages.

Exploring further Search popular media sites for accounts of two or more acts of individual heroism, altruism or bravery. How are these behaviours explained in the popular media accounts? Read on and see how these popular explanations compare with those developed by social psychologists.

Positive psychology A movement within psychology that emphasizes how positive aspects of human nature and experience can be enhanced. It is informed by the philosophical position of humanism, which assumes that human nature is ultimately good.

As social psychologists, we are interested in what leads so many people to perform these amazing acts of kindness. Just as the worst of human behaviours needs to be explained and controlled, so do the best of behaviours. In this chapter, our concern is how to realize some of the best, noblest impulses of human beings – to make sacrifices in order to help others and to love and defend justice. To some extent, then, this is where social psychology intersects with **positive psychology** – a humanistic tradition that focuses on the best aspects of human nature and experience rather than the worst (Seligman and Csikszentmihalyi, 2000).

Although generosity and striving for justice represent some of the most noble aspects of human psychology, this chapter is by no means devoid of studies that document human failings. Often, and under predictable circumstances, people do not act according to these prosocial motivations. Sometimes, as we shall see, these motivations ironically lead people to engage in antisocial behaviour, such as the blame and derogation of the victims of injustice. Also, we shall see how even prosocial behaviours, such as helping others, may be inspired by selfish motives, such as the desire to feel better about ourselves. The 'good' and the 'evil' in human nature appear to be more closely related than most people would normally think. In this chapter, we begin by examining the social psychological literature on altruism, in which we consider the human capacity to sacrifice one's own interests to benefit others. We then consider the importance of social justice to people and the effect – sometimes paradoxical – this has on the way they think, feel and act towards others.

Altruism

Altrusim An action that is performed to benefit a person without benefiting the self.

Helping behaviour An action that is performed to help another person.

Prosocial behaviour An action that is positively valued by society.

Altruism refers to an action that is performed to benefit another person without benefiting the self. It is a more specific example of **helping behaviour**, which is an action that is performed with the explicit intention of helping another person. The key difference between the two is that altruistic behaviour, unlike helping behaviour, does not benefit, and can sometimes be to the detriment of, the self. Both are examples of an even broader category of behaviour known as **prosocial behaviours**. These are behaviours that are valued by others in society – in contrast with behaviours that are antisocial.

Two great puzzles have motivated research on human altruism. First, it is unclear why human beings are as altruistic as they are. The science of economics has long been built on the assumption that people pursue their own interests, selecting courses of action according to whether they maximize benefits and minimize costs to themselves. This notion of self-interest is at the heart of capitalism (e.g., Buchholz, 2009; Smith, [1759]2007), which is now the dominant mode of political and economic organization worldwide (Hall and Soskice, 2001). However, if we accept this starting position, it is not obvious why people would act in defiance of their own self-interest in order to help other people. In particular, one puzzling finding is that lower income individuals tend to give more money to charity than high-income earners (Greve, 2009; Piff, Kraus, Côté et al.,

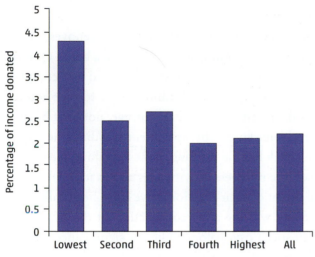

FIGURE 14.1 Income level and giving to charity Findings suggest that those with the lowest levels of income give proportionally more to charity than high-income earners. For example, the figures show that the lowest income earners (earning an average of $10,531 per year) gave 4.3% of their salary to charity, whereas the highest income earners (earning an average of $158,888 per year) gave only 2.1%. The national average was 2.2%.

Source: Greve, 2009

2010) (see Figure 14.1). Why would they do this? Similarly, evolutionary biologists have struggled to explain altruistic behaviour, which poses a threat to the survival of an individual organism for the benefit of other organisms – even organisms with which it may be competing to survive and reproduce. These major intellectual traditions tend to assume that individuals must be supremely selfish.

Conversely, although people are sometimes helpful in ways that are hard to relate to dominant understandings of human nature, historians and social psychologists alike have documented many cases in which people have shown a shocking failure to help others, even in ways that would cost them very little and even in circumstances where failure to help has potentially lethal consequences. These examples confound our commonsense understanding of people as possessing empathy, conscience and a desire to do the right thing. And, of course, they pose a practical problem for social psychologists, whose collective job, arguably, is to employ psychological methods and concepts in order to improve socially valued outcomes such as helping behaviour.

Time to reflect Why are the poor the most charitable when this does not fulfil human self-serving tendencies?

The study of altruism has focused on three key themes. First, there has been extensive study of bystander intervention. Second, there has been a lot of research on the situational and dispositional determinants of helping behaviour more generally. Third, there has been a great deal of research on helping behaviour in the context of social dilemmas, where people must decide either to help themselves or to help the collective of which they are a part.

Bystander intervention

Bystander intervention The act of helping a person in danger or distress by people who are not its cause.

When people witness the suffering of others, they have two basic choices – to help or do nothing. Under what circumstances do they help? Social psychologists' interest in altruism was captured by the phenomenon of **bystander intervention**. Research on bystander intervention was triggered by a tragic and shocking case in which it appeared that many people chose to do nothing while a woman was raped and murdered right outside their homes.

In 1964, at about 3.15am on a cold New York night, Kitty Genovese drove back to her apartment block after a night working as a manager of a bar in Queens. While walking from her car to the building, she was brutally stabbed by a complete stranger, who left the scene, only to return some 10 minutes later to rape and kill her in a stairwell. Media reports of the attack caused an outrage, not least because it was reported that some 38 residents in nearby apartment buildings heard her cries for help and witnessed the attack but did nothing, not even taking the trouble to call the police. As we shall see, the numbers of witnesses and exactly what they knew about the attack, and the extent of their inaction, have since been called into question. Nonetheless, so shocking was the apparent inaction of the bystanders that, in the popular press and in social psychology alike, its significance came to overshadow the appalling and apparently sexually motivated murder itself (e.g., Latané and Darley, 1968). The alleged failure of these 38 witnesses to act became an emblem of the all-too-frequent failure of bystanders to intervene. Further, it inspired a plethora of studies that demonstrated the failure of bystanders to intervene in a number of simulated emergencies (Manning, Levine and Collins, 2007).

These studies also yielded valuable insights into the reasons underlying the apathy of bystanders, and the factors that encourage bystander intervention. The first experimental research into bystander intervention in the wake of the Kitty Genovese case was conducted by Darley and Latané (1968). Participants were seated in rooms alone and communicated with other participants through an intercom. One 'participant' was actually a confederate of the experimenters, who during the experiment pretended to have a seizure, asked for help and then began to choke. Participants believed that just they, one other participant, or four other participants could hear the emergency unfolding. The dependent variable was whether the participant made an attempt to help the confederate. As Figure 14.2 shows, participants' willingness to help sharply declined as the number of other bystanders increased. Further, participants hesitated for much longer as group size increased.

FIGURE 14.2 Bystander intervention depends on the number of bystanders The number of bystanders who helped in Darley and Latané's (1968) experiment (a), and how long it took them to begin helping (b), as a function of the number of bystanders (including themselves) they believed were witnessing the emergency.

Source: Data from Darley and Latané, 1968

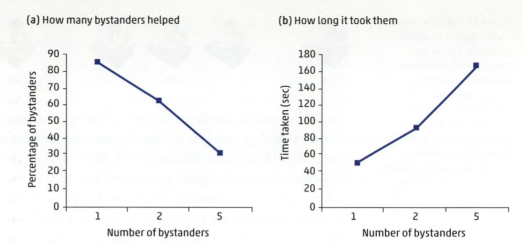

(a) How many bystanders helped

(b) How long it took them

FIGURE 14.3 Decision model of bystander intervention Latané and Darley argued that, at any point in time, the presence of other bystanders creates distractions or diversions that inhibit people from helping.

Source: Latané and Darley, 1968. Copyright © 1968 by the American Psychological Association. Adapted with permission

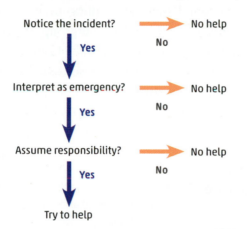

Diffusion of responsibility One explanation why bystanders do not intervene is the perception that someone else will.

Pluralistic ignorance The phenomenon whereby people wrongly assume, based on others' actions, that they endorse a particular norm.

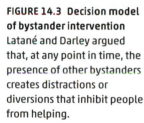

Why does the presence of other bystanders stop people from helping? Latané and Darley (1968) thought that as the number of bystanders increased, people were less likely to notice the incident, less likely to interpret it as a problem at all, and less likely to assume responsibility for taking action (see Figure 14.3).

More specifically, this adverse effect of group size points to the notion that bystander intervention is impaired by the **diffusion of responsibility** – the perception that 'it's none of my business' or that 'someone else will deal with this' (Darley and Latané, 1968). This is rather like the phenomenon of social loafing encountered in Chapter 10, where you are likely to pull harder in a tug-of-war if it is just you against one other person than if you are in a large team. Other studies have shown that diffusion of responsibility is not the only reason why bystanders fail to intervene. Another reason is **pluralistic ignorance** – the situation where people wrongly assume, based on others' actions, that they endorse a particular norm (Latané and Rodin, 1969; Prentice and Miller, 1996). In other words, if you observe others standing by doing nothing about an unfolding emergency, you may wrongly infer that they believe intervention is not necessary. The problem is, they may be committing the same error, and inferring from your inaction that you think intervention is not necessary. In the worst-case scenario, the collective effect of this fallacy is that nobody does anything. Latané and Darley (1968) demonstrated this by pumping large quantities of smoke into a room in which participants were completing questionnaires (see Figure 14.4). When participants were alone in the room, 75% of them reported the smoke. When the room contained three participants, only 38% reported the smoke. When the room contained the participant and two passive confederates, just 10% reported the smoke.

75%   38%   10%

FIGURE 14.4 **Where there's smoke, there's pluralistic ignorance** Latané and Darley (1968) conducted an experiment where a large amount of smoke was pumped into a room while participants were completing a questionnaire. When in the room alone, 75% of participants reported the smoke, compared to 38% when there were two other participants and only 10% when they were in the room with two unresponsive confederates.

Still other studies implicate further barriers to bystander intervention. If people are in a hurry, they help less, perhaps because they are less likely even to notice the emergency (Darley and Batson, 1973). Even if they do notice an emergency unfolding, motivated cognition processes may kick in that are designed to minimize anxiety and distress (as we saw in Chapters 2, 3 and 4). This means, for example, that people are sometimes inclined to interpret emergencies in ways that downplay their seriousness, just as some of the witnesses in the Kitty Genovese case assumed that a domestic dispute or minor assault was occurring (Wilson and Petruska, 1984). Conversely, research has uncovered factors that promote bystander intervention. Groups of individuals who have drunk alcohol (Steele, Critchlow and Liu, 1985) or who are friends (Rutkowski, Gruder and Romer, 1983) are less inhibited about intervening. Bystanders are more likely to help if they believe those around them are willing to intervene, particularly if these bystanders are 'ingroup' as opposed to 'outgroup' (Levine, Cassidy, Brazier and Reicher, 2002). However, as we shall see in the Critical focus box, there is controversy over the facts of the Kitty Genovese case and the mark it has made on social psychological thinking about altruism.

CRITICAL FOCUS

Bystander intervention and the tragic case of Kitty Genovese

In a review article, Manning, Levine and Collins (2007) examined the role the Kitty Genovese story has played in social psychology, both in research on helping and in textbook coverage. They found that the original media reports contained inaccuracies, unsubstantiated reports and omissions, which together exaggerate the extent of bystander intervention in the Kitty Genovese case. For example:

- Despite the number of witnesses (38) cited in media reports, no list of these was ever made.
- The public prosecutor in the case could find only 'about half a dozen witnesses that saw what was going on, that we could use'.
- The first and second attack on Kitty Genovese took place in different locations, meaning that few people could have seen the whole episode and understood its magnitude.

- Trial witnesses reported that they believed they were witnessing the aftermath of an assault, rather than a stabbing.
- Witnesses later claimed that they or others had reported the first attack to the police. At the time, there was no emergency number (911) system in place. Police had a reputation for hostile or indifferent responses to some emergency calls, and received many calls for affrays associated with a bar on the street on which Kitty Genovese was murdered. After the attack, the emergency call system was reformed.
- The murderer left the scene after one witness had shouted out of his window to scare him off.

The attack occurred after 3am, when people had their windows closed and were unlikely to be able to identify the noises they might have heard as a cry for help. All this in an inner-city street accustomed to disturbances in the middle of the night. However tragic, lamentable and even inexcusable the inaction of some local residents may have been, there is no evidence that a large number of people were aware of what was happening to Kitty Genovese but did nothing. Manning et al. (2007, p. 561) describe the Kitty Genovese story, as it was reported, as 'a stubborn and intractable urban myth', which, for them, 'makes its continued presence at the heart of the social psychology of helping even more unfortunate'.

In addition, Manning et al. (2007, p. 555) argue that despite the undoubted quality and importance of the research on bystander intervention, which media reports of this case inspired, those reports have also contributed to a biased view of helping behaviour in social psychology:

> We suggest that, almost from its inception, the story of the 38 witnesses became a kind of modern parable – the antonym of the parable of the good Samaritan. Whereas the good Samaritan parable venerates the individual who helps while others walk by, the story of the 38 witnesses in psychology tells of the malign influence of others to overwhelm the will of the individual. The power of the story comes from the moral lesson about the dangers of the group and how the presence of others can undermine the bonds of neighborly concern. We argue that the repeated telling of the parable of the 38 witnesses has served to curtail the imaginative space of helping research in social psychology.

What Manning et al. (2007) mean is that the effect of the mistold Kitty Genovese story has been to constrain the way researchers, textbook authors and students of social psychology think about helping behaviour. The notion that people are unwilling to help, especially when in the presence of others, has taken an undue hold on social psychological thinking. It has caused less attention to be paid to the possibility that under some conditions, the presence of others, especially when those others comprise a meaningful 'group', may be a boon to bystander intervention and helping behaviour more generally.

Indeed, Levine and Crowther (2008) argued that under some circumstances, group size may actually increase helping behaviour. When people in a bystander situation feel that helping is normative – the expected, normal thing to do – they are more likely to help. For example, friends are accustomed to helping and supporting each other, and so when the other bystanders are your friends, rather than strangers, a norm of helping is likely to be more salient to you. Likewise, when the victim is an ingroup rather than an outgroup member, the norm that one helps other ingroup members (see Chapter 11) may be reinforced by the presence of other bystanders who belong to the same group. Thus, the presence of bystanders who are friends and who, like you, share group membership with the victim may actually increase bystander intervention. Levine and Crowther conducted studies to test these predictions and found they were supported. In one study, British undergraduates indicated they would be more likely to help in a bystander intervention scenario if they were with a group of five *friends* rather than just one friend. Conversely, echoing the Latané and Darley (1968) findings, participants indicated they would be less likely to help when in the presence of five *strangers* as opposed to one. In another study, increasing the group size of women led to increased helping of a female confederate, whereas increasing the group size of men did not.

Levine and Crowther were not the first to demonstrate that the presence of others can promote helping. In a rather extreme version of the bystander intervention paradigm, Harari, Harari and White (1985) staged a simulated rape in the corner of a car park. They found that male bystanders were significantly more likely to intervene when they were accompanied by other men than when they were alone. Presumably, in some situations where it might be dangerous for people to act alone, they feel empowered to intervene by the presence of other people, whose help they might be able to recruit.

Manning et al. (2007) point out a lesson that can be drawn about social psychology more generally from bystander research. One way of doing social psychology is not only to test hypotheses derived from a particular theoretical argument and accept or reject the argument accordingly, but also to think about each argument as being balanced by an opposing position. This is what Billig (1987) calls a *rhetorical* approach to social psychology, in which knowledge of the subject is understood as the balance of opposing arguments. In principle, each argument has an opposite. It can enrich our understanding enormously if we are prepared at least to entertain the opposite of our position. So, Manning et al. (2007, p. 561) write: 'In the helping tradition, the argument that groups inhibit helping should be haunted by the possibility (at least) of the opposite – that groups can facilitate helping.' Among other benefits, this helps us clarify the scope of our ideas and identify cases where opposing arguments hold – as in Levine and Crowther's (2008) studies.

More generally, here we have another case in which, throughout the 1950s and 60s, when many of the most important breakthroughs were being made in social psychology, there was a strong tendency to assume that groups were a pernicious influence on society. Not only in the case of altruism but also in the literatures on aggression, prejudice and decision making, groups were seen to corrupt or override the rationality and morality of the individual. More recently, in particular since the advent of social identity theory (Tajfel and Turner, 1986), social psychologists have paid more careful attention to the positive, facilitating and enabling effect that groups can have on our lives. Thus, if we apply the terms of Billig's (1987) rhetorical framework, the generally unspoken sentiment that 'groups are bad' is now being balanced by more attention to the opposite assertion that 'groups are good'. Both sentiments capture important aspects of social life but neither can be said to be entirely true or entirely false.

Questions

1 We recommend this as a useful approach to your thinking. Entertaining an opposite view to many of the claims you encounter helps you think critically and creatively about the limits of an idea. Are there situations in which you could obtain completely different results than have been obtained in the article you have just read, for example? Find and read an article and try it for yourself. It may also help you find studies and theories in the literature that draw different conclusions.

2 Read the article by Harari, Harari and White (1985). We invite you to reflect on the ethics of this experiment, based on the ethical principles discussed in Chapter 1.

Question to consider Reread question 1 at the start of the chapter. What conditions would make it easier for you to help the victim?

Determinants of altruism

Helpfulness is not only important in the case of emergency bystander situations. In a host of other situations and in other ways, we can choose whether or not to help, for example by donating to the needy, offering support to family members or friends going through difficult times, or volunteering time to work for charitable causes. A great deal of research has examined what causes people to offer these kinds of help. The research has centred around three key questions. First, is the personality or the situation a more important determinant of helping behaviour? Second, in what sense (if any) is helping behaviour truly altruistic, designed to help with no thought for any benefit to the helper? And third, might the human willingness to help under some circumstances have evolved?

Personality and situational factors that give rise to helping

Some of the early research on altruism was inspired by a sliver of light that emerged from the moral darkness of the Second World War. Specifically, what caused some individuals to risk their own lives in order to shelter Jewish people from the Holocaust, while others did nothing to intervene or even collaborated with the Nazis (Oliner, 2004)? These stark differences between people in their response to the Holocaust led early thinkers to postulate that there must be some important personality variables at play. Theory and research were devoted to determining whether there was such a thing as an 'altruistic personality', that is, a stable psychological makeup that predisposes people to help others. Research attention was also paid to finding out what traits this altruistic personality might be made up of (Oliner and Oliner, 1988; Rushton, 1980; Rushton, Chrisjohn and Fekken, 1981; Staub, 1978). Much of the research involved correlational studies in which researchers attempted to find relationships between personality characteristics, other individual factors, and helpful behaviours. The following have been identified:

Machiavellianism Individual differences variable associated with the tendency to manipulate others for personal gain.

Belief in a just world The belief that the world is a just place in which people get what they deserve.

1 **Machiavellianism:** This personality trait is associated with a willingness and preparedness to exploit or manipulate others in the pursuit of one's own goals. As we might expect, it is negatively correlated with willingness to help – as Machiavellianism goes up, helping goes down (McHoskey, 1999).

2 **The belief in a just world:** People who believe the world is a just place in which people get what they deserve are, in some cases, more inclined to help others. However, the belief in a just world may only encourage helping behaviour among people who are awaiting an important outcome for themselves. Under such conditions, people may help others, guided by a superstitious and probably unconscious belief that doing so will help them. This was exactly what Zuckerman (1975) observed. University students who scored high on a scale measuring the strength of just world beliefs were more likely to help (e.g., by volunteering to participate in experiments or act as a reader for a blind student) than those who scored low on the same scale. However, this difference only emerged shortly before their examinations and was not present in the middle of term (Zuckerman, 1975). In general, the belief in a just world is likely to discourage people from doing wrong or failing in moral duties (Hafer, 2000; Sutton and Winnard, 2007), but is less likely to encourage people to help when they do not feel they have a strong obligation to do so (Dalbert, 1999; Strelan and Sutton, 2011).

Empathy The ability of people to take the perspective of others.

Empathic concern An emotional reaction to the suffering of others which results from taking their perspective, and which is thought by many researchers to motivate helping behaviour.

3 **Empathy:** People are more helpful when they empathize with a victim who is in need of help. This involves taking the perspective of the victim, and is associated with emotional reactions such as compassion, tenderness, soft-heartedness and sympathy, which together can be termed **empathic concern** (Batson and Shaw, 1991). Personality psychologists have shown that people who are generally prone to empathic concern tend be able to take the perspective of others, and also to be more helpful across situations (Bierhoff, Klein and Kramp, 1991; Eisenberg and Miller, 1987). For example, people who score high on empathy tend to donate to charity more (Davis, 1983) and take the place of a person who is engaging in an upsetting task (Carlo, Eisenberg, Troyer et al., 1991). Individual differences in empathy and perspective-taking show up in childhood (Knight, Johnson, Carlo and Eisenberg, 1994) and are therefore argued to have some genetic basis.

Moral reasoning The extent to which people compare their own needs with overarching moral standards.

4 **Moral reasoning:** The extent to which a person's willingness to help is a function of their own needs versus overarching moral standards (Eisenberg and Miller, 1987). People who use higher level reasoning to solve moral dilemmas tend to show greater empathy and altruism. For example, children who watched a video of an injured child and were then given the opportunity to play with

some toys, or organize toys to be sent to a hospital, chose the latter option more to the extent that they used higher level moral reasoning (Miller, Eisenberg, Fabes and Shell, 1996).

Extensivity A person's sense that they are obligated to help others, both close and distant.

DONATIONS

5 *Widened feelings of responsibility:* Oliner and Oliner (1988) argued that **extensivity** is a characteristic of helpful people. Part of extensivity is a person's sense that they are obligated to help not just those in their immediate social circle, such as close friends and family, but also those more distant from themselves. In other words, extensivity is the belief that 'I should help everyone in my society, not just those close to me'. Einolf (2010) developed a measure of extensivity (see the Try it yourself feature below) and found scores to be associated with helping behaviours such as donations of time and money to various causes. Later in this chapter, we will encounter a related idea, namely Opotow's (1990) concept of moral inclusion and exclusion. We all consider some beings as worthy of moral regard, who have moral rights and who can be wronged. We differ in how closely to ourselves we draw the line – at the ingroup, at certain outgroups, at humans, or at animals more generally.

6 *Religiosity:* In some research, religious beliefs have been associated with more altruistic behaviour. For example, Hansen, Vandenberg and Patterson (1995) showed that university students who described themselves as more religious spent more time volunteering with various university organizations. However, this is not always the case. For example, Jackson and Esses (1997) found that people holding strong conservative religious beliefs (e.g., fundamentalists) were likely to help some people, but not others. Their willingness to help was determined by perceived deservingness of help. Specifically, people were likely to help those they felt were deserving, but not those whose behaviour went against their religious beliefs (e.g., homosexuals) (see also Batson, Floyd, Meyer and Winner, 1999; Skitka and Tetlock, 1993).

7 *Gender:* Findings suggest that men and women differ considerably in their likelihood of helping in various types of situations (Becker and Eagly, 2004; Eagly, 1987). For example, men tend to show more acts of altruism than women in situations where heroism and bravery are involved (e.g., saving someone from a fire) and this finding generalizes across cultures (Johnson, Danko, Darvill et al., 1989). One explanation for these gender differences comes from an evolutionary perspective. Specifically, Kelly and Dunbar (2001) argue that women prefer men who are brave over those who are less brave – men are aware of this preference and are therefore motivated to act bravely. On the other hand, women appear to be more likely to help in situations that call for long-term care and volunteering (Becker and Eagly, 2004). However, gender differences like these can also be explained in terms of socially constructed norms and gender roles.

8 *Mood:* Research suggests that both positive and negative moods can lead to helping. For example, if people are put into a good mood by being offered a biscuit (Isen and Levin, 1972) or listening to uplifting music (North, Tarrant and Hargreaves, 2004), they tend to be more helpful. These findings suggest that people act altruistically in order to maintain a positive mood. Thus, people

who are in a good mood may help in order not to have their mood 'brought down' by others' suffering (Wegener and Petty, 1994). Perhaps, people in a good mood focus more generally on the positives rather than the negatives, which leads to increased helping. Or, being in a good mood may make people more aware of their values (e.g., Batson et al., 1999). This may all sound good, but other findings suggest that bad moods can increase altruistic behaviour (Regan, Williams and Sparling, 1972). As we will see later, people who are made to feel guilty are more likely to help (Regan, 1971). One reason why this may occur is because being in a bad mood makes people more motivated to make up for whatever happened to induce the negative feeling. However, as we will also see later, sometimes being in a bad mood can make people less altruistic. In particular, being ostracized makes people less likely to want to help (Twenge, Baumeister, DeWall et al., 2007).

9 *Having positive role models:* Some findings suggest that people are more altruistic if they have witnessed altruistic behaviour from role models such as parents and peers (Schroeder, Penner, Dovidio and Piliavin, 1995). Seeing others perform helping behaviour provides people with strong examples of how to behave and reinforces positive prosocial norms and the social value of helping. For example, Bryan and Test (1967) showed that people were 10 times more likely to stop for a woman with a flat tyre on the side of the road if a quarter of a mile earlier they saw someone being helped in a similar situation.

Try it yourself How extensive are you? Indicate your feelings of obligation to perform each of the behaviours below (0 = no obligation at all, 10 = a very great obligation). Compare your scores with the means reported by Einolf (2010).

Drop plans for child	To drop your plans when your children seem very troubled?	8.9	1.8
Contact child	To call, write, or visit your adult children on a regular basis?	7.8	2.3
Take child in home	To take your divorced or unemployed adult child back into your home?	7.4	2.6
Call parents	To call your parents on a regular basis?	8.0	2.5
Drop plans for spouse	To drop your plans when your spouse seems very troubled?	8.6	2.3
Raise friend's child	To raise the child of a close friend if the friend died?	7.2	2.7
Take friend in home	To take a friend into your home who could not afford to live alone?	6.1	2.7
Give money to friend	To give money to a friend in need, even if this made it hard to meet your own needs?	6.4	2.6
Do more on job	To do more than most people would do on your kind of job?	8.0	2.0
Work hard	To work hard even if you didn't like or respect your employer or supervisor?	8.2	2.9
Work overtime	To cancel plans to visit friends if you were asked, but not required, to work overtime?	6.7	2.6
Vote	To vote in local and national elections?	8.0	2.7
Jury duty	To serve on a jury if called?	7.2	3.0
Stay informed	To keep fully informed about national news and public issues?	7.1	2.4
Testify in court	To testify in court about an accident you witnessed?	8.0	2.2
Volunteer or donate	To volunteer time or money to social causes you support?	6.3	2.6
Vote for redistributive tax	To vote for a law that would help others worse off than you but would increase your taxes?	5.4	2.9
Pay more for health care	To pay more for your health care so that everyone had access to health care?	5.8	2.9
Collect money for charity	To collect contributions for heart or cancer research if asked to do so?	5.8	2.9

Source: Einolf, 2010. Copyright 2010, reprinted with permission from Elsevier

However, there are also situational factors that determine helping behaviour, such as culture and similarity, which we discuss briefly here:

1 *Culture:* The likelihood of helping behaviour differs significantly across cultures. Levine, Norenzayan and Philbrick (2001) examined three types of helping behaviour in 23 different countries – assisting a blind person across the street, picking up a dropped pen, and picking up magazines for an injured person. They found that helping behaviour was strongest in Brazil (100%, 100% and 80% for the different scenarios respectively), followed by Costa Rica, Malawi and India. Malaysia was at the bottom (53%, 26% and 41% for the different scenarios respectively), with the USA a close second last, and Singapore in third last place. One factor that appears to determine cultural differences in altruism is productivity. Specifically, countries in which people earn more actually help less. Those who witness economic deprivation more often are perhaps more able to empathize with others and thus help more. Religion could also be a factor in determining cultural differences in helping behaviour. Differences may also be the result of different cultural norms for helping behaviour. For example, cultures differ with respect to the norm of reciprocity (Miller and Bersoff, 1994), with some countries such as the USA seeing reciprocity as a matter of choice, but others seeing it as a matter of obligation. We will return to culture throughout this chapter, especially when we discuss the topic of justice.

2 *Similarity:* As you learned in Chapter 7, similarity is a significant factor in determining who we like. It is probably not surprising therefore that people are also more empathic and helpful towards people who are similar to them (Miller, Kozu and Davis, 2001; Stürmer, Snyder, Kropp and Siem, 2006). For example, students who have been through a romantic breakup feel more empathy for someone who has had a similar experience (Batson, Sympson, Hindman et al., 1996). People are more likely to help those who are similar in dress, nationality and various attitudes (Dovidio and Morris, 1975; Holloway, Tucker and Hornstein, 1977). DeBruine (2002) morphed participants' faces with strangers' faces to make a composite face and found that participants were more generous to the composite face rather than the stranger's face, presumably because it was more similar to the self. One important type of similarity relates to the groups we belong to. For example, in a study by Levine, Prosser, Evans and Reicher (2005), Manchester United football supporters completed a series of questionnaires and were then asked to walk to a different part of the building to complete the next part of the study. As they walked down a hallway, they saw another person (a confederate) slip and fall, appearing to have hurt their ankle. In one condition, the person was wearing a Manchester United jersey, in another condition they wore a Liverpool jersey (a rival football team) and in a control condition, the victim wore a generic shirt with no name on it. Levine et al. then examined whether the participants stopped to help the person. As they expected, participants were more likely to help someone who was wearing a Manchester United jersey rather than either of the others. Specifically, 92% of those wearing the

Manchester United jersey were helped, in comparison with 33% of those wearing Liverpool shirts and 30% with no-name shirts. Ingroup similarity is therefore a key factor in determining a person's willingness to help another.

3 *The power of the situation:* Guided by the prevailing notion of 'the power of the situation' that had led social psychologists to examine how normal people could perform monstrous acts (e.g., Milgram, 1965; see Chapter 9), researchers in the 1970s began to examine how social situations could lead people to help or not, whatever their character. As we have seen, one strand of this research focused on bystander intervention. Other lines of research examined what might drive individuals to help in more private settings. Regan (1971) led participants to believe that the experiment in which they were taking part had been ruined. Half the participants were also led to believe that this was their fault. Compared to control participants, they subsequently donated more to a charity. Later, Regan, Williams and Sparling (1972) replicated this effect under more realistic conditions in a field experiment. Female shoppers were approached by a male experimenter who asked if they could take his photograph. The camera failed to work. The experimenter led half the women to think *they* had broken the camera (this was the experimental condition), and the control group of women to believe it was not their fault. Soon afterwards, a female experimenter walked across the women's path, carrying a broken shopping bag from which groceries were spilling. Over half (55%) of the women in the experimental group went out of their way to tell her, whereas only 15% of control group women did. Apparently, the incidental experience of guilt was powerful enough to more than triple the incidence of altruism. These experiments shaped later research on helping behaviour in two key ways. First, they demonstrated the power of the situation to shape helping behaviour. As a result, most researchers since have taken an experimental approach, examining the situational factors that influence helping. Second, they seemed to show that people help others for a selfish reason – to make themselves feel better. Much of the research has followed up this paradoxical result.

Exploring further Use a search engine or database such as PsycINFO to find some recent research on personality traits and individual differences associated with prosocial behaviour.

Altruism: inspired by empathy or more selfish motives?

Some researchers, most notably Cialdini (1991) and Cialdini, Brown, Lewis et al. (1997), reached an unsettling conclusion – if people help others in order to help themselves, there may be no such thing as 'true' or 'pure' altruism, which is supposed to have no thought for the self. In direct contrast, other researchers, most notably Batson (1987) and Batson and Shaw (1991), sought to show that at least sometimes, people are truly motivated to help others with no regard for themselves. In particular, Batson argued that helping behaviour is sometimes motivated purely by empathic concern for the welfare of others. According to this

Empathy-altruism hypothesis
Hypothesis that when people feel empathy for others, they will be more likely to help that person at a personal cost to the self.

empathy-altruism hypothesis, some helpful actions are genuinely motivated by a desire to do something good for someone else.

This controversy over whether there is such a thing as truly unselfish empathic helping generated many research and review papers. Both sides of the debate seemed to gain some support from research findings. For example, an early study of the 'empathy' view showed that helping behaviour increased after participants were asked directly to take the perspective of the victim (Toi and Batson, 1982). Other studies seemed to suggest that both empathic concern and selfish motives have a role to play. This is consistent with Batson's (1991) view of altruism, because he admits that selfish motives can be important. Where Batson differs from Cialdini is that he argues that in the right conditions, purely selfless altruism will also emerge, whereas Cialdini (1991) argues that there is always some kind of self-interest involved in a decision to help.

One study that seemed to uncover a mixture of selfless and selfish motives for altruism was conducted by Carlo et al. (1991). These researchers exposed participants to a woman who seemed to be distressed as a result of reading a highly upsetting account of an assault. Two features of this situation were manipulated. First, the woman's distress seemed either to be strong or weak. Second, participants' ability to escape from the situation was varied. In the easy-escape condition, participants were told that they could choose not to watch any more of the woman's suffering. In the difficult-escape condition, they were told they would have to watch the woman read 15 upsetting assault accounts. As we might expect from Cialdini's (1991) approach to altruism, those who could not easily escape from the situation were most helpful, especially when the woman's distress seemed to be intense. As we might expect from Batson's (1991) approach to altruism, those who had scored highly on proneness to empathy and other altruistic personality traits were especially likely to help when escape was easy. Altruistic personality traits were less powerful predictors of helping when escape was difficult. Thus, the results suggested that there are some people who are dispositionally ready to help even in distressing situations from which they could easily walk away. But, they also suggest that the situation determines when altruistic personality traits will promote helping. If situational cues are powerful enough and provide people with enough incentive to help, it does not necessarily matter whether or not they are innately helpful.

Still other studies appear to offer strong support for the hypothesis that, ultimately, it is self-interest that drives people to help others. A classic experiment conducted by Cialdini, Schaller, Houlihan et al. (1987) is a case in point. They had participants watch an upsetting (but fictional) video about the plight of a university student who had broken both her legs and needed the help of a student, such as the participants themselves, to take lecture notes for her. To test the hypothesis that people help in order to improve their mood, they gave an experimental group of participants a pill immediately after watching the video. The pill was a placebo with no active ingredients, but participants were told that it was a mood-fixing pill – it would 'freeze' their current emotional state, meaning that it could not be changed for the next half hour or so. So, these participants had been led to believe that helping the woman in the video would not help them feel any better. Results showed that despite reporting high levels of empathic distress, participants given this mood-fixing 'drug' agreed to help the injured woman much less than control participants who might still have imagined that helping would make them feel better. Further, empathic concern no longer affected helping behaviour.

As the authors of this textbook, one of our jobs is to help you consider which of two competing arguments is more plausible in the light of mixed findings. Usually, the key to resolving apparently contradictory results is to look closely at the methods employed by different studies. Typically, you will find that a certain methodological feature causes results to go one way, and if this is changed, results go another, allowing you to make sense of mixed results and what processes might be responsible for them. Alas, this does not seem to be the case in this area of research. For example, a study much like the one by Carlo et al. (1991), set up in a similar way, produced quite different findings – empathic concern was related to helping behaviour when escape was difficult, rather than easy (Batson, Bolen, Cross and Neuringer-Benefiel, 1986). Likewise, a study employing similar methods to Cialdini et al. (1987) produced very different results, showing that leading participants to think their mood was fixed did *not* change helping behaviour (Schroeder, Dovidio, Sibicky et al., 1988). We do not have an easy take-home message, therefore, about whether Batson (1991) or Cialdini (1991) are right.

However, we think we can place these different results in an overall context that makes some sense. In short, it may not matter ultimately whether people help others in order to make themselves feel better. Indeed, it may be a conceptual mistake to assume that this apparently 'selfish' motive makes helping behaviour any less altruistic. The point is, people who help in order to make themselves feel better are pursuing an internal, rather than an external reward. And it feels good to help only because people are equipped with deeply moral capacities. One of these moral capacities is the ability to feel empathy for the plight of others, even to experience a sense of 'oneness' with them (Cialdini et al., 1997; Maner, Luce, Neuberg et al., 2002). Another moral capacity we have is to respond emotionally to our own actions and their outcomes – feeling good if we help and bad if we do not, especially if we think we could have done something. Thus, we need to consider people in their entirety. If they are prepared to help others without concern for external rewards like money or reputation, they are being altruistic. If they experience internal rewards for altruistic behaviour, this is because moral capacities are ingrained in their character (see Figure 14.5).

Exploring further You may be familiar with the TV programme *The Secret Millionaire*, where each week, a wealthy individual takes time out of their privileged life to live in an impoverished community. At the end of the programme, the secret millionaire donates money to a worthy cause (or causes) they have identified throughout the programme. They also identify themselves as the altruist at the end of the programme. Based on what you have read so far, what do you see as the motives for their actions?

External rewards

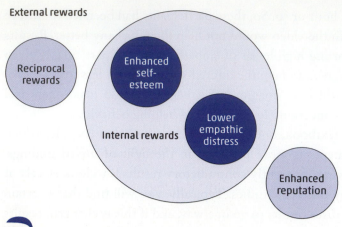

Reciprocal rewards

Enhanced self-esteem

Lower empathic distress

Internal rewards

Enhanced reputation

FIGURE 14.5 Simple model of the internal and external rewards of altruism If individuals are motivated by the rewards they expect to receive from the person they are helping, or from others, by gaining a positive reputation, their helping behaviour does not count as 'altruism'. A person without any built-in moral capacities, such as empathy or conscience, might help others in order to accrue such rewards. However, individuals also appear to be motivated by internal rewards, such as the prospect that their empathic distress would be relieved by helping, or that they would feel better about themselves if they helped. Such internal rewards can be seen as evidence that the normal human personality is effectively engineered to be altruistic.

Time to reflect Giving presents makes us feel happy. Using the knowledge you have gained so far, can you say why this is the case?

Indeed, some thinkers such as Staub (1978, p. 10) have put forward exactly this view of altruism:

> A prosocial act may be judged altruistic if it appears to have been intended to benefit others rather than to gain either material or social rewards. Altruistic prosocial acts are likely to be associated, however, with internal rewards (and the expectation of such rewards) and with empathic reinforcing experiences.

FIGURE 14.6 Altruism and sharing in nature Altruism is not a characteristic limited only to humans, but is also displayed by animals, who will call out to each other to warn of predators, share food and protect each other.

© PHOTODISC

We therefore think that altruism should be defined as behaviour to help others without thought of *external reward*. The important question is not *whether* internal rewards matter – researchers generally agree that they do – but *why*? Why are we equipped with the moral capacities that make us willing to help others even when doing so may be costly and thankless? Many theorists have argued that evolution has played a role in this phenomenon (e.g., Bowles, 2006; Fehr and Fischbacher, 2003; Trivers, 1971). At first glance, this hypothesis does not make sense. If evolution favours organisms who survive long enough to reproduce and nurture their offspring, how can it cause organisms to sacrifice their own interests to help others? Intuitively, for many people at least, it would seem that uniquely human characteristics such as empathy are required in order for altruism to triumph over our innately selfish, animal nature. However, studies of animal behaviour show that they do engage in acts of altruism. Birds will incur risks by crying out a warning to nearby birds when they spot a predator, animals will share food with relatives (see Figure 14.6), or defend them from attack (Hamilton, 1963; Trivers, 1971). Chimpanzees act in much the same way as young human children and demonstrate spontaneous acts of helping and kindness towards unrelated individuals (Warneken, Hare, Melis et al., 2007).

Question to consider Reread question 2 at the start of the chapter. Do you think that Ziva's donation to charity was purely selfless?

Exploring further One interesting example of altruistic behaviour is that of volunteering – spontaneous altruism for the common good. You may be familiar with high-profile examples of volunteering, such as Bob Geldof and Midge Ure who organized the Live Aid concert in 1985 to raise funds for the Ethiopian famine. Some researchers argue that volunteering is a difficult task that should be seen as a case of genuine altruism (Clary and Snyder, 1991, 1999; Omoto and Snyder 2002). However, people's motives for making even the grandest and most difficult humanitarian gestures are often questioned. Are even the noblest volunteers, at some level, being self-serving? Familiarize yourself with the literature on volunteerism and decide whether community volunteering can be driven by egoistic motives.

The discovery of altruistic behaviour in nonhuman animals led early evolutionary theorists to identify two reasons why they, as well as humans, help each other. The first is that by helping one's relatives or kin, one is promoting the successful reproduction of one's own genes. This is because we share many of our genes with our relatives. As we discussed in Chapter 13, evolutionary theory does not entail the survival of the fittest organisms, but of the fittest genes (Dawkins, 1976). For this model, **kin selection** is important. Genes that programme animals to help their relatives will be more likely to be successfully copied. There is strong evidence that nonhuman animals are selectively altruistic towards their relatives (Clutton-Brock, 2002). Human beings also prefer to help those who are more closely related to them (Burnstein, Crandall and Kitayama, 1994) (see Figure 14.7), but, as we have seen, show remarkable willingness to help even strangers.

Kin selection Acting differently towards members of the same species depending on their degree of genetic relatedness to the self. Kin selection can deter animals from mating, for example, but can encourage them to act altruistically.

FIGURE 14.7 People are more inclined to help their relatives, especially in life or death, rather than everyday, situations

Source: Data from Burnstein et al., 1994

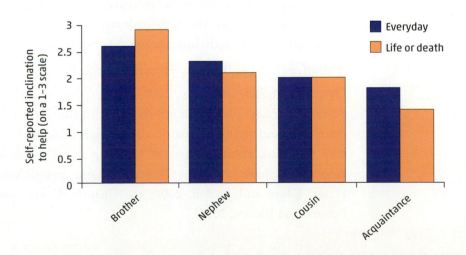

Reciprocal altruism Animals act altruistically towards members of the same species that have already helped them. This principal gives animals an incentive to help other animals, because it heightens the prospects that they will be rewarded.

The second reason why animals may make sacrifices to help each other is that their altruism may be repaid. This is the principal of **reciprocal altruism**. If animals evolve a preference to help others who will help them and to help others who have helped them before, then the prospects of mutual survival are enhanced. Leider, Möbius, Rosenblat and Do (2009) ran a study on Facebook in which participants were able to exchange money with strangers or friends in a range of 'social dilemma' games that we will encounter later in this chapter. Predictably, participants were 52 per cent more likely to donate money to friends than strangers. This is consistent with the principle of reciprocal altruism, because friends are more likely to reciprocate one's acts of generosity than strangers. Leider et al. (2009) also manipulated whether participants expected to interact with each other in the future. This prospect of future interaction increased giving by a further 24 per cent.

Although these studies show that altruism is more commonly directed at relatives or those who are likely to reciprocate, altruism does not disappear when these conditions are not met. Human beings selectively make sacrifices to help ingroup rather than outgroup members, even when ingroup members are not able to reciprocate (Bernhard, Fischbacher and Fehr, 2006). De Waal (2008) argues that the adaptive value of altruism has shaped our emotional and cognitive makeup, so that we have evolved the capacity for empathy. Success in reproduction and parenthood requires us, and other mammalian species, to have the capacity to form emotional ties and develop empathic concern for children very quickly (MacLean, 1985). This ability to empathize and quickly care for others may then have generalized to other cases. Indeed, de Waal (2008) argues that in most situations confronting our ancestors, who lived in small, interrelated groups, the people they had opportunities to help were somewhat related to them and were likely to reciprocate. The tendency to feel empathic concern for others has taken on a motivational life of its own. As de Waal (2008, p. 281) puts it:

> Once evolved, behavior often assumes motivational autonomy, that is, its motivation becomes disconnected from its ultimate goals. A good example is sexual behavior, which arose to serve reproduction. Since animals are, as far as we know, unaware of the link between sex and reproduction, they must be engaging in sex (as do humans much of the time) without progeny in mind.

A similar argument has often been run with the emotion of disgust (Haidt, 2003; Oaten, Stevenson and Case, 2009; Phillips, Young, Senior et al., 1997). Disgust deterred our ancestors from interacting with slimy, rotten things that could make them sick, and the same emotional machinery has now generalized to shape the way we think about outgroups (Fincher and Thornhill, 2012; Inbar, Pizarro, Knobe and Bloom, 2009; see Chapter 12), other people's moral violations (Schnall, Haidt, Clore and Jordan, 2008; see Chapter 4) and political ideology (Inbar, Pizarro and Bloom, 2008).

Time to reflect Knowing what you know about altruism, imagine you are trying to get members of your university to donate blood. What techniques would work best, and why?

Who gets help?

Research suggests that aspects of the person significantly influence whether or not they receive help. Specifically, factors like age, gender, attractiveness and personality determine the degree of help received:

© PHOTOALTO

1 *Age:* As we get older, we become more reluctant to seek help. For example, research shows that children are very willing to seek and accept help, arguably because they need it more, but also because they do not regard it as a sign of weakness. Unfortunately, this is not true of older children and adults, who may be less likely to get help when they need it, because they do not ask (Shell and Eisenberg, 1992).

2 *Gender:* Research suggests that women are more likely to receive help than men (Bruder-Mattson and Hovanitz, 1990). For example, strangers are more likely to respond to simple questions (e.g., asking for the time) if they are made by women rather than men (Pearce, 1980). One of the suspected reasons for this tendency is that it is more difficult for men to accept help than it is for women (Bruder-Mattson and Hovanitz, 1990). For men, it is argued that accepting help is a sign of weakness and has more personal costs than it does for women.

3 *Attractiveness:* Attractive people receive more help than unattractive people (Wilson and Dovidio, 1985). For example, people are more likely to receive directions (and people take longer to give directions) if the recipient is attractive (Harrell, 1978). Interestingly, this happens in cases where there may or may not be a benefit for the help-giver. One might assume that attractive people receive more help because people perceive the possibility of future interactions with them, but this does not appear to be the case (Benson, Karabenick and Lerner, 1976).

4 *Personality:* Personality influences the likelihood of receiving help. For example, people who are socially anxious receive less support from their peers (Caldwell and Reinhart, 1988). However, some studies suggest that people who are high in self-esteem receive less help, mainly because they do not ask for it, or need it (Nadler, Altman and Fisher, 1979). On the other hand, people with high self-esteem benefit more from social support networks (Caldwell and Reinhart, 1988).

Social dilemmas

The study of altruism has an important implication that extends beyond situations in everyday life where we can choose whether or not to help a victim. In particular, a kind of altruism is crucial to the very success of our society. In many situations, what is best for the individual is not best for the group as a whole. Very often, if the group is going to achieve its goals for the benefit of all, it requires individuals to pool together and sacrifice their own interests. These situations are known as **social dilemmas** (Dawes, 1980). When people put aside their own interests in order to help the group as a whole, their behaviour is termed **cooperation**, and when they act in their own interests at the expense of the group, their behaviour is termed **defection**.

Real-life examples of social dilemmas abound. In war, soldiers' interests and indeed their very lives may be better protected if they desert the field of battle, but the interests of their group – their platoon, or their entire nation – normally require that they fight. Recycling and environmental behaviours can be expensive for the individual but benefit wider society. Team sports often require that a player sacrifice their own performance to ensure the success of their team, rather than going for individual glory. In cricket, for example, when a team needs to score many runs quickly to win, individual batters are expected to risk getting out, potentially damaging their own career statistics, in pursuit of quick runs. Another less entertaining but probably more important example is taxation. Individuals are materially better off if they can avoid paying tax. However, without tax revenue, it would be difficult, if not impossible, to finance hospitals, schools, roads or the streetlights to illuminate them. These are just a few of the goods and services provided by governments for the good of all, using tax revenue.

Social dilemmas Situations in which the interests of the individual are at odds with the interests of the group.

Cooperation Decisions that sacrifice the person's interests for the sake of the group.

Defection Decisions that pursue the person's interests at the expense of the group.

Exploring further Using a search engine or database such as PsycINFO, search the literature and list the types of social dilemmas studied by social psychologists.

Types of social dilemma

Experimental social psychologists (and researchers in related fields such as behavioural economics and evolutionary biology) attempt to distil the essence of these real-life dilemmas into experimental games. The simplest and most studied is the **prisoner's dilemma**. This is played by two people, who are asked to imagine that they are suspects caught by the police and charged with a joint crime. The police offer each of them a bargain. Each is told that if they confess to the joint crime, effectively betraying their partner as well as themselves, they will receive a reduced sentence. If one prisoner confesses and their partner does not, the confessor's sentence will be greatly reduced, and their partner's will be increased. If they both confess, they will receive a somewhat shorter sentence of intermediate length. If neither confesses, they will both receive quite short sentences (see Figure 14.8).

This is a social dilemma because the overall interests of this 'group' of two people, defined as the total amount of time served in prison, are better served if

Prisoner's dilemma Simulated social dilemma used in social psychological research. 'Prisoners' have to choose between confessing or not, risking a heavy or light sentence for them and a partner.

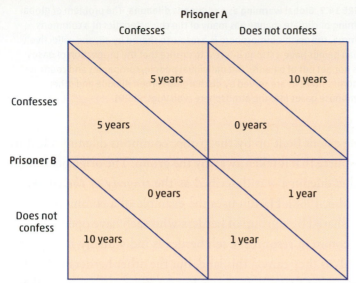

Prisoner A

FIGURE 14.8 **The prisoner's dilemma game** Each of the four rectangles represents the prison sentence that prisoner A will receive (above the diagonal line) and the sentence that prisoner B will receive if one, both or neither confesses.

each prisoner does not confess. On the other hand, each individual prisoner is always better off if they confess. Therefore, refusing to confess is an example of 'cooperation', serving the group's interest, whereas confession is 'defection', in which the individual does what is best for them despite the overall interests of the group.

Try it yourself To help illustrate why not confessing is the cooperative choice in the prisoner's dilemma, calculate the total amount of prison time served by both prisoners in all combinations. The mean sentence served by both is an index of their joint interests. The lower this is, the better off they are as a 'group' of two people. Your calculations should show that, on average, both are better off if they do not confess, but one prisoner is always personally better off confessing. This is why the prisoner's dilemma is truly a social dilemma, pitting individual interests against those of the whole group.

Thus far, we have looked at the prisoner's dilemma from the perspective of the prisoner who is immediately faced with a decision – do I betray my partner to save my own skin? But the flipside of this perspective is that as well as being a *moral agent* who has to make their own decision, each prisoner is a *moral patient* whose fate depends on the other's decision. As you can see in Figure 14.8, regardless of their own decision, a prisoner is better off if their partner decides to cooperate. Many social situations are rather like that – you can enjoy a park, use a road or a hospital that others have paid for, regardless of whether you have personally contributed to it through taxes, for example. Thus, the prisoner's dilemma is sometimes described as a two-person **public goods dilemma** (e.g., Andreoni, 1988). A public good is one that people cannot feasibly be prevented from using, even if they have not paid their share – such as a park or a public hospital. The group as a whole is better off if everybody cooperates by contributing to such goods, but each individual within the group is better off, at least in material terms, if they avoid paying their share. The parks, roads and hospitals will still be there, and are unlikely to be noticeably worse off because one individual does not cooperate. Defection in a public goods dilemma is termed *free riding* – benefiting from others' contribution while choosing not to follow their example (e.g., Yamagishi and Sato, 1986).

The other type of social dilemma that has received a lot of attention is the **commons dilemma**. Whereas public goods dilemmas involve a resource that is to

Public goods dilemma A dilemma in which individuals are better off if they do not contribute but the group as a whole is worse off.

Commons dilemma A dilemma in which individual interests are served by using a resource but collective interests suffer because the resource is depleted.

FIGURE 14.9 Global warming as a commons dilemma The problem of global warming or climate change has many of the characteristics of a commons dilemma. The earth's atmosphere is a resource shared by all, and collectively human beings have a strong interest to ensure that the proportion of gases does not get out of balance. But individual people, companies and countries' economic interests are served by discharging carbon dioxide and other greenhouse gases into the atmosphere (van Vugt, 2009).

some extent built up by the group, commons dilemmas feature a resource that is taken away by the group. The original example of this dilemma was described as the *tragedy of the commons* (Hardin, 1968). Hardin uses the example of a common grazing land shared by a group of herders who each have open access to this common resource. Each herder is individually better off if they graze as many animals as they can on this land, but the other herders will suffer as a result of the damage caused to the common by the excess of animals. If too many herders graze more than their share, eventually the common is exhausted and may even be permanently destroyed by overuse. It is easy to think of real-life commons dilemmas, such as global warming (see Figure 14.9) and the depletion of global fish stocks. Each fishing boat, and each country, benefits by overfishing. Doing so, however, both reduces the resources available for others and threatens to destroy the resource altogether, because intense overfishing makes it impossible for the fish population to replenish itself through breeding.

Time to reflect Can you think of other examples of commons dilemmas or specific situations of dilemmas? What happened in these cases?

Encouraging cooperation

Learning to build and share resources for the common good is one of the most fundamental challenges facing human beings, and is likely to be ever more pressing now that there are more and more of 'us', the human population having recently reached seven billion. Thus, it is apt that social psychologists have spent a good deal of effort identifying conditions that facilitate cooperation for the common good. Broadly speaking, four types of factors seem to be helpful:

- if people in a social dilemma value the common interest as well as their own
- if they have a strong sense of identification with the wider group
- if they are able to communicate with each other and establish principles and ground rules before they have to make decisions
- if their own strategic decisions effectively reward cooperators and punish defectors as the social dilemma unfolds.

Encouraging prosocial versus pro-self orientation

Situational factors determine behaviour in social dilemmas, but personality factors also play a role. Some people will tend to cooperate across social dilemmas,

Social value orientation The extent to which an individual is 'pro-self' or 'prosocial', which determines the extent to which people will be cooperative.

whereas others will defect in the same situations. One personality variable that captures this difference between people is known as **social value orientation** (van Lange and Liebrand, 1991). Essentially, some people are 'pro-self', and indicate on questionnaires that given the choice, they will prioritize getting resources for themselves without concern for the resources that others gain (Liebrand and McClintock, 1988). Indeed, some pro-self individuals may actively seek to ensure that others get less than themselves (van Lange, Otten, de Bruin and Joireman, 1997). In contrast, others are 'prosocial', indicating concern with maximizing the resources available to others as well as themselves (van Lange, 1999). It may not surprise you to learn that pro-self individuals are much less likely to cooperate in social dilemmas than prosocial people (for reviews, see Bogaert, Boone and Declerck, 2008; van Lange, de Cremer, van Dijk and van Vugt, 2007). One implication of these findings is that people who are in charge of group situations such as work teams, which have the characteristics of a group dilemma – people sometimes have to sacrifice their own interests for the sake of the group – might do well to select individuals who are prosocial, rather than pro-self. Another implication is that the group's interests would be served if it were somehow possible to 'make' people more prosocial, whether temporarily or permanently, but no research has examined whether this is possible (see the Blind spot in social psychology exercise at the end of this chapter).

Try it yourself Are you pro-self or prosocial? Use a search engine to find a copy of a measure of social value orientation. You can complete it, score yourself, and see how you fall relative to the means reported in the articles.

Encouraging strong social identification

In this chapter, we have already seen how bystanders' sense of shared social identification with a victim can encourage helping behaviour. A strong sense of social identification with the group also encourages people to cooperate in public goods dilemmas. This is especially true of people who are pro-self, suggesting that social identification increases cooperation by encouraging people to see helping the group as tantamount to helping themselves. De Cremer and van Vugt (1999) obtained support for this hypothesis with a study of behaviour in public goods dilemmas among students at Southampton University in the UK. De Cremer and van Vugt pretested the social value orientation of their participants according to their choices in hypothetical social dilemmas. On the basis of the pretest, 61 per cent of the participants were classified as prosocial, and 24 per cent as pro-self. Before participants played the public goods dilemma game, the researchers manipulated the level of group identification by describing the experiment either as a comparison of the behaviour of different individuals in such games (low identification) or of the behaviour of students at different universities (high identification, the group in question being Southampton University students). Pro-self participants contributed more money when in the high, rather than the low, identification condition. In fact, in the high group identification condition, they donated as much money as prosocial participants. In the low group identification condition, pro-

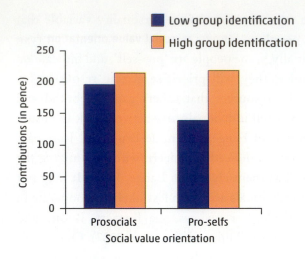

FIGURE 14.10 Cooperation as a function of social identity and social value orientation Pro-self participants contributed more money in the high group identification condition than in the low identification condition. Prosocial participants were unaffected by the manipulation.

These results suggest that cooperation can be increased by encouraging people to see helping the group as really helping the self.

Source: De Cremer and van Vugt, 1999. Copyright © 1999 by the American Psychological Association. Reproduced with permission

self participants gave significantly less money than prosocial participants, as we might normally expect. For their part, prosocial participants were unaffected by the group identification manipulation (see Figure 14.10).

Communication

Part of the problem facing participants in social dilemmas is their uncertainty about how others will behave. Presumably, most people would like to live in a world where people do not behave with absolute selfishness but also take into account the common good. However, a significant problem is that we cannot necessarily trust others to do that, and perhaps because of that mistrust, we are more inclined to pursue our own interests. No one likes to lose out, and no one likes to find their prosocial behaviour exploited by others (Yamagishi, Cook and Watabe, 1998). This mistrust can be resolved by communication. In an early demonstration of this effect, Dawes, McTavish and Shaklee (1977) put participants into groups of eight and either gave them a chance to communicate about how they should behave in an upcoming commons dilemma, to communicate about irrelevant topics, or deprived them of the opportunity to communicate before playing the game. Cooperation was significantly higher in the 'relevant communication' condition than in the other two conditions. Communicating about irrelevant topics did not increase cooperative behaviour. It seems that cooperative behaviour can be increased if people have a chance to discuss the ground rules and establish a norm of cooperative behaviour. Associated with this change is an increased trust that others will cooperate. The finding that communicating about irrelevant topics does not increase cooperative behaviour suggests that the effect of communication does not boil down simply to participants getting to know each other.

Subsequent research has suggested that the beneficial effect of communication only works under some conditions. Specifically, communication most effectively increases cooperation when:

- group members discuss appropriate behaviour and advocate cooperation in a constructive way, rather than merely taking the opportunity to threaten those who would defect (Stech and McClintock, 1981)
- the social dilemma is relatively easy to understand or 'demonstrable', so that group members can explain to each other how their common interest is served by cooperation (Hopthrow and Hulbert, 2005; Laughlin, 1980)
- individuals make clear and emphatic personal promises to cooperate, and establish a strong norm of cooperation (Kerr and Kaufman-Gilliland, 1994).

Under the right conditions, communication can be powerful in bringing cooperation about, as demonstrated by a recent study with English undergraduate students. Hopthrow and Abrams (2010) conducted a pretest to determine whether each of the participants in this study favoured cooperation or defection as a strategy in a social dilemma. They then put participants together in groups of six, several of which were *unanimously opposed to cooperation* at the start of the experiment. Surprisingly, even these groups showed high levels of cooperation in a subsequent dilemma if they were first given a chance to communicate with each other. This is a remarkable exception to the group polarization effect we have seen in earlier chapters (notably Chapter 10), where groups tend to act in line with a stronger version of their members' initial attitudes. Communication had this striking effect of overturning members' initial attitudes only if the social dilemma was demonstrable, making the benefits of cooperation easy to explain to group members.

Strategies during the game: punishing others' defection and rewarding their cooperation

Participants in a social dilemma often have the chance to modify each others' behaviour during the game even if they have not first had a chance to lay down the norms and ground rules through communication. They can do this by making strategic decisions that tend to reward cooperators and punish defectors. A simple example is the so-called *tit-for-tat strategy*. In a two-person social dilemma such as the prisoner's dilemma, a player can opt to cooperate if the other player has just cooperated, and to defect if they have just defected. This simple strategy is an example of the principle of reciprocity – responding in kind to others' cooperation and defection. The strategy works because it encourages other players to cooperate. Indeed, the tit-for-tat strategy has consistently been shown to be the best, or 'optimal' strategy in the prisoner's dilemma, especially when the dilemma is set up so that players take alternating turns (e.g., Wedekind and Milinski, 1996). Indeed, the success of tit for tat has led some theorists to suggest that it may have evolved in humans and other animals (e.g., Axelrod and Hamilton, 1981) – one study even showed that fish use this strategy (Milinski, 1987).

Doing unto others as they do unto others: indirect reciprocity and altruistic punishment

As we have seen, biologists, economists and psychologists have long been puzzled by the extent to which people are altruistic (e.g., cooperate), when they would be better off, at least in purely material terms, if they defected. Scientists' understanding of this puzzle has been greatly advanced by recent research into altruistic punishment and indirect reciprocity. In social dilemmas, people frequently choose to punish defections by other member of the group, even at personal expense. For example, a person may sacrifice €1 of their own payoff to reduce a defector's payoff by €2. This is known as **altruistic punishment**, because of its self-sacrificing quality (e.g., Fehr and Gächter, 2002). Also, people incur personal costs to reward cooperative behaviour and punish defection. They do this, for example, by donating money to people who have previously donated to others, even when they know the person they are donating to will have no chance to give them money in turn. This behaviour is known as **indirect reciprocity** (e.g., Wedekind and

Altruistic punishment This involves incurring a personal cost in order to harm a person who has defected.

Indirect reciprocity This involves incurring a personal cost in order to reward a person who has cooperated with other group members.

Milinski, 2000). It can be distinguished from **direct reciprocity** – the form of reciprocal altruism we learned about earlier in this chapter. In direct reciprocity, an altruist is rewarded by the beneficiary of their altruism – not by a third party.

Time to reflect Before you read on, what do you think might motivate people to sacrifice their own interests to punish defectors?

Direct reciprocity The case where a person incurs personal cost to reward a person who has cooperated with them personally. Both altruistic punishment and indirect reciprocity encourage people to cooperate rather than defect.

In a classic series of experiments, Fehr and Gächter (2002) showed that altruistic punishment may be commonplace and has the effect of increasing cooperative behaviour. Fehr and Gächter's (2002) public goods dilemmas ran in blocks of six rounds. In some of these blocks, participants were able to punish other players who had defected. Each unit of their own money they spent to do this cost the punished member three units of their money. Punishment was performed anonymously – other group members could not tell who was doing the punishment. In these blocks, punishment was frequent, with over 84 per cent of participants choosing to punish at least once, and it was harsh. For example, imagine you are playing in round five or six, by which time punishment systems are entrenched, and you pay approximately 15 fewer monetary units to the group than the other participants. In this case, your 'crime' definitely does not pay – you can expect to pay just about double your original underpayment – nearly 30 monetary units – in punishments imposed by the rest of the group. In blocks of rounds where this kind of punishment was possible, cooperation levels across the group gradually increased (see Figure 14.11). In stark contrast, blocks in which participants were deprived of the opportunity to punish saw cooperation levels gradually decrease from round to round. In the final round of a block of trials, the average contribution to the group in each round was around three times greater if punishment was allowed than if it was not.

Here, then, is a case of an 'altruistic' behaviour that is a deliberate infliction of harm on another person. Indeed, it qualifies as an act of *aggression*, according to the definition we adopted in Chapter 13. If it deserves to be called altruistic, it is because it is self-sacrificing, and because it appears to be an attempt to preserve the interests of the group by discouraging

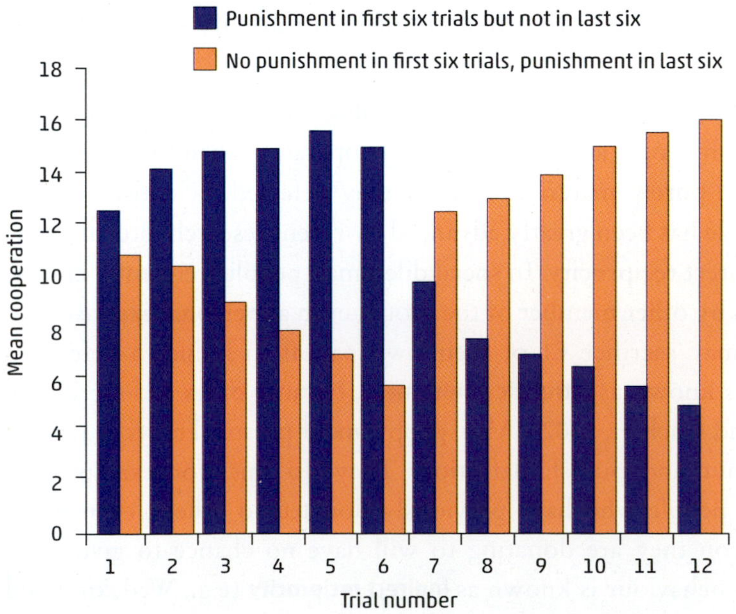

FIGURE 14.11 The power of altruistic punishment to increase cooperation When participants initially have the ability to punish each other, cooperation levels are high and increase over time. When this ability is taken away (on the seventh trial), cooperation levels drop dramatically and keep dropping. Conversely, when participants are initially unable to punish, cooperation starts at a reasonably good level but declines over trials. When the ability to punish is introduced, cooperation levels rise and keep increasing. These results vividly demonstrate the power of altruistic punishment to increase cooperation.

Source: Data from Fehr and Gächter, 2002

defection. Thus, it would seem that altruistic punishment is an attempt at being 'cruel to be kind'. However, while it is obviously cruel in a sense to the punished individual, it is not yet entirely clear whether it is really kind to the group in the way that punishers presumably intend.

One problem was raised by Dreber, Rand, Fudenberg and Nowak (2008), who ran prisoner's dilemma games under two different conditions. In one condition, participants could either cooperate (paying one unit for the other player to get two or three units) or defect (gaining one unit at a cost to the other person of one unit), with no opportunity to punish. In the other condition, participants had a third option of punishing (spending one unit for the other player to lose four units). Dreber et al. (2008) found that cooperation was increased in the punishment condition, as it was in Fehr and Gächter's (2002) studies. Crucially though, this did not seem to do anyone much good. The problem is that punishment is costly, reducing the payoffs received by those who punish and who are punished alike. This cost counteracts the effect of increased cooperation on the average payoffs received by participants in the dilemma. In the case of the experiments by Dreber et al. (2008) and some others they reviewed, the net effect was to reduce the average payoff received by participants, compared to the no-punishment condition. Far from benefiting the group, altruistic punishment harmed it in material terms.

As Dreber et al. (2008) acknowledged, there could well be circumstances in which altruistic punishment does increase the average payoff received by all group members, for example in games where the price of cooperation, defection and punishments is changed, or where games continue for longer. However, one key finding is bad news for the idea that evolutionary forces may have equipped human beings with a disposition towards altruistic punishment. Specifically, among Dreber et al.'s (2008) participants, those who punished received substantially smaller payoffs than those who refrained from punishment. The best strategy was 'tit for tat' – to respond with cooperation after the other player cooperates, and with defection when they defect. Thus, altruistic punishment may not benefit the group, and costs the punishers dearly. In light of these results, it is difficult to see how altruistic punishment may have been favoured by natural selection.

Still, we think there is room to believe that it might have been. Notably, the experimental games conducted thus far, however ingenious, elegant and tightly controlled, differ from many real-life contexts in important respects. One is that the currency of punishment in these experiments is exactly the same as the currency of cooperation and defection – money. In reality, the range of human motivation and emotion equips us with many more ways to punish effectively, including violence, ostracism, malicious gossip and disdain. These forms of punishment do not necessarily cost the punisher or even the punished individual in the same way. Thus, a group whose primary goal is to make money is likely to do better if it has available to it a punishment scheme that is effective but does not require the expenditure of money. Indeed, one study suggests that the use of a non-monetary punishment can increase monetary cooperation. Specifically, participants in a social dilemma contribute more to the group if they believe they will be ostracized if they do not (Ouwerkerk, Kerr, Gallucci and van Lange, 2005) (see the Blind spot in social psychology at the end of Chapter 8). By definition, because punishing by means of ostracism costs no money and because average payoffs increase as cooperation increases, the group is better off in monetary terms. Further, there are perhaps less tangible benefits of altruistic punishment, such as improved satisfaction with the group and increased adherence to its norms and its leadership. These might stand groups in good stead in less narrow, more realistic circumstances than those found in the experimental social dilemmas conducted thus far. Imagine, for example, that a group has to confront a collective crisis such as a flood or an invasion of its territory – those with strongly enforced norms of cooperation are more likely to win through. These less tangible benefits are of great interest to social psychologists and probably to participants themselves, but typically are not measured as outcomes in the experiments.

A specific feature of the experiments by Dreber et al. (2008) also suggests that altruistic punishment may be more obviously beneficial in other social situations. Specifically, their social dilemma was the dyadic (that is, two-player) prisoner's dilemma. If you punish the other player, they are hardly going to be impressed with you, which may undermine their cooperation with you. However, if you punish a defector in a larger group, the third, fourth, fifth and any other players may be impressed with your firm action. In this case, they may be inclined to reward you, much as they reward those who make generous donations to others (Wedekind and Milinski, 2000). Indeed, when given the opportunity, they may choose to punish you if you fail to punish a defector. If you are in a social dilemma, your reputation can be important to you. Concern about your reputation, and therefore how others will treat you, is likely to motivate you to cooperate and punish those who do not. Computer simulations suggest that altruistic punishment will have a marginal effect on cooperation in dyadic dilemmas, but a large effect in dilemmas involving 16 people (Fehr and Fischbacher, 2003).

Time to reflect What parallels or similarities can you draw between this research and what else you have learned about behaviour within groups (e.g., social facilitation, social loafing)?

Question to consider Reread question 3 at the start of the chapter. Why did Jane uncover the cheat when she stood to lose from doing so?

The social psychology of justice

Justice This is said to exist when people treat each other as they are entitled or deserve to be treated.

We have seen that altruism and cooperation are important principles of social organization in human life. Another principle is also important – justice. **Justice** is a broad term with many meanings and nuances, but at heart, it exists when people treat each other as they are entitled or deserve to be treated. Entitlement refers to the positive treatments (e.g., respect, autonomy, inheritances) people should receive according to agreed upon laws, customs and moral principles. Deservingness refers to the treatments, positive or negative, that a person is perceived to have earned because of their good or bad behaviour (Feather, 2003, 2008). **Distributive justice** is concerned with the apportionment of privileges, duties and goods in consonance with the merits of the individual and in the best interest of society. **Procedural justice** is concerned with the fairness of the procedures that resolve disputes and allocate resources. Normally, fair procedures produce fair outcomes, but not always. It is possible, for example, for a referee to incorrectly rule a penalty. This violates a principle of distributive justice. However, if the referee's mistake is an honest one, and they explain the basis for the decision clearly, then there has been no violation of procedural justice (see Figure 14.12).

Distributive justice Concern with the justness of the outcomes that people receive.

Procedural justice Concern with the fairness of the processes used to distribute justice.

FIGURE 14.12 Procedurally vs. distributively fair refereeing This referee's decision may be mistaken, and so violates principles of distributive justice. But if it is made honestly and according to correct procedures, then it is not a violation of procedural justice.

Justice permeates all aspects of our lives. For example, we think about justice and injustice in the context of the criminal justice system, in the allocation of economic resources and costs such as taxes and benefits, in discrimination and equality between groups, in education (have you always felt your marks and comments were fair?) and in our personal lives. Why is it that justice is such an ever present concern to human beings? According to most theories that have addressed this question, justice has two important functions. First, if people are, or think they have been, treated justly in life, their own functioning is improved; for example, they are happier, less prone to negative affect and anxiety, more confident that if they work hard and respect social norms they will receive good outcomes and so on (Jost and Banaji, 1994; Lerner, 1980). Second, justice has a benefit to the collective if people work hard, respect social rules, are not motivated to abuse others and so on (Jost and Kay, 2010; Tyler, 2007).

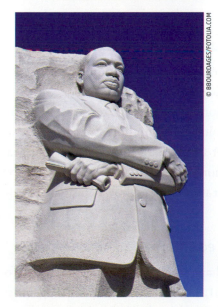

FIGURE 14.13 Martin Luther King Jr said: 'Injustice anywhere is a threat to justice everywhere'

Culture and justice

Culture plays a crucial role in shaping perceptions of the treatment that people are entitled or deserve to receive. In some cultures, for example, theft is seen as a crime deserving amputation of hands or even execution, whereas in others, thieves are required to meet and discuss their offence with their victims. Nonetheless, some basic, universally regarded principles of justice seem to underpin these widely varying cultural practices. Deutsch (1975) articulated three key principles of justice – the equity, equality and need principles (see also Rai and Fiske, 2011):

Equity principle The principle that the outcomes people receive should be proportional to their merit and contribution.

Equality principle The principle that resources should be distributed equally.

Need principle The principle that the focus should be on what people need to survive and thrive.

- According to the **equity principle**, the outcomes that people receive should be proportional to their merit and contribution. So, the harder you work or the more you produce, the more you should be rewarded.
- According to the **equality principle**, resources should be distributed equally in the community.
- According to the **need principle**, the focus should be on what people need to survive and thrive.

Thus, regardless of how hard people work or their moral qualities, the need principle would suggest they should receive support from others. Although people in all cultures seem to invoke these principles and regard them as important, their relative importance varies (Bond, Leung and Schwartz, 1992). In collectivist cultures, where harmony within a community is given the highest priority, equality assumes more importance (Leung and Bond, 1984). On the other hand, where the focus is on the job of maximizing wealth and productivity, the equity principle tends to be most important. And when the group confronts grave shortages of resources or threats to its survival, need may become a more important principle (Deutsch, 1975).

Exploring further Using an internet search engine, can you find examples of people complaining that money or some other resource is not being distributed fairly? In the cases you find, do the perceived violations of justice seem to be violations of equity, principle or need?

The importance of justice for human beings

In the following pages, we review in more detail some of the leading theories of the universal psychological importance of justice. In so doing, we pay attention to two important questions at the heart of research on justice. The first is, what effect does the deep psychological commitment to justice have on people's behaviour – how do they attempt to preserve justice when it appears to be threatened? The second, related but more general question is, what are some of the factors that lead people to act justly or unjustly, and how can social psychologists play their part in promoting justice?

Social exchange and equity theories

Of all the theoretical approaches to the human desire for justice, social exchange theory (Homans, 1961; Thibaut and Kelley, 1959) is most consistent with the view of classical economics and evolutionary biology that people pursue their own interests first and foremost. Like those frameworks, social exchange theory assumes that people try to maximize personal benefits and minimize personal costs in their social relationships. People see relationships with others as incurring costs to themselves and accruing benefits. In a romantic relationship, the benefits might include the warm feelings, intimacy and pleasure of spending time with your partner; the costs might include the arguments and the time you invest in the relationship at the expense of other activities you enjoy (see Chapter 7). In a working relationship, the benefits might include the pay you get and the recognition you receive, and the costs include the time and energy you sink into your work. The principal of reciprocity is therefore at the heart of social exchange theory – we invest in relationships and expect our partners to invest in kind.

To varying degrees, people expect the benefits of relationships to outweigh the costs. Thibaut and Kelley (1959) describe this expectation as a comparison level. If you have a high comparison level, you expect the benefits of a social relationship to greatly outweigh its costs. If you have a low comparison level, you might expect to just about 'break even'. Either way, if the relationship does not meet with your expectations, you are likely to be dissatisfied. This motivates you to change the relationship to make it more personally rewarding, or to leave it altogether (and so to seek a new job or a new companion). You are especially likely to walk away if you have a high comparison level for alternatives, that is, if you feel there is an alternative relationship available to you that will be more rewarding (see Chapter 7).

Where social exchange theory differs from some economic perspectives is that it does not view the decision-making process as entirely rational or cold-blooded. A major factor that prevents people from simply walking away from underrewarding relationships is their previous investment in the relationship. Ironically, the more people feel they have invested in the relationship – the jobs they turned down, the hard work they put in at the beginning, for example – the more attached they feel to the relationship (Rusbult and Buunk, 1993). Having invested heavily in a relationship, your heart may tell you to stay, even though your head knows that it is no longer rewarding. Also, people often feel a sense of mutual fate with their relationship partners, and understand that each partner needs to make some sacrifices so that the relationship can bring everyone rewards. In other words, social exchange theory acknowledges that people often feel that they are better off in relationships of all kinds rather than going it alone.

Emotions and concerns with justice are also important, as was made clear by Adams' (1965) equity theory, which builds on core principles of social exchange theory. According to equity theory, people compare and evaluate the net benefits they are receiving with those received by their relationship partners. In doing so, they calculate something like the ratio below:

$$\frac{\text{My rewards}}{\text{My contributions}} : \frac{\text{Their rewards}}{\text{Their contributions}}$$

Of course, it is distressing to people when they feel they are underbenefiting – when they get fewer rewards, in proportion to the contribution they make, than their partner does. But also, it is distressing to people when they feel they are overbenefiting – that is, doing better out of the relationship than the other person. This is decidedly not what a classical economic framework, which assumes that people are only concerned to maximize personal gain, would predict. And it happens, according to equity theory, because people are fundamentally concerned with the fairness of the relationships they are in. A fair distribution of resources is one expressed in the following equation:

$$\frac{\text{My rewards}}{\text{My contributions}} = \frac{\text{Their rewards}}{\text{Their contributions}}$$

More specifically, when partners feel they are underbenefiting, they feel angry and resentful. When they feel they are overbenefiting, they feel guilty. In either case, people will try to restore equity if they feel they can. Crucially, this means that if people feel they are overbenefiting, they will try to reduce the rewards they receive or increase their contributions. Research findings largely support this prediction. For example, people in romantic relationships will seek to restore equity whether they feel they are over- or underbenefiting in some way (e.g., Walster, Traupmann and Walster, 1978).

© CORBIS

However, people are not necessarily perfectly selfless in their reactions to unfairness. For one thing, as we saw in Chapter 2, people tend to be somewhat self-serving and so overestimate their contribution to relationships, distorting their perception of fairness. Ross and Sicoly (1979) separately interviewed men and women in married couples, asking them to list the jobs around the house they did and those their spouses did. Participants indicated that they did more jobs (approximately 11) than their spouse (approximately 9). When asked to indicate what proportion of the housework they did overall, the scores of the husbands and wives added up to more than 100 per cent, suggesting that either the husbands, the wives, or both were overestimating their own contribution. Thus, people in relationships that might be described as objectively equitable may feel that they are underbenefiting; those who are overbenefiting may feel that their relationship is equitable.

Further, reactions to overbenefiting are more complicated than reactions to underbenefiting. If you are getting too much out of a relationship, you may indeed feel guilty, but at some level it is also intrinsically satisfying to be doing well. According to some theorists, self-interest has a fast, largely unconscious, gut-level effect on our satisfaction levels, whereas it takes more cognitive effort to process and evaluate information about fairness and unfairness (Moore and Lowenstein, 2004). Consistent with this reasoning, people are less likely to express dissatisfaction with being overpaid when they are under cognitive load, that is, distracted by a second task such as trying to remember the following string of symbols: @*%#?$±§ (van den Bos, Peters, Bobocel and Ybema, 2006). Presumably, cognitive load deprives overpaid people of the cognitive resources they need to fully realize, and feel bad about, the injustice of their privileged position.

Time to reflect   As we shall see below, a recent study by Callan, Sutton and Dovale (2010) showed that people tend to construe outcomes as just when under cognitive load. In keeping with Lerner's (1980) just world theory, they suggest that people preconsciously interpret events as if the world were a just place. Do you think this offers a viable alternative interpretation of the findings by van den Bos et al. (2006)? How?

Along the same lines, Peters, van den Bos and Karremans (2008) measured the time it took for people to make judgements about the fairness or unfairness of their pay. When they were being underpaid, they were relatively quick to indicate that their pay was unfair, but when they were being overpaid, it took them longer. Apparently, the inherent ambivalence of being overpaid – it is nice to have lots of money but not nice that it is not necessarily fair – creates mixed emotions that slow people's reactions down. There is an emotional reason to say 'Yes, it is fair' and another to say 'It is not fair', and the conflict causes delay.

Social exchange and equity theories have been widely applied in the science of management and organizational behaviour (Cohen-Charash and Spector, 2001), as well as the science of intimate personal relationships, where they have been successful in predicting which marriages and long-term partnerships last and which fail (e.g., Frisco and Williams, 2003). However, there are some problems facing these theories. Most importantly, they explain why people are concerned when they appear to be being unfairly treated compared to people who are in some kind of relationship with us, but do not readily explain why we care more generally about the justice received by people with little or no connection to us (Lerner, 1980; van den Bos and Lind, 2001). They also do not explain why we react to injustices that appear to occur outside the context of ongoing social relationships – such as when people are struck down undeservedly with disease, injury or famine. These concerns motivated the formulation of the most influential of all theories of justice, the just world theory.

Just world theory

According to Lerner's (1980) just world theory, people have a deep-seated need to perceive the world as a just place. For Lerner (1980), this need arises early in life, at the stage where parents are socializing their children to follow rules and work towards their goals. Influenced by Freud's theorizing about human development, Lerner speculated that at a certain stage in childhood, children switch from living according to the *pleasure principle*, in which they pursue immediate gratification regardless of the longer term consequences, to the *reality principle*, in which they learn to delay and moderate gratification in order to avoid punishments and earn rewards in the longer term. To illustrate, a very young child will probably follow the pleasure principle by simply taking a toy or a sweet, regardless of whether it belongs to someone else or if they have been told not to do it. In contrast, an older child is more likely to refrain from doing so, because they realize that such behaviour is likely to be punished. Lerner suggests that around this time, children form an implicit 'personal contract' with the world, in which they commit to following moral rules, but expect to receive good (that is, deserved) outcomes in exchange for doing so.

Effectively, the essence of just world theory is that in childhood, most people make a commitment to live according to the principles of justice. Faith in the personal contract – that life will treat them fairly – becomes an organizing principle in their lives. It gives them the confidence to make and pursue goals, expecting their lives to be orderly, meaningful and controllable. In turn, this expectation promotes mental health, meaning that the belief in a just world (BJW) can be seen as a 'positive illusion' (Taylor and Brown, 1988). Indeed, research links it to many measures of psychological health, including positive affect (Dalbert, 1999), optimism (Littrell and Beck, 1999), effective coping with stress (Tomaka and Blascovich, 1994), better sleep (Jensen, Dehlin, Hagberg et al., 1998), low levels of depression (Ritter, Benson and Synder, 1990) and less loneliness (Jones, Freemon and Goswick, 2006).

However, according to this theory, BJW is a double-edged sword because its psychological benefits motivate individuals to defend it against contradictory evidence, thereby minimizing the injustices they see happening to others. Where possible, observers may do this by actively helping victims (e.g., Zuckerman, 1975), but where not, individuals may adopt cognitive strategies such as blame and derogation to minimize the apparent injustice being suffered (Lerner and Miller, 1978).

This tendency was illustrated in a classic experiment by Lerner and Simmons (1966). Women volunteers watched a female confederate who seemed to be a participant in a learning experiment and who was receiving painful electric shocks when she got the answers wrong (the task was difficult, so that observers would not be tempted to think the confederate was stupid). Lerner and Simmons wanted to test the idea that observers would compensate the suffering victim where they could, but would devalue and reject her if they could not defend justice in this behavioural way. To up the ante, Lerner and Simmons informed their participants that they would have to watch a second session of the learning experiment, that is, witness more of the victim's suffering. Results supported their predictions. When observers could help the victim, they did so (by assigning her to a condition where she received money rather than shocks), and did not devalue or reject her. However, when observers were told there was nothing they could do to help the victim, their attitudes towards her were more harsh.

Lerner and Simmons (1966) also included a condition in which the victim seemed to be especially undeserving of the suffering she was going through. Specifically, they led participants to believe that the victim was taking the shocks so as to prevent them from going through a similar experience. This creates a situation in which bad things seem to be happening to a good person, which is especially threatening to the BJW. Under these conditions, attitudes to the victim were, ironically, the harshest of all. Other early experiments supported the core idea that people will help when they can, but restore the 'just world' with distorted thinking about victims when they could not (for reviews, see Hafer and Bègue, 2005; Lerner and Miller, 1978).

This line of thought has important implications for charities; ironically, if they ask the public for help to solve huge problems, such as mass famine or eradicating widespread and devastating diseases, the public may think there is little they can do to help, which, far from encouraging helping behaviour, is likely to lead to devaluation of the victims. On the other hand, if they ask the public to help just one victim, they are much more likely to do so. It is probably for this reason that charitable appeals often ask us to 'adopt a polar bear' rather than do something small to save them all. Indeed, Miller (1977) found that Canadian participants who believed strongly in a just world were more likely to help the victims of a rare rather than a common disease, or a temporary financial setback rather than ongoing poverty. Those who did not believe so strongly in a just world were not affected by whether the problems they were asked to help solve were large or small. It seems that making a small contribution to alleviate a big problem is unattractive to many people because it provides a painful reminder that there is a lot of injustice in the world; resolving a small, local injustice feels more like making the world a just place.

Exploring further Look at advertisements for charity appeals for some major environmental, animal welfare, medical and children's charities. Research suggests that these appeals may be more successful when, instead of presenting a huge, widespread problem, they invite the public to help just one victim of the problem. To what extent do they 'personalize' or 'particularize' the problems they are trying to solve in this way?

© PHOTOALTO

FIGURE 14.14 The bigger the problem seems, the less we help The problem of homelessness is so big. What can I do? Just world research suggests that in such situations, the victims can become devalued. Helping behaviour actually decreases.

In line with these experimental findings, research shows that individuals who have a strong BJW also tend to be prejudiced towards a range of disadvantaged groups, including refugees (Montada, 1998), people with AIDS (Connors and Heaven, 1990), the unemployed (Reichle, Schneider and Montada, 1998), the elderly (Lipkus and Siegler, 1993) and the poor (Furnham and Gunter, 1984). Thus, there seems to be something like a social dilemma at play – believing in a just world is good for the individual, but may, in some respects, be bad for the group, insofar as it can breed prejudice towards the most vulnerable and disadvantaged in society.

However, recent research suggests that in principle, this dilemma can be resolved. Specifically, researchers have distinguished between the belief that the world is a just place to the self (BJW-self) and the belief that it is a just place for other people generally (BJW-others). Lipkus, Dalbert and Siegler (1996) measured BJW-self and BJW-others with 16 closely matched items (e.g., 'I feel that I get what I deserve' and 'I feel that people get what they deserve'). These two spheres of BJW are positively correlated, but only moderately so. Among relatively privileged samples such as professionals and university students in developed economies, scores on the BJW-self scale were much higher than on the BJW-others scale (Bègue, 2002; Bègue and Bastounis, 2003). Crucially, it turns out that BJW-self is correlated with psychological wellbeing but not harsh social attitudes. In contrast, BJW-others is correlated with harsh social attitudes but not wellbeing (Bègue and Bastounis, 2003; Dalbert, 2001; Lipkus et al., 1996; Sutton and Douglas, 2005). Indeed, the two spheres of belief are sometimes associated with the same outcomes but in opposite directions. For example, a study of at-risk British teenagers found that strong beliefs in the justice of the world to the self were associated with reduced intentions to engage in antisocial behaviour, whereas the more strongly teenagers believed the world was a just place for others, the more they intended to be antisocial (Sutton and Winnard, 2007). Moreover, a study of Australian students showed that BJW-self is positively correlated with the tendency to forgive those who do us wrong, whereas BJW-others is negatively correlated with forgiveness and is associated with the desire to take revenge or cut the transgressor out of our lives (Strelan and Sutton, 2011; see also Lucas, Young, Zhdanova and Alexander, 2010). Thus, in principle, it seems that individuals can 'have their cake', by endorsing BJW-self and accruing psychological benefits, and 'eat it too', by rejecting BJW-others and its harsher social connotations (see Figure 14.15). This makes sense from the perspective of just world theory, because it is the personal contract that matters. Thus the belief that 'I get what I deserve' is of primary psychological interest. This belief is related to, but separate from, the belief that others get what they deserve.

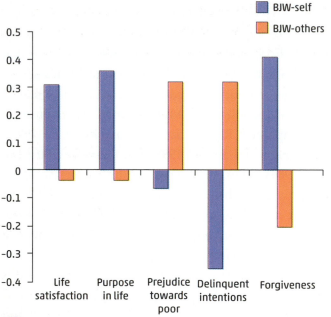

FIGURE 14.15 Correlation between outcome measures and the two spheres of BJW (measured in standardized beta weights) Although BJW-self and BJW-others are positively related to each other, they are related to quite different variables, and sometimes related to the same variable in opposite directions. BJW-self but not BJW-others is related to indices of psychological wellbeing, including life satisfaction (Sutton and Douglas, 2005) and purpose in life (Sutton, Douglas, Wilkin et al., 2008). BJW-others but not BJW-self is related to intergroup attitudes that justify inequality and the misfortunes of lower status groups such as the poor (Sutton and Douglas, 2005). BJW-self is negatively related to antisocial behavioural tendencies, such as delinquent intentions among at-risk youth, whereas BJW-others is positively related to them (Sutton and Winnard, 2007). Finally, BJW-self is positively related to forgiveness, whereas BJW-others is negatively related to the same variable (Strelan and Sutton, 2011). The overall pattern of these results suggests that BJW-self is adaptive, bringing both social and psychological benefits, whereas BJW-others is maladaptive, incurring social costs with no apparent psychological benefit.

Time to reflect Research on the effects of the belief in a just world is correlational: individual differences in the strength of this belief are measured and then related to outcome variables of interest. Of course, this leaves the crucial question of causality open. Do you think the belief in a just world can be experimentally manipulated? How much does longitudinal research help? You can search the research literature to help you, if you like.

Just world theory has undoubtedly been one of the most influential and successful theories in social psychology, able to relate variables as diverse as altruism, impression formation, prejudice, physical and psychological health, and even gambling (Callan, Ellard Shead and Hodgins, 2008) to an underlying human commitment to justice. That said, the theory has not been without its controversies. One issue has been whether the belief in the just world is really delusional. It is clear that the human need for justice influences our behaviour in surprising and sometimes unfortunate ways, which can ironically sometimes cause us to compound the original injustice. But it is not clear that these reactions are necessarily out of touch with reality.

Let us illustrate with one of the most striking and convincing tests of just world theory. Hafer (2000) had participants watch an upsetting video in which a young woman recounted how she had contracted HIV as a result of bad luck (a condom broke). Before watching the video, an experimental group of participants had been asked to list their long-term life goals. According to just world theory, the personal contract is at the heart of just world beliefs – people need to plan in order to reap long-term rewards; this, in turn, requires a certain degree of faith in justice – that our efforts and sacrifices will pay off. Thus, planning for the future should make people even more motivated to somehow construe the innocent victim's situation as just. And that is what happened. Compared to control participants, the experimental group were more prone to attributing blame and negative personality characteristics to the victim. Undoubtedly, this is strong evidence for just world theory, but the issue we are considering here is whether the claim that just world beliefs are delusional is warranted. A problem is that in this as in other experiments, there is no right or wrong answer on the scales that participants complete. Rather, participants are required to circle a number from one to seven, say, which best represents their opinion.

ETHICS AND RESEARCH METHODS

Eliciting distress in studies of the 'just world'

In Chapter 9, we considered the ethics of Milgram's (1974) well-known studies of obedience. Participants displayed signs of intense anxiety and emotional distress. Zimbardo's Prison Experiment was also intensely distressful for participants, and Zimbardo (2006) himself criticized Haslam and Reicher's (2006a, 2006b, 2007, 2008) BBC Prison Study on the grounds that it was unethical to run such a study again. In these studies of social influence, however, the distress that participants experienced was not the outcome the experimenters wanted to elicit. It was more or less a by-product, although interesting in its own right, of processes such as obedience, tyranny and intergroup conflict.

In contrast, research on the justice motive, particularly research concerned with the blame and derogation of victims, often sets out to cause participants distress. The reason for this is that theory assumes people consciously acknowledge that the world is an unjust place, but at a less rational, preconscious level, they defend their implicit faith in the justice of the world by any means they can. Intense emotional impact is therefore assumed to be required in order to break through the veneer of rationality. Lerner (1998, p. 389) stated that in experiments that do not emotionally impact participants sufficiently:

> With little at stake to be gained or lost, the participants' main incentives are not to re-establish justice ... but rather to manage their impressions. For the most part, they try to be cooperative participants, and, of course, not do anything that would threaten their self or public esteem by appearing foolish or embarrassing.

Many just world studies require participants to blame and derogate innocent victims of misfortune, such as rape survivors (Bal and van den Bos, 2010; Kleinke and Meyer, 1990), people living with HIV/AIDS (Hafer, 2000) and children who suffer horrendous injuries as a result of electrocution (Correia, Vala and Aguiar, 2007). To overtly blame and derogate such people cuts strongly against social and moral norms and so comprises a threat to participants' self-image, and probably seems to them to threaten their image in the eyes of the experimenter, too.

Thus, to disrupt socially desirable responding, and motivate people to defend the belief in a just world, researchers set out to create materials that are emotionally impactful and distressing. They use videos in which victims, sometimes real people rather than actors, recount upsetting personal stories of misfortune, loss and ongoing suffering (Callan, Kay, Davidenko and Ellard, 2009; Hafer, 2000) or place participants directly in front of a victim who appears to be suffering intensely (Lerner and Simmons, 1966).

Is this ethically warranted? A key issue is *informed consent*. Participants need to know they are signing up for a potentially distressing experience. The problem is that by telling participants this, researchers may make participants aware that intense emotions are an intrinsic part of the scientific theory behind the experiment. This might cause them to hold *privately held hypotheses* about the experiment that can interfere with their responses (cf. Silver, Wortman and Klos, 1982). Neither is it scientifically acceptable to alert participants to the fact that they will be asked to blame and derogate the victims, even though this is likely to come across as a nasty surprise to many participants. By signalling to participants that the study is about perceived justice, researchers are likely to invalidate their studies since participants' normal efforts to present themselves as rational, decent people are likely to be bolstered (Lerner, 1998). As far as possible, researchers

need to inform participants about the nature and even the aims of the study in advance, but they cannot do so with complete candour, otherwise the scientific integrity of the experiment is lost. To inform participants that they may experience distress in the experiment is an absolute must, but to inform them exactly how or why they might find their experience distressing is, unfortunately, not possible.

Questions

1   What other ethical considerations are important in determining whether these studies are ethically warranted? What ethical safeguards should researchers build in to such studies? You might want to reread the section on ethics in Chapter 1.

2   Although Lerner (1998) distinguishes between low-impact and high-impact studies, which elicit moderate or high levels of psychological distress, there has not been a study that systematically manipulates the emotional impact of an experiment and determines whether this affects victim derogation and other forms of just world defence. Also, no study to our knowledge has even correlated the extent of emotional arousal with just world defences. So, we do not have the kind of firm evidence that emotional impact matters that we would normally require to accept a scientific hypothesis. What ethical implications does this have for the conduct of just world studies?

Fortunately for just world theory, recent studies suggest that the concern with justice can indeed cause people to distort reality. For example, Callan, Powell and Ellard (2007) asked participants to look at a photo of a young woman and told them they would have to identify her later on. They then told participants that there had been a fire at her house and she had either suffered greatly or not very much. Finally, they presented a set of photographs that were digitally altered versions of the original they had earlier seen. The researchers had subtly altered these photographs in order to make the woman more or less physically attractive. When asked which photograph was the original they had seen, participants selected photographs in which the woman was significantly less attractive than the original. Put differently, they misremembered the woman, thinking she was less attractive than she was in reality. This is true victim derogation – evaluating a victim more negatively than is objectively warranted.

In a follow-up paper, Callan et al. (2009) found that participants misremembered the amount won by a lottery winner, recalling a sum of money too low if they had learned that the winner was a 'bad' person. Participants especially did this if their justice beliefs had already been threatened by watching a distressing video of a victim (see Figure 14.16). These findings are in line with suggestions that memory is essentially a constructive process in which a reality is built rather than faithfully reproduced. They show specifically that it is a process in which a just world can be created without our awareness.

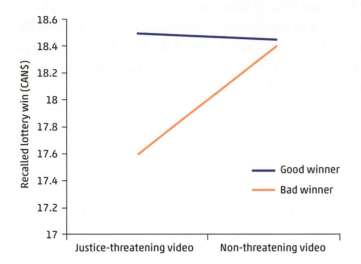

FIGURE 14.16 Recall and justice beliefs Participants were told that a man had won CAN$18.42 million in a lottery, and were given information that he was of good or bad moral character (friendly and a good tipper, or an unfriendly non-tipper). Later, they were asked to recall this number. They recalled a lower number when the lottery winner was 'bad' and after watching an apparently unrelated video that threatened the just world (a videoed interview with a young woman who had contracted HIV/AIDS because a condom broke, and for whom antiviral drugs were not effective; a manipulation borrowed from a study by Hafer, 2000, we read about earlier). In all except this condition, participants accurately recalled the size of the lottery win (the mean recalled win was not significantly different than the actual win).
Source: Data from Callan et al., 2009

Although responses to individual victims can be shown to be irrational, to date there is no real evidence that people consciously endorse just world beliefs that are irrational. Again, BJW questionnaires ask participants to make responses on scales in which there is no right or wrong answer. At first glance, the finding that people endorse the BJW-self view more than the BJW-others view looks like delusional thinking – another manifestation of the self-enhancing biases we noted in Chapter 2. How can the world be especially just to you, while being unjust to others? However, these findings are typically obtained from privileged samples who may have a point – they are immune from the famine, diseases and political oppression that affect many of the less fortunate people in the world. Indeed, when we ask less privileged samples about the justice of the world, they do not show this bias (Sutton and Winnard, 2007). Further, even privileged individuals do not think they are unique in their receipt of justice – they rate the world as more just to themselves than to others generally, but do not think they get any more justice than other people in the same social demographic as themselves (Sutton et al., 2008).

Recent versions of just world theory explain why people sometimes look like they have irrational worldviews but other times seem to be able to acknowledge that the world is not necessarily a just place. The key is that people's commitment to justice is deep-rooted since childhood and by adulthood is largely preconscious or automatic (Lerner, 1998; Lerner and Clayton, 2011). They are confronted with evidence of injustice almost every day of their lives, through personal experience and the media, and it would be absurd – and undesirable – to say out loud that, in general, victims deserve what they get or are not worthy of concern. Thus, at a conscious level, we are able to acknowledge that, at least as far as other people are concerned, the world is not a just place. But unconsciously, we are inclined to construe events as if they were just. Thus, if our cognitive resources are over-whelmed by strong emotions or we are cognitively busy, the tendency to see the world as a just place should be heightened.

Recent research supports this view. Callan et al. (2010) presented carefully constructed fake newspaper reports of an accident to participants, complete with photographs. For example, a story related how a swimming coach had been killed when a tree fell onto his car. The newspaper story mentioned either that the swimming coach was much beloved by his community for all the work he did, or that he was in disgrace, having been caught stealing from his class. Clearly, there was no plausible causal relationship between the moral character of the swimming coach and the freak accident that killed him. Nonetheless, participants made this link, agreeing that the accident was a consequence of his behaviour more when he had been stealing than when his conduct had been unimpeachable. This is an example of **immanent justice reasoning** – the superstitious attribution of good and bad outcomes to unrelated good and bad deeds, which was once thought to be the preserve of children (Jose, 1990; Piaget, 1932), but has more recently been shown to be a pitfall into which adults fall, too (e.g., Raman and Winer, 2004). Further, this effect was only significant when participants were under cognitive load, that is, trying to mentally rehearse a 12-digit as opposed to a 2-digit number in order to recall it later. Thus, when we consciously think things through in a calm and collected way, we do not necessarily conclude that, in general terms, justice reigns and people get what they deserve. When we do not think things through, we appear to be prone to an automatic tendency to appraise events as if they were just.

The group-value model

Just world theory has shaped later theorizing about the need for justice in particular contexts. One such theory is the **group-value model** proposed by Lind and Tyler (1988; also Tyler, 1994). According to this model, people care about justice not only because of the outcomes they expect to receive (as assumed by equity theory), but also because their social identity is important. In particular, people care about the status and respect they receive within their social groups. The fairness of the outcomes they experience (distributive justice) and the processes they are subjected to (procedural justice) tell them about their status. If they are treated fairly, they assume they are held in high regard. As a result, they are more likely to identify with the group and work hard in the interests of the group, making sacrifices for it if necessary. If they are not treated fairly, they experience a state of threat in which they are not confident about their status within the group. Many research findings support this model. For example, employees who perceive that they receive procedural justice are more likely to perform so-called 'extra-role' behaviours, working harder than they are obliged to in order to serve the organization for which they work (Moorman, Blakely and Niehoff, 1998). Receiving more procedural justice from authorities such as the police and managers makes people more inclined to respect their authority and comply with their requests, crucially, because it also encourages them to identify more strongly with the group (Tyler and Blader, 2003).

Immanent justice reasoning
The superstitious attribution of good and bad outcomes to unrelated good and bad deeds.

Group-value model Model explaining that people care about the status and respect they receive within their social groups. The fairness of outcomes (distributive justice) and the processes (procedural justice) are an indicator of their status.

The moral is clear for all authorities – treat people with fairness, or, at the very least, convince them that you are treating them fairly.

Although the distinction between distributive and procedural justice is interesting and important (e.g., Leonardelli and Toh, 2011; Lucas et al., 2010; Tyler, 2012), people do not always have enough knowledge to determine whether their outcomes are fair. If you do not know how much the person in the office next to you is getting paid, or the grades that other students are getting for similar work, then you cannot evaluate the distributive justice of your outcomes. In such cases, there is a good chance that you will rely on information as to whether the process by which your pay and grades are determined appears to be fair. For example, were you given feedback with your grade? Did a second person also mark your work, or check the grade? In such situations, if you feel that you have received procedural justice, you will also tend to assume that you have received distributive justice, that is, your final outcome was fair, relative to other people. Van den Bos, Lind, Vermunt and Wilke (1997) demonstrated this effect in a study with Dutch students from Leiden University. Participants worked on tasks, ostensibly in pairs, in order to earn lottery tickets. Some participants were given 'voice' – a chance to express their opinion on how the lottery tickets should be divided between themselves and their partner. Other students were given no 'voice' and so were not able to express this opinion. 'Voice' is a key aspect of procedural justice – people tend to perceive processes that give them voice as fair, and processes that do not give them voice as unfair (Lind, Kanfer and Earley, 1990). Results showed that after receiving their payment, participants relied on whether or not they had 'voice' to evaluate the outcome itself, but only when they had no idea how much their partner had been paid. When they knew whether their partner had been paid, they relied on social comparison to determine whether their payments were just or not, and their satisfaction with the payment they received did not depend on whether or not they had voice. Thus, van den Bos et al. (1997) argued that people use procedural justice indicators as a *heuristic* (Chapter 3), because they often – even typically – lack all the information they need to evaluate the distributive justice (Figure 14.17).

FIGURE 14.17 The fair process effect When participants did not know how much the other person had received, they lacked the information needed to judge whether their own outcome was fair. In this condition, they relied on their knowledge of procedural justice – whether they had been given 'voice', meaning the chance to express their opinion. This is the 'fair process effect', in which judgements of distributive justice are made on the basis of procedural justice. The fair process effect disappeared when participants knew how much the other person had received, and so could evaluate distributive justice independently.

Source: Van den Bos et al., 1997

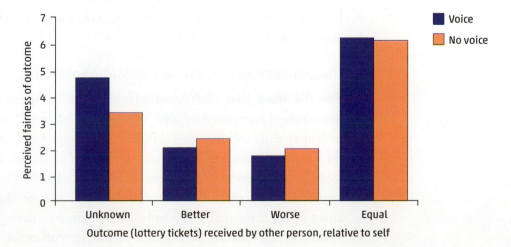

System justification theory

System justification theory
Theory that people's dependence on social systems for wealth and security motivates them to justify those social systems and see them as fair.

Another major theory spawned by the just world theory is **system justification theory** (Jost and Banaji, 1994). The core idea of this theory is that people's dependence on social systems for wealth and security motivates them to justify those social systems – to see them as essentially fair and functional. Thus, dissonance is aroused when there is a patent defect in the system, so that people are subject to unfair inequalities, for example.

Early work on system justification focused on how people in low status groups react to the injustices they experience. As much or even more than high status group members, members of low status groups often internalize negative stereotypes of their group that serve to justify their lowly position (as in, 'no wonder we are poor – look how lazy we are!'), to believe that the government acts in the interests of the people, and that economic inequality is legitimate and necessary (Jost, Pelham, Sheldon and Sullivan, 2003). As if justifying the tendency for women to be paid less than men for the same work, female participants display a **depressed entitlement effect** (Callahan-Levy and Meese, 1979; Major, 1994). In a study, when given the chance to determine their own pay for work done in an experimental task, they paid themselves less than male participants, even though independent judges rated their work as being of the same quality (Jost, 1997).

Depressed entitlement effect
The tendency for women, when given the chance to determine their own pay in an experimental task, to pay themselves less than men.

More recently, research on system justification has gone beyond the reactions of low status individuals to their plight. For example, one way that people justify a system, regardless of their own status, is to use complementary stereotyping – as in 'poor but happy'. These stereotypes imply that 'poverty has its rewards and affluence its drawbacks', making economic inequality feel somewhat more legitimate (Kay and Jost, 2003, p. 823). Other work highlights how the motive to justify social systems is especially strong when one depends on the system and it is seen as something that cannot be changed. In a set of experiments by Kay, Gaucher, Peach et al. (2009), for example, Canadians were more likely to endorse current inequalities in Canadian society if they were reminded how much their lives depended on the political system in Canada ('system dependence'), if they were led to believe that it was relatively difficult to leave Canada ('system inescapability'), and if they were exposed to a passage suggesting that the Canadian system was not working ('system threat').

The communication and social construction of justice

For the most part, the social psychological perspectives on justice we have encountered are concerned with why individuals 'need' to perceive that the world and/or specific social systems are just. More specifically, they are concerned with how and why individuals defend their beliefs in justice, and the specific psychological consequences of beliefs in justice and injustice. However, justice is not 'all in the mind'. As system justification theory points out (Jost and Banaji, 1994; Jost and van der Toorn, 2012), people also benefit by sharing a perception that their system is just. Sharing perceptions of justice with others not only bolsters your own certainty, but allows you to feel that you have a basis for reality. One implication of this is that people collaborate to *socially construct* a just world. In addition to all the thinking processes that uphold a just world, there are also likely to be communication processes that contribute to the shared assumption that our lives are basically just.

Researchers in experimental social psychology are beginning to investigate these processes. Alves and Correia (2008) found that participants rated a fictional person higher if they had expressed a high, rather than low, belief in a just world. Such people are rated as more trustworthy, a better leader and co-worker, more likeable and so on. This effect is independent of participants' own level of BJW (Alves and Correia, 2010). It is not that participants are more likely to agree with others who express a high belief in a just world. Rather, they are seen as more constructive, socially desirable and socially useful people.

Researchers in the discourse analysis tradition (Durrheim, Quayle, Whitehead and Kriel, 2005; Potter and Wetherell, 1987; van Dijk, 1993, 2011; Wetherell, Stiven and Potter, 1987) have always been concerned with the use of language to establish the legitimacy of social arrangements. Wetherell et al. (1987) argue that people's use of language when discussing inequality, gender roles and other topics related to social hierarchy and specialization embodies and reveals 'practical ideologies'. These are not coherent, rigidly formulated bodies of knowledge, but rather 'montages of incoherently related themes' or 'fragmentary complexes of notions, norms and models which guide conduct and allow for its justification and rationalization' (p. 60). We saw in Chapter 11 how Pakeha (White) interviewees in New Zealand used contradictory statements as part of discourses to establish that they were not racist, while justifying the disadvantages of Māori in New Zealand. The use of discourse enables people to legitimize the social status quo and their own position in relation to it.

Wetherell et al. (1987) illustrated how people use discourse in sophisticated ways to justify social inequality in a study of final-year students at the University of St Andrews in Scotland. They were asked to discuss gender and employment opportunities. Participants were generally keen to establish that they supported the principle of equality. Thus, 'Male Three' in the study said:

> I've never been a male chauvinist so I mean I just, on the business side, women are just as good as men, I mean if not better, I mean obviously perfectly equal. (p. 62)

At the same time, participants gave voice to the discourse that gender differences are natural and may explain inequality, as voiced by 'Female Two':

> I [was talking] … to some friends the other night who have got children … and one of them was high up in management but once her children came along that was it, she just, all these maternal urges came surging out of her and she just couldn't go back again. (p. 62)

Sometimes conflicts between cultural notions force people into awkward positions and lead them to contradict themselves fairly obviously. Take this extract:

Interviewer: So if it was a decision between you and your wife as to who was to stay at home, you would rather go to work than stay at home?

Male One: Well, no, that would have to be a unanimous decision, in other words if my wife was adamant that she wanted to go out to work, uh and if I were 90 per cent convinced that I wanted to go out to work, then it is possible that I would look after the children. But I would say that it's unlikely that I would marry a person who would be so closeted in her views anyway. So you know, it's not really likely to happen. I will be going to work. (p. 63)

Later, the same interviewee said 'there should be equalities for both men and women at the workplace', and 'I think they [women] should look after the children'. Through these and several other ways of using language and argument, participants in this study both distanced themselves from inequality in the context of gender roles and said things that justified it. The study of talk – what people say – reveals how the status quo can be justified in everyday conversation.

Question to consider Reread question 4 at the start of the chapter. How can we explain why female students think they will be paid less than their male counterparts after they graduate?

SOCIAL PSYCHOLOGY IN THE REAL WORLD

Economic inequality and economic crisis

In the world's developed economies, economic inequality – the difference between the wealth of the richest and poorest sections of society – has risen steadily over recent decades (Galbraith, 2012; Western, Bloome, Sosnaud and Tach, 2012). In a sustained investigation of the effects that this might have, sociologists Wilkinson and Pickett (2010) explored correlations between the extent of inequality in 25 of the world's richest countries and a range of important outcomes. It turns out that many so-called 'modern ills' are closely associated with inequality. Inequality was correlated with mental illness ($r = .73$), lower levels of trust ($r = .66$), shorter life expectancy ($r = .44$), infant mortality ($r = .42$), obesity ($r = .57$), poor children's educational performance ($r = .45$), teenage births ($r = .73$), homicides ($r = .47$) and imprisonment rates ($r = .75$). These correlation coefficients (r values) reflect much larger effect sizes than we are used to seeing in social psychology (see Chapter 15 for discussion of typical effect sizes). Squaring them suggests that anything between 20 and 50 per cent of the differences between

© JASMIN MERDAN/FOTOLIA.COM

countries on these measures of wellbeing are explained by differences in social inequality. The relationship between inequality and reduced wellbeing holds even when poverty levels in societies are controlled for. Thus, the increasing levels of poverty that are associated with inequality do not account for their results. Also, even richer citizens of countries with high levels of inequality tend to suffer more from these 'modern ills' than their rich equivalents in more egalitarian countries. However, it is not entirely clear why inequality is such a problem.

Social psychology suggests a few answers to this question. As we have seen, people across cultures value equality (Deutsch, 1975; Schwarz, 1992). It is strongly associated in people's minds with fairness and justice (Chen, 1999), is a crucial concept in the field of human rights (Conte, Davidson and Burchill, 2004), and is a simple and popular rule for allocating resources (Samuelson and Allison, 1994). In experimental games involving decisions about the allocation of money, people will pay money out of their own accounts in order to ensure that allocations are reasonably equal (Camerer, 2003). A recent survey showed that Americans underestimated the extent of wealth inequality in their country, yet wanted it to be still more equal than their rose-tinted beliefs suggested (Norton and Ariely, 2011). In keeping with a line from Shakespeare's *Hamlet* (Act II, Scene II) that 'there is nothing good or bad, but thinking makes it so', many negative outcomes of inequality arise because, in general, people do not like it.

System justification theory and just world theory both suggest that people are threatened by the perceived injustice associated with high levels of inequality (social dominance theory does not necessarily make this presumption). Processes of motivated social cognition (see Chapters 2 and 3) cause them to think in ways that minimize the perceived size or unfairness of inequality (O'Brien and Major, 2005; Sutton et al., 2008; Jost and van der Toorn, 2012). Thus, increases in inequality may strengthen the motivation to blame and derogate the less well-off in society, not just by those better off, but also by themselves. It may also demotivate people from perceiving injustice and resolving to change it through protest and other forms of collective action (van Zomeren, Spears and Leach, 2008) (see Chapter 12). There is considerable evidence that inequality and relative deprivation are more distressing for people who perceive them as unjust (Kessler and Mummendey, 2002; Napier and Jost, 2008). This led Sutton, Cichocka and van der Toorn (2012, p. 132) to argue that 'the essential dilemma facing individuals is a choice between coping with inequality and combating inequality', since 'psychological mechanisms that support one tend to be at odds with those that support the other'.

This argument suggests that inequality can be self-perpetuating – as it increases, so does the desire to legitimize and comply with society's hierarchies. There are other ways in which inequality perpetuates itself.

Some evidence suggests that people experimentally assigned to a powerful 'leader' role subsequently act less morally but evaluate themselves as more moral than those assigned to a 'subordinate' role. In other words, inequality may promote the hypocrisy of elites, causing them to act in their own interests without realizing they are doing so (Lammers, Stapel and Galinsky, 2010). Consistent with this notion that privilege may erode moral motivation, we saw earlier in this chapter that richer people tend to give proportionally less of their income to charity than poorer people (Greve, 2009; Piff et al., 2010). Also, in social dilemma games, people are less cooperative if their initial allocations of money are unequal than if they are all given the same amount (Anderson, Mellor and Milyo, 2008). This may happen because inequality undermines the trust that is essential for social cooperation (Putnam, 2000). Less sharing in social dilemmas means less for all – and also means that players will end up with more unequal sums of money. Further, as inequality increases, children and adolescents from less wealthy backgrounds tend increasingly to disengage from education (Teachman, 1987).

There is controversy about whether economic inequality is the price we have to pay for economic growth. Correlations between inequality and growth are mixed and depend on factors such as the type of government a country has (Banerjee and Duflo, 2003; Bjørnskov, 2008; Forbes, 2000). However, research by economic historians suggests that periods of heightened inequality tend to precipitate economic crises (Reich, 2010). Greater wealth inequality means there is more capital available for risky, speculative investments and 'bubbles', in which assets become increasingly overpriced until they crash in value. Research like that of Lammers et al. (2010) also suggests that it may erode the moral judgements of those in charge of the resources.

This appears to have been the backdrop for the recent international banking crisis, which continues to have disastrous effects on the finances of many countries. In September 2008, the global financial crisis that had been brewing for a year went critical. A cascade of bad debts meant that the value of financial assets evaporated, and normal lending between banks ceased. It was widely thought within government and banking circles that within days, if not hours, ATMs would be unable to dispense money (Brown, 2011). Thanks to the actions of world governments, this looming cataclysm was avoided.

But in averting disaster, governments suspended principles such as justice and equality. Instead, governments took on the bad debts of investment banks. In this way, bank debts were transferred to taxpayers, who were also to be affected by the resulting cuts in public services. To illustrate, after the Irish government agreed to bail out its banks, the average Irish person owed something in the order of US$500,000 to international lenders (CNBC, 2011). Sutton et al. (2012, p. 116) conclude that 'just as violence begets violence, inequality tends to breed still more inequality'.

Questions

1 There must be some limit to the rather pessimistic conclusion of Sutton, Cichocka and van der Toorn (2012) that inequality is self-perpetuating, since history shows that levels of inequality peak and then fall again. Based on what you have read in this chapter (much of Chapter 12 is also relevant), what factors do you think might help reduce inequality again?

2 There is remarkably little experimental evidence that inequality causes reductions in wellbeing. The evidence cited by Wilkinson and Pickett (2010) is overwhelmingly correlational. What barriers are there to manipulating inequality and seeing what effects it has? How might you do this in experiments?

3 Search the internet for 'skyscrapers economic crisis' to find interesting material on the correlation between high-rise building developments and subsequent crashes.

© BIKEWORLDTRAVEL/FOTOLIA.COM

FIGURE 14.18 The Shard skyscraper in London Research suggests that periods of heightened development of such buildings prefigure major financial crises. The correlation between skyscrapers and subsequent crashes is surely spurious; strictly speaking, skyscrapers do not cause markets to crash. The common 'third cause' may be economic inequality. As inequality increases, so do skyscrapers, bubbles and risky, injudicious forms of speculation. These factors lead to economic perdition.

Chapter summary

In this chapter, we considered the positive social psychological phenomenon of altruism and the reasons why people make personal sacrifices for others. We also discussed how people respond to social dilemmas and how cooperation can be encouraged. Finally, we considered why justice is such an important factor for people. You will have learned that:

- Altruism is an action that is performed to benefit another person without benefiting the self. It is a specific example of the more general phenomena of helping behaviour and prosocial behaviour.

- Social psychologists' interest in altruism was captured by the phenomenon of bystander intervention – why do people often stand by and fail to help when something terrible happens? Theorists have argued that as bystander numbers increase, people are less likely to interpret the situation as a problem and are therefore less likely to assume responsibility (diffusion of responsibility). Another reason is pluralistic ignorance, where people wrongly assume, based on others' actions, that they endorse a particular norm of 'standing by'.

- Early theorists argued that there may be an 'altruistic personality', or a stable psychological makeup that predisposes people to help others. Several individual differences characteristics such as Machiavellianism, empathy and the belief in a just world have been found to correlate with altruistic behaviours. However, situational factors such as culture and perceived similarity of the target to the self also influence altruistic behaviour.

- Some researchers have concluded that people often help others in order to help themselves, therefore there is no such thing as 'true' or 'pure' altruism. However, other theorists have argued that the act of altruism can indeed be 'pure', and driven by empathic concern for the welfare of others. There is evidence for both perspectives. Altruism may serve internal rather than external rewards.

- Some theorists posit that altruism has an evolutionary origin and that people are altruistic (to their own kin) as a way of promoting the successful reproduction of their own genes. Others argue that altruism occurs because it is also repaid.

- Aspects of the target requiring help significantly influence whether or not they receive it. In particular, age, gender, attractiveness and personality determine the degree of help received.

- The study of altruism is also influenced by the study of how people deal with social dilemmas such as the prisoner's dilemma, public goods dilemmas and commons dilemmas. When they set aside their own interests for the collective, they are cooperating, whereas when they act in their own interests at the expense of the collective, they are defecting. Both situational and personality factors determine behaviour in social dilemmas. A strong sense of identification with the group also encourages cooperation. Mistrust can be resolved by communication. Cooperation can also be improved by rewarding cooperators and punishing defectors, even at personal expense to the self (e.g., altruistic punishment).

- Justice exists when people treat each other as they are entitled or deserve to be treated. Distributive justice refers to the justice of the outcome and procedural justice refers to the justice of the procedures. Theorists argue that justice has two important functions – it improves functioning and benefits the collective. Culture plays a crucial role in shaping perceptions of justice, but three key principles (equity, equality and need) of justice appear to be universal.

- Social psychological theories explain the importance of justice to people. Social exchange theory explains that people try to maximize personal benefits and minimize personal costs. People invest and so that things are fair, they expect that others will do the same. Equity theory explains that people compare and evaluate the net benefits they receive compared to those received by others. Fairness means that nobody over- or underbenefits. According to just world theory, people have a deep-seated need to perceive the world as a just place. In childhood, people make a 'personal contract' with the world to commit to the rules of justice. The belief in a just world predicts many psychological and health outcomes. However, it may not always be good for the group insofar as it can breed prejudice towards the disadvantaged. Belief in a just world for the self and for others predicts different outcomes. According to the group-value model, people's social identity is important to their perception of justice. The fairness of the outcomes they experience and the process tell people about their status within the group. System justification theory proposes that people's dependence on social systems for wealth and security motivates them to justify those social systems as fair and just.

- People also collaborate to socially construct a just world through communication processes, as can be seen in work from the discourse analysis tradition on the role of language in legitimizing social arrangements.

Essay questions

At the beginning of the chapter, we asked you to consider these questions:

1 You are out one evening and while walking through the city streets, you notice a heated argument between a man and a woman. The man is shouting and looks like he is about to hit the woman, who is clearly distressed. Rather than helping, everyone appears to be walking past, ignoring the woman's plight. Is this unusual, and why is it happening? Under what conditions are people more likely to help?

2 Ziva describes why she gives to a charity in support of famine victims. 'Once I saw those starving children on TV, I just knew I'd feel awful if I didn't do something. I feel much better now that I've given a bit of money away.' Was Ziva's donation a selfless act of charity, or was she being selfish?

3 Jane is working in a competition between two teams and discovers that one of her own teammates is cheating in order to win the competition. Risking her own fate in the competition, she tells the organizer about her teammate's

dishonesty. What social psychological processes might help explain Jane's behaviour?

4   A university teacher asks her students to write down their expected income after they graduate. She compares what males think they might earn with what the female students think they would earn and finds a significant difference – the males think they will earn more; or looked at differently – the female students think they would earn less. What social psychological theory might help explain this finding?

Having read this chapter, these questions could also be framed as the following essay questions, which you can attempt in preparation for your examinations:

1   Critically evaluate social psychological theory and research on bystander intervention.

2   Are people ever completely altruistic? Discuss with reference to social psychological theory and research on prosocial, helping and altruistic behaviour.

3   Based on theory and research on how people deal with social dilemmas, explain why people often punish others for their defection, even at personal risk to the self.

4   Describe and critically evaluate the research supporting social dominance theory.

Further reading

Batson, C.D. (1998) Altruism and prosocial behaviour. In D.T. Gilbert, S.T. Fiske and G. Lindzey (eds) *The Handbook of Social Psychology* (4th edn, vol. 2, pp. 282–316). New York: McGraw-Hill. Scholarly overview of the social psychological literature on prosocial behaviour.

Batson, C.D., van Lange, P.A.M., Ahmad, N. and Lishner, D.L. (2003) Altruism and helping behavior. In M.A. Hogg and J. Cooper (eds) *The Sage Handbook of Social Psychology* (pp. 279–95). London: Sage. Accessible overview of research on altruism and helping behaviour.

Jost, J.T. and Kay, A. (2010) Social justice: History, theory and research. In D.T. Gilbert, S.T. Fiske and G. Lindzey (eds) *The*

Handbook of Social Psychology (5th edn, vol. 2, pp. 1122–65). New York: McGraw-Hill. Up-to-date coverage of the social psychological literature on social justice.

Snyder, M. and Omoto, A.M. (2007) Social action. In A.W. Kruglanski and E.T. Higgins (eds) *Social Psychology: Handbook of Basic Principles* (2nd edn, pp. 940–61). New York: Guilford Press. Detailed discussion of prosocial behaviour.

Van Trijp, H. (ed.) (2012) *Encouraging Sustainable Behavior: Psychology and the Environment*. New York: Psychology Press. Brings together a range of social scientific perspectives on how to encourage sustainable behaviour.

 Visit the companion website at www.palgrave.com/psychology/suttondouglas for access to a wide range of resources to help you get to grips with this chapter.

Applying social psychology

Encouraging energy saving among students

Ultimately, everybody wins if people save energy. However, when people engage in prosocial behaviour such as this, there are also personal prices to pay. For example, energy saving can be inconvenient because it can interfere with everyday activities. Also, going out of one's way to save energy can feel rather fruitless if one feels that others are not pulling their

weight to do the same. Of course, there are personal as well as group-level advantages. For example, homeowners who conserve energy also save money on their bills. Energy-saving campaigners can therefore appeal to people's desire to keep their costs down. But what about university students, for whom such incentives may be less relevant? Perhaps these individuals are renting student property and have no say in the types of light bulbs they use. Perhaps they are unable to personally control thermostats. Potentially, they share bills with other students and cannot limit the amount of energy used by others. How does one design an intervention to reduce energy use among students?

Imagine you are a social psychology consultant who has been approached by the local council. The council has observed that university students in the town are relatively high energy users and would like to design an intervention to reduce energy usage among this group. Your job is to help the council, with your knowledge and expertise in social psychology, to put together this intervention.

In a job such as this, your first task is typically to search the psychological literature for theory and evidence on the topic. Based on this knowledge, you would then make recommendations for an intervention based on what appears to be the most promising and effective principles of intervention.

The following questions are designed to guide you through this type of process:

1 Conduct an internet search using a database such as Google Scholar to find at least three energy use interventions that have been designed in the past 10 years. What search terms would you use?

2 Read the articles and take some notes about the nature of the interventions. For example, what theories did the researchers draw upon? What was involved in the interventions? Were the interventions successful? How did the researchers measure the success of the interventions?

3 Crucially, who were the targets (that is, participants) of the interventions? Note again that you have been asked to design an intervention to apply to *university students*. In what ways are students potentially different from the samples tested in the studies concerned? Specifically, are students' energy-saving concerns and behaviours likely to be different from previously tested samples? Would the interventions you have found be relevant to students, or could they be modified to apply to students? In thinking about these issues, consider carefully what students are able to do to reduce the amount of energy they use. It may be useful to find a list of behaviours that are recommended to reduce energy use in general (e.g., closing curtains, switching off lights in empty rooms, using thermostats correctly, using tumble dryers less), and think about the feasibility of recommending each of these to students.

4 Think about other features of the intervention. For example, if the intervention involves recommending that students switch off lights and so on, what is the reason for them to do so? Will an argument that appeals to the fight against climate change be more likely to succeed? Or, would students respond better to an argument based on a financial incentive (that is, saving money)? On what evidence are you basing this choice?

5 Decide exactly what you plan to do and why.

6 Now, write a brief summary of a report you would provide to the council. This should fit on two sides of an A4 page. Your report summary should include:
   - A title.
   - Theoretical accounts that have dealt with energy-saving behaviour and the barriers to energy-saving behaviour.
   - An evaluation of different approaches to intervention – which is most likely to be effective? In particular, what should be involved in a potential intervention for a student sample?
   - Recommendations for steps that the council should take to reduce energy use among students.
   - Recommendations for how the council should test the success of its intervention.
   - A reference list (citations should be made in text, in APA format).

Blind spot in social psychology

Changing social value orientation: Can people be made more prosocial?

As we learned earlier in the chapter, an individual's social value orientation (van Lange and Liebrand, 1991) can predict how they behave in social dilemmas. Research suggests that some people are more pro-self and are less likely to cooperate (Liebrand and McClintock, 1988), whereas others are more prosocial and are more likely to cooperate (van Lange, 1999). Thus, the interests of groups would appear to be served better if its members were more prosocial. So, one question is whether it would be possible to 'make' people more prosocial, either temporarily or permanently. In doing so, it may be possible to influence people to become more cooperative in social dilemmas, with many positive consequences. At present, however, no research has examined this possibility. In particular, there is no research that has treated pro-self and prosocial orientation as a dependent measure to examine whether or not it can be influenced by the manipulation of other variables. We would like you to think about this issue here.

1   Do you think it is possible to change a person's social value orientation? In other words, do you think it is a stable trait, or would it be responsive to situational variables? It might help you to search this textbook, or the internet, to see whether some variables can be seen as both stable personality variables and as sensitive to the situation or context.

2   Do you think it would be possible to do so permanently, or only temporarily?

3   Think about specific strategies that might work in changing a person's social value orientation. For example, you will remember from Chapter 3 on social cognition that the priming of stimuli can activate particular concepts. What stimuli might prime a prosocial value orientation? Do you think that doing this would 'make' a person more prosocial? Alternatively, can you think of other manipulations to make people more prosocial? Would norm manipulations (e.g., telling people that prosocial norms are prevalent within a group) be effective? Could you somehow manipulate empathy to influence a person's social value orientation? Perhaps focus on one or two of these ideas, and come up with some methods to change people's social value orientation. Or, perhaps you have a novel way of manipulating social value orientation.

4   Finally, how would you measure the effectiveness of your manipulation?

Student project

The psychology of 'retail therapy'

Stephanie Barrows studied as an undergraduate student at the University of Essex and her final-year dissertation was supervised by Dr Mitch Callan. Her research investigates whether the feeling of relative deprivation – a consequence, in part, of economic inequality, and a driver of feelings of injustice – can be linked to impulsive consumerism.

My topic and aims

Working in retail, I have always been intrigued by the psychological aspects of impulsiveness, which prompted me to consider the concept of 'retail therapy' and how therapeutic it is. Impulsive purchases appear to provide immediate relief from anxiety and emotional discomfort, where the primary intention is to improve the buyer's affect temporarily. Along these lines, my project explored the extent to which personal relative deprivation predicts an individual's tendency to engage in impulsive buying depending on their ability to delay gratification. Previous research suggests that feeling relatively deprived predicts the urge to gamble, but little research had explored the link between relative deprivation and impulsive buying. I investigated whether the ability to delay gratification interacts with personal relative deprivation on impulsive buying, and predicted that the relation between relative deprivation and impulsive buying depends on an individual's willingness to delay gratification.

My methods

One hundred volunteers from the University of Essex completed a paper-based questionnaire containing validated scales measuring personal relative deprivation, willingness to delay gratification, and impulsive buying. Participants were informed that the questionnaire measured their consumer intentions and behaviours.

My findings and their implications

Contrary to the hypothesis, overall there was no interaction between relative deprivation and willingness to delay gratification on impulse buying. Interestingly, however, further analyses revealed that the expected interaction pattern occurred for women but not for men. Personal relative deprivation positively predicted impulsive buying only among women who were less willing to delay gratification. Women who had a higher willingness to delay gratification did not engage in impulsive buying as a function of their relative deprivation levels. Thus, a willingness to delay gratification is a limiting factor to the effects of relative deprivation and appears to act as a buffer for women who are able to delay gratification. This pattern was not observed for men, which opens the possibility that men may respond to their feelings of relative deprivation in ways other than impulsive buying.

My journey

I always had an interest in the application of psychology to banking and finance so I decided to continue my education by pursing a Masters degree in occupational psychology at the University of Hertfordshire. I then had the opportunity to apply my knowledge in my first role as a sales consultant for a banking software firm pitching to banks and selling services. Six months later, I moved into a financial consultancy role working as a consultant on various projects for some of the largest financial institutions. Psychology has given me many transferable skills and the ability to successfully manage people in demanding environments. In the future, I aim to earn more responsibility by moving up the management chain and, ultimately, I expect my company to grow where I am a critical player of its success. The plan for this goal is continuous learning and determination – key skills learnt throughout my degree.

My project was my own piece of work, which I researched, analysed and wrote throughout nine months. During those months, I learnt how to be extremely disciplined in managing my time around other work commitments. Using SPSS to analyse my data allowed me to revisit statistics, skills that have aided me in my current role. I was able to be creative in certain parts of the project, encouraging me to think out of the box and make important decisions. I was surprised to see how well my written skills had developed through drafts of the project and I

quickly learnt that attention to detail is vital. This has led me to ensure I proofread more than once. Receiving a first class mark for my project has given me the confidence to apply the skills I learnt to my job and career.

My advice

I believe my project was successful because I was organized and interested in my research proposal. Focus on something you're interested in, and having a supervisor who is helpful is valuable. Look at some project examples as they can build a picture of what your final piece will look like. Before I started, I ensured I had a collection of previous studies and understood the literature as a whole. It's always best to set yourself smaller goals and focus on certain headings. I began on the introduction first and lastly the abstract. Finally, do your best – there are opportunities to get your project published which would look fantastic on your CV.

15 Social psychology: an overview

Now that you have encountered the major concerns, concepts and methods of social psychology, it is time to take an overview. In this chapter, we consider the wisdom of social psychology. In doing so, we outline some overarching principles you can apply not only to your study of the discipline but to your future lives. We consider the major limitations of the discipline and the challenges confronting it, and consider future directions for the discipline. Finally, we highlight some of the many skills and benefits that students of social psychology take away with them and discuss career options and opportunities for students of social psychology.

Topics covered in this chapter

○ The wisdom of social psychology

○ Some challenges and limitations

○ Current and future directions in social psychology

○ Social psychology and you

Key features

Critical focus Sampling bias in social psychology

Ethics and research methods Crowdsourcing social psychology

Social psychology in the real world Nudge theory

Questions to consider

1 Imagine you are having a conversation with your friend in which you discuss an interesting social psychological finding you have just read about – specifically, that meat eaters deny mental qualities to animals they eat as a way of justifying their meat eating (Bastian, Loughnan, Haslam and Radke, 2012). Your friend says this is rubbish because they are a meat eater and they love animals. As an expert on social psychology research methodologies, how might you respond to your friend's statement?

2 Imagine reading about another interesting finding that people are often influenced by conspiracy theories – theories arguing that secret plots and deals determine major political events – without their awareness (Douglas and Sutton, 2008). Your friend again says that this cannot be the case. People would know if they had been influenced. Is this true?

3 The discussion with your friend takes an unpleasant turn and they say to you: 'Social psychology is a pseudo-science.' What would you say in response?

As we have seen throughout this book, social psychology has cast light on many aspects of human thought, feeling and behaviour. Its insights are being applied to help people deal with depression, improve their personal relationships, reduce aggression, conserve natural resources, and improve relationships within and between communities. Social psychology has informed social debate, raising popular awareness of social identity processes, sexism, and system justification (e.g., Hanson, 2009). A number of social psychologists have published bestselling books outlining what social psychology has to offer to topics such as how to persuade people (Cialdini, 2008), how to be happy (Gilbert, 2007), the power of unconscious thought (Wilson, 2002) and the limits of classical economic theory (Ariely, 2011).

The contribution of social psychology has been based on a set of unique strengths. Compared to other social sciences, it has an emphasis on building relatively simple explanations of human behaviour and social phenomena. As a branch of psychology, it has retained the virtues of using experiments and related methods to test causal explanations of behaviour. Rather like physics, it strives to relate the very large and the very small, attempting to explain interactions between complex social and political processes and the intimate details of individual lives and minds (see Figure 15.1). This means that social psychology has a lot to offer to the efforts of policy makers, who are trying to address the social causes and cumulative effects of individual decision making in domains such as crime, taxation and health.

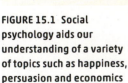

FIGURE 15.1 Social psychology aids our understanding of a variety of topics such as happiness, persuasion and economics

By now, you have read about the theories and concepts of social psychology. The journey you have been on is not just a process of accumulating knowledge to get you through your coursework and examinations. Along the way, we hope, guided by your teachers, peers, our writing and the exercises we have suggested for you, you have developed a set of thinking and problem-solving tools. In your hands, these tools can enrich whatever professional and personal journey you take in the future. One of the reasons we have written this chapter is to help you reflect on everything you have learned. What are the key insights of social psychology to date?

What concepts, skills and perspectives can you take forward into the next phase of your lives? We also hope that this chapter will enhance your critical reflection on the discipline of social psychology as a whole. In so doing, we hope that your ability to critically evaluate specific theories and findings within social psychology will be enhanced. This is likely to help you in your coursework, and, in the future, help you evaluate claims about human behaviour, relationships and society.

In the first section of this chapter, we attempt to distil some of the most important items of wisdom that have emerged from social psychology. We think all readers may find these useful. We also think you are likely to find these items of wisdom useful in providing you with an overview of social psychology, considered both as a body of knowledge and as a set of processes by which knowledge is produced. In the second section, we consider some of the most important problems confronting the discipline. In the third section, we consider some of the future directions that social psychology is likely to take over the next years and decades. The chapter concludes with a discussion of career and further study opportunities available to students of social psychology.

Time to reflect Make a list of some of the social issues that can potentially benefit from social psychological theories and findings. Jot down a few points to explain why social psychology is relevant and how insights from social psychology could help.

The wisdom of social psychology

Lying behind the many theories that social psychology has produced, and the findings that have been obtained, what does the study of social psychology teach us? In the following paragraphs, we have tried to distil some of the key pieces of wisdom that we feel we have acquired over a decade and a half of studying social psychology. We expect that the wisdom of social psychology is relevant to the personal and professional lives of just about anyone who has picked up this book. We therefore hope that the wisdom of social psychology will enrich your life, even if the course you are taking will be your last formal contact with the discipline. In the meantime, while you are studying social psychology, we also think that understanding its key themes will help you approach specific theories, findings and pieces of coursework wisely.

This could never be an exhaustive list of the insights and pieces of wisdom that you can expect to acquire from the study of social psychology. No doubt some social psychologists would disagree with some of the items in our list, and would want to see other items in their place. Indeed, some social psychologists are extremely critical of the discipline and are inclined not to put faith in most of its findings. But this list reflects the way we see it. Based on our experiences of doing social psychological research, reading about it, and talking to colleagues at home and abroad, we think that *most* social psychologists would essentially agree with the following take-home principles.

Do not succumb to mysticism: social psychology can be studied scientifically

Inchoate Not articulated; difficult or impossible to articulate.

You may often hear it said that psychology, still less social psychology, is not a legitimate scientific subject. Love, hatred, envy, sexual desire, happiness, culture and personal philosophies are too intangible, intricate or **inchoate** to be properly studied by scientific means. Many people have a strong intuition that the private and unique character of each person's individual experiences make them impossible for other people to study. Take the example of love, which we considered in Chapter 7. Intuitively, there is no topic more magical, subjective and resistant to scientific analysis. But, as we have learned, qualitative methods allow participants to articulate their experiences of love and relationships. Self-report questionnaires capture meaningful variation in the intensity and nature of love. Correlational and experimental studies have uncovered some of the factors that determine how intense love is and how long it lasts. However imperfectly or incompletely, even this aspect of human behaviour can be explained, scientifically studied and modified.

The intuition that social psychological topics such as love cannot be scientifically studied probably stems from two principal sources. The first is the uneven reach of introspection. We are aware of many of our thoughts, feelings and behaviours, but we lack introspective awareness of many of the psychological processes that shape them (Nisbett and Wilson, 1977). In other words, we have a much better grasp of *what* we are thinking, feeling and doing, than *why*. Our thoughts, feelings and actions at any given time may be more or less unique, but the processes that shape them are, by and large, similar to those that shape other people's. This bias in experience leads people to doubt the existence of many psychological processes and to consider themselves as unique, rather than governed by much the same processes as other people are. This is a manifestation of *naive realism*: the tendency to assume that one's own perceptions and judgements are objective, comprehensive reflections of reality (Liberman, Minson, Bryan and Ross, 2011; Pronin, Gilovich and Ross, 2004; Ross and Ward, 1985).

The second source is a misunderstanding of science. People typically underestimate the uncertainty, imprecision and controversy inherent in science (Miller, 2001; Osborne, 2010). When scientists disagree, or do not know the answer to important questions, they are still scientists. It is true that some unique challenges confront the social sciences. As social and cultural forces change, so will many aspects of social behaviour. Thus, in social psychology we are studying a 'moving target' – theories and findings that work in one period of time, in one social context, may not work in another. For example, the prejudice and discrimination facing racial minorities today is different in many ways from that faced 50, 20 and even 10 years ago, and social psychological work reflects these changes. Thus, studies of 'old-fashioned' racism, in which certain groups were overtly seen as less intelligent, are now outnumbered by studies of concepts such as 'modern' and 'aversive' racism, which are concerned with the allegedly special treatment that minority groups receive (Chapter 11). Further, social science is reactive, in that concepts such as self-esteem, prejudice and other variables percolate into public consciousness and change the way people think, feel and act (Moscovici, 1988).

For example, public awareness of prejudice and discrimination towards minorities has led to various reforms in employment practices and language use in everyday life (Chapters 11 and 12). Thus, in social psychology and other social sciences, we are also moving the target – our findings and concepts change the way people think, feel and behave. But this does not mean that social psychology is not a science, or that scientific progress is impossible.

Exploring further Think of a current topic of scientific debate. This can be anything from the debate over the existence of climate change, explanations for apoptosis or 'programmed cell suicide', or the debate over the theory of plate tectonics – what drives the movement of the earth's tectonic plates? Such topics have generated much interest, heated debate and media interest. But they have also generated a great deal of scientific investigation. Examine one of these topics for yourself using internet searches and decide whether disagreement and debate has made its study any less scientific.

Be realistic: scientific explanations are incomplete, imperfect and in flux

One thing you must have noticed about social psychology as you have been reading this book is that there are often several explanations for the same phenomenon. Take aggression (Chapter 13) as an example. We discussed explanations for aggressive behaviour that invoked genes, specific hormones and neurotransmitters, gender roles, alcohol, frustration, learning from others, cultural scripts, attributions, and ideologies. Many of these specific causes of aggression are theoretically related to two underlying views of aggression and, through aggression, human behaviour more generally. These, essentially, are nature and nurture – the view that human behaviour is primarily determined by biologically determined causes (nature) or people's social and cultural experiences (nurture).

It is important to understand that any one explanation of human behaviour is not invalidated by the presence of other explanations. This is true even when other explanations are plausible and supported by evidence. This is because human behaviour is affected by many causes, including those to be found under the umbrellas of nature and nurture, or personality and situation. It is also affected by interactions between these causes. Further, the effects of one variable on another are typically small. In social psychology, the average effect size enables researchers to say that just a little more than 4 per cent of the variance in a dependent variable can be explained in terms of a given cause (Richard, Bond and Stokes-Zoota, 2003). Thus, there is plenty of room for the operation of other causes. To say that 'theory X does not explain behaviour Z, because theory Y has been shown to explain Z' is generally not valid, since no theory is likely to explain *all* of Z.

Of course, theories sometimes make competing predictions, and can be tested against each other. For example, recall from Chapter 13 how social learning theory predicts increased aggression among fans of a winning team, whereas the frustration-aggression hypothesis predicts increased aggression among losing teams. Critical tests like this are vital for the development of theory. However, they do not always mean that the 'losing' theory should be discarded altogether. Often, one theory provides a good model of human behaviour under a particular set of circumstances, and another theory works better in different situations. For example, you may remember that social facilitation explains how people can perform optimally in groups when they are being observed or evaluated (Zajonc, 1965), but that social loafing explains why people perform poorly in groups when they are not being observed or evaluated (see also Latané, Williams and Harkins, 1979) (see Chapter 10). As different findings emerge, theories are modified or integrated, rather than rejected completely.

The fact that human behaviour is so adaptable, diverse and changeable means that, in principle, findings obtained with one sample, in one context, can easily be altered. Introduce different cultural, situational or personality factors and quite different, even reversed patterns might be observed. It also means that exceptions do not necessarily falsify rules. Thus, it is not a powerful criticism of theory X if you, a friend or anyone you know clearly bucks its predictions. (Of course, it is a serious, and perhaps fatal problem if people *on average* do not conform to a theory's prediction.) The flipside is that one can seldom use theory and evidence to predict with great confidence what a *given person* will do in a *given situation*. But when theories of human behaviour are built logically and insightfully, when they are tested well, and the results are interpreted properly, you can begin to explain and predict what people will *tend* to do with levels of confidence that are vastly superior to chance.

Question to consider Reread question 1 at the start of this chapter. What would you say in response to such a statement?

People are not billiard balls: they interpret and react to influence attempts

One of the reasons that theories in social psychology can explain only a minority of the variance in people's behaviour is that in laboratory studies, as in real-life contexts, people are not easily manipulated. In general, autonomy and distinctiveness are important to people (Chapter 2). As a result, they do not like to be manipulated, and to protect their autonomy, they will often produce behaviour change that is diametrically opposed to that which was intended (e.g., Imhoff and Erb, 2008; Snyder and Fromkin, 1980). As we know from Chapter 9, this 'reverse psychology' phenomenon, known as 'reactance' (Brehm, 1966), occurs especially when influence attempts are blatant or obvious.

People are generally skilled at detecting when an attempt at manipulation has been made, even when the attempt is fairly subtle. When people are motivated to cooperate, this can facilitate social influence (Chapter 6). However, many influence attempts fail because of people's fundamental desire for control and distinctiveness, coupled with their ability to detect attempts to influence them. This unique human skill presents a significant challenge for social psychology. If people can so readily detect challenges to their autonomy, how can researchers ever hope to achieve attitude or behaviour change? How can they be sure that the attitudes and behaviours they are measuring reflect participants' true inclinations, or reactions against the researchers' wishes? To complicate matters further, research participants may be motivated to give the researcher exactly the responses they want, so that the response set is subject to demand characteristics (Chapter 1). Social psychologists need to carefully craft their investigations with these factors in mind; as do governments and other agencies, as we suggest in our analysis of **nudge theory** in the Social psychology in the real world box later in this chapter.

Nudge theory Theory of social influence arguing that people's behaviour can be shifted relatively easily and cheaply in a more socially desirable direction, by relatively small, subtle situational cues.

This is not the only barrier that confronts attempts to change people's behaviours. Health behaviours, such as diet, smoking and exercise, may be embedded in cherished social identities (Tarrant and Butler, 2011). Many attempts to change behaviour in domains such as health and the environment rely on fear and other negative emotions. These campaigns can be effective, but often trigger anxiety and 'threat appraisals', in which people feel unable to change their behaviour (O'Neill and Nicholson-Cole, 2009; Tomaka, Blascovich, Kelsey and Leitten, 1993).

Social cognition is creative and motivated

Much of the early research in social cognition set out to show that human beings are prone to all sorts of mistakes (e.g., see the 'Heuristics and biases' section of Chapter 3). This programme uncovered many limitations in the way people process information. However, in recent years, researchers have demonstrated that people are capable of being more rational than these early studies suggested. Errors in attribution such as the 'fundamental attribution error' may reflect some degree of cognitive bias, but also reflect mistakes made by researchers, who did not give participants enough information to make unbiased attributions.

It is also important to remember that people have many goals in life, only some of which involve being truthful and logical. Other 'rational' goals include meeting the apparent expectations of others in social situations, which, for participants in laboratory studies, include those of experimenters. This desire to behave in ways that seem to be expected can lead people to do bizarre things, such as walking more slowly in response to words related to the elderly (Doyen, Klein, Pichon and Cleeremans, 2012), and to commit logical fallacies (Dulany and Hilton, 1991; Slugoski and Wilson, 1998). Another includes preserving the global coherence of one's belief system, at the expense of local contradictions. For example, people who harbour extreme prejudice towards Jewish people may hold simultaneous, contradictory beliefs about them – they are believed to be clannish and insular, but also rootless and cosmopolitan (Adorno et al., 1950). People who have extreme distrust in authority may simultaneously entertain multiple, mutually inconsistent 'conspiracy' theories. So, for example, the more participants believe that Princess Diana faked her own death, the more they tend to believe that Princess Diana was murdered by the MI6. Likewise, the more they believe that Osama bin Laden is still alive, the more they appear to believe that he was already dead at the time of the American forces' raid in 2011 (Wood, Douglas and Sutton, in press).

This research demonstrates that people forsake one type of 'rationality' for another, depending on the goals they are pursuing in a specific social situation (Fiedler and Wänke, 2009). They do not necessarily prioritize traditional standards of truth or logic. People's ability to choose from standards of rationality highlights the creativity of their thinking. Since the cognitive revolution in psychology in the 1960s, we have known that people do not passively process information received from the environment, but instead actively manipulate, synthesize and create information in their minds (Baars, 1986; Gardner, 1987; Miller, 2003). In so doing, they invest their environment with meaning. Crucially, people's ability to suspend truth or logic as their other goals require means that they tend to believe what they want to believe. This basic principle of motivated social cognition is one of the core lessons of social psychology. In this book, we have seen how people use attention, inference and memory to preserve optimistic views of their personalities, control over life events and future prospects (Chapter 2), their intimate partners and relationships (Chapter 7), their social groups (Chapters 8 and 11) and the society in which they live (Chapter 14). Other relevant goals include finding people to blame, to defend cherished worldviews, and to stave off the fear of death (Chapter 4). It is increasingly clear that processes such as stereotyping do not simply reflect the need to take simplifying shortcuts in the face of limited time and cognitive resources (c.f. Pendry and Macrae, 1994). They also reflect myriad other needs, including constructing a positive image of the self, the ingroup, and justifying the inequalities of society (Chapter 11).

Reality is socially constructed

Although individuals are capable of much creativity in their interpretation of their world, they do not do this unaided. They inherit a vast reservoir of knowledge from their culture, in the form of what have been called 'social representations' (Moscovici, 1988). People not only passively adopt collective beliefs, but also actively collaborate to construct them (see Chapter 3). Beliefs, memories and decisions are formed collectively as well as individually (Mesoudi, Whiten and Laland, 2006; Smith and Collins, 2009). Ideologies that provide a shared sense of what is right and wrong, such as political conservatism and liberalism, sexism and racism, wax, wane and mutate over time. They change people's perceptions of what *is* so, as well as what *ought* to be so. For example, conservatives are less likely than liberals to believe that the world's climate is changing as a result of human activity (Feygina, Jost and Goldsmith, 2010).

Returning to stereotypes, these have been seen as the products of faulty or biased thinking, but equally are perpetuated by the biased way that people share information with each other (Sutton, 2010) (see Chapters 5 and 11). For example, recall from Chapter 5 how people describe the negative behaviours of rival groups, and the positive behaviour of their own group abstractly (we are kind, they are violent). Conversely, they describe the negative behaviour of their own group, and the positive behaviour of rival groups concretely (we hit, they donated) (Maass, 1999). Recall, also from Chapter 5, how Australian participants in 'communication chains' tended to relay information from stories that was consistent with shared stereotypes and to omit information that contradicted stereotypes (Lyons and Kashima, 2003). Thus, they passed on details of the oafish, more than the poetic, behaviour of football fans.

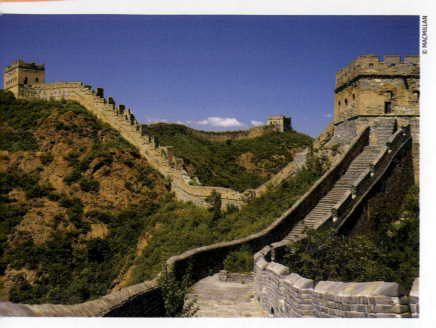

© MACMILLAN

FIGURE 15.2 Iconic monuments are enduring manifestations of the intrinsically social nature of human beings The construction of monuments was achieved collectively, involving the coordinated efforts of hundreds if not thousands of people. In most cases, they symbolize some collective ideal or striving. Some of these are lost to history, but some are known, if not necessarily current, such as the optimistic modernism of the Eiffel Tower. Since they have been constructed, they are recognized by many, and symbolize for many the values and anxieties of present-day cultures, such as national identity, national decline and ecological destruction. Their iconic fame allows them to form part of the texture of cultural 'common ground' and 'shared reality' that binds societies, cultures and social groups together.

Interestingly, this collective construction of reality sometimes seems to be part of an effort to serve the collective. For example, biased descriptions of behaviour often appear to be motivated by perceived threats from the outgroup, which motivate people to portray 'them' negatively compared to 'us' (Maass, 1999). However, sometimes people bolster socially shared realities in the pursuit of small, personal goals such as being understood (Lyons and Kashima, 2003) or liked (Clark and Kashima, 2007). Here, people implicitly understand that saying things that cohere with, rather than challenge, socially shared understandings is more likely to help them in their day-to-day lives. Likewise, people perpetuate ideologies without necessarily meaning to do so, because thinking, feeling and acting in line with ideologies helps them solve personal dilemmas and pursue personal goals. Thus, conservative ideology may help people to cope with fear and uncertainty (Jost and van der Toorn, 2012). Nonetheless, under certain conditions, people will take concerted, collective action to deliberately generate, contest and change ideologies, as we saw in Chapter 12 (Dixon, Levine, Reicher and Durrheim, in press).

In recent human history, the advent of mass media has accelerated the social construction of reality. Recall, for example, the fascinating study by Weisbuch, Pauker and Ambady (2009) encountered in Chapter 4. They analysed US television shows and found that the nonverbal behaviour of white characters towards black characters displayed a subtly negative, avoidant bias. After watching excerpts from these shows, white participants' racial prejudice increased. Television and the internet represent an enormously powerful mechanism of social influence, which cause millions of people to share the same reality – even in ways they cannot consciously recognize. The point that people are not self-contained individuals is at the heart of social psychology, and is underlined further by our next point – the self-perpetuating nature of social reality.

Social reality is self-perpetuating

The social psychological experiment is, at its heart, concerned with simple A causes B relationships, where independent variables have more or less immediate effects on dependent variables. But causal relationships in real life are much more complicated. Once a behavioural pattern, a thinking style, or a set of relationships takes hold, it tends to perpetuate itself. Habits are one mechanism by which this happens. Habits of thought and decision carve neural pathways in our brains and hijack or bypass the deliberative mental processes (Verplanken, 2006; Wood and Neal, 2007) (see Chapter 4). Distrust (Brewer and Kramer, 1985), loneliness (Bartholomew, 1990), aggression (Huesmann, 1986) and inequality (Sutton,

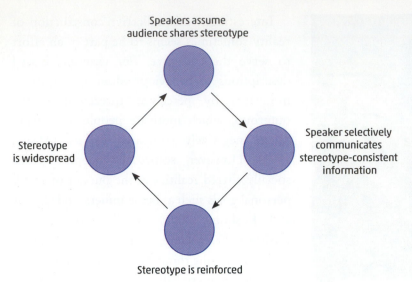

Speakers assume
audience shares stereotype

Speaker selectively
communicates
stereotype-consistent
information

Stereotype
is widespread

Stereotype is reinforced

FIGURE 15.3 A positive feedback loop implied by work on serial communication This highlights not only how people collaborate to build or reinforce social realities, but also how these social realities are self-perpetuating. Once a social stereotype has formed (e.g., football fans are uncultured), then communicators recognize that the people they are communicating with probably share that stereotype. They then select information that is consistent with that stereotype (e.g., a story about the mindless behaviour of a football fan) over information that contradicts it (e.g., a story about a sensitive and erudite poem written by a football fan). By selectively communicating this stereotype-consistent information, they reinforce the stereotype in their own and others' minds, and so on and so on (Clark and Kashima, 2007; Lyons and Kashima, 2003).

Cichocka and van der Toorn, 2012) all create self-perpetuating cycles of thought, emotion and action. As we have just seen, stereotypes also create self-perpetuating patterns of communication, causing people to communicate information that supports stereotypes more often and more abstractly. A social psychological experiment in which A causes B is always a snapshot of some broader, more intricate causal process involving A, B and other variables (see Figure 15.3).

This means that often, without concerted action, undesirable patterns of thought, feeling and action at all levels, from the individual, to relationships, groups and societies, are likely to persist. An interesting and important manifestation of this self-perpetuating quality of social reality is the self-fulfilling prophecy encountered in Chapter 1. Again and again, we have encountered evidence that people are prone to behaving in line with their own or others' expectancies (Merton, 1948). When people seem to act in line with stereotypes, this is often because they are expected to. We saw this, for example, in the research on stereotype threat effects in Chapter 11. If people are conscious that they belong to a group that is stereotypically assumed to be worse at a task, then their performance suffers. So, women and girls do less well at maths, and people from disadvantaged socioeconomic backgrounds do worse at a range of academic tests. For example, if people are expected to be kind, or cruel, then there is a good chance they will pick up on this effect. If parents think their children will grow up to be drinkers, the odds are increased, all else being equal, that they will (Madon, Guyll, Spoth and Willard, 2004). In this book, we have seen evidence that the effects of alcohol, fatigue and blood sugar are prone to the power of self-fulfilling prophecies. For example, people who think that alcohol is strongly disinhibiting are more likely to become violent when drunk (Chapter 13). People who think that self-control is a limited resource are more prone to ego depletion effects, in which after exercising self-control for a considerable length of time, people show reduced self-control on a second task (Chapter 2). So when people's behaviour seems to confirm expectations, whether in an experiment or in a real-life context, and whether the expectations are based on situational factors, personal factors, group-based stereotypes or ideologies, always ask yourself, could this be an example of a self-fulfilling prophecy?

Exploring further The placebo effect is a supreme example of the power of self-fulfilling prophecies and is by no means confined to drug trials. Look up mechanisms underlying the placebo effect or find out about the magnitude of placebo effects.

The power of the group

Although we are all individuals with our unique characteristics, thoughts, feelings and beliefs, the study of social psychology has another clear message: group memberships and social identities largely define who we are. This is another way in which social psychology punctures the individualistic assumptions of Western societies. We are members of groups in almost every facet of life, from our daily work (e.g., project teams, research groups) to our social lives (e.g., friends, sports groups). When we think and talk about ourselves, we refer to things like our gender, race and occupation and the important social identities that make us who we are. In turn, these social identities influence what we think and do. As we saw in Chapter 8, we are guided by explicit and implicit social norms that provide useful frames of reference from which to judge and recalibrate our own behaviour in social situations (Cialdini, Reno and Kallgren, 1990). We are also guided by social roles such as gender roles (e.g., Eagly and Steffen, 2000; Twenge, 2001) and status within groups and organizations – roles that often arise as a result of social comparisons with other group members (Festinger, 1954).

It is also clear from the study of social psychology that people need groups. Deviant group members who do not adhere to the norms and standards of the group are often disliked and derogated (Marques et al., 1988). People who pose as group members when in fact they are not (e.g., occasional meat-eating 'vegetarians') are dealt with harshly by the group (Jetten et al., 2005). And as we know from the research on social exclusion (Chapter 8), being left out of groups – even groups we dislike – can have disastrous consequences for individuals' psychological wellbeing (Williams, 2001). Being left out of a group can cause significant psychological stress, which – as shown by studies of brain activity – resembles the same processes as physical pain (Eisenberger et al., 2003). Once in groups, people work together to solve problems and pursue goals that cannot be realized by any individual acting alone (Chapter 10).

The power of the situation

People do not only act in line with their personal attitudes, values and traits. The 'power of the situation' (e.g., Benjamin and Simpson, 2009) was originally demonstrated by the classic studies of Solomon Asch, in which participants would proffer answers they must have known were false in order to conform to the opinions being voiced by other people. This tradition followed in Milgram's and Zimbardo's shocking studies of obedience and tyranny. As we have outlined in our critical discussion of these studies (especially in Chapter 9), they involved situations that were carefully designed to manipulate participants' behaviour. Since individuals designed and commanded these situations, just like those of real-world tyrannies, we cannot blame the situation entirely for the behaviour people displayed (Mandel, 1998).

More generally, different people respond in different ways to the same situation. Thus, the most comprehensive models of human behaviour are interactionist, specifying the interplay between personality and situational variables (Carnahan and McFarland, 2007; Haslam and Reicher, 2007; Mischel and Shoda, 1995; Shibutani, 1961). However, these studies remain iconic, vivid demonstrations that the situation powerfully shapes our behaviour.

Other lines of research also corroborate this central take-home message of social psychology. Every time we conduct an experiment in social psychology, we are exploiting the power of the situation to reveal something about why people think, feel and act the way they do. Situational factors like a lack of blood sugar (Chapter 2), the brief appearance of words or pictures related to stereotypes (Chapter 3), the body language of the people we interact with (Chapters 4 and 5), standing on a wobbly bridge (Chapter 7), the film we have just watched or the game we have just played (Chapter 12), and thinking that we have just broken a computer (Chapter 14) can affect how racist, aggressive, kind, sexually attracted and sexually attractive we are. Goals, beliefs and emotions are primed by situations, and our bodily responses to situations also play a key role in influencing our responses to them.

The fact that we can adapt to the situations we find ourselves in is enormously helpful to us. Think what life would be like if we were incapable of flexibly responding to the different demands that situations place on us. At the same time, our responses to situations are often so rapid, subtle and automatic that we do not notice them and are unable to control them. It also means that in our personal and professional lives, we should not assume that a person's behaviour in a given situation reflects who they really are.

Be conscious of the unconscious

People cannot always tell what influences them (Nisbett and Wilson, 1977). Consider the results of an interesting study in environmental social psychology. When asked what kinds of messages would cause them to save energy in their homes, people thought they would be most responsive to the message that saving energy will save them money. But when this message was displayed in people's homes, it did not influence their behaviour. The message that did cause householders to save energy was simply the information that their neighbours were doing so. Participants had earlier dismissed the idea that this social norm information would be enough to change their behaviour (Nolan, Schultz, Cialdini et al., 2008).

These studies suggest that people cannot always tell what is going to influence them. As we have seen, they cannot always tell when they have been influenced either. Their attitudes can be changed by persuasive messages (Douglas and Sutton, 2004, 2008) and other sources of social influence, such as peer pressure, without their awareness (Pronin, Berger and Molouki, 2007). This means that situations and social systems can alter the way people think, feel and behave in ways that escape their attention. As we saw in Chapters 3 and 4, people form and pursue goals of which they are not conscious. And as we saw in Chapter 5, people unconsciously hold attitudes towards social objects, including other people and groups, which may be at odds with their conscious attitudes (Nisbett and Wilson, 1977).

Thus, it is important not to be complacent about your own goals, beliefs, actions and the things that influence you. You may not think you are being changed by the company you keep, the place you work or the media you consume, but this does not mean that you are not being changed. You may not be aware that you harbour stereotypes and prejudice, but this does not guarantee that you do not. And do not take people's accounts of their own goals, beliefs and actions at face value either. Even if they sincerely want to tell the truth, they may not be able to. A final implication of the unconsciousness of human psychology is that we should take our intuitions with a pinch of salt. Intuitions can be valuable and accurate, but it is not a criticism of a theory, or a finding, that it runs counter to our intuitions.

Question to consider Reread question 2 at the start of this chapter. Just how good are people at detecting when they have been influenced by pieces of information? In general, how aware are people of social psychological phenomena that determine their thoughts, feelings and behaviours?

Behaviour matters

Social psychological research suggests that our behaviours have the power to influence who we are and what we think. For example, as we saw in Chapter 4, the theory of cognitive dissonance suggests that when there is a discrepancy between beliefs and behaviours, something must change (Festinger, 1957; Festinger and Carlsmith, 1959). Self-perception theory suggests that we infer our own attitudes from our behaviour. Thus, you are more likely to enjoy exercising if you make large sacrifices to do so, and you are more likely to adopt green attitudes if you recycle and save energy. Thus, social psychologists have conclusively demonstrated that beyond the commonsense understanding that our attitudes shape our behaviour, our behaviour changes our attitudes. Social psychologists have witnessed similar effects in communication, as we saw in Chapter 5. For example, the 'saying is believing' effect demonstrates that in articulating an argument for an audience, people's opinions change to become more in line with what they said to their audience, irrespective of what they originally thought (Echterhoff, Higgins and Levine, 2009; Hausmann, Levine and Higgins, 2008). For example, if we dislike a group, saying that we like them (for whatever reason) may subsequently cause us to change our minds about them, even if only a little.

© BANANASTOCK

In short, our behaviour is crucial. Not only is behaviour the central means by which social psychologists and laypeople alike understand human nature, but it also has the power to change what we think and who we are. Therefore, another message of social psychology is that it may not always be wise to rely on winning hearts and minds – whether your own or others'. One implication of the social psychological phenomena mentioned above is that you sometimes ought to 'do' what you want to be.

Human beings are not disembodied

In the heyday of the cognitive revolution in psychology (Baars, 1986), and the development of computers in the years following the Second World War, the computer was adopted as a powerful metaphor for the human being. Like computers, humans had a short-term memory (analogous to random access memory), a long-term memory (analogous to information stored permanently on a disk or flash drive), and an executive system, like a central processing unit, that organized the whole system (e.g., Boden, 1998; Broadbent, 1987; Neisser, 1963). In this view, the fact that the computer runs on a physical platform of silicon and the human mind inhabits a brain made of water, fats and other chemicals hardly matters. This model of human nature was always controversial. Philosophers such as Koestler ([1967]1990) and Ryle (1949) argued that what we call the 'mind' cannot be sharply separated from the brain, and the entire body, in which it resides. Emotions and thoughts are based in bodily events.

With the passing of time, research has increasingly revealed the social psychological importance of the body. We are not information processors whose motivations and behaviours are shaped only by socialization. To illustrate, we are more prone to impulsivity and stereotyping when blood sugar levels are low (Chapter 2), and the extent to which we like other people depends on the movements of our arms and facial muscles. Although not conclusive, there is evidence that our attitudes, including our left–right political orientation, are partly hereditable, that is, influenced by genes (see Chapter 4). There is strong evidence that aggression levels are hereditable in other animals, which means that the same is likely to be true of human beings – a conclusion supported by studies of twins (Chapter 13). Different aspects of our brains are specialized for aspects of judging other people's traits, emotions and intentions (Chapter 3). The presence of 'mirror neurons' has been demonstrated in human beings, which cause us to automatically engage in empathic mimicry of others (Chapter 4).

None of these effects are straightforward. They tend to be small and dependent on other variables. As we have just discussed in relation to self-fulfilling prophecies, the effects of some bodily variables such as circadian rhythms and blood sugar may depend on people's beliefs about their effects, in a kind of placebo effect (Chapter 2). Not only does alcohol lead to aggressive behaviour, but people who are feeling aggressive seek alcohol, perhaps because they think it will allow them to aggress (Chapter 13). Further, the extent to which we embrace biological explanations for behaviour is highly controversial. One reason for this is that we run into severe political problems when we argue that differences between ethnic groups (see Chapter 13 on the 'warrior gene') and gender groups (see the Critical focus box in Chapter 8 on gender roles) are determined by biology, since this can be used as a justification of stereotypes and inequality (Reicher, 2011). However, the study of evolutionary and biological processes in social psychology does not require us to postulate or study biological differences between social groups. Setting aside this specific research question, social psychologists cannot ignore the biological and bodily basis of behaviour. Research has suggested all kinds of interesting interactions between bodily, mental and social processes.

Some challenges and limitations

Having talked about the achievements, value and potential of social psychology, it is important to recognize some of its limitations and controversies. These are important to bear in mind when considering the history of the discipline and its future directions. Again, this list by no means exhausts the criticisms that have been levelled at social psychology. Our conclusions may be strongly disputed by some social psychologists. Nonetheless, we think this is a reasonable summary of some of the main criticisms frequently levelled at social psychology as it stands. One of the main limitations of social psychological research thus far has been an overreliance on so-called 'convenience samples' of undergraduate university students. We deal with this limitation in the Critical focus box below.

CRITICAL FOCUS

Sampling bias in social psychology

One of the key limitations of mainstream social psychology over the past few decades is that researchers have relied too heavily on convenience samples of undergraduate university students, who are typically aged 17–25. Sears (1986) found that 82 per cent of studies published in three of the leading journals of social psychology used student samples (*Journal of Personality and Social Psychology*, *Personality and Social Psychology Bulletin* and *Journal of Experimental Social Psychology*). Reviewing the literature on changes through the life span, Sears (1986) argued that this cross-section of society, compared to older adults, are likely to have less crystallized attitudes and self-concepts, stronger cognitive capabilities, and less stable peer group relationships. Sears (1986) therefore concluded that sampling bias may help explain why so many studies in social psychology have found people to be compliant, quick to change their attitudes, behave inconsistently with their attitudes, and use situational cues rather than introspection to make inferences about themselves.

Other authors have added weight to Sears' (1986) troubling critique of sampling bias in social psychology. Arnett (2008) reviewed the samples found in studies published in the *Journal of Personality and Social Psychology*, the most prestigious outlet in social psychology. He found that 67 per cent of samples from the USA were students. Much has been written about the differences between social psychology as it is conducted in America versus elsewhere, but this is not peculiarly a US problem. In fact, 80 per cent of the samples from non-American papers were students. This gives rise to a striking statistic. A randomly selected American university student is over *4,000 times more likely* to participate in a study published in the *Journal of Personality and Social*

Psychology than a person selected randomly from the populations of non-Western countries. This is the most prestigious journal devoted to the publication of research in social and personality psychology, meaning that the most influential findings tend to be based on samples that are non-representative of the global population.

If Arnett (2008) highlighted the scale of the sampling bias in social psychology, Peterson (2001) underlined its importance. Peterson conducted a systematic review of meta-analyses comparing student and non-student samples and found a range of differences. In some cases, effects found in student samples were completely reversed in non-student samples. For example, Byrnes, Miller and Schafer (1999) found that in studies of students, women showed a greater propensity to engage in risky sexual and drink-driving behaviour than men. In studies of other sections of the community, men were found to take more risks than women (Byrnes et al., 1999).

More recently, Heinrich, Heine and Norenzayan (2010) published perhaps the most far-reaching and troubling critique of sampling bias in the behavioural sciences, including social psychology. They argue that social scientists have grossly overrelied on WEIRD participants – WEIRD standing for Western, educated, industrialized, rich and democratic. The middle classes of Western countries represent a relatively small minority of the world's population but a large majority of the samples in published articles. This group show remarkable differences to other portions of the world's population in terms of their self-concept, styles of thought and perception, and social behaviours. It is therefore difficult to make generalizations about human nature across the board on the basis of the evidence that social psychologists and other social scientists have accrued. This is especially important, given that experimental procedures are often designed for WEIRD samples and tried out on other populations later (Bennis and Medin, 2010).

This is a major challenge to the validity of the social psychology you have been learning about. However, studies have shown that there are some cross-cultural universals in human behaviour. We have seen an example in the criteria that people use to choose mates (Chapter 7). Across cultures, men report placing greater emphasis than women on physical characteristics (the waist-to-hip ratio of 0.70 being an example), and less emphasis on status-related characteristics such as intelligence or wealth. Across cultures, people are also willing to make personal sacrifices in order to punish defectors in social dilemmas (as we saw in Chapter 14). Thus, it is by no means certain that a finding obtained from WEIRD participants will differ markedly when tested on a different sample. While we cannot glibly assume that findings will generalize across cultures, neither should we assume that findings will not. In forming hypotheses about whether a particular finding will apply across cultures, we should be guided by theories implying that findings will hold or will differ. We should not be overly confident that findings will, or will not, generalize until we have tested these hypotheses.

Other things can be said in defence of social psychology in light of its sampling bias. For one thing, when you are concerned with a specific behaviour characteristic of reasonably affluent Westerners, you may not have any practical need to worry about whether findings from such samples generalize to other people. Also, if one has good theoretical and empirical reasons to believe that little variability should exist across diverse populations in a particular domain, then it may be reasonable to infer that a process is universal based on an investigation utilizing a WEIRD sample. Further, globalization means that more and more people in the world find themselves living in Western-style cultures with similar economic and political models, so it is likely that WEIRD samples have become, and will become, relevant to more and more of the world's population (Rozin, 2010). Also, some cultural differences may be superficially different but have similar functions. For example, markedly different cultural rituals, such as circumcision, sex acts and debutant balls, may fulfil essentially the same social psychological purpose. In each of these cases, the rituals are an initiation of young people into adulthood (Gaertner, Sedikides, Cai and Brown, 2010).

Finally, different experimental results obtained across cultures may not always reflect genuine differences in psychological processes. Instead, they may reflect different interpretations of the experimental task – what the task means and what is required of participants. Baumard and Sperber (2010) illustrate this point with an example from studies of behaviour during economic games. In such experiments, people are given money and are asked to share it with someone they do not know. For a start, both are unusual events that do not typically occur in everyday life. Many things are unclear in such a study. For example, is the money to be given as a gift? Who owns it? Who is the other participant and what is their right to the money? Such ambiguities inherent in the research methodology raise the possibility that cultural differences on such tasks are not down to psychological differences per se, but are instead the result of different interpretations of the situation. The authors cite some interesting findings whereby, for example, participants from collective hunter-gatherer societies are typically generous in economic games, perhaps because they see the money as jointly owned by the participants in the study. On the other hand, findings from solitary horticulturalist societies are less generous, arguably because they may see the money as their own property and are therefore unwilling to share it. Going back to WEIRD samples, reluctance to share the money may be a result of contextual factors (e.g., living in large capitalist societies) and may reflect different assumptions about economic games rather than fundamental psychological processes that differ across cultures. All in all, we think the sampling bias in social psychology should be a cause of serious concern, but not a total loss of confidence in the discipline.

Questions

1. Of course, we cite many, many studies in this textbook. We do not always describe the samples that were recruited. If you pick a random selection of, say, 10 pages from this textbook (not Chapters 1 or 15), how many studies do we describe, and for how many of these studies do we indicate whether a student sample was employed?

2. Can you identify a finding described in this textbook, obtained with a sample of undergraduate students, that you think would be different if it were conducted on a different sample? Can you articulate why?

3. If you wanted to test whether people from a Western European country differed from people from, say, a North African sample on some variable, let us say in their attachment style (Chapter 7), how would you go about it? What problems would you expect to encounter when designing the materials for the study and in interpreting its results?

Exploring further Women now outnumber men by roughly 58:42 at university. This ratio is significantly larger among psychology students, who are overrepresented as participants in psychological research. Using an internet database or search engine, find recent research, published within the last 10 years or so, reviewing the magnitude and nature of gender differences. To what extent, and in what ways, are female-dominated samples unrepresentative of the population as a whole?

Narrow methods and assumptions

As you will have noticed through reading this book (and as we discussed in Chapter 1), social psychologists use a variety of research methods, but tend to use some more than others. For example, experimental and correlational research designs tend to dominate mainstream social psychological research. Thus, much of our knowledge of social psychology is derived from investigations that use similar methods. Social psychological research also tends to employ question-naires more than any other empirical tool. Researchers who are trained in a particular method and perspective are prone to sticking to what they know. Of course, most of the time this reflects a researcher's methodological expertise. Much like scholars in other disciplines and professions, social psychologists specialize in certain topics and research methods. For example, an experimentalist may not attempt a conversational analysis simply because they will not know where to begin. However, researchers' preference for particular research methods means that specific research questions tend to be examined in a fairly uniform manner. We have seen, for example, that the laboratory experiment has dominated the study of prejudice reduction techniques (Paluck and Green, 2009). This raises two issues. First, can we be sure that the methods used to examine a specific research question are the most optimal methods? Could other methods do a better job? Attachment to a particular method may mean that the insights and findings poten-tially gained by using other methods can be overlooked.

Another issue is the ecological validity of social psychological studies. Specifi-cally, many studies attempt to simulate real-life thoughts and contexts and apply the findings to non-simulated situations. For example, a significant body of research on social power tends to ask people to imagine a time when they were in a position of power or one when they were not in a position of power (see Galinsky, Gruenfeld and Magee, 2003; Guinote and Vescio, 2010; Guinote, Weick and Cai, 2012). We have learned a great deal from such findings, but to what extent is it possible to generalize them to real-life situations where people have, or lack, power? Similar questions could be asked about research on prejudice, attitudes and, indeed, most other areas of social psychology. In general, mainstream social psychologists tend to rely heavily on the use of experiments, which often have limited ecological validity or take insufficient account of moderating factors in the situation or sample.

Exploring further Ecological validity may or may not be an issue in many areas of social psychology. Take some time to read around an area such as social power, prejudice or attitudes. To what extent does it rely on experiments conducted in laboratory settings? Make up your own mind about whether or not this is problematic.

Publication bias The tendency for researchers to report positive results (or those that show a significant finding) differently from those that show negative results (or those that show non-significant findings).

Finally, it is arguably easier to publish social psychological research if it finds 'closure' on a research question and provides the reader with a coherent and compelling 'story'. Again, this phenomenon is not unique to social psychology. This **publication bias** – or tendency to report experimental results that are positive or show a significant finding differently from those that are negative – is well known across the sciences and social sciences (Rosenthal, 1979). Indeed, it has been reported in clinical trials research that statistically significant results are three times more likely to be published than research that affirms a null result (Dickersin, Chan, Chalmers et al., 1987). This means that many potentially important findings – particularly those that fail to find support for hypotheses – are not in the public domain. As an attempt to decrease this problem, some medical journals now require registration of trials before they begin so that negative results are not withheld from publication. However, such a strategy does not exist within social psychology at this point. The bias not only applies to research that is published, but also extends to work that researchers are prepared to submit for publication in the first place. Typically, researchers will not even attempt to publish non-significant findings, leading to what is commonly known as the **file drawer effect** – many studies are simply not reported because they either yield non-significant results or yield results that run contrary to established research findings (Rosenthal, 1979). It is important, therefore, to question whether what is published on a topic reflects the truth. The epistemic drive towards certainty could lead to a bias in the way social psychologists report their work (Billig, 1996).

File drawer effect The phenomenon whereby studies are not submitted for publication because they either yield non-significant results or results that run contrary to established research findings.

Insufficient attention to behaviour

Attitudes are important for individuals to satisfy their various psychological needs and motivational drives (see Chapter 4). So it is unsurprising that attitudes and the measurement of attitudes figure prominently in social psychological research. However, attitudes are only one facet of social psychology. Behaviours and social action are also important. One criticism often levelled at social psychology is its overreliance on measures of attitudes over behaviours and social action (Durrheim, in press). This reliance on attitudes is largely motivated by practical rather than theoretical concerns. It is relatively easy for a researcher to ask someone what their attitudes are in an interview or survey. It tends to be more difficult, time-consuming and expensive to measure behaviour. Therefore, for practical reasons, social psychological studies of attitudes are more common than observational studies that measure behaviour. A major worry is that researchers are paying less attention to behaviour than they used to. Over half the studies published by the leading *Journal of Personality and Social Psychology* in the 1960s and 70s included behavioural measures. By the 2000s, this proportion had dropped to something like 20 per cent (Baumeister, Vohs and Funder, 2007). In a pithy, witty conclusion, Baumeister et al. (p. 402) wrote:

> There is no need to stop asking for ratings or analyzing reaction times, but perhaps psychologists could all push themselves to include an occasional study that includes direct observation of what Knee et al. (2005) poignantly called 'actual behavior.'

We are happy to report that since this plea was published, there have been serious moves to bring behaviour more into the centre of social psychology. Journal editors are increasingly calling for behavioural measures (e.g., Simpson, 2009).

However, as we know from the research outlined in Chapter 4, there is ample evidence from mainstream social psychology that attitudes do predict behaviour. So, using attitudes as a proxy for what people do may not always be a major problem. Critical social psychologists disagree, arguing that mainstream attitude–behaviour research is based on a fallacy that attitudes somehow belong to individuals. From this perspective, attitudes are constructed by people in the course of their interactions with others and cannot be studied at the level of individuals. Indeed, critical social psychologists argue that the construction of meaning through talk is a type of social action (e.g., Billig, 1992, 1996; Durrheim, in press; Potter, 1996). We think talk is different from other types of behaviour, and since many studies of talk come from specific contexts such as interviews with researchers, we are not sure that it necessarily counts as social action any more than does (say) the completion of a survey. But it is clear that mainstream social psychology needs to pay greater attention to behaviour.

Time to reflect Many attitude scales are subjected to examinations of test-retest reliability. They are taken once, and some weeks or months later they are taken again by the same participants. The scores between the two tests are then correlated. The resulting indices of test-retest reliability are often impressive, showing correlations of over 0.50 or 0.60. What does this mean for the argument made by critical social psychologists that attitudes cannot be considered to be stable or associated with individuals?

Disciplinary isolation and fragmentation

As we discussed in Chapter 1, social psychology is a subject that bridges some of the gaps between psychology and sociology. Indeed, social psychologists and

sociologists are concerned with some of the same issues and, in the 1940s and 50s, social psychologists and sociologists frequently worked together. However the two disciplines have become increasingly isolated from each other, as each has become more specialized and focused on different methods of data collection. Typically nowadays, sociologists are more concerned with 'macro-social' variables, such as social structure, hierarchy, power and historical contexts, whereas social psychologists focus more on 'micro-social' variables, such as features of individuals and small groups that determine social behaviours and outcomes (Oishi, Kesebir and Snyder, 2009).

A good example of the difference in sociological and psychological perspectives is to be found in the case of racism. Social psychologists generally regard racism as the product of individual-level variables, such as the desire to achieve cognitive closure and identification with a racial ingroup, whereas sociologists might look for the 'ways in which institutions encourage racist acts by motivating people to behave in a racist manner or behave in a manner that motivates others to do so' (Frymer, 2005, p. 373). Institutional racism is different from individual racism. As we have seen, social psychologists do examine genuinely social predictors of racism such as group norms and ideologies. However, we typically do so through the lens of individual differences in measures of endorsement of these ideologies and norms, or in what individuals say in qualitative research interviews. We tend not to study the specific practices of institutions (e.g., hiring practices, implicit messages in training) and how these affect the psychology of the individual. As a result of these issues, it could be argued that a weakness of social psychology is that it has lost its concept of the 'bigger picture'. While it seeks to relate the very large and the very small, it does not offer a very rich or detailed account of how the two are related by specific institutional and social practices.

Another area of concern is that there are many ongoing divisions within social psychology. One example is the division between American and European approaches to social psychology. As a general rule, American social psychologists have historically been more concerned with processes occurring at the level of the individual, whereas European social psychologists have focused their research more on processes occurring within or between groups. The two approaches rarely met. This is perhaps less of a concern in more recent years, as increasing globalization has allowed communities of scholars to associate with each other more effectively. The publication process has also become more globalized. American and European researchers are under similar pressures to publish in similar journals with similar reputations, impact factors, and oriented to similar issues and methods. This has meant that their research has become more similar over time (Smith, 2005).

However, other significant divisions exist within the discipline. For example, in Chapter 1 we discussed the ongoing conflict between researchers who conduct qualitative research and those who conduct quantitative research. Also, researchers in the quantitative tradition tend to be seen either as personality or social psychologists. For years, bitter wrangles were fought over the power of the situation versus personality variables to predict our behaviour (Mischel, 1990). This is strange, given that papers in social and personality psychology study much the same psychological phenomena and test similar theories. The principle difference is simply that correlational methods tend to be preferred by personality psychologists, and experimental methods are preferred by social psychologists (Tracy, Robins and Sherman, 2009). Also, social psychologists often describe the same phenomena and processes in different ways depending on the research grouping they come from. For example, the heuristic-systematic model of information processing by Chaiken (1980) and Petty and Cacioppo's (1986) elaboration likelihood model of persuasion describe almost identical processes using completely different terminology. Social identity scholars and those closely aligned with the more recent self-categorization theory (Turner et al., 1987) argue the finer points of both theories that essentially describe the same phenomena in very similar ways.

Exploring further Although there is an important distinction between critical and mainstream social psychology, which typically use qualitative and quantitative research methodologies respectively, some researchers are involved in both types of research. Look up some of these researchers (e.g., Olivier Klein, Stephen Reicher) and see if you can find more. The extent to which the two 'camps' are divided may sometimes be overestimated. Some researchers also call for a fusion of the two types of research (e.g., Jost and Kruglanski, 2002).

Divisions within a discipline need not be a bad thing. Dissension can be healthy in science. However, there is a tendency to think in 'us' and 'them' terms, and dismiss the validity of alternative perspectives. Here is an example from a recent paper in social psychology:

> To use evolution as a proximal explanation of human social behaviour is to overextend the approach, to take social kinds as natural kinds, and to reify all the imperfections and inequalities of our contemporary world … Evolutionary theories themselves, lest they be tempted by the prospect of extending their explanatory reach, should recall that hubris is the anvil on which every great empire is destroyed. (Reicher, 2011, p. 393)

In this book, we have encountered many examples of evolutionary social psychology, few of which attempt to explain the social positions or roles of different groups in society. More of these investigations concern the ultimate (and seldom the proximal) causes of empathy, altruism, love, and the desire for cognitive consistency, none of which are directly relevant to the inequalities and systemic imperfections of human society. This quote touches on important and legitimate criticisms that can be levelled at evolutionary social psychology, but in our opinion glosses over crucial distinctions between specific theories within this tradition.

Exploring further Can you find examples of evolutionary social psychology that are politically dubious, for example which suggest that women are less suited than men to high status roles?

Another example features a similar use of metaphor and emotive rhetoric when discussing a rival point of view:

> the field [of social psychology] remains tethered to cognitive constructivist assumptions regarding causality … This old view of cognition as being about representation is incompatible with the embodied principle of 'behavior before brain.' (Marsh, Johnston, Richardson and Schmidt, 2009, p. 1217)

Here, advocates of embodiment in social psychology suggest that social psychology should somehow liberate itself from the traditional cognitivist assumptions that mental representations and schemas are important. The word 'old' in this quote is pejorative. It means outdated, out of vogue, and wrong. In general, criticism and debate are healthy for a discipline, but it is important that the potential contributions of alternative approaches are not unduly dismissed.

Exploring further Until relatively recently, European and American social psychology were divided. So you can see this for yourself, go to the library and find old (e.g., 1970s) editions of a major US journal such as the *Journal of Personality and Social Psychology* and also select some more recent editions (e.g., 2000s). Look through the author affiliations. What is the proportion of American to European scholars represented in each edition? Has this changed over the years? Do the same for one of the major European journals such as the *European Journal of Social Psychology*.

Academic politics and reward systems

As we briefly alluded to in the previous section, some of the changes in social psychology have brought the various different traditions closer together in some ways. For example, academics in general – not just social psychologists – are required to meet certain performance standards such as publishing in 'high impact' journals and winning research grants. This brings consistency to academia in general – everyone knows what they are supposed to do – but it also creates problems. One problem is that the field becomes more competitive. There are limited numbers of pages in social psychology journals and many social psychologists who want to publish their work in the most visible and prestigious place possible. Getting published in the more prestigious and higher impact journals is therefore a competitive business, which can again expose divisions within the different research and methodological 'camps' in social psychology.

The pressure on social psychologists to produce (lots of) high impact work has also prompted a recent change in the publication process. In recent years, many of the major journals in social psychology, including the *Journal of Experimental Social Psychology*, the *British Journal of Social Psychology* and the *European Journal of Social Psychology*, have introduced the acceptance of short reports of typically less than 5,000 words. While this is positive in some respects, in that researchers can quickly disseminate novel findings without the necessity for lengthy delays in the review process, and it creates more space in the journals, it can also encourage researchers to publish research they have not yet replicated or fully explained (note the Ethics and research methods box on replication in

Chapter 3). The pressure to publish innovative and novel findings can mean that researchers overlook some of the weaknesses of their work. It may also mean, either intentionally or unintentionally, that researchers 'spin' their research so that it is exciting and newsworthy but perhaps stretches the truth. As Jonathan Schooler, a psychologist at the University of California, Santa Barbara said in an interview with the *New York Times* (Carey, 2011):

> The big problem is that the culture is such that researchers spin their work in a way that tells a prettier story than what they really found … It's almost like everyone is on steroids, and to compete you have to take steroids as well.

The most unscrupulous response to this pressure is to publish falsified (made up or dishonestly altered) data. In September 2011, the prominent Dutch social psychologist Diederik Stapel was suspended on suspicion that he had published falsified data. A committee report later concluded that he had faked data for at least 30 of his publications, including papers in highly prestigious journals such as *Science*, the *Journal of Personality and Social Psychology* and *Psychological Science*, which have since been retracted. Falsifying data is an extremely serious breach in a discipline that is motivated to find the truth. Falsified data not only misleads researchers and practitioners but wastes their time, as they seek to replicate and extend effects that were not real to begin with.

Of course, allegations of academic misconduct are not unique to social psychology. Neither is there any evidence that the practice is widespread. There are serious efforts to reduce the risk that falsified data are going to be published. You will find that such problems exist in many of the sciences, social sciences and humanities. Dishonest people and pressure to succeed exist in every sphere of life. However, as a student of the discipline, it is important to appreciate that the context in which contemporary social psychologists work means that their work is not always free of bias or exempt from pressure. As we have noted throughout this chapter, it is always important to think critically about what you read. This does not mean dismissing novel or surprising findings out of hand, and it is not helpful to entertain the possibility that a finding is fake. However, bias and sheer chance will produce findings that are not robust, and which are nonetheless published. Replication is always crucial before we place too much weight on a finding. Considering the various weaknesses and limitations of the discipline is important too.

Current and future directions in social psychology

Thus far, we have reviewed some of the great strengths and weaknesses of social psychology. In this section, we will discuss where the discipline is likely to go in the future. Predicting the future is an enterprise littered with failure. Nevertheless, it is possible to identify some of the forces that have shaped the discipline in the past and are likely to affect its course in the future. In particular, some factors influence the things that social psychologists *can* do. For example, new technologies, intellectual developments within the field, new statistics and research techniques, and new insights from other fields influence what researchers are able to do, but not necessarily what they ought to do. On the other hand, some factors influence the things that social psychologists *choose* to do, or what they feel they *ought* to do, within the changing limits of what is possible. For example, governments, charities, businesses and the public are likely to demand certain types of research (on particular topics). Such factors are typically related to social and economic forces. We highlight some of these 'supply' and 'demand' factors in the following sections, first focusing on the use of the internet for research in social psychology.

The internet

We have already encountered a significant limitation of social psychological research to date in that it relies too much on samples of willing and readily available volunteers, who are typically university students. In the past decade or so, the internet has provided an extremely valuable resource for social psychologists, providing access to samples of a size and quality that was hitherto difficult to achieve. Gaining access to a reasonably representative sample of, say, 1,000 participants or more has traditionally required researchers to hire market research and polling companies who typically charge significant sums of money per participant. For international samples, a great deal of time-consuming and expensive coordination was required, involving several groups of researchers. Using the internet, researchers are able to mount experiments and surveys online. A great advantage of internet-based studies is that they offer access to participants distributed across the globe, and may free researchers from overreliance on convenient, but local, samples (Gosling, Sandy, John and Potter, 2010). Studies have shown that research mounted on the internet produces similar findings to comparable studies run in the laboratory with participants recruited in traditional ways (Gosling, Vazire, Srivastava and John, 2004).

Of course, the internet has its limitations as a means of recruiting participants. Many research questions cannot, at least at present, be examined in this way (Johnson and Gosling, 2010). For example, if you want to study participants' body language, or the way they respond to people in the same physical space as them, then the internet is not the best medium of choice. Meaningful interaction between the experimenter and participants is too difficult. This may help rule out some experimenter effects (Paolacci, Chandler and Ipeirotis, 2010), but also makes it more difficult for researchers to get feedback from participants about how they experienced an experimental or survey procedure. Such information can be an invaluable aid to the interpretation of results and the refinement of experiments (Aronson, Wilson and Brewer, 1998). When experiments are potentially distressing to participants, the lack of contact also has a negative ethical implication. Specifically, it is hard for

FIGURE 15.4 The internet has created many opportunities, but also challenges, for data collection in social psychology

© BANANASTOCK

researchers to discuss with participants the distress and other negative effects that the research procedure may have caused. Another downside of internet-based studies is that it can be difficult to stop the flow of information from debriefed participants, who know what the study was about, to new participants. All it takes is for participants to post information on a blog or discussion board, and new participants may enter the study with a good deal of knowledge about the aims and objectives of the experiment. Nonetheless, the potential to obtain more results from larger and more globally representative samples is an exciting prospect for the discipline.

ETHICS AND RESEARCH METHODS

Crowdsourcing social psychology

Although the internet makes it easier to access a potential audience of millions, researchers using this tool are confronted with much the same problem – how to motivate people to take part in their research. Apart from a minority of people who are willing to volunteer, for studies that take up more of participants' time and require larger samples, it is usually necessary to offer some monetary incentive. This can be expensive, and transferring money to participants over the internet poses logistical and security difficulties. In recent years, a promising solution to this problem has emerged – **crowdsourcing** services. One such service, Amazon's Mechanical Turk, had over 100,000 subscribers by 2010, who take part in various tasks for small monetary rewards. It allows researchers to recruit from this pool for payments of less than a US dollar. The subscribers to this service tend to be reasonably representative of the population as a whole – somewhat more educated, but earning slightly less than average. Studies run on Mechanical Turk appear to produce similar findings to those run in other ways (Paolacci et al., 2010; Burhmester, Kwang and Gosling, 2011).

Questions

1 You are asked to evaluate the ethics of a study into attitudes to rape survivors (e.g., Abrams et al., 2003). The questionnaire presents a scenario involving a rape, and asks participants to rate the extent to which the perpetrator and the victim were responsible for the attack. The researchers propose to run their study using online survey software and recruit participants remotely on Mechanical Turk. What are the ethical advantages and disadvantages of running sensitive studies like this on anonymous online sites, versus face-to-face laboratory settings?

2 Paying people to participate in psychological studies, not only on Mechanical Turk but in any setting, raises ethical issues. Some people see it as akin to a type of coercion, in that people who lack money may feel compelled to take part (Head, 2009; Malouff and Schutte, 2005). What do you think, bearing in mind the ethical guidelines of professional psychological societies? Search 'ethics participant payment' to obtain a range of views.

Crowdsourcing A means of achieving complex, labour-intensive tasks by recruiting many people to contribute to the tasks over the internet.

Exploring further Find recently published articles that have used Mechanical Turk or some other crowdsourcing software to recruit participants. Summarize the three you find most interesting or relevant to your assignments. What were the sample characteristics and main findings? Do you think the research would have been difficult or expensive to conduct without this service? Do you think that the findings would have been different if they had been conducted in a more traditional way such as testing a group of undergraduate participants?

New research tools provided by information technology

Data mining The process of automatically searching large volumes of data for patterns.

Advances in information technology (IT) also provide exciting avenues for conducting social psychological research. One example is the technique of **data mining**, which is the process of automatically searching large volumes of data for patterns, extracting useful information from large data sets or databases. To give a simple example, imagine that a retail department tracks the purchases of a particular customer and notes that they purchase a large number of shoes. A data mining system will detect a correlation between that particular customer and shoes. This information can be used by the company to target their sales efforts towards that customer in future – they may want to sell them even more shoes or direct them towards other products. You can probably imagine how, on a larger scale, this technique could be useful to social psychologists. Essentially, data mining allows the user to identify correlations or patterns among many different fields in large sets of data. One interesting use of this technique can be seen in a study by Thelwall, Wilkinson and Uppal (2010), who examined the extent to which emotion was present in MySpace accounts (a commonly used social networking site). Using data mining and content analysis, they randomly sampled 819 public comments from American users, finding that females were more likely to give and receive emotionally positive comments than males, but that there was no difference for negative comments. Although traditionally used in marketing research, data mining holds a lot of potential to answer social psychological questions.

Online social networking sites (e.g., MySpace, Facebook) also provide new possibilities for social psychological research. Indeed, analysing social networking behaviour is becoming increasingly popular in social psychology. For example, Buffardi and Campbell (2008) found social networking sites a useful forum in which to study narcissism, finding that narcissism predicts higher levels of social activities online and more self-promoting content (see also DeWall, Buffardi, Bonser and Campbell, 2011). Using social networking sites allows researchers to examine differences between online and offline relationships (e.g., Carpenter, Green and LaFlam, 2011), and even changes in personality and self-views as a function of internet use (Gentile, Twenge, Freeman and Campbell, 2012). At a practical level too, social networking sites allow researchers to recruit participants quickly and easily, although perhaps from a rather limited sample of younger adults.

It is also possible to examine spontaneous behaviour on web discussions that are largely archived, thus opening up a wide range of data for analysis. For example, Bordia and Rosnow (1998) examined the transmission of rumours online by studying posts on an electronic discussion board after a rumour had recently surfaced about the shady behaviour of an IT service provider. The researchers analysed the posts using categories developed from theories of rumour transmission and followed their prevalence over time. Monitoring the development and communication of this rumour online provided the researchers with a novel and unobtrusive way of studying rumour transmission – an area that had traditionally only been possible to study in artificial laboratory settings (Bordia, 1996). Thus, the archival study of rumour transmission provides a good example of how using IT can open up new and realistic ways of examining social phenomena.

Skitka and Sargis (2005) pointed to other ways in which social psychologists have used developments in IT to advance their research. For example, Shohat and Musch (2003) studied discrimination by analysing behaviour on online auctions. They found that sellers with Turkish names (who are a minority group in Germany) took longer to receive winning bids than those who had German names. Also notable is research by Glaser, Dixit and Green (2002), who posted varying 'problems' on white supremacist discussion lists to examine whether participants supported different levels of violence depending on the content of the problem. They found that participants advocated more violence when the researchers posed as someone whose (white) sister was considering getting married to a black man, compared to someone who faced competition for a job from a black man. In the future, the creative use of technological advances will, undoubtedly, allow social psychologists to answer a wide variety of research questions.

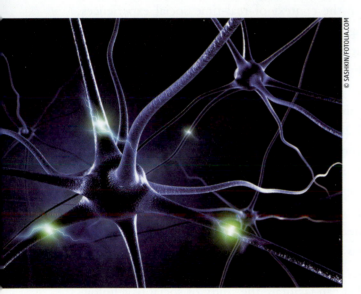

© SASHKIN/FOTOLIA.COM

FIGURE 15.5 New technologies make social neuroscience easier to do, and shape this rapidly growing sub-discipline of social psychology

Transcranial magnetic stimulation Technique that induces weak electric currents in the brain to allow the study of brain function.

Electrocardiography The measure of electrical activity in the heart.

Neuroscience and psychophysiology

As we discussed in Chapter 1, social neuroscience aims to understand how biological systems implement social processes and behaviour. It also uses biological theories, concepts and methods to inform and refine theories of social behaviour and social processes. Developments in psychophysiological and neuroscientific methods and theories have greatly facilitated the study of social neuroscience (see Figure 15.5). For example, functional magnetic resonance imaging (fMRI) measures brain activity by detecting associated changes in blood flow. Recently, this technique has been used broadly in social psychology to study topics such as social exclusion (Eisenberger et al., 2003), knowledge about the self (Kelley, Macrae, Wyland et al., 2002), person perception (Cloutier, Gabrieli, O'Young and Ambady, 2011) and cross-cultural differences in the representations of significant others (Ng, Han, Mao and Lai, 2010), to name but a few examples. **Transcranial magnetic stimulation** induces weak electric currents in the brain using a rapidly changing magnetic field. In doing so, it causes activity in targeted parts of the brain, allowing researchers to study brain function. It has been used in social psychology to study the experience of emotions such as anger and fear (Carver and Harmon-Jones, 2009), responses to emotional pictures (Hajcak, Molnar, George et al., 2007) and the relationship between anger and aggression (Hortensius, Schutter and Harmon-Jones, 2012).

Advances in existing methods, such as **electrocardiography** (measuring electrical activity of the heart), have also allowed advances in social psychology. For example, Vick, Seery, Blascovich and Weisbuch (2008) measured physiological responses to stereotype threat and found that cardiovascular patterns for women in a gender-biased condition reflected a threatened motivational state compared to

Event-related potentials The measure of brain response at the onset of a stimulus.

those in a gender-fair condition. Further, enhanced software associated with the measure of **event-related potentials** has allowed social psychologists to answer specific questions about brain responses as a direct result of specific sensory events, such as distinguishing between automatic and controlled processing of emotional stimuli (Hajcak, MacNamara and Olvet, 2010) and cultural differences in self-construal (Lewis, Goto and Kong, 2008). There are now dedicated journals for the study of social neuroscience (*Social Neuroscience* and *Social Cognitive and Affective Neuroscience*), plus the *Journal of Personality and Social Psychology* published a special issue on social neuroscience in 2003. This is a rapidly emerging field and will continue to be responsive to technological developments.

Nonverbal and co-verbal behaviour

The study of nonverbal behaviour allows social psychologists to rely less and less on self-report data, and to answer a wide variety of research questions. Studying social phenomena via nonverbal behaviour also adds ecological validity, since behaviour is often being studied in the context of real-time social experiences. Technological advances are making this type of research easier and easier. For example, **electromyography** (measuring electrical activity of the muscles), and particularly facial electromyography, is increasingly used in social psychology. In particular, it has been used extensively to study changes in emotional facial expressions as a result of various social stimuli (e.g., Otte, Habel, Schulte-Rüther et al., 2011; Philipp, Storrs and Vanman, 2012). For example, Dimberg, Thunberg and Elmehed (2000) revealed that when people were exposed to emotional facial expressions, they responded with emotional expressions themselves, as measured by changes in muscular activity in emotion-relevant facial muscles. As we know from Chapter 5, people often unconsciously mimic the bodily postures and expressions of others, and using electromyography is a way to measure spontaneous changes in behaviour (see also Foroni and Semin, 2009; Halberstadt, Winkielman, Niedenthal and Dalle, 2009).

Electromyography The measure of electrical activity in the muscles.

Eye tracking The process of measuring either the point of gaze (that is, where a person is looking), or the motion of the eyes relative to the head.

Eye tracking is another method that can facilitate the study of social psychological research questions. This method involves measuring either the point of gaze (that is, where a person is looking), or eye movements relative to the position of the head. An eye tracker is a device used to measure eye movements and eye positions and these are interpreted with the help of computer software. One example of how this technique has been used in social psychology can be seen in the research of Süssenbach, Bohner and Eyssel (in press). They asked participants to read a short text concerning a rape case and then view an apparent police photograph of the plaintiff's living room where the rape allegedly occurred. Their eye movements were measured while they viewed the photograph. Crucially, the photograph contained two cues that are consistent with typical rape myths – one being expected for the situation (wine bottle and glasses), whereas the other was unexpected (a poster of a naked man). Results of one study showed that participants who scored high in a measure of rape myth acceptance (RMA) fixated on the expected cue earlier (and for less time) and took longer to view the unexpected cue. The authors argued that this indicates hypervigilance and greater ease of processing. In other words, for people who endorse rape myths to a greater extent, it is easier to process cues that are consistent with rape myths (e.g., that the victim probably had too much to drink and that rape was therefore unlikely). In a second study, the researchers manipulated participants' levels of RMA, which significantly influenced eye movement patterns for the expected cue. Thus, by using the method of eye tracking, it was possible for the authors to examine how a social phenomenon (RMA) influences visual attention. It should be noted that the processing differences were also responsible for judgements of the plaintiff's blame, indicating that eye movements reflect real social processes.

In a recent study by Callan, Ferguson and Bindeman (in press), participants were asked to listen to auditory scenarios that varied as to whether the characters engaged in morally bad or morally good behaviours. While they engaged in this task, participants' eye movements were tracked around a set of visual scenes depicting positive or negative outcomes. Results revealed that the good behaviour of the characters influenced gaze preference for positive outcomes just prior to the actual outcomes being revealed to the participants. On the other hand, the bad behaviour of the characters influenced gaze preference for negative outcomes. These findings suggest that beliefs about a person's morality encourage observers to anticipate the 'deserved' outcome as the event unfolds. The findings support research demonstrating that people are motivated to maintain the belief that the world is a just place in which good things happen to good people and bad things happen to bad people (Lerner, 1980) (see also Chapter 14). They also comprise another example of eye tracking to study social psychological phenomena.

As it is becoming easier to study nonverbal behaviours through techniques such as electromyography and eye tracking, it is also becoming simpler to study co-verbal behaviours, or behaviours that are associated with speech. You may remember in Chapter 5 that we talked about the concept of vocal pitch and the finding that elevated pitch tends to be associated with lower perceptions of power (Scherer, 1979; for a review, see Krauss and Chiu, 1998; also see the Try it yourself exercise on this topic in Chapter 5). Enhanced measurement and software techniques allow for more objective ways of recording and coding behaviour such as this, which may take the study of social psychology and communication into new and exciting directions. Indeed, the measurement of vocal pitch is increasingly being used in evolutionary psychology examinations of mate choice and mate preference (e.g., O'Connor and Feinberg, 2012; O'Connor, Fraccaro and Feinberg, in press). Interestingly, some research suggests that men can detect ovulation in women based on changes in their vocal pitch (Haselton and Gildersleeve, 2011), so the range of phenomena that may be studied by measuring co-verbal behaviour could be vast. Further, traditional qualitative methodologies that have examined talk in real time can potentially be merged with mainstream social psychological experiments that use these objective measures of behaviour. Overall, the study of nonverbal behaviour and technological advances in this area make for promising research opportunities in social psychology.

Age

The world's population is ageing. In 1950, 8% of the world's population was aged 60 years or older. This figure currently stands at a little over 10%, but by 2050 is forecast to reach 21%. By then, older people (60+) will outnumber children and younger adolescents (under 16) for the first time in human history (UN, 2001). In developed economies such as in Europe, North America, East Asia and Australasia, the trends are even starker. In the UK, for example, there are currently 10.3 million people aged over 65, representing some 15% of the total population and an 80% increase since 1951. This number is predicted to increase to 12.7 million in 2018, and by 2035, it is estimated there will be 4 million people more aged over 65 than under 16 (Rutherford, 2012).

This fact raises several challenges and opportunities for social psychologists. The study of social psychological processes related to ageing will become increasingly important. One important process is prejudice and discrimination against older adults, or ageism, which we considered in Chapter 11. Ageism appears to be the most widespread form of discrimination in Europe (Age UK, 2011), yet is rated as more socially acceptable than other forms of prejudice and discrimination such as sexism, racism and homophobia (Abrams, Eilola and Swift, 2009). It is a particularly ironic form of prejudice since most young people aspire to live to a ripe old age. Adding to this irony, stereotypically associating age with infirmity and poor memory can become self-fulfilling, increasing the risk of heart attacks and strokes (Levy et al., 2009), and cognitive deficits (Swift, Abrams and Marques, in press). Intervening to reduce ageism, by innovative extensions of techniques we described in Chapter 12, is an important challenge. This may occur in the context of increasing resentment of older adults by the working-age population, which increasingly may feel that it is subsidizing their pensions and healthcare. Other problems associated with ageing including social exclusion and loneliness (Victor, Scambler, Bowling and Bond, 2005).

Ageing is not only associated with negative outcomes, however. On average, older people experience more positive affect and are less egocentric than younger people. Rather than being pathologized, a more balanced picture of ageing may reveal opportunities for older adults, and society, to exploit the benefits that it brings. The older population can be viewed as a resource as well as a burden.

Exploring further Using the internet, can you find examples of other social psychological processes and outcomes that may occur with increasing frequency as the population of your country, and the entire world, ages?

Culture

As globalization and technology afford new levels of contact between cultures, there is an increasing need to understand how relations between people are affected by cultural differences, and how valuable aspects of culture can be preserved. The increasing frequency of contact is not only a challenge, but also an opportunity. Recent work highlights the benefits of exposure to cultural diversity;

it can make people more creative, tolerant and productive (Crisp and Meleady, 2012; Crisp and Turner, 2011).

Intercultural contact has other benefits. The accumulated cultural wisdom of one people can be adapted fruitfully by people from other cultures. This has happened in the case of the custom of *restorative justice* found among New Zealand Māori and some other indigenous cultures (Maxwell and Morris, 2006; Sullivan and Tifft, 2006). Rather than focusing principally on punishing people for their transgressions, with retribution and deterrence in mind, restorative justice brings offenders and their victims together with other vested members of their community. The focus is on dialogue, apology and mutual understanding, which often includes some element of forgiveness (Braithwaite, 2002; Peachey, 1989; Roche, 2003; Wenzel, Okimoto, Feather and Platow, 2008). Some agreed punishment is often a feature of restorative justice, but its main aim is to repair and reinforce the moral norms of the community (Okimoto and Wenzel, 2009). Informal practices of restorative justice – meeting, dialogue, apology, forgiveness – are common to everyday life across cultures (e.g., Wenzel and Okimoto, 2010). However, as part of a formal justice system, restorative justice is a recent innovation or remains absent from many countries. The concept was tried out in New Zealand in the context of youth justice in order to make the justice system more culturally sensitive (Morris, 2002). Its practices, such as conferences between the families of victims and offenders, have been exported from the shores of New Zealand in large part because social psychologists and social scientists stood up and paid attention to it. Their research accumulated to show that the practice has many benefits, and so it has gradually been incorporated around the world (Latimer, Dowden and Muise, 2005; van Ness and Heetderks Strong, 2010). Attention to cultural practices has enriched theorizing about justice in social psychology and, in so doing, has translated into real-world applications.

Although we have seen the existence of many cultural universals in social psychological practices, there are also many differences that tend not to be emphasized in social psychology. An entire field of study, cross-cultural psychology, is interested in charting some of these specific differences. Also, psychologists are interested in identifying the deeper, underlying dimensions on which cultures differ. This means that many cultural differences are organized and explained by variables that are universal to human beings. One of these is individualism and collectivism, which we encountered in Chapter 2: some cultures are more oriented to individuals and their qualities, rights and achievements, whereas some emphasize the interests of the collective and the responsibilities of individuals (Markus and Kitayama, 1991; Triandis, 1995). Another is an analytic versus holistic cognitive style: Western European cultures tend to promote a focus on specific objects or features of interests in a stimulus field, whereas other cultures promote attention to the whole stimulus field and the relationships between them. As we saw in Chapter 13, cultures also differ in the extent to which the honour of families and individuals is valued (Nisbett and Cohen, 1996), how religious they are and how hierarchical they are (Jeffries, Hornsey, Sutton et al.,

2012; Shavitt, Torelli and Riemer, 2010). These cultural differences mean that some of the most well-known effects in social psychology, such as the hindsight bias and the fundamental attribution error (see Chapter 3), are not to be found in many of the world's cultures (Nisbett, Peng, Choi and Norenzayan, 2001).

Exploring further Access the table of contents of the leading specialist journal, the *Journal of Cross-Cultural Psychology*. Sample the titles and abstracts of a few issues. What trends do you notice? For example, which cultures are most often compared?

Research on culture is not only gathering momentum but is taking new perspectives. One new perspective is *indigenous social psychology*. Overlapping with anthropology, this variety of social psychology puts culture at the forefront of investigation. It is interested in investigating cultural practices and concepts that are not acknowledged by mainstream social psychology. It implies that not only the content but the methodology of social psychology may need to be modified or reinvented to make investigations pertinent to particular cultures (Adair, 2005; Moghaddam, 1987; D. Sinha, 1984, 1997; J. Sinha, 1984). Another newer perspective on culture is to examine not how culture shapes, but how it is shaped by, everyday thoughts, feelings, behaviours and relationships. Over time, for example, the gossip and stories we exchange in everyday life shape and strengthen stereotypes and shared understandings of right and wrong (Boyd and Richerson, 1985; Kashima, 2000; Schaller and Crandall, 2004). Culture depends on everyday enactment and renewal, and on transmission between generations, and in this sense is constantly being produced and reproduced. Further, recent research suggests that daily exposure to specific cultural practices also causes culture to become hard-wired into the brain. So, for example, there are identifiable brain differences between those immersed in independent (individualistic) as opposed to interdependent (collectivist) cultures (Kitayama and Uskul, 2011).

Social psychology and you

We have already described some of the main points of wisdom that arise from the study of social psychology. More generally, however, the study of social psychology has the potential to change you, as a person. It may even change you for the better, even if you are not aware of the changes. In this section, we outline some of the main skills and attributes you can expect to have acquired, and should consider acquiring, as you study social psychology. Specifically, we outline some of the transferable skills you will be able to take with you into your careers. More generally, we talk about career prospects for students of social psychology.

Critical thinking skills

One of the major differences between social psychology as opposed to, say, cell division, organic chemistry or particle physics is that people with no training in the discipline have a rich array of knowledge, beliefs and investments in its subject matter. There are far fewer discussions in taxis and family gatherings about RNA, oxalic acid and gluons than there are about social influence (e.g., celebrity culture, peer pressure), intergroup processes (e.g., racism, gender roles), justice and relationships. We touched on this at the beginning of Chapter 1, when we discussed the popular debate about the causes of riots and social disorder. All sorts of people have an opinion and are often prepared to voice them in strong and unqualified terms, despite their lack of professional or scientific expertise.

In short, people think they know a lot about the things that social psychologists study; and, in many respects, they do. Years of personal experience, millennia of culture, and perhaps the biological inheritance of specific social skills and understandings equip us with a rich knowledge about minds, relationships and social systems that allow us to navigate through social life (Fletcher, 1995; Malle, 2005, 2008). This knowledge, however, has important limitations. As we have seen time and time again, people are often completely unaware of the situational forces and the psychological processes that influence them (Chapter 3). People overestimate the significance of personality variables and attitudes in shaping behaviour. They are surprisingly unable to predict their own emotional reactions to life events or the behaviour of others.

One of the reasons that laypeople's beliefs about social psychology can be so limited and wrong is that they are not informed by research findings. Theories in the discipline of social psychology are informed and constrained by systematically obtained and evaluated evidence in ways that the theories of laypeople are not. As you know well by now, social psychological research has thrown up a lot of surprising findings. Recall Milgram's (1961) observation of striking levels of compliance with instructions to deliver apparently excruciating, dangerous and even lethal doses of electricity to an innocent stranger (Chapter 9). Roughly two-thirds of participants went all the way, flatly contradicting the intuition – even social scientists' intuition – that only a tiny minority of people would do this (Milgram, 1965). These results not only falsify specific intuitions about what people would do in a particular experimental task. They also pose an immense challenge to general notions about the resistance of the individual to obedience, the power of norms, values and attitudes to constrain behaviour, and, ultimately, the view that the perpetrators of group-based atrocities must have been exceptionally evil people. Of course, we saw in Chapter 9 that there has been considerable and renewed debate about exactly what these findings mean. Nonetheless, they have profoundly transformed social psychological theorizing about human nature and the specific causes of human behaviour.

Finally, as we have seen, laypeople's claims about what people do, and why they do it, are often motivated. To some extent, people believe what they want to believe, as we saw in our coverage of the concept of *motivated social cognition* in Chapter 3 (but also see in almost every other chapter in the book). People tend to believe claims that support their own self-image (Chapter 2), the superiority of their ingroup (Chapter 11) and their preferred ideological position, which often entails the perpetuation of the social status quo (Chapter 14). Finally, of course, people (often on behalf of the companies, governments or other vested interests they represent) make claims about social and psychological phenomena they do not necessarily believe, because they are trying to influence you (Chapter 6).

Therefore, before accepting any claim about human behaviour, you should evaluate it carefully. Claims of fact, and explanations of fact, should be clear, unambiguous and testable. Before accepting them, you should consider whether they are supported by evidence and logic. These criteria are seldom met in everyday discussions about relationships, motivations, social problems, or anything else impinging on social psychology. If you hold on to what you have learned in the study of this discipline, and recall some of the key messages of social psychology reviewed in this chapter, you are well equipped to be an informed sceptic, applying new levels of critical thinking skills to your everyday and professional life. Learning to think critically in one domain, such as social psychology, will help you think critically in all areas of your life (Sá, West and Stanovich, 1999).

While you continue to pursue academic study, you will also encounter overblown, unsupported and illogical claims. Academic ideas are sometimes marketed with terminology that is greatly out of step with the evidence that supports them. Recall, for example, the 'warrior gene' hypothesis encountered in Chapter 13. To have the 'warrior gene' is not to be consigned by one's DNA to a life of violence, but is to be one of 34 per cent of ethnically Caucasian people. Academic claims are usually much less silly than this, but there is almost always room for critical doubt about whether claims hold up in the light of evidence, and whether evidence is not subject to alternative interpretations. In the Critical focus boxes of each chapter, we have encountered theoretical claims that are open to question. For example, in Chapter 5, we critically examined whether facial expressions are culturally determined, having evolved over the millennia, while in Chapter 8, we did much the same thing for gender roles. In Chapter 9, we critically evaluated the long-accepted hypothesis that the presence of other people inhibits the tendency of the individual to help a victim.

If someone says that contact benefits intergroup relations (Chapter 12), ask, is this based on correlational or experimental evidence? A negative correlation between contact and prejudice proves little, because very often, people who are less prejudiced towards an outgroup are less averse to contact with it. Thus, more contact does not necessarily mean less prejudice. Experiments in which people are found to have lower prejudice after contact with the outgroup than a control group who have not had the contact provide much stronger evidence of causality. But even then, manipulations of contact in these experiments may not be realistic models of contact in everyday life (see Figure 15.6). The dependent measures in these experiments may omit or misrepresent the effect that contact has in natural settings.

As these examples suggest, there are many reasons to question what we read and hear about in social psychology.

FIGURE 15.6 Contact benefits intergroup relations Research associated with the contact hypothesis demonstrates that people become less prejudiced if they have contact with the outgroup. The study of social psychology encourages students to think critically about such findings and the studies from which they were found. Ultimately, you can decide for yourself, based on the evidence and arguments, if contact really makes a difference to prejudice and intergroup relations more generally. Sometimes, essay questions will ask you to critically evaluate research in an area such as this, so it is always good to think critically about everything you learn.

© ISTOCK

Even the most rigorously designed experiments cannot, and should not, escape scholarly enquiry and scrutiny. As a student of social psychology, you are therefore encouraged to evaluate what you learn critically, take it apart (argument, findings, interpretations and conclusions), and critically appraise everything you learn. In doing so, you will have a clearer picture of a research topic and will take an important skill with you into the next phase of your lives.

Critical thinking is often a difficult concept to define, but it embraces the ability and willingness to *analyse* arguments or evidence (break them down into parts, to categorize them), *synthesize* them (to incorporate multiple pieces of evidence into one argument, or to put together aspects of different arguments), and *evaluate* them (to determine whether arguments are logical, and evidence is sound) (Moseley, Elliott, Gregson and Higgins, 2005). Griggs, Jackson, Marek and Christopher (1998, p. 256), after reviewing many definitions of critical thinking, describe it in these terms:

> a process of evaluating evidence for certain claims, determining whether presented conclusions logically follow from this evidence, and considering alternative explanations. Critical thinkers exhibit open-mindedness, tolerance of ambiguity; and a sceptical, questioning attitude.

Time to reflect It is interesting that critical thinking is often defined in terms that incorporate some of the social psychological constructs we have encountered in this book, including open vs. closed-mindedness and tolerance of ambiguity (Chapters 4 and 11 respectively). This illustrates how the study of social psychology is reactive – ideas from social psychology percolate into other disciplines, such as education, and ultimately into public consciousness. Strikingly, although these constructs are not inherently political, they have political implications in practice. As we saw in the Social psychology in the real world box in Chapter 4, people who are closed-minded tend to be more right-wing. So, let us consider a controversial question. Could this explain why professional social scientists tend to be left-wing, rather than right-wing (Cardiff and Klein, 2005; Klein and Stern, 2005; Tierney, 2011)? And can it explain why left-wing social scientists tend to win promotion more quickly than right-wing social scientists (Rothman, Lichter and Nevitte, 2005)? What we mean is that the predominance (and pre-eminence) of left/liberal academics may stem from an association between their political orientation and an open-minded, integrative thinking style that is likely to lend itself to successful research.

We think a crucial element of critical thinking is also *informed* thinking – the ability not just to do things with information, but to find information (Halpern, 1998). This is why we have included so many exercises in this textbook that require you to find information for yourself – including academic papers but also all sorts of other information. In your critical thinking about issues touching on social psychology, it is always useful to bear some of its key messages in mind. For example, considering what the evidence is for a claim, since claims about human behaviour, emotion and society should be testable and can be tested, is crucial. Looking past the surface differences between people and groups is also crucial, and considering critically what social and mental processes might produce them is important too. In a much-cited paper on critical thinking, Halpern (1998) also suggests some practical techniques for enhancing your critical thinking skills as a student:

1 *Draw a diagram or other graphic display that organizes the information:* This can make the structure of a problem or argument clear.

2 *Ask: 'What additional information do I need before answering the question?':* Sometimes, you need further information to interpret the question (e.g., to read about the theory you are being asked to evaluate), but you always need to locate the information that will enable you to begin answering.

3 *State the problem you are trying to solve (e.g., an essay question) in at least two ways:* A lot of essay questions, and especially a lot of interesting and important real-world problems, are rather open-ended. Seeing the problem from different perspectives, and being able to find ways to narrow it down, is an essential part of critical thinking (Buunk and van Vugt, 2008).

4 *Ask which information is most important, and which is least important:* This focuses your mind on the value of different sorts of information, such as research findings versus anecdotes.

5 *Categorize research findings in a meaningful way:* Grouping findings together or labelling them will often help you notice underlying similarities and differences.

6 *List two solutions for a problem. Present two arguments that support a conclusion and two that do not support a conclusion:* Halpern's (1998) suggestion is that you should entertain both sides of an argument. This may lead you to adopt some new, third position, because you can see the limitations of both sides. Even if you come down clearly on one side of an argument, you will be in a much better position to defend your preferred side from counterarguments and apparently contradictory evidence. In Chapter 14, we saw an excellent example of this from Manning, Levine and Collins (2007). Applying Billig's (1996) dialectic approach to knowledge, they suggest that a useful approach to social psychology is that any given argument 'should be haunted by the possibility (at least) of the opposite'. This is an excellent basis for critical thinking, especially about theory, in social psychology. It encourages you to think about how the results of a study could have been completely different if something about the context, the independent variables or the dependent variables were different.

7 *Ask what two actions would you take to improve the design of a study that was described:* As we have seen in this chapter, sampling characteristics can be an important source of bias in studies. But, equally, in our experience, students sometimes focus too much on the sample when critically evaluating studies, or on the fact that a study was done in the laboratory, at the expense of other important characteristics of a study. In particular, as we saw in Chapter 1, it is always important to consider whether the manipulations and measures of experiments really reflect the variables they are supposed to represent. Might something other than the intended variables be reflected in the scores? One example of this is the confound in twin studies, intended to study the effects of genetic similarity on ideologies or behaviour (e.g., Chapter 4 on the apparent heritability of ideology, and Chapter 13 on the apparent heritability of aggression). The confound is that genetic similarity is associated with environmental similarity: people who look identical and are equally physically attractive, for example, are treated more similarly.

Exploring further As part of your social psychology training, you will be invited to work on your critical thinking skills. You will learn to read research articles and book chapters, and critically evaluate the claims being made. As you read social psychology material, you will notice different styles of writing and different ways of making claims. For example, some sources report empirical findings and the authors make claims based on the objective data they have collected. Others write book chapters, which are partly based on research data while some of the claims are made from extrapolating from data and/or are formed from personal opinions and experiences. As a student of social psychology, it is important to be able to separate fact from interpretations, which can be subject to bias. To help you understand this process, read two to three different newspaper reports on the same topic (e.g., an event such as the 9/11 attacks on the World Trade Center or the 2011 UK riots). Identify the factual claims made in the articles. After you have done this, identify the claims that are based not on facts but on interpretation or personal opinion. What can you conclude from these articles? Are the articles significantly different from each other and which one do you believe holds the most weight? How do factors such as the credibility of the source also influence your judgement?

Psychological literacy

Psychological literacy A set of skills including critical thinking, ethics and social responsibility.

The study of social psychology equips the learner with what is known broadly as **psychological literacy**. According to McGovern, Corey and Cranney et al. (2010, p. 10), psychologically literate citizens are 'critical scientific thinkers and ethical and socially responsible participants in their communities'. Thus, critical thinking is a key aspect of psychological literacy. Other aspects of psychological literacy are presented in Table 15.1 (see also Cranney and Dunn, 2011). Although we will not cover all these in this chapter, we will draw out some key examples and highlight their relevance to social psychology.

Technological, research and statistical skills

Throughout your studies, you will (if you have not already) become familiar with some more advanced IT skills. Your work will be produced via word processing and spreadsheets, much of your literature search will be conducted through academic search engines and databases, you may develop research materials using online questionnaire software or crowdsourcing techniques, and you will analyse data using statistical software packages. You will learn to retrieve relevant information for your essays and reports and handle the information critically (see above). You will learn to solve complex problems. Further, you will learn a wide range of data collection techniques, both qualitative and quantitative, as described in Chapter 1, as well as a broad range of data analytic techniques. You will learn to understand, analyse and present complex data effectively.

TABLE 15.1 Aspects of psychological literacy

Having a well-defined vocabulary and basic knowledge of the critical subject matter of psychology
Valuing the intellectual challenges required to use scientific thinking and the disciplined analysis of information to evaluate alternative courses of action
Taking a creative and amiable sceptic approach to problem solving
Applying psychological principles to personal, social and organizational issues in work, relationships and the broader community
Acting ethically
Being competent in using and evaluating information and technology
Communicating effectively in different modes and with many different audiences
Recognizing, understanding and fostering respect for diversity
Being insightful and reflective about one's own and others' behaviour and mental processes

Source: McGovern et al., 2010, p. 11

Exploring further Social psychologists use a range of methods and data analytical techniques. The next time you read a social psychology paper, pay special attention to the research method they used and how they analysed their data. Could they have conducted their investigation differently?

Understanding diversity

Studying social psychology will equip you with a strong understanding of the issues raised by increasing social and cultural diversity in modern societies. It will help you understand the processes that have shaped modern societies and the diversity issues (e.g., immigration and multiculturalism) they are currently facing. It will equip you with a broad understanding of intergroup relations, which, in understanding diversity, involves studying what happens when people migrate from one place to another, how they adapt or acculturate, and how 'host' cultures are influenced by their presence. You will have a solid understanding of how inequality and prejudice work. Thus, the study of social psychology will give you a practical understanding of diversity issues as they exist where you live.

Connection between science and wider social and policy debates

Much of social psychology relates to real-life questions and problems. For example, how do we explain and reduce prejudice? Why do people deny the existence of climate change? In examining questions such as these that have wide implications for society, social psychologists have the opportunity to inform policy. Indeed, there are many cases where social psychological findings have directly informed public policy. For example, Carol Dweck's research on how children respond to feedback in educational settings has brought about changes in the way children are taught to think about their own intelligence and abilities. Specifically, this work has helped practitioners understand what kinds of praise and criticism help students to stay motivated and focus on their learning. Her intervention – the 'Brainology' program – has been implemented widely across the USA in an effort to promote children's motivation and achievement (see the Social psychology in the real world box in Chapter 1). Further, in 2007 a team of UK and European social psychologists led by Greg Maio worked with the UK government to tackle obesity and inform interventions for people to make lifestyle changes. These are only two examples of the many ways that social psychologists contribute their expertise to important social issues.

SOCIAL PSYCHOLOGY IN THE REAL WORLD

Nudge theory

In July 2010, the British government established a Behavioural Insights Team to 'find intelligent ways to encourage, support and enable people to make better choices for themselves' (Cabinet Office, 2012, p. 3). The idea behind the initiative is to bring about significant changes in society (e.g., increased organ donation, environmental consciousness and healthier eating) by applying insights from behavioural science – and, to a large extent, social psychology – to influence people's behaviour in inexpensive, non-coercive ways. This initiative is influenced by 'nudge theory', which was advanced by Thaler and Sunstein (2008) in a popular book. Nudge theory may not qualify as a 'theory' in the normal social psychological sense of the word. For example, it does not put forward a unique set of psychological processes to explain social behaviour. Neither does it generate a unique set of predictions that allow it to be tested. Nonetheless, it is an interesting collection of ideas about how to apply the lessons of social psychology and other approaches to human behaviour.

Nudge theory builds on several of the central insights of social psychological research; for example, that much of behaviour is shaped by unconscious processes and does not live up to commonly understood standards of rationality. Thaler and Sunstein (2008) point out that governments typically attempt to influence behaviour by coercing people, via laws and regulations, or else by appealing to rationality. For example, tax agencies point out that dire consequences will follow if people do not file their tax returns, and health agencies highlight the consequences of overeating. The central idea of nudge theory is that these interventions have limited impact precisely because deliberative, conscious thinking is not the only shaper of our behaviour, and that unconscious, reflexive psychological processes are often equally or more powerful (see Chapters 3 and 4). Thus, small behavioural interventions or 'nudges' might elicit the kinds of behavioural changes that governments have been struggling to achieve.

In 2012, the UK government published the results of several randomized experimental trials to test some ideas based on this broad, 'nudge' perspective on behaviour change. The results are generally promising, although they have not yet been subjected to peer review and published in academic journals, and several were 'interim' results. In one trial, a letter to taxpayers sent by HMRC, the UK government tax office, was experimentally manipulated. Taxpayers received either a traditional letter, in the control group, or messages in which social norms (see Chapter 5) were highlighted. Specifically, the letter said that '9 out of 10 people in Britain pay their tax on time'. Additional variants of the letter stated that most people in the taxpayer's postcode, or town, had already paid. These letters had the desired effect, increasing the extent to which people paid tax – from 67.5 per cent in the control group to 83 per cent in the most successful experimental group.

As an approach to social policy, this has several strengths. It is evidence based, using experimental methodology to test the success of interventions. It takes account of research and theory in social psychology, rather than relying on the intuitions of government staff or consultants. However, it is not without its problems and controversies. These are laid out in some detail in a report

commissioned by the UK Parliament (House of Lords Science and Technology Select Committee, 2011). This involved interviews with more than 80 witnesses from academia and the civil service, including noted social psychologists such as Gregory Maio and Geoff Haddock (whose work you will find cited in this book). The gist of many of the criticisms is that 'nudging' people is unlikely to work on its own. Social problems are not just attributable to individual behaviour. Obesity is a case in point. Although 'nudge' interventions focus on simplifying the communication of dietary information, or placing fatty foods in less obvious places in school tuck shops, obesity is an endemic problem in Western societies, caused not just by bad decision making by individuals, but by the convenience of public transport, long working hours and food production (e.g., Roberts and Edwards, 2010; Swinburn et al., 2011). Too much focus on 'nudging' individuals is likely to have little effect in the light of these larger forces, and may indeed mislead people as to the causes of obesity.

Another problem is although people are far from perfectly rational, or perfectly conscious, important life decisions and long-lasting behaviour changes are often accompanied by systematic conscious thought. Witness, for example, the importance of chronic egalitarian motivations in reducing prejudice that we saw in Chapter 12. Actively trying not to be prejudiced, over the long run, appears to be effective. Also consider how long-term persuasion often requires the systematic presentation of logic and evidence, in the so-called 'central route to persuasion'. In contrast, short-term, one-shot interventions such as nudges may not be enough to induce lasting change. Still, on balance, it seems to us that in conjunction with regulations and other tools of social policy, a focus on properly evaluated, carefully designed behavioural interventions such as 'nudges' have a promising role to play.

Questions

1 You can download the Cabinet Office's report on trials of nudge theory at: http://www.cabinetoffice.gov.uk/sites/default/files/resources/BIT_FraudErrorDebt_accessible.pdf. It is an interesting read for students of social psychology who are interested in how its insights are being applied by governments. Some results appear to be quite promising, but many do not seem to support the starting assumptions of the

researchers, and show that 'nudges' designed with social psychological principles in mind do not always work. You should read it with a critical mindset, both in terms of whether the results support the claims being made and whether the interventions are being tested with appropriate methodologies.

2 Take a close look, for example, at the methodology employed in Trial 6. Looking at the results displayed in the graph, does the trial appear to have been a success? Looking at the results, what are the experimental conditions in this trial? How many changes do there seem to be in the letters, between conditions? If there is more than one change between any two conditions, then there is a confound, and it is impossible to determine exactly why results are different – or the same – between the two conditions.

3 We can see trials like these as applications of social psychology. However, we can also see them as extensions of social psychology, in that they add to what we know about people's social cognition, attitudes, emotions and behaviours. Assuming trials like this are well conducted, what specifically might they offer to social psychology?

Try it yourself Imagine that you are an employer and you have recently moved your staff to a new office. Your employees have a habit of eating lunch at their desks, which makes the office messy. You would rather they didn't do this in the new office. You are trying to work out how best to make this request of your employees. Write down a list of things you might say or do. Which are the most likely to succeed? Why?

Exploring further Research 'impact' is becoming increasingly important in academia. Governments, who typically fund academic research, need to know that their funds are being used for research that makes a difference in some way. This is not to say that non-applied (basic) research has less value. Of course it does and the insights gained from basic social psychological research continue to increase our knowledge of many facets of human social processes. This is called 'academic impact'. However, as we have discussed throughout this chapter, social psychology can make a difference to society in many ways too. As an exercise to help you appreciate this contribution more, take some time to look for examples of social psychological impact on social policy. Think of a topic (e.g., prejudice, persuasion, healthy eating, climate change, any issue you can think of) and spend some time researching social psychologists' social or policy impact on these topics.

Social psychological findings are also frequently reported in the media and contribute to debates about prominent social issues. If you conduct an internet search on the names of prominent social psychologists, it is very likely that you will come across media reports highlighting and debating their findings. For example, several social psychologists commented on the UK riots in 2011, talking about topics such as crowd behaviour, aggression and gang violence (Reicher and Stott, 2011). Others have contributed to the public debate on climate change, and social psychologists frequently offer their expertise on public debates related to prejudice and persuasion and other topics such as domestic violence. A great deal of social psychological research deals with issues that are relevant to people's everyday lives and so it has great potential to engage the public with science and scientific findings.

© PHOTOALTO

FIGURE 15.7 Media reporting of social psychologists' research Social psychologists deal with a range of topical subjects and, as such, their research is frequently reported in the media

Communication skills

Studying social psychology provides students with an opportunity to develop communication skills. Effective communication involves developing a clear, logical argument that is supported by relevant evidence and written in an appropriate style for its audience. Throughout your degree, you will have the opportunity to develop these skills through experiences such as making oral presentations to groups. However, for the most part, social psychology work involves writing. Your studies will therefore enable you to develop your written communication skills. By the end of your degree, you should be able to present an argument effectively. Of course, some people write more fluently than others, but if you write carefully and deliberately, the quality of your ideas should be evident. Write simply and to the best of your ability, drafting your work in advance. When writing, use empathy – put yourself in your reader's perspective. Consider who your audience is and what does, and does not, need to be explained to them. Crucially, always write to the brief – carefully read and listen to any instructions on your written assignments you are given. Read the assignment carefully and ensure you are answering the question that has been set. Respect the due dates, word lengths, and formatting and submission requirements absolutely. If some instruction by your tutor seems to contradict anything we have written here, follow your tutor's instruction.

Of interest, social psychologist Michael Billig (2011) has identified several pitfalls that are encountered in social psychological writing. In particular, he critiques writing in social psychological journals and undergraduates alike. He offers the following advice:

1 Try to use simple language and to avoid technical terms as much as possible. Sometimes, technical terms are not as clear as the ordinary ones and it is often more difficult to write without jargon. But it is much easier to read writing that is free of (unnecessary) jargon. Interestingly, Billig recommends that we should not become 'personally attached to technical terms' (p. 18). As instructors, we often find that students overuse technical language in their essays. Instructors understand the pressure students feel to demonstrate that they have mastered technical terms. However, we are generally much more impressed by clear writing, sound logic, good use of evidence and critical thinking than we are by the use of terminology. We feed back to students that they overused terminology and elevated language more often than we comment that their language was too simple and did not employ enough terminology.

2 Avoid writing in passive sentences where possible. Writing 'It was found … (Manning et al., 2007)' is much less clear and efficient than writing 'Manning et al. (2007) found …'.

3 Treat these recommendations as aspirations rather than rigid rules. Sometimes, at a key point in your work, it may be necessary to break one of these rules. There may be an area of literature that is so riddled with terminology, for example, that it is all but impossible to avoid it. Still, you should avoid producing long tracts of writing that break these rules.

Billig (2011, p. 14) highlights a couple of adjacent sentences from a recent article to illustrate his points. The first sentence reads:

> Whereas intergroup anxiety is by now an established mediator of intergroup contact and cross-group friendship, the present study also sought to explore cognitions of rejection as a cognitive mediator predicted by cross-group friendship, and predictive of intergroup anxiety, as well as a range of attitudes towards the outgroup.

This is the second sentence:

> Specifically, we propose that people with cross-group friends cease to expect outgroup members to reject their attempts at contact and friendship.

The second sentence is not only shorter and crisper but is also written, as Billig (2011, p. 14) puts it, 'in terms of people and what they might do and feel'. It is relatively free of jargon, and is much clearer in its use of active voice, clearly establishing who is doing what. Mastering the art of simple, accurate writing will allow you to communicate complex ideas to a range of audiences, and is a valuable skill, no matter what career you choose.

Research projects

As an undergraduate student in psychology, you will probably be required to undertake a research project as part of your degree. Throughout this book, we have highlighted some projects that students have done over the course of their studies, comprising a range of projects across social psychology. We hope that this has made the prospect of conducting your own research less daunting. All these students – just like you – had to start somewhere. Here, we would like to offer some small pieces of advice in conducting your own undergraduate projects. Also, in the Some further reading section, we have cited a book that may help you with your project.

First, it is advisable to be realistic about the amount of work you can achieve in your project. Some of you will be required to work for a year on a project. Some will have more time and some will have less time. Some students will be permitted to work with other students and others will be required to work alone. Be mindful of the requirements of your specific institution and, when in doubt, take the advice of your supervisor. In meetings with your supervisor, be professional, punctual and polite. Likewise, observe professional standards when dealing with research participants. Do not attempt to influence your participants. It is crucial that you adhere to the ethical guidelines of your institution or professional association (e.g., British Psychological Society). Be scrupulous and thorough in this respect (see Chapter 1).

When deciding on a topic and designing your research, apply critical reasoning skills and spend a good amount of time researching the relevant literature. We strongly advise that you aim to be incremental; that is, look for one new piece of knowledge in your research rather than trying to invent a whole new research area for yourself. Novelty is key, but do not leave yourself stranded in an entirely new research area with no literature from which to draw upon. Likewise, you should introduce methodological innovation only where necessary. This means using manipulations and measures devised by other researchers where possible. This will save time and avoid mistakes, and you will find it easier to interpret your findings if you adapt others' procedures and materials. It is important that you plan your time carefully to avoid any pitfalls associated with conducting research. It is also important that you design your project mindful of how you plan to analyse the results.

Having given all these words of caution, it is important that you also be curious and open-minded. Typically, marks on project work are awarded according to the quality of your research, your professionalism in running it, and the quality of your write-up, not your results. So, do not be disappointed if your project produces non-significant findings. This is very common for student projects and does not mean that you will receive a low mark.

Time to reflect It is never too early to start thinking about your research project. Conducting an undergraduate project is an opportunity for you to conduct a unique investigation into a topic that interests you. Now that you have a broad knowledge of social psychology, perhaps have a go at generating some ideas for a research project. The first step is to think of a general topic. To do this, take some time to list the topics in social psychology that interest you the most. Then, narrow this down to a specific research area. For example, if you are interested in prejudice, what type of prejudice is most interesting to you (e.g., race, gender, sexuality)? Are you interested in understanding prejudice or reducing prejudice? Once you have got this far, it is time to think of some potential questions you might ask. Do you notice any gaps in the literature? For example, what can social psychological research tell us about reducing prejudice and what can it not tell us yet? This is where you begin to generate your unique research question. The steps that follow involve deciding on what you will do, what you will predict, and what you will be able to conclude based on your investigation. This may seem a daunting task but broken down into a series of smaller steps, it need not be a scary process. Again, this is a unique opportunity for you to make your mark on a research topic, so enjoy it. For other information and advice on conducting your research project, do read the Student projects at the end of Chapters 1–14.

Careers and employability

It is widely known that many psychology graduates do not seek employment as professional psychologists. Specifically, it was recently noted that 80 per cent of psychology graduates in the UK are employed in other types of careers (QAA, 2010). Of course, professional bodies in many countries, such as the British Psychological Society, need to ensure that degrees adhere to the topics and standards that would allow graduates to ultimately become professional psychologists. However, the Quality Assurance Agency psychology benchmark in the UK stresses that 'due to the wide range of generic skills, and the rigour with which they are taught, training in psychology is widely accepted as providing an excellent preparation for many careers' (QAA, 2010, p. 2). Specifically, because psychology graduates develop so many different kinds of transferable skills, as we discussed earlier (e.g., computer literacy, numeracy, teamwork, critical thinking), they are viewed as highly desirable employees (Trapp, Banister, Ellis et al., 2011).

Whether you are planning a career in psychology or elsewhere, or whether you are not consciously planning one, it is worth reflecting on the skills and attributes that will help open doors for you later in life. Landrum and Harrold (2003) report that employers of psychology graduates rated the following attributes as most important (1 = most important):

1 listening skills
2 teamwork skills
3 ability to get along with others
4 wanting and being able to learn
5 in particular, being willing to learn new and important skills
6 having a focus on customers or clients
7 strong interpersonal relationship skills
8 being adaptable to changing situations
9 having the ability to suggest solutions to problems
10 being able to implement solutions to problems.

Time to reflect Think about Landrum and Harrold's (2003) list of attributes desired by employers and the key points of psychological literacy we identified earlier in the chapter. How do these relate to each other?

Obtaining a university degree does not guarantee that you will have the attributes that will set you up in a career. Employers in the USA took a rather dim view of university graduates, according to one survey (AACandU, cited in Trapp et al., 2011). Specifically, employers rated:

- 33% of graduates as having insufficient skills and knowledge to succeed in relatively basic or 'entry-level' positions
- 42% as lacking self-direction
- 37% as having poor writing skills
- 31% as lacking critical thinking skills
- 30% as lacking adaptability
- 26% as lacking the ability to accurately appraise their strengths and weaknesses.

It is useful to consider this list of concerns together with Landrum and Harrold's list of qualities that employers are looking for in psychology graduates. Looking at these two lists, you can develop a clear picture of the qualities you might want to develop in the course of your studies. Critical thinking and social skills, including the ability to communicate effectively in different ways to different audiences, are crucial. How can you develop these skills? Some methods are very traditional. Attend available classes, listen to lectures in order to develop your ability to listen to others and to speak effectively. Take available opportunities to work in teams, and do so with enthusiasm and diplomacy. Be critical and curious. Read widely, both to increase your knowledge and also to enhance your writing skills. The more you encounter how others express complex psychological concepts in writing, the easier you will find it to do the same. The take-home message here is that a degree in psychology – of which social psychology plays a crucial part – gives students the opportunity to develop a range of skills that will equip them to succeed in a broad variety of careers.

Chapter summary

In this chapter, we have invited you to reflect on everything you have learned throughout reading this book. What are the key insights of social psychology? What concepts, skills and ideas can you take forward into your careers? We argued that there are several take-home principles or messages of social psychology:

- Despite much popular thinking, social psychology can be studied scientifically. Common misunderstandings about what can and cannot be studied in social psychology often stem from a misunderstanding of science.
- Scientific explanations are incomplete and imperfect. Any one explanation of human behaviour is not invalidated by the presence of other explanations.
- People need groups – group memberships and social identities largely define who we are.
- People are not easily manipulated. They often react strongly to attempts to change their opinions and influence their behaviours. They are creative and reactive.
- Be aware of self-fulfilling prophecies. When people's behaviour seems to confirm expectations, always ask if this could be an example of a self-fulfilling prophecy.
- People are not always aware of factors that will influence them. Also, they cannot always tell when they have been influenced.
- Behaviour is crucial. Not only is it the central means by which we can understand human nature, it also has the power to change what we think and who we are.
- Critical thinking is key. Before accepting any claim about human behaviour, evaluate it carefully. Claims of fact, and explanations of fact, should be clear, unambiguous and testable.

We also argued that the study of social psychology presents several challenges and limitations:

- Social psychology suffers significantly from the sampling bias. Researchers rely too heavily on convenience samples of undergraduate students.
- The discipline is dominated by a small number of research methods such that the majority of social psychological findings are derived from correlational and experimental studies.
- Social psychological research often attempts to simulate real-life thoughts and contexts and apply findings to the real world. Some work may lack the ecological validity to do so.

- As in other disciplines, there is a publication bias in favour of positive findings that report significant results.
- Social psychology relies heavily on studies of attitudes and probably not enough on studies of behaviours and actions.
- Some argue that social psychology has lost sight of the 'bigger picture' as it focuses on basic questions about human nature.
- Ongoing divisions within social psychology (e.g., European vs. American; quantitative vs. qualitative) create problems within the discipline.
- Like other disciplines, social psychology is a competitive academic subject, which means that findings may not always be free of bias resulting from the pressure to publish.

We also outlined some current directions in social psychology:

- The internet provides a valuable resource for social psychologists, enabling them to access samples of a size and quality that was hitherto very difficult.
- Advances in information technology such as data mining and social networking also provide exciting avenues for conducting social psychological research.
- Developments in psychophysiological and neuroscientific methods (e.g., fMRI, transcranial magnetic stimulation) and theories have greatly facilitated the study of social neuroscience.
- The non-invasive study of nonverbal behaviour (e.g., electromyography, eye tracking) allows social psychologists to rely less on self-report data and to answer a wide variety of research questions.
- An ageing population makes the study of social psychological processes related to ageing (e.g., ageism, changes in affect) increasingly important.
- As globalization and technology afford new levels of contact between cultures, there is an increasing need to understand how relations are influenced by cultural differences, and how valuable aspects of culture can be preserved.

In the final section, we discussed some of the skills you will take forward with you from your study of social psychology, such as psychological literacy, technological, research and statistical skills, an understanding of diversity, the connection between science and wider social policy debates, and communication skills. We discussed how to use these skills in your student projects and in your future careers. Now that you have reached the end of this book, we wish you all the very best in these future adventures.

Essay questions

At the beginning of the chapter, we asked you to consider these questions:

1 Imagine you are having a conversation with your friend in which you discuss an interesting social psychological finding you have just read about – specifically, you read that meat eaters deny mental qualities to animals they eat as a way of justifying their meat eating (Bastian et al., 2012). Your friend says this is rubbish because they are a meat eater and they love animals. As an expert on social psychology research methodologies, how might you respond to your friend's statement?

2 Imagine reading about another interesting finding that people are often influenced by conspiracy theories – theories arguing that secret plots and deals determine major political events – without their awareness (Douglas and Sutton, 2008). Your friend again says that this cannot be the case. People would know if they had been influenced. Is this true?

3 The discussion with your friend takes an unpleasant turn and they say to you: 'Social psychology is a pseudo-science.' What would you say in response?

Having read this chapter, these questions could also be framed as the following essay questions, which you can attempt in preparation for your examinations:

1 If a study shows that meat eaters tend to be less likely to see animals as having minds, does this mean that all meat eaters will do this? Explain how a social psychologist might have reached such a conclusion (what research methods and analyses) and discuss some of the common misconceptions about social psychological research.

2 Are people always aware that they are being influenced? If not, what does this mean about the value of intuition?

3 Discuss the claim that social psychology is not a science.

Some further reading

Special section: Celebrating the BJSP's 50th Anniversary, of the *British Journal of Social Psychology*, September 2011, 50(3). Edited by Jolanda Jetten and John Dixon, this special issue contains articles from some of the foremost contributors to this leading journal. It surveys developments in the field of social psychology, particularly as it has been done in Europe, the UK and the Commonwealth over the past 50 years. We do not agree with everything the contributors have to say, but all the articles are impassioned, insightful and thought-provoking.

McGarty, C. and Haslam, S.A. (eds) (1997) *The Message of Social Psychology: Perspectives on Mind in Society*. London: Blackwell. Although compiled in 1997, this remains a unique and insightful collection of perspectives on the principal lessons to be learned from the study of social psychology. Twenty-five eminent social psychologists share their views on

the message of social psychology and the practice of conducting social psychological research.

Smith, J.R. and Haslam, S.A. (2012) *Social Psychology: Revisiting the Classic Studies*. London: Sage. Smith and Haslam have assembled a group of leading social psychologists to 'rediscover' some of the classic studies in social psychology discussed throughout this book. It will encourage you to think critically about the findings and carefully reflect on the conclusions that were drawn.

Smyth, T.R. (2007) *The Psychology Thesis: Research and Coursework*. Basingstoke: Palgrave Macmillan. Provides students with clear advice on how to plan, design, research and write a psychology thesis (or project).

 Visit the companion website at www.palgrave.com/psychology/suttondouglas for access to a wide range of resources to help you get to grips with this chapter.

References

AAUW (American Association of University Women) Educational Foundation (1998) *Gender Gaps: Where Schools Still Fail Our Children.* Washington, DC: AAUW Educational Foundation.

Aberson, C.L. and Haag, S.C. (2007) Contact, perspective taking, and anxiety as predictors of stereotype endorsement, explicit attitudes, and implicit attitudes. *Group Processes and Intergroup Relations*, 10, 179–201.

Aboud, F.E. (2005) The development of prejudice in childhood and adolescence. In J.F. Dovidio, P. Glick and L.A. Rudman (eds) *On the Nature of Prejudice: Fifty Years after Allport* (pp. 310–26.) Malden, MA: Blackwell.

Aboud, F.E. and Dolye, A.-B. (1996) Parental and peer influences on children's racial attitudes. *International Journal of Intercultural Relations*, 20, 371–83.

Abrams, D. and Hogg, M.A. (1988) Comments on the motivational status of self-esteem in social identity and intergroup discrimination. *European Journal of Social Psychology*, 18, 317–34.

Abrams, D., Crisp, R.J., Marques, S. et al. (2008) Threat inoculation: Experienced and imagined intergenerational contact prevents stereotype threat effects on older people's math performance. *Psychology and Aging*, 23, 934–9.

Abrams, D., Eilola, T. and Swift, H. (2009) *Attitudes to Age in Britain 2004–08.* Research Report No 599, on behalf of Department for Work and Pensions. Norwich: HMSO.

Abrams, D., Eller, A. and Bryant, J. (2006) An age apart: The effects of intergenerational contact and stereotype threat on performance and intergroup bias. *Psychology and Aging*, 21, 691–702.

Abrams, D., Rutland, A., Cameron, L. and Ferrell, J. (2007) Older but wilier: In-group accountability and the development of subjective group dynamics. *Developmental Psychology*, 43, 134–48.

Abrams, D., Viki, T., Masser, B. and Bohner, G. (2003) Perceptions of stranger and acquaintance rape: The role of benevolent and hostile sexism in victim blame and rape proclivity. *Journal of Personality and Social Psychology*, 84, 111–25.

Abrams, D., Wetherell, M., Cochrane, S. et al. (1990) Knowing what to think by knowing who you are: Self-categorization and the nature of norm formation, conformity and group polarization. *British Journal of Social Psychology*, 29, 97–119.

Abramson, L.Y., Metalsky, G.I. and Alloy, L.B. (1989) Hopelessness depression: A theory-based subtype of depression. *Psychological Review*, 96, 358–72.

Achtziger, A., Gollwitzer, P.M. and Sheeran, P. (2008) Implementation intentions and shielding from unwanted thoughts and feelings. *Personality and Social Psychology Bulletin*, 34, 381–93.

Acitelli, L.K., Kenny, D.A. and Weiner, D. (2001) The importance of similarity and understanding of partners' marital ideals to relationship satisfaction. *Personal Relationships*, 8, 167–85.

Adair, J.G. (2005) An introduction to the special issue. Social psychology around the world: Origins and subsequent development. *International Journal of Psychology*, 40, 209–12.

Adam, H. and Galinsky, A.D. (2012) Enclothed cognition. *Journal of Experimental Social Psychology*, 48, 918–25.

Adams, J.M. and Jones, W.H. (1997) The conceptualization of marital commitment: An integrative analysis. *Journal of Personality and Social Psychology*, 72, 1177–69.

Adams, J.S. (1965) Inequity in social exchange. In L. Berkowitz (ed.) *Advances in Experimental Social Psychology* (2nd edn, pp. 267–99). New York: Academic Press.

Adams, R.B. Jr, Franklin, R.G., Rule, N.O. et al. (2010) Culture, gaze and the neural processing of fear expressions. *Social Cognitive and Affective Neuroscience*, 5, 340–8.

Adler, N.J. and Bartholomew, S. (1992) Managing globally competent people. *Academy of Management Executive*, 6, 52–65.

Adolphs, R., Tranel, D. and Damasio, A.R. (1998) The human amygdala in social judgment. *Nature*, 393, 470–4.

Adorno, T.W., Frenkel-Brunswik, E., Levinson, D.J. and Sanford, R.N. (1950) *The Authoritarian Personality.* Norton, NY: Harper & Row.

Age Concern (2006) *How Ageist is Britain*? London: Age Concern.

Age UK (2011) *A Snapshot of Ageism in the UK and Across Europe.* London: Age UK.

Agthe, M., Sporrle, M. and Maner, J. (2011) Does being attractive always help? Positive and negative effects of attractiveness on social decision making. *Personality and Social Psychology Bulletin*, 37, 1042–54.

Ahn, W., Kalish, C.W., Medin, D.L. and Gelman, S.A. (1995) The role of covariation versus mechanism information in causal attribution. *Cognition*, 54, 299–352.

Ainsworth, M.D.S. (1973) The development of infant–mother attachment. In B.M. Caldwell and H.N. Ricciuti (eds) *Review of Child Development Research* (vol. 3, pp. 1–94). Chicago, IL: University of Chicago Press.

Ainsworth, M.D.S. (1979) Infant–mother attachment. *American Psychologist*, 34, 932–7.

Ainsworth, M.D.S., Blehar, M., Waters, E. and Wall, S. (1978) *Patterns of Attachment: A Psychological Study of the Strange Situation.* Hillsdale, NJ: Erlbaum.

Aitchison, J. (2003) *Words in the Mind: An Introduction to the Mental Lexicon.* London: Blackwell.

Ajzen, I. (1985) From intentions to actions: A theory of planned behavior. In J. Kuhl and J. Beckmann (eds) *Action-control: From Cognition to Behavior* (pp. 1 l–39). Heidelberg: Springer.

Ajzen, I. (1988) *Attitudes, Personality, and Behavior*. Chicago, IL: Dorsey Press.

Ajzen, I. (1991) The theory of planned behavior. *Organizational Behavior and Human Decision Processes*, 50, 179–211.

Ajzen, I. and Fishbein, M. (1980) *Understanding Attitudes and Predicting Social Behavior*. Englewood Cliffs, NJ: Prentice Hall.

Ajzen, I. and Fishbein, M. (2005) The influence of attitudes on behavior. In D Albarracín, B.T. Johnson and M.P. Zanna (eds) *The Handbook of Attitudes* (pp. 173–221). Mahwah, NJ: Erlbaum.

Ajzen, I. and Madden, T.J. (1986) Prediction of goal-directed behavior: Attitudes, intentions, and perceived behavioral control. *Journal of Experimental Social Psychology*, 22, 453–74.

Ajzen, I., Czasch, C. and Flood, M.G. (2009) From intentions to behavior: Implementation intention, commitment, and conscientiousness. *Journal of Applied Social Psychology*, 39, 1356–72.

Albarracin, D., Johnson, B.T., Fishbein, M. and Muellerleile, P.A. (2001) Theories of reasoned action and planned behavior as models of condom use: A meta-analysis. *Psychological Bulletin*, 127, 142–61.

Albert, S. (1977) Temporal comparison theory. *Psychological Review*, 84, 485–503.

Albright, L. and Forziati, C. (1995) Cross-situational consistency and perceptual accuracy in leadership. *Personality and Social Psychology Bulletin*, 21, 1269–76.

Albright, L., Kenny, D.A. and Malloy, T.E. (1988) Consensus in personality judgments at zero acquaintance. *Journal of Personality and Social Psychology*, 55, 387–95.

Alexander, C.N. Jr, Zucker, L.G. and Brody, C.L. (1970) Experimental expectations and autokinetic experiences: Consistency theories and judgemental convergence. *Sociometry*, 33, 108–22.

Alicke, M.D. and Largo, E. (1995) The role of self in the false consensus effect. *Journal of Experimental Social Psychology*, 31, 28–47.

Alicke, M.D, LoSchiavo, F.M., Zerbst, J. and Zhang, S. (1997) The person who outperforms me is a genius: Maintaining perceived competence in upward social comparison. *Journal of Personality and Social Psychology*, 73, 781–9.

Alicke, M.E. (1985) Global self-evaluation as determined by the desirability and controllability of trait adjectives. *Journal of Personality and Social Psychology*, 49, 1621–30.

Allen, B.P. (1996) African Americans' and European Americans' mutual attributions: Adjective generation technique (AGT) stereotyping. *Journal of Applied Social Psychology*, 26, 884–912.

Allen, J.B., Kenrick, D.T., Linder, D.E. and McCall, M.A. (1989) Arousal and attraction: A response-facilitation alternative to misattribution and negative-reinforcement models. *Journal of Personality and Social Psychology*, 57, 261–70.

Allen, K. (2003) Are pets a healthy pleasure? The influence of pets on blood pressure. *Current Directions in Psychological Science*, 12, 236–9.

Allen, K., Shykoff, B.E. and Izzo, J.L. Jr (2001) Pet ownership, but not ACE inhibitor therapy, blunts home blood pressure responses to mental stress. *Hypertension*, 38, 815–20.

Allen, V.L. (1965) Situational factors in conformity. In L. Berkowitz (ed.) *Advances in Experimental Social Psychology* (vol. 2, pp. 133–75). New York: Academic Press.

Allen, V.L. and Levine, J.M. (1971) Social support and conformity: The role of independent assessment of reality. *Journal of Experimental Social Psychology*, 7, 48–58.

Allport, F.H. (1920) The influence of the group upon association and thought. *Journal of Experimental Psychology*, 3, 159–82.

Allport, F.H. (1924) *Social Psychology*. Boston, MA: Houghton Mifflin.

Allport, G.W. (1954) The historical background of modern social psychology. In G. Lindzey (ed.) *Handbook of Social Psychology* (vol. 1, pp. 3–56). Reading, MA: Addison-Wesley.

Allport, G.W. (1954) The historical background of social psychology. In G. Lindzey and E. Aronson (eds) *Handbook of Social Psychology* (vol. 1, pp. 1–46). New York: Random House.

Allport, G.W. (1954) *The Nature of Prejudice*. Reading, MA: Addison-Wesley.

Allport, G.W. (1968) The historical background of modern social psychology. In G. Lindzey and E. Aronson (eds) *Handbook of Social Psychology* (2nd edn, vol. 1, pp. 1–80). Reading, MA: Addison-Wesley.

Alnuaimi, O.A., Robert, L.P. and Maruping, L.M. (2010) Team size, dispersion, and social loafing in technology-supported teams: A perspective on the theory of moral disengagement. *Journal of Management Information Systems*, 27, 203–30.

Altabe, M. and Thompson, J.K. (1996) Body image: A cognitive self-schema construct? *Cognitive Therapy and Research*, 20, 171–93.

Altemeyer, B. (1981) *Right-wing Authoritarianism*. Winnipeg, Canada: University of Manitoba Press.

Altemeyer, B. (1998) The other 'authoritarian personality'. In M. Zanna (ed.) *Advances in Experimental Social Psychology* (vol. 30, pp. 47–92). San Diego, CA: Academic Press.

Altman, I. and Taylor, D. (1973) *Social Penetration: The Development of Interpersonal Relationships*. New York: Holt, Rinehart & Winston.

Alves, H. and Correia, I. (2008) On the normativity of expressing the belief in a just world: Empirical evidence. *Social Justice Research*, 21, 106–18.

Alves, H. and Correia, I. (2010) Personal and general belief in a just world as judgement norms. *International Journal of Psychology*, 45, 221–31.

Amancio, L. (1989) Social differentiation between 'dominant' and 'dominated' groups: Toward an integration of social stereotypes and social identity. *European Journal of Social Psychology*, 19, 1–10.

Ambady, N. and Gray, H.M. (2002) Sad and mistaken: Mood effects on the accuracy of thin-slice judgments. *Journal of Personality and Social Psychology*, 83, 947–61.

Ambady, N. and Rosenthal, R. (1992) Thin slices of expressive behavior as predictors of interpersonal consequences: A meta-analysis. *Psychological Bulletin*, 111, 256–74.

Ambady, N. and Rosenthal, R. (1993) Half a minute: Predicting teacher evaluations from thin slices of nonverbal behavior and physical attractiveness. *Journal of Personality and Social Psychology*, 64, 431–41.

Ambady, N. and Weisbuch, M. (2010) Nonverbal behavior. In. S.T. Fiske, D.T. Gilbert and G. Lindzey (eds) *Handbook of Social Psychology* (5th edn, vol. 1, pp. 464–97). New York: Wiley.

Ambady, N., Hallahan, M. and Conner, B. (1999) Accuracy of judgments of sexual orientation from thin slices of behavior. *Journal of Personality and Social Psychology*, 77, 538–47.

Ambady, N., Hallahan, M. and Rosenthal, R. (1995) On judging and being judged accurately in zero-acquaintance situations. *Journal of Personality and Social Psychology*, 69, 518–29.

Ambady, N., Koo, J., Lee, F. and Rosenthal, R. (1996) More than words: Linguistic and nonlinguistic politeness in two cultures. *Journal of Personality and Social Psychology*, 70, 996–1011.

Ambady, N., Krabbenhoft, M.A. and Hogan, D. (2006) The 30-sec sale: Using thin-slice judgments to evaluate sales effectiveness. *Journal of Consumer Psychology*, 16, 4–13.

Ames, D. (2004) Inside the mind-reader's toolkit: Projection and stereotyping in social inference. *Journal of Personality and Social Psychology*, 87, 340–53.

Ames, D.R., Kammrath, L.K., Suppes, A. and Bolger, N. (2010) No so fast: The (not-quite-complete) dissociation between accuracy and confidence in thin-slice impressions. *Personality and Social Psychology Bulletin*, 36, 264–77.

Amir, Y. (1965) Contact hypothesis in ethnic relations. *Psychological Bulletin*, 71, 319–42.

Amodio, D.M. (2009) Intergroup anxiety effects on the control of racial stereotypes: A psychoneuroendocrine analysis. *Journal of Experimental Social Psychology*, 45, 60–7.

Amodio, D.M. and Frith, C.D. (2006) Meeting of minds: The medial frontal cortex and social cognition. *Nature Reviews Neuroscience, 7*, 268–77.

Amodio, D.M. and Harmon-Jones, E. (2012) Neuroscience approaches in social and personality psychology. In K. Deaux and M. Snyder (eds) *The Oxford Handbook of Personality and Social Psychology* (pp. 111–50). Oxford: Oxford University Press.

Amodio, D.M. and Showers, C. (2005) 'Similarity breeds liking' revisited: The moderating role of commitment. *Journal of Social and Personal Relationships*, 22, 817–36.

Amodio, D.M., Harmon-Jones, E., Devine, P.G. et al. (2004) Neural signals for the detection of unintentional race bias. *Psychological Science*, 15, 88–93.

Andersen, S.M., Reznik, I. and Manzella, L.M. (1996) Eliciting facial affect, motivation, and expectancies in transference: Significant-other representations in social relations. *Journal of Personality and Social Psychology*, 71, 1108–29.

Anderson, C.A. (2002) Violent video games and aggressive thoughts, feelings, and behaviors. In S.L. Calvert, A.B. Jordan and R.R. Cocking (eds) *Children in the Digital Age* (pp. 101–19). Westport, CT: Praeger.

Anderson, C.A. and Bushman, B.J. (2002) Human aggression. *Annual Review of Psychology*, 53, 27–51.

Anderson, C.A., Bushman, B.J. and Groom, R.W. (1997) Hot years and serious and deadly assault: Empirical tests of the heat hypothesis. *Journal of Personality and Social Psychology*, 73, 1213–23.

Anderson, C.A., Deuser, W.E. and DeNeve, K.M. (1995) Hot temperatures, hostile affect, hostile cognition and arousal: Tests of a general model of affective aggression. *Personality and Social Psychology Bulletin*, 21, 434–48.

Anderson, C.M., Riddle, B.L. and Martin, M.M. (1999) Socialization processes in groups. In L.R. Frey (ed.) D.S. Gouran and M.S. Poole (eds) *The Handbook of Group Communication Theory and Research* (pp. 139–66). Thousand Oaks, CA: Sage.

Anderson, E. (1994) The code of the streets. *Atlantic Monthly*, 273, 81–94.

Anderson, J.R. (1990) *Cognitive Psychology and its Implications* (3rd edn). New York: Freeman.

Anderson, L.R., Mellor, J.M. and Milyo, J. (2008) Inequality and public good provision: An experimental analysis. *The Journal of Socio-Economics*, 37, 1010–28.

Anderson, N.H. (1965) Primacy effects in personality impression formation using a generalized order effect paradigm. *Journal of Personality and Social Psychology*, 2, 1–9.

Anderson, N.H. (1965) Averaging versus adding as a stimulus-combination rule in impression formation. *Journal of Experimental Social Psychology*, 70, 394–400.

Anderson, N.H. (1971) Integration theory and attitude change. *Psychological Review*, 78, 171–206.

Anderson, N.H. (1974) Cognitive algebra: Integration theory applied to social attribution. *Advances in Experimental Social Psychology*, 7, 1–101.

Anderson, N.H. (1975) On the role of context effects in psychophysical judgement. *Psychological Review*, 82, 462–82.

Anderson, N.H. (1996) *A Functional Theory of Cognition*. Mahwah, NJ: Erlbaum.

Anderson, R.A., Bancroft, J. and Wu, F.C. (1992) The effects of exogenous testosterone on sexuality and mood of normal men. *Journal of Clinical Endocrinology and Metabolism*, 75, 1503–7.

Andreoni, J. (1988) Why free ride? Strategies and learning in public goods experiments. *Journal of Public Economics*, 37, 291–304.

Andreoni, J. and Vesterlund, L. (2001) Which is the fair sex? Gender differences in altruism. *The Quarterly Journal of Economics*, 116, 293–312.

Anthony, D.B., Holmes, J.G. and Wood, J.V. (2007) Social acceptance and self-esteem: Tuning the sociometer to interpersonal value. *Journal of Personality and Social Psychology*, 92, 1024–39.

Archer, D., Iritani, B., Kimes, D.D. and Barrios, M. (1983) Face-ism: Five studies of sex differences in facial prominence. *Journal of Personality and Social Psychology*, 45, 725–35.

Archer, J. (1991) The influence of testosterone on human aggression. *British Journal of Psychology*, 82, 1–28.

Archer, J. (2009) Does sexual selection explain human sex differences in aggression? *Behavioral and Brain Sciences*, 32, 249–311.

Arendt, H. (1963) *Eichmann in Jerusalem: A Report on the Banality of Evil*. London: Penguin.

Argyle, M. (1987) *The Psychology of Happiness*. London: Methuen.

Argyle, M. (1990) *Bodily Communication* (2nd edn). London: Routeledge.

Argyle, M. (2003) Causes and correlates of happiness. In D. Kahneman, E. Diener and N. Schwarz (eds) *Wellbeing: The Foundations of Hedonic Personality* (pp. 353–73). New York: Russell Sage Foundation.

Argyle, M. and Dean, J. (1965) Eye-contact, distance and affiliation. *Sociometry*, 28, 289–304.

Argyle, M. and Henderson, M. (1985) *The Anatomy of Relationships*. Harmondsworth: Penguin.

Argyle, M. and Ingham, R. (1972) Gaze, mutual gaze, and proximity. *Semiotica*, 6, 32–49.

Ariely, D. (2011) *The Upside of Irrationality: The Unexpected Benefits of Defying Logic at Work and at Home*. London: Harper.

Arkes, H.R., Boehm, L.E. and Xu, G. (1991) Determinants of judged validity. *Journal of Experimental Social Psychology*, 27, 576–605.

Arkes, H.R., Faust, D., Guilmette, T.J. and Hart, K. (1988) Eliminating the hindsight bias. *Journal of Applied Psychology*, 73, 305–7.

Arkes, H.R., Wortman, R.L., Saville, P.D. and Harkness, A.R. (1981) Hindsight bias among physicians weighing the likelihood of diagnoses. *Journal of Applied Psychology*, 66, 252–4.

Arkin, R.M. and Duval, S. (1975) Focus of attention and causal attributions of actors and observers. *Journal of Experimental Social Psychology*, 11, 427–38.

Arkin, R.M. and Hermann, A.D. (2000) Constructing desirable identities – self-presentation in psychotherapy and daily life: Comment on Kelly (2000) *Psychological Bulletin*, 126, 501–4.

Arkin, R.M., Cooper, H.M. and Kolditz, T.A. (1980) A statistical review of the literature concerning the self-serving attribution bias in interpersonal influence situations. *Journal of Personality*, 48, 435–48.

Armitage, C.J. and Conner, M. (2001) Efficacy of the theory of planned behaviour: A meta-analytic review. *British Journal of Social Psychology*, 40, 471–99.

Armitage, C.J. and Talibudeen, L. (2010) Test of a brief theory of planned behaviour-based intervention to promote adolescent safe sex intentions. *British Journal of Psychology, 101*, 155–72.

Arnett, J. (2008) The neglected 95%: Why American psychology needs to become less American. *American Psychologist*, 63, 602–14.

Aron, A., Fisher, H., Mashek, D.J. et al. (2005) Reward, motivation, and emotion systems associated with early-stage intense romantic love. *Journal of Neurophysiology*, 94, 327–37.

Aronson, E. (1968) Dissonance theory: Progress and problems. In R.P. Abelson, E. Aronson, W.J. McGuire et al. (eds) *Theories of Cognitive Consistency: A Sourcebook* (pp. 5–27). Chicago, IL: Rand McNally.

Aronson, E. (1997) Back to the future: Retrospective review of Leon Festinger's 'A theory of cognitive dissonance.' *The American Journal of Psychology*, 110, 127–37.

Aronson, E. and Mills, J. (1959) The effect of severity of initiation on liking for a group. *The Journal of Abnormal and Social Psychology*, 59, 177–81.

Aronson, E., Blaney, N., Stephan, C. et al. (1978) *The Jigsaw Classroom*. Beverly Hills, CA: Sage.

Aronson, E., Fried, C. and Stone, J. (1991) Overcoming denial and increasing the intention to use condoms through the induction of hypocrisy. *American Journal of Public Health*, 81, 1636–8.

Aronson, E., Wilson, T.D. and Brewer, M.B. (1998) Experimentation in social psychology. In D.T. Gilbert, S.T. Fiske and G. Lindzey (eds) *The Handbook of Social Psychology* (pp. 99–142). New York: McGraw-Hill.

Aronson, J., Jannone, S., McGlone, M. and Johnson-Campbell, T. (2009) The Obama effect: An experimental test. *Journal of Experimental Social Psychology*, 45, 957–60.

Arriaga, X.B. and Agnew, C.R. (2001) Being committed: Affective, cognitive, and conative components of relationship commitment. *Personality and Social Psychology Bulletin*, 27, 1190–203.

Arrow, H., McGrath, J.E. and Berdahl, J.L. (2000) *Small Groups as Complex Systems: Formation, Coordination, Development, and Adaptation*. Thousand Oaks, CA: Sage.

Article 19 (1996) *Broadcasting Genocide: Censorship, Propaganda and State-sponsored Violence in Rwanda 1990–1994*. London: Article 19.

Arvey, R.D., Bouchard, T.J., Segal, N.L. and Abraham, L.M. (1989) Job satisfaction: Environmental and genetic components. *Journal of Applied Psychology*, 74, 187–92.

Arvey, R.D., Rotundo, M., Johnson, W. et al. (2006) The determinants of leadership role occupancy: Genetic and personality factors. *Leadership Quarterly*, 17, 1–20.

Arvey, R.D., Zhang, Z., Avolio, B.J. and Krueger, R.F. (2007) Developmental and genetic determinants of leadership role occupancy among women. Journal of Applied Psychology, 92, 693–706.

Asch, S.E. (1946) Forming impressions of personality. *Journal of Abnormal and Social Psychology*, 41, 258–90.

Asch, S.E. (1951) Effects of group pressure on the modification and distortion of judgements. In H. Guetzkow (ed.) *Groups, Leadership and Men* (pp. 177–90). Pittsburgh, PA: Carnegie Press.

Asch, S.E. (1952) *Social Psychology*. Englewood Cliffs, NJ: Prentice Hall.

Asch, S.E. (1955) Opinions and social pressure. *Scientific American*, 193, 31–5.

Asch, S.E. (1956) Studies of independence and conformity: I. A minority of one against a unanimous majority. *Psychological Monographs: General and Applied*, 70, 1–70.

Ashburn-Nardo, L., Voils, C.I. and Monteith, M.J. (2001) Implicit associations as the seeds of intergroup bias: How easily do they take root? *Journal of Personality and Social Psychology*, 81, 789–99.

Ashforth, B.E. and Mael, F. (1989) Social identity theory and the organization. *Academy of Management Review*, 14, 20–39.

Ashforth, B.E., Sluss, D.M. and Saks, A.M. (2007) Socialization tactics, proactive behavior, and newcomer learning: Integrating socialization models. *Journal of Vocational Behavior*, 70, 447–62.

Attrill, A. and Jalil, R. (2011) Revealing only the superficial me: Exploring categorical self-disclosure online. *Computers in Human Behaviour*, 27, 1634–42.

Attrill, A. and Semper, H. (2012) Loving friends and friendly love: Validation of the attitude toward online relationship formation scale. Unpublished manuscript, DeMontfort University.

Austin, J.L. (1962) *How to do Things with Words*. Oxford: Clarendon Press.

Axelrod, R. and Hamilton, D.R. (1981) The evolution of cooperation. *Science*, 211, 1390–6.

Ayar, A.A. (2006) Road rage: Recognizing a psychological disorder. *Journal of Psychiatry and Law*, 34, 123–50.

Ayduk, O., Mendes, W.B., Akinola, M. and Gyurak, A. (2008) Self-esteem and blood pressure reactivity to social acceptance and rejection: Self-verification processes revealed in physiological responses. Unpublished manuscript, University of California, Berkeley.

Ayres, I. (2001) *Pervasive Prejudice? Unconventional Evidence of Race and Gender Discrimination*. Chicago, IL: University of Chicago Press.

Baars, B.J. (1986) *The Cognitive Revolution in Psychology*. New York: Guilford Press.

Baas, M., de Dreu, K.K.W and Nijstad, B.A. (2008) A meta-analysis of 25 years of mood-creativity research: Hedonic tone, activation, or regulatory focus? *Psychological Bulletin*, 134, 779–806.

Baccus, J.R., Baldwin, M.W. and Packer, D.J. (2004) Increasing implicit self-esteem through classical conditioning. *Psychological Science*, 15, 498–502.

Back, M.D., Schmukle, S.C. and Egloff, B. (2008) How extraverted is honey.bunny77@hotmail.de? Inferring personality from e-mail addresses. *Journal of Research in Personality*, 42, 1116–22.

Bagenstos, S.R. (2007) Implicit bias, 'science' and antidiscrimination law. *Harvard Law & Policy Review*, 1, 477–93.

Bailey, D.S. and Taylor, S.P. (1991) Effects of alcohol and aggressive disposition on human physical aggression. *Journal of Research in Personality*, 25, 334–42.

Baise, H.R. and Schroeder, J.E. (1995) Personality and mate selection in personal ads: Evolutionary preferences in a public mate selection process. *Journal of Social Behavior and Personality*, 10, 517–36.

Baker, P.E. (1934) *Negro–White Adjustment*. New York: Association Press.

Bal, M. and van den Bos, K. (2010) The role of perpetrator similarity in reactions toward innocent victims. *European Journal of Social Psychology*, 40, 957–69.

Baldwin, J.M. (1897) *Social and Ethical Interpretations in Mental Development: A Study in Social Psychology*. New York: Macmillan & Co.

Bales, R.F. (1950) *Interaction Process Analysis*. Cambridge, MA: Addison Wesley.

Ball-Rokeach, S.J., Rockeach, M. and Grube, J.W. (1984) *The Great American Values Test: Influencing Behavior and Belief Through Television*. London: Free Press.

Banaji, M.R. and Heiphetz, L. (2010) Attitudes. In S.T. Fiske, D.T. Gilbert and G. Lindzey (eds) *Handbook of Social Psychology* (5th edn, vol. 1, pp. 353–92). Hoboken: Wiley.

Bandura, A. (1977) *Social Learning Theories*. Englewood Cliffs, NJ: Prentice Hall.

Bandura, A. (1978) Social learning theory of aggression. *Journal of Communication*, 28, 12–29.

Bandura, A., Ross, D. and Ross, S.A. (1961) Transmission of aggression through imitation of aggressive models. *Journal of Abnormal and Social Psychology*, 63, 575–82.

Banerjee, A.V. and Duflo, E. (2003) Inequality and growth: What can the data say? *Journal of Economic Growth*, 8, 267–99.

Banks, J.A., Cookson, P., Gay, G. et al. (2001) Diversity within unity: Essential principles for teaching and learning in a multicultural society. *The Phi Delta Kappan*, 83, 196–8, 200–3.

Banuazizi, A. and Movahedi, S. (1975) Interpersonal dynamics in a simulated prison: A methodological analysis. *American Psychologist*, 30, 152–60.

Bar-Anan, Y., de Houwer, J. and Nosek, B.A. (2010) Evaluative conditioning and conscious knowledge of contingencies: A correlational investigation with large samples. *Quarterly Journal of Experimental Psychology*, 63, 2313–35.

Barber, B.L., Eccles, J.S. and Stone, M.R. (2001) Whatever happened to the jock, the brain and the princess? Young adult pathways linked to adolescent activity involvement and social identity. *Journal of Adolescent Research*, 16, 429–55.

Barber, N. (2010) Pity the poor murderer, his genes made him do it. Retrieved from http://www.psychologytoday.com/blog/the-human-beast/201007/pity-the-poor-murderer-his-genes-made-him-do-it, 24 October 2011.

Barden, J., Maddux, W.W., Petty, R.E. and Brewer, M.B. (2004) Contextual moderation of racial bias: The impact of social roles on controlled and automatically activated attitudes. *Journal of Personality and Social Psychology*, 87, 5–22.

Bardi, A. and Schwartz, S.H. (2003) Values and behavior: Strength and structure of relations. *Personality and Social Psychology Bulletin*, 29, 1208–20.

Bardwick, J.M. (1971) *Psychology of Women: A Study of Bio-cultural Conflicts*. New York: Harper & Row.

Bargh, J.A. (1994) The four horsemen of automaticity: Awareness, efficiency, intention, and control in social cognition. In R.S. Wyer Jr and T.K. Srull (eds) *Handbook of Social Cognition* (2nd edn, pp. 1–40). Hillsdale, NJ: Erlbaum.

Bargh, J.A. and McKenna, K.Y.A. (2004) The internet and social life. *Annual Review of Psychology*, 55, 573–90.

Bargh, J.A., Chen, M. and Burrows, L. (1996) Automaticity of social behavior: Direct effects of trait construct and stereotype activation on action. *Journal of Personality and Social Psychology*, 71, 230–44.

Bargh, J.A., Gollwitzer, P.M., Lee-Chai, A. et al. (2001) The automated will: Nonconscious activation and pursuit of behavioral goals. *Journal of Personality and Social Psychology*, 81, 1014–27.

Bargh, J.A., McKenna, K.Y.A. and Fitzsimons, G.M. (2002) Can you see the real me? Activation and expression of the 'true self' on the internet. *Journal of Social Issues*, 58, 33–48.

Barkan, E. (2000) *The Guilt of Nations: Restitution and Negotiating Historical Injustices*. New York: W.W. Norton.

Barley, S.R. and Bechky, B.A. (1994) In the backrooms of science: The work of technicians in science labs. *Work and Occupations*, 21, 85–126.

Barner-Barry, C. (1986) Rob: Children's tacit use of peer ostracism to control aggressive behavior. *Ethology and Sociobiology*, 7, 281–93.

Baron, R.A. and Byrne, D. (2003) *Social Psychology* (10th edn). Boston: Allyn & Bacon.

Baron, R.S. (1986) Distraction-conflict theory: Progress and problems. *Advances in Experimental Social Psychology*, 19, 1–40.

Barrett, L., Dunbar, R. and Lycett, J. (2002) *Human Evolutionary Psychology*. Princeton: Princeton University Press.

Barrett, P.T. and Eysenck, S.B.G. (1992) Predicting EPQR full scale scores from the short form version. *Personality and Individual Differences*, 13, 851–3.

Barsalou, L.W. (1999) Perceptual symbol systems. *Behavioral and Brain Sciences*, 22, 577–660.

Bartels, A. and Zeki, S. (2004) The neural correlates of maternal and romantic love. *NeuroImage*, 21, 1155–66.

Bartholomew, K. (1990) Avoidance of intimacy: An attachment perspective. *Journal of Social and Personal Relationships*, 7, 147–78.

Bartholow, B.D. and Heinz, A. (2006) Alcohol and aggression without consumption: Alcohol cues, aggressive thoughts, and hostile perception bias. *Psychological Science*, 17, 30–7.

Baruch, G.K. and Barnett, R.C. (1986) Role quality, multiple role involvement, and psychological well being in midlife women. *Journal of Personality and Social Psychology*, 51, 578–85.

Baruch, Y. (2005) Bullying on the net: Adverse behavior on email and its impact. *Information & Management*, 42, 361–71.

Bassett, J.F., Cate, K.L. and Dabbs, J.M. (2002) Individual differences in self-presentation style: Driving an automobile and meeting a stranger. *Self & Identity*, 1, 281–8.

Bastian, B., Jetten, J. and Fasoli, F. (2011) Cleansing the soul by hurting the flesh: The guilt-reducing effect of pain. *Psychological Science*, 22, 334–35.

Bastian, B., Loughnan, S., Haslam, N. and Radke, H.R.M. (2012) Don't mind meat? The denial of mind to animals used for human consumption. *Personality and Social Psychology Bulletin*, 38, 247–56.

Batalha, L., Reynolds, K.J. and Newbigin, C.A. (2011) All else being equal: Are men always higher in social dominance orientation than women? *European Journal of Social Psychology*, 41, 796–806.

Batson, C.D. (1987) Prosocial motivation: Is it ever truly altruistic? In L. Berkowitz (ed.) *Advances in Experimental Social Psychology* (vol. 20, pp. 65–122). New York: Academic Press.

Batson, C.D. (1991) *The Altruism Question*. Hillsdale, NJ: Erlbaum.

Batson, C.D. and Shaw, L.L. (1991) Evidence for altruism: Toward a pluralism of prosocial motives. *Psychological Inquiry*, 2, 107–22.

Batson, C.D., Bolen, M.H., Cross, J.A. and Neuringer-Benefiel, H.E. (1986) Where is the altruism in the altruistic personality? *Journal of Personality and Social Psychology*, 50, 212–20.

Batson, C.D., Floyd, R.B., Meyer, J.M. and Winner, A.L. (1999) 'And who is my neighbour?': Intrinsic religion as a source of universal compassion. *Journal for the Scientific Study of Religion*, 38, 445–57.

Batson, C.D., Schoenrade, P. and Ventis, L. (1993) *Religion and the Individual*. New York: Oxford University Press.

Batson, C.D., Sympson, S.C., Hindman, J.L. et al. (1996) 'I've been there, too': Effect of empathy of prior experience with a need. *Personality and Social Psychology Bulletin*, 22, 474–82.

Baumard, N. and Sperber, D. (2010) Weird people, yes, but also weird experiments. *Behavioral and Brain Sciences*, 33, 84–5.

Baumeister, R.F. (1982) A self-presentational view of social phenomena. *Psychological Bulletin*, 91, 3–26.

Baumeister, R.F. (1998) The self. In D.T. Gilbert, S.T. Fiske and G. Lindzey (eds) *Handbook of Social Psychology* (4th edn, pp. 680–740). New York: McGraw-Hill.

Baumeister, R.F. and Bratslavsky, E. (1999) Passion, intimacy, and time: Passionate love as a function of change in intimacy. *Personality and Social Psychology Review*, 3, 49–67.

Baumeister, R.F. and Leary, M.R. (1995) The need to belong: Desire for interpersonal attachments as a fundamental human motivation. *Psychological Bulletin*, 117, 497–529.

Baumeister, R.F. and Wotman, S.R. (1992) *Breaking Hearts: The Two Sides of Unrequited Love*. New York: Guilford Press.

Baumeister, R.F., Bratslavsky, E., Muraven, M. and Tice, D.M. (1998) Ego depletion: Is the active self a limited resource? *Journal of Personality and Social Psychology*, 74, 1252–65.

Baumeister, R.F., Campbell, J.D., Krueger, J.I. and Vohs, K.D. (2003) Does self-esteem cause better performance, interpersonal success, happiness, or healthier lifestyle? *Psychological Science in the Public Interest*, 4, 1–44.

Baumeister, R.F., Smart, L. and Boden, J.M. (1996) Relation of threatened egotism to violence and aggression: The dark side of self-esteem. *Psychological Review*, 103, 5–33.

Baumeister, R.F., Tice, D.M. and Hutton, D.G. (1989) Self-presentational motivations and personality differences in self-esteem. *Journal of Personality*, 57, 547–79.

Baumeister, R.F., Twenge, J.M. and Nuss, C.K. (2002) Effects of social exclusion on cognitive processes: Anticipated aloneness reduces intelligent thought. *Journal of Personality and Social Psychology*, 83, 817–27.

Baumeister, R.F., Vohs, K.D. and Funder, D.C. (2007) Psychology as the science of self-reports and finger movements. *Perspectives on Psychological Science*, 2, 396–403.

Baumeister, R.F., Wotman, S.R. and Stillwell, A.M. (1993) Unrequited love: On heartbreak, anger, guilt, scriptlessness, and humiliation. *Journal of Personality and Social Psychology*, 64, 377–94.

Baumgardner, S.R. (1977) Critical studies in the history of social psychology. *Personality and Social Psychology Bulletin*, 3, 681–7.

Baumrind, D. (1964) Some thoughts on ethics of research: After reading Milgram's 'behavioral study of obedience'. *American Psychologist*, 19, 421–3.

Baumrind, D. (1985) Research using intentional deception: Ethical issues revisited. *American Psychologist*, 40, 165–74.

Baumrind, D. (1991) The influence of parenting style on adolescent competence and substance use. *Journal of Adolescence*, 11, 56–95.

Bavelas, J.B., Black, A., Chovil, N. et al. (1988) Form and function in motor mimicry: Topographic evidence that the primary function is communicative. *Human Communication Research*, 14, 275–99.

Bavelas, J.B., Black, A., Lemery, C.R. and Mullett, J. (1986) 'I *show* how you feel': Motor mimicry as a communicative act. *Journal of Personality and Social Psychology*, 50, 322–9.

Baxter, L.A. (1984) Trajectories of relationship disengagement. *Journal of Social and Personal Relationships*, 1, 29–49.

Beaman, A.L., Klentz, B., Diender, E. and Svanum, S. (1979) Self-awareness and transgression in children: Two field studies. *Journal of Personality and Social Psychology*, 37, 1835–46.

Beck, A.T., Rush, A.J., Shaw, B.F. and Emery, G. (1979) *Cognitive Therapy of Depression*. New York: Guilford Press.

Becker, J.C., Wagner, U. and Christ, O. (2011) Consequences of the 2008 financial crisis for intergroup relations: The role of perceived threat and causal attributions. *Group Processes and Intergroup Relations*, 6, 871–85.

Becker, S.W. and Eagly, A.H. (2004) The heroism of women and men. *American Psychologist*, 59, 173–8.

Bègue, L. (2002) Beliefs in justice and faith in people: Just world, religiosity and interpersonal trust. *Personality and Individual Differences*, 32, 375–82.

Bègue, L. and Bastounis, M. (2003) Two spheres of belief in justice: Extensive support for the bidimensional model of belief in a just world. *Journal of Personality*, 71, 435–63.

Bègue, L. and Muller, D. (2006) Belief in a just world as a moderator or hostile attribution bias. *British Journal of Social Psychology*, 45, 117–26.

Bègue, L. and Subra, B. (2008) Alcohol and aggression: Perspectives on controlled and uncontrolled social information processing. *Social and Personality Psychology Compass*, 2, 511–38.

Bègue, L., Subra, B., Arvers, P. et al. (2009) A message in a bottle: Extrapharmacological effects of alcohol on aggression. *Journal of Experimental Social Psychology*, 45, 137–42.

Bekoff, M. (2003) Consciousness and self in animals: Some reflections. *Zygon*, 38, 229–46.

Belyaev, D.K. (1979) Destabilizing selection as a factor in domestication. *Journal of Heredity*, 70, 301–8.

Bem, D.J. (1967) Self-perception: An alternative interpretation of cognitive dissonance phenomena. *Psychological Review*, 74, 183–200.

Bem, D.J. (1972) Constructive cross-situational consistencies in behaviour: Some thoughts on Alker's critique of Mischel. *Journal of Personality*, 40, 17–26.

Bem, D.J. (1972) Self-perception theory. *Advances in Experimental Social Psychology*, 6, 1–62.

Bem, D.J. and Allen, A. (1974) On predicting some of the people some of the time: The search for cross-situational consistencies in behavior. *Psychological Review*, 81, 506–20.

Bem, D.J. and McConnell, H.K. (1970) Testing the self-perception explanation of dissonance phenomena: On the salience of premanipulation attitudes. *Journal of Personality and Social Psychology*, 14, 23–31.

Benjamin, L.T. and Simpson, J.A. (2009) The power of the situation: The impact of Milgram's obedience studies on personality and social psychology. *American Psychologist*, 64, 12–19.

Bennis, W. (1984) The 4 competencies of leadership. *Training and Development Journal*, 38, 14–19.

Bennis, W.M. and Medin, D.L. (2010) Weirdness is in the eye of the beholder. *Behavioral and Brain Sciences*, 33, 85–6.

Benson, P.L., Karabenick, S.A. and Lerner, R.M. (1976) Pretty pleases: The effects of attractiveness, race, and sex on receiving help. *Journal of Experimental Social Psychology*, 12, 409–15.

Benton, A.A., Kelley, H.H. and Leibling, B. (1972) Effects of extremity of offers and concession rate on the outcomes of bargaining. *Journal of Personality and Social Psychology*, 24, 73–83.

Berg, J.A. (2009) Core networks and whites' attitudes toward immigrants and immigration policy. *Public Opinion Quarterly*, 73, 7–31.

Berger, C.R. and Calabrese, R.J. (1975) Some explorations in initial interaction and beyond: Toward a developmental theory of interpersonal communication. *Human Communication Research*, 1, 99–112.

Berger, J., Fisek, M.H., Norman, R.Z. and Zelditch, M. (1997) *Status Characteristics and Social Interaction: An Expectation States Approach*. New York: Elsevier Science.

Berglas, S. and Jones, E.E. (1978) Drug choice as a self-handicapping strategy in response to noncontingent success. *Journal of Personality and Social Psychology*, 36, 405–17.

Berk, M.S. and Andersen, S.M. (2000) The impact of past relationships on interpersonal behavior: Behavioral confirmation in the social–cognitive process of transference. *Journal of Personality and Social Psychology*, 79, 546–62.

Berkowitz, L. (1954) Group standards, cohesiveness, and productivity. *Human Relations*, 7, 509–19.

Berkowitz, L. (1982) Aversive conditions as stimuli to aggression. *Advances in Experimental Social Psychology*, 15, 249–95.

Berkowitz, L. (1988) Frustrations, appraisals and aversively stimulated aggression. *Aggressive Behavior*, 14, 3–11.

Berkowitz, L. (1990) On the formation and regulation of anger and aggression: A cognitive–neoassociationistic analysis. *American Psychologist*, 45, 494–503.

Berkowitz, L. and LePage, A. (1967) Weapons as aggression-eliciting stimuli. *Journal of Personality and Social Psychology*, 7, 202–7.

Berman, M.E., McCloskey, M.S., Fanning, J.R. et al. (2009) Serotonin augmentation reduces response to attack in aggressive individuals. *Psychological Science*, 20, 714–20.

Berman, M.E., Tracy, J.I. and Coccaro, E.F. (1997) The serotonin hypothesis of aggression revisited. *Clinical Psychology Review*, 17, 651–65.

Bernard, M.M., Maio, G.R. and Olson, J.M. (2003a) Effects of introspection about reasons for values: Extending research on values-as-truisms. *Social Cognition*, 21, 1–25.

Bernard, M.M., Maio, G.R. and Olson, J.M. (2003b) The vulnerability of values to attack: Inoculation of values and value-relevant attitudes. *Personality and Social Psychology Bulletin*, 29, 63–75.

Berndsen, M., McGarty, C., van der Plight, J. and Spears, R. (2001) Meaning-seeking in the illusory correlation paradigm: The active role of participants in the categorization process. *British Journal of Social Psychology*, 40, 209–33.

Bernhard, H., Fischbacher, U. and Fehr, E. (2006) Parochial altruism in humans. *Nature*, 442, 912–15.

Bernieri , F. (1991) Interpersonal sensitivity in teaching interactions. *Personality and Social Psychology Bulletin*, 71, 98–103.

Bernstein, D.M., Erdfelder, E., Meltzoff, A.N. et al. (2011) Hindsight bias from 3 to 95 years of age. *Journal of Experimental Psychology: Learning, Memory, and Cognition*, 37, 378–91.

Bernstein, I.S., Rose, R.M., Gordon, T.P. and Grady, C.L. (2006) Agonistic rank, aggression, social context, and testosterone in male pigtail monkeys. *Aggressive Behavior*, 5, 329–39.

Bernthal, P.R. and Insko, C.A. (1993) Cohesiveness without groupthink: The interactive effects of social and task cohesion. *Group Organization Management*, 18, 66–87.

Berry, D.S. and Brownlow, S. (1989) Were the physiognomists right? Personality correlates of facial babyishness. *Personality and Social Psychology Bulletin*, 15, 266–79.

Berscheid, E. (1994) Interpersonal relationships. *Annual Review of Psychology*, 45, 79–129.

Berscheid, E. and Meyers, S.A. (1996) A social categorical approach to a question about love. *Personal Relationships*, 3, 19–43.

Berscheid, E. and Reis, H.T. (1998) Attraction and close relationships. In D.T. Gilbert, S.T. Fiske and G. Lindzey (eds) *The Handbook of Social Psychology* (4th edn, vol. 2, 193–281). New York: Wiley.

Berscheid, E. and Walster, E.H. (1987) *Interpersonal Attraction* (2nd edn). Reading, MA: Addison-Wesley.

Berscheid, E., Dion, E.K., Walster, E. and Walster, G.W. (1971) Physical attractiveness and dating choice: A test of the matching hypothesis. *Journal of Experimental Social Psychology*, 7, 173–89.

Berscheid, E., Graziano, W., Monson, T. and Dermer, M. (1976) Outcome dependency: Attention, attribution, and attraction. *Journal of Personality and Social Psychology*, 34, 978–89.

Bettencourt, B.A. and Sheldon, K. (2001) Social roles as mechanisms for psychological need satisfaction within social groups. *Journal of Personality and Social Psychology*, 81, 1131–43.

Beukeboom, C.J. (2009) When words feel right: How affective expressions of listeners change a speaker's language use. *European Journal of Social Psychology*, 39, 747–56.

Beukeboom, C.J. and de Jong, E.M. (2008) When feelings speak: How affective and proprioceptive cues change language abstraction. *Journal of Language and Social Psychology*, 27, 110–22.

Beukeboom, C.J. and Semin, G.R. (2005) Mood and representations of behaviour: The how and why. *Cognition and Emotion*, 19, 1242–51.

Beukeboom, C.J. and Semin, G.R. (2006) How mood turns on language. *Journal of Experimental Social Psychology*, 42, 553–66.

Bianco, M., Harris, B., Garrison-Wade, D. and Leech, N. (2011) Gifted girls: Gender bias in gifted referrals. *Roeper Review*, 33, 170–81.

Bierhoff, H.W., Klein, R. and Kramp, P. (1991) Evidence for the altruistic personality from data on accident research. *Journal of Personality*, 59, 263–80.

Biernat, M., Crandall, C.S., Young, L.V. et al. (1998) All that you can be: Stereotyping of self and others in a military context. *Journal of Personality and Social Psychology*, 75, 301–17.

Biernat, M., Vescio, T.K. and Green, M.L. (1996) Selective self-stereotyping. *Journal of Personality and Social Psychology*, 71, 1194–209.

Billig, M. (1973) Normative communication in a minimal inter-group situation. *European Journal of Social Psychology*, 3, 339–43.

Billig, M. (1987) *Arguing and Thinking: A Rhetorical Approach to Social Psychology.* Cambridge: Cambridge University Press.

Billig, M. (1988) Social representations, objectification and anchoring: A rhetorical analysis. *Social Behaviour*, 3, 1–16.

Billig, M. (1992) *Talking about the Royal Family*. London: Routledge.

Billig, M. (1996) *Arguing and Thinking*. Cambridge: Cambridge University Press.

Billig, M. (1997) The dialogic unconscious: Psychoanalysis, discursive psychology and the nature of repression. *British Journal of Social Psychology*, 36, 139–59.

Billig, M. (2011) Writing social psychology: Fictional things and unpopulated texts. *British Journal of Social Psychology*, 50, 4–20.

Billig, M. and Tajfel, H. (1973) Social categorization and similarity in intergroup behaviour. *European Journal of Social Psychology*, 3, 27–55.

Bjork, J.M., Dougherty, D.M., Moeller, F.G. et al. (1999) The effects of tryptophan depletion and loading on laboratory aggression in men: Time course and a food-restricted control. *Psychopharmacology*, 142, 24–30.

Björkqvist, K. (1994) Sex differences in physical, verbal, and indirect aggression: A review of recent research. *Sex Roles*, 30, 177–88.

Bjorkqvist, K., Lagerspetz, K.M. and Osterman, K. (2002) Sex differences in covert aggression. *Aggressive Behavior*, 20, 27–33.

Björkqvist, K., Nygren, T., Björkland, A. and Björkqvist, S. (1994) Testosterone intake and aggressiveness: Real effect or anticipation? *Aggressive Behavior*, 20, 17–26.

Bjørnskov, C. (2008) The growth-inequality association: Government ideology matters. *Journal of Development Economics*, 87, 300–8.

Blackhart, G.C., Nelson, B.C., Knowles, M.L. and Baumeister, R.F. (2010) Rejection elicits emotional reactions but neither causes immediate distress nor lowers self-esteem: A meta-analytic review of 192 studies on social exclusion. *Personality and Social Psychology Review*, 13, 269–309.

Blair, R.J.R., Jones, L., Clark, F. and Smith, M. (1997) The psychopathic individual: A lack of responsiveness to distress cues? *Psychophysiology*, 34, 192–8.

Blake, R.R. and Mouton, J.S. (1961) Reactions to intergroup competition under win/lose conditions. *Management Science*, 7, 420–35.

Blank, H., Musch, J. and Pohl, R.F. (2008) Hindsight bias: On being wise after the event. *Social Cognition*, 25, 1–9.

Blank, R.H. (2005) The brain, aggression, and public policy. *Politics and the Life Sciences*, 24, 12–25.

Blankenship, K.L. and Holtgraves, T. (2005) The role of different markers of linguistic powerlessness in persuasion. *Journal of Language and Social Psychology*, 24, 3–24.

Blanton, H., Crocker, J. and Miller, D.T. (1999) The effects of in-group versus out-group social comparison on self-esteem in the context of a negative stereotype. *Journal of Experimental Social Psychology*, 36, 519–30.

Blascovich, J., Medes, W.B., Hunter, S.B. et al. (2001) Perceiver threat in social interactions with stigmatized others. *Journal of Personality and Social Psychology*, 80, 253–67.

Blascovich, J., Mendes, W.B., Hunter, S.B. and Salomon, K. (1999) Social 'facilitation' as challenge and threat. *Journal of Personality and Social Psychology*, 77, 68–77.

Blass, T. (1991) Understanding behavior in the Milgram obedience experiment: The role of personality, situations, and their interactions. *Journal of Personality and Social Psychology*, 60, 398.

Blass, T. (1992) The social psychology of Stanley Milgram. In M.P. Zanna (ed.) *Advances in Experimental Social Psychology* (pp. 227–328). San Diego: Academic Press.

Blass, T. (2004) *The Man Who Shocked the World: The Life and Legacy of Stanley Milgram*. New York: Basic Books.

Blatz, C.W. and Philpot, C.R. (2010) On the outcomes of intergroup apologies: A review. *Social and Personality Psychology Compass*, 4, 995–1007.

Blatz, C.W., Schumann, K. and Ross, M. (2009) Government apologies for historical injustices. *Political Psychology*, 30, 219–41.

Bleich, E. (2011) The rise of hate speech and hate crime laws in liberal democracies. *Journal of Ethnic and Migration Studies*, 6, 917–34.

Bless, H., Bohner, G., Schwarz, N. and Strack, F. (1990) Mood and persuasion. *Personality and Social Psychology Bulletin*, 16, 331–45.

Bliuc, A.M., McGarty, C., Reynolds, K.

and Muntele, D. (2007) Opinion-based group membership as a predictor of commitment to political action. *European Journal of Social Psychology*, 37, 19–32.

Block, L.G. and Keller, P.A. (1995) When to accentuate the negative: The effects of perceived efficacy and message framing on intentions to perform a health-related behavior. *Journal of Marketing Research*, 2, 192–203.

Blumer, H. (1969) *Symbolic Interactionism: Perspective and Method*. Englewood Cliffs, NJ: Prentice Hall.

Blumer, H.M. (1939) The nature of race prejudice. *Social Process in Hawaii*, 5, 11–21.

Boden, M. (1998) Creativity and artificial intelligence. *Artificial Intelligence*, 103, 347–56.

Bodenhausen, B.V., Sheppard, L.A. and Kramer, G.P. (1994) Negative affect and social judgment: The differential impact of anger and sadness. *European Journal of Social Psychology*, 24, 45–62.

Bodenhausen, G.V. (1990) Stereotypes as judgemental heuristics: Evidence of circadian variations in discrimination. *Psychological Science*, 1, 319–22.

Bodenhausen, G.V. (1993) *Emotions, Arousal, and Stereotypic Judgements: A Heuristic Model of Affect and Stereotyping*. New York: Academic Press.

Boeckmann, R.J. and Turpin-Petrosino, C. (2002) Understanding the harm of hate crime. *Journal of Social Issues*, 58, 207–25.

Bogaert, S., Boone, C. and Declerck, C. (2008) Social value orientation and co-operation in social dilemmas: A review and conceptual model. *British Journal of Social Psychology*, 47, 453–80.

Bohner, G. and Wänke, M. (eds) (2002) *Attitudes and Attitude Change*. Hove: Psychology Press.

Bohner, G., Chaiken, S. and Hunyadi, P. (1994) The role of mood and message ambiguity in the interplay of heuristic and systematic processing. *European Journal of Social Psychology*, 24, 207–21.

Bohner, G., Moskowitz, G.B. and Chaiken, S. (1995) The interplay of heuristic and systematic processing of social information. *European Review of Social Psychology*, 6, 33–68.

Bohner, G., Weisbrod, C., Raymond, P. et al. (1993) Salience of rape affects self-esteem: The moderating role of gender and rape myth acceptance. *European Journal of Social Psychology*, 23, 561–79.

Boldt, M. (1976) *Report of the Task Force on Suicides to the Minister of Social Services and Community Health*. Edmonton: Government of Alberta.

Bond, A.J., Wingrove, J. and Critchlow, D.G. (2001) Tryptophan depletion increases aggression in women during the premenstrual phase. *Pscyhopharmacology*, 156, 477–80.

Bond, C.F. Jr (1982) Social facilitation: A self-presentational view. *Journal of Personality and Social Psychology*, 42, 1042–50.

Bond, C.F. and Titus, L.J. (1983) Social facilitation: A meta-analysis of 241 studies. *Psychological Bulletin*, 94, 265–92.

Bond, C.F., Berry, D.S. and Omar, A. (1994) The kernal of truth in judgements of deceptiveness. *Basic and Applied Social Psychology*, 15, 523–34.

Bond, M.H. (1983) How language variation affects intercultural differentiation of values by Hong Kong bilinguals. *Journal of Language and Social Psychology*, 2, 57–67.

Bond, M.H., Leung, K. and Schwartz, S. (1992) Explaining choices in procedural and distributive justice across cultures. *International Journal of Psychology*, 27, 211–25.

Bond, R. and Smith, P.N. (1996) Culture and conformity: A meta-analysis of studies using Asch's (1952b, 1956) line judgment task. *Psychological Bulletin*, 119, 111–37.

Bones, A.K. and Johnson, N.R. (2007) Measuring the immeasurable: Or 'Could Abraham Lincoln take the implicit association test'? *Perspectives on Psychological Science*, 2, 406–11.

Bonta, B.D. (1997) Cooperation and competition in peaceful societies. *Psychological Bulletin*, 121, 299–320.

Book, A.S., Starzyk, K.B. and Quinsey, V.L. (2001) The relationship between testosterone and aggression: A meta-analysis. *Aggression and Violent Behavior*, 6, 579–99.

Booth, A., Shelly, G., Mazur, A. et al. (1989) Testosterone, and winning and losing in human competition. *Hormones and Behavior*, 23, 556–71.

Bordia, P. (1996) Studying verbal interaction on the Internet: The case of rumour transmission research. *Behavior Research Methods*, 28, 149–51.

Bordia, P. and Rosnow, R.L. (1998) Rumor rest stops on the information highway: Transmission patterns in a computer-mediated rumor chain. *Human Communication Research*, 25, 163–79.

Borg, I., Groenen, P.J.F., Jehn, K.A. et al. (2011) Embedding the organizational culture profile into Schwartz's theory of universals in values. *Journal of Personnel Psychology*, 10, 1–12.

Borkenau, P., Brecke, S., Möttig, C. and Paelecke, M. (2009) Extraversion is accurately perceived after a 50-ms exposure to a face. *Journal of Research in Personality*, 43, 703–6.

Bornstein, G., Rapoport, A., Kerpel, L. and Katz, T. (1989) Within and between group communication in intergroup competition for public goods. *Journal of Experimental Social Psychology*, 25, 422–36.

Bornstein, R.F. (1989) Exposure and affect: Overview and meta-analysis of research, 1968–1987. *Psychological Bulletin*, 106, 265–89.

Bornstein, R.F. and D'Agostino, P.R. (1992) Stimulus recognition and the mere exposure effect. *Journal of Personality and Social Psychology*, 63, 545–52.

Bornstein, R.F. and D'Agostino, P.R. (1994) The attribution and discounting of perceptual fluency: Preliminary tests of a perceptual fluency/attributional model of the mere exposure effect. *Social Cognition*, 12, 103–28.

Bosveld, W., Koomen, W. and Vogelaar, R. (1997) Construing a social issue: Effects on attitudes and the false consensus effect. *British Journal of Social Psychology*, 36, 263–72.

Bouas, K.S. and Komorita, S.S. (1996) Group discussion and cooperation in social dilemmas. *Personality and Social Psychology Bulletin*, 22, 1144–50.

Bouchard, T.J., Segal, N.L., Tellegan, A. et al. (2003) Evidence for the construct validity and heritability of the Wilson-Patterson conservatism scale: A reared-apart twins study of social attitudes. *Personality and Individual Differences*, 34, 959–69.

Bourgault, L.M. (1995) *Mass Media in Sub-Saharan Africa*. Bloomington, IN: Indiana University Press.

Bourhis, R.Y. and Giles, H. (1977) The language of intergroup distinctiveness. In H. Giles (ed.) *Language, Ethnicity and Intergroup Relations* (pp. 119–35). London: Academic Press.

Bourhis, R.Y., Giles, H. and Lambert, W.E. (1975) Social consequences of accommodating one's style of speech: A cross-cultural investigation. *International Journal of the Sociology of Language*, 6, 55–72.

Bowers, L., Smith, P.K. and Binney, V. (1994) Perceived family relationships of bullies, victims and bully/victims in middle childhood. *Journal of Social and Personal Relationships*, 11, 215–32.

Bowlby, J. (1969) *Attachment and Loss*, vol. 1: *Attachment*. New York: Basic Books

Bowlby, J. (1973) Self-reliance and some conditions that promote it. *Support, Innovation, and Autonomy*. London: Tavistock.

Bowlby, J. (1980) *Loss: Sadness and Depression*. New York: Basic Books.

Bowlby, J. (1988) *A Secure Base: Parent-child Attachment and Healthy Human Development*. New York: Hogarth Press.

Bowles, S. (2006) Group competition, reproductive levelling, and the evolution of human altruism. *Science*, 314, 1569–752.

Boyd, R. and Richerson, P.J. (1985) *Culture and the Evolutionary Process*. Chicago, IL: University of Chicago Press.

Boyden, T., Carroll, J.S. and Maier, R.A.

(1984) Similarity and attraction in homosexual males: The effects of age and masculinity-femininity. *Sex Roles*, 10, 939–48.

Boyes, W., Mounts, W.S. and Sowell, C. (2004) Monitoring and moral hazard in restaurant tipping. *Journal of Applied Social Psychology*, 34, 2616–28.

Boyle, K. (2001) What's natural about killing? Gender, copycat violence and natural born killers. *Journal of Gender Studies*, 10, 311–21.

Bradac, J. (1990) Language attitudes and impression formation. In H. Giles and W. Robinson (eds) *Handbook of Language and Social Psychology* (pp. 387–412). Chichester: Wiley.

Bradfield, A. and Wells, G.L. (2005) Not the same old hindsight bias: Outcome information distorts a broad range of recollections. *Memory and Cognition*, 33, 120–30.

Bradford, S.A., Feeney, J.A. and Campbell, L. (2002) Links between attachment orientations and dispositional and diary-based measures of disclosure in dating couples: A study of actor and partner effects. *Personal Relationships*, 9, 491–506.

Braginsky, B.M. and Braginsky, D.D. (1967) Schizophrenic patients in the psychiatric interview: An experimental study of the manipulative tactics of mental patients. *Journal of Consulting Psychology*, 31, 543–7.

Braithwaite, J. (2002) *Restorative Justice and Responsive Regulation*. Oxford: Oxford University Press.

Brandon, D.P. and Hollingshead, A.B. (2007) Characterizing online groups. In A. Joinson, K. McKenna, T. Postmes and U.-D. Reips (eds) *Oxford Handbook of Internet Psychology* (pp. 105–19). Oxford: Oxford University Press.

Brandstätter, V., Lengfelder, A. and Gollwitzer, P.M. (2001) Implementation intentions and efficient action initiation. *Journal of Personality and Social Psychology*, 81, 946–50.

Branscombe, N.R. and Doosje, B. (eds) (2004) *Collective Guilt: International Perspectives*. Cambridge: Cambridge University Press.

Brauer, M., Judd, C.M. and Gliner, M.D. (1995) The effects of reoperated expressions on attitude polarization during group discussion. *Journal of Personality and Social Psychology*, 68, 1014–29.

Brauer, M., Judd, C.M. and Jacquelin, V. (2001) The communication of social stereotypes: The effects of group discussion and information distribution on stereotypic appraisals. *Journal of Personality and Social Psychology*, 81, 463–75.

Braun, V. and Clarke, V. (2006) Using thematic analysis in psychology. *Qualitative Research in Psychology*, 3, 77–101.

Brehm, J.W. (1956) Postdecision changes in the desirability of alternatives. *Journal of Abnormal and Social Psychology*, 52, 384–9.

Brehm, J.W. (1966) *A Theory of Psychological Reactance*. New York: Academic Press.

Brehm, S.S. and Brehm, J.W. (1981) *Psychological Reactance: A Theory of Freedom and Control*. New York: Academic Press.

Brekler, S.J. (1984) Empirical validation of affect, behavior and cognition as distinct components of attitude. *Journal of Personality and Social Psychology*, 47, 1191–205.

Brendgen, M., Dionne, G., Girard, A. et al. (2005) Examining genetic and environmental effects on social aggression: A study of 6-year-old twins. *Child Development*, 76, 930–46.

Brennan, K.A. and Shaver, P.R. (1995) Dimensions of adult attachment, affect regulation, and romantic relationship functioning. *Personality and Social Psychology Bulletin*, 21, 267–83.

Brewer, M.B. (1968) Determinants of social distance among east African tribal groups. *Journal of Personality and Social Psychology*, 10, 279.

Brewer, M.B. (1991) The social self: On being the same and different at the same time. *Personality and Social Psychology Bulletin*, 17, 475–82.

Brewer, M.B. (1993) Social identity, distinctiveness, and in-group homogeneity. *Social Cognition*, 11, 15–164.

Brewer, M.B. (1999) The psychology of prejudice: Ingroup love or outgroup hate? *Journal of Social Issues*, 55, 429–44.

Brewer, M.B. and Kramer, R.M. (1985) The psychology of intergroup attitudes and behavior. *Annual Review of Psychology*, 36, 219–43.

Brewer, M.B. and Kramer, R.M. (1986) Choice behavior in social dilemmas: Effects of social identity, group size, and decision framing. *Journal of Personality and Social Psychology*, 50, 543–9.

Brewer, M.B. and Miller, N. (1984) Beyond the contact hypothesis: Theoretical perspectives on segregation. In N. Miller and M.B. Brewer (eds) *Groups in Contact: The Psychology of Desegregation* (pp. 281–302). Orlando, FL: Academic Press.

Brewer, M.B. and Weber, J.G. (1994) Self-evaluation effects of interpersonal versus intergroup social comparison. *Journal of Personality and Social Psychology*, 66, 268–75.

Briñol, P. and Petty, R.E. (2005) Individual differences in persuasion. In D. Albarracin, B.T. Johnson and M.P. Zanna (eds) *The Handbook of Attitudes and Attitude Change* (pp. 575–616). Hillsdale, NJ: Erlbaum.

Brinthaupt, T.M., Moreland, R.L. and Levine, J.M. (1991) Sources of optimism among prospective group members. *Personality and Social Psychology Bulletin*, 17, 36–43.

Brislin, R.W. (1993) *Understanding Culture's Influence on Behavior*. Fort Worth, TX: Harcourt Brace.

Britt, T.W., Boniecki, K.A., Vescio, T.K. et al. (1996) Intergroup anxiety: A person X situation approach. *Personality and Social Psychology Bulletin*, 22, 1177–88.

Broadbent, D.E. (1987) *Perception and Communication*. Oxford: Oxford University Press.

Brockner, J. (1979) The effects of self-esteem, success-failure, and self-consciousness on task performance. *Journal of Personality and Social Psychology*, 37, 1732–41.

Brodbeck, F. and Greitemeyer, T. (2000) A dynamic model of group performance: Considering the group members' capacity to learn. *Group Processes and Intergroup Relations*, 3, 159–82.

Bronson, F.H. and Desjardins, C. (1968) Aggression in adult mice: Modification by neonatal injections of gonadal hormones. *Science*, 161, 705–6.

Brooks, R.L. (1999) *When Sorry isn't Enough: The Controversy over Apologies and Reparations for Human Injustice*. New York: NYU Press.

Brown, G. (2011) Take back the future. *Newsweek*. Available at http://www.newsweek.com/2011/05/15/take-back-the-future.html, accessed 13 June 2011.

Brown, P. (1993) Gender, politeness and confrontation in Tenejapa. In D. Tannen (ed.) *Gender and Conversational Interaction* (pp. 144–64). New York: Oxford University Press.

Brown, P. and Levinson, S.C. (1978) Universals in language usage: Politeness phenomena. In E.N. Goody (ed.) *Questions and Politeness: Strategies in Social Interaction* (pp. 56–311). Cambridge: Cambridge University Press.

Brown, P. and Levinson, S.C. (1987) *Politeness: Some Universals in Language Usage*. Cambridge: Cambridge University Press.

Brown, R. (1965) The basic dimensions of interpersonal relationships. In R. Brown (ed.) *Social Psychology* (pp. 51–100). New York: Free Press.

Brown, R. and Gilman, A. (1989) Politeness theory and Shakespeare's four major tragedies. *Language in Society*, 18, 159–212.

Brown, R.J. (1978) Divided we fall: An analysis of relations between sections of a factory workforce. In H. Tajfel (ed.) *Differentiation Between Social Groups: Studies in the Social Psychology of Intergroup Relations* (pp. 395–429). London: Academic Press.

Brown, R.J. (1995) *Prejudice: Its Social Psychology*. Oxford: Blackwell.

Brown, R.J. (2000) *Group Processes: Dynamics Within and Between Groups* (2nd edn). Oxford: Blackwell.

Brown, R.J. and Hewstone, M. (2005) An integrative theory of intergroup contact. *Advances in Experimental Social Psychology*, 37, 255–343.

Brown, R.J. and Zagefka, H. (2005) Intergroup affiliations and prejudice. In J.F. Dovidio, P. Glick and L.A. Rudman (eds) *On the Nature of Prejudice: Fifty Years after Allport* (pp. 54–70). Malden, MA: Blackwell.

Brown, R.J., Condor, S., Mathews, A. et al. (1986) Explaining intergroup differentiation in an industrial organization. *Journal of Occupational and Organizational Psychology*, 59, 273–86.

Brown, R.J., González, R., Zagefka, H. et al. (2008) Nuestra culpa: Collective guilt and shame as predictors of reparation for historical wrongdoing. *Journal of Personality and Social Psychology*, 94, 75–90.

Brown, R.P., Wohl, M.J.A. and Exline, J.J. (2008) Taking up offenses: Secondhand forgiveness and group identification. *Personality and Social Psychology Bulletin*, 34, 1406–19.

Brown, S.L., Coyne, S.M., Barlow, A. and Qualter, P. (2010) Alcohol-related image-priming and aggression in adolescents aged 11–14. *Addictive Behaviors*, 35, 791–4.

Brown, V.R. and Paulus, P.B. (2002) Making group brainstorming more effective: Recommendations from an associative memory perspective. *Current Directions in Psychological Science*, 11, 208–12.

Browning, C. (1992) *Ordinary Men*. London: Penguin.

Brownmiller, S. (1975) *Against our Will: Men, Women, and Rape*. London: Secker & Warburg.

Bruder-Mattson, S.F. and Hovanitz, C.A. (1990) Coping and attributional styles as predictors of depression. *Journal of Clinical Psychology*, 46, 557–65.

Brunell, A.B., Gentry, W.A., Campbell, W.K. et al. (2008) Leader emergence: The case of the narcissistic leader. *Personality and Social Psychology Bulletin*, 34, 1663–76.

Bruner, G.C. (1990) Music, mood and marketing. *Journal of Marketing*, 54, 94–104.

Bruner, J. (1990) *Acts of Meaning*. Cambridge, MA: Harvard University Press.

Brusco, M. and Steinley, D. (2010) K-balancing partitioning: An exact method with applications to generalized structural balance and other psychological contexts. *Psychological Methods*, 15, 145–57.

Bryan, J.H. and Test, M.A. (1967) Models and helping: Naturalistic studies in aiding behavior. *Journal of Personality and Social Psychology*, 6, 400–7.

Bryant, F.B. and Guilbault, R.L. (2002) 'I knew it all along' eventually: The development of hindsight bias in reaction to the Clinton impeachment verdict. *Basic and Applied Social Psychology*, 24, 27–41.

Buchholz, R.A. (2009) *Rethinking Capitalism: Community and Responsibility in Business*. London: Routledge.

Buck, R. (1984) *The Communication of Emotion*. New York: Guilford Press.

Buckley, K.E., Winkel, R.E. and Leary, M.R. (2004) Reactions to acceptance and rejection: Effects of level and sequence of relational evaluation. *Journal of Experimental Social Psychology*, 40, 14–28.

Buehler, R., Griffin, D. and Ross, M. (1994) Exploring the 'planning fallacy': Why people underestimate their task completion times. *Journal of Personality and Social Psychology*, 67, 366–81.

Bueno de Mesquita, E. and Dickson, E.S. (2007) The propaganda of the deed: Terrorism, counterterrorism, and mobilization. *American Journal of Political Science*, 51, 364–81.

Buffardi, L.E. and Campbell, W.K. (2008) Narcissism and social networking sites. *Personality and Social Psychology Bulletin*, 34, 1303–14.

Bugental, D.E., Love, L.R. and Gianetto, R.M. (1971) Perfidious feminine faces. *Journal of Personality and Social Psychology*, 17, 314–18.

Bunge, C.O. (1903) *Principes de psychologie individuelle et sociale*. Paris: Alcan.

Burger, J.M. (1986) Increasing compliance by improving the deal: The that's-not-all technique. *Journal of Personality and Social Psychology*, 51, 277–83.

Burger, J.M. (1987) Increased performance with increased personal control: A self-presentation interpretation. *Journal of Experimental Social Psychology*, 23, 350–60.

Burger, J.M. (2009) Replicating Milgram: Would people still obey today? *American Psychologist*, 64, 1–11.

Burger, J.M., Reed, M., DeCesare, K. et al. (1999) The effects of initial request size on compliance: More about the that's-not-all technique. *Basic and Applied Social Psychology*, 21, 243–49.

Burgoon, J.K., Buller, D.B. and Woodall, W.G. (1989) *Nonverbal Communication: The Unspoken Dialogue*. New York: Harper & Row.

Burhmester, M., Kwang, T. and Gosling, S.D. (2011) Amazon's Mechanical Turk: A new source of inexpensive, yet high-quality, data? *Perspectives on Psychological Science*, 6, 3–5.

Burke, P.J. (1991) Identity processes and social stress. *American Sociological Review*, 56, 836–49.

Burleson, B.R. (1994) Comforting messages: Features, functions, and outcomes. In J.A. Daly and J.M. Wiemann (eds) *Strategic Interpersonal Communication* (pp. 135–61). Hillsdale, NJ: Lawrence Erlbaum.

Burleson, B.R. and Samter, W. (1996) Similarity in the communication skills of young adults: Foundations of attraction, friendship, and relationship satisfaction. *Communication Reports*, 9, 127–39.

Burman, E. (2011) Psychology, women, and political practice in Britain. In A. Rutherford, R. Capdevila, V. Undurti and I. Palmary (eds) *Handbook of International Feminisms, International and Cultural Psychology* (pp. 219–43). New York: Springer.

Burnstein, E. and Vinokur, A. (1977) Persuasive argumentation and social comparison as determinants of attitude polarization. *Journal of Experimental Social Psychology*, 13, 315–32.

Burnstein, E. and Worschel, S. (1962) Arbitrariness of frustration and its consequences for aggression in a social situation. *Journal of Personality*, 30, 528–41.

Burnstein, E., Crandall, C. and Kitayama, S. (1994) Some neo-Darwinian decision rules for altruism: Weighing cues for inclusive fitness as a function of the biological importance of the decision. *Journal of Personality and Social Psychology*, 67, 773–89.

Bush, G., Luu, P. and Posner, M.I. (2000) Cognitive and emotional influences in anterior cingulate cortex. *Trends in Cognitive Sciences*, 4, 215–22.

Bush, L.K., Barr, C.L., McHugo, G.J. and Lanzetta, J.T. (1989) The effects of facial control and facial mimicry on subjective reactions to comedy routines. *Motivation and Emotion*, 13, 31–52.

Bushman, B. and Baumeister, R.F. (1998) Threatened egotism, narcissism, self-esteem, and direct and displaced aggression: Does self-love or self-hate lead to violence? *Journal of Personality and Social Psychology*, 75, 219–29.

Bushman, B.J. and Anderson, C.A. (1998) Methodology in the study of aggression: Integrating experimental and nonexperimental findings. In R. Geen and E. Donnerstein (eds) *Human Aggression: Theories, Research and Implications for Policy* (pp. 23–48). San Diego, CA: Academic Press.

Bushman, B.J. and Anderson, C.A. (2001) Media violence and the American public: Scientific facts versus media misinformation. *American Psychologist*, 56, 477–89.

Bushman, B.J. and Cantor, J. (2003) Media ratings for violence and sex: Implications for policy makers and parents. *American Psychologist*, 58, 130–41.

Bushman, B.J. and Huesmann, L.R. (2006) Short-term and long-term effects of violent media on aggression in children and adults. *Archives of Pediatrics and Adolescent Medicine*, 160, 348–52.

Bushman, B.J. and Whitaker, J.L. (2010) Like a magnet: Catharsis beliefs attract angry people to video games. *Psychological Science*, 21, 790–2.

Bushman, B.J., Baumeister, R.F. and Phillips, C.M. (2001) Do people aggress to improve their mood? Catharsis beliefs, affect regulation opportunity, and aggressive responding. *Journal of Personality and Social Psychology*, 81, 17–32.

Buss, A.H. (1980) *Self-consciousness and Social Anxiety*. San Francisco: Freeman.

Buss, D.M. (1989) Sex differences in human mate preferences: Evolutionary hypotheses tested in 37 cultures. *Behavioral and Brain Sciences*, 12, 1–49.

Buss, D.M. (1995) Psychological sex differences: Origins through sexual selection. *American Psychologist*, 50, 164–8.

Buss, D.M. (2000) The evolution of happiness. *American Psychologist*, 55, 15–23.

Buss, D.M. (2003) *The Evolution of Desire: Strategies of Human Mating* (2nd edn). New York: Basic Books.

Buss, D.M. (2009) How can evolutionary psychology successfully explain personality and individual differences? *Perspectives on Psychological Science*, 4, 359–66.

Buss, D.M. and Schmitt, D.P. (1993) Sexual strategies theory: An evolutionary perspective on human mating. *Psychological Review*, 100, 204–54.

Buston, P.M. and Emlen, S.T. (2003) Cognitive processes underlying human mate choice: The relationship between self-perception and mate preference in western society. *Proceedings of the National Academy of Sciences*, 100, 8805–10.

Butler, D. and Geis, F.L. (1990) Nonverbal affect responses to male and female leaders: Implications for leadership evaluations. *Journal of Personality and Social Psychology*, 58, 48–59.

Butler, J.L. and Baumeister, R.F. (1998) The trouble with friendly faces: Skilled performance with a supportive audience. *Journal of Personality and Social Psychology*, 75, 1213–30.

Buunk, A.P. and van Vugt, M. (2008) *Applying Social Psychology: From Problems to Solutions*. London: Sage.

Buunk, B.P. and Schaufeli, W.B. (1999) Reciprocity in interpersonal relationships: An evolutionary perspective on its importance for health and well-being. *European Review of Social Psychology*, 10, 259–91.

Buunk, B.P. and van Yperen, N.W. (1991) Referential comparisons, relational comparisons, and exchange orientation: Their relation to marital satisfaction. *Personality and Social Psychology Bulletin*, 17, 709–17.

Buunk, B.P., Zurriaga, R., Peiro, J.M. et al. (2005) Social comparisons at work as related to a cooperative social climate and to individual differences in social comparison orientation. *Applied Psychology*, 54, 61–80.

Bylsma, W.H. and Major, B. (1994) Social comparisons and contentment: Exploring the psychological costs of the gender wage gap. *Psychology of Women Quarterly*, 18, 241–9.

Byrne, D. (1997) An overview (and underview) of research and theory within the attraction paradigm. *Journal of Social and Personal Relationships*, 14, 417–31.

Byrne, D. and Clore, G.L. (1970) A reinforcement model of evaluative responses. *Personality: An International Journal; Personality: An International Journal*, 1, 103–28.

Byrne, D. and Nelson, D. (1965) Attraction as a linear function of proportion of positive reinforcements. *Journal of Personality and Social Psychology*, 1, 659–63.

Byrne, D.E. (1971) *The Attraction Paradigm*. New York: Academic Press.

Byrne, G. (2000) Road rage. *New Scientist*, 168, 38–41.

Byrnes, J.P., Miller, D C. and Schafer, W.D. (1999) Gender differences in risk taking: A meta-analysis. *Psychological Bulletin*, 125, 367–83.

Cabinet Office (2012) *Applying Behavioural Insights to Reduce Fraud, Error and Debt*. Behavioural Insights Team, February, www.cabinetoffice.gov.uk.

Cacioppo, J.T. and Petty, R.E. (1979) Attitudes and cognitive response: An electrophysiological approach. *Journal of Personality and Social Psychology*, 37, 2181–99.

Cacioppo, J.T. and Petty, R.E. (1982) The need for cognition. *Journal of Personality and Social Psychology*, 42, 116–31.

Cacioppo, J.T., Petty, R.E. and Kao, C.F. (1984) The efficient assessment of need for cognition. *Journal of Personality Assessment*, 48, 306–7.

Cacioppo, J.T., Petty, R.E. and Morris, K.J. (1983) Effects of need for cognition on message evaluation, recall, and persuasion. *Journal of Personality and Social Psychology*, 45, 805–18.

Cacioppo, J.T., Petty, R.E., Feinstein, J.A. and Jarvis, W.B.G. (1996) Dispositional differences in cognitive motivation: The life and times of individuals varying in need for cognition. *Psychological Bulletin*, 119, 197–253.

Cacioppo, J.T., Petty, R.E., Losch, M.E. and Kim, H.S. (1986) Electromyographic activity over facial muscle regions can differentiate the valence and intensity of affective reactions. *Journal of Personality and Social Psychology*, 50, 260–8.

Cacioppo, J.T., Priester, J.R. and Berntson, G.G. (1993) Rudimentary determinants of attitudes. II: Arm flexion and extension have differential effects on attitudes. *Journal of Personality and Social Psychology*, 65, 5–17.

Cacioppo, J.T., Sandman, C.A. and Walker, B.B. (1978) The effects of operant heart rate conditioning on cognitive elaboration and attitude change. *Psychophysiology*, 15, 330–8.

Caldwell, R.A. and Reinhart, M.A. (1988) The relationship of personality to individual differences in the use of, type, and source of social support. *Journal of Social and Clinical Psychology*, 6, 140–6.

Callahan-Levy, C.M. and Meese, L.A. (1979) Sex differences in the allocation of pay. *Journal of Personality and Social Psychology*, 37, 433–46.

Callan, M.J., Ellard, J.H., Shead, N.W. and Hodgins, D.C. (2008) Gambling as a search for justice: Examining the role of personal relative deprivation in gambling urges and gambling behaviour. *Personality and Social Psychology Bulletin*, 34, 1514–29.

Callan, M.J., Ferguson, H.J. and Bindemann, M. (in press) Eye movements to audio-visual scenes reveal expectations of a just-world. *Journal of Experimental Psychology: General*

Callan, M.J., Kay, A.C., Davidenko, N. and Ellard, J.H. (2009) The effects of justice motivation on memory for self- and other-relevant events. *Journal of Experimental Social Psychology*, 45, 614–23.

Callan, M.J., Powell, N.G. and Ellard, J.H. (2007) The consequences of victim physical attractiveness on reactions to injustice: The role of observers' belief in a just world. *Social Justice Research*, 20, 433–56.

Callan, M.J., Sutton, R.M. and Dovale, C. (2010) When deserving translates into causing: The effect of cognitive load on immanent justice reasoning. *Journal of Experimental Social Psychology*, 46, 1097–100.

Callaway, M.R. and Esser, J.K. (1984) Groupthink: Effects of cohesiveness and problem-solving procedures on group decision-making. *Social Behavior and Personality*, 12, 157–64.

Calogero, R.M. (2004) A test of objectification theory: The effect of the male gaze on appearance concerns in college women. *Psychology of Women Quarterly*, 28, 16–21.

Calogero, R.M. and Jost, J.T. (2011) Self-subjugation among women: Exposure to sexist ideology, self-objectification, and the protective function of the need to avoid closure. *Journal of Personality and Social Psychology*, 100, 211–28.

Calogero, R.M. and Pina, A. (2011) Body guilt: Preliminary evidence for a further subjective experience of self-objectification. *Psychology of Women Quarterly*, 35, 428–40.

Calogero, R.M., Bardi, A. and Sutton, R.M. (2009) A need basis for values: Associations between the need for cognitive closure and value orientations. *Personality and Individual Differences*, 46, 154–9.

Calogero, R.M., Davis, W.N. and Thompson, J.K. (2005) The role of self-objectification in the experience of women with eating disorders. *Sex Roles*, 52, 43–50.

Camerer, C.F. (2003) *Behavioral Game Theory: Experiments in Strategic Interaction*. Princeton, NJ: Princeton University Press.

Cameron, L. and Rutland, A. (2006) Extended contact through story reading in school: Reducing children's prejudice toward the disabled. *Journal of Social Issues*, 62, 469–88.

Cameron, L., Rutland, A., Brown, R. and Douch, R. (2006) Changing children's intergroup attitudes toward refugees: Testing different models of intergroup contact. *Child Development*, 77, 1208–19.

Campbell-Kibler, K. (2007) Accent, (ING), and the social logic of listener perceptions. *American Speech*, 82, 32–64.

Campbell, D.T. (1958) Common fate, similarity and other indices of the status of aggregates of persons as social entities. *Behavioral Sciences*, 3, 14–25.

Campbell, D.T. (1967) Stereotypes and the perception of group differences. *American Psychologist*, 22, 817–29.

Campbell, J.D. (1990) Self-esteem and clarity of the self-concept. *Journal of Personality and Social Identity*, 59, 538–49.

Campbell, J.D. and Fairey, P.J. (1989) Informational and normative routes to conformity: The effect of faction size as a function of norm extremity and attention to the stimulus. *Journal of Personality and Social Psychology*, 57, 457–68.

Campbell, J.D., Trapnell, P.D., Heine, S.J. et al. (1996) Self-concept clarity: Measurement, personality correlates, and cultural boundaries. *Journal of Personality and Social Psychology*, 70, 141–56.

Campbell, M.C. and Keller, K.L. (2003) Brand familiarity and advertising repetition effects. *Journal of Consumer Research*, 30, 292–304.

Campbell, W.K., Bosson, J.K., Goheen, T.W. et al. (2007) Do narcissists dislike themselves 'deep down inside'? *Psychological Science*, 18, 227–9.

Caplan, S.E. (2002) Problematic internet use and psychosocial well-being: Development of a theory-based cognitive-behavioral measurement instrument.

Computers in Human Behavior, 18, 553–75.

Cappella, J.N. (1997) Behavioral and judged coordination in adult informal social interactions: Vocal and kinesic indicators. *Journal of Personality and Social Psychology*, 72, 119–31.

Cappella, J.N. and Planalp, S. (1981) Talk and silence sequences in informal conversations III: Interspeaker influence. *Human Communication Research*, 7, 117–32.

Card, N.A., Stucky, B.D., Sawalani, G.M. and Little, T.D. (2008) Direct and indirect aggression during childhood and adolescence: A meta-analytic review of gender differences, intercorrelations, and relations to maladjustment. *Child Development*, 79, 1185–229.

Cardiff, C.F. and Klein, D.B. (2005) Faulty partisan affiliations in all disciplines: A voter-registration study. *Critical Review*, 17, 237–55.

Carey, B. (2011) Fraud case seen as red flag for psychology research. *New York Times*, http://www.nytimes.com/2011/11/03/health/research/noted-dutch-psychologist-stapel-accused-of-research-fraud.html.

Carli, L.L. (1990) Gender, language, and influence. *Journal of Personality and Social Psychology*, 59, 941.

Carli, L.L. (1999) Cognitive reconstruction, hindsight, and reactions to victims and perpetrators. *Personality and Social Psychology Bulletin*, 25, 966–79.

Carli, L.L. and Eagly, A.H. (1999) Gender effects on social influence and emergent leadership. In G.N. Powell (ed.) *Handbook of Gender and Work* (pp. 203–22). Thousand Oaks, CA: Sage.

Carlo, G., Eisenberg, N., Troyer, D. et al. (1991) The altruistic personality: In what contexts is it apparent? *Journal of Personality and Social Psychology*, 61, 450–8.

Carlsmith, J.M. and Gross, A.E. (1969) Some effects of guilt on compliance. *Journal of Personality and Social Psychology*, 11, 232–9.

Carlston, D.E. and Skowronski, J.J. (1994) Savings in the relearning of trait information as evidence for spontaneous inference generation. *Journal of Personality and Social Psychology*, 66, 840–56.

Carnagey, N.L., Anderson, C.A. and Bartholow, B.D. (2007) Media violence and social neuroscience. *Current Directions in Psychological Science*, 16, 178–82.

Carnaghi, A. and Maass, A. (2007) In-group and out-group perspectives in the use of derogatory group labels: Gay versus fag. *Journal of Language and Social Psychology*, 26, 142–56.

Carnaghi, A., Maass, A., Gresta, S. et al. (2008) Nomina sunt omina: On the inductive potential of nouns and

adjectives in person perception. *Journal of Personality and Social Psychology*, 94, 839–59.

Carnahan, T. and McFarland, S. (2007) Revisiting the Stanford prison experiment: Could participant self-selection have led to the cruelty? *Personality and Social Psychology Bulletin*, 33, 603–14.

Carney, D. and Banaji, M. (2008) First is Best. Unpublished manuscript, Harvard University.

Carney, D.R., Colvin, C.R. and Hall, J.A. (2007) A thin slice perspective on the accuracy of first impressions. *Journal of Research in Personality*, 41, 1054–72.

Carney, D.R., Cuddy, A.J.C. and Yap, A.J. (2010) Power posing: Brief nonverbal displays affect neuroendocrine levels and risk tolerance. *Psychological Science*, 21, 1363–8.

Carpenter, J.M., Green, M.C. and LaFlam, J. (2011) People or profiles: Individual differences in online social networking use. *Personality and Individual Differences*, 50, 538–41.

Carré, J.M. and McCormick, C.M. (2008) In your face: Facial metrics predict aggressive behaviour in the laboratory and in varsity and professional hockey players. *Proceedings of the Royal Society of London, Section B*, 275, 2651–6.

Carré, J.M., Morrissey, M.D., Mondloch, C.J. and McCormick, C.M. (2010) Estimating aggression from emotionally neutral faces: Which facial cues are diagnostic? *Perception*, 39, 356–77.

Carroll, J.S., Bazerman, M.H. and Maury, R. (1988) Negotiator cognitions: A descriptive approach to negotiators' understanding of their opponents. *Organizational Behavior and Human Decision Processes*, 41, 352–70.

Carruthers, P. (2010) Introspection: Divided and partly eliminated. *Philosophy and Phenomenological Research*, 80, 76–111.

Carter, C.S. (1998) Neuroendocrine perspectives on social attachment and love. *Psychoneuroendocinology*, 23, 779–818.

Carver, C.S. and Harmon-Jones, E. (2009) Anger is an approach-related affect: Evidence and implications. *Psychological Bulletin*, 135, 183–204.

Carver, C.S. and Scheier, M.F. (1981) Analyzing shyness: A specific application of broader self-regulatory principles. In W.H. Jones, J.M. Cheek and S.R. Briggs (eds) *Shyness: Perspectives on Research and Treatment* (pp. 173–85). New York: Plenum Press.

Carver, C.S. and Scheier, M.F. (1981) *Attention and Self-regulation*. New York: Springer-Verlag.

Carver, C.S. and Scheier, M.F. (1998) *On the Self-regulation of Behavior*. New York: Cambridge University Press.

Casper, J.D., Benedict, K. and Perry, J.L.

(1989) Juror decision making, attitudes, and the hindsight bias. *Law and Human Behavior*, 13, 291–310.

Caspi, A., McClay, J., Moffitt, T.E. et al. (2002) Role of genotype in the cycle of violence in maltreated children. *Science*, 297, 5582.

Cassidy, J. (2000) Adult romantic attachments: A developmental perspective on individual differences. *Review of General Psychology*, 4, 111–31.

Castano, E., Paladino, M.P., Coull, A. and Yzerbyt, V.Y. (2002) Protecting the ingroup stereotype: Ingroup identification and the management of deviant ingroup members. *British Journal of Social Psychology*, 41, 365–85.

Castano, E., Yzerbyt, V., Paladino, M. and Sacchi, S. (2002) I belong, therefore, I exist: Ingroup identification, ingroup entitativity, and ingroup bias. *Personality and Social Bulletin*, 28, 135–43.

Castelli, L., Pavan, G., Ferrari, E. and Kashima, Y. (2009) The stereotyper and the chameleon: The effects of stereotype use on perceivers' mimicry. *Journal of Experimental Social Psychology*, 45, 835–9.

Castelli, L., Zogmaister, C. and Tomelleri, S. (2009) The transmission of racial attitudes within the family. *Developmental Psychology*, 45, 586–91.

Cavazza, N. and Mucchi-Faina, A. (2008) Me, us, or them: Who is more conformist? Perception of conformity and political orientation. *The Journal of Social Psychology*, 148, 335–46.

Cesarani, D. (2005) *Eichmann: His Life and Crimes*. New York: Vintage Books.

Chacko, T.I. (1982) Women and equal employment opportunity: Some unintended effects. *Journal of Applied Psychology*, 67, 119–23.

Chaiken, S. (1979) Communicator physical attractiveness and persuasion. *Journal of Personality and Social Psychology*, 37, 1387–97.

Chaiken, S. (1980) Heuristic versus systematic information processing and the use of source versus message cues in persuasion. *Journal of Personality and Social Psychology*, 39, 752–66.

Chaiken, S. (1987) The heuristic model of persuasion. In M.P. Zanna, J.M. Olson and C.P. Herman (eds) *Social Influence: The Ontario Symposium* (vol. 5, pp. 3–39). Hillsdale, NJ: Erlbaum.

Chaiken, S. and Eagly, A.H. (1976) Communication modality as a determinant of message persuasiveness and message comprehensibility. *Journal of Personality and Social Psychology*, 34, 605–14.

Chaiken, S. and Eagly, A.H. (1983) Communication modality as a determinant of persuasion: The role of communicator salience. *Journal of Personality and Social Psychology*, 45, 241–56.

Chaiken, S. and Maheswaran, D. (1994) Heuristic processing can bias systematic processing: Effects of source credibility, argument ambiguity, and task importance on attitude judgement. *Journal of Personality and Social Psychology*, 66, 460–73.

Chaiken, S., Giner-Sorolla, R. and Chen, S. (1996) Beyond accuracy: Defense and impression motives in heuristic and systematic information processing. In P.M. Gollwitzer and J.A. Bargh (eds) *The Psychology of Action: Linking Cognition and Motivation to Behavior* (pp. 553–78). New York: Guilford Press.

Chaiken, S, Liberman, A and Eagly, A.H. (1989) Heuristics and systematic information processing within and beyond the persuasion context. In J.S. Uleman and J.A. Bargh (eds) *Unintended Thought: Limits of Awareness, Intention, and Control* (pp. 212–52). New York: Guilford Press.

Chan, D.K.S. and Cheng, G.H.L. (2004) A comparison of offline and online friendship qualities at different stages of relationship development. *Journal of Social and Personal Relationships*, 21, 305–20.

Chandra, S. (1973) The effects of group pressure in perception: A cross-cultural conformity study in Fiji. *International Journal of Psychology*, 8, 37–9.

Chang, C.S. and Swann, W.B. (2012) The benefits of self-verifying social feedback. In R. Sutton, M. Hornsey and K. Douglas (eds) *Feedback: The Handbook of Praise, Criticism, and Advice* (pp. 29–42). New York: Peter Lang.

Chang, L., Lu, H.J., Li, H. and Li, T. (2011) The face that launched a thousand ships: The mating-warring association in men. *Personality and Social Psychology Bulletin*, 37, 976–84.

Chartrand, T.L. and Bargh, J.A. (1999) The chameleon effect: The perception-behavior link and social interaction. *Journal of Personality and Social Psychology*, 76, 893–910.

Chasteen, A.L., Park, D C. and Shwarz, N. (2001) Implementation intentions and facilitation of prospective memory. *Psychological Science*, 12, 457–61.

Chatterjee, A. and Hambrick, D.C. (2007) It's all about me: Narcissistic chief executive officers and their effects on company strategy and performance. *Administrative Science Quarterly*, 52, 351–86.

Chemers, M.M., Hays, R.B., Rhodewalt, F. and Wysocki, J. (1985) A person-environment analysis of job stress: A contingency model explanation. *Journal of Personality and Social Psychology*, 49, 628–35.

Chen, F.F. and Kenrick, D.T. (2002) Repulsion or attraction?: Group membership and assumed attitude similarity. *Journal of Personality and Social Psychology*, 83, 111–25.

Chen, L.H., Baker, S., Braver, E.R. and Li, G. (2000) Carrying passengers as a risk factor for crashes fatal to 16- and 17-year old drivers. *The Journal of the American Medical Association*, 283, 1578–82.

Chen, M. and Bargh, J.A. (1997) Nonconscious behavioral confirmation processes: The self-fulfilling consequences of automatic stereotype activation. *Journal of Experimental Social Psychology*, 33, 541–60.

Chen, M. and Bargh, J.A. (1999) Consequences of automatic evaluation: Immediate behavioral predispositions to approach or avoid the stimulus. *Personality and Social Psychology Bulletin*, 25, 215–24.

Chen, M.K. and Risen, J.L. (2010) How choice affects and reflects preferences: Revisiting the free-choice paradigm. *Journal of Personality and Social Psychology*, 99, 573–94.

Chen, S., Lee-Chai, A.Y. and Bargh, J.A. (2001) Relationship orientation as a moderator of the effects of social power. *Journal of Personality and Social Psychology*, 80, 173–87.

Chen, S.C. (1937) Social modification of the activity of ants in nest-building. *Physiological Zoology*, 10, 420–36.

Chen, X.P. (1999) Work team cooperation: The effects of structural and motivational changes. In M. Foddy and M. Smithson (eds) *Resolving Social Dilemmas: Dynamic, Structural, and Intergroup Aspects* (pp. 181–92). Philadelphia, PA: Psychology Press.

Cheng, P.W. (1997) From covariation to causation: A causal power theory. *Psychological Review*, 104, 367–405.

Cheng, P.W. and Novick, L.R. (1990) A probabilistic contrast model of causal induction. *Journal of Personality and Social Psychology*, 58, 545–67.

Choi, I. and Nisbett, R.E. (2000) Cultural psychology of surprise: Holistic theories and recognition of contradiction. *Journal of Personality and Social Psychology*, 79, 890–905.

Choi, I., Nisbett, R.E. and Norenzayan, A. (1999) Causal attribution across cultures: Variation and universality. *Psychological Bulletin*, 125, 47–63.

Choma, B.L., Busseri, M.A. and Sadava, S.W. (2009) Liberal and conservative political ideologies: Different routes to happiness? *Journal of Research in Personality*, 43, 502–5.

Chomsky, N. (1957) *Syntactic Structures*. The Hague: Mouton.

Chrisler, J.C. (2002) Hormone hostages: The cultural legacy of PMS as a legal defense. In L.H. Collins, M.R. Dunlap and J.C. Chrisler (eds) *Charting a New Course for Feminist Psychology* (pp. 238–52). Santa Barbara, CA: Greenwood.

Chrisler, J.C. and Levy, K.B. (1990) The media construct a menstrual monster: A content analysis of PMS articles in the popular press. *Women and Health*, 16, 89–104.

Christiansen, M.H. and Chater, N. (2008) Language as shaped by the brain. *Behavioral and Brain Sciences*, 31, 489–558.

Chua, A. (2011) *Battle Hymn of the Tiger Mother*. Harmondsworth: Penguin.

Cialdini, R.B. (1984) *Influence: How and Why People Agree to Things.* New York: Quill.

Cialdini, R.B. (1991) Altruism or egoism? That is (still) the question. *Psychological Inquiry*, 2, 124–6.

Cialdini, R.B. (1993) *Influence: The Psychology of Persuasion.* New York: Collins Business.

Cialdini, R.B. (2001) Harnessing the science of persuasion. *Harvard Business Review*, 79, 72–9.

Cialdini, R.B. (2008) *Influence: Science and Practice*. Boston: Pearson.

Cialdini, R.B. and Petty, R.E. (1979) Anticipatory opinion effects. In R.E. Petty, T.M. Ostrom and T.C. Brock (eds) *Cognitive Response in Persuasion* (pp. 217–35). Hillsdale, NJ: Erlbaum.

Cialdini, R.B., Borden, R.J., Thorne, A. et al. (1976) Basking in reflected glory: Three (football) field studies. *Journal of Personality and Social Psychology*, 34, 366–75.

Cialdini, R.B., Brown, S.L., Lewis, B.P. et al. (1997) Reinterpreting the empathy-altruism relationship: When one into one equals oneness. *Journal of Personality and Social Psychology*, 73, 481–94.

Cialdini, R.B., Cacioppo, J.T., Bassett, R. and Miller, J.A. (1978) Low-ball procedure for producing compliance: Commitment then cost. *Journal of Personality and Social Psychology*, 36, 463–76.

Cialdini, R.B., Petty, R.E. and Cacioppo, J.T. (1981) Attitude and attitude change. *Annual Review of Psychology*, 32, 357–404.

Cialdini, R.B., Reno, R.R. and Kallgren, C.A. (1990) A focus theory of normative conduct: Recycling the concept of norms to reduce littering in public places. *Journal of Personality and Social Psychology*, 58, 1015–26.

Cialdini, R.B., Schaller, M., Houlihan, D. et al. (1987) Empathy-based helping: Is it selflessly or selfishly motivated? *Journal of Personality and Social Psychology*, 52, 749–58.

Cialdini, R.B., Trost, M.R. and Newsom, J.T. (1995) Preference for consistency: The development of a valid measure and the discovery of surprising behavioral implications. *Journal of Personality and Social Psychology*, 69, 318–28.

Cialdini, R.B., Vincent, J.E., Lewis, S.K. et al. (1975) Reciprocal concessions procedure for inducing compliance: The door-in-the-face technique. *Journal of Personality and Social Psychology*, 31, 206–15.

Cicerello, A. and Sheehan, E.P. (1995) Personal advertisements: A content analysis. *Journal of Social Behavior & Personality*, 10, 751–6.

Cini, M., Moreland, R.L. and Levine, J.M. (1993) Group staffing levels and responses to prospective and new group members. *Journal of Personality and Social Psychology*, 65, 723–34.

Clark, A. (1996) Linguistic anchors in the sea of thought. *Pragmatics and Cognition*, 4, 93–103.

Clark, A.E. and Kashima, Y. (2007) Stereotypes help people connect with others in the community: A situated functional analysis of the stereotype consistency bias in communication. *Journal of Personality and Social Psychology*, 93, 1028–39.

Clark, D.M. (1986) A cognitive approach to panic. *Behaviour Research and Therapy*, 24, 461–70.

Clark, L.A., Kochanska, G. and Ready, R. (2000) Mothers' personality and its interaction with child temperament as predictors of parenting behavior. *Journal of Personality and Social Psychology*, 79, 274–85.

Clary, E.G. and Snyder, M. (1991) A functional analysis of altruism and prosocial behavior: The case of volunteerism. In M.S. Clark (ed.) *Review of Personality and Social Psychology:* vol. 12, *Prosocial Behavior* (pp. 119–148). Newbury Park, CA: Sage.

Clary, E.G. and Snyder, M. (1999) The motivation to volunteer: Theoretical and practical considerations. *Current Directions in Psychological Science*, 8, 156–69.

Clifford, M.M. and Walster, E. (1973) The effect of physical attractiveness on teacher expectations. *Sociology of Education*, 46, 248–58.

Clore, G.L. (1976) Interpersonal attraction: An overview. In J.W. Thibaut, J.T. Spence and R.C. Carson (eds) *Contemporary Topics in Social Psychology* (pp. 135–75). Morristown, NJ: General Learning Press.

Clore, G.L. (1992) Cognitive phenomenology: Feelings and the construction of judgment. In L.L. Martin and A. Tesser (eds) *The Construction of Social Judgments* (pp. 133–63). Hillsdale, NJ: Erlbaum.

Clore, G.L. and Byrne, D. (1974) A reinforcement-affect model of attraction. In T.L Huston (ed.) *Foundations of Interpersonal Attraction* (pp. 143–70). New York: Academic Press.

Clore, G.L. and Parrott, W.G. (1991) Moods and their vicissitudes: Thoughts and feelings as information. In J.P.P. Forgas (ed.) *Emotion and Social Judgments: International Series in Experimental Social Psychology* (pp. 107–23). Elmsford: Pergamon.

Cloutier, J., Gebrieli, J.D.E., O'Young, D. and Ambady, N. (2011) An fMRI study of violations of social expectations: When people are not who we expect them to be. *NeuroImage*, 57, 583–8.

Clutton-Brock, T. (2002) Breeding together: Kin selection and mutualism in cooperative vertebrates. *Science*, 296, 69–72.

CNBC (2011) World's biggest debtor nations. Available at http://www.cnbc.com/id/30308959?slide=1, accessed 13 June 2011.

Coch, L. and French, J.R.P. Jr (1948) Overcoming resistance to change. *Human Relations*, 1, 512–32.

Codol, J.P. (1975) On the so-called 'superior conformity of the self' behavior: Twenty experimental investigations. *European Journal of Social Psychology*, 5, 457–501.

Codol, J.P. (1984) Social differentiation and non-differentiation. In H. Tajfel (ed.) *The Social Dimension: European Developments in Social Psychology* (pp. 314–37). Cambridge: Cambridge University Press.

Cohen, D. and Nisbett, R.E. (1994) Self-protection and the culture of honor: Explaining southern violence. *Personality and Social Psychology Bulletin*, 20, 551–67.

Cohen, D. and Nisbett, R.E. (1997) Field experiments examining the culture of honor: The role of institutions in perpetuating norms about violence. *Personality and Social Psychology Bulletin*, 23, 1188–99.

Cohen, D., Nisbett, R.E., Bowdle, B.F. and Schwartz, N. (1996) Insult, aggression, and the Southern culture of honor: An 'experimental ethnography'. *Journal of Personality and Social Psychology*, 70, 945–60.

Cohen, E.G. (1982) Expectation states and interracial interaction in school settings. *Annual Review of Sociology*, 8, 209–35.

Cohen, S. and Wills, T.A. (1985) Stress, social support, and the buffering hypothesis. *Psychological Bulletin*, 98, 310–57.

Cohen-Charash, Y. and Spector, P.E. (2001) The role of justice in organizations: A meta-analysis. *Organizational Behavior and Human Decision Processes*, 86, 278–321.

Collins, C.L., Fields, S.K. and Comstock, R.D. (2008) When the rules of the game are broken: What proportion of high school sports-related injuries are related to illegal activity? *Injury Prevention*, 14, 34–8.

Collins, N.L. (1996) Working models of attachment: Implications for explanation, emotion, and behavior. *Journal of Personality and Social Psychology*, 71, 810–32.

Collins, N.L. and Miller, L.C. (1994) Self-disclosure and liking: A meta-analytic review. *Psychological Bulletin*, 116, 457–75.

Collins, N.L. and Read, S.J. (1990) Adult attachment, working models, and relationship quality in dating couples. *Journal of Personality and Social Psychology*, 58, 644–63.

Collins, R.L. (1996) For better or worse: The impact of upward social comparison on self evaluations. *Psychological Bulletin*, 119, 51–69.

Condon, J.W. and Crano, W.D. (1988) Inferred evaluation and the relation between attitude similarity and interpersonal attraction. *Journal of Personality and Social Psychology*, 54, 789–97.

Condor, S. (1988) Race stereotypes and racist discourse. *Text*, 8, 69–90.

Conner, M., Kirk, S.F.L., Cade, J.E. and Barrett, J.H. (2003) Environmental influences: Factors influencing a woman's decision to use dietary supplements. *Journal of Nutrition*, 133, 1978S–82.

Conner, M., Warren, R., Close, S. and Sparks, P. (1999) Alcohol consumption and the theory of planned behavior: An examination of the cognitive mediation of past behaviors. *Journal of Applied Social Psychology*, 29, 1676–704.

Connors, J. and Heaven, P.C. (1990) Belief in a just world and attitudes towards AIDS sufferers. *Journal of Social Psychology*, 130, 559–60.

Conte, A., Davidson, S. and Burchill, R. (2004) *Defining Civil and Political Rights: The Jurisprudence of the United Nations Human Rights Committee*. Burlington: Ashgate.

Cooley, C.H. (1902) *Human Nature and the Social Order*. New York: Scribner's.

Cooper, E. and Jahoda, M. (1947) The evasion of propaganda: How prejudiced people respond to anti-prejudice propaganda. *Journal of Psychology: Interdisciplinary and Applied*, 23, 15–25.

Cooper, J. and Brehm, J.W. (1971) Prechoice awareness of relative deprivation as a determinant of cognitive dissonance. *Journal of Experimental Social Psychology*, 7, 571–81.

Cooper, J. and Fazio, R.H. (1984) A new look at dissonance theory. *Advances in Experimental Social Psychology*, 17, 229–66.

Cooper, J., Fazio, R.H. and Rhodewalt, F. (1978) Dissonance and humor: Evidence for the undifferentiated nature of dissonance arousal. *Journal of Personality and Social Psychology*, 36, 280–5.

Corballis, M.C. (1999) The gestural origins of language. *American Scientist*, 87, 138–45.

Corballis, M.C. (2003) *From Hand to Mouth: The Origins of Language*. Princeton, NJ: Princeton University Press.

Corballis, M.C. (2004) The origins of modernity: Was autonomous speech the critical factor? *Psychological Review*, 111, 543–52.

Corbetta, P., Cavazza, N. and Roccato, M. (2009) Between ideology and social representations: Four theses plus (a new) one on the relevance and the meaning of the political left and right. *European Journal of Political Research*, 48, 622–41.

Corneille, O. and Judd, C.M. (1999) Accentuation and sensitization effects in the categorization of multifaceted stimuli. *Journal of Personality and Social Psychology*, 77, 927–41.

Correia, I., Vala, J. and Aguiar, P. (2007) Victim's innocence, social categorization, and the threat to the belief in a just world. *Journal of Experimental Social Psychology*, 43, 31–8.

Correll, J., Park, B., Judd, C.M. and Wittenbrink, B. (2002) The police officer's dilemma: Using ethnicity to disambiguate potentially threatening individuals. *Journal of Personality and Social Psychology*, 83, 1314–29.

Cosmides, L. (1989) The logic of social exchange: Has natural selection shaped how humans reason? Studies with the Wason selection task. *Cognition*, 31, 187–276.

Cosmides, L. and Tooby, J. (1992) Cognitive adaptations for social exchange. In J.H. Barkow, L. Cosmides and J. Tooby (eds) *The Adapted Mind: Evolutionary Psychology and the Generation of Culture* (pp. 163–228). New York: Oxford University Press.

Cotterell, N., Eisenberger, R. and Speicher, H. (1992) Inhibiting effects of reciprocation wariness on interpersonal relationships. *Journal of Personality and Social Psychology*, 62, 658–68.

Cottrell, C.A., Richards, D.A.R. and Nichols, A.L. (2010) Predicting policy attitudes from general prejudice versus specific intergroup emotions. *Journal of Experimental Social Psychology*, 46, 247–54.

Cottrell, N.B., Wack, D.L., Sekerak, G.J. and Rittle, R.M. (1968) Social facilitation of dominant responses by the presence of an audience and the mere presence of others. *Journal of Personality and Social Psychology*, 9, 245–50.

Coupland, N. (2010) Accommodation theory. In J. Jaspers, J. Verschueren and J.-O. Ostman (eds) *Society and Language Use* (pp. 21–7). Amsterdam: John Benjamins.

Coupland, N., Bishop, H., Evans, B. and Garrett, P. (2006) Imagining Wales and the Welsh language: Ethnolinguistic subjectivities and demographic flow. *Journal of Language and Social Psychology*, 25, 351–76.

Coyne, J.C. (1976) Toward an inter-actional description of depression. *Psychiatry*, 39, 28–40.

Craig, C.S., Sternthal, B. and Leavitt, C. (1976) Advertising wearout: An experimental analysis. *Journal of Marketing Research*, 13, 365–72.

Craig, J.A., Koestner, R. and Zuroff, D.C. (1994) Implicit and self-attributed intimacy motivation. *Journal of Social and Personal Relationships*, 11, 491–507.

Craig, K.M. and Waldo, C.R. (1996) 'So, what's a hate crime anyway? Young adults' perceptions of hate crimes, victims, and perpetrators. *Law and Human Behavior*, 20, 113–29.

Crampton, P. and Parkin, C. (2007) Warrior genes and risk-taking science. *The New Zealand Medical Journal*, 120, 1250.

Crandall, C.S. (1994) Prejudice against fat people: Ideology and self-interest. *Journal of Personality and Social Psychology*, 66, 882–94.

Crandall, C.S. and Eshleman, A. (2003) A justification-suppression model of the expression and and experience of prejudice. *Psychological Bulletin*, 129, 414–46.

Crandall, C.S., Eshleman, A. and O'Brien, L. (2002) Social norms and the expression and suppression of prejudice: The struggle for internalization. *Journal of Personality and Social Psychology*, 82, 359–78.

Crandall, C.S., Silvia, P.J., N'Gbala, A. et al. (2007) Balance theory, unit relations, and attribution: The underlying integrity of Heiderian theory. *Review of General Psychology*, 11, 12–30.

Cranney, J. and Dunn, D.S. (eds) (2011) *The Psychologically Literate Citizen: Foundations and Global Perspectives*. Oxford: Oxford University Press.

Crano, W.D. (1995) Attitude strength and vested interest. In R.E. Petty and J.A. Krosnick (eds) *Attitude Strength: Antecedents and Consequences* (pp. 131–57). Mahwah, NJ: Erlbaum.

Crano, W.D. and Prislin, R. (2006) Attitudes and persuasion. *Annual Review of Psychology*, 57, 345–74.

Crawford, J.T., Jussim, L., Madon, S. et al. (2011) The use of stereotypes and individuating information in political person perception. *Personality and Social Psychology Bulletin*, 37, 529–42.

Crelia, R.A. and Tesser, A. (1996) Attitude heritability and attitude reinforcement: A replication. *Personality and Individual Differences*, 21, 803–8.

Crick, N.R. and Dodge, K.A. (1994) A review and reformulation of social-information-processing mechanisms in children's social adjustment. *Psychological Bulletin*, 115, 74–101.

Crick, N.R., Bigbee, M.A. and Howes, C. (1996) Gender differences in children's normative beliefs about aggression: How do I hurt thee? Let me count the ways. *Child Development*, 67, 1003–14.

Crisp, R.J. (2005) Recognizing complexity in intergroup relations. *The Psychologist*, 21, 206–9.

Crisp, R.J. and Beck, S.R. (2005) Reducing intergroup bias: The moderating role of ingroup identification. *Group Processes and Intergroup Relations*, 8, 173–86.

Crisp, R.J. and Hewstone, M. (2007) Multiple social categorization. *Advances in Experimental Social Psychology*, 39, 163–254.

Crisp, R.J. and Meleady, R. (2012) Adapting to a multicultural future. *Science*, 336, 853–5.

Crisp, R.J. and Turner, R.N. (2009) Can imagined interactions produce positive perceptions? Reducing prejudice through simulated social contact. *American Psychologist*, 64, 231–40.

Crisp, R.J. and Turner, R.N. (2011) Cognitive adaptation to the experience of social and cultural diversity. *Psychological Bulletin*, 137, 242–66.

Crisp, R.J., Stone, C.H. and Hall, N.R. (2006) Recategorization and subgroup identification: Predicting and preventing threats from common ingroups. *Personality and Social Psychology Bulletin*, 32, 230–43.

Crisp, R.J., Walsh, J. and Hewstone, M. (2006) Crossed categorization in common ingroup contexts. *Personality and Social Psychology Bulletin*, 32, 1204–18.

Crites, S.L. and Cacioppo, J.T. (1996) Electrocortical differentiation of evaluative and nonevaluative categorizations. *Psychological Science*, 7, 318–21.

Crocker, J. and Park, L.E. (2004) The costly pursuit of self-esteem. *Psychological Bulletin*, 130, 392–414.

Crocker, J. and Wolfe, C.T. (2001) Contingencies of self-worth. *Psychological Review*, 108, 593–623.

Crocker, J., Voelkl, K., Testa, M. and Major, B. (1991) Social stigma: The affective consequences of attributional ambiguity. *Journal of Personality and Social Psychology*, 53, 397–410.

Croizet, J. and Claire, T. (1998) Extending the concept of stereotype threat to social class: The intellectual underperformance of students from low socioeconomic backgrounds. *Personality and Social Psychology Bulletin*, 24, 588–94.

Cronin, P. and Reicher, S. (2009) Accountability processes and group dynamics: A SIDE perspective on the policing of an anti-capitalist riot. *European Journal of Social Psychology*, 39, 237–54.

Crosby, F. (1976) A model of egoistical relative deprivation. *Psychological Review*, 83, 85–113.

Croyle, R.T. and Cooper, J. (1983) Dissonance arousal: Physiological evidence. *Journal of Personality and Social Psychology*, 45, 782–91.

Cunningham, W.A., Espinet, S.D.,

DeYoung, C.G. and Zelazo, P.D. (2005) Attitudes to the right and left: Frontal ERP asymmetries associated with stimulus valence and processing goals. *NeuroImage*, 28, 827–34.

Cunningham, W.A., Raye, C.L. and Johnson, M.K. (2004) Implicit and explicit evaluation: fMRI correlates of valence, emotional intensity, and control in the processing of attitudes. *Journal of Cognitive Neuroscience*, 16, 1717–29.

Curry, T.G. and Emerson, R.M. (1970) Balance theory: A theory of interpersonal attraction? *Sociometry*, 33, 216–38.

Custers, R. and Aarts, H. (2010) The unconscious will: How the pursuit of goals operates outside of conscious awareness. *Science*, 329, 47–50.

Cvetkovich, G. and Löfstedt, R. (eds) (1999) *Social Trust and the Management of Risk*. London: Earthscan.

Dalbert, C. (1999) The world is more just for me than generally: About the personal belief in a just world's validity. *Social Justice Research*, 12, 79–98.

Dalbert, C. (2001) *The Justice Motive as a Personal Resource: Dealing with Challenges and Critical Life Events*. New York: Kluwer Academic/Plenum.

Daly, M. and Wilson, M. (1990) Killing the competition: Female/female and male/male homicide. *Human Nature*, 1, 81–107.

Damasio, A. (2006) *Descartes' Error: Emotion, Reason, and the Human Brain*. London: Vintage.

Damasio, H., Grabowski, T., Bechara, A. et al. (2000) Subcortical and cortical brain activity during the feeling of self-generated emotions. *Nature Neuroscience*, 3, 1049–56.

Damberg, M. (2005) Transcriptionfactor AP-2 and monoaminergic functions in the central nervous system. *Journal of Neural Transmission*, 112, 1281–96.

Dardenne, B., Dumont, M. and Bollier, T. (2007) Insidious dangers of benevolent sexism: Consequences for women's performance. *Journal of Personality and Social Psychology*, 93, 764–79.

D'Argembeau, A., Stawarczyk, D., Majerus, S. et al. (2010) Modulation of medial prefrontal and inferior parietal cortices when thinking about past, present, and future selves. *Social Neuroscience*, 5, 187.

Darley, J.M. (1992) Social organization for the production of evil. *Psychological Inquiry*, 3, 199–218.

Darley, J.M. and Batson, C.D. (1973) From Jerusalem to Jericho: A study of situational and dispositional variables in helping behavior. *Journal of Personality and Social Psychology*, 27, 100–8.

Darley, J.M. and Berscheid, E. (1967) Increased liking as a result of the anticipation of personal contact. *Human Relations*, 20, 29–40.

Darley, J.M. and Latané, B. (1968) Bystander intervention in emergences: Diffusion of responsibility. *Journal of Personality and Social Psychology*, 8, 377–83.

Darley, J.M., Carlsmith, K.M. and Robinson, P.H. (2000) Incapacitation and just deserts as motives for punishment. *Law and Human Behavior*, 24, 659–83.

Darwin, C. ([1859]1996) *On The Origin of Species*. Oxford: Oxford University Press.

Darwin, C. (1872) *The Expression of Emotions in Man and Animals*. Chicago, IL: Chicago University Press.

Dasgupta, S.D. (1998) Gender roles and cultural continuity in the Asian Indian immigrant community in the US. *Sex Roles*, 38, 953–74.

Dashiell, J.F. (1930) An experimental analysis of some group effects. *Journal of Abnormal and Social Psychology*, 25, 190–9.

David, B. and Turner, J.C. (1996) Studies in self-categorization and minority conversion: Is being a member of the out-group an advantage? *British Journal of Social Psychology*, 35, 179–99.

David, B. and Turner, J.C. (1999) Studies in self-categorization and minority conversion: The in-group minority in intragroup and intergroup contexts. *British Journal of Social Psychology*, 38, 115–34.

David, B. and Turner, J.C. (2001) Majority and minority influence: A single process self-categorization analysis. In C.K.W. De Dreu and N.K. Vries (eds) *Group Consensus and Minority Influence: Implications for Innovation* (pp. 91–121). Oxford: Blackwell.

Davidson, A.R. and Jaccard, J.J. (1979) Variables that moderate the attitude-behavior relation: Results of a longitudinal survey. *Journal of Personality and Social Psychology*, 37, 1364–76.

Davidson, R.J., Putnam, K.M. and Larson, C.L. (2000) Dysfunction in the neural circuitry of emotion regulation: A possible prelude to violence, *Science*, 289, 591–4.

Davies, J.E. and Gibson, T. (1978) Injuries in rugby union football. *British Medical Journal*, 2, 1759–61.

Davis, D.D. and Harless, D.W. (1996) Group vs. individual performance in a price-searching experiment. *Organizational Behavior and Human Decision Processes*, 66, 215–27.

Davis, J.I., Senghas, A., Brandt, F. and Oschner, K.N. (2010) The effects of BOTOX injections on emotional experience. *Emotion*, 10, 433–40.

Davis, M.H. (1983) Measuring individual differences in empathy: Evidence for a multidimensional approach. *Journal of Personality and Social Psychology*, 44, 113–26.

Davison, W.P. (1983) The third-person

effect in communication. *Public Opinion Quarterly, 47,* 1–15.

Dawes, R.M. (1980) Social dilemmas. *Annual Review of Psychology, 31,* 169–93.

Dawes, R.M. (1991) Probabilistic versus causal reasoning. In D. Cicchetti and W.M. Grove (eds) *Thinking Clearly about Psychology,* vol. 1: *Matters of Public Interest* (pp. 235–64). Minneapolis, MN: University of Minnesota Press.

Dawes, R.M. and Smith, T.L. (1985) Attitude and opinion measurement. In G. Lindzey and E. Aronson (eds) *Handbook of Social Psychology* (3rd edn, vol. 1, pp. 509–66). New York: Random House.

Dawes, R.M., McTavish, K. and Shaklee, H. (1977) Behavior, communication, and assumptions about other people's behavior in a commons dilemma situation. *Journal of Personality and Social Psychology, 35,* 1–11.

Dawkins, R. (1976) *The Selfish Gene.* New York: Oxford University Press.

Dawkins, R. (1997) Three herring gull chicks … the reason juries don't work. *The Observer,* 16 November. Also available at http://lucite.org/lucite/archive/atheism_-_dawkins_articles/trial%20by%20jury.pdf.

De Almeida, R.M.M., Saft, D.M., Rosa, M.M. and Miczek, K.A. (2010) Flunitrazepam in combination with alcohol engenders high levels of aggression in mice and rats. *Pharmacology, Biochemistry, and Behavior, 95,* 292–7.

Dean, L.M., Wills, F.N. and Hewitt, J. (1975) Initial interaction distance among individuals equal and unequal in military rank. *Journal of Personality and Social Psychology, 32,* 294–9.

Deaux, K., Reid, A., Mizrahi, K. and Ethier, K.A. (1995) Parameters of social identity. *Journal of Personality and Social Psychology, 68,* 280–91.

DeBold, J.F. and Miczek, K.A. (1985) Testosterone modulates the effects of ethanol on male mouse aggression. *Psychopharmacology, 86,* 286–90.

DeBono, K.G. and Snyder, M. (1995) Acting on one's attitudes: The role of a history of choosing situations. *Personality and Social Psychology Bulletin, 21,* 629–36.

DeBruine, L.M. (2002) Facial resemblance enhances trust. *Proceedings of the Royal Society B: Biological Sciences, 269,* 1307–12.

Dechêne, A., Stahl, C., Hansen, J. and Wänke, M. (2009) Mix me a list: Context moderates the truth effect and the mere-exposure effect. *Journal of Experimental Social Psychology, 45,* 1117–22.

Deci, E.L. (1975) *Intrinsic Motivation.* New York: Plenum.

Deci, E.L. and Ryan, R.M. (2000) The 'what' and 'why' of goal pursuits: Human needs and the self-determination of behaviour. *Psychological Inquiry, 11,* 227–68.

De Cremer, D. (1999) Trust and fear of exploitation in a public goods dilemma. *Current Psychology, 18,* 153–63.

De Cremer, D. and Leonardelli, G.J. (2003) Cooperation in social dilemmas and the need to belong: The moderating effect of group size. *Group Dynamics: Theory, Research, and Practice, 7,* 168–74.

De Cremer, D. and Sedikides, C. (2005) Self-uncertainty and responses to procedural injustice. *Journal of Experimental Social Psychology, 41,* 157–73.

De Cremer, D. and van Vugt, M. (1999) Social identification effects in social dilemmas: A transformation of motives. *European Journal of Social Psychology, 29,* 871–93.

DeDonder, J., Corneille, O., Yzerbyt, V. and Kuppens, T. (2010) Evaluative conditioning of high-novelty stimuli does not seem to be an automatic form of associative learning. *Journal of Experimental Social Psychology, 46,* 1118–21.

De Dreu, C.K.W. and de Vries, N.K. (1996) Differential processing and attitude change following majority and minority arguments. *British Journal of Social Psychology, 35,* 77–90.

DeFleur, M.L. and Petranoff, R.M. (1959) A televised test of subliminal persuasion. *Public Opinion Quarterly, 23,* 168–80.

DEFRA (Department for Environment, Food and Rural Affairs) (2009) *Dangerous Dogs Law: Guidance for Enforcers.* DEFRA: London.

Degner, J. and Wentura, D. (2008) The extrinsic affective Simon task as an instrument for indirect assessment of prejudice. *European Journal of Social Psychology, 38,* 1033–43.

DeHart, T., Pelham, B.W. and Tennen, H. (2006) What lies beneath: Parenting style and implicit self-esteem. *Journal of Experimental Social Psychology, 42,* 1–17.

De Hoog, N., Stroebe, W. and de Wit, J.B.F. (2007) The impact of vulnerability to and severity of a health risk on processing and acceptance of fear-arousing communications: A meta-analysis. *Review of General Psychology, 11,* 258–85.

De Houwer, J., Thomas, S. and Baeyens, F. (2001) Associative learning of likes and dislikes: A review of 25 years of research on human evaluative conditioning. *Psychological Bulletin, 127,* 853–69.

Delgado, J.M. (1967) Social rank and radio-stimulated aggressiveness in monkeys. *Journal of Nervous and Mental Diseases, 144,* 383–90.

Demie, F. and Lewis, K. (2011) White working class achievement: An ethnographic study of barriers to learning in schools. *Educational Studies, 37.*

Denissen, J.J.A., Penke, L., Schmitt, D.P. and van Aken, M.A.G. (2008) Self-esteem reactions to social interactions: Evidence for sociometer mechanisms across days, people, and nations. *Journal of Personality and Social Psychology, 95,* 181–96.

Dennett, D.C. (1991) *Consciousness Explained.* London: Penguin.

DePaulo, B.M. (1992) Nonverbal behavior and self-presentation. *Psychological Bulletin, 111,* 203–43.

DePaulo, B.M. and Friedman, H.S. (1998) Nonverbal communication. In D.T. Gilbert, S.T. Fiske and G. Lindzey (eds) *The Handbook of Social Psychology* (4th edn, vol. 2, pp. 3–40). New York: McGraw-Hill.

DePaulo, B.M. and Rosenthal, R. (1979) Telling lies. *Journal of Personality and Social Psychology, 37,* 1713–22.

DePaulo, B.M. and Rosenthal, R. (1982) Measuring the development of sensitivity to nonverbal communication. In C.E. Izard and P.B. Read (eds) *Measuring Emotions in Infants and Children* (pp. 208–50). New York: Cambridge University Press.

DePaulo, B.M., Kirkendol, S.E., Tang, J. and O'Brien, T. (1988) The motivational impairment effect in the communication of deception: Replications and extensions. *Journal of Nonverbal Behavior, 12,* 177–202.

DePaulo, B.M., Lindsay, J.J., Malone, B.E. et al. (2003) Cues to deception. *Psychological Bulletin, 129,* 74–118.

DePaulo, B.M., Stone, J.I. and Lassiter, G.D. (1985) Deceiving and detecting deceit. In B.R. Schenkler (ed.) *The Self and Social Life* (pp. 323–70). New York: McGraw-Hill.

Derks, D., Bos, A.E.R. and von Grumbkow, J. (2004) Emoticons en sociale interactie via internet: Het belang van de sociale context. In D. Wigboldus, M. Dechesne, E. Gordijn and E. Kluwer (Red) *Jaarboek Sociale Psychologie 2003.* Delft: Eburon.

DeSteno, D., Petty, R.E., Wegener, D.T. and Rucker, D.D. (2000) Beyond valence in the perception of likelihood: The role of emotion specificity. *Journal of Personality and Social Psychology, 78,* 397–416.

Deutsch, M. (1975) Equity, equality, and need: What determines which value will be used as the basis of distributive justice? *Journal of Social Issues, 31,* 137–49.

Deutsch, M. and Gerard, H.B. (1955) A study of normative and informational social influences upon individual judgement. *The Journal of Abnormal and Social Psychology, 51,* 629.

De Veer, M.W. and van den Bos, R. (1999) A critical review of methodology and interpretation of self-recognition research in nonhuman primates. *Animal Behavior*, 58, 459–68.

De Vet, A.J. and de Dreu, C.K.W. (2007) The influence of articulation, self-monitoring ability, and sensitivity to others on creativity. *European Journal of Social Psychology*, 37, 747–60.

Devine, P.G. (1989) Stereotypes and prejudice: Their automatic and controlled components. *Journal of Personality and Social Psychology*, 56, 5–18.

Devine, P.G. and Sharp, L.B. (2009) Automaticity and control in stereotyping and prejudice. In T.D. Nelson and L.B. Sharp (eds) *Handbook of Prejudice, Stereotyping, and Discrimination* (pp. 61–87). New York: Psychology Press.

Devine, P.G., Hamilton, D.L. and Ostrom, T.M. (eds) (1994) *Social Cognition: Impact on Social Psychology*. San Diego, CA: Academic Press.

Devine-Wright, H. and Devine-Wright, P. (2009) Social representations of electricity network technologies: Exploring processes of anchoring and objectification through the use of visual research methods. *British Journal of Social Psychology*, 48, 357–73.

Devos-Comby, L. and Salovey, P. (2002) Applying persuasion strategies to alter HIV-relevant thoughts and behavior. *Review of General Psychology*, 6, 287–304.

De Waal, F.B.M. (2008) Putting the altruism back into altruism: The evolution of empathy. *Annual Review of Psychology*, 59, 279–300.

DeWall, C.N., Buffardi, L.E., Bonser, I. and Campbell, W.K. (2011) Narcissism and implicit attention seeking: Evidence from linguistic analyses of social networking and online presentation. *Personality and Individual Differences*, 51, 57–62.

DeWall, C.N., Bushman, B.J., Giancola, P.R. and Webster, G.D. (2010) The big, the bad, and the boozed-up: Weight moderates the effect of alcohol on aggression. *Journal of Experimental Social Psychology*, 46, 619–23.

DfE (Department for Education) (2009) *Special Educational Needs in England, January 2009*. Retrieved from http://www.education.gov.uk/rsgateway/DB/SFR/s000852/sfr14-2009.pdf on 29 June 2012.

DfE (2010a) *Key Stage 1 Attainment by Pupil Characteristics in England, 2009/2010*. Retrieved from http://www.education.gov.uk/rsgateway/DB/SFR/s000968/sfr33-2010.pdf on 29 June 2012.

DfE (2010b) *GCSE and Equivalent Attainment by Pupil Characteristics in England, 2009/2010*. Retrieved from http://www.education.gov.uk/rsgateway/DB/SFR/s000977/sfr37-2010.pdf on 29 June 2012.

DfE (2011) *Permanent and Fixed Period Exclusions from Schools and Exclusion Appeals in England, 2009/2010*. Retrieved from http://www.education.gov.uk/rsgateway/DB/SFR/s001016/sfr17-2011.pdf on 29 June 2012.

DfES (Department for Education and Skills) (2007) *Gender and Education: The Evidence on Pupils in England*. Retrieved from https://www.education.gov.uk/publications/eOrderingDownload/00389-2007BKT-EN.pdf on 29 June 2012.

Dhawan, N., Roseman, I.J., Naidu, R.K. et al. (1995) Self-concepts across two cultures: India and the United States. *Journal of Cross Cultural Psychology*, 26, 606–21.

Diamond, L.M. (2003) What does sexual orientation orient? A biobehavioral model distinguishing romantic love and sexual desire. *Psychological Review*, 110, 173–92.

Diamond, L.M. (2004) Emerging perspectives on distinctions between romantic love and sexual desire. *Current Directions in Psychological Science*, 13, 116–19.

Dickersin, K., Chan, S., Chalmers, T.C., Sacks, H.S. and Smith, H. Jr (1987) Publication bias and clinical trials. *Controlled Clinical Trials*, 8, 343–53.

Dickey, C. (2012) Marseille's melting pot. *National Geographic Magazine*, March.

Diehl, M. (1990) The minimal group paradigm: Theoretical explanations and empirical findings. *European Review of Social Psychology*, 1, 263–92.

Diehl, M. and Stroebe, W. (1987) Productivity loss in brainstorming groups: Toward the solution of a riddle. *Journal of Personality and Social Psychology*, 53, 497–509.

Diener, E. (1979) Deindividuation, self-awareness, and disinhibition. *Journal of Personality and Social Psychology*, 37, 1160–71.

Diener, E. (1980) Deindividuation: The absence of self-awareness and self-regulation in group members. In P.B. Paulhus (ed.) *Psychology of Group Influence* (pp. 209–42). Hillsdale, NJ: Erlbaum.

Diener, E. and Wallbom, M. (1976) Effects of self-awareness on antinormative behavior. *Journal of Research in Personality*, 10, 107–11.

Diener, E., Fraser, S.C., Beaman, A.L. and Kelem, R.T. (1976) Effects of deindividuation variables on stealing among Halloween trick-or-treaters. *Journal of Personality and Social Psychology*, 33, 178–83.

Dijker, A.J. and Koomen, W. (1996) Stereotyping and attitudinal effects under time pressure. *European Journal of Social Psychology*, 26, 61–74.

Dijksterhuis, A. and van Knippenberg, A. (1998) The relation between perception and behavior, or how to win a game of Trivial Pursuit. *Journal of Personality and Social Psychology*, 74, 854–77.

Dijksterhuis, A., Aarts, H. and Smith, P.K. (2005) The power of the subliminal: On subliminal persuasion and other potential applications. In R. Hassin, J. Ulemann and J. Bargh (eds) *The New Unconscious* (pp. 77–106). New York: Oxford University Press.

Dijksteruis, A., van Knippenberg, A., Kruglanski, A.W. and Schaper, C. (1996) Motivated social cognition: Need for closure effects on memory and judgment. *Journal of Experimental Social Psychology*, 32, 254–70.

Dijkstra, J.K., Lindenberg, S., Verhulst, F.C. et al. (2009) The relation between popularity and aggressive, destructive, and norm-breaking behaviors: Moderating effects of athletic abilities, physical attractiveness, and prosociality. *Journal of Research on Adolescence*, 19, 401–13.

DiMatteo, M.R. (1993) Solving the mysteries of medical communication. *PsycCRITIQUES*, 38, 1065.

DiMatteo, M.R., Hays, R.D. and Prince, L.M. (1986) Relationship of physicians' nonverbal communication skill to patients satisfaction, appointment noncompliance, and physician workload. *Health Psychology*, 5, 581–94.

Dimberg, U. (1982) Facial reactions to facial expressions. *Psychophysiology*, 19, 643–7.

Dimberg, U., Thunberg, M. and Elmehed, K. (2000) Unconscious facial reactions to emotional facial expressions. *Psychological Science*, 11, 86–9.

Dindo, M., Whiten, A. and de Waal, F.B.M. (2009) Social facilitation of exploratory foraging behavior in capuchin monkeys (*Cebus apella*). *American Journal of Primatology*, 71, 419–26.

Dion, K.K. (1972) Physical attractiveness and evaluation of children's transgressions. *Journal of Personality and Social Psychology*, 24, 207–13.

Dion, K.K. (1973) Young children's stereotyping of facial attractiveness. *Developmental Psychology*, 9, 183–8.

Dion, K.K. and Berscheid, E. (1974) Physical attractiveness and peer perception among children. *Sociometry*, 37, 1–12.

Dion, K.K. and Dion, K.L. (1985) Personality, gender, and the phenomenology of romantic love. In P. Shaver (ed.) *Self, Situation, and Social Behavior: Review of Personality and Social Psychology* (vol. 6, pp. 209–39). Beverly Hills, CA: Sage.

Dion, K.K. and Dion, K.L. (1991) Psychological individualism and romantic love. *Journal of Social Behavior & Personality*, 6, 17–33.

Dion, K.K. and Stein, S. (1978) Physical

attractiveness and interpersonal influence. *Journal of Experimental Social Psychology*, 14, 97–108.

Dion, K.K., Berscheid, E. and Walster, E. (1972) What is beautiful is good. *Journal of Personality and Social Psychology*, 24, 285–90.

Dion, K.L. (2000) Group cohesion: From 'field of forces' to multidimensional construct. *Group Dynamics: Theory, Research and Practice*, 4, 7–26.

Dion, K.L. and Dion, K.K. (1988) Romantic love: Individual and cultural perspectives. In R. Sternberg and M. Barnes (eds) *The Psychology of Love* (pp. 264–92). New Haven: Yale University Press.

Dion, K.L. and Dion, K.K. (1993) Gender and ethnocultural comparisons in styles of love. *Psychology of Women Quarterly*, 17, 463–73.

Dipboye, R.L., Arvey, R.D. and Terpstra, D.E. (1977) Sex and physical attractiveness of raters and applicants as determinants of resumé evaluations. *Journal of Applied Psychology*, 62, 288–94.

Dittes, J.E. and Kelley, H.H. (1956) Effects of different conditions of acceptance upon conformity to group norms. *The Journal of Abnormal and Social Psychology*, 53, 100–7.

Ditto, P.H., Munro, G.D., Apanovitch, A.M. et al. (2003) Spontaneous scepticism: The interplay of motivation and expectation in responses to favorable and unfavorable medical diagnoses. *Personality and Social Psychology Bulletin*, 29, 1120–32.

Dixon, J. and Durrheim, K. (2000) Displacing place-identity: A discursive approach to locating self and other. *British Journal of Social Psychology*, 39, 27–44.

Dixon, J. and Durrheim, K. (2003) Contact and the ecology of racial division: Some varieties of informal segregation. *British Journal of Social Psychology*, 42, 1–23.

Dixon, J., Durrheim, K. and Tredoux, K. (2005) Beyond the optimal contact strategy: A reality check for the contact hypothesis. *American Psychologist*, 60, 697–711.

Dixon, J., Levine, M., Reicher, S. and Durrheim, K. (in press) Beyond prejudice: Are negative evaluations the problem? Is getting us to like one another more the solution? *Behavioral and Brain Sciences*.

Dodd, D. (1985) Robbers in the classroom: A deindividuation exercise. *Teaching of Psychology*, 72, 89–91.

Dodge, K.A. (1986) A social information processing model of social competence in children. In M. Perlmutter (ed.) *Minnesota Symposium on Child Psychology* (vol. 18, pp. 77–125). Hillsdale, NJ: Erlbaum.

Doll, J. and Ajzen, I. (1992) Accessibility and stability of predictors in the theory of planned behavior. *Journal of Personality and Social Psychology*, 63, 754–65.

Dollard, J., Doob, L.W., Miller, N.E. et al. (1939) *Frustration and Aggression*. New Haven, CT: Yale University Press.

Donnellan, M.B., Trzesniewski, K.H., Robins, R.W. et al. (2005) Low self-esteem is related to aggression, antisocial behaviour, and delinquency. *Psychological Science*, 16, 328–35.

D'Onofrio, B.M.D., Eaves, L.J., Murrelle, L. et al. (1999) Understanding biological and social influences on religious affiliation, attitudes, and behaviors: A behavior genetic perspective. *Journal of Personality*, 67, 953–84.

Doob, L.W. (1935) *Propaganda: Its Psychology and Technique*. Oxford: Holt.

Doosje, B. and Branscombe, N.R. (2003) Attributions for the negative historical actions of a group. *European Journal of Social Psychology*, 33, 235–48.

Doosje, B., Branscombe, N.R., Spears, R. and Manstead, A.S.R. (1998) Guilty by association: When one's group has a negative history. *Journal of Personality and Social Psychology*, 75, 872–86.

Doosje, B., Rojahn, K. and Fischer, A. (1999) Partner preferences as a function of gender, age, political orientation and level of education. *Sex Roles*, 40, 45–60.

Douglas, K.M. (2007) Psychology, discrimination and hate groups online. In A.N. Joinson, K. McKenna, T. Postmes and U. Reips (eds) *The Oxford Handbook of Internet Psychology* (pp. 155–64). Oxford: Oxford University Press.

Douglas, K.M. (2008) Antisocial communication on electronic mail and internet. In E.A. Konijn, M.A. Tanis, S. Utz and S. Barnes (eds) *Mediated Interpersonal Communication* (pp. 200–14). London: Routledge.

Douglas, K.M. and McGarty, C. (2001) Identifiability and self-presentation: Computer-mediated communication and intergroup interaction. *British Journal of Social Psychology*, 40, 399–416.

Douglas, K.M. and McGarty, C. (2002) Internet identifiability and beyond: A model of the effects of identifiability on communicative behavior. *Group Dynamics: Theory, Research and Practice*, 6, 17–26.

Douglas, K.M. and Sutton, R.M. (2003) Effects of communication goals and expectancies on language abstraction. *Journal of Personality and Social Psychology*, 84, 692–6.

Douglas, K.M. and Sutton, R.M. (2004) Right about others, wrong about ourselves? Actual and perceived self-other differences in resistance to persuasion. *British Journal of Social Psychology*, 43, 585–603.

Douglas, K.M. and Sutton, R.M. (2006) When what you say about others says something about you: Language abstraction and inferences about describers' attitudes and goals. *Journal of Experimental Social Psychology*, 42, 500–8.

Douglas, K.M. and Sutton, R.M. (2008) The hidden impact of conspiracy theories: Perceived and actual influence of theories surrounding the death of Princess Diana. *Journal of Social Psychology*, 148, 210–21.

Douglas, K.M. and Sutton, R.M. (2011) Constructive or cruel? Positive or patronizing? Reactions to expressions of positive and negative stereotypes of the mentally ill. *British Journal of Psychology*, 102, 97–107.

Douglas, K.M. and Sutton, R.M. (2011) Does it take one to know one? Endorsement of conspiracy theories is influenced by willingness to conspire. *British Journal of Social Psychology*, 50, 544–52.

Douglas, K.M., McGarty, C., Bliuc, A.M. and Lala, G. (2005) Understanding cyberhate: Social competition and social creativity in on-line white-supremacist groups. *Social Science Computer Review*, 23, 68–76.

Douglas, K.M., Sutton, R.M. and Stathi, S. (2010) Why am I less persuaded than you: People's intuitive understanding of the psychology of persuasion. *Social Influence*, 5, 133–48.

Douglas, K.M., Sutton, R.M. and Wilkin, K. (2008) Could you mind your language? An investigation of communicators' ability to inhibit linguistic bias. *Journal of Language and Social Psychology*, 27, 123–39.

Dovidio, J.F. and Gaertner, S.L. (1998) On the nature of contemporary prejudice: The causes, consequences, and challenges of aversive racism. In J.L. Eberhardt and S.T. Fiske (eds) *Confronting Racism: The Problem and the Response* (pp. 3–32). Thousand Oaks, CA: Sage.

Dovidio, J.F. and Morris, W.N. (1975) Effects of stress and commonality of fate on helping behavior. *Journal of Personality and Social Psychology*, 31, 145–9.

Dovidio, J.F., Brigham, J.C., Johnson, B.T. and Gaertner, S.L. (1996) Stereotyping, prejudice, and discrimination: Another look. In C.N. Macrae, C. Stangor and M. Hewstone (eds) *Stereotypes and Stereotyping* (pp. 276–322). New York: Guilford Press.

Dovidio, J.F., Gaertner, S. and Kawakami, K. (2003) Intergroup contact: The past, present, and future. *Group Processes and Intergroup Relations*, 6, 5–20.

Dovidio, J.F., Kawakami, K. and Gaertner, S.L. (2002) Implicit and explicit prejudice and interracial interaction. *Journal of Personality and Social Psychology*, 82, 62–8.

Downs, A.C. and Lyons, P.M. (1991) Natural observations of the links between attractiveness and initial legal judgements. *Personality and Social Psychology Bulletin*, 17, 541–7.

Doyen, S., Klein, O., Pichon, C.L. and Cleeremans, A. (2012) Behavioral priming: It's all in the mind, but whose mind? *PLoS ONE*, 7, e29081.

Dreben, E.K., Fiske, S.T. and Hastie, R. (1979) The independence of evaluative and item information: Impression and recall order effects in behavior-based impression formation. *Journal of Personality and Social Psychology*, 37, 1758–68.

Dreber, A., Rand, D.G., Fudenberg, D. and Nowak, M. (2008) Winners don't punish. *Nature*, 452, 348–51.

Drew, P. (2005) Conversation analysis. In K.L. Fitch and R.E. Sanders (eds) *Handbook of Language and Social Interaction* (pp. 71–102). Mahwah, NJ: Lawrence Erlbaum.

Driskell, J.E. and Mullen, B. (1990) Status, expectations, and behavior. *Personality and Social Psychology Bulletin*, 16, 541–53.

Drury, J. and Reicher, S.D. (2005) Explaining enduring empowerment: A comparative study of collective action and psychological outcomes. *European Journal of Social Psychology*, 35, 35–58.

Drury, J., Reicher, S. D. and Stott, C. (2012) Crowds and change. In B. Wagoner, E. Jensen and J. A. Oldmeadow (eds) *Culture and Social Change: Transforming Society through the Power of Ideas* (pp. 19–38). Charlotte, NC: Information Age Publishing.

Dubé-Simard, L. and Guimond, S. (1986) Relative deprivation and social protest: The personal group issue. In J. Olson, C. Herman and M. Zanna (eds) *Relative Deprivation and Social Comparison: The Ontario Symposium* (vol. 4, pp. 201–16). Hillsdale, NJ: Erlbaum.

Duck, J.M., Terry, D.J. and Hogg, M.A. (1995) The perceived influence of AIDS advertising: Third-person effects in the context of positive media content. *Basic and Applied Social Psychology*, 17, 305–25.

Duck, J.M., Terry, D.J. and Hogg, M.A. (1998) Perceptions of a media campaign: The role of social identity and the changing intergroup context. *Personality and Social Psychology Bulletin*, 24, 3–16.

Duck, S.W. (1998) *Human Relationships*. Thousand Oaks, CA: Sage.

Duckitt, J. (2001) A dual-process cognitive-motivational theory of ideology and prejudice. *Advances in Experimental Social Psychology*, 33, 41–113.

Duckitt, J. (2006) Differential effects of right wing authoritarianism and social dominance orientation on outgroup attitudes and their mediation by threat from and competitiveness to outgroups. *Personality and Social Psychology Bulletin*, 32, 684–96.

Duckitt, J. and Fisher, K. (2003) The

impact of social threat on worldview and ideological attitudes. *Political Psychology*, 24, 199–222.

Duckworth, A. and Seligman, M.E. (2006) Self-discipline gives girls the edge: Gender in self-discipline, grades, and achievement test scores. *Journal of Educational Psychology*, 98, 198–208.

Dula, C.S. (2011) A social-cognitive model of driver aggression: Taking situations and individual differences into account. *Current Psychology*, 30, 324–34.

Dulany, D.E. and Hilton, D.J. (1991) Conversational implicature, conscious representation, and the conjunction fallacy. *Social Cognition*, 9, 67–84.

Dunbar, R.I.M. (1993) Co-evolution of neocortex size, group size and language in humans. *Behavioral and Brain Sciences*, 16, 681–735.

Dunbar, R.I.M. (1998) The social brain hypothesis. *Evolutionary Anthropology*, 6, 178–90.

Dunn, J. and McGuire, S. (1992) Sibling and peer relationships in childhood. *Journal of Child Psychology and Psychiatry*, 33, 78–105.

Dunning, D. and Sherman, D.A. (1997) Stereotypes and tacit inference. *Journal of Personality and Social Psychology*, 73, 459–71.

Duran, A. (2006) Flash mobs: Social influence in the 21st century. *Journal of Social Influence*, 4, 301–15.

Durante, K.M., Li, N.P. and Haselton, M.G. (2008) Changes in women's choice of dress across the ovulatory cycle: Naturalistic and laboratory task-based evidence. *Personality and Social Psychology Bulletin*, 34, 1451–60.

Duriez, B. and van Hiel, A. (2002) The march of modern fascism: A comparison of social dominance orientation and authoritarianism. *Personality and Individual Differences*, 32, 1199–213.

Duriez, B., Klimstra, T.A., Luyckx, K. et al. (in press) Right-wing authoritarianism: Protective factor against or risk factor for depression? *European Journal of Personality*.

Durkheim, E. ([1912]2001) *The Elementary Forms of Religious Life*. Oxford: Oxford University Press.

Durrheim, K. (in press) Discourse, action, rhetoric: From a perception to an action paradigm in social psychology. *British Journal of Social Psychology*.

Durrheim, K., Quayle, M., Whitehead, K. and Kriel, A. (2005) Denying racism: Discursive strategies used by the South African media. *Critical Arts: South-North Cultural and Media Studies*, 19, 167–86.

Dutton, D.G. and Aron, A.P. (1974) Some evidence for heightened sexual attraction under conditions of high anxiety. *Journal of Personality and Social Psychology*, 30, 510–17.

Dutton, D.G. and Lake, R.A. (1973) Threat of own prejudice and reverse discrimination in interracial situations. *Journal of Personality and Social Psychology*, 28, 94–100.

Duval, S. and Wicklund, R.A. (1972) *A Theory of Objective Self-awareness*. Oxford: Academic Press.

Dvorak, R.D. and Simons, J.S. (2009) Moderation of resource depletion in the self-control strength model: Differing effects of two modes of self-control. *Personality and Social Psychology Bulletin*, 35, 572–83.

Dweck, C.S. (1999) *Self-theories: Their Role in Motivation, Personality, and Development*. Philadelphia: Psychology Press.

Eagly, A.H. (1978) Sex differences in influenceability. *Psychological Bulletin*, 85, 86.

Eagly, A.H. (1987) *Sex Differences in Social Behavior: A Social Role Interpretation*. Hillsdale, NJ: Erlbaum.

Eagly, A.H. and Carli, L.L. (1981) Sex of researchers and sex-typed communications as determinants of sex differences in influenceability: A meta-analysis of social influence studies. *Psychological Bulletin*, 90, 1.

Eagly, A.H. and Chaiken, S. (1975) An attribution analysis of the effect of communicator characteristics on opinion change: The case of communicator attractiveness. *Journal of Personality and Social Psychology*, 32, 136–44.

Eagly, A.H. and Chaiken, S. (1993) *The Psychology of Attitudes*. Fort Worth, TX: Harcourt Brace.

Eagly, A.H. and Chaiken, S. (1998) Attitude structure and function. In D.T. Gilbert, S.T. Fiske and G. Lindzey (eds) *The Handbook of Social Psychology* (vol. 1, pp. 269–322). New York: McGraw-Hill.

Eagly, A.H. and Karau, S.J. (2002) Role congruity theory of prejudice toward female leaders. *Psychological Review*, 109, 573–98.

Eagly, A.H. and Mladinic, A. (1994) Are people prejudiced against women? Some answers from research on attitudes, gender stereotypes, and judgements of competence. *European Review of Social Psychology*, 5, 1–35.

Eagly, A.H. and Steffen, V.J. (2000) Gender stereotypes stem from the distribution of women and men into social roles. In C. Stangor (ed.) *Stereotypes and Prejudice: Essential Readings. Key Readings in Social Psychology* (pp. 142–60). New York: Psychology Press.

Eagly, A.H. and Wood, W. (1985) Gender and influenceability: Stereotype versus behavior. In V.E. O'Leary, R.K. Unger and B.S. Wallston (eds) *Women, Gender, and Social Psychology* (pp. 225–56). Hillsdale, NJ: Erlbaum.

Eagly, A.H. and Wood, W. (1999) The origins of sex differences in human behavior: Evolved dispositions versus social roles. *American Psychologist*, 54, 408–23.

Eagly, A.H., Chen, S., Chaiken, S. and Shaw-Barnes, K. (1999) The impact of attitudes on memory: An affair to remember. *Psychological Bulletin*, 125, 64–89.

Eagly, A.H., Karau, S.J. and Makhijani, M.G. (1995) Gender and the effectiveness of leaders: A meta-analysis. *Psychological Bulletin*, 117, 125–45.

Eagly, A.H., Kulesa, P., Brannon, L.A. et al. (2000) Why counterattitudinal messages are as memorable as proattitudinal messages: The importance of active defense against attack. *Personality and Social Psychology Bulletin*, 26, 1392–408.

Eagly, A.H., Makhijani, M.G. and Klonsky, B.G. (1992) Gender and the evaluation of leaders: A meta-analysis. *Psychological Bulletin*, 111, 3–22.

Eagly, A.H., Wood, W. and Chaiken, S. (1978) Causal inferences about communicators and their effect on opinion change. *Journal of Personality and Social Psychology*, 36, 424–35.

Eagly, A.H., Wood, W. and Fishbaugh, L. (1981) Sex differences in conformity: Surveillance by the group as a determinant of male nonconformity. *Journal of Personality and Social Psychology*, 40, 384.

Earle, M.J. (1969) A cross-cultural and cross-language comparison of language scores. *Journal of Social Psychology*, 79, 19–24.

Earley, P.C. (1989) Social loafing and collectivism: A comparison of United States and the People's Republic of China. *Administrative Science Quarterly*, 34, 565–81.

Earley, P.C. (1993) East meets West meets Mideast: Further explorations of collectivistic and individualistic work groups. *Academy of Management Journal*, 36, 319–48.

Easterbrook, J.A. (1959) The effect of emotion on cue utilization and the organization of behavior. *Psychological Review*, 66, 183–201.

Eastwick, P.W., Finkel, E.J., Mochon, D. and Ariely, D. (2007) Selective versus unselective romantic desire: Not all reciprocity is created equal. *Psychological Science*, 18, 317–19.

Eaton, A.A. (2009) Prescriptions for persuasion: The relationship between sex role norms and gender differences in persuadability. Doctoral dissertation, University of Chicago.

Eatough, V. and Smith, J. (2006) 'I was like a wild wild person': Understanding feelings of anger using interpretative phenomenological analysis. *British Journal of Psychology*, 97, 483–98.

Ebert, I.D., Steffens, M.C., von Stülpnagel, R. and Jelenec, P. (2009) How to like yourself better, or chocolate less:

Changing implicit attitudes with one IAT task. *Journal of Experimental Social Psychology*, 45, 1098–104.

Ebstein, R.P. (2006) The molecular genetic architecture of human personality: beyond self-report questionnaires. *Molecular Psychiatry*, 11, 427–45.

Eccles, J.S. and Barber, B.L. (1999) Student council, volunteering, basketball, or marching band: What kind of extracurricular involvement matters? *Journal of Adolescent Research*, 14, 10–43.

Eccles, J.S., Barber, B.L., Stone, M. and Hunt, J. (2003) Extracurricular activities and adolescent development. *Journal of Social Issues*, 59, 865–89.

Echterhoff, G., Higgins, E.T. and Levine, J.M. (2009) Shared reality: Experiencing commonality with others' inner states about the world. *Perspectives on Psychological Science*, 4, 496–521.

Eckert, P. and McConnell-Ginet, S. (1999) New generalizations and explanations in language and gender research. *Language and Society*, 28, 185–201.

Edelman, G.M. (1993) *Bright Air, Brilliant Fire: On the Matter of the Mind*. New York: Basic Books.

Eder, A.B., Fiedler, K. and Hamm-Eder, S. (2011) Illusory correlations revisited: The role of pseudocontingencies and working-memory capacity. *The Quarterly Journal of Experimental Psychology*, 64, 517–32.

Edmondson, A. (2004) Psychological safety, trust, and learning in organizations: A group lens. In R.M. Kramer and K.S. Cook (eds) *Trust and Distrust in Organizations: Dilemmas and Approaches* (pp. 239–72). New York: Russell Sage.

Edwards, A.L. (1983) *Techniques of Attitude Scale Construction*. New York: Irvington.

Edwards, D. (1997) *Discourse and Cognition.* London: Sage.

Edwards, D. (1999) Emotion discourse. *Culture and Psychology*, 5, 271–91.

Edwards, D. (2005) Moaning, whinging and laughing: The subjective side of complaints. *Discourse Studies*, 7, 4–29.

Edwards, D. and Potter, J. (eds) (1992) *Discursive Psychology*. London: Sage.

Edwards, D. and Potter, J. (1993) Language and causation: A discursive action model of description and attribution. *Psychological Review*, 100, 23–41.

Edwards, D. and Potter, J. (2001) Discursive psychology. In A.W. McHoul and M. Rapley (eds) *How to Analyse Talk in Institutional Settings: A Casebook of Methods* (pp. 12–24.). London: Continuum International.

Edwards, K. (1990) The interplay of affect and cognition in attitude formation and change. *Journal of Personality and Social Psychology*, 59, 202–16.

Effron, D.A., Cameron, J.S. and Monin,

B. (2009) Endorsing Obama licenses favoring Whites. *Journal of Experimental Social Psychology*, 45, 590–3.

Egan, L.C., Bloom, P. and Santos, L.R. (2010) Choice induced preferences in the absence of choice: Evidence from a blind two choice paradigm with young children and capuchin monkeys. *Journal of Experimental Social Psychology*, 46, 204–7.

Egan, L.C., Santos, L. R. and Bloom, P. (2007) The origins of cognitive dissonance: Evidence from children and monkeys. *Psychological Science*, 18, 978–83.

Ehrlinger, J., Gilovich, T. and Ross, L. (2005) Peering into the bias blind spot: People's assessments of bias in themselves and others. *Personality and Social Psychology Bulletin*, 31, 680–92.

Eidelman, S., Crandall, C.S., Goodman, J.A. and Blanchar, J.C. (2012) Low-effort thought promotes political conservatism. *Personality and Social Psychology Bulletin*, 36, 808–20.

Einolf, C.J. (2010) Does extensivity form part of the altruistic personality? An empirical test of Oliner and Oliner's theory. *Social Science Research*, 39, 142–51.

Eisenberg, N. and Miller, P.A. (1987) The relation of empathy to prosocial and related behaviors. *Psychological Bulletin*, 101, 91–119.

Eisenberger, N.I., Lieberman, M.D. and Satpute, A.B. (2005) Personality from a controlled processing perspective: An fMRI study of neuroticism, extraversion, and self-consciousness. *Cognitive, Affective, and Behavioral Neuroscience*, 5, 169–81.

Eisenberger, N.I., Lieberman, M.D. and Williams, K.D. (2003) Does rejection hurt? An fMRI study of social exclusion. *Science*, 302, 290–2.

Eiser, C., Eiser, J.R. and Greco, V. (2004) Surviving childhood cancer: Quality of life and parental regulatory focus. *Personality and Social Psychology Bulletin*, 30, 123–33.

Ekman, P. (1971) Universals and cultural differences in facial expressions of emotion. In J.K. Cole (ed.) *Nebraska Symposium on Motivation* (vol. 19, pp. 207–84). Lincoln, NE: University of Nebraska Press.

Ekman, P. (1973) Cross cultural studies of facial expression. In P. Ekman (ed.) *Darwin and Facial Expression* (pp. 169–222). New York: Academic Press.

Ekman, P. (1982) *Emotion and the Human Face.* New York: Cambridge University Press.

Ekman, P. (1993) Facial expression of emotion. *American Psychologist*, 48, 384–92.

Ekman, P. and Friesen, W.V. (1971) Constants across cultures in the face and emotion. *Journal of Personality and Social Psychology*, 17, 124–9.

Ekman, P. and Friesen, W.V. (1972) Hand movements. *Journal of Communication*, 22, 353–74.

Ekman, P. and Friesen, W.V. (1974) Detecting deception from the body or face. *Journal of Personality and Social Psychology*, 29, 188–98.

Ekman, P. and Friesen, W.V. (1975) *Unmasking the Face*. Englewood Cliffs, NJ: Prentice Hall.

Ekman, P., Friesen, W.V. and Scherer, K.R. (1976) Body movement and voice pitch in deceptive interaction. *Semiotica*, 16, 23–7.

Ekman, P., Friesen, W.V., O'Sullivan, M. et al. (1987) Universals and cultural differences in the judgements of facial expressions of emotion. *Journal of Personality and Social Psychology*, 53, 712–17.

Ekman, P., Levenson, R.W. and Friesen, W.V. (1983) Autonomic nervous system activity distinguishes between emotions. *Science*, 221, 1208–10.

El-Alayli, A., Lystad, A.L., Webb, S.R. et al. (2006) Reigning cats and dogs: A pet-enhancement bias and its link to pet attachment, pet-self similarity, self-enhancement, and wellbeing. *Basic and Applied Social Psychology,* 28, 131–43.

Elcheroth, G., Doise, W. and Reicher, S. (2011) On the knowledge of politics and the politics of knowledge: How a social representations approach helps us rethink the subject of political psychology. *Political Psychology*, 32, 729–58.

Elder, T.J., Douglas, K.M. and Sutton, R.M (2006) Perceptions of social influence when messages favour 'us' versus 'them': A closer look at the social distance effect. *European Journal of Social Psychology*, 36, 353–65.

Elfenbein, H.A. and Ambady, N. (2002) On the universality and cultural specificity of emotion recognition: A meta-analysis. *Psychological Bulletin*, 128, 203–35.

Elliot, A.J. and Devine, P.G. (1994) On the motivational nature of cognitive dissonance: Dissonance as psychological discomfort. *Journal of Personality and Social Psychology*, 67, 382–94.

Elliot, M.A., Armitage, C.J. and Baughan, C.J. (2003) Drivers' compliance with speed limits: An application of the theory of planned behaviour. *Journal of Applied Psychology*, 88, 964–72.

Ellis, D.S. (1967) Speech and social status in America. *Social Forces*, 45, 431–7.

Ellison-Potter, P., Bell, P. and Deffenbacher, J. (2001) The effects of trait driving anger, anonymity, and aggressive stimuli on aggressive driving behavior. *Journal of Applied Social Psychology*, 31, 431–43.

Elms, A.C. and Milgram, S. (1966) Personality characteristics associated with obedience and defiance toward

authoritative command. *Journal of Experimental Research in Personality*, 1, 282–9.

Emmons, R.A. (1996) Striving and feeling: Personal goals and subjective well-being. In J.A. Bargh and P.M. Gollwitzer (eds) *The Psychology of Action: Linking Motivation and Cognition to Behavior* (pp. 314–37). New York: Guilford Press.

Engell, A.D., Haxby, J.V. and Todorov, A. (2007) Implicit trustworthiness decisions: Automatic coding of face properties in the human amygdala. *Journal of Cognitive Neuroscience*, 19, 1508–19.

Engell, A.D., Todorov, A. and Haxby, J.V. (2010) Common neural mechanisms for the evaluation of facial trustworthiness and emotional expressions as revealed by behavioral adaptation. *Perception*, 30, 931–41.

Epley, N. and Gilovich, T. (2004) Are adjustments insufficient? *Personality and Social Psychology Bulletin*, 30, 447–60.

Epley, N. and Whitchurch, E. (2008) Mirror, mirror on the wall: Enhancement in self-recognition. *Personality and Social Psychology Bulletin*, 34, 1159–70.

Erb, H.P. and Bohner, G. (2007) Social influence and persuasion: Recent theoretical developments and integrative attempts. In K. Fiedler (ed.) *Social Communication* (pp. 191–221). New York: Psychology Press.

Erb, H.P., Bohner, G., Hewstone, M. et al. (2006) Large minorities and small majorities: Interactive effects of inferred and explicit consensus on attitudes. *Basic and Applied Social Psychology*, 28, 221–31.

Ericsson, K.A. and Simon, H.A. (1980) How to study thinking in everyday life: Contrasting think-aloud protocols with descriptions and explanations of thinking. *Mind, Culture and Activity*, 5, 178–86.

Erikson, R.S., Luttberg, N.R. and Tedin, K.T. (1988) *American Public Opinion* (3rd edn). New York: Macmillan.

Eron, L.D. (1963) Relationship of TV viewing habits and aggressive behavior in children. *Journal of Abnormal and Social Psychology,* 67, 193–6.

Esmer, Y. and Petterson, T. (eds) (2007) *Measuring and Mapping Cultures: 25 Years of Comparative Value Research*. Leiden: Koninklijke Brill.

Esses, V.M. and Dovidio, J.F. (2002) The role of emotions in determining willingness to engage in intergroup contact. *Personality and Social Psychology Bulletin*, 19, 1202–14.

Etcoff, N.L. (1989) Asymmetries in recognition of emotion. In F. Boller and J. Grafman (eds) *Handbook of Neuropsychology* (vol. 3, pp. 363–82). New York: Elsevier.

European Professional Women's Network (2006) *Second Bi-annual European PWN*

Board Women Monitor 2006: Scandinavia Strengthens its Lead. Retrieved from http://www.europeanpwn.net/files/boardwomen_press_release120606_1.pdf on 20 August 2012.

Exum, M.L. (2006) Alcohol and aggression: An integration of findings from experimental studies. *Journal of Criminal Justice*, 34, 131–45.

Fabrigar, L.R. and Petty, R.E. (1999) The role of the affective and cognitive bases of attitudes in susceptibility to affectively and cognitively based persuasion. *Personality and Social Psychology Bulletin*, 25, 363–81.

Fajardo, D.M. (1985) Author race, essay quality, and reverse discrimination. *Journal of Applied Social Psychology*, 15, 255–68.

Falk, E.B., Rameson, L., Berkman, E.T. et al. (2010) The neural correlates of persuasion: A common network across cultures and media. *Journal of Cognitive Neuroscience*, 22, 2447–59.

Fast, N.J., Heath, C. and Wu, G. (2009) Common ground and cultural prominence: How conversation reinforces culture. *Psychological Science*, 20, 904–11.

Fawcett, C.A. and Markson, L. (2010) Children reason about shared preferences. *Developmental Psychology*, 46, 299–309.

Fazio, R.H. (1986) How do attitudes guide behaviour? In R.M. Sorrentino and E.T. Higgins (eds) *Handbook of Motivation and Cognition: Foundations of Social Behavior* (pp. 204–43). New York: Guilford Press.

Fazio, R.H. (1989) On the power and functionality of attitudes: The role of attitude accessibility. In A.R. Pratkanis, S.J. Breckler and A.G. Greenwald (eds) *Attitude Structure and Function* (pp. 153–79). Hillsdale, NJ: Erlbaum.

Fazio, R.H. and Powell, M.C. (1997) On the value of knowing one's likes and dislikes: Attitude accessibility, stress, and health in college. *Psychological Science*, 8, 430–36.

Fazio, R.H. and Zanna, M.P. (1981) Direct experience and attitude-behavior consistency. *Advances in Experimental Social Psychology*, 14, 161–202.

Fazio, R.H., Blascovich, J. and Driscoll, D.M. (1992) On the functional value of attitudes: The influence of accessible attitudes on the ease and quality of decision making. *Personality and Social Psychology Bulletin*, 18, 388–401.

Fazio, R.H., Ledbetter, J.E. and Towles-Schwen, T. (2000) On the costs of accessible attitudes: Detecting that the attitude object has changed. *Journal of Personality and Social Psychology*, 78, 197–210.

Fazio, R.H., Roskos-Ewoldsen, D.R. and Powell, M.C. (1994) Attitudes, perception, and attention. In P.M. Niedenthal and S. Kitayama (eds) *The Heart's Eye: Emotional Influences in Perception and Attention* (pp. 197–216). San Diego, CA: Academic Press

Feather, N.T. (1991) Human values, global self-esteem, and belief in a just world. *Journal of Personality*, 59, 83–107.

Feather, N.T. (2003) Distinguishing between deservingness and entitlement: Earned outcomes versus lawful outcomes. *European Journal of Social Psychology*, 33, 367–85.

Feather, N.T. (2008) Perceived legitimacy of a promotion decision in relation to deservingness, entitlement, and resentment in the context of affirmative action and performance. *Journal of Applied Social Psychology*, 38, 1230–54.

Feeney, J.A. (1994) Attachment style, communication patterns, and satisfaction across the life cycle of marriage. *Personal Relationships*, 1, 333–48.

Feeney, J.A. and Noller, P. (1990) Attachment style as a predictor of adult romantic relationships. *Journal of Personality and Social Psychology*, 58, 281–91.

Fehr, B. (1994) Prototype-based assessment of laypeople's views of love. *Personal Relationships*, 1, 309–31.

Fehr, B. and Russell, J.A. (1991) The concept of love viewed from a prototype perspective. *Journal of Personality and Social Psychology*, 60, 425–38.

Fehr, B. and Sprecher, S. (2009) Compassionate love: Conceptual, measurement, and relational issues. In B. Fehr, S. Sprecher and L.G. Underwood (eds) *The Science of Compassionate Love: Theory, Research, and Applications* (pp. 27–52). Malden, MA: Wiley-Blackwell.

Fehr, E. and Fischbacher, U. (2003) The nature of human altruism. *Nature*, 425, 785–91.

Fehr, E. and Gächter, S. (2002) Altruistic punishment in humans. *Nature*, 415, 137–40.

Feingold, A. (1994) Gender differences in personality: A meta-analysis. *Psychological Bulletin*, 116, 429–56.

Feldman, R.S., Philippot, P. and Custrini, R. (1991) Social competence and nonverbal behavior. In R.S. Feldman and B. Rimé (eds) *Fundamentals of Nonverbal Behavior* (pp. 329–50). Cambridge: Cambridge University Press.

Felmlee, D., Sprecher, S. and Bassin, E. (1990) The dissolution of intimate relationships: A hazard model. *Social Psychology Quarterly*, 53, 13–30.

Fenichel, O. (1945) *The Psychoanalytic Theory of Neurosis*. New York: Norton.

Fenigstein, A. (1979) Self-consciousness, self-attention, and social interaction. *Journal of Personality and Social Psychology*, 37, 75–86.

Fenigstein, A., Scheier, M.F. and Buss, A.H. (1975) Public and private self-consciousness: Assessment and theory. *Journal of Consulting and Clinical Psychology*, 43, 522–7.

Fergusson, D.M., Horwood, L.J. and Shannon, F.T. (1984) A proportional hazards model of family breakdown. *Journal of Marriage and the Family*, 46, 539–49.

Festinger, L. (1950) Informal social communication. *Psychological Review*, 57, 271.

Festinger, L. (1954) A theory of social comparison processes. *Human Relations*, 7, 117–40.

Festinger, L. (1957) *A Theory of Cognitive Dissonance*. Evanston, IL: Row, Peterson.

Festinger, L. and Carlsmith, J.M. (1959) Cognitive consequences of forced compliance. *Journal of Abnormal and Social Psychology*, 58, 203–10.

Festinger, L., Pepitone, A. and Newcomb, T.M. (1952) Some consequences of deindividuation in a group. *Journal of Personality and Social Psychology*, 47, 382–9.

Festinger, L., Schachter, S. and Back, K. (1950) *Social Pressures in Informal Groups: A Study of a Housing Project*. New York: Harper & Bros.

Feygina, I., Jost, J.T. and Goldsmith, R. (2010) System justification, the denial of global warming, and the possibility of 'system-sanctioned change'. *Personality and Social Psychology Bulletin*, 36, 326–38.

Fiedler, F.E. (1967) *A Theory of Leadership Effectiveness*. New York: McGraw-Hill.

Fiedler, F.E. (1978) The contingency model and the dynamics of the leadership process. *Advances in Experimental Social Psychology*, 11, 59–112.

Fiedler, K. (1991) The tricky nature of skewed frequency tables: An information loss account of distinctiveness-based illusory correlations. *Journal of Personality and Social Psychology*, 60, 24–36.

Fiedler, K. (2004) Illusory correlation. In R. Pohl (ed.) *Cognitive Illusions: A Handbook on Fallacies and Biases in Thinking, Judgement and Memory* (pp. 98–116). Hove: Psychology Press.

Fiedler, K. (2008) Language: A toolbox for sharing and influencing social reality. *Perspectives on Psychological Science*, 3, 38–47.

Fiedler, K. (2009) On embodied cognition and mental simulation: A meta-theoretical comment to Zwaan's treatise. *European Journal of Social Psychology*, 39, 1156–9.

Fiedler, K. and Wänke, M. (2009) The cognitive-ecological approach to rationality in social psychology. *Social Cognition*, 27, 699–732.

Fiedler, K., Bluemke, M., Friese, M. and Hofmann, W. (2003) On the different uses of linguistic abstractness: From LIB to LED and beyond. *European Journal of Social Psychology*, 33, 441–53.

Fiedler, K., Messner, C. and Bluemke, M. (2006) Unresolved problems with the 'I', the 'A', and the 'T': A logical and psychometric critique of the Implicit Association Test (IAT), *European Review of Social Psychology*, 17, 74–147.

Fields, S.K., Collins, C.L. and Comstock, R.D. (2007) Conflict on the courts: A review of sports-related violence literature. *Trauma, Violence & Abuse*, 8, 359–69.

Fields, S.K., Collins, C.L. and Comstock, R.D. (2010) Violence in youth sports: Hazing, brawling and foul play. *British Journal of Sports Medicine*, 44, 32–7.

Fincham, F.D., Paleari, F.G. and Regalia, C. (2002) Forgiveness in marriage: The role of relationship quality, attributions, and empathy. *Personal Relationships*, 9, 27–37.

Fincher, C.L. and Thornhill, R. (2012) Parasite-stress promotes in-group assortative sociality: The cases of strong family ties and heightened religiosity. *Behavioral and Brain Sciences*, 35, 1–19.

Fine, M.A. and Harvey, J.H. (2006) *Handbook of Divorce and Relationship Dissolution*. Mahwah, NJ: Lawrence Erlbaum.

Fischer, A.H., Rodriguez Mosquera, P.M., van Vianen, A.E.M. and Manstead, A.S.R. (2004) Gender and culture differences in emotion. *Emotion*, 4, 87–94.

Fischer, D.H. (1989) *Albion's Seed: Four British Folkways in America*. New York: Oxford University Press.

Fischhoff, B. (1975) Hindsight is not equal to foresight: The effect of outcome knowledge on judgment under uncertainty. *Journal of Experimental Psychology: Human Perception and Performance*, 1, 288–99.

Fischhoff, B., Gonzalez, R.M., Lerner, J.S. and Small, D.A. (2005) Evolving judgements of terrorism's risks: Foresight and hindsight. *Journal of Experimental Psychology: Applied*, 11, 124–39.

Fishbein, M. (1967) Attitude and the prediction of behavior. In M. Fishbein (ed.) *Readings in Attitude Theory and Measurement* (pp. 477–92). New York: Wiley.

Fishbein, M. (1982) Social psychological analysis of smoking behaviour. In J.R. Eiser (ed.) *Social Psychology and Behavioural Medicine* (pp. 179–97). Chichester: Wiley.

Fisher, H.E. (2004) *Why We Love: The Nature and Chemistry of Romantic Love*. New York: Henry Holt.

Fisher, R.J. (1990) *The Social Psychology of Intergroup and International Conflict Resolution*. New York: Springer.

Fishman, J.A. (1989) *Language and Nationalism*. Rowley, MA: Newbury House.

Fiske, A.P., Kitayama, S., Markus, H.R. and Nisbett, R.E. (1998) The cultural matrix of social psychology. In D.T. Gilbert, S. Fiske and G. Lindzey (eds) *Handbook of Social Psychology* (4th edn, vol. 2, pp. 915–81). New York: McGraw-Hill.

Fiske, S.T. (1980) Attention and weight in person perception: The impact of negative and extreme behavior. *Journal of Personality and Social Psychology*, 38, 889–906.

Fiske, S.T. (1998) Stereotyping, prejudice and discrimination. In D.T. Gilbert, S.T. Fiske and G. Lindzey (eds) *The Handbook of Social Psychology* (4th edn, vol. 2, pp. 357–414). New York: McGraw-Hill.

Fiske, S.T. and Neuberg, S.L. (1990) A continuum model of impression formation, from category-based to individuating processes: Influences of information and motivation on attention and interpretation. *Advances in Experimental Social Psychology*, 23, 1–74.

Fiske, S.T. and Taylor, S.E. (1991) *Social Cognition* (2nd edn). London: McGraw-Hill.

Fiske, S.T. and Taylor, S.E. (2008) *Social Cognition: From Brains to Culture*. New York: McGraw-Hill.

Fiske, S.T., Cuddy, A.J.C., Glick, P. and Xu, J. (2002) A model of (often mixed) stereotype content: Competence and warmth respectively follow from perceived status and competition. *Journal of Personality and Social Psychology*, 82, 878–902.

Fitzpatrick, A.R. and Eagly, A.H. (1981) Anticipatory belief polarization as a function of the expertise of a discussion partner. *Personality and Social Psychology Bulletin*, 7, 636–42.

Fletcher, G.J.O. (1995) *The Scientific Credibility of Folk Psychology*. Hillsdale, NJ: Erlbaum.

Fletcher, G.J.O. (1995) Two uses of folk psychology: Implications for psychological science. *Philosophical Psychology*, 8, 221–38.

Fletcher, G.J.O. and Ward, C. (1988) Attribution theory and processes: A cross-cultural perspective. In M.H. Bond (ed.) *The Cross-cultural Challenge to Social Psychology* (vol. 11, pp. 230–44). Thousand Oaks, CA: Sage.

Fletcher, G.J.O., Simpson, J.A. and Thomas, G. (2000) Ideals, perceptions, and evaluations in early relationship development. *Journal of Personality and Social Psychology*, 79, 933–40.

Fletcher, G.J.O., Simpson, J.A., Thomas, G. and Giles, L. (1999) Ideals in intimate relationships. *Journal of Personality and Social Psychology*, 76, 72–89.

Flowers, M.L. (1977) A laboratory test of some implications of Janis's groupthink hypothesis. *Journal of Personality and Social Psychology*, 35, 888–96.

Flynn, F.J. and Amanatullah, E. (2012) Psyched up or psyched out: The impact of coactor status on individual performance. *Organization Science*, 23, 402–15.

Foa, U.G. and Foa, E.B. (1975) *Resource Theory of Social Exchange*. Morristown, NJ: General Learning Press.

Foddy, M., Platow, M.J. and Yamagishi, T. (2009) Group-based trust in strangers: The role of stereotypes and expectations. *Psychological Science*, 20, 419–22.

Fodor, E.M. and Smith, T. (1982) The power motive as an influence on group decision making. *Journal of Personality and Social Psychology*, 42, 178–85.

Forbes, H.D. (1997) *Ethnic Conflict: Commerce, Culture and the Contact Hypothesis*. New Haven, CT: Yale University Press.

Forbes, H.D. (2004) Ethnic conflict and the contact hypothesis. In Y.T. Lee, C. McAuley, F. Moghaddam and S. Worchel (eds) *The Psychology of Ethnic and Cultural Conflict* (pp. 69–88). Westport, CT: Praeger.

Forbes, K.J. (2000) A reassessment of the relationship between inequality and growth. *American Economic Review*, 90, 869–87.

Ford, W.S. (1986) Favorable intergroup contact may not reduce prejudice: Inconclusive journal evidence, 1960–1984. *Sociology and Social Research*, 70, 256–8.

Forgas, J.P. (1983) What is social about social cognition? *British Journal of Social Psychology*, 22, 129–44.

Forgas, J.P. (1995) Mood and judgment: The affect infusion model (AIM). *Psychological Bulletin*, 17, 39–66.

Forgas, J.P. (1998) On being happy but mistaken: Mood effects on the fundamental attribution error. *Journal of Personality and Social Psychology*, 75, 318–31.

Forgas, J.P. (1999) Feeling and speaking: Mood effects on verbal communication strategies. *Personality and Social Psychology Bulletin*, 25, 850–63.

Forgas, J.P. (2000) Affect and information processing strategies: An interactive relationship. In J.P. Forgas (ed.) *Feeling and Thinking: The Role of Affect in Social Cognition* (pp. 253–80). Cambridge: Cambridge University Press.

Forgas, J.P. (2007) When sad is better than happy: Negative affect can improve the quality and effectiveness of persuasive messages and social influence strategies. *Journal of Experimental Social Psychology*, 43, 513–28.

Forgas, J.P. and Moylan, S. (1987) After the movies: Transient mood and social judgments. *Personality and Social Psychology Bulletin*, 13, 467–77.

Foroni, F. and Semin, G.R. (2009) Language that puts you in touch with your bodily feelings: The multimodal responsiveness of affective expressions. *Psychological Science*, 20, 974–80.

Förster, J. and Strack, F. (1997) Motor actions in retrieval of valenced information: A motor congruence effect. *Perceptual and Motor Skills*, 85, 1419–27.

Förster, J. and Strack, F. (1998) Motor actions in retrieval of valenced information II: Boundary conditions for motor congruence effects. *Perceptual and Motor Skills*, 86, 1423–6.

Försterling, F. (1989) Models of covariation and attribution: How do they relate to the analogy of analysis of variance? *Journal of Personality and Social Psychology*, 57, 615–25.

Försterling, F. and Rudolph, U. (1988) Situations, attributions, and the evaluation of reactions. *Journal of Personality and Social Psychology*, 54, 225–32.

Foshee, V.A., Bauman, K.E. and Fletcher, L. (1999) Family violence and the perpetration of adolescent dating violence: Examining social learning and social control processes. *Journal of Marriage and the Family*, 61, 331–42.

Foss, R.D. and Dempsey, C.B. (1979) Blood donation and the foot-in-the-door technique: A limiting case. *Journal of Personality and Social Psychology*, 37, 580–90.

Foster, C.A., Witcher, B.S., Campbell, W.K. and Green, J.D. (1998) Arousal and attraction: Evidence for automatic and controlled processes. *Journal of Personality and Social Psychology*, 74, 580–90.

Foster, D. and Finchilescu, G. (1986) Contact in a 'non-contact' society: The case of South Africa. In M. Hewstone and R. Brown (eds) *Contact and Conflict in Intergroup Encounters* (pp. 119–36). Oxford: Blackwell.

Fox, S. and Hoffman, M. (2002) Escalation behavior as a specific case of goal-directed activity: A persistence paradigm. *Basic and Applied Social Psychology*, 24(4), 273–85.

Fox-Kales, E. (2011) *Body Shots: Hollywood and the Culture of Eating Disorders*. Albany, NY: State University of New York Press.

Fragale, A.R. and Heath, C. (2004) Evolving informational credentials: The (mis) attribution of believable facts to credible sources. *Personality and Social Psychology Bulletin*, 30, 225–36.

Francik, E.P. and Clark, H.H. (1985) How to make requests that overcome obstacles to compliance. *Journal of Memory and Language*, 24, 560–8.

Franco, F. and Maass, A. (1996) Implicit vs. explicit strategies of outgroup discrimination: The role of intentional control in biased language use and reward allocation. *Journal of Language and Social Psychology*, 15, 335–59.

Franco, F.M. and Maass, A. (1999) Intentional control over prejudice: When the choice of the measure matters. *European Journal of Social Psychology*, 29, 469–77.

Frank, M.G. and Gilovich, T. (1988) The dark side of self- and social perception: Black uniforms and aggression in professional sports. *Journal of Personality and Social Psychology*, 54, 74–85.

Fredrickson, B.L. (1998) What good are positive emotions? *Review of General Psychology*, 2, 300–19.

Fredrickson, B.L. (2001) The role of positive emotions in positive psychology: The broaden-and-build theory of positive emotions. *American Psychologist*, 56, 218–26.

Fredrickson, B.L. and Roberts, T. (1997) Objectification theory: Toward understanding women's lived experiences and mental health risks. *Psychology of Women Quarterly*, 21, 173–206.

Fredrickson, B.L., Roberts, T., Noll, S.M. et al. (1998) That swimsuit becomes you: Sex differences in self-objectification, restrained eating, and math performance. *Journal of Personality and Social Psychology*, 75, 269–84.

Freedman, J.L. and Fraser, S.C. (1966) Compliance without pressure: The foot-in-the-door technique. *Journal of Personality and Social Psychology*, 4, 195–202.

French, M.T. (2002) Physical appearance and earnings: Further evidence. *Applied Economics*, 34, 569–72.

Freud, S. ([1930]2004) *Civilisation and its Discontents* (trans. D. McLintock). London: Penguin.

Friedman, J.N.W., Oltmanns, T.F. and Turkheimer, E. (2007) Interpersonal perception and personality disorders: Utilization of a thin-slice approach. *Journal of Research in Personality*, 41, 667–88.

Friedman, R.S. and Förster, J. (2000) The effects of approach and avoidance motor actions on the elements of creative insight. *Journal of Personality and Social Psychology*, 79, 477–92.

Friedman, R.S. and Förster, J. (2001) The effects of promotion and prevention cues on creativity. *Journal of Personality and Social Psychology*, 81, 1001–13.

Friedmann, E., Katcher, A.H., Lynch, J.J. and Thomas, S.A. (1980) Animal companions and one-year survival after discharge from a coronary care unit. *Public Health Reports*, 95, 307–12.

Friedrich, J., Fetherstonhaugh, D., Casey, S. and Gallagher, D. (1996) Argument integration and attitude change: Suppression effects in the integration of one-sided arguments that vary in persuasiveness. *Personality and Social Psychology Bulletin*, 22, 179–91.

Frieze, I.H., Olson, J.E. and Russell, J. (1991) Attractiveness and income for men and women in management. *Journal of Applied Social Psychology*, 21, 1039–57.

Frinter, M.P. and Rubinson, L. (1993) Acquaintance rape: The influence of alcohol, fraternity membership, and sports team membership. *Journal of Sex Education and Therapy*, 19, 272–84.

Frisco, M.L. and Williams, K. (2003) Perceived housework equity, marital happiness, and divorce in dual-earner households. *Journal of Family Issues*, 24, 51–73.

Fritsche, I., Jonas, E., Fischer, P. et al. (2007) Mortality salience and the desire for offspring. *Journal of Experimental Social Psychology*, 43, 753–62.

Froming, W.J., Allen, L. and Jensen, R. (1985) Altruism, role-taking and self-awareness: The acquisition of norms governing altruistic behaviour. *Child Development*, 56, 1223–8.

Fromme, K., Stroot, E. and Kaplan, D. (1993) Comprehensive effects of alcohol: Development and psychometric assessment of a new expectancy questionnaire. *Psychological Assessment*, 5, 19–26.

Frymer, P. (2005) Racism revised: Courts, labor law, and the institutional construction of racial animus. *American Political Science Review*, 99, 373–87.

Funder, D.C. (1995) On the accuracy of personality judgement: A realistic approach. *Psychological Review*, 102, 652–70.

Fung, H.H. and Carstensen, L.L. (2003) Sending memorable messages to the old: Age differences in preferences and memory for advertisements. *Journal of Personality and Social Psychology*, 85, 163–78.

Furnham, A. (1990) Language and personality. In H. Giles and W.P. Robinson (eds) *Handbook of Language and Social Psychology* (pp. 73–95). Chichester: John Wiley & Sons.

Furnham, A. and Gunter, B. (1984) Just world beliefs and attitudes towards the poor. *British Journal of Social Psychology*, 23, 265–9.

Gabrenya, W.K., Wang, Y.E. and Latané, B. (1985) Social loafing on an optimizing task: Cross-cultural differences among Chinese and Americans. *Journal of Cross-Cultural Psychology*, 16, 223–42.

Gaertner, L. and Schopler, J. (1998) Perceived ingroup entitativity and intergroup bias: An interconnection of self and others. *European Journal of Social Psychology*, 28, 963–80.

Gaertner, L., Sedikides, C. and Graetz, K. (1999) In search of self-definition: Motivational primacy of the individual self, motivational primacy of the collective self, or contextual primacy? *Journal of Personality and Social Psychology*, 76, 5–18.

Gaertner, L., Sedikides, C., Cai, H. and Brown, J.D. (2010) It's not WEIRD, it's WRONG: When researchers overlook underlying genotypes, they will not detect universal processes. *Behavioral and Brain Sciences*, 33, 93–4.

Gaertner, S.L. and Dovidio, J.F. (1986) The aversive form of racism. In J.F. Dovidio and S.L. Gaertner (eds) *Prejudice, Discrimination, and Racism* (pp. 61–89). Orlando, FL: Academic Press.

Gaertner, S.L. and Dovidio, J.F. (2000) *Reducing Intergroup Bias: The Common Ingroup Identity Model*. Philadelphia: Psychology Press.

Gaertner, S.L., Dovidio, J.F., Rust, M.C. et al. (1999) Reducing intergroup bias: Elements of intergroup cooperation. *Journal of Personality and Social Psychology*, 76, 388–402.

Gaertner, S.L., Mann, J.A., Murrell, A. and Dovidio, J.F. (1989) Reducing intergroup bias: The benefits of recategorization. *Journal of Personality and Social Psychology*, 57, 239–49.

Gaertner, S.L., Rust, M.C., Dovidio, J.F. et al. (1994) The contact hypothesis: The role of a common ingroup identity on reducing intergroup bias. *Small Group Research*, 25, 224–49.

Gailliot, M.T., Plant, E.A., Butz, D.A. and Baumeister, R.F. (2007) Increasing self-regulatory strength can reduce the depleting effect of suppressing stereotypes. *Personality and Social Psychology Bulletin*, 33, 281–94.

Galbraith, J.K. (2012) *Inequality and Instability: A Study of the World Economy Just Before the Great Crisis*. Oxford: Oxford University Press.

Galinsky, A.D. and Moskowitz, G.B. (2000) Perspective-taking: Decreasing stereotype expression, stereotype accessibility, and in-group favoritism. *Journal of Personality and Social Psychology*, 78, 708–824.

Galinsky, A.D. and Mussweiler, T. (2001) First offers as anchors: The role of perspective-taking and negotiator focus. *Journal of Personality and Social Psychology*, 81, 657–69.

Galinsky, A.D., Gruenfeld, D.H. and Magee, J.C. (2003) From power to action. *Journal of Personality and Social Psychology*, 85, 453–66.

Galinsky, A.D., Stone, J. and Cooper, J. (2000) The reinstatement of dissonance and psychological discomfort following failed affirmations. *European Journal of Social Psychology*, 30, 123–47.

Gallo, I.S., McCulloch, K.C. and Gollwitzer, P. (2012) Differential effects of various types of implementation intentions on the regulation of disgust. *Social Cognition*, 30, 1–17.

Gallup, G.G. (1977) Self-recognition in primates. *American Psychologist*, 32, 329–38.

Gallupe, R.B., Cooper, W.H., Grisé, M.L.

and Bastianutti, L.M. (1994) Blocking electronic brainstorms. *Journal of Applied Psychology*, 79, 77–86.

Gallupe, R.B., Dennis, A.R., Cooper, W.H. et al. (1992) Electronic brainstorming and group size. *Academy of Management Journal*, 35, 350–69.

Galton, F. ([1870]1952) *Hereditary Genius*. New York: Appleton.

Gangestad, S.W. and Simpson, J.A. (2000) The evolution of human mating: Trade-offs and strategic pluralism. *Behavioral and Brain Sciences*, 23, 573–87.

Gangestad, S.W., Simpson, J.A., Cousins, A.J. et al. (2004) Women's preferences for male behavioral displays change across the menstrual cycle. *Psychological Science*, 15, 203–7.

Gannon, T.A. (2006) Increasing honest responding on cognitive distortions in child molesters: The bogus pipeline procedure. *Journal of Interpersonal Violence*, 21, 358–75.

Garcia-Moreno, C., Heise, L., Jansen, H.A. et al. (2005) Violence against women. *Science*, 310, 1282–3.

Gardner, H.E. (1987) *The Mind's New Science: A History of the Cognitive Revolution*. New York: Basic Books.

Gardner, W.L. and Knowles, M.L. (2008) Love makes you real: Favorite television characters are perceived as 'real' in a social facilitation paradigm. *Social Cognition*, 26, 156–68.

Gardner, W.L., Gabriel, S. and Lee, A.Y. (1999) 'I' value freedom but 'we' value relationships: Self-construal priming mirrors cultural differences in judgement. *Psychological Science*, 10, 321–6.

Garfinkel, H. (1967) *Studies in Ethnomethodology*. Englewood Cliffs, NJ: Prentice Hall.

Garfinkel, H. (2002) *Ethnomethodology's Program: Working out Durkheim's Aphorism*. Lanham, MD: Rowman & Littlefield.

Gast, A. and Rothermund, K. (2011) What you see is what will change: Evaluative conditioning effects depend on a focus on valence. *Cognition and Emotion*, 25, 89–110.

Gates, M.F. and Allee, W.C. (1933) Conditioned behavior of isolated and grouped cockroaches on a simple maze. *Journal of Comparative Psychology*, 15, 331–58.

Gaunt, R. (2006) Couple similarity and marital satisfaction: Are similar spouses happier? *Journal of Personality*, 74, 1401–20.

Gawronski, B. and Bodenhausen, G.V. (2006) Associative and propositional processes in evaluation: An integrative review of implicit and explicit attitude change. *Psychological Bulletin*, 132, 692–731.

Gawronski, B. and Bodenhausen, G.V. (2007) Unraveling the processes underlying evaluation: Attitudes from the perspective of the APE model. *Social Cognition*, 25, 687–717.

Gawronski, B. and Bodenhausen, G.V. (2011) The associative-propositional evaluation model: Theory, evidence, and open questions. *Advances in Experimental Social Psychology*, 44, 59–127.

Gawronski, B., Deutsch, R., Mbirkou, S. et al. (2008) When 'just say no' is not enough: Affirmation versus negation training and the reduction of automatic stereotype activation. *Journal of Experimental Social Psychology*, 44, 370–7.

Geen, R.G. (1983) Evaluation apprehension and the social facilitation/inhibition of learning. *Motivation and Emotion*, 7, 203–12.

Geen, R.G. (1990) *Human Aggression* (2nd edn). Buckingham: Open University Press.

Geen, R.G. (1991) Social motivation. *Annual Review of Psychology*, 42, 377–99.

Geen, R.G. and Gange, J.J. (1983) Social facilitaton: Drive theory and beyond. In H.H. Blumberg, A.P. Hare, V. Kent and M. Davies (eds) *Small Groups and Social Interaction* (vol. 1, pp. 141–53). London: Wiley.

Geen, R.G. and Quanty, M.B. (1977) The catharsis of aggression: An evaluation of a hypothesis. In L. Berkowitz (ed.) *Advances in Experimental Social Psychology* (vol. 10, pp. 1–37). New York: Academic Press.

Gentile, B., Twenge, J.M., Freeman, E.C. and Campbell, W.K. (2012) The effect of social networking websites on positive self-views: An experimental investigation. *Computers in Human Behavior*, 28, 1929–33.

George, J.M. (1990) Personality, affect, and behavior in groups. *Journal of Applied Psychology*, 75, 107–16.

Gerard, H.B. and Mathewson, G.C. (1966) The effects of severity of initiation on liking for a group: A replication. *Journal of Experimental Social Psychology*, 2, 278–87.

Gerard, H.N. and Hoyt, M.F. (1974) Distinctiveness of social categorization and attitude towards ingroup members. *Journal of Personality and Social Psychology*, 29, 836–42.

Gerbner, G., Gross, L., Eleey, M.F. et al. (1977) TV violence profile no. 8: The highlights. *Journal of Communication*, 27, 171–80.

Gergen, K.J. (1965) Interactions goals and personalistic feedback as factors affecting the presentations of self. *Journal of Personality and Social Psychology*, 1, 413–24.

Gergen, K.J. (1973) Social psychology as history. *Journal of Personality and Social Psychology*, 26, 309–20.

Gergen, K.J. (1989) Social psychology and the wrong revolution. *European Journal of Social Psychology*, 19, 463–84.

Gergen, K.J. (1999) *An Invitation to Social Construction*. London: Sage.

Gergen, M.M. and Gergen, K.J. (1984) The social construction of narrative accounts. In K.J. Gergen and M.M. Gergen (eds) *Historical Social Psychology* (pp. 173–89). Hillsdale, NJ: Lawrence Erlbaum.

Gersick, C.J.G. and Hackman, J.R. (1990) Habitual routines in task-performing groups. *Organizational Behavior and Human Decision Processes*, 47, 65–97.

Gibbon, P. and Durkin, K. (1995) The third person effect: Social distance and perceived media bias. *European Journal of Social Psychology*, 25, 597–602.

Gibbons, A. (2004) American Association of Physical Anthropologist's meeting: Tracking the evolutionary history of a 'warrior' gene. *Science*, 304, 818.

Gibbs, R.W. (1986) On the psycholinguistics of sarcasm. *Journal of Experimental Psychology: General*, 115, 3–15.

Giddens, A. (1981) *The Class Structure of the Advanced Societies*. London: Hutchinson.

Gilbert, D.T. (1998) Ordinary psychology. In D.T. Gilbert, S.T. Fiske and G. Lindzey (eds) *The Handbook of Social Psychology* (4th edn, vol. 1, pp. 89–150). New York: McGraw-Hill.

Gilbert, D.T. (1999) What the mind's not. In S. Chaiken and Y. Trope (eds) *Dual Process Theories in Social Psychology* (pp. 3–11). New York: Guilford Press.

Gilbert, D.T. (2002) Inferential correction. In T. Gilovich, D.W. Griffin and D. Kahneman (eds) *Heuristics and Biases: The Psychology of Intuitive Judgment* (pp. 167–84). New York: Cambridge University Press.

Gilbert, D.T. (2007) *Stumbling on Happiness*. London: Harper.

Gilbert, D.T. and Hixon, J.G. (1991) The trouble of thinking: Activation and application of stereotypic beliefs. *Journal of Personality and Social Psychology*, 60, 509–17.

Gilbert, D.T. and Malone, P.S. (1995) The correspondence bias. *Psychological Bulletin*, 117, 21–38.

Gilbert, D.T. and Osborne, R.E. (1989) Thinking backward: Some curable and incurable consequences of cognitive busyness. *Journal of Personality and Social Psychology*, 57, 940–9.

Gilbey, A., McNicholas, J. and Collis, G.M. (2007) A longitudinal test of the belief that companion animal ownership can help reduce loneliness. *Anthrozoös*, 20, 345–53

Giles, H. (1970) Evaluative reactions to accents. *Educational Review*, 22, 211–27.

Giles, H. and Coupland, N. (1991) *Language: Contexts and Consequences*. Milton Keynes: Open University Press.

Giles, H. and Ogay, T. (2007) Communication accommodation theory. In B.B.

Whaey and W. Samter (eds) *Explaining Communication: Contemporary Theories and Exemplars* (pp. 325–44). New York: Psychology Press.

Giles, H. and Powesland, P.F. (1975) *Speech Style and Social Evaluation*. London: Academic Press.

Giles, H. and Smith, P. (1979) Accommodation theory: Optimal levels of convergence. In H. Giles and R.N. St Clair (eds) *Language and Social Psychology* (pp. 45–65). Baltimore, MD: University Park Press.

Giles, H., Bourhis, R.Y. and Taylor, D.M. (1977) Towards a theory of language in ethnic group relations. In H. Giles (ed.) *Language, Ethnicity and Intergroup Relations* (pp 307–48). London: Academic Press.

Giles, H., Coupland, J. and Coupland, N. (eds) (1991) *Contexts of Accommodation: Developments in Applied Sociolinguistics.* Cambridge: Cambridge University Press.

Giles, H., Coupland, N., Henwood, K. et al. (1990) The social meaning of RP: An intergenerational perspective. In S. Ramsaran (ed.) *Studies in the Pronunciation of English: A Commemorative Volume in Honour of A.C. Gimson* (pp. 191–211). London: Routledge.

Giles, H., Mulac, A., Bradac, J.J. and Johnson, P. (1987) Speech accommodation theory: The next decade and beyond. In M. McLaughlin (ed.) *Communication Yearbook* (vol. 10, pp. 13–48). Newbury Park, CA: Sage.

Giles, H., Taylor, D.M. and Bourhis, R.Y. (1973) Towards a theory of interpersonal accommodation through language: Some Canadian data. *Language in Society*, 2, 177–92.

Gilovich, T., Medvec, V.H. and Savitsky, K. (2000) The spotlight effect in social judgment: An egocentric bias in estimates of the salience of one's own actions and appearance. *Journal of Personality and Social Psychology*, 78, 211–22.

Giner-Sorolla, R., Castano, E., Espinosa, P. and Brown, R. (2008) Shame expressions reduce the recipient's insult from outgroup reparations. *Journal of Experimental Social Psychology*, 44, 519–26.

Glaser, J., Dixit, J. and Green, D.P. (2002) Studying hate crime with the Internet: What makes racists advocate racial violence? *Journal of Social Issues*, 58, 177–93.

Glick, P. and Fiske, S.T. (1996) The Ambivalent Sexism Inventory: Differentiating hostile and benevolent sexism. *Journal of Personality and Social Psychology*, 70, 491–512.

Glick, P., Fiske, S.T., Mladinic, A. et al. (2000) Beyond prejudice as simple antipathy: Hostile and benevolent sexism across cultures. *Journal of Personality and Social Psychology*, 79, 763–75.

Glick, P., Lameiras, M., Fiske, S.T. et al. (2004) Bad but bold: Ambivalent attitudes toward men predict gender inequality in 16 nations. *Journal of Personality and Social Psychology*, 86, 713–28.

Godin, G., Valois, P., Lepage, L. and Desharnais, R. (1992) Predictors of smoking behaviour: An application of Ajzen's theory of planned behaviour. *Addiction*, 87, 1335–43.

Goethals, G.R. and Nelson, R.E. (1973) Similarity in the influence process: The belief-value distinction. *Journal of Personality and Social Psychology*, 25, 117–22.

Goffman, E. (1955) On face-work. *Psychiatry: Journal for the Study of Interpersonal Processes*, 18, 213–31.

Goffman, E. (1959) *The Presentation of Self in Everyday Life*. New York: Anchor Books.

Gold, J.A., Ryckman, R.M. and Mosley, N.R. (1984) Romantic mood induction and attraction to a dissimilar other. *Personality and Social Psychology Bulletin*, 10, 358–68.

Goldin-Meadow, S. and Singer, M.A. (2003) From children's hands to adults' ears: Gesture's role in teaching and learning. *Developmental Psychology*, 39, 509–20.

Goldman, A. and de Vignemont, F. (2009) Is social cognition embodied? *Trends in Cognitive Sciences*, 13, 154–9.

Goldman, J. (1967) A comparison of sensory modality preference of children and adults. Unpublished PhD thesis, Yeshiva University.

Goldman, M., Creason, C.R. and McCall, C.G. (1981) Compliance employing a two-feet-in-the-door procedure. *The Journal of Social Psychology*, 114, 259–65.

Golec de Zavala, A., Cichocka, A., Eidelson, R. and Jayawickreme, N. (2009) Collective narcissism and its social consequences. *Journal of Personality and Social Psychology*, 97, 1074–96.

Gollwitzer, M. and Denzler, M. (2009) What makes revenge sweet: Seeing the offender suffer or delivering a message? *Journal of Experimental Social Psychology*, 45, 840–4.

Gollwitzer, M., Rothmund, T., Pfeiffer, A. and Ensenbach, C. (2009) Why and when justice sensitivity leads to pro- and antisocial behavior. *Journal of Research in Personality*, 43, 999–1005.

Gollwitzer, P.M. (1993) Goal achievement: The role of intentions. *European Review of Social Psychology*, 4, 141–85.

Gollwitzer, P.M. (1999) Implementation intentions: Strong effects of simple plans. *American Psychologist*, 54, 493–503.

Gollwitzer, P.M. and Sheeran, P. (2006) Implementation intentions and goal achievement: A meta-analysis of effects

and processes. *Advances in Experimental Social Psychology*, 38, 69–119.

Gómez, Á., Dovidio, J.F., Huici, C. et al. (2008) The other side of we: When outgroup members express common identity. *Personality and Social Psychology Bulletin*, 34, 1613–26.

Goncalo, J.A., Flynn, F.J. and Kim, S.H. (2010) Are two narcissists better than one? The link between narcissism, perceived creativity, and creative performance. *Personality and Social Psychology Bulletin*, 36, 1484–95.

Gonsalkorale, K. and Williams, K.D. (2007) The KKK won't let me play: Ostracism even by a despised outgroup hurts. *European Journal of Social Psychology*, 37, 1176–86.

Gonzaga, G.C., Turner, R.A., Keltner, D. et al. (2006) Romantic love and sexual desire in close relationships. *Emotion*, 6, 163–79.

Gonzales, M.H. (1992) A thousand pardons: The effectiveness of verbal remedial tactics during account episodes. *Journal of Language and Social Psychology*, 3, 133–51.

Gonzalez-Bono, E., Salvador, A., Serrano, M.A. and Ricarte, J. (1999) Testosterone, cortisol, and mood in a sports team competition. *Hormones and Behavior*, 35, 55–62.

Gordon, R.A. (1996) Impact of ingratiation on judgements and evaluations: A meta-analytic investigation. *Journal of Personality and Social Psychology*, 71, 54–70.

Gorn, G.J. (1982) The effects of music in advertising on choice behavior: A classical conditioning approach. *The Journal of Marketing*, 46, 94–101.

Gosling, S.D., John, O.P., Craik, K.H. and Robins, R.W. (1998) Do people know how they behave? Self-reported act frequencies compared with on-line codings by observers. *Journal of Personality and Social Psychology*, 74, 1337–49.

Gosling, S.D., Sandy, C.J., John, O.P. and Potter, J. (2010) Wired but not WEIRD: The promise of the Internet in reaching more diverse samples. *Behavioral and Brain Sciences*, 33, 94–5.

Gosling, S.D., Vazire, S., Srivastava, S. and John, O. (2004) Should we trust web-based studies? A comparative analysis of six preconceptions about internet questionnaires. *American Psychologist*, 59, 93–104.

Gottman, J.M. (1998) Psychology and the study of marital processes. *Annual Review of Psychology*, 49, 169–97.

Gould, S.J. (1996) *The Mismeasure of Man* (2nd edn). New York: Norton.

Gouldner, A.W. (1960) The norm of reciprocity: A preliminary statement. *American Sociological Review*, 25, 161–78.

Graham, J., Haidt, J. and Nosek, B.A.

(2009) Liberals and conservatives rely on different sets of moral foundations. *Journal of Personality and Social Psychology*, 96, 1029–46.

Graham, K. (2000) Collective responsibility. In T. van den Beld (ed.) *Moral Responsibility and Ontology* (pp. 49–61). Dordrecht: Kluwer.

Graham, K. and Wells, S. (2003) 'Somebody's gonna get their head kicked in tonight': Aggression among young males in bars – a question of values? *British Journal of Criminology*, 43, 546–66.

Grammer, K. and Thornhill, R. (1994) Human (homo sapiens) facial attractiveness and sexual selection: The role of symmetry and averageness. *Journal of Comparative Psychology*, 108, 233–42.

Gray, J. (1992) *Men are from Mars, Women are from Venus: A Practical Guide for Improving Communication and Getting What You Want in Your Relationships.* New York: HarperCollins.

Graziano, W.G., Bruce, J., Tobin, R.M. and Sheese, B.E. (2007) Attraction, personality, and prejudice: Liking none of the people most of the time. *Journal of Personality and Social Psychology*, 93, 565–82.

Greenberg, J., Pyszczynski, T. and Solomon, S. (1986) The causes and consequences of the need for self-esteem: A terror management theory. In R.F. Baumeister (ed.) *Public Self and Private Self* (pp. 189–212). New York: Springer-Verlag.

Greenberg, J., Pyszczynski, T., Solomon, S. et al. (1990) Evidence for terror management theory II: The effects of mortality salience on reactions to those who threaten or bolster the cultural worldview. *Journal of Personality and Social Psychology*, 58, 308–18.

Greenberg, J., Solomon, S. and Pyszczynski, T. (1997) Terror management theory of self-esteem and cultural worldviews: Empirical assessments and conceptual refinements. *Advances in Experimental Social Psychology*, 29, 61–139.

Greene, J. and Haidt, J. (2002) How (and where) does moral judgment work? *Trends in Cognitive Sciences*, 6, 517–23.

Greene, J.D., Sommerville, R.B., Nystrom, L.E. et al. (2001) An fMRI investigation of emotional engagement in moral judgement. *Science*, 293, 2105–8.

Greenhaus, J.H. and Powell, G.N. (2006) When work and family are allies: A theory of work-family enrichment. *Academy of Management Review*, 31, 72–92.

Greenwald, A.G., McGhee, D.E. and Schwartz, J.L.K. (1998) Measuring individual differences in implicit cognition: The Implicit Association Test. *Journal of Personality and Social Psychology*, 74, 1464–80.

Greenwald, A.G., Nosek, B.A. and Banaji, M.R. (2003) Understanding and using the Implicit Association Test: I. An improved scoring algorithm. *Journal of Personality and Social Psychology*, 85, 197–216.

Greenwald, A.G., Poehlman, T.A., Uhlmann, E.L. and Banaji, E.L. (2009) Understanding and using the Implicit Association Test: III. Meta-analysis of predictive validity. *Journal of Personality and Social Psychology*, 97, 17–41.

Gregg, A.P., Seibt, B. and Banaji, M.R. (2006) Easier done than undone: Asymmetry in the malleability of implicit preferences. *Journal of Personality and Social Psychology*, 90, 1–20.

Gregory, R. (1970) *The Intelligent Eye.* New York: McGraw-Hill.

Greve, F. (2009) America's poor are its most generous givers. McClatchy newspapers. Retrieved from http://www.mcclatchydc.com/2009/05/19/68456/americas-poor-are-its-most-generous.html on 23 July 2011.

Grice, H.P. (1975) Logic and conversation. In P. Cole and J.L. Morgan (eds) *Syntax and Semantics: Speech Acts* (vol. 3, pp. 41–58). New York: Academic Press.

Grice, H.P. (1989) *Studies in the Way of Words.* Cambridge, MA: Harvard University Press.

Griffitt, W. (1970) Environmental effects on interpersonal affective behavior: Ambient effective temperature and attraction. *Journal of Personality and Social Psychology*, 15, 240–4.

Griggs, R.A., Jackson, S.L., Marek, P. and Christopher, A.N. (1998) Critical thinking in introductory psychology texts and supplements. *Teaching of Psychology*, 25, 254–66.

Grumm, M., Nestler, S. and Collani, G. (2009) Changing explicit and implicit attitudes: The case of self-esteem. *Journal of Experimental Social Psychology*, 45, 327–35.

Grush, J.E. (1980) Impact of candidate expenditures, regionality, and prior outcomes on the 1976 democratic presidential primaries. *Journal of Personality and Social Psychology*, 38, 337–47.

Gruys, M.L. and Sackett, P.R. (2003) Investigating the dimensionality of counterproductive work behavior. *International Journal of Selection and Assessment*, 11, 30–42.

Guadagno, R.E. and Cialdini, R.B. (2002) Online persuasion: An examination of gender differences in computer-mediated interpersonal influence. *Group Dynamics: Theory, Research, and Practice*, 6, 38–51.

Guinote, A. (2007) Power and goal pursuit. *Personality and Social Psychology Bulletin*, 33, 1076–87.

Guinote, A. and Vescio, T.K. (eds) (2010) *The Social Psychology of Power.* New York: Guilford Press.

Guinote, A., Weick, M. and Cai, A. (2012) Does power magnify the expression of dispositions? *Psychological Science*, 23, 475–82.

Gulian, E., Matthews, G., Glendon, A.I. et al. (1989) Dimensions of driver stress. *Ergonomics*, 32, 585–602.

Gunther, A.C. (1995) Overrating the X-rating: The third-person perception and support for censorship of pornography. *Journal of Communication*, 45, 27–38.

Guo, G., Ou, X.M., Roettger, M. and Shih, J.C. (2008) The VNTR 2 repeat in MAOA and delinquent behaviour in adolescence and young adulthood: Associations and MAOA promoter activity. *European Journal of Human Genetics*, 16, 626–34.

Gupta, U. and Singh, P. (1982) An exploratory study of love and liking and type of marriages. *Indian Journal of Applied Psychology*, 19, 92–7.

Gustafson, R. (1994) Alcohol and aggression. *Journal of Offender Rehabilitation*, 21, 41–80.

Guy, G.R. (1988) Language and social class. In F.J. Newmeyer (ed.) *Linguistics: The Cambridge Survey* (vol. 4, pp. 37–63). Cambridge: Cambridge University Press.

Haberstroh, S., Oyserman, D., Schwarz, N. et al. (2002) Is the interdependent self more sensitive to question context than the independent self? Self-construal and the observation of conversational norms. *Journal of Experimental Social Psychology*, 38, 323–9.

Hackman, J.R. (1986) The psychology of self-management in organizations. In M.S. Pallak and R.O. Perloff (eds) *Psychology and Work: Productivity, Change and Employment* (vol. 5, pp. 89–136). Washington, DC: American Psychological Association.

Hadar, U., Wenkert-Olenik, D., Krauss, R. and Soroker, N. (1998) Gesture and the processing of speech: Neuropsychological evidence. *Brain and Language*, 62, 107–26.

Haddock, G., Maio, G.R., Arnold, K. and Huskinson, T. (2008) Should persuasion be affective or cognitive? The moderating effects of need for affect and need for cognition. *Personality and Social Psychology Bulletin*, 34, 769–78.

Haddock, G., Rothman, A.J., Reber, R. and Shwarz, N. (1999) Forming judgments of attitude certainty, intensity, and importance: The role of subjective experiences. *Personality and Social Psychology Bulletin*, 25, 771–82.

Hafer, C.L. (2000) Investment in long-term goals and commitment to just means drive the need to believe in a just world. *Personality and Social Psychology Bulletin*, 26, 1059–73.

Hafer, C.L. and Bègue, L. (2005) Experimental research on just-world theory: Problems, developments, and future challenges. *Psychological Bulletin*, 131, 128–67.

Hagger, M.S., Wood, C., Stiff, C. and Chatzisarantis, N.L.D. (2010) Ego depletion and the strength model of self-control: A meta-analysis. *Psychological Bulletin*, 136, 495–525.

Haidt, J. (2001) The emotional dog and its rational tail: A social intuitionist approach to moral judgment. *Psychological Review*, 108, 814–34.

Haidt, J. (2003) The moral emotions. In R.J. Davidson, K.R. Scherer and H.H. Goldsmith (eds) *Handbook of Affective Sciences* (pp. 852–70). Oxford: Oxford University Press.

Haidt, J. and Hersh, M.A. (2001) Sexual morality: The cultures and emotions of conservatives and liberals. *Journal of Applied Social Psychology*, 31, 191–221.

Haidt, J., Koller, S.H. and Dias, M.G. (1993) Affect, culture, and morality, or is it wrong to eat your dog? *Journal of Personality and Social Psychology*, 65, 613–28.

Hajcak, G., MacNamara, A. and Olvet, D.M. (2010) Event-related potentials, emotion, and emotion regulation: An integrative review. *Developmental Neuropsychology*, 35, 129–55.

Hajcak, G., Molnar, C., George, M.S. et al. (2007) Emotion facilitates action: A transcranial magnetic stimulation study of motor cortex excitability during picture viewing. *Psychophysiology*, 44, 91–7.

Halberstadt, J. and Rhodes, G. (2000) The attractiveness of nonface averages: Implications for an evolutionary explanation of the attractiveness of average faces. *Psychological Science*, 11, 285–9.

Halberstadt, J. and Rhodes, G. (2003) It's not just average faces that are attractive: Computer-manipulated averageness makes birds, fish, and automobiles attractive. *Psychonomic Bulletin & Review*, 10, 149–56.

Halberstadt, J., Winkielman, P., Niedenthal, P.M. and Dalle, N. (2009) Emotional conception: How embodied emotion concepts guide perception and facial action. *Psychological Science*, 20, 1254–61.

Hale, C. (1996) Fear of crime: A review of the literature. *International Journal of Victimology*, 4, 79–150.

Hall, E.T. (1966) *The Hidden Dimension*. New York: Doubleday.

Hall, J.A. (1984) *Nonverbal Sex Differences: Communication Accuracy and Expressive Style*. Baltimore, MD: Johns Hopkins University Press.

Hall, P.A. and Soskice, D. (2001) An introduction to varieties of capitalism. In P.A. Hall and D. Soskice (eds) *Varieties of Capitalism: The Institutional Foundations of Comparative Advantage* (pp. 1–70). New York: Oxford University Press.

Halpern, D.F. (1998) Teaching critical thinking for transfer across domains: Disposition, skills, structure training, and metacognitive monitoring. *American Psychologist*, 53, 449–55.

Hamaguchi, E. (1985) A contextual model of the Japanese: Toward a methodological innovation in Japan studies. *Journal of Japanese Studies*, 11, 289–321.

Hamermesh, D.S. and Parker, A. (2005) Beauty in the classroom: Instructors' pulchritude and putative pedagogical productivity. *Economics of Education Review*, 24, 369–76.

Hamilton, D.L. and Gifford, R.K. (1976) Illusory correlation in interpersonal personal perception: A cognitive basis of stereotype judgments. *Journal of Experimental Social Psychology*, 12, 392–407.

Hamilton, D.L. and Sherman, S.J. (1996) Perceiving persons and groups. *Psychological Review*, 103, 336–55.

Hamilton, D.L. and Zanna, M.P. (1974) Context effects in impression formation: Changes in connotative meaning. *Journal of Personality and Social Psychology*, 29, 649–54.

Hamilton, D.L., Sherman, S.J. and Lickel, B. (1998) Perceiving social groups: The importance of the entitativity continuum. In C. Sedikides, J. Schopler and C.A. Insko (eds) *Intergroup Cognition and Intergroup Behavior* (pp. 47–74). Mahwah, NJ: Lawrence Erlbaum.

Hamilton, D.L., Stroessner, S.J. and Driscoll, D.M. (1994) Social cognition and the study of stereotyping. In P.G. Devine, D.L. Hamilton and T.M. Ostrom (eds) *Social Cognition: Impact on Social Psychology* (pp. 291–321). San Diego, CA: Academic Press.

Hamilton, W.D. (1963) The evolution of altruistic behavior. *American Naturalist*, 97, 354–6.

Hancock, J.T., Curry, L., Goorha, S. and Woodworth, M.T. (2008) On lying and being lied to: A linguistic analysis of deception in computer-mediated communication. *Discourse Processes*, 45, 1–23.

Haney, C., Banks, C. and Zimbardo, P. (1973) Interpersonal dynamics in a simulated prison. *International Journal of Criminology and Penology*, 1, 69–97.

Hannes, R.P., Franck, D. and Liemann, F. (1984) Effects of rank order fights on whole-body and blood concentrations of androgens and corticosteroids in the male swordtail (*Xiphophoborus helleri*). *Zietshrift für Tierpsychologie*, 65, 53–65.

Hansen, D.E., Vandenberg, B. and Patterson, M.L. (1995) The effects of religious orientation on spontaneous and nonspontaneous helping behaviors. *Personality and Individual Differences*, 19, 101–4.

Hansen, J. and Wänke, M. (2009) Liking what's familiar: The importance of unconscious familiarity in the mere-exposure effect. *Social Cognition*, 27, 161–82.

Hansen, J., Winzeler, S. and Topolinski, S. (2010) When the death makes you smoke: A terror management perspective on the effectiveness of cigarette on-pack warnings. *Journal of Experimental Social Psychology*, 46, 226–8.

Hanson, J. (2009) Thanksgiving as 'system justification': Is there a downside to giving thanks? http://www.psychologytoday.com/blog/minding-the-law/200911/thanksgiving-system-justification?page=2.

Harari, H., Harari, O. and White, R.V. (1985) The reaction to rape by American male bystanders. *Journal of Social Psychology*, 125, 653–8.

Harber, K.D. (1998) Is feedback to minorities positively biased? *Psychological Science Agenda*, 11, 8–9.

Harber, K.D. (1998) Feedback to minorities: Evidence of a positive bias. *Journal of Personality and Social Psychology*, 74, 622–28.

Harber, K.D., Stafford, S. and Kennedy, K.A. (2010) The positive feedback bias as a response to self-image threat. *British Journal of Social Psychology*, 49, 207–18.

Hardin, C. and Higgins, E.T. (1996) Shared reality: How social verification makes the subjective objective. In E. T. Higgins and R.M. Sorrentino (eds) *Handbook of Motivation and Cognition: The Interpersonal Context* (vol. 3, pp. 28–79). New York: Guilford Press.

Hardin, G. (1968) The tragedy of the commons. *Science*, 162, 1243–8.

Haridakis, P.M. and Rubin, A.M. (2005) Third-person effects in the aftermath of terrorism. *Mass Communication and Society*, 8, 39–59.

Harkins, S.G. and Szymanski, K. (1987) Social loafing and social facilitation: New wine in old bottles. In N.C. Hendrick (ed.) *Review of Personality and Social Psychology: Group Processes and Intergroup Relations* (vol. 9, pp. 167–88). Newbury Park, CA: Sage.

Harley, E.M. (2007) Hindsight bias in legal decision making. *Social Cognition*, 25, 48–63.

Harlow, H.F. (1932) Social facilitation of feeding in the albino rat. *The Pedagogical Seminary and Journal of Genetic Psychology*, 41, 211–21.

Harlow, H.F. (1958) The nature of love. *American Psychologist*, 13, 673–85.

Harlow, H.F. and Harlow, M.K. (1965) The affectional systems. *Behavior of Nonhuman Primates*, 2, 287–334.

Harmon-Jones, E. (2000) Cognitive dissonance and experienced negative affect: Evidence that dissonance increases experienced negative affect even in the absence of aversive consequences. *Personality and Social Psychology Bulletin*, 26, 1490–501.

Harmon-Jones, E. and Allen, J.J.B. (2001) The role of affect in the mere exposure effect: Evidence from psycho-physiological and individual differences approaches. *Personality and Social Psychology Bulletin*, 27, 889–98.

Harmon-Jones, E., Simon, L., Greenberg, J. et al. (1997) Terror management theory and self-esteem: Evidence that increased self-esteem reduces mortality salience effects. *Journal of Personality and Social Psychology*, 72, 24–36.

Harré, R. (1979) *Social Being: A Theory for Social Psychology*. Oxford: Blackwell.

Harré, R. (1997) Forward to Aristotle: The case for a hybrid ontology. *Journal for the Theory of Social Behaviour*, 27, 173–91.

Harrell, W.A. (1978) Physical attractiveness, self-disclosure, and helping behavior. *Journal of Social Psychology*, 104, 15–17.

Harrington, J. (2006) An acoustic analysis of 'happy-tending' in the Queen's Christmas broadcasts. *Journal of Phonetics*, 34, 439–57.

Harris, M. (1991) *Cultural Anthropology* (3rd edn). New York: HarperCollins.

Harris, M.J. and Rosenthal, R.R. (1985) The mediation of interpersonal expectancy effects: 31 meta-analyses. *Psychological Bulletin*, 97, 363–86.

Harrison, K. (2001) Ourselves, our bodies: Thin-ideal media, self-discrepancies, and eating disorder symptomatology in adolescents. *Journal of Social and Clinical Psychology*, 20, 289–323.

Hart, P.T. (1990) *Groupthink in Government: A Study of Small Groups and Policy Failure*. Lisse: Swets & Zeitlinger.

Hart, P.T. (1998) Preventing groupthink-revisited: Evaluating and reforming groups in government. *Organizational Behavior and Human Decision Processes*, 73, 306–26.

Harth, N.S., Hornsey, M.J. and Barlow, F.K. (2011) Emotional responses to rejection of gestures of intergroup reconciliation. *Personality and Social Psychology Bulletin*, 37, 815–29.

Harwood, R.L., Schölmerich, A. and Schulze, P.A. (2000) Homogeneity and heterogeneity in cultural belief systems. *New Directions for Child and Adolescent Development*, 87, 41–57.

Haselton, M.G. and Gildersleeve, K. (2011) Can men detect ovulation? *Current Directions in Psychological Science*, 20, 87–92.

Haslam, N. (2006) Dehumanization: An integrative review. *Personality and Social Psychology Review*, 10(3), 252–64.

Haslam, N. and Bain, P. (2007) Humanizing the self: Moderators of the attribution of lesser humanness to others. *Personality and Social Psychology Bulletin*, 33, 57–68.

Haslam, N., Loughnan, S., Kashima, Y. and Bain, P. (2008) Attributing and denying humanness to others. *European Review of Social Psychology*, 19, 55–85.

Haslam, S.A. (2001) *Psychology in Organizations: The Social Identity Approach*. London: Sage.

Haslam, S.A. and Reicher, S. (2006a) Debating the psychology of tyranny: Fundamental issues of theory, perspective and science. *British Journal of Social Psychology*, 45, 55–63.

Haslam, S.A. and Reicher, S. (2006b) Stressing the group: Social identity and the unfolding dynamics of responses to stress. *Journal of Applied Psychology*, 91, 1037–52.

Haslam, S.A. and Reicher, S. (2007) Beyond the banality of evil: Three dynamics of an interactionist social psychology of tyranny. *Personality and Social Psychology Bulletin*, 33, 615–22.

Haslam, S.A. and Reicher, S.D. (2008) Questioning the banality of evil. *The Psychologist*, 21, 16–19.

Haslam, S.A., Jetten, J., Postmes, T. and Haslam, C. (2009) Social identity, health and well-being: An emerging agenda for applied psychology. *Applied Psychology*, 23, 1–23.

Haslam, S.A., McGarty, C. and Turner, J.C. (1996) Salient group memberships and persuasion: The role of social identity in the validation of beliefs. In J. Nye and A. Brower (eds) *What's Social about Social Cognition? Research on Socially Shared Cognition in Small Groups* (pp. 29–56). Newbury Park, CA: Sage.

Haslam, S.A., Postmes, T. and Ellemers, N. (2003) More than a metaphor: Organizational identity makes organizational life possible. *British Journal of Management*, 14, 357–69.

Hassin, R. and Trope, Y. (2000) Facing faces: Studies on the cognitive aspects of physiognomy. *Journal of Personality and Social Psychology*, 78, 837–52.

Hastie, R. (1988) A computer simulation model of person memory. *Journal of Experimental Social Psychology*, 24, 423–47.

Hastie, R. and Park, B. (1986) The relationship between memory and judgment depends on whether the judgment task is memory-based or online. *Psychological Review*, 93, 258–68.

Hatfield, E. (1987) Passionate and companionate love. In R.J. Sternberg and M.L. Barnes (eds) *The Psychology of Love* (pp. 191–217). New Haven, CT: Yale University Press.

Hatfield, E. and Sprecher, S. (1986) *Mirror, Mirror: The Importance of Looks in Everyday Life*. Albany, NY: State University of New York Press

Hatfield, E. and Walster, G.W. (1981) *A New Look at Love*. Reading, MA: Addison-Wesley.

Hatfield, E., Aronson, E., Abrahams, D. and Rottman, L. (1966) The importance of physical attractiveness in dating behavior. *Journal of Personality and Social Psychology*, 4, 508–16.

Hatfield, E., Cacioppo, J.T. and Rapson, R.L. (1994) *Emotional Contagion*. New York: Cambridge University Press.

Hatfield, E., Walster, G.W. and Berscheid, E. (1978) *Equity: Theory and Research*. Boston, MA: Allyn & Bacon.

Haugtvedt, C.P. and Petty, R.E. (1992) Personality and persuasion: Need for cognition moderates the persistence and resistance of attitude changes. *Journal of Personality and Social Psychology*, 63, 308–19.

Haugtvedt, C.P. and Wegener, D.T. (1994) Message order effects in persuasion: An attitude strength perspective. *Journal of Consumer Research*, 21, 205–18.

Hausmann, L.R.M., Levine, J.M. and Higgins, E.T. (2008) Communication and group perception: Extending the 'saying is believing' effect. *Group Processes and Intergroup Relations*, 11, 539–54.

Havas, D.A., Glenberg, A.M., Gutowski, K.A. et al. (2010) Cosmetic use of Botulinum Toxin-A affects processing of emotional language. *Psychological Science*, 14, 895–900.

Hawkins, S.A. and Hastie, R. (1990) Hindsight: Biased judgments of past events after the outcomes are known. *Psychological Bulletin*, 10, 311–27.

Haynes, T.L., Daniels, L.M., Stupnisky, R.H. et al. (2008) The effect of attributional retraining on mastery and performance motivation among first-year college students. *Basic and Applied Social Psychology*, 30, 198–207Hazan, C. and Shaver, P.R. (1987) Romantic love conceptualized as an attachment process. *Journal of Personality and Social Psychology*, 52, 511–24.

Hazan, C. and Shaver, P.R. (1994) Attachment as an organizational framework for research on close relationships. *Psychological Inquiry*, 5, 1–22.

Hazan, C., Gur-Yaish, N. and Campa, M. (2004) What does it mean to be attached? In W.S. Rholes and J.A. Simpson (eds) *Adult Attachment: Theory, Research, and Clinical Implications* (pp. 55–85). New York: Guilford Press.

Head, E. (2009) The ethics and implications of paying participants in qualitative research. *International Journal of Social Research Methodology*, 12, 335–44.

Headey, B. and Grabka, M. (2011) Health correlates of pet ownership from national surveys. In P. McCardle, S. McCune, J.A. Griffin and V. Maholmes (eds) *How Animals Affect Us: Examining the Influence of Human–Animal Interaction on Child Development and Human Health* (pp. 153–62). Washington, DC: American Psychological Association.

Heatherton, T.F., Macrae, C.N. and Kelley, W.M. (2004) What the social brain sciences can tell us about the self. *Current Directions in Psychological Science*, 13, 190–3.

Heaven, P. and Conners, J. (2001) A note on the value correlates of social dominance orientation and right wing authoritarianism. *Personality and Individual Differences*, 31, 925–30.

Hebl, M.R. and Mannix, L.M. (2003) The weight of obesity in evaluating others: A mere proximity effect. *Personality and Social Psychology Bulletin*, 29, 28–38.

Heflick, N.A. and Goldenberg, J.L. (2009) Objectifying Sarah Palin: Evidence that objectification causes women to be perceived as less competent and less fully human. *Journal of Experimental Social Psychology*, 45, 298–301.

Heider, F. (1958a) *The Psychology of Interpersonal Relations*. New York: Wiley.

Heider, F. (1958b) Perceiving the other person. In R. Tagiuri and L. Petrullo (eds) *Personal Perception and Interpersonal Behavior* (pp. 22–6). Stanford, CA: Stanford University Press.

Heider, F. and Simmel, M. (1944) An experimental study of apparent behavior. *American Journal of Psychology*, 13.

Heilman, M.E. and Stopeck, M.H. (1985) Being attractive: advantage or disadvantage? Performance-based evaluations and recommended personnel actions as a function of appearance, sex, and job type. *Organizational Behavior and Human Decision Processes*, 35, 202–15.

Heilman, M.E., Block, C.J. and Lucas, J.A. (1992) Presumed incompetent? Stigmatization and affirmative action efforts. *Journal of Applied Psychology*, 77, 536–44.

Heimpel, S.A., Wood, J.V., Marshall, M.A. and Brown, J.D. (2002) Do people with low self-esteem really want to feel better?: Self-esteem differences in motivation to repair negative moods. *Journal of Personality and Social Psychology*, 82, 128–47.

Heine, S.J. and Lehman, D.R. (1997) The cultural construction of self-enhancement: An examination of group-serving biases. *Journal of Personality and Social Psychology*, 72, 1268–83

Heine, S.J. and Ruby, M.B. (2010) Cultural psychology. *Wiley Interdisciplinary Reviews: Cognitive Science*, 1, 254–66.

Heine, T.T., Takemoto, T., Moskalenko, S. et al. (2008) Mirrors in the head: Cultural variation in objective self-awareness. *Personality and Social Psychology Bulletin*, 34, 879–87.

Heinrich, J., Heine, S.J. and Norenzayan, A. (2010) The weirdest people in the world? *Behavioral and Brain Sciences*, 33, 61–135.

Helmrich, R.L. (1997) Managing human error in aviation. *Scientific American*, May, 62–7.

Hendrick, C. and Costantini, A.F. (1970) Effects of varying trait inconsistency and response requirements on the primacy effect in impression formation. *Journal of Personality and Social Psychology*, 15, 158–64.

Hendrick, C., Hendrick, S., Foote, F.H. and Slapion-Foote, M.J. (1984) Do men and women love differently? *Journal of Social and Personal Relationships*, 1, 177–95.

Hendrick, S.S. and Hendrick, C. (1995) Gender differences and similarities in sex and love. *Personal Relationships*, 2, 55–65.

Hendrick, S.S., Hendrick, C. and Adler, N.L. (1988) Romantic relationships: Love, satisfaction, and staying together. *Journal of Personality and Social Psychology*, 54, 980–8.

Hendy, D. (2000) *Radio in the Global Age*. Cambridge: Polity Press.

Henley, N.M. (1973) Status and sex: Some touching observations. *Bulletin of the Psychonomic Society*, 2, 91–3.

Henley, N.M. and Harmon, S. (1985) The nonverbal semantics of power and gender: A perceptual study. In S.L. Ellyson and I.F. Dovidio (eds) *Power, Dominance, and Nonverbal Behavior* (pp. 151–64). New York: Springer-Verlag.

Hennigan, K.M., Del Rosario, M.L., Heath, L. et al. (1982) Impact of the introduction of television on crime in the United States: Empirical findings and theoretical implications. *Journal of Personality and Social Psychology*, 42, 461–77.

Henriksen, L., Dauphinee, A., Wang, Y. and Fortmann, S. (2006) Industry sponsored anti-smoking ads and adolescent reactance: Test of a boomerang effect. *Tobacco Control*, 15, 13–18.

Henry, P.J., Sidanius, J., Levin, S. and Pratto, F. (2005) Social dominance orientation, authoritarianism, and support for intergroup violence between the Middle East and America. *Political Psychology*, 26, 569–83.

Heritage, J. (2005) Conversation analysis and institutional talk. In K.L. Fitch and R.E. Sanders (eds) *Handbook of Language and Social Interaction*. New York: Psychology Press.

Herzog, H. (2010) *Some We Love, Some We Hate, Some We Eat: Why it's so Hard to Think Straight about Animals*. New York: Harper.

Herzog, H. (2011) The impact of pets on human health and psychological wellbeing: Fact, fiction, or hypothesis. *Current Directions in Psychological Science*, 20, 236–9.

Heslin, R. (1978) Responses to touching as an index of sex-role norms and attitudes. Paper presented at the meeting of the American Psychological Association, Toronto, Canada.

Heslin, R. and Alper, T. (1983) Touch: A bonding gesture. In J.M. Wiemann and R.P. Harrison (eds) *Nonverbal Interaction* (pp. 47–75). Beverly Hills, CA: Sage.

Heslin, R. and Patterson, M.L. (1982) *Nonverbal Behavior and Social Psychology*. New York: Plenum Press.

Hewstone, M. (1996) Contact and categorization: Social psychological interventions to change intergroup relations. In C.N. Macrae, C. Stangor and M. Hewstone (eds) *Stereotypes and Stereotyping* (pp. 323–68). New York: Guilford Press.

Hewstone, M. and Brown, R.J. (1986) Contact is not enough: An intergroup perspective on the 'contact hypothesis'. In M. Hewstone and R. Brown (eds) *Contact and Conflict in Intergroup Encounters* (pp. 1–44). Oxford: Blackwell.

Hewstone, M. and Jaspers, J. (1982) Intergroup relations and attribution processes. In H. Tajfel (ed.) *Social Identity and Intergroup Relations* (pp. 99–133). Cambridge: Cambridge University Press.

Hewstone, M., Cairns, E., Voci, A. et al. (2006) Intergroup contact, forgiveness, and experience of 'The Troubles' in Northern Ireland. *Journal of Social Issues*, 62, 99–120.

Hewstone, M., Islam, M.R. and Judd, C.M. (1993) Models of crossed categorization and intergroup relations. *Journal of Personality and Social Psychology*, 64, 779–93.

Higgins, E.T. (1987) Self-discrepancy: A theory relating to self and affect. *Psychological Review*, 94, 319–40.

Higgins, E.T. (1997) Beyond pleasure and pain. *American Psychologist*, 52, 1280–300.

Higgins, E.T. (1998) Promotion and prevention: Regulatory focus as a motivational principle. *Advances in Experimental Social Psychology*, 30, 1–46.

Higgins, E.T. and Silberman, I. (1998) Development of regulatory focus: Promotion and prevention as ways of living. In J. Heckhausen and C.S. Dweck (eds) *Motivation and Self-regulation Across the Life Span* (pp. 78–113). New York: Cambridge University Press.

Higgins, E.T. and Tykocinski, O. (1992) Self-discrepancies and biographical memory: Personality and cognition at the level of psychological situation. *Personality and Social Psychology Bulletin*, 18, 527–35.

Higgins, E.T., Bond, R.N., Klein, R. and Strauman, T. (1986) Self-discrepancies and emotional vulnerability: How magnitude, accessibility, and type of discrepancy influence affect. *Journal of Personality and Social Psychology*, 51, 5–15.

Higher Education Statistics Agency (2011) *Students in Higher Education Institutions*. Retrieved from http://www.hesa.ac.uk/index.php/content/view/1974/278/ on 29 June 2012.

Hill, C.E., Gelso, C.J. and Mohr, J.J. (2000) Client concealment and self-presentation in therapy: Comment on Kelly (2000). *Psychological Bulletin*, 126, 495–500.

Hilton, D.J. and Slugoski, B.R. (2001) The conversational perspective in reasoning and explanation. In A. Tesser and N. Schwarz (eds) *Blackwell Handbook of Social Psychology*, vol, 1, *Interpersonal Processes* (pp. 181–206). Oxford: Blackwell.

Hinde, R.A. (ed.) (1972) *Nonverbal Communication*. Cambridge, MA: Cambridge University Press.

Hintzman, D.L. (1986) 'Schema abstraction' in a multiple-trace memory model. *Psychological Review*, 93, 411–28.

Hobbes, T. ([1651]2007) *Leviathan*. Available online at http://ebooks.adelaide.edu.au/h/hobbes/thomas/h68l/.

Hodgins, H.S. and Liebeskind, E. (2003) Apology versus defence: Antecedents and consequences. *Journal of Experimental Social Psychology*, 39, 297–316.

Hodson, G. and Busseri, M.A. (2012) Bright minds and dark attitudes: Lower cognitive ability predicts greater prejudice through right-wing ideology and low intergroup contact. *Psychological Science*, 23, 187–95.

Hoffman, C., Lau, I. and Johnson, D.R. (1986) The linguistic relativity of person cognition: An English-Chinese comparison. *Journal of Personality and Social Psychology*, 51, 1097–105.

Hoffman, C., Mischel, W. and Mazze, K. (1981) The role of purpose in the organization of information about behaviour: Trait-based versus goal-based categories in person perception. *Journal of Personality and Social Psychology*, 40, 211–25.

Hoffman, M.L. (1977) Sex differences in empathy and related behaviours. *Psychological Bulletin*, 84, 712–22.

Hoffman, W. and Friese, M. (2008) Impulses got the better of me: Alcohol moderates the influence of implicit attitudes toward food cues on eating behavior. *Journal of Abnormal Psychology*, 117, 420–7.

Hoffrage, U., Hertwig, R. and Gigerenzer, G. (2000) Hindsight bias: A by-product of knowledge updating? *Journal of Experimental Social Psychology*, 26, 566–81.

Hofling, C.K., Brotzman, E., Dalrymple, S. et al. (1966) An experimental study in nurse-physician relationships. *The Journal of Nervous and Mental Disease*, 143, 171.

Hofstede, G. (1980) *Culture's Consequences: International Differences in Work-related Values*. Beverly Hills, CA: Sage.

Hogan, R., Curphy, G.J. and Hogan, J. (1994) What we know about leadership: Effectiveness and personality. *American Psychologist*, 49, 493–504.

Hogg, M.A. (1992) *The Social Psychology of Group Cohesiveness: From Attraction to Social Identity*. New York: New York University Press.

Hogg, M.A. (2001) A social identity theory of leadership. *Personality and Social Psychology Review*, 5, 184–200.

Hogg, M.A. (2007) Uncertainty-identity theory. *Advances in Experimental Social Psychology*, 39, 69–126.

Hogg, M.A. and Hains, S.C. (1998) Intergroup relations and group solidarity: Effects of group identification and social beliefs on depersonalized attraction. *Journal of Personality and Social Psychology*, 70, 295–309.

Hogg, M.A. and Hardie, E.A. (1991) Social attraction, personal attraction, and self-categorization: A field study. *Personality and Social Psychology Bulletin*, 17, 175–80.

Hogg, M.A. and Smith, J.R. (2007) Attitudes in social context: A social identity perspective. *European Review of Social Psychology*, 18, 89–131.

Hogg, M.A., Hohman, Z.P. and Rivera, J.E. (2008) Why do people join groups? Three motivational accounts from social psychology. *Social and Personality Psychology Compass*, 2, 1269–80.

Hogg, M.A., Sherman, D.K., Dierselhuis, J. et al. (2007) Uncertainty, entitativity, and group identification. *Journal of Experimental Social Psychology*, 43, 135–42.

Hokanson, J.E. (1974) An escape-avoidance view of catharsis. *Criminal Justice and Behavior*, 1, 195–223.

Holland, R.W., Verplanken, B. and van Knippenberg, A. (2002) On the nature of attitude-behavior relations: The strong guide, the weak follow. *European Journal of Social Psychology*, 32, 869–76.

Hollander, E.P. (1961) Some effects of perceived status on responses to innovative behavior. *The Journal of Abnormal and Social Psychology*, 63, 247–50.

Holloway, S., Tucker, L. and Hornstein, H.A. (1977) The effects of social and non-social information on interpersonal behavior of males: The news makes news. *Journal of Personality and Social Psychology*, 35, 514–22.

Holtgraves, T. (2010) Social psychology and language: Words, utterances and conversations. In S.T. Fiske, D.T. Gilbert and G. Lindzey (eds) *Handbook of Social Psychology* (5th edn, vol. 2, pp. 1386–422).

Holtgraves, T. and Kashima, Y. (2008) Language, meaning, and social cognition. *Personality and Social Psychology Review*, 12, 73–94.

Holtgraves, T. and Yang, J. (1990) Politeness as universal: Cross-cultural perceptions of request strategies and inferences based on their use. *Journal of Personality and Social Psychology*, 59, 719–29.

Homans, G.C. (1961) *Social Behavior and its Elementary Forms*. New York: Harcourt, Brace and World.

Homer, P.M. and Kahle, L.R. (1988) A structural equation test of the value-attitude-behavior hierarchy. *Journal of Personality and Social Psychology*, 54, 638–46.

Hong, Y.Y., Chiu, C.Y. and Kung, T.M. (1997) Bringing culture out in front: Effects of cultural meaning system activation on social cognition. In K. Leung, Y. Kashima, U. Kim and S. Yamaguchi (eds) *Progress in Asian Social Psychology* (vol. 1, pp. 135–46). Singapore: Wiley.

Hong, Y.Y., Morris, M.W., Chiu, C.Y. and Benet-Martinez, V. (2000) Multicultural minds: A dynamic constructivist approach to culture and cognition. *American Psychologist*, 55, 709–20.

Hooghe, M. (2002) Watching television and civic engagement: Disentangling the effects of time, programs, and stations. *The International Journal of Press/Politics*, 7, 84–104.

Hoon, H. and Tan, T.M.L. (2008) Organizational citizenship behavior and social loafing: The role of personality, motives and contextual factors. *The Journal of Psychology: Interdisciplinary and Applied*, 142, 89–112.

Hoorens, V. and Ruiter, S. (1996) The optimal impact phenomenon: Beyond the third person effect. *European Journal of Social Psychology*, 26, 599–610.

Hopkins, N., Reicher, S. and Levine, M. (1997) On the parallels between social cognition and the 'new racism'. *British Journal of Social Psychology*, 36, 305–29.

Hopthrow, T. and Abrams, D. (2010) Group transformation: How demonstrability promotes intra-group cooperation in social dilemmas. *Journal of Experimental Social Psychology*, 46, 799–803.

Hopthrow, T. and Hulbert, L.G. (2005) The effect of group decision making on cooperation in social dilemmas. *Group Processes and Intergroup Relations*, 8, 89–100.

Hornsey, M.J. and Hogg, M.A. (2000) Subgroup relations: A comparison of mutual intergroup differentiation and common ingroup identity models of prejudice reduction. *Personality and Social Psychology Bulletin*, 26, 242–56.

Hornsey, M.J. and Imani, A. (2004)

Criticizing groups from the inside and the outside: A social identity perspective on the intergroup sensitivity effect. *Personality and Social Psychology Bulletin*, 30, 365–83.

Hornsey, M.J. and Jetten, J. (2003) Not being what you claim to be: Imposters as sources of group threat. *European Journal of Social Psychology*, 33, 639–57.

Hornsey, M.J. and Jetten, J. (2004) The individual within the group: Balancing the need to belong with the need to be different. *Personality and Social Psychology Review*, 8, 248–64.

Hornsey, M.J., Oppes, T. and Svensson, A. (2002) It's OK if we say it, but you can't: Responses to intergroup and intragroup criticism. *European Journal of Social Psychology*, 32, 293–307.

Hornsey, M.J., Trembath, M. and Gunthorpe, S. (2004) 'You can criticize because you care': Identity attachment, constructiveness, and the intergroup sensitivity effect. *European Journal of Social Psychology*, 34, 499–518.

Hortensius R., Schutter D.J.L.G. and Harmon-Jones, E. (2012) When anger leads to aggression: Induction of relative left frontal cortical activity with transcranial direct current stimulation increases the anger-aggression relationship, *Social Cognitive and Affective Neuroscience*, 7, 342–7.

Hostetter, A.B. and Alibali, M.W. (2008) Visible embodiment: Gestures as simulated action. *Psychonomic Bulletin and Review*, 15, 495–514.

Houben, K., Schoenmakers, T.M. and Wiers, R.W. (2010) I didn't feel like drinking but I don't know why: The effects of evaluative conditioning on alcohol-related attitudes, craving, and behavior. *Addictive Behaviors*, 35, 1161–3.

House of Lords Science and Technology Select Committee (2011) *Behaviour Change: 2nd Report of Session 2010–12*, www.parliament.uk/hlscience.

House, R.J. and Singh, J.V. (1987) Organizational behavior: Some new directions for I/O psychology. *Annual Review of Psychology*, 38, 669–718.

House, R.J., Hanges, P.J., Javidan, M. et al. (2004) *Culture, Leadership, and Organizations: The GLOBE Study of 62 Societies*. Thousand Oaks, CA: Sage.

Hovland, C.I. and Weiss, W. (1951) The influence of source credibility on communication effectiveness. *Public Opinion Quarterly*, 15, 635–50.

Hovland, C.I., Janis, I.L. and Kelley, H.H. (1953) *Communication and Persuasion: Psychological Studies of Opinion Change*. New Haven, CT: Yale University Press.

Howard, J.A. (2000) Social psychology of identities. *Annual Review of Sociology*, 26, 367–93.

Høigaard, R., Fuglestad, S., Peters, D.M. et al. (2010) Role satisfaction mediates the relation between role ambiguity and social loafing among elite women handball players. *Journal of Applied Sport Psychology*, 22, 408–19.

Huang, L.C. and Harris, M.B. (1973) Conformity in Chinese and Americans. *Journal of Cross-Cultural Psychology*, 4, 427–34.

Huesmann, L.R. (1986) Psychological processes promoting the relation between exposure to media violence and aggressive behavior by the viewer. *Journal of Social Issues*, 42, 125–39.

Huesmann, L.R. (1998) The role of social information processing and cognitive schema in the acquisition and maintenance of habitual aggressive behavior. In R. Geen and E. Donnerstin (eds) *Human Aggression: Theories, Research and Implications for Policy* (pp. 73–109). New York: Academic Press.

Huesmann, L.R. (2007) The impact of electronic media violence: Scientific theory and research. *Journal of Adolescent Health*, 41, S6–S13.

Huesmann, L.R., Moise-Titus, J., Podolski, C.-L. and Eron, L.D. (2003) Longitudinal relations between children's exposure to TV violence and their aggressive and violent behavior in young adulthood: 1977–1992. *Developmental Psychology*, 39, 201–21.

Hughes, D., Rodriguez, J., Smith, E.P. et al. (2006) Parents' ethnic-racial socialization practices: A review of research and directions for future study. *Developmental Psychology*, 42, 747–70.

Hughes, G.D. (1992) Realtime response measures redefine advertising wearout. *Journal of Advertising Research*, 32, 61–77.

Hume, D. ([1741]1985) *A Treatise of Human Nature: Being an Attempt to Introduce the Experimental Method of Reasoning into Moral Subjects*. London: Penguin.

Hummon, N.P. and Doreian, P. (2003) Some dynamics of social balance processes: Bringing Heider back into balance theory. *Social Networks*, 25, 17–49.

Hundley, G. and Kim, J. (1997) National culture and the factors affecting perceptions of pay fairness in Korea and the United States. *The International Journal of Organizational Analysis*, 5, 325–41.

Hunt, A.M. (1935) A study of the relative value of certain ideals. *Journal of Abnormal and Social Psychology*, 30, 222–8.

Huo, Y.J., Smith, H.H., Tyler, T.R. and Lind, A.E. (1996) Superordinate identification, subgroup identification, and justice concerns: Is separatism the problem: Is assimilation the answer? *Psychological Science*, 7, 40–5.

Huston, A.C., Donnerstein, E., Fairchild, H. et al. (1992) *Big World, Small Screen: The Role of Television in American Society*. Lincoln, NE: University of Nebraska Press.

Huston, T.L. and Chorost, A.F. (1994) Behavioral buffers on the effect of negativity on marital satisfaction: A longitudinal study. *Personal Relationships*, 1, 223–39.

Hyman, H.H. (1954) *Interviewing in Social Research*. Chicago, IL: University of Chicago Press.

Iacoboni, M. (2009) Imitation, empathy, and mirror neurons. *Annual Review of Psychology*, 60, 653–70.

Iacoboni, M., Lieberman, M.D., Knowlton, B.J. et al. (2004) Watching social interactions produces dorsomedial prefrontal and medial parietal BOLD fMRI signal increases compared to a resting baseline. *Neuroimage*, 21, 1167–73.

Ibáñez, A., Haye, A., González, R. et al. (2009) Multi-level analysis of cultural phenomena: The role of ERPs approach to prejudice. *Journal for the Theory of Social Behaviour*, 39, 81–110.

Ickes, W. (1984) Compositions in black and white: Determinants of interaction in interracial dyads. *Journal of Personality and Social Psychology*, 47, 330–41.

Ickes, W., Snyder, M. and Garcia, S. (1997) Personality influences on the choice of situations. In R. Hogan, J. Johnson and S. Briggs (eds) *Handbook of Personality Psychology* (pp. 165–95). San Diego, CA: Academic Press.

Ijzerman, H. and Semin, G.R. (2009) The thermometer of social relations: Mapping social proximity on temperature. *Psychological Science*, 20, 1214–20.

Imhoff, R. and Erb, H.P. (2009 What motivates nonconformity? Uniqueness seeking blocks majority influence. *Personality and Social Psychology Bulletin*, 35, 309–20.

Inbar, Y., Pizarro, D. A. and Bloom, P. (2009) Conservatives are more easily disgusted than liberals. *Cognition & Emotion*, 23, 714–25.

Inbar, Y., Pizarro, D.A., Knobe, J. and Bloom, P. (2009) Disgust sensitivity predicts intuitive disapproval of gays. *Emotion*, 9, 435–9.

Ingham, A.G., Levinger, G., Graves, J. and Peckham, V. (1974) The Ringelmann effect: Studies of group size and group performance. *Journal of Experimental Social Psychology*, 10, 371–84.

Inglehart, R. and Welzel, C. (eds) (2005) *Modernization, Cultural Change and Democracy: The Human Development Sequence*. Cambridge: Cambridge University Press.

Inglehart, R. and Welzel, C. (2011) The WVS cultural map of the world. Accessed at www.worldvaluessurvey.org.

Insko, C.A. (1965) Verbal reinforcement

of attitude. *Journal of Personality and Social Psychology*, 2, 621–3.

Insko, C.A., Songer, E. and McGarvey, W. (1974) Balance, positivity, and agreement in the Jordan paradigm: A defense of balance theory. *Journal of Experimental Social Psychology*, 10, 53–83.

Ioannidis, J.P.A. (2005) Why most published research findings are false. *PLoS Medicine*, 2, 696–701.

Isen, A.M. (1993) Positive affect and decision making. In M. Lewis and J.M. Haviland (eds) *Handbook of Emotions* (pp. 261–77). New York: Guilford Press.

Isen, A.M. and Levin, P.F. (1972) Effect of feeling good on helping: Cookies and kindness. *Journal of Personality and Social Psychology*, 21, 384–8.

Isen, A.M., Daubman, K.A. and Nowicki, G.P. (1987) Positive affect facilitates creative problem solving. *Journal of Personality and Social Psychology*, 52, 1122–31.

Islam, M.R. and Hewstone, M. (1993) Intergroup attributions and affective consequences in majority and minority groups. *Journal of Personality and Social Psychology*, 64, 936–50.

Isozaki, M. (1984) The effects of discussion on polarization of judgements. *Japanese Psychological Research*, 26, 187–93.

Iyer, A. (2008) Emotion in inter-group relations. *European Review of Social Psychology*, 19, 86–125.

Iyer, A., Jetten, J., Tsivrikos, D. et al. (2009) The more (and the more compatible) the merrier: Multiple group memberships and identity compatibility as predictors of adjustment after life transitions. *British Journal of Social Psychology*, 48, 707–33.

Iyer, A., Schmader, T. and Lickel, B. (2007) Why individuals protest the perceived transgressions of their country: The role of anger, shame, and guilt. *Personality and Social Psychology Bulletin*, 33, 572–87.

Jackson, J. (2009) A psychological perspective on vulnerability in the fear of crime. *Psychology, Crime & Law*, 15, 365–90.

Jackson, J. and Harkins, S.G. (1985) Equity in effort: An explanation of the social loafing effect. *Journal of Personality and Social Psychology*, 49, 1199–206.

Jackson, L.M. and Esses, V.M. (1997) Of scripture and ascription: The relation between religious fundamentalism and intergroup helping. *Personality and Social Psychology Bulletin*, 23, 893–906.

Jacobs, R.C. and Campbell, D.(1961) The perpetuation of an arbitrary tradition through several generations of a laboratory microculture. *The Journal of Abnormal and Social Psychology*, 62, 649–58.

Jacoby, L.L. (1983) Perceptual enhance-ment: Persistent effects of an experience. *Journal of Experimental Psychology: Learning, Memory, and Cognition*, 9, 21–38.

Jahoda, G. (1988) Critical notes and reflections on 'social representations'. *European Journal of Social Psychology*, 18, 195–209.

James, W. (1890) *Principles of Psychology*, vol. 2. New York: Holt.

James, W.T. (1953) Social facilitation of eating behavior in puppies after satiation. *Journal of Comparative and Physi-ological Psychology*, 46, 427–8.

Jameson, F. (1991) *Postmodernism, or the Cultural Logic of Late Capitalism*. Durham, NC: Duke University Press Books.

Janis, I.L. (1967) Effects of fear arousal on attitude change: Recent developments in theory and experimental research. *Advances in Experimental Social Psychology*, 3, 166–224.

Janis, I.L. (1971) Groupthink. *Psychology Today*, November, 43–6, 74–6.

Janis, I.L. (1982) *Groupthink: Psycho-logical Studies of Policy Decisions and Fiascoes* (2nd edn). Boston, MA: Houghton Mifflin.

Janis, I.L., Kaye, D. and Kirschner, P. (1965) Facilitating effects of 'eating-while-reading' on responsiveness to persuasive communications. *Journal of Personality and Social Psychology*, 1, 181–6.

Jankowiak, W.R. and Fischer, E.F. (1992) A cross-cultural perspective on romantic love. *Ethnology*, 31, 149–55.

Jarvis, W.B.G. and Petty, R.E. (1996) The need to evaluate. *Journal of Personality and Social Psychology*, 70, 172–94.

Jassawalla, A., Sashittal, H. and Malshe, A. (2009) Students' perceptions of social loafing: Its antecedents and consequences in undergraduate business classroom teams. *Academy of Manage-ment Learning and Education*, 8, 42–54.

Jeffries, C., Hornsey, M.J., Sutton, R.M., Douglas, K.M. and Bain, P. (2012) The David and Goliath principle: Cultural, ideological and attitudinal underpinnings of the normative protection of low status groups from criticism. *Personality and Social Psychology Bulletin*, 38, 1053–65.

Jellison, J.M. and Arkin, R.M. (1977) Social comparison of abilities: A self-presentational approach to decision making in groups. In J.M. Suls and R.L. Miller (eds) *Social comparison processes* (pp. 235–57). New York: Halsted.

Jensen, E., Dehlin, O., Hagberg, B. et al. (1998) Insomnia in an 80-year-old population: Relationship to medial, psychological and social factors. *Journal of Sleep Research*, 7, 183–9.

Jetten, J. and Spears, R. (2003) The divisive potential of differences and similarities: The role of intergroup distinctiveness in intergroup differentiation. *European Review of Social Psychology*, 14, 203–41.

Jetten, J., Summerville, N., Hornsey, M.J. and Mewse, A. (2005) When differences matter: Intergroup distinctiveness and the evaluation of imposters. *European Journal of Social Psychology*, 35, 609–20.

Ji, L.J., Peng, K. and Nisbett, R.E. (2000) Culture, control, and perception of relationships in the environment. *Journal of Personality and Social Psychology*, 78, 943–55.

Job, V., Dweck, C.S. and Walton, G.M. (2010) Ego depletion – it is all in your head? Implicit theories about willpower affect self-regulation. *Psychological Science*, 21, 1686–93.

Johannesen-Schmidt, M.C. and Eagly, A.H. (2002) Another look at sex differ-ences in preferred mate characteristics: The effects of endorsing the traditional female gender role. *Psychology of Women Quarterly*, 26, 322–8.

Johnson, B.T. (1994) Effects of outcome-relevant involvement and prior information on persuasion. *Journal of Experimental Social Psychology*, 30, 556–79.

Johnson, D.W. and Johnson, E.P. (1987) *Joining Together: Group Theory and Group Skills* (3rd edn). Englewood Cliffs, NJ: Prentice Hall.

Johnson, J.A. and Gosling, S.D. (2010) How to use this book. In S.D. Gosling and J.A. Johnson (eds) *Advanced Methods for Conducting Online Behav-ioral Research* (pp. 3–7). Washington, DC: American Psychological Association.

Johnson, M.P. (1991) Commitment to personal relationships. In W.H. Jones and D.W. Perlman (eds) *Advances in Personal Relationships* (vol. 3, pp. 117–43). London: Jessica Kingsley.

Johnson, R.C., Danko, G.P., Darvill, T.J. et al. (1989) Cross-cultural assessment of altruism and its correlates. *Personality and Individual Differences*, 10, 855–68.

Johnson, R.D. and Downing, L.L. (1979) Deindividuation and valence of cues: Effects on prosocial and antisocial behavior. *Journal of Personality and Social Psychology*, 37, 1532–8.

Johnston, V.S. (2000) Female facial beauty: The fertility hypothesis. *Pragmatics & Cognition*, 8, 107–22.

Johnstone, B., Ferrara, K. and Bean, J.M. (1992) Gender, politeness, and discourse management in same-sex and cross-sex opinion-poll interviews. *Journal of Pragmatics*, 18, 405–30.

Joinson, A.N. (2001) Self-disclosure in computer-mediated communication: The role of self-awareness and visual anonymity. *European Journal of Social Psychology*, 31, 177–92.

Joinson, A.N. and Paine, C.B. (2007) Self-disclosure, privacy and the internet. In A.N. Joinson, K. McKenna, T. Postmes and U.-D. Reips (eds) *The Oxford Handbook of Internet Psychology* (pp. 237–52). Oxford: Oxford University Press.

Joinson, A.N., McKenna, K., Postmes, T. and Reips, U.-D. (eds) (2007) *Oxford Handbook of Internet Psychology*. Oxford: Oxford University Press.

Jokela, M. (2009) Physical attractiveness and reproductive success in humans: Evidence from the late 20th century united states. *Evolution and Human Behavior*, 30, 342–50.

Jolls, C. and Sunstein, C.R. (2006) Debiasing through law. *Journal of Legal Studies*, 35, 199–242.

Jonas, E., Schimel, J., Greenberg, J. and Pyszczynski, T. (2002) The Scrooge effect: Evidence that mortality salience increases prosocial attitudes and behavior. *Personality and Social Psycholgy Bulletin*, 28, 1342–53.

Jones, B.C., DeBruine, L.M., Perrett, D.I. et al. (2008) Effects of menstrual cycle phase on face preferences. *Archives of Sexual Behavior*, 37, 78–84.

Jones, C.R., Fazio, R.H. and Olson, M.A. (2009) Implicit misattribution as a mechanism underlying evaluative conditioning. *Journal of Personality and Social Psychology*, 96, 933–48.

Jones, E.E. (1979) The rocky road from acts to dispositions. *American Psychologist*, 34, 107–17.

Jones, E.E. and Berglas, S. (1978) Control of attributions about the self through self-handicapping strategies: The appeal of alcohol and the role of under-achievement. *Personality and Social Psychology Bulletin*, 4, 200–6.

Jones, E.E. and Davis, K.E. (1965) From acts to dispositions: the attribution process in person perception. In L. Berkowitz (ed.) *Advances in Experimental Social Psychology* (vol. 2, pp. 219–66). New York: Academic Press.

Jones, E.E. and Harris, V.A. (1967) The attribution of attitudes. *Journal of Experimental Social Psychology*, 3, 1–24.

Jones, E.E. and Nisbett, R.E. (1971) *The Actor and the Observer: Divergent Perceptions of the Causes of Behavior*. New York: General Learning Press.

Jones, E.E. and Pittman, T. (1982) Toward a general theory of strategic self-presentation. In J. Suls (ed.) *Psychological Perspectives on the Self* (pp. 231–62). Hillsdale, NJ: Erlbaum.

Jones, E.E. and Sigall, H. (1971) The bogus pipeline: A new paradigm for measuring affect and attitude. *Psychological Bulletin*, 76, 349–64.

Jones, E.E., Rock, L., Shaver, K.G. et al. (1968) Pattern of performance and ability attribution: An unexpected primacy effect. *Journal of Personality and Social Psychology*, 10, 317–40.

Jones, J.M. and Jetten, J. (2011) Recovering from strain and enduring pain: Multiple group memberships promote resilience in the face of physical challenges. *Social Psychological and Personality Science*, 3, 239–44.

Jones, J.M., Williams, W.H., Jetten, J. et al. (2012) The role of psychological symptoms and social group memberships in the development of post-traumatic stress after traumatic injury. *British Journal of Health Psychology*, 17, 798–811.

Jones, J.T. and Cunningham, J.D. (1996) Attachment styles and other predictors of relationship satisfaction in dating couples. *Personal Relationships*, 3, 387–99.

Jones, J.T., Pelham, B.W., Carvallo, M. and Mirenberg, M.C. (2004) How do I love thee? Let me count the Js: Implicit egotism and interpersonal attraction. *Journal of Personality and Social Psychology*, 87, 665–83.

Jones, P.E. (2004) False consensus in social context: Differential projection and perceived social distance. *British Journal of Social Psychology*, 43, 417–29.

Jones, R.A. and Brehm, J.W. (1970) Persuasiveness of one-and two-sided communications as a function of awareness there are two sides. *Journal of Experimental Social Psychology*, 6, 47–56.

Jones, W.H., Freemon, J.E. and Goswick, R.A. (2006) The persistence of loneliness: Self and other determinants. *Journal of Personality*, 49, 27–48.

Jordan, C.H., Spencer, S.J., Zanna, M.O. et al. (2003) Secure and defensive high self-esteem. *Journal of Personality and Social Psychology*, 85, 969–78.

Jose, P.E. (1990) Just-world reasoning in children's immanent justice judgments. *Child Development*, 61, 1024–33.

Josey, C.S. (2010) Hate speech and identity: An analysis of neo racism and the indexing of identity. *Discourse and Society*, 21, 27–39.

Jost, J.J. and Banaji, M.R. (2004) A decade of system justification theory: Accumulated evidence of conscious and unconscious bolstering of the status quo. *Political Psychology*, 25, 881–919.

Jost, J.J., Pelham, B.W., Sheldon, O. and Sullivan, B.N. (2003) Social inequality and the reduction of ideological dissonance on behalf of the system: Evidence of enhanced system justification among the disadvantaged. *European Journal of Social Psychology*, 33, 13–36.

Jost, J.T. (1997) An experimental replication of the depressed-entitlement effect among women. *Psychology of Women Quarterly*, 21, 387–93.

Jost, J.T. (2006) The end of the end of ideology. *American Psychologist*, 61, 651–70.

Jost, J.T. and Banaji, M. (1994) The role of stereotyping in system-justification and the production of false consciousness. *British Journal of Social Psychology*, 33, 1–27.

Jost, J.T. and Kay, A.C. (2005) Exposure to benevolent sexism and complementary gender stereotypes: Consequences for specific and diffuse forms of system justification. *Journal of Personality and Social Psychology*, 88, 498–509.

Jost, J.T. and Kay, A.C. (2010) Social justice: History, theory and research. In S.T. Fiske, D.T. Gilbert and G. Lindzey (eds) *Handbook of Social Psychology* (vol. 2, pp. 1122–65). New York: Wiley.

Jost, J.T. and Kruglanski, A.W. (2002) The estrangement of social constructionism and experimental social psychology: History of the rift and prospects for reconciliation. *Personality and Social Psychology Review*, 6, 168–87.

Jost, J.T. and van der Toorn, J. (2012) System justification theory. In P.A.M. van Lange, A.W. Kruglanski and E.T. Higgins (eds) *Handbook of Theories of Social Psychology* (pp. 313–43). London: Sage.

Jost, J.T., Federico, C.M. and Napier, J.L. (2009) Political ideology: Its structure, functions, and elective affinities. *Annual Review of Psychology*, 60, 307–37.

Jost, J.T., Glaser, J., Kruglanski, A.W. and Sulloway, F.J. (2003) Political conservatism as motivated social cognition. *Psychological Bulletin*, 129, 339–75.

Jost, J.T., Ledgerwood, A. and Hardin, C.D. (2008) Shared reality, system justification, and the relational basis of ideological beliefs. *Social and Personality Psychology Compass*, 2, 171–86.

Jost, J.T., Pelham, B.W., Sheldon, O. and Sullivan, B.N. (2003) Social inequality and the reduction of ideological dissonance on behalf of the system: Evidence of enhanced system justification among the disadvantaged. *European Journal of Social Psychology*, 33, 13–36.

Judd, C.M. and Lusk, C.M. (1984) Knowledge structures and evaluative judgments: Effects of structural variables on judgment extremity. *Journal of Personality and Social Psychology*, 46, 1193–207.

Judd, C.M., Blair, I.V. and Chapleau, K.M. (2004) Automatic stereotypes vs. automatic prejudice: Sorting out the possibilities in the Payne (2001) weapon paradigm. *Journal of Experimental Social Psychology*, 40, 75–81.

Judd, C.M., Park, B., Ryan, C.S. et al. (1995) Stereotypes and ethnocentrism: Diverging interethnic perceptions of African American and White American youth. *Journal of Personality and Social Psychology*, 69, 460–81.

Judge, T.A., Bono, J.E., Ilies, R. and Gerhardt, M.W. (2002) Personality and leadership: A qualitative and quantitative review. *Journal of Applied Psychology*, 87, 765–80.

Kacmar, K.M. and Baron, R.A. (1999) Organizational politics: The state of the field, links to related processes, and an agenda for future research. In G.R. Ferris (ed.) *Research in Personnel and Human Resources Management* (pp. 1–39). Greenwich, CT: JAI Press.

Kahneman, D. and Treisman, A. (1984) Changing views of attention and automaticity. In R. Parasuraman and R. Davies (eds) *Varieties of Attention* (pp. 29–61). San Diego, CA: Academic Press.

Kahneman, D. and Tversky, A. (1973) On the psychology of prediction. *Psychological Review*, 80, 237–51.

Kaiser, C.R., Drury, B.J., Spalding, S. et al. (2009) The ironic consequences of Obama's election: Decreased support for social justice. *Journal of Experimental Social Psychology*, 45, 556–9.

Kaiser, F.G., Byrka, K. and Hartig, T. (2010) Reviving Campbell's paradigm for attitude research. *Personality and Social Psychology Review*, 14(4), 351–67.

Kallgren, C.A., Reno, R.R. and Cialdini, R.B. (2000) A focus theory of normative conduct: When norms do and do not affect behavior. *Personality and Social Psychology Bulletin*, 26, 1002–12.

Kamarck, T.W., Shiffman, S.M., Smithline, L. et al. (1998) Effects of task strain, social conflict, and emotional activation on ambulatory cardiovascular activity: Daily life consequences of recurring stress in a multiethnic adult sample. *Health Psychology*, 17, 17–29.

Kamins, M.L. and Dweck, C.S. (1999) Person versus process praise and criticism: Implications for contingent self-worth and coping. *Developmental Psychology*, 35, 835–47.

Kanagawa, C., Cross, S.E. and Markus, H.R. (2001) 'Who am I?' The cultural psychology of he conceptual self. *Personality and Social Psychology Bulletin*, 27, 90–103.

Kanazawa, H. and Loveday, L. (1988) The Japanese immigrant community in Brazil: Language contact and shift. *Journal of Multilingual and Multicultural Development*, 9, 423–35.

Kang, J. and Banaji, M.R. (2006) Fair measures: A behavioral realist revision of 'affirmative action'. *California Law Review*, 94, 1063–118.

Kanouse, D.E. and Hanson, L.R. (1972) Negativity in evaluations. In E.E. Jones, D.E. Kanouse, H.H. Kelly et al. (eds) *Attribution: Perceiving the Causes of Behaviour* (pp. 27–46). New York: General Learning Press.

Kaplan, H.S. and Robson, A.J. (2002) The emergence of humans: The coevolution of intelligence and longevity with inter-generational transfers. *Proceedings of the National Academy of Sciences of the United States of America*, 99, 10221–6.

Karau, S.J. and Williams, K.D. (1993) Social loafing: A meta-analytic review and theoretical integration. *Journal of Personality and Social Psychology*, 65, 681–706.

Karau, S.J. and Williams, K.D. (1997) The effects of group cohesiveness on social loafing and social compensation. *Group Dynamics: Theory, Research and Practice*, 1, 156–68.

Karp, D., Jin, N., Yamagishi, T. and Shinotsuka, H. (1993) Raising the minimum in the minimal group paradigm. *Japanese Journal of Experimental Social Psychology*, 32, 231–40.

Karpinski, A. and Hilton, J.L. (2001) Attitudes and the Implicit Association Test. *Journal of Personality and Social Psychology*, 81, 774–88.

Karpinski, A. and von Hippel, W. (1996) The role of the linguistic intergroup bias in expectancy maintenance. *Social Cognition*, 14, 141–64.

Karremans, J.C., Stroebe, W. and Claus, J. (2006) Beyond Vicary's fantasies: The impact of subliminal priming and brand choice. *Journal of Experimental Social Psychology*, 42, 792–8.

Kashima, Y. (2000) Conceptions of culture and person for psychology. *Journal of Cross-Cultural Psychology*, 31, 14–32.

Kashima, Y. and Kashima, E.S. (2003) Individualism, GNP, climate, and pronoun drop: Is individualism determined by affluence and climate, or does language use play a role? *Journal of Cross-Cultural Psychology*, 34, 125–34.

Kashima, Y., Kashima, E.S., Kim, Y. and Gelfand, M. (2006) Describing the social world: How is a person, a group, and a relationship described in the East and the West? *Journal of Experimental Social Psychology*, 42, 388–96.

Kashima, Y., Klein, O. and Clark, A. (2007) Grounding: Sharing information in social interaction. In K. Fiedler (ed.) *Social Communication* (pp. 27–77). New York: Psychology Press.

Kassin, S.M. (1997) The psychology of confession evidence. *American Psychologist*, 52, 221–33.

Katz, D. (1960) The functional approach to the study of attitudes. *Public Opinion Quarterly*, 24, 163–204.

Katz, D. and Kahn, R.L. (1978) *The Social Psychology of Organisations* (2nd edn). New York: John Wiley & Sons.

Katz, J.E. and Aakhus, M.A. (2002) Making meaning of mobiles: A theory of apparatgeist. In J.E. Katz and M. Aakhus (eds) *Perpetual Contact: Mobile Communication, Private Talk, Public Performance* (pp. 301–18). Cambridge: Cambridge University Press.

Kavanagh, L.C., Suhler, C.L., Churchland, P.S. and Winkielman, P. (2011) When it's an error to mirror: The surprising reputational costs of mimicry. *Psychological Science*, 22, 1274–6.

Kay, A.C. and Jost, J.T. (2003) Complementary justice: Effects of 'poor but happy' and 'poor but honest' stereotype exemplars on system justification and implicit activation of the justice motive. *Journal of Personality and Social Psychology*, 85, 823–37.

Kay, A.C., Gaucher, D., Napier, J. et al. (2008) God and the government: Testing a compensatory control mechanism for he support of external systems. *Journal of Personality and Social Psychology*, 95, 18–35.

Kay, A.C., Gaucher, D., Peach, J.M. et al. (2009) Inequality, discrimination, and the power of the status quo: Direct evidence for a motivation to see the way things are as the way they should be. *Journal of Personality and Social Psychology*, 97, 421–34.

Kay, A.C., Whitson, J.A., Gaucher, D. and Galinsky, A.D. (2009) Compensatory control: Achieving order through the mind, our institutions, and the heavens. *Current Directions in Psychological Science*, 18, 264–8.

Keller, J. (2002) Blatant stereotype threat and women's math performance: Self-handicapping as a strategic means to cope with obtrusive negative performance expectations. *Sex Roles*, 47, 193–8.

Keller, L.M., Bouchard, T.J., Arvey, R.D. et al. (1992) Work values: Genetic and environmental influences. *Journal of Applied Psychology*, 77, 79–88.

Kelley, H.H. (1950) The warm-cold variable in first impressions of persons. *Journal of Personality*, 18, 431–9.

Kelley, H.H. (1952) Two functions of reference groups. In G.E. Swanson, T.M., Newcomb and E.L. Hartley (eds) *Readings in Social Psychology* (2nd edn, pp. 410–14). New York: Holt, Rinehart & Winston.

Kelley, H.H. (1967) Attribution theory in social psychology. *Nebraska Symposium on Motivation*, 15, 192–238.

Kelley, H.H. and Thibaut, J.W. (1978) *Interpersonal Relations: A Theory of Interdependence*. New York: Wiley.

Kelley, W.M., Macrae, C.N., Wyland, C.L. et al. (2002) Finding the self? An event-related fMRI study. *Journal of Cognitive Neuroscience*, 14, 785–94.

Kelly, A.E. (1998) Clients' secret keeping in outpatient therapy. *Journal of Counseling Psychology*, 45, 50–7.

Kelly, A.E. (2000) Helping construct desirable identities: A self-presentational view of psychotherapy. *Psychological Bulletin*, 126, 475–94.

Kelly, S. and Dunbar, R.I.M. (2001) Who dares, wins: Heroism versus altruism in women's mate choice. *Human Nature*, 12, 89–105.

Kelman, H.C. (1997) Social-psychological dimensions of international conflict. In I.W. Zartman and J.L. Rasmussen (eds)

Peacemaking in International Conflict: Methods and Techniques (pp. 191–236). Washington, DC: US Institute of Peace.

Kelman, H.C. and Hovland, C.I. (1953) 'Reinstatement' of the communicator in delayed measurement of opinion change. *The Journal of Abnormal and Social Psychology*, 48, 3276–335.

Keltner, D. and Haidt, J. (1999) Social functions of emotions at four levels of analysis. *Cognition and Emotion*, 13, 505–21.

Keltner, D., Ellsworth, P.C. and Edwards, K. (1993) Beyond simple pessimism: Effects of sadness and anger on social perception. *Journal of Personality and Social Psychology*, 64, 740–52.

Kenny, D.A. and DePaulo, B.M. (1993) Do people know how others view them? An empirical and theoretical account. *Psychological Bulletin*, 114, 145–61.

Kenny, D.A. and Nasby, W. (1980) Splitting the reciprocity correlation. *Journal of Personality and Social Psychology*, 38, 249–56.

Kenworthy, J.B., Turner, R.N., Hewstone, M. and Voci, A. (2005) Intergroup contact: When does it work, and why? In J.F. Dovidio, P. Glick and L.A. Rudman (eds) *On the Nature of Prejudice: Fifty Years After Allport* (pp. 278–92). Malden: Blackwell.

Kernis, M.H. and Paradise, A.W. (2002) Distinguishing between fragile and secure forms of high self-esteem. In E.L. Deci and R.M. Ryan (eds) *Handbook of Self-determination Research* (pp. 339–60). Rochester, NY: University of Rochester Press.

Kerr, N.L. (1983) Motivation losses in small groups: A social dilemma analysis. *Journal of Personality and Social Psychology*, 45, 819–28.

Kerr, N.L. and Brunn, S.E. (1983) Dispensability of member effort and group motivation losses: Free-rider effects. *Journal of Personality and Social Psychology*, 44, 78–94.

Kerr, N.L. and Kaufman-Gilliland, C.M. (1994) Communication, commitment, and cooperation in social dilemma. *Journal of Personality and Social Psychology*, 66, 513–29.

Kessler, T. and Mummendey, A. (2002) Sequential or parallel processing? A longitudinal field study concerning determinants of identity-management strategies. *Journal of Personality and Social Psychology*, 82, 75–88.

Khoo, P.N. and Senn, C.Y. (2004) Not wanted in the inbox!: Evaluations of unsolicited and harassing e-mail. *Psychology of Women Quarterly*, 28, 204–14.

Kiesler, C.A. and Pallak, M.S. (1976) Arousal properties of dissonance manipulations. *Psychological Bulletin*, 83, 1014–25.

Kiesler, S., Siegel, J. and McGuire, T.W. (1984) Social psychological aspects of computer-mediated communication. *American Psychologist*, 39, 1123–34.

Kirkpatrick, L.A. and Hazan, C. (1994) Attachment styles and close relationships: A four-year prospective study. *Personal Relationships*, 1, 123–42.

Kirkpatrick, L.A., Waugh, C.E., Valencia, A. and Webster, G.D. (2002) The functional domain specificity of self-esteem and the differential prediction of aggression. *Journal of Personality and Social Psychology*, 82, 756–67.

Kirschner, D. (1992) Understanding adoptees who kill: Dissociation, patricide, and the psychodynamics of adoption. *International Journal of Offender Therapy and Comparative Criminology*, 36, 323–33.

Kisley, M.A., Wood, S. and Burrows, C.L. (2007) Looking at the sunny side of life: Age-related change in an event-related potential measure of the negativity bias. *Psychological Science*, 18, 838–43.

Kitayama, S. and Uskul, A.K. (2011) Culture, mind, and the brain: Current evidence and future directions. *Annual Review of Psychology*, 62, 419–49.

Kitayama, S., Markus, H.R., Matsumoto, H. and Norasakkunkit, V. (1997) Individual and collective processes in the construction of the self: Self-enhancement in the United States and self-criticism in Japan. *Journal of Personality and Social Psychology*, 72, 1245–67.

Kitayama, S., Mesquita, B. and Karasawa, M. (2006) Cultural affordances and emotional experience: Socially engaging and disengaging emotions in Japan and the United States. *Journal of Personality and Social Psychology*, 91, 890–903.

Kitzmann, K.M., Cohen, R. and Lockwood, R.L. (2002) Are only children missing out? Comparison of the peer-related social competence of only children and siblings. *Journal of Social and Personal Relationships*, 19, 299–316.

Kjaer, T.W., Nowak, M. and Lou, H.C. (2002) Reflective self-awareness and conscious states: PET evidence for a common midline parietofrontal core. *Neuroimage*, 17, 1080–6.

Klein, C., DiazGranados, D., Salas, E. et al. (2009) Does team building work? *Small Group Research*, 40, 181–222.

Klein, D.B. and Stern, C. (2005) Professors and their politics: The policy views of social scientists. *Critical Review*, 17, 257–303.

Klein, O., Spears, R. and Reicher, S. (2007) Social identity performance: Extending the strategic side of the SIDE model. *Personality and Social Psychology Review*, 11, 28–45.

Klein, W.M. and Kunda, Z. (1992) Motivated person perception: Constructing justifications for desired beliefs. *Journal of Experimental Social Psychology*, 28, 145–68.

Kleinke, C.L. (1977) Compliance to requests made by gazing and touching experimenters in field settings. *Journal of Experimental Social Psychology*, 13, 218–23.

Kleinke, C.L. (1986) Gaze and eye contact: A research review. *Psychological Bulletin*, 100, 78–100.

Kleinke, C.L. and Meyer, C. (1990) Evaluation of a rape victim by men and women with high and low belief in a just world. *Psychology of Women Quarterly*, 14, 343–53.

Kleinke, C.L., Bustos, A.A., Meeker, F.B. and Staneski, R.A. (1973) Effects of self-attributed and other-attributed gaze on interpersonal evaluations between males and females. *Journal of Experimental Social Psychology*, 9, 154–63.

Klen, O., Clark, A.E. and Lyone, A. (2010) When the social becomes personal: Exploring the role of common ground in stereotype communication. *Social Cognition*, 28, 329–52.

Klopfer, P.H. (1958) Influence of social interaction on learning rates in birds. *Science*, 128, 903.

Klucharev, V., Smidts, A. and Fernández, G. (2008) Brain mechanisms of persuasion: How 'expert power' modulates memory and attitudes. *Social Cognitive and Affective Neuroscience*, 3, 353–66.

Knapp, M.L., Hart, R.P. and Dennis, H.S. (1974) An exploration of deception as a communication construct. *Human Communication Research*, 1, 15–29.

Knee, C.R., Lonsbary, C., Canevello, A. and Patrick, H. (2005) Self-determination and conflict in romantic relationships. *Journal of Personality and Social Psychology*, 89, 997–1009.

Knetsch, J.L. (2010) Values of gains and losses: Reference states and choice of measure. *Environmental and Resource Economics*, 46, 179–88.

Knight, G.P., Johnson, L.G., Carlo, G. and Eisenberg, N. (1994) A multiplicative model of the dispositional antecedents of a prosocial behavior: Predicting more of the people more of the time. *Journal of Personality and Social Psychology*, 66, 178–83.

Knight, J.A. and Vallacher, R.R. (1981) Interpersonal engagement in social perception: The consequences of getting into the action. *Journal of Personality and Social Psychology*, 40, 990.

Knowles, E.D., Lowery, B.S. and Schaumberg, R.L. (2009) Anti-egalitarians for Obama? Group-dominance motivation and the Obama vote. *Journal of Experimental Social Psychology*, 45, 965–9.

Knowles, E.D., Morris, M.W., Chiu, C.Y. and Hong, Y.Y. (2001) Culture and the process of person perception: evidence for automaticity among East Asians in correcting for situational influences on behaviour. *Personality and Social Psychology Bulletin*, 27, 1344–56.

Koehler, J.J. (1996) The base rate fallacy reconsidered: Descriptive, normative, and methodological challenges. *Behavioral and Brain Sciences*, 19, 1–53.

Koenig, A.M. and Eagly, A.H. (2005) Stereotype threat in men on a test of social sensitivity. *Sex Roles*, 52, 489–96.

Koestler, A. ([1967]1990) *The Ghost in the Machine*. London: Penguin.

Koestner, R. and Aube, J. (1995) A multifactorial approach to the study of gender characteristics. *Journal of Personality*, 63, 681–710.

Koestner, R. and Wheeler, L. (1988) Self-presentation in personal advertisements: The influence of implicit notions of attraction and role expectations. *Journal of Social and Personal Relationships*, 5, 149–60.

Konecni, V.J. and Doob, A.N. (1972) Catharsis through displacement of aggression. *Journal of Personality and Social Psychology*, 23, 379–87.

Konijn, E.A., Utz, S., Tanis, M. and Barnes, S.B. (2008) *Mediated Interpersonal Communication*. New York: Routledge.

Koole, S. and van't Spijker, M. (2000) Overcoming the planning fallacy through willpower: Effects of implementation intentions on actual and predicted task-completion times. *European Journal of Social Psychology*, 30, 873–88.

Kors, D.J., Linden, W. and Gerin, W. (1997) Evaluation interferes with social support: Effects on cardiovascular stress reactivity in women. *Journal of Social and Clinical Psychology*, 16, 1–23.

Kouchaki, M. (2011) Vicarious moral licensing: The influence of others' past moral actions on moral behavior. *Journal of Personality and Social Psychology*, 101, 702–15.

Kraus, S.J. (1995) Attitudes and the prediction of behavior: A meta-analysis of the empirical literature. *Personality and Social Psychology Bulletin*, 21, 58–75.

Krauss, R.M. (1998) Why do we gesture when we speak? *Current Directions in Psychological Science*, 7, 54–60.

Krauss, R.M. and Chiu, C. (1998) Language and social behavior. In D.T. Gilbert, S.T. Fiske and G. Lindzey (eds) *The Handbook of Social Psychology* (4th edn, vol. 2, pp. 41–88). New York: McGraw-Hill.

Krauss, R.M., Curran, N.M. and Ferleger, N. (1983) Expressive conventions and the cross-cultural perception of emotion. *Basic and Applied Social Psychology*, 4, 295–305.

Kraut, R., Patterson, M., Lundmark, V. et al. (1998) Internet paradox: A social technology that reduces social involve-

ment and psychological well-being? *American Psychologist*, 53, 1017–31.

Kravitz, D.A. and Martin, B. (1986) Ringelmann rediscovered: The original article. *Journal of Personality and Social Psychology*, 50, 936–41.

Kristof, N. (1995) Japanese women begin to find their own voices. *Vancouver Sun*, 23 December.

Krizan, Z. and Baron, R.S. (2007) Group polarization and choice-dilemmas: How important is self-categorization? *European Journal of Social Psychology*, 37, 191–201.

Krosnick, J.A. (1988) The role of attitude importance in social evaluation: A study of policy preferences, presidential candidate evaluations, and voting behavior. *Journal of Personality and Social Psychology*, 55, 196–210.

Krosnick, J.A. (1989) Attitude importance and attitude accessibility. *Personality and Social Psychology Bulletin*, 15, 297–308.

Krosnick, J.A. and Alwin, D.F. (1989) Aging and susceptibility to attitude change. *Journal of Personality and Social Psychology*, 57, 416–25.

Krosnick, J.A. and Smith, W.R. (1994) Attitude strength. In V.S. Ramachandran (ed.) *Encyclopedia of Human Behavior* (pp. 279–89). San Diego: Academic Press.

Krosnick, J.A., Betz, A.L., Jussim, L.J. and Lynn, A.R. (1992) Subliminal conditioning of attitudes. *Personality and Social Psychology Bulletin*, 18, 152–62.

Krueger, J. and Rothbart, M. (1990) Contrast and accentuation effects in category learning. *Journal of Personality and Social Psychology*, 56, 866–75.

Krueger, J., Rothbart, M. and Siriam, N. (1989) Category learning and change: Differences in sensitivity to information that enhances or reduces intercategory distinctions. *Journal of Personality and Social Psychology*, 56, 866–75.

Kruglanski, A.W. (1990) Lay epistemic theory in social-cognitive psychology. *Psychological Inquiry: An International Journal for the Advancement of Psychological Theory*, 1, 181–97.

Kruglanski, A.W. (1990) Motivations for judging and knowing: Implications for causal attribution. In E.T. Higgins and R.M. Sorrentino (eds) *The Handbook of Motivation and Cognition: Foundations of Social Behavior* (vol. 2, pp. 333–68). New York: Guilford Press.

Kruglanski, A.W. (2006) *The Psychology of Closed-mindedness*. New York: Psychology Press.

Kruglanski, A.W. and Thompson, E.P. (1999) Persuasion by a single route: A view from the unimodel. *Psychological Inquiry*, 10, 83–109.

Kruglanski, A.W., Chen, X., Pierro, A. et al. (2006) Persuasion according to the unimodel: Implications for

cancer communication. *Journal of Communication*, 56, 105–22.

Kruglanski, A.W., Webster, D.M. and Klem, A. (1993) Motivated resistance and openness to persuasion in the presence or absence of prior information. *Journal of Personality and Social Psychology*, 65, 861–76.

Kugihara, N. (1999) Gender and social loafing in Japan. *Journal of Social Psychology*, 139, 516–26.

Kulich, C., Ryan, M.K. and Haslam, S.A. (2007) Where is the romance for women leaders? The effects of gender on leadership attributions and performance-based pay. *Applied Psychology: An International Review*, 56, 582–601.

Kumkale, G.T. and Albarracin, D. (2004) The sleeper effect in persuasion: A meta-analytic review. *Psychological Bulletin*, 130, 143–72.

Kunda, Z. (1990) The case for motivated reasoning. *Psychological Bulletin*, 108, 480–98.

Kunich, J.C. (2000) Natural born copycat killers and the law of shock torts. *Washington University Law Quarterly*, 78, 1157–270.

Kurdek, L.A. (1998) Relationship outcomes and their predictors: Longitudinal evidence from heterosexual married, gay cohabiting, and lesbian cohabiting couples. *Journal of Marriage and the Family*, 60, 553–68.

Kurdek, L.A. (2000) Attractions and constraints as determinants of relationship commitment: Longitudinal evidence from gay, lesbian, and heterosexual couples. *Personal Relationships*, 7(3), 245–62.

Kwang, T. and Swann, W.B. Jr (2010) Do people embrace praise even when they feel unworthy? A review of critical tests of self-enhancement versus self-verification. *Personality and Social Psychology Review*, 14, 263–80.

LaFrance, M. (1979) Nonverbal synchrony and rapport: Analysis by the cross lag panel technique. *Social Psychology Quarterly*, 42, 66–70.

LaFrance, M. and Mayo, C. (1976) Racial differences in gaze behavior during conversations: Two systematic observational studies. *Journal of Personality and Social Psychology*, 33, 547–52.

Lagerspetz, K.M.J. (1979) Modification of aggressiveness in mice. In S. Feshbach and A. Fraçzek (eds) *Aggression and Behavior Change: Biological and Social Processes* (pp. 66–82). New York: Praeger.

Lagerspetz, K.M.J. and Lagerspetz, K.Y.H. (1971) Changes in the level of aggressiveness of mice as results of isolation, learning, and selective breeding. *Scandinavian Journal of Psychology*, 12, 241–48.

Lakoff, G. and Johnson, M. (1980) *Metaphors We Live By*. Chicago, IL: University of Chicago Press.

Lakoff, G. and Johnson, M. (1999) *Philosophy in the Flesh: The Embodied Mind and its Challenge to Western Thought.* New York: Basic Books.

Lakoff, R. (1973) Language and woman's place. *Language in Society*, 2, 45–80.

Lakoff, R. (1975) *Language and Woman's Place.* New York: Colophon/Harper & Row.

Lambert, P.J., Millimet, D.L. and Slottje, D. (2003) Inequality aversion and the natural rate of subjective inequality. *Journal of Public Economics*, 87, 1061–90.

Lammers, J., Stapel, D.A. and Galisnky, A.D. (2010) Power increases hypocrisy: Moralizing in reasoning, immorality in behavior. *Psychological Science*, 21, 737–44.

Landau, M.J., Meier, B.P. and Keefer, L.A. (2010) A metaphor-enriched social cognition. *Psychological Bulletin*, 136, 1045–67.

Landis, D., Hope, R.O. and Day, H.R. (1984) Training for desegregation in the military. In N. Miller and M.B. Brewer (eds) *Groups in Contact: The Psychology of Desegregation* (pp. 258–78). Orlando, FL: Academic Press.

Landrum, R.E. and Harrold, R. (2003) What employers want from psychology graduates. *Teaching of Psychology*, 30, 131–3.

Landy, D. and Sigall, H. (1974) Beauty is talent: Task evaluation as a function of the performer's physical attractiveness. *Journal of Personality and Social Psychology*, 29, 299–304.

Lane, J.D. and DePaulo, B.M. (1999) Completing Coyne's cycle: Dysphoric's ability to detect deception. *Journal of Research in Personality*, 33, 311–29.

Langer, E.J. (1975) The illusion of control. *Journal of Personality and Social Psychology*, 32, 311–28.

Langer, E.J. and Rodin, J. (1976) The effects of choice and enhanced personal responsibility for the aged: A field experiment in an institutional setting. *Journal of Personality and Social Psychology*, 34, 191–8.

Langlois, J.H. and Roggman, L.A. (1990) Attractive faces are only average. *Psychological Science*, 1, 115–21.

Langlois, J.H., Kalakanis, L., Rubenstein, A.J. et al. (2000) Maxims or myths of beauty? A meta-analytic and theoretical review. *Psychological Bulletin*, 126, 390–423.

Langlois, J.H., Roggman, L.A. and Musselman, L. (1994) What is average and what is not average about attractive faces? *Psychological Science*, 5, 214–20.

Langlois, J.H., Roggman, L.A., Casey, R.J. et al. (1987) Infant preferences for attractive faces: Rudiments of a stereotype? *Developmental Psychology*, 23, 363–9.

Lansford, J.E., Malone, P.S., Castellino, D.R. et al. (2006) Trajectories of internalizing, externalizing, and grades for children who have and have not experiences their parents' divorce or separation. *Journal of Family Psychology*, 20, 292–301.

Lansford, J.E., Malone, P.S., Dodge, K.A. et al. (2006) A 12-year prospective study of patterns of social information processing problems and externalizing behaviors. *Journal of Abnormal Child Psychology*, 34, 715–24.

LaPiere, R.T. (1934) Attitudes vs. actions. *Social Forces*, 13, 230–7.

Larsen, R.J., Diener, E. and Emmons, R.A. (1986) Affect intensity and reactions to daily life events. *Journal of Personality and Social Psychology*, 51, 803–14.

Larsson, K. (1956) *Conditioning and Sexual Behavior in the Male Albino Rat.* Stockholm: Almqvist & Wiksell.

Latané, B. and Darley, J.M. (1968) Group inhibition of bystander intervention in emergencies. *Journal of Personality and Social Psychology*, 10, 215–21.

Latané, B. and Darley, J.M. (1970) *The Unresponsive Bystander: Why Doesn't He Help?* New York: Appleton-Century-Crofts.

Latané, B. and Rodin, J. (1969) A lady in distress: Inhibiting effects of friends and strangers on bystander intervention. *Journal of Experimental Social Psychology*, 5, 189–202.

Latané, B. and Wolf, S. (1981) The social impact of majorities and minorities. *Psychological Review*, 88, 438–53.

Latané, B., Williams, K.D. and Harkins, S.G. (1979) Many hands make light the work: The causes and consequences of social loafing. *Journal of Personality and Social Psychology*, 37, 822–32.

Latham, G.P., Stajkovic, A.D. and Locke, E.A. (2010) The relevance and viability of subconscious goals in the workplace. *Journal of Management*, 36, 234–55.

Latimer, J., Dowden, C. and Muise, D. (2005) The effectiveness of restorative justice practices: A meta-analysis. *The Prison Journal*, 85, 127–44.

Latner, J.D., Rosewall, J.K. and Simmonds, M.B. (2007) Childhood obesity stigma: Association with television, videogame, and magazine exposure. *Body Image*, 4, 147–55.

Laughlin, P.R. (1980) Social combination processes of cooperative problem solving groups on verbal intellective tasks. In M. Fishbein (ed.) *Progress in Social Psychology* (pp. 127–55). Hillsdale, NJ: LEA.

Laughlin, P.R. and Adamopoulos, J. (1980) Social combination processes and individual learning for six-person cooperative groups on an intellective task. *Journal of Personality and Social Psychology*, 38, 941–7.

Lavallee, L.F. and Campbell, J.D. (1995) Impact of personal goals on self-regulation processes elicited by daily negative events. *Journal of Personality and Social Psychology*, 69, 341–52.

Le, B. and Agnew, C.R. (2003) Commitment and its theorized determinants: A meta-analysis of the investment model. *Personal Relationships*, 10, 37–57.

Lea, M. and Spears, R. (1995) Love at first byte? Building personal relationships over computer networks. In J.T. Wood and S. Duck (eds) *Under-studied Relationships: Off the Beaten Track. Understanding Relationship Processes Series* (vol. 6, pp. 197–233). Thousand Oaks, CA: Sage.

Lea, M., O'Shea, T., Fung, P. and Spears, R. (1992) 'Flaming' in computer-mediated communication: Observations, explanations, implications. In M. Lea (ed.) *Contexts of Computer-mediated Communication* (pp. 30–65). Hemel Hempstead: Harvester Wheatsheaf.

Lea, M., Spears, R. and Rogers, P. (2003) Social processes in electronic teamwork: The central issue of identity. In S.A. Haslam, D. van Knippenberg, M.J. Platow and N. Ellemers (eds) *Social Identity at Work: Developing Theory for Organizational Practice* (pp. 99–115). New York: Psychology Press.

Lea, R. and Chambers, G. (2007) Monoamine oxidase, addiction, and the 'warrior' gene hypothesis. *The New Zealand Medical Journal*, 120, 1250.

Lea, S.E. and Kiley-Worthington, M. (1996) Can animals think? In V. Bruce (ed.) *Unsolved Mysteries of the Mind: Tutorial Essays in Cognition* (pp. 211–44). Oxford: Erlbaum.

Leach, C.W., Iyer, A. and Pedersen, A. (2006) Anger and guilt about ingroup advantage explain the willingness for political action. *Personality and Social Psychology Bulletin*, 32, 1232–45.

Leader, T.I., Mullen, B. and Abrams, D. (2007) Without mercy: The immediate impact of group size on lynch mob atrocity. *Personality and Social Psychology Bulletin*, 33, 1340–52.

Leader, T.I., Mullen, B. and Rice, D. (2009) Complexity and valence in ethnophaulisms and exclusion of ethnic out-groups: What puts the 'hate' into hate speech? *Journal of Personality and Social Psychology*, 96, 170–82.

Leana, C.R. (1985) A partial test of Janis's groupthink model: Effects of group cohesiveness and leader behavior on defective decision making. *Journal of Management*, 11, 5–17.

Leaper, C. and Robnett, R.D. (2011) Women are more likely than men to use tentative language, aren't they? A meta-analysis testing for gender differences and moderators. *Psychology of Women Quarterly*, 35, 129–42.

Leary, M.R. (1995) *Self-presentation: Impression Management and Interper-*

sonal Behavior. Madison, WI: Brown & Benchmark.

Leary, M.R. (2004) The function of self-esteem in terror management theory and sociometer theory: Comment on Pyszczynski et al. *Psychological Bulletin*, 130, 478–82.

Leary, M.R. and Baumeister, R.F. (2000) The nature and function of self-esteem: Sociometer theory. *Advances in Experimental Social Psychology*, 32, 1–62.

Leary, M.R. and Kowalski, R.M. (1990) Impression management: A literature review and two-component model. *Psychological Bulletin*, 107(1), 34–47.

Leary, M.R., Cottrell, C.A. and Phillips, M. (2001) Deconfounding the effects of dominance and social acceptance on self-esteem. *Journal of Personality and Social Psychology*, 81, 898–909.

Leary, M.R., Tambor, E.S., Terdal, S.K. and Downs, D.L. (1995) Self-esteem as an interpersonal monitor: The sociometer hypothesis. *Journal of Personality and Social Psychology*, 68, 518–30.

Leavitt, J.D. and Christenfeld, N.J.S. (2011) Story spoilers don't spoil stories. *Psychological Science*, 22, 1152–4.

Le Bon, G. ([1896]1908) *The Crowd: A Study of the Popular Mind.* London: Unwin.

LeDoux, J.E. (2000) Emotion circuits in the brain. *Annual Review of Neuroscience*, 23, 155–84.

Lee, J. (2003) The salience of race in everyday life: Black customers' shopping experiences in black and white neighbourhoods. *Work and Occupations*, 27, 353–76.

Lee, J.A. (1973) *The Colors of Love: An Exploration of the Ways of Loving.* Don Mills, Ontario: New Press.

Lee, J.A. (1976) *Lovestyles.* London: JM Dent & Sons.

Lee, Y.P. and Bond, M.H. (1998) Personality and roommate friendship in Chinese culture. *Asian Journal of Social Psychology*, 1, 179–90.

Leichty, G. and Applegate, J.L. (1991) Social-cognitive and situational influences on the use of face-saving persuasive strategies. *Human Communication Research*, 17, 451–84.

Leider, S., Möbius, M.M., Rosenblat, T. and Do, Q.A. (2009) Directed altruism and enforced reciprocity in social networks. *Quarterly Journal of Economics*, 124, 1815–51.

Lemyre, L. and Smith, P.M. (1985) Intergroup discrimination and self-esteem in the minimal group paradigm. *Journal of Personality and Social Psychology*, 49, 660–70.

Leonardelli, G.J. and Toh, S.M. (2011) Perceiving expatriate coworkers as foreigners encourages aid: Social categorization and procedural justice together improve intergroup cooperation

and dual identity. *Psychological Science*, 22, 110–17.

Lerner, J.S. and Keltner, D. (2001) Fear, anger, and risk. *Journal of Personality and Social Psychology*, 81, 146–59.

Lerner, J.S., Goldberg, J.H. and Tetlock, P.E. (1998) Sober second thought: The effects of accountability, anger, and authoritarianism on attributions of responsibility. *Personality and Social Psychology Bulletin*, 24, 563–74.

Lerner, J.S., Gonzalez, R.M., Small, D.A. and Fischhoff, B. (2003) Effects of fear and anger on perceived risks of terrorism: A national field experiment. *Psychological Science*, 14, 144–50.

Lerner, M.J. (1980) *The Belief in a Just World: A Fundamental Delusion.* New York: Plenum.

Lerner, M.J. (1998) The two forms of belief in a just world: Some thoughts on why and how people care about justice. In L. Montada and M.J. Lerner (eds) *Responses to Victimization and Belief in a Just World* (pp. 247–69). New York: Plenum.

Lerner, M.J. and Clayton, S. (2011) *Justice and Self-interest: Two Fundamental Motives.* Cambridge: Cambridge University Press.

Lerner, M.J. and Miller, D.T. (1978) Just world research and the attribution process: Looking back and ahead. *Psychological Bulletin*, 85, 1030–51.

Lerner, M.J. and Simmons, C.H. (1966) Observers' reaction to the 'innocent victim': Compassion or rejection? *Journal of Personality and Social Psychology*, 4, 203–10.

Leshner, A.I. (1983) The hormonal responses to competition and their behavioral significance. In B.B. Svare (ed.) *Hormones and Aggressive Behaviour* (pp. 393–404). New York: Plenum.

Leung, K. and Bond, M.H. (1984) The impact of cultural collectivism on reward allocation. *Journal of Personality and Social Psychology*, 47, 793–804.

Levenson, R.W. (1994) Human emotions: A functional view. In P. Ekman and R.J. Davidson (eds) *The Nature of Emotion: Fundamental Questions* (pp. 123–6). New York: Oxford University Press.

Levenson, R.W., Ekman, P. and Friesen, W.V. (1990) Voluntary facial action generates emotion-specific autonomic nervous system activity. *Psychophysiology*, 27, 363–84.

Leventhal, H., Watts, J.C. and Pagano, F. (1967) Effects of fear and instructions on how to cope with danger. *Journal of Personality and Social Psychology*, 6, 313–21.

Levine, J.M. and Moreland, R L. (1990) Progress in small group research. *Annual Review of Psychology*, 41, 585–634.

Levine, J.M. and Moreland, R.L. (1994) Group socialization: Theory and

research. *European Review of Social Psychology*, 5, 305–36.

Levine, J.M., Higgins, E.T. and Choi, H.-S. (2000) Development of strategic norms in groups. *Organizational Behavior and Human Decision Processes*, 82, 88–101.

Levine, M. and Crowther, S. (2008) The responsive bystander: How social group membership and group size can encourage as well as inhibit bystander intervention. *Journal of Personality and Social Psychology*, 95, 1429–39.

Levine, M., Cassidy, C., Brazier, G. and Reicher, S. (2002) Self-categorization and bystander non-intervention: Two experimental studies. *Journal of Applied Social Psychology*, 32, 1452–63.

Levine, M., Prosser, A., Evans, D. and Reicher, S. (2005) Identity and emergency intervention: How social group membership and inclusiveness of group boundaries shape helping behavior. *Personality and Social Psychology Bulletin*, 31, 443–53.

Levine, R.V., Norenzayan, A. and Philbrick, K. (2001) Cross-cultural differences in helping strangers. *Journal of Cross-cultural Psychology*, 32, 543–60.

Levinger, G. (1980) Toward the analysis of close relationships. *Journal of Experimental Social Psychology*, 16, 510–44.

Levy, B.R., Zonderman, A.B., Slade, M.D. and Ferrucci, L. (2009) Age stereotypes held earlier in life predict cardiovascular events in later life. *Psychological Science*, 20, 296–8.

Levy, S.R., Chiu, C. and Hong, Y. (2006) Lay theories and intergroup relations. *Group Processes and Intergroup Relations*, 9, 5–24.

Lewandowski, G.W. Jr, Nardone, N. and Raines, A.J. (2010) The role of self-concept clarity in relationship quality. *Self and Identity*, 9, 416–33.

Lewicki, P. (1985) Nonconscious biasing effects of single instances on subsequent judgements. *Journal of Personality and Social Psychology*, 48, 563–74.

Lewin, K. (1936) The psychological worlds and the physical world. In K. Lewin and F. Heider (eds) *Principles of Topological Psychology* (pp. 66–75). New York: McGraw-Hill.

Lewin, K. (1943) Defining the 'field at a given time'. *Psychological Review*, 50, 292–310.

Lewin, K. (1948) *Resolving Social Conflicts.* New York: Harper & Row.

Lewis, H.D. (1948) Collective responsibility. *Philosophy*, 24, 3–18.

Lewis, M. and Brooks-Gunn, J. (1981) Visual attention at three months as a predictor of cognitive functioning at two years of age. *Intelligence*, 5, 131–40.

Lewis, M. and Brooks-Gunn, J. (1978) Self-knowledge and emotional development. In M. Lewis and L. Rosenblum (eds) *The Development of Affect*, vol. 1, *Genesis of Behaviour* (pp. 205–26). New York: Plenum Press.

Lewis, R.S., Goto, S.G. and Kong, L. (2008) Culture and context: East Asian American and European American differences in P3 event-related potentials. *Personality and Social Psychology Bulletin*, 34, 623–34.

Leyens, J.P., Desert, M., Croizet, J.C. and Darcis, C. (2000) Stereotype threat: Are lower status and history of stigmatization preconditions of stereotype threat? *Personality and Social Psychology Bulletin*, 26, 1189–99.

Li, D. (2004) Echoes of violence: Considerations of radio and genocide in Rwanda. *Journal of Genocide Research*, 6, 9–27.

Liberman, A. and Chaiken, S. (1992) Defensive processing of personally relevant health messages. *Personality and Social Psychology Bulletin*, 18, 669–79.

Liberman, V., Minson, J.A., Bryan, C. J. and Ross, L. (2011) Naïve realism and capturing the 'wisdom of dyads'. *Journal of Experimental Social Psychology*, 48, 507–12.

Lickel, B., Hamilton, D.L., Wieczorkowska, G. et al. (2000) Varieties of groups and the perception of group entitativity. *Journal of Personality and Social Psychology*, 78, 223–46.

Lieberman, J.D., Arndt, J., Personius, J. and Cook, A. (1999) Vicarious annihilation: The effect of mortality salience on perceptions of hate crimes. *Law and Human Behavior*, 25, 547–66.

Lieberman, M.D. (2007) Social cognitive neuroscience: A review of core processes. *Annual Review of Psychology*, 58, 259–89.

Liebkind, K. and McAlister, A. (1999) Extended contact through peer modeling to promote tolerance in Finland. *European Journal of Social Psychology*, 29, 765–80.

Liebrand, W.B. and McClintock, C.G. (1988) The ring measure of social values: A computerized procedure for assessing individual differences in information processing and social value orientation. *European Journal of Personality*, 2, 217–30.

Likert, R. ([1932]1974) The method of constructing an attitude scale. In G.M. Maranell (ed.) *Scaling: A Sourcebook for Behavioral Scientists* (pp. 233–43). Chicago, IL: Aldine.

Lim, T.S. and Bowers, J.W. (1991) Facework solidarity, approbation, and tact. *Human Communication Research*, 17, 415–50.

Lin, M.C. and Harwood, J. (2003) Accommodation predictors of grandparent–grandchild relational solidarity in Taiwan. *Journal of Social and Personal Relationships*, 20, 537–63.

Lind, E.A. and O-Barr, W.M. (1979) The social significance of speech in the courtroom. In H. Giles and R.N. St Clair (eds) *Language and Social Psychology* (pp. 66–87). Oxford: Blackwell.

Lind, E.A. and Tyler, T.R. (1988) *The Social Psychology of Procedural Justice*. New York: Plenum.

Lind, E.A., Kanfer, R. and Earley, P.C. (1990) Voice, control, and procedural justice: Instrumental and noninstrumental concerns in fairness judgments. *Journal of Personality and Social Psychology*, 59, 952–9.

Linder, D.E., Cooper, J. and Jones, E.E. (1967) Decision freedom as a determinant of the role of incentive magnitude in attitude change. *Journal of Personality and Social Psychology*, 6, 245–54.

Lindskold, S. (1981) Styles of announcing conciliation. *Journal of Conflict Resolution*, 25, 145–55.

Linville, P.W. (1985) Self-complexity and affective extremity: Don't put all of your eggs in one cognitive basket. *Social Cognition*, 3, 94–120.

Linville, P.W. (1987) Self-complexity as a cognitive buffer against stress-related illness and depression. *Journal of Personality and Social Psychology*, 52, 663–76.

Linz, D., Donnerstein, E. and Adams, S.M. (1989) Physiological desensitization and judgments about female victims of violence. *Human Communication Research*, 15, 509–22.

Lipkus, I.M. and Siegler, I.C. (1993) The belief in a just world and perceptions of discrimination. *Journal of Social Psychology*, 127, 465–74.

Lipkus, I.M., Dalbert, C. and Siegler, I.C. (1996) The importance of distinguishing the belief in a just world for self versus others: Implications for psychological well-being. *Personality and Social Psychology Bulletin*, 22, 666–77.

Lipps, T. (1907) Das wissen von fremden ichen. *Psychologische Untersuchnung*, 1, 694–722.

Little, A.C. and Perrett, D.I. (2002) Putting beauty back in the eye of the beholder. *The Psychologist*, 15, 28–32.

Little, A.C., Burt, D.M. and Perrett, D.I. (2006) Assortative mating for perceived facial personality traits. *Personality and Individual Differences*, 40, 973–84.

Little, A.C., Saxton, T.K., Roberts, S.C. et al. (2010) Women's preferences for masculinity in male faces are highest during reproductive age-range and lower around puberty and post-menopause. *Psychoneuroendrocrinology*. 35, 912–20.

Littleford, L.N., O'Dougherty Wright, M. and Sayoc-Parial, M. (2005) White students' intergroup anxiety during same-race and interracial interactions: A multimethod approach. *Basic and Applied Social Psychology*, 27, 85–94.

Littrell, J. and Beck, E. (1999) Perceiving oppression: Relationships with resilience, self-esteem, depressive symptoms, and reliance on God in African-American homeless men. *Journal of Sociology and Social Welfare*, 26, 127–58.

Liu, J.H. and Hilton, D.J. (2005) How the past weighs on the present: Social representations of history and their role in identity politics. *British Journal of Social Psychology*, 44, 537–56.

Liu, J.H., Campbell, S.M. and Condie, H. (1995) Ethnocentrism in dating preferences for an American sample: The ingroup bias in social context. *European Journal of Social Psychology*, 25, 95–115.

Liverta-Sempio, O. and Marchetti, A. (1997) Cognitive development and theories of mind: Towards a contextual approach. *European Journal of Psychology of Education*, 12, 3–22.

Lock, A. (ed.) (1978) *Action, Gesture and Symbol: The Emergence of Language*. London: Academic Press.

Lock, A. (1980) *The Guided Reinvention of Language*. London: Academic Press.

Locke, E.A. and Latham, G.P. (1990) *A Theory of Goal Setting and Task Performance*. Englewood Cliffs, NJ: Prentice Hall.

Locke, E.A. and Latham, G.P. (2009) Has goal setting gone wild, or have its attackers abandoned good scholarship? *Academy of Management Perspectives*, 23, 17–23.

Locksley, A., Borgida, E., Brekke, N. and Hepburn, C. (1980) Sex stereotypes and social judgment. *Journal of Personality and Social Psychology*, 39, 821–31.

Lockwood, P. and Kunda, Z. (1997) Superstars and me: Predicting the impact of role models on the self. *Journal of Personality and Social Psychology*, 73, 91–103.

Lockwood, P. and Kunda, Z. (1999) Increasing the salience of one's best selves can undermine inspiration by outstanding role models. *Journal of Personality and Social Psychology*, 76, 214–28.

Logan, B. (2010) The rise of the rape joke, *The Guardian*, 10 September, accessible at www.guardian.co.uk/lifeandstyle/2010/sep/10/rape-jokes-in-comedy.

Long, K. and Spears, R. (1997) The self-esteem hypothesis revisited: Differentiation and the disaffected. In R. Spears, P.J., Oakes, N. Ellemers and S.A. Haslam (eds) *The Social Psychology of Stereotyping and Group Life* (pp. 296–317). Oxford: Blackwell.

López-Claros, A. and Zahidi, S. (2005) *Women's Empowerment: Measuring the Global Gender Gap*. Geneva: World Economic Forum.

Lord, C.G., Ross, L. and Lepper, M.R. (1979) Biased assimilation and attitude polarization: The effects of prior theories on subsequently considered evidence.

Journal of Personality and Social Psychology, 37, 2098–109.

Lord, R.G., DeVader, C.L. and Alliger, G.M. (1986) A meta-analysis of the relation between personality traits and leadership perceptions: An application of validity generalization procedures. *Journal of Applied Psychology*, 71, 402–410.

Lorenz, K. (1966) *On Aggression*. New York: Harcourt, Brace and World.

Losch, M.E. and Cacioppo, J.T. (1990) Cognitive dissonance may enhance sympathetic tonus, but attitudes are changed to reduce negative affect rather than arousal. *Journal of Experimental Social Psychology*, 26, 289–304.

Lott, A.J. and Lott, B.E. (1972) The power of liking: Consequences of interpersonal attitudes derived from a liberalized view of secondary reinforcement. *Advances in Experimental Social Psychology*, 6, 109–48.

Lott, A.J., Aponte, J.F., Lott, B.E. and McGinley, W.H. (1969) The effect of delayed reward on the development of positive attitudes toward persons. *Journal of Experimental Social Psychology*, 5, 101–13.

Loughnan, S., Leidner, B., Doron, G. et al. (2010) Universal biases in self-perception: Better and more human than average. *British Journal of Social Psychology*, 49, 627–36.

Löve, J., Grimby-Ekman, A.P., Eklöf, M. et al. (2010) 'Pushing oneself too hard: Performance-based self-esteem as a predictor of sickness presenteeism among young adult women and men: A cohort study. *Journal of Occupational and Environmental Medicine*, 52, 603–9.

Lowe, J.B., Windsor, R.A., Adams, B. et al. (1986) Use of a bogus pipeline method to increase accuracy of self-reported alcohol consumption among pregnant women. *Journal of Studies on Alcohol*, 47, 173–5.

Lowenstein, L.F. (1997) Research into causes and manifestations of aggression in car driving. *Police Journal*, 70, 263–70.

Lozowick, Y. (2003) *Right to Exist: A Moral Defense of Israel's Wars*. New York: Doubleday.

Lucas, T., Young, J.D., Zhdanova, L. and Alexander, S. (2010) Self and other justice beliefs, impulsivity, rumination and forgiveness: Justice beliefs can both prevent and promote forgiveness. *Personality and Individual Differences*, 49, 851–6.

Luchins, A.S. (1957) Primacy-recency in impression formation. In C.I. Hovland (ed.) *The Order of Presentation in Persuasion* (pp. 33–61). New Haven, CT: Yale University Press.

Luo, M. (2004) Excuse me. May I have your seat? *The New York Times*, 14 September.

Luo, S. and Klohnen, E.C. (2005) Assortative mating and marital quality in newlyweds: A coupled-centered approach. *Journal of Personality and Social Psychology*, 88, 304–26.

Lüschen, G. (ed.) (1970) *The Cross-cultural Analysis of Sport and Games*. Champaign: Stipes.

Lyons, A. and Kashima, Y. (2003) How are stereotypes maintained through communication? The influence of stereotype sharedness. *Journal of Personality and Social Psychology*, 85, 989–1005.

Lyons, C.J. (2006) Stigma or sympathy? Attributions of fault to hate crime victims and offenders. *Social Psychology Quarterly*, 69, 39–59.

Maass, A. (1999) Linguistic intergroup bias: Stereotype-perpetuation through language. In M. Zanna (ed.) *Advances in Experimental Social Psychology* (vol. 31, pp. 79–121). New York: Academic Press.

Maass, A. and Clark, R.D. III (1984) Hidden impact of minorities: Fifteen years of minority influence research. *Psychological Bulletin; Psychological Bulletin*, 95, 428–50.

Maass, A. and Clark, R.D. III (1986) Conversion theory and simultaneous majority/minority influence: Can reactance offer an alternative explanation? *European Journal of Social Psychology*, 16, 305–9.

Maass, A., Ceccarelli, R. and Rudin, S. (1996) The linguistic intergroup bias: Evidence for ingroup-protective motivation. *Journal of Personality and Social Psychology*, 71, 512–26.

Maass, A., Karasawa, M., Politi, F. and Suga, S. (2006) Do verbs and adjectives play different roles in different cultures? A cross-linguistic analysis of person perception. *Journal of Personality and Social Psychology*, 90, 734–50.

Maass, A., Salvi, D., Acuri A. and Semin, G. (1989) Language use in intergroup contexts: The linguistic intergroup bias. *Journal of Personality and Social Psychology*, 57, 981–93.

McArthur, L.Z. (1972) The how and what of why: Some determinants and consequences of causal attributions. *Journal of Personality and Social Psychology*, 22, 171–93.

McAuliffe, B.J., Jetten, J., Hornsey, M.J. and Hogg, M.A. (2003) Individualist and collectivist norms: When it's ok to go your own way. *European Journal of Social Psychology*, 33, 57–70.

McCauley, C. (1989) The nature of social influence in group-think: Compliance and internalization. *Journal of Personality and Social Psychology*, 57, 250–60.

McCauley, C. (1998) Group dynamics in Janis's theory of groupthink: Backward and forward. *Organizational Behavior and Human Decision Processes*, 73, 142–62.

McCauley, C.R. and Segal, M.E. (1987) Social psychology of terrorist groups. In C. Hendrick (ed.) *Group Processes and Intergroup Relations: Review of Personality and Social Psychology* (vol. 9, pp. 231–56). Thousand Oaks, CA: Sage.

McClure, J. (1998) Discounting causes of behavior: Are two reasons better than one? *Journal of Personality and Social Psychology*, 74, 7–20.

McClure, J. and Hilton, D.J. (1997) For you can't always get what you want: When preconditions are better explanations than goals. *British Journal of Social Psychology*, 36, 223–40.

McClure, J., Meyer, L.H., Garisch, J. et al. (2011) Students' attributions for their best and worst marks: Do they relate to achievement? *Contemporary Educational Psychology*, 36, 71–81.

Maccoby, E.E. (2002) Gender and group processes: A developmental perspective. *Current Directions in Psychological Science*, 11, 54–8.

McConahay, J.B. (1986) Modern racism, ambivalence, and the Modern Racism Scale. In J.F. Dovidio and S.L. Gaertner (eds) *Prejudice, Discrimination, and Racism* (pp. 91–125). San Diego: Academic Press.

McConnell, A.R. and Liebold, J.M. (2001) Relations between the Implicit Association Test, explicit racial attitudes, and discriminatory behavior. *Journal of Experimental Social Psychology*, 37, 435–42.

McCrea, S.M. and Hirt, E.R. (2001) The role of ability judgements in self-handicapping. *Personality and Social Psychology Bulletin*, 27, 1378–89.

McCullough, M.E., Worthington, E.L. Jr and Rachal, K.C. (1997) Interpersonal forgiving in close relationships. *Journal of Personality and Social Psychology*, 73, 321–36.

McDevitt, J., Levin, J. and Bennett, S. (2002) Hate crime offenders: An expanded typology. *Journal of Social Issues*, 58, 303–17.

MacDonald, G. and Leary, M.R. (2005) Why does social exclusion hurt? The relationship between social and physical pain. *Psychological Bulletin*, 131, 202–23.

MacDonald, J.M. (1975) *Armed Robbery: Offenders and their Victims*. Springfield, IL: Charles C Thomas.

McDougall, W. (1919) *An Introduction to Social Psychology*. London: Methuen.

McDougall, W. (1920) *The Group Mind*. London: Cambridge University Press.

McFadyen, R. (2011) Gender, status and 'powerless' speech: Interactions of students and lecturers. *British Journal of Social Psychology*, 35, 353–67.

McFarlane, J., Martin, C.L. and Williams, T.M. (1988) Mood fluctuations: Women versus men and menstrual versus other cycles. *Psychology of Women Quarterly*, 12, 201–23.

McFarlane, J., Martin, C.L. and Williams, T.M. (1988) Women versus men and menstrual versus other cycles. *Psychology of Women Quarterly*, 12, 201–23.

McGarty, C. (1999) *Categorization in Social Psychology*. London: Sage.

McGarty, C. and de la Haye, A.M. (1997) Stereotype formation: Beyond illusory correlation. In R. Spears, P.J. Oakes, N. Ellemers and S.A. Haslam (eds) *The Social Psychology of Stereotyping and Group Life* (pp. 144–70). Oxford: Blackwell.

McGarty, C. and Penny, R.E.C. (1988) Categorization, accentuation and social judgement. *British Journal of Social Psychology*, 22, 147–57.

McGarty, C., Haslam, S.A., Turner, J.C. and Oakes, P.J. (1993) Illusory correlation as accentuation of actual intercategory difference: Evidence for the effect with minimal stimulus information. *European Journal of Social Psychology*, 23, 391–410.

McGarty, C., Turner, J.C., Hogg, M.A. et al. (1992) Group polarization as conformity to the prototypical group member. *British Journal of Social Psychology*, 31, 1–20.

McGillicuddy, N.B., Welton, G.K. and Pruitt, D G. (1987) Third-party intervention: A field experiment comparing three different models. *Journal of Personality and Social Psychology*, 53, 104–12.

McGlynn, R.P., McGurk, D., Effland, V.S. et al. (2004) Brainstorming and task performance in groups constrained by evidence. *Organizational Behavior and Human Decision Processes*, 93, 75–87.

McGlynn, R.P., Tubbs, D.D. and Holzhausen, K.G. (1995) Hypothesis generation in groups constrained by evidence. *Journal of Experimental Social Psychology*, 31, 64–81.

McGonagle, K.A., Kessler, R.C. and Schilling, E.A. (1992) The frequency and determinants of marital disagreements in a community sample. *Journal of Social and Personal Relationships*, 9, 507–24.

McGovern, T.V., Corey, L.A., Cranney, J. et al. (2010) Psychologically literate citizens. In D.F. Halpern (ed.) *Undergraduate Education in Psychology: A Blueprint for the Future of the Discipline* (pp. 9–27). Washington, DC: American Psychological Association.

McGrath, J.E., Arrow, H. and Berdhal, J.L. (2000) The study of groups: Past, present and future. *Personality and Social Psychology Review*, 4, 95–105.

McGregor, I., Nash, K., Mann, N. and Phills, C.E. (2010) Anxious uncertainty and reactive approach motivation (RAM). *Journal of Personality and Social Psychology*, 99, 133–47.

McGuire, S., McHale, S.M. and Updegraff, K. (1996) Children's perceptions of the sibling relationship in middle childhood: Connections within and between family relationships. *Personal Relationships*, 3, 229–39.

McGuire, W.J. (1961) Resistance to persuasion conferred by active and passive prior refutation of the same and alternative counterarguments. *The Journal of Abnormal and Social Psychology*, 63, 326–32.

McGuire, W.J. (1964) Inducing resistance to persuasion. In L. Berkowitz (ed.) *Advances in Experimental Social Psychology* (vol. 1, pp. 192–227). New York: Academic Press.

McGuire, W.J. (1969) The nature of attitudes and attitude change. *The Handbook of Social Psychology*, 3, 136–314.

McGuire, W.J. and Papageorgis, D. (1961) The relative efficacy of various types of prior belief-defense in producing immunity against persuasion. *The Journal of Abnormal and Social Psychology*, 62, 327–37.

McHoskey, J.W. (1999) Machiavellianism, intrinsic versus extrinsic goals, and self-interest: A self-determination theory analysis. *Motivation and Emotion*, 23, 267–83.

Mack, D. and Rainey, D. (1990) Female applicants' grooming and personnel selection. *Journal of Social Behavior & Personality*, 5, 399–407.

Mackie, D. and Cooper, J. (1984) Attitude polarization: Effects of group membership. *Journal of Personality and Social Psychology*, 46, 575–85.

Mackie, D.M. (1987) Systematic and nonsystematic processing of majority and minority persuasive communications. *Journal of Personality and Social Psychology*, 53, 41–52.

Mackie, D.M. and Smith, E.R. (2002) Beyond prejudice: Moving from positive and negative evaluations to differentiated reactions to social groups. In D.M. Mackie and E.R. Smith (eds) *From Prejudice to Intergroup Emotions: Differentiated Reactions to Social Groups* (pp. 1–12). New York: Psychology Press.

Mackie, D.M. and Smith, E.R. (eds) (2004) *From Prejudice to Intergroup Emotions: Differentiated Reactions to Social Groups*. New York: Psychology Press.

Mackie, D.M. and Worth, L.T. (1989) Processing deficits and the mediation of positive affect in persuasion. *Journal of Personality and Social Psychology*, 57, 27–40.

Mackie, D.M. and Worth, L.T. (1991) Feeling good, but not thinking straight: The impact of positive mood on persuasion. In J. Forgas (ed.) *Emotion and Social Judgement* (pp. 201–20). Oxford, England: Pergamon.

Mackie, D.M., Devos, T. and Smith, E.R. (2000) Intergroup emotions: Explaining offensive action tendencies in an intergroup context. *Journal of Personality and Social Psychology*, 79, 602–16.

Mackie, D.M., Gastardo-Conaco, M.C. and Skelly, J.J. (1992) Knowledge of the advocated position and the processing of in-group and out-group persuasive messages. *Personality and Social Psychology Bulletin*, 18, 145–51.

Mackie, D.M., Smith, E.R. and Ray, D.G. (2008) Intergroup emotions and intergroup relation. *Social and Personality Psychology Compass*, 2, 1866–80.

Mackie, D.M., Worth, L.T. and Asuncion, A.G. (1990) Processing of persuasive in-group messages. *Journal of Personality and Social Psychology*, 58, 812–22.

McKenna, K.Y.A. (2007) Through the internet looking glass: Expressing and validating the true self. In A.N. Joinson, K. McKenna, T. Postmes and U.-D. Reips (eds) *The Oxford Handbook of Internet Psychology* (pp. 203–20). Oxford: Oxford University Press.

McKenna, K.Y.A. and Bargh, J.A. (2000) Plan 9 from cyberspace: The implications of the internet for personality and social psychology. *Personality and Social Psychology Review*, 4, 57–75.

McKenna, K.Y.A., Green, A.S. and Gleason, M.E.J. (2002) Relationship formation on the internet: What's the big attraction? *Journal of Social Issues*, 58, 9–31.

McKillop, K.J. and Schlenker, B.R. (1988) Audience effects on the internalization of depressed vs. nondepressed self-presentations. Paper presented at the annual meeting of the American Psychological Association, Atlanta.

MacLean, P.D. (1985) Brain evolution relating to family, play, and the separation call. *Archives of General Psychiatry*, 42, 405–17.

McLernon, F., Cairns, E., Hewstone, M. and Smith, R. (2004) The development of intergroup forgiveness in Northern Ireland. *Journal of Social Issues*, 60, 587–601.

MacNeil, M.K. and Sherif, M. (1976) Norm change over subject generations as a function of arbitrariness of prescribed norms. *Journal of Personality and Social Psychology*, 34, 762–73.

Macrae, C.N., Alnwick, K.A., Milne, A.B. and Schloerscheidt, A.M. (2002) Person perception across the menstrual cycle: Hormonal influences on social-cognitive functioning. *Psychological Science*, 13, 532–6.

Macrae, C.N., Bodenhausen, G.V., Milne, A.B. and Jetten, J. (1994) Out of mind but back in sight: Stereotypes on the rebound. *Journal of Personality and Social Psychology*, 67, 808–17.

Macrae, C.N., Mitchell, J.P. and Pendry, L.F. (2002) What's in a forename? Cue familiarity and stereotypical thinking. *Journal of Experimental Social Psychology*, 38, 186–93.

Madden, T.J., Ellen, P.S. and Ajzen, I. (1992) A comparison of the theory of planned behavior and the theory of reasoned action. *Personality and Social Psychology Bulletin*, 18, 3–9.

Madjar, N., Oldham, G.R. and Pratt, M.G. (2002) There's no place like home? The contributions of work and nonwork creativity support to employees' creative performance. *Academy of Management Journal*, 45, 757–67.

Madon, S., Guyll, M., Spoth, R. and Willard, J. (2004) Self-fulfilling prophecies: The synergistic accumulative effect of parents' beliefs on children's drinking behavior. *Psychological Science*, 15, 837–45.

Madon, S., Jussim, L. and Eccles, J. (1997) In search of the powerful self-fulfilling prophecy. *Journal of Personality and Social Psychology*, 72, 791–809.

Maheswaran, D. and Chaiken, S. (1991) Promoting systematic processing in low-motivation settings: Effect of incongruent information on processing and judgement. *Journal of Personality and Social Psychology*, 61, 13–25.

Maio, G.R. (2010) Mental representations of social values. In M.P. Zanna (ed.) *Advances in Experimental Social Psychology* (vol. 42, pp. 1–43). Burlington, MA: Academic Press.

Maio, G.R. and Olson, J.M. (1995) Relations between values, attitudes, and behavioral intentions: The moderating role of attitude function. *Journal of Experimental Social Psychology*, 31, 266–85.

Maio, G.R. and Olson, J.M. (2000) What *is* a value-expressive attitude? In G.R. Maio and J.M. Olson (eds) *Why we Evaluate: Functions of Attitudes* (pp. 249–69). Mahwah, NJ: Erlbaum.

Maio, G.R., Esses, V.M. and Bell, D.W. (1994) The formation of attitudes toward new immigrant groups. *Journal of Applied Social Psychology*, 24, 1762–76.

Maitner, A.T., Mackie, D.M. and Smith, E.R. (2006) Evidence for the regulatory function of intergroup emotion: Emotional consequences of implemented or impeded intergroup action tendencies. *Journal of Experimental Social Psychology*, 42, 720–8.

Maitner, A.T., Mackie, D.M. and Smith, E.R. (2007) Antecedents and consequences of satisfaction and guilt following ingroup aggression. *Group Processes and Intergroup Relations*, 10, 225–39.

Major, B. (1994) From social inequality to personal entitlement: The role of social comparisons, legitimacy appraisals, and group membership. *Advances in Experimental Social Psychology*, 26, 293–355.

Major, B. and Adams, J.B. (1983) Role of gender, interpersonal orientation, and self-presentation in distributive-justice behavior. *Journal of Personality and Social Psychology*, 45, 598–608.

Major, B. and Deaux, K. (1982) Individual differences in justice behavior. In J. Greenberg and R.L. Cohen (eds) *Equity and Justice in Social Behavior* (pp. 43–76). London: Academic Press.

Malamuth, N.M. and Addison, T. (2001) Integrating social psychological research on aggression within an evolutionary-based framework. In G.J.O. Fletcher and M.S. Clark (eds) *Blackwell Handbook of Social Psychology: Interpersonal Processes* (pp. 129–61). Malden: Blackwell.

Malle, B.F. (2004) *How the Mind Explains Behavior: Folk Explanations, Meaning, and Social Interaction*. Cambridge, MA: MIT Press.

Malle, B.F. (2005) Folk theory of mind: Conceptual foundations of human social cognition. In R. Hassin, J.S. Uleman and J.A. Bargh (eds) *The New Unconscious* (pp. 225–55). New York: Oxford University Press.

Malle, B.F. (2006) The actor-observer asymmetry in attribution: A (surprising) meta-analysis. *Psychological Bulletin*, 132, 895–919.

Malle, B.F. (2008) The fundamental tools, and possibly universals, of human social cognition. In R.M. Sorrentino and S. Yamaguchi (eds) *Handbook of Motivation and Cognition Across Cultures* (pp. 267–96). San Diego, CA: Elsevier.

Malle, B.F. and Knobe, J. (1997) Which behaviors do people explain? A basic actor-observer asymmetry. *Journal of Personality and Social Psychology*, 72, 288–304.

Malle, B.F. and Pearce, G.E. (2001) Attention to behavioral events during interaction: Two actor-observer gaps and three attempts to close them. *Journal of Personality and Social Psychology*, 81, 278–94.

Malle, B.F., Knobe, J. and Nelson, S.E. (2007) Actor-observer asymmetries in explanations of behaviour: New answers to an old question. *Journal of Personality and Social Psychology*, 93, 491–514.

Mallick, S.K. and McCandless, B.R. (1966) A study of catharsis of aggression. *Journal of Personality and Social Psychology*, 4, 591–6.

Malouff, J. and Schutte, N. (2005) Academic psychologists' perspectives on the human research ethics review process. *Australian Psychologist*, 40, 57–62.

Mandel, D.R. (1998) The obedience alibi: Milgram's account of the Holocaust reconsidered. *Analyse & Kritik*, 20, 74–94.

Mandler, G. (1980) Recognizing: The judgement of previous occurrence. *Psychological Review*, 87, 252–71.

Maner, J.K., Luce, C.L., Neuberg, S.L. et al. (2002) The effect of perspective taking on motivations for helping: Still no evidence for altruism. *Personality and Social Psychology Bulletin*, 28, 1601–10.

Mann, L. (1981) The baiting crowd in episodes of threatened suicide. *Journal of Personality and Social Psychology*, 41, 703–9.

Mann, S., Vrij, A. and Bull, R. (2004) Detecting true lies: Police officers' ability to detect suspects' lies. *Journal of Applied Psychology*, 89, 137–49.

Manning, R., Levine, M. and Collins, A. (2007) The Kitty Genovese murder and the social psychology of helping. *American Psychologist*, 62, 555–62.

Mansted, A.S.R. (1992) Gender differences in emotion. In A. Gale and M.W. Eysenck (eds) *Handbook of Individual Differences: Biological Perspectives* (pp. 355–87). Oxford: Wiley.

Manstead, A.S.R. and Semin, G.R. (1980) Social facilitation effects: Mere enhancement of dominant responses? *British Journal of Clinical Psychology*, 19, 119–35.

Manuck, S.B., Flory, J.D., Ferrell, R.E. and Muldoon, M.F. (2004) Socio-economic status covaries with central nervous system serotonergic responsivity as a function of allelic variation in the serotonin transporter gene-linked polymorphic region. *Psychoneuroendocrinology*, 29, 651–68.

Marcus, S. (1974) Book review of *Obedience to authority* by Stanley Milgram. *The New York Times Book Review*, 2, 1–3.

Marková, I. (2000) Amédée or How to get rid of it: Social representations from a dialogical perspective. *Culture & Psychology*, 6, 419–60.

Marks, M.L., Mirvis, P.H., Hackett, E.J. and Grady, J.F. (1986) Employee participation in a quality circle program: Impact on quality of work life, productivity and absenteeism. *Journal of Applied Psychology*, 71, 61–9.

Markus, H.R. (1977) Self-schemata and processing information about the self. *Journal of Personality and Social Psychology*, 35, 63–78.

Markus, H.R. (1978) The effect of mere presence on social facilitation: An unobtrusive test. *Journal of Experimental Social Psychology*, 14, 389–97.

Markus, H.R. and Kitayama, S. (1991) Culture and the self: Implications for cognition, emotion, and motivation. *Psychological Review*, 98, 224–53.

Markus, H.R. and Kitayama, S. (1994) A collective fear of the collective: Implication for selves and theories of selves. *Personality and Social Psychology Bulletin*, 20, 568–79.

Markus, H.R. and Nurius, P. (1986) Possible selves. *American Psychologist*, 41, 954–69.

Markus, H.R. and Sentis, K. (1982) The

self in social information processing. In J. Suls (ed.) *Psychological Perspectives on the Self* (pp. 51–70). Hillsdale, NJ: Erlbaum.

Markus, H.R. and Zajonc, R.B. (1985) The cognitive perspective in social psychology. In G. Lindzey and E. Aronson (eds) *Handbook of Social Psychology* (pp. 137–229). New York: Random House.

Markus, H.R., Hamill, R. and Sentis, K.P. (1987) Thinking fat: Self-schemas for body weight and the processing of weight relevant information. *Journal of Applied Social Psychology*, 17, 50–71.

Marlow, M.L. and Giles, H. (2008) 'Who you tink You, talkin propah?' Hawaiian Pidgin demarginalized. *Journal of Multicultural Discourses*, 2, 53–69.

Marlow, M.L. and Giles, H. (2010) 'We won't get ahead speaking like that!' Expressing and managing criticism in Hawaii. *Journal of Multilingual and Multicultural Development*, 31, 237–51.

Marlowe, F. and Wetsman, A. (2001) Preferred waist-to-hip ratio and ecology. *Personality and Individual Differences*, 30, 481–9.

Marques, J., Abrams, D. and Serodio R.G. (2001) Being better by being right: Subjective group dynamics and derogation of in-group deviants when generic norms are undermined. *Journal of Personality and Social Psychology*, 81, 436–47.

Marques, J.M. and Yzerbyt, V.Y. (1988) The black sheep effect: Judgemental extremity towards ingroup members in inter- and intra- group situations. *European Journal of Social Psychology*, 18, 287–92.

Marques, J.M., Yzerbyt, V.Y. and Leyens, J.P. (1988) The 'black sheep effect': Extremity of judgments towards ingroup members as a function of group identification. *European Journal of Social Psychology*, 18, 1–16.

Marsh, D., Hart, P. and Tindall, K. (2010) Celebrity politics: The politics of the late modernity? *Political Studies Review*, 8, 322–40.

Marsh, K.L., Johnston, L., Richardson, M.J. and Schmidt, R.C. (2009) Toward a radically embodied, embedded social psychology. *European Journal of Social Psychology*, 39, 1217–25.

Marshall, P.D. (2006) New media – new self: The changing power of celebrity. In P.D Marshall (ed.) *The Celebrity Culture Reader* (pp. 634–44). Routledge: London.

Martin, N.G., Eaves, L.J., Heath, A.C. et al. (1986) Transmission of social attitudes. *Proceedings of the National Academy of Science*, 83, 4364–8.

Martin, R. (1996) Minority influence and argument generation. *British Journal of Social Psychology*, 35, 91–103.

Martin, R. and Hewstone, M. (2008) Majority versus minority influence, message processing and attitude change: The source-context-elaboration model. *Advances in Experimental Social Psychology*, 40, 237–326.

Martin, R., Hewstone, M. and Martin, P.Y. (2003) Resistance to persuasive messages as a function of majority and minority source status. *Journal of Experimental Social Psychology*, 39, 585–93.

Martin, R., Hewstone, M., Martin, P.Y. and Gardikiotis, A. (2008) Persuasion from majority and minority groups. In W. Crano and R. Prislin (eds) *Attitudes and Attitude Change* (pp. 361–84). New York: Psychology Press.

Martinez, M.A., Zeichner, A., Reidy, D.E. and Miller, J.D. (2008) Narcissism and displaced aggression: Effects of positive, negative, and delayed feedback. *Personality and Individual Differences*, 44, 140–9.

Marvelle, K. and Green, S.K. (1980) Physical attractiveness and sex bias in hiring decisions for two types of jobs. *Journal of the National Association of Women Deans, Administrators and Counselors*, 44, 3–6.

Marx, D.M., Ko, S.J. and Friedman, R.A. (2009) The 'Obama effect': How a salient role model reduces race-based performance differences. *Journal of Experimental Social Psychology*, 45, 953–6.

Marx, K. and Engels, F. ([1848]1998) *The Communist Manifesto: A Modern Edition*. London: Verso.

Masciampo, E.J. and Baumeister, R.F. (2008) Toward a physiology of dual-process reasoning and judgement: Lemonade, willpower, and expensive rule-based analysis. *Psychological Science*, 19, 255–60.

Maslow, A.H. and Mintz, N.L. (1956) Effects of esthetic surroundings: I. Initial effects of three esthetic conditions upon perceiving 'energy' and 'well-being' in faces. *The Journal of Psychology*, 41, 247–54.

Massey, G., Scott, V. and Dornbusch, S. (1975) Racism without racists: Institutional racism in urban schools. *Black Scholar*, 7, 10–19.

Masuda, T. and Nisbett, R.E. (2001) Attending holistically versus analytically: Comparing the context sensitivity of Japanese and Americans. *Journal of Personality and Social Psychology*, 81, 922–34.

Mathes, E.W. and Kozak, G. (2008) The exchange of physical attractiveness for resource potential and commitment. *Journal of Evolutionary Psychology*, 6, 43–56.

Mathews, J.S., Morrison, F.J. and Ponitz, C.C. (2009) Early gender differences in self-regulation and academic achievement. *Journal of Educational Psychology*, 101, 689–704.

Matsumoto, D. (2004) Pauk Ekman and the legacy of universals. *Journal of Research in Personality*, 38, 45–51.

Matsumoto, D. (2006) Culture and nonverbal behavior. In V. Manusov and M.L. Patterson (eds) *The Sage Handbook of Nonverbal Communication*. Thousand Oaks, CA: Sage.

Matsumoto, D. and Yoo, S.H. (2006) Toward a new generation of cross-cultural research. *Perspectives on Psychological Science*, 1, 234–50.

Matthews, V.P., Kronenberger, W.G., Want, Y. et al. (2005) Media violence exposure and frontal lobe activation measure by functional magnetic resonance imaging in aggressive and nonaggressive adolescents. *Journal of Computer Assistant Tomography*, 29, 287–92.

Maxwell, G. and Morris, A. (2006) Youth justice in New Zealand: Restorative justice in practice? *Journal of Social Issues*, 62, 239–58.

Maxwell, J.P. and Visek, A.J. (2009) Unsanctioned aggression in rugby union: Relationships among aggressiveness, anger, athletic identity, and professionalization. *Aggressive Behavior*, 35, 237–43.

Mayo, C.W. and Crockett, W.H. (1964) Cognitive complexity and primacy-recency effects in impression formation. *Journal of Abnormal and Social Psychology*, 68, 335–8.

Mayor, E., Eicher, V., Bangerter, A. et al. (in press) Dynamic social representations of the 2009 H1N1 pandemic: Shifting patterns of sense-making and blame. *Public Understanding of Science*.

Mazur, A. and Lamb, T.A. (1980) Testosterone, status and mood in human males. *Hormones and Behavior*, 14, 236–46.

Mead, G.H. (1934) *Mind, Self, and Society*. Chicago, IL: University of Chicago Press.

Meade, R.D. and Barnard, W.A. (1973) Conformity and anticonformity among Americans and Chinese. *The Journal of Social Psychology*, 89, 15–24.

Mealey, L., Bridgstock, R. and Townsend, G.C. (1999) Symmetry and perceived facial attractiveness: A monozygotic co-twin comparison. *Journal of Personality and Social Psychology*, 76, 151–8.

Meertens, R.W. and Pettigrew, T.F. (1997) Is subtle prejudice really prejudice? *Public Opinion Quarterly*, 61, 54–71.

Mehrabian, A. and Piercy, M. (1993) Differences in positive and negative connotations of nicknames and given names. *The Journal of Social Psychology*, 133, 737–9.

Mehrabian, A. and Stefl, C. (1995) Basic temperament components of loneliness, shyness, and conformity. *Social Behavior and Personality: An International Journal*, 23, 253–64.

Meier, B.P., Hauser, D.J., Robinson, M.D.

et al. (2007) What's 'up' with God? Vertical space as a representation of the divine. *Journal of Personality and Social Psychology*, 93, 699–710.

Meier, B.P., Robinson, M.D., Carter, M.S. and Hinsz, V.B. (2010) Are sociable people more beautiful? A zero-acquaintance analysis of agreeableness, extraversion, and attractiveness. *Journal of Research in Personality*, 44, 293–6.

Meier, B.P., Robinson, M.D. and Clore, G.L. (2004) Why good guys wear white: Automatic inferences about stimulus valence based on brightness. *Psychological Science*, 15, 82–7.

Meltzoff, A.N. and Moore, M.K. (1977) Imitation of facial and manual gestures by human neonates. *Science*, 198, 75–8.

Meltzoff, A.N. and Moore, M.K. (1989) Imitation in newborn infants: Exploring the range of gestures imitated and the underlying mechanisms. *Developmental Psychology*, 25, 954–62.

Mendoza, S.A., Gollwitzer, P.M. and Amodio, D.M. (2010) Reducing the expression of implicit stereotypes: Reflexive control through implementation intentions. *Personality and Social Psychology Bulletin*, 36, 512–23.

Merrell, K.W., Gueldner, B.A., Ross, S.W. and Isava, D.M. (2008) How effective are school bullying intervention programs? A meta-analysis of intervention research. *Social Psychology Quarterly*, 23, 26–47.

Merriman, T. and Cameron, V. (2007) Risk-taking: Behind the warrior gene story. *The New Zealand Medical Journal*, 120, 1250.

Merton, R.K. (1948) The self-fulfilling prophecy. *The Antioch Review*, 8, 193–210.

Mesoudi, A., Whiten, A. and Laland, K.N. (2006) Towards a unified science of cultural evolution. *Behavioral and Brain Sciences*, 29, 329–83.

Meyer, I.H. (2003) Prejudice, social stress and mental health in lesbian, gay, and bisexual populations: Conceptual issues and research evidence. *Psychological Bulletin*, 129, 674–97.

Michaels, J.W., Blommel, J.M., Brocato, R.M. et al. (1982) Social facilitation and inhibition in a natural setting. *Replications in Social Psychology*, 2, 21–4.

Michotte, A. (1962) *The Perception of Causality*. Andover, MA: Methuen.

Middlemist, R., Knowles, E. and Matter, C. (1976) Personal space invasions in the lavatory: Suggestive evidence for arousal. *Journal of Personality and Social Psychology*, 33, 541–6.

Middleton, D. and Edwards, D. (eds) (1990) *Collective Remembering*. London: Sage.

Miles, D.R. and Carey, G. (1997) Genetic and environmental architecture of human aggression. *Journal of Personality and Social Psychology*, 72, 207–17.

Milgram, S. (1961) Nationality and conformity. *Scientific American*, December, 45–51.

Milgram, S. (1965) Some conditions of obedience and disobedience to authority. *Human Relations*, 18, 57–76.

Milgram, S. (1974) *Obedience to Authority*. New York: Harper & Row.

Milgram, S. (1992) *The Individual in a Social World: Essays and Experiments* (2nd edn). New York: McGraw-Hill.

Milgram, S. (2009) *Obedience to Authority: An Experimental View* (3rd edn). New York: Harper Perennial Modern Classics.

Milgram, S., Bickman, L. and Berkowitz, L. (1969) Note on the drawing power of crowds of different size. *Journal of Personality and Social Psychology*, 13, 79.

Milinski, M. (1987) Tit for tat in stickle-backs and the evolution of co-operation. *Nature*, 325, 433–5.

Miller, A.G. (1986) *The Obedience Experiments*. New York: Praeger.

Miller, A.G. (2009) Reflections on 'replicating Milgram' (Burger, 2009). *American Psychologist*, 64, 20–7.

Miller, D.T. (1977) Altruism and threat to a belief in a just world. *Journal of Experimental Social Psychology*, 13, 113–24.

Miller, D.T. and McFarland, C. (1987) Pluralistic ignorance: When similarity is interpreted as dissimilarity. *Journal of Personality and Social Psychology*, 53, 298–305.

Miller, D.T. and Ross, M. (1975) Self-serving biases in the attribution of causality: Fact or fiction? *Psychological Bulletin*, 82, 213–25.

Miller, G., Tybur, J.M. and Jordan, B.D. (2007) Ovulatory cycle effects on tip earnings by lap dancers: Economic evidence for human estrus? *Evolution and Human Behavior*, 28, 375–81.

Miller, G.A. (2003) The cognitive revolution: A historical perspective. *Trends in Cognitive Science*, 7, 141–4.

Miller, J.G. (1984) Culture and the development of everyday social explanation. *Journal of Personality and Social Psychology*, 46, 961–78.

Miller, J.G. and Bersoff, D.M. (1994) Cultural influences on the moral status of reciprocity and the discounting of endogenous motivation. *Personality and Social Psychology Bulletin*, 20, 592–602.

Miller, L.C., Murphy, R. and Buss, A.H. (1981) Consciousness of body: Private and public. *Journal of Personality and Social Psychology*, 41, 397–406.

Miller, N. (2002) Personalization and the promise of contact theory. *Journal of Social Issues*, 58, 387–410.

Miller, N. and Brewer, M.B. (eds) (1984) *Groups in Contact: The Psychology of Desegregation*. Orlando, FL: Academic Press.

Miller, N. and Campbell, D.T. (1959) Recency and primacy in persuasion as a function of the timing of speeches and measurements. *The Journal of Abnormal and Social Psychology*, 59, 1–9.

Miller, N., Brewer, M.B. and Edwards, K. (1985) Cooperative interaction in deseg-regated settings: A laboratory analogue. *Journal of Social Issues*, 41, 63–79.

Miller, N., Maruyama, G., Beaber, R.J. and Valone, K. (1976) Speed of speech and persuasion. *Journal of Personality and Social Psychology*, 34, 615–24.

Miller, N.E. (1941) The frustration-aggression hypothesis. *Psychological Bulletin*, 48, 337–42.

Miller, P.A., Eisenberg, N., Fabes, R.A. and Shell, R. (1996) Relations of moral reasoning and vicarious emotion to young children's prosocial behavior toward peers and adults. *Developmental Psychology*, 32, 210–19.

Miller, P.A., Kozu, J. and Davis, A.C. (2001) Social influence, empathy, and prosocial behavior in cross-cultural perspective. In W. Wosinska, R.B. Cialdini, D.W. Barrett and J. Reykowski (eds) *The Practice of Social Influence in Multiple Cultures* (pp. 63–77). Mahwah, NJ: Erlbaum.

Miller, P.J.E. and Rempel, J.K. (2004) Trust and partner-enhancing attributions in close relationships. *Personality and Social Psychology Bulletin*, 30, 695–705.

Miller, S. (2001) Public understanding of science at the crossroads. *Public Understanding of Science*, 10, 115–20.

Milne, S., Orbell, S. and Sheeran, P. (2002) Combining motivational and volitional interventions to promote exercise participation: Protection motivation theory and implementation intentions. *British Journal of Health Psychology*, 7, 163–84.

Miltiades, H. and Shearer, J. (2011) Attachment to pet dogs and depression in rural older adults. *Anthrozoös*, 24, 147–54.

Mischel, W. (1969) Continuity and change in personality. *American Psychologist*, 24, 1012.

Mischel, W. (1990) Personality disposi-tions revisited and revised: A view after three decades. In Pervin, L.A. (ed.) *Handbook of Personality: Theory and Research* (pp. 111–34). New York: Guilford Press.

Mischel, W. and Shoda, Y. (1995) A cognitive-affective system theory of personality: Reconceptualizing situations, dispositions, dynamics, and invariance in personality structure. *Psychological Review*, 102, 246–68.

Mitchell, G. and Tetlock, P.E. (2006) Antidiscrimination law and the perils of mindreading. *Ohio State University Law Review*, 67, 1023–122.

Mitchell, L.A., MacDonald, R.A.R. and

Brodie, E.E. (2004) Temperature and the cold pressor test. *The Journal of Pain*, 5, 233–7.

Mobius, M.M. and Rosenblat, T.S. (2006) Why beauty matters. *The American Economic Review*, 96, 222–35.

Moghaddam, F.M. (1987) Psychology in the three worlds: As reflected by the crisis in social psychology and the move towards indigenous third-world psychology. *American Psychologist*, 42, 912–20.

Moghaddam, F.M. (2005) The staircase to terrorism: A psychological exploration. *American Psychologist*, 60, 161–9.

Monahan, J. L., Murphy, S.T. and Zajonc, R.B. (2000) Subliminal mere exposure: Specific, general, and diffuse effects. *Psychological Science*, 11, 462–6.

Monin, B. (2003) The warm glow heuristic: When liking leads to familiarity. *Journal of Personality and Social Psychology*, 85, 1035–48.

Monin, B. and Miller, D.T. (2001) Moral credentials and the expression of prejudice. *Journal of Personality and Social Psychology*, 81, 33–43.

Monin, B. and Norton, M.I. (2003) Perceptions of a fluid consensus: Uniqueness bias, false consensus, false polarization, and pluralistic ignorance in a water conservation crisis. *Personality and Social Psychology Bulletin*, 29, 559–67.

Monsour, M., Betty, S. and Kurzweil, N. (1993) Levels of perspectives and the perception of intimacy in cross-sex friendships: A balance theory explanation of shared perceptual reality. *Journal of Social and Personal Relationships*, 10, 529–50.

Montada, L. (1998) Belief in a just world: A hybrid of justice motive and self-interest. In L. Montada and M.J. Lerner (eds) *Responses to Victimization and Belief in a Just World* (pp. 217–46). New York: Plenum.

Monteith, M.J. (1993) Self-regulation of prejudiced responses: Implications for progress in prejudice-reducing efforts. *Journal of Personality and Social Psychology*, 65, 469–85.

Monteith, M.J., Ashburn-Nardo, L., Voils, C.I. and Czopp, A.M. (2002) Putting the brakes on prejudice: On the development and operation of cues of control. *Journal of Personality and Social Psychology*, 83, 1029–50.

Monteith, M.J., Sherman, J.W. and Devine, P.G. (1998) Suppression as a stereotype control strategy. *Personality and Social Psychology Review*, 2, 63–82.

Montoya, R.M. and Insko, C.A. (2008) Toward a more complete understanding of the reciprocity of liking effect. *European Journal of Social Psychology*, 38, 477–98.

Moons, W.G. and Mackie, D.M. (2007) Thinking straight while seeing red. *Personality and Social Psychology Bulletin*, 33, 706–20.

Moons, W.G., Mackie, D.M. and Garcia-Marques, T. (2009) The impact of repetition-induced familiarity on agreement with weak and strong arguments. *Journal of Personality and Social Psychology*, 96, 32–44.

Moore, D.A. and Lowenstein, G. (2004) Self-interest, automaticity, and the psychology of conflict of interest. *Social Justice Research*, 17, 189–202.

Moore, J.S., Graziano, W.G. and Millar, M.G. (1987) Physical attractiveness, sex role orientation, and the evaluation of adults and children. *Personality and Social Psychology Bulletin*, 13, 95–102.

Moore, M. (2004) *Stupid White Men … and Other Sorry Excuses for the State of the Nation!* New York: HarperCollins.

Moore, S.C., Shepherd, J.P., Eden, S. and Sivarajasingam, V. (2007) The effect of rugby match outcome on spectator aggression and intention to drink alcohol. *Criminal Behaviour and Mental Health*, 17, 118–27.

Moore, T.M., Scarpa, A. and Raine, A. (2002) A meta-analysis of serotonin metabolite 5-HIAA and antisocial behavior. *Aggressive Behavior*, 28, 299–316.

Moorman, R.H., Blakely, G.L. and Niehoff, B.P. (1998) Does perceived organizational support mediate the relationship between procedural justice and organizational citizenship behavior? *Academy of Management Journal*, 41, 351–7.

Mor, N. and Winquist, J. (2002) Self-focused attention and negative affect: A meta-analysis. *Psychological Bulletin*, 128, 638–62.

Moreland, R.L. and Beach, S.R. (1992) Exposure effects in the classroom: The development of affinity among students. *Journal of Experimental Social Psychology*, 28, 255–76.

Moreland, R.L. and Levine, J.M. (1982) Socialization in small groups: Temporal changes in individual–group relations. In L. Berkowitz (ed.) *Advances in Experimental Social Psychology* (vol. 15, pp. 137–92). New York: Academic Press.

Moreland, R.L. and Levine, J.M. (1984) Role transitions in small groups. In V. Allen and E. van de Vliert (eds) *Role Transitions: Explorations and Explanations* (pp. 181–95). New York: Plenum.

Moreland, R.L. and Levine, J.M. (1989) Newcomers and oldtimers in small groups. In P. Paulus (ed.) *Psychology of Group Influence* (2nd edn, pp. 143–86). Hillsdale, NJ: Erlbaum.

Moreland, R.L. and Levine, J.M. (2001) Socialization in organizations and work groups. In M.E. Turner (ed.) *Groups at Work: Theory and Research* (pp. 69–112). Mahwah, NJ: Erlbaum.

Moreland, R.L. and McGinn, J. (1999) Gone but not forgotten: Loyalty and betrayal among ex-members of small groups. *Personality and Social Psychology Bulletin*, 25, 1476–86.

Moreland, R.L. and Zajonc, R.B. (1982) Exposure effects in person perception: Familiarity, similarity, and attraction. *Journal of Experimental Social Psychology*, 18, 395–415.

Morgan, E.M., Richards, T.C. and VanNess, E.M. (2010) Comparing narratives of personal and preferred partner characteristics in online dating advertisements. *Computers in Human Behavior*, 26, 883–8.

Morris, A. (2002) Critiquing the critics: A brief response to critics of restorative justice. *British Journal of Criminology*, 42, 596–615.

Morris, D. (1977) *Manwatching: A Field Guide to Human Behavior*. New York: Harry N. Abrams.

Morris, M.W. and Larrick, R.P. (1995) When one cause casts doubt on another: A normative analysis of discounting in causal attribution. *Psychological Review*, 102, 331–55.

Morris, M.W. and Peng, K. (1994) Culture and cause: American and Chinese attributions for social and physical events. *Journal of Personality and Social Psychology*, 67, 949–71.

Morrison, E.W. and Herlihy, J.M. (1992) Becoming the best place to work: Managing diversity at American Express. In S.E. Jackson and associates (eds) *Diversity in the Workplace: Human Resources Initiatives* (pp. 203–16). New York: Guilford Press.

Morton, T.L. (1978) Intimacy and reciprocity of exchange: A comparison of spouses and strangers. *Journal of Personality and Social Psychology*, 36, 72–81.

Moscovici, S. (1961) *La psychanalyse: Son image et son public*. Paris: Presses Universitaires de France.

Moscovici, S. (1963) Attitudes and opinions. *Annual Review of Psychology*, 14, 231–60.

Moscovici, S. (1972) Society and theory in social psychology. In J. Israel and H. Tajfel (eds) *The Context of Social Psychology: A Critical Assessment* (pp. 17–68). London: Academic Press.

Moscovici, S. (1976) *La psychanalyse: Son image et son public*. Paris: Presses Universitaires de France.

Moscovici, S. (1980) Toward a theory of conversion behavior. In L. Berkowitz (ed.) *Advances in Experimental Social Psychology* (13th edn, pp. 209–39). New York: Academic Press.

Moscovici, S. (1982) The coming era of social representations. In J.P. Codol and

J.P. Leyens (eds) *Cognitive Approaches to Social Behaviour* (pp. 115–50). The Hague: Nijhoff.

Moscovici, S. (1983) The phenomenon of social representations. In R.M. Farr and S. Moscovici (eds) *Social Representations* (pp. 3–69). Cambridge: Cambridge University Press.

Moscovici, S. (1988) Notes towards a description of social representations. *European Journal of Social Psychology*, 18, 211–50.

Moscovici, S. and Lage, E. (1976) Studies in social influence III: Majority versus minority influence in a group. *European Journal of Social Psychology*, 6, 149–74.

Moscovici, S. and Zavalloni, M. (1969) The group as a polarizer of attitudes. *Journal of Personality and Social Psychology*, 12, 125–35.

Moscovici, S., Lage, E. and Naffrechoux, M. (1969) Influence of a consistent minority on the responses of a majority in a color perception task. *Sociometry*, 32, 365–80.

Moseley, D., Elliott, J., Gregson, M. and Higgins, S. (2005) Thinking skills frameworks for use in education and training. *British Educational Research Journal*, 31, 367–90.

Moskowitz, G.B., Gollwitzer, P.M., Wasel, W. and Schaal, B. (1999) Preconscious control of stereotype activation through chronic egalitarian goals. *Journal of Personality and Social Psychology*, 77, 167–84.

Moss, N.E. (2002) Gender equity and socioeconomic inequality: A framework for the patterning of women's health. *Social Science & Medicine*, 54, 649–61.

Moya, M., Glick, P., Exposito, F. et al. (2007) It's for your own good: Benevolent sexism and women's reactions to protectively justified restrictions. *Personality and Social Psychology Bulletin*, 33, 1421–34.

Moyer, K.E. (1976) *The Psychobiology of Aggression*. New York: Harper & Row.

Mugny, G., Papastamou, S. and Sherrard, C. (1982) *The Power of Minorities*. London: Academic Press.

Mullen, B. (1986) Atrocity as a function of lynch mob composition: A self-attention perspective. *Personality and Social Psychology Bulletin*, 12, 187–97.

Mullen, B. and Baumeister, R.F. (1987) Group effects on self-attention and performance: Social loafing, social facilitation and social impairment. In C. Hendrick (ed.) *Group Processes and Intergroup Relations: Review of Personality and Social Psychology* (vol. 9, pp. 189–206). Newbury Park, CA: Sage.

Mullen, B. and Suls, J. (1982) 'Know thyself': Stressful life changes and the ameliorative effect of private self-consciousness. *Journal of Experimental Social Psychology*, 18, 43–55.

Mullen, B., Brown, R.J. and Smith,

C. (1992) Ingroup bias as a function of salience, relevance and status: An integration. *European Journal of Social Psychology*, 22, 103–22.

Mullen, B., Bryant, B. and Driskell, J.E. (1997) The presence of others and arousal: An integration. *Group Dynamics*, 1, 52–64.

Mullen, B., Calogero, R.M. and Leader, T.I. (2007) A social psychological study of ethnonyms: Cognitive representation of the in-group and intergroup hostility. *Journal of Personality and Social Psychology*, 92, 612–30.

Mullen, B., Johnson, C. and Salas, E. (1991) Productivity loss in brainstorming groups: A meta-analytic integration. *Basic and Applied Social Psychology*, 12, 3–23.

Muller, D., Atzeni, T. and Butera, F. (2004) Coaction and upward social comparison reduce the illusory conjunction effect: Support for distraction-conflict theory. *Journal of Experimental Social Psychology*, 40, 659–65.

Mummendey, A., Kessler, T., Klink, A. and Mielke, R. (1999) Strategies to cope with negative social identity: Predictions by social identity theory and relative deprivation theory. *Journal of Personality and Social Psychology*, 76, 229–45.

Murphy, A.O., Sutton, R.M., Douglas, K.M. and McClellan, L.M. (2011) Ambivalent sexism and the 'do's and 'don't's of pregnancy: Examining attitudes toward proscriptions and the women who flout them. *Personality and Individual Differences*, 51, 812–16.

Murphy, G. and Murphy, L.B. (1931) *Experimental Social Psychology*. New York: Harper.

Murphy, S.K., Wayne, S.J., Liden, R.C. and Erdogan, B. (2003) Understanding social loafing: The role of justice perceptions and exchange relationships. *Human Relations*, 56, 61–84.

Murray, D.M. and Perry, C.L. (1987) The measurement of substance use among adolescents: When is the 'bogus pipeline' method needed? *Addictive Behaviors*, 12, 225–33.

Murray, H.A. and McAdams, D.P. (2007) *Explorations in Personality*. Oxford: Oxford University Press.

Murray, S.L. and Holmes, J.G. (1999) The (mental) ties that bind: Cognitive structures that predict relationship resilience. *Journal of Personality and Social Psychology*, 77, 1228–44.

Murray, S.L., Haddock, G. and Zanna, M. (1996) On creating value expressive attitudes: An experimental approach. In C. Seligman, J.M. Olson and M.P. Zanna (eds) *Values: The Ontario Symposium* (vol. 8, pp. 107–34). Mahwah, NJ: Erlbaum.

Murstein, B.I. (1986) *Paths to Marriage*. New York: Sage.

Myers, D.G. and Bishop, G.D. (1970) Discussion effects on racial attitudes. *Science*, 169, 778–9.

Myrdal, G. (1944) *An American Dilemma: The Negro Problem and Modern Democracy*. New York: Harper.

Nadler, A. and Livitian, I. (2006) Intergroup reconciliation: Effects of adversary's expressions of empathy, responsibility, and recipients' trust. *Personality and Social Psychology Bulletin*, 32, 459–70.

Nadler, A., Altman, A. and Fisher, J.D. (1979) Helping is not enough: Recipients' reactions to aid as a function of positive and negative information about the self. *Journal of Personality*, 47, 615–28.

Nail, P.R. (1986) Toward an integration of some models and theories of social response. *Psychological Bulletin*, 100, 190–206.

Napier, J.L. and Jost, J.T. (2008) Why are conservatives happier than liberals? *Psychological Science*, 19, 565–72.

Neal, D.T. and Chartrand, T.L. (2011) Embodied emotion perception: Amplifying and dampening facial feedback modulates emotion perception accuracy. *Social Psychological and Personality Science*, 2, 673–8.

Neisser, U. (1963) The imitation of man by machine. *Science*, 139, 193–7.

Nelissen, R.M.A. (2012) Guilt induced self-punishment as a sign of remorse. *Social Psychological and Personality Science*, 3, 139–44.

Nelson, T.D. (ed.) (2002) *Ageism: Stereotyping and Prejudice against Older People*. Cambridge, MA: MIT Press.

Nelson, T.D. (2005) Ageism: Prejudice against our feared future self. *Journal of Social Issues*, 61, 207–21.

Nemeth, C.J. (1986) Differential contributions of majority and minority influence. *Psychological Review*, 93, 23–32.

Nemeth, C.J. (1995) Dissent as driving cognition, attitudes, and judgements. *Social Cognition*, 13, 273–91.

Nemeth, C.J. and Chiles, C. (1988) Modelling courage: The role of dissent in fostering independence. *European Journal of Social Psychology*, 18, 275–80.

Nemeth, C.J. and Wachtler, J. (1974) Creating the perceptions of consistency and confidence: A necessary condition for minority influence. *Sociometry*, 37, 529–40.

Nemeth, C.J., Swedlund, M. and Kanki, B. (1974) Patterning of the minority's responses and their influence on the majority. *European Journal of Social Psychology*, 4, 53–64.

Nestler, S., Blank, H. and von Collani, G. (2008) Hindsight bias doesn't always come easy: Causal models, cognitive effort, and creeping determinism. *Journal of Experimental Psychology: Learning, Memory and Cognition*, 34, 1043–54.

Neto, F., Mullet, E., Deschamps, J.C. et al. (2000) Cross-cultural variations in attitudes toward love. *Journal of Cross-Cultural Psychology*, 31, 626–35.

Neuberg, S.L. and Newsom, J.T. (1993) Personal need for structure: Individual differences in the desire for simpler structure. *Journal of Personality and Social Psychology*, 65, 113–31.

Neuberg, S.L., Kenrick, D.T. and Schaller, M. (2011) Human threat management systems: Self-protection and disease avoidance. *Neuroscience & Biobehavioral Reviews*, 35, 1042–51.

Neumann, R. and Strack, F. (2000) 'Mood contagion': The automatic transfer of mood between persons. *Journal of Personality and Social Psychology*, 79, 211–23.

Newcomb, T.M. (1956) The prediction of interpersonal attraction. *American Psychologist*, 11, 575–86.

Newcomb, T.M. (1961) *The Acquaintance Process*. New York: Holt, Rinehart & Winston.

New Zealand Women's Refuge (2011) Whether we win or lose, please don't take it out on your families! Available at https://womensrefuge.org.nz/.

Nezlek, J.B. and Plesko, R.M. (2001) Day-to-day relationships among self-concept clarity, self-esteem, daily events, and mood. *Personality and Social Psychology Bulletin*, 27, 201–11.

Ng, S.H. (1990) Androgenic coding of man and his memory by language users. *Journal of Experimental Social Psychology*, 26, 455–64.

Ng, S.H. and Bradac, J.J. (1993) *Power in Language: Verbal Communication and Social Influence*. Newbury Park, CA: Sage.

Ng, S.H., Han, S., Mao, L. and Lai, J.C. (2010) Dynamic bicultural brains: fMRI study of their flexible representation of self and significant others in response to culture primes. *Asian Journal of Social Psychology*, 13, 83–91.

Nicholson, L.J. (1990) *Feminism/Postmodernism*. New York: Routledge.

Niedenthal, P.M. (2007) Embodying emotion. *Science*, 316, 1002–5.

Niedenthal, P.M., Barsalou, L.W., Winkielman, P. et al. (2005) Embodiment in attitudes, social perception, and emotion. *Personality and Social Psychology Review*, 9, 184–211.

Niedenthal, P.M., Brauer, M., Halberstadt, J.B. and Ines-Ker, Å.H. (2001) When did her smile drop? Facial mimicry and the influences of emotional state on the detection of change in emotional expression. *Cognition and Emotion*, 15, 853–64.

Niedenthal, P.M., Ric, F. and Krauth-Gruber, S. (2002) Explaining emotion congruence and its absence in terms of perceptual simulation. *Psychological Inquiry*, 13, 80–3.

Niedenthal, P.M., Winkielman, P., Mondillon, L. and Vermeulen, N. (2009) Embodiment of emotion concepts. *Journal of Personality and Social Psychology*, 96, 1120–36.

Nienhuis, A.E., Manstead, A.S.R. and Spears, R. (2001) Multiple motives and persuasive communication: Creative elaboration as a result of impression motivation and accuracy motivation. *Personality and Social Psychology Bulletin*, 27, 118–32.

Nightingale, D.J. and Crombie, J. (1999) *Social Constructionist Psychology: A Critical Analysis of Theory and Practice*. Buckingham: Open University Press.

Nisbett, R.E. (1993) Violence and US regional culture. *American Psychologist*, 48, 441–9.

Nisbett, R.E. and Ross, L. (1980) *Human Inference: Strategies and Shortcomings of Social Judgment*. Englewood Cliffs, NJ: Prentice Hall.

Nisbett, R.E. and Wilson, T.D. (1977) Telling more than we can know: Verbal reports on mental processes. *Psychological Review*, 84, 231–59.

Nisbett, R.E., Peng, K., Choi, I. and Norenzayan, A. (2001) Culture and systems of thought: Holistic versus analytic cognition. *Psychological Review*, 108, 291–310.

Nolan, J.M., Shultz, P.W., Cialdini, R.B. et al. (2008) Normative social influence is underdetected. *Personality and Social Psychology Bulletin*, 34, 913–23.

Noller, P. and Fitzpatrick, M.A. (1990) Marital communication in the eighties. *Journal of Marriage and the Family*, 52, 832–43.

Norenzayan, A. and Nisbett, R.E. (2000) Culture and causal cognition. *Current Directions in Psychological Science*, 9, 132–5.

Norman, P. and Conner, M. (2006) The theory of planned behaviour and binge drinking: Assessing the moderating role of past behaviour within the theory of planned behaviour. *British Journal of Health Psychology*, 11, 55–70.

North, A.C., Hargreaves, D.J. and McKendrick, J. (1999) The influence of in-store music on wine selections. *Journal of Applied Psychology*, 84, 271–6.

North, A.C., Tarrant, M. and Hargreaves, D.J. (2004) The effects of music on helping behavior: A field study. *Environment & Behavior*, 36, 266–75.

Northcraft, G.B. and Neale, M.A. (1987) Experts, amateurs, and real estate: An anchoring-and-adjustment perspective on property pricing decisions. *Organizational Behaviour and Human Decision Processes*, 38, 84–97.

Norton, M.I. and Ariely, D. (2011) Building a better America – one wealth quintile at a time. *Perspectives on Psychological Science*, 6, 9–12.

Norton, M.I., Frost, J.H. and Ariely, D. (2007) Less is more: The lure of ambiguity, or why familiarity breeds contempt. *Journal of Personality and Social Psychology*, 92, 97–105.

Nosek, B.A. and Banaji, M.R. (2001) The go/no-go association task. *Social Cognition*, 19, 625–64.

Notarius, C. and Markman, H. (1993) *We Can Work It Out: Making Sense of Marital Conflict*. New York: Putnam.

Novaco, R. (1998) Roadway aggression. *ITS Review*, 21, 1–3.

Nunnally, J.C. (1978) *Psychometric Theory*. New York: McGraw-Hill.

Oakes, P.J., Haslam, S.A. and Turner, J.C. (1994) *Stereotyping and Social Reality*. Oxford: Blackwell.

Oaten, M., Stevenson, R.J. and Case, T.I. (2009) Disgust as a disease-avoidance mechanism. *Psychological Bulletin*, 135, 303–21.

O'Brien, L.T. and Major, B. (2005) System-justifying beliefs and psychological well-being: The roles of group status and identity. *Personality and Social Psychology Bulletin*, 31, 1718–29.

Ochsner, K.N. and Lieberman, M.D. (2001) The emergence of social cognitive neuroscience. *American Psychologist*, 56, 717–34.

O'Connor, J.J.M. and Feinberg, D.R. (2012) The influence of facial masculinity and voice pitch on jealousy and perceptions of intrasexual rivalry. *Personality and Individual Differences*, 52, 369–73.

O'Connor, J.J.M., Fraccaro, P.J. and Feinberg, D.R. (in press) The influence of male voice pitch on women's perceptions of relationship investment. *Journal of Evolutionary Psychology*.

O'Donovan, D. (1969) Detection of simulation on the MPI by subjects given the rational of the lie scale. *British Journal of Psychology*, 60, 535–41.

O'Dwyer, A., Berkowitz, N.H. and Alfeld-Johnson, D. (2002) Group and person attributions in response to criticism of the in-group. *British Journal of Social Psychology*, 41, 563–88.

OECD (Organisation for Economic Co-operation and Development) (2010) *The High Cost of Low Educational Performance: The Long-run Economic Impact of Improving PISA Outcomes*. Paris: OECD.

Office of Law Reform (2004) *Civil Partnership: A Legal Status for Committed Same-Sex Couples in Northern Ireland: Analysis of Responses*. Belfast: Office of Law Reform, Department of Finance and Personnel.

O'Hegarty, M., Pederson, L.L., Nelson, D. et al. (2007) Peer reviewed: Young adults' perceptions of cigarette warning labels in the United States and Canada. *Preventing Chronic Disease*, 4, A27.

Oishi, S., Kesebir, S. and Snyder, B.H.

(2009) Sociology: A lost connection in social psychology. *Personality and Social Psychology Review*, 13, 334–53.

Okimoto, T.G. and Wenzel, M. (2009) Punishment as restoration of group and offender values following a transgression: Value consensus through symbolic labelling and offender reform. *European Journal of Social Psychology*, 39, 346–67.

Oliner, P.M. (2004) *Saving the Forsaken: Religious Culture and the Result of Jews in Nazi Europe*. New Haven, CT: Yale University Press.

Oliner, S.P. and Oliner, P.M. (1988) *The Altruistic Personality*. New York: Free Press.

Olson, J.M., Vernon, P.A., Harris, J.A. and Jang, K.L. (2001) The heritability of attitudes: A study of twins. *Journal of Personality and Social Psychology*, 80, 845–60.

Olson, M. (1965) *The Logic of Collective Action: Public Goods and the Theory of Groups*. Cambridge: Harvard University Press.

Olson, M.A. and Fazio, R.H. (2001) Implicit attitude formation through classical conditioning. *Psychological Science*, 12, 413–17.

Olson, M.A. and Fazio, R.H. (2006) Reducing automatically activated racial prejudice through implicit evaluative conditioning. *Personality and Social Psychology Bulletin*, 32, 421–33.

Olweus, D. (1993) *Bullying at School: What We Know and What We Can Do*. Oxford: Blackwell.

Omoto, A.M. and Snyder, M. (2002) Considerations of community: The context and process of volunteerism. *American Behavioral Scientist*, 45, 846–67.

O'Neill, S.J. and Nicholson-Cole, S. (2009) Fear won't do it: promoting positive engagement with climate change through imagery and icons. *Science Communication*, 30, 355–79.

ONS (Office for National Statistics) (2009) Smoking related behaviour and attitudes. Retrieved from http://www.statistics.gov.uk/hub/health-social-care/health-of-the-population/lifestyles-and-behaviours/index.html.

ONS (2010) Divorces in England and Wales 2010. Retrieved from http://www.ons.gov.uk/ons/rel/vsob1/divorces-in-england-and-wales/2010/stb-divorces-2010.html on 29 June 2012.

ONS (2011) Baby names in England and Wales, 2011. Retrieved from http://www.ons.gov.uk/ons/rel/vsob1/baby-names-england-and-wales/2011/index.html on 29 June 2012.

Oosterhof, N.N. and Todorov, A. (2008) The functional basis of face evaluation. *Proceedings of the National Academy of Sciences*, 105, 11087–92.

Oosterwijk, S., Rotteveel, M., Fischer, A.H. and Hess, U. (2009) Embodied emotion concepts: How generating words about pride and disappointment influences posture. *European Journal of Social Psychology*, 39, 457–66.

Opie, K. and Power, C. (2008) Grandmothering and female coalitions: A basis for matrilineal priority? In N.J. Allen, H. Callan, R. Dunbar and W. James (eds) *Early Human Kinship: From Sex to Social Reproduction* (pp. 168–86). Malden, MA: Blackwell.

Opotow, S. (1990) Moral exclusion and injustice: An introduction. *Journal of Social Issues*, 46, 1–20.

Orano, P. (1901) *Psicologia Sociale*. Bari: Lacerta.

Orbell, S. and Sheeran, P. (2000) Motivational and volitional processes in action initiation: A field study of the role of implementation intentions. *Journal of Applied Social Psychology*, 30, 780–97.

Orbuch, T.L. (1992) *Close Relationship Loss: Theoretical Approaches*. New York: Springer.

Orobio de Castro, B., Veerman, J.W., Koops, W. et al. (2002) Hostile attribution of intent and aggressive behaviour: A meta-analysis. *Child Development*, 73, 916–34.

Ortony, A., Clore, G.L. and Collins, A. (1988) *The Cognitive Structure of Emotions*. Cambridge: Cambridge University Press.

Orvis, B.R., Cunningham, J.D. and Kelley, H.H. (1975) A closer examination of causal inference: The roles of consensus, distinctiveness, and consistency. *Journal of Personality and Social Psychology*, 32, 605–16.

Osborne, J. (2010) Arguing to learn in science: The role of collaborative, critical discourse. *Science*, 328, 463–6.

Osgood, C.E. (1962) *An Alternative to War or Surrender*. Urbana, IL: University of Illinois Press.

Östman, M. and Kjellin, L. (2002) Stigma by association: Psychological factors in relatives of people with mental illness. *British Journal of Psychiatry*, 181, 494–8.

Otte, E., Habel, U., Schulte-Rüther, M., Konrad, K. and Koch, I. (2011) Interference in simultaneously perceiving and producing facial expressions: Evidence from electromyography. *Neuropsychologia*, 49, 124–30.

Ouwerkerk, J.W., Kerr, N.L., Gallucci, M. and van Lange, P.E.M. (2005) Avoiding the social death penalty: Ostracism and cooperation in social dilemmas. In K.D. Williams, J.P. Forgas and W. von Hippel (eds) *The Social Outcast: Ostracism, Social Exclusion, Rejection, and Bullying* (pp. 321–32). New York: Psychology Press.

Overall, N.C., Fletcher, G.J.O. and Simpson, J.A. (2006) Regulation processes in intimate relationships: The role of ideal standards. *Journal of Personality and Social Psychology*, 91, 662–85.

Overall, N.C., Fletcher, G.J.O., Simpson, J.A. and Sibley, C.G. (2009) Regulating partners in intimate relationships: The costs and benefits of different communication strategies. *Journal of Personality and Social Psychology*, 96, 620–39.

Oviatt, D.P. and Iso-Ahola, S.E. (2008) Social facilitation and motor/athletic performance: A meta-analysis. In J.H. Humphrey (ed.) *Sports and Athletics Developments* (pp. 1–28). Hauppauge, NY: Nova Science.

Oyserman, D., Coon, H.M. and Kemmelmeier, M. (2002) Rethinking individualism and collectivism: Evaluation of theoretical assumptions and meta-analyses. *Psychological Bulletin*, 128, 3–73.

Packer, D.J. (2008) Identifying systematic disobedience in Milgram's obedience experiments: A meta-analytic review. *Perspectives on Psychological Science*, 3, 301–4.

Packer, D.J. (2008) On being both with us and against us: A normative conflict model of dissent in social groups. *Personality and Social Psychology Review*, 12, 50–72.

Packer, D.J. and Chasteen, A.L. (2010) Loyal deviance: Testing the normative conflict model of dissent in social groups. *Personality and Social Psychology Bulletin*, 36, 5–18.

Páez, D. (2010) Official or political apologies and improvement of intergroup relations: A neo-Durkheimian approach to official apologies as rituals. *Revista de Psicología Social*, 25, 101–15.

Paluck, E.L. (2009) Reducing intergroup prejudice and conflict using the media: A field experiment in Rwanda. *Journal of Personality and Social Psychology*, 96, 574–87.

Paluck, E.L. (2010) Is it better not to talk? Group polarization, extended contact, and perspective-taking in eastern Democratic Republic of Congo. *Personality and Social Psychology Bulletin*, 36, 1170–85.

Paluck, E.L. and Green, D.P. (2009) Prejudice reduction: What works? A review and assessment of research and practice. *Annual Review of Psychology*, 60, 339–67.

Pancer, S.M. (1997) Social psychology: The crisis continues. In D. Fox and I. Prilleltensky (eds) *Critical Psychology: An Introduction* (pp. 150–65). London: Sage.

Panksepp, J. (1998) *Affective Neuroscience: The Foundations of Human and Animal Emotions*. Oxford: Oxford University Press.

Paolacci, G., Chandler, J. and Ipeirotis, P.G. (2010) Running experiments on Amazon Mechanical Turk. *Judgment and Decision Making*, 5, 411–19.

Paolini, S., Hewstone, M., Cairns, E. and Voci, A. (2004) Effect of direct and indirect cross-group friendships on judgments of Catholics and Protestants in Northern Ireland: The mediating role of an anxiety-reduction mechanism. *Personality and Social Psychology Bulletin*, 30, 770–86.

Papastamou, S. and Mugny, G. (1990) Synchronic consistency and psychologization in minority influence. *European Journal of Social Psychology*, 20, 85–98.

Park, W.W. (1990) A review of research on groupthink. *Behavioral Decision Making*, 3, 229–45.

Parker, D., Manstead, A.S.R. and Stradling, S.G. (1995) Extending the theory of planned behaviour: The role of personal norm. *British Journal of Social Psychology*, 34, 127–38.

Parker, G., Gayed, A., Owen, C. et al. (2010) Survival following an acute coronary syndrome: A pet theory put to the test. *Acta Psychiatrica Scandinavica*, 121, 65–70.

Parker, I. (2005) *Qualitative Psychology: Introducing Radical Research*. Buckingham: Open University Press.

Parker, J.H. (1968) The interaction of negroes and whites in an integrated Church setting. *Social Forces*, 46, 359–66.

Parkinson, B. (1985) Emotional effects of false automatic feedback. *Psychological Bulletin*, 98, 471–94.

Parkinson, B. (2001) Anger on and off the road. *British Journal of Social Psychology*, 92, 507–26.

Parks, C.D. and Rumble, A.C. (2001) Elements of reciprocity and social value orientation. *Personality and Social Psychology Bulletin*, 27, 1301–9.

Parrott, W.G. and Smith, R.H. (1993) Distinguishing the experiences of envy and jealousy. *Journal of Personality and Social Psychology*, 64, 906–20.

Patchen, M. (1982) *Black-white Contact in Schools*. West Lafayette, IN: Purdue University Press.

Patterson, M.L. (1983) *Nonverbal Behavior: A Functional Perspective*. New York: Springer.

Patterson, M.L. (2003) Commentary: Evolution and nonverbal behavior: Functions and mediating processes. *Journal of Nonverbal Behavior*, 27, 201–7.

Paulus, P.B., Larey, T.S. and Ortega, A.H. (1995) Performance and perceptions of brainstormers in an organizational setting. *Basic and Applied Social Psychology*, 17, 249–65.

Pavelchak, M.A., Moreland, R.L. and Levine, J.M. (1986) Effects of prior group memberships on subsequent reconnaissance activities. *Journal of Personality and Social Psychology*, 50, 56–66.

Pavlov, I.P. ([1927]1960) *Conditional Reflexes*. New York: Dover.

Payne, B.K. (2001) Prejudice and perception: The role of automatic and controlled processes in misperceiving a weapon. *Journal of Personality and Social Psychology*, 81, 181–92.

Payne, B.K., Lambert, A.J. and Jacoby, L.L. (2002) Best laid plans: Effect of goals on accessibility bias and cognitive control in race-based misperceptions of weapons. *Journal of Experimental Social Psychology*, 38, 384–96.

Pays, O., Dubot, A.L., Jarman, P.J. et al. (2009) Vigilance and its complex synchrony in the red-necked pademelon, *Thylogale thetis*. *Behavioral Ecology*, 20, 22–9.

Peachey, D.E. (1989) The Kitchener experiment. In M. Wright and B. Galaway (eds) *Mediation and Criminal Justice: Victims, Offenders and Community* (pp. 14–26). London: Sage.

Pearce, P.L. (1980) Strangers, travelers, and Greyhound terminals: A study of small-scale helping behaviors. *Journal of Personality and Social Psychology*, 38, 935–40.

Pearson, K.A., Watkins, E.R., Kuyken, W. and Mullan, E.G. (2010) The psychosocial context of depressive rumination: Ruminative brooding predicts diminished relationship satisfaction in individuals with a history of past major depression. *British Journal of Clinical Psychology*, 49, 275–80.

Pei, M. (1965) *The Story of Language* (2nd edn). Philadelphia, PA: Lippincott.

Pelham, B.W. and Swann, W.B. (1989) From self-conceptions to self-worth: On the sources and structure of global self-esteem. *Journal of Personality and Social Psychology*, 57, 672–80.

Pendry, L.F. and Macrae, C.N. (1994) Stereotypes and mental life: The case of the motivated but thwarted tactician. *Journal of Experimental Social Psychology*, 30, 303–25.

Penton-Voak, I.S. and Perrett, D.I. (2001) Male facial attractiveness: Perceived personality and shifting female preferences for male traits across the menstrual cycle. *Advances in the Study of Behavior*, 30, 219–59.

Pepitone, A. (1981) Lessons from the history of social psychology. *American Psychologist*, 36, 972–85.

Peplau, L.A. and Fingerhut, A.W. (2007) The close relationships of lesbians and gay men. *Annual Review of Psychology*, 58, 405–24.

Perloff, R.M. (1989) Ego-involvement and the third person effect of televised news coverage. *Communication Research*, 16, 236–62.

Perrett, D. (2010) *In Your Face: The New Science of Human Attraction*. Basingstoke: Palgrave Macmillan.

Perrett, D., May, K. and Yoshikawa, S. (1994) Facial shape and judgements of female attractiveness. *Nature*, 368, 239–42.

Perry, D.G., Perry, L.C. and Rasmussen, P. (1986) Cognitive social learning mediators of aggression. *Child Development*, 57, 700–11.

Perry, P.J., Anderson, K.H. and Yates, W.R. (1990) Illicit anabolic steroid use in athletes: A case series analysis. *American Journal of Sports and Medicine*, 18, 422–8.

Persaud, R. (2005) The man who shocked the world: The life and legacy of Stanley Milgram. *British Medical Journal*, 331, 356.

Pervin, L.A. and Yatko, R.J. (1965) Cigarette smoking and alternative methods of reducing dissonance. *Journal of Personality and Social Psychology*, 2, 30–6.

Peters, S.L., van den Bos, K. and Bobocel, D.R. (2004) The moral superiority effect: Self versus other differences in satisfaction with being overpaid. *Social Justice Research*, 17, 257–73.

Peters, S.L., van den Bos, K. and Karremans, J.C. (2008) On the psychology of the advantaged: How people react to being overpaid. *Social Justice Research*, 21, 179–91.

Peterson, R.A. (2001) On the use of college students in social science research: Insights from a second-order meta-analysis. *Journal of Consumer Research*, 28, 450–61.

Peterson, R.S. and Nemeth, C.J. (1996) Focus versus flexibility majority and minority influence can both improve performance. *Personality and Social Psychology Bulletin*, 22, 14–23.

Petkova, K.G., Ajzen, I. and Driver, B.L. (1995) Salience of anti-abortion beliefs and commitment to an attitudinal position: On the strength, structure, and predictive validity of anti-abortion beliefs. *Journal of Applied Social Psychology*, 25, 463–83.

Pettigrew, T.F. (1998) Intergroup contact theory. *Annual Review of Psychology*, 49, 65–85.

Pettigrew, T.F. and Tropp, L.R. (2006) A meta-analytic test of intergroup contact theory. *Journal of Personality and Social Psychology*, 90, 751–83.

Pettigrew, T.F. and Tropp, L.R. (2008) How does intergroup contact reduce prejudice? Meta-analytic tests of three mediators. *European Journal of Social Psychology*, 38, 922–34.

Petty, R.E. and Briñol, P. (2008) Persuasion: From single to multiple to metacognitive processes. *Perspectives on Psychological Science*, 3, 137–47.

Petty, R.E. and Cacioppo, J.T. (1979) Issue involvement can increase or decrease persuasion by enhancing message-relevant cognitive responses. *Journal of Personality and Social Psychology*, 37, 1915–26.

Petty, R.E. and Cacioppo, J.T. (1984) Source factors and the elaboration likelihood model of persuasion. *Advances in Consumer Research*, 11, 668–72.

Petty, R.E. and Cacioppo, J.T. (1986a) *Communication and Persuasion: Central and Peripheral Routes to Attitude Change*. New York: Springer-Verlag.

Petty, R.E. and Cacioppo, J.T. (1986b) The elaboration likelihood model of persuasion. *Advances in Experimental Social Psychology*, 19, 123–205.

Petty, R.E. and Krosnick, J.A. (1995) *Attitude Strength: Antecedents and Consequences*. Mahwah, NJ: Erlbaum.

Petty, R.E. and Wegener, D.T. (1998a) Attitude change: Multiple roles for persuasion variables. In D.T. Gilbert, S.T. Fiske and G. Lindzey (eds) *The Handbook of Social Psychology* (4th edn, vol. 1, pp. 323–90). New York: McGraw Hill.

Petty, R.E. and Wegener, D.T. (1998b) Matching versus mismatching attitude functions: Implications for scrutiny of persuasive messages. *Personality and Social Psychology Bulletin*, 24, 227–40.

Petty, R.E. and Wegener, D.T. (1999) The elaboration likelihood model: Current status and controversies. In S. Chaiken and Y. Trope (eds) *Dual-process Theories in Social Psychology* (pp. 41–72). New York: Guilford Press.

Petty, R.E., Cacioppo, J.T. and Goldman, R. (1981) Personal involvement as a determinant of argument-based persuasion. *Journal of Personality and Social Psychology*, 41, 847–55.

Petty, R.E., Haugtvedt, C.P. and Smith, S.M. (1995) Elaboration as a determinant of attitude strength: Creating attitudes that are persistent, resistant, and predictive of behavior. In R.E. Petty and J.A. Krosnik (eds) *Attitude Strength: Antecedents and Consequences* (4th edn, pp. 93–130). Hillsdale, NJ: Lawrence Erlbaum.

Petty, R.E., Tormala, Z.L., Briñol, P. and Jarvis, W.B.G. (2006) Implicit ambivalence from attitude change: An exploration of the PAST model. *Journal of Personality and Social Psychology*, 90, 21–41.

Petty, R.E., Wells, G.L. and Brock, T.C. (1976) Distraction can enhance or reduce yielding to propaganda: Thought disruption versus effort justification. *Journal of Personality and Social Psychology*, 34, 874–84.

Pezzo, M.V. and Beckstead, J.W. (2008) The effects of disappointment on hindsight for real-world outcomes. *Applied Cognitive Psychology*, 22, 491–506.

Pezzo, M.V. and Pezzo, S.P. (2007) Making sense of failure: A motivated model of hindsight bias. *Social Cognition*, 25, 147–64.

Pfungst, O. (1911) *Clever Hans (The Horse of Mr. von Osten): A Contribution to Experimental Animal and Human Psychology*. New York: Henry Holt.

Philipp, M., Storrs, K. and Vanman, E. (2012) Sociality of facial expressions in immersive virtual environments: A facial EMG study. *Biological Psychology*, 91, 17–21.

Phillips, A. and Hranek, C. (2011) Is beauty a gift or a curse? The influence of an offender's physical attractiveness on forgiveness. *Personal Relationships*, 19, 420–30.

Phillips, M.L., Young, A.W., Senior, C. et al. (1997) A specific neural substrate for perceiving facial expressions of disgust. *Nature*, 389, 495–8.

Philpot, C.R. and Hornsey, M.J. (2008) What happens when groups say sorry: The effect of intergroup apologies on their recipients. *Personality and Social Psychology Bulletin*, 34, 474–87.

Philpot, C.R. and Hornsey, M.J. (2011) Memory for intergroup apologies and its relationship with forgiveness. *European Journal of Social Psychology*, 41, 96–106.

Philpot, C.R., Balvin, N., Mellor, D. and Bretherton, D. (2011) Exploring the benefits and limitations of collective apologies: The case of Australia's apology to its Aboriginal peoples. Unpublished manuscript, University of Queensland.

Phinney, J.S., Lochner, B.T. and Murphy, R. (1990) Ethnic identity development in adolescence. In A.R. Stiffman and L.E. Davis (eds) *Ethnic Issues in Adolescent Mental Health* (pp. 53–72). Newbury Park, CA: Sage.

Piaget, J. (1932) *The Moral Judgment of the Child*. London: Kegan, Paul, Trench, Trubner.

Piff, P., Kraus, M.W., Côté, S. et al. (2010) Having less, giving more: The influence of social class on prosocial behavior. *Journal of Personality and Social Psychology*, 99, 771–84.

Pinker, S. (1994) *The Language Instinct: How the Mind Creates Language*. New York: HarperCollins.

Pinto, I.R., Marques, J.M., Levine, J.M. and Abrams, D. (2010) Membership status and subjective group dynamics: Who triggers the black sheep effect? *Journal of Personality and Social Psychology*, 99, 107–19.

Plant, E.A. and Devine, P.G. (1998) Internal and external motivation to respond without prejudice. *Journal of Personality and Social Psychology*, 75, 811–32.

Plant, E.A., Devine, P.G., Cox, W.T.L. et al. (2009) The Obama effect: Decreasing implicit prejudice and stereotyping. *Journal of Experimental Social Psychology*, 45, 961–4.

Platow, M.J., Grace, D.M. and Smithson, M.J. (2012) Examining the preconditions for psychological group membership: Perceived social interdependence as the outcome of self-categorization. *Social Psychological and Personality Science*, 3, 5–13.

Platow, M.J., Haslam, S.A., Both, A. et al. (2005) 'It's not funny if they're laughing': Self-categorization, social influence, and responses to canned laughter. *Journal of Experimental Social Psychology*, 4, 542–50.

Platow, M.J., Voudouris, N.J., Coulson, M. et al. (2007) In-group reassurance in a pain setting produces lower levels of physiological arousal: Direct support for a self-categorization analysis of social influence. *European Journal of Social Psychology*, 37, 649–60.

Pollock, C.L., Smith, S.D., Knowles, E.S. and Bruce, H.J. (1998) Mindfulness limits compliance with the that's-not-AU technique. *Personality and Social Psychology Bulletin*, 24, 1153–7.

Pomerantz, A. and Mandelbaum, J.S. (2005) Conversation analytic approaches to the relevance and uses of relationship categories in interaction. In K.L. Fitch and R.E. Sanders (eds) *Handbook of Language and Social Interaction* (pp. 149–73). Mahwah, NJ: Erlbaum.

Pomerantz, E.M., Altermatt, E.R. and Saxon, J.L. (2002) Making the grade but feeling distressed: Gender differences in academic performance and internal distress. *Journal of Educational Psychology*, 94, 396–404.

Pomerantz, E.M., Chaiken, S. and Tordesillas, R.S. (1995) Attitude strength and resistance processes. *Journal of Personality and Social Psychology*, 69, 408–19.

Popper, K. (1959) *The Logic of Scientific Discovery*. London: Hutchinson.

Porges, S.W. (1998) Love: An emergent property of the mammalian autonomic nervous system. *Psychoneuroendocrinology*, 23, 837–61.

Pornari, C.D. and Wood, J. (2010) Peer and cyber aggression in secondary school students: The role of moral disengagement, hostile attribution bias, and outcome expectancies. *Aggressive Behavior*, 36, 81–94.

Postmes, T. (2007) The psychological dimensions of collective action online. In A.N. Joinson, K. McKenna, T. Postmes and U.-D. Reips (eds) *The Oxford Handbook of Internet Psychology* (pp. 165–84). Oxford: Oxford University Press.

Postmes, T. and Spears, R. (1998) Deindividuation and anti-normative behavior: A meta-analysis. *Psychological Bulletin*, 123, 238–59.

Postmes, T. and Spears, R. (2000) Refining the cognitive redefinition of the group: Deindividuation effects in common bond vs. common identity groups. In T. Postmes, R. Spears, M. Lea and

S. Reicher (eds) *SIDE Effects Centre Stage: Recent Developments in Studies of Deindividuation in Groups* (pp. 63–78). Amsterdam: KNAW.

Postmes, T., Spears, R. and Cihangir, S. (2001) Quality of decision making and group norms. *Journal of Personality and Social Psychology*, 80, 918–30.

Postmes, T., Spears, R., Sakhel, K. and de Groot, D. (2001) Social influence in computer-mediated communication: The effects of anonymity on group behaviour. *Personality and Social Psychology Bulletin*, 27, 1243–54.

Potter, J. (1996) *Representing Reality: Discourse, Rhetoric and Social Construction.* London: Sage.

Potter, J. and Litton, I. (1985) Some problems underlying the theory of social representations. *British Journal of Social Psychology*, 24, 81–90.

Potter, J. and Wetherell, M.S. (1987) *Discourse and Social Psychology: Beyond Attitudes and Behaviour.* London: Sage.

Poutvaara, P., Jordahl, H. and Berggren, N. (2009) Faces of politicians: Baby-facedness predicts inferred competence but not electoral success. *Journal of Experimental Social Psychology*, 45, 1132–35.

Powell, G.N. and Greenhaus, J.H. (2010) Sex, gender, and the work-to-family interface: Exploring negative and positive interdependencies. *Academy of Management Journal*, 53, 513–34.

Pratkanis, A.R., Eskenazi, J. and Greenwald, A.G. (1994) What you expect is what you believe (but not necessarily what you get): A test of the effectiveness of subliminal self-help audiotapes. *Basic and Applied Social Psychology*, 15, 251–76.

Pratkanis, A.R., Greenwald, A.G., Leippe, M.R. and Baumgardner, M.H. (1988) In search of reliable persuasion effects: III. The sleeper effect is dead: Long live the sleeper effect. *Journal of Personality and Social Psychology*, 54, 203–18.

Pratto, F., Sidanius, J., Stallworth, L.M. and Malle, B.F. (1994) Social dominance orientation: A personality variable predicting social and political attitudes. *Journal of Personality and Social Psychology*, 67, 741–63.

Prentice-Dunn, S. and Rogers, R.W. (1980) Effects of deindividuating situational cues and aggressive models on subjective deindividuation and aggression. *Journal of Personality and Social Psychology*, 39, 104–13.

Prentice-Dunn, S. and Rogers, R.W. (1982) Effects of public and private self-awareness on deindividuation and aggression. *Journal of Personality and Social Psychology*, 43, 503–13.

Prentice-Dunn, S. and Rogers, R.W. (1983) Deindividuation in aggression. In R.G. Geen and E.I. Donnerstein (eds) *Aggression: Theoretical and Empirical Reviews* (vol. 2, pp. 155–71). San Diego, CA: Academic Press.

Prentice, D.A. and Miller, D.T. (1993) Pluralistic ignorance and alcohol use on campus: Some consequences of misperceiving the social norm. *Journal of Personality and Social Psychology*, 64, 243–56.

Prentice, D.A. and Miller, D.T. (1996) Pluralistic ignorance and the perpetuation of social norms by unwitting actors. *Advances in Experimental Social Psychology*, 28, 161–209.

Prentice, D.A., Miller, D.T. and Lightdale, J.R. (1994) Asymmetries in attachments to groups and to their members: Distinguishing between common-identity and common-bond groups. *Personality & Social Psychology Bulletin*, 20, 484–93.

Prestwich, A., Lawton, R. and Conner, M. (2003) The use of implementation intentions and the decision balance sheet in promoting exercise behaviour. *Psychology & Health*, 18, 707–21.

Preuss, G.S. and Alicke, M.D. (2009) Everybody loves me: Self-evaluations and metaperceptions of dating popularity. *Personality and Social Psychology Bulletin*, 35, 937–50.

Price, R.A. and Vandenberg, S.G. (1979) Matching for physical attractiveness in married couples. *Personality and Social Psychology Bulletin*, 5, 398–400.

Priester, J.R. and Petty, R.E. (2001) Extending the bases of subjective attitudinal ambivalence: Interpersonal and intrapersonal antecedents of evaluative tension. *Journal of Personality and Social Psychology*, 80, 19–34.

Pronin, E., Berger, J. and Molouki, S. (2007) Alone in a crowd of sheep: Asymmetric perceptions of conformity and their roots in an introspection illusion. *Journal of Personality and Social Psychology*, 92, 585–95.

Pronin, E., Gilovich, T. and Ross, L. (2004) Objectivity in the eye of the beholder: Divergent perceptions of bias in self versus others. *Psychological Review*, 111, 781–99.

Pronin, E., Wegner, D.M., McCarthy, K. and Rodriguez, S. (2006) Everyday magical powers: The role of apparent mental causation in the overestimation of personal influence. *Journal of Personality and Social Psychology*, 91, 218–31.

Provine, R.R. (1989) Faces as releasers of contagious yawning: An approach to face detection using normal human participants. *Bulletin of the Psychonomic Society*, 27, 211–14.

Provine, R.R. (1992) Contagious laughter: Laughter is sufficient stimulus for laughs and smiles. *Bulletin of the Psychonomic Society*, 30, 1–4.

Pruitt, D.G. (1981) *Negotiation Behavior.* New York: Academic Press.

Pruitt, D.G. (1998) Social conflict. In D.T. Gilbert, S.T. Fisk and L. Gardner (eds) *The Handbook of Social Psychology* (4th edn, vol. 2, pp. 470–503). New York: McGraw-Hill.

Pruitt, D.G. and Kimmel, M.J. (1977) Twenty years of experimental gaming: Critique, synthesis, and suggestions for the future. *Annual Review of Psychology*, 28, 363–92.

Pruitt, D.J. and Insko, C.A. (1980) Extension of the Kelley attribution model: The role of comparison-object consensus, distinctiveness, and consistency. *Journal of Personality and Social Psychology*, 39, 39–58.

Putnam, L. and Krauss, R. (1991) Affective valence, arousal, and attention and their relationship to physiological response. *Psychophysiology*, 28, S45.

Putnam, R. (2000) *Bowling Alone: The Collapse and Revival of American Community.* New York: Simon & Schuster.

Putrevu, S. (2008) Consumer responses toward sexual and nonsexual appeals: The influence of involvement, need for cognition (NFC), and gender. *Journal of Advertising*, 37(2), 57–69.

Pyszczynski, T., Greenberg, J. and Solomon, S. (1999) A dual process model of defense against conscious and unconscious death-related thoughts: An extension of terror management theory. *Psychological Review*, 106, 835–45.

Pyszczynski, T., Greenberg, J., Solomon, S. et al. (2004) Why do people need self-esteem? A theoretical and empirical review. *Psychological Bulletin*, 130, 435–68.

QAA (Quality Assurance Agency) (2010) *Subject Benchmark Statement: Psychology.* Gloucester: QAA.

Queller, S., Schell, T. and Mason, W. (2006) A novel view of between-categories contrast and within-category assimilation. *Journal of Personality and Social Psychology*, 91, 406–22.

Quigley-Fernandez, B. and Tedeschi, J.T. (1978) The bogus pipeline as lie detector: Two validity studies. *Journal of Personality and Social Psychology*, 36, 247–56.

Rabbie, J.M. and Horwitz, M. (1988) Categories versus groups as explanatory concepts in intergroup relations. *European Journal of Social Psychology*, 18, 117–23.

Rafiq, U., Jobanuptra, N. and Muncer, S. (2006) Comparing the perceived causes of the second Iraq war: A network analysis approach. *Aggressive Behavior*, 32, 321–9.

Rai, T.S. and Fiske, A.P. (2011) Moral psychology is relationship regulation: Moral motives for unity, hierarchy, equality, and proportionality. *Psychological Review*, 118, 57–75.

Raine, A. (1993) *The Psychopathology of*

Crime: Criminal Behaviour as a Clinical Disorder. San Diego: Academic Press.

Raine, A., Buchsbaum, M. and LaCasse, L. (1997) Brain abnormalities in murderers indicated by positron emission tomography. *Biological Psychiatry*, 42, 495–508.

Rajala, A.Z., Reininger, K.R., Lancaster, K.M. and Populin, L.C. (2010) Rhesus monkeys (Macaca mulatta) do recognize themselves in the mirror: implications for the evolution of self-recognition. *PLoS ONE*, 5, e12865.

Raman, L. and Winer, G.A. (2004) Evidence of more immanent justice responding in adults than children: A challenge to traditional developmental theories. *British Journal of Developmental Psychology*, 22, 255–74.

Ramirez, J.M. (2003) Hormones and aggression in childhood and adolescence. *Aggression and Violent Behavior*, 8, 621–44.

Ramírez-Esparza, N., Gosling, S.D., Benet-Martínez, V. et al. (2006) Do bilinguals have two personalities? A special case of cultural frame switching. *Journal of Research in Personality*, 40, 99–120.

Rapoport, A. and Chammah, A.M. (1965) *Prisoners' Dilemma.* Ann Arbor, MI: University of Michigan Press.

Rathvon, N. (2008) *Effective School Interventions: Evidence-based Strategies for Improving Student Outcomes* (2nd edn). New York: Guilford Press.

Reeves, R.A., Baker, G.A., Boyd, J.G. and Cialdini, R.B. (1991) The door-in-the-face technique: Reciprocal concessions vs. self-presentational explanations. *Journal of Social Behavior and Personality*, 6, 545–58.

Regan, D.T. (1971) Effects of a favor and liking on compliance. *Journal of Experimental Social Psychology*, 7, 627–39.

Regan, D.T. (1971) Voluntary expiation of guilt: A field experiment. *Journal of Personality and Social Psychology*, 24, 42–5.

Regan, D.T. and Fazio, R. (1977) On the consistency between attitudes and behavior: Look to the method of attitude formation. *Journal of Experimental Social Psychology*, 13, 28–45.

Regan, D.T., Williams, M. and Sparling, S. (1972) Voluntary expiation of guilt: A field experiment. *Journal of Personality and Social Psychology*, 24, 42–4.

Regan, P.C. and Berscheid, E. (1999) *Lust: What we Know about Human Sexual Desire.* Thousand Oaks, CA: Sage.

Regan, P.C., Snyder, M. and Kassin, S.M. (1995) Unrealistic optimism: Self-enhancement or person positivity? *Personality and Social Psychology Bulletin*, 21, 1073–82.

Reich, R. (2010) *Aftershock: The Next Economy and America's Future.* New York: Random House.

Reicher, S.D. (1984a) Social influence in the crowd: Attitudinal and behavioural effects of de-individuation in conditions of high and low group salience. *British Journal of Social Psychology*, 23, 341–50.

Reicher, S.D. (1984b) The St. Pauls' riot: An explanation of the limits of crowd action in terms of a social identity model. *European Journal of Social Psychology*, 14, 1–21.

Reicher, S.D. (1987) Crowd behaviour as social action. In J.C. Turner, M.A. Hogg, P.J. Oakes et al. (eds) *Rediscovering the Social Group: A Self-categorization Theory* (pp. 171–202). Oxford: Blackwell.

Reicher, S.D. (1996) 'The battle of Westminster': Developing the social identity model of crowd behaviour in order to explain the initiation and development of collective conflict. *European Journal of Social Psychology*, 26, 115–34.

Reicher, S.D. (2001) The psychology of crowd dynamics. In M.A. Hogg and R.S. Tindale (eds) *Blackwell Handbook of Social Psychology: Group Processes* (pp. 182–207). Oxford: Blackwell.

Reicher, S.D. (2004) The context of social identity: Domination, resistance, and change. *Political Psychology*, 25, 921–45.

Reicher, S.D. (2011) Promoting a culture of innovation: BJSP and the emergence of new paradigms in social psychology. *British Journal of Social Psychology*, 50, 391–8.

Reicher, S.D. and Levine, M. (1994a) Deindividuation, power relations between groups and the expression of social identity: The effects of visibility to the out-group. *British Journal of Social Psychology*, 33, 145–63.

Reicher, S.D. and Levine, M. (1994b) On the consequences of deindividuation manipulations for the strategic communication of self: Identifiability and the presentation of social identity. *European Journal of Social Psychology*, 24, 511–24.

Reicher, S.D. and Stott, C. (2011) *Mad Mobs and Englishmen? Myths and Realities of the 2011 Riots.* London: Constable & Robinson.

Reicher, S.D, Haslam, S.A. and Rath, R. (2008) Making a virtue of evil: A five-step social identity model of the development of collective hate. *Social and Personality Psychology Compass*, 2, 1313–44.

Reicher, S.D., Spears, R. and Postmes, T. (1995) A social identity model of deindividuation phenomena. *European Review of Social Psychology*, 6, 161–98.

Reichle, B., Schneider, A. and Montada, L. (1998) How do observers of victimization preserve their belief in a just world cognitively or actionally? In L. Montada and M.J. Lerner (eds) *Responses to Victimization and Belief in a Just World* (pp. 55–86). New York: Plenum.

Reid, S.A. and Ng, S.H. (1999) Language, power and intergroup relations. *Journal of Social Issues*, 55, 119–39.

Reid, S.A., Byrne, S., Brundidge, J.S. et al. (2007) A critical test of self-enhancement, exposure, and self-categorization explanations for first- and third-person perceptions. *Human Communication Research*, 33, 143–62.

Reidy, D.E., Foster, J.D. and Zeichner, A. (2010) Narcissism and unprovoked aggression. *Aggressive Behavior*, 36, 414–22.

Reis, H.T. and Collins, W.A. (2004) Relationships, human behavior, and psychological science. *Current Directions in Psychological Science*, 13, 233–7.

Reis, H.T. and Shaver, P. (1988) Intimacy as an interpersonal process. In S. Duck (ed.) *Handbook of Personal Relationships: Theory, Research and Interventions* (pp. 367–89). New York: Wiley.

Reis, H.T., Collins, W.A. and Berscheid, E. (2000) The relationship context of human behavior and development. *Psychological Bulletin*, 126, 844–72.

Reiss, D. and Marino, L. (2001) Mirror self-recognition in the bottlenose dolphin: A case of cognitive convergence. *Proceedings of the National Academy of Sciences of the United States of America*, 98, 5937–42.

Renfrew, J.W. (1993) *Aggression and its Causes: A Biopsychosocial Approach.* New York: Oxford University Press.

Reno, R.R., Cialdini, R.B. and Kallgren, C.A. (1993) The transsituational influence of social norms. *Journal of Personality and Social Psychology*, 64, 104.

Renzetti, C.M. (1992) *Violent Betrayal: Partner Abuse in Lesbian Relationships.* Newbury Park, CA: Sage.

Reynolds, C.R. and Richmond, B.O. (1979) Factor structure and construct validity of 'What I think and feel': The Children's Manifest Anxiety Scale. *Journal of Personality Assessment*, 43, 281–3.

Rhode, D.L. (1989) *Justice and Gender: Sex Discrimination and the Law.* Cambridge, MA: Harvard University Press.

Rhodes, G. (1996) *Superportraits: Caricatures and Recognition.* Hove: Psychology Press.

Rhodes, G. (2006) The evolutionary psychology of facial beauty. *Annual Review of Psychology*, 57, 199–226.

Rhodes, G. and Tremewan, T. (1996) Averageness, exaggeration, and facial attractiveness. *Psychological Science*, 7, 105–10.

Rhodes, G. and Zebrowitz, L.A. (2002) *Facial Attractiveness: Evolutionary, Cognitive, and Social Perspectives.* Westport, CT: Ablex.

Rhodes, G., Halberstadt, J., Jeffery, L. and

Palermo, R. (2005) The attractiveness of average faces is not a generalized mere exposure effect. *Social Cognition*, 23, 205–17.

Rhodes, G., Sumich, A. and Byatt, G. (1999) Are average facial configurations attractive only because of their symmetry? *Psychological Science*, 10, 52–8.

Rhodes, G., Yoshikawa, S., Clark, A. et al. (2001) Attractiveness of facial averageness and symmetry in nonwestern cultures: In search of biologically based standards of beauty. *Perception*, 30, 611–26.

Rhodes, J. and Smith, J.A. (2010) 'The top of my head came off': An interpretative phenomenological analysis of the experience of depression. *Counselling Psychology Quarterly*, 23, 399–409.

Rhodewalt, F. and Davison, J. (1983) Reactance and the coronary-prone behavior pattern: The role of self-attribution in responses to reduced behavioral freedom. *Journal of Personality and Social Psychology*, 44, 220–8.

Rhodewalt, F. and Strube, M.J. (1985) A self attribution reactance model of recovery from injury in type A individuals. *Journal of Applied Social Psychology*, 15, 330–44.

Rhodewalt, F., Morf, C., Hazlett, S. and Fairfield, M. (1991) Self-handicapping: The role of discounting and augmentation in the preservation of self-esteem. *Journal of Personality and Social Psychology*, 61, 122–31.

Rholes, W.S., Simpson, J.A. and Blakely, B.S. (1995) Adult attachment styles and mothers' relationships with their young children. *Personal Relationships*, 2, 35–54.

Richard, F.D., Bond, C.F. and Stokes-Zoota, J.J. (2001) 'That's completely obvious … and important': Lay judgements of social psychological findings. *Personality and Social Psychology Bulletin*, 27, 497–505.

Richard, F.D., Bond, C.F. Jr and Stokes-Zoota, J.J. (2003) One hundred years of social psychology quantitatively described. *Review of General Psychology*, 7, 331–63.

Richeson, J.A. and Nussbaum, R.J. (2004) The impact of multiculturalism versus color-blindness on racial bias. *Journal of Experimental Social Psychology*, 40, 417–23.

Richter, L. and Kruglanski, A.W. (1998) Seizing on the latest: Motivationally driven recency effects in impression formation. *Journal of Experimental Social Psychology*, 34, 313–29.

Ridgeway, C.L. and Berger, J. (1986) Expectations, legitimation and dominance behavior in task groups. *American Sociological Review*, 51, 603–17.

Riger, S. and Gordon, M.T. (1981) The fear of rape: A study in social control. *Journal of Social Issues*, 37, 71–92.

Ringelmann, M. (1913) Recherches sur les moteurs animés: Travail de l'homme. *Annales de l'Institut National Agronomique*, 2, 1–40.

Riordan, C. and Ruggiero, J. (1980) Producing equal-status interracial interaction: A replication. *Social Psychology Quarterly*, 43, 131–6.

Risen, J.L. and Chen, M.K. (2010) How to study choice-induced attitude change: Strategies for fixing the free-choice paradigm. *Social and Personality Psychology Compass*, 4, 1151–64.

Riskind, J.H. (1984) They stoop to conquer: Guiding and self-regulatory functions of physical posture after success and failure. *Journal of Personality and Social Psychology*, 47, 479–93.

Ritchie, T.D., Sedikides, C., Wildschut, T. et al. (2011) Self-concept clarity mediates the relationship between stress and subjective well-being. *Self and Identity*, 10, 493–508.

Ritov, I. (1996) Anchoring in simulated competitive market negotiation. *Organizational Behaviour and Human Decision Processes*, 67, 16–25.

Ritter, C., Benson, D.E. and Synder, C. (1990) Belief in a just world and depression. *Sociological Perspectives*, 33, 235–52.

Rizzolatti, G., Fadiga, L., Fogassi, L. and Gallese, V. (2002) From mirror neurons to imitation: Facts and speculations. In A.N. Meltzoff and W. Prinz (eds) *The Imitative Mind: Development, Evolution and Brain Bases* (pp. 247–65). Cambridge: Cambridge University Press.

Ro, T., Russell, C. and Lavie, N. (2001) Changing faces: A detection advantage in the flicker paradigm. *Psychological Science*, 12, 94–9.

Roberts, I. and Edwards P. (2010) *The Energy Glut: The Politics of Fatness in an Overheating World*. London: Zed Books.

Roberts, K.A. (2007) Relationship attachment and the behaviour of fans towards celebrities. *Applied Psychology in Criminal Justice*, 3, 54–74.

Robins, R.W., Trzesniewski, K.H., Tracy, J.L. et al. (2002) Global self-esteem across the life span. *Psychology and Aging*, 17, 423–34.

Robinson, J.W. and Preston, J.D. (1976) Equal status contact and modification of racial prejudice: A reexamination of the contact hypothesis. *Social Forces*, 54, 911–24.

Roccas, S. and Brewer, M.B. (2002) Social identity complexity. *Personality and Social Psychology Review*, 6, 88–106.

Roche, D. (2003) *Accountability in Restorative Justice*. Oxford: Oxford University Press.

Rockloff, M.J. and Dyer, V. (2007) An experiment on the social facilitation of gambling behaviour. *Journal of Gambling Studies*, 23, 1–12.

Röder, S., Brewer, G. and Fink, B. (2009) Menstrual cycle shifts in women's self-perception and motivation: A daily report method. *Personality and Individual Differences*, 47, 616–19.

Rodriguez Mosquera, P.M., Manstead, A.S.R. and Fischer, A.H. (2002) Honor in the Mediterranean and Northern Europe. *Journal of Cross-cultural Psychology*, 33, 16–36.

Roese, N.J. and Jamieson, D.W. (1993) Twenty years of bogus pipeline research: A critical review and meta-analysis. *Psychological Bulletin*, 114, 363–75.

Roese, N.J. and Olson, J.M. (1996) Counterfactuals, causal attributions, and the hindsight bias: A conceptual integration. *Journal of Experimental Social Psychology*, 32, 197–227.

Roets, A. and van Hiel, A. (2011) Item selection and validation of a brief, 15-item version of the need for closure scale. *Personality and Individual Differences*, 50, 90–4.

Rogler, L.H., Cortes, D.E. and Malgady, R.G. (1991) Acculturation and mental health status among Hispanics: Convergence and new directions for research. *American Psychologist*, 46, 585–97.

Rohrer, J.H., Baron, S.H., Hoffman, E. and Swander, D. (1954) The stability of autokinetic judgements. *The Journal of Abnormal and Social Psychology*, 49, 595–7.

Roizen, J. (1997) Epidemiological issues in alcohol-related violence. In M. Galanter (ed.) *Recent Developments in Alcoholism* (vol. 13, pp. 7–40). New York: Plenum Press.

Rokeach, M. (1956) On the unity of thought and belief. *Journal of Personality*, 25, 224–50.

Rokeach, M. (1960) *The Open and Closed Mind: Investigations into the Nature of Belief Systems and Personality Systems*. New York: Basic Books.

Rokeach, M. (1973) *The Nature of Human Values*. New York: Free Press.

Rolfe, A., Dalton, S., Krishnan, M. et al. (2006) Alcohol, gender, aggression and violence: Findings from the Birmingham Untreated Heavy Drinkers Project. *Journal of Substance Use*, 11, 343–58.

Rollie, S.S. and Duck, S. (2006) Divorce and dissolution of romantic relationships: Stage models and their limitations. In M. Fine and J. Harvey (eds) *Handbook of Divorce and Dissolution of Romantic Relationships* (pp. 176–93). Mahwah, NJ: Lawrence Erlbaum.

Romero-Sánchez, M., Durán, M., Carretero-Dios, H. et al. (2010) Exposure to sexist humor and rape proclivity: The moderator effect of aversiveness ratings. *Journal of Interpersonal Violence*, 25, 2339–50.

Rose, J.D. (2011) Diverse perspectives on the groupthink theory: A literary review. *Emerging Leadership Journeys*, 4, 37–57.

Rosenbaum, M.E. (1986) Comment on a proposed two-stage theory of relationship formation: First, repulsion, then attraction. *Journal of Personality and Social Psychology*, 51, 1171–72.

Rosenberg, M.J. (1968) *The Logic of Survey Analysis.* New York: Basic Books.

Rosenberg, M.J. (1969) The conditions and consequences of evaluation apprehension. In R. Rosenthal and R.L. Rosnow (eds) *Artifact in Behavioral Research* (pp. 280–349). New York: Academic Press.

Rosenthal, R. (1979) The 'file drawer problem' and the tolerance for null results. *Psychological Bulletin*, 86, 638–41.

Rosenthal, R. and DePaulo, B.M. (1979) Sex differences in eavesdropping on nonverbal cues. *Journal of Personality and Social Psychology*, 37, 273–85.

Rosenthal, R., Hall, J.A., DiMatteo, M.R. et al. (1979) *Sensitivity to Nonverbal Communication: The PONS Test.* Baltimore, MD: Johns Hopkins University Press.

Rosip, J.C. and Hall, J.A. (2004) Knowledge of nonverbal cues, gender, and nonverbal decoding accuracy. *Journal of Nonverbal Behavior*, 28, 267–86.

Roskos-Ewoldsen, D.R., Roskos-Ewoldsen, B. and Carpentier, F.R.D. (2002) Media priming: A synthesis. In J. Bryant and D. Zillman (eds) *Media Effects: Advances in Theory and Research* (pp. 97–120). Mahwah, NJ: Erlbaum.

Ross, D.F., Read, J.D. and Toglia, M.P. (eds) (1994) *Adult Eyewitness Testimony: Current Trends and Developments.* Cambridge: Cambridge University Press.

Ross, L. and Ward, A. (1995) Psychological barriers to dispute resolution. *Advances in Experimental Social Psychology*, 27, 255–304.

Ross, L. and Ward, A. (1996) Naïve realism in everyday life: Implications for social conflict and misunderstanding. In T. Brown, E. S. Reed and E. Turiel (eds) *Values and Knowledge* (pp. 103–35). Hillsdale, NJ: Erlbaum.

Ross, L., Greene, D. and House, P. (1977) The 'false consensus effect': An egocentric bias in social perception and attribution processes. *Journal of Experimental Social Psychology*, 13, 279–301.

Ross, L., Lepper, M. and Ward, A. (2010) History of social psychology: Insights, challenges, and contributions to theory and application. In S.T. Fiske, D.T. Gilbert and G. Lindzey (eds) *Handbook of Social Psychology* (5th edn, vol. 1, pp. 3–50). Hoboken, NJ: Wiley.

Ross, M. and Sicoly, F. (1979) Egocentric biases in availability and attribution. *Journal of Personality and Social Psychology*, 37, 322–36.

Roter, D.L. and Hall, J.A. (1992) *Doctors Talking to Patients/Patients Talking to Doctors: Improving Communication in Medical Visits.* Westport, CT: Auburn House.

Rothbart, M. (1981) Memory processes and social beliefs. In D.L. Hamilton (ed.) *Cognitive Processes in Stereotyping and Intergroup Behavior* (pp. 73–122). New York: Random House.

Rothman, S., Lichter, S.R. and Nevitte, N. (2005) Politics and professional advancement among college faculty. *The Forum*, available at http://www.cwu.edu/~manwellerm/academic%20bias.pdf.

Rousseau, J.J. ([1762]1998) *The Social Contract.* Ware: Wordsworth.

Rovio, E., Eskola, J., Kozub, S.A. et al. (2009) Can high cohesion be harmful? A case study of a junior ice-hockey team. *Small Group Research*, 40, 421–35.

Rowatt, W.C., Cunningham, M.R. and Druen, P.B. (1999) Lying to get a date: The effect of facial physical attractiveness on the willingness to deceive prospective dating partners. *Journal of Social and Personal Relationships*, 16, 209–23.

Rozin, P. (2010) The weirdest people in the world are a harbinger of the future of the world. *Behavioral and Brain Sciences*, 33, 108–9.

Rozin, P. and Millman, L. (1987) Family environment, not heredity, accounts for family resemblances in food preferences and attitudes: A twin study. *Appetite*, 8, 125–34.

Rozin, P. and Nemeroff, C. (1990) A psychological analysis of similarity and contagion. In J.W. Stigler, R.A. Schweder and G. Herdt (eds) *Cultural Psychology: Essays on Comparative Human Development* (pp. 205–32). Cambridge: Cambridge University Press.

Rozin, P. and Royzman, E.B. (2001) Negativity bias, negativity dominance, and contagion. *Personality and Social Psychology Review*, 5, 296–300.

Rozin, P., Lowery, L., Imada, S. and Haidt, J. (1999) The CAD triad hypothesis: A mapping between three moral emotions (contempt, anger, disgust) and three moral codes (community, autonomy, divinity). *Journal of Personality and Social Psychology*, 76, 574–86.

Rozin, P., Millman, L. and Nemeroff, C. (1986) Operation of the laws of sympathetic magic in disgust and other domains. *Journal of Personality and Social Psychology*, 50, 703–12.

Rubin, J.Z. and Brown, B.R. (1975) *The Social Psychology of Bargaining and Negotiation.* New York: Academic Press.

Rubin, Z. (1970) Measurement of romantic love. *Journal of Personality and Social Psychology*, 16, 265–73.

Rubini, M. and Menegatti, M. (2008) Linguistic bias in personnel selection. *Journal of Language and Social Psychology*, 27, 168–81.

Rucker, D.D., Polifroni, M., Tetlock, P.E. and Scott, A.L. (2004) On the assignment of punishment: The impact of general-societal threat and the moderating role of severity. *Personality and Social Psychology Bulletin*, 30, 673–84.

Rudman, L.A. and Fairchild, K. (2004) Reactions to counterstereotypic behavior: The role of backlash in cultural stereotype maintenance. *Journal of Personality and Social Psychology*, 87, 157–76.

Rudman, L.A. and Glick, P. (2001) Prescriptive gender stereotypes and backlash toward agentic women. *Journal of Social Issues*, 57, 743–62.

Rudman, L.A. and Kilianski, S.E. (2000) Implicit and explicit attitudes toward female authority. *Personality and Social Psychology Bulletin*, 26, 1315–28.

Rule, N.O. and Ambady, N. (2008) Brief exposures: Male sexual orientation is accurately perceived at 50ms. *Journal of Experimental Social Psychology*, 44, 1100–5.

Runciman, W.G. (1966) *Relative Deprivation and Social Justice: A Study of Attitudes to Social Inequality in Twentieth-century England.* London: Routledge.

Rusbult, C.E. (1983) A longitudinal test of the investment model: The development (and deterioration) of satisfaction and commitment in heterosexual involvements. *Journal of Personality and Social Psychology*, 45, 101–17.

Rusbult, C.E. and Buunk, B.P. (1993) Commitment processes in close relationships: An interdependence analysis. *Journal of Social and Personal Relationships*, 10, 175–204.

Rusbult, C.E. and van Lange, P.A.M. (2003) Interdependence, interaction, and relationships. *Annual Review of Psychology*, 54, 351–75.

Rusbult, C.E. and Zembrodt, I.M. (1983) Responses to dissatisfaction in romantic involvements: A multidimensional scaling analysis. *Journal of Experimental Social Psychology*, 19, 274–2.

Rusbult, C.E., Johnson, D.J. and Morrow, G.D. (1986) Determinants and consequences of exit, voice, loyalty, and neglect: Responses to dissatisfaction in adult romantic involvements. *Human Relations*, 39, 45–63.

Rusbult, C.E., Martz, J.M. and Agnew, C.R. (1998) The investment model scale: Measuring commitment level, satisfaction level, quality of alternatives, and investment size. *Personal Relationships*, 5, 357–87.

Rusbult, C.E., Morrow, G.D. and Johnson, D.J. (1987) Self-esteem and problem-solving behaviour in close relationships. *British Journal of Social Psychology*, 26, 293–303.

Rusbult, C.E., Olsen, N., Davis, J.L. et al. (2001) Commitment and relationship maintenance mechanisms. In J.H. Harvey and A. Wenzel (eds) *Close Romantic Relationships: Maintenance and Enhancement* (pp. 87–113). Mahwah, NJ: Erlbaum.

Ruscher, J.B. (1998) Prejudice and stereotyping in everyday communication. *Advances in Experimental Social Psychology*, 30, 241–307.

Rushton, J.P. (1980) *Altruism, Socialization, and Society*. Englewood Cliffs, NJ: Prentice Hall.

Rushton, J.P., Chrisjohn, R.D. and Fekken, G.C. (1981) The altruistic personality and the self-report altruism scale. *Personality and Individual Differences*, 2, 293–302.

Russell, G.W. (2008) *Aggression in the Sports World: A Social Psychological Perspective*. New York: Oxford University Press.

Russell, J.A. (1994) Is there a universal recognition of emotion from facial expressions? A review of the cross-cultural studies. *Psychological Bulletin*, 115, 102–41.

Russell, J.A., Bachorowski, J.A. and Fernandez-Dols, J.M. (2003) Facial and vocal expressions of emotion. *Annual Review of Psychology*, 54, 329–49.

Russell, R.L., Stokes, J.M., Jones, M.E. et al. (1993) The role of nonverbal sensitivity in children's psychopathology. *Journal of Nonverbal Behavior*, 17, 69–83.

Rutherford, T. (2012) *Population Ageing: Statistics*. House of Commons, SN/SG/3228.

Rutkowski, G.K., Gruder, C.L. and Romer, D. (1983) Group cohesiveness, social norms, and bystander intervention. *Journal of Personality and Social Psychology*, 44, 542–52.

Ryan, E.B., Giles, H. and Sebastian, R.J. (1982) An integrative perspective for the study of attitudes toward language variation. In E.B. Ryan and H. Giles (eds) *Attitudes Towards Language Variation* (pp. 1–19). London: Edward Arnold.

Ryan, J. (2007) The four P-words of militant Islamist radicalization and recruitment: Persecution, precedent, piety, and perseverance. *Studies in Conflict & Terrorism*, 30, 985–1011.

Ryan, L. (1996) *The Aboriginal Tasmanians*. Sydney: Allen & Unwin.

Ryan, M.K. and Haslam, S.A. (2005) The glass cliff: Evidence that women are over-represented in precarious leadership positions. *British Journal of Management*, 16, 81–90.

Ryan, M.K. and Haslam, S.A. (2007) The glass cliff: Exploring the dynamics surrounding the appointment of women precarious leadership positions. *Academy of Management Review*, 32, 549–72.

Rydell, R.J., McConnell, A.R. and Mackie, D.M. (2008) Consequences of discrepant explicit and implicit attitudes: Cognitive dissonance and increased information processing. *Journal of Experimental Social Psychology*, 44, 1526–32.

Rydell, R.J., Mackie, D.M., Maitner, A.T. et al. (2008) Arousal, processing, and risk taking: Consequences of intergroup anger. *Personality and Social Psychology Bulletin*, 34, 1141–52.

Ryle, G. (1949) *The Concept of Mind*. Harmondsworth: Penguin.

Sá, W.C., West, R.F. and Stanovich, K.E. (1999) The domain specificity and generality of belief bias: Searching for a generalizable critical thinking skill. *Journal of Educational Psychology*, 91, 497–510.

Sachs, C.J. and Chu, L.D. (2000) The association between professional football games and domestic violence in Los Angeles County. *Journal of Interpersonal Violence*, 15, 1192–201.

Sacks, H., Schegloff, E.A. and Jefferson, G. (1974) The simplest systematic for the organization of turn-taking for conversation. *Language*, 50, 696–735.

Sadler, P. and Woody, E. (2003) Is who you are who you're talking to? Interpersonal style and complementarily in mixed-sex interactions. *Journal of Personality and Social Psychology*, 84, 80.

Sagarin, B.J., Cialdini, R.B., Rice, W.E. and Serna, S.B. (2002) Dispelling the illusion of invulnerability: The motivations and mechanisms of resistance to persuasion. *Journal of Personality and Social Psychology*, 83, 526–41.

Saguy, T., Tausch, N., Dovidio, J.F. and Pratto, F. (2009) The irony of harmony: Intergroup contact can produce false expectations for equality. *Psychological Science*, 20, 114–21.

Saks, M.J. (1978) Social psychological contributions to a legislative subcommittee on organ and tissue transplants. *American Psychologist*, 33, 680–90.

Salmivalli, C., Kaukiainen, A. and Voeten, M. (2005) Anti-bullying intervention: Implementation and outcome. *British Journal of Educational Psychology*, 75, 465–87.

Saltzstein, H.D. and Sandberg, L. (1979) Indirect social influence: Change in judgemental process or anticipatory conformity? *Journal of Experimental Social Psychology*, 15, 209–16.

Samuelson, C.D. and Allison, S.T. (1994) Cognitive factors affecting the use of social decision heuristics in resource-sharing tasks. *Organizational Behavior and Human Decision Processes*, 58, 1–27.

Sanders, G.S. (1981) Driven by distraction: An integrative review of social facilitation theory and research. *Journal of Experimental Social Psychology*, 17, 227–51.

Sanders, G.S., Baron, R.S. and Moore, D.L. (1978) Distraction and social comparison as mediators of social facilitation effects. *Journal of Experimental Social Psychology*, 14, 291–303.

Sandler, W., Meir, I., Padden, C. and Aronoff, M. (2005) The emergence of grammar: Systematic structure in a new language. *Proceedings of the National Academy of Sciences of the United States of America*, 102, 2661–5.

Sani, F. and Reicher, S. (1998) When consensus fails: An analysis of the schism within the Italian Communist Party (1991). *European Journal of Social Psychology*, 28, 623–45.

Sani, F. and Reicher, S. (1999) Identity, argument and schism: Two longitudinal studies of the split in the Church of England over the ordination of women to the priesthood. *Group Processes & Intergroup Relations*, 2, 279–300.

Sani, F. and Reicher, S. (2000) Contested identities and schisms in groups: Opposing the ordination of women as priests in the Church of England. *British Journal of Social Psychology*, 39, 95–112.

Sanna, L.J. (1992) Self-efficacy theory: Implications for social facilitation and social loafing. *Journal of Personality and Social Psychology*, 62, 774–86.

Sassenberg, K. (2002) Common bond and common identity groups on the Internet: Attachment and normative behavior in on-topic and off-topic chats. *Group Dynamics*, 6, 27–37.

Sassenberg, K. and Boos, M. (2003) Attitude change in computer-mediated communication: Effects of anonymity and category norms. *Group Processes and Intergroup Relations*, 6, 405–23.

Sassenberg, K. and Jonas, K.J. (2007) Attitude change and social influence on the net. In A.N. Joinson, K. McKenna, T. Postmes and U.-D. Reips (eds) *The Oxford Handbook of Internet Psychology* (pp. 273–89). Oxford: Oxford University Press.

Saucier, G. (2000) Isms and the structure of social attitudes. *Journal of Personality and Social Psychology*, 78, 366–85.

Saygin, A.P., Cicekli, I. and Akman, V. (2000) Turing test: 50 years later. *Minds and Machines*, 463–518.

Schachter, S. (1959) *The Psychology of Affiliation: Experimental Studies of the Sources of Gregariousness*. Stanford, CA: Stanford University Press.

Schafer, R.B. and Keith, P.M. (1980) Equity

and depression among married couples. *Social Psychology Quarterly*, 43, 430–5.

Schaller, M. and Crandall, C.S. (2004) *The Psychological Foundations of Culture.* Mahwah, NJ: Erlbaum.

Schaller, M., Boyd, C., Yohannes, J. and O'Brien, M. (1995) The prejudiced personality revisited: Personal need for structure and formation of erroneous group stereotypes. *Journal of Personality and Social Psychology*, 68, 544–55.

Schegloff, E.A. (2007) *Sequence Organization in Interaction: A Primer in Conversation Analysis*, vol. 1. Cambridge: Cambridge University Press.

Scheier, M.F. and Carver, C.S. (1977) Self-focused attention and the experience of emotion: Attraction, repulsion, elation, and depression. *Journal of Personality and Social Psychology*, 35, 625–36.

Scheier, M.F. and Carver, C.S. (1980) Private and public self-attention, resistance to change, and dissonance reduction. *Journal of Personality and Social Psychology*, 39, 390–405.

Scheier, M.F. and Carver, C.S. (1981) Private and public aspects of the self. In L. Wheeler (ed.) *Review of Personality and Social Psychology* (vol. 2, pp. 189–216). Beverly Hills, CA: Sage.

Scherer, K.R. (1979) Non-linguistic indicators of emotion and psychopathology. In C.E. Izard (ed.) *Emotions in Personality and Psychopathology* (pp. 495–529). New York: Plenum Press.

Scherer, K.R. and Giles, H. (eds) (1979) *Social Markers in Speech.* Cambridge: Cambridge University Press.

Schlenker, B.R. (1980) *Impression Management: The Self Concept, Social Identity, and Interpersonal Relations.* Monterey, CA: Brooks/Cole.

Schlenker, B.R. and Forsyth, D.R. (1977) On the ethics of psychological research. *Journal of Experimental Social Psychology*, 13, 369–96.

Schlenker, B.R., Dlugolecki, D.W. and Doherty, K.J. (1994) The impact of self-presentations on self-appraisals and behaviors: The power of public commitment. *Personality and Social Psychology Bulletin*, 20, 20–33.

Schmeichel, B.J., Gailliot, M.T., Filardo, E. et al. (2009) Terror management theory and self-esteem revisited: The roles of implicit and explicit self-esteem in mortality salience effects. *Journal of Personality and Social Psychology*, 96, 77–1087.

Schmid, J. and Fiedler, K. (1996) Language and implicit attributions in the Nuremberg trials analyzing prosecutors' and defense attorneys' closing speeches. *Human Communication Research*, 22, 371–98.

Schmid, J. and Fiedler, K. (1998) The backbone of closing speeches: The impact of prosecution versus defense language on judicial attributions. *Journal of Applied Social Psychology*, 28, 1140–72.

Schmitt, B.H., Gilovich, T., Goore, N. and Joseph, L. (1986) Mere presence and social facilitation: One more time. *Journal of Experimental Social Psychology*, 22, 242–8.

Schmitt, D.P., Alcalay, L. Alik, J. et al. (2003) Universal sex differences in the desire for sexual variety: Tests from 52 nations, 6 continents, and 13 islands. *Journal of Personality and Social Psychology*, 85, 85–104.

Schnall, S., Haidt, J., Clore, G.L. and Jordan, A.H. (2008) Disgust as embodied moral judgment. *Personality and Social Psychology Bulletin*, 34, 1096–109.

Schneider, D.J., Hastorf, A.H. and Ellsworth, P.C. (1979) *Person Perception.* Reading, MA: Addison-Wesley.

Schoemann, A.M. and Branscombe, N.R. (2011) Looking young for your age: Perceptions of anti-aging actions. *European Journal of Social Psychology*, 41, 86–95.

Schofield, J.W. and Eurich-Fulcer, R. (2001) When and how school desegregation improves intergroup relations. In R. Brown and S.L. Gaertner (eds) *Blackwell Handbook of Social Psychology: Intergroup Processes* (pp. 475–94). Malden, MA: Blackwell.

Schofield, T.J., Parke, R.D., Castañeda, E.K. and Coltrane, S. (2008) Patterns of gaze between parents and children in European American and Mexican American families. *Journal of Nonverbal Behavior*, 32, 171–86.

Schopler, J. and Insko, C.A. (1999) The reduction of the inter-individual-intergroup discontinuity effect: The role of future consequences. In M. Foddy (ed.) *Resolving Social Dilemmas: Dynamic, Structural, and Intergroup Aspects* (pp. 281–94). New York: Psychology Press.

Schroeder, D.A., Dovidio, J.F., Sibicky, M.E. et al. (1988) Empathic concern and helping behavior: Egoism or altruism? *Journal of Experimental Social Psychology*, 24, 333–53.

Schroeder, D.A., Penner, L.A., Dovidio, J.F. and Piliavin, J.A. (1995) *The Psychology of Helping and Altruism: Problems and Puzzles.* New York: McGraw-Hill.

Schubert, T.W. (2004) The power in your hand: Gender differences in bodily feedback from making a fist. *Personality and Social Psychology Bulletin*, 30, 757–69.

Schubert, T.W. and Semin, G.R. (2009) Embodiment as a unifying perspective for psychology. *European Journal of Social Psychology*, 39, 1135–41.

Schwartz, S.H. (1992) Universals in the content and structure of values: Theoretical advances and empirical tests in 20 countries. *Advances in Experimental Social Psychology*, 25, 1–65.

Schwartz, S.H. (1994) Are there universal aspects in the content and structure of values? *Journal of Social Issues*, 50, 19–45.

Schwartz, S.H. (2011) Studying values: Personal adventure, future directions. *Journal of Cross-Cultural Psychology*, 42, 307–19.

Schwarz, N. (1998) Accessible content and accessibility experiences: The interplay of declarative and experiential information in judgement. *Personality and Social Psychology Review*, 2, 87–99.

Schwarz, N. and Brand, J.F. (1983) Effects of salience of rape on sex role attitudes, trust, and self-esteem in non-raped women. *European Journal of Social Psychology*, 13, 71–6.

Schwarz, N. and Clore, G.L. (1983) Mood, misattribution, and judgments of well-being: Informative and directive functions of affective states. *Journal of Personality and Social Psychology*, 45, 513–23.

Schwarz, N., Bless, H. and Bohner, G. (1991) Mood and persuasion: Affective states influence the processing of persuasive communications. *Advances in Experimental Social Psychology*, 24, 161–99.

Schwarz, N., Bless, H., Strack, F. et al. (1991) Ease of retrieval as information: Another look at the availability heuristic. *Journal of Personality and Social Psychology*, 61, 195–202.

Schwarz, N., Groves, R.M. and Schuman, H. (1998) Survey methods. In D.T. Gilbert, S.T. Fiske and G. Lindzey (eds) *The Handbook of Social Psychology* (vol. 1, pp. 143–79). New York: McGraw-Hill.

Schwarz, N., Knauper, B., Hippler, H.J. et al. (1991) Rating scales: Numeric values may change the meaning of scale labels. *Public Opinion Quarterly*, 55, 570–82.

Schwarz, N., Strack, F. and Mai, H.P. (1991) Assimilation and contrast effects in part-whole question sequences: A conversational-logic analysis. *Public Opinion Quarterly*, 55, 3–23.

Schwarz, N., Strack, F., Hilton, D.J. and Naderer, G. (1991) Base-rates, representativeness, and the logic of conversation. *Social Cognition*, 9, 67–84.

Schwarz, S. (1992) Universals in the content and structure of values: Theoretical advances and empirical tests in 20 countries. *Advances in Experimental Social Psychology*, 25, 1–66.

Schwarz, S. and Hassebrauck, M. (2008) Self-perceived and observed variations in women's attractiveness throughout the menstrual cycle – a diary study. *Evolution and Human Behavior*, 29, 282–8.

Schwarzer, R., Bowler, R. and Rauch, S. (1985) Psychological indicators of acculturation: Self-esteem, racial tension and inter-ethnic contact. In L. Ekstrand (ed.) *Ethnic Minorities and Immigrants in a*

Cross-cultural Perspective (pp. 211–29). Lisse: Swets & Zeitlinger.

Schwarzwald, J., Koslowsky, M. and Shalit, B. (1992) A field study of employees' attitudes and behaviors after promotion decisions. *Journal of Applied Psychology*, 77, 511–14.

Scott, W. (1883) *The Works of John Dryden*. Edinburgh: William Paterson.

Searle, J.R. (1975) Indirect speech acts. *Syntax and Semantics*, 3, 59–82.

Sears, D.O. (1986) College sophomores in the laboratory: Influences of a narrow data base on social psychology's view of human nature. *Journal of Personality and Social Psychology*, 51, 515–30.

Sedikides, C. (1993) Assessment, enhancement and verification determinants of the self-evaluation process. *Journal of Personality and Social Psychology*, 65, 317–38.

Sedikides, C. and Gregg, A.P. (2003) Portraits of the self. In M.A. Hogg and J. Cooper (eds) *Sage Handbook of Social Psychology* (pp. 110–38). London: Sage

Sedikides, C. and Ostrom, T.M. (1988) Are person categories used when organizing information about unfamiliar sets of persons? *Social Cognition*, 6, 252–67.

Sedikides, C., Rudich, E.A., Gregg, A.P. et al. (2004) Are normal narcissists psychologically healthy? Self-esteem matters. *Journal of Personality and Social Psychology*, 87, 400–16.

Seligman, M.E.P. (2002) *Authentic Happiness*. New York: Free Press.

Seligman, M.E.P. and Csikszentmihalyi, M. (2000) Positive psychology: An introduction. *American Psychologist*, 55, 5–14.

Seligman, M.E.P., Steen, T.A., Park, N. and Peterson, C. (2005) Positive psychology progress: Empirical validation of interventions. *American Psychologist*, 60, 410–21.

Semin, G.R. (2000) Agenda 2000 – communication: Language as an implementational device for cognition. *European Journal of Social Psychology*, 30, 595–612.

Semin, G.R. and Fiedler, K. (1988) The cognitive functions of linguistic categories in describing persons: Social cognition and language. *Journal of Personality and Social Psychology*, 54, 558–68.

Semmler, C. and Brewer, N. (2002) Effects of mood and emotion on juror processing and judgements. *Behavioral Sciences and the Law*, 20, 423–36.

Senghas, A. and Coppola, M. (2001) Children creating language: How Nicaraguan sign language acquired a spatial grammar. *Psychological Science*, 12, 323–8.

Seta, J.J. (1982) The impact of comparison processes on coactors' task performance. *Journal of Personality and Social Psychology*, 42, 281–91.

Shackelford, T.K. and Larsen, R.J. (1997) Facial asymmetry as an indicator of psychological, emotional, and physiological distress. *Journal of Personality and Social Psychology*, 72, 456–66.

Shah, J., Higgins, E.T. and Friedman, R.S. (1998) Performance incentives and means: How regulatory focus influences goal attainment. *Journal of Personality and Social Psychology*, 74, 285–93.

Shapiro, D.A. and Firth, J.A. (1987) Prescriptive vs. exploratory psychotherapy: Outcomes of the Sheffield Psychotherapy Project. *British Journal of Psychiatry*, 151, 790–9.

Shapiro, J.P., Baumeister, R.F. and Kessler, J.W. (1991) A three component model of children's teasing: Aggression, humor, and ambiguity. *Journal of Social and Clinical Psychology*, 10, 459–72.

Sharot, T., Velasuez, C.M. and Dolan, R.J. (2010) Do decisions shape preference? Evidence from blind choice. *Psychological Science*, 21, 1231–5.

Shaver, P.R. and Hazan, C. (1993) Adult romantic attachment: Theory and evidence. *Advances in Personal Relationships*, 4, 29–70.

Shavitt, S., Torelli, C.J. and Riemer, H. (2010) Horizontal and vertical individualism and collectivism: Implications for understanding psychological processes. In M.J.Gelfand, C.Y. Chiu and Y.Y. Hong (eds) *Advances in Culture and Psychology* (vol. 1, pp. 309–250). Oxford: Oxford University Press.

Shaw, G.B. ([1916]1951) *Pygmalion*. New York: Brentano.

Shaw, M.E., Rothschild, G.H. and Strickland, J.F. (1957) Decision processes in communication nets. *The Journal of Abnormal and Social Psychology*, 54, 323.

Sheeran, P. (2002) Intention–behavior relations: A conceptual and empirical review. *European Review of Social Psychology*, 12, 1–36.

Sheeran, P. and Orbell, S. (2000) Using implementation intentions to increase attendance for cervical cancer screening. *Health Psychology*, 19, 283–9.

Sheeran, P. and Taylor, S. (1999) Predicting intentions to use condoms: A meta-analysis and comparison of the theories of reasoned action and planned behavior. *Journal of Applied Social Psychology*, 29, 1624–75.

Sheldon, K.M. (1999) Learning the lessons of tit-for-tat: Even competitors can get the message. *Journal of Personality and Social Psychology*, 77, 1245–53.

Shell, R.M. and Eisenberg, N. (1992) A developmental model of recipients' reactions to aid. *Psychological Bulletin*, 111, 413–33.

Shelton, J.N. (2003) Interpersonal concerns in social encounters between majority and minority group members. *Group Processes and Intergroup Relations*, 6, 171–85.

Shepperd, J.A. and Taylor, K.M. (1999) Social loafing and expectancy-value theory. *Personality and Social Psychology Bulletin*, 25, 1147–58.

Sherif, M. (1935) A study of some social factors in perception. *Archives of Psychology*, 27, 1–60.

Sherif, M. (1936) *The Psychology of Social Norms*. New York: Harper Collins.

Sherif, M. (1937) An experimental approach to the study of attitudes. *Sociometry*, 1, 90–8.

Sherif, M. (1966) *Group Conflict and Cooperation*. London: Routledge & Kegan Paul.

Sherif, M. and Sherif, C.W. (1953) *Groups in Harmony and Tension*. New York: Harper.

Sherif, M. and Sherif, C.W. (1969) *Social Psychology*. New York: Harper & Row.

Sherif, M., Harvey, O.J., White, B.J. et al. ([1954]1961) *Intergroup Conflict and Cooperation: The Robbers Cave Experiment*. Norman, OK: University of Oklahoma Book Exchange.

Sherman, D.A.K., Nelson, L.D. and Steele, C.M. (2000) Do messages about health risks threaten the self? increasing the acceptance of threatening health messages via self-affirmation. *Personality and Social Psychology Bulletin*, 26, 1046–58.

Sherman, G.D. and Clore, G.L. (2009) The color of sin: White and black are perceptual symbols of moral purity and pollution. *Psychological Science*, 20, 1019–25.

Sherman, J.W., Kruschke, J.K., Sherman, S.J. et al. (2009) Attentional processes in stereotype formation: A common model for category accentuation and illusory correlation. *Journal of Personality and Social Psychology*, 96, 305–23.

Shevlin, M., Walker, S., Davies, M.N. et al. (2003) Can you judge a book by its cover? Evidence of self-stranger agreement on personality at zero-acquaintance. *Personality and Individual Differences*, 35, 1373–83.

Shibutani, T. (1961) *Society and Personality*. Englewood Cliffs, NJ: Prentice Hall.

Shin, G.W., Freda, J. and Yi, G. (1999) The politics of ethnic nationalism in divided Korea. *Nations and Nationalism*, 5, 465–84.

Shohat, M. and Musch, J. (2003) Online auctions as a research tool: A field experiment on ethnic discrimination. *Swiss Journal of Psychology*, 62, 139–45.

Shotter, J. (1984) *Social Accountability and Selfhood*. Oxford: Blackwell.

Sia, C.L., Tan, B.C.Y. and Wei, K.K. (2002) Group polarization and computer-mediated communication: Effects of communication cues, social presence, and anonymity. *Information Systems Research*, 13, 70–90.

Sibley, C.G., Liu, J.H., Duckitt, J. and Khan, S.S. (2008) Social representations of history and the legitimation of social inequality: The form and function of historical negation. *European Journal of Social Psychology*, 38, 542–65.

Sidanius, J. and Pratto, F. (1999) *Social Dominance: An Intergroup Theory of Social Hierarchy and Oppression*. New York: Cambridge University Press.

Sidanius, J., Pratto, F. and Bobo, L. (1994) Social dominance orientation and the political psychology of gender: A case of invariance? *Journal of Personality and Social Psychology*, 67, 998–1011.

Sidanius, J., Pratto, F. and Levin, S. (2006) Social dominance theory and the dynamic of inter group relations: Taking stock and looking forward. *European Review of Social Psychology*, 17, 271–320.

Siegel, A. and Siegel, S. (1957) Reference groups, membership groups, and attitude change. *Journal of Abnormal and Social Psychology*, 55, 360–4.

Siegel, A.E. (1956) Film-mediated fantasy aggression and strength of aggressive drive. *Child Development*, 27, 365–78.

Siegel, J., Dubrovsky, V., Kiesler, S. and McGuire, T.W. (1986) Group processes in computer-mediated communication. *Organizational Behavior and Human Decision Processes*, 37, 157–87.

Silver, R.L., Wortman, C.B. and Klos, D.S. (1982) Cognitions, affect, and behavior following uncontrollable outcomes: A response to current human helplessness research. *Journal of Personality*, 50, 480–514.

Simpson, J.A. (1987) The dissolution of romantic relationships: Factors involved in relationship stability and emotional distress. *Journal of Personality and Social Psychology*, 53, 683–92.

Simpson, J.A. (2009) Editorial. *Journal of Personality and Social Psychology*, 96, 60.

Singer, J.E., Brush, C.A. and Lublin, S.C. (1965) Some aspects of deindividuation: Identification and conformity. *Journal of Experimental Social Psychology*, 1, 356–78.

Singh, D. (1993) Adaptive significance of female physical attractiveness: Role of waist-to-hip ratio. *Journal of Personality and Social Psychology*, 65, 293–307.

Singh, D. and Young, R.K. (1995) Body weight, waist-to-hip ratio, breasts, and hips: Role in judgements of female attractiveness and desirability for relationships. *Ethology and Sociobiology*, 16, 483–507.

Singh, R. and Ho, S.Y. (2000) Attitudes and attraction: A new test of the attraction, repulsion and similarity-dissimilarity asymmetry hypotheses. *British Journal of Social Psychology*, 39, 197–211.

Singh, R. and Simons, J.J. (2010) Attitudes and attraction: Optimism and weight as explanations for the similarity-dissimilarity asymmetry. *Social and Personality Psychology Compass*, 12, 1206–19.

Sinha, D. (1984) Psychology in the context of third world development. *International Journal of Psychology*, 19, 17–29.

Sinha, D. (1997) Current status of applied psychology in India. In Q. Hasan (ed.) *Applied Psychology: Indian Perspective* (pp. 35–46). New Delhi: Gyan.

Sinha, J.B.P. (1984) Towards partnership for relevant research in the third world. *International Journal of Psychology*, 19, 169–77.

Sipes, R.G. (1973) Sports and aggression: An empirical test of two rival theories. *American Anthropologist*, 75, 64–86.

Sistrunk, F. and McDavid, J.W. (1971) Sex variable in conforming behavior. *Journal of Personality and Social Psychology*, 17, 200.

Sivacek, J. and Crano, W.D. (1982) Vested interest as a moderator of attitude-behaviour consistency. *Journal of Personality and Social Psychology*, 43, 210–21.

Sivarajasingam, V., Moore, S.C. and Shepherd, J.O. (2005) Winning, losing, and violence. *Injury Prevention*, 11, 69–70.

Skinner, B.F. (1938) *The Behavior of Organisms: An Experimental Analysis*. Oxford: Appleton-Century.

Skipper, Y. and Douglas, K. (2011) Is no praise good praise? Effects of positive feedback on children's and university students' responses to subsequent failures. *British Journal of Educational Psychology*, 82, 327–39.

Skitka, L.J. and Sargis, E.G. (2005) Social psychological research and the Internet: The promise and peril of a new methodological frontier. In Y. Amichai-Hamburger (ed.) *The Social Net: The Social Psychology of the Internet* (pp. 1–29). Oxford: Oxford University Press.

Skitka, L.J. and Tetlock, P.E. (1993) Providing public assistance: Cognitive and motivational processes underlying liberal and conservative policy preferences. *Journal of Personality and Social Psychology*, 65, 1205–23.

Skowronski, J.J. and Carlston, D.E. (1989) Negativity and extremity biases in impression formation: A review of explanations. *Psychological Bulletin*, 105, 131–42.

Skowronski, J.J., Carlston, D.E., Mae, L. and Crawford, M.T. (1998) Spontaneous trait transference: Communicators take on the qualities they describe in others. *Journal of Personality and Social Psychology*, 87, 482–93.

Slater, M., Antley, A., Davison, A. et al. (2006) A virtual reprise of the Stanley Milgram obedience experiments. *PLOS One*, 1, e39.

Slotter, E.B., Gardner, W.L. and Finkel, E.J. (2010) Who am I without you? The influence of romantic breakup on the self-concept. *Personality and Social Psychology Bulletin*, 36, 147–60.

Slovic, P. and Fischhoff, B. (1977) On the psychology of experimental surprises. *Journal of Experimental Psychology: Human Perception and Performance*, 3, 544–51.

Slugoski, B.R. and Turnbull, W. (1988) Cruel to be kind and kind to be cruel: Sarcasm, banter and social relations. *Journal of Language and Social Psychology*, 7, 101–21.

Slugoski, B.R. and Wilson, A.E. (1998) Contribution of conversational skills to the production of judgmental errors. *European Journal of Social Psychology*, 28, 575–601.

Smith, A. ([1759]2007) *The Theory of Moral Sentiments*. New York: Cosimo Classics.

Smith, A. and Williams, K.D. (2004) R U there? Ostracism by cell phone text messages. *Group Dynamics: Theory, Research and Practice*, 8, 291–301.

Smith, D.L., Pruitt, D.G. and Carnevale, P.J. (1982) Matching and mismatching: The effect of own limit, other's toughness, and time pressure on concession rate in negotiation. *Journal of Personality and Social Psychology*, 42, 876–83.

Smith, E.R. (1991) Illusory correlation in a simulated exemplar-based memory. *Journal of Experimental Social Psychology*, 27, 107–23.

Smith, E.R. (1993) Social identity and social emotions: Toward new conceptualizations of prejudice. In D.M. Mackie and D.L. Hamilton (eds) *Affect, Cognition, and Stereotyping: Interactive Processes in Group Perception* (pp. 297–315). San Diego, CA: Academic Press.

Smith, E.R. (1999) Affective and cognitive implications of a group becoming part of the self: New models of prejudice and of the self- concept. In D. Abrams and M.A. Hogg (eds) *Social Identity and Social Cognition* (pp. 183–96). Oxford: Basil Blackwell.

Smith, E.R. and Collins, E.C. (2009) Contextualizing person perception: Distributed social cognition. *Psychological Review*, 116, 343–64.

Smith, H.J. and Tyler, T.R. (1996) Justice and power: When will justice concerns encourage the advantaged to support policies which redistribute economic resources and the disadvantaged to willingly obey the law? *European Journal of Social Psychology*, 26, 171–200.

Smith, J.A. (2011) Evaluating the contribution of interpretative phenomenological analysis. *Health Psychology Review*, 5, 9–27.

Smith, J.A., Flowers, P. and Larkin, M. (2009) *Interpretive Phenomenological*

Analysis: Theory, Method and Research. London: Sage.

Smith, M.B., Bruner, J.S. and White, R.W. (1956) *Opinions and Personality*. New York: Wiley.

Smith, N. and Joffe, H. (in press) How the public engages with global warming: A social representations approach. *Public Understanding of Science*.

Smith, P.B. (2005) Is there an indigenous European social psychology? *International Journal of Psychology*, 40, 254–62.

Smith, P.B., Bond, M.H. and Kağıtçıbaşı, Ç. (2006) *Understanding Social Psychology across Cultures: Living and Working in a Changing World*. London: Sage.

Smith, R.H. and Kim, S.H. (2007) Comprehending envy. *Psychological Bulletin*, 133, 46–64.

Smith, S.M. and Shaffer, D.R. (1991) Celerity and cajolery: Rapid speech may promote or inhibit persuasion through its impact on message elaboration. *Personality and Social Psychology Bulletin*, 17, 663–9.

Smith, T.W. and Greenberg, J. (1981) Depression and self-focused attention. *Motivation and Emotion*, 5, 323–31.

Smith, W.R. and Torstensson, M. (1997) Gender differences in risk perception and neutralizing fear of crime: Toward resolving the paradoxes. *British Journal of Criminology*, 37, 608–29.

Smrt, D.L. and Karau, S.J. (2011) Protestant work ethic moderates social loafing. *Group Dynamics: Theory, Research and Practice*, 15, 267–74.

Snowden, A., White, C.A., Christie, Z. et al. (2011) The clinical utility of the Distress Thermometer: A review. *British Journal of Nursing*, 20, 152–9.

Snowden, A., White, C.A., Christie, Z. et al. (2012) Helping the clinician help me: Towards listening in cancer care. *British Journal of Nursing* (Oncology Supplement), 21, S18–26.

Snyder, C.R. and Fromkin, H.L. (1980) *Uniqueness: The Human Pursuit of Difference*. New York: Plenum.

Snyder, M. (1974) Self-monitoring of expressive behavior. *Journal of Personality and Social Psychology*, 30, 526–37.

Snyder, M. and Ickes, W. (1985) Personality and social behavior. In G. Lindzey and E. Aronson (eds) *Handbook of Social Psychology* (3rd edn, pp. 883–948). Reading, MA: Addison-Wesley.

Snyder, M. and Swann, W.B. (1976) When actions reflect attitudes: The politics of impression management. *Journal of Personality and Social Psychology*, 34, 1034–42.

Snyder, T.D. and Dillow, S.A. (2011) *Digest of Education Statistics 2010*. Washington, DC: National Center for Education Statistics, US Department of Education.

Solomon, S., Greenberg, J. and Pyszczynski, T. (1991) A terror management theory of social behavior: The psychological functions of self-esteem and cultural worldviews. *Advances in Experimental Social Psychology*, 24, 91–159.

Spain, J.S., Eaton, L.G. and Funder, D.C. (2000) Perspectives on personality: The relative accuracy of self versus others for the prediction of emotion behaviour. *Journal of Personality*, 68, 837–67.

Spears, R. and Lea, M. (1994) Panacea or panopticon? The hidden power in computer-mediated communication. *Communication Research*, 21, 427–59.

Spears, R., Ellemers, N. and Doosje, B. (2009) Strength in numbers or less is more? A matter of opinion and a question of taste. *Personality and Social Psychology Bulletin*, 35, 1099–111.

Spears, R., Lea, M. and Lee, S. (1990) De-individuation and group polarization in computer-mediated communication. *British Journal of Social Psychology*, 29, 121–34.

Spears, R., Lea, M. and Postmes, T. (2007) Computer-mediated communication and social identity. In A. Joinson, K. McKenna, T. Postmes and U.-D. Reips (eds) *Oxford Handbook of Internet Psychology* (pp. 253–70). Oxford: Oxford University Press.

Spears, R., Lea, M., Postmes, T. and Wolbert, A. (2011) A SIDE look at computer-mediated interaction. Power and the gender divide. In Z. Birchmeier, B. Dietz-Uhler and G. Stasser (eds) *Strategic Uses of Social Technology* (pp. 16–39). Cambridge: Cambridge University Press.

Spector, P.E. (1986) Perceived control by employees: A meta-analysis of studies concerning autonomy and participation at work. *Human Relations*, 39, 1005–16.

Spencer, S.J., Steele, C.M. and Quinn, D.M. (1999) Stereotype threat and women's math performance. *Journal of Experimental Social Psychology*, 35, 4–28.

Sperber, D. and Wilson, D. (1986) *Relevance: Communication and Cognition*. Cambridge, MA: Harvard University Press.

Spivey, C.B. and Prentice-Dunn, S. (1990) Assessing the directionality of deindividuated behavior: Effects of deindividuation, modeling, and private self-consciousness on aggressive and prosocial responses. *Basic and Applied Social Psychology*, 11, 387–403.

Sporer, S.L., Malpass, R.S. and Koehnken, G. (eds) (1996) *Psychological Issues in Eyewitness Identification*. Hillsdale, NJ: Lawrence Erlbaum.

Sprecher, S. (1987) The effects of self-disclosure given and received on affection for an intimate partner and stability of the relationship. *Journal of Social and Personal Relationships*, 4, 115–27.

Sprecher, S. (1998) Insiders' perspectives on reasons for attraction to a close other. *Social Psychology Quarterly*, 61, 287–300.

Sprecher, S. (1999) 'I love you more today than yesterday': Romantic partners' perceptions of changes in love and related affect over time. *Journal of Personality and Social Psychology*, 76, 46–53.

Sprecher, S. (2001) A comparison of emotional consequences of and changes to equity over time using global and domain-specific measures of equity. *Journal of Social and Personal Relationships*, 18, 477–501.

Sprecher, S., and Fehr, B. (1998) The dissolution of close relationships. In J.H. Harvey (ed.) *Perspectives on Loss: A Sourcebook* (pp. 99–112). Philadelphia, PA: Taylor & Francis.

Sprecher, S. and Schwartz, P. (1994) Equity and balance in the exchange of contributions in close relationships. In M.J. Lerner and G. Mikula (eds) *Entitlement and the Affectional Bond: Justice in Close Relationships* (pp. 11–41). New York: Plenum Press.

Sprecher, S. and Toro-Morn, M. (2002) A study of men and women from different sides of earth to determine if men are from Mars and women are from Venus in their beliefs about love and romantic relationships. *Sex Roles*, 46, 131–47.

Sprecher, S., Zimmerman, C. and Abrahams, E.M. (2010) Choosing compassionate strategies to end a relationship: Effects of compassionate love for a partner and the reason for the breakup. *Social Psychology*, 41, 66–75.

Sproull, L. and Kiesler, S. (1986) Reducing social context cues: Electronic mail in organizational communications. *Management Science*, 32, 1492–512.

Srivastava, S. and Beer, J.S. (2005) How self-evaluations relate to being liked by others: Integrating sociometer and attachment perspectives. *Journal of Personality and Social Psychology*, 89, 966–77.

Srull, T.K. and Wyer, R.S. (1989) Person memory and judgment. *Psychological Review*, 96, 58–83.

Srull, T.K. and Wyer, R.S. Jr (1979) The role of category accessibility in the interpretation of information about persons: Some determinants and implications. *Journal of Personality and Social Psychology*, 37, 1660–7.

St Claire, L. and Turner, J.C. (1982) The role of demand characteristics in the social categorization paradigm. *European Journal of Social Psychology*, 12, 307–14.

Stainton Rogers, W. (2011) *Social Psychology*. Milton Keynes: Open University Press.

Stambush, M.A. and Mattingly, B.A. (2010) When being liked makes us dislike ourselves: Self-rated attractiveness as influenced by an attractive or unattractive other's romantic interest in the self. *North American Journal of Psychology*, 12, 341–54.

Stathi, S. and Crisp, R.J. (2008) Imagining intergroup contact promotes projection to outgroups. *Journal of Experimental Social Psychology*, 44, 943–57.

Staub, E. (1978) *Positive Social Behavior and Morality:* vol. 1, *Social and Personal Influences*. New York: Academic Press.

Staub, E. (1996) Breaking the cycle of violence: Helping victims of genocidal violence heal. *Journal of Personal and Interpersonal Loss*, 1, 191–7.

Staub, E. (2000) Genocide and mass killing: Origins, prevention, healing and reconciliation. *Political Psychology*, 21, 379.

Staub, E., Pearlman, L.A. and Miller, V. (2003) Healing the roots of genocide in Rwanda. *Peace Review: A Journal of Social Justice*, 15, 287–94.

Staub, E., Pearlman, L.A., Gubin, A. and Hagengimana, A. (2005) Healing, reconciliation, forgiving and the prevention of violence after genocide or mass killing: An intervention and its experimental evaluation in Rwanda. *Journal of Social and Clinical Psychology*, 24, 297–334.

Stech, F. and McClintock, C.G. (1981) Effects of communication timing on duopoly bargaining outcomes. *Journal of Personality and Social Psychology*, 40, 664–74.

Steele, C.M. (1988) The psychology of self-affirmation: Sustaining the integrity of the self. *Advances in Experimental Social Psychology*, 21, 261–302.

Steele, C.M. (1997) A threat in the air: How stereotypes shape intellectual identity and performance. *American Psychologist*, 52, 613–29.

Steele, C.M. and Aronson, J. (1995) Stereotype threat and the intellectual test-performance of African Americans. *Journal of Personality and Social Psychology*, 69, 797–811.

Steele, C.M. and Josephs, R.A. (1990) Alcohol myopia: Its prized and dangerous effects. *American Psychologist*, 45, 921–33.

Steele, C.M., Critchlow, B. and Liu, T.J. (1985) Alcohol and social behavior II: The helpful drunkard. *Journal of Personality and Social Psychology*, 48, 35–46.

Steele, C.M., Southwick, L.L. and Critchlow, B. (1981) Dissonance and alcohol: Drinking your troubles away. *Journal of Personality and Social Psychology*, 41, 831–46.

Steffens, M.C. (2004) Is the Implicit Association Test immune to faking? *Experimental Psychology*, 51, 165–79.

Steffens, M.C. and Buchner, A. (2003) Implicit Association Test: Separating

transsituationally stable and variable components of attitudes toward gay men. *Experimental Psychology*, 50, 33–48.

Steiner, I.D. (1972) *Group Processes and Productivity.* New York: Academic Press.

Steiner, I.D. (1976) Task-performing groups. In J.W. Thibaut and I.T. Spence (eds) *Contemporary Topics in Social Psychology* (pp. 393–422). Morristown, NJ: General Learning Press.

Stel, M. and van Knippenberg, A. (2008) The role of facial mimicry in the recognition of affect. *Psychological Science*, 19, 984–5.

Stephan, W.G. (1987) The contact hypothesis in intergroup relations. In C. Hendrick (ed.) *Group Processes and Intergroup Relations: Review of Personality and Social Psychology* (vol. 9, pp. 13–33). Newbury Park, CA: Sage.

Stephan, W.G. and Stephan, C.W. (1984) The role of ignorance in intergroup relations. In N. Miller and M.B. Brewer (eds) *Groups in Contact: The Psychology of Desegregation* (pp. 229–56). Orlando, FL: Academic Press.

Stephan, W.G. and Stephan, C.W. (1985) Intergroup anxiety. *Journal of Social Issues*, 41, 157–75.

Stephan, W.G. and Stephan, C.W. (2001) *Improving Intergroup Relations*. Thousand Oaks, CA: Sage.

Stephan, W.G., Berscheid, E. and Hatfield, E. (1971) Sexual arousal and heterosexual perception. *Journal of Personality and Social Psychology*, 20, 93–100.

Stephan, W.G., Boniecki, K.A., Ybarra, O. et al. (2002) The role of threats in the racial attitudes of blacks and whites. *Personality and Social Psychology Bulletin*, 28, 1242–54.

Stephan, W.G., Diaz-Loving, R. and Duran, A. (2000) Integrated threat theory and intercultural attitudes: Mexico and the United States. *Journal of Cross-Cultural Psychology*, 31, 240–9.

Stephan, W.G., Stephan, C.W. and Gudykunst, W.B. (1999) Anxiety in intergroup relations: A comparison of anxiety/uncertainty management theory and integrated threat theory. *International Journal of Intercultural Relations*, 23, 613–28.

Stepper, S. and Strack, F. (1993) Proprioceptive determinants of emotional nonemotional feelings. *Journal of Personality and Social Psychology*, 64, 211–20.

Stern, S.E. and Faber, J.E. (1997) The Internet as a psychological data gathering tool: Lost letters, web page experiments, and more. *Council on Undergraduate Research Quarterly*, 17, 30–3.

Sternberg, R.J. (1988) Triangulating love. In R.J. Sternberg and M.L. Barnes (eds) *The Psychology of Love* (pp. 119–38). New Haven, CT: Yale University Press.

Sternberg, R.J. (1998) *Cupid's Arrow:*

The Course of Love Through Time. Cambridge: Cambridge University Press.

Sternberg, R.J. and Vroom, V. (2002) The person versus the situation in leadership. *The Leadership Quarterly*, 13, 301–23.

Sterzer, P., Stadler, C., Krebs, A. et al. (2003) Reduced anterior cingulated activity in adolescents with antisocial conduct disorder confronted with affective pictures. *NeuroImage*, 19(Suppl. 1), 123.

Stevens, G., Owens, D. and Schaefer, E.C. (1990) Education and attractiveness in marriage choices. *Social Psychology Quarterly*, 53, 62–70.

Stewart, A.E. (2005) Attributions of responsibility for motor vehicle crashes. *Accident Analysis and Prevention*, 37, 681–8.

Stewart, B.D. and Payne, B.K. (2008) Bringing automatic stereotyping under control: Implementation intentions as efficient means of thought control. *Personality and Social Psychology Bulletin*, 34, 1332–45.

Stice, R. (2002) Risk and maintenance factors for eating pathology: A meta-analytic review. *Psychological Bulletin*, 128, 825–48.

Stockard, J. and Johnson, M.M. (1992) *Sex and Gender in Society* (2nd edn). Englewood Cliffs, NJ: Prentice Hall.

Stokoe, E. (2010) 'I'm not gonna hit a lady': Conversation analysis, membership categorization and men's denials of violence towards women. *Discourse and Society,* 21, 59–82.

Stone, J., Lynch, C.I., Sjomeling, M. and Darley, J.M. (1999) Stereotype threat effects on black and white athletic performance. *Journal of Personality and Social Psychology*, 77, 1213–27.

Stone, J., Wiegand, A.W., Cooper, J. and Aronson, E. (1997) When exemplification fails: Hypocrisy and the motive for self-integrity. *Journal of Personality and Social Psychology*, 72, 54–65.

Stoner, J.A.F. (1961) A comparison of individual and group decisions including risk. Unpublished Master's thesis, Massachusetts Institute of Technology, Boston.

Storms, M.D. (1973) Videotape and the attribution process: Reversing actors' and observers' points of view. *Journal of Personality and Social Psychology*, 27, 165–75.

Stott, C. and Reicher, S. (1998) Crowd action as intergroup process: Introducing the police perspective. *European Journal of Social Psychology*, 28, 509–29.

Stott, C., Adang, O., Livingstone, A. and Schreiber, M. (2007) Variability in the collective behaviour of England fans at Euro2004: 'Hooliganism', public order policing and social change. *European Journal of Social Psychology*, 37, 75–100.

Strack, F., Martin, L. and Stepper, S. (1988)

Inhibiting and facilitating conditions of the human smile: A non-obtrusive test of the facial feedback hypothesis. *Journal of Personality and Social Psychology*, 53, 768–77.

Strack, F., Schwarz, N. and Gschneidinger, E. (1985) Happiness and reminiscing: The role of time perspective, affect, and mode of thinking. *Journal of Personality and Social Psychology*, 49, 1460–9.

Strahan, E.J., Spencer, S.J. and Zanna, M.P. (2002) Subliminal priming and persuasion: Striking while the iron is hot. *Journal of Experimental Social Psychology*, 38, 556–68.

Strassberg, D.S., Roback, H.B., Anchor, K.N. and Abramowitz, S.I. (1975) Self-disclosure in group therapy with schizophrenics. *Archives of General Psychiatry*, 32, 1259–61.

Strelan, P. and Hargreaves, D. (2005) Reasons for exercise and body esteem: Men's responses to self-objectification. *Sex Roles*, 53, 495–503.

Strelan, P. and Mehaffy, S.J. (2003) Self-objectification and esteem in young women: The mediating role of reasons for exercise. *Sex Roles*, 48, 89–95.

Strelan, P. and Sutton, R.M. (2011) When just-world beliefs promote and when they inhibit forgiveness. *Personality and Individual Differences*, 50, 163–8.

Striegel-Moore, R.H., Silberstein, L.R. and Rodin, J. (1993) The social self in bulimia nervosa: Public self-consciousness, social anxiety, and perceived fraudulence. *Journal of Abnormal Psychology*, 102, 297–303.

Strodtbeck, F.L., James, R.M. and Hawkins, C. (1957) Social status in jury deliberations. *American Sociological Review*, 22, 713–19.

Stroebe, W. (2000) *Social Psychology and Health* (2nd edn). Buckingham: Open University Press.

Stroebe, W. and Diehl, M. (1994) Why groups are less effective than their members: On productivity losses in idea-generating groups. *European Review of Social Psychology*, 5, 271–303.

Stroebe, W., Insko, C.A., Thompson, V.D. and Layton, B.D. (1971) Effects of physical attractiveness, attitude similarity, and sex on various aspects of interpersonal attraction. *Journal of Personality and Social Psychology*, 18, 79–91.

Student Monitor (2010) Lifestyle and media. Retrieved from http://studentmonitor.com/lifestyle.php#SlideFrame_2 on 29 June 2012.

Stürmer, S., Snyder, M., Kropp, A. and Siem, B. (2006) Empathy-motivated helping: The moderating role of group membership. *Personality and Social Psychology Bulletin*, 32, 943–56.

Subbotsky, E., Hysted, C. and Jones, N. (2010) Watching films with magical content facilitates creativity in children. *Perceptual and Motor Skills*, 111, 261–77.

Sue, S. (1999) Science, ethnicity and bias: Where have we gone wrong? *American Psychologist*, 54, 1070–7.

Suler, J. (1996) *The Psychology of Cyberspace*. Online treatise at http://www-usr.rider.edu/~suler/psycyber/psycyber.html.

Sullivan, D. and Tifft, L. (eds) (2006) *Handbook of Restorative Justice: A Global Perspective*. New York: Routledge.

Sumner, W.G. (1906) *Folkways*. Boston, MA: Ginn.

Süssenbach, P., Bohner, G. and Eyssel, F. (in press) Schematic influences of rape myth acceptance on visual information processing: An eye-tracking approach. *Journal of Experimental Social Psychology*.

Sutton, R.M. (2010) The creative power of language in social cognition and intergroup elations. In H. Giles, S. Reid and J. Harwood (eds) *Dynamics of Intergroup Communication: Language as Social Action*, 8 (pp. 105–15). New York: Peter Lang.

Sutton, R.M. and Douglas, K.M. (2005) Justice for all, or just for me? More support for self-other differences in just world beliefs. *Personality and Individual Differences*, 39, 637–45.

Sutton, R.M. and Farrall, S. (2008) Untangling the web: Deceptive responding in fear of crime research. In S. Farrall and M. Lee (eds) *Critical Voices in an Age of Anxiety* (pp. 108–24). London: Taylor & Francis.

Sutton, R.M. and Farrall, S.D. (2005) Gender, socially desirable responding and the fear of crime: Are women *really* more anxious about crime? *British Journal of Criminology*, 45, 212–24.

Sutton, R.M. and McClure, J. (2001) Covariational influences on goal-based explanation: An integrative model. *Journal of Personality and Social Psychology*, 80, 222–36.

Sutton, R.M. and Winnard, E.J. (2007) Looking ahead through lenses of justice: The relevance of just-world beliefs to intentions and confidence in the future. *British Journal of Social Psychology*, 46, 649–66.

Sutton, R.M., Cichocka, A. and van der Toorn, J. (2012) The corrupting power of inequality: Social-psychological causes, consequences, and solutions. In A. Golec de Zavala and A. Cichocka (eds) *The Social Psychology of Social Problems* (pp.115–40). Basingstoke: Palgrave Macmillan.

Sutton, R.M., Douglas, K.M. and McClellan, L.M. (2011) Benevolent sexism, perceived health risks, and the inclination to restrict pregnant women's freedoms. *Sex Roles*, 65, 596–605.

Sutton, R.M., Douglas, K.M., Elder, T.J. and Tarrant, M. (2007) Social identity and social convention in responses to criticisms of groups. In Y. Kashima, K. Fiedler and P. Freytag (eds) *Stereotype Dynamics: Language-based Approaches to Stereotype Formation, Maintenance, and Transformation* (pp. 345–72). Mahwah, NJ: Lawrence Erlbaum.

Sutton, R.M., Douglas, K.M., Elder, T.J. and Tarrant, M. (2008) Social identity and social convention in response to criticism of groups. In Y. Kashima, K. Fiedler and P. Freytag (eds) *Stereotype Dynamics: Language-based Approaches to the Formation, Maintenance, and Transformation of Stereotypes* (pp. 339–66). New York: Lawrence Erlbaum.

Sutton, R.M., Douglas, K.M., Wilkin, K.J. et al. (2008) Justice for whom exactly? Beliefs in justice for the self and various others. *Personality and Social Psychology Bulletin*, 34, 528–41.

Sutton, R.M., Elder, T.J. and Douglas, K.M. (2006) Reactions to internal and external criticism of outgroups: Social convention in the intergroup sensitivity effect. *Personality and Social Psychology Bulletin*, 32, 563–75.

Sutton, R.M., Robinson, B. and Farrall, S.D. (2011) Gender, fear of crime, and self-presentation: An experimental investigation. *Psychology, Crime and Law*, 17, 421–33.

Svenson, O. (1981) Are we all less risky and more skillful than our fellow drivers? *Acta Psychologica, 47*, 143–8.

Swami, V., Chamorro-Premuzic, T., Bridges, S. and Furnham, A. (2009) Acceptance of cosmetic surgery: Personality and individual difference predictors. *Body Image*, 6, 7–13.

Swami, V., Furnham, A. and Joshi, K. (2008) The influence of skin tone, hair length, and hair colour on ratings of women's physical attractiveness, health and fertility. *Scandinavian Journal of Psychology*, 49, 429–37.

Swami, V., Gray, M. and Furnham, A. (2007) The female nude in Rubens: Disconfirmatory evidence of the waist-to-hip ratio hypothesis of female physical attractiveness. *Imagination, Cognition and Personality*, 26, 139–47.

Swami, V., Pietschnig, J., Stieger, S. and Voracek, M. (2011) Alien psychology: Associations between extraterrestrial beliefs and paranormal ideation, superstitious beliefs, schizotypy, and the big five personality factors. *Applied Cognitive Psychology*, 25, 647–53.

Swann, W.B. Jr (1997) The trouble with change: Self-verification and allegiance to the self. *Psychological Science*, 8, 177–80.

Swann, W.B. Jr, Hixon, J.G. and De La Ronde, C. (1992) Embracing the bitter 'truth': Negative self-concepts and marital commitment. *Psychological Science*, 3, 118–21.

Swann, W.B. Jr, Rentfrow, P.J. and Guinn,

J.S. (2003) Self-verification: The search for coherence. In M.R. Leary and J.P. Tangney (eds) *Handbook of Self and Identity* (pp. 365–83). New York: Guilford Press.

Swann, W.B. Jr, Stein-Seroussi, A. and Giesler, B. (1992) Why people self-verify. *Journal of Personality and Social Psychology*, 62, 392–401.

Swap, W.C. (1977) Interpersonal attraction and repeated exposure to rewarders and punishers. *Personality and Social Psychology Bulletin*, 3, 248–51.

Swift, H.J., Abrams, D. and Marques, S. (in press) Threat or boost: Social comparison affects older people's performance differently depending on task domain. *Journals of Gerontology, Series B*.

Swim, J.K., Ferguson, M.J. and Hyers, L.L. (1999) Avoiding stigma by association: Subtle prejudice against lesbians in the form of social distancing. *Basic and Applied Social Psychology*, 21, 61–8.

Swinburn, B.A., Sacks, G., Hall, K.D. et al. (2011) The global obesity pandemic: Shaped by global drivers and local environments. *The Lancet*, 378, 804–14.

Symons, D. (1979) *The Evolution of Human Sexuality*. New York: Oxford University Press.

Szymanski, K. and Harkins, S. (1987) Social loafing and self-evaluation with a social standard. *Journal of Personality and Social Psychology*, 53, 891–7.

Tabernero, C., Chambel, M.J., Curral, L. and Arana, J.M. (2009) The role of task-oriented versus relationship-oriented leadership on normative contract and group performance. *Social Behavior and Personality: An International Journal*, 37, 1391–404.

Tajfel, H. (1959) Quantitative judgement in social perception. *British Journal of Social Psychology*, 50, 16–29.

Tajfel, H. (1972) Experiments in a vacuum. In J. Israel and H. Tajfel (eds) *The Context of Social Psychology: A Critical Assessment* (pp. 69–119). London: Academic Press.

Tajfel, H. and Turner, J.C. (1979) An integrative theory of intergroup conflict. In W.G. Austin and S. Worchel (eds) *The Social Psychology of Intergroup Relations* (pp. 33–47). Monterey, CA: Brooks/Cole.

Tajfel, H. and Turner, J.C. (1986) The social identity theory of intergroup behavior. In S. Worchel and W. Austin (eds) *Psychology of Intergroup Relations* (2nd edn, pp. 7–24). Chicago, IL: Nelson-Hall.

Tajfel, H. and Wilkes, A.L. (1963) Classification and quantitative judgement. *British Journal of Psychology*, 54, 101–14.

Tajfel, H., Billig, M.G., Bundy, R.P. and Flament, C. (1971) Social categorization and intergroup behaviour. *European Journal of Social Psychology*, 1, 149–77.

Takaki, R. (1993) *A Different Mirror: A History of Multicultural America*. Boston: Little, Brown.

Tal-Or, N. (2007) Age and third-person perception in response to positive product advertisements. *Mass Communication and Society*, 10, 403–22.

Tam, T., Hewstone, M., Cairns, E. et al. (2007) The impact of intergroup emotions on forgiveness in Northern Ireland. *Group Processes & Intergroup Relations*, 10, 119–36.

Tan, D.T.Y. and Singh, R. (1995) Attitudes and attraction: A developmental study of the similarity-attraction and dissimilarity-repulsion hypotheses. *Personality and Social Psychology Bulletin*, 21, 975–86.

Tan, R., Overall, N.C. and Taylor, J.K. (2012) Let's talk about us: Attachment, relationship-focused disclosure, and relationship quality. *Personal Relationships*, 19(3), 521–34.

Tangney, J.P., Miller, R.S., Flicker, L. and Barlow, D.H. (1996) Are shame, guilt and embarrassment distinct emotions? *Journal of Personality and Social Psychology*, 70, 1256–69.

Tangney, J.P., Wagner, P.E., Hill-Barlow, D. et al. (1996) Relation of shame and guilt to constructive versus destructive responses to anger across the lifespan. *Journal of Personality and Social Psychology*, 70, 797–809.

Tanis, M. (2007) Online social support groups. In A. Joinson, K. McKenna, T. Postmes and U.-D. Reips (eds) *The Oxford Handbook of Internet Psychology* (pp. 139–54). New York: Oxford University Press.

Tanis, M. and Postmes, T. (2003) Social cues and impression formation in CMC. *Journal of Communication*, 53, 676–93.

Tanner, R.J., Ferraro, R., Chartrand, T.L. et al. (2008) Of chameleons and consumption: The impact of mimicry on choice and preferences. *Journal of Consumer Research*, 34, 754–66.

Tarde, G. (1890) *Les lois de l'imitation*. Paris: Libraire Felix Alcan.

Tarrant, M. and Butler, K. (2011) Effects of self-categorization on orientation towards health. *British Journal of Social Psychology*, 50, 121–39.

Tarrant, M. and Campbell, E. (2007) Responses to within-group criticism: Does past adherence to group norms matter? *European Journal of Social Psychology*, 37, 1187–202.

Taylor, D.M. and Brown, R.J. (1979) Towards a more social psychology? *British Journal of Social and Clinical Psychology*, 18, 173–80.

Taylor, L.D., Davis-Kean, P. and Malanchuk, O. (2007) Self-esteem, academic self-concept, and aggression at school. *Aggressive Behavior*, 33, 130–6.

Taylor, L.S., Fiore, A.T., Mendelsohn,

G. and Cheshire, C. (2011) 'Out of my league': A real-world test of the matching hypothesis. *Personality and Social Psychology Bulletin*, 37, 942–54.

Taylor, S. Jr (2008) Racism marginalized – even if Obama loses. *National Journal*, www.nationaljournal.com.

Taylor, S.E. (1981) The interface of cognitive and social psychology. In J.H. Harvey (ed.) *Cognition, Social Behavior and the Environment* (pp. 189–211). Hillsdale, NJ: Erlbaum.

Taylor, S.E. (1998) The social being in social psychology. In D.T. Gilbert, S.T. Fiske and G. Lindzey (eds) *The Handbook of Social Psychology* (4th edn, vol. 1, pp. 58–95). New York: McGraw-Hill.

Taylor, S.E. and Brown, J.D. (1988) Illusion and well-being: A social psychological perspective on mental health. *Psychological Bulletin*, 103, 193–210.

Taylor, S.P. and Gammon, C.B. (1975) Effects of type and dose of alcohol on human physical aggression. *Journal of Personality and Social Psychology*, 32, 169–75.

Teachman, J. (1987) Family background, educational resources and educational attainment. *American Sociological Review*, 52, 548–57.

Tedeschi, J.T. and Quigley, B.M. (1996) Limitations of laboratory paradigms for studying aggression. *Aggression and Violent Behavior*, 1, 163–77.

Tellegen, A., Lykken, D.T., Bouchard, T.J. et al. (1988) Personality similarity in twins reared apart and together. *Journal of Personality and Social Psychology*, 6, 1031–9.

Tellis, G.J. (1987) Consumer purchasing strategies and the information in retail prices. *Journal of Retailing*, 63, 279–97.

Terry, D.J. and O'Brien, A.T. (2001) Status, legitimacy, and ingroup bias in the context of an organizational merger. *Group Processes and Intergroup Relations*, 4, 271–89.

Terry, D.J., Carey, C.J. and Callan, V.J. (2001) Employee adjustment to an organizational merger: An intergroup perspective. *Personality and Social Psychology Bulletin*, 27, 267–80.

Tesser, A. (1988) Toward a self-evaluation maintenance model of social behavior. In L. Berkowitz (ed.) *Advances in Experimental Social Psychology* (vol. 21, pp. 181–227). New York: Academic Press.

Tesser, A. (1991) Emotion in social comparison and reflection processes. In J. Suls and T.A. Wills (eds) *Social Comparison: Contemporary Theory and Research* (pp. 117–48). Hillsdale, NJ: Lawrence Erlbaum.

Tesser, A. (1993) The importance of heritability in psychological research: The case of attitudes. *Psychological Review*, 100, 129–42.

Tesser, A. and Collins, J.E. (1988) Emotion

in social reflection and comparison situations: Intuitive, systematic, and exploratory approaches. *Journal of Personality and Social Psychology*, 55, 695–709.

Tesser, A. and Martin, L. (1996) The psychology of evaluation. In E.T. Higgins and A.W. Kruglanski (eds) *Social Psychology: Handbook of Basic Principles* (pp. 400–32). New York: Guilford Press.

Tesser, A. and Shaffer, D.R. (1990) Attitudes and attitude change. *Annual Review of Psychology*, 41, 479–523.

Tesser, A., Martin L. and Mendolia, M. (1995) The impact of thought on attitude extremity and attitude-behavior consistency. In R.E. Petty and J.A. Krosnick (eds) *Attitude Strength: Antecedents and Consequences* (pp. 73–92). Mahwah, NJ: Erlbaum.

Tetlock, P.E. (1979) Identifying victims of groupthink from public statements of decision makers. *Journal of Personality and Social Psychology*, 37, 1314–24.

Tetlock, P.E. (1984) Cognitive style and political belief systems in the British House of Commons. *Journal of Personality and Social Psychology*, 46, 365–75.

Tetlock, P.E., Petersen, R.S., McGuire, C. et al. (1992) Assessing political group dynamics: A test of the groupthink model. *Journal of Personality and Social Psychology*, 63, 403–25.

Thaler, R. and Sunstein, C. (2008) *Nudge: Improving Decisions about Health, Wealth, and Happiness*. London: Yale University Press.

Thayer, S. and Saarni, C. (1975) Demand characteristics are everywhere (anyway): A comment on the Stanford prison experiment. *American Psychologist*, 30, 1015–16.

Thelwall, M., Wilkinson, D. and Uppal, S. (2010) Data mining emotion in social network communication: Gender differences in MySpace. *Journal of the American Society for Information Science and Technology*, 61, 190–9.

Thibaut, J.W. and Kelley, H.H. (1959) *The Social Psychology of Groups*. New York: Wiley.

Thibaut, J.W. and Strickland, L.H. (1956) Psychological set and social conformity. *Journal of Personality*, 25, 115–29.

Thoits, P.A. (1983) Multiple identities and psychological well-being: A reformulation and test of the social isolation hypothesis. *American Sociological Review*, 48, 174–87.

Thomas, E.F., McGarty, C. and Mavor, K.I. (2009a) Transforming 'apathy into movement': The role of prosocial emotions in motivating action for social change. *Personality and Social Psychology Review*, 13, 310–33.

Thomas, E.F., McGarty, C. and Mavor, K.I. (2009b) Aligning identities, emotions, and beliefs to create commitment to sustainable social and political

action. *Personality and Social Psychology Review*, 13, 194–218.

Thomas, M.H., Horton, R.W., Lippincott, E.C. and Drabman, R.S. (1977) Desensitization to portrayals of real life aggression as a function of television violence. *Journal of Personality and Social Psychology*, 35, 450–8.

Thompson, A. (2007) *The Media and the Rwandan Genocide*. London: Pluto Press.

Thompson, J.B. (1990) *Ideology and Modern Culture: Critical Social Theory in the Era of Mass Communication*. London: Wiley.

Thompson, L. (1990) Negotiation behavior and outcomes: Empirical evidence and theoretical issues. *Psychological Bulletin*, 109, 515–32.

Thompson, M.M., Naccarato, M.E. and Parker, K.E. (1989) Assessing cognitive need: The development of the personal need for structure and personal fear of invalidity scales. Paper presented at the annual meeting of the Canadian Psychology Association, Halifax, Canada.

Thornhill, R. and Gangestad, S.W. (1993) Human facial beauty. *Human Nature*, 4, 237–69.

Thornton, G. (2011) For richer, for poorer? What's yours is mine, and what's mine is out of sight. Matrimonial survey 2011. Retrieved from www.grant-thornton.co.uk/pdf/matrimonial_survey_2011.pdf on 29 June 2012.

Tice, D.M. (1992) Self-presentation and self-concept change: The looking glass self as a magnifying glass. *Journal of Personality and Social Psychology*, 63, 435–51.

Tidwell, M.C.O., Reis, H.T. and Shaver, P.R. (1996) Attachment, attractiveness, and social interaction: A diary study. *Journal of Personality and Social Psychology*, 71, 729–45.

Tierney, J. (2011) Social scientist sees bias within. *New York Times*, 7 February. Retrieved from http://www.nytimes.com/2011/02/08/science/08tier.html?_r=1&ref=science on 29 June 2012.

Tinbergen, N. (1952) 'Derived' activities; their causation, biological significance, origin, and emancipation during evolution. *The Quarterly Review of Biology*, 27, 1–32.

Todorov, A. and Uleman, J.S. (2003) The efficiency of binding spontaneous trait inferences to actors' faces. *Journal of Experimental Social Psychology*, 39, 549–62.

Todorov, A., Mandisodza, A.N., Goren, A. and Hall, C.C. (2005) Inferences of competence from faces predict election outcomes. *Science*, 308, 1623–6.

Toi, M. and Batson, C.D. (1982) More evidence that empathy is a source of altruistic motivation. *Journal of Personality and Social Psychology*, 43, 281–92.

Tolman, C.W. (1964) Social facilitation of

feeding behaviour in the domestic chick. *Animal Behavior*, 12, 245–51.

Tom, G., Pettersen, P., Lau, T. et al. (1991) The role of overt head movement in the formation of affect. *Basic and Applied Social Psychology*, 12, 281–9.

Tomaka, J. and Blascovich, J. (1994) Effects of justice beliefs on cognitive appraisal and subjective, physiological and behavioral responses to potential stress. *Journal of Personality and Social Psychology*, 67, 732–40.

Tomaka, J., Blascovich, J., Kelsey, R.M. and Leitten, C.L. (1993) Subjective, physiological, and behavioral effects of threat and challenge appraisal. *Journal of Personality and Social Psychology*, 65, 248–60.

Tooby, J. and Cosmides, L. (1990) The past explains the present: Emotional adaptations and the structure of ancestral environments. *Ethology and Sociobiology*, 11, 375–424.

Tormala, Z.L. and Clarkson, J.J. (2007) Assimilation and contrast in persuasion. *Personality and Social Psychology Bulletin*, 33, 559–71.

Tormala, Z.L. and Petty, R.E. (2002) What doesn't kill me makes me stronger: The effects of resisting persuasion on attitude certainty. *Journal of Personality and Social Psychology*, 83, 1298–313.

Tormala, Z.L. and Petty, R.E. (2004) Resistance to persuasion and attitude certainty: The moderating role of elaboration. *Personality and Social Psychology Bulletin*, 30, 1446–57.

Tormala, Z.L., Briñol, P. and Petty, R.E. (2006) When credibility attacks: The reverse impact of source credibility on persuasion. *Journal of Experimental Social Psychology*, 42, 684–91.

Tormala, Z.L., Clarkson, J.J. and Petty, R.E. (2006) Resisting persuasion by the skin of one's teeth: The hidden success of resisted persuasive messages. *Journal of Personality and Social Psychology; Journal of Personality and Social Psychology*, 91, 423–35.

Tourangeau, R. and Yan, T. (2007) Sensitive questions in surveys. *Psychological Bulletin*, 133, 859–83.

Tourangeau, R., Rips, L. and Rasinski, K. (2000) *The Psychology of Survey Response*. Cambridge: Cambridge University Press.

Traclet, A., Rascle, O., Souchon, N. et al. (2009) Aggression in soccer: An exploratory study of accounts preference. *Research Quarterly for Exercise and Sport*, 80, 398–402.

Tracy, J.L., Robins, R.W. and Sherman, J.W. (2009) The practice of psychological science: Searching for Cronbach's two streams in social-personality psychology. *Journal of Personality and Social Psychology*, 96, 106–1225.

Trafimow, D. (2000) Habit as both a direct

cause of intention to use a condom and as a moderator of the attitude-intention and subjective norm-intention relations. *Psychology and Health*, 15, 383–93.

Trafimow, D., Triandis, H.C. and Goto, S.G. (1991) Some tests of the distinction between the private self and the collective self. *Journal of Personality and Social Psychology,* 60, 649–55.

Trapp, A., Banister, P., Ellis, J. et al. (2011) *The Future of Undergraduate Psychology Education in the United Kingdom.* York: Higher Education Academy.

Trappey, C. (1996) A meta-analysis of consumer choice and subliminal advertising. *Psychology and Marketing*, 13, 517–30.

Trend, D. (2007) *The Myth of Media Violence: A Critical Introduction.* Malden, MA: Blackwell.

Triandis, H.C. (1989) The self and social behaviour in differing cultural contexts. *Psychological Review*, 96, 269–89.

Triandis, H.C. (1994) *Culture and Social Behavior.* New York: McGraw-Hill.

Triandis, H.C. (1995) *Individualism and Collectivism.* Boulder, CO: Westview Press.

Triplett, N. (1898) The dynamogenic factors in pacemaking and competition. *American Journal of Psychology*, 9, 507–33.

Trivers, R.L. (1971) The evolution of reciprocal altruism. *Quarterly Review of Biology*, 46, 35–57.

Trivers, R.L. (1972) Parental investment and sexual selection. In B. Campbell (ed.) *Sexual Selection and the Descent of Man: 1871–1971* (pp. 136–19). Chicago, IL: Aldine.

Trope, Y. (1986) Identification and inferential processes in dispositional attribution. *Psychological Review*, 93, 239–57.

Trope, Y. and Thompson, E.P. (1997) Looking for truth in all the wrong places? Asymmetric search of individuating information about stereotyped group members. *Journal of Personality and Social Psychology*, 73, 229–41.

Tropp, L.R. and Mallett, R.K. (eds) (2011) *Moving Beyond Prejudice Reduction: Pathways to Positive Intergroup Relation.* Washington, DC: American Psychological Association.

Trut, L.N. (1999) Early canid domestication: the farm-fox experiment. *American Scientist*, 87, 160–8.

Tucker, J.S., Friedman, H.S., Schwartz, J.E. et al. (1997) Parental divorce: Effects on individual behavior and longevity. *Journal of Personality and Social Psychology*, 73, 381–91.

Tuckman, B.W. (1965) Developmental sequence in small groups. *Psychological Bulletin*, 63, 384–99.

Tuckman, B.W. and Jensen, M.A.C. (1977) Stages of small-group development

revisited. *Group and Organization Studies*, 2, 419–27.

Tuckman, J. and Lorge, I. (1953) Attitudes towards old people. *Journal of Social Psychology*, 37, 249–60.

Turing, A.M. (1950) Computing machinery and intelligence. *Mind*, 49, 433–60.

Turner, J.C. (1982) Towards a cognitive redefinition of the social group. In H. Tajfel (ed.) *Social Identity and Intergroup Relations* (pp. 15–40). Paris: Editions de la Maison des Sciences de l'Homme.

Turner, J.C. (1984) Social identification and psychological group formation. In H. Tajfel (ed.) *The Social Dimension: European Developments in Social Psychology* (vol. 2, pp. 518–38). Cambridge: Cambridge University Press.

Turner, J.C. (1985) Social categorization and the self-concept: A social cognitive theory of group behavior. In E.J. Lawler (ed.) *Advances in Group Processes* (vol. 2, pp. 77–122). Greenwich, CT: JAI Press.

Turner, J.C. (1991) *Social Influence.* Belmont, CA: Thomson Brooks/Cole.

Turner, J.C. and Oakes, P.J. (1989) Self-categorization theory and social influence. In P.B. Paulus (ed.) *The Psychology of Group Influence* (2nd edn, pp. 233–75). Hillsdale, NJ: Lawrence Erlbaum.

Turner, J.C., Hogg, M.A., Oakes, P.J. et al. (1987) *Rediscovering the Social Group: A Self-categorization Theory.* Cambridge, MA: Blackwell.

Turner, J.C., Wetherell, M.S. and Hogg, M.A. (1989) Referent informational influence and group polarization. *British Journal of Social Psychology*, 28, 135–47.

Turner, M.E., Pratkanis, A.R., Probasco, P. and Leve, C. (1992) Threat, cohesion, and group effectiveness: Testing a social identity maintenance perspective on groupthink. *Journal of Personality and Social Psychology*, 63, 781–96.

Turner, R.H. and Killian, L.M. (1987) *Collective Behavior* (3rd edn). Englewood Cliffs, NJ: Prentice Hall.

Turner, R.H. and Killian, L.M. (1993) *Collective Behavior* (4th edn). Englewood Cliffs, NJ: Prentice Hall.

Turner, R.N. and Crisp, R.J. (2010) Imagining intergroup contact reduces implicit prejudice. *British Journal of Social Psychology*, 49, 129–42.

Turner, R.N., Crisp, R.J. and Lambert, E. (2007) Imagining intergroup contact can improve intergroup attitudes. *Group Processes and Intergroup Relations*, 10, 427–41.

Turner, R.N., Hewstone, M., Voci, A. and Vonofakou, C. (2008) A test of the extended intergroup contact hypothesis: The mediating role of intergroup anxiety, perceived ingroup and outgroup norms, and inclusion of the outgroup in the

self. *Journal of Personality and Social Psychology*, 95, 843–60.

Turner, R.N., West, K. and Christie, Z. (in press) Outgroup trust, intergroup anxiety, and outgroup attitude as mediators of the effect of imagined intergroup contact on intergroup behavioural tendencies. *Journal of Applied Social Psychology*.

Tuvblad, C., Raine, A., Zheng, M. and Baker, L.A. (2009) Genetic and environmental stability differs in reactive and proactive aggression. *Aggressive Behavior*, 35, 437–52.

Tversky, A. and Kahneman, D. (1974) Judgment under uncertainty: Heuristics and biases. *Science*, 185, 1124–31.

Tversky, A. and Kahneman, D. (1983) Extensional versus intuitive reasoning: The conjunction fallacy in probability judgment. *Psychological Review*, 90, 293–315.

Twenge, J.M. (1997) Changes in masculine and feminine traits over time: A meta-analysis. *Sex Roles*, 36, 305–25.

Twenge, J.M. (2001) Changes in women's assertiveness in response to status and roles: A cross-temporal meta-analysis, 1931–1993. *Journal of Personality and Social Psychology*, 81, 133–45.

Twenge, J.M. (2006) *Generation Me: Why Today's Young Americans are More Confident, Assertive, Entitled – and More Miserable than Ever Before.* New York: Free Press.

Twenge, J.M. and Campbell, W.K. (2009) *The Narcissism Epidemic: Living in the Age of Entitlement.* New York: Free Press.

Twenge, J.M., Baumeister, R.F., DeWall, C.N. et al. (2007) Social exclusion decreases prosocial behavior. *Journal of Personality and Social Psychology*, 92, 56–66.

Twenge, J.M., Baumeister, R.F., Tice, D.M. and Stucke, T.S. (2001) If you can't join them, beat them: Effects of social exclusion on aggressive behavior. *Journal of Personality and Social Psychology*, 81, 1058–69.

Tyler, J.M. and Burns, K.C. (2009) Triggering conservation of the self's regulatory resources. *Basic and Applied Social Psychology*, 31, 255–66.

Tyler, T.R. (1994) Psychological models of the justice motive: Antecedents of distributive and procedural justice. *Journal of Personality and Social Psychology*, 67, 850–3.

Tyler, T.R. (2007) *Psychology and the Design of Legal Institutions.* Nijmegen: Wolf Legal.

Tyler, T.R. (2012) Justice theory. In P.A.M. van Lange, A.W. Kruglanski and E.T. Higgins (eds) *Handbook of Theories of Social Psychology* (vol. 2, pp. 344–61). Thousand Oaks, CA: Sage.

Tyler, T.R. and Blader, S.L. (2003) The

group engagement model: Procedural justice, social identity, and cooperative behavior. *Personality and Social Psychology Review*, 7, 349–61.

Tyler, T.R. and Schuller, R.A. (1991) Aging and attitude change. *Journal of Personality and Social Psychology*, 61, 689–97.

Uhlmann, E.L., Brescoll, V.L. and Paluck, E.L. (2006) Are members of low status groups perceived as bad, or badly off? Egalitarian negative associations and automatic prejudice. *Journal of Experimental Social Psychology*, 42, 491–9.

Umberson, D. and Hughes, M. (1987) The impact of physical attractiveness on achievement and psychological well-being. *Social Psychology Quarterly*, 50, 227–36.

UN (United Nations) (2001) *World Population Monitoring 2001: Population, Environment and Development*. New York: UN.

Unkelbach, C., Forgas, J.P. and Denson, T.F. (2008) The turban effect: The influence of Muslim headgear and indirect affect on responses in the shooter bias paradigm. *Journal of Experimental Social Psychology*, 44, 1409–13.

Unzueta, M.M., Gutierrez, A.S. and Ghavami, N. (2010) How believing in affirmative action affects white women's self-image. *Journal of Experimental Social Psychology*, 46, 120–6.

Updegraff, J.A., Emanuel, A.S., Suh, E.M. and Gallagher, K.M. (2010) Sheltering the self from the storm: Self-construal abstractness and the stability of self-esteem. *Personality and Social Psychology Bulletin*, 36, 97–108.

Uslaner, E.M. (2002) Social capital, television, and the 'Mean World': Trust, optimism, and civic participation. *Political Psychology*, 19, 441–67.

Uziel, L. (2007) Individual differences in the social facilitation effect: A review and meta-analysis. *Journal of Research in Personality*, 41, 579–601.

Valenza, E., Simion, F., Cassia, V.M. and Umiltaa, C. (1996) Face preference at birth. *Journal of Experimental Psychology: Human Perception and Performance*, 22, 892–903.

Valins, S. and Nisbett, R.E. (1971) Attribution processes in the development and treatment of emotional disorders. In E.E. Jones, D.E. Kanouse, H.H. Kelley et al. (eds) *Attribution: Perceiving the Causes of Behavior* (pp. 137–50). Morristown, NJ: General Learning Press.

Vallacher, R.R. and Solodky, M. (1979) Objective self-awareness, standards of evaluation, and moral behavior. *Journal of Experimental Social Psychology*, 15, 254–62.

Vallone, R.P., Ross, L. and Lepper, M.R. (1985) The hostile media phenomenon: Biased perception and perceptions of media bias in coverage of the Beirut massacre. *Journal of Personality and Social Psychology*, 49, 577–85.

Van Baaren R.B., Maddux, W.W., Chartrand, T.L. et al. (2003) It takes two to mimic: Behavioural consequences of self-construals. *Journal of Personality and Social Psychology*, 84, 1093–102.

Van Baaren, R.B., Holland, R.W., Kawakami, K. and van Knippenberg, A. (2004) Mimicry and prosocial behavior. *Psychological Science*, 15, 71–4.

Van Baaren, R.B., Holland, R.W., Steenaert, B. and van Knippenberg, A. (2003) Mimicry for money: Behavioral consequences of imitation. *Journal of Experimental Social Psychology*, 39, 393–8.

Van Dellen, M.R., Campbell, W.K., Hoyle, R.H. and Bradfield, E.K. (2011) Compensating, resisting, and breaking: A meta-analytic examination of reactions to self-esteem threat. *Personality and Social Psychology Review*, 15, 51–74.

Van den Beld, T. (2002) Can collective responsibility for perpetrated evil persist over generations? *Journal of Ethics*, 1, 181–200.

Van den Bos, K. and Lind, E.A. (2001) The psychology of own versus others' treatment: Self-oriented and other-oriented effects on perceptions of procedural justice. *Personality and Social Psychology Bulletin*, 27, 1324–33.

Van den Bos, K. and Spruijt, N. (2002) Appropriateness of decisions as a moderator of the psychology of voice. *European Journal of Social Psychology*, 32, 57–72.

Van den Bos, K., Lind, E.A., Vermunt, R. and Wilke, H.A.M. (1997) How do I judge my outcome when I do not know the outcome of others? The psychology of the fair process effect. *Journal of Personality and Social Psychology*, 72, 1034–46.

Van den Bos, K., Peters, S.L., Bobocel, D.R. and Ybema, J.F. (2006) On preferences and doing the right thing: Satisfaction with advantageous inequity when cognitive processing is limited. *Journal of Experimental Social Psychology*, 42, 273–89.

Van den Bos, K., van Lange, P.A.M., Lind, E.A. et al. (2011) On the benign qualities of behavioral disinhibition: Because of the prosocial nature of people, behavioral disinhibition can weaken pleasure with getting more than you deserve. *Journal of Personality and Social Psychology*, 101, 791–811.

Van de Ven, P., Bornholt, L. and Bailey, M. (1996) Measuring cognitive, affective, and behavioral components of homophobic reaction. *Archives of Sexual Behavior*, 25, 155–79.

Van Dick, R., Tissington, P.A. and Hertel, G. (2009) Do many hands make light work? How to overcome social loafing and gain motivation in work teams. *European Business Review*, 21, 233–45.

Van Dierendonck, M.C., de Vries, H. and Schilder, M.B.H. (1995) An analysis of dominance, its behavioural parameters and possible determinants in a herd of Icelandic horses in captivity in the Netherlands. *Journal of Zoolology*, 45, 362–85.

Van Dijk, T.A. (1993) *Elite Discourse and Racism: Ethnic Prejudice in Thought and Talk*. Newbury Park, CA: Sage.

Van Dijk, T.A. (1993) Principles of critical discourse analysis. *Discourse and Society*, 4, 249–83.

Van Dijk, T.A. (ed.) (2011) *Discourse Studies: A Multidisciplinary Introduction*. London: Sage.

Van Duynslaeger, M., Sterken, C., van Overwalle, F. and Verstraeten, E. (2008) EEG components of spontaneous trait inferences. *Social Neuroscience*, 3, 164–77.

Van Gelder, L. (1985) 'The strange case of the electronic lover'. *Ms Magazine*, October. Reprinted in C. Dunlop and R. Kling (eds) (1991) *Computerization and Controversy: Value Conflicts and Social Choices*. San Diego, CA: Academic Press.

Van Gyn, G.H., Wenger, H.A. and Gaul, C.A. (1990) Imagery as a method of enhancing transfer from training to performance. *Journal of Sport and Exercise Psychology*, 12, 366–75.

Van Hiel, A. and Brebels, L. (2011) Conservatism is good for you: Cultural conservatism protects self-esteem in older adults. *Personality and Individual Differences*, 50, 120–3.

Van Houtte, M. (2004) Why boys achieve less at school than girls: The difference between boys' and girls' academic culture. *Educational Studies*, 30, 159–73.

Van Knippenberg, D. and Wilke, H. (1992) Prototypicality of arguments and conformity to ingroup norms. *European Journal of Social Psychology*, 22, 141–55.

Van Lange, P.A.M. (1999) The pursuit of joint outcomes and equality in outcomes: An integrative model of social value orientation. *Journal of Personality and Social Psychology*, 77, 337–49.

Van Lange, P.A.M. and Liebrand, W.B.G. (1991) Social value orientation and intelligence: A test of the goal-prescribes-rationality principle. *European Journal of Social Psychology*, 21, 273–92.

Van Lange, P.A.M. and Visser, K. (1999) Locomotion in social dilemmas: How people adapt to cooperative, tit-for-tat, and noncooperative partners. *Journal of Personality and Social Psychology*, 77, 762–73.

Van Lange, P.A.M., de Cremer, D., van Dijk, E. and van Vugt, M. (2007) Self-interest and beyond: Basic principles of social interaction. In A.W. Kruglanski and E.T. Higgins (eds) *Social Psychology: Handbook of Basic Principles* (pp. 540–61). New York: Guilford Press.

Van Lange, P.A.M., Otten, W., de Bruin, E. and Joireman, J.A. (1997) Development of prosocial, individualistic, and competitive orientations: Theory and preliminary evidence. *Journal of Personality and Social Psychology*, 73, 733–46.

Van Lange, P.A.M., Ouwerkerk, J.W. and Tazelaar, M.J.A. (2002) How to overcome the detrimental effects of noise in social interaction: The benefits of generosity. *Journal of Personality and Social Psychology*, 82, 768–80.

Van Ness, D.W. and Heetderks Strong, K. (2010) *Restoring Justice: An Introduction to Restorative Justice*. New Providence, NJ: Matthew Bender.

Van Rooy, D., van Overwalle, F., Vanhoomissen, T. et al. (2003) A recurrent connectionist model of group biases. *Psychological Review*, 110, 536–63.

Van Stekelenburg, J. and Klandermans, B. (2012) Social conflict and social protest. In A. Golec de Zavala and A. Cichocka (eds) *The Social Psychology of Social Problems* (pp. 141–71). Basingstoke: Palgrave Macmillan.

Van Vugt, M. (2009) Averting the tragedy of the commons: Using social psychological science to protect the environment. *Current Directions in Psychological Science*, 18, 169–73.

Van Vugt, M. and Hart, C.M. (2004) Social identity as social glue: The origins of group loyalty. *Journal of Personality and Social Psychology*, 86, 585–98.

Van Vugt, M., de Cremer, D. and Janssen, D.P. (2007) Gender differences in cooperation and competition: The male-warrior hypothesis. *Psychological Science*, 18, 19–23.

Van Yperen, N.W. and Buunk, B.P. (1990) A longitudinal study of equity in intimate relationships. *European Journal of Social Psychology*, 20, 297–309.

Van Zomeren, M., Postmes, T. and Spears, R. (2008) Toward an integrative social identity model of collective action: A quantitative research synthesis of three socio-psychological perspectives. *Psychological Bulletin*, 134, 504–35.

Van Zomeren, M., Spears, R. and Leach, C.W. (2008) Exploring psychological mechanisms of collective action: Does relevance of group identity influence how people cope with collective disadvantage? *British Journal of Social Psychology*, 47, 353–72.

Vangelisti, A.L. and Perlman, D. (2006) *The Cambridge Handbook of Personal Relationships*. New York: Cambridge University Press.

Vartanian, L.R. and Hopkinson, M.M. (2010) Social connectedness, conformity, and internalization of societal standards of attractiveness. *Body Image*, 7, 86–9.

Vasquez, K., Keltner, D., Ebenbach, D.H. and Banaszynski, T.L. (2001) Cultural variation and similarity in moral rhetorics: Voices from the Philippines and the United States. *Journal of Cross-Cultural Psychology*, 32, 93–120.

Vauclair, C.M. and Fischer, R. (2011) Do cultural values predict individuals' moral attitudes? A cross-cultural multilevel approach. *European Journal of Social Psychology*, 41, 645–57.

Vennard, J. (1984) Disputes within trials over the admissibility and accuracy of incriminating statements: Some research evidence. *Criminal Law Review*, 15, 21.

Verplanken, B. (1991) Persuasive communication of risk information: A test of cue versus message processing effects in a field experiment. *Personality and Social Psychology Bulletin*, 17, 188–93.

Verplanken, B. (2006) Beyond frequency: Habit as mental construct. *British Journal of Social Psychology*, 45, 639–56.

Verplanken, B. and Holland, R.W. (2002) Motivated decision making: Effects of activation and self-centrality of values on choices and behavior. *Journal of Personality and Social Psychology*, 82, 434–47.

Vick, S.B., Seery, M.D., Blascovich, J. and Weisbuch, M. (2008) The effect of gender stereotype activation on challenge and threat motivational states. *Journal of Experimental Social Psychology*, 44, 624–30.

Vick, S.J., Waller, B.M., Parr, L.A. et al. (2007) A cross-species comparison of facial morphology and movement in humans and chimpanzees using the Facial Action Coding System (FACS). *Journal of Nonverbal Behavior*, 31, 1–20.

Victor, C.R., Scambler, S.J., Bowling, A. and Bond, J. (2005) The prevalence of, and risk factors for, loneliness in later life: a survey of older people in Great Britain. *Ageing and Society*, 25, 357–76.

Vignoles, V.L., Chryssochoou, X. and Breakwell, G.M. (2000) The distinctiveness principle: Identity, meaning and the bounds of cultural relativity. *Personality and Social Psychological Review*, 4, 337–54.

Viki, G.T. and Abrams, D. (2002) But she was unfaithful: Benevolent sexism and reactions to rape victims who violate traditional gender role expectations. *Sex Roles*, 47, 289–93.

Vinokur, A. and Burnstein. E. (1974) Effects of partially shared persuasive arguments on group-induced shifts: A group-problem-solving approach. *Journal of Personality and Social Psychology*, 29, 305–15.

Vinokur, A.D., Price, R.H. and Caplan, R.D. (1996) Hard times and hurtful partners: How financial strain affects depression and relationship satisfaction of unemployed persons and their spouses. *Journal of Personality and Social Psychology*, 71, 166–79.

Visser, P.S. and Krosnick, J.A. (1998) Development of attitude strength over the life cycle: Surge and decline. *Journal of Personality and Social Psychology*, 75, 1389–409.

Voelklein, C. and Howarth, C. (2005) A review of controversies about social representations theory: A British debate. *Culture and Psychology*, 11, 431–54.

Vogel, T., Kutzner, F., Fiedler, K. and Freytag, P. (2010) Exploiting attractiveness in persuasion: Senders' implicit theories about receivers' processing motivation. *Personality and Social Psychology Bulletin*, 36, 830–42.

Vohs, K.D. and Baumeister, R.F. (2004) Understanding self-regulation: An introduction. In R.F. Baumeister and K.D. Vohs (eds) *Handbook of Self-regulation: Research, Theory and Applications* (pp. 1–9). New York: Guilford Press.

Von Hippel, W. and Trivers, R. (2011) The evolution and psychology of self-deception. *Behavioral and Brain Sciences*, 34, 1–56.

Vonk, R. (1998) The slime effect: Suspicion and dislike of likeable behavior toward superiors. *Journal of Personality and Social Psychology*, 74, 849–64.

Vrij, A. (2000) *Detecting Lies and Deceit: The Psychology of Lying and the Implications for Professional Practice*. New York: John Wiley.

Vrij, A., Mann, S., Robbins, E. and Robinson, M. (2006) Police officers ability to detect deception in high stakes situations and in repeated lie detection tests. *Applied Cognitive Psychology*, 20, 741–55.

Wagner, W. (1998) Social representations and beyond: Brute facts, symbolic coping and domesticated worlds. *Culture and Psychology*, 4, 297–329.

Walby, S. and Allen, J. (2004) *Domestic Violence, Sexual Assault and Stalking: Findings from the British Crime Survey*. Home Office Research Study 276. London: Home Office.

Walker, A. (1995) Theory and methodology in premenstrual syndrome research. *Social Science and Medicine*, 41, 793–800.

Walker, I. (2001) The changing nature of racism: From old to new? In M. Augoustinos and K.J. Reynolds (eds) *Understanding Prejudice, Racism, and Social Conflict* (pp. 24–42). London: Sage.

Walker, M., Harriman, S. and Costello, S. (1980) The influence of appearance on compliance with a request. *The Journal of Social Psychology*, 112, 159–60.

Wallace, H.M., Baumeister, R.F. and Vohs, K.D. (2005) Audience support and choking under pressure: A home disadvantage? *Journal of Sports Sciences*, 23, 429–38.

Wallach, M.A., Kogan, N. and Bem, D.J. (1962) Group influence on individual risk taking. *Journal of Abnormal and Social Psychology*, 85, 75–86.

Wallbott, H.G. (1991) Recognition of emotion from facial expression via imitation? Some indirect evidence for an old theory. *British Journal of Social Psychology*, 30, 207–19.

Waller, N.G., Kojetin, B.A., Bouchard T.J. Jr et al. (1990) Genetics and environmental influences on religious interests, attitudes, and values: A study of twins reared together and apart. *Psychological Science*, 1, 138–42.

Walster, E. and Festinger, L. (1962) The effectiveness of 'overheard' persuasive communications. *The Journal of Abnormal and Social Psychology*, 65, 395–402.

Walster, E., Traupmann, J. and Walster, G.W. (1978) Equity and extramarital sexuality. *Archives of Sexual Behavior*, 7, 127–42.

Walther, E. (2002) Guilty by mere association: Evaluative conditioning and the spreading attitude effect. *Journal of Personality and Social Psychology*, 82, 919–34.

Walther, E. and Nagengast, B. (2006) Evaluative conditioning and the awareness issue: Assessing contingency awareness with the Four-Picture Recognition Test. *Journal of Experimental Psychology: Animal Behavior Processes*, 32, 454–9.

Walther, J.B. and D'Addario, K.P. (2001) The impacts of emoticons on message interpretation in computer-mediated communication. *Social Science Computer Review*, 19, 324–47.

Walton, G.M. and Cohen, G.L. (2003) Stereotype lift. *Journal of Experimental Social Psychology*, 39, 456–67.

Wang, Q. (2006) Culture and the development of self-knowledge. *Psychological Science*, 15, 182–7.

Wang, Q., Shao, Y. and Li, Y.J. (2010) 'My way or mom's way?' The bilingual and bicultural self in Hong Kong Chinese children and adolescents. *Child Development*, 81, 555–67.

Wann, D.L., Carlson, J.D., Holland, L.C. et al. (1999) Beliefs in symbolic catharsis: The importance of involvement with aggressive sports. *Social Behavior and Personality*, 27, 155–64.

Ward, T. (2000) Sexual offenders' cognitive distortions as implicit theories. *Aggression and Violent Behavior*, 5, 491–507.

Warneken, F., Hare, B., Melis, A.P. et al. (2007) Spontaneous altruism by chimpanzees and young children. *PLoSBiology*, 5, e184.

Warner, R., Hornsey, M.J. and Jetten, J. (2007) Why minority group members resent imposters. *European Journal of Social Psychology*, 37, 1–17.

Warnick, D.H. and Sanders, G.S. (1980) Why do eyewitnesses make so many mistakes? *Personality and Social Psychology Bulletin*, 8, 60–7.

Warr, M. and Stafford, M.C. (1983) Fear of victimization: A look at the proximate causes. *Social Forces*, 61, 1033–43.

Warren, G., Schertler, E. and Bull, P. (2009) Detecting deception from emotional and unemotional cues. *Journal of Nonverbal Behavior*, 33, 59–69.

Watson, A.W.S. (1994) Sports injuries during one academic year in 6799 Irish school children. *American Journal of Sports Medicine*, 12, 65–71.

Watson, D., Klohnen, E.C., Casillas, A. et al. (2004) Match makers and deal breakers: Analyses of assortative mating in newlywed couples. *Journal of Personality*, 72, 1029–68.

Waugh, C.E. and Fredrickson, B.L. (2006) Nice to know you: Positive emotions, self-other overlap, and complex understanding in the formation of a new relationship. *Journal of Positive Psychology*, 1, 93–106.

Webb, T.L. (2011) Advice taking as an unobtrusive measure of prejudice. *Behavior Research Methods*, 43, 953–63.

Webb, T.L. and Sheeran, P. (2007) How do implementation intentions promote goal attainment? A test of component processes. *Journal of Experimental Social Psychology*, 43, 295–302.

Webb, T.L., Ononaiye, M.S.P., Sheeran, P. et al. (2010) Using implementation intentions to overcome the effects of social anxiety on attention and appraisals of performance. *Personality and Social Psychology Bulletin*, 36, 612–27.

Webb, T.L., Sheeran, P. and Pepper, J. (2010) Gaining control over responses to implicit attitude tests: Implementation intentions engender fast responses on attitude-incongruent trials. *British Journal of Social Psychology*, 51, 13–32.

Weber, R., Ritterfeld, U. and Mathiak, K. (2006) Does playing violent video games induce aggression? Empirical evidence of a functional magnetic resonance imaging study. *Media Psychology*, 8, 39–60.

Webster, D.M. and Kruglanski, A. (1994) Individual differences in the need for cognitive closure. *Journal of Personality and Social Psychology*, 67, 1049–62.

Webster, D.M., Kruglanski, A.W. and Pattinson, D.A. (1997) Motivated language use in intergroup contexts. Need-for-closure effects on the linguistic intergroup bias. *Journal of Personality and Social Psychology*, 72, 1122–31.

Webster, G.D., Urland, G.R. and Correll, J. (2012) Can uniform color color aggression? Quasi-experimental evidence from professional ice hockey. *Social Psychological and Personality Science*, 3, 274–81.

Wedekind, C. and Milinski, M. (1996) Human cooperation in the simultaneous and the alternating prisoner's dilemma: Pavlov versus generous tit-for-tat. *Proceedings of the National Academy of Sciences*, 93, 2686–9.

Wedekind, C. and Milinski, M. (2000) Cooperation through image scoring in humans. *Science*, 288, 850–2.

Wegener, D. and Petty, R.E. (1994) Mood management across affective states: The hedonic contingency hypothesis. *Journal of Personality and Social Psychology*, 66, 1034–8.

Wegener, D.T. and Petty, R.E. (1998) The naive scientist revisited: Naive theories and social judgement. *Social Cognition*, 16, 1–7.

Wegener, D.T., Petty, R.E. and Smith, S.M. (1995) Positive mood can increase or decrease message scrutiny: The hedonic contingency view of mood and message processing. *Journal of Personality and Social Psychology*, 69, 5–15.

Wegner, D.M. (1994) Ironic processes of mental control. *Psychological Review*, 101, 34–52.

Wegner, D.M. (2002) *The Illusion of Conscious Will*. London: MIT Press.

Wegner, D.M. (2009) How to think, say, or do precisely the worst thing for any occasion. *Science*, 325, 48–50.

Wegner, D.M. and Wheatley, T. (1999) Apparent mental causation: Sources of the experience of will. *American Psychologist*, 54, 480–92.

Weiner, B. (1985) An attributional theory of achievement motivation and emotion. *Psychological Review*, 92, 548–73.

Weisbuch, M. and Ambady, N. (2009) Unspoken cultural influence: Exposure to and influence of nonverbal bias. *Journal of Personality and Social Psychology*, 96, 1104–19.

Weisbuch, M., Pauker, K. and Ambady, N. (2009) The subtle transmission of race bias via televised nonverbal behavior. *Science*, 326, 1711–14.

Weitz, S. (1972) Attitude, voice and behavior: A repressed affect model of interracial interaction. *Journal of Personality and Social Psychology*, 24, 14–21.

Wells, G.L. and Petty, R.E. (1980) The effects of overt head movements on persuasion: Compatibility and incompatibility of responses. *Basic and Applied Social Psychology*, 1, 219–30.

Wenzel, M. and Okimoto, T.G. (2010) How acts of forgiveness restore a sense of justice: Addressing status/power and value concerns raised by transgressions. *European Journal of Social Psychology*, 40, 401–17.

Wenzel, M., Okimoto, T.G., Feather, N.T. and Platow, M.J. (2008) Retributive and restorative justice. *Law and Human Behavior*, 32, 375–89.

Werner, C.M., Stoll, R., Birch, P. and White, P.H. (2002) Clinical validation and cognitive elaboration: Signs that encourage sustained recycling. *Basic and Applied Social Psychology*, 24, 185–203.

Werth, L., Strack, F. and Förster, J. (2002) Certainty and uncertainty: The two faces of the hindsight bias. *Organizational Behavior and Human Decision Processes*, 87, 323–41.

West, C. (1984) Medical misfired: Mishearings, misgivings, and misunderstandings in physician-patient dialogues. *Discourse Processes*, 7, 107–34.

West, C. (1984) When the doctor is a 'lady': Power, status and gender in physician-patient encounters. *Symbolic Interaction*, 7, 87–106.

West, K., Holmes, E. and Hewstone, M. (2011) Enhancing imagined contact to reduce prejudice against people with schizophrenia. *Group Processes and Intergroup Relations*, 14, 407–28.

West, P. (1999) Boys' underachievement in school: Some persistent problems and some current research. *Issues in Educational Research*, 9, 33–54.

Westen, D., Blagov, P.S., Harenski, K. et al. (2006) Neural bases of motivated reasoning: An fMRI study of emotional constraints on partisan political judgment in the 2004 U.S. presidential election. *Journal of Cognitive Neuroscience*, 18, 1947–58.

Western, B., Bloome, D., Sosnaud, B. and Tach, L. (2012) Economic insecurity and social stratification. *Annual Review of Sociology*, 38, 341–59.

Wetherell, M. and Maybin, J. (1996) The distributed self: A social constructionist perspective. In R. Stevens (ed.) *Understanding the Self* (pp. 219–79). London: Sage/Open University Press.

Wetherell, M. and Potter, J. (1992) *Mapping the Language of Racism: Discourse and the Legitimation of Exploitation.* London: Harvester Wheatsheaf.

Wetherell, M., Stiven, H. and Potter, J. (1987) Unequal egalitarianism: A preliminary study of discourses concerning gender and employment opportunities. *British Journal of Social Psychology*, 26, 59–71.

Whatley, M.A., Webster, J.M., Smith, R.H. and Rhodes, A. (1999) The effect of a favor on public and private compliance: How internalized is the norm of reciprocity? *Basic and Applied Social Psychology*, 21, 251–9.

Wheeler, L. and Kim, Y. (1997) What is beautiful is culturally good: The physical attractiveness stereotype has different content in collectivistic cultures. *Personality and Social Psychology Bulletin*, 23, 795–800.

Wheeler, M.E. and Fiske, S.T. (2005) Controlling racial prejudice: Social-cognitive goals affect amygdala and stereotype activation. *Psychological Science*, 16, 56–63.

Whitcher, S.J. and Fisher, J.D. (1979) Multi-dimensional reaction to therapeutic touch in a hospital setting. *Journal of Personality and Social Psychology*, 37, 87–96.

White, G.F., Katz, J. and Scarborough, K.E. (1992) The impact of professional football games on battering. *Violence and Victims*, 7, 157–71.

White, G.L. (1980) Physical attractiveness and courtship progress. *Journal of Personality and Social Psychology*, 39, 660–8.

White, G.L., Fishbein, S. and Rutsein, J. (1981) Passionate love and the misattribution of arousal. *Journal of Personality and Social Psychology*, 41, 56.

White, J.R. (1991) *Terrorism: An Introduction.* Pacific Grove, CA: Brooks/Cole.

White, P.A. (1988) Causal processing: Origins and development. *Psychological Bulletin*, 104, 36–52.

White, P.A. (1991) Ambiguity in the internal/external distinction in causal attribution. *Journal of Experimental Social Psychology*, 27, 259–70.

White, P.A. (1995) Use of prior beliefs in the assignment of causal roles: Causal powers versus regularity-based accounts. *Memory and Cognition*, 23, 243–54.

Whitson, J.A. and Galinsky, A.D. (2008) Lacking control increases illusory pattern perception. *Science*, 322, 115–17.

Whittaker, J.O. and Meade, R.D. (1967) Social pressure in the modification and distortion of judgement. A cross-cultural study. *International Journal of Psychology*, 2, 109–13.

Whitty, M.T. (2007) The art of selling one's self on an online dating site: The BAR approach. In M.T. Whitty, A.J. Baker and J.A. Inman (eds) *Online Matchmaking* (pp. 57–69). Basingstoke: Palgrave Macmillan.

Whitty, M.T. (2008) Revealing the 'real' me, searching for the 'actual' you: Presentations of self on an internet dating site. *Computers in Human Behavior*, 24, 1707–23.

Whitty, M.T. and Gavin, J. (2001) Age/sex/location: Uncovering the social cues in the development of online relationships. *CyberPsychology & Behavior*, 4, 623–30.

Whitty, M.T. and Joinson, A.N. (2008) *Truth, Trust and Lies on the Internet.* New York: Routledge.

Whorf, B.L. (1956) *Language, Thought, and Reality.* Cambridge, MA: MIT Press.

Wicker, A.W. (1969) Attitudes versus actions: The relationship of verbal and overt behavioral responses to attitude objects. *Journal of Social Issues*, 25, 41–78.

Wicker, B., Keysers, C., Plailly, J. et al. (2003) Both of us disgusted in *my* insula: The common neural basis of seeing and feeling disgust. *Neuron*, 40, 655–64.

Wieselquist, J., Rusbult, C.E., Foster, C.A. and Agnew, C.R. (1999) Commitment, pro-relationship behavior, and trust in close relationships. *Journal of Personality and Social Psychology*, 77, 942–66.

Wiesenfeld, B.M., Swann, W.B. Jr, Brockner, J. and Bartel, C. (2007) Is more fairness always preferred? Self-esteem moderates reactions to procedural justice. *Academy of Management Journal*, 50, 1235–53.

Wigboldus, D.H.J. and Douglas, K.M. (2007) Language, expectancies and intergroup relations. In K. Fiedler (ed.) *Social Communication* (pp. 79–106). New York: Psychology Press.

Wigboldus, D.H.J., Dijksterhuis, A. and van Knippenberg, A. (2003) When stereotypes get in the way: Stereotypes obstruct stereotype-inconsistent trait inferences. *Journal of Personality and Social Psychology*, 84, 470–84.

Wigboldus, D.H.J., Semin, G.R. and Spears, R. (2000) How do we communicate stereotypes? Linguistic bases and inferential consequences. *Journal of Personality and Social Psychology*, 78, 5–18.

Wilder, D.A. (1977) Perception of groups, size of opposition, and social influence. *Journal of Experimental Social Psychology*, 13, 253–68.

Wilder, D.A. (1990) Some determinants of the persuasive power of in-groups and out-groups: Organization of information and attribution of independence. *Journal of Personality and Social Psychology*, 59, 1202–13.

Wildschut, T., Insko, C.A. and Gaertner, L. (2002) Intragroup social influence and intergroup competition. *Journal of Personality and Social Psychology*, 82, 975–92.

Wilkinson, R. and Pickett, K. (2010) *The Spirit Level: Why Equality is Better for Everyone.* London: Penguin.

Williams, E.F. and Gilovich, T. (2008) Do people really believe they are above average? *Journal of Experimental Social Psychology*, 44, 1121–8.

Williams, K.D. (2001) *Ostracism: The Power of Silence.* New York: Guilford Press.

Williams, K.D. (2009) Ostracism: A temporal need-threat model. *Advances in Experimental Social Psychology*, 41, 275–314.

Williams, K.D. and Karau, S.J. (1991) Social loafing and social compensation: The effects of expectations of coworker performance. *Journal of Personality and Social Psychology*, 61, 570–81.

Williams, K.D. and Sommer, K.L. (1997) Social ostracism by coworkers: Does rejection lead to loafing or compensation? *Personality and Social Psychology Bulletin*, 23, 693–706.

Williams, K.D., Bourgeois, M.J. and

Croyle, R.T. (1993) The effects of stealing thunder in criminal and civil trials. *Law and Human Behavior*, 17, 597–609.

Williams, K.D., Cheung, C.K. and Choi, W. (2000) Cyberostracism: Effects of being ignored over the internet. *Journal of Personality and Social Psychology*, 79, 748–62.

Williams, K.D., Govan, C.L., Croker, V. et al. (2002) Investigations into differences between social and cyberostracism. *Group Dynamics: Theory, Research, and Practice*, 61, 65–77.

Williams, K.D., Nida, S.A., Baca, L.D. and Latané, B. (1989) Social loafing and swimming: Effects of identifiability on individual and relay performance of intercollegiate swimmers. *Basic and Applied Social Psychology*, 10, 73–81.

Williams, L.E. and Bargh, J.A. (2008) Experiencing physical warmth promotes interpersonal warmth. *Science*, 322, 606–7.

Wills, T.A. (1981) Downward comparison principles in social psychology. *Psychological Bulletin*, 90, 245–71.

Wilson, A.E. and Ross, M. (2000) The frequency of temporal-self and social comparisons in people's personal appraisals. *Journal of Personality and Social Psychology*, 78, 928–42.

Wilson, A.E. and Ross, M. (2001) From chump to champ: People's appraisals of their earlier and present selves. *Journal of Personality and Social Psychology*, 80, 572–84.

Wilson, M. and Dovidio, J.F. (1985) Effects of perceived attractiveness and feminist orientation on helping behavior. *Journal of Social Psychology*, 125, 415–20.

Wilson, T.D. (2002) *Strangers to Ourselves: Discovering the Adaptive Unconscious*. London: Belknap Press.

Wilson, T.D. and Dunn, D.S. (1986) Effects of introspection on attitude-behavior consistency: Analyzing reasons versus focusing on feelings. *Journal of Experimental Social Psychology*, 22, 249–63.

Wilson, T.D. and Petruska, R. (1984) Motivation, model attributes, and prosocial behavior. *Journal of Personality and Social Psychology*, 46, 458–68.

Wilson, T.D., Lindsey, S. and Schooler, T.Y. (2002) A model of dual attitudes. *Psychological Review*, 107, 101–26.

Wingfield, J.C. (1985) Short-term changes in plasma levels of hormones during establishment and defense of breeding territory in male song sparrows, *Melospiza melodia*. *Hormones and Behavior*, 19, 174–87.

Winkielman, P. and Kavanagh, L. (2012) How do emotions move us? Embodied and disembodied influences of affect and emotions on social thinking and interper-

sonal behavior. In J.P.P. Forgas, K. Fiedler and C. Sedikides (eds) *Social Thinking and Interpersonal Behavior* (pp. 127–42). New York: Psychology Press.

Winkielman, P., Halberstadt, J., Fazendeiro, T. and Catty, S. (2006) Prototypes are attractive because they are easy on the mind. *Psychological Science*, 17, 799–806.

Winston, J.S., Strange, B.A., O'Doherty, J. and Dolan, R.J. (2002) Automatic and intentional brain responses during evaluation of trustworthiness of faces. *Nature Neuroscience*, 5, 277–83.

Winton, W.M., Putnam, L.E. and Krauss, R.M. (1984) Facial and autonomic manifestations of the dimensional structure of emotion. *Journal of Experimental Social Psychology*, 20, 195–216.

Wisman, A. and Goldenberg, J.L. (2005) From the grave to the cradle: Evidence that mortality salience engender a desire for offspring. *Journal of Personality and Social Psychology*, 89, 46–61.

Wisman, A. and Koole, S.L. (2003) Hiding in the crowd: Can mortality salience promote affiliation with others who oppose one's worldviews? *Journal of Personality and Social Psychology*, 84, 511–26.

Witte, K., Berkowitz, J.M., Cameron, K.A. and McKeon, J.K. (1998) Preventing the spread of genital warts: Using fear appeals to promote self-protective behaviors. *Health Education and Behavior*, 25, 571–85.

Wohl, M.J.A. and Branscombe, N.R. (2008) Remembering historical victimization: Collective guilt for current ingroup transgressions. *Journal of Personality and Social Psychology*, 94, 988–1006.

Wohl, M.J.A., Branscombe, N.R. and Klar, Y. (2006) Collective guilt: Emotional reactions when one's group has done wrong or been wronged. *European Review of Social Psychology*, 17, 1–37.

Wohl, M.J.A., Hornsey, M.J. and Bennett, S.H. (2012) Why group apologies succeed and fail: Intergroup forgiveness and the role of primary and secondary emotions. *Journal of Personality and Social Psychology*, 102, 306–22.

Wohl, M.J.A., Hornsey, M.J. and Philpot, C.R. (2011) A critical review of official public apologies: Aims, pitfalls, and a staircase model of effectiveness. *Social Issues and Policy Review*, 5, 70–100.

Wojciszke, B., Bazinska, R. and Jaworski, M. (1998) On the dominance of moral categories in impression formation. *Personality and Social Psychology Bulletin*, 24, 1251–63.

Wolf, A. (2000) Emotional expression online: Gender differences in emoticon use. *Cyberpsychology and Behavior*, 3, 827–33.

Wong, R.Y.M. and Hong, Y.Y. (2005) Dynamic influences on culture on

cooperation in the prisoner's dilemma. *Psychological Science*, 16, 429–34.

Wood, J.V. (1989) Theory and research concerning social comparisons of personal attributes. *Psychological Bulletin*, 106, 231–48.

Wood, J.V., Heimpel, S.A. and Michela, J.L. (2003) Savoring versus dampening: Self-esteem differences in regulating positive affect. *Journal of Personality and Social Psychology*, 85, 566–80.

Wood, J.V., Heimpel, S.A., Newby-Clark, I. and Ross, M. (2005) Snatching defeat from the jaws of victory: Self-esteem differences in the experience and anticipation of success. *Journal of Personality and Social Psychology*, 89, 764–80.

Wood, J.V., Perunovic, E. and Lee, J.W. (2010) Positive self-statements: Power for some, peril for others. *Psychological Science*, 20, 860–6.

Wood, M., Douglas, K.M. and Sutton, R.M. (2012) Dead and alive: Belief in contradictory conspiracy theories. *Social Psychological and Personality Science*, 3, 767–73.

Wood, W. (2000) Attitude change: Persuasion and social influence. *Annual Review of Psychology*, 51, 539–70.

Wood, W. and Eagly, A.H. (1981) Stages in the analysis of persuasive messages: The role of causal attributions and message comprehension. *Journal of Personality and Social Psychology*, 40, 246–59.

Wood, W. and Eagly, A.H. (2010) Gender. In S.T. Fiske, D.T. Gilbert and G. Lindzey (eds) *Handbook of Social Psychology* (5th edn, vol. 1, pp. 629–67). New York: Wiley.

Wood, W. and Neal, D.T. (2007) A new look at habits and the habit–goal interface. *Psychological Review*, 114, 843–63.

Wood, W., Kallgren, C.A. and Preisler, R.M. (1985) Access to attitude-relevant information in memory as a determinant of persuasion: The role of message attributes. *Journal of Experimental Social Psychology*, 21, 73–85.

Wood, W., Christensen, P.N., Hebl, M.R. and Rothgerber, H. (1997) Conformity to sex-typed norms, affect, and the self-concept. *Journal of Personality and Social Psychology*, 73, 523–35.

Woodman, T., Roberts, R., Hardy, L. et al. (2011) There is an 'I' in TEAM: Narcissism and social loafing. *Research Quarterly for Exercise and Sport*, 82, 285–90.

Woodside, A.G. and Chebat, J. (2001) Updating Heider's balance theory in consumer behaviour: A Jewish couple buys a German car and additional buying-consuming transformation stories. *Psychology and Marketing*, 18, 475–95.

Worchel, S. (1996) Emphasizing the social nature of groups in a developmental framework. In J.L. Nye and A.M.

Brower (eds) *What's Social about Social Cognition* (pp. 261–82). London: Sage.

Worchel, S., Lee, J. and Adewole, A. (1975) Effects of supply and demand on ratings of object value. *Journal of Personality and Social Psychology*, 32, 906–14.

Worchel, S., Rothgerber, H., Day, E.A. et al. (1998) Social identity and individual productivity with groups. *British Journal of Social Psychology*, 37, 389–413.

Word, C.O., Zanna, M.P. and Cooper, J. (1974) The nonverbal mediation of self-fulfilling prophecies in interracial interaction. *Journal of Experimental Social Psychology*, 10, 109–20.

World Bank (1993) *World Development Report 1993: Investing in Health*. New York: Oxford University Press.

Wright, J.D., Kritz-Silverstein, D., Morton, D.J. et al. (2007) Pet ownership and blood pressure in old age. *Epidemiology,* 18, 613–17.

Wright, S.C., Aron, A. and Tropp, L.R. (2002) Including others (and groups) in the self: self-expansion and intergroup relations. In J.P. Forgas and K.D. Williams (eds) *The Social Self: Cognitive, Interpersonal, and Intergroup Perspectives* (pp. 343–63). New York: Psychology Press.

Wright, S.C., Aron, A., McLuaghlin-Volpe, T. and Ropp, S. (1997) The extended contact effect: Knowledge of cross-group friendships and prejudice. *Journal of Personality and Social Psychology*, 73, 73–90.

Wu, C. and Shaffer, D.R. (1987) Susceptibility to persuasive appeals as a function of source credibility and prior experience with the attitude object. *Journal of Personality and Social Psychology*, 52, 677–88.

Wyer, R.S. Jr and Frey, D. (1983) The effects of feedback about self and others on the recall and judgements of feedback-relevant information. *Journal of Experimental Social Psychology*, 19, 540–59.

Yamada, A.-M. and Singelis, T.M. (1999) Biculturalism and self-construal. *International Journal of Intercultural Relations*, 23, 697–709.

Yamagishi, T. and Kiyonari, T. (2000) The group as the container of generalized reciprocity. *Social Psychology Quarterly*, 63, 116–32.

Yamagishi, T. and Sato, K. (1986) Motivational bases of the public goods problem. *Journal of Personality and Social Psychology*, 50, 67–73.

Yamagishi, T., Cook, K.S. and Watabe, M. (1998) Uncertainty, trust, and commitment formation in the United States and Japan. *American Journal of Sociology*, 104, 165–94.

Yamagishi, T., Makimura, Y., Foddy, M. et al. (2005) Comparisons of Australians and Japanese on group-based coopera-

tion. *Asian Journal of Social Psychology*, 8, 173–90.

Yardi, S. and Boyd, D. (2010) Dynamic debates: An analysis of group polarization over time on Twitter. *Bulletin of Science, Technology and Society*, 30, 316–27.

Yarmouk, U. (2000) The effect of presentation modality on judgements of honesty and attractiveness. *Social Behavior and Personality*, 28, 269–78.

Ybarra, M.L. and Mitchell, K.J. (2004) Youth engaging in online harassment: Associations with caregiver-child relationships, internet use, and personal characteristics. *Journal of Adolescence*, 27, 319–36.

Yik, M.S.M., Bond, M.H. and Paulhus, D.L. (1998) Do Chinese self-enhance or self-efface? It's a matter of domain. *Personality and Social Psychology Bulletin*, 24, 399–406.

Yinger, J.M. (1994) *Ethnicity: Source of Strength? Source of Conflict?* Albany, NY: SUNY Press.

Yovetich, N.A. and Rusbult, C.E. (1994) Accommodative behavior in close relationships: Exploring transformation of motivation. *Journal of Experimental Social Psychology*, 30, 138–164.

Yu, Y.W., Tsi, S.J., Hong, C.J. et al. (2005) Association study of a monoamine oxidase-a polymorphism with major depressive disorder and antidepressant response. *Neuropsychopharmacology*, 30, 1719–23.

Yukl, G.A. (1974) Effects of situational variables and opponent concessions on a bargainer's perception, aspirations, and concessions. *Journal of Personality and Social Psychology*, 29, 227–36.

Zadro, L., Williams, K.D. and Richardson, R. (2004) How low can you go? Ostracism by a computer is sufficient to lower self-reported levels of belonging, control, self-esteem and meaningful existence. *Journal of Experimental Social Psychology*, 40, 560–7.

Zajonc, R.B. (1965) Social facilitation. *Science*, 149, 269–74.

Zajonc, R.B. (1968) Attitudinal effects of mere exposure. *Journal of Personality and Social Psychology Monograph Supplement*, 9, 1–27.

Zajonc, R.B. (1970) The effects of frequency and duration of exposure on response competition and affective ratings. *The Journal of Psychology: Interdisciplinary and Applied*, 75, 163–9.

Zajonc, R.B. (1980) Feeling and thinking: Preferences need no inferences. *American Psychologist*, 35, 151–75.

Zajonc, R.B. (1989) Styles of explanation in social psychology. *European Journal of Social Psychology*, 19, 345–68.

Zajonc, R.B. (2001) Mere exposure: A gateway to the subliminal. *Current Directions in Psychological Science*, 224–8.

Zajonc, R.B. (2003) *The Selected Works of Robert Zajonc*. New York: Wiley.

Zajonc, R.B., Adelmann, P.K., Murphy, S.T. and Niedenthal, P.M. (1987) Convergence in the physical appearance of spouses. *Motivation and Emotion*, 11, 335–46.

Zajonc, R.B., Heingartner, A. and Herman, E.M. (1969) Social enhancement and impairment of performance in the cockroach. *Journal of Personality and Social Psychology*, 13, 83–92.

Zald, D.H. (2003) The human amygdala and the emotional evaluation of sensory stimuli. *Brain Research Reviews*, 41, 88–123.

Zanna, M.P. and Rempel, J.K. (1988) Attitudes: A new look at an old concept. In D. Bar-Tal and A.W. Kruglanski (eds) *The Social Psychology of Knowledge* (pp. 315–34). Cambridge: Cambridge University Press.

Zanna, M.P., Kiesler, C.A. and Pilkonis, P.A. (1970) Positive and negative attitudinal affect established by classical conditioning. *Journal of Personality and Social Psychology*, 14, 321–28.

Zebrowitz, L.A., Hall, J.A., Murphy, N.A. and Rhodes, G. (2002) Looking smart and looking good: Facial cues to intelligence and their origins. *Personality and Social Psychology Bulletin*, 28, 238–49.

Zeng, M. and Chen, X.P. (2003) Achieving cooperation in multiparty alliances: A social dilemma approach to partnership management. *Academy of Management Review*, 28, 587–605.

Zerjal, T., Xue, Y., Bertorelle, G. et al. (2003) The genetic legacy of the Mongols. *American Journal of Human Genetics*, 23, 717–21.

Zhong, C. and Leonardelli, G.J. (2008) Cold and lonely: Does social exclusion literally feel cold? *Psychological Science*, 19, 838–42.

Zhou, X., Wildschut, T., Sedikides, C. et al. (2012) Heartwarming memories: Nostalgia maintains physiological comfort. *Emotion*, 12, 678–84.

Zillman, J. (1972) *A Study of Some Aspects of the Radiation and Heat Budgets of the Southern Hemisphere Oceans*. Canberra: Australian Government Publishing Service

Zimbardo, P.G. (1969) The human choice: Individuation, reason, and order versus deindividuation, impulse and chaos. *Nebraska Symposium on Motivation*, 17, 237–307.

Zimbardo, P.G. (1970) The human choice: Individuation, reason and order versus deindividuation, impulse and chaos. In W.J. Arnold and D. Levine (eds) *Nebraska Symposium on Motivation 1969* (vol. 17, pp. 237–307). Lincoln, NE: University of Nebraska Press.

Zimbardo, P.G. (2006) On the psychology of imprisonment: Alternative perspectives from the laboratory and TV studio. *British Journal of Social Psychology*, 45, 47–53.

Zimbardo, P.G. (2007) *The Lucifer Effect: Understanding How Good People Turn Evil*. New York: Random House.

Zimbardo, P.G., Haney, C., Banks, W.C. and Jaffe, D. (1982) The psychology of imprisonment. In J.C. Brigham and L. Wrightsman (eds) *Contemporary Issues of Social Psychology* (4th edn, pp. 230–5). Monterey, CA: Brooks/Cole.

Zimmerman, D.H. and West, C. (1975) Sex roles, interruptions and silences in conversation. In B. Thorne and N.

Henley (eds) *Language and Sex: Difference and Dominance*. Rowley, MA: Newbury House.

Zuckerman, M. (1975) Belief in a just world and altruistic behavior. *Journal of Personality and Social Psychology*, 31, 972–6.

Zuckerman, M. (1979) Attribution of success and failure revisited, or: The motivational bias is alive and well in attributional theory. *Journal of Personality*, 47, 245–87.

Zuckerman, M. and Tsai, F. (2005) Costs of self-handicapping. *Journal of Personality*, 73, 411–42.

Zuckerman, M., DePaulo, B.M. and Rosenthal, R. (1981) Verbal and nonverbal communication of deception. In N. Berkowitz (ed.) *Advances in Experimental Social Psychology* (vol. 14, pp. 2–60). New York: Academic Press.

Zuwerink, J.R. and Devine, P.G. (1996) Attitude importance and resistance to persuasion: It's not just the thought that counts. *Journal of Personality and Social Psychology*, 70, 931–44.

Zwaan, R.A. (2009) Mental simulation in language comprehension and social cognition. *European Journal of Social Psychology*, 39, 1142–50.

Subject index

Author index